2001

2001

WOMEN IN WORLD HISTORY

A Biographical Encyclopedia

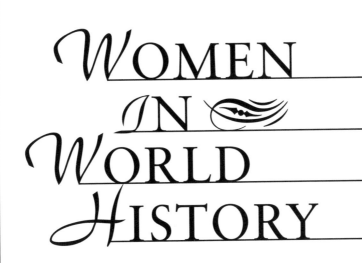

WOMEN IN WORLD HISTORY

A Biographical Encyclopedia

VOLUME
8
Jab-Kyt

Anne Commire, Editor
Deborah Klezmer, Associate Editor

YORKIN PUBLICATIONS

GALE GROUP

Detroit
New York
San Francisco
London
Boston
Woodbridge, CT

Yorkin Publications

Anne Commire, *Editor*
Deborah Klezmer, *Associate Editor*
Barbara Morgan, *Assistant Editor*

Eileen O'Pasek, Gail Schermer, Patricia Coombs, James Fox,
Catherine Cappelli, Karen Rikkers, *Editorial Assistants*
Karen Walker, *Assistant for Genealogical Charts*

Special acknowledgment is due to Peg Yorkin who made this project possible.

Thanks also to Karin and John Haag, Bob Schermer, and to
the Gale Group staff, in particular Dedria Bryfonski, Linda Hubbard, John Schmittroth, Cynthia Baldwin,
Tracey Rowens, Randy Bassett, Christine O'Bryan, Rebecca Parks, and especially Sharon Malinowski.

The Gale Group

Sharon Malinowski, *Senior Editor*
Rebecca Parks, *Editor*
Linda S. Hubbard, *Managing Editor*

Margaret A. Chamberlain, *Permissions Specialist*
Mary K. Grimes, *Image Cataloger*

Mary Beth Trimper, *Production Director*
Evi Seoud, *Assistant Production Manager*

Cynthia Baldwin, *Product Design Manager*
Tracey Rowens, *Cover and Page Designer*
Michael Logusz, *Graphic Artist*

Barbara Yarrow, *Graphic Services Manager*
Randy Bassett, *Image Database Supervisor*
Robert Duncan, *Imaging Specialist*
Christine O'Bryan, *Graphics Desktop Publisher*
Dan Bono, *Technical Support*

Library of Congress Catalog Card Number 99-24692
A CIP record is available from the British Library

ISBN 0-7876-4067-0
Printed in the United States of America.

Library of Congress Cataloging-in-Publication Data

Women in world history : a biographical encyclopedia / Anne Commire, editor, Deborah Klezmer, associate editor.
    p. cm.
    Includes bibliographical references and index.
    ISBN 0-7876-3736-X (set). — ISBN 0-7876-4064-6 (v. 5). —
ISBN 0-7876-4065-4 (v. 6) — ISBN 0-7876-4066-2 (v. 7) — ISBN 0-7876-4067-0 (v. 8) — ISBN 0-7876-4068-9 (v. 9)
    1. Women—History Encyclopedias. 2. Women—Biography Encyclopedias.
    I. Commire, Anne. II. Klezmer, Deborah.
    HQ1115.W6 1999
    920.72'03—DC21   99-24692

10 9 8 7 6 5 4 3 2 1

𝒥

Jaburkova, Jozka (d. 1944)

Czechoslovakian feminist and patriot. Died in 1944.

A journalist and author by trade, Jozka Jaburkova edited *The Disseminator* magazine, wrote children's books, and published three novels about working women. She was also an early leader in the women's progressive movement and a member of the Prague City Council. During the 1930s, Jaburkova joined the Communist Party, campaigning for employment equity for women as well as for nurseries and schools for their children. She was sent to Ravensbrück concentration camp at the onset of the German occupation, where shortly before her death in 1944, she organized a resistance movement. At the end of World War II, Jaburkova was a national hero, and in 1965 a statue was erected to her memory in Prague.

Jachmann-Wagner, Johanna (1826–1894).

See Wagner, Johanna.

Jackson, Alice (1887–1974)

Australian journalist. Born Alice Archibald on October 15, 1887, in Ulmarra, New South Wales; died on October 28, 1974; one of eight children of William Archibald (a schoolteacher) and Clara Amelia (Baker) Archibald; married Samuel Henry Jackson (an accountant and businessman); children: one daughter; one son.

One of Australia's leading magazine editors in the early 20th century, Alice Jackson was a schoolteacher in the years before her marriage to Samuel Henry Jackson, with whom she had two children. She began her career in journalism by contributing short stories and feature articles to several major newspapers in Sydney, including the *Bulletin* and *Triad*. Her early years also included a stint on the staff of the *Sunday Times* and as editor of the women's page at the *Telegraph*. In 1933, Jackson joined the newly established *Australian Women's Weekly*, becoming editor in 1939. By some accounts, she actually took over the job in 1934, when editor George Warnecke left on an extended trip overseas. Under Jackson, the *Weekly*—a blend of service features, fiction, and news—grew to command Australia's largest readership.

Jackson added heft to the paper's regular mix of food, fashion, beauty, child care, and fiction, with features on distinguished women, including sports figures. She also covered the more controversial issues of her day, such as women's problems in marriage and in the workplace, and the refusal of the Chief Protector of Aborigines to permit an Aboriginal woman to marry the man of her choice. During the war, the paper devoted many of its pages to the women on the home front, but in an effort to bring the war closer to her readers, Jackson also toured army camps, including operational areas in New Guinea. Following the war, the *Weekly* took a more glamorous turn, though Jackson retained an edge with an occasional controversial article, such as the one advising the textile industry that they might be able to remedy their labor shortages by establishing a policy of equal pay.

In 1950, under increasing pressure from new owners, Jackson left the *Weekly* to start *Woman's Day and Home*, a Melbourne-based paper owned by Keith Murdoch. The formula that had served her so well in the past, however, was no longer successful, and she resigned after a year and returned to Sydney. One of her last jobs was in public relations, doing promotions for a fashionable restaurant. When Alice Jackson died in October 1974, her status as one of Australia's greatest magazine editors had long been ignored.

SOURCES:
Radi, Heather, ed. *200 Australian Women*. NSW, Australia: Women's Redress Press, 1988.

Barbara Morgan,
Melrose, Massachusetts

Jackson, Anne (1926—)

American actress of stage, film, and television. Born Anna Jane Jackson in rural Millvale, Pennsylvania, on

1

the outskirts of Pittsburgh, on September 3, 1926; youngest of three daughters of John Ivan Jackson (a hairdresser) and Stella Germaine (Murray) Jackson; graduated from Franklin K. Lane High School, Brooklyn, New York, 1943; attended New School for Social Research, New York City, summer 1943; attended Neighborhood Playhouse School of the Theater, New York City, 1943–44, and member of Actors Studio from 1948; married Eli Wallach (an actor), on March 5, 1948; children: **Roberta Wallach** (an actress); **Katherine Wallach** (an actress); Peter Wallach (an artist and filmmaker).

Selected theater: made professional debut as Anya in a touring production of The Cherry Orchard (September 1944); appeared as Alice Stewart in the pre-Broadway tryout of Signature (Forrest Theater, Philadelphia, February 1945); appeared with Eva Le Gallienne's American Repertory Theater (New York City, 1946–47); appeared as Judith in The Last Dance (Belasco Theater, New York City, January 1948), Nellie in Summer and Smoke (Music Box Theater, New York City, October 1948), Nita in Magnolia Alley

*A*nne *J*ackson

(Mansfield Theater, New York City, April 1949), Margaret Anderson in Love Me Long (48th St. Theater, New York City, November 1949), Mildred in Oh, Men! Oh, Women! (Henry Miller Theater, New York City, December 1953), the Daughter in Middle of the Night (ANTA, February 1956); succeeded Glynis Johns in the title role of Major Barbara (Martin Beck Theater, New York City, October 1956); appeared as Laura in The Glass Menagerie (Westport Country Playhouse, Connecticut, summer 1959), Daisy in Rhinoceros (Longacre Theater, New York City, January 1961); appeared in The Typist and The Tiger (Orpheum Theater, New York City, February 1963, London, 1964); appeared as the Actress in The Exercise (Berkshire Festival, Stockbridge, Massachusetts, summer 1967, and John Golden Theater, New York City, April 1968), Molly Malloy in revival of The Front Page (Ethel Barrymore Theater, New York City, May 1969), *Ethel Rosenberg* in Inquest (Music Box Theater, New York City, April 1970); appeared as Mother H., Grandmother H., Doris, and Joan in Promenade, All! (Alvin Theater, New York City, April 1972), Madame St. Pé in The Waltz of the Toreadors (Eisenhower Theater, Kennedy Center, Washington, D.C., as well as national tour and Circle in the Square Theater, September 1973), Madame Ranevskaya in The Cherry Orchard (Stage Company, Hartford, December 1974), Mrs. McBride in Marco Polo Sings a Solo (Public Theater, New York City, January 1977), Mrs. Frank in The Diary of Anne Frank (Theater Four, New York City, December 1978), Anna Cole in Cafe Crown (Brooks Atkinson Theater, New York City, February 1989); succeeded *Irene Worth* as Grandma Kurnitz in Lost in Yonkers (Richard Rogers Theater, New York City, 1991); appeared in In Persons (Kaufman Theater, New York City, September 1993); appeared as Esther in The Flowering Peach (Lyceum Theater, March 1994).

Filmography: So Young So Bad (1950); The Journey (1959); Tall Story (1960); The Tiger Makes Out (1967); How to Save a Marriage and Ruin Your Life (1968); The Secret Life of an American Wife (1968); Zigzag (1970); (cameo) The Angel Levine (1970); Lovers and Other Strangers (1970); Dirty Dingus Magee (1970); (as Abigail Adams) Independence (1976); Nasty Habits (UK, 1976); The Bell Jar (1979); The Shining (1980); Sam's Son (1984); (documentary) Sanford Meisner (1985); Funny About Love (1989); Folks! (1992).

Born in 1926 in rural Millvale, Pennsylvania, on the outskirts of Pittsburgh, Anne Jackson was the youngest of three daughters of **Stella**

Murray Jackson, an Irish Catholic from a coal-mining family, and John Jackson, a restless Croatian immigrant who, in 1931, opened one of the country's first unisex hairdressing establishments. In her autobiography *Early Stages*, Jackson recalled the somewhat tense relationship between her "ill-matched" parents and the frequent flights with her mother to her maternal grandmother's house. "Although I didn't like it when my parents fought, I loved running home to Ma'am's with our suitcase, for Mom's relatives were a colorful lot. They were constantly birthing, burying, and backbiting. They wet-kissed, were maudlin and sentimental. Mom was very much at home with them."

A shy youngster with red hair and freckles, Jackson called her eldest sister Katherine her "mentor and stage mother." It was Katherine who read stories to the younger girls and led them in reenactments of movies. In 1933, the family moved to New York, settling in a tenement in Brooklyn. Jackson responded to city life with a personality change. "I no longer hid behind my mother's skirts, but emerged from a quiet, timid child into a show-off and hellion," she wrote. As she advanced into adolescence, she became more and more enraptured with the movies, memorizing large chunks of dialogue and entertaining her sisters with elaborate impersonations of her favorite stars. At age 11, she won an amateur night at a local movie house, after which she was called upon to perform for local civic and church groups. Live audiences became an enormous source of affirmation. "The power of making an audience laugh was joyous," she later said. "And you never forget it once you do it."

Jackson went through a difficult period in junior high school when her mother had a nervous breakdown, but a sympathetic English teacher kept her busy preparing monologues for the weekly assembly program. After graduating from high school in the winter of 1943, she held down a series of jobs (insurance tracer, elevator operator, and salesgirl in a chocolate shop) while studying drama at night with Herbert Berghof at the New School for Social Research. "Herbert Berghof's classes whetted my appetite and increased my craving to act," she wrote, "though I still thought of the theater as an escape from reality. Berghof would help me discover how the two are inextricably entwined." Through Berghof, she also met Sanford Meisner, an acting coach at the Neighborhood Playhouse, where she obtained a scholarship to study acting full-time. In 1944, ignoring overtures from movie scouts, Jackson launched her stage career with a 16-week road tour as Anya in Anton Chekhov's *The Cherry Orchard*.

Jackson's first outing on Broadway was in the melodrama *Signature* (1945), which closed after two performances. In 1946, while performing in a showcase production of Tennessee Williams' one-act *This Property is Condemned*, she met her future husband, actor Eli Wallach. The two then joined *Eva Le Gallienne's American Repertory Theater where Jackson had small roles in *Henry VIII*, *What Every Woman Knows*, and *Androcles and the Lion*. The couple married in 1948, after which Jackson continued to build her credentials in a series of what she describes as "smash flops." Her first solid Broadway hit was *Oh, Men! Oh, Women!* (1953), a sex farce by Edward Chodorov in which, as psychiatric patient Mildred Turner, she delivered a hilarious 20-minute monologue while lying on the doctor's couch. During the 1950s, Jackson continued to hone her skills by studying with method acting teacher Lee Strasberg and with frequent performances on live television dramas, including "Armstrong Circle Theater," "Philco Playhouse," and "Goodyear Playhouse."

Jackson returned to Broadway in 1956, playing the daughter in Paddy Chayefsky's *Middle of the Night* and, in 1957, replaced ✥➤ Glynis Johns in the title role of Shaw's *Major Barbara*. Other notable actors in the Shaw production included *Cornelia Otis Skinner, Burgess Meredith, Charles Laughton and her husband Eli Wallach, with whom Jackson frequently appeared. "The kind of thing that happens on stage between us is very good," she explained to Jerry Parker of *Newsday* (August 6, 1970). "With other actors, I'm less certain. With some actors a lot of time is spent just creating a relationship so that we can work together. But I know Eli's range. I know how he works, what he will discover about a play."

The Jackson-Wallach team scored a number of subsequent successes, including Ionesco's *Rhinoceros* (1961) and a double bill, *The Typist and the Tiger*, of Murray Schisgal's one-act plays, *The Typist*, which recounts the lives of two office workers, and *The Tiger*, a satire about a lonely postman who kidnaps a discontented suburban housewife. Jackson made her London stage debut in the Schisgal plays in May 1964 at the famed Globe Theatre. For her performance in *The Tiger*, which was later recreated for television and made into a movie (*The Tiger Makes Out*, 1967), Jackson also received the 1963 Village Voice Obie award for Best Actress in an Off-Broadway Play. The Jackson-Wallach team

✥᪣
Johns, Glynis.
See Bergner,
Elisabeth for
sidebar.

scored again in Schisgal's first full-length play *Luv* (1964) and were also paired in the 1972 David Robinson comedy *Promenade, All!*, about six generations of an American family in which Jackson played all four of the female roles.

Jackson and Wallach enjoyed perhaps their greatest triumph in the revival of Jean Anouilh's *The Waltz of the Toreadors*, which toured nationally in 1973 and 1974. In it, Jackson played the shrewish, bedridden wife of the foolish, aging roué, General St. Pé (Wallach). *The New York Times* critic Clive Barnes likened the actress to "a poisoned Isolde." "She takes her one big scene," he wrote, "and, looking like a kewpie doll with temper tantrums, makes it into a beautifully virtuostic thing." In 1978, in an Off-Off-Broadway production of *The Diary of Anne Frank*, Jackson (as Mrs. Frank) and Wallach appeared with their daughters Roberta and Katherine. Although some critics felt that Jackson's portrayal of Mrs. Frank was too low-key, Martin Gottfried found it the most powerful of her career.

On her own, Jackson performed in numerous television specials throughout the 1970s, including a superb PBS production of **Helene Hanff**'s "84 Charing Cross Road," and on stage portrayed Mrs. McBride, the transsexual, in John Guare's *Marco Polo Sings a Solo* (1977) at the New York Shakespeare Festival. In 1977, she also played Diana, a defeated woman who suspects her husband of adultery, in the American premiere of Alan Ayckbourn's *Absent Friends* at the Long Wharf Theater in New Haven, Connecticut, a performance that showcased a fully matured acting talent. "Her nerve ends seem to glitter through an only nearly opaque charm," wrote Clive Barnes, "and her social graces, even her efforts to keep afloat her subsiding marriage, have the small poetry of genteel despair."

In addition to her stage and television career, Jackson also appeared sporadically in films, including *So Young, So Bad* (1950), *Tall Story* (1960), and *The Secret Life of an American Wife* (1968). She did several with her husband: *How to Save a Marriage—And Ruin Your Life* (1968), *Zig-Zag* (1970), and *The Angel Levine* (1970). Jackson and Wallach also appeared as **Abigail Adams* and Benjamin Franklin, respectively, in John Huston's *Independence* (1976), a half-hour film celebrating the American Bicentennial. In 1993, they produced *In Persons* (scenes from plays in which they had performed over the years), which ran Off-Broadway at the Kaufman Theater. Jackson, who is generally characterized as direct and good-humored, attributes the longevity of her marriage to luck. "We seem to have in a very modest sense the same talent quota. And a similar idea about homelife and marriage. . . . We're fairly independent as people, stubborn as people, [and] we hold on to our own identities."

SOURCES:

Jackson, Anne. *Early Stages: Scenes from a Life*. Boston, MA: Little, Brown, 1979.

Katz, Ephraim. *The Film Encyclopedia*. NY: Harper-Collins, 1994.

McGill, Raymond D., ed. *Notable Names in the American Theater*. Clifton, NJ: James T. White, 1976.

Moritz, Charles, ed. *Current Biography 1980*. NY: H.W. Wilson, 1980.

Barbara Morgan,
Melrose, Massachusetts

Jackson, Barbara (1914–1981).

See Ward, Barbara.

Jackson, Bessie (1897–1948).

See Bogan, Lucille.

Jackson, Cordell (1923—)

American guitarist and rockabilly star. Born Cordell Miller in Pontotoc, Mississippi, in 1923.

Born in Pontotoc, Mississippi, in 1923, Cordell Jackson was a talented performer who played guitar, wrote her own material, ran her own record label, and avoided the mainstream because she valued her freedom. As a teenager, Jackson performed with her father's band, the Pontotoc Ridge Runners. In 1943, after graduating from high school, she made her way to Memphis, where she joined the Fisher Air Craft Band. In 1956, Jackson launched her own record label, Moon Records, with her hit single "Rock 'n' Roll Christmas" with "Beboppers' Christmas" on the flip side. While holding down a series of outside jobs, she continued to produce records by outside performers as well as her own. Notable among her hits was "Football Widow" and a 1983 album *Knockin' 60*. She also produced a contemporary Christian radio show, "Let's Keep the Family Together, America." Jackson enjoyed some popularity in 1991 when she performed a dueling guitar sequence with Brian Setzer of the Stray Cats in a Budweiser beer commercial.

Jackson, Glenda (1936—)

British actress and politician. Born in Birkenhead, Cheshire, England, on May 9, 1936; eldest of four daughters of Harry Jackson (a bricklayer turned

Glenda Jackson

building contractor) and Joan Jackson; attended Hoylake Church School and West Kirby Country Grammar School for Girls; graduated with honors from the Royal Academy of Dramatic Art, London; married Roy Hodges (an actor-director), in 1958 (divorced); children: one son, Daniel.

Selected theater: made stage debut at Worthing in Separate Tables *(February 1957); made London debut as Ruby in* All Kinds of Men *(Arts Theater, September 1957); appeared as Alexandra in* The Idiot *(Lyric, Hammersmith Theater, March 1962), Siddie in* Alfie *(Mermaid Theater, London, June 1963); joined the*

Royal Shakespeare Company in 1964; appeared in the experimental Theater of Cruelty (January 1964); appeared as Princess of France in Love's Labour's Lost *(RSC, 1965),* Ophelia *in* Hamlet *(RSC, August 1965), Charlotte Corday in* Marat/Sade *(RSC, November 1965); made New York debut in same role (Martin Beck Theater, December 1965); appeared as Masha in* The Three Sisters *(Royal Court Theater, London, April 1967), Tamara in* Fanghorn *(Fortune Theater, London, November 1967), Katherine Winter in* Collaborators *(Duchess Theater, London, April 1973), Solange in* The Maids *(Greenwich Theater, London, February 1974), the title role in* Hedda Gabler *(Aldwych Theater, London, July 1975), then toured U.S. and Australia in the role; appeared as Vittoria Corombona in* The White Devil *(Old Vic, July 1976); the title role in* Stevie *(Vaudeville Theater, London, March 1977); the title role in* Rose *(Duke of York's Theater, London March 1980); appeared in* Strange Interlude *(1984),* The House of Bernarda Alba *(1986),* Macbeth *(1988); appeared in the title role in* Mother Courage *(Citizens Theater, Glasgow, May 1990); appeared as Christine Mannon in* Mourning Becomes Electra *(Citizens Theater, Glasgow, April 1991).*

Filmography: This Sporting Life *(1966);* The Persecution and Assassination of Jean-Paul Marat as Performed by the Inmates of the Asylum of Charenton under the Direction of the Marquis de Sade *(Marat/Sade for short, 1967);* Tell Me Lies *(1968);* Negatives *(1968);* Women in Love *(1969);* The Music Lovers *(1971);* Sunday, Bloody Sunday *(1971);* Mary Queen of Scots *(1971);* The Boy Friend *(1971);* Triple Echo *(1973);* A Bequest to the Nation *(The Nelson Affair, 1973);* A Touch of Class *(1973);* The Maids *(1974);* The Romantic Englishwoman *(1975);* The Devil is a Woman *(UK/It., 1975);* Hedda *(1975);* The Incredible Sarah *(1976);* Nasty Habits *(1976);* House Calls *(US, 1978);* Stevie *(Can., 1978);* The Class of Miss MacMichael *(1978, released in US, 1979);* Hopscotch *(US, 1980);* Giro City *(And Nothing But the Truth, 1982);* Return of the Soldier *(1983);* Turtle Diary *(1985);* Beyond Therapy *(US, 1987);* Business as Usual *(1987);* Salome's Last Dance *(1988);* The Rainbow *(1989).*

Distinguished by her flinty personality and an intense approach to her craft, British actress Glenda Jackson has always viewed acting as hard work. "I was taught to earn my pleasures and to earn through work," she has said. "To work at my best I have to be interested, and what interests me more than anything are the difficulties the work presents. Even if I am working in rub-

bish, the strictures I place on myself make the acting difficult." In reviewing Jackson in her breakthrough movie *Women in Love*, Stanley Kauffmann (*New Republic,* April 18, 1970) also noted that she had no interest in the trappings of stardom. "She is not an actress in order to be loved," he wrote, "but in order to act."

The eldest of the four daughters of a bricklayer, Jackson was born in 1936 in Birkenhead, Cheshire, England, and raised in a working-class home. As a girl, she aspired to become a ballet dancer but eventually grew too tall. She left school at 16, taking a job at a drugstore and spending her evenings performing in amateur productions at the local YMCA. On a whim, she applied for a scholarship at the Royal Academy of Dramatic Art (RADA) in London and was accepted. "I had no real ambitions about acting," she later told Peter Buckley (*TWA Ambassador,* July 1971). "But . . . I knew there had to be something better than the bloody chemist's shop." Although she graduated with honors from RADA, Jackson's career got off to a slow start. During the 1950s, she acted and stage-managed for various repertory companies in England and Scotland; she also married Roy Hodges, a fellow actor. Between acting assignments, Jackson worked as a waitress, receptionist, and file clerk to help make ends meet.

In 1963, after three previous unsuccessful auditions, Jackson was accepted into the Royal Shakespeare Company and spent her first season with the company's experimental Theater of Cruelty, under the direction of Peter Brook. During her early days at Stratford, Jackson became known for her quirky characterizations. As Ophelia in *Hamlet,* she was described by critic Hugh Leonard as "a regular man-eater: a highly sexed young woman, cracking under the strain of a disintegrating love affair." Her unconventional approach to the role prompted another critic to suggest that the production be retitled "Ophelia." In 1964, Jackson received international acclaim playing *Charlotte Corday in Peter Weiss' avant-garde psychological drama The Persecution and Assassination of Jean Paul Marat as Performed by the Inmates of the Asylum of Charenton under the Direction of the Marquis de Sade, a play-within-a-play better known by its shortened title* Marat/Sade. Directed by Peter Brook, the play was brought to New York in December 1965, where it won the Drama Critics' Circle Award and four Tony awards. Although the role in *Marat/Sade* was pivotal for Jackson (she won a Tony nomination and a Variety poll award as the most promising new actress of 1965–66), she found the play distasteful. "I loathe and detest everything about this production," she told Rex Reed in a *New York Times* interview, "We all loathe it. . . . It's a play that breeds sickness, with no release for the tension." The play was also filmed with the original cast and released by United Artists in 1967. In the meantime, Jackson returned to London, appearing as Masha in *The Three Sisters* (1967) and as Tamara Fanghorn in *Fanghorn* (1967), a play described by Michael Billington as "an arbitrary mixture of *Iris Murdoch and J.M. Barrie: a piece of black whimsy."

Having made an auspicious screen debut in *Marat/Sade,* Jackson's film career blossomed with her Oscar-winning performance in *Women in Love* (1970), a screen adaptation of the D.H. Lawrence novel directed by Ken Russell and costarring Oliver Reed. Her portrayal of the liberated sculptress Gudrun Brangwen (whom Lawrence reportedly modeled on the writer *Katherine Mansfield), was praised as intelligent, sensual, and self-assured. "She bursts upon the screen like a young sturdier version of *Katharine Hepburn, with all of her animal magnetism," wrote Arthur Knight (*Saturday Review,* March 21, 1970). "It was a magnificent performance." In addition to an Oscar, Jackson won the Variety Award of Great Britain for the Best Film Actress of 1970, as well as the Best Actress award from the New York Film Critics and the National Society of Film Critics in the United States. Following a stunning performance in a second Ken Russell film, *The Music Lovers* (1971), Jackson broke away from her usual neurotic characters to play a cultured divorcée in *Sunday, Bloody Sunday* (1971), based on an original screenplay by **Penelope Gilliat.** She then captured a second Oscar for her performance in her first comedy, *A Touch of Class* (1973), which was followed by a riveting portrayal of Queen *Elizabeth I in *Mary Queen of Scots* (1971), a role she also played in the BBC television six-part biography, "Elizabeth R." Later television credits include her portrayal of actress *Patricia Neal in "The Patricia Neal Story" (1981) and that of *Elena Bonner** in "Sakharov" (1984).

Jackson returned to the stage in 1973 in the unsuccessful *Collaborators,* followed by a turn as Solange in Genet's *The Maids.* In 1976, her portrayal of Vittoria Corombona (*Vittoria Accoramboni) in *The White Devil* was seen as overwhelmingly cynical by David Zane Mairowitz, who reviewed the play for *Plays and Players.* "Once again, Jackson gives the impression she knows the entire plot from the outset, so that we never get Vittoria's freshness or vitality," he wrote. Jackson went on to great success

in the title role of *Stevie* (1977), about the eccentric English poet *Stevie Smith, and also starred in the film version in 1978. Returning to the RSC, Jackson played the Egyptian queen *Cleopatra VII in *Antony and Cleopatra* and, in 1980, won acclaim as a discontented, middle-aged teacher in Andrew Davies' *Rose,* which also played on Broadway the following year.

Jackson's later career included the leading role in Bothe Strauss' controversial play *Great and Small* (1983), centering on a middle-aged bag lady, and the lead in a London revival of Eugene O'Neill's five-hour marathon *Strange Interlude,* which also enjoyed a Broadway run in 1985. In New York again in 1988, she portrayed Lady Macbeth (*Gruoch) and, in 1990, played the title role in Brecht's *Mother Courage* in Glasgow and London. "Glenda Jackson makes of the heroine a snarling, caustically snappish fishwife," wrote Joe Farrell in *Plays and Players,* "who punches out her intolerant contempt for those around her in a rasping, metallic voice. More than any other actor, she has a remarkable ability to make every line count, to give equal value to each successive mood."

In person, Jackson is slightly less formidable than on stage, although **Vera Lustig,** who interviewed the actress in a backstage dressing room for a 1990 article in *Plays and Players,* was still intimidated. "It's somewhat unnerving to meet at close quarters that famous salty drawl, those narrowed, scrutinising eyes and that chin puckered as though eating a sour fruit," she wrote. Though Jackson's marriage to Roy Hodges ended in divorce, she remained devoted to her son, Daniel, born in 1969. Like many working mothers, she felt a sense of guilt over being away from home so much while he was growing up. "I've had to learn to live with that guilt and hope that it doesn't become too punitive," she said.

Throughout her long career, Jackson suffered from extreme stage fright. "The longer I carried on, the greater the fear became." In 1990, she gave up the stage, transferring her energy to the political arena. A staunch Socialist, she was a parliamentary candidate for the Labour Party in 1990 and elected a Labour member of Parliament for Hampstead and Highgate in 1992; she then served seven years in the House of Commons. Jackson was also London's junior transport minister under Prime Minister Tony Blair until 1999, when she resigned to make a bid to become London's first directly elected mayor.

SOURCES:

Farrell, Joe. "Mother Courage," in *Plays & Players.* July 1990, p. 32.

Hartnoll, Phyllis, and Peter Found. *The Concise Oxford Companion to the Theater*. Oxford and NY: Oxford University Press, 1993.

Katz, Ephraim. *The Film Encyclopedia*. NY: Harper-Collins, 1994.

Lustig, Vera. "Who's Afraid. . . ?," in *Plays & Players*. May 1990.

Moritz, Charles, ed. *Current Biography 1971*. NY: H.W. Wilson, 1971.

Morley, Sheridan. *The Great Stage Stars*. London: Angus & Robertson, 1986.

"Star Tracks," in *People Weekly*. May 25, 1998, p. 16.

Barbara Morgan,
Melrose, Massachusetts

Jackson, Grace (1961—)

Jamaican track and field athlete. Born on June 14, 1961, in St. Ann, Jamaica; educated in Jamaican public schools; attended Alabama A&M and conducted graduate studies at Queens College in New York City.

Won the silver medal in the 200-meters in the 1988 Olympics in Seoul, Korea.

Born in the Jamaican village of St. Ann on June 14, 1961, Grace Jackson demonstrated a strong interest in athletics as well as considerable ability at an early age. Encouraged during her school years, she began her formal training after winning an athletic scholarship to Alabama A&M. She later enrolled in graduate studies in computer science at Queens College, New York City, while running as a member of the Atoms Track Club of Brooklyn. According to Jackson, it was there that she matured into a serious competitive runner; prior to Brooklyn, "If my coach said, 'You can take a week off,' I'd take a week off. . . . Now if he says, 'You can take a week off,' I know that means, 'You can come in and jog.'"

In 1988, competing in London at the International Amateur Athletic Federation Mobil Grand Prix track and field meet, Jackson turned in a time of 22.40 seconds to win the women's 200-meter run. She also beat Cuba's *Ana Quirot* in the 400-meter run with a time of 49.57 seconds, the second-best time recorded worldwide for that race during 1988. At the Olympics that year in Seoul, South Korea, Jackson won the silver medal in the 200-meters with a time of 21.72, just behind gold medalist *Florence Griffith Joyner*'s time of 21.34.

SOURCES:

The New York Times Biographical Service. March 1984.

Page, James A. *Black Olympian Medalists*. Englewood, CO: Libraries Unlimited, 1991.

Don Amerman,
freelance writer, Saylorsburg, Pennsylvania

Jackson, Helen Fiske (1830–1885).

See Jackson, Helen Hunt.

Jackson, Helen Hunt (1830–1885)

Prolific American poet, novelist, and activist who documented the conditions of Native Americans in A Century of Dishonor *(1881), a scathing critique of government policy that went largely ignored, then recast the same material into the novel* Ramona, *which became the most popular romance of the late 19th century. Name variations: Helen Fiske Jackson; Helen Fiske Hunt; (pseudonyms) H.H., Marah, Rip Van Winkle, Saxe Holm, and No-Name. Born Helen Maria Fiske on October 15, 1830 (her obituary in the New York Tribune cites October 18, 1831), in Amherst, Massachusetts; died on August 12, 1885, in San Francisco, California; daughter of Nathan Welby Fiske (a professor) and Deborah Waterman (Vinal) Fiske; attended private schools, including the Ipswich Female Seminary and the Springler Institute in New York City; married Lieutenant Edward Bissell Hunt, on October 28, 1852 (died 1863); married William Sharpless Jackson, on October 22, 1875; children: Murray (1853–1854); Warren Horsford (nicknamed Rennie, 1856–1865).*

After marriage to Hunt, moved to Washington (1852); death of infant son Murray (1854); death of husband in explosion (October 1863); death of son Rennie (April 1865); after move to Newport, began writing poems that were published in the New York Evening Post, the Nation, Atlantic, and elsewhere (1870–79); married Jackson and moved West (1875); on visit back East, attended lecture about the fate of the Ponca Indian tribe that became the turning point for her Indian crusade (1879).

Selected publications: Versus (1870, 1873, 1879); Bits of Travel (1872); Mercy Philbrick's Choice (1876); Hetty's Strange Story (1877); Nelly's Silver Mine (1878); A Century of Dishonor (1882); Ramona (1884).

In the autumn of 1879, Helen Hunt Jackson was well known in America as a writer of children's books and poetry, as well as articles that had appeared in virtually every popular magazine, but she was not known as a person easily drawn to causes. She was then in the fourth year of her second marriage, living in Colorado Springs, but a homesickness for her native New England led her to make a prolonged trip back East, with plans to be there until December for the celebration of the 70th birthday of her longtime friend, essayist and novelist Oliver Wendell Holmes. That November, she was in Boston, where she attended a lecture organized by Thomas Henry Tibbles, an editor at the *Omaha Herald,* the purpose of which was to describe the plight of the Ponca Indian tribe of Nebraska. The evening featured the Ponca Indian chief Standing Bear, dressed in traditional garb, and a moving oration delivered by *Susette LaFlesche Tibbles, a striking young woman, more than six feet tall, billed that night as "Bright Eyes." Standing before her audience, the articulate and statuesque Native American recounted the story of broken treaties and the horrors of the Poncas' forcible removal to Indian Territory in Oklahoma by the U.S. Army in 1878.

The billing of "Bright Eyes" lent a quality of simplicity to the speaker who was in fact anything but simple. Susette LaFlesche had been educated at the mission school on her Nebraska reservation until 1869, then at the Elizabeth Institute for Young Ladies in New Jersey, where she proved to be an excellent writer. Her works were published in a New York newspaper before her graduation in 1875. It was not the first time Jackson had been drawn to a woman of forceful personality, and in this case she was swept up by the speaker's tragic tale. She and LaFlesche became friends, and Jackson soon turned her extraordinary energies to the cause of exposing U.S. government abuses of Indian tribes and treaties, in the hope of bringing about reform.

Helen Maria Fiske was born on October 15, 1830, in Amherst, Massachusetts, the second of four children of Nathan Welby Fiske and **Deborah Vinal Fiske**; only Helen and her younger sister **Ann** would survive infancy. Deborah Fiske had talent as a writer for children and "showed a power of expression and a purity of form mingled with genuine humor" in publications that included *Letters from a Cat.* Helen's father was the son of Massachusetts farmers and had planned for a career in the Congregational ministry, before turning to the teaching of moral philosophy, Latin, and Greek at Amherst College. The Fiskes remained staunch Calvinists, providing their children with a strictly moral and structured household, which young Helen tested at every opportunity.

In spite of—or perhaps because of—the stern and pious atmosphere, Jackson demonstrated a "will of iron." She was vivacious, impetuous, and, as her mother noted in a journal, hard to handle: "Helen is so wild—jumping rope, dressing up in odd things, and jumping out behind doors." At age eight, she ran away with a playmate to a nearby town, where they interrupted a funeral in session by jumping on the bier. Hauled home by a search party, Helen announced, "Oh, Mother, I've had a perfectly lovely time." Confined in the attic with a large Bible after the escapade, Jackson chose a whipping rather than repent. But her unruly temperament was accompanied by a gift for vivid recall and creative storytelling, and her writing began as a record of her childhood journeys and escapades, kept in completest detail.

When Helen was 13, family tragedy began to set her adrift. In 1844, her mother died of tuberculosis; three years later, her father succumbed to the same disease. Jackson went to Falmouth, on Cape Cod, to live with her Aunt Hooker, while Ann lived in Boston with their Aunt Vinal. The sisters' finances were taken over by their grandfather, David Vinal, and they became his beneficiaries. A brandy drinker with a love for money and an acumen for business, he encouraged Helen in her flamboyant behavior while promoting her self-esteem, laying the groundwork for her adventurous spirit and good business sense as an adult. These influences were further buoyed during Jackson's attendance at the Ipswich Female Seminary in Massachusetts and the Springler Institute in New York City.

*D*ear friend, can you walk, were the last words that I wrote her. Dear friend, I can fly—her immortal reply.

—Emily Dickinson, on the death of Helen Hunt Jackson

Jackson grew up in an era that heralded the "cult of domesticity," according to historian **Barbara Welter**, in which a woman's sphere was within the home. The four qualities that a "true" or "good" woman embodied were purity, piety, submissiveness, and domesticity. But the Springler Institute, run by the brothers John and Gorham Abbott, important pioneers in the improvement of women's education, was operated in contradiction to the cult of domesticity's ideals. In an era when the ideal physical attributes for women were paleness and anemia, this progressive school housed a large playground for girls and provided equipment for athletics; the students were self-governed and no punishments were meted out. On the whole, however, the educational opportunities for girls that began to expand in the 1830s (primarily for upper- and middle-class women) were not aimed at extending women's sphere, but at making them better mothers. As an adult, Jackson's life demonstrated some of this dichotomy, in that her writings tout the ideals of domesticity, especially the nurturing of children, and yet she made telling choices of travel and friendship with women over the love of home and husband.

By age 20, it was not unusual for Jackson to find herself the most sought-after and attended-to woman at any function. Blonde, graceful, vivacious, she was not actually beautiful but had perfect taste in dress, and her green eyes, her most arresting feature, were described as "beaming and candid." One gentleman thought them "more alive than those of any one else I ever knew." Flirting demurely and laughing without inhibition, she made conquests wherever she went. It was at a ball given by the governor of New York that she met and charmed his brother, Lieutenant Edward Bissell Hunt, and they married in Boston on October 28, 1852.

Edward Hunt was an army engineer, a career that did not permit the couple a permanent home. Helen called their uprooted and helter-skelter existence together "scatterdom." They also frequently held opposing views, though Jackson could be persuaded to change her mind. She was a staunch supporter, for instance, of the views of abolitionist *Harriet Beecher Stowe, author of Uncle Tom's Cabin, in opposition to Lieutenant Hunt; but around the time of the birth of their first child, when Helen "had her own slave girl for five dollars a month," she found herself more pragmatic about the institution of slavery. Some friends found this willingness to vacillate in her opinions a frustrating aspect of Jackson in later life.

The marriage was fraught with personal tragedy. Helen's first son Murray, born in Washington, D.C., on September 30, 1853, died in August of the following year, of a brain tumor. Jackson, who blamed herself, fell gravely ill, but her grief was eased with the birth of a second son, Warren Horsford, nicknamed Rennie, on December 11, 1856. Shortly after Rennie's birth, she met *Sarah Chauncey Woolsey, who became her closest friend. Though summer was the only time her husband was at home, Jackson chose to spend the season doing volunteer work with Woolsey at the Knight Hospital; during the last five years of her marriage, she spent little time with Hunt. Biographer Ruth Odell suggests that Jackson and Woolsey had little in common, but that they shared "a view of romance . . . a sort of eager sparkle . . . although never permitted to show on the surface."

In September 1863, in the midst of the Civil War, Edward Hunt was experimenting with a "sea miner," which he had designed, when the device exploded; he was killed by its lethal fumes. Two years later, Jackson faced the most heartfelt tragedy of her life when her beloved son Rennie, only nine years old, died of malignant diphtheria. The mother and child had shared a deep bond, which included a belief in the supernatural. Before Rennie died, he exacted a promise from her that she would not take her own life, while he promised in turn to communicate with her after death. By this time Jackson was living among friends in Newport, Rhode Island, but in her intense grief, coupled with her desire to communicate with Rennie, she became so isolated that friends worried about her sanity. She tried to take comfort in her sister's children and begged her sister and her brother-in-law to let her adopt their little girl. Jackson wrote "pathetic and tender little notes" to the child which foreshadowed the writings for children she would later produce.

At the same time, she had also begun to write professionally. In October 1865, her first paid work appeared in the New York Evening Post. She preferred the Atlantic Monthly, but using the business sense inherited from her grandfather, she sold to the highest bidder. According to one biographer, "if selling were an honorable business for men, she didn't see why it wasn't for women and children." She also experimented with book translations and juvenile literature, writing for the Galaxy and the Riverside Magazine for Young People.

Helen Hunt Jackson had many connections to the literary world. For one thing, she had known *Emily Dickinson since childhood, and they maintained a lifelong contact; she was also a close friend of *Anne C.L. Botta, who hosted "the first important salon in the history of American letters"; Jackson was influenced by both Oliver Wendell Holmes and Thomas Wentworth Higginson, another popular essayist. Learning her craft around such literary figures, she found her writing projects well received back at Amherst, but her rise to fame was also partially engendered by the quantity of work she produced. The Civil War years (1861–65) spawned a barren period in American literature, and, in conservative Newport society, the key to literary credibility was quantity, not quality. Jackson became a prolific writer, churning out 371 articles for the New York Independent alone and writing poetry for the New York Evening Post and the Nation. Under Higginson's tutelage, her style began to please editors of popular magazines like the Atlantic.

In November 1868, Jackson traveled with Woolsey to Europe and recorded the journey in articles and letters to friends. Excerpts were pub-

Helen
Hunt
Jackson

lished as *Bits of Travel* (1872). Shunning personal celebrity, Jackson adopted various pseudonyms, such as "H.H," "Rip Van Winkle," and "Saxe Holm," or escaped into total anonymity with unsigned reviews and novels signed "No-Name." Though writing was one of the few ways acceptable for women to make money, the social climate toward women writers remained hostile, and she did not want to be identified "as one of the detestable ink-stained women"; Charles Dickens derisively called them "Scribbling Women."

During the European trip, Jackson may also have shrunk from the public eye and rebelled against prescribed cultural dictates. In Rome, she rejected the accepted custom of neighborly visiting, leaving Woolsey to uphold their social obligations while she smuggled herself into off-limit places like the Quirinal Palace, where she sat in the pope's chair when nobody was looking and put "her heretic feet" on his footstool. At the Etruscan Museum, she persuaded her reluctant guide to allow her to light a 3,000-year-old candle, displaying traces of her childhood antics.

Back in the U.S., Jackson's thoughts turned to a much-longed-for trip to California. The publications of her collections were sufficiently lucrative to make the trip possible. After the *Independent* offered to buy her account of the journey, and Woolsey agreed to accompany her, Jackson set off from New York by rail in the spring of 1872; the descriptions she gathered crossing the countryside would appear a decade later in *Ramona*. En route, the women toured Salt Lake City, where Jackson was repulsed by the "ugliness of the whole Mormon philosophy," particularly the practice of polygamy. In support of its abolition, she renounced her former stance against women's public speaking by openly promoting a woman's speaking tour. Jackson and Woolsey then toured Yosemite with and without guides, riding horseback over dizzying trails and fording swollen streams. She loved Native American place names rather than their Anglicized translations. It was here that her sensitivity began for the tribal people whose plight would become her life struggle.

Since her trip to Europe, Jackson had repeatedly suffered incapacitating attacks of sore throat, and in 1873 she became more seriously ill with what was diagnosed as diphtheria and dysentery. After convalescing for a while at the home of Emily Dickinson, Jackson's worsening condition led a homeopathic doctor in Amherst to prescribe treatment in the dry climate of the Rocky Mountains. Following his advice, she relocated, and it was at the Colorado Springs Hotel that she met William Sharpless Jackson. A Quaker banker six years her junior, he had made a fortune as promoter of the Denver and Rio Grande Railroad. On October 22, 1875, the two were married at the house of Helen's sister Ann, in Wolfeboro, New Hampshire, then returned to their home in Colorado Springs, the finest house in town and the first that Jackson could truly call her own. The couple entertained frequently. William Jackson was a charming host and loved to have his house filled with friends. His wife found immense pleasure in her new life, but it did not diminish her love of travel.

The relief that the marriage gave Jackson from the need to earn money also released the creative powers that were to produce her best works. Based on childhood memories, she soon wrote the "No-Name" book, *Mercy Philbrick's Choice*, published in 1876, whose protagonist bore a strong resemblance to her longtime friend Emily Dickinson, with her "orchid-like face," morbid shyness, and sheaves of unpublished poems. *Hetty's Strange History* (1877) and *Nelly's Silver Mine* (1878) followed, but despite Jackson's productivity and success, she began to show signs of depression. Isolated from her East Coast friends, she longed for New England, and her zest for Colorado waned. In the late summer of 1879, Jackson left Colorado for Mt. Desert, Maine, planning to remain in the East until December. That November, she was in Boston when she heard the lecture that gave a new direction to her life.

It was then suggested to Jackson that she was the proper person to undertake what William Justin Horsha's Native American novel, *Ploughed Under*, failed to do. If she would take up the Indian cause, such a story would do for the Indians what Harriet Beecher Stowe's novel did for blacks. After a lifetime of indifference to reform, Jackson became fascinated with her new, all-engaging cause. As she wrote to a friend, she was now what she had always considered to be "the most odious thing in the world, 'a woman with a hobby.'"

For several months, Jackson diligently researched the files of Americana at the Astor Library in New York City. It was a sign of her national stature that she was admitted every morning before the library doors were officially open. In 1881, Jackson published *A Century of Dishonor*, a scathing and accusatory account of the government's treatment of American tribes that spared no one. Bound in blood red to give visual impact to her fury, copies of the document were sent at her expense to every important official concerned with Indian issues, including members of Congress. She also waged war against then secretary of the interior Carl Schurz, arousing national attention. The report produced no governmental action to right the wrongs Jackson cited, but in 1882 she received a commission from the Department of the Interior to travel to southern and coastal California and document the conditions of the remnant Indian tribes on the lands that had once belonged to the California missions.

Abbott Kinney was selected to assist Jackson as chaperon and interpreter, as well as to intimidate white squatters responsible for the dispossession and eviction of the mission Indians. They arrived in California in the winter of 1881–82 and made a five-week tour of Native American settlements in the three southernmost counties of the state, during which Jackson roused the enmity of many who crossed her path. While staying at Horton House in San Diego, she evoked criticism for interfering with the manager's rearing of his children and for demanding "one thing after another in the interest of her own comfort." Undoubtedly motivated by her experience with the hotel manager, she simultaneously churned out four essays on child training. She also fought bitterly with every government official who dared question her recommendations.

More important, while gathering the material for her report, Jackson became acquainted with places and characters that were to appear later in *Ramona*. From her San Diego hotel, she made drives to the villages and missions of Saboba, the Serrano tribe in the San Jacinto Valley, Temecula Valley, the Pauma, the Potraro, the Rincon, San Luis Rey, San Juan Capistrano, and San Antonio de Pala—all sites reproduced in the novel with great exactitude. Her excursions were detailed in articles released while she traveled, and in July 1883, her 56-page document produced for the government, *Report on the Conditions and Needs of the Mission Indians*, was sent off to Washington.

When the government still showed no sign of response, Jackson resurrected the idea of the novel. "It came in the middle of the night," she wrote. "The story came at white heat. I did not write *Ramona*; it was written through me. My life-blood went into it—all I had thought, felt and suffered for five years on the Indian question." For her protagonist, she chose a woman of Spanish and Native American ethnicity, but it is likely that the character was modeled after Susette LaFlesche, whose story had affected her so deeply.

Published in 1884, *Ramona* became the best-selling romance novel of the 19th century. The story lacked the scope and power of Stowe's *Uncle*

From the movie Ramona, based on the novel by Helen Hunt Jackson.

Tom's Cabin. The many intricate issues of conflict between Indians and whites were distorted by oversimplification, and the unlikely ending was anticlimactic, weakening its impact as protest fiction. But the story is important for its portrayal of old Spanish society in California on the brink of dissolution, and it successfully characterizes the victimization of the mission Indians by white squatters and officials. The book sold steadily through more than 300 printings, and to date there have been at least four movie versions made, three in the silent-film era. In Hemet, California, the romantic tragedy has been performed annually in an outdoor amphitheater since the 1920s.

Her own mission accomplished, Jackson returned to Colorado to redecorate her house. By now, she had become very heavy, and, after a fall down a flight of stairs resulted in a compound fracture of her hip, she never walked again. But she still wrote and continued to travel, stopping in Los Angeles and Long Beach. By the time she reached San Francisco, she was seriously ill with cancer but managed to write parting thoughts and wishes to her friends and to leave instructions that all her letters and manuscripts be burned. From her deathbed, she wrote to President Grover Cleveland, thanking him for what he had already done for the Indians and suggesting that he read *A Century of Dishonor.* Ten days after her husband arrived in San Francisco, Jackson died at age 54, a year after the publication of *Ramona.* That she always forgot herself and devoted her strength to the cause of others explains why her friend Emily Dickinson, upon learning of her death, could say, "Helen of Troy will die, but Helen of Colorado, never."

A great flood of tributes praised Jackson for her personal magnetism, love of nature, and zest for living. She was buried in a favorite spot, beneath a cairn on Cheyenne Mountain overlooking Colorado Springs, but in 1891 a spate of vandalism made it necessary to move her casket to Evergreen Cemetery, her final resting place. Although she did not live to see the mission Indians of southern California vindicated, her writings and activism were instrumental in leading to the work of the Women's National Indian Association, the Indian Rights Association, and the Lake Mohonk Conference.

SOURCES:

Banning, Evelyn I. *Helen Hunt Jackson.* NY: Vanguard Press, 1973.

Jackson, Helen (H.H.). *A Century of Dishonor: A Sketch of the United States Government's Dealings with some of the Indian Tribes.* Minneapolis, MN: Ross & Haines (repr. in 1964).

———. *Ramona.* Boston, MA: Little, Brown, 1884.

Mathes, Valerie Sherer. *Helen Hunt Jackson and Her Indian Reform Legacy.* Edited by William H. Goetzmann. 1st ed. American Studies Series, Austin, TX: University of Texas Press, 1990.

Odell, Ruth. *Helen Hunt Jackson (H.H.).* NY: D. Appleton-Century, 1939.

SUGGESTED READING:

Armitage, Susan, and Elizabeth Jameson, eds. *The Women's West.* OK: University of Oklahoma Press, 1987.

Schlissel, Lillian, Vicki L. Ruiz, and Janice Monk, eds. *Western Women: Their Land, Their Lives.* NM: University of New Mexico Press, 1988.

RELATED MEDIA:

Ramona (silent film), starring *Mary Pickford** and Henry B. Walthall, produced by D.W. Griffith for Biograph, 1910.

Ramona (12-reel silent film), starring **Adda Gleason** and Monroe Salisbury, produced by William H. Clune, 1916.

Ramona (silent film), starring ***Dolores Del Rio** and Roland Drew, United Artists, 1928.

Ramona (sound film), starring ***Loretta Young** and Don Ameche, 20th Century-Fox, 1936.

A yearly stage production of *Ramona* is performed in Hemet, California.

Roberta A. Hobson,
author of "In Search of Herself, Judith McDaniel," in *Contemporary Lesbian Writers of the United States* (Greenwood Press, 1993)

Jackson, Julia (fl. 19th c.)

Voodoo woman of New Orleans. Flourished in the 19th century.

In 19th-century New Orleans, Julia Jackson was one of the most notorious practitioners of voodoo, a form of animism involving sorcery, fetishes, and trances. A resident of the city's red-light district known as Storyville, Jackson reportedly stood six feet tall, was cross-eyed, and possessed incredible skills, including the ability to cause spontaneous pregnancies or abortions. New Orleans' prostitutes feared her most, however, for her alleged "sealing power," the voodoo to induce a case of venereal disease that could put a lady of the night out of business. The Storyville prostitutes, known for their in-fighting, would often taunt a rival with threats to hire Jackson to "close her up."

Jackson, Lady (1914–1981).

See Ward, Barbara.

Jackson, Laura (1901–1991).

See Riding, Laura.

Jackson, Mahalia (1911–1972)

American gospel and spiritual singer, known as the Gospel Queen, who extended black music from cabarets into the homes of the white middle class. Born in New Orleans, Louisiana, on October 26, 1911; died of heart failure in Evergreen Park, Illinois, on January 27, 1972; daughter of Charity Clark (a laundress and maid) and Johnny Jackson (a Baptist preacher, barber, and longshoreman); married Isaac "Ike" Hockenhull (an entrepreneur), in 1936 (divorced); married Sigmond Galloway (a musician), in 1965 (divorced).

Mahalia Jackson was an optimist by nature. When told she could have been a great blues singer, she replied, "Blues are the songs of despair. Gospel songs are the songs of hope. When you sing gospel, you have the feeling there's a cure for what's wrong. When you're through with the blues, you've got nothing to rest on." Her optimistic attitude was at odds with some in the black community throughout much of her career. From the beginning, hers was a different route to fame and fortune than many black entertainers. She never bought a ticket to the theater or a movie house, much less performed in a nightclub. Launching her career in black churches, she moved easily into mainstream America where her spirituals and gospel songs were greatly loved. As a result, she became a wealthy woman who seemingly escaped the discrimination other blacks suffered at the hands of the white entertainment world. Black music was simply too marvelous to remain in the confines of one culture, a fact Jackson recognized and exploited. Her audacity, sense of purpose, and business abilities made her an American star.

Mahalia Jackson was born in 1911 in New Orleans and grew up in a three-room shack on Water Street between the railroad tracks and the Mississippi River levee, the cradle of black music. Her absent father Johnny Jackson was a stevedore who preached on Sundays and moonlighted as a barber. Her upbringing was very religious. Her mother **Charity Jackson** and her Aunt Duke had no use for the blues and what they represented. Some members of the family were in show business, however. Two cousins toured with *Ma Rainey, but they were the exception. Mahalia was five when her mother died, and her Aunt Duke made certain that family standards were upheld. She went to the Mount Moriah Baptist Church where her father sometimes preached on Sundays. "I loved best to sing in the congregation," noted Jackson.

> All around me I could hear the foot-tapping and hand-clapping. That gave me the bounce. I liked it better than being up in the choir singing anthems. I liked to sing songs which testify to the glory of the Lord. Those anthems are too dead and cold for me. As David said in the Bible: "Make a joyous noise unto the Lord." That's me.

A devout Baptist, Jackson was drawn to the uninhibited fervor in the Holiness Church next door. The physical involvement induced by the music inspired her and left a permanent mark on her performance style. Jackson recounted:

> These people had no choir or no organ. They used the drum, the cymbal, the tambourine and the steel triangle. Everybody in there sang, and they clapped and stomped their feet, and sang with their whole bodies. They had a beat, a rhythm we held on to from slavery days, and their music was so strong and expressive. It used to bring tears to my eyes. . . . [When] these Holiness people tore into "I'm So Glad Jesus Lifted me Up!" they came out with real jubilation. I say: Don't let the devil steal the beat from the Lord! The Lord don't like us to act dead. If you feel it, tap your feet a little—dance to the glory of the Lord.

As a distinctive form of music, gospel has a recent history, dating back only to the 1930s. It was a combination of spirituals and the revivalist hymns sung by 18th-century white settlers. *Amazing Grace*, probably the quintessential gospel song, is loved by blacks and whites alike. But blacks freed these hymns from their European constraints, combining them with an African song style to create a national music in which African elements dominate. Gospel made jazz, blues, and rock more acceptable to white audiences.

When Mahalia Jackson moved to Chicago in 1927, at age 16, black music was thriving in a city filled with immigrants from the South. Gospel and blues were a soothing balm for the homesick. She was soon the lead singer at the Greater Salem Baptist Church on Sundays, supporting herself as a maid and laundress during the week. By the mid-1930s, she was touring with the Johnson Gospel Singers, led by the son of the pastor of her church. Her first recording for Decca-Coral (1937) was "God's Gonna Separate the Wheat from the Tares" which was an immediate hit. By the 1940s, she was traveling throughout America with Thomas A. Dorsey, the "Father of Gospel Music." By 1946, "Move On Up a Little Higher" had sold a million copies, establishing her as the Gospel Queen.

For decades, blacks had performed only where they were allowed—in Southern vaudeville and tent shows, clubs in Harlem and Chicago, and in some theaters. Breaking into the white world was not easy. When black entertainers were invited, it was through the back door. The

Daughters of the American Revolution refused to let *Marian Anderson sing in Washington's Independence Hall in the 1930s, typical of a form of discrimination black entertainers suffered time and again.

In the early 1950s, however, things were changing, and new doors were opening into the white world. On October 4, 1950, Mahalia Jackson soloed at Carnegie Hall with the National Baptist Convention. "I stood there," she recalled, "gazing out at the thousands of men and women who had come to hear me—a baby nurse and washer woman—on the stage where great artists like Caruso and *Lily Pons and Marian Anderson had sung, and I was afraid I wouldn't be able to make a sound." But the more she sang, "the more people in the audience cried out for joy. As the beat picked up, hands started flying and feet started tapping and folks began to shout all over the great hall."

In 1952, her song "I Can Put My Trust in Jesus" won her a prestigious French award and soon she was touring Europe. By 1954, she had her own television program, "The Mahalia Jackson Show," and was leaving Apollo for Columbia Records. Jazz musician John Hammond warned her at the time, "Mahalia, if you want ads in *Life,* and to be known to the white audience, do it. But if you want to keep on singing for the black audience, forget singing with Columbia, because they don't know the black market at all." But this contract opened up a new world to Mahalia Jackson.

With expanding opportunities, she soon became a wealthy woman, making eight records which sold over a million copies each. Everyone knew her songs, which included "I Believe," "Precious Lord, Take My Hand," "How Great Thou Art," "It's No Secret What God Can Do," "He's Got the Whole World in His Hands," and "When I Wake Up in Glory." Unlike some stars, she managed her money extremely well. Early in her career, Jackson had taken a course in beauty culture at Madame *C.J. Walker's and opened Mahalia's Beauty Salon in Chicago. She bought a florist shop and later opened Mahalia Jackson Chicken Dinners. She invested heavily in real estate and made money. Extravagant spending was never her style; she wanted economic security. Joe Goldberg, the producer of her television show, recalled meeting Jackson at the Garrick Theater in Chicago:

> I expected some sort of Daddy Grace routine, with the Rolls Royce and the ermine and the entourage. There was no one in the theater except a big woman in an old overcoat sitting and eating a bag of popcorn. I asked her if she knew where I would find Miss Jackson. "I'm Mahalia, honey," she said. "Are we gonna work together?"

In 1969, she told Max Jones in London, "I don't work for money. I sing because I love to sing."

Some never forgave Mahalia Jackson for crossing over. Writes Tony Heilbut: "One regrets the transmutation of Mahalia Jackson from shouter to huckster." In the same vein, John Hammond griped: "I grew very disenchanted with Mahalia. She was more talented than anybody, but she wanted to do that phony religious stuff that white folks like." Had she followed their advice, the world would have never enjoyed her marvelous renditions of "Danny Boy," "Silent Night," "Trees," "Summertime," and "The Lord's Prayer." Perhaps this is a debate which can never be settled. Did Mahalia Jackson leave her roots or did she expand them?

The public adored her, buying her records, watching her on television, attending her shows. Jackson never saw a conflict between her faith and her career. Born in poverty, she was glad to be able to afford a decent life. She used her money wisely, establishing the Mahalia Jackson Scholarship Foundation to help others. She also encouraged the careers of **Aretha Franklin** and **Della Reese**. But Jackson was not a politically passive bystander. A strong supporter of the civil-rights movement, she was highly visible during the 1956 bus boycott in Montgomery, Alabama, and delivered her own charged version of "We Shall Overcome." She also sang at President John F. Kennedy's inauguration in 1961, and, as a loyal friend of Martin Luther King, Jr.'s, sang "How I Got Over" in front of the Lincoln Memorial during the 1963 "March on Washington" rally. At King's funeral, she sang his last request, "Precious Lord."

When Mahalia Jackson died in 1972, 40,000 mourners filed past her open coffin in Greater Salem Baptist Church. Because of the size of the crowd, her service was held at Chicago's McCormick Place Convention Center; it was probably the largest funeral ever seen in that city. The international press remembered her accomplishments, and the president of the United States eulogized her. To those who had criticized her for bringing jazz into the church, she had generally responded with scripture: "Oh, clap your hands, all ye people! Shout unto the Lord with the voice of a trumpet!" Gospel songs, she said, made "a joyful noise unto the Lord." Indeed, Mahalia Jackson made a joyful noise.

𝓜ahalia
𝒥ackson

SOURCES:

Anderson, Robert, and Gail North. *Gospel Music Encyclopedia*. NY: Sterling, 1979.

Parachin, Victor M. "Mahalia Jackson," in *American History*. October 1994.

Pleasants, Henry. *The Great American Popular Singers*. NY: Simon and Schuster, 1974.

Smith, Jessie Carney. *Notable Black American Women*. Detroit, MI: Gale Research, 1992.

SUGGESTED READING:

Goreau, Laurraine. *Just Mahalia, Baby*. Gretna, LA: Pelican, 1975.

Jackson, Mahalia, with Evan McLeod Wylie. *Movin' On Up*. NY: Hawthorne, 1966.

Schwerin, Jules. *Got to Tell It: Mahalia Jackson, Queen of Gospel*. Oxford University Press, 1992.

RELATED MEDIA:

Imitation of Life (125 min. film), starring **Lana Turner, **Juanita Moore, **Sandra Dee**, and John Gavin, featured Mahalia Jackson singing "Trouble of the World," Universal, 1959.

Mahalia! (90 min. documentary), produced by Jules Victor Schwerin, 1983 (centers around Jackson's triumphant 1972 Christian musical tour of Europe; songs include "Didn't It Rain").

Mahalia Jackson and *Elizabeth Cotten: Two Remarkable Ladies (58 min. documentary), CBS-Mastervision, 1974.

Mahalia Jackson (34 min, film), produced by Jules Victor Schwerin, 1974.

St. Louis Blues (93 min. film), based on the life and music of W.C. Handy, starring Mahalia Jackson, **Ella Fitzgerald, **Eartha Kitt, **Pearl Bailey, **Ruby Dee, Cab Calloway and Nat King Cole, with costumes by **Edith Head, Paramount, 1958.

John Haag,
Associate Professor of History,
University of Georgia, Athens, Georgia

Jackson, Marjorie (1931—)

Australian runner. Name variations: Marjorie Nelson. Born Marjorie Jackson on September 13, 1931, in Coffs Harbor, New South Wales, Australia; brought up in Lithgow; married Peter Nelson (an Olympic cyclist), in 1953 (died 1977).

Set four world records (1950); won sprints at the Auckland British Empire games (1950); won Olympic gold medals in the 100 meters and 200 meters (1952); tied world and Olympic records in the 100 meters with 11.5 second time (1952); improved the 100-meter mark to 11.4 seconds (1952); set and broke the 200-meter world record with 23.6 second and 23.4 second times (1952); broke the world 100-yard mark three times (1950, 1951, 1958); won gold medals in the 100-yard, 220-yard, and 4x110-yard relay at Vancouver Commonwealth Games (1954).

Australian champion Marjorie Jackson had to prepare for the 1952 Olympics in Helsinki, Finland, in the "Lithgow fog" of New South Wales by lighting up the track with beams from car lights. In 1949, the 18-year-old runner had beaten **Fanny Blankers-Koen in a 100-meter race in Sydney. Having set four world records in 1950, Jackson was known as the Lithgow flash. In Helsinki, she took both sprints, becoming the first Australian woman to win an Olympic gold medal in track and field. She won the 100 meters with a world record 11.5, while her teammate **Shirley Strickland arrived third for the bronze. "It was a terrific moment," said Jackson. "To stand on the dais and know that for fifty-six years you were the first one

to put the flag up there. . . . I always felt that one was for Australia, the second one was for me."

In the 200 meters, Jackson's time was 23.7, tying a 17-year-old record set by **Stella Walsh. Her closest competitor, **Bertha Brouwer** of the Netherlands, was four yards behind her. Jackson's only bad moment was dropping the baton in the 4x100 relay, with the Australians in the lead. The U.S. team, spurred by **Mae Faggs, took the gold, while the Australians came in fifth. On returning home, Jackson was named Australia Broadcasting's Sportsman of the Year, elected to the Helms Hall of Fame in 1952, and was awarded the MBE in 1953. After another successful year in 1954, she retired at 22.

After her husband Peter Nelson, an Olympic cyclist, died of leukemia in 1977, Jackson founded the Peter Nelson Leukaemia Appeal in honor of his courage. Six years later, she had raised about 75% of its million-dollar objective. Jackson saw her talents as a gift from God and felt that lending her famous name to the Appeal was a way of returning that gift.

SOURCES:

Hemery, David. *The Pursuit of Sporting Excellence*. Champaign, IL: Human Kinetics Books, 1986.

Jackson, Nell (1929–1988)

African-American track champion, coach, and educator. Born on July 1, 1929, in Athens, Georgia; died on April 1, 1988, in Vestal, New York; only daughter and middle of three children of Burnette L. Jackson and Wilhemina G. Jackson; graduated from Tuskegee High School, Tuskegee, Alabama; B.S. in physical education from Tuskegee University; M.S. in physical education from Springfield College, Springfield, Massachusetts, 1953; Ph.D. from the University of Iowa, 1962; never married; no children.

Born in 1929 in Athens, Georgia, Nell Jackson grew up in Tuskegee, Alabama, where her family moved when she was a child. A graduate of Tuskegee University, she received a master's degree in physical education from Springfield College in 1953 and a doctorate from the University of Iowa in 1962.

Jackson's interest in athletics began in grade school, where she competed in basketball, tennis, swimming, and track. In eighth grade, she was on the basketball team when the coach noticed her speed on the court and suggested that she go out for track. Jackson specialized in the 200-meter sprint, mainly because women were excluded from long-distance competitions.

"There were a lot of so-called 'studies' around then showing how 'dangerous' it was for women to run longer distances, that they would upset their chemical and physical make up," she explained. "It didn't make a great deal of sense to me, but there was nothing I could do about it." Joining the newly formed Tuskegee Institute Track-and-Field Club, Jackson also ran as anchor on the 400-meter relay team, which won the relay title for five years in a row.

Jackson was one of 11 women track-and-field competitors to win a spot on the 1948 U.S.

Olympic team, though she did not place in her two events—the 200-meter and 400-meter relay. (The women's track-and-field competition was dominated that year by *Fanny Blankers-Koen, the Dutch mother of four who captured four gold medals.) Unfortunately, Jackson reached the height of her competitive career between Olympiads. In 1949, she won the national 200-meter title in 24.2 seconds, beating the 14-year American record by two-tenths of a second. In 1950, she successfully defended her national title, running the dash in 25 seconds. At the first Pan-American games held in Buenos Aires in

Nell
Jackson

1951, Jackson won a silver medal in the 200 meter and a gold in the 400-meter relay. That gold medal became a prized possession. "It wasn't an Olympic medal," she said, "but it still gave me great satisfaction."

After receiving her master's degree in the summer of 1953, Jackson returned to Tuskegee Institute, where she taught physical education and coached the women's track-and-field team from 1954 to 1962. Her outstanding work brought her to the attention of the Olympic Organization, which in 1956 made her the first black woman head coach of an Olympic track-and-field team. At the Melbourne Games that year, she had the satisfaction of seeing one of the Tuskegee women, *Mildred McDaniel, win a gold medal in the high jump with a world-record leap.

Resuming her education at the University of Iowa in 1960, Jackson returned to Tuskegee in 1962 with her Ph.D., rejoining the faculty as an assistant professor of physical education. Her teaching career subsequently took her to Illinois State University and to the University of Illinois at Champaign, where she organized and coached the Illinois Track Club for Girls, the first track-and-field team for women at the university. She also published numerous papers and articles, as well as a highly regarded textbook, *Track and Field for Girls and Women*.

In 1968, Jackson chaired both the U.S. Women's Track and Field and the AAU Women's Track and Field Committees and also served as a member of the board of directors of the U.S. Olympic Committee. In 1972, she was off to Munich to coach another women's track-and-field Olympic team.

In 1973, Jackson was hired as director of women's athletics at Michigan State University, becoming the first black woman to head athletics at a major university. Jackson downplayed the race issue. "I think the people who hired me thought I was the best qualified for the job. I've never had a single problem with any young women athletes I've coached that had anything to do with race." During her tenure at Michigan

Rachel Jackson

State, Jackson expanded women's sports to a full-scale program and quadrupled the budget allotted to women's athletics, though the amount spent was still considerably less than the huge sum spent on men's athletics. Jackson left Michigan State in 1981 to become director of physical education and intercollegiate athletics at the State University of New York (SUNY). She died on April 1, 1988, after a short illness.

SOURCES:

Bortstein, Larry. *After Olympic Glory.* NY: Frederick Warne, 1978.

Smith, Jessie Carney. *Notable Black American Women.* Detroit, MI: Gale Research, 1992.

Barbara Morgan,
Melrose, Massachusetts

Jackson, Rachel Donelson
(1767–1828)

American frontier woman who died shortly before taking her place as first lady of the United States. Name variations: Rachel Robards. Born on June 17, 1767, in Pittsylvania County, Virginia; died on December 22, 1828, in Nashville, Tennessee; fourth daughter and tenth of twelve children of Colonel John Donelson (an iron master and surveyor) and Rachel (Stockley) Donelson; married Lewis Robards, on March 1, 1785, in Harrodsburg, Kentucky (divorced); married Andrew Jackson (7th president of the United States), on August 18, 1791, in Natchez, Mississippi (remarried on January 17, 1794, in Nashville, Tennessee); children: (adopted) Andrew Jackson, Jr.

In March 1829, when Andrew Jackson entered the Capitol building for his inauguration as the seventh president of the United States, he wore a miniature portrait of his wife around his neck and a band of mourning on his sleeve. Rachel Jackson had been buried in her inaugural gown the previous Christmas Eve, victim of a heart attack and the scandal that had punctuated their marriage.

One of 12 children, Rachel was 12 years old when her father John Donelson led 120 Virginians, including his family, on a perilous six-month journey to found a settlement in the Cumberland Basin. After floods and Indian raids destroyed their first encampment near Nashville, the family moved to a farm near Harrodsburg, Kentucky. John Donelson was killed four year later, and the family opened their home as a roadhouse to support themselves.

In 1785, Rachel married Captain Lewis Robards, the son of a prominent local family, and, from all reports, an alcoholic given to drunken periods of unfounded jealousy and rage. In 1788, Robards accused Rachel of returning the advances of another man and sent her back to her family, complaining, "She did not behave with the discretion he had the right to expect." While staying with her mother, Rachel met and befriended Andrew Jackson, then a young lawyer boarding with the Donelsons. Jackson, though attracted to Rachel, kept a respectable distance. Robards came to claim his wife in 1790, but the reconciliation failed, and he filed for divorce. Mistakenly thinking a divorce had been finalized, Rachel and Andrew pursued a courtship and married in 1791, only to learn two years later that the divorce had only been sanctioned, not granted. Robards subsequently completed the proceedings on the grounds that Rachel "doth still live in adultery with another man." The Jacksons quietly remarried in 1794, but questions surrounding Rachel's matrimonial history would persist throughout her life.

While Jackson distinguished himself in the War of 1812 and pursued a political career, Rachel's happiest moments were spent managing the family farm, the Hermitage, near Nashville, Tennessee. Childless, the couple opened their home to the children of Rachel's many relatives, and even raised the sons of friends who had appointed Jackson guardian. They formally adopted a nephew, naming him Andrew Jackson, Jr. Rachel also found comfort in religion, occasioned by her conversion by a frontier Presbyterian minister.

Jackson's successful campaign against John Quincy Adams for the presidency in 1828 provided his enemies with another opportunity to parade the questions surrounding the Jackson marriage before the public, and detractors had a field day. Handbills and newspapers declared Jackson an "immoral homewrecker" and Rachel an "illiterate adulteress." Emotionally wounded by the ordeal, Rachel had little enthusiasm for her upcoming role as first lady. Stricken with a heart attack in Nashville, where she had traveled to purchase her inaugural gown, she died on December 22, 1828, and was buried in a favorite garden spot at the Hermitage. Jackson was buried beside her when he died in 1845.

SOURCES:

Klapthor, Margaret Brown. *The First Ladies.* Washington, DC: The White House Historical Association, 1979.

Melick, Arden David. *Wives of the Presidents.* Maplewood, NJ: Hammond, 1977.

Paletta, LuAnn. *The World Almanac of First Ladies.* NY: World Almanac, 1990.

RELATED MEDIA:

The President's Lady (96 min., b/w film), starring *Susan Hayward* and Charlton Heston, based on Irving Stone's fictionalized account of Rachel Jackson's life, 20th Century-Fox, 1953.

Barbara Morgan,
Melrose, Massachusetts

Jackson, Rebecca Cox (1795–1871)

African-American mystic. Born on February 15, 1795, in Hornstown, Pennsylvania; died in 1871; daughter of Jane Wisson (or Wilson); married Samuel S. Jackson; no children.

A free-born African-American, Rebecca Cox Jackson was born outside of Philadelphia in 1795. What little is known of her early life has been gleaned from her surviving spiritual writings. She knew nothing about her father; her mother was married at least twice before her death in 1808. At that time, Jackson was taken in by her brother Joseph Cox, the minister of an African Methodist Episcopal church in Philadelphia. After her marriage to Samuel S. Jackson, she continued to live with her brother, caring for his four children and earning her own living as a seamstress.

Jackson experienced a dramatic religious conversion at the age of 35, after which she claimed to have dreams or visions in which she could heal the sick, make the sinful holy, speak with angels, and even fly. The conversion and her subsequent dreams led her to flee her husband's bed so as to live a life of "Christian perfection." Jackson was further guided by an inner voice, which, among other directives, led her to leave home "to travel some and speak to the people." At first, she related her visionary experiences and conducted prayer meetings in private homes. During this time, Jackson, who had never attended school, was entirely dependent on her brother for assistance. While mourning her illiteracy, and praying for the gift of reading and writing, she claimed she was answered by God: "And when I looked on the word, I began to read. And when I found I was reading I was frightened—then I could not read one word. I closed my eyes again in prayer and then opened my eyes, began to read."

Jackson's ability to read allowed her access to the revelations of the Bible, through which she defended her practice of "holy living" against intense criticism from her husband, her brother, as well as the clergy of the African Methodist Episcopal church, who objected to women preaching in general and to Jackson's specific renouncement of "the flesh." By 1837, at the height of accusations against her, Jackson requested a formal trial for heresy from Methodist and Presbyterian ministers. When this request was refused, she completely severed her relationship with the church and her family.

Throughout the late 1830s and early 1840s, Jackson traveled through Pennsylvania, northern Delaware, New Jersey, southern New England, and New York, testifying to her powers and preaching. In 1847, she and her friend and disciple, **Rebecca Perot**, joined a Shaker community at Watervliet, near Albany, attracted by the sect's practice of celibacy and their recognition of the motherhood as well as the fatherhood of God. Jackson stayed with the community until 1851, then returned to Philadelphia where she established a small, predominately black and female, Shaker family around the time of the start of the Civil War. Little is known of how the family fared, as Jackson's diary entries ended in 1864. She died in 1871 and was taken to a Shaker community in New Lebanon, New York, for burial. Following Jackson's death, Shakers from the Watervliet and New Lebanon communities visited the Philadelphia family, which apparently survived until as late as 1908.

In 1980, Jackson's writings were collected in a single volume, titled *Gifts of Power*.

SOURCES:
Smith, Jessie Carney. *Notable Black American Women*. Detroit, MI: Gale Research, 1992.

Barbara Morgan,
Melrose, Massachusetts

Jackson, Shirley (1916–1965)

American novelist and short-story writer who gained a reputation as a master of gothic horror and psychological suspense. Born on December 14, 1916, in San Francisco, California; died on August 8, 1965, in North Bennington, Vermont; daughter of Leslie Jackson and Geraldine (Bugbee) Jackson; attended Syracuse University; married Stanley Edgar Hyman (a critic), on August 13, 1940; children: Laurence Hyman (b. 1942); Joanne Hyman (b. 1945); Sarah Hyman (b. 1948); Barry Hyman (b. 1951).

Began writing at an early age, composing poetry and short stories by the time she graduated from high school; enrolled as an English major at Syracuse University (1937); published nearly 20 pieces in the school humor magazine, became its fiction editor, and established a literary magazine before her graduation (1940); married (1940) and moved with husband to North Bennington, Vermont (1945); wrote her most famous short story, "The Lottery," which was published amid much controversy in The New Yorker *(1948).*

Selected writings: published six novels and some 45 short stories, including The Haunting of Hill House *(1959);* We Have Always Lived in the Castle *(1962); (autobiographical)* Life Among the Savages *(1953); (autobiographical)* Raising Demons; *(never before published short stories compiled by two of her children)* Just an Ordinary Day *(Bantam, 1997).*

One late spring day in 1948, a curious short story—only nine pages long, less than 5,000 words—arrived on the fiction editor's desk at *The New Yorker* from an author whose work the magazine had been publishing for five years. It was immediately obvious that this new story was the best thing submitted by the writer to date, but its subject matter was so disturbing and its effect so chilling that the magazine felt obliged to offer additional space in which the author could explain her reasons for writing it. The author declined. "It's just a story," she said. But "The Lottery" would unleash a flood of shocked letters and telephone calls to the magazine and catapult Shirley Jackson to national attention from the remote obscurity of rural Vermont, which had provided the story's setting and, more ominously, its preoccupation with lurking disorder and creeping evil.

Jackson had been painfully aware since early childhood of the sense, as she once described it, "of a human and not very rational order struggling inadequately to keep in check forces of great destruction." It was a peculiar way to view the prosperous San Francisco enclave of Ashbury Park, where Shirley was born on December 14, 1916, to Leslie and **Geraldine Bugbee Jackson**. While her mother was solidly upper-middle class and grimly dedicated to its social rituals and privileges, Leslie Jackson's background may have provided the early nourishment for his daughter's troubling visions of chaos held barely at bay. The Jacksons of San Francisco had originally been the Henchalls of England but had been forced from their homeland in the 1890s by a scandal so ruinous that they had lost not only their name but their considerable fortune. Although the trouble had arisen when Leslie was just a small boy, it remained a forbidden topic at the time of Shirley's birth and a mystery to her as an adult.

Geraldine had become pregnant almost immediately after her marriage in March 1916 and was not prepared for the rigors of child-rearing or the restless, high-strung daughter to which she gave birth. She had been expecting a quiet, obedient girl destined for the debutante balls and sorority parties which had been a part of her own upbringing. Mother and daughter were so markedly different that Shirley's brother Barry, born almost two years later, thought Shirley's arrival in the world had been "like a goldfish giving birth to a porpoise." Like the hidden troubles of her father's family, the emotional distance between Shirley and her mother would eventually work its way onto the page. Almost all of Jackson's fictional heroines would be outsiders who somehow never fit in.

Geraldine's sense that her daughter was somehow different deepened when Shirley began describing to her the "strange man with a beard" that only she could see or the odd music she would hear wafting through the California sunshine. "How can anyone handle things if her head is full of voices and her world is full of things no one else can see?" one of Jackson's characters wonders in her unfinished novel *Come Along With Me*, and Geraldine may have wondered the same thing. Then, too, there was Shirley's passionate attraction to writing and reading, a predilection not immediately obvious elsewhere in her family. By the time her father had prospered well enough as an executive at a label-making company to move his family to the manicured San Francisco suburb of Burlingame, his daughter could always be found in her room with a book or scribbling on a pad. "Writing," Jackson said many years later, "used to be a delicious, private thing, done in my own room with the door locked, in constant terror of the maternal knock and the summons to bed."

In 1933, Jackson's father was assigned to oversee the merger of his company with another in Rochester, New York. The move to Rochester was important in several ways, not the least of which was its effect on Shirley's deepening sense of isolation as she entered a strange high school in a cold climate for her last year of public education. Particularly hurtful was Jackson's rejection for membership in a sorority that had at first seemed to accept her. "Shirley . . . wasn't what they used to call a 'popular' type of girl," one of her classmates recalled. "I think she never learned the techniques of being a more accepted person." Her writing became an even more critical sanctuary; Jackson lost herself for hours each day in a flurry of short stories and sketches, many of them with a strong element of the supernatural. Witchcraft held a special fascination for her. She found in the supernatural a convenient "shorthand statement of the possibilities of human adjustment to what seems at best to be an inhuman world," Jackson would later write. By the time she had enrolled at the University of Rochester in 1934, she had invented on the page an entire pantheon of ghostly figures and sinister personalities drawn from folklore. The half-satyr,

half-human Pan was a particular favorite, as well as the French folklore character Harlequin, introduced to Jackson by a French exchange student who became a close friend and who encouraged her writing as a balm for her loneliness.

Jackson dropped out of college after two years, perhaps anticipating a pending dismissal due to poor grades, but continued to pour out a thousand words a day amid rumors that she had suffered a mild breakdown. During the summer of 1937, however, Jackson announced she had applied to Syracuse University, the nearest college to the University of Rochester. Although her parents were concerned about its reputation for leftist politics, the school's chief attractions for Shirley were its strong journalism and creative writing departments, its respected student newspaper, and its widely read humor magazine, *The Syracusan*. Her hopes for the school proved well-founded, for she had at last discovered a place filled with others who felt as passionately about writing as she did and who accepted her into their circle. Even this group, however, felt there was something different about Jackson. "She was a little more mystical than the rest of us," one of them remembered, while another thought that, at times, Shirley seemed to become overexcited, nearly hysterical, for no apparent reason. "She would get very shrill, words would come tumbling out," this particular acquaintance said, recalling how at these moments Shirley would ask somebody to hit her and calm her down.

I could see what the cat saw.

—Shirley Jackson

Jackson's first published work appeared in her sophomore year at Syracuse. "Janice," a one-page dialogue in which the title character describes a suicide attempt to a friend, was unlike anything else in the collection of works from one of her writing classes that was passed around campus in March of 1938. While her classmates' characters epitomized lofty idealism or socialist dogma, Jackson's character talks of locking herself in the garage and turning on the car engine. Among the many admirers of "Janice" was a fellow student named Stanley Edgar Hyman, one of a group of radical intellectuals much talked about on campus, and one of the school's few Jews. A devoted socialist from a poor Brooklyn family, Hyman was as extroverted and boisterous as Jackson was introspective and secretive, but nonetheless the two fell in love. "It was nuclear fission," a mutual friend described their first meeting, "and after that, everything was different. Once she met him, she became completely involved."

Hyman's influence on Jackson's writing was apparent to all who knew her, for Hyman took her literary development in hand by choosing her reading lists and her professors and introducing her to new styles of expressive writing. "He talked a lot, but she wrote better all the time," one of the faculty noted of this period. "His essays were blustering, polemical—hers were more literate." Jackson's work was published frequently in *The Syracusan* to much admiration, and by 1939 she had been named fiction editor of the magazine—a short-lived appointment, as it turned out, when the university administration decided to cease publication. Undaunted, Shirley and Stanley convinced the school to sponsor a new fiction magazine which they called *The Spectre,* of which Jackson was again the editor. In one year and four issues, the magazine managed to become the talk of the campus for its sexually liberal content and artwork, and, under Hyman's influence, its frank and often angry discussions of racism and anti-Semitism. The last straw for the college administration was the magazine's scathing review, written by Jackson, of a volume of poetry published by one of the most-respected members of the college's faculty. *The Spectre* was summarily closed down.

In her senior year, Jackson sported a two-dollar ring bought at a thrift shop as a defense against the fact that she and Hyman were living together. She told friends that Hyman was responsible for holding her insanity at bay, despite frequent arguments over Hyman's philandering. Both of them dealt as best they could with the objections of their respective families to their relationship. Hyman's orthodox father disowned him for his consorting with a non-Jew, while the Jackson family's middle-class anti-Semitism was compounded by their displeasure with Hyman's socialism.

After graduating from Syracuse in June of 1940 (Hyman magna cum laude), the couple defied both sets of parents and moved to New York's Greenwich Village, long the favored nesting site for East Coast political and creative malcontents. Jackson took a job writing commercials for a radio station and, later, selling books at Macy's. Hyman found work at a factory that manufactured shoulder straps until he was offered a position as an editorial assistant at *The New Republic* after winning an essay contest with an article lampooning Charles Lindbergh's political conservatism. With the steady income the job provided, the two were married in a civil ceremony at a friend's apartment on August 13, 1940.

No one gave the marriage much of a chance, and not only because of Hyman's continued casual affairs with other women. While Hyman found New York exhilarating, Jackson found it oppressive and threatening, developing a particular phobia of pieces of buildings falling off and crushing her. The couple's precarious finances troubled her, too. She complained loudly to friends about Hyman's frugality and his insistence, for example, on "using the same coffee grounds for three days running. And who ever heard," she further pointed out, "of giving up smoking!," a habit she would refuse to abandon throughout her life. Of some comfort was the intellectual stimulation of their circle of literary friends, Ralph Ellison among them, and the lively discussions of the approaching war in Europe that went on long into the evenings. After a year in which making a living overshadowed their dreams of literary careers, Jackson convinced Hyman to spend 12 months living in the country on their meager savings to allow both of them the time to write. Her instincts were right. When she and Hyman returned to New York a year later from their rented cabin in Keene, New Hampshire, Jackson had published her first short story in *The New Republic,* while Hyman had landed a job as a staff writer at *The New Yorker* and had begun to get his own literary critiques into print.

The couple's first child, a son they named Laurence, was born in October of 1942, shortly after their return to New York. "Laurie," as they took to calling him, provided a further anchor for Jackson's troubled flights of imagination and would become a leading character in the two humorous autobiographical works Shirley would in publish in later years. It seemed, in fact, that the demands of motherhood acted as a catalyst for Jackson's writing career, for the next year marked the beginning of her long relationship with *The New Yorker,* which had published eight of her short stories by the time Laurie was two years old. Although the supernatural element was missing, these early stories still revolved around something unexpected disrupting everyday middle-class life. "After You, My Dear Alphonse," for example, is about a boy from a placid, white, conservative suburb, not unlike Burlingame or Ashbury Park, who brings a black friend home for lunch; while "Come Dance With Me in Ireland" concerns three refined society women who are verbally abused by a tramp to whom they have ministered as part of their charity work. As the reputations of Jackson and her husband grew, invitations to the couple's parties became much sought after by the Greenwich Village elite, who delighted in the word games invented by their

Shirley Jackson

hosts and in the mischief of Shirley's presentations at the dining table, including steaks dyed blue served with red-tinted mashed potatoes.

Jackson was pregnant with their second child in early 1945 when Hyman received an offer of a teaching position in the literature department of Bennington College in Vermont. By the time their daughter Joanne was born in November of that year, Jackson and Hyman had rented a rambling old 14-room house in the village of North Bennington, Shirley insisting that they live off campus and in the midst of what she saw as a promising field of study for her fiction. Even though the Bennington campus and its relative cosmopolitanism was less than a mile away over twisting country roads, North Bennington was populated exclusively by the type of white, middle-class Christians who were the chief characters of Jackson's fiction, inhabiting a world narrowly bound by agricultural cycles, church festivals and a deep suspicion of outsiders. Jackson had, in fact, succeeded in casting herself as one of her early fictional heroines, out of step and an uneasy fit with the world around her.

But the fascinations of her new environment, the eccentric charms of the house Jackson described as "old, and noisy, and full" and the rigors of running a household that now included a three-year-old and a newborn, captured Shirley's spirit and her creative instincts. The house soon filled with books, cats and old furniture, she wrote, and "the paraphernalia of our living—sandwich bags, typewriters, little wheels off things." She produced a stream of amusing short pieces about their life in Vermont for *Good Housekeeping* and other magazines directed at women and, more important, began work on a novel, *The Road Through the Wall*, which appeared in 1948 to critical praise but only moderate sales. The book, a troubling coming-of-age story, presented two young girls—one overweight and unpopular, the other equally an outcast for being a Jew. Jackson readily admitted that the two characters were different aspects of herself and that the story was drawn from her memories of Burlingame and her family's conformist ethic. "The first book is the book you have to write to get back at your parents," she said in later years. "Once you get that out of your way, you can start writing books." But it was her short story "The Lottery" that cleared the way for her later success.

"She's written a real masterpiece," Hyman told one of his college associates, "and I don't know where it came from." But tales abound of just how Jackson came to write her dark, powerful story of a ritual stoning in a small farming village. Jackson herself said she got the idea from a book her husband gave her about ancient rites of human sacrifice, but also told one of her college professors who wrote to congratulate her on the story that the idea had come to her during one of his folklore classes. Hyman, on the other hand, preferred to say that Jackson had written the story during a gap in a bridge game in which she held the dummy hand and had little to do. Even the villagers of North Bennington got into the act, allowing a rumor that several school-boys had once thrown stones at Shirley to spread unchecked. (In fact, Jackson recounts in *Life Among the Savages* an incident in which her son Laurie supposedly threw a stone at a school bully.) Jackson skated closer to the truth in saying that the idea for the story had been born from an overheard anti-Semitic comment delivered by a local shopkeeper. Although the villagers treated the Hymans with polite respect to their faces, certain elements resented the presence of the flamboyant city folk in their midst; certain others harbored outright hatred of the Hymans because of Stanley's Judaism and because of Shirley's well-known interest in the occult. One village woman regularly dumped her trash in the Hymans' hedges; soaped swastikas would sometimes appear on their windows; and there was the usual hate mail warning them to leave. "We were kind of aliens in our hometown," **Sarah Hyman**, born in October of 1948, recalled after her mother's death. "We were disliked, each of us in our own way."

But "The Lottery," whatever its specific genesis, is entirely in keeping with Jackson's earlier work, before the move to rural Vermont. The story's brisk, deceptively sunny prose barely conceals the horror which bursts through in its last paragraphs, as the villagers crowd around the annual victim chosen by lottery and Old Man Warner hurls the first stone, urging "Come on, come on, everyone" to the others. The story, complained hundreds of *The New Yorker*'s readers after receiving their issues for June 26, 1948, was in "incredibly bad taste" and was "a new low in human viciousness." A reader from Toronto warned the magazine to "tell Miss Jackson to stay out of Canada!," while another demanded a personal apology from the author and yet another sniffed, "We would expect something like this in *Esquire*, but *not* in *The New Yorker*." Jackson was still receiving letters about the story 15 years after its publication, its notoriety ensuring it was included in several collections of her short fiction issued during her most prolific years. It is the story for which she is still chiefly remembered. If her goal in writing it was, as she told an interviewer some years after its first appearance, "to shock the readers with a graphic dramatization of the pointless violence and general inhumanity in their own lives," she certainly succeeded.

Except for a two-year stay in Westport, Connecticut, where Stanley Hyman briefly moved his family to be closer to his beloved New York, Shirley would enjoy her new-found celebrity from the relative isolation of North Bennington. The birth of her son Barry in November of 1951 may have added to the general confusion of the raucous Hyman household and its air of, as one visitor put it, a "genial mess," but Jackson's creative powers seemed to thrive all the more. Her writing continued to serve as a potent outlet for the fears and paranoia that still troubled her dreams and her few private moments—so much so that one reviewer thought portions of her 1951 novel *Hangsaman* were as "strange and obscure as nightmares of a mad psychoanalyst." Jackson explored multiple personalities in 1954's *The Bird's Nest,* her most commercially successful novel to that point and the first to be translated to the screen as 1957's *Lizzie* (which had the misfortune to be released at the same time as *The Three Faces of Eve*), and delved once again into the hidden horrors of a small town in *The Sundial,* written after Jackson's vituperative campaign against a teacher her children accused of physically abusing them turned most of North Bennington against her and her family. In between the novels, she produced her two autobiographical works, *Life Among the Savages* and *Raising Demons.* Both were praised for their wry humor, and few remarked on the underlying scenes of hostile outsiders and threatened chaos that were Jackson's trademarks. Jackson merely chose to apply a humorous veneer to these two works, producing what one critic thought was "a fine lemon flavor, nothing of the chocolate cream." In the fall of 1959, Jackson published her best-known work after "The Lottery," *The Haunting of Hill House.* She spent nearly a year researching haunted houses and ghosts in general before writing the novel, noticing that while hardly anyone she asked had actually seen a ghost, most people were afraid they *might* if they were not careful. *The Haunting of Hill House* plays so skillfully on this sense of nervous expectancy that Stephen King later called it the greatest horror novel ever written and dedicated his own *Firestarter* to the woman he said "never had to raise her voice" to produce her effects. The book was a bestseller and became a successful MGM film, 1963's *The Haunting,* directed by Robert Wise, and starring *Julie Harris** and **Claire Bloom.**

Amid all the praise, Jackson's struggles with both her mental and physical health were known only to her family. Her weight had always been problematical, but by the time she began work on her last complete novel she had ballooned to over 200 pounds, suffered from arthritis in her fingers, and was increasingly troubled by asthma. She had also come to depend on tranquilizers for the episodes of acute anxiety that were becoming more frequent and which made concentrating on her writing difficult. *We Have Always Lived in the Castle,* published in the summer of 1962, took her three laborious years to produce and left her emotionally exhausted. "It's exactly like having one of the kids leave home," she said when it was finished. The book tells the story of two sisters living in a large house in the now familiar village, one of whom, it is suggested, has killed their parents. Increasingly estranged from the outside world, the sisters end up trapped and alone in the house in which they will probably die. It was a theme at which Jackson had begun to hint in *The Haunting of Hill House,* where Eleanor Vance comes to believe she is "disappearing inch by inch into this house" and eventually becomes one of its ghosts. With the publication of *We Have Always Lived in the Castle,* Jackson, too, felt herself unable to break free of her own demons. One of her husband's numerous affairs which she discovered at this point only made things worse. By Thanksgiving of 1962, Jackson was terrified to leave the house. "Sometimes she'd make it out to the car, intending to go to the store," her daughter Sarah later remembered, "but then she'd grip the steering wheel and start to cry. The fear of people is a real thing."

For the next three months, Jackson refused to set foot outside. Her confused diary entries during this time indicate that the most troubling aspect of her illness was her inability to work. "i used to be able to write but no one even thinks of me anymore when it's writing no one includes me," she typed in a desperate rush on one page. "i am a writer i used to be a good writer and now no one even stanley says to students that i used to be." Finally, early in 1963, Jackson agreed to see a psychoanalyst in New York, who diagnosed what he saw as a classic case of "acute anxiety." Slowly, the darkness seemed to retreat, although her physical condition changed little. "One day I am fine," she wrote in her journal many months later, "the next depressed and desolate, with no cause at all." But she forced herself back into the world, starting with brief shopping trips to the village, then by inviting friends for lunch or dinner and, at last, by starting a new novel, its relatively bright tone in marked contrast to the despair and gloom of *We Have Always Lived in the Castle.* On the afternoon of August 8, 1965, Jackson lay down for her usual afternoon nap but failed to respond when one of her daughters came to wake her for dinner. She had died of a heart attack as she slept.

Her last short story, "The Possibility of Evil," appeared in the *Saturday Evening Post* four months later. In 1968, Stanley Hyman published her uncollected short fiction and the completed portions of her last novel as *Come Along With Me.* The finished segments of Jackson's last book display her usual preoccupation with the supernatural, but this time there is a lightheartedness to her story, as if she had finally come to terms with her inner turmoil. The last words of her diary, too, indicate a new-found peace. "Laughter is possible," she had written, "laughter is possible laughter is possible. . . ."

SOURCES:

Jackson, Shirley. *Life Among the Savages.* NY: Farrar, Straus and Young, 1953.

Lethem, Jonathan. "Monstrous Acts and Little Murders," in *Salon Magazine.* January 1997.

Oppenheimer, Judy. *Private Demons: The Life of Shirley Jackson.* NY: Putnam, 1988.

RELATED MEDIA:

The Haunting, film starring Julie Harris and Claire Bloom, directed by Robert Wise, MGM, 1963.

The Haunting (1 hr., 53 min.), film starring **Lili Taylor**, **Catherine Zeta-Jones**, and Liam Neeson, Dreamworks Home Entertainment, 1999.

Lizzie (81 min. film), based on the novel *The Bird's Nest,* starring *Eleanor Parker, Richard Boone, and *Joan Blondell, MGM, 1957.

Wanda Jackson

We Have Always Lived in the Castle (play) opened at the Ethel Barrymore Theater in October 1966, starring **Shirley Knight.**

Norman Powers,
writer-producer, Chelsea Lane Productions,
New York, New York

Jackson, Wanda (1937—)

American rockabilly singer of the late 1950s and 1960s. Born Wanda Lavonne Jackson in Maud, Oklahoma, on October 20, 1937; married Wendell Goodman.

Selected LPs: Rockin' with Wanda *(Capitol, 1960);* Two Sides of Wanda *(Capitol, 1964);* Reckless Love Affair *(Capitol, 1965);* You'll Always Have My Love *(Capitol, 1967);* Many Moods of Wanda *(Capitol, 1969);* Portrait *(Capitol, 1970);* A Woman Lives for Love *(Capitol, 1970);* Praise the Lord *(Capitol, 1973);* Country Gospel *(Word, 1974);* When It's Time to Fall in Love *(Myrrh, 1975–76);* Now I Have Everything *(Myrrh, 1975–76);* Make Me Like a Child Again *(Myrrh, 1975–76);* I'll Still Love You *(DJM, 1977);* Closer to Jesus *(Word, 1978);* Greatest Hits *(Gusto, 1979);* Let's Have a Party *(Charly UK, 1986).*

The undisputed queen of the hybrid musical genre known as rockabilly, Wanda Jackson was known for a trademark style that, according to one observer, sometimes sounded like she had "gargled with nitroglycerine." Born in 1937, Jackson learned to play the piano and guitar as a youngster and hosted a radio show on Oklahoma's station KLPR when she was 13. After high school, she toured with Hank Thompson and his Brazos Valley Boys and with Elvis Presley, who, along with Gene Vincent of "Be-Bop-A-Lula" fame, influenced her later style. In 1954, she signed her first recording contract with Decca, and had her first hit with "You Can't Have My Love," a duet with bandleader Billy Gray that reached number eight on the country and western chart.

Jackson switched to Capitol in 1956 and made her mark with "Let's Have a Party," a hit in both the United States and Great Britain. Also notable were renditions of "Mean Mean Man" (one of several songs she wrote), "Right or Wrong," and "In the Middle of a Heartache." Jackson was also popular in Holland, Germany, and Japan and cut versions of some of her hit songs, like the explosive "Fujiyama Mama," in three languages. As the rockabilly craze faded, she returned to country music, and with her husband Wendell Goodman and her own band, The Party Timers, had a series of hits during the

1960s. During the 1970s, Jackson moved into gospel, although she continued to perform her old favorites on tour. "My lifestyle is a Christian lifestyle," she explained, "but I have no problems doin' those early rock things."

Barbara Morgan,
Melrose, Massachusetts

Jackson, Zina Garrison (b. 1963).

See Garrison, Zina.

Jackson-Coppin, Fanny (1837–1913).

See Coppin, Fanny Jackson.

Jackson of Lodsworth, Baroness (1914–1981).

See Ward, Barbara.

Jaclard, Anna (1843–1887).

See Kovalevskaya, Sophia for sidebar.

Jacob, Mary Phelps (1892–1970).

See Crosby, Caresse.

Jacob, Rosamund (1888–1960)

Irish journalist, author, and campaigner on feminist, nationalist, pacifist and humanitarian issues. Name variations: Rose or Rosa Jacob; (pseudonym) F. Winthrop. Born Rosamund Jacob in 1888 in County Waterford, Ireland; died in Dublin on October 11, 1960; never married; no children.

Selected writings: Callaghan (1920); The Rise of the United Irishmen (1937); The Rebel's Wife (1957); The Raven's Glen (1960).

Born in 1888 into a County Waterford Quaker family, Rosamund Jacob inherited a tradition of social concern, a strong sense of justice, and independence of mind. Arriving in Dublin in the first decade of the 20th century, she was quickly drawn into the multiplicity of movements which characterized the city during those years. As a convinced feminist, she was inevitably attracted to the suffrage campaign, becoming a member of the militant Irish Women's Franchise League, founded in 1908 by *Margaret Cousins and *Hanna Sheehy-Skeffington, and contributing regularly to the IWFL journal, *The Irish Citizen*. Simultaneously, Jacob developed an enthusiasm for the revival of Gaelic music and culture, and became involved in nationalist politics. She was a prominent member of the nationalist women's organization, Cumann na mBan, and of the separatist nationalist party, Sinn Fein, and was a leading defender of feminist claims to equal representation within an independent state. As

one of the few women delegates to the Sinn Fein Convention of October 1917, Jacob was instrumental in achieving a tacit commitment to female suffrage, which was honored when in 1922 the Irish Free State guaranteed political rights on an equal basis to all citizens.

With the signing of the Anglo-Irish Treaty in 1921, there was a split in the nationalist movement between those who accepted, and those who opposed, the agreement. On the outbreak of civil war in 1922, Jacob was selected as a member of a women's peace committee which met representatives from both the government and anti-Treaty sides in an unsuccessful effort to achieve a ceasefire. She was resolutely opposed to the Treaty and in early 1923 was briefly imprisoned for her republican activities.

The defeat of the anti-Treaty forces left Rosa disillusioned with mainstream nationalist politics, and from the mid-1920s she devoted herself to republican causes and to other campaigns, including the Women's International League for Peace and Freedom (WILPF), which had been founded in 1915 with the objective of abolishing war and promoting peaceful cooperation between nations. With her longtime friend and colleague **Lucy Kingston**, Jacob represented Ireland at the 1921 International Congress of WILPF in Vienna and, as secretary of the Irish branch, played a leading part in the organization of the fifth International Congress, which took place in Dublin in July 1926. As the first international gathering to be held in the Irish Free State since independence, the conference succeeded in drawing together the opposing parties in Ireland, when the Taoiseach (prime minister), W.T. Cosgrave, and the anti-Treaty leader, Eamon de Valera, both attended its opening session, the first occasion on which the two had appeared together in public since the outbreak of the civil war.

Throughout the following decades, Jacob was associated with a range of feminist, humanitarian, animal welfare and radical causes. She was, for instance, a member of the Irish Women Citizens' Association (IWCA), founded in 1923 to monitor the condition and status of women in the new Irish state, and was involved in Hanna Sheehy-Skeffington's short-lived women's political party, the Women's Social and Progressive League. As a member of the IWCA and of the Irish Housewives Association (IHA), with which the IWCA merged in 1947, she lent her support to campaigns for improved health care for women and children, equal pay, and the encouragement of women in public life. During the 1957 General Election, she canvassed vigorously in her own area on behalf of a candidate nominated by the IHA. Though unsuccessful, the experience has been described by the historian of the association as a valuable experience, which "drew attention to the need for representation of women by women and the gross imbalance of the sexes in government."

In addition to these commitments, Jacob maintained a career as a journalist and author. In 1920, she published her first novel, *Callaghan,* under a pseudonym, F. Winthrop; two other works, *The Rise of the United Irishmen* (1937) and *The Rebel's Wife* (1957), dealt with events in Irish history. The former was described by the critic Stephen Gwynne as "a work of real importance" which "no student of the period . . . can neglect," while *The Rebel's Wife,* the story of **Matilda Tone,** made a useful contribution to the slender body of writing on Irish women's history.

The Raven's Glen (1960) was a children's book set in the Dublin mountains. The book reflected her love of children and of the area, where she often went on walking expeditions. Among those whom she befriended was the young Owen Sheehy-Skeffington, Hanna's son. A noted liberal himself, Owen was later to acknowledge Jacob's influence, describing her as "a realistic romantic, unafraid to see nobility in human beings, undismayed by human turpitude."

In 1959, Rosa Jacob suffered a deep personal loss when her beloved brother Tom died. Not long afterwards, on September 25, 1960, she was hit by a car while walking in Dublin and died in the hospital on October 11. The large attendance at her funeral included delegates from the many groups and individuals with whom she had been associated, as well as an emissary of President Eamon de Valera. It was, as Lucy Kingston noted, an appropriately "representative" farewell for one whose life had been given to so many causes, but which had been consistent in its moral integrity and in its commitment to public service.

SOURCES:

Sheehy-Skeffington, Andree. "A coterie of lively suffragists," in *Writers, Raconteurs and Notable Feminists.* Edited by Alf MacLochlainn and Andree Sheehy-Skeffington. Dublin: National Library of Ireland Society, 1993.

———. *Skeff: The Life of Owen Sheehy-Skeffington.* Dublin: Lilliput Press, 1991.

Swanton, Daisy Lawrenson. *Emerging from the Shadow: The Lives of Sarah Anne Lawrenson and Lucy Olive Kingston.* Dublin: Attic Press, 1994.

Tweedy, Hilda. *A Link in the Chain.* Dublin: Attic Press, 1992.

Ward, Margaret. *In Their Own Voice: Women and Irish Nationalism.* Dublin: Attic Press, 1995.

Rosemary Raughter,
freelance writer in women's history, Dublin, Ireland

Jacoba.

Variant of Jacqueline.

Jacoba di Settesoli (d. about 1273)

Saint. Name variations: Jacqueline of Settesoli; Saint Jacoba. Died around 1273; married Gratian Frangipini; children: two sons. Her feast day is February 8.

As a loyal friend, Jacoba di Settesoli was second only to *Clare of Assisi in the eyes St. Francis of Assisi. Francis, who met the Roman noblewoman around 1212, affectionately called her "Brother Jacoba." She was the widow of Gratian Frangipini and would have undoubtedly entered the religious life following the death of her husband had she not had been left with two sons to care for. As it was, she entered the third order (the lay branch of the religious order).

Known for her intelligence and vitality, Jacoba often entertained the Poverello (poor man) during his visits to Rome, preparing for him a cream confection called *motairol,* made of almonds, sugar, and other ingredients ground with a mortar and pestle. To thank her for her hospitality, he presented her with the gift of a lamb, which, according to St. Bonaventure, "seemed to have been educated by him in the spiritual life." The lamb gently awakened Jacoba for devotions and followed her to church, remaining by her side while she prayed. Just before his death, the Poverello sent a note to Jacoba saying: "Set out then as soon as possible, if you wish to see me once more. Bring with you what is necessary for my burial, and some of the good things which you gave me to eat when I was sick in Rome." Following his instructions, Jacoba brought to him a burial veil, a cushion on which his head would rest on the bier, and a sheet of haircloth to cover his body. She also brought the confection he desired, although he could manage only a taste.

Jacoba, who survived her children and grandchildren, spent her last years in Assisi to be close to those who had known St. Francis. Following her death, she was buried in the Great Umbrian basilica, not far from her dear friend.

Jacoba of Bavaria (1401–1436).

See Jacqueline of Hainault.

Jacoba von Beijeren (1401–1436).

See Jacqueline of Hainault.

Jacobi, Lotte (1896–1990)

German-born American photographer, a major figure in the history of photography, whose portraits of many of the greatest individuals of the 20th century are an archive of the modern age. Born Johanna Alexandra Jacobi on August 17, 1896, in Thorn, West Prussia, Germany (now Torun, Poland); died in Concord, New Hampshire, in May 6, 1990; daughter of Sigismund Jacobi and Marie (Mia) Lublinski Jacobi; sister of Alexander and Ruth Jacobi; received honorary doctorate in fine arts from the University of New Hampshire, 1974; married Siegbert Fritz Honig; married Erich Reiss; children: (first marriage) one son, Jochen (known as John Frank Hunter after emigrating to the United States).

Headed a photography studio in Berlin (1927–35) and photographed many of the brilliant personalities of the Weimar Republic; fled Nazism (1935) and continued career in America.

Lotte Jacobi came from a premier family of photographers. In the early 1840s, her great-grandfather went to Paris to learn about photography from the new sensation's inventor, Louis Daguerre. Sensing a promising business opportunity, he purchased equipment and a license to use the Daguerre process, returning to Germany and a successful lifelong career as a photographer. Her grandfather and father also became professional photographers. "I was born to photography," said Jacobi.

She was born in 1896 in Thorn, West Prussia, and grew up in Posen (now Poznan, Poland) in a supportive, assimilated German-Jewish family. Delighting her parents (and annoying her brother and sister) with early signs of intellectual independence, Lotte showed an interest in working at her father's photography studio by age 12. Sigismund Jacobi allowed her to assist him with making wet plates for reproductions. She also observed the manner in which he sensitized his own paper, because the photographic paper commercially available was not up to Jacobi studio standards.

Before long, she expressed a desire for her own camera. Fine, said Sigismund, but first she would have to make her own, a pinhole camera; with his assistance, she built one and set about making prints. Her efforts, long lost, were the best photographs she ever made, she would later claim. Her enthusiasm for photography contin-

Lotte Jacobi (self-portrait, 1930)

ued to grow, and within a year her father presented her with a 12-cm. Erneman camera. Although for a short period during her late teens Jacobi hoped to become an actress, she was fated for a future in photography. She did, however, retain a strong fascination with the stage, an interest that would be revived when she moved to Berlin. For the next few years, she continued taking photographs for her own private pleasure. In 1916, she appeared to have chosen a life of domesticity, marrying Siegbert Fritz Honig, the son of a prosperous Posen merchant. A son Jochen (later known as John Frank Hunter) was born to the couple, who had a troubled marriage from the start. Lotte and Siegbert separated for the last time in 1924, and their divorce was finalized in 1926.

Life for the Jacobi family changed dramatically in 1921 when Posen became part of the newly established Republic of Poland. Lotte moved to Berlin with her family, where the Jacobi photo studio, which her father had established in the German capital some years earlier, prospered as the German economy began to revive. With the end of her marriage, Lotte decided to train professionally as a photographer, enrolling at Munich's Bavarian State Academy for Photography. She studied various aspects of photography and film, working closely with the noted photographer **Hanna Seewald**. In 1927, with the completion of her studies, Jacobi moved back to Berlin where she began working at her father's studio.

> *I* am opinionated. I am a born rebel and a troublemaker.

> —Lotte Jacobi

Berlin in the 1920s was a virtual festival of the arts. The Weimar spirit, bursting with the energies of modernity, would leave its mark on the remainder of the 20th century. As a talented young photographer and theater enthusiast, Jacobi found herself moving in the most brilliant circles in town. The quality of her work came to the attention of older photographers, including Otto Renger-Patsch who would serve as her patron. She would photograph most of the leading artistic and intellectual personalities of Germany during the next six years, including Albert Einstein, *Käthe Kollwitz, Kurt Weill, *Lotte Lenya, Bertolt Brecht, Gerhart Hauptmann, Heinrich Mann, Karl Valentin and ◄ Liesl Karlstadt, George Grosz, Carl von Ossietzky, Lion Feuchtwanger, Fritz Lang, Karl Kraus, Erwin Piscator, Emil Jannings and Peter Lorre. These portraits captured the essence of the sitters, who are often caught slightly off-guard. Displaying a quasi-snapshot quality which looks to have been achieved with ease, these works are in fact the result of immense skill and talent.

Jacobi purchased an Ermanox 9x12 cm. camera in 1928, one of the newest and best cameras then on the German market. Fitted with a 16.5 cm. Ernostar 1:1.8 lens, it was the fastest available, and only nine of these extraordinary made-to-order instruments were ever produced. One reason for this acquisition was the camera's performance during live theater events. Among the many historic evenings in German theater history that Jacobi documented was the premiere performance of *Marieluise Fleisser's *Pioneers in Ingolstadt*. She was also on hand to photograph the premiere performance of Bertolt Brecht and Kurt Weill's *Die Dreigroschenoper* (*The Threepenny Opera*).

Although not active in party politics during the Weimar Republic, Jacobi followed political developments with great interest and was sympathetic to the Left. Many of the artists she photographed, and whose circles she moved in, were Communists or sympathetic to Communism. Starting in 1930, when Adolf Hitler's Nazis began taking center stage in German public life, many saw Marxism as the only realistic alternative to fascism. During these years, a pilgrimage to Moscow was virtually obligatory for the world's anti-fascists. While Jacobi was again in the Soviet Union during the summer of 1930, Italian-born photographer *Tina Modotti became an acquaintance and offered use of her studio darkroom in Moscow. Jacobi also organized an exhibition of Modotti's work in her own studio during her fellow photographer's brief sojourn in Berlin.

During 1932, the last year of pre-Nazi Germany, Jacobi's involvement in politically charged events increased. She documented the prosecution of Carl von Ossietzky, a courageous anti-Nazi editor of the journal *Die Weltbühne*, who was sentenced to prison for alleged high treason. Her photographs of Ossietzky during his trial and afterwards remain a powerful view of a democracy in its death throes. Ossietzky would die in 1938 as a result of the treatment he received in a Nazi concentration camp. In 1932, Jacobi also photographed Ernst Thälmann, leader of the German Communist Party, who was also to die in a Nazi concentration camp. She would accept no honorarium from Thälmann for her services, suggesting to him instead that she would be grateful if he could arrange a trip to the Soviet Union for her. Surprisingly, he remembered her request and by September 1932, Jacobi was in the Soviet Union taking photographs. Among the most memorable was a portrait of the veteran Bolshevik Karl Radek, who was purged and died in Stalin's gulag in 1939. Another legendary revolutionary, Max Hoelz, whom she had photographed around the

---

◄ Karlstadt, Liesl (1892–1960)

German cabaret performer. Name variations: Lisl Karlstadt. Born in 1892; died in 1960.

German cabaret performer Liesl Karlstadt, along with Karl Valentin, set the tone of popular culture in Munich for a generation.

SUGGESTED READING:

Dimpfl, Monika. *Immer veränderlich: Liesl Karlstadt (1892–1960)*. Munich: Monacensia A-1 Verlag, 1996.

Unterstoeger, Hermann. "Das Geheimnis der Girafftorte. Immer veränderlich—eine Ausstellung über Leben und Leiden der Liesl Karlstadt," in *Süddeutsche Zeitung*. March 28, 1996.

Albert Einstein,
Caputh,
Germany, 1928,
by Lotte Jacobi.

same time in Berlin, was also to be liquidated by Stalin, in this case in a "boating accident."

By the time Jacobi returned to Berlin in February 1933, Adolf Hitler had become Germany's chancellor and the edifice of the Nazi dictator-ship was rapidly being erected. She refused at first to even consider the idea of leaving Germany and initially employed a strategy of adaptation to the new atmosphere of political terror and anti-Semitism. She hoped that by giving her studio a more "Aryan" name, it might survive.

Several name changes took place, including "Jacobi and Bender," but this one had to be dropped when it was discovered that her partner Bender had a Jewish ancestor. Such stratagems were of little use, and by 1934 Jacobi was banned from exhibiting her work. After her father's death in March 1935, she and her mother resolved to leave Germany.

After a brief stay in London, she arrived in New York City on September 9, 1935. Her sister **Ruth Jacobi**, also a photographer, had been living there with her husband for some time and offered temporary accommodations. For a while, the two sisters worked out of the same studio in Manhattan, located on the corner of Sixth Avenue and 57th Street. Soon, however, Jacobi was able to establish her own studio. Because of the strength of her Berlin reputation (which was already known to leading American photographers)—and the fact that more and more of her friends, acquaintances and clients from Berlin had now settled in New York City as refugees from Nazism—she was quickly back at work as a portraitist of note. Before long, she established productive contacts with leading photographers in her new country, including *Berenice Abbott, *Barbara Morgan, and Alfred Stieglitz. Jacobi also became known to American newspapers and magazines, with her work appearing in *Life, The New York Times,* and the *New York Herald-Tribune.* Not all editors, however, appreciated the candor and spontaneity of her portraiture, and she would never be published in as many mass-circulation periodicals in the United States as she had been in pre-Nazi Germany.

In addition to photographing news, Jacobi occasionally made news herself. In 1938, she became the first woman ever to be permitted to photograph on the trading floor of the New York Stock Exchange during regular business hours. Mostly, however, she continued in her best-known field of portraiture. Starting in the 1930s, she photographed fellow exiles from Germany, including Thomas Mann, Max Reinhardt, *Helene Thimig, Alexander Granach, Paul Tillich, *Karen Horney, Hubertus Prinz von Löwenstein, and Oskar Maria Graf. Her most famous photograph of an exile celebrity is her 1938 portrait of a relaxed Albert Einstein wearing a leather jacket. Among the many other luminaries she photographed during her first decade in the United States were *Eleanor Roosevelt, *Margaret Mead, W.H. Auden, Benjamin Britten, Paul Robeson, Theodore Dreiser, Erskine Caldwell, Robert Frost, and *Billie Holiday.

In 1940, Jacobi married Erich Reiss, a fellow refugee from Nazism who had been one of Berlin's most innovative publishers before 1933. Always experimenting with new photographic techniques, in the mid-1940s Jacobi began to create cameraless abstract images produced either by playing light beams over a sheet of sensitized paper or by exposing to a fixed or moving light source various translucent and opaque objects placed in patterns on sensitized paper. Calling the new art form "photogenics," she joined **Carlotta Corpron** and other photographers who boldly sailed into uncharted waters.

After the death of her husband in 1951, Jacobi needed a change of scene. Her son and his wife had long lived in New Hampshire, and in 1955 she moved to that state to concentrate on "freedom and nature." To an interviewer she confided that her pleasures in rural Deering included keeping bees (a dream she'd had since her youth), gardening, watching birds and being a natural foods enthusiast. In her mid-60s, she learned to drive so she could attend classes at the University of New Hampshire, where she studied not only graphic arts and art history, but also French, educational television and horticulture.

Mentally alert and physically spry, Jacobi remained active in her personal and professional pleasures during the final decades of her life. Travel included a trip to Europe to visit her hometowns of Thorn and Posen (now Torun and Poznan in Poland), as well as stays in Berlin and other German cities. During an extended visit to Paris, she studied etching and engraving with William Stanley Hayter. Back in New Hampshire, in 1963 she opened an art gallery to bring attention to the works of talented young artists and photographers. Refusing to slow down, in her 80s she visited Peru to see antiquities and, not surprisingly, to take advantage of opportunities to photograph. She also became active in local and national politics. As a committed Democrat, she spoke out in conventions and meetings on a great variety of subjects and maintained that she had been able to introduce art as a plank on the party platform "because they are afraid of a cranky old lady."

Honors were showered on Jacobi during her final years. In 1974, she received an honorary doctorate in fine arts from the University of New Hampshire. In 1979, President Jimmy Carter extended a personal invitation to the White House. That year, when she was 83, Jacobi was seen wearing a black leather jacket of the Hell's Angels. "I am opinionated. I am a born rebel and a troublemaker," she told critic **Vicki Goldberg**

(*American Photographer,* March 1979). As a photographer, she said, "You can't see what I do. I don't need any background or anything special. I make it simple and try never to complicate things." Lotte Jacobi died of pneumonia on May 6, 1990, at the Havenwood-Heritage Heights Retirement Center in Concord, New Hampshire.

SOURCES:

"Artist and Activist, Photography Great Lotte Jacobi Dies," in *The Union Leader.* May 8, 1990, p. 1.

Beckers, Marion, and Elisabeth Moortgat. *Atelier Lotte Jacobi Berlin New York.* Berlin: Das verborgene Museum/Nicolai, 1998.

Fraser, C. Gerald. "Lotte Jacobi, 93; Photographer Made Portraits of Artists," in *The New York Times Biographical Service.* May 1990, p. 429.

Halley, Anne. "Photographs by Lotte Jacobi: Shaker Women in New Hampshire," in *The Massachusetts Review.* Vol. 24, no. 1. Spring 1983, pp. 113–124.

Jacobi, Lotte. *Berlin-New York: Schriftsteller in den 30er Jahren.* Edited by Walter P.H. Scheffler. 2nd rev. ed. Marbach am Neckar and Stutttgart: Deutscher Literaturarchiv/ Cotta, 1983.

———. *Russland 1932/33: Moskau, Tadschikistan, Usbekistan.* Edited by Marion Beckers and Elisabeth Moortgat. Berlin: Nishen, 1988.

———. *Theater and Dance Photographs.* Introduction by Cornell Capa. Woodstock, VT: Countryman Press, 1982.

Milton, Sybil. "The Refugee Photographers, 1933–1945," in Helmut F. Pfanner, ed. *Kulturelle Wechselbeziehungen im Exil—Exile across Cultures.* Bonn: Bouvier Verlag Herbert Grundmann, 1986, pp. 279–293.

Mitchell, Margaretta K. "Jacobi, Lotte (Johanna)," in Martin M. Evans, ed. *Contemporary Photographers.* 3rd ed. NY: St. James Press, 1995, pp. 545–547.

———. *Recollections: Ten Women of Photography.* NY: Viking Press, 1979.

Pfanner, Helmut, and Gary Samson. "Lotte Jacobi: German Photographer and Portraitist in Exile," in *The Germanic Review.* Vol. 62, no. 3. Summer 1967, pp. 109—.

Rosenblum, Naomi. *A World History of Photography.* 3rd ed. NY: Abbeville Press, 1997.

Tarshis, Jerome. "German Photography Between the Wars," in *Portfolio: The Magazine of the Visual Arts.* Vol. 3, no. 2. March–April, 1981, pp. 62–67.

Whelan, Richard. "Are Women *Better* Photographers Than Men?," in *Art News.* Vol. 79, no. 8. October 1980, pp. 80–88.

Wise, Kelly, ed. *Lotte Jacobi.* Introduction by James Fasanelli. Danbury, NH: Addison House, 1978.

COLLECTIONS:

Lotte Jacobi Papers and Collection, Dimond Library, University of New Hampshire, Durham, New Hampshire.

RELATED MEDIA:

A Conversation with Lotte Jacobi, Washington, DC: PBS Video, 1977.

Lotte Jacobi: Portrait, Chicago: Loyola University Media Services, 1981.

John Haag,
Associate Professor of History,
University of Georgia, Athens, Georgia

Jacobi, Mary Putnam (1842–1906)

First woman admitted to the renowned École de Médecine in Paris (1868) and foremost woman physician of her era, whose career won the respect of her male colleagues and inspired many women physicians. Name variations: Mary Putnam, Minnie. Pronunciation: Ja-KOH-bee. Born Mary Corinna Putnam on August 31, 1842, in London, England; died in New York City on June 10, 1906; daughter of George Palmer Putnam (a publisher) and Victorine (Haven) Putnam; educated at home until she entered public school at age 15; graduated from the Twelfth Street School in New York City, 1859; graduated from the New York College of Pharmacy, 1863; graduated from the Female Medical College of Pennsylvania, 1864; graduated from the École de Médecine in Paris, 1871; married Dr. Abraham Jacobi, on July 22, 1873; children: Ernst (1875–1883); **Marjorie Jacobi** (b. 1878).

Awards: bronze medal for her thesis at the École de Médecine (1871); Boyleston Prize for a research paper, Harvard University (1876); first woman elected to membership in the New York Academy of Medicine (1880).

Family returned to New York from England (1848); had first article published in Atlantic Monthly (1860); interned at the New England Hospital for Women and Children (1864); did clinical, laboratory, and course work in Paris (1866–71); was professor of materia medica and therapeutics at the Woman's Medical College of the New York Infirmary (1871–89); had private medical practice (1871–1902); served as president of the Association for the Advancement of Medical Education for Women (1874–1903); was a clinical lecturer on children's diseases at the Post-Graduate Medical School (1882–85); was president of the Alumnae Association of the Woman's Medical College of Pennsylvania (1888 and 1894); helped found the Consumer's League (1890); helped found the League for Political Education (1894); was a member of the New York County Medical Society, Medical Library and Journal Association, New York Pathological Society, New York Neurological Society, Therapeutical Society of New York, New York Academy of Medicine, and Women's Medical Association of New York City (1871–1906).

Publications: over 120 articles and scientific papers in various newspapers, magazines, and medical journals (1860–1903).

In the middle of the 19th century, the medical profession in the United States was considered disreputable. Almost anyone who wished to declare himself a physician could start a medical practice, even without a college education or medical degree. New proprietary medical schools proliferated, organized by physicians who offered only the most elementary of medical courses over a period of a few months to two years. In this atmosphere of freedom from regulation, women began to enter the field of medicine, often motivated by a perception of their special role and influence in the care of women and children. Because women were generally excluded from orthodox medical colleges, they usually attended women's medical schools. The first and most prominent of these was the Female (later Woman's) Medical College of Pennsylvania, established in 1850 by Philadelphia Quakers.

If you cannot learn to act without masters, you evidently will never become the real equals of those who do.

—Mary Putnam Jacobi

When Mary Corinna Putnam arrived in Philadelphia in 1863 to attend the Female Medical College, her father George Palmer Putnam, a publisher who had always encouraged his eldest child's independence and inquiring mind, felt compelled to give her some fatherly advice. "Now Minnie," George Putnam wrote:

> you know very well that I am proud of your abilities and am willing that you should apply them even to the repulsive pursuit (for so it is in spite of oneself) of Medical Science. But *don't* let yourself be absorbed and gobbled up in that branch of the animal kingdom ordinarily called strong-minded women! Don't let them intensify your self will and independence, for they are strong enough already. . . . Be a lady from the dotting of your i's to the color of your ribbons— and if you must be a doctor and a philosopher, be an attractive and agreeable one.

Mary was fortunate to have unusually broad-minded parents, for daughters were normally expected to limit their aspirations to marriage and children. **Victorine Putnam**, a lively, charming woman whose life was centered on her husband and 11 children, also indulged her daughter's intellectual curiosity and independence. Taking charge of her daughter's education at home, Victorine had Mary read aloud from great works of literature and encouraged her to write stories and essays. Mary treasured the memory of the day in 1860 when her first article, "Found and Lost," was accepted by the *Atlantic Monthly*, and her father dropped $80 in gold pieces into her hand one by one. Her literary talent was a strong factor in her later success, for she became a prolific author of articles, lectures, and scientific papers.

When George and Victorine Putnam decided that their daughter needed a more formal education, Mary was enrolled at the Twelfth Street School in New York City, where she graduated in 1859 after two years. She then resolved to attend the New York College of Pharmacy where she could obtain a scientific background in preparation for medical school, although most women in that era had very little exposure to science before beginning medical studies. Mary's plans were postponed for several years, however, when her father persuaded her that she was needed at home to help her mother and younger siblings after the outbreak of the Civil War. During this period, Mary and one of her sisters studied the classics in private lessons with a professor from Poland, and Mary in turn taught the younger children.

Mary demonstrated her unusual self-reliance when her brother Haven, who was stationed with federal forces in New Orleans, became ill with malaria. Not yet 21 years old, she traveled on one of the federal transports to New Orleans where she lived for several months with the Holabird family. It was extraordinary that Mary's parents approved such an venture for a lone young woman, and an indication of their confidence in her.

After graduating from the New York College of Pharmacy in 1863, Mary began her studies at the Female Medical College of Pennsylvania. Because her work in pharmacy and her private instruction counted toward a degree, she received her medical certificate in one year (1864) instead of the normal two. Despite her solid preparation for medical school, Mary felt ill-prepared after graduation to assume the responsibilities of patient care, and she went to Boston for a few months to obtain more clinical experience at the New England Hospital for Women and Children under the supervision of women physicians on the staff. Her experience there convinced her that she was temperamentally unsuited for private medical practice and that she preferred scientific research.

Returning to New York, she lived at home and had a small private practice while she studied chemistry with a Professor Mayer; she was his only pupil. Although George Putnam placed his son Bishop in the same laboratory, ostensibly as a chemistry student but also as a chaperon, the close collaboration of Mary and Professor Mayer ignited a romance, and Mary was soon engaged to be married. Within a short time, however, she began to have second thoughts and implored her father to help break the engagement. "I am not sure that his intellect or character are as strong as mine," she wrote. "I influence him a great deal, he scarcely influences me at all; in a word, I can manage him, and that makes him far less interesting than if he, by superior power, controlled and magnetized me." Clearly, it would take an exceptional man to capture her attention. George Putnam determined that "the whole thing must end now, once for all—and unconditionally."

Her freedom regained, Mary, like many other medical graduates of that period, decided she needed the kind of scientific training available only in the great European medical schools. She set her sights on the venerable École de Médecine in Paris, which had never admitted a woman. In September of 1866, just after her 24th birthday, she sailed for France.

With a few letters of introduction, Mary made herself at home in Paris. After taking French lessons, she felt comfortable enough to begin medical work and obtained permission to assist at several hospitals as well as attend lectures at the Jardin des Plantes and the College of France. Within two months, she wrote to her parents that she was devoting half her time to chemistry and half to medical studies, and that she had now decided medicine would take precedence after all. She saw more possibilities for success in clinical medicine than in scientific chemistry, and, even though she still felt that a purely scientific life would better suit her, she wanted to be able to help her family, the main anchor in her life.

Mary was especially devoted to her parents and grateful to them for giving her the freedom to make choices. In February 1867, she wrote her father, thanking him for "the large liberty in which you have always left me. . . . It would be perfectly distracting to have a man fussing and directing everything. . . . I should have been stifled." To her mother, she wrote of her gratitude for Victorine's example of charm and loveliness: "Thanks to your blood in my veins, I, also, am sometimes able to amuse people, which is a most valuable faculty for getting along in the world."

Mary's Parisian friends and medical associates were intrigued by this independent young American, and they occasionally interceded with authorities to open opportunities as her studies expanded. She worked with male students and interns, and her obvious competence won the respect of many male physicians. But, because she was a woman, the faculty of the École de Médecine rejected her application for admission. When she heard that the Minister of Public In-

Mary
Putnam
Jacobi

struction was interested in the question of women physicians, Mary saw her opening. With the help of a few influential friends, she petitioned the minister and finally received permission simply to attend a course at the École. Once inside the amphitheater, she reasoned, all objections to her presence would fade, and she would eventually be accepted for a degree.

The scenario played out as she had predicted. On January 23, 1868, she began a histology course at the École, entering the room by a side door and sitting in a chair near the professor. Because most of the students knew Mary by sight from her work at other institutions, the uproar envisioned by opposing faculty members did not occur. In a triumphant letter to her parents, she wrote: "Day before yesterday, for the first time since its foundation several centuries ago, a petticoat might be seen in the august amphitheater of the École de Médecine." Even American newspapers took note of her attainment, and one article mentioned how the civility of French medical students contrasted with the boorish behavior of University of Pennsylvania medical students, who had jeered and taunted women from the Female Medical College of Pennsylvania on their arrival at Penn to attend a lecture.

Thanks to the support of the Minister of Public Instruction, Mary was soon thoroughly established at the École and sanctioned as a regular student. Her American diploma was accepted for credit, and she needed only to pass a series of six examinations and write a thesis to receive a medical degree. In preparation for her first oral examination in June of 1868, she exercised tremendous mental discipline, studying intensely up to ten hours a day and repeating information aloud to ensure that her French was precise. She passed the examination with a high mark, "as telling and effective an achievement as for the moment any woman could accomplish," she noted in a letter to her parents. But her plans to obtain her degree within two years were disrupted by the Franco-Prussian war between July 1870 and May 1871.

During the period of political ferment, Mary wrote an article for *Scribner's Monthly* entitled "Some of the French Leaders: The Provisional Government of the Fourth of September," which was described by the magazine's editor as "one of the ablest ever printed in an American magazine." Her articles for American magazines, newspapers, and the *Medical Record* were a main source of income during her five years in Paris. Her writing was logical, precise, and expressive—a true reflection of her extraordinary mind.

In July of 1871, Mary finally received her medical degree from the École de Médecine. Her thesis, submitted in competition with all theses for the year, received the bronze medal. It was dedicated: "To the professor, whose name I do not know, who was the only one to vote for my admission to the school, thus protesting against the prejudice which would exclude women from advanced studies." She was the second woman to graduate, however, rather than the first. Mary's admission to the École had opened the door for *Elizabeth Garrett (Anderson), an English physician who had been in medical practice for several years. Garrett accelerated her studies and was able to graduate in 1870.

When Mary returned from Paris in September of 1871, there were only four hospitals in the United States where a woman could be an attending physician—all were women's hospitals. She chose to work at the New York Infirmary for Women and Children, established in 1858 by Drs. *Elizabeth and *Emily Blackwell. At the same time, Mary set up an office for a private practice and began teaching materia medica and therapeutics at the Woman's Medical College of the New York Infirmary. Mary was a stimulating professor who demanded that her students have the will to learn, but she was shocked by the poor preparation of women for medical school. After her first few lectures, she was so frustrated by her students' inadequate education that she wrote to Elizabeth Blackwell in England for advice. Dr. Blackwell urged her to reacquaint herself with America now that Mary had become so thoroughly French. To adapt to American expectations, she must simplify her course in materia medica and see how she could "gradually vivify that course" rather than try to change established ways abruptly. "Do, my dear Mary," wrote Blackwell, "be very prudent and patient! You are young enough to wait for brilliant success, *but you must not fail now.*"

Mary's path to success in the male medical establishment in New York began with her acceptance as a member of the New York County Medical Society in November of 1871, just a few months after the acceptance of Emily Blackwell, the first woman member. The president of the Society at the time was Dr. Abraham Jacobi (1830–1919), a German-Jewish physician who had been imprisoned in Germany for two years during the 1848 revolution. After his escape from prison, he made his way to New York, where he became known as an authority on the diseases of children. When he met Dr. Mary Putnam, he was a professor of pediatrics at the College of Physicians and Surgeons.

Mary and Abraham Jacobi were married on July 22, 1873. Despite the death of their first baby in 1874, the next ten years were happy and productive. While continuing her teaching, private practice, research and writing, Jacobi had two more children, Ernst in 1875 and Marjorie in 1878, and began to focus on improving women's medical education. From 1873 to 1903, she served as president of the Association for the Advancement of Medical Education for Women, which she organized in 1872. It was her conviction that standards of medical education needed to be raised for women so that they could prove themselves equal to men in the medical profession. To achieve this goal, women required access to the same classroom and clinical training that men received.

The main objections to the higher education of women were summarized in a book published in 1873 by a Harvard professor, Dr. E.H. Clarke, who contended that the stress of higher education disrupted the proper development of a woman's reproductive system. Also, he asserted, women could not be relied on in medical emergencies because menstruation incapacitated them for one week each month. When the topic for

Harvard's celebrated Boyleston essay was announced—"Do women require mental and bodily rest during menstruation, and to what extent?"—several women physicians urged Jacobi to enter the competition to win credit for all women by obtaining the Boyleston prize in 1876. She sent out questionnaires to women and summarized her findings in a scientific paper submitted anonymously. Her paper won the $200 prize and refuted Clarke's arguments unequivocally.

Both Mary and Abraham Jacobi were interested in post-graduate study for physicians. When the faculty of the New York University Medical College founded the Post-Graduate Medical School in 1882 for men and women, Mary was appointed clinical lecturer on children's diseases. She also became a student once again, with a particular interest in the treatment of the mentally ill and methods of preventing insanity. She wrote *Essays on Hysteria and Brain Tumors* in 1888, as well as other papers on neurological subjects, an area that would later be of personal concern and eventually lead to her death.

After ten golden years, the most devastating blow of her life came in 1883 when her son Ernst died of diphtheria at the age of seven years, ten months. The children's nurse was found to have been harboring the disease. It was a bitter loss as well for Abraham Jacobi, who never really recovered from the death of his son.

Mary's interest in the rights of women expanded in the 1890s to encompass social and political issues. She helped organize the Consumer's League in 1890, which was concerned with the working conditions of saleswomen, cashiers, and other women employed in the retail stores of New York City. In 1894, she was selected to represent the women of New York City in a speech before the New York Constitutional Convention, which was considering the issue of voting rights for women. When the franchise for women was defeated, Mary Jacobi helped organize the League for Political Education and expanded her speech into a booklet entitled *"Common Sense" Applied to Woman Suffrage.*

Until the age of 54, Jacobi had enjoyed perfect health. During the winter of 1896, while she and her daughter were vacationing in Greece, Mary began to have brief, sharp headaches for several minutes each morning. After four years, the headaches increased in severity and duration, and she began to have other symptoms of a brain tumor. By 1902, she was forced to close her medical practice. Perfectly aware of the nature of the meningeal tumor slowly compressing her brain, she wrote one final paper in 1903, this time with herself as the subject. In it, she described the extraordinary mental clarity she had experienced throughout her life:

> It seemed to me often as if I lived in a glass house on the summit of a lofty mountain where I could see in every direction an almost illimitable distance looking through an atmosphere of blue and gold. The delight I experienced in the clearness of this view was immense. On account of it I was never conscious of depression or of irritation for more than a few moments at a time. I lived in an equable golden calm as in a sunrise or sunset cloud.

Mary Jacobi died at her home in New York City three years later, on the 23rd anniversary of her son's death. By that time, many gains had been made in the status of women in the medical profession. Her male and female colleagues attributed much of this success to Mary Putnam Jacobi's efforts and example as the leading woman physician of her era in the United States.

SOURCES:

Putnam, Ruth, ed. *Life and Letters of Mary Putnam Jacobi.* NY: Putnam, 1925.

Truax, Rhoda. *The Doctors Jacobi.* Boston, MA: Little, Brown, 1952.

The Women's Medical Association of New York City, ed. *Mary Putnam Jacobi, M.D.: A Pathfinder in Medicine.* NY: Putnam, 1925.

SUGGESTED READING:

Abram, Ruth J. *"Send Us a Lady Physician": Women Doctors in America, 1835–1920.* NY: W.W. Norton, 1985.

Morantz-Sanchez, Regina Markell. *Sympathy and Science: Women Physicians in American Medicine.* NY: Oxford University Press, 1985.

Walsh, Mary Roth. *Doctors Wanted: No Women Need Apply: Sexual Barriers in the Medical Profession, 1835–1975.* New Haven, CT: Yale University Press, 1979.

COLLECTIONS:

Correspondence and writings located in the Schlesinger Library, Radcliffe College, Cambridge, Massachusetts.

Katherine G. Haskell,
freelance writer and medical editor,
Philadelphia, Pennsylvania

Jacobini, Maria (1890–1944)

Italian actress. Born in Rome, Italy, on February 17, 1890; died in 1944; niece of Cardinal Jacobini, minister of state to Pope Leo XIII.

Selected films: Lucrezia Borgia *(1910);* Beatrice Cenci *(1910);* La Fugitiva *(1912);* Vampe di Gelosia *(1912);* Giovanna d'Arco *(1913);* La Corsara *(1915);* Resurrezione *(1917);* La Signora Arlecchino *(1918);* Addio Giovinezza *(1918);* La Vergine Folle *(1919);* Il Viaggio *(1921);* Amore rosso *(1922);* La Vie de Bohème *(1923);* Orinte *(1924);* Transatlantico *(1926);* Il Carnavale di Venezia *(1926)*; Unfug der Liebe *(Ger., 1918)*; Villa Falconieri *(Ger., 1928)*; The Living Corpse *(USSR, 1929)*; Maman Colbiri *(Fr., 1929)*; La Scala *(1931)*; Giuseppe Verdi *(1938)*; Melodie eterne *(Eternal Melodies, 1940)*; La Donna della Montagna *(1943)*.

One of the most revered European stars of her day, Maria Jacobini was born in Rome in 1890 into a distinguished family and studied at Rome's Academy of Dramatic Arts. She made both her stage and screen debuts in 1910 and quickly became one of Italy's leading "divas" of the silent screen. Starring mostly in Italian historical spectacles and social dramas, Jacobini also appeared in German, Austrian, and French productions. In 1920, she performed in Fedor Ozep's Soviet screen adaptation of Leo Tolstoy's *The Living Corpse*. Jacobini's sisters, **Bianca** (b. 1888) and **Diomira** (b. 1896), also appeared in films.

Jacobs, Aletta (1854–1929)

Dutch physician who was an international leader in family planning, women's rights, and pacifism. Born Aletta Henriette Jacobs on February 9, 1854, in Sappemeer, Holland; died on August 10, 1929, in Baarn, Holland; eighth of eleven children of Abraham Jacobs (a physician) and Anna (de Jongh) Jacobs; married Carel Gerritsen (a Dutch politician), on April 28, 1892; children: son (b. 1893 but lived only one day); (foster son) Charles Jacobs (son of Aletta's deceased brother Julius).

Received medical degree (1879); opened birth control clinic (1882); translated Women and Economics *by Charlotte Perkins Gilman (1900); led Dutch Association for Woman Suffrage (1903–19); organized International Woman Suffrage Alliance conference (1908); translated* Women and Labor *by Olive Schreiner; went on speaking tour of Africa and Asia (1911–12); ran for political office (1918); published autobiography (1924).*

A pioneer and activist in medicine, women's rights, and the international peace movement, the Dutch physician Aletta Henriette Jacobs was the eighth of eleven children of **Anna de Jongh Jacobs** and Abraham Jacobs, a poor Jewish doctor. Born in the small town of Sappemeer, Holland, Jacobs and her siblings were well educated by their father, a liberal-minded intellectual who advocated professional careers for his daughters as well as his sons. Aletta Jacobs excelled at her local public school and showed an early determination to follow her father into the medical profession, despite the fact that medical schools were closed to Dutch

women and there were no female doctors in Holland. At first her parents discouraged her, hoping she would pursue a career in teaching, one of the few professional paths open to women. Jacobs refused to change her mind and eventually won her father's support, although her mother continued to oppose her plans as being improper for a woman. Jacobs then attended a finishing school for young women, but its focus on preparing girls for marriage and motherhood rather than academics caused her to quit after two weeks. Since further schooling seemed unavailable, Jacobs was apprenticed to a dressmaker, a dreary job which only made her more determined to become a doctor.

In 1870, she was one of the first women to take the state pharmacist's assistant exam. Her father then secured special permission for Jacobs to continue her education at the local boys' high school, where she concentrated in the sciences and Latin, in addition to learning English, French, and German. When she learned that a man had recently used his pharmacist's diploma to apply for an exemption from the state university admissions exam, Jacobs decided to apply as well. Abraham Jacobs wrote to the liberal prime minister, Johan Thorbecke, to allow his daughter exemption from the normal university admissions requirements. Although it took a year for Thorbecke to act on the request, in April 1871 Aletta received permission to attend classes at the nearby University of Groningen. In her autobiography, Jacobs claims that at the time she was unaware of the symbolic meaning that her admission to the university would have for Dutch women, although she also writes that even as a girl she was intensely interested in the women's rights movements emerging across Europe.

Jacobs' experiences at Groningen were, according to her autobiography, generally positive, because she was fortunate to have several professors and classmates who supported her goals. Yet she also describes numerous incidents of hostile professors and students trying to humiliate her or force her to leave Groningen. She also found herself the subject of editorials and letters in local and national newspapers which condemned her desire to intrude on a male profession. Even some members of her family felt that she was dishonoring the Jacobs family by her actions. For a young woman—she was 17 in 1871—Jacobs' persistence in the face of this private and public hostility is remarkable. She refused to be segregated from her classmates during and between classes or to receive lessons in private, as the administration wished, and instead insisted on equal treatment. In 1874, after three years of study in anatomy and physics, Jacobs passed her physician's exams, but her intense work took a toll on her health. Nonetheless, she began a hospital internship, where she mostly treated poor working-class women, an experience which made her aware of the hardships and injustices suffered by poor women, especially prostitutes. Jacobs was shocked to learn of the regulation of prostitution by the Dutch government which included forced medical exams designed to prevent the spread of venereal disease. Her outrage at the callous treatment of these women and the hypocrisy of treating only the prostitute and not her clients would later lead Jacobs into political activism against the regulation of prostitution.

In 1876, she transferred to the University of Amsterdam to complete her training following a bout of malaria. She barely survived an attack of typhus in 1877 but returned to her studies. Finally, Jacobs passed her clinical examinations in April 1878 and returned home to Sappemeer to work on her thesis. Although she had to take over her father's practice for a while after he suffered a stroke, by March 1879 she had submitted her thesis and received her medical degree.

A cash gift from a friend allowed Jacobs to continue her studies in London, where she became acquainted with some of the leading socialist and freethinking activists of England, attending meetings of the socialist-utopian Fabian society and of female suffragists. She also met activists promoting family planning, an issue which would soon take on new significance for her.

Jacobs stayed only four months in London, but the trip introduced her to the emerging progressive reform movements whose values she shared, and to the possibility of women's political activism on behalf of other women. She returned to Amsterdam in September 1879 to attend an international medical conference; her presence brought her considerable public notice (as well as numerous offers of marriage from other doctors). This positive experience convinced her to open a private practice in Amsterdam. She had many patients, but once again Jacobs encountered opposition and hostility from some physicians, who advised her, for example, that she should charge lower fees than they did since she was not as good as male doctors. She flatly rejected this advice; she could, she argued, justify charging even more than men, simply because she was the only woman doctor in Holland. Some also opposed her membership in the all-male public library which had the medical journals and books she needed to refer to in her

practice. Yet again Jacobs' determination prevailed, a success which can in part be ascribed to her skill in locating those in authority who could best help her, and making rational appeals designed to win their support. Jacobs never accepted quietly that which she felt was unjust, a trait which would be apparent later in her years of political activism.

When the time comes, I will feel free to say that I have contributed to making the world I leave a better place than the world I entered.
—Aletta Jacobs

In 1880, Jacobs began teaching free classes in hygiene and child care to working-class women. This led to the establishment of a free clinic for poor women and children which she would operate for 14 years, in addition to her thriving private practice. She also found time to join the Union, a progressive workers' organization, and to make house calls to the slums where many of her free clinic patients lived. Although she had never intended to specialize in gynecology, Jacobs found herself drawn to the sufferings of these women and saw contraception as the necessary solution to the economic and physical problems of multiple unwanted pregnancies. She began offering her patients a contraceptive device similar to the modern cervical cap, known then as the Mensinga pessary but today called the Dutch pessary because of Jacobs' promotion of it. For distributing the device, Jacobs faced open condemnation and slander by much of the medical establishment, who opposed contraception on moral and religious grounds despite its legal status in Holland. Yet she continued dispensing contraceptives and birth-control information in an era when sex and sexuality were taboo as topics of discussion.

In the late 1880s and 1890s, Aletta Jacobs became actively involved in several causes related to women's health care and political equality. Her longest association was with the movement for women's suffrage, in which she would be a leading figure for the rest of her life. In 1883, she filed a lawsuit contending that Dutch law did not specifically exclude women from suffrage and thus she should be able to vote. The Dutch Supreme Court rejected her case, and in 1887, a new constitution explicitly granted voting rights to male citizens only. Jacobs' one-woman campaign again brought her widespread hostility by both men and women, but it also brought her into contact with suffragists across Europe and the United States.

Jacobs also promoted improvements in the working conditions of "shop girls," who were forced to stand at their counters for 12 to 14 hours at a time with only a few short breaks. Although she had the support of the shop clerks and the inspector of labor in Amsterdam, shop owners resisted her call for shorter hours and seating arrangements. However, she and her supporters refused to give up the cause, and in 1902, after much debate, including Jacobs' testimony before Parliament, a law was finally passed requiring chairs for shop clerks.

More controversial were Jacobs' efforts to end the state regulation of prostitution and state-run brothels. Having treated many working-class prostitutes in her free clinic, Jacobs was well aware of the health risks such women faced, and regarded prostitution as a social evil which no civilized people could condone. She joined other liberals campaigning for the deregulation of prostitution. This would end the humiliating medical exams and legal double standard in the fight against the spread of venereal disease; it would also end the registration of prostitutes with local police, which stigmatized them and made it difficult for them to find "honest" employment. Jacobs published essays on the subject in newspapers and magazines, and from 1895 on she spoke publicly for deregulation, again facing vocal public disapproval for discussing such "indecent" topics. She persevered, however, and as late as 1909 she spoke to an international medical conference in Budapest on deregulation and the prevention of prostitution through increased economic opportunities for poor women.

In April 1892, Jacobs married her longtime friend, the Dutch politician Carel Gerritsen, in a civil ceremony in Amsterdam. Jacobs had first become aware of the shy Gerritsen when he sent a congratulatory note after her first medical exams. He continued to correspond with her occasionally through her years at college and sent her letters of introduction to use when she traveled to London. Yet it was only after she established her practice in Amsterdam that Gerritsen and Jacobs met in person. During Jacobs' years in Amsterdam, the two became friends, a relationship which deepened when Gerritsen helped Jacobs through her grief after the death of her father in 1881. Gerritsen, an active social reformer who held progressive democratic and feminist views, had been elected to the governing body of Amsterdam from the Radical Union Party in 1888. In 1893, he became the first Radical member of the Dutch Parliament.

The relationship between Jacobs and Gerritsen developed slowly but steadily during the 1880s. They shared similar world views and goals for political and social reform; they wrote essays and speeches together and supported each other's ambitions. They also shared an antipathy to religion and embraced the ideology of freethinking; Gerritsen had been raised as a Calvinist but rejected it as an adult. Likewise, Jacobs' family was Jewish, but she does not mention any religious observation or beliefs in her autobiography. She does not seem to have identified as a Jew either, and her letters and writings clearly show that she was an atheist by her early 20s.

Gerritsen and Jacobs had considered marriage in the early 1880s but rejected it at first as an institution demeaning to women. Yet by 1892, they were spending most of their time together and became increasingly concerned that by not marrying, they risked public disapproval which could damage Jacobs' practice and Gerritsen's political career. They wanted to be able to live together and raise a family, but did not want to burden their children with the stigma of illegitimacy. Finally they decided to marry but maintain economic independence and separate living quarters within their home, forming what was known as a "companionate marriage," a union of equals.

Jacobs gave birth to a son in September 1893, but the baby survived only one day. She mourned the death deeply and noted in her autobiography that it took years to recover emotionally from her loss. It was after the baby's death that Jacobs, whose mental and physical health had suffered, decided to close her free clinic and curtail her private practice. She and Gerritsen spent much of the rest of the decade traveling in France, Germany, and Austria-Hungary, usually to organize with activists from other regions who shared their goals of universal suffrage and family planning. In 1895, the couple once again became parents, when Jacobs' young nephew Charles became their foster son. Charles Jacobs was the son of her brother Julius, who had recently died in the Dutch East Indies. Jacobs and Gerritsen raised Charles as their own and sent him to a private boarding school in 1900. He returned in 1905, when Jacobs was widowed, and lived with her until he started law school in 1910. It is interesting to note that Jacobs never mentions her foster son in her autobiography. As an adult Charles broke off their relationship completely after an argument, although the details of their difficult relationship and the reason for his estrangement are unknown.

In the years of her marriage, Jacobs focused more and more on her work for women's political rights. In 1895, she became head of the Amsterdam section of the Association for Woman Suffrage, serving as president after 1903. In 1899, both she and Gerritsen participated in the first international women's suffrage conference in London, sponsored by the International Council of Women, later known as the International Woman Suffrage Alliance (IWSA). At the conference, Jacobs met three American women who influenced her work, and in turn were influenced by her work—*Susan B. Anthony, *Carrie Chapman Catt, and *Charlotte Perkins Gilman. Moved by Gilman's analysis of married women's economic dependence as one of the keys to women's oppression, Jacobs translated Gilman's *Women and Economics* into Dutch to make it available to her colleagues.

In 1904, Carel Gerritsen's failing health and her own political commitments led Jacobs to shut down her private practice for good, after 24 years of providing health care and education to the women of Amsterdam. In June, she and Gerritsen traveled to the United States for the Interparliamentary Union meeting in St. Louis, followed by a tour across America. It was to be Gerritsen's last trip abroad. They returned to Holland in January 1905; Gerritsen died of cancer six months later. In her grief, Jacobs found it impossible to work at all for many months; her own health suffered badly, and she took an extended trip to Switzerland to regain her strength.

By 1906, Jacobs had returned to her political activism. In 1908, she organized the large IWSA conference in Amsterdam. Over the next two years, Jacobs, age 55 in 1909, was too ill and overworked to travel or speak much, yet she managed to produce a constant stream of writings—essays, letters, and editorials on suffrage, prostitution, and birth control, a collection of travel writings by herself and Gerritsen, and the Dutch translation of South African feminist *Olive Schreiner's *Women and Labor*.

Her health restored, Jacobs set off on a world tour of colonial Africa and Asia in July 1911. Her traveling companion was the American suffragist Carrie Chapman Catt, who had first suggested the idea several years earlier. For 16 months, the two women traveled by ship, train, and carriage to major cities in South Africa, Egypt, Palestine, India, Indonesia, China, Japan, and Russia. At each stop, they met contacts in suffrage movements, organized speaking engagements on women's rights, and observed women's cultural and political positions. By the time she returned to Holland, Jacobs had come to believe that it was not enough to petition a government to extend suffrage rights; the suffragists needed to show the government that the public supported universal voting rights. In consequence, the Association for Woman Suffrage began a series of public events and demonstrations which brought the message of suffrage rights to the people of Holland.

At the outbreak of World War I in 1914, Jacobs' long-held pacifist and anti-military views and the prospect of a Europe torn apart by war led her to add antiwar organizing to her suffrage work. She felt strongly that women had a mission to protest the suffering and sacrifice of war, rather than easing its burden through nursing and other traditional tasks, and joined the international women's groups petitioning for peace. The large International Congress of Women held in The Hague in 1915, primarily organized by Jacobs and the American social reformer *Jane Addams, was dedicated to promoting pacifism among the nations of Europe. Following the conference, Jacobs and Addams were sent to submit the Congress' resolutions for world peace to the leaders of Western nations involved in the conflict as well as neutral countries. This mission took them from Holland to personal meetings with heads of state in London, Paris, Bern, Rome, and Washington, D.C., where they met with Woodrow Wilson. The receptions they received were usually polite but nowhere did they receive a positive commitment to peace.

Yet Jacobs did not neglect the slow progress towards women's suffrage in Holland even during the war years. To the contrary, her associations became ever more vocal and public in their demands for equality. In 1918, the adoption of a revised constitution allowed Dutch women to run for political office; Jacobs was one of the first female candidates to run for Parliament, although she did not win. In September 1919, the goal she and many others had sought for decades was achieved when the Dutch Parliament finally voted to allow women full suffrage rights.

Aletta Jacobs soon returned to two other issues of concern to her, international peace and family planning, publishing articles and attending conferences across Europe well into the 1920s. She also maintained her contacts with the IWSA, which was continuing its work in other countries, and began writing her autobiography, which she hoped might inspire younger women to a life of activism. But her personal life was suffering from her total commitment to political causes. Jacobs had had virtually no income of her own since she had ceased practicing medicine, and a series of financial setbacks apparently caused by poor investments led her to file for bankruptcy in 1922. For her remaining years, she lived off the generosity of friends in The Hague, but her economic problems could not keep her from her social and political work.

An elaborate public celebration in honor of her 70th birthday, held at The Hague in February 1924, confirmed her status as a nationally and internationally respected physician and equal rights activist. At the end of the year, her autobiography *Memories* appeared. Despite failing health and her advanced age, Aletta Jacobs continued traveling and attending international conferences on women's rights, peace, and family planning until a few weeks before her death on August 10, 1929. She was deeply mourned by feminists and pacifists around the world for her lifetime of achievement, and is still honored as a national hero in the Netherlands.

SOURCES:

Bosch, Mineke. *Politics and Friendship: Letters from the International Woman Suffrage Alliance, 1902–1942.* Columbus: Ohio State University Press, 1990.

Jacobs, Aletta, *Memories: My Life as an International Leader in Health, Suffrage, and Peace.* Ed. by Harriet Feinberg. NY: The Feminist Press, 1996.

SUGGESTED READING:

Addams, Jane, et al. *Women at the Hague: The International Congress of Women and Its Results.* NY: Macmillan, 1915.

Bonner, Thomas N. *To the Ends of the Earth: Women's Search for Education in Medicine.* Cambridge, MA: Harvard University Press, 1992.

Feinberg, Harriet. "A Pioneering Dutch Feminist Views Egypt: Aletta Jacobs' Travel Letters," in *Feminist Issues.* Vol. 10, 1990, pp. 65–77.

McLaren, Angus. *A History of Contraception.* Oxford: Basil Blackwell, 1990.

COLLECTIONS:

Aletta Jacobs Papers in the International Archive for the Women's Movement, International Information Center and Archive for the Women's Movement, Amsterdam.

Laura York, M.A. in history,
University of California, Riverside, California

Jacobs, Frances Wisebart

(1843–1892)

American welfare worker. Born in Harrodsburg, Kentucky, on March 29, 1843; died in Denver, Colorado, on November 3, 1892; first daughter and second of seven children of Leon Henry Wisebart (a tailor) and Rosetta (Marx) Wisebart; attended schools in Cincinnati, Ohio; married Abraham Jacobs (a merchant), on February 18, 1863; children: a daughter and two sons, one of whom died in childhood.

Known as Colorado's "Mother of the Charities," Frances Jacobs was born in 1843 in Harrodsburg, Kentucky, and as a child moved with her family to Cincinnati, Ohio. She was educated in that city and taught school before her marriage in 1863 to Abraham Jacobs, who took his young wife to the booming mining town of Central City, Colorado. Abraham ran a store with his brother until 1874, when a fire destroyed Central City. The family went to live in Denver.

Jacobs quickly became active in Denver's burgeoning charitable community, beginning with the Hebrew Benevolent Ladies Aid Society, of which she was elected president. In 1874, she was a founding officer of the non-sectarian Ladies' Relief Society and, in 1877, became a leading force in establishing the Charity Organization Society, a federation of Denver's charitable groups which coordinated fund-raising efforts and allocated proceeds among affiliates. Jacobs served as secretary of the federation until her death.

Jacobs approached her charitable work with hands-on dedication, risking both her health and her reputation in order to call on families in need. Making up to 15 visits a day, she generally arrived with a bar of soap, convinced that any home that needed food probably needed soap as well. Jacobs also took an interest in the kindergarten movement and organized a kindergarten association in Denver shortly before her death in 1892, at age 49. Eulogized by leading citizens, including the governor of Colorado, Jacobs was also the only woman among 16 Colorado pioneers memorialized in a stained-glass portrait in the state capitol dome.

SOURCES:

James, Edward T., ed. *Notable American Women 1607–1950.* Cambridge, MA: The Belknap Press of Harvard University Press, 1971.

McHenry, Robert, ed. *Famous American Women.* NY: Dover, 1983.

Barbara Morgan,
Melrose, Massachusetts

Jacobs, Harriet A. (1813–1897)

American abolitionist and writer who was born into slavery and spent nearly seven years hiding in an attic before escaping to freedom. Name variations: (pseudonym) Linda Brent. Born Harriet Ann Jacobs into slavery in the autumn of 1813 (exact date unrecorded), in Edenton, North Carolina; died in Washington, D.C., on March 7, 1897; daughter of slave parents Daniel Jacobs (a carpenter) and Delilah; never attended school; taught to read and write by first owner, then was self-educated; never married; children: Joseph (b. 1829); Louisa Matilda (b. 1833).

Mother died (1819); first owner died and bequeathed Jacobs to three-year-old niece (1825); father died (1826); after ongoing threats of rape by owner Dr. James Norcom, began a relationship with white neighbor Samuel Sawyer; gave birth to son by Sawyer (1829); daughter by Sawyer born (1833); sent to a plantation and ran away, eventually hiding under roof of grandmother's house where she would remain for seven years; Sawyer purchased son and daughter (1835); escaped to the North and worked in New York as nursemaid to Willis family (1842); fleeing slave hunters, went to Boston with daughter and worked as seamstress (1844); worked in Anti-Slavery Reading Room in Rochester, New York (1849); moved to New York and worked for Willis family again (1850); purchased and freed by Cornelia Grinnell Willis (1852); approached Harriet Beecher Stowe about writing her story and decided to write the book herself, while working for the Willis family (1853); Incidents in the Life of a Slave Girl *published anonymously, with white abolitionist Lydia Maria Child as editor (1861); throughout Civil War and aftermath, took part in relief work and efforts to help freed slaves (1862–68).*

Despite the language of liberty and equality in its founding documents, the United States at its very inception recognized and permitted slavery. U.S. law defined slaves as chattel, property that could be bought and sold at will. Seemingly standard biographical information—like name, family, marital status, education—is often difficult to unearth for women and men who were slaves, because the laws of slavery worked to deny such information. Not considered citizens or even legal persons, under the Constitution slaves were counted as three-fifths of a person for purposes of congressional representation. They could not vote or hold office. According to the laws of most slave states, they could not own property, attend school, or marry. Because their children were also considered property, slaves could not control their children's destinies, or even stop an infant from being sold. They could be brutally beaten, raped, or otherwise abused without legal recourse. The limited protections that did exist were essentially unenforceable, since slaves (and in many cases free blacks) were not allowed to testify against white people. The laws attempted to deny slaves a voice in myriad other ways. In many states, it was illegal for a slave to learn or to teach reading and writing, punishable by fines, imprisonment or whipping. It was into this America that Harriet Ann Jacobs was born a slave who would one day commit the powerful, subversive act of writing her own story.

Weeks before the Civil War began, *Incidents in the Life of a Slave Girl, Written by Herself* appeared in print. Written by Jacobs, the book had a first-person narrator named Linda Brent, and the only name on the title page was that of editor *Lydia Maria Child. While Jacobs remained anonymous, the book revealed details of her life, particularly her struggles under slavery and her ultimately successful efforts to free herself and her children. Although her narrator is not identical to Jacobs, the book clearly is an autobiographical narrative, both using and subverting techniques of sentimental fiction to launch an extended critique of Southern slavery and Northern complicity.

"*The* bill of sale!" Those words struck me like a blow. So I was *sold* at last! A human being *sold* in the free city of New York! The bill of sale is on record, and future generations will learn from it that women were articles of traffic in New York, late in the nineteenth century of the Christian religion.

—Harriet A. Jacobs, *Incidents in the Life of a Slave Girl*

Harriet Jacobs was born into slavery in Edenton, North Carolina, in 1813 (the precise date of her birth is not recorded). Jacobs' family members lived on the margins of freedom. Her father, Daniel Jacobs, was a slave, but he was permitted to hire himself out as a carpenter while paying his owner for the "privilege." What little money he kept, he saved in the hopes of one day buying his children out of slavery. Harriet's mother **Delilah** (there is no record of a last name) belonged to a different owner than her husband, but the two were permitted to live together. Under slave law, owners were not required to recognize slave marriage in any way. Although very little is known about Delilah, more is known about Delilah's mother **Molly Horniblow**. At a young age, Horniblow was freed when her owner-father died and emancipated the family, but while sailing to Britain during the Revolutionary War the family was captured once again and sold back into slavery. Like Harriet's father, Molly Horniblow also eventually worked for her own money. Under her new owner, she sold goods that she baked and tried to save the cash needed to free her family members. Though she was to be freed when her mistress died, the executor of the will (the man who was to become Harriet Jacobs' owner and nemesis) instead put her on the auction block. An illiterate old woman—sister of the deceased mistress—bought her for a few dollars, signing the bill of sale with an X, and freed her. Horniblow continued to work as a baker and lived in her own home near her grandchildren, providing Harriet Jacobs and her brother with food, clothing, and a safe haven whenever possible. Even though free, Molly Horniblow had few rights as a black woman. Nevertheless, she was well-respected in the community, among both blacks and whites, and she was a strong moral force for her family and in the community at large. Jacobs' grandmother provided her with physical and spiritual sustenance throughout her years in slavery, and Jacobs writes about her with great respect in the narrative.

One of Jacobs' central arguments in *Incidents* is that slavery itself is evil, and that the kindness of individuals is fleeting and does not protect against the injustices of slavery, under which all slaves ultimately are merely property. Harriet was only six when her mother Delilah died, and the death led Harriet to her first awareness that she was a slave. She describes her first mistress as having been kind to her in her childhood, and it was this owner who taught the young Jacobs to read and write. But when the mistress died in 1825, a deathbed postscript to her will bequeathed twelve-year-old Jacobs, along with a bureau and work table, to her three-year-old niece **Mary Norcom**. Jacobs spent the rest of her slave years under the legal and physical control of the girl's father, Dr. James Norcom. Harriet's father Daniel, a slave on a nearby plantation, died in 1826, one year after Harriet and her brother John had moved into the Norcom household. Although they received a certain degree of protection from their grandmother, they faced the horror of slavery that was all around them, on their own and nearby plantations, as slaves were beaten and tortured as well as subjected to daily abuse by back-breaking labor, hunger, and other deprivations.

Unlike the majority of Southern slaves—male and female—Jacobs did not engage in field-work, but Norcom was a harsh and lecherous master. From a very young age, Jacobs was subjected to his advances and threats, which prompted jealousy and hostility from Norcom's wife. While *Incidents* was intended as an appeal to white women to be allies, Jacobs also acknowledges the difficulties of such alliances. She uses sarcasm throughout her narrative to condemn the hypocrisy of a slaveholding society that invents delicate standards of white womanhood while permitting white women to be brutal slaveowners and permitting black women to be brutalized. Jacobs' narrator notes that her

owner, "like many southern women, was totally deficient in energy. She had not strength to superintend her household affairs; but her nerves were so strong, that she could sit in her easy chair and see a woman whipped, till the blood trickled from every stroke of the lash."

While denying slaves the ability to legally marry, slave law also failed to protect slave women against rape by owners or other white men. Jacobs was under constant harassment and threat of rape from Norcom, with no legal recourse. Norcom also denied her request to marry a free black man. She writes of his abuse:

> But I now entered on my fifteenth year—a sad epoch in the life of a slave girl. My master began to whisper foul words in my ear. Young as I was, I could not remain ignorant of their import. . . . He tried his utmost to corrupt the pure principles my grandmother had instilled. He peopled my young mind with unclean images, such as only a vile monster could think of. I turned from him with disgust and hatred. But he was my master. I was compelled to live under the same roof with him—where I saw a man forty years my senior daily violating the most sacred commandments of nature. He told me I was his property; that I must be subject to his will in all things. My soul revolted against the mean tyranny. But where could I turn for protection?

In an effort to repel her pursuer, Jacobs entered a relationship with an apparently sympathetic white man, Samuel Sawyer. She was fully aware that by entering a sexual relationship outside of marriage she had violated her day's societal standards of female behavior; she was also aware, however, that the dominant standards of womanhood inherently excluded slave women. In her narrative, careful in telling readers of her choice, she places her decision in the context of slavery, appealing to her white female readers while simultaneously pointing out the differences in their situations:

> O, ye happy women, whose purity has been sheltered from childhood, who have been free to choose the objects of your affection, whose homes are protected by law, do not judge the poor desolate slave girl too severely! If slavery had been abolished, I, also, could have married the man of my choice; I could have had a home shielded by the laws.

Jacobs both invoked and critiqued the patriarchal standards of womanhood that condemned her for her relationship with Sawyer. Upon finding that Harriet was pregnant, her grandmother was dismayed at what she regarded as a moral failure: "[H]as it come to this? I had rather see you dead than to see you as you now are. You are a disgrace to your dead mother. . . . Go away! . . . and never come to my house, again."

Jacobs chose this relationship with Sawyer strategically—to protect herself from Norcom and to protect any children she might have. She hoped that her owner might become so angry at her behavior that he would sell her. Reconciling with her grandmother, she gave birth in 1829 to a son by Sawyer, Joseph Jacobs, in her grand-mother's house, and later to a daughter by Sawyer, **Louisa Matilda Jacobs** (1833).

Rather than prompt Norcom to sell her as she had hoped, Jacobs' relationship with Sawyer led Norcom to continue to pursue, curse, and threaten her, actions to which he now added threats against her children. According to the laws of slavery, Jacobs' children were the prop-erty of her owner, even though the father was free. Jacobs was fully aware of this law linking children to their mother's status, a regulation that particularly affected the children of women impregnated by their masters. When the Nor-com character in Jacobs' narrative makes a threat to sell the children, the narrator states: "I knew the law gave him power to fulfil it; for slaveholders have been cunning enough to enact that 'the child shall follow the condition of the *mother*,' not of the *father*; thus taking care that licentiousness shall not interfere with avarice." In fact, many male slaveholders increased their "property" by impregnating their female slaves, institutionalizing rape as an economic benefit to the slaveholding class.

Children were also used as tools of manipu-lation. As punishment for her lack of response to his advances, Norcom sent Jacobs to his son's plantation, separating her from her children, who remained living with Molly Horniblow. Norcom also threatened that her children would be sold off when Jacobs' official owner, his daughter Mary Norcom, married, unless Jacobs became his mistress. If she consented, he promised to allow her to live with her children in a cottage. Unwilling to let him determine the fate of her children, Jacobs made the difficult de-cision to run away. She writes in *Incidents:*

> My mind was made up; I was resolved that I would foil my master and save my children, or I would perish in the attempt. . . . My grandmother was much cast down. I had my secret hopes; but I must fight my battle alone. I had a woman's pride, and a moth-er's love for my children; and I resolved that out of the darkness of this hour a brighter dawn should rise for them. My master had power and law on his side; I had a deter-mined will. There is might in each.

Harriet A. Jacobs

When Jacobs learned that Norcom planned to send the children, who were still very young, to his brutal son's plantation to have them put to work and "broken in," she escaped and hid in a friend's home. Advertisements seeking her cap-ture were posted on every corner and in all public places within miles. Norcom ran the following ad on Tuesdays, Thursdays, and Saturdays for two weeks in Norfolk, Virginia's *American Beacon:*

$100 REWARD

Will be given for the approhension [sic] and delivery of my Servant Girl HARRIET. She is a light mulatto 21 years of age, about 5 feet 4 inches high, of a thick and corpulent habit, having on her head a thick covering of black hair that curls naturally, but which can be easily combed straight. She speaks easily and fluently, and has an agreeable car-riage and address. Being a good seamstress, she has been accustomed to dress well, and has a variety of very fine clothes, made in the prevailing fashion, and will probably ap-pear, if abroad, tricked out in gay and fash-ionable finery. As this girl absconded from the plantation of my son without any known cause or provocation, it is probable she designs to transport herself to the North.

The above reward, with all reasonable charges, will be given for apprehending her, or securing her in any prison or jail within the U. States.

All persons are hereby forewarned against harboring or entertaining her, or being in any way instrumental in her escape, under the most rigorous penalties of the law.

JAMES NORCOM
Edenton, N.C. June 30

Instead of running to the North, Jacobs eventually concealed herself in a small crawlspace in her grandmother's house. Starting in 1835, at the age of 21, she found refuge for nearly seven years in that small hidden space between the ceiling and the sloped roof, nine feet by seven feet, and only about three feet high at its tallest point. Her family—except for her children, who were not told where she was—spoke to her and gave her food through a small trap door, but only in the darkness of night. She made a small hole in the wall, giving her enough light to sew and read, and permitting her to watch the street below, often seeing her children and others who thought she was miles away. While voluntarily imprisoned in her grandmother's attic, Jacobs used her ability to write to wage psychological warfare against her owner Norcom. Holed up just yards from him, she wrote phony letters and had friends mail them back to North Carolina from as far away as New York and Canada. When Norcom would come across the letters, as Jacobs intended, he often would set off in search of her. He was convinced that he could outsmart her, when in fact she was orchestrating his unsuccessful efforts. In *Incidents in the Life of a Slave Girl*, Jacobs recognized the power of writing in many ways. Her descriptions were intended to persuade a Northern audience of the evils of slavery. In one scene in the book, told through the characters of Linda Brent and Dr. Flint (Norcom), the escaped slave overhears Flint reading to the grandmother his own falsified version of one of the slave's faked letters. In *his* version, the fugitive Linda is miserable, regretful, and wants to return to slavery from her exile in the North. The grandmother listens, knowing her granddaughter is crouched above, and knowing that the respected doctor is lying. Eventually, thinking Jacobs was long gone, Norcom sold the children, and their father, Sawyer, purchased them. Jacobs, her limbs numb and atrophied, still needed to find a way to get herself and her children safely to the North.

Part of the plan was for Sawyer to free his children, but he failed to do so immediately, frustrating Jacobs who was both physically and legal-ly helpless. Sawyer had since married and been elected to Congress, and, like many seemingly well-meaning owners who promised freedom to their slaves, he persisted in claiming their labors a little longer. Jacobs was faced with two profound obstacles: Norcom, who claimed the sale was never legal and the children still belonged to his family, and Sawyer, who intended to send the children to his own family in the North instead of freeing them. "So, then," concludes the narrator in *Incidents*, "after all I had endured for their sakes, my poor children were between two fires; between my old master and their new master! And I was powerless. There was no protecting arm of the law for me to invoke."

Orchestrating everything to the best of her ability from her tiny prison, Jacobs eventually arranged to have both children sent to the North and later, in 1842, fled to the North herself. After Jacobs finally left North Carolina, Norcom and his family continued to try to track her down and return her to slavery. She supported herself and her children by working as a nursemaid for a white family in New York. Under pursuit by slave catchers, Jacobs was chased from New York to Boston and back several times between 1843 and 1846. She eventually returned to work for the Willis family in New York, and it was Nathaniel Parker Willis' second wife, **Cornelia Grinnell Willis**, who purchased and emancipated her in 1852, 17 years after Jacobs had first fled from slavery. While relieved to be finally free, Jacobs was appalled at the idea of being bought and sold like a piece of merchandise to gain the freedom that should have been her right. In her book, the narrator describes hearing about the bill of sale, the legal record of her freedom that horrified her as much as it freed her:

"The bill of sale!" Those words struck me like a blow. So I was *sold* at last! A human being *sold* in the free city of New York! The bill of sale is on record, and future generations will learn from it that women were articles of traffic in New York, late in the nineteenth century of the Christian religion.

Grateful to her benefactor, Jacobs also acknowledged how this debt of gratitude kept her in a sense bound to her employer.

The North, Jacob found, was not simply a safe haven: slave hunters sought out fugitive slaves to return them to the South, and slaves and free blacks alike were subjected to Northern racism. In her narrative, she describes the discrimination and segregation that ran rampant in the "free" North. She reports riding in segregated train cars and steam boats, staying in segregated hotels, and encountering racist work-places. After being told that black Americans could not ride in first class, the narrator compares this affront to treatment in the South: "Colored people were allowed to ride in a filthy box, behind white people, at the south, but they were not required to pay for the privilege. It made me sad to find how the North aped the customs of slavery." She also indicts the arbitrariness of racist policy in the North. For example, the narrator describes the discrimination her son suddenly faced at his workplace in Boston: "[O]ne day they accidentally discovered a fact they had never before suspected—that he was colored! This at once transformed him into a different being." The American and Irish-American co-workers find it "offensive to their dignity to have a 'nigger' among them," the narrator reports, adding, "after they had been told that he *was* a 'nigger.'"

Realizing that the fight was in no way over, Jacobs became involved in abolitionist activities in the North. She worked for a period in the abolitionist reading room run by her brother, and she was involved in a circle of abolitionist and feminist women. Among her friends were white abolitionist **Amy Post** and black abolitionist William Nell, activists who were also involved in women's rights. Jacobs decided that telling her story publicly, although she was uneasy about revealing some of the details (particularly her decision to embark upon a sexual relationship with Sawyer), could help her cause. "I would never consent to give my past life to any one for I would not do it with out giving the whole truth," Jacobs wrote in a letter to Amy Post, as she struggled with the dilemma of revealing her past to the public. She continued, "if it could help save another from my fate it would be selfish and unchristian in me to keep it back."

Post helped Jacobs contact *Harriet Beecher Stowe (author of the influential antislavery novel *Uncle Tom's Cabin*), sending her a summary of Jacobs' story and requesting Stowe's help in producing a dictated narrative of Jacobs' life. To Jacobs' surprise, the famous abolitionist Stowe responded very inadequately, doubting Jacobs' authenticity and offering at best to include parts of Jacobs' story in her own book. Jacobs refused Stowe's offer. Instead, she decided to write her own story, first in letters to abolitionist newspapers and then as the full narrative. It took several years for her to complete *Incidents in the Life of a Slave Girl,* because she was supporting her family by working full-time as a live-in nursemaid for the Willis family. She wrote only late at night after her work was done, hid-ing her efforts from her employer. Although an endorsement from Stowe or Willis would have helped Jacobs publish her book—since slave narratives generally needed authorization from a well-known white citizen—Jacobs did not approach either of these people. Instead, William Nell introduced her to white abolitionist Lydia Maria Child, who agreed to be the editor of Jacobs' book and to write the introduction that would help "validate" Jacobs to a skeptical (and often racist) white audience.

After her book was published (1861) and the Civil War began, Jacobs remained active in numerous ways. She spent the years of the war and Reconstruction helping former slaves. The year after her book was published, she went to Washington, D.C., to aid escaped slaves there. She performed relief work and wrote about the conditions of these refugees in the abolitionist newspaper the *Liberator.* After the Emancipation Proclamation was signed in 1863, bringing even more blacks to the North, Jacobs also worked in Alexandria, Virginia, where over a thousand former slaves were living. Her daughter, Louisa Matilda Jacobs, joined her, and they provided clothing, health care and education. Jacobs continued to confront racist assumptions, as when whites tried to take over a school that the freed slaves had established. She helped arrange for blacks to keep control of the school and for her daughter to be one of the teachers. "I do not object to white teachers," she wrote in a letter to **Hannah Stevenson** of the New England Freedmen's Aid Society, "but I think it has a good effect upon these people to convince them their own race can do something for their elevation. It inspires them with confidence to help each other." After the war, Jacobs visited Edenton, North Carolina, where she had spent her years in slavery. She brought relief supplies for the newly freed blacks, including clothing and seeds, and she worked to teach the women subsistence gardening. She and her daughter also did relief work in Savannah, Georgia, and they traveled to England to raise money for an orphanage and other efforts in Savannah. In 1868, the year the 14th Amendment was passed (giving black men the right to vote), Jacobs was in Cambridge, Massachusetts, running a boardinghouse.

Her son Joseph, disgusted with racism in the North, tried to make his living elsewhere, traveling to California and Australia. Jacobs learned he was sick overseas in 1863 and never heard from him again. She remained close to her daughter, with whom she worked during the war and Reconstruction years, and moved to Washington, D.C., in 1885. Jacobs died in Washington in her 80s, having spent her life not only trying to change her own circumstances, but also fighting to improve the conditions of others. Her act of writing her story, and her other forms of activism, challenged the racist and sexist assumptions of her time.

Because she wrote under a pseudonym, and because the lives of slaves are difficult to document, for over a hundred years Harriet Jacobs' name was virtually forgotten. Her narrative was republished as recently as the 1970s under the name Linda Brent, and many readers assumed that editor Lydia Maria Child was the real author. Scholar **Jean Fagan Yellin** has recovered extensive documentation verifying Jacobs' identity and the details of her story, publishing a highly documented version of *Incidents in the Life of a Slave Girl*. Jacobs' book is taught in history, literature and a range of other classes. Her narrative stands as one of the strongest indictments of the institution of slavery—both of its practitioners and those who stood by and did nothing. It is also one of the most powerful testimonies of the experiences of a woman under slavery, unswerving in its condemnation of both racism and patriarchy.

SOURCES:

Carby, Hazel. "'Hear My Voice, Ye Careless Daughters': Narratives of Slave and Free Women before Emancipation," in *Reconstructing Womanhood: The Emergence of the Afro-American Woman Novelist*. NY: Oxford University Press, 1987.

*Davis, Angela. *Women, Race and Class*. NY: Vintage Books, 1983.

Deck, Alice A. "Whose Book is This?: Authorial versus Editorial Control of Harriet Brent Jacobs's *Incidents in the Life of a Slave Girl: Written by Herself*," in *Women's Studies International Forum*. Vol. 10, 1987, pp. 33–40.

Jacobs, Harriet Ann. *Incidents in the Life of a Slave Girl, Written by Herself*. Edited and with an introduction by Jean Fagan Yellin. 1861. Cambridge: Harvard University Press, 1987.

———. *Incidents in the Life of Slave Girl, Written by Herself*. Edited by Lydia Maria Child. New introduction and notes by Walter Teller. NY: Harcourt Brace Jovanovich, 1973.

———. *Incidents in the Life of a Slave Girl*. Introduction by Valerie Smith. NY: Oxford University Press, 1988.

Sterling, Dorothy. *We Are Your Sisters: Black Women in the Nineteenth Century*. NY: W.W. Norton, 1984.

Stroud, George M. *A Sketch of the Laws Relating to Slavery in the Several States of the United States of America*, 1856. NY: Negro Universities Press, 1968.

Yellin, Jean Fagan. *Women and Sisters: The Anti-Slavery Feminists in American Culture*. New Haven, CT: Yale University Press, 1990 (chapter 4).

———. "Written by Herself: Harriet Jacobs' Slave Narrative," in *American Literature*. Vol. 53, no. 3, 1981, pp. 479–486.

———, and Cynthia D. Bond, comps. *The Pen is Ours: A Listing of Writings by and about African-American*

Women before 1910 With Secondary Bibliography to the Present. NY, Oxford: Oxford University Press, 1991.

SUGGESTED READING:

Foster, Frances Smith. "Writing Across the Color Line: Harriet Jacobs and *Incidents in the Life of a Slave Girl*," in *Written by Herself: Literary Production by African American Women, 1746–1892*. Indianapolis, IN: Indiana University Press, 1993.

Yellin, Jean Fagan. "Sojourner Truth and Harriet Jacobs," in *Women and Sisters: The Antislavery Feminists in American Culture*. New Haven, CT: Yale University Press, 1989.

COLLECTIONS:

The letters of Harriet Jacobs to Amy Post are housed in the Post Papers at the University of Rochester.

Christina Accomando,
Assistant Professor of English,
California State University, Humboldt,
and **Sharon Barnes**, Ph.D. candidate,
University of Toledo, Toledo, Ohio

Jacobs, Helen Hull (1908–1997)

American tennis player and author who won four consecutive U.S. women's singles titles. Name variations: "Little Helen." Born Helen Hull Jacobs in Globe, Arizona, on August 6, 1908; died in East Hampton, New York, on June 2, 1997; daughter of Roland Herbert Jacobs and Eula (Hull) Jacobs; attended Anna Head School for Girls (Berkeley); attended the University of California at Berkeley, 1926–29; attended William and Mary College, 1942; never married; no children.

National junior tennis champion (1924–25); was first to win four consecutive U.S. women's singles championships (1932, 1933, 1934, 1935); won the U.S. women's doubles championship (1932, 1933, 1934); won the Wimbledon singles championship (1936); was a six-time Wimbledon finalist; was a member of the American Wightman Cup team for 13 successive years; ranked in the world's top ten (1928–40).

Designer of sports clothes, New York City; senior editor, Grolier Book of Knowledge, New York City; served on Republican National Committee (1932); served as lieutenant in the U.S. Naval Reserve (1954), becoming Commander USNR, retired.

Selected publications: Modern Tennis (1933); (autobiography) Beyond the Game (1936); Laurel for Judy; Tennis (1941); By Your Leave, Sir (1943); Gallery of Champions (1949); Center Court (1950); Judy, Tennis Ace (1951); Proudly She Serves (1953); Storm Against the Wind (1954); Famous Women Athletes (1964); The Young Sportsman's Guide to Tennis (1965).

Famous for her historical matches against her nemesis *Helen Wills, Helen Hull Jacobs was nonetheless a champion in her own right,

Helen
Hull
Jacobs

winning four consecutive U.S. women's singles championships between 1932 and 1935, a record equaled only by *Molla Mallory and *Chris Evert. For three years (1932–34), she was also the U.S. women's doubles champion. Popular with players and fans, in 1933 Jacobs was the first woman to break with tradition by wearing man-tailored shorts at Wimbledon.

Helen Hull Jacobs was born in Globe, Arizona, in 1908, the daughter of Roland Herbert Jacobs and **Eula Hull Jacobs**. The family moved to San Francisco shortly before World War I, then to Berkeley, California, where Helen Wills also lived. Helen Jacobs learned to play tennis at the Berkeley Tennis Club under Pop Fuller. She won her first title in 1924, becoming the National Junior Tennis champion, a victory she repeated the following year. For 13 years, she was a member of the American Wightman Cup team, and she brought the crown home to America in 1936, when she won the women's singles at Wimbledon. She would not win again at Wimbledon, although she was a finalist in the games there from 1929 through 1938.

Jacobs' rivalry with Helen Wills began when she was just 14, at a practice set arranged by Fuller. The older Wills won the set 6-0, and, although Jacobs was eager to play another, Wills declined. From then on, an uneasiness existed between the women whenever they appeared together on the court, even though they both repeatedly denied a feud. "During all the years in which we were both playing, we never once exchanged an unpleasant word!," said Jacobs (known as Little Helen). Wills (known as Queen Helen) also noted that Jacobs "was hardly an enemy." Regardless, Britain's *Kay Stammers, a leading player during the 1930s, felt that something was amiss. "There was *definite* friction between them—particularly, I think, on Helen Wills' side. They met when they played tennis: but apart from that, I don't think they had a great deal to do with one another." Wills dominated the rivalry, allowing Jacobs only one win in seven major championship finals (1936), but Jacobs was a fighter. George Lott, an American doubles player, believed that part of what made Jacobs so popular was her perseverance. "I always thought she got the furthest with the leastest," he wrote. "She had a forehand chop, a sound backhand, and lots and lots of stomach muscles. She was buffeted from pillar to post by Helen Wills and still came back for more."

After retiring from tennis, Jacobs' career took some interesting twists and turns. In 1943, following a year at William and Mary College, she joined the WAVES during World War II and served as public relations officer at the U.S. Training School in the Bronx and the Naval Station in Dalgren, Virginia. In 1953, she became Officer in Charge of Enlisted Personnel (inactive) in New York City. After leaving the service, Jacobs remained in New York City, where she was a designer of sports clothes for women, and in 1961, she joined Grolier Company as a senior editor for their *Book of Knowledge*. Over the years, Jacobs also authored some 19 books, including *Young Sportsman's Guide to Tennis*, several tennis novels, and her autobiography, *Beyond the Game* (1936). Jacobs did not pick up a tennis racket, however, after 1947, when she tore the Achilles tendon in her leg and was advised not to attempt the game again.

SOURCES:

King, Billie Jean. *We Have Come a Long Way*. NY: McGraw-Hill, 1988.

Lamparski, Richard. *Whatever Became of . . .?* 1st and 2nd Series. NY: Crown, 1967.

Barbara Morgan,
Melrose, Massachusetts

Jacobs-Bond, Carrie.

See Bond, Carrie Jacobs.

Jacobson, Louise (1924–1943)

French correspondent whose Lettres de Louise Jacobson *was adapted for the theater. Born in Paris, France, on December 24, 1924; died in Auschwitz in 1943; daughter of* Olga Jacobson (d. 1943).

Louise Jacobson was born in Paris on December 24, 1924. In 1942, as a 17-year-old, she was studying for her baccalaureate exam at the Hélène Boucher lycée in Vincennes, during the German Occupation of France. When orders went out from the German high command for Jews to wear the yellow star, Jacobson defied the edict. On September 1, 1942, she was arrested as a political prisoner and taken to the Parisian prison, Fresnes. There, while she was interned for around two months, she wrote often to schoolfriends in a tiny script on hard-to-obtain paper. In her first letter, she wrote: "(I'm going to tell you something that will make you blush) I'm the only virgin here and the only political prisoner (!!!) The others are in for theft, prostitution, vagrancy."

Jacobson was moved to Drancy where she spent her 18th birthday (1942). She wrote her sister **Nadia**: "The life I'm living tempers me and forces me to manage on my own. Despite a few inconveniences all will not have been lost and I will have learned certain things." Friends sent her photos of her family and books for which she was extremely thankful.

Jacobson and the other young prisoners of Drancy determined to eradicate the scene around them by exploring the intellect. "I've finished *The Physiology of Instinct and Intelligence*," she wrote Nadia. "I read it with Mallina and we both memorized the sections on the brain, which was a little tricky." On February 13, 1943, Louise Jacobson was deported to

Auschwitz on French convoy 48 which included 1,000 Jews of French birth, 153 of them children. Her mother would follow on French convoy 62. There, both perished, though Nadia escaped deportation and survived the war. Like *Anne Frank, Louise Jacobson's legacy was an articulate record of her thoughts and experiences, which was later published by Serge Klarsfeld in France in 1989 as *Lettres de Louise Jacobson* and adapted for the theater.

Jacobsson, Ulla (1929–1982)

Swedish actress. Born on May 23, 1929, in Göteborg, Sweden; died of bone cancer on August 20, 1982, in Vienna, Austria; married an Austrian scientist; no children.

Selected filmography: Rolling Sea *(1951);* One Summer of Happiness *(1951);* All the Joy of the Earth *(1953);* Eternal Love *(1954);* Sir Arne's Treasure *(1954);* Smiles of a Summer Night *(1955);* The Sacred Lie *(1955);* Crime et Châtiment *(Crime and Punishment, Fr., 1956);* Song of the Scarlet Flower *(1956);* Unruhige Nacht *(The Restless Night, Ger., 1958);* The Phantom Carriage *(1958);* Riviera Story *(1961);* Love Is a Ball *(US, 1963);* Zulu *(UK, 1964);* The Heroes of Telemark *(UK, 1965);* Nightmare *(1965);* The Double Man *(UK, 1967);* Bamse *(Teddy Bear, 1969);* The Servant *(1970);* Faustrecht der Freiheit *(Fist-Right of Freedom or* Fox and His Friends, *Ger., 1975).*

After an early stage career, Swedish actress Ulla Jacobsson gained international attention with her second movie, *One Summer of Happiness* (1951), directed by Arne Mattsson. She subsequently appeared in *Smiles of a Summer Night* (1955), the breakthrough film of famed Swedish director Ingmar Bergman. During the 1960s, Jacobsson also starred in British, French, and German movies. Her only American film was *Love Is a Ball* (1963). The actress, who was married to an Austrian scientist, died of bone cancer in 1982, at the age of 53.

Jacqueline.

Variant of Jacoba.

Jacqueline Felicie de Almania (fl. 1322).

See de Almania, Jacqueline Felicie.

Jacqueline of Bavaria (1401–1436).

See Jacqueline of Hainault.

Jacqueline of Hainault (1401–1436)

Countess of Hainault and Holland. Name variations: Jacqueline of Bavaria; Jacqueline of Holland; Jacoba or *Jakobäa of Bavaria; Jacoba von Beijeren; (family name) Wittelsbach. Born on July 25, 1401 (some sources cite 1402), in Hainault, a Flemish province; died on October 9, 1436, in Teylingen, Netherlands; buried at The Hague; created countess in 1417; daughter of William VI, count of Hainault and Holland, and* *Margaret of Burgundy (c. 1376–1441); married John (1398–1417), duke of Touraine and dauphin of France, in July 1416; married John IV, duke of Brabant (r. 1415–1427), on March 10, 1418 (annulled around 1422); married Humphrey, duke of Gloucester, in 1422 (annulled 1428); married Francis of Borselen also known as Franz von Borselen or Franz de Borselle, count of Ostrevent, in July 1432.*

A powerful noblewoman, Jacqueline of Hainault was also a talented military leader. When she was about 15 years old, her father, Count William of Hainault, died and left his titles and vast estates to her; among other titles, Jacqueline became countess of Hainault and Holland. It was reported that Jacqueline excelled in all the accomplishments thought important for a woman of her status, including hunting with falcons.

Like many other medieval noblewomen, Jacqueline of Hainault married several times. Her first husband was John, duke of Touraine, whom she married in 1416. John died before they had been wed a year, and Jacqueline married John IV, duke of Brabant, in 1418. The duke was much older than Jacqueline, who was only 17, and after a few years the couple separated. As an heiress, Jacqueline had more say in her marriage plans than most women of her time; it is thought that she was much more adamant about the annulment than the duke. In 1422, Jacqueline wed Humphrey, duke of Gloucester. At this time Jacqueline encountered resistance to her independence from the pope, who declared her latest marriage invalid in 1428.

Eventually a war began between Jacqueline of Hainault and Philip the Good, duke of Burgundy. When Philip successfully wrenched control of Hainault from Jacqueline and Humphrey, Jacqueline was captured and imprisoned by his forces. Undaunted, she disguised herself as a pageboy and managed to escape. Returning to Holland, she again took up the fight for the right to rule her inheritance. She eventually had to concede defeat and signed the Treaty of Delft, which made Philip her guardian and guaranteed him the right to her lands upon her death. Although the treaty specifically gave Philip the right to choose Jacqueline's next husband, she married the man of her choice, Franz von Borselen, soon after signing the treaty.

The war for Hainault and Holland continued until Franz was captured. Philip offered to spare Franz's life if she signed over all of her properties to him. Jacqueline, who either truly loved her husband or could see no way to triumph over Philip's superior armies, agreed to his conditions. Little is known of Jacqueline after Philip took over as duke of Hainault and Holland.

SOURCES:

Echols, Anne, and Marty Williams. *An Annotated Index of Medieval Women.* NY: Markus Wiener, 1992.

Salmonson, Jessica. *The Encyclopedia of Amazons.* NY: Doubleday, 1991.

Laura York,
Riverside, California

Jacqueline of Holland (1401–1436).

See Jacqueline of Hainault.

Jacqueline of Settesoli (d. about 1273).

See Jacoba di Settesoli.

Jacquet de la Guerre, Elisabeth-Claude (c. 1666–1729)

French composer and musician. Name variations: Elisabeth de la Guerre. Born Elisabeth-Claude Jacquet around 1666; died on June 27, 1729, in Paris, France; daughter of musician Claude Jacquet; married Marin de la Guerre, in 1684 (died 1704); children: one son (died young).

Elisabeth-Claude Jacquet was born around 1666 into a family of Parisian instrument makers and musicians. She and her siblings were trained in music by her father, an organist and harpsichord maker. Widely regarded as a prodigy, she first performed on the harpsichord before King Louis XIV when she was four. Her talent won her the lifelong support and protection of Louis and the subsequent admiration of Paris. In 1677, an article calling Elisabeth-Claude "the marvel of our century" appeared in a Parisian magazine, noting that she had already distinguished herself as a singer, harpsichordist, and composer. She continued to play frequently at the royal court, where the king placed her under the protection of his mistresses, *Madame de Montespan and *Madame de Maintenon, and provided her an annual stipend.

In 1682, Elisabeth-Claude declined the king's invitation to move with his court to Versailles, preferring to remain in Paris, where she enjoyed a long and successful career which brought her considerable wealth. In 1684, she married a Parisian organist, Marin de la Guerre, with whom she had one son who died as an infant. Neither marriage, motherhood, nor widowhood (her husband died in 1704) affected the pursuit of her music. She composed for the harpsichord and for ballet scores, performed professionally as a singer and musician, mostly in the salons of the nobility but also in popular public recitals. She became widely known for her improvisational techniques. She also wrote at least one opera, *Cephale et Procris* (1694), along with sonatas and Biblical cantatas. Although she wrote a book of harpsichord music around 1687 and a ballet in 1691, these works have been lost. However, her opera and several later books of music, published after 1700, have survived.

Elisabeth-Claude Jacquet de la Guerre continued to write and give concerts in Paris until her retirement in 1717, after almost 50 years as a performer. A commemorative medal was struck in her honor after her death in 1729, at age 63.

SOURCES:

Borroff, Edith. *An Introduction to Elisabeth-Claude Jacquet de la Guerre.* NY: Institute of Medieval Music, 1966.

Schleifer, Martha, and Sylvia Glickman, eds. *Women Composers: Music Through the Ages.* Vol. 2. NY: McGraw-Hill, 1996.

Laura York,
Riverside, California

Jacquetta of Luxemburg (c. 1416–1472).

See Woodville, Elizabeth for sidebar.

Jacubowska, Wanda (b. 1907).

See Jakubowska, Wanda.

Jaculin.

Variant of Jacqueline.

Jaczynowska, Katarzyna (1875–1920)

Polish pianist. Born in Stawle, Poland, in 1875; died in 1920; studied with Anton Rubinstein.

Born in Stawle, Poland, in 1875, Katarzyna Jaczynowska's talent brought her to the attention of Anton Rubinstein, and she studied with him from 1883 through 1894. She studied an additional two years with Leschetizky in Vienna. She then embarked on a very successful virtuoso career throughout Central Europe. Starting in 1912, she taught a master class at the Warsaw Conservatory.

John Haag,
Athens, Georgia

Jadwiga.

Variant of Hedwig or Hedvig.

Jadwiga (1374–1399)

Queen of Poland whose reign is seen as the beginning of the golden age in Poland's history and whose policies and foundations continued to bear fruit after her death. Name variations: Hedwig, Hedwiga, Hedvigis; Jadwiga of Anjou. Born in Hungary on February 18, 1374; died in Poland from complications of childbirth three days after the death of her only child on July 17, 1399; buried with her daughter in the cathedral on Wawel Hill, Cracow; youngest daughter of Louis I the Great, king of Hungary (r. 1342–1382) and Poland (r. 1370–1382) and Elizabeth of Bosnia (c. 1345–1387); married Jagello or Jagiello (1377–1434), grand duke of Lithuania, who became Vladislav also known as Ladislas II (or V) Jagello, king of Poland (r. 1386–1434), on February 18, 1386, in the cathedral on Wawel Hill, Cracow, Poland; children: Elizabeth Bonifacio (June 22, 1399–July 14, 1399).

Crowned king [sic] of Poland (October 15, 1384) in the cathedral on Wawel Hill, Cracow; refounded Cracow University; beatified by Pope John Paul II during his visit to Poland (1979).

Jadwiga died a queen, venerated as a saint, in July 1399, at the age of 25 years. As a queen, she is acknowledged to have been "one of Poland's great rulers." Her concern for the spiritual well-being of her nation and her devotion to the poor and to charitable works earned her the love of her people and the special recognition and continuing support of the Catholic Church. Her personal sacrifice in giving up her betrothed, William of Austria, in order to marry Jagiello, grand duke of Lithuania, and so unite their two countries under the banner of Roman Catholicism, pushed forward the frontier of Western civilization and made possible the emergence of that region described as Central East Europe. Although of tender years, she exhibited a remarkable strength of character, skilled diplomacy, and inspired political acumen. She was a model of Christian virtue in both her public and private life and dedicated to solving her country's problems by peaceful means. Her purely human approach to legal issues and her charitable care for the poor contributed to the popularity of the diarchy. Her premature death was mourned by all, not least by Jagiello, who wore her ring for the remainder of his days, despite three further marriages. Her reign is seen as the beginning of the golden age in Poland's history.

The great events that followed her death were the result of her personal efforts. In the waning days of the 20th century, she was still a hero of the Polish people, and her canonization was being actively pursued in the Vatican.

Jadwiga was born on February 18, 1374, at the Hungarian court, probably at Buda, her father's capital, and lived there for the first four years of her life. She was the youngest daughter and last-born child of Louis I, king of Hungary (r. 1342–1382) and Poland (r. 1370–1382), and his second wife, ✥▶ **Elizabeth of Bosnia**. Her ancestry contained both kings and saints, and monarchy and sainthood went hand in hand throughout her life. Through her father, she was a direct descendant of the house of Anjou, which at the time of her birth ruled over France, Hungary, and Poland. Her paternal grandparents were of the Polish Piast dynasty. She was named for her ancestress, St. Jadwiga of Silesia (*Hedwig of Silesia), who was renowned for her ascetic piety, and she also numbered Louis IX, king of France, *Elizabeth of Hungary (1207–1231), *Salome of Hungary and other saints among her antecedents. It was both as a queen and as a saint that Jadwiga left her own mark on history.

Her father, Louis I of Hungary, was a strong influence on her early life. He was the son of Charles I, king of Hungary (r. 1308–1342), and *Elizabeth of Poland (c. 1310–1386), daughter of Ladislas I Lokietek, king of Poland (r. 1306–1333), and sister of Casimir the Great, king of Poland (r. 1333–1370). In Hungary, Louis I was respected as a ruler who was a clever politician and had been a distinguished soldier. He was also a champion of the Roman Catholic Church with a special devotion to *Mary the Virgin. Scholars, writers, artists, and musicians from all over Europe were attracted to his court, which revolved around the services and rites demanded by his religion. Mass was said daily and fasting

---

✥▶ **Elizabeth of Bosnia** (c. 1345–1387)

Queen and regent of Hungary. Born before 1345; executed in January 1387; daughter of Stefan Kotromanic of Bosnia (a district governor); became second wife of Louis I the Great, king of Hungary (r. 1342–1382) and Poland (r. 1370–1382), betrothed in 1353; children: unnamed daughter (1365–1365); Catherine (1370–1378); *Maria of Hungary (1371–1395); *Jadwiga (1374–1399), queen of Poland (r. 1384–1399).

and feasting were faithfully observed according to the Church calendar. Jadwiga was therefore familiar from an early age with the cultures and traditions and religion of the Western civilized world. She was surrounded by young people of her own age and country as well as children from visiting royal families. She learned many languages including Latin, Hungarian, French, and German, as well as Polish and probably Italian. Her father encouraged a love of books and literature, music, and dancing. She became an expert needlewoman. These early experiences bore fruit in her adult life. As queen of Poland, Jadwiga pioneered the translation of books and manuscripts, including religious texts, into the vernacular; she inaugurated church choirs and music, and personally stitched altar cloths and vestments for her various foundations.

Jagiello's forces had looted and pillaged the area. When Jadwiga heard of it, she was distraught, and, to ease her distress, Jagiello made recompense for damage caused and possessions lost. But "who will give them back their tears?" she asked.

—Margaret Lynch

Her mother Elizabeth of Bosnia was the daughter of Stefan Kotromanic of Bosnia, who held the position of *ban*, that is a district governor who takes command in time of war. Jadwiga had Serbian and Croatian roots. In contrast to her father, her mother had few admirable qualities, and it was fortunate that she took little interest in the upbringing of her daughters. Although commended as a devout woman, Elizabeth of Bosnia was reputedly of a deceitful, conniving nature. The marriage of Elizabeth and Louis was a relatively happy one. Louis had chosen her as his second wife in 1353 in the hope that her father, the *ban*, would aid him in his efforts to bring his Croatian subjects under control. The greatest disappointment of their union was their failure to produce a male heir. By 1374, they had three surviving daughters, Catherine born in 1370, *Maria of Hungary in 1371, and Jadwiga in 1374. Their first-born, an unnamed daughter, had been born in 1365, dying one year later.

It was from her paternal grandmother that Jadwiga, destined to live and rule in Poland, learned of its language, traditions, culture, myths and legends. Elizabeth of Poland was an energetic woman and a strong moral influence on the young Jadwiga. Her marriage in 1320 to

the king of Hungary had made allies of their two countries. When her brother, Casimir the Great, had died in a hunting accident in 1370, without leaving an heir, the crown of Poland had passed to her son, Louis.

In 1374, therefore, Jadwiga's father ruled over both Hungary and Poland. But where in Hungary he was highly regarded, in Poland he was resented, since he spared little time for the Poles, not bothering to learn their language and rarely visiting them. Instead, Louis had entrusted the regency of Poland to his mother, Elizabeth of Poland. From 1370 to 1375, 1376 to 1377, and 1379 to 1380, she had exercised real power on her son's behalf, but overall her rule had been unhappy and ineffectual since the Poles had disliked being governed by a woman, even if she was of Polish Piast descent, and had considered her to be too old to cope with the problems arising from the power struggles taking place within the various factions of nobility encouraged by the apparent laxity in government.

The origins of the Poles are obscure since little documentary evidence has survived, but they are believed to be Slavic in nature. The country's earliest history is based mostly on myth and legend. It was Christianized in the 10th century and has had close relations with the West, especially the Roman Catholic Church, ever since. Its geographical features and its location have always had a profound influence on its development and character. It is, effectively, a huge flat plain—the name Poland is derived from *pole* meaning "plain"—and lacks any natural boundaries, except the Carpathian Mountains which separate it from Hungary and Slovakia. Poland, therefore, was difficult to defend, an easy target, open to attack from her enemies, but, at the same time, it could itself encroach upon its neighbors. The boundaries were ever-changing. As a result, in the 14th century, Poland had become cosmopolitan, tolerant, and hospitable to visitors and a refuge for the persecuted. By the reign of Casimir the Great, it had a well-developed monarchial system of government, was highly cultured, a part of Western civilization, and strongly supportive of Roman Catholicism. Casimir had followed the policies of his father, Ladislas I Lokietek, king of Poland, in making allies of Bavaria and Hungary, in striving to curb the spread of the power of the Teutonic Order and Bohemia, and in seeking to exert Poland's control towards the south and the east. Domestic policy had been centered around the need to keep harmony between the four principal sovereignties of Silesia, Little Poland, Greater Poland, and Mazovia. Their uneasy relationship threatened to disintegrate during Louis' reign, and it was the power struggles between these factions that had stretched Elizabeth of Poland beyond her capability and threatened civil order. That the youthful Jadwiga should succeed in reconciling these factions under one banner during her reign is a tribute to her character and her moderate policies. After his mother's death in 1380, Louis set up a Council of Five headed by the bishop of Cracow, but the personal ambitions of the bishop denied it any chance of success.

As 1374 progressed, and it seemed unlikely that Louis would have any more children, it became increasingly important that he should settle the question of his successor. The Polish nobility made it clear that they would not accept another regent, they wanted their own ruler. Louis summoned their representatives to a meeting in Koszyce (or Kassa) in northern Hungary. The result of their deliberations is recorded in the privilege of Koszyce dated September 17, 1374. Louis offered the Poles one of his daughters as their next monarch, and the conditions under which they agreed to this are laid down in this important document. It guaranteed all the rights of the Polish nobility and exempted them from all taxes except for the traditional tax of twopence per acre on landed property, and promised that only nobles from the province concerned would be appointed to office in that province, and that only Poles would be appointed as *starosta* or governors of the royal castles. The Polish nobility had never been granted so much before. Louis named his eldest daughter Catherine as the next ruler of Poland. But Catherine died, aged eight years, in 1378. Maria was designated to take her place. At the same time, it was announced that Jadwiga would inherit the crown of Hungary.

The marriage alliances Louis had arranged for his daughters would, he hoped, provide them with the necessary support when they came to claim their inheritances. Catherine's betrothed was Louis Valois, duke of Orleans, son of Charles V, king of France; Maria was betrothed to Sigismund of Luxemburg, the margrave of Brandenburg, son of Holy Roman Emperor Charles IV; and Jadwiga to another German, William of Habsburg, the eight-year-old son of King Leopold III of Austria, Hungary's Western neighbor. Jadwiga and William's betrothal took place in Austria in June 1378 in the cathedral of Hainburg on the river Danube. The solemn ceremony was conducted by the Cardinal Archbishop Demetrius, and the contract was binding in every respect, lacking only consummation (sexual maturity was considered to begin at the age of

Jadwiga

12 years). Only the pope could annul it. As was customary, Jadwiga was sent to Vienna to continue her education under the care of the Austrians while William remained in Buda; both were young hostages to the marriage alliance. Compensation for failure of either side to consummate the marriage was set at 200,000 florins for Jadwiga and 300,000 florins for William.

At the Austrian court in Vienna, Jadwiga was fortunate to be placed in the care of Albrecht, brother of King Leopold. Albrecht was a good teacher, well-versed in the arts and sciences, and a devout and caring man. He was a complete contrast to Leopold who had earned the reputation of leading a corrupt court and of being a blatant opponent of the pope. Jadwiga lived here for the next four years, seeing William on occasional exchange visits and apparently untainted by the immorality around her. Jadwiga grew to know and to love William whom she regarded as her future husband. Her affection for him made her personal sacrifice in agreeing to marry another much older than herself all the more poignant. In 1382, Jadwiga was recalled to Buda when her father suddenly fell ill and died on September 11 at Nagy Zombat in northern Hungary.

Jadwiga's world was turned upside down for, only three days after her father's death, it was her sister Maria of Hungary, not herself, who was crowned king of Hungary. Elizabeth of Bosnia, acting in her capacity as regent and queen mother, had acted swiftly, taking advantage of the absence of Sigismund, whom she disliked, and putting Maria on the throne instead of the younger and less experienced Jadwiga. She also hoped that, since the Hungarians had no liking for the German either, Sigismund would be refused reentry into Hungary, and Maria could rule alone while another husband was found. Sigismund, however, did return, and Elizabeth, with the apparent support of Maria, continued to intrigue against him and, disregarding their betrothal, sought a French marriage for Maria.

In Poland, the situation became more acute as the Poles waited for the conditions of Koszyce to be implemented, but they no longer wanted Maria of Hungary as their king. The German Sigismund was far from popular there too, and they were not prepared to accept another absentee monarch. They asked rather that Jadwiga be sent to Poland. Elizabeth agreed to their request but in various ways contrived to let two full years elapse before Jadwiga finally left Buda for Cracow. She traveled alone except for her attendants. She was ten years old.

On October 15, 1384, her name-day, Jadwiga was crowned king of Poland in Wawel Cathedral in Cracow, a title that raised her to an exceptional position. On the following day, October 16, wearing her crown and coronation robes, she descended the hill into the city where she received the homage of the burghers of Cracow. Within days, she was signing official documents and sending money and gifts to found a convent. This would be the pattern for the rest of her life; service to the state and to the Church at one and the same time.

Jadwiga had received a tremendous welcome and had been accepted, but the welcome did not extend to William of Austria, her betrothed. Public opinion was hostile to the idea of a king of German birth, and Austria was at that time engaged in a hopeless struggle against the Swiss which was unlikely to be of any benefit to Poland. Her marriage to William was to be put aside and a replacement husband urgently sought before Jadwiga reached her 12th birth-

day. There were two eligible candidates, Ziemovit II of Mazovia, a Piast and a Christian, who had strong support from Greater Poland, and Jagiello, the grand duke of Lithuania, who, despite his lack of Christian faith, was favored by those nearest to the queen. It was Jagiello's suit that gained momentum as Jadwiga's reign began, since union of Poland with Lithuania would be of enormous benefit to both countries. But Jagiello and his compatriots would have to become Christians.

Jagiello was the seventh son of Olgierd, grand prince of Lithuania (died 1377), and *Julianna of Ruthenia. Olgierd, a strong and vigorous leader, had conquered much of Russia and had successfully defended his country against the Knights of the Teutonic Order. Lithuania, which was still pagan, despite the fact that her leaders had married Christian princesses, was seen as a legitimate target by the Knights, and many prominent representatives of European noble families had, over the years, joined their crusades, attracted by the ideal of fighting pagans and saving souls. But now in 1384, Jagiello, having succeeded his father, found himself heavily involved in domestic crises, and increasingly vulnerable to attacks by the Order and by Russia, with the ever-growing threat from the Ottoman Empire. Union with Poland could save Lithuania from possible extinction and, at the same time, bring it into the sphere of Western civilization with all the advantages that would offer. Further, Christianization would put it forever beyond the reach of the crusaders.

To the young Jadwiga there was no need for a contest. She was "married" to William. Vows made before God were binding. But when William arrived in Cracow to take his place by her side, he found the gates of the city barred against him. There is much of Jadwiga's story that has become legendary. Few documents have survived, and those that have must be considered with care. It is very difficult sometimes to disentangle fact from fiction. This is one of those occasions. Legend has it that Jadwiga not only met with William at a Franciscan monastery but that she arranged to flee with him to Austria. It is said that she was only prevented from taking such drastic action by the intervention of an elder diplomat, Demetrius of Goraj, treasurer of the kingdom, who respectfully asked her to reconsider her decision. The dramatic potential of this scene, during which Jadwiga is supposed to have asked for an axe to break down the door no one would open for her, has inspired many writers and artists, as has the aftermath when, after spending the night in prayer at the foot of a standing cross, she acceded to the pleas of her counselors and agreed to a marriage with Jagiello. This same cross is preserved in the cathedral of Cracow. In fact, it is doubtful whether she could ever have done otherwise. She was fully aware of the responsibility of her position, having been trained for leadership from a child. Devotion to God and to her duty had, likewise, been instilled from an early age. Flight with William would have betrayed these ideals. However, it would be wrong to underestimate the magnitude of the personal sacrifice she made or the strength of mind required to make it. Jagiello was quite unknown to her and, at 36, was three times her age. Moreover, as a child she had listened to the heroic tales of the crusades against the formidable heathen Lithuanians; crusades, indeed, in which her own father had participated.

On August 14, 1385, at Krewo, near Vilno in Lithuania, Jagiello further strengthened his cause by promising to unite his Lithuanian and Ruthenian lands with the crown of Poland forever. By this Treaty of Krewo, he also promised to restore Poland's lost lands, to release all Polish prisoners of war, to defend a united Poland and Lithuania against the Teutonic Order, and to pay the forfeit of 200,000 florins to the Austrians. But most important, he promised to become a Christian and all his people with him. This must have been the deciding factor for Jadwiga. Reared on the stories of her ancestor saints and their battles to save souls, she could not have held out any more. William was banished from Poland, and her envoy was sent to Pope Urban VI to request an annulment of her marriage to him. This was eventually granted on March 12, 1388, two years after her marriage, when the pope had received confirmation of the Christianization of Lithuania.

In 1386, Jagiello arrived in Poland, at Lublin, where, on February 2, according to official records, he was "unanimously accepted as king and lord of Poland." Ten days later, he entered the capital, Cracow, with his brothers, cousins, and associates. Jadwiga and Jagiello met for the first time. Ceremonies followed rapidly one after another. On February 15, Jagiello was baptized and received the Christian name of Ladislas; on February 18, Jadwiga's 12th birthday, they were married; on March 4, 1386, he was crowned Ladislas II, king of Poland, and, as Jadwiga had done, the following day he received the homage of the burghers in the city of Cracow. During the 16 days between marriage and coronation, the Polish nobles were granted the privileges they had held under Louis of Hungary and were compensated for their ex-

penses and losses due to military service, especially for fighting outside Poland. From 1386 to 1399, there was a diarchy in Poland, that is two rulers both crowned as king. Jadwiga's generosity of spirit and complete lack of selfishness were major factors in its success. She demanded and received from her people complete loyalty to Jagiello as her co-ruler, as indeed she herself gave him her loyalty. At the same time, the Poles, more significantly, promised, at her insistence, that they would continue to serve him should she die before he did.

The reign was characterized by their different personalities, which complemented each other. As Jadwiga matured as a diplomat, so Jagiello's faith deepened. Jadwiga had little interest in the nobility and was always more concerned for the spiritual and material needs of the poor, while Jagiello looked for support from the nobles as a means to advance his dynasty. Jagiello settled his problems with a show of force but the sight of Jadwiga was sufficient for men to lay down their arms and pay homage instead. Jadwiga always favored the peaceful solution. Particular problems were created for them by the distances and diversities of their countries and by the ambitions of their subjects and of Jagiello's family. They needed regents they could trust to govern in the provinces and these were rarely found. Thus constant control and vigilance were demanded. They were always on the move, more often than not separately. In the spring of 1387, Jagiello went to Vilno, the capital of Lithuania, to oversee his country's conversion and to initiate the process whereby the Lithuanians would in time achieve those privileges accorded to their Polish counterparts; at the same time, Jadwiga traveled to Lwow in Ruthenia. The borderlands of Ruthenia had long been a source of friction between Poland, Lithuania, and Hungary. Jadwiga's purpose was to establish Polish authority specifically in Volhynia, lately Lithuanian, and Halicz, which had a Hungarian governor. Although accompanied by her personal bodyguard and at the head of an army, a force of arms was not necessary as everywhere she was welcomed and honored. She issued charters granting new privileges and promised them that they would always be part of Poland. Hungary was in no position to protest as, since 1385, civil war had been raging there.

Elizabeth of Bosnia was as unpopular a regent and queen mother as Louis had been a popular monarch. Nothing could illustrate better the sense and maturity of Jadwiga's domestic policies based on negotiation which led to peace and increased her popularity in Poland than the bitter strife in Hungary caused by the aggressive policies and subterfuges employed there by her mother. The strongest challenge to her daughter Maria as queen came from the Croatians who supported the Angevin Charles, duke of Durazzo, who, they claimed, had a more legitimate right to the Hungarian throne. Maria of Hungary, acting on Elizabeth of Bosnia's instructions, set a trap for him by appearing to agree and invited him to Buda, where arrangements were made for his election and coronation as the king of Hungary. Maria and her mother surrendered their crowns and swore allegiance to him. Within days, he was attacked by assassins of Elizabeth of Bosnia's choosing and died from the wounds he received. Status quo was restored and at last Elizabeth withdrew her objection to Maria's marriage to Sigismund. But the unrest continued, now fuelled by the fury of Charles' former supporters. While seeking refuge in southern Hungary, Maria and her mother were ambushed by Croatians and thrown into prison. A court found Elizabeth of Bosnia guilty of inciting murder, and she was executed in the prison in January 1387 in the presence of her daughter. Maria remained in prison until June 4 when she was freed by her husband and they returned together to Buda. Although technically a diarchy as in Poland, Maria was dominated by her husband, and it was Sigismund who ruled in Hungary. In August 1387, Sigismund concluded an armistice with Jagiello, and, while Jadwiga lived, Hungary and Poland were at peace with each other. Maria died in 1395 following a fall from her horse. Her unborn child died with her. As there were no other children, Sigismund ruled alone. Until and unless he remarried and had issue, Jadwiga was heir to the crown of Hungary.

Jagiello's relations also threatened the security of the Polish diarchy. Vitold, cousin to Jagiello, had expected to be awarded a position of authority in Lithuania. When this was not forthcoming, his reaction was to attempt to take the administrative capital, Vilno, by force. Unsuccessful, he fled in 1389 to Prussia and sought help from the Knights of the Teutonic Order. Although suspicious of Vitold's motives, they seized perhaps their last chance to attack their old enemy and test the strength of its new conviction. Further, equally unsuccessful, attempts were made to gain control of Vilno. For two years, the situation remained critical. Only the intervention of Polish forces saved Vilno. Jadwiga's prudence and moderation held the key to the solution. Through the mediation of his wife, Jagiello offered his cousin an administrative role in Lithuania, subject only to the Polish crown. In 1392, at Ostrow, Vitold

was reconciled with the queen and king and accepted the position. But he would continue to cause concern, ever seeking to increase his authority, and during the summer of 1399 would align himself with the Knights against the Tartars led by Tamerlane in the hope of increasing his landholding farther east. In August, after Jadwiga's death, he would meet the Tartar army at Worskla River and be defeated. Jadwiga had foreseen the catastrophe and had protested against it. Her words had gone unheeded, and the resulting fiasco would close the shores of the Black Sea to Poland forever.

The problem of the Teutonic Order of Knights remained. Unwilling to accept that they were already in decline and deaf to criticisms of corruption, they continued to harass Lithuania, and even approached Sigismund of Hungary for aid. From as early as 1395, Jadwiga had attempted to negotiate with the Order. In 1397, she went in person to treat with the Grand Master of the Order, then Conrad von Jungingen. She was successful in as much as while she lived there was no further bloodshed. She is reported to have warned him in words, which echoed those of St. *Bridget of Sweden, that "so long as I live, the Crown will bear your lawlessness with patience. But after my death the punishment of Heaven for all the wrongs you have done to Poland shall fall upon you. War that cannot be averted will destroy you." Her words would come true in 1410 when at Grunwald (or Tannenberg) Jagiello met with the Knights face to face and destroyed them.

Up to 1388, when the pope finally gave his blessing to their union, Jadwiga's marriage had to withstand accusations of a more personal nature. The Habsburgs, in the name of William and supported by the Teutonic Order, continued to challenge Urban VI on its validity. An embittered William asserted that consummation had taken place and, in fact, refused to marry as long as Jadwiga lived. (He did marry, in 1401, *Joanna II of Naples, the sister and heiress of the king of Naples and distant cousin of Jadwiga, and died about five years later.) The Habsburg petition carried little weight since Jadwiga's marriage to the Lithuanian had brought much to Rome. The influence of the Catholic Church was now spread as far as the Baltic Sea, and with Jadwiga's well-known purity of spirit and devotion to Catholicism, the papal decision in favor of her marriage to Jagiello was a foregone conclusion. The slanderous accusations made in the same vein by Gniewosz of Dalewice against Jadwiga were strongly denied by the queen herself who was prepared to swear in open court that her marriage to Jagiello was not bigamous. Faced with such a showdown, Gniewosz was forced to retract his words.

Following the tradition of her saintly ancestors, Jadwiga was a zealous saver of souls. The Church had such confidence in her that she was able to nominate her own prelates and repaid the trust by choosing wisely and well. She was anxious to promote the religious development of Poland and Lithuania, and, in order to further this ideal, throughout her reign she founded innumerable churches, libraries, colleges, and schools. During the last years of her life, she began the refounding of Cracow University. The original foundation in 1364 by Casimir the Great had been modeled on the Italian universities of Bologna and Padua. He had envisaged it as a law school, but the revival by Jadwiga included a theological faculty to provide for Poland's missionary activities in the east. Reorganized on the lines of the Sorbonne, it opened, after Jadwiga's death, in 1400. This "Jagellonian" university became the intellectual center of Poland and the basis of its influence on Eastern Europe. In her will, she bequeathed half the proceeds from the sale of her jewelry and belongings to its completion; the other half, she left to the poor and needy. She inaugurated the foundation of a theological college for young Lithuanians at the University of Prague, known as Jadwiga College. With Jagiello, she founded a cathedral in Vilno for the spiritual care of the new Christians of Lithuania. She did not live to see any of her foundations come to fruition.

One thing marred her marriage and her reign, Jadwiga's failure to conceive. Then, after 13 years of marriage, the miracle happened, and Jadwiga announced her pregnancy. There was general rejoicing; a jubilant Jagiello made arrangements for both the birth and the christening of the child who would be heir not only to the crown of Poland but also to that of Hungary if Sigismund died childless. Pope Boniface IX sent congratulations and consented to be the child's godfather. But as the weeks passed, Jadwiga's health declined. A lifelong regime of self-denial had taken its toll. As her reign had progressed and her piety had deepened, she had adopted an even more penitent style, wearing simple plain clothing and increasing the number of days a week when she ate only bread and water. Earlier, as her infertility had become more of a problem, so she had increased the fasting in the hope of finding favor with God, and, when her prayers were answered, she continued to fast as a means of thanking Him for the miracle of birth and in the mistaken belief that He would

grant her a safe delivery and a healthy baby. At the same time, her royal duties and responsibilities were heavier than usual because of Vitold's ambitious plans and the ever-increasing menace of the Ottoman Empire.

The child, a daughter, named Elizabeth Bonifacia, was born prematurely on June 22, 1399, in the castle of Cracow. The baby was weak, and the mother exhausted. The Polish people knelt in the cobbled streets surrounding the castle and prayed for their recovery. The child died on July 14, 1399. Three days later, Jadwiga died with her baby's dead body beside her. They were buried in the same coffin, together with the last letters sent by the pope, and placed beneath the stone slabs on the Gospel side of the High Altar in the cathedral on Wawel Hill, Cracow. In accordance with Jadwiga's wishes, the funeral rites and memorials were simple. Her body lay in state for four weeks while all over Europe masses were said for her soul. The last of the funeral ceremonies took place on August 14, 1399, the feast of the Assumption of the Blessed Virgin Mary. A black stone tablet now marks the spot where she lies. In 1796, the following was inscribed on it in gold letters: "Jadwiga, daughter of Louis, King of Hungary and Poland, great-niece of Casimir the Great, wife of Ladislas Jagiello, died in the year of Our Lord 1399. Behind this marble she awaits the last day."

Almost immediately her burial place became a site of pilgrimage, and miracles were said to be effected there, though no miracle could be more astounding to her contemporaries than her own achievements as queen. A cult began soon after her death and certainly during her husband's lifetime. Jadwiga was venerated as a saint. Calls for her to be canonized began in the 15th century based on her achievements in the name of Christ. The intense interest in her caused her grave to be opened, first in 1887, when it was noted that she had been "of unusual height," and second in July 1949 on the 550th anniversary of her death when the seals from the papal letters were discovered to be intact.

In 1979, Queen Jadwiga was beatified by Pope John Paul II during his official visit to Poland. Her relics were solemnly placed on the altar of the Holy Cross in Wawel Cathedral in Cracow. In February 1991, Francis Cardinal Macharski, archbishop metropolitan of Cracow, stated in a letter that the canonization of the Blessed Jadwiga was being actively pursued in the Vatican with the warm support of the pope.

After Jadwiga's death, Jagiello had himself reelected and recrowned as king of Poland in his own right. And, following Jadwiga's advice given to him on her deathbed, he took as his second wife, **Anna of Cilli**, who was, as Jadwiga had been, a descendant of the Piast dynasty, being a granddaughter of Casimir the Great, and as such could transfer hereditary rights of the Polish crown to Jagiello and his children. But Jagiello was to remarry twice further, including *Sophia of Kiev, before he had sons to succeed him.

Jadwiga's express wish for no monuments was observed. She remains a hero to the Poles, however, and they keep her memory alive; her acts of mercy and compassion are faithfully commemorated and recalled in legends told and artifacts preserved. Her compassion is illustrated by the following episode that occurred at Gniezno during the joint visit of Jadwiga and Jagiello to Greater Poland in the autumn of 1386. Jagiello had been ill-advised that a show of strength was necessary, and his forces had, accordingly, looted and pillaged the area. When Jadwiga heard of it, she was distraught, and, to ease her distress, Jagiello made recompense for damage caused and possessions lost. But "who" she is famously said to have said, "will give them back their tears?" In the place of tangible memorials there is, for example, a sculptured plaque set in the wall of the Carmelite monastery in Cracow said to be the imprint of her shoe recalling the time and place where she rested her foot in order to tear the golden buckle from her shoe and give it to a stonemason to buy food for his sick wife. The cross where she accepted her destiny to marry Jagiello is preserved in Cracow cathedral. When a coppersmith dies, a silk mantle is thrown over the coffin in remembrance of the occasion when Jadwiga threw her cloak over a drowned boy, son of a coppersmith, whereupon he breathed again. This tattered cloak was for many years the banner of the Guild of Coppersmiths.

But there is no doubt at all about her political achievements. During her reign, the young queen-saint had successfully preserved the union of Poland and Lithuania, reinforced her country's hold on its peripheral territories (for example, those of Ruthenia), held the Teutonic Order in check, and left instructions that would secure the succession. Her policies and her foundations continued to bear fruit after her death.

Oscar Halecki, Jadwiga's devoted biographer, saw, in the 1989 downfall of the Communist regime in Poland, supported by such creative moral leaders as Pope John Paul II and Lech Walesa, the survival of the heritage of Jadwiga. He believed that her joint ideals of duty to her country and devotion to God remained an inspiration.

SOURCES:

Halecki, Oscar. "From the Union with Hungary to the Union with Lithuania: Jadwiga, 1374–99" in W.F. Reddaway, J.H. Penson, and O. Halecki, eds. *The Cambridge History of Poland, from origins to Sobieski.* Cambridge University Press, 1950, pp. 188–209.

———. *Jadwiga of Anjou and the Rise of East Central Europe.* Edited by Thaddeus V. Gromada. East European Monographs. No. CCCVIII. NY: Columbia University Press, 1991.

SUGGESTED READING:

Davies, N. *God's Playground: A History of Poland.* Vol. 1. Clarendon Oxford Press, 1951.

Gardner, M.M. *Queen Jadwiga of Poland.* London, 1934.

Halecki, O. *A History of Poland.* Rev. ed. Routledge, 1983.

Kellogg, C. *Jadwiga, Poland's Great Queen.* N.Y., 1931, reissued 1971.

Thomson, S. Harrison. *Europe in Renaissance and Reformation.* R. Hart Davis, 1963, pp. 191–195.

Margaret Lynch, M.A.,
Teaching Fellow in the Department of History at Lancaster University, Lancaster, United Kingdom, and an independent scholar

Jadwiga of Anjou (1374–1399).

See Jadwiga.

Jadwiga of Glogow (fl. late 1300s)

*Queen of Poland. Flourished in the late 1300s; fourth wife of Kazimierz III also known as Casimir III the Great, king of Poland (r. 1333–1370); children: possibly Elizabeth (who married Boguslaw V of Slupsk); Cunegunde; Anna. Casimir III was first married to *Aldona of Lithuania, Adelaide of Hesse, and *Krystyna Rokiczanska.*

Jadwiga of Silesia (1174–1243).

See Hedwig of Silesia.

Jael (fl. 1125 BCE).

See Deborah for sidebar.

Jagan, Janet (1920—)

Jewish-American Guyanese politician and president, known as the "matriarch of Guyanese sovereignty." Born Janet Rosenberg on October 20, 1920, in Chicago, Illinois; attended University of Detroit, Wayne State University, Michigan State College (now University), Cook County School of Nursing; married Cheddi Jagan (a dentist and East Indian from Guyana), in 1943 (died, March 1997); children: Nadira Jagan; Cheddi Jagan, Jr.

Awards: Order of Excellence of Guyana; Women of Achievement, University of Guyana; Gandhi Gold Medal for Peace, Democracy, and Women's Rights.

Married Cheddi Jagan and moved to Guyana (1943); co-founded the Women's Political and Economic Organization and the Political Affairs Committee (1946); co-founded the People's Progressive Party (1950); served as general secretary of the PPP (1950–70); served as deputy speaker of the Legislature (1953); jailed for six months (1955); served as minister of Labour, Health and Housing (1957); served as minister of Home Affairs and Senate (1963–64); served on the Guyana Elections Commission (1967–68); was president, Union of Guyanese Journalists (1970–97); worked as editor of the Mirror *(1973–97); was first lady of the Republic and acting ambassador to the United Nations (1993); was prime minister and vice-president (1997); elected president of Guyana (December 1997); resigned office because of ill health (August 1999).*

The first American woman to serve as president of Guyana, Janet Rosenberg was born to Jewish-Americans in Chicago in 1920. She arrived in Guyana in December 1943, following her husband to his South American homeland. She had met Cheddi Jagan while he was studying dentistry in the United States; against the wishes of both of their parents, they had married.

Once in Guyana, Jagan put her nursing training to use, assisting Cheddi in his dental practice. The Jagans, however, soon looked for avenues to develop their political ideas. While Cheddi converted men in the living room, Janet converted women in the kitchen. Together, they attended discussion groups in Georgetown, collecting around them a group of radical activists. Later, while Cheddi made speeches in the legislative assembly, Janet recorded meetings, strategized, and organized the party. They became a formidable partnership. "We complemented and assisted each other," said Cheddi. "She concentrating on organisational and administrative work and I on research, propaganda and public speaking."

In 1946, Guyana was the only British colony in South America. Using African slaves and Indians, Chinese and Portuguese as indentured servants, the British had exploited the country's natural resources while creating a grossly unjust society. Together with other Europeans, each immigrant group and the indigenous Amerindians occupied a distinct place in the colonial hierarchy. Globally, independence movements in Ghana and India were successfully challenging the established order of colonialism.

To this "land of six races," the Jagans brought their ideas of change, self-determination, and an end to colonialism. From the abstract discussions of the progressive groups, Janet moved to the domestic workers' union, and Cheddi went to the plantations. By 1946, a group that included **Jocelyn Hubbard**, Ashton Chase, and the Jagans had come together to form the Political Affairs Committee. Janet Jagan was the editor of "The Bulletin," a critical part of the PAC's campaign during the limited franchise elections of 1947. Although she failed to win a seat, her campaign made final her commitment to the future of Guyana.

Before the elections, Janet Jagan, **Winifred Gaskin**, and others formed the Women's Political and Economic Organization, "the first real political grouping of women." By then Jagan had already angered the conservatives with her outspoken support for women's rights to abortion and birth control. By partnering with Gaskin, an African Guyanese, Jagan was also building bridges across the deep racial divisions in the society.

Two years after the 1948 strikes at Demerara, the PAC was transformed into the People's Progressive Party (PPP), a mass participation political party. For the next 20 years, Janet Jagan served as general secretary of the PPP. In 1953, the PPP won the elections, and Jagan became the first female deputy speaker of the Legislature. However, PPP policies proved to be too radical for the British, and the constitution was suspended. Janet Jagan spent six months in jail and

Janet Jagan

was subsequently restricted to Georgetown. This did not lessen the popularity of the Jagans, and when elections were held again in 1957, Janet won her seat.

In the early 1960s, the British gave in to the campaign for independence. They then manipulated the transition in order to prevent the pro-Marxist PPP from forming the first independent government. Forbes Burnham had split the PPP during the 1950s and formed the People's National Congress. The PNC would govern Guyana until 1992, despite the continued popularity of the PPP. Corruption and violence were part of the PNC rule; the economy was stifled and many Guyanese went into exile.

After Burnham's death, pressure from the international community brought about changes to the electoral process. Jimmy Carter, former president of the United States, was one of the moderators of the reform. In 1992, Cheddi Jagan finally became president of Guyana. When Cheddi died in March 1997, Janet Jagan stepped forward and ran for president of Guyana as a candidate of the People's Progressive Party (PPP). She won the election in December of that same year. Her victory was not without controversy. There were still those who labeled her an outsider, despite the 54 years she committed to Guyanese nationalism, and Desmond Hoyte, aging leader of the Afro-Guyanese People's National Congress (PNC), refused to recognize her presidency, despite an independent audit that upheld her election win. During her watch, there were also street protests, mini-riots, and a 55-day civil servant strike, but Jagan had extended the hand of reconciliation to her Caribbean neighbors. In July 1999, she suffered a mild heart attack. That August, Jagan resigned her office because of ill health. Her 20 months as president, she said, had left her "a little more battered and a little wiser." Hoyte promptly predicted that he would not recognize her successor, either.

SOURCES:

Jagan, Cheddi. *The West on Trial: The Fight for Guyana's Freedom.* NY: International Publishers, 1972.

The People's Progressive Party, Georgetown, Guyana.

Simms, Peter. *Trouble in Guyana: An account of People, Personalities and Politics as they were in British Guiana.* London: George Allen & Unwin, 1966.

SUGGESTED READING:

Burrowes, Reynold A. *The Wild Coast: An Account of Politics in Guyana.* Cambridge, MA: Schenkman, 1984.

Despres, Leo. *Cultural Pluralism and Nationalist Politics in British Guiana.* Chicago, IL: Rand McNally, 1967.

Muhonjia Khaminwa,
freelance writer, Cambridge, Massachusetts

Jagello, Catherine (1525–1583).

See Catherine Jagello.

Jagellonica, Catherine (1525–1583).

See Catherine Jagello.

Jagemann, Karoline (1777–1848)

German actress and singer. Name variations: Caroline; Frau von Heygendorf; Madame Kegendorf. Born in Weimar, Germany, on January 5, 1777; died in Dresden, Germany, on July 10, 1848; daughter of Christian Joseph Jagemann (1735–1804, a German scholar); sister of Ferdinand Jagemann (1780–1820, a portrait painter); children: (with Charles Augustus, grand duke) two sons.

A noted German singer, Karoline Jagemann made her debut in 1795 at Mannheim. At Weimar the following year, she was such a sensation that she caught the attention of Goethe and Schiller. In 1801, she had another success in Berlin. On her return to Goethe's theater in Weimar in 1809, she became the mistress of the grand duke Charles Augustus, who began to refer to her as Frau von Heygendorf. Jagemann's close relations with the duke, with whom she had two children, gave her such powerful influence that she often hampered Goethe's work, causing the poet to resign from directing in the theater in April 1817 to avoid her. She remained at Weimar until the death of the grand duke, when she retired to Dresden.

Jahel (fl. 1125 BCE).

See Deborah for sidebar on Jael.

Jaipur, maharani of.

See Gayatra Devi (b. 1919).

Jakoba or Jakobäa.

Variant of Jacoba or Jacqueline.

Jakubowska, Wanda (1907—)

Noted Polish film director whose career featured the 1948 film The Last Stop, *depicting life in the German concentration camp at Auschwitz. Name variations: Jacubowska. Pronunciation: Ya-koo-BOV-ska. Born on November 10, 1907, in Warsaw, Poland, then a part of the Russian empire; studied art history at the University of Warsaw.*

Was a founding member of START (1929); completed first documentary (1930); completed first feature film (1939); captured by the Nazi authorities in Poland (1942); sent to the concentration camp at

Auschwitz (1943); returned to Auschwitz to make The Last Stop *(1945–47); won International Peace Prize for* The Last Stop *(1951).*

Filmography: Report One *(1930);* Report Two *(1931);* Impressions, The Sea *(1932);* We Build *(1934);* On the Banks of the Niemen *(1939);* The Last Stop *(*The Last Stage, *1948);* The Atlantic Story *(1955);* Soldier of Victory *(1953);* Farewell to the Devil *(1956);* King Matthew I *(1958);* Encounter in the Shadows *(*Encounters in the Dark, *1960);* It Happened Yesterday *(1960);* The End of Our World *(1964);* The Hot Line *(1965);* At 150 Kilometers Per Hour *(1971);* Ludwik Warynski *(1978);* Dance in Chains *(*The Mazurka Danced at Dawn, *1979);* Invitation to Dance *(*Invitation, *1986);* Colors of Love *(1987).*

Wanda Jakubowska's career as one of Poland's most important film directors was marked by the spectacular success of *The Last Stop* (also known as *The Last Stage* or in Poland *Ostatni etap*), which she completed in 1947. Like several contributors to Poland's lively post-World War II cinema, Jakubowska began her career in the 1930s. But the war gave her an intense and unforgettable set of experiences. Drawing on her own time as a prisoner in the Nazi concentration camps of Auschwitz and Ravensbrück, Jakubowska created a memorable picture of the horrors and dehumanization of these victims of Nazism and of the heroism of those who tried to resist.

This film was emblematic of Jakubowska's work in cinema from the early 1930s, since she and her colleagues in the innovative, left-wing START movement were characterized by their political engagement. It also reflected the relatively free artistic climate that existed during the immediate post-World War II period in Poland. As Communist control first intensified then weakened after the death of Joseph Stalin in 1953, Jakubowska's work was influenced by these new political currents in her country.

The Poland in which Jakubowska grew up and worked as a film director was one of the most troubled countries of the 20th century. At

Wanda Jakubowska

the time of her birth, Poland was still divided, as it had been since the close of the 18th century, among its three powerful neighbors: Russia, Austria, and Germany. While Jakubowska was still a child, Polish territory became a chief battleground in World War I. By the fall of 1915, powerful German and Austrian assaults had pushed Russia out of its Polish territories for the remainder of the conflict. A revived Poland was born at the close of World War I when the three countries that had been its occupiers all suffered defeat and revolution. In 1920, an invasion by Russian forces, now the army of the new Soviet state, was defeated at the gates of Warsaw.

In the 1920s, Poland went from being a nominal democracy to a military dictatorship under General Joseph Pilsudski. When he died in 1935, only to be succeeded by other military leaders, the revival of both Russian and German strength was beginning to threaten the existence of the new Poland. The threat became reality when the first campaign of World War II in September 1939 put much of Poland under the brutal dictatorship of Adolf Hitler with the eastern part of the country under the rule of Soviet dictator Joseph Stalin.

[Jakubowska's The Last Stop] was the first full-length film to bring international attention to the existence of Polish cinema.

—Frank Bren

Poland experienced almost six horrendous years under German occupation. A key feature of the period was the German attempt to crush Polish culture, partly carried out by the murder or imprisonment of the Polish intellectual class. When Poland was liberated by the Soviet Union in 1944 and 1945, it soon fell under its domination. Up until 1953, this meant brutal repression and strict controls on Polish cultural life. Thereafter, with the death of Stalin, Poland was permitted an increasing—although often interrupted—process of cultural liberalization.

Wanda Jakubowska was born in Warsaw, then located in the Polish provinces of the Russian Empire, on November 10, 1907. Little has been recorded about her family background and early life before she attended the University of Warsaw as a student of art history. It was there she became interested in film and found a circle of colleagues likewise enthusiastic about film's potential as a medium of political enlightenment.

There was little place for such individuals in the conventional Polish film industry that had begun shortly after the start of the 20th century.

In the years following World War I, Polish filmmakers produced a large stock of full-length films. For the most part, these were popular melodramas designed for a mass audience and heavily dependent on the model set by Hollywood. Historical films often featured anti-German or, more frequently, anti-Russian themes, becoming what Frank Bren calls "grudge-movies." A relatively distinguished example of the genre which received some international praise was *Hurricane,* a 1928 production directed by Joseph Lejtes and set during Poland's 1863 revolt against Russian domination.

In fact, most of the movies Polish audiences saw came directly from abroad with American productions dominating the scene. The Polish government had no particular interest in filmmaking. When it was not actively censoring works with a left-wing coloration, it offered occasional help—such as the use of army facilities—but only for bombastic patriotic films. The industry was dominated by fly-by-night entrepreneurs who rarely finished more than a handful of films before fading from sight.

Wanda Jakubowska, along with future luminaries of the Polish cinema like Alexander Ford, was a founding member of START, the "Organization for the Promotion of Artistic Films," which appeared in the fall of 1929. START aimed at creating a film school and other activities designed to promote a new era in Polish filmmaking. These politically active young artists looked to the Soviet film of their era as an example of what they wished to accomplish: the use of the mass medium as a tool for social improvement. Writes Bren, "START attacked the dullness of the national cinema and also its technical poverty," and it sought "to root Polish films in reality."

Poland's conservative military governments were hostile to anything of the sort. Thus, START's credo, "Fight for films for the public good," proclaimed in 1932, was unlikely to please the authorities. The Polish dictatorship's suspicious censorship office permitted the organization to be registered. The censor required, however, that the politically suggestive word "Promotion" be replaced by "Friends." The organization grew to include 300 members, but it did not last more than a few years. Internal conflicts led to its demise in 1935, though it was reconstituted two years later. Despite its shaky origins, START provided a base from which the postwar cinema emerged.

In addition to Ford and Jakubowska, the members of START included such future celebrities of the Polish film world as Jerzy Toeplitz and Stanislaw Wohl. Beginning with a desire for social activism, they tended to produce work in the form of documentaries, such as Ford's *The Way of Youth*. Completed in 1936, this powerful study of a sanitorium for Jewish children provoked the censor to ban the film in Poland. Jakubowska followed this pattern, completing a number of documentaries throughout the course of the 1930s. She was able to take on the task of making a feature film, *On the Banks of the Niemen,* a work based on the novel by *Eliza Orzeszkowa,* only at the close of the decade. Among the members of START, only Ford was able to make full-length films during the entire course of the 1930s.

Jakubowska's career was abruptly suspended by the outbreak of World War II in September 1939. Her now completed feature film, *On the Banks of the Niemen,* had been scheduled for its premier on September 15, but the work could not be shown in the midst of Poland's desperate defense of its territory against German attacks. The film has been lost, apparently forever, since

Jakubowska entrusted parts of the negative to three friends, not one of whom survived the war and the German occupation of Poland.

By the wartime years, according to some sources, Jakubowska was now a member of the Polish Workers' Party, the core of the future Polish Communist Party. In this period, filmmaking became impossible due to the conditions of the occupation and the removal of equipment from Poland to Nazi Germany. As a political activist, Jakubowska managed to work against the Nazis by helping to operate an underground press, until, in October 1942, she was arrested and shipped off to confinement. Held for six months in the notorious Gestapo Pawiak prison in Warsaw, she was then sent to Auschwitz, a concentration camp in her own country, where she spent most of the following years of the war. Jakubowska was evacuated to the Ravensbrück concentration camp in Germany during the conflict's final months. In later years, Jakubowska claimed that she owed her survival in these two concentration camps to her ability to transform her experiences in her mind into the raw material for a future

From the movie
The Last Stop,
directed by
Wanda
Jakubowska.

documentary. She was determined that she would make a film on this hideous subject.

In the aftermath of the war, Jakubowska found that a new film industry was emerging. The wartime period had nearly destroyed the Polish film industry, with its leading figures either going into exile, like Stanislaw Wohl, or, like Jakubowska, suffering imprisonment under the Nazis. Three-quarters of Poland's movie theaters closed in the years of World War II, and filmmaking—except for shooting clandestine documentary footage showing the horrors of the occupation—came to a halt.

The revival took the form of a nationalized endeavor, sponsored by the government. A government of the left, containing a substantial number of Communists, came into power in 1945; this meant substantial official support for the country's nationalized film industry, Film Polski. The model was the Soviet Union. There, the founder for the revolutionary state V.I. Lenin had early recognized the propaganda potential of film. The new center of the industry became Lodz, which had suffered far less destruction during the war than the capital city of Warsaw. Hundreds of new theaters opened, and a film workshop was started in Cracow; subsequently relocated to Lodz, it developed into the Higher School of Film. Its founder was Antoni Bohdziewicz, who had worked underground during the war years to shoot documentary film. Wohl recalled traveling to Berlin and visiting the smaller studios, whose equipment, unlike that of the major German studios, had not yet been seized by Soviet troops. He managed to amass about $2 million worth of cameras, recording devices, and other key tools for cinematography.

Jakubowska also found that a period of relative artistic freedom existed in the years immediately after 1945, with the full weight of a Stalinist-style Polish dictatorship coming only at the close of the decade. The combination of government support—in place of the right-wing censorship of the interwar period—and a relatively relaxed cultural climate led to a number of distinguished films about the wartime years coming from Film Polski. Key figures from START were now able to operate with resources unknown in the 1930s, and the prewar organization dominated the new Polish film. Ford's 1949 film *Border Street* set out to show the bond between Polish Catholics and Jews in occupied Warsaw, and Jakubowska, the previous year, came out with *The Last Stop*, her most memorable film.

The Last Stop had been put into production in May 1945 and work on it was completed in May 1947. It fit into a larger trend in postwar Polish filmmaking that focused on the immense effects and the vivid memories of World War II. The first feature film to come out of these stressful conditions was director Leonard Buczkowski's *Forbidden Songs* in 1947. Set in wartime Warsaw, *Forbidden Songs,* which centered on a Polish musician collecting the popular songs sung in the streets during the Nazi years, was criticized for presenting less than a total condemnation of the German occupying authorities. According to Frank Turaj, the film managed to "exemplify the indomitable nature and tough humor of the common man," but it had to be withdrawn for ideological revisions. Nonetheless, its initial showing drew enormous crowds and showed the hunger in Polish audiences for art and entertainment that reflected their recent, horrendous experiences.

Jakubowska used vastly different materials to create *The Last Stop,* employing her own experiences along with historical documentation in the form of German records and the memoirs of other prisoners. The screenplay from which she worked was done in collaboration with **Gerda Schneider**, a German woman who had been a fellow prisoner at Auschwitz. Jakubowska had first conceived the idea of a film about Auschwitz immediately upon arriving at the dreaded camp. Working with two talented young assistants, Jerzy Kawalerowicz and Jan Rybkowski, she presented a restrained picture of camp life that combined the suffering of the inmates with their will to live and their solidarity with one another.

Made with a combination of documentary and dramatic elements, *The Last Stop* did not try to tell a linear story. Rather, it abandoned the unity of a single person's experience to bring together numerous characters and plots. As Turaj writes, it was "as if someone were narrating in a voice choked with emotion, not able to tell something in a linear way." In a low-key but compelling fashion, the film presents the women prisoners arriving at Auschwitz and the way in which most of them were immediately selected to be gassed and then burned in the camp's crematoria. A particularly harrowing scene in the film shows camp officials torturing a woman who is going through childbirth. A note of hope comes at the film's close when several inmates manage to escape.

Jakubowska's great film drew particular strength from the fact that many of the performers, like Jakubowska herself, had been confined in Auschwitz. Its production crew consisted largely of women, many of whom had also been prisoners at Auschwitz, and there were noted performances from actresses **Barbara Krapińska** and **Wanda Bartówna** with **Aleksandra Slaska** and **Alina Janowska** in supporting roles. *The Last Stop* had its world premier on March 5, 1948, in Prague at a festival of Slavic film, and was subsequently hailed at the 1948 Marienbad Film Festival. Shown in 60 countries, the film demonstrated to an international audience some of the potential of a reviving Polish film industry. *The Last Stop* earned its director the Communist bloc's International Peace Prize in 1951, but it was also an achievement Jakubowska was never able to match even though her career continued for four decades. Nevertheless, writes Ephraim Katz, her films were "influential in the development of post-WWII Polish cinema."

The state monopoly that had been created after World War II became increasingly heavy-handed in the 1940s and early 1950s. In these years, Soviet control over Eastern Europe tightened, Communist parties were purged of anyone suspected of disloyalty to Moscow, and the artistic world was expected to toe the line. At a filmmakers' conference in Wila in southern Poland in 1949, top political leaders set the harsh guidelines for Polish cinema. "Socialist realism," with its obligation to reeducate society using positive heroes waging a victorious class struggle under the direction of the Communist Party, had to become the central approach. Notes Turaj: "Few filmmakers, under the circumstances, could rise above mediocrity."

Jakubowska apparently found it impossible to escape the strictures of the time. Alexander Ford did so by making historical epics such as *Chopin's Youth*, which appeared in 1952. By contrast, Jakubowska's second postwar film, made in these years of political repression, was *Soldier of Victory*, completed in 1953. The film included all of the political cliches of the time, and it stands in sad contrast to the achievement of *The Last Stop*. It tells the story of General Karol Swierczewski, a Pole living in the Soviet Union who rises to the rank of general in the Soviet army before being assassinated by Ukrainian nationalists after the conclusion of World War II.

The harsh political climate of the Stalinist years softened in the mid-1950s, and Polish cinema experienced change as the government decentralized its control of the industry. What had been a state monopoly was now transformed into separate, semiautonomous film units. Dominated by a distinguished director, each unit could

work without onerous government control. The government retained the right to approve the script and, after the film's completion, to control its distribution and promotion. Jakubowska and other veterans of START, such as Alexander Ford and Jerzy Toeplitz, obtained the leadership of some units in May 1955. This relatively relaxed system eventually grew to allow films increasingly critical of the state to be completed and presented to an international audience.

Although younger filmmakers began to dominate the scene in the 1960s, and the reform currents begun in the 1950s were at times reversed, Jakubowska continued to make films at regular intervals during the various stages of Poland's political evolution. She turned away from politics in 1958 with *King Matthew I*, a technicolor film made for children. In 1960, she returned to the topic of World War II with *Encounter in the Shadows*, which told the story of Magdalena, a Polish pianist touring Germany. The young woman finds herself in the same city to which she had been sent as a slave laborer during the course of the war.

Wanda Jakubowska returned to Auschwitz to make a second picture about the concentration camp. Entitled *The End of the World*, it was completed in 1964. Like her other work, it failed in the eyes of most critics to reach the level achieved in *The Last Stop*. She continued to make films in the next two decades. *The Mazurka Danced at Dawn* was finished in 1979, and, at the apparent close of her career, *Invitation to the Dance* appeared in 1986 and *Colors of Love* in 1987.

SOURCES:

Bren, Frank. *World Cinema 1: Poland.* London: Flicks Books, 1986.

Foster, Gwendolyn Audrey. *Women Film Directors: An International Bio-critical Dictionary.* Westport, CT: Greenwood Press, 1995.

Karcz, Danuta. *Wanda Jakubowska.* Berlin: Henschelverlag, 1967 (in German).

Katz, Ephraim. *The Film Encyclopedia.* NY: Harper, 1994.

Michalek, Boleslaw, and Frank Turaj. *The Modern Cinema of Poland.* Bloomington, IN: Indiana University Press, 1988.

Slater, Thomas, ed. *Handbook of Soviet and East European Films and Filmmakers.* NY: Greenwood Press, 1992.

Smith, Sharon. *Women Who Make Movies.* NY: Hopkins and Blake, 1975.

SUGGESTED READING:

Dziewanowski, M.K. *Poland in the Twentieth Century.* NY: Columbia University Press, 1977.

Quart, Barbara Koenig. *Women Directors: The Emergence of a New Cinema.* NY: Praeger, 1988.

Neil M. Heyman,
Professor of History, San Diego State University,
San Diego, California

Jalinto, A. (1862–1934).

See Almeida, Julia Lopes de.

James, Alice (1848–1892)

Youngest of the five children of Henry James, Sr., and a chronic invalid, whose diary and letters shine a revealing light on the life of a Victorian "hysteric" and on her exceptional family. Born Alice James in New York, New York, on August 7, 1848; died in Campden Hill, Kensington, England, on March 6, 1892; daughter of Henry James, Sr. (1811–1882, a writer and lecturer) and Mary Walsh James (1810–1882); sister of William James (1842–1910, a philosopher and psychologist) and Henry James (1843–1916, a novelist and short story writer); never married; no children.

Selected writings: (edited and with an introduction by Leon Edel) The Diary of Alice James *(NY: Dodd, Mead, 1964).*

Alice James

Alice James was the youngest of five exceptional children born to a prosperous Victorian family in New England. Her two elder brothers were among the premier intellectuals of the late 19th and early 20th centuries, William James as a philosopher and psychologist, Henry James, Jr., as a novelist. The two younger brothers, Robertson and Garth, fought in the Civil War and ran an experimental farm in the Reconstruction South. Alice, by contrast, published nothing, had no career, and spent most of her life as an invalid, dying at the age of 44 in an English sanitarium. However, her many brilliant letters and the diary she kept during the last three years of her life have been recognized as shrewd commentaries on the famous family, and on the nature of an invalid woman's life in that era.

Alice James was born in New York in 1848. Her family, of Irish Protestant descent, traveled widely through Europe during her childhood, and the five children were educated by a succession of governesses and educational experimenters in London, Paris, and Geneva. Alice was as fluent in French as in English by the age of eight. Their father, Henry James, Sr., was himself a writer and lecturer, open-minded, unconventional, a friend of the Transcendentalists and a convert to Swedenborgianism. He was an eager traveler despite having lost one of his legs in an accident during his teens, but although he was intellectually daring he shared the common 19th-century view that women were by nature more virtuous but less intelligent than men. He thought of virtue as something that men had to strive for but women were endowed with from birth. Her mother ❧▶ **Mary Walsh James** was more down to earth than the often impractical Henry, Sr., but Alice sought above all her father's good opinion. She was teased good-naturedly by her four older brothers, who kept up a bantering tone with each other throughout their lives. William described her as a "cherry-lipped, apricot-nosed, double-chinned little Sister."

The James family returned to America and settled at Newport, Rhode Island, just before the Civil War, moving to Cambridge, Massachusetts, when the war ended. Alice would remain there until her parents' deaths in the early 1880s. Her health appears to have been fine in childhood, but from the onset of puberty she suffered increasingly from stomach pains, fainting fits, facial neuralgia, and even occasional paralysis, breaking down completely at the age of 19. A certain "delicacy" was fashionable in young ladies, and fictional heroines (including those of her brother Henry) often had ailments which enhanced their beauty. The reality of a nervous breakdown was another matter—terrifying and disorienting. Psychoanalysis had not yet been developed, and numerous doctors pondered her symptoms. Over the following decades, her anxious parents tried dozens of experimental remedies but although she often rallied for a time, she inevitably relapsed. She came to regard herself as a classic Victorian "hysteric," one whose illness seemed more serious than the identifiable symptoms. Sometimes something as slight as an oath or angry remark could make her faint away. She wrote that she was unable to work in a sustained way without the danger of a "violent revolt in my head," which, "from just behind the eyes . . . feels like a dense jungle into which no ray of light has ever penetrated." Her brothers Robertson and William also suffered from nervous ailments—a breakdown made William question his vocation to medicine in the late 1860s.

Some of Alice's recoveries were quite long lasting, but never complete, and she seems to have realized that her life would be restricted. She played an active role in a women's sewing bee that made clothes for the Boston poor in the late 1860s and early 1870s. Comprised of the sisters of many prominent Bostonians, it doubled as a social and intellectual group—she served a term as its president in the early 1870s. As the members married one by one, however (the group had begun as a teenagers' medical support group during the Civil War), she was left behind, aware that her health was making her marginal to the usual woman's life of the era. Her letters sometimes suggest that she was jealous of her contemporaries' marriages, and to one friend who was being courted in London, she admitted: "I am becoming ardently matrimonial, and if I could get any sort of man to be impassioned about me I should not let him escape." Such a man never appeared, and she tried to compensate by finding work. Growing more serious about the possibility, and necessity for, social reform, she befriended *Elizabeth Palmer Peabody (1804–1894), a leading figure among female reformers (much satirized by Alice's father and brothers), and joined her in running a local charity, the Female Humane Society.

In 1872, when she was 24, Alice went on a five-month tour of Europe with Henry Jr. and her maternal Aunt Kate (Catherine Walsh). It was Alice's first sojourn in Europe since the family's return to America, when she had been 12. She proved to be an eager tourist and thrived on her journeys through England, France, Switzerland, Italy, Austria, and southern Germany. Henry, delighted in her apparently robust health during the trip, wrote that "change . . . seems to me to have been the great agent in her marvelous improvement." She was, he wrote, "like a per-

son coming at last into the faculty and pleasure of movement and it is the most active part of her life here which does her the most good and leaves the most substantial effects behind it." Her biographer Jean Strouse comments that of all her brothers Henry, the novelist, was closest to her and that "throughout their lives they shared a deeper intellectual and spiritual kinship than either felt with any other member of the family." Although he was not troubled by the nervous debility from which Alice suffered, Henry also remained unmarried and apparently celibate throughout his life and felt unable to compete in the "manly" world of that era. In the spring of 1873, back in America, Alice was well enough to make a walking tour all the way from Cambridge, Massachusetts, to New York City.

In 1875, she even briefly got a job at *Anna Eliot Ticknor's Society to Encourage Studies at Home. In an age when even wealthy young women had few educational opportunities, it was an attempt to give them a form of education by correspondence course, and Alice—widely if informally educated, and extremely interested in history—became a history teacher via correspondence. In the year of her 30th birthday, 1878, however, she suffered another severe breakdown, was terribly depressed, and even contemplated suicide, which she discussed with her father. He calmly approved it for anyone who found life unendurable, knowing that in practice it was not something she would attempt. She continued to discuss it in letters and conversation but never made an attempt. In her view, a suicide openly admitted (rather than hushed up, as was then usual) would be a kind of social triumph. "What a pity to hide it," she wrote, "every educated person who kills himself does something towards lessening the superstition. . . . How heroic to be able to suppress one's vanity to the extent of confession that the game

❦▶ **James, Mary Walsh** (1810–1882)
*American society woman and mother of the brilliant Jameses. Born in New York, New York, in 1810; died in Cambridge, Massachusetts, in 1882; daughter of James Walsh and Elizabeth (Robertson) Walsh; married Henry James, Sr., in 1840; sister of Catherine Walsh (b. 1812); children: William James (1842–1910, a philosopher and psychologist); Henry James (1843–1916, a novelist); Garth Wilkinson James (1845–1883); Robertson James (1846–1910); *Alice James (1848–1892, a diarist).*

[of life] is too hard." She hated the perpetual uncertainty of her health, recognizing the inability of herself or anyone to diagnose it adequately, and despising the numerous doctors who tried to make sense of her ailment. She wrote of the "ignorant asininity of the medical profession in its treatment of nervous disorders" and of "those doctors who tell you that you will die or recover." After years of invalidism and hearing declarations like this, she wrote: "I am neither dead nor recovered."

In 1882, her mother, who throughout her life had been the most dependably healthy and stable force in the family, suddenly died at the age of 72. It had the effect of causing Alice to rally to the care of her father, who was suddenly alone, and for a year she was bright and vigorous. But he died too, apparently having lost the will to live without his wife, and as soon as he had gone Alice relapsed into her own sick bed. After experimenting with several unsatisfactory cures, she traveled, in 1884, to England, with the encouragement of Henry and in the company of her loyal friend **Katherine Loring**, whom she had met in connection with the correspondence school. Alice shifted between London and a sanitarium in Leamington Spa, in the Midlands, but never again got back to America. Loring's sister **Louisa**, another invalid, had come on the voyage too, and the James brothers realized that Alice was jealous of her as a rival. Luckily for Alice, Louisa recovered, enabling Katherine to turn her full affection on her friend. Henry James wrote to William: "I may be wrong in the matter but it rather strikes me as an effect that Katherine Loring has upon her—that as soon as they get together Alice takes to her bed." Henry, as close to Alice as ever and her most regular visitor, was grateful to Loring for her fidelity, but could not help noticing the way in which she, in effect, authorized his sister's permanently sickly condition.

It was in England that Alice began her diary—at first more of a commonplace book in which she copied out snatches of verse, sayings, and aphorisms. On May 31, 1889, she began writing it as a journal, remarking that writing a little every day might help her "lose a little of the sense of loneliness and desolation which abides with me." The diary was not entirely private because often, when she was too sick to write, she dictated it to her nurse or Katherine Loring. It included numerous clippings from the newspapers, on which she then commented acerbically, and it was packed with humorous remarks about the odd ways of the English among whom she was now living. She reported a conversation with her nurse about the difference between American and British women: the nurse told her that American women were "far less 'aughty." She found much that was crass and vulgar about Britain, and was dismayed by the passivity of the lower classes, who, as it seemed to her, let themselves be trodden down by people they wrongly thought of as their superiors. Although she admitted that living on the income from investments as she did made her a "bloated capitalist," she was nevertheless glad that a large May Day demonstration of working men "made emperors, kings, presidents and millionaires tremble." And of the British Empire, then expanding rapidly in Africa and Asia, she wrote that Britons were ridiculous in their "conviction that outlying regions [of the world] are their preserves, [and that] they alone of the human races massacre savages out of pure virtue." She followed with interest the debate, then in progress, over Home Rule for Ireland, from which her ancestors had emigrated to America, and sympathized with Irish nationalism.

Her diary's engaged and ironic tone, and the detached way in which she writes about herself and her illness, make her seem to modern readers strong and shrewd rather than frail and fainting. It includes many passages in which she attempts to diagnose the battle going on between her body and her will. Looking back on her earlier episodes "of hysteria," she wrote that she had always been self-aware, always struggling with one half of her mind to maintain control over the other half. "It used to seem to me that the only difference between me and the insane was that I had not only all the horrors and suffering of insanity, but the duties of doctor, nurse, and strait-jacket imposed upon me too."

During her better phases, she welcomed visitors, including distinguished members of the American expatriate community in England and English admirers of America, such as *Fanny Kemble. Most of them found her witty, entertaining, and a good companion. Her brother William wrote that she rebuffed all expressions of sympathy, "having her own brave philosophy, which was to keep her attention turned to things outside her sick-room and away from herself."

When Alice James was diagnosed in 1891 with a breast cancer tumor, she wrote about it pleasurably in her diary, "I have longed for some palpable disease, no matter how conventionally dreadful a label it might have," and a few days later she wrote about it as an achievement comparable to her brothers' books and plays. She died on March 6, 1892, having kept her diary to the bitter end, writing in it within a few hours of her final lapse into unconsciousness. Her brother Henry, who was there, also wrote a long description of her last days, with his customary literary vividness, in a letter to William. Loring took Alice's ashes back to America where they were buried in a family plot in Cambridge, Massachusetts.

Katherine Loring later typed the diary manuscript, as Alice had requested, and gave a copy to each of the three surviving brothers. She believed that Alice had wanted to have it published, but Henry discouraged the project because several passages consisted of London gossip he had passed on to Alice, which she in turn had exaggerated for dramatic effect. He feared that the book, if published, would alienate half his fashionable friends at a stroke. Even so, he admired it as "a revelation of a moral and personal picture, heroic in its individuality, its independence—its face-to-face with the universe . . . and the beauty and eloquence with which she often expresses this." In light of his anxieties, the diary was not published until 1934, after the death of nearly all the principal characters involved. At first, it was regarded chiefly as a source for studies of the two famous brothers, but the creation of feminist scholarship in the 1970s and 1980s made Alice James a source of fascination in her own right. Feminists have been particularly struck by Alice James' way of finding her special niche in society and **Ruth B. Yeazell** has wittily entitled her study *The Death and Letters of Alice James* in parody of the common Victorian title "Life and Letters of . . . ." Alice James appears, she says, to have turned her death into a kind of virtuoso experience of its own.

SOURCES AND SUGGESTED READING:

Edel, Leon, ed. *The Diary of Alice James*. NY: Dodd, Mead, 1964.
Matthiessen, F.O. *The James Family*. NY: Knopf, 1947.
Strouse, Jean. *Alice James: A Biography*. Boston, MA: Houghton Mifflin, 1980.
Yeazell, Ruth B. *The Death and Letters of Alice James*. Berkeley, CA: University of California Press, 1981.

COLLECTIONS:

Houghton Library, Harvard University

Patrick Allitt,
Professor of History, Emory University, Atlanta, Georgia

James, Alice Gibbens (1849–1922)

American society woman, wife of philosopher William James, and sister-in-law of Alice James. Born in Weymouth, Massachusetts, in 1849; died in Cambridge, Massachusetts, in 1922; daughter of Daniel Lewis Gibbens and Eliza (Putnam) Gibbens; married William James (1842–1910), the psychologist and progressive thinker, in 1878; sister-in-law of *Alice

James (1848–1892); children: Henry James (1879–1947); William James (1882–1961); Herman James (1884–1885); Margaret Mary James (Porter) (1887–1950); Alexander James (1890–1946).

James, Florence (b. 1904).

See Franklin, Miles for sidebar.

James, Hilda (b. 1904).

See Ederle, Gertrude for sidebar.

James, Mary Walsh (1810–1882).

See James, Alice for sidebar.

James, P.D. (1920—)

British mystery writer known as the "Queen of Crime." Name variations: Phyllis Dorothy James; Phyllis Dorothy James White; Baroness James of Holland Park. Born Phyllis Dorothy James on August 3, 1920, in Oxford, England; daughter of Sidney Victor James (an Inland Revenue officer) and Dorothy May (Hone) James; educated at Cambridge Girls' High School, 1931–37; married Ernest Connor Bantry White, in 1941 (died 1964); children: two daughters.

Selected writings: Cover Her Face (London: Faber & Faber, 1962); A Mind to Murder (London: Faber & Faber, 1963); Unnatural Causes (London: Faber & Faber, 1967); Shroud for a Nightingale (London: Faber & Faber, 1971); An Unsuitable Job for a Woman (London: Faber & Faber, 1972); The Black Tower (London: Faber & Faber, 1975); Death of an Expert Witness (London: Faber & Faber, 1977); Inno-

*P.D.
James*

cent Blood *(London: Faber & Faber, 1980); The Skull Beneath the Skin (London: Faber & Faber, 1982); A Taste for Death (London: Faber & Faber, 1986); Devices and Desires (London: Faber & Faber, 1989); The Children of Men (London: Faber & Faber, 1992); Original Sin (London: Faber & Faber, 1994); A Certain Justice (London: Faber & Faber, 1997).*

Phyllis Dorothy James White, who is better known to legions of mystery fans as P.D. James, the "Queen of Crime," was born in Oxford, England, on August 3, 1920, the daughter of Sidney, an official of the Inland Revenue, and **Dorothy Hone James**. The family moved to Cambridge, where Phyllis attended school at the Cambridge High School for Girls. James recalls that from an early age she knew that she wanted to write and had a gift for it; the problem would be to figure out how to use this gift. She has described her childhood as "reasonably happy," not the sort of traumatic youth that some might think a prerequisite for producing tales filled with violent deaths.

Forced to quit school at age 16, James went to work in a tax office. A few years later, she managed to escape the bureaucratic world and became an assistant stage manager at the Festival Theater of Cambridge. In 1941, she married Ernest Conner White, a physician serving in the Royal Army Medical Corps during World War II. White returned from the war in 1945 mentally incapacitated and was hospitalized until his death in 1964. In 1949, with two young daughters to support, James began work for the National Health Service, and medical administration became her career. James' understanding of medical matters, gained through personal experiences during these years, later proved valuable for clinical settings in many of her stories. In 1968, she entered the Home Office and served first as a principal in the Police Department and later in the Criminal Policy Department, again experiences that later made their way into her crime novels. She also served as a magistrate in London.

James did not get around to putting her writing skills to work until she was almost 40, but she knew from the start that it would be a crime story. Because mysteries were then popular, James felt she would have a better chance of getting her work published; she also liked the constraints involved in the craft of writing detective fiction. Although mystery writers are often criticized for using a formulaic process, James found these restrictions liberating, and she was fascinated by the variety of writers who could use the so-called formula successfully. Her first book, *Cover Her Face* (1962), featured Inspector Adam Dalgliesh, her most popular and well-known character, who goes on to solve a number of cases in later books: *A Mind to Murder* (1963), *Unnatural Causes* (1967), *Shroud for a Nightingale* (1971), *The Black Tower* (1975), *Death of an Expert Witness* (1977) and *Devices and Desires* (1989). James' other famous literary creations include private detective Cordelia Gray, featured in *An Unsuitable Job for a Woman* (1972) and *The Skull Beneath the Skin* (1982), and Kate Miskin, detective inspector, who appears in *A Taste for Death* (1986) and *A Certain Justice* (1997). James chose to use her maiden name as her pen name because it was "genderless," and because she thought "it would look good on the dust jacket, if it ever got on a dust jacket."

Phyllis James had a relatively small following for her crime stories until her eighth novel, *Innocent Blood* (1980). After that, the popularity of her books, which share similar settings, a sense of the Gothic, preoccupation with architectural structures, and meticulous, complex character and story lines, increased immensely. She not only enjoyed an international reputation but was granted honorary doctorates at five universities and became a member of the House of Lords (Baroness James of Holland Park). She also served as a governor of the BBC and was a member of the Arts Council, the Society of Authors, and the Booker Prize panel.

James won numerous awards and prizes for her writing. In 1983, she was awarded the OBE (Officer, Order of the British Empire) and, in 1985, was elected a fellow of the Royal Society of Arts and an associate fellow of Downing College, Cambridge. James won Silver Daggers from the Crime Writers' Association of Great Britain for *Shroud for a Nightingale, The Black Tower*, and *A Taste for Death*, and, in 1987, received the Diamond Dagger for outstanding lifetime contributions to crime writing.

SOURCES:

Basbanes, Nicholas A. "The Queen of Crime brings Dalgliesh Back," in *The Day* [New London, CT]. February 1, 1998.

Gussow, Mel. "P.D. James: Murder, She Wrote, and Why She Did," in *The New York Times News Service*. February 8, 1998.

Jo Anne Meginnes,
freelance writer, Brookfield, Vermont

James, Zerelda (c. 1824–1911)

Mother of notorious American outlaw Jesse James. Name variations: Mrs. Robert James; Mrs. Zerelda Samuel; Mrs. James-Samuel. Born Zerelda Cole in Kentucky, around 1824; died in Oklahoma City, Ok-

Zerelda
James

lahoma, on February 10, 1911; married Robert James (a preacher), on December 28, 1841 (died August 1851); married Benjamin Simms (a farmer), on September 30, 1852 (died); married Dr. Reuben Samuel (a physician), in 1857; children: (first marriage) Frank James (b. 1844); Jesse James (b. 1847); Susan James (b. 1849); (third marriage) Sallie, Johnnie, and Archie (who died in childhood).

Zerelda James, the mother of the notorious James brothers, was born in Kentucky around 1824, but little is known of her childhood. By most accounts, she was orphaned at a young age and was living in a Catholic convent in Lexington, Kentucky, when she met young theological student Robert James. The two were married at the home of her guardian James M. Lindsay (a relative of her mother's), near Stamping Ground, Kentucky, on December 28, 1841. After Robert finished his studies at Georgetown University, the couple settled in Missouri and, from the summer of 1843, resided in Kearney, where Robert divided his time between farming and preaching. Their first child, Frank James, was born on January 19, 1844, with the more celebrated Jesse James arriving on September 5, 1847. A daughter, **Susan James**, followed two years later, in November 1849, just as gold was being discovered in California. In 1851, the desire for riches overtook Robert who left his family to join the migration west. He died of a mysterious fever, however, before he could make his fortune.

Zerelda James found widowhood extremely difficult and wed a neighbor farmer, Benjamin Simms, in 1852. The marriage was unhappy and short-lived, due to Simms' death, and Zerelda once again went by the name of Mrs. Robert James. In 1857, she married Reuben Samuel, a soft-spoken doctor four years her junior. Although Zerelda ruled the relationship, Samuel was said to have been a kind man who was good to his stepchildren. The couple expanded their family with another three children: Sallie, Johnnie, and Archie.

According to Carl W. Breihan, who wrote a biography of Jesse James in 1953, Zerelda was a raw-boned, stern-looking woman, who bore her difficult life with little complaint. Although she brought up her children strictly, as was the manner in backwoods Missouri, Zerelda somewhat idolized her children, particularly Frank, whom she referred to as "Mister Frank." Both the James boys were strong-willed even as children, and Zerelda had her hands full. They became skilled with shotguns and pistols at an early age and were leaders in the youthful pranks of the neighborhood. As the boys matured and advanced to more serious crimes, Zerelda became more resolute in her defense of them. The boys apprenticed as guerrilla fighters during the Civil War before graduating to the string of holdups that kept them on the run for 15 years. Throughout that time, Zerelda provided a safe haven for her sons whenever necessary and even offered advice about prospective members of the outlaw band, although she was seldom paid much attention.

In 1874, after a string of robberies, several banks and railroads banded together and engaged the Pinkerton Detective Agency to capture the outlaws. When Pinkerton agent J.W. Whicher was found dead a week after he had been assigned to the case, Jesse James was thought to be responsible. In retaliation, the Pinkerton men tossed a bomb into the Samuel home, hoping to kill Jesse while he slept. Jesse, however, knowing he was in danger, had long since fled. When the bomb exploded, it killed young Archie and tore off Zerelda's right arm below the elbow. After the botched attack, the community rallied around the James family. Sentiment in favor of the James boys was so strong that, in March 1875, General Jeff Jones of Callaway County introduced a bill into the Missouri House of Representatives offering amnesty to them for crimes committed during the Civil War, if they agreed to surrender and stand trial for subsequent crimes. The bill failed to pass.

When Jesse James was killed on April 3, 1882, in St. Joseph, Missouri—shot in the back of the head by a member of his own gang—Zerelda identified his body and accompanied her son by train to the family home in Kearney, Missouri. After the funeral, which was attended by several thousand (mostly curiosity seekers), he was buried in the yard of the Samuel homestead, because Zerelda and her family feared that the body might be stolen if placed in a more public location. Later, in 1900, Zerelda consented to have the body removed to the family cemetery at Kearney. Over the years, however, so many tourists have chipped pieces from the stone marker that the gravestone is barely distinguishable.

Zerelda remained loyal to her son Frank, who escaped conviction for his many crimes and divided his time between the family homestead at Kearney and his ranch at Fletcher. While returning from a visit to the ranch, Zerelda was stricken by a massive heart attack and taken off the train in Oklahoma City. She died there on February 10, 1911. Frank died soon after, in 1915.

SOURCES:
Breihan, Carl W. *Complete and Authentic Life of Jesse James*. NY: Frederick Fell, 1953.

SUGGESTED READING:
Love, Robertus. *The Rise and Fall of Jesse James*. Lincoln, NE: University of Nebraska Press, 1990.

> **Barbara Morgan,**
> Melrose, Massachusetts

Jameson, Anna Brownell

(1794–1860)

Irish writer. Name variations: Mrs. Jameson; Anna Bronwell Jameson. Born Anna Brownell Murphy in Dublin, Ireland, on May 17, 1794; died in Ealing,

London, England, on March 17, 1860; eldest of five daughters of D(enis) Brownell Murphy (a noted Irish miniaturist and enamel painter) and an English mother; married Robert Jameson (a lawyer), in 1825 (separated September 1837; he died in 1854).

Selected writings: The Diary of an Ennuyée *(1826);* Loves of the Poets *(1829);* Celebrated Female Sovereigns *(1831);* Characteristics of Women *(1832);* Winter Studies and Summer Rambles in Canada *(1838); (translator)* Social Life in Germany *(1840);* Companion to the Public Picture Galleries of London *(1842);* Memoirs of Early Italian Painters *(1845);* Memoirs and Essays on Art, Literature and Morals *(1846); (edited)* Sacred and Legendary Art *(4 vols., 1848–60);* Sisters of Charity *(1855);* The Communion of Labor *(1856).*

Chiefly known for her works on travel and art, Anna Brownell Jameson was the daughter of D. Brownell Murphy, an Irish patriot and miniature-painter-in-ordinary to the Princess *Charlotte Augusta (1796–1817). Murphy had probably been fleeing the Irish rebellion of 1798 when he moved his family to Cumberland, in the north of England; they eventually settled in Hanwell, near London.

Young Anna's education was haphazard, as was that of most girls in 19th-century England. Independent and impetuous, she amused her four sisters with stories and instigated a revolt against their governess. By age 16, she had become a governess in the family of the Marquis of Winchester where she remained for several years. There, she met her future husband, Robert Jameson, a lawyer with an artistic bent, around 1820. Though an engagement was immediately made and broken and a grand tour of the Continent as governess-companion to a young charge in the family of Lord Hatherton intervened, they were married in 1825. The newlyweds had been settled in London for only a week when Anna Jameson knew that the marriage was a monumental mistake. Robert Jameson proved thoughtless and inconsiderate.

Fortunately, Anna Jameson would have a large contingent of friends. A journal, written in a fictitious narrative and kept while she had been abroad, came to the attention of an eccentric bookseller who had taught her to play the guitar. Jameson agreed to have it printed in exchange for a Spanish guitar. The *Diary of an Ennuyée* was an immediate success and brought her a host of intense friendships with the literary great, including *Fanny Kemble, ✥➤ Lady Noel Byron, *Jane Welsh Carlyle, *Elizabeth Barrett

Browning, George Eliot (*Mary Anne Evans), *Elizabeth Gaskell, and *Mary Russell Mitford. Jameson's many sojourns in Germany added other friends: Ottilie von Goethe, the critic Ludwig Tieck, the painter Moritz Retzsch, and Friedrich von Schlegel.

In 1829, when Robert Jameson was appointed puisne judge (judge of inferior rank) on the island of Dominica, he went alone. He returned to England in 1833 but, with the help of her powerful friends, was assigned a post in Canada; again, he went alone. Anna Jameson lived with and would travel with her father.

In the winter of 1836, against her better judgment, she boarded a ship to join her husband in Toronto, where he had been appointed chancellor of the province. When he failed to meet her ship as it docked in New York, Jameson had to make her way to Canada, a difficult trek during the wintry season. While there, she undertook a journey to Indian settlements, explored Lake Huron, and saw much of emigrant and Indian life that was then unknown to travelers. Eight months later, the couple separated, and she returned to England. The result was *Winter Studies and Summer Rambles in Canada* (1838), in which she evoked the physical setting of Canada juxtaposed with a woman's inner journey. When Robert Jameson died in 1854, he left no provision for his wife in his will. She lived on an annuity of £100 raised by her friends as well as a royal pension.

Anna Jameson began to devote her attention to writing. Her first work was *Characteristics of Women* (1832), analyses of Shakespeare's heroines. She then began her four-volume series of *Sacred and Legendary Art*. When she died at Ealing, London, of bronchial pneumonia—complications from a cold she refused to take seriously—the last of the series was in preparation. It was completed under the title *The History of Our Lord in Art* by Lady *Elizabeth Eastlake.

Besides writing other books on travel, biography, and art criticism, Jameson took a keen interest in questions affecting the education, occupations, and support of women. Hospitals, penitentiaries, prisons, and workhouses all caught her eye. Her private lectures before friends became well-springs for many later reformers and philanthropists. In her later years (1855–56), Jameson became interested in the Sisters of Charity and spent much of her time abroad investigating their methods. Upon returning to England, she lectured on the Sisters and the role of women as reformers. She also

◀✥ *Byron, Lady Noel.* See *Lovelace, Ada Byron* for sidebar on Anne Milbanke.

sponsored feminist reformers *Barbara Bodichon and *Adelaide Procter.

SUGGESTED READING:

Fowler, M. *The Embroidered Tent: Five Gentlewomen in Early Canada.* General Publishing, 1982.

Kemble, Fanny. *Records of a Girlhood* (1878).

MacPherson, G. *Memoirs of the Life of Anna Jameson.*

Martineau, Harriet. *Biographical Sketches.*

Nestor, Pauline. *Female Friendships and Communities: Charlotte Brontë, George Eliot, Elizabeth Gaskell.*

Thomas, Clara. *Love and Work Enough: The Life of Anna Jameson.* 1967.

Jameson, Betty (1919—)

American golfer, and first woman to score below 300 in a 72-hole event, who was a founder and charter member of the LPGA. Born Elizabeth Jameson in Norman, Oklahoma, on May 9, 1919.

Betty Jameson was born in Norman, Oklahoma, in 1919. Since few girls played golf in her high school, she was the only female on the boys' golf team. Her amateur career was impressive. Jameson won the Trans-Amateur championships twice, the Texas state championship four times, the Trans-Mississippi, Texas Open, U.S. Amateur, and Western Amateur each twice.

Betty Jameson

In 1942, she took the Western Open and the Western Amateur, the first player to win both titles at the same time.

Jameson turned pro in 1945. On the LPGA tour, she won the U.S. Women's Open in 1947 with a 295 total, the first woman to score below 300 in a 72-hole event. Always interested in helping women play professional golf, Jameson was a founder and charter member of the LPGA (Ladies Professional Golf Association), along with *Patty Berg, *Babe Didrikson Zaharias, Helen Dettweiler, Betty Hicks, and Betty Mims Danoff. In 1951, Jameson was inducted into the Women's Golf Hall of Fame. In 1952, she donated the Vare Trophy, named for *Glenna Collett Vare, which is awarded to the player with the lowest scoring average in a minimum of 70 official rounds of tournament play.

Karin Loewen Haag,
Athens, Georgia

Jameson, Margaret (1891–1986).

See Jameson, Storm.

Jameson, Storm (1891–1986)

British novelist, playwright, literary critic, editor, and administrator who, as the first woman president of the English Center of International P.E.N., worked vigorously to help writers escape from Nazi Germany and Eastern European countries before and during the Second World War. Name variations: (pseudonyms) James Hill and William Lamb. Born Margaret Storm Jameson on January 8, 1891, in Whitby, Yorkshire, England; died in Cambridge, England, on September 30, 1986; daughter of Hannah Margaret (Gallilee) Jameson and William Storm Jameson (a sea captain); first woman graduate in English, Leeds University, B.A. (first class honors), 1912; King's College, London, M.A., 1914; married second husband Guy Patterson Chapman (a writer and historian), on February 1, 1926 (died 1972); children: (first marriage) Charles William Storm Clark.

Awards, honors: John Ruteau fellowship (1912–13); D.Litt., Leeds University (1948); English Center of International P.E.N. award (1974) for There Will Be a Short Interval.

Worked as a copywriter for the Carlton Agency, a London advertising firm (1918–19); was editor of New Commonwealth, London (1919–21); served as English representative and later co-manager for Alfred A. Knopf, a New York publishing firm (1925–28); served as president of English Center of International P.E.N., an international writers' organization (1938–45); au-

thored over 45 books, contributor of short stories, arti- cles, and prefaces to numerous publications.

Selected writings—fiction: The Pot Boils *(1919);* The Happy Highways *(1920);* The Clash *(1922);* The Pitiful Wife *(1923);* Lady Susan and Life: An Indis- cretion *(1923); (translator from French) Guy de Maupassant,* Mont-Oriol *(1924); (translator from French) de Maupassant,* Horla and Other Stories *(1925);* Three Kingdoms *(1926);* The Lovely Ship *(1927);* Farewell to Youth *(1928);* Full Circle *(one- act play, 1929); (translator with Ernest Boyd) de Maupassant,* Eighty-Eight Short Stories *(1930);* The Voyage Home *(1930);* A Richer Dust *(1931);* The Triumph of Time: A Trilogy *(includes* The Lovely Ship, A Voyage Home, A Richer Dust, *1932);* That Was Yesterday *(1932);* The Single Heart *(1933);* A Day Off *(1933);* Women Against Men *(includes* A Day Off, Delicate Monster, The Single Heart, *1933);* Company Parade *(1934);* Love in Winter *(1935);* In the Second Year *(1936);* None Turn Back *(1936);* Delicate Monster *(1937); (under pseudonym William Lamb)* The World Ends *(1937); (under pseudonym James Hill)* Loving Memory *(1937);* The Moon Is Making *(1937); (under pseudonym James Hill)* No Victory for the Soldier *(1938);* Here Comes a Candle *(1938);* The Captain's Wife *(1939);* Europe to Let: The Memoirs of an Obscure Man *(1940);* Cousin Honoré *(1940);* The Fort *(1941); (editor)* London Calling *(1942);* Then We Shall Hear Singing: A Fan- tasy in C Major *(1942);* Cloudless May *(1943);* The Journal of Mary Hervey Russell *(1945);* The Other Side *(1946);* Before the Crossing *(1947);* The Black Laurel *(1947);* The Moment of Truth *(1949);* The Green Man *(1953);* The Hidden River *(published se- rially as* The House of Hate, *1955);* The Intruder *(1956);* A Cup of Tea for Mr. Thorgill *(1957);* One Ulysses Too Many *(1958);* A Day Off: Two Short Novels and Some Stories *(1959);* Last Score; Or, The Private Life of Sir Richard Ormston *(published seri- ally as* The Lion and the Dagger, *1961);* The Road from the Monument *(1962);* A Month Soon Goes *(1963);* The Blind Heart *(1964);* The Early Life of Stephen Hind *(1966);* The White Crow *(1968);* There Will Be a Short Interval *(1973).*

Nonfiction: Modern Drama in Europe *(1920);* The Georgian Novel and Mr. Robinson *(1929);* The Decline of Merry England *(1930); (editor)* Challenge to Death *(1934);* The Soul of Man in the Age of Leisure *(1935);* The Novel in Contemporary Life *(1938);* Civil Journey *(essays, 1939);* The End of This War *(1941);* The Writer's Situation and Other Essays *(1950);* Morley Roberts: The Last Eminent Victorian *(1961);* Parthian Words *(1970); (editor)* A Kind of

Survivor: The Autobiography of Guy Chapman *(1975);* Speaking of Stendhal *(1979).*

Autobiography: No Time Like the Present *(1933);* Journey from the North: Autobiography of Storm Jameson *(2 vols., 1969–70).*

In June 1938, during an International P.E.N. Conference in Prague, **Jiřina Tůmová**, author and secretary of the Czech Center, speaking to Storm Jameson, author and president of the Eng- lish Center, asked: "My darling . . . tell me please, why does your government not say to Hitler, 'These dull sober obstinate Czechs are our friends, do not threaten them?' Why?" In her ac- claimed autobiography, *Journey from the North,* Storm Jameson records her excruciating inter- views with Eastern European writers who were desperately facing Nazi invasion before the Sec- ond World War. Many would subsequently suffer imprisonment in concentration camps, torture, and murder. Tůmová was herself imprisoned; her husband, a physician, was displayed bruised and broken, then killed in front of her.

> *W*hat I do not know, and cannot even hope to understand before I die, is why human beings are willfully, coldly, matter-of-factly cruel to each other.
>
> —Storm Jameson

In the book, Jameson refers frequently to Tůmová's ordeals, believing, as she had ex- pressed in *No Time Like the Present* (1933), that "literature is the living nerve between past and future—the continuity of human experience, the mind which experiences and the mind which re- members." Jameson was president of P.E.N. from 1938 to 1945, from the period before the abandonment of Poland and Czechoslovakia to Nazi Germany until the period after the war's end when she returned to ravaged Warsaw and disillusioned Prague. Imagining herself into the experiences of her European compatriots, she had created a body of anti-fascist fiction, includ- ing *Europe to Let* (1940), *Cousin Honoré* (1940), *Cloudless May* (1943), and *The Black Laurel* (1947).

Margaret Storm Jameson was born on Janu- ary 8, 1891, in Whitby, a northern sea village in Yorkshire, England; it was a profoundly influen- tial early environment, as she attested in her au- tobiography written when she was 70 years old:

> I could not live in Whitby again, but in a sense I live nowhere else, since only there and nowhere else except in the lowest level of my being, do I touch and draw energy from a few key images, sea, distant lights,

the pure line of a coast, first images and last,
source of such strength as I have. Source,
too, of my talent for happiness.

Her father William Storm Jameson spent 61
years at sea as a ship captain and was seldom
home during her childhood. Her mother **Margaret Jameson**, a daughter of a shipowner, accompanied her husband on voyages to foreign
ports before becoming confined to home with
children, conveying to Jameson her yearning for
adventure and disappointment in life. Margaret
Jameson was a harsh and punitive mother, beating her six-month-old daughter each time she
stubbornly and repeatedly attempted to crawl
upstairs: "If I looked closely enough, I might see
that what made me loathe Fascism was only my
hatred of authority, only a mute rebellion
against my violently feared and loved mother."

Nonetheless, Storm Jameson attributes her
ambition for fame, "to be somebody," to her
mother: she "was zealous for my future." In
1908, Margaret took Jameson, aged 16 years, to
the Municipal School in Scarborough, assuming
she would receive necessary training in one year
to qualify as recipient of one of three North Riding County scholarships. At Municipal, Jameson
remembers gratefully that she was no longer persecuted as a "freak." She made friends with the
brothers Sydney and Oswald Harland, later to
share a flat with them in London, remaining
friends throughout life. They read and argued
ideas with her—anarchical, socialist, atheist, a
torrent. At year's end, as her mother had expected, she was awarded the County scholarship; it
provided enough money to cover fees at a
provincial university.

Between 1909 and 1912, Jameson studied
English literature at Leeds University, where, despite being "self-absorbed and undisciplined,"
she wrote an honors thesis about William Blake
and earned a first in English. She was the first
woman to graduate in English at Leeds. In London in 1913, the recipient of a scholarship,
Jameson studied for a short time at London University before transferring to King's College,
which had fewer than a dozen women students.
Her roommates, the Harland brothers and
Archie White, invited Jameson to join a King's
College discussion group, the Eikonoklasts; she
was the only woman participant, discovering in
herself "the promptings of a shrewd nonconformist." While writing her thesis on modern
European drama, she volunteered to tutor at a
newly founded Working Women's College. Impoverished, sometimes hungry, often unable to
afford transportation, Jameson and her three
companions tramped the streets of London—hi-

larious, intellectually exhilarated, free. In one of
her first novels, *The Happy Highways* (1920),
and in her first autobiography, *No Time Like the
Present* (1933), she recorded her memories of
this confident, optimistic moment before the
First World War.

Jameson married in 1913, the year before
the beginning of the war that would slaughter
and "push under the earth" her cohort generation of young men. She confessed, however, that
she was far more preoccupied with her private
life than she was with the war. From the beginning of her marriage, she was unhappy. She gave
birth to her son, Charles William Clark, called
Bill, on June 20, 1915, leaving him, aged 4, in
the keeping of a paid caretaker, while she
worked as a copywriter for the Carlton Agency,
a London advertising firm. Thus began several
years of weekly train trips between Whitby and
London. Jameson's autobiography is permeated
with deep regret about the decision she had
made as a young woman to leave her beloved
son, prompting her to write:

> I am deeply convinced—so deeply that it
> will be no use citing against me married
> women who are famous scientists or architects or financiers—that a woman who
> wishes to be a creator of anything except
> children should be content to be a nun or a
> wanderer on the face of the earth. She cannot be writer and woman in the way a male
> writer can be also husband and father. The
> demands made on her as a woman are destructive in a particularly disintegrating
> way—if she consents to them.

Jameson did not "consent" to conventional,
gendered marital expectations. She preferred all
of her life to live in hotel rooms, as she would
for months at a time, rather than organize a
house for which she was responsible: "My hatred of settled domestic life was, is, an instinct,
and borders on mania." Divorced from her first
husband, she then, on February 1, 1926, married Guy Patterson Chapman, a novelist and historian. On occasion in the ensuing years, Jameson's son Bill lived with her, sometimes in the
country, sometimes in London. Of their footloose existence, Guy Chapman wrote before he
died in 1972:

> Until the last nine or ten years we have never
> lived for long in any place. Whose fault is it?
> Mine in so far as I never made a determined
> attempt to settle anywhere. My wife's restlessness—no, she must speak for herself.
> The centre holds. I have lived in her, and
> she, I think, in me. I ask for nothing more.

Between 1919 and 1921, Storm Jameson
edited an obscure periodical entitled the *New*

Commonwealth. A novel she had started to write while pregnant, *The Pot Boils,* was published in 1919, followed by her published master's thesis, *Modern Drama in Europe* (1920), which caused a literary stir. She produced several novels: *The Happy Highways* (1920), *The Clash* (1922), *The*

Pitiful Wife (1923). Jameson became an established literary figure in the 1920s, associating with *Rose Macaulay and her companion ❧➤ Naomi Royde-Smith, editor of the *Saturday Westminster,* among others, including Michael Sadleir, Middleton Murray, Walter de la Mare, Frank Swinner-

◀❧
Royde-Smith, Naomi. *See Macaulay, Rose for sidebar.*

ton, and Q.D. Leavis. Jameson's novels were financially successful; she bought a fur coat for her mother and in 1921 gave her editorship of the *New Commonwealth* to her first husband who was unable to find work.

The New York publishers Alfred and *Blanche Knopf hired Jameson as their English representative in 1923, expanding their operation in 1926 when they established a British office. Storm Jameson and her second husband, Guy Patterson, were co-managers of British Knopf until 1928. Shy and retiring by nature, Jameson was a public person against her will: "During these years I came to know so many people that I almost died of it."

Meanwhile, she was translating from the French stories of Guy de Maupassant, writing literary criticism and novels, striving now for an honest, spare, non-emotional style. In this more disciplined vein were *The Lovely Ship* (1927), *The Voyage Home* (1930), and *A Richer Dust* (1931), collected in a trilogy entitled *The Triumph of Time*—a chronicle of a woman shipbuilder who prospered during the 19th century on the Yorkshire coast. One of Storm Jameson's contemporaries noted that her "feminism is so profound that she takes it for granted."

Storm Jameson is regularly listed with those authors of the '30s who were knowledgeable about European politics and prescient about the crisis of impending war. **Elaine Feinstein**, poet and biographer, notes that many "of her best books came to be written from a deepening comprehension of the nightmare that was developing in Europe through the '30s. Among them, *Cousin Honoré*, draws a portrait of the province of Alsace as a microcosm of the forces undermining European civilization as a whole." Several of Jameson's novels of this period were reproduced by the feminist press, Virago, in the 1980s, including *Women Against Men* (1933) and *The Mirror in Darkness* trilogy: *Company Parade* (1934), *Love in Winter* (1935), and *None Turn Back* (1936) in which the fate of the Yorkshire woman and writer, Mary Hervey Russell, is tangled with the General Strike masters and workers, fascists and communists, politicians and trade unionists during the '20s. Politically, Jameson was a socialist who was motivated by concern for poverty: "There is little to choose between the ancient custom of exposing unwanted babies and ours allowing an accident of birth to decide which child shall be carefully nurtured and which grow up in a slum."

By 1933, Jameson was deeply involved in anti-fascist committee work. She hated and dreaded the prospect of war, having lost her younger brother, a pilot, in the First World War. (Her loved younger sister was killed by a bomb during the Second World War.) Jameson was a pacifist in the early '30s, organizing a Peace Symposium which included *Rebecca West, Rose Macaulay, and *Winifred Holtby. Contributing an article of her own, Jameson edited a volume of essays against war, *Challenge to Death* (1935). At first, she held to her pacifism despite the deepening flood of refugees streaming out of Nazi Germany. A young German socialist, **Lilo Linke**, lived with her, then immigrated to Ecuador where she became a renowned liberal activist.

By 1940, Jameson shifted her position and began to support Britain's participation in the war:

> I could not cry with the pacifists: Submit, submit. The price was too high; the smell from the concentration camps, from cells where men tortured men, from trains crammed to suffocation with human cattle, choked the words back in my throat.

Between 1938 and 1945, Storm Jameson was the elected president of the English Center of International P.E.N., the first woman to hold this office. She was at the center of a community of European writers living in exile, witnessing firsthand Nazi persecution of writers and intellectuals. Before war was declared, she visited Prague, where she met Tůmová, and Budapest, where her host, a Jewish journalist, described anti-Semitic brutalities. He did not survive the war. She worked, literally, day and night throughout the war, securing visas for escaping authors, aiding German immigrants interned in England as potential spies, providing a welcoming community for desolate refugees. She "never felt separate from an exile by more than a thin membrane," writes Feinstein, who describes Storm Jameson as a "gallant and humane" president of P.E.N.

After the war, Jameson first traveled to Warsaw, now in ruins, and then Prague, where she accompanied Tůmová on a visit to give bread to an imprisoned German woman who had been Tůmová's prison guard during the war. Jameson toured German prison rooms still containing guillotines once used for executing political prisoners. She inspected inhumane Czech internment camps for German citizens. Forty years later, she mused, "The ways to be cruel, to inflict pain, are countless: all have been or will be tried. Why? Why? What nerve has atrophied in the torturer, or—worse—is sensually moved?"

After the war, Jameson moved with her husband to Leeds where she rented rooms in a hotel and continued to write. Guy Chapman was appointed professor of modern history at Leeds University. In 1949, Jameson and Chapman lived in the United States, he lecturing on history, she teaching creative writing at the University of Pittsburgh. She remained an energetic participant in P.E.N. throughout the Cold War, a politician behind the scenes working for Anglo-French relations and helping writers escape from the totalitarian Communist countries in the Soviet bloc.

Although Storm Jameson's novels published through the Second World War were bestsellers and well-received by reviewers, those written after the war were misunderstood and disparaged; her readership dwindled as taste sought new voices. In 1962, the critic W.S. White wrote:

> The present, mature Storm Jameson is a social satirist of keen perception, a skillful writer, who has an ability to comment with ironic detachment, a figure of literary distinction and integrity which makes the merely angry young British writers seem pallid and puerile.

Storm Jameson died in Cambridge, England, aged 95, on September 30, 1986.

SOURCES:

Adcock, St. John. *The Glory That Was Grub Street: Impressions of Contemporary Authors.* NY: Frederick A. Stokes, 1928.

Chapman, Guy. *A Kind of Survivor: The Autobiography of Guy Chapman.* Edited by Storm Jameson. London: Victor Gollancz, 1975.

Feinstein, Elaine. "Introductions," in *Women Against Men* (London: Virago, 1982), *Love in Winter* (London: Virago, 1984), *None Turn Back* (London: Virago, 1984).

Jameson, Storm. *Journey from the North: Autobiography of Storm Jameson, Volumes I and II.* London: Virago, 1984.

———. *No Time Like the Present.* London: Cassell, 1933.

SUGGESTED READING:

Cunningham, Valentine. *British Writers of the Thirties.* Oxford: Oxford University Press, 1989.

Jameson, Storm. *That Was Yesterday.* London: Knopf, 1932.

COLLECTIONS:

Manuscripts: *The Journal of Mary Hervey Russell,* the Pennsylvania Public Library; *A Richer Dust,* the Central Library in Leeds; *That Was Yesterday,* St. Andrew University; *No Time Like the Present,* Wellesley College; *The Voyage Home,* Kenyon College.

Jill Benton,
author of *Naomi Mitchison: A Biography,* and
Professor of English and World Literature
at Pitzer College, Claremont, California

Jamieson, Penny

New Zealand bishop. Name variations: Penelope Jamieson. Born in England; married Ian Jamieson.

Penny Jamieson grew up in England, emigrating to New Zealand when she was 22. After some years as a cleric, she was named bishop of the Diocese of Dunedin in 1989. Upon assuming this post, she became the first woman diocesan bishop in the Anglican Communion. "It was clearly seen as an enormous triumph, not for me personally, for I had been but a passive player in the process, but for women in general," Jamieson wrote in *Living at the Edge.* "I discerned some ambiguity in it all. Was the sense of triumph, of achievement, because a woman had gained a position that was defined, at least historically, as one of the most powerful that society has created? Or was it because a woman had broken the stranglehold that men have held on the episcopal leadership of a church which is undoubtedly one of the most patriarchal institutions in the history of Western society? . . . I began to tremble."

SUGGESTED READING:

Campbell, Douglas A. *The Call to Serve: Biblical and Theological Perspectives on Ministry in Honour of*

Penny Jamieson

Bishop Penny Jamieson. Sheffield, U.K.: Sheffield Academic Press, 1996.

Jamieson, Penny. Living at the Edge: Sacrament and Solidarity in Leadership. Mowbray, 1997.

Jamison, Judith (1943—)

African-American dancer and choreographer. Born on May 10, 1943, in Philadelphia, Pennsylvania; only daughter and one of two children of John Jamison (a sheet-metal mechanic) and Tessie (Bell) Jamison (a part-time teacher); attended Philadelphia public schools; studied dance at the Judimar School of Dance, Philadelphia; attended the Philadelphia Dance Academy and John Kerr's Dance School; married Miguel Godreau (a dancer), in December 1972 (divorced).

Described as regal in stature and glorious in motion, the 5'10" Judith Jamison made her mark during the 1960s as a principal dancer with the Alvin Ailey Dance Theater, an integrated but largely black company founded by choreographer Alvin Ailey. In addition to her "commanding presence," Jamison was acclaimed for her impeccable technique and her individualistic style, the result of a somewhat eclectic training program that included classical ballet and a wide variety of modern-dance disciplines. Leaving the Ailey company in 1980, Jamison pursued independent ventures, including the formation of her own company, the Jamison Project. Upon Ailey's death in 1989, she was named artistic director of both the Alvin Ailey American Dance Theater and the Alvin Alley American Dance Center, the company's official school. As one of the few women to head up a major dance company, she remains a powerful force in the dance world.

Born in Philadelphia, Pennsylvania, on May 10, 1943, Judith Jamison was a musical child who took formal violin lessons and was taught to play the piano by her father, a part-time musician and singer who had longed to be a concert performer. When she was six, her parents enrolled her in dance lessons as part of an effort to deal with her developing gangliness. At the Judimar School of Dance, she concentrated on ballet under the direction of Marion Cuyjet, but also received instruction in tap, acrobatics, jazz, and primitive dance. During her 11 years with teachers **Dolores Brown**, John Jones, Melvin Brooms, and John Hines, Jamison also benefited from guest instructors from the professional world, such as Anthony Tudor, Vincenzo Celli, and **Maria Swoboda**. Despite her years of dance training, Jamison graduated from high school without any clear-cut goals. "I never thought of dancing as a career," she told Robert Wahls in a 1972 interview for *The New York Sunday Times*. "It was simply the hobby giving me the most pleasure." Jamison received a scholarship to Fisk University and began studying for a degree in psychology, but she spent a large part of her time "mooning around the music room." After three semesters, she realized she wanted to dance and left college to enroll at the Philadelphia Dance Academy, where she continued ballet studies under **Nadia Chilkovsky**, James Jamieson, and Juri Gottschalk. She rounded out her program with the study of Labanotation (a system of dance symbols based on movement of various parts of the body) and classes in the Lester Horton technique at John Kerr's Dance School.

In 1964, Jamison caught the attention of *Agnes de Mille who was at the Philadelphia Dance Academy to teach a master class. De Mille invited her to dance the role of Mary Seaton in her new ballet *The Four Marys*, which premiered in February 1965, during the American Ballet Theater's run at Lincoln Center in New York. Following that season, Jamison remained in New York so she would be available to audition for other companies. To help pay the rent, she took a job at the World's Fair as an assistant operator of the Log-Flume Ride.

Another break came in 1965, when Jamison auditioned for Donald McKayle for a projected Harry Belafonte television special. Although she did not get a part, she caught the eye of choreographer Alvin Ailey, who was visiting the audition and thought she was "extraordinary." Three days later, he called and invited her to join his company. Jamison made her debut with the Dance Theater in *Conga Tango Palace* at the Harper Festival in Chicago later in 1965, and, in December of that year, she danced in Ailey's *Revelations* at a dance series at Hunter College in New York. She then joined the troupe on a whirlwind tour of Western Europe, with a side trip to the First World Festival of Negro Arts in Dakar, Senegal, at which the Ailey troupe was the only integrated company to perform.

In 1966, when the Ailey company temporarily disbanded due to financial difficulties, Jamison joined the Harkness Ballet for several months; she also undertook further ballet training with **Patricia Wilde** and Raymond Segarra. Performing opportunities for Jamison were limited with the Harkness troupe, although she did dance in several works with Tim Harum, one of the tallest men in ballet at the time. Her association with the Harkness ended when she injured her ankle in a fall on a slippery floor.

After recuperating, Jamison rejoined the Ailey company for its 1967 European tour. Over the course of the next 13 years, she reached her zenith as a dancer, performing in a number of memorable roles, some of which were created especially for her. An early role was that of Voudoun Erzuile in Geoffrey Holder's *The Prodigal Prince,* which she danced at its premiere at Hunter College in January 1968 and at the Brooklyn Academy of Music that April. "Miss Jamison is a marvelous all-around performer," wrote **Deborah Jowitt** in the *Village Voice* (April 11, 1968), "extravagantly tall with a purring

kind of strength and a leap that looks as if she had been poured upward." Jamison was also memorable as the Mother in Ailey's new work *Knoxville: Summer of 1915,* which premièred at the Edinburgh Festival in September 1968.

By the time the Ailey troupe made its initial appearance on Broadway in 1969, Jamison had attracted quite a following. In that short, sell-out season, she performed in Talley Beatty's *The Black Belt* and fairly dazzled audiences as the Sun in Lucas Hoving's *Icarus.* At the Brooklyn Academy's Festival of Dance in the winter of

Judith Jamison

1969–70, Jamison excelled in two new works: Michael Smuin's *Panambi*, and Ailey's controversial *Masakela Language*. Walter Terry's review of the latter piece in the *Saturday Review* (December 13, 1969) was one among many glowing notices. "Her solo of agonized, but curiously contained loneliness was brilliantly conceived—but that might have been expected of a young woman who is darkly beautiful, whose technique is dazzling, and whose artistry makes her the undisputed prima of the Ailey company."

Another high point for Jamison was her performance of Ailey's *Cry,* a solo piece created especially for her and dedicated to "all black women everywhere—especially our mothers." In the dance, which depicts the experiences of black women, Jamison was lauded by Clive Barnes, critic for *The New York Times* (May 1, 1971). "Miss Jamison dances with great control, and although her work has obviously been greatly influenced, via Ailey, by the Lester Horton West Coast Style, . . . it is also strongly tinged with classic dance. The result, added to her lithe and statuesque physique, is fascinating." Ailey created other notable roles for Jamison, including one in *Mary Lou's Mass,* a piece choreographed to *Mary Lou Williams'* jazz Mass, and another in *The Lark Ascending,* which she danced with Clive Thompson. In 1972, at the height of her performing career, Jamison received the Dance Magazine Award, and was also honored by President Richard Nixon, who appointed her an advisor to the National Council of the Arts.

In 1980, Jamison left the Ailey company to perform in the Broadway musical *Sophisticated Ladies.* She was also a guest performer with a number of other companies and pursued her interest in creating her own choreography. Ailey encouraged her in this endeavor, having his company perform her first piece, *Divining,* in 1984. Jamison went on to form her own dance company, the Jamison Project, which made its debut in 1988.

In 1989, when Jamison succeeded Alvin Ailey as director of the Alvin Ailey American Dance Theater, any anxieties about the future of the company were put to rest. Viewing her goal as "not to stand in Alvin's shadow, but on his shoulders," Jamison embraced the company's historic mission of preserving works by pioneering black choreographers. Ailey's legacy was evident in the repertory for the 1990–91 season, the first under Jamison's direction. It included a revival of Ailey's *Hidden Rites* and his *Revelations* and *Blues Suites,* as well as Kris World's *Read Matthew 11.28,* created in 1988 for the Jamison

Project, Lar Lubovitch's *North Star,* *Pearl Primus'* *Impinyuza,* and Jamison's own *Forgotten Time.* Jamison also continued Ailey's efforts to bring women to the forefront of the company's work, collaborating with and commissioning women choreographers and dancers, and presenting works portraying women. She wrote a moving memory piece about Ailey called *Hymn,* with a libretto by **Anna Deveare Smith**.

Along with directing the dance company, Jamison took over the responsibility for the Alvin Ailey American Dance Center, a satellite school attended by over 3,000 students. During her tenure, Jamison has worked to establish short-term residencies in various cities, with the goal of providing classes in dance, creative writing, and stage production to underprivileged youths. She has also overseen fund-raising efforts for the company, the school, and the Alvin Ailey Repertory Ensemble, seeking funds from corporate as well as private contributors.

Throughout the 1990s, Jamison's efforts were rewarded with several ground-breaking achievements, including an emotional 15-day tour of South Africa in June 1997, the first time the company had visited the African nation. South African officials called the visit, which included hands-on workshops along with performances, an inspiration and an "end of a long drought." The trip was a dream of Jamison's since Nelson Mandela's release from prison in 1990. "This is my homeland, my lineage. South Africans are not the same as African Americans, but we greet each other as brothers and sisters because we've both been through turmoil and we understand that. We have so much to learn from them, and they have a lot to learn about us."

Jamison was among the recipients of the Kennedy Center Honors and was awarded an honorary degree from the University of Massachusetts, both 1999. "I've got a million heartbeats in me," she has said. "My folks have been dancing since the beginning of time, so I've got this advantage."

SOURCES:

Grant, Diane C. "The Women of Ailey," in *The Boston Globe.* April 23, 1995.

Moritz, Charles, ed. *Current Biography 1973.* NY: H.W. Wilson, 1973.

Sancton, Thomas. "Back to Their Roots" in *Time.* June 30, 1997, pp. 69–70.

Smith, Jessie Carney. *Notable Black American Women.* Detroit, MI: Gale Research, 1992.

SUGGESTED READING:

Jamison, Judith, with Howard Kaplan. *Dancing Spirit.* NY: Doubleday, 1993.

Barbara Morgan,
Melrose, Massachusetts

Janauschek, Fanny (1829–1904)

Czech actress. Name variations: Fanny Janauscheck. Born Francesca or Franziska Magdalena Romana Janauschek in Prague, Bohemia (now Czech Republic), on July 20, 1829; died at the Brunswick Home in Amityville, Long Island, New York, on November 28, 1904; fourth in a family of nine children; her father was a tailor; her mother was a theater laundress; married Frederick J. Pillot (died July 1884).

A celebrated actress, Fanny Janauschek gave evidence of dramatic talent from childhood and, by 16, was playing lead roles in Prague. After a series of successful engagements in European cities, Janauschek became a European star, touring throughout Germany, Austria, and Russia for the next 20 years.

Though she spoke only a few words of English, she arrived in America in 1867 with her own troupe of actors, playing in New York and elsewhere, in the German language. When producer Augustin Daly promised her that she would be a great success if she learned English, she went "into the country," said Janauschek, "took four professors, one for reading, one for grammar, one for pronunciation, and the other to go over my roles with me. I studied twelve and fifteen hours a day." Daly then presented her to the American public in numerous roles, including that of Lady Macbeth (*Gruoch) and *Elizabeth I, queen of England. By the 1870s, she was, indeed, a great success. After several visits to Europe and Australia, Janauschek finally settled in the United States, where she continued to appear until her retirement in 1898.

An actress of the highest order, Janauschek was gifted with a patrician voice and gave fiery performances. The majesty and pathos of her *Mary Stuart, queen of Scots, and *Marie Antoinette were long remembered, while her characterizations of Medea, Meg Merrilies, and Lady Macbeth were considered outstanding. She also gave marvelously contrasted portrayals of the dual roles of Hortense, the French maid, and Lady Dedlock, in a dramatic version of Dickens' *Bleak House.*

Jane.

Variant of Jean and Joan.

Jane, countess of Montfort
(c. 1310–c. 1376).

See Jeanne de Montfort.

Jane, queen of Naples.

See Joanna I.

Jane, queen of Scotland (c. 1410–1445).

See Beaufort, Joan.

Jane I of Naples.

See Joanna I of Naples.

Jane II of Naples.

See Joanna II of Naples.

Jane Grey, Lady (1537–1554).

See Grey, Jane, Lady.

Jane of Bourbon-Vendome
(d. 1511)

*Countess of Auvergne. Name variations: Jane Bourbon; Jane de Bourbon-Vendôme; Jane de la Tour. Died on January 22, 1511 (some sources cite 1512); daughter of John II, count of Vendome, and Isabeau, duchess de La Roche-sur-Yon; became second wife of John II (1426–1488), duke of Bourbon (r. 1456–1488), in June 1487; married John II de la Tour, count of Auvergne, on January 11, 1495; children: (first marriage) Mathieu of Bourbon; Charles of Bourbon; Hector of Bourbon; (second marriage) *Anne de la Tour (c. 1496–1524); *Madeline de la Tour d'Auvergne (1501–1519).*

Jane of Flanders (c. 1310–c. 1376).

See Jeanne de Montfort.

Jane of France (1343–1373)

*Queen of Navarre. Name variations: Joanna of France; Jane Valois. Born in 1343; died in 1373; daughter of John II the Good (1319–1364), king of France (r. 1350–1364), and *Bona of Bohemia (1315–1349); sister of Charles V (1337–1380), king of France (r. 1364–1380), and *Isabelle of France (1349–1372); married Charles II (1332–1387), king of Navarre (r. 1349–1387), in 1352; children: *Joanna of Navarre (c. 1370–1437, who married Henry IV, king of England); Charles III, king of Navarre; Pierre.*

Jane Seymour (c. 1509–1537).

See Six Wives of Henry VIII.

Jane Shore (c. 1445–c. 1527).

See Shore, Jane.

Janeway, Elizabeth (1913—)

American author, critic and lecturer. Born Elizabeth Hall on October 7, 1913, in Brooklyn, New York; daughter of Charles H. Hall (a naval architect) and Jeanette F. (Searle) Hall; attended Swarthmore Col-

lege, 1930–31; Barnard College, B.A., 1935; married Eliot Janeway (an economist and author), October 29, 1938; children: Michael Charles, William Hall.

Recipient of Delta Kappa Gamma Educators award (1972); D. Lit. from Simpson College (1972), Cedar Crest College, and Villa Maria College; Distinguished Alumna award, Barnard College (1979).

Selected writings: The Walsh Girls *(1943);* Daisy Kenyon *(1945);* The Question of Gregory *(1949);* The Vikings *(1951);* Leaving Home *(1953);* The Early Days of the Automobile *(1956);* The Third Choice *(1958);* Accident *(1964);* Ivanov VII *(1967); (ed. with others)* Discovering Literature *(1968); (ed.)* The Writer's World *(1969);* Man's World-Woman's Place: A Study in Social Mythology; *(ed.)* Women: Their Changing Roles *(1973);* Between Myth and Morning: Women Awakening *(1974);* Powers of the Weak *(1980).*

Elizabeth Janeway

Born on October 7, 1913, in Brooklyn, New York, to Charles H. and **Jeanette Searle Hall**, Elizabeth Janeway was educated in local schools

and then enrolled at Barnard College of Columbia University. Intent on a literary career, she took a short-story course repeatedly in order to force herself to write a certain number of words each term. Her diligence appears to have been successful because in 1935 she won *Story Magazine*'s Intercollegiate Short Story Contest. Janeway, who was forced to leave college during the Depression due to her family's financial losses, continued to write, turning out persuasive advertisements for a department store's bargain basement. She was eventually able to return to Barnard and graduated in June 1935.

After graduation and a short courtship, Elizabeth Hall married Eliot Janeway, an economist, author, and one of the editors of *Life* and *Fortune* magazines, on October 29, 1938. During this period, Elizabeth Janeway began working on a short story which, on the third attempt, was finished and published as *The Walsh Girls* in 1943. A psychological study of two New England sisters, Janeway's first novel attracted attention and critical acclaim from many. Others, although agreeing that she was a "new and brilliant young writer," with much to be expected from her future work, found her characters somewhat lackluster. Janeway devoted herself to improving her writing and, during the 1940s and 1950s, turned out several novels, including *Daisy Kenyon* (1945), *The Question of Gregory* (1949), *Leaving Home* (1953), and *The Third Choice* (1958). She also penned two children's books, *The Vikings* (1951) and *Ivanov VII* (1967). Although her novels and later works, including *Man's World-Woman's Place: A Study in Social Mythology* (1971) and *Between Myth and Morning: Women Awakening* (1974), helped earn Janeway praise for her contribution to feminist literature, these works are considered by many to be low key and noncontroversial. Janeway was also a regular contributor to numerous literary and popular journals.

SOURCES:
Current Biography. NY: H.W. Wilson, 1944.

Jo Anne Meginnes,
freelance writer, Brookfield, Vermont

Janine-Marie de Foix (fl. 1377).

See Foix, Janine-Marie de.

Janis, Elsie (1889–1956)

American actress, musical comedy star, and author. Born Elsie Bierbower in Columbus, Franklin County, Ohio, on March 16, 1889; died at her Beverly Hills home on February 25, 1956; buried beside her mother at Forest Lawn Memorial Park, Glendale, California; daughter of John E. Bierbower and Jane Elizabeth (Cockrell) Bierbower; married Gilbert Wilson (an actor), in 1931.

Elsie Janis was born in Columbus, Ohio, in 1889. Guided firmly by her mother **Jane Bierbower**, Janis first trod the boards at age eight, making her Columbus debut as the boy Cain in *The Charity Ball*. The following year, she appeared in Cincinnati stock company productions of *Little Lord Fauntleroy, East Lynne,* and *The Galley Slave.* Under the management of E.E. Rice, Janis was off to New York in 1900, working the vaudeville stage at the Casino Theater Roof Garden as "Little Elsie"; she followed that with a three-year tour. Her first substantial hit came in 1905, when she appeared at the New York Theater Roof Garden in *When We Were Forty-One,* in which her imitations of popular actors of the day created a furor.

In 1906, Janis starred on Broadway as Dorothy Willetts in *The Vanderbilt Cup,* which had a seasonal run and subsequent tour. The following year, she was again successful playing Joan Talbot in *The Hoyden* at the Knickerbocker Theater. She was also seen as Cynthia Bright in *The Fair Co-Ed* (1908), as Princess Kalora in *The Slim Princess* (1909), and as Cinderella in *The Lady of the Slipper* (1912). Her London debut came in 1914, when she portrayed Kitty O'Hara in *The Passing Show* at the Palace. Again, she met with phenomenal success.

During World War I, the 18-year-old Janis toured the trenches of France for some months, becoming known as the "sweetheart of the American Expeditionary Force" as she entertained the troops. In New York, she starred in *Miss Information* (1915), *The Century Girl* (1916), *Miss 1917* (1919), *Elsie Janis and her Gang* (1922), and *Puzzles of 1925* and *Oh, Kay!* (1925). She also took her *La Revue de Elsie Janis* to the Apollo in Paris (1921). By then, she had long been an international celebrity.

In 1939, Elsie Janis made her farewell stage appearance in Frank Fay's vaudeville *Laugh Time*; she also gave a series of Sunday night performances of songs and impersonations. The multitalented Janis appeared in silent and talkie films, composed over 50 songs, penned the screenplay for *Close Harmony,* starred in her own revues and plays *A Star for a Night* (1911) and *It's All Wrong* (1920), for which she was also co-composer, staged *New Faces of 1934,* and wrote several books (*Love Letters of an Actress, If I Know What I Mean,* as well as her au-

tobiography *So Far So Good,* 1932). Her only marriage, which ended in separation, came at age 42 to actor Gilbert Wilson.

Elsie Janis

Jannsen, L. (1843–1886).

See Koidula, Lydia.

Janotha, Natalia (1856–1932)

Polish pianist and teacher of Ignacy Jan Paderewski. Name variations: Nathalie Janotha. Born Maria Cecylia Natalia Janotha in Warsaw, Poland, on June 8, 1856; died at The Hague, Netherlands, on June 9, 1932; her father was a professor at the Warsaw Conservatorium; studied with Clara Schumann.

Natalia Janotha studied with *Clara Schumann and was considered one of her most gifted pupils; her debut took place in Leipzig in 1874. George Bernard Shaw thought highly of her 1879 London performance of Beethoven's Fourth Piano Concerto, but on her return in 1891 his opinion of her art had cooled considerably, noting that her playing had lost its freshness and had gained little in maturity. Besides receiving many honors as a pianist, she composed piano pieces, including a series of *Mountain Scenes,* which was dedicated to Clara Schumann. Janotha also taught; her most famous student was Ignacy Jan Paderewski. In 1885, she was appointed pianist to the Prussian court, a post she held until 1916. An eccentric, Janotha insisted that her dog Prince White Heather be on stage within her view during her recitals; she also placed a prayer book ostentatiously on the piano. In 1905, she made four recordings, one of which was of Chopin's unpublished fugue; she owned the manuscript of the student work. She also wrote several books on Chopin as well as translating into English Tarnowski's biography of Chopin.

SOURCES:

Chechlinska, Zofia. "Janotha, (Maria Cecylia) Natalia," in *New Grove Dictionary of Music and Musicians.* Vol. 9, pp. 500–501.

"Janotha Natalia," in *Wielka Encyklopedia Powszechna PWN.* Warsaw: Panstwowe Wydawnictwo Naukowe, 1965, vol. 5, p. 202.

John Haag,
Athens, Georgia

Janowitz, Gundula (1937—)

German soprano. Born on August 2, 1937, in Berlin, Germany; studied with Herbert Thöny at the Graz Conservatory.

Made debut at the Vienna Staatsoper (1959); appeared at Bayreuth (1960–63); was a member of the Frankfurt Opera (1963–66); made Metropolitan Opera debut (1976), Paris Opéra (1973), Covent Garden (1976); was a director of the Graz Opera (1990).

At age 22, Gundula Janowitz won a student contract at the Vienna State Opera. Two years later, she had appeared not only in Vienna but also at Bayreuth and Glyndebourne, and came to the attention of Herbert von Karajan who was a major influence in her career. Janowitz appeared on the stages of international opera houses, but divided most of her time between Berlin and Vienna. Her voice was characterized by purity of tone, cleanness of line, and aristocratic phrasing. Hers was a pure "white" soprano usually associated with Central European sopranos. For most of her career, Janowitz never tried to push her voice beyond its capabilities, choosing only the lighter Wagnerian roles, but Von Karajan persuaded her to sing Sieglinde for his Salzburg *Ring* in 1967 which was a triumph. Describing herself as "a very normal kind of person," Janowitz was not flamboyant onstage which caused some to criticize her acting as cold and impersonal. Janowitz also performed in concerts and recitals, achieving great distinction.

She retired in 1990 to become director of the Graz Opera.

John Haag,
Athens, Georgia

Jans, Annetje (c. 1605–1663)

American Dutch settler. Born in the Netherlands around 1605; died in New York in 1663; married Roeloef Janssen (died around 1636); married Dominie Bogardus (a minister), in 1638; children: (first marriage) three daughters and two sons; (second marriage) four sons.

Annetje Jans was one of the many exceptional Dutch women who immigrated to New York during the 17th century. Independent, well-educated, and traditionally included in business affairs, these women often acquired large parcels of property that became extremely valuable after their deaths. Although many of Jans' contemporaries have been forgotten, she is remembered because of a 200-year dispute over her valuable Manhattan holdings.

Jans' family, including her husband Roeloef Janssen, her three daughters, her widowed mother, and her unmarried sister, immigrated to America in 1630, when the New Netherlands colony in New York was just a few years old. Jans' sister **Tryntje Jonas**, a midwife and nurse, was purportedly the first woman to practice medicine in New York. The family first settled on a farm in Fort Orange (now Albany), but in 1635, moved to the farming village of New Amsterdam, where they acquired 62 acres of land (running along what is now Broadway, between Fulton and Canal Streets). Shortly after the move, Jans' husband died, leaving her with five children to support (two boys were born in America). In 1638, before her second marriage to the colony's minister, Dominie Bogardus, Jans drew up a prenuptial agreement to insure her financial independence. When her second husband died at sea in 1642, Jans, whose family had increased with the addition of four more boys, added his estate to her considerable holdings.

With assistance from her mother, Jans raised and educated her children, including her daughters. Her oldest daughter Sara was a talented linguist who worked as an interpreter with the Algonquin natives. Annetje expanded her real estate holdings and took steps to insure that her land stayed within the family, even to the point of drawing up prenuptial agreements for her daughters. When she died in 1663, her estate was divided equally among her children and grandchildren. Some 75 years later, a descendant of a Bogardus son began a series of well-publicized lawsuits over the property that lasted well into the 20th century. Although they proved fruitless in the end, the lawsuits did insure Annetje Jans her place in the history of early New York.

Jansen, Elly (1929—)

Dutch-born social worker. Born in Holland in 1929; sixth in a family of nine children.

A leading figure in the field of mental health, Elly Jansen was born in Holland, where she studied psychology, trained as a nurse, and worked with disturbed children. In 1955, she went to England to train as a missionary, which, over the next few years, led her into social work with the mentally ill. She realized that help was needed for those newly discharged from mental hospitals to adjust to day-to-day living. In 1959, she rented a house in Richmond, put up a notice in the local hospital, and waited three months before the first applicant appeared. The house became her first therapeutic community, or halfway house, for mental patients. Its success led Jansen to establish the Richmond Fellowship, through which she promoted the re-integration of mental health patients into mainstream society. The fellowship, of which Jansen later became international director, grew to include some 50 houses in Britain, and another 50 scattered throughout nations of the world, including Australia, New Zealand, Austria, India, Pakistan, Bangladesh, Nepal, and the United States. Her publications include *The Therapeutic Community Outside the Hospital* and *Towards a Whole Society.* Jansen was made an OBE in 1980.

Jansson, Tove (1914—)

Finnish artist, author, and illustrator who created the "Moomins." Born on August 9, 1914, in Helsinki, Finland; daughter of Viktor (a sculptor) Jansson and Signe (Hammarsten) Jansson (an artist); studied book design in Stockholm, 1930–33; painting in Helsinki, 1933–36; and at Atelier Adrien Holy, Paris, France, 1938, and in Florence, Italy; never married; no children.

Awards, honors: Stockholm Award for best children's book (1952), Nils Holgersson plaque (1953), and Selma Lagerlof Medal (1953), all for Hur gick det sen? *(The Book about Moomin, Mymble and Little My);* Moominsummer Madness *was nominated by the Swedish section of the International Board on Books for Young People for the International Hans Christian Andersen Award (1956); an award from the Academy*

(Finland), Hans Christian Andersen Diploma of the International Council of Youth (Florence), Rudolf Koivu plaquette (Finland), and the Elsa Beskow Award (all 1958), all for Trollvinter *(Moominland Midwinter); Swedish Culture Prize (Helsinki) for body of work (1958, 1963, and 1970); Hans Christian Andersen Diploma of the International Council of Youth for* Who Will Comfort Toffle? *(1962) and* Tales from Moominvalley *(1964); Langman's Prize (1965); Hans Christian Andersen Medal, Author Award (1966);* Expressen *(Stockholm's daily paper) Winnie-the-Pooh Prize for* Moominvalley in November *(1970); prize of the Finnish State for* Moominvalley in November *(1971); Selma Lagerlof prize for* Sculptor's Daughter *(1972); Bonniers Publishing House, Sweden, scholarship award (1972); prize of Swedish Academy (1972); Werner Soderstrom Publishing House and Grafia Society (Finland) scholarship and medal for illustration (1973); given the "Order of Smile" medal by the Polish children (1976); Austrian State Prize for Children's and Juvenile Literature (1978), for* Wer soll den Lillan trosten? *(Austrian edition of* Vem ska trosta Knyttet?*); honorary doctorate from Abo Academy (1978); Le Grand Prix des Treize for* Sommarboken *(The Summer Book, 1979); awarded the "Prize of Dunce's Hat" by the Finnish Comic Strip Society (1980).*

Selected writings—all juvenile self-illustrated, except as noted: Smaatrollen och den stora oversvamningen *("The Small Trolls and the Large Flood," Soderstrom, 1945);* Kometjakten *(Soderstrom, 1945, published in Sweden as* Mumintrollet pa Kometjakt, *Sorlins, 1946, translated by Elizabeth Portch and published in England, 1951, rev. ed. published as* Kometen Kommer, *Schildt, 1968, published in America as* Comet in Moominland, *Walck, 1968);* Trollkarlens hatt *(Schildt, 1949, published in England as* The Finn Family Moomintroll, *Benn, 1950, published in America as* The Happy Moomins, *Bobbs-Merrill, 1952, and as* The Finn Family Moomintroll, *Walck, 1965);* Moominpappans bravader *(Schildt, 1950, published in America as* The Exploits of Moominpappa, *Walck, 1966, rev. ed., published as* Muminpappans memoarer, *Schildt, 1968);* Hur gick det sen? *(Schildt, 1952, published in England as* The Book About Moomin, Mymble and Little My, *Benn, 1953);* Farlig midsommar *(Schildt, 1954, published in America as* Moominsummer Madness, *Walck, 1961);* Trollvinter *(Schildt, 1957, translated by T. Warburton, published in England as* Moominland Midwinter, *Benn, 1958, published in America, Walck, 1962);* Vem ska trosta Knyttet? *(Schildt, 1960, translated by Kingsley Hart, published in England as* Who Will Comfort Toffle?,

Tove
Jansson

Benn, 1961, published in America, Walck, 1969); Det osynliga barnet och andra berattelser (Schildt, 1962, translated by Thomas Warburton, published in America as Tales from Moominvalley, Walck, 1964); Pappan och Havet (Schildt, 1965, translated by K. Hart, published in America as Moominpappa at Sea, Walck, 1967); (autobiographical) Bildhuggarens Dotter (Schildt, 1968, published in England as Sculptor's Daughter, Benn, 1969, translated by K. Hart, published in America, Avon, 1976); Sent i November (Schildt, 1970, translated by K. Hart, published in America as Moominvalley in November, Walck,

1971); (adult short stories) Lyssnerskan *("The Listener," Schildt, 1971); (adult fiction)* Sommarboken *(Schildt, 1972, translated by Thomas Teal, published in America as* The Summer Book, *Pantheon, 1975); (adult fiction)* Solstaden *(Schildt, 1974, translated by T. Teal, published in America as* Sun City, *Pantheon, 1976);* Den Farliga Resan *(Schildt, 1977, translated by K. Hart, published in England as* The Dangerous Journey, *Benn, 1978); (adult short stories)* Dockskapet *(Schildt, 1978);* Moominstroll *(contains Volume 1,* Comet in Moominland, *Volume 2,* Finn Family Moomintroll, *Volume 3,* Moominland Midwinter, *Volume 4,* Moominpappa at Sea, *Volume 5,* Moominsummer Madness, *Volume 6,* Moominvalley in November, *Volume 7,* Tales from Moominvalley, *Avon, 1978);* Skurken i Muminhuset *(Schildt, 1980); (adult novel)* Den A'rliga Bedragaren *(Schildt, 1982); (adult novel)* Stenakern *(Schildt, 1984). Writer of two plays for children; writer and designer of strip-cartoon, "Moomin,"* The Evening News, *London, 1953–60.*

The daughter of artists (a sculptor and a designer), Tove Jansson was born in 1914 and grew up in a large, dilapidated studio in Helsinki, Finland. She remembers pitying other children who had to live in more conventional households. Jansson later recalled that her upbringing was remarkably complex, although she never noticed it at the time. "My parents gave their children the impression of growing up in a wealthy, generous, problem-free home, although one comes to understand in later years how 'troublesome' it really was, both financially and in other ways. . . . My mother, especially, had an unusual quality; a mixture of strict morals and almost endless unparalleled tolerance." Since her mother frequently designed book covers, Jansson was an avid reader from an early age, devouring the free samples her mother brought home, as well as the stories of Rudyard Kipling, Robert Louis Stevenson, Joseph Conrad, *Selma Lagerlöf, Jack London, and Edgar Allan Poe.

From 1930 to 1936, Jansson studied book design and then painting in Stockholm, Helsinki, Paris, and Florence. Over the years, she would have many exhibitions of her paintings in Helsinki. In 1939, she wrote and illustrated her first children's book and, in 1945, published the first of her enchanting "Moomin" books, a series of troll stories set in the bizarre "Moominworld" for which she became known. The books, which were first written in Swedish then translated into Finnish, English, and other languages, were inspired by an island off the coast of Finland, where the family went when she was

a child. "Much later, I moved out to that same island and sat listening to the gales in my cabin, and one day I felt the urge to write about trolls," she explained. "I called them Moomintrolls. Perhaps I wrote mostly for myself, as a sort of secret game and a way to return to my adventurous summers of long ago."

Between 1952 and 1953, Jansson won three prestigious awards: the Stockholm Award, the Nils Holgersson Plaque, and the Selma Lagerlöf Medal, all for *The Book about Moomin, Mymbie and Little My.* Although Jansson said at the time that she wrote primarily for herself and not for children, she did admit that her stories would probably be most appealing to the person who has difficulty fitting in, "those on the fringe, the lost ones." In 1966, she won the Hans Christian Andersen Medal for the "Moomintroll" books, which over the years have won countless other awards and have been translated into 27 languages. Her beloved characters were also seen in the comic-strip "Moomin," which she wrote and drew for *The* [London] *Evening News* from 1953 to 1960.

In later years. Jansson made a successful transition to adult books with her autobiography *Sculptor's Daughter* (1968), several collections of short stories, including *The Listener* (1971), and *The Doll's House* (1978), and a few adult novels.

SOURCES:
Commire, Anne, ed. *Something about the Author.* Vol. 41. Detroit, MI: Gale Research.

Barbara Morgan,
Melrose, Massachusetts

Januaria (1822–1901)

*Princess Imperial of Brazil and countess of Aquila. Name variations: Januária. Born Januária María Joana de Bragança on March 11, 1822, in Rio de Janeiro, Brazil; died on March 13, 1901, in Nice; daughter of *Leopoldina of Austria (1797–1826) and Pedro I, emperor of Brazil (also known as Peter IV, king of Portugal, and Peter I of Brazil); married Luigi Carlo Maria Giuseppe of Sicily, count of Aquila, on April 28, 1844.*

Janvier, Catherine Ann (1841–1922).

See Beaux, Cecilia for sidebar on Catherine Ann Drinker.

Japan, empress of.

See Jingū (c. 201–269).
See Suiko (554–628).
See Kōgyoku-Saimei (594–661).

See Jitō (645–702).
See Gemmei (c. 661–721).
See Gensho (680–748).
See Kōken-Shōtoku (718–770).
See Onshi (872–907).
See Sadako (r. 976–1001).
See Meisho (1624–1696).
See Go-Sakuramachi (1740–1813).
See Yoshiko.
See Haruko (1850–1914).
See Sadako (1885–1951).
See Nagako (b. 1903).
See Michiko (b. 1934).

Japha, Louise (1826–1889)

German pianist. Born in Hamburg, Germany, in 1826; died in 1889; married Friedrich Langhans (divorced 1874).

Like her lifelong friend Johannes Brahms, Louise Japha was born in Hamburg. She studied there first and later with *Clara Schumann. On her many European tours, Japha was particularly appreciated in Paris for her performances of the music of Robert Schumann. In 1868, she participated in the first public performance in Paris of the Brahms Piano Quintet in F minor, Op. 34. After divorcing the violinist Friedrich Langhans in 1874, she lived in Wiesbaden as a teacher.

John Haag,
Athens, Georgia

Jarboro, Caterina (1903–1986).
See Price, Leontyne for sidebar.

Jarman, Frances Eleanor (c. 1803–1873).
See Ternan, Frances Eleanor.

Jarrett, Eleanor Holm (b. 1913).
See Holm, Eleanor.

Jarvis, Anna M. (1864–1948)

American founder of Mother's Day. Born in Grafton, West Virginia, on May 1, 1864; died in West Chester, Pennsylvania, on November 24, 1948; attended Mary Baldwin College; never married; no children.

Due to the efforts of Anna M. Jarvis, the second Sunday in May is celebrated across much of the world as Mother's Day. Born to a prosperous family in Grafton, Virginia, in 1864, Jarvis was an attractive, well-educated woman who never married. Following her mother's death in 1905, she began a one-woman campaign to set aside one day a year to honor mothers everywhere. Although it was not an original idea (*Julia Ward Howe had suggested it as early as 1872), Jarvis had the commitment to turn it into a reality. Indeed, it became an obsession, occupying her entire life and depleting her modest inheritance.

On May 10, 1908, in tribute to her mother who had died on that date three years earlier, Jarvis organized simultaneous church services honoring mothers in her hometown of Grafton and in Philadelphia, Pennsylvania, where she then lived. She also initiated the custom of wearing carnations on that day. She then embarked on a massive letter-writing campaign to state officials, legislators, and congressional representatives, which resulted in several states proclaiming official Mother's Day celebrations. In May 1914, a bill was introduced in Congress to set aside the second Sunday in May as a national Mother's Day. The legislation passed unanimously and was authorized by President Woodrow Wilson the following year. Jarvis then incorporated herself as the Mother's Day International Association and continued her efforts to extend the holiday internationally. Her correspondence grew to such a volume that she had to purchase the house next door for storage.

Jarvis deplored the commercialization of Mother's Day by florists, card companies, and candy makers and spent her later years in an effort to maintain the purity of the holiday. Although she did succeed in stopping a commercial celebration in New York City by threatening a law suit, her attempts were largely met with indifference. She spent her final years in ill health and died in a sanitarium in West Chester, Pennsylvania, in 1948. Later, the Andrews Methodist Church in Grafton, where the holiday began, memorialized Jarvis and her mother in two stained-glass windows. A small museum there also sells Mother's Day cards the year round, a practice that Jarvis would likely frown upon.

SOURCES:
Felton, Bruce, and Mark Fowler. *Famous Americans You Never Knew Existed.* NY: Stein and Day, 1980.
McHenry, Robert, ed. *Famous American Women.* NY: Dover, 1993.

Barbara Morgan,
Melrose, Massachusetts

Jarvis, Lucy (1919—)

American television producer, known for her NBC documentaries during the 1950s and 1960s. Born Lucile Howard in New York City in 1919; only daughter and youngest of the two children of Herman Howard and Sophie (Kirsch) Howard; Cornell University, B.S.

in home economics, 1938; Columbia University Teachers College, M.S., 1941; attended New School for Social Research, New York, 1942; married Serge Jarvis (a specialist in corporation and international law), on July 18, 1940; children: Barbara Ann Jarvis; Peter Leslie Jarvis.

Selected production credits for NBC: "The Kremlin" (1963); "Museum Without Walls" (1963); "The Louvre" (1964); "Who Shall Live?" (1965); "Mary Martin: Hello Dolly! Around the World" (1965); "Dr. Barnard's Heart Transplant Operations" (1968); "Khrushchev in Exile: His Opinions and Revelations" (1967); "Bravo, Picasso!" (1967); "Cry Help!" (1970); "Trip to Nowhere" (1970); "Scotland Yard: The Golden Thread" (1971). Independent credits: "Family Reunion" (1981–82).

One of the first women to produce for prime-time network television, Lucy Jarvis credits her mother with giving her the confidence to turn her dreams into reality. "She used to say, 'I want you and your brother to be able to walk into a room anywhere in the world and feel comfortable and be able to cope,' and that is exactly what she did." Jarvis' path into television was a meandering one, beginning at Cornell University where she studied home economics. After graduating in 1938, she worked for a year as a dietitian at New York Hospital-Cornell Medical Center before taking a job in special promotions for the Beech-Nut Company. In 1940, the same year she married, Jarvis joined the staff of *McCall's* magazine as a food editor. While there, she attended Columbia University's Teachers College, receiving her M.S. degree in 1941. Jarvis left her job in 1943, for the birth of her first child. She and her husband moved to Connecticut, and she became a stay-at-home mom until her two children, Peter and Barbara, were teenagers. Jarvis filled her free time with volunteer work, serving as an instructor for the American Red Cross and as national vice-president of the women's division of the Organization for Rehabilitation through Training (1944–51).

Lucy Jarvis re-entered the job force in the early 1950s, working on various production staffs in radio and television. By 1955, she was assistant producer for David Susskind's Talent Associates, an enterprise that packaged special programs for television. She then worked for a year as a TV editor for Pathé News. In 1957, she joined *Martha Rountree (creator of "Meet the Press") to help launch and coproduce "Capitol Close-up," a syndicated radio program which aired daily and featured important events and notable personalities in government. Their guests on the first three shows were Dwight Eisenhower, Richard Nixon, and J. Edgar Hoover.

Jarvis began her association with the National Broadcasting Company in 1960, working in the creative projects unit. Over the next 16 years, she created and produced a series of innovative documentaries for NBC, including programs on the Kremlin (1963), the Louvre (1964), and the Ming Tombs of the Forbidden City (1973). She presented the first program on kidney dialysis in 1965 and took audiences behind the scene of Dr. Christiaan Barnard's pioneering heart transplant operations in 1968. "I became known as the whirlwind of Rockefeller Plaza," she later recounted, "because I was bringing television crews into places that never before permitted cameras."

It was not always easy for Jarvis to convince the executives at NBC to support her venturesome projects, but as her successes multiplied, the task took less effort. Her first documentary on the Kremlin was a decided coup: NBC had tried unsuccessfully for two years to get a film crew inside the tightly guarded Soviet Union. Jarvis, who prepared herself with a course in spoken Russian, spent five months in Russia, first negotiating through a bureaucratic labyrinth in order to obtain the necessary permission, and then serving as associate producer to George Vicas, in the actual shooting of the documentary, which was aired on May 21, 1963. The program won an Emmy Award in cinematography and the Golden Mike Award. "We were very careful to keep politics out of it," said Jarvis. "Instead, we put our emphasis on history, art, music, architecture and stories, even when we brought it up to modern times."

Continually motivated by her belief that television is a tool of enlightenment and change, Jarvis also produced several documentaries on medical and social welfare issues, the first of which, "Who Shall Live?," examined the medical, moral, and economic dilemmas posed by the use of the artificial kidney and in the selection of patients for dialysis treatment. Viewer response to the show, which aired in November 1965, brought a flood of angry letters to government officials expressing indignation over the nation's failure to provide funding for kidney patients. As a result, the federal government made $6 million available for dialysis centers across the country. A spokesperson for the National Dialysis Committee called Jarvis an inspiration: "Each new patient treated with the therapy of dialysis on the artificial kidney will owe some portion of his life to the camera and cutting shears of Lucy Jarvis." Jarvis also stimulated public interest in the problem of mental illness among young people with the documentary "Cry Help!" (1970), which was filmed at the state mental hospital in Napa, California. "It is a plea; it is an emergency cry," said Jarvis, "for society to help our children."

In 1963, Jarvis produced the first NBC-TV special using a communications satellite in "Museum Without Walls," which presented a simultaneous view of the Louvre in Paris and the National Gallery in Washington, D.C. The famous Paris museum was also the subject of a more in-depth project, "The Louvre: The Golden Prison" (1964). Television audiences were able to view the largest collection of the works of Picasso in the documentary "Bravo, Picasso" (1967), described in the *Los Angeles Times* (February 7, 1976), as an "artistic triumph for NBC staff." Other firsts included a look inside Scotland Yard, and a film version of the Peking Opera's "Red Detachment of Women," presented in 1972.

As the years went by, large-scale documentaries eventually gave way to magazine shows, and Jarvis' budgets began to get smaller. In 1976, she left NBC to produce independently. Jarvis produced two shows for her long-time friend *Barbara Walters, who left NBC at the same time to work for ABC. The relationship did not work out, and Jarvis left to try her hand at producing movies and series, the first of which was "Family Reunion" (1981), a four-hour mini-series starring *Bette Davis. The project, which Jarvis explained was "based on reality," grew from a study done by the *Ladies' Home Journal* on the growing interest in annual family reunions.

Jarvis received numerous awards throughout her career. In 1967, she was the first recipient of the Golden Mike Award, presented by the American Women in Radio and Television. In 1968, she was decorated by the French government for her programs on French history and culture. She was named among America's most prominent women in a poll by the *Ladies' Home Journal* in 1971 and that same year was included in the *Harper's Bazaar* list of One Hundred Women in Tune with the Times. In 1999, age 80, Lucy Jarvis was pressuring U.S. bureaucrats to allow her to take the Ballet Hispanico troupe to Cuba and film them "visiting the roots of their influence."

SOURCES:

Brown, Les. *Les Brown's Encyclopedia of Television*. Detroit, MI: Visible Ink Press, 1992.

Diamonstein, Barbaralee. *Open Secrets*. NY: Viking, 1970.

Gilbert, Lynn, and Gaylen Moore. *Particular Passions*. NY: Clarkson Potter, 1981.

Kissel, Howard. "They Love Lucy," in [New York] *Daily News*. July 25, 1999.

Moritz, Charles, ed. *Current Biography 1972*. NY: H.W. Wilson, 1972.

Barbara Morgan,
Melrose, Massachusetts

Jasnorzewska, Maria Pawlikowska (1891–1945).

See Pawlikowska, Maria.

Jayakar, Pupul (1915–1999)

Considered by many to be the tsarina of Indian culture. Born on September 11, 1915, at Etawah in Uttar Pradesh, India; died of cardiac arrest at her home in South Bombay, India; graduate of London School of Economics; married Manmohan M. Jayakar, a lawyer.

Selected writings: Children of a Barren Woman: Essays, Investigations, Stories *(1994)*; Indira Gandhi: A Biography *(1995)*; J. Krishnamurti: A Biography *(1996)*; Textiles and Ornaments of India *(1972)*.

Pupul Jayakar was born into a Gujarati Brahmin family on September 11, 1915, at Etawah in Uttar Pradesh, India. Following her graduation from the London School of Economics, she began her career in public life as an assistant secretary in the National Planning Committee, which at that time was chaired by prime minister Jawaharlal Nehru. Jayakar was soon recognized as the tsarina of Indian culture. She was particularly noted for popularizing Indian art, culture and heritage by promoting Festivals of India abroad. Jayakar was also active in elevating Indian handicrafts and served as the executive director and later chair of the Handicrafts and Handloom Corporation of India. As well, she chaired the All India Handicrafts Board for a period of three years beginning in 1974. Involved in many other cultural movements in India as well, Jayakar was appointed vice-president of the Indian Council for Cultural Relations in 1982. In 1984, she founded the Indian National Trust for Art and Cultural Heritage (INTACH), and for a period of five years, beginning in 1985, she served as vice-chair of the Indira Gandhi Memorial Trust as well as an adviser on heritage and cultural resources to the prime minister. She was a close friend of *Indira Gandhi and a disciple of philosopher Jiddu Krishnamurti, writing biographies of both. Pupul Jayakar died in South Bombay, India, of cardiac arrest in 1999.

Jo Anne Meginnes,
freelance writer, Brookfield, Vermont

Jeakins, Dorothy (1914—)

American costume designer. Born on January 11, 1914 in San Diego, California; attended Otis Art Institute, 1931–34; children: Stephen Sydney Dane; Peter Jeakins Dane.

Selected films as costume designer, alone or in collaboration: ***Joan of Arc** *(1948);* Samson and Delilah *(1949–50);* The Greatest Show on Earth *(1952);* My Cousin Rachel *(1952);* The Outcasts of Poker Flat *(1952);* Niagara *(1952);* Titanic *(1952);* Three Coins in the Fountain *(1954);* Friendly Persuasion *(1956);* The Ten Commandments *(1956);* South Pacific *(1958);* Let's Make Love *(1960);* The Children's Hour *(1961);* All Fall Down *(1962);* The Music Man *(1962);* The Best Man *(1964);* The Night of the Iguana *(1964);* The Sound of Music *(1965);* Hawaii *(1966);* Reflections in a Golden Eye *(1967);* Finian's Rainbow *(1968);* True Grit *(1969);* Little Big Man *(1970);* Fat City *(1972);* The Way We Were *(1973);* Young Frankenstein *(1974);* The Hindenburg *(1975);* The Yakuza *(1975);* Audrey Rose *(1977);* The Betsy *(1978);* North Dallas Forty *(1979);* The Postman Always Rings Twice *(1981);* On Golden Pond *(1981);* The Dead *(1987).*

Born in San Diego, California, in 1914, Dorothy Jeakins trained at Otis Art Institute and designed for the stage before arriving in Hollywood in the late 1940s. Jeakins frequently collaborated with ***Edith Head** and also worked with Charles LeMaire during the 1950s. The designer shared Academy Awards for *Joan of Arc* (1948), *Samson and Delilah* (1950), and *The Night of the Iguana* (1964). She also designed costumes for network television.

Jean, Gloria (1926—)

American actress and singer. Born Gloria Jean Schoonover, in Buffalo, New York, on April 14, 1926; the youngest of the four daughters of Ferman Schoonover (a music store owner) and Eleanor Schoonover; married, 1962–66; children: one son, Angelo.

Filmography: The Under-Pup *(1939);* If I Had My Way *(1940);* A Little Bit of Heaven *(1940);* Never Give a Sucker an Even Break *(1941);* What's Cookin'? *(1942);* Get Hep to Love *(1942);* When Johnny Comes Marching Home *(1943);* It Comes Up Love *(1943);* Mister Big *(1943);* Moonlight in Vermont *(1943);* Follow the Boys *(1944);* Pardon My Rhythm *(1944);* Ghost Catchers *(1944);* The Reckless Age *(1944);* Destiny *(1944);* I'll Remember April *(1945);* River Gang *(1945);* Easy to Look At *(1945);* Copacabana *(1947);* I Surrender Dear *(1948);* An Old-Fashioned Girl *(1949);* Manhattan Angel *(1949);* There's a Girl in My Heart *(1950);* Air Strike *(1955);* The Ladies' Man *(1961);* The Madcaps *(1961).*

Gloria Jean was born Gloria Jean Schoonover in Buffalo, New York, in 1926 but raised in Scranton, Pennsylvania, where her family settled when she was a baby. She made her singing debut at age three (billed as Baby Schoonover) and by age five had her own radio program in Scranton. In 1939, after Joe Pasternak heard her sing, she was signed by Universal Pictures with hopes that she would succeed megastar ***Deanna Durbin**, who was getting too old for teenage roles. Jean's first film, *The Under-Pup* (1939), a story about a poor girl who wins a vacation to summer camp with a group of rich girls, was promising. *Variety* praised Jean's poise, winsome personality, and remarkable screen presence. "She also has vocal ability which is demonstrated briefly in several sequences. Gloria Jean is well qualified for starring responsibilities in the future." Her next film, *If I Had My Way* (1940), with Bing Crosby, gave her more opportunity to show off her soprano

Gloria Jean

voice and was probably the most popular of her movies. Well on her way with her third effort, W.C. Fields' *Never Give a Sucker an Even Break* (1941), Jean also made guest appearances on a number of radio shows and sang at President Franklin D. Roosevelt's birthday party in 1940.

Beginning in 1942, Gloria Jean was paired with Donald O'Connor in a series of low-budget musicals that began with *What's Cookin'?* (1942) and ended with *Moonlight in Vermont* (1943). By now, Universal was losing interest in their promising star, and she closed out her contract with mediocre roles. In 1945, she embarked on a lengthy personal appearance tour, returning to the screen in *Copacabana* (1947), in which she was pretty much upstaged by Groucho Marx and *Carmen Miranda. A second lead in *There's a Girl in My Heart* (1949) led to a six-year hiatus from movies.

During the 1950s, she undertook another tour of the United States, but it ended badly when her appearance at the London Casino was so poorly received that she broke down on stage. Returning to Hollywood, she made a few television appearances and starred in the low-budget programmer *Air Strike* (1955) and the little-seen comedy *The Madcaps* (1962). Jean then retired from films and took a job as a hostess in a restaurant. In 1965, she began work as a receptionist in a cosmetics firm in Van Nuys and, aside from an occasional television appearance, has since remained pretty much out of the public eye.

SOURCES:

Katz, Ephraim. *The Film Encyclopedia.* NY: Harper-Collins, 1994.

Lamparski, Richard. *Whatever Became of . . . ?* 4th series. NY: Crown, 1973.

Parish, James Robert, and Michael R. Pitts. *Hollywood Songsters.* NY: Garland, 1990.

Barbara Morgan,
Melrose, Massachusetts

Jeanes, Anna Thomas (1822–1907)

American Quaker philanthropist. Born in Philadelphia, Pennsylvania, on April 7, 1822; died at Stapeley Hall, a Friends home in Germantown, Pennsylvania, on September 24, 1907; youngest of ten children of Isaiah Jeanes (a shipping merchant and Quaker) and Anna (Thomas) Jeanes (died 1826); never married; no children.

Anna Thomas Jeanes led a quiet life, with a predilection for the philosophy of Buddhism. When the last of her brothers and sisters died in 1894, she inherited over $2 million and spent the remaining years of her life dispersing the funds. Her benefactions included $200,000 to the Spring Garden Institute, a technical school, $100,000 to the Hicksite Friends, and $200,000 to the Pennsylvania Home for Aged Friends, a Quaker institution where she spent the closing years of her own life. In 1907, she left the sum of $1 million to be used exclusively for the benefit of African-American elementary schools in the South and to develop improved means of education for blacks. "Jeanes teachers" traveled from school to school to advise local teachers.

COLLECTIONS:

Letters in the Friends Historical Library, Swarthmore, Pennsylvania.

Jeanmaire, Renée (b. 1924).

See Jeanmaire, Zizi.

Jeanmaire, Zizi (1924—)

French ballerina and film actress. Name variations: Renée Jeanmaire; Zizi Petit. Born Renée Jeanmaire in Paris, France, on April 29, 1924; daughter of Marcel Jeanmaire (owner of a Paris chromium factory) and Olga (Brunus) Jeanmaire; studied ballet at the Paris Opera Ballet School; married Roland Petit (a dancer and director of Les Ballets des Champs Elysées), on December 29, 1954; children: one daughter, Valentine Petit.

Selected films: Hans Christian Andersen *(US, 1952);* Anything Goes *(US, 1956);* Folies-Bergère *(1956);* Charmants Garçons *(1957);* Guinguette *(1958);* Un Deux Trois *(Les Collants noirs or Black Tights, 1960).*

Born in Paris, France, in 1924, Zizi Jeanmaire entered the famed Paris Opera Ballet School at the age of nine and studied under Alexandre Volinine and Boris Kniaseff. As a young student, she also met Roland Petit, who would later influence both her career and personal life. At 17, after leaving the Paris Opera, she spent several seasons with the de Basil and de Guevas Russian ballets, then became an original member of Les Ballets de Champs-Elysées, a company formed by Petit in October 1945. She left the group in 1948 to join Petit's newly formed Les Ballets de Paris de Roland Petit, a troupe of 15 solo dancers. During the company's initial season, Jeanmaire danced the leading roles in *Que le Diable l'Emporte, Études Symphoniques,* and *Carmen,* three new ballets choreographed by Petit. Following a successful Paris engagement, the company toured Western Europe, appearing in London for the first time in February 1949.

On the occasion of the company's debut in New York on October 6, 1949, Jeanmaire dazzled American audiences with her unconventional interpretation of Carmen. The elfin star also received enthusiastic notices from the American critics, one of whom called her short-cropped hair and exotic eye make-up "sensual and bold." Louis Biancolli, writing for the *New York World-Telegram*, thought Jeanmaire's Carmen "one of the most amazing portrayals of the modern stage. Using almost strictly classical technique, abetted by a shrewd sense of subtly graded pantomime, she manages to depict the whole tantalizing personality of Don Jose's femme fatale." After 118 performances of the ballet in New York, the company went on to tour other eastern cities as well as Canada.

In 1949, Jeanmaire suffered a leg injury which required surgery and a six-month recuperation period. She then returned to dance in yet another new ballet by Petit, *La Croqueuse de Diamants* (The Diamond Cruncher), which tells the story of a woman who has an insatiable appetite for diamonds (for eating, rather than wearing). In the ballet, which toured the United States in 1951, the principals sang and spoke as well as danced, an innovation that met with varying degrees of acceptance among the critics. In the leading role, Jeanmaire revealed a knack for comedy and a charming singing voice reminiscent of *chanteuse* *Edith Piaf. "She dances, mimes, and sings with an intensity that makes the most fantastic episodes seem wholly natural," noted the reviewer for *Musical America* (November 15, 1950), "and she tosses off the technically difficult solos and duets with the utmost ease."

While touring with the ballet on the West Coast, Jeanmaire signed a movie contract with Howard Hughes (whose plans to film *Carmen* never materialized) and, in 1952, was loaned to Samuel Goldwyn to star in the film *Hans Christian Andersen* with Danny Kaye. The movie's end contains a 17-minute ballet choreographed by Petit, the most elaborate ever staged by Goldwyn. Jeanmaire went on to star in several French movies and also appeared on Broadway in *The Girl in Pink Tights* (1953).

The dancer married Roland Petit in 1954 and had a daughter, **Valentine Petit**. During her later career, Jeanmaire combined singing and acting with dancing and starred in the stage shows *Revue des Ballets de Paris* (1956), *Le Patron* (1959), and *An Evening with Zizi*, which came to the United States in 1964. "There is nothing interesting about me personally," she

Zizi Jeanmaire

once said. "But when people see me dance, they understand me. That is the important thing."

SOURCES:

Candee, Marjorie Dent, ed. *Current Biography*. NY: H.W. Wilson, 1952.

Katz, Ephraim. *The Film Encyclopedia*. NY: Harper-Collins, 1994.

Barbara Morgan,
Melrose, Massachusetts

Jeanne.

Variant of Joan and Juana.

Jeanne, Pope (d. 858).

See Joan (d. 858).

Jeanne I (1273–1305).

See Joan I of Navarre.

Jeanne I (d. 1346)

Countess of Dreux. Born in Dreux, France; died in 1346; daughter of Robert V, count of Dreux (r. 1309–1329); sister of Jean III, count of Dreux (r.

1329–1331); sister of Pierre, count of Dreux (r. 1331–1345).

Jeanne I succeeded her deceased brothers, ruling Dreux from 1345 until her death in 1346; she was replaced by her aunt, *Jeanne II.

Jeanne II (r. 1346–1355)

Countess of Dreux. Born in Dreux, France; reigned from 1346 to 1355; second daughter of Jean II, count of Dreux (r. 1282–1309); sister of Robert V, count of Dreux (r. 1309–1329); married Louis, vicomte de Thouars; children: Simon de Thouars, count of Dreux (r. 1355–1365).

Jeanne II was the sister of Robert V, count of Dreux. She succeeded her niece *Jeanne I in 1346 and reigned until 1355. The fief of Dreux was sold in 1377 to Charles VI, king of France, who then conferred it on the House of Albret.

Jeanne I de Navarre (1273–1305).

See Joan I of Navarre.

Jeanne II de Navarre (1309–1349).

See Joan II of Navarre.

Jeanne I of Burgundy (c. 1291–1330)

*Queen of France. Name variations: Jeanne de Bourgogne; Joan I, countess of Artois; Joan of Burgundy. Born around 1291; died in 1330 (some sources cite 1325); daughter of Count Otto IV of Burgundy, and *Mahaut (c. 1270–1329), countess of Artois; married Philip V the Tall (1294–1322), king of France (r. 1316–1322), in 1306 or 1307; children: *Jeanne II of Burgundy (1308–1347); *Margaret of Artois (d. 1382, who married Louis II of Flanders); Isabelle Capet (who married Guigne VIII of Viennois).*

Jeanne II of Burgundy (1308–1347)

*Countess of Artois. Name variations: Joan II, countess of Artois; Jeanne II of Artois; Jeanne II of Bourgogne. Born on May 2, 1308; died on August 13, 1347; daughter of *Jeanne I of Burgundy (c. 1291–1330) and Philip V (c. 1294–1322), king of France (r. 1316–1322); married Eudes IV, duke of Burgundy, on June 18, 1318; children: Philip Capet (d. 1346); and five other sons who died in infancy.*

Jeanne III d'Albret (1528–1572).

See Jeanne d'Albret.

Jeanne d'Albret (1528–1572)

One of the first members of the French nobility to convert to Protestantism, who became a leader of the Huguenot movement, and whose son Henry IV became king of England and founder of the Bourbon Dynasty. Name variations: Joan III, Queen of Navarre; Jeanne III d'Albret. Born in 1528; died in Paris in 1572; daughter of Henry or Henri II d'Albret, king of Navarre, and Margaret of Angoulême (1492–1549); niece of Francis I, king of France (r. 1515–1547); married Guillaume de la March also known as William, duke of Cleves, in 1541 (annulled); married Antoine also known as Anthony (1518–1562), duke of Bourbon and Vendôme, in 1548; children: (second marriage) Henri or Henry of Navarre (1553–1610, later Henry IV, king of France, r. 1589–1610); Catherine of Bourbon (c. 1555–1604).

From the moment of her birth in 1528, Jeanne d'Albret seemed destined to become a pawn in the sophisticated game of French politics. Her mother was *Margaret of Angoulême, sister of Renaissance French king Francis I. Her father, Henry II d'Albret, was king of Navarre, a title that had become a mere courtesy since 1512 when Ferdinand II of Aragon had annexed most of Navarre to his kingdom of Spain. Henry II d'Albret married Margaret in hopes that her brother Francis I would help him regain the lost provinces of Navarre. Francis arranged the marriage in hopes that it would prevent Henry d'Albret from coming to an agreement with the Spanish which would allow them to break through the Pyrenees into France. Thus, as was customary among the noble class in that day, Jeanne's parents were married for political convenience. It was expected that Jeanne's marriage would also be dictated by political expediency.

When it became obvious that she was to be the only child of Henry d'Albret and Margaret to survive infancy, Jeanne's future was plotted with special care. Until she was ten, she lived a carefree life at her mother's castle in Angoulême, where she had the run of a large park as well as a bevy of animals and a little girl to entertain her. During these years, her father Henry d'Albret had repeatedly failed to persuade Francis I to send the promised soldiers to his aid, and so Henry d'Albret began plotting to obtain a betrothal between his daughter Jeanne and Prince Philip (II) of Spain. However, Henry d'Albret's wife Margaret had loyalties to her brother, not her ill-matched husband. Margaret lived mostly apart from her indifferent and often unfaithful spouse, and she remained determined to put

Jeanne's future in the hands of her brother, Francis I. (Margaret of Angoulême's influence on Jeanne extended into literature, and Jeanne is credited with seeing that her mother's greatest work, *L'Heptaméron,* unfinished at the time of Margaret's death, was published true to her mother's concept. Of her own writing, Jeanne left a number of poems written in a form of French which was spoken in medieval times. She also left a manuscript of her memoirs.)

When Francis negotiated a match for her, Jeanne showed the first spark of the inflexible will that she would later bravely exhibit as a mature woman. She was to be wed to William, duke of Cleves, a dull and ponderous young man whose only advantage lay in his connection to the German princes, with whom Francis I wished to ally against the formidable power of the Habsburg family. Under Charles V, the Habsburgs ruled the Holy Roman Empire, Spain, and the Low Countries. Thirteen-year-old Jeanne protested the match, but she was given no choice and, succumbing to dire threats, bowed to the inevitable. Dressed fabulously in cloth of gold, Jeanne was married to William in an elaborate ceremony in June 1541. In view of the bride's tender years, the marriage was not consummated, and Jeanne went back home to France while her new husband embarked on a military crusade to save his lands from Habsburg encroachment.

Stubbornly refusing to accept the marriage, Jeanne had a document drafted, signed and witnessed in which she swore to have been coerced into the nuptials and never to have given her free consent. It was, however, a futile gesture. Her fortunes did take a turn for the better when William proved himself to be completely inept on the battlefield. Within a few years, Charles V forced William to publicly capitulate, and Francis I took immediate steps to have Jeanne's marriage annulled. Her document of protest was brought before the courts, which ruled that it provided sufficient evidence to invalidate the marriage.

Now that Jeanne was free, her father Henry d'Albret reopened marriage negotiations with the Spanish. Meanwhile, Francis I died and was succeeded by his son Henry II. Catching wind of Henry d'Albret's plans, Henry II pressed his aunt Margaret to have Jeanne married quickly to a French suitor. Soon, Jeanne fell in love with one of her admirers, Antoine, duke of Bourbon. Though he was ten years her senior, she appreciated his quick mind and affectionate nature. Margaret was skeptical; although, as duke of Bourbon, Antoine was a Prince of the Blood (di-

rectly related to the French royal family), his family was neither wealthy nor powerful. But Henry II, delighted that Jeanne and Antoine showed such a liking for each other, convinced Jeanne's parents to acquiesce to the match by promising to send an army to her father Henry d'Albret to help him conquer Navarre and by providing him with a stipend of 15,000 livres. (In fact, the promised army never materialized, and the stipend was paid only once.) Jeanne was ecstatic over the surprising turn of events. Henry II noted at her wedding in October of 1649 that "she does nothing but laugh."

The early years of Jeanne d'Albret's marriage were truly happy. Antoine was often absent, usually in the field fighting the Spanish on the border, but they exchanged many warm and tender letters. Antoine assured her, "I never would have believed that I should love you as much as I do," claiming that he could no more live without her than could a body without a soul. Within two years of their marriage, Jeanne gave birth to a son. Sadly, the child died in infancy, a tragedy all too common in an age when roughly one-third of all children did not survive to their fifth birthday.

> $\mathcal{Q}$ueen of her people and the savior of the Huguenots, busying herself with their causes, righting their wrongs, pleading for compassion and toleration on their behalf.
>
> —Irene Mahoney

But Jeanne quickly conceived again. Her mother, suffering from chronic ill health, had died soon after the wedding. Her father, increasingly aware of his own mortality, became obsessed with the need for a male heir. Although he had shown little interest in his daughter except as a political pawn, he insisted that she travel to his seat in Bearn to have the child. Alarmed by persistent rumors that her father was considering marrying again in an attempt to produce a male heir, Jeanne dutifully traveled to his estate. Henry d'Albret drew up his will, leaving all of his estate to her, and placed it in a gold box. He promised to deliver the will to his daughter as soon as the baby was born, provided that, while she was in labor, she sing a traditional song sung by Bearnais women to the Virgin when praying for a son. In December 1553, when Jeanne gave birth to a fine, healthy boy, her father immediately snatched up the child, rubbed its lips with garlic, and put a cup of local Jurancon wine to its mouth. When the baby did not cry but wiggled his head with delight, Henry d'Albret gleefully exclaimed, "Thou wilt be a true Bearnais!" He fulfilled his promise and gave his will to his daughter. The baby was named Henry (of Navarre), in his honor.

Old Henry d'Albret did not survive much longer, dying in May 1555. Since Antoine was still away most of the time, Jeanne threw herself into raising her son. Little Henry was nursed by the sturdy local peasant women, and when he was older he ran around barefoot with the local boys, living on black bread and cheese. From a young age, Henry of Navarre showed great energy, reckless courage, and a shrewd mind. When he was three, Jeanne and Antoine took him to Paris to present him to King Henry II and his queen *Catherine de Medici. Henry II was impressed with the boy, and even made an informal agreement to betroth little Henry of Navarre to his daughter *Margaret of Valois (1553–1615), then three-and-a-half.

By 1559, the first tremors of the political upheavals which would eventually plunge France into civil war could be felt. While Henry II was jousting in a tournament held to celebrate the marriage of his eldest daughter *Elizabeth of Valois to Philip of Spain, a lance slipped through his visor and penetrated his eye. After several days of torment, he died. Henry II left behind four young sons. The eldest, at 16, succeeded as Francis II. As a child, Francis had been married to *Mary Stuart (1542–1587), queen of Scotland. Mary was the niece of the dukes of Guise, who led an ambitious faction intent on securing political power. Francis' accession gave the Guise their chance. Francis was declared old enough to rule without a regency, but the crown weighed heavily upon his young and sickly frame. Francis' mother Catherine de Medici was determined not to lose her influence over her son. In this struggle between Catherine and the Guise faction, the Princes of the Blood, including Jeanne's husband Antoine, were pushed away from their rightful place of influence. Antoine, like his late father-in-law, was concerned first and foremost with regaining the Navarre provinces. When he gave up all hope of obtaining help from the French Crown, Antoine began to look for other avenues to achieve his goals. One such which presented itself was through the "reformed religion," a growing faction in France that called themselves Huguenots.

Huguenots were followers of John Calvin, a famous Reformation theologian who had set up a community of followers in Geneva, Switzerland. Calvin and his disciples broke away from the Catholic Church and established a new, con-gregational church structure as opposed to the hierarchical schema of the Catholic Church. Calvinists emphasized direct communication with God and preached the doctrine of election, wherein certain "elect" men and women are pre-ordained to be saved. Although Calvinism was a harsh doctrine, it had great appeal because of its stress on sincere piety at a time when the bloated and corrupt Catholic Church was making little attempt to address the spiritual needs of its members. Throughout the 16th century, the number of Huguenots multiplied rapidly, and the reformed religion spread even into the aristocratic class. French nobles embraced the Huguenot religion for yet another reason—practicing Protestantism gave them leverage against the Roman Catholic Church and indirectly gave them a measure of independence from the authority of the Crown.

But religious toleration did not exist in French law, and heretics were subjected to fines, imprisonment, and even burning at the stake. Calvinist leaders sent missionaries to France hoping to convert a sufficient number of the nobility to force a relaxation of the laws against Huguenots. One of the nobles they approached was Jeanne's husband Antoine de Bourbon. Although Antoine entertained the Huguenots' message with interest, he was not the man to champion the Protestant cause; an opportunist at heart, he was unwilling to suffer the consequences which a public conversion might bring. But Jeanne d'Albret, queen of Navarre in her own right, heard the message of the Huguenots and came to believe that they preached spiritual truth. On Christmas Day, 1561, she made her formal confession in the Calvinist faith and began openly worshipping as a Huguenot.

Immediately, Jeanne became a guiding light in the Huguenot movement. She daily received preachers and leaders of the reformed religion in her home and helped plan an organization of Huguenots on a national scale. She was "receiv'd everywhere by the heretics with great enthusiasm, as though she were a messiah."

The 1560s were a time of turmoil in France. Francis II died in December 1560, leaving the throne to his brother Charles IX. Catherine de Medici, desperately trying to maintain her power over her son, played the Huguenots against the Guise faction, which remained staunchly Catholic. In order to balance the Catholic faction against the Protestant faction, Catherine pushed through legislation guaranteeing religious liberty to the Huguenots.

Jeanne d'Albret

Furious, the Guise faction left the court and began plotting to undermine the recent Huguenot victories. They approached Antoine full of lush promises backed by Spain: Antoine was to have another kingdom to compensate him for the loss of Navarre—if only he would live as a faithful Catholic and bring his recalcitrant wife back into the Holy Mother Church. This would not be an easy task; Jeanne was a sincere convert to the Protestant faith. Antoine commanded her to attend mass. When she refused, he resorted to threats and finally banished her from court.

Thus, Jeanne's religious conversion ended her happy relationship with Antoine. The price she paid for refusing to renounce her new faith was separation from her young son. Although only nine years old, little Henry of Navarre had learned much from his mother. She had admonished him to attend only the worship of the reformed religion. When his father tried to force him to attend Catholic mass, Henry of Navarre endured scoldings, threats and beatings for two months before finally bowing to the inevitable.

Open warfare broke out between Catholics and Huguenots after the duke of Guise ordered the massacre of a Huguenot assembly at Vassey. The Prince of Condé, Antoine's brother, publicly announced his conversion and took over leadership of the Huguenot cause on the battlefield. In November 1562, Antoine died of battle wounds. After his death, Jeanne tried to regain custody of Henry of Navarre, but Catherine de Medici insisted that Henry of Navarre remain at court with his cousins in Paris. The duke of Guise was assassinated in the spring of 1763, and a temporary cease-fire was called. Soon after, Pope Pius V called Jeanne before the Inquisition, threatening excommunication and confiscation of her titles and property if she refused to appear. Help came from an unexpected quarter. Catherine de Medici wrote to the pope on Jeanne's behalf, threatening intervention of the French Crown if he dared try to exert his authority against a French subject. Jeanne, grateful for the queen mother's intervention, accepted her invitation to join the court, where she was allowed to see her son, although she could not take him to Huguenot services.

Catherine de Medici continued to refuse Jeanne's request to take Henry of Navarre from the court until 1567. When mother and son finally left, civil war erupted anew. Charles IX revoked the edict of toleration, but this only encouraged the Huguenots to fight back with greater force. Jeanne joined her brother-in-law, the Prince of Condé, at the Huguenot stronghold at La Rochelle, where she gave Henry of Navarre over to his uncle for military training. Within months, Condé was killed by a group of Catholics after being taken prisoner following battle. Condé's death left 15-year-old Henry of Navarre as the nominal leader of the Huguenot faction. As the intermittent war raged on, a new duke of Guise, also named Henry, began to take control of the Catholic forces. Charles IX's younger brother, Henry de Valois, also distinguished himself as a military leader and completed the triumvirate which made up the War of the Three Henrys.

By 1571, the country was heartily tired of the violence and destruction of civil war, and the royal treasury was empty. Despite the pope's continuing insistence that "there can be no harmony between light and darkness," Charles IX and Catherine de Medici began negotiating for peace with the Huguenots. A marriage between Jeanne's son Henry of Navarre and Catherine's daughter Margaret of Valois seemed a perfect means to secure tranquility. Although stalwart Huguenots and Catholics disapproved of a marriage between partners of different faiths, Charles IX favored the match as an omen of peace. On April 11, 1572, Charles IX, Catherine de Medici, and Jeanne d'Albret all signed a contract of marriage between Henry of Navarre and Margaret of Valois. The wedding was scheduled to take place that summer.

To await her son's arrival and to make plans for the upcoming wedding, Jeanne traveled to the ancestral Bourbon home, where she fell seriously ill. By June, she took to her bed with a high fever. Rumors that she had been poisoned were carried to Paris; she, however, blamed her sudden illness on a chronic pulmonary disorder. By June 6, she was told she was dying. In her typical practical nature, she carefully prepared her will, including a codicil that her son must uphold the reformed religion and asking that he give protection to his younger sister *Catherine of Bourbon. Two days later, Jeanne d'Albret was dead. According to her request, no candles were set at her casket, and her funeral was performed without the familiar Catholic rituals: "no priests, no cross, nor any holy water." Her death was sudden even by the standards of the day. When her son Henry of Navarre was informed of her death on June 13, he wrote: "I have just received the saddest news that has ever been brought to me, the death of the Queen my mother whom God called a few days ago." Henry was now king of Navarre and the undisputed leader of the Huguenot movement in France. He proclaimed: "Now that my mother is dead, I succeed her and must take as my duty all that was in her charge."

The proposed wedding between Henry of Navarre and Margaret of Valois did not end the fighting between Catholics and Huguenots in France. No sooner were the festivities concluded in August, than Catherine de Medici and the Catholics hatched a plot to end the Huguenot movement in France once and for all. On the evening of St. Bartholomew's Day, the Catholics in Paris rose up in the middle of the night and attacked all the Huguenots who had come to Paris for the wedding. Thousands of Huguenots were massacred, and the streets ran with blood. Henry of Navarre escaped and fled to the countryside where he took control of the remaining Huguenot forces. The civil war raged until 1589. By the end of the War of the Three Henrys, both Henry, duke of Guise, and Henry de Valois (who had succeeded as Henry III after Charles IX's death) had been killed. Henry of Navarre was the closest heir to the throne, and he succeeded as Henry IV in August of 1589. Although it took nine more years of fighting and Henry IV's conversion to Catholicism to end the civil wars, eventually Jeanne d'Albret's son brought peace to France and founded the royal dynasty of Bourbon, which would rule France for almost two centuries, until the French Revolution in 1789.

SOURCES:

Mahoney, Irene. *Royal Cousin: The Life of Henri IV of France*. NY: Doubleday, 1970.

Memoirs of Henry the Great and of the Court of France During His Reign. Vol. I. London: Harding, Triphook and Lepard, 1824.

Roelker, Nancy Layman. *Queen of Navarre: Jeanne d'Albret*. Cambridge, MA: Harvard Univ. Press, 1968.

Sedgwick, Henry Dwight. *Henry of Navarre*. Indianapolis, IN: Bobbs-Merrill, 1930.

SUGGESTED READING:

Nabonne, Bernard. *Jeanne d'Albret*. Paris, 1945.

Rochambeau, Marquis de. *Lettres de Antoine de Bourbon et Jeanne d'Albret*. Paris: Societe de l'Histoire de France, 1877.

Kimberly Estep Spangler,
Assistant Professor of History and Chair of the Division of Religion and Humanities at Friends University, Wichita, Kansas

Jeanne d'Arc (c. 1412–1431).

See Joan of Arc.

Jeanne d'Autriche (1535–1573).

See Joanna of Austria.

Jeanne de Belleville (fl. 1343)

French noblewoman and pirate. Name variations: Jeanne de Clisson. Flourished in 1343 in France and England; married Olivier III, lord of Clisson (died 1343); married Gautier de Bentley, an English courtier; children: at least three, including Olivier IV, lord of Clisson.

A French noblewoman, Jeanne de Belleville's rebellion against Philip VI, king of France, gained her a reputation for being vicious, bloodthirsty, and vengeful. She lived rather quietly as a younger woman, marrying Olivier III, lord of Clisson, and bearing several children. But when her husband was executed for treason in 1343 on the king's orders, Jeanne revolted, gathering other discontented petty nobles and beginning a bloody rampage against the king's followers. With the troops of King Philip close after them, the rebels rode across the kingdom, killing all the royalist nobles they could find.

Her revolt found support from Edward III, king of England, who, in his desire to weaken the French king in any way possible, agreed to loan Jeanne some arms and English warships. From the coast of Brittany, Jeanne and her supporters conducted skirmishes against French soldiers. After 1344, Jeanne escaped to the protection of the English king and lived at his court, eventually marrying Gautier de Bentley, a courtier.

SOURCES:

Echols, Anne, and Marty Williams. *An Annotated Index of Medieval Women*. NY: Markus Wiener, 1992.

Salmonson, Jessica. *The Encyclopedia of Amazons*. NY: Doubleday, 1991.

Laura York,
Riverside, California

Jeanne de Bourbon (1338–1378)

Queen of France. Name variations: Joan of Bourbon. Born on February 3, 1338, in Bourbon (some sources erroneously cite 1326 or 1327); died on February 6, 1378, in Paris; daughter of Pierre or Peter I, duke of Bourbon, and Isabelle of Savoy (d. 1383); married

Coronation of Jeanne de Bourbon at Rheims, 1364.

Charles V (1338–1380), king of France (r. 1364–1380), in 1350; children: Charles VI the Mad (1368–1422), king of France (r. 1380–1422); Louis (1372–1407), duke of Orléans (assassinated in 1407); Isabelle (1378–1378); **Catherine of France** *(who married John of Montpensier).*

Born in 1338, Jeanne de Bourbon was the daughter of *Isabelle of Savoy and Pierre I of Bourbon. In 1350, a marriage took place between the 12-year-old girl and the French king, Charles V (r. 1364–1380). During her life, Jeanne was primarily recognized for her important religious patronage and generosity to convents. She founded a Celestine monastery among others, and was also a benevolent patron of the arts. She commissioned numerous paintings and sculptures, mostly on religious topics, including a statue of pure gold carved in the image of **Mary the Virgin** to adorn one of her religious houses. Like many queens, Jeanne did not assist in the administration of the kingdom, but rather spent her time presiding over a large and intellectual court. She was also noted as an avid book collector and often commissioned works to be copied for her. However, all her life she was plagued by bouts of mental instability of unknown origin. It is believed her son, King Charles VI, inherited his weak mental condition from her. Jeanne died from complications of childbirth at age 40.

SOURCES:
Anderson, Bonnie S., and Judith P. Zinsser. *A History of Their Own.* Vol. I. NY: Harper and Row, 1988.
LaBarge, Margaret. *A Small Sound of the Trumpet: Women in Medieval Life.* Boston: Beacon Press, 1986.

Laura York,
Riverside, California

Jeanne de Bourgogne (1293–1348).

See Jeanne of Burgundy.

Jeanne de Castile (r. 1366–1374)

Co-ruler of Vendôme. *Name variations: Castille; Jeanne of Vendôme or Vendome; Juana of Castile. Reigned in Vendôme with her son Bouchard VII from 1366 to 1374; married Jean VI, count of Vendôme (r. 1336–1366); children:* **Catherine of Vendôme** *(r. 1374–1412); Bouchard VII, count of Vendôme (r. 1366–1374).*

Jeanne de Chatillon (d. 1292)

Countess of Blois. *Reigned from 1279 to 1292; died in 1292; daughter of Jean de Chatillon, count of Blois and Chartres (r. 1241–1279); married Pierre, count d'Alençon.*

Jeanne de Clisson (fl. 1343).

See Jeanne de Belleville.

Jeanne de Dammartin (d. 1279).

See Eleanor of Castile (1241–1290) for sidebar.

Jeanne de France (1464–1505).

See Anne of Beaujeu for sidebar.

Jeanne de Laval (d. 1498)

Duchess of Lorraine and Guise. *Name variations: Duchess of Lorraine and Bar; duchess of Provence; duchess of Anjou and Guise. Died in 1498; became second wife of René I the Good (1408–1480), duke of Lorraine and Bar, duke of Provence, duke of Anjou and Guise (r. 1431–1480), and king of Naples (r. 1435–1442), in 1454. René's first wife was *Isabelle of Lorraine (1410–1453).*

Jeanne de Lestonac (1556–1640)

Saint. *Name variations: Baroness de Landiras. Born in Bordeaux, France, in 1556; died in 1640; niece of Michel de Montaigne; married the baron de Landiras; children: seven.*

Widowed at age 41, Saint Jeanne de Lestonac was a novice for five months at the Feuillantines of Toulouse before founding, with the help of two Jesuits, the Institute of the Daughters of Our Lady. Her feast day is on February 2.

Jeanne de Montfort (c. 1310–c. 1376)

Countess of Montfort and duchess of Brittany. *Name variations: Jane or Joan of Flanders; Jane, countess of Montfort; Jeanne of Flanders. Born around 1310 in Flanders; died around 1376 in England; daughter of Louis de Nevers, count of Flanders; married Jean de Montfort also known as John III (IV) de Montfort (d. 1345), duke of Brittany (r. 1341–1345); children: Jean also seen as John IV (or V) the Valiant or John IV de Montfort (1339–1399), 5th duke of Brittany (r. 1364–1399).*

Daughter of the count of Flanders, Jeanne de Montfort was born around 1310 and spent much of her life warring against claimants to her husband's estates. Historians describe her as a woman of great valor, capable of leadership that would rival the most experienced general. She married John III de Montfort, becoming countess of Montfort and later duchess of Brittany, and gave birth to at least one son in 1339. Throughout Jeanne's married life, the French king Philip VI made war on the dukes of Brittany, seeking to annex that rich province and place his nephew, Charles of Blois, on the ducal throne. After her husband was captured by the French and imprisoned in Paris in 1342, Jeanne de Montfort was forced to continue the war to save Brittany from Charles of Blois and his formidable wife, *Jeanne de Penthièvre.

To protect her property from falling into the hands of her enemies, Jeanne de Montfort assembled an army of supporters from neighboring towns to take up arms in her behalf. From the castle of Hennebonne (or Hennobont) on the coast of Brittany, she led a remarkable defense against constant attack from Charles of Blois, who thought a war conducted by a woman would mean an easy victory. Much has been written of Jeanne de Montfort's valor, strategic capabilities, and quick intellect. Accounts portray her in full armor, sword in hand, standing resolute amid violent assaults. Under her leadership, the dispirited Bretons rallied to the cause of saving their native land from French rule.

After three years in prison, Jeanne's husband escaped from Paris but died during the siege of Hennebonne in 1345, shortly after making his way home to Brittany. The widow Jeanne refused to give up the fight. After her own army had suffered numerous losses and was exhausted from battle, she finally received reinforcements from some English troops. At one point, she mounted a nighttime attack on Charles of Blois' encampment, dispatched his army, and took him hostage. Her military skills, as well as a strong alliance with the English king Edward III, eventually led her to victory. Ultimately, Charles of Blois was killed in the battle of Auray, fought on September 27, 1364, and the disputes in Brittany ended. Finally acknowledged by Charles V, king of France, Jeanne's son inherited the duchy as Duke John IV de Montfort, regaining his rightful properties and title, even though he was a fierce supporter of England. He would marry *Joanna of Navarre in 1386.

Jeanne de Montfort did not put away her sword after Charles V conceded defeat; she appears in later chronicles fighting in a naval battles off the coast of Guernsey. The historian Roujoux called her "a new Penthesilea [the legendary daughter of Orithia, co-ruler of Amazonia], with all the grandeur of a noble character."

SOURCES:

Salmonson, Jessica. *The Encyclopedia of Amazons*. NY: Doubleday, 1991.

Tuchman, Barbara. *A Distant Mirror: The Calamitous Fourteenth Century*. NY: Ballantine, 1978.

Laura York,
Riverside, California

Jeanne de Penthièrre (c. 1320–1384).

See Jeanne de Penthièvre.

Jeanne de Penthièvre (c. 1320–1384)

French noblewoman and countess of Blois. Name variations: Jeanne de Penthièrre or Penthierre or Penthievre; Joan of Blois. Born around 1320; died in 1384 in France; daughter of Guy of Brittany and Jeanne of Avaugour; married Charles of Blois, 1337 (killed 1364).

Jeanne de Penthièvre was a French noblewoman who became the primary enemy of *Jeanne de Montfort. Both women had legitimate claims to the duchy of Brittany, causing a long-lasting feud between them. In 1337, Jeanne de Penthièvre married Charles of Blois, and together they fought against Jeanne de Montfort and her husband John III de Montfort for the right to the duchy of Brittany. During the war, English forces led by Jeanne de Montfort took Charles hostage, but his wife was not willing to give up the fight. Instead, Jeanne de Penthièvre became the commander of Charles' supporters, even leading troops into battle herself. When Charles was slain in 1364 at the battle of Auray, Jeanne de Penthièvre was forced to sign a treaty relinquishing her claims to Brittany. Little is known of her life after the war's conclusion in 1364.

Laura York,
Riverside, California

Jeanne de Sarmaize (fl. 1456)

Impersonator of Joan of Arc. Name variations: Jeanne of Sarmaize; Joan, the Maid of Sarmaize. Flourished in 1456 in France; real name unknown.

Jeanne de Sarmaize was one of several French women who claimed to be *Joan of Arc following the real Joan's death in 1431. Jeanne, whose real name is unknown, was a young peasant woman from the small town of Sarmaize, who must have seen Joan of Arc's continuing popularity as an opportunity to gain a better life. Like the real Joan, Jeanne wore men's clothing; many French people, including a few who had actually known Joan, believed she was truly the reincarnation of their heroine, and some believers even accompanied Jeanne as she traveled across France. Jeanne disappears from the records after 1456.

Laura York,
Riverside, California

Jeanne des Anges.

See French "Witches."

Jeanne des Armoises (fl. 1438)

Captain in the French army. Name variations: Joan of Armoises. Flourished in 1438 in France; married and mother of two.

A few years after the death of ***Joan of Arc,** another Joan came to prominence in France's fight against England. Mother of two and married when she began her military career, Jeanne des Armoises was a soldier from the peasantry. Whether her inspiration to join in the war was true patriotism or a chance for an adventurous life far removed from the drudgery of the peasant woman's life is not known; either way, she fought well and the king's marshal rewarded her by making her a captain in the army.

Jeanne had the support of the soldiers she led as well as the support of the people, but her warrior life did not please the clergy, who successfully pushed for the king to arrest her as an impostor of Joan of Arc. Ironically, the lives of Jeanne des Armoises and Joan of Arc are indeed similar, in that both women risked their lives for the benefit of their country, and both were arrested and condemned for it.

Laura York,
Riverside, California

Jeanne de Valois (c. 1294–1342).
See Jeanne of Valois.

Jeanne de Valois (c. 1304–?).
See Jeanne of Valois.

Jeanne de Valois (c. 1464–1505).
See Anne of Beaujeu for sidebar on Jeanne de France.

Jeanne Hachette (c. 1454–?).
See Hachette, Jeanne.

Jeanne of Boulogne (1326–1360).
See Blanche of Boulogne.

Jeanne of Bourbon (1434–1482)

Duchess of Bourbon. Name variations: Jeanne de France or Jeanne of France. Born in 1434; died on May 4, 1482; daughter of ***Marie of Anjou** (1404–1463) and Charles VII (1403–1461), king of France (r. 1422–1461); sister of Louis XI, king of France (r. 1461–1483); became first wife of Jean also known as John II (1426–1488), duke of Bourbon (r. 1456–1488), on March 11, 1447; no children. John II's second wife was ***Jane of Bourbon-Vendome** (d. 1511).

Jeanne of Bourbon (d. 1493)

Princess of Orange. Name variations: Jeanne de Bourbon. Died on July 10, 1493; daughter of ***Agnes of Burgundy** (d. 1476) and Charles I, duke of Bourbon (r. 1434–1456); married John IV the Good, prince of Orange, on October 21, 1467.

Jeanne of Burgundy (1293–1348)

Queen of France. Name variations: Jeanne de Bourgogne; Joan of Burgundy; countess of Valois; called The Lame. Born in 1293; died on September 12, 1348, in Paris, France (some sources cite 1349); daughter of Robert II, duke of Burgundy, and ***Agnes Capet** (1260–1327, daughter of Louis IX of France); sister of ***Margaret of Burgundy** (1290–1315); became first wife of Philip VI of Valois (1293–1350), king of France (r. 1328–1350), in July 1313; children; Jean also known as John II the Good or Le Bon (1319–1364), king of France (r. 1350–1364); Louis (d. 1328); Louis (d. 1330); Jean or John (d. 1333); Philip (1336–1375), count of Beaumont, count of Valois, duke of Orléans. Philip VI's second wife was ***Blanche of Navarre** (1331–1398).

Jeanne of Burgundy (1344–1360)

French princess. Name variations: Joan of Burgundy. Born in 1344; died in 1360 in Larrey-en-Montagne; daughter of ***Blanche of Boulogne** (1326–1360) and Philip Capet (d. 1346); stepdaughter of John II (1319–1364), king of France (r. 1350–1364).

Jeanne of Chalon (1300–1333)

Countess of Tonnerre. Name variations: Jeanne de Chalon. Born in 1300; died on October 15, 1333; daughter of **Eleonore of Savoy** (d. 1324) and William, count of Auxerre and Tonnerre; married Robert of Burgundy (1302–1334), count of Tonnerre, on June 8, 1321.

Jeanne of Flanders (c. 1310–c. 1376).
See Jeanne de Montfort.

Jeanne of Lorraine (1458–1480)

Countess of Maine and Provence. Name variations: Jeanne of Vaudemont-Lorraine. Born in 1458 (some sources cite 1448); died on January 25, 1480; daughter of *Yolande of Vaudemont (1428–1483) and Ferrey de Vaudemont also known as Frederick, count of Vaudemont; married Charles II of Anjou (1436–1481), count of Maine and Provence.

Jeanne of Navarre (1273–1305).

See Joan I of Navarre.

Jeanne of Navarre (1309–1349).

See Joan II of Navarre.

Jeanne of Nemours (d. 1724)

Duchess and regent of Savoy. Name variations: Giovanna Battista; Jeanne de Nemours; Jeanne-Baptist de Savoie-Nemours; Jean de Savoie-Nemours; Marie-Jeanne-Baptiste; Marie de Savoy-Nemours; Marie of Savoy-Nemours; Madame Royale. Born Marie Jeanne Baptiste de Savoie-Nemours around 1648; regent from 1675 to 1684; died in 1724 in Savoy; daughter of Charles Amadeus of Savoy-Nemours also known as Charles Amedeé of Savoy (who was killed in a celebrated duel with his brother-in-law, François de Vendome, duke of Beaufort) and Elizabeth de Bourbon; sister of *Marie Françoise of Savoy (1646–1683); became second wife of Charles Emmanuel II (1634–1675), duke of Savoy (r. 1638–1675), in 1664; children: Victor Amadeus II (1666–1732), duke of Savoy (r. 1675–1713), king of Sicily (r. 1713–1718) and Sardinia (r. 1718–1730). Charles Emmanuel's first wife was *Françoise d'Orleans (fl. 1650).

Born into the Franco-Italian nobility around 1648, Jeanne of Nemours was the daughter of Charles Amadeus, a younger son of the duke of Nemours, and **Elizabeth de Bourbon**. Little is known about her childhood; in 1664, Jeanne became the second wife of her fourth cousin, Charles Emmanuel, duke of Savoy. He was 15 years her senior. The duke had, with the aid of his mother, ***Christine of France**, ruled over the small but politically important state of Savoy since 1638. Rich in resources and strategically located in the Alps between France and northwest Italy, Savoy was sought as an ally by the Spanish, French, and Italian states.

Jeanne of Nemours gave birth to only one child, Victor Amadeus. Her life at the Savoy court, centered in Turin, was typical of a Western European duchess: she presided over the court's administration and activities but took no overt political role herself. However, this was to change on the death of Duke Charles at age 41 in 1675. Victor Amadeus became duke in name, but as he was only nine years old, Duke Charles Emmanuel had named Jeanne regent of Savoy. He also named a council of advisors to aid her in administering the duchy.

Jeanne's nine-year regency has been seen by some historians as a period of decline for the state, and she has been viewed as an unloving mother who usurped her son's authority. Yet seen in the context of the unstable circumstances she faced, Jeanne must be credited for maintaining Savoy's independence against its internal and external enemies. Ambitious and politically astute, Jeanne recognized the dangers and instability of her position; regencies were always temporary political situations, and without a strong, stable ruler in place, nobles and rival rulers often tried to increase their power at the regent's expense. Her situation was exacerbated by her son's extremely poor health, for few expected

Jeanne of Nemours

him to survive childhood. He was also showing signs of a violent and rash disposition and a secretive nature, which Jeanne observed with apprehension. Her letters concerning him show little maternal tenderness but reveal her anxiety over his character and his potential as a ruler. In addition to these concerns, Savoy was facing strong pressure from foreign powers, most notably the kings of France and Spain, as well as hostility between the pro-French and pro-Spanish factions of the Savoyard nobility.

However, Jeanne immediately demonstrated that she intended to govern directly by dismissing her husband's council and naming her own advisors, several of whom are believed to have been her lovers. Referred to in court records as Madame Royale, Jeanne took her position seriously and spent most of her time in routine administrative and policy business. She attempted to appease the nobles, who grew more openly partisan each day, with financial rewards for their loyalty, giving rise to complaints over her vast expenditures. She also attempted to keep her volatile son from being exposed to the politics of the court, but this failed and led Victor Amadeus to resent his mother's attempt to keep him from an active political role.

The weakness of her position led Jeanne to accept the financial and military support of King Louis XIV of France. At first, she viewed it as a mutually beneficial relationship; Savoy needed the protection of the French against its Italian and Spanish enemies, and the French wanted Savoy to pursue a pro-French foreign policy. Yet Jeanne eventually became convinced that France was more of a threat than an ally. Louis was moving his troops in and around Savoy's borders, causing suspicion that he planned to seize the state. However, Savoy did not have the troops or the money necessary to break away from France entirely. Resentment against the French grew at court and among the Savoy people, resentment also aimed at the regent for her pro-French stance.

Matters came to a crisis point for the regency in 1681–82; the army could not put down the rebellion known as the "Salt War," a peasant uprising in Mondovi in opposition to the salt tax, and open opposition to her rule was spreading. In addition, both her son and the pro-Spain faction at court opposed the marriage Jeanne had planned for Victor to her niece **Isabel Luisa Josefa** (1669–1690), the princess of Portugal. The alliance would have made Victor Amadeus king of Portugal, but he believed that his mother was trying to remove him from Savoy so that she could

rule there permanently. Victor Amadeus had reached the age of majority in 1681, but Jeanne did not make any move to transfer the government to him. These problems were followed by a series of insurrections led by nobles against the regent. Although they failed, they demonstrated a general lack of respect for her authority.

Eventually Jeanne had to give in to the demands of the rebelling peasants. She also had to cancel the marriage contract with Portugal. In 1682, King Louis of France used the regent's period of weakness to force a formal alliance between Savoy and France, ostensibly to protect Savoy. He also began to court the favor of Jeanne's son, who was beginning to assert his own power. The regent tried to resist Louis' offer of his niece, ◄❧ **Anne-Marie d'Bourbon-Orleans** (1669–1728), as a bride for Victor Amadeus, knowing that once he was married he would be unwilling to let his mother rule for him.

However, by 1684 Jeanne was given a choice by the French ambassador: allow Victor Amadeus' marriage to the French princess or face French troops in Savoy. She gave in and allowed the marriage to occur, and in March she finally transferred the duchy's administration over to him. Although some historians have suggested that Jeanne was banished from Savoy after her son began his personal rule, Victor Amadeus made no such dramatic gesture against his mother. On the contrary, Jeanne simply withdrew from court once she was out of power, as many regents did. However, Victor Amadeus may have shown some ill feeling towards his mother when he reduced her pension and cut her household staff. She played no active political role in her son's administration after 1684, and instead spent her remaining years in retirement. She died about age 75, in 1724.

SOURCES:

Claretta, Gaudenzio. *Storia del Regno e dei Tempo di Carlo Emanuele II, duca di Savoia.* Genoa: Luigi Ferrari, 1877.

Symcox, Geoffrey. *Victor Amadeus II: Absolutism in the Savoyard State 1675–1730.* Berkeley, CA: University of California Press, 1983.

SUGGESTED READING:

A Princess of Intrigue. NY: Putnam, 1907.

Williams, H. Noel. *A Rose of Savoy: Marie Adélaïde of Savoy, Duchesse de Bourgogne, Mother of Louis XV.* London: Methuen, 1909.

Laura York,
Riverside, California

Jeanne of Valois (c. 1294–1342)

Countess of Hainault and Holland. Name variations: Jeanne de Valois; Joan Valois; Joan of Valois. Born

Anne-Marie d'Bourbon-Orleans. *See Henrietta Anne for sidebar.*

around 1294; died on March 7, 1342; daughter of Charles III (1270–1325, son of Philip III of France), duke of Anjou and count of Valois, and *Margaret of Anjou (c. 1272–1299); sister of Philip VI, king of France (r. 1328–1350); married William III the Good, count of Hainault and Holland, on May 19, 1305; children: William IV, count of Hainault and Holland (d. 1345); *Margaret of Holland (d. 1356); *Joan of Hainault (c. 1310–?); *Philippa of Hainault (1314–1369).

Jeanne of Valois (c. 1304–?)

*Countess of Beaumont. Name variations: Jeanne de Valois. Born around 1304; daughter of *Catherine de Courtenay (d. 1307) and Charles of Valois also known as Charles I (1270–1325), count of Valois (son of Philip III the Bold, king of France); half-sister of Philip VI of Valois (1293–1350), king of France (r. 1328–1350), and *Jeanne of Valois (c. 1294–1342, mother of *Philippa of Hainault); married Robert III of Artois, count of Beaumont.*

Jeanne of Vaudemont-Lorraine (1458–1480).

See Jeanne of Lorraine.

Jeanne of Vendôme (r. 1366–1374).

See Jeanne de Castile.

Jeans, Isabel (1891–1985)

English actress of stage and screen for more than 60 years. Born in London, England, on September 16, 1891; died in London on September 4, 1985; daughter of Frederick George Jeans and Esther (Matlock) Jeans; married Claude Rains (an actor), in 1913 (divorced 1920); married Gilbert Edward Wakefield (a playwright-screenwriter).

Selected theater: made stage debut as Daffodil in Pinkie and the Fairies (His Majesty's Theater, London, December 1909); had first speaking role as Peggy Bannister in The Greatest Wish (Garrick Theater, London, March 1913); toured the U.S. with Granville Barker's company, playing Titania in A Midsummer Night's Dream, Fanny in Fanny's First Play, and Mlle de la Carandière in The Man Who Married a Dumb Wife (1915–16); appeared as Celia in Volpone for the Phoenix Society (Lyric Hammersmith Theater, London, January 1921), Aspathia in The Maid's Tragedy (Lyric Hammersmith Theater, London, November 1921), the First Constantia in The Chances (Shaftesbury Theater, London, January 1922), Abigail in The Jew of Malta (Daly's Theater, London, November 1922), Cloe in The Faithful Shep-

herdess (Shaftesbury Theater, London, June 1923), and Margery Pinchwife in The Country Wife; appeared as Zélie de Chaumet in The Rat (Prince of Wales' Theater, London, June 1924), Amytis in The Road to Rome (Strand Theater, London, May 1928), Crystal Wetherby in The Man in Possession (Booth Theater, New York, November 1930), Leslie in Counsel's Opinion (Strand Theater, London, April 1931), Mrs. Wislack in On Approval (Strand Theater, London, April 1933), Victoria in Home and Beauty (Playhouse Theater, London, November 1942), Lady Utterwood in Heartbreak House (Cambridge, March 1943), Mrs. Erlynne in Lady Windermere's Fan (Haymarket Theater, London, August 1945), Mme. Arkadina in The Seagull (Lyric Hammersmith Theater, London, October 1949), Mrs. Allonby in A Woman of No Importance (Savoy Theater, London, February 1953), Mrs. Malaprop in The Rivals (Haymarket Theater, London, June 1967), Lady Bracknell in The Importance of Being Earnest (Haymarket Theater, London, February 1968), and Madame Desmortes in Ring Round the Moon (Haymarket Theater, London, October 1968).

Selected films: The Profligate (UK, 1917); Tilly of Bloomsbury (UK, 1921); The Triumph of the Rat (UK, 1926); Downhill (UK, 1927); Easy Virtue (UK, 1928); Sally Bishop (UK, 1932); The Love Affair of the Dictator (Loves of a Dictator, UK, 1935); The Crouching Beast (UK, 1935); Tovarich (US, 1937); Fools for Scandal (US, 1938); Garden of the Moon (US, 1938); Secrets of an Actress (US, 1938); Youth Takes a Fling (US, 1938); Hard to Get (US, 1938); Good Girls Go to Paris (US, 1939); Man About Town (US, 1939); Suspicion (US, 1941); Great Day (UK, 1945); Gigi (US, 1958); A Breath of Scandal (US, 1960); Heavens Above! (UK, 1963); The Magic Christian (UK, 1969).

In a career that spanned 60 years, British actress Isabel Jeans was one of England's most versatile and hard-working stage personalities. Born in London in 1891, she made her stage debut in 1909 as Daffodil in *Pinkie and the Fairies* at His Majesty's Theater. During her early career, she toured the United States with Granville Barker's noted British company. She was also a member the Phoenix Society, a London group founded in 1919 and dedicated to reviving early English plays, many of which, aside from the works of Shakespeare, were seldom produced. For the Phoenix, Jeans appeared as Celia in Ben Jonson's *Volpone* (1921), Cloe in John Fletcher's *The Faithful Shepherdess* (1923), and Margery Pinchwife in William Wycherley's

The Country Wife (1924). She also performed in modern works, including *The Rat* (1924), by Ivor Novello and *Constance Collier, and *The Road to Rome* (1928), by Robert Sherwood. In 1931, she appeared as Leslie in *Counsel's Opinion,* written by her second husband Gilbert Wakefield. (An earlier marriage to actor Claude Rains had ended in divorce in 1920.)

Throughout her career, Jeans, who had a particular gift for high comedy, remained in demand for both classic and modern roles. As the years progressed, she made a graceful transition into character roles, including Mrs. Malaprop in *The Rivals* (1967), and Lady Bracknell in *The Importance of Being Earnest* (1968), one of her favorite roles. Her last stage appearance was as Madame Desmortes in *Ring Round the Moon* (1968).

Jeans had a sporadic film career, starring in 1917 with *The Profligate*. Her American film roles included that of Mrs. Newsham in *Suspicion* (1941) and Aunt Alicia in *Gigi* (1957). Jeans made her television debut in "The Confidential Clerk," in July 1955. The actress died in London in September 1985.

Jeans, Ursula (1906–1973)

British actress. Born Ursula McMinn on May 5, 1906, in Simla, India; died in a nursing home near London, England, on April 21, 1973; daughter of C.H. McMinn and Margaret Ethel (Fisher) McMinn; educated in England; studied for the stage at the Royal Academy of Dramatic Art, London; married Robin Irvine (deceased); married Roger Livesey (an actor).

Selected theater: stage debut as Sophie Binner in Cobra *(Theater Royal, Nottingham, August 1925); London debut as Angela in* The Firebrand *(Wyndham's Theater, February 1926); the Girl of the Town in* Escape *(Ambassadors' Theater, August 1926); Toby in* The Fanatics *(Ambassadors' Theater, March 1927); Dagmar Krumbak in* Samson and Delilah *(Arts Theater, July 1927); Jill Osborne in* Chance Acquaintance *(Strand Theater, September 1927); Monica Grey in* The Second Man *(Playhouse Theater, January 1928); Pearl Pretty in* Mud and Treacle *(Globe Theater, May 1928); Miss Carruthers in* Passing Brompton Road *(Criterion Theater, July 1928); Evelyn Seymour in* High Treason *(Strand Theater, November 1928); Ilona Szabo in* The Play's the Thing *(St. James's Theater, December 1928); Cora Wainwright in* The Five O'clock Girl *(London Hippodrome, March 1929); Elsie Fraser in* The First Mrs. Fraser *(Haymarket Theater, June 1929); Barbara Olwell in* Apron Strings *(Vaudeville Theater, July 1931);*

Flaemmchen in Grand Hotel *(Adelphi Theater, September 1931); Glad in* I Lived With You *(Prince of Wales' Theater, March 1932); Trudy Hanks in* The Multabello Road *(St. Martin's Theater, April 1932); New York debut as Pauline Murray in* Late One Evening *(Plymouth Theater, New York City, January 1933); with Old Vic-Sadler's Wells Company played Viola in* Twelfth Night, *Anya in* The Cherry Orchard, *Anne Boleyn in* Henry VIII, *Mariana in* Measure for Measure, *Cecily Cardew in* The Importance of Being Earnest, *Angelica in* Love for Love, *and Miranda in* The Tempest *(1938); Sarah Traille in* Lovers' Leap *(Vaudeville Theater, October 1934); The Sphinx in* The Machine of the Gods *(Grafton Theater, March 1935); Olive Allingham in* The Benefit of the Doubt *(Arts Theater, June 1935); Nina Popinot in* Vintage Wine *(Victoria Palace, August 1935); Penelope Marsh in* Short Story *(Queen's Theater, November 1935); Alithea in* The Country Wife *(Old Vic, October 1936); Karen in* The Children's Hour *(Gate Theater, November 1936); Sally Grosvenor in* They Came by Night *(Globe Theater, July 1937); Shena March in* People of Our Class *(New Theater, May 1938); with Old Vic played Kate Hardcastle in* She Stoops to Conquer, *Petra in* The Enemy of the People, *and Katherine in* The Taming of the Shrew *(1939); Joanna in* Dear Brutus *(Globe Theater, January 1941); toured as Elvira in* Blithe Spirit *(1942); Helen in* Ever Since Paradise *(New Theater, June 1947); Mary Bernard in* Man of the World *(Lyric, Hammersmith, February 1950); with Old Vic appeared as Olivia in* Twelfth Night, *Dame Overdo in* Bartholomew Fair, *Lady Cicely Waynflete in* Captain Brassbound's Conversion, *and Mistress Ford in* The Merry Wives of Windsor *(1950); Jean Moreland in* Third Person *(Arts Theater, October 1951); Lady Pounce-Pellott in* The Blaikie Charivari *(Citizen's Theater, Glasgow, October 1952); Margaret Bell in* The Teddy Bear *(St. Martin's Theater, April 1953); Stella Hampden in* Escapade *(48th St. Theater, New York, November 1953); Barbara Leigh in* Uncertain Joy *(Court Theater, March 1955); Mrs. Tarleton in* Misalliance *(Lyric, Hammersmith, February 1956); with husband, toured Australia and New Zealand in* The Reluctant Debutante, *and* The Great Sebastians *(1956–58); Lady Touchwood in* The Double-Dealer *(Old Vic, September 1959); Juliette Dulac in* Head of the Family *(Hampstead Theater Club, January 1962); Irette in* The Twelfth Hour *(Oxford Playhouse, May 1964); Mrs. Pocock in* The Elephant's Foot *(Nottingham Playhouse, April 1965); Lady Markby in* An Ideal Husband *(Strand Theater, December 1965); toured South Africa in* Oh, Clarence *(July 1970).*

Selected films: The Gypsy Cavalier *(1922);* The Virgin Queen *(1923);* S.O.S. *(1928);* The Love Habit *(1931);* The Crooked Lady *(1932);* Cavalcade *(1933);* Friday the 13th *(1933);* Dark Journey *(1937);* Storm in a Teacup *(1937);* The Life and Death of Colonel Blimp *(1943);* Mr. Emmanuel *(1944);* Gaiety George *(Show-time, 1946);* The Woman in the Hall *(1947);* The Weaker Sex *(1948);* The Dam Busters *(1955);* North West Frontier *(Flame Over India, 1959);* The Green Helmet *(1961);* The Battle of the Villa Fiorita *(1965).*

Born Ursula McMinn in Simla, India, in 1906, to British parents, C.H. McMinn and **Margaret Fisher McMinn**, actress Ursula Jeans was educated in London and studied acting at the Royal Academy of Dramatic Art. She made her first stage appearance in 1925 and debuted in London in 1926, playing Angela in *The Firebrand.* Although primarily a stage actress, Jeans also made occasional films beginning in 1922 with *The Gypsy Cavalier.* She made only two appearances in New York: the first in 1933 at the Plymouth Theater in *Late One Evening*; the second in 1953 at the 48th Street Theater in *Escapade.* After the death of her first husband, Jeans married actor Roger Livesey, with whom she toured Australia and New Zealand from 1956 to 1958, co-starring in *The Reluctant Debutante* and *The Great Sebastians.* Ursula Jeans died in a nursing home in London, age 66, in 1973.

Barbara Morgan,
Melrose, Massachusetts

Jebb, Eglantyne (1876–1928)

English philanthropist who founded the Save the Children Fund. Born Eglantyne Jebb in Ellesmere, Shropshire, England, in 1876; died in Geneva, Switzerland, in 1928; sister of Dorothy Buxton; graduated from Lady Margaret Hall, Oxford, in 1898; never married; no children.

Born into a prosperous Shropshire landowning family in 1876, Eglantyne Jebb was an athletic dreamer as a child. She loved riding, swimming, boating, and the books in her father's large library. She also hated the effects of the class system. "Respect accorded to [people] should not depend upon the way in which they spend their working hours," she would later say. "In a social sense there should be only one class—the great class of humanity."

Jebb took advantage of the educational opportunities then afforded to women in Victorian England. In 1895, she entered Lady Margaret Hall in Oxford to study history, graduating in 1898; she then trained at Stockwell in London for a career as an elementary school teacher. Her first assignment was at a school in Marlborough but, within 18 months, ill health forced Jebb to return to her mother's house in Cambridge. During this period, she wrote poetry, traveled, and began working for local charities. In 1906, she produced a study, "Cambridge: A Study in Social Questions," showing a firm grasp of how philanthropies worked.

In 1913, at the request of the Macedonian Relief Fund in London, Jebb went to Macedonia to organize aid for the millions of children left destitute following the Balkan wars. In 1914, at the outbreak of World War I, she was working for the Agricultural Organization Society. In 1915, her sister **Dorothy Buxton**, concerned with the lack of reportage on the realities of life in wartime Europe, began publishing a newsletter which contained translated extracts from European newspapers, including those of the enemy nations—Austria and Germany. Jebb joined her endeavor in 1917.

The people of Europe were starving and, though the end of the war was near, the Allies continued their blockade to force the defeated powers to quickly agree to a peace treaty. Eglantyne and Dorothy were aware of the devastation; they knew that there was such a shortage of linen that newborn babies had to be wrapped in newspapers; that families were living on cabbage and turnips; and that six-year-olds were so malnourished they looked like two-year-olds.

Those who felt the blockade should be lifted founded the Fight the Famine Council, and Jebb and Buxton took part. It was an unpopular position in a country still at war. While handing out a leaflet with a picture of a starving Austrian baby under the heading "Our Blockade Has Caused This," Jebb was arrested and fined for publishing it without reference to the censor.

Soon aware that the Council was too focused on campaigning for direct action, Jebb set up a separate fund, Save the Children, for immediate help of the thousands in distress. The fund was earmarked for children, "beyond any consideration of race, nationality, or creed." At a public meeting at Royal Albert Hall on May 19, 1919, Jebb spoke to a large crowd that had gathered. "The public arrived supplied with rotten apples destined to be thrown at the head of 'the traitors who wanted to raise money for enemy children,'" reported an associate who viewed the scene. "But they did not insult Eglantyne Jebb; they were forced to listen to her. She began hesitantly, then, gaining by the fervor of her mission, her voice became louder. Did she convince you? It was not by the arguments, but by the passionate conviction for the cause that she defended."

Jebb worked as her own publicist and fund raiser, often pushing herself to the point of exhaustion. At her insistence, the Fund hired a professional publicist, and page-length advertisements were placed in national newspapers. Charities had never advertised on such a massive scale, and Jebb was chastised by outsiders for wasting the charity's money. "We have to devise a means," she countered, "of making known the facts in such a way as to touch the imagination of the world." The fund expanded quickly, allowing her to feed and provide for children in Greece, Bulgaria, Romania, Armenia, and Poland. In 1921, when the world learned of extensive famine in Russia, Save the Children organized an operation to feed up to 650,000.

During the last years of her life, Eglantyne Jebb was based in Geneva. In 1924, at the Declaration of Geneva, her Children's Charter was adopted by the United Nations, the first Declaration of the Rights of the Child. The document, of international importance, was also central to the work of her fund. The Fund's journal, *The World's Children*, became a record of children's welfare in many countries, and summer schools in Geneva were held for staff and supporters. Eglantyne Jebb wanted to organize a conference on the needs of the children of Africa; she wanted to provide an alternative to child labor in China and began to learn Chinese. But she died in 1928, age 52.

Martha Jefferson

SUGGESTED READING:

Wilson, F.M. *Eglantyne Jebb: Rebel Daughter of a Country House,* 1967.

Jecholiah

Biblical woman. Pronunciation: Jek-uh-LIGH-uh. Married King Amaziah; children: King Azariah (or Uzziah).

Jedidah

Biblical woman. Pronunciation: juh-DIGH-duh. Married Amon, king of Judah; children: Josiah, who succeeded his father to the throne at the age of eight.

Jefferson, Martha (1748–1782)

Wife of Thomas Jefferson who died before he was president of the United States. Name variations: Martha Skelton. Born Martha Wayles in October 1748 (the specific day is in dispute) in Charles City County, Virginia; died on September 6, 1782, in Monticello, Virginia; daughter of John Wayles (a planter and lawyer) and Martha (Eppes) Wayles; half-sister of Sally Hemings (1773–1835); married Bathurst Skelton, on November 20, 1766, in Williamsburg, Virginia (died 1768); married Thomas Jefferson (1743–1826, third president of the United States), on January 1, 1772, in Williamsburg, Virginia; children: (first marriage) one son who died in infancy; (second marriage) five daughters and one son—only two daughters, Martha Jefferson Randolph (1775–1836) and Maria Jefferson Eppes (1778–1804), lived to adulthood; both served as White House hostesses during Jefferson's administration, 1801–09.

When Thomas Jefferson became president in 1801, his beloved wife Martha had been dead for 19 years. Although he never recorded their life together, and apparently destroyed her letters, historians agree that she was a great love of his life and had a lasting influence on him.

Martha Wayles was born in October 1748 to a prosperous Virginia lawyer and planter, John Wayles, and the first of his three wives, **Martha Eppes Wayles**. Her only sibling was a half-sister, *Sally Hemings, daughter of John Wayles and his slave **Betty Hemings**. As was the custom of the day, Martha was tutored at home, but at an early age became an avid reader and a talented musician, singing and playing both the pianoforte and the harpsichord. At age 18, she married Bathurst Skelton, a planter, who died less than two years later, leaving her with an infant son.

It may have been Thomas Jefferson's love of books or his facility on the violin that endeared him to Martha, who as a wealthy and beautiful young widow had her choice of suitors. Their courtship was filled with music and plans for the magnificent home Jefferson was building at Monticello. The two were married New Year's Day 1772, after a wedding postponement to grieve the death of Martha's young son. During their honeymoon trip to Monticello, a fierce snowstorm forced them to abandon their carriage and finish the last leg of the journey up a treacherous mountainside on horseback. Arriving late and half frozen at their barely habitable new home, the only welcome was a bottle of wine found hidden on a shelf behind some books.

During the next ten years, Martha gave birth to six children, four of whom died in infancy. Two daughters, ***Martha Jefferson Randolph** and ❧➤ **Maria Jefferson Eppes,** lived to adulthood. Although Jefferson referred to his marriage as "unchequered happiness," his wife's delicate health and mental anguish over the deaths of her children was a factor in his career. Refusing a foreign appointment, he served in the Virginia House of Delegates and later as governor.

Shortly after New Year's Day 1781, a British invasion forced Martha and her newborn daughter, Lucy Elizabeth, to flee their residence in the Governor's House in Richmond. As a result of the journey, the baby later died. Jefferson resigned the governorship and promised his inconsolable wife he would not seek public office again. The grieving Martha became pregnant once more and gave birth to her last daughter in May of 1792. She never recovered her health and Jefferson remained at her bedside until her death on September 6, at the age of 34. Martha Jefferson was laid to rest at Monticello with four of her children.

Thomas Jefferson found his way back into politics but never remarried. For years, many believed that Martha's half-sister Sally Hemings became his mistress and gave birth to his son. In 1999, DNA tests provided conclusive evidence that Hemings' progeny had a blood link to Jefferson. Martha and Thomas' daughters, Martha and Maria, served alternately as White House hostesses during the eight years of Jefferson's presidency. Occasionally, ***Dolley Madison,** wife of the then secretary of state, filled in for the sisters. Martha Jefferson Randolph also tended to her father's household during his retirement at Monticello. Thomas Jefferson died there in 1826.

SOURCES:

Healy, Diana Dixon. *America's First Ladies: Private Lives of the Presidential Wives.* NY: Atheneum, 1988.

Klapthor, Margaret Brown. *The First Ladies.* Washington, DC: The White House Historical Association, 1979.

Melick, Arden David. *Wives of the Presidents.* Maplewood, NJ: Hammond, 1977.

Paletta, LuAnn. *The World Almanac of First Ladies.* NY: World Almanac, 1990.

SUGGESTED READING:

McLaughlin, Jack. *Jefferson and Monticello: The Biography of a Builder.* NY: Henry Holt, 1988.

Jeffery, Dorothy (1685–1777).

See Pentreath, Dolly.

Jehosheba (fl. 9th c).

See Athaliah for sidebar.

❧➤ **Eppes, Maria Jefferson** (1778–1804)

White House hostess during her father's administration. Name variations: known as Polly in her youth; Mary Jefferson Eppes. Born Mary Jefferson in 1778; died in 1804; daughter of *Martha Jefferson *(1748–1782) and Thomas Jefferson (1743–1826, third president of the U.S.); married her cousin John Wales Eppes; children: several, including Frances Eppes and* **Maria Eppes** *(who died in childbirth at age 25).*

Jehudijah

Biblical woman. Pronunciation: jee-huh-DIGH-juh. One of the two wives of Mered; children: Jered, Heber, and Jekuthiel.

Jekyll, Gertrude (1843–1932)

Distinguished English garden designer and expert on plants who has had a profound and continuing influence on English and American horticulture. Name variations: (nickname) Aunt Bumps. Pronunciation: JEE-kl. Born on November 29, 1843, in London; died at her home at Munstead Wood, Surrey, on December 8, 1932; daughter of Edward Joseph Hill Jekyll (a retired military officer) and Julia (Hammersley) Jekyll (a member of a prominent banking family); educated at home and at Kensington School of Art, 1861–63; never married; no children.

Moved to Bramley, Surrey (1848); traveled in Greece, Italy, and Algeria (1863–74); family settled at Wargrave Hill, Berkshire (1868); met William Robinson (1875); family returned to West Surrey (1876); published first article in Robinson's magazine, The Garden *(1881); met architect Edwin Lutyens (1889); forced to give up painting and other artistic activities because of weak eyesight (1891); moved into her permanent home of Munstead Wood and honored by Royal Horticultural Society (1897); became joint editor of* The Garden *(1900); designed garden in Provence, her first on foreign soil (1902); awarded Veitch Memorial Gold Medal (1922); had issue of* Botanical Magazine *dedicated to her and received George Robert White Medal of Honor from the Massachusetts Horticultural Society (1929).*

Major works: Wood and Garden *(1899);* Home and Garden *(1900);* Wall and Water Gardens *(1901);* Old West Surrey *(1904);* Color in the Flower Garden *(1908);* Gardens for Small Country Houses *(1912);* Old English Household Life *(1925).*

Gertrude Jekyll was a leading horticulturist from the last decades of the 19th century through the first three decades of the 20th century. Born to an affluent and well-connected English family, she pursued a number of artistic interests until, nearly 50 years old, she was encouraged by failing eyesight to curtail such activities as painting. At that point, she joined the rising young architect Edwin Lutyens, designing gardens to enhance the country houses he was planning. Together, they produced 100 such country houses with accompanying gardens; working on her own, Jekyll designed an additional 300 gardens, many of them located in the United States.

Gardening was not a craft or even a science to her—it was an art.

—Harold Faulkner

At the same time, Jekyll's writings and activities as a consultant made her the foremost authority on gardening of her time. She presented a vast and adoring public, in both Britain and the U.S., with 15 books and 2,000 articles. In recent years, the established picture of Jekyll as a potentially great artist thwarted by poor eyesight as well as a Victorian figure with a carefully controlled personality has been challenged by biographer **Sally Festing**. For her, Jekyll was "far more complicated, abrasive, autocratic, impatient, fun-loving and lovable than she is made out to be."

Gertrude Jekyll took the gardening practices of her country in a new direction. In contrast to the formal style of garden design that had come to prominence in the mid-19th century—with ribbon borders, raised flower beds, and great pyramids of flowers—an alternate approach was emerging under the aegis of William Robinson, a proponent of a free and natural style of gardening. Jekyll was a crucial figure in combining and harmonizing the two styles; her designs, for example, often called for a formal garden near the house, with a more natural one emerging as the woods encroached.

Jekyll's most eloquent view of her work came in her introduction to *Wood and Garden*: "The best purpose of a garden is to give delight and to give refreshment of mind, to soothe, to refine, and to lift up the heart in a spirit of praise and thankfulness." In that same spirit, she expressed her respect for modest gardens, notably the cottage gardens to be found in the English countryside. "The size of a garden has very little to do with its merit," she wrote, since such things depended upon the accident of the owner's wealth. "It is the size of his heart and brain and goodwill," according to Jekyll, "that will make his garden either delightful or dull." The small gardens planted by the owners of roadside cottages she saw as wonderful sources of horticultural lore. There, one found flowers that had been rejected from the more formal landscape gardens of the first half of the 19th century. Thus, the accidental pairing of plants, or the casual innovation practiced by a country garden's owner, brought her a wealth of practical experience.

The future horticulturist was born in London on November 29, 1843, one of six children and the second daughter of Edward Joseph Jekyll and **Julia Hammersley Jekyll**. Her father was an independently wealthy man who was able to serve, in his early years, as an officer in the fashionable Grenadier Guards. He married Julia Hammersley, the daughter of a banker, and the two of them spent much of their life living in the countryside. As the daughter of a privileged family, Jekyll was unusually free to pursue her interests. Noted Festing: "Gertrude was the product of a time when most of the best things in life, wealth, property and social position, belonged to those [like her] who were born to them." By her own recollection, Jekyll was interested in flowers at the age of four or so, clashing with her nurse when the older woman refused to allow Gertrude to take common dandelions home from the park.

In 1848, she found herself in West Surrey, the part of England in which she would do her most distinguished work as a gardener, when her family moved to a new home near the town of Guildford. As she later recalled, around the age of seven she first stumbled upon a copse of primroses, a flower that was later to stand at the center of her gardening. It was an experience that she remembered leaving a profound impression upon her mind. Similarly she recalled spending hours in the family home's large garden. When she was nine, the family governess provided her with a book on wildflowers, thus beginning Gertrude's process of self-education in the matter of plants.

Steeped in a family atmosphere that revered art and music—her mother was an intrepid artist as well as a serious pianist who had studied with Felix Mendelssohn, a family friend—Gertrude Jekyll at the age of 17 took the slightly daring step of enrolling at the Kensington School of Art. For a young girl of her social background, a serious pursuit of art was still considered eccentric. She divided her time between her art studies in London and her country home in Surrey. The acute sense of color that characterized her work as a garden designer may well have come from her academic study of art.

Her world also expanded as she undertook a series of trips in the company of married friends to other parts of Europe and to the eastern Mediterranean. In 1863–64, for example, her travels took her to Greece, Rhodes, and Asia Minor. She visited Paris in 1866, made an extended trip to Italy in 1868, and, in 1873–74, accompanied a friend to Algeria. Throughout her life, she traveled abroad a dozen times, mainly in Europe.

Jekyll encountered eligible men, but without romantic results. A large young woman with a receding chin who already wore spectacles for her nearsightedness, she struck her father as "a queer fish," and a taste for solitude was a large part of her personal makeup. "No one called her pretty," writes Festing, "and there are indications that she never entirely accepted her physical self." Thus, the young woman passed through the years in which her contemporaries married without attaching herself to a spouse. Instead, her energies went into her painting. Her artistic interests and her circle of friends brought her into contact with John Ruskin in the mid-1860s. Ruskin, the reigning art critic and cultural guide of the time, praised her painting, and between 1865 and 1870 she put ten of her watercolors on exhibit. Much of her life centered around the family of Jacques Blumenthal, composer and pianist to Queen *Victoria. Through him, she met the painter Hercules Brabazon and Princess *Louise (1848–1939), duchess of Argyle, the daughter of Victoria.

While her interests centered on painting, Gertrude Jekyll helped acquaintances with their interior decorating and plunged into a range of other activities such as gardening, wood-inlaying, and embroidering. In the mid-1880s, she took up photography. Such activities reflected her acquaintance with William Morris, who promoted the production of nobly made handcrafts to counteract the shabby goods poured out in profusion by the industrial revolution.

Gertrude
Jekyll

According to Festing, "Gertrude Jekyll did not, as legend suggests, somewhere in mid-life exchange her paintbrush for a spade." Instead, in her late 20s, "she was [already] perusing cottage gardens, returning home laden with seeds and cuttings." A new friendship with William Robinson, editor of *The Garden*, began in 1875 and also paved the way for what was to become the center of her life as she now began to contribute articles to his magazine.

The Jekyll family had lived in Berkshire from 1868 to 1876, returning to West Surrey after the death of Gertrude's father when the house in Berkshire went to her eldest brother. In her new family home at Munstead Heath in West Surrey, Gertrude followed the precepts of William Morris and became increasingly interested in crafts, such as designing and making ornamental dishes, with her painting taking less and less of her time. She also spent many of her hours exploring the nearby countryside in her small carriage. Jekyll's travels in the Surrey countryside, with its profusion of wild vegetation, came to play a large role in the development of her ideas about gardening. Like her mentor Robinson, she grew convinced that the best gardens did not artificially alter nature.

The intensity of Jekyll's interest in gardening grew in the 1880s. She submitted 19 articles to Robinson's *The Garden* in 1881 alone, and her growing reputation as a gardener led to a role as judge at the annual Horticultural Society show in London's Regent Park. Her own garden, which she often described in her articles, became a magnet for visiting horticultural experts, and she was in increasing demand as a consultant for those planning gardens. In 1883, she contributed an important chapter on color to Robinson's pioneering book *The English Flower Garden*.

At the close of the 1880s and the start of the following decade, as Jekyll approached the age of 50, this active, artistically minded woman found her life changed by two new elements. First came the beginning of a warm friendship with the young architect Edwin Lutyens; she met him initially in Surrey in 1889 at the home of a neighbor and fellow gardener. In 1891, after becoming increasingly uncomfortable with her weak eyesight, she consulted a noted eye specialist in Germany. He gave her the crushing news that her eyesight would never improve; in order to prevent her sight from weakening further, she must, he insisted, abandon such favorite activities as painting and embroidery. In Festing's view, Jekyll was "a mediocre painter, a gifted craftswoman and a unique garden designer,"

and her passion for excellence made it relatively easy for her to concentrate her energies in the gardening work in which her talents had full play. Moreover, in the preceding decade, she had already moved away from other activities to concentrate on gardening.

Biographer **Betty Massingham** interpreted these events differently and more dramatically. She saw Jekyll's life forced to take an abrupt new turn; and she stressed how Jekyll was crushed by the news the eye specialist gave her. Nonetheless, in this view, Jekyll was saved by her ability to turn to the new activity of gardening: "She had this other string to her bow. . . . [S]he had not neglected the gardening side of her life, which was now to come to her aid in a practical manner." Jekyll was aided by her family's affluence and the absence of a need to earn a living. As well, Massingham points to a distaste for self-pity and a strong religious belief that also aided a shaken Gertrude Jekyll.

Lutyens' friendship with Jekyll took the form of frequent visits to Surrey in which the young man and the elderly woman explored Surrey and nearby Sussex to study the area's picturesque architecture. She was able to help the novice architect by recommending him to family friends and clients for whom she was doing garden designs. For example, she bolstered his career by introducing him to Princess Louise, now the wife of the Marquess of Lorne. She also became his firm supporter as he reached up the social scale in a successful effort to marry Lady **Emily Lytton**, daughter of the former viceroy of India and sister of Lady *Constance Lytton.

In her initial work with Lutyens, Jekyll merely offered the young architect some advice about the garden to accompany a country house he was designing at a location near the town of Farnham. Their collaboration became an intense one in the mid-1890s: Gertrude's mother had died in 1895, Gertrude's brother took over the family home of Munstead Heath, and she pushed forward to plan with Lutyens her own house nearby, named Munstead Wood. They had already worked together in planning eight gardens and two country cottages.

In 1897, the year she moved into Munstead Wood, Jekyll received a signal honor. The Royal Horticultural Society chose her as one of 60 eminent gardeners to be awarded a Victoria Medal of Honor on the occasion of the monarch's Diamond Jubilee. In this commemoration of the queen's 60 years on the British throne, Jekyll was one of only two women to receive the distinction.

"Laburnum Arch," photo and garden design by Gertrude Jekyll.

A longtime contributor to gardening journals, Gertrude Jekyll soon heightened her reputation by publishing two important books, *Wood and Garden* (1899) and *Home and Garden* (1900). As Festing notes, passages in *Wood and Garden* demonstrate in vivid fashion Jekyll's privilege-laden view of the English class system and the workers who aided her. The common working gardener lacked the chances to develop his mind, Jekyll insisted; thus he could bring only a limited imagination to his task. Such servants could only do as they were told; they could, she wrote, "set up the canvas and grind the colours and even set the palette, but the master alone can paint the pictures."

In the following years, Jekyll began to produce works prodigiously, and, by 1908, she had completed ten books. In 1900, she had also taken on the task of joint editor of *The Garden*, although her poor eyesight compelled her to serve in this post for only two years. Asked for advice on gardens from all over the world—one request came from South Africa concerning the garden of Cecil Rhodes—Jekyll continued her collaboration with Lutyens until an architectural cliché of the time became "a Lutyens house with a Jekyll garden." She expressed the spirit of their collaboration in her book *Wall and Water Gardens*: in order to work together well, the architect and the landscape designer with "much knowledge on both sides" must understand each other's work to some extent, but "each must regard with feelings of kindly reverence the unknown domains of the other's higher knowledge."

Jekyll wrote notably about flower arrangement. As Massingham put it, "She suggests certain flowers being used together as a painter would suggest colours to be used from his paintbox." Moreover, her travels around the countryside had made her into a storehouse of information about local crafts, and she had gathered a large collection of utensils from Surrey homes. She drew together her encyclopedic knowledge of Surrey's village society—its speech, manners, songs, and artifacts—in her book *Old West Surrey, Some Notes and Memories*. Consistent with her general views about class relations, Jekyll presented here an idealized view of the country village with its picturesque population satisfied to be the workers at the base of a structured society. Three years later, she donated much of her collection of village artifacts to the newly opened museum of the Surrey Archaeological Society.

What some biographers consider her greatest achievement in the development of English gardening, her book *Color Scheme in the Flower Garden*, appeared in 1908. Her guiding principle was simple: "Planting ground is painting a landscape with living things." Thus, she claimed, the gardener had an obligation to the garden "to use the plants that they shall form beautiful pictures." To this end, she recommended grouping together flowers that bloom at the same time. There should be no effort to cover an entire garden with blooming plants, since "groups of flower-beauty are all the more enjoyable . . . [with] stretches of intervening greenery." By now a skilled and experienced photographer, she illus-

trated the text with 85 of her own pictures. In 1907, one of her books was translated into German, and, but for the outbreak of war in 1914, several of her works would have appeared in French from a Belgian press.

Jekyll's burst of activity and her on-going collaboration with Lutyens took place against the background of her increasing age and fading energies. In the years before 1914 and the outbreak of World War I, she no longer tried to travel abroad, and even extended trips within England were tiring for her. She presented her schemes in the form of extensive paper drawings accompanied by detailed written instructions for the gardeners on the scene.

Despite her age, Gertrude Jekyll responded to the war by plunging into a number of new activities. She collected plants needed for the war effort, turned many of her flower beds into vegetable gardens to produce food for a nearby military hospital, and opened her home to visiting soldiers. This noted authority on flowers wrote articles in *The Gardener* advising British women on how to substitute parsnips and turnips for potatoes to help the country through its wartime food shortage. She also played an advisory role in the planning of the great collection of postwar British military cemeteries. Lutyens, whose reputation had already led to the honor of designing the new British capital of India at Delhi, undertook the task of the cemetery designs. His old friend and collaborator Gertrude Jekyll reviewed and approved his concepts.

Even in the postwar period, when she was in her 80s and Lutyens had now reached the pinnacle of the architectural profession, Jekyll continued their longstanding collaboration. And her activity remained prodigious. Her health was so fragile that her doctor required her to spend one day per week in bed, but she wrote numerous articles for various general-interest and gardening publications, while sending her old books out in new and revised editions. In 1923 alone, she worked on 13 projects including a memorial garden at Winchester College. The previous year, she had been honored with the Veitch Memorial Medal of the Royal Horticultural Society. She was now recognized in the United States as well as in Europe, and she received commissions—along with lavish praise in American gardening publications—from wealthy gardening connoisseurs across the Atlantic. Her books were published in the United States from 1900 onward, and, in 1929, she added the George Robert White Medal of Honor from the Massachusetts Horticultural Society to her other honors.

In her last years, Jekyll was almost completely blind and largely unable to move about. She visited her garden by using a wheelchair. Although her work continued—almost to the day of her death, Jekyll wrote articles and revised her now-classic books on gardening—she was shaken by the death of her closest relative, her beloved brother Herbert, in late September 1932. On December 8, 1932, just after her 89th birthday, she too succumbed at Munstead Wood, her longtime home in Surrey.

Judith B. Tankard, an American admirer, summed up Jekyll's accomplishment in an article written on the 150th anniversary of the gardener's birth. "Her sophisticated yet practical advice for artistically grouping textural plans with coordinated color sequences has challenged gardeners for years." Jekyll "reveled in the use of green as a garden color . . . planting in sweeps of harmonious colors rather than stiff rows of overly bright curiosities."

SOURCES:

Brown, Jane. *Gardens of a Golden Afternoon: The Story of a Partnership: Edwin Lutyens and Gertrude Jekyll*. NY: Van Nostrand Reinhold, 1982.

Festing, Sally. *Gertrude Jekyll*. London: Viking, 1991.

Massingham, Betty. *Miss Jekyll: Portrait of a Great Gardener*. London: Country Life, 1966.

Tankard, Judith B. "Celebrating Gertrude Jekyll," in *Horticulture: The Magazine of American Gardening*. November 29, 1993, p. 11.

SUGGESTED READING:

Bisgrove, Richard. *The Gardens of Gertrude Jekyll*. Boston, MA: Little, Brown, 1992.

Hussey, Christopher. *The Life of Sir Edwin Lutyens*. Woodbridge, Suffolk, England: Antique Collectors' Club, 1984.

Hyams, Edward. *A History of Gardens and Gardening*. NY: Praeger, 1971.

Tooley, Michael, ed. *Gertrude Jekyll: Artist Gardener Craftswoman: A Collection of Essays to Mark the 50th Anniversary of Her Death*. Witton-Le-Wear, England: Michaelmas Books, 1984.

Weideger, Paula. "A Budding Genius: The Growing Legend of Landscape Artist Gertrude Jekyll," in *Ms*. March 1989, pp. 48–49.

Neil M. Heyman,
Professor of History, San Diego State University, San Diego, California

Jellett, Mainie (1897–1944)

Irish artist. Born in Dublin, Ireland, on April 29, 1897; died of pancreatic cancer at St. Vincent's Hospital, Dublin, on February 16, 1944; eldest of four daughters of William Morgan Jellett and Janet (Stokes) Jellett; educated at home and subsequently studied art at Dublin Metropolitan School of Art, Westminster School of Art, and with André Lhote and Albert Gleizes in France.

Mainie Jellett was born in Dublin in 1897, the eldest of four daughters of William Morgan Jellett and **Janet Stokes Jellett**. She had her first painting lessons when she was 11 and attended classes given by *Elizabeth Yeats, daughter of the artist J.B. Yeats and sister of the poet W.B. Yeats. Mainie also took classes with **Sarah Cecilia Harrison** and **May Manning** and visited France in 1911 and 1913. She studied for three years under William Orpen at the Dublin Metropolitan Art School and in January 1917 went to London to study with Walter Sickert at the Westminster Art School. In her essay "An Approach to Painting," she claimed that Sickert's influence, and especially his compositional techniques and use of line and realism, was the first of the three revolutions in her work, style and ideas.

It was while she was working with Sickert that she met *Evie Hone who became a lifelong friend and colleague. Jellett and Hone visited Spain in 1920, and later that year they went to Paris to study with André Lhote and Albert Gleizes, the other two "revolutions" in Jellett's work. With Lhote, "I learned how to use natural forms as a starting point towards the pure creation of form for its own sake." Gleizes sent her right back to the beginning and gave her the "severest type of exercises in pure form and colour. . . . I now felt I had come to essentials and though the type of work I had embarked upon would mean years of misunderstanding and walls of prejudice to break through, yet I felt I was on the right track."

Jellett soon experienced this misunderstanding and prejudice when, on her return to Dublin, she exhibited some of her Cubist paintings in 1923 and 1924. Despite the hostile reaction from the more conservative sections of the Irish art world, she continued to exhibit regularly in Dublin and also in London and Paris. She was a founder member of the Abstraction-Création group, which led the European abstract movement in the 1930s. She could have made her career in London or Paris but preferred to stay in Ireland. Thanks to the force of her personality and through her incisive teaching, lectures and broadcasts, Jellett gradually spread the gospel of modernism and won acceptance for her work and the work of other modern artists. In 1930, she exhibited at the Royal Hibernian Academy, which was the bastion of conservatism. She also designed for the stage, particularly at the Edwards-MacLiammóir Gate Theater in Dublin. Major recognition for her work came in 1938–39 when the Irish government commissioned Jellett to decorate the Irish Pavilions at

Mainie
Jellett

the Glasgow Exhibition and at the New York World Fair.

At the outbreak of the Second World War, a number of foreign artists arrived in Ireland, including members of the London-based White Stag Group. Jellett helped many of these artists and in 1940 gave a series of lectures to members of the White Stag. Out of this came the idea for the 1943 Irish Exhibition of Living Art which became an annual event and would be a dominant influence in Irish art up to the 1970s. In

1942, Jellett had written despairingly about that year's Royal Hibernian Academy exhibition: "Every year I go . . . in a spirit of hopefulness expecting there may be some new young head pushing itself up through the miasma of vulgarity and self-satisfaction, which is the general impression I unfortunately register every year." Jellett was appointed the first chair of Living Art but missed the exhibition because of her deteriorating health. She died in February 1944. *Elizabeth Bowen, who had known Jellett since they were children growing up in Dublin, wrote a moving tribute to her in *The Bell* (December 1944). "The greatness of Mainie Jellett was to be felt in many ways: but not least in her simplicity. She was not only easy but, which is rarer, easing to be with. She not only calmed one, but re-lit lamps which seemed to be going out. I felt very much her junior, in vision, in virtue, in experience of what is truly life."

In "An Approach to Painting" which was published the year before her death, Jellett summed up her views on the role of the artist in society. "The idea of an artist being a special person, an exotic flower set apart from other people is one of the errors resulting from the industrial revolution, and the fact of artists being pushed out of their lawful position in the life and society of the present day. . . . Their present enforced isolation from the majority is a very serious situation and I believe it is one of the many causes which has resulted in the present chaos we live in. The art of a nation is one of the ultimate facts by which its spiritual health is judged and appraised by posterity."

SOURCES:
Arnold, Bruce. *Mainie Jellett and the Modern Movement in Ireland*. New Haven, CT: Yale University Press, 1991.
Frost, Stella. *A Tribute to Evie Hone and Mainie Jellett*. Dublin: Browne and Nolan, 1957.
Snoddy, Theo. *Dictionary of Irish Artists: 20th Century*. Dublin: Wolfhound Press, 1996.
Walker, Dorothy. *Modern Art in Ireland*. Dublin: Lilliput Press, 1997.

Deirdre McMahon,
lecturer in history at Mary Immaculate College,
University of Limerick

Jellicoe, Anne (1823–1880)

Irish educationalist who improved the schooling and employment opportunities available to middle-class women. Born Anne Mullin in Mountmellick, County Laois, in 1823; died in Birmingham on October 18, 1880; daughter of William Mullin (a schoolmaster); mother's name unknown; probably educated at home; married John Jellicoe, in 1846 (died 1862); no children.

When Anne Jellicoe died suddenly in 1880, the movement to improve educational provision for middle-class Irish girls had already made a number of notable gains. Two years earlier, state-run examinations had been opened to girls as well as to boys, while at about the same time, the government established the Royal University of Ireland, whose degrees and scholarships were open to both men and women. Women's ability to take advantage of these opportunities, however, depended on the existence of secondary schools which would prepare girls for competitive examinations and for university entrance. While few contemporary girls' schools met these requirements, a few pioneering institutions had been established during the previous decade, of which one of the most celebrated and successful was Alexandra College in Dublin.

Founded in 1866, in order "to afford an education more sound and solid . . . and better tested, than is at present easily to be obtained by women of the middle and upper classes in this country," Alexandra College was the brainchild of Anne Jellicoe. As the daughter of a Quaker schoolmaster, the young Anne Mullin had grown up with a firm belief in the value of education for every individual, regardless of sex or social standing, and as a young woman was involved in a scheme to establish an embroidery industry for women in her native Mountmellick. In 1846, she married John Jellicoe, a flour miller, and two years later moved with him to Clara, County Offaly. Noting the extent of female unemployment in the town, she made use of her previous experience to set up embroidery and lace crochet schools, and when in 1858 the Jellicoes moved to Dublin she continued her interest in education by involving herself in the running of infant schools for poor children.

Philanthropic efforts of this kind were not uncommon among middle-class women of the time, but Jellicoe went further than most in her conviction that conditions could be improved by fundamental social change. In 1861, in a paper "On the conditions and prospects of young women employed in the manufactories in Dublin," she argued for the introduction of protective legislation and for the employment of female overseers in factories where women were employed. Also in 1861, she founded the Irish Society for Promoting the Training and Employment of Educated Women, later known as the Queen's Institute, which offered training in various skills to "distressed gentlewoman," with the objective of equipping them to support themselves. By 1870, the institute had found employment for 862 of its 1,786 pupils, had extended its syllabus from technical to academic subjects, and had, it claimed, played a part in removing the stigma on women working for pay.

Jellicoe soon discovered, however, that many of the women coming to the institute lacked even the most basic elementary education and, in order to tackle this problem, proposed the establishment of a training college for governesses. She found an influential ally in the new archbishop of Dublin, Dr. Trench, and together they drew up plans for a college which would offer a liberal education to university level, not merely to future governesses but to middle-class women in general. Subscriptions were solicited, a house was bought in Earlsfort Terrace, and Alexandra College opened in October 1866, with Jellicoe as Lady Superintendent, a position which she was to hold until her death.

Prior to the foundation of Alexandra, most girls' schools paid little attention to academic learning, and many of the college's new pupils were found to be in need of elementary classes in subjects such as English, history and mathematics. While tackling these difficulties, the college offered a wider range of subjects than its competitors, and to a much higher level. Lectures were given by professors from Dublin's Trinity College, and in 1869, at Jellicoe's suggestion, a course of Saturday lectures on astronomy, Greek literature, and English poetry was instituted in Trinity, with over 200 women attending each year. The college itself continued to expand, with the establishment in 1872 of Alexandra School for younger girls. This had the effect of improving the educational standard of college entrants, while the profits from the school ensured the survival of the college. Meantime, in founding the Governess Association of Ireland (1869), Jellicoe had taken steps to improve the training of women teachers, and thus to improve the standard of education in girls' schools throughout Ireland.

According to one of those who worked closely with her, Jellicoe took "no active part" in the women's rights movement of her time. The only "women's right" for which she contended was, to quote her own words, "their right to be educated." Aware that there was "opposition to be conciliated, prejudice to be overcome, and the fear of what is new to be soothed," her instinct was to seek consensus rather than confrontation. Yet her efforts put middle-class Irish women in a position to take advantage of the educational reforms of the 1870s, and to press for further improvements in the status of women generally.

SOURCES:

Breathnach, Eibhlin. "Women and Higher Education in Ireland, 1879–1910," in *Crane Bag*. Vol. IV, 1980, pp. 47–54.

Luddy, M. *Women in Ireland 1800–1918: A Documentary History*. Cork University Press, 1995, pp. 137–138.

O'Connor, Anne V. "Anne Jellicoe." *Women, Power and Consciousness in 19th-Century Ireland*. Edited by M. Cullen and M. Luddy. Dublin: Attic Press, 1995, pp 125–159.

———. "Influences affecting girls' secondary education in Ireland, 1860–1910," in *Archivium Hibernicum*. Vol. XLI, 1986.

———, and Susan Parkes. *Gladly Learn and Gladly Teach: A History of Alexandra College and School, Dublin, 1866–1966*. Dublin: 1983.

COLLECTIONS:

Archives of Alexandra College and material in Friends' Historical Library, Dublin.

Rosemary Raughter,
freelance writer in women's history, Dublin, Ireland

Jemima

Biblical woman. Name variations: Jemimah. Born in the land of Uz; eldest of Job's three daughters.

Job's three daughters were born after his period of great suffering. He named the first Jemima, which means "handsome as the day" in Hebrew and "dove" in Arabic. Her sisters were named *Keziah and *Kerenhappuch. "And in all the land were no women found so fair as the daughters of Job" (*Job* xlii, 14 and 15).

Jemison, Alice Lee (1901–1964)

Native American political leader and journalist. Born Alice Mae Lee on October 9, 1901, at Silver Creek, New York (just off of the Cattaraugus Reservation); died on March 6, 1964, in Washington, D.C.; daughter of Daniel A. Lee and Elnora E. Seneca; educated at Silver Creek High School; married LeVerne Leonard Jemison, on December 6, 1919 (separated, December 1928); children: LeVerne "Jimmy" Lee (b. 1920); Jeanne Marie Jemison (b. 1923).

Alice Jemison was born on October 9, 1901, the first of three children of Daniel A. Lee and **Elnora Seneca**. Though her cabinetmaker father was Cherokee, Alice grew up in the matrilineal society of her Seneca mother. Much of Alice's confidence in her later activist work stemmed from the ancient Iroquois tradition of female political participation. Her family's financial instability limited Alice's education to the Silver Creek High School, and she worked in the evenings as an usher and a beautician until she graduated in 1919.

Alice married LeVerne Jemison, a steelworker from her reservation, on December 6, 1919. After their marriage ended in 1928, Alice Jemison was left to support her two children and her mother. Over the next two years, she was employed as a factory worker, a clerk, a peddler, a dressmaker, a practical nurse, a secretary, a paralegal researcher, and a freelance journalist. In 1930, she became an employee for the Bureau of the Census.

Increasingly concerned about the plight of the poverty-stricken Seneca Nation, Jemison became the secretary to Ray Jimerson, the president of the Nation. She was instrumental in the defense of two Seneca women arrested for the murder of a white woman in Buffalo, New York, in 1930. Jemison wrote letters to public figures and articles for the Buffalo newspapers in defense of the women, who were eventually released. From 1932 to 1934, Jemison was a syndicated columnist for the North American Newspaper Alliance. In her writings, she expressed a firm belief in the sanctity of Indian treaty rights and advocated the abolishment of the Bureau of Indian Affairs (BIA). The writings of Carlos Montezuma, the prominent Pan-Indian leader, profoundly influenced her stance on the BIA and her criticism of Commissioner of Indian Affairs John Collier.

In 1935, Jemison became the spokesperson for Joseph Bruner, president of the American Indian Federation. As such, she functioned as the organization's main lobbyist on Capitol Hill. Attending more congressional hearings than any other Indian in the late 1930s, she fought for the repeal of the Indian Reorganization Act of 1934, which had been established by Collier as a way to fashion home rule among the nation's tribes. Jemison resented federal intervention in Native American affairs and opposed government imposition on every side. She disagreed with the herd reduction program among the Navaho, lobbied against the construction of the Blue Ridge Parkway through Cherokee land, and charged the BIA with incompetence. She resigned from this position in 1939.

Occasionally known to denounce opponents as communists or atheists, Jemison gained acceptance from right-wing critics of the Roosevelt administration. In 1938 and 1940, determined in her battle against the BIA, she was willing to appear before the House Committee on Un-American Activities at the same hearings with self-proclaimed fascists. Jemison also showed formidable opposition to the Selective Service Act in 1940, and these activities opened the door for the Interior Department to successfully label her an "Indian Nazi," even though she passed the most rigorous FBI loyalty checks. Despite constant government harassment, she continued to call for the abolishment of the BIA.

Alice Jemison remained in Washington, D.C. for the rest of her life, keeping her connection with the Seneca through her uncle Cornelius Seneca, president of the Seneca Nation. She died of cancer on March 6, 1964, and was buried on the Cattaraugus Indian Reservation.

SOURCES:

Sicherman, Barbara, and Carol Hurd Green, ed. *Notable American Women: The Modern Period.* Boston, MA: Belknap Press of Harvard University, 1980.

Karina L. Kerr, M.A.,
Ypsilanti, Michigan

Jemison, Mae C. (b. 1956).

See Astronauts: Women in Space.

Jemison, Mary (1742–1833)

Captive of the Iroquois Indians in the French and Indian War who, having decided to stay with the Senecas following the war, survived tremendous hardship during the American Revolution and became a great, though temporary, landowner in western New York. Name variations: Dickewamis (Di-keh-WAH-mes), Dehewamis (Deh-he-WA-mes), Dehgewanus (Deh-ge-WAH-nus). Born Mary Jemison in 1742 aboard the ship William and Mary *en route to America; died at the Buffalo Creek Reservation, near Buffalo, New York, on September 19, 1833; daughter of Thomas Jemison (an Irish-born farmer) and Jane (Erwin) Jemison; married Delaware warrior Sheninjee, in 1760 (died); married Seneca warrior Hiokatoo, around 1766; children: (first marriage) Thomas; (second marriage) John, Nancy, Betsey, Polly, Jane, Jesse.*

Family moved to western Pennsylvania soon after their landing in Philadelphia (1742); captured by a French and Indian raiding party and adopted by the Seneca (1758); migrated with Seneca to town of Wiishto (1760); moved with Seneca brothers to Genishau in Genessee Valley, western New York (1763); moved to Gardow Flats with five of her then six children (1779); decided to stay with the Seneca following the Revolution; given possession of Gardow Flats by Iroquois chiefs at Council of Big Tree (1797); naturalized and given title to land by special act of New York Legislature (1817); sold all of reservation except 4,000 acres with approval of council of chiefs and U.S. Commissioner of Indian Lands in exchange for $300 per-

petual annuity (1823); gave narrative of her life to Dr. James Seaver (1823); exchanged perpetual annuity and remaining 4,000 acres for lump sum payment and removed to Buffalo Creek Reservation, New York (1831); converted to Christianity shortly before her death (1833).

Women in the Iroquois Confederacy of northern New York enjoyed many powers. They aided in the selection of chiefs, decided whether war prisoners would be killed or adopted to replace slain family members, and prepared children for their expected future roles. Sons were trained to be hunters and warriors, as their mothers allowed them to torture prisoners, and daughters were taught child-rearing and corn-raising techniques. Iroquois women were so powerful because they alone raised the corn crop, which was the Iroquois' chief staple, while men hunted, waged war, and conducted foreign affairs. This traditional picture of Iroquois life changed, however, in the late 18th and early 19th centuries, when most Iroquois faced the encroachment of whites and the restriction of reservations. In this time of crisis, one woman took initiative and entered the men's councils as a respected landowner, thus attaining power rare to any New York woman, white or Iroquois. Her name was Mary Jemison. In 1823, she gave an account of her life to Dr. James Seaver; the narrative reveals the impact of war and white encroachment on the Iroquois Confederacy.

Mary Jemison's life was constantly related to social and political change. She was the fourth child of Thomas and **Jane Jemison**, who, according to Mary's narrative, left their native Ireland because of the "intestine divisions, civil wars, and ecclesiastical rigidity and domination" which plagued that country. Mary was born on the ship *William and Mary* during the voyage to America. After landing in Philadelphia, the family settled in western Pennsylvania around Marsh Creek, where Thomas Jemison established a farm. The French and Indian War, begun in 1754 when Virginians under Colonel George Washington tried to make good their claims on the Ohio country, soon shattered the Jemisons' quiet frontier life. In the spring of 1758, a party of four Frenchmen and six Shawnee Indians attacked the Jemisons' house, killed a neighbor, and took Mary, her parents, her two younger brothers and older sister, and the neighbor's wife and three children prisoner. Mary's two older brothers escaped to Virginia, where their uncle lived.

Except for Mary and a son of the neighboring family, all of these prisoners were killed and scalped, as the French and Indian party feared the ongoing pursuit of other neighbors. Before her death, Jane Jemison became a model of strength, noted her daughter. She "manifested a great degree of fortitude, and encouraged us to support our troubles without complaining." Jemison's father, however, was "absorbed in melancholy" and "lost all his ambition" as soon as they were captured.

Several days later, the raiding party arrived at Fort Duquesne (in modern-day Pittsburgh). There Mary's young neighbor was taken away by the French, while two Seneca squaws, seeking an enemy's scalp or a prisoner to avenge the loss of their brother in the war, claimed Mary and took her to a nearby Seneca town on the Ohio River. There, in a deeply mournful ceremony, they adopted her into their family. Jemison reported that the Seneca name then given her was Dickewamis, meaning "pretty girl," but Seaver and historian Charles Milliken later gave other variations of this name, Dehewamis or Dehgewanus, which can be translated as "Two-Females-Letting-Words-Fall."

At this time, Mary was about 16 years old. She told Seaver that her capture and adoption occurred in 1755, the same year, according to her, when the British captured Fort Duquesne from the French. The seizure of the fort, however, occurred in 1758, and this date is generally accepted as the start of her captivity.

As a teenager among the Iroquois, Jemison was expected to help care for children and, along with other children, to carry game for hunters. Children of both sexes could thus be exposed to the violence of the hunt, but Seneca women had no place in war; instead, their duty was to help keep village harmony and maintain the corn crop. Several years later, when Mary's Seneca sisters wished her to witness the burning of a prisoner, her adoptive mother admonished her two natural daughters: "Our task is quite easy at home, and our business needs our attention. With war we have nothing to do."

In her first summer with the Seneca, Jemison also tended the corn crop, but she tried to maintain her European identity. That spring, when she and many Senecas traveled to Fort Duquesne (newly named Fort Pitt) to negotiate peace with the British, some of the English took an interest in her situation. Her Seneca sisters, not wanting to lose her, took Jemison away from the fort, and Mary was temporarily disheartened. At that time, she still longed for rescue, reciting her catechism privately in English so that she would not forget the language. As time went on, however, she became more comfortable with the Iroquois way of life.

In 1760, her Seneca family moved to their summer home, the town of Wiishto in the Ohio country, over 300 miles below Pittsburgh on the Ohio River. In the winter, they moved to better hunting grounds on the nearby Sciota River. There her adoptive family arranged her marriage to Sheninjee, a Delaware. Jemison expressed her genuine love for Sheninjee, with whom she had two children, a daughter, who died shortly after birth, and a son, Thomas. About three years later, her "anxiety to get away, to be set at liberty, and leave them," said Jemison, "had almost subsided." She began to think that her lot as an adopted Iroquois was better than that of white women, seeing benefits in the steady routine of female-directed Iroquois agriculture:

> Our labor was not severe; and that of one year was exactly similar . . . to that of the others, without that endless variety that is to be observed in the common labor of the white people. . . . [W]e . . . had no master to . . . drive us, so that we could work as leisurely as we pleased.

In the early summer of 1763, Jemison left Wiishto with Sheninjee, two of her adoptive brothers, and her infant son Thomas to trade furs at Fort Pitt. Another adoptive brother met them on the way and convinced them to live at Genishau (near Geneseo) on the Genessee River in western New York, where her adoptive Seneca mother and two adoptive sisters had moved two summers earlier. Mary took Thomas along, but Sheninjee remained behind to continue the trading mission. Though Jemison received a warm welcome at Genishau, she was anxious about her husband's fate. In her second summer there, she learned that Sheninjee had become ill and died the previous winter.

At Genishau, Jemison demonstrated her unwillingness to return to white society. After the conclusion of the French and Indian War in 1763, the British Crown offered a bounty for returned war prisoners. John Van Sice, a Dutch trader, wanted to redeem Jemison at Fort Niagara, but Mary fled until Van Sice gave up the chase. Soon after, the "old King" at Genishau also wanted to redeem Mary, but, forewarned by an adoptive brother, she hid in the woods until the "old King" left with the prisoners he already had. About 1766, Jemison was married to Hiokatoo, a fierce warrior 34 years her senior. The couple had six children: four girls, Jane, Nancy, Betsey, and Polly, and two boys, John and Jesse.

According to Jemison, between the end of the French and Indian War and the beginning of the Revolution the Iroquois led "happy" lives, the men "hunting" and the women attending "to agriculture, their families, and a few domestic concerns of little consequence . . . with but little labor." Before the widespread use of "spiritous liquors" among the Seneca after the Revolution, "Their fidelity was perfect . . . ; they were strictly honest; they despised deception and falsehood. . . . They were temperate in their desires, moderate in their passions."

But the conduct of the Iroquois chiefs around the time of the Revolution belied Jemison's characterization. Moravian missionaries recorded widespread use of alcohol among the Seneca in the 1740s and 1750s, and Jemison stated that British promises of rum and riches convinced the Iroquois chiefs to break their pledged neutrality and fight against the American colonists. This unfortunate side of Iroquois life, alcohol consumption, would also lead to the death of her sons in the 1810s.

Jemison helped the Iroquois war effort in support of the British, preparing food and supplies for Mohawk leader Colonel Joseph Brant. The Seneca, however, would suffer for their breach of neutrality, and during this trial Jemison would earn great respect from Iroquois chiefs.

In the fall of 1779, the American army under General John Sullivan advanced on the Genessee region and destroyed Seneca houses and fields, leaving little food for the Seneca upon their return. Mary Jemison had fled from the advancing troops with one child on her back, another on horseback, and three on foot. With food scarce when she returned to Geneseo, she seized the initiative. Carrying her two youngest children on her back, she led her three other children on foot to the nearby Gardow Flats in one night. There she discovered two fugitive black slaves living in a cabin. In exchange for a share to feed her family through the harsh winter, she agreed to help them harvest their corn crop. The escaped slaves also let Jemison and her children live in their cabin until she constructed her own shelter the following spring. When the former slaves abandoned the flats three years later, they left the land in Jemison's control.

After the Peace of 1783, Jemison's adoptive Seneca brother Kaujisestaugeau offered her the opportunity to return to white society. Jemison, however, expressed her desire to stay. She did not want to be separated from her adult son Thomas, whom the chiefs would not let go because of his leadership potential, nor did she want her Iroquois children to be treated with "cold indifference" in white society. Kaujisestaugeau then decided that for her loyalty over the years Jemison should receive compensation. He spoke to the Seneca chiefs at Buffalo about conferring a tract of land to his sister at the next great council.

When this council finally convened in 1797 at Big Tree (near Geneseo), all of the Seneca lands west of the Genessee River—except for several reservations totalling 310 square miles—was sold for $100,000 to Robert Morris and the Holland Land Company. The money was to be divided among certain Senecas in annuities. Chief Farmer's Brother also presented Jemison's claim, but another chief, the orator Red Jacket (who got his name for his service as messenger for the British during the Revolution), opposed the claim, likely because it frustrated his own visions of gain. Farmer's Brother won the day, however, and Jemison was given the 17,927-acre Gardow Tract, where she had lived since 1779. For two years, Red Jacket refused to surrender Mary's share of the $100,000 until Jasper Parrish, a U.S. Indian agent and former Iroquois captive, convinced him that white officials recognized her claim. Finding the tract too large for her and her daughters to farm, Jemison gained permission from the chiefs to lease small parcels of land to white settlers. The leases and annuity provided Mary with a generous income.

Jemison tried to promote peace within her village. She hid and fed Ebenezer Allen, a white fugitive who had frustrated British and Iroquois plans to attack white American settlements. Allen had misrepresented his own wampum string to American officials as an Iroquois peace offering, which, though fraudulent, the Iroquois would not dishonor. The Senecas, including Jemison, supported Allen, but the British and other Iroquois nations kept up the pursuit. Though Allen was eventually captured, he was acquitted of any crime.

Jemison had trouble keeping peace in her own family, however. Her two oldest sons had many disagreements over the years, as the often drunk Thomas strongly disapproved of half-brother John's bigamy and even accused John of witchcraft. Thomas had also struck John's father Hiokatoo, thus aggravating the hatred. Though Mary beseeched them to "become reconciled to each other," in July 1811, the "somewhat intoxicated" Thomas started another quarrel with his half-brother. John had had enough. Suddenly seizing Thomas, he killed him with his tomahawk. In council, the Seneca chiefs acquitted

John of any wrongdoing because of Thomas' constant "abuses." But other Senecas shunned John, including younger brother Jesse, whom Mary favored because of his frequent assistance with household chores. In May 1812, John fatally stabbed Jesse after an argument. Mary was "overcome with grief" following Jesse's death, especially as it came so soon after the deaths of Thomas and Hiokatoo the previous November.

Jemison also had to worry about the growing presence of whites unsympathetic to Iroquois interests. In 1810, for example, a man by the name of George Jemison—in debt and nearly destitute—came to Gardow Flats claiming to be Mary's cousin. A trusting and sympathetic Mary gave him a parcel of land, horses, livestock, furniture, farming implements, and supported George Jemison for eight years. Nonetheless, in George's sixth or seventh year at Gardow, a supposed friend of Mary's convinced her to give George 40 more acres of land. In fact, the deed which they presented for Mary's signature was for 400 acres, of which George had conspired to give the friend half. Though the friend eventually gave his ill-gotten land back to Mary, George sold his 200 acres. Mary finally persuaded George to leave Gardow; she later became certain that he was not her cousin.

Meanwhile, her son John continued his dangerous ways. In May 1817, while drinking "freely" with two other Iroquois named Doctor and Jack, he quarrelled with them and was beaten to death because of his earlier crimes. Though Mary felt that John's murder was "just," she insisted that the two killers be exiled. Soon after this binding order, Jack committed suicide; the Doctor died of consumption two years later.

Meanwhile, Jemison still faced the growing presence of whites. Through federal government purchases, the Iroquois were gradually losing control of their lands and moving onto reservations, such as Buffalo Creek. There was also the pressure of white immigration. In 1816, Micah Brooks, a lawyer from Ontario County, New York, offered to procure a special act of the New York Legislature which would protect Jemison's property rights. In exchange for his services, Brooks wanted half of the Gardow Flats. Jemison then consulted her neighbor Thomas Clute and his brother Jellis Clute, Esq., who agreed with Brooks to present a petition on Jemison's behalf to Congress. Brooks, however, petitioned the State Legislature, which passed the special act naturalizing Jemison and confirming the title to her land on April 19, 1817.

Even though the legislation was probably motivated by self-interest (as Brooks and Jellis Clute eventually bought Jemison's land), it was remarkable. As New York law stood until 1848, women's property rights were limited. For the most part, unmarried and widowed women acquired land only through inheritance, and once married or remarried their property went to their husband (unless the spouses made a prenuptial agreement). Since the Iroquois had also been selling their lands, Jemison's security of tenure as a Seneca and a woman was extraordinary.

With the consent of her daughters, who also lived on the Flats, Jemison decided to sell most of her land, feeling too old to manage it. In September 1823, with the approval of a council of Iroquois chiefs and a U.S. Commissioner of Indian Lands, she sold all but 4,000 acres (about two square miles) to Brooks, Jellis Clute, and Canandaigua banker H.B. Gibson, in exchange for a $300 perpetual annuity. However, finding herself increasingly surrounded by white settlements, Jemison in 1831 sold her annuity and her remaining two square miles at Gardow for a lump sum and moved to Buffalo Creek Reservation. She converted to Christianity a few months before her death on September 19, 1833.

In 1874, William Letchworth, a prominent businessman and Genessee Valley landowner, moved Jemison's remains to his estate, now Letchworth State Park. There he also placed her Gardow house and commissioned a statue of Jemison from H.K. Bush-Brown. The statue, representing Jemison and her infant son Thomas during their trek to the Genesee Valley, was dedicated in 1910. Letchworth State Park is on Mt. Morris Lake, about ten miles southwest of the modern-day town of Geneseo.

Most of the information concerning Mary Jemison comes from Dr. James Seaver's *A Narrative of the Life of Mrs. Mary Jemison,* which was first published in 1824 and went through 21 editions over the next 100 years. The story was later made into a children's book and adapted for chamber theater. As **June Namias** points out in *White Captives,* the intense interest in Mary Jemison's story may have stemmed from white society's desire to see how a white woman preserved "civilized" manners while living with "savages." Milliken asserts that many readers were interested in Indian society's response to growing white encroachment.

Whatever the reason, readers must take care to distinguish fact from fiction. Beginning with Seaver, many accounts of Jemison assume that she believed white culture superior to that of the Iroquois. The *Narrative* is, after all, a second-hand report, told through James Seaver, who embellished the story somewhat. Given Mary Jemison's preference for the Seneca way of life, it becomes questionable that she would think of her life as a "reduction from a civilized to a savage state." In fact, she maintained that Iroquois and white societies were distinct, not inferior or superior to each other: "I have seen . . . the effects of [white] education upon some of our Indians," she wrote, "but I have never seen one of those but was an Indian in every respect after he returned."

Lois Lenski's children's story, *Indian Captive: The Story of Mary Jemison,* published in 1941 and adapted into a play by **Gertrude Breen** in 1961, also depicts Jemison as a continually resistant member of Seneca society. In these versions, the 12-year-old Jemison, treated badly by a "cross" adoptive sister, frequently tries to run away and hides and cries in the woods. She also asks a white trader Fallenash to help her escape. Only after she learns about her family's murder does she consent to remain with the Seneca. Of course, this account differs from Jemison's narrative. Though she initially wanted to be rescued, she was not abused by her adoptive sisters, and she went into the woods to work, not to run away. She also foiled the trader Van Sice's attempt to return her to white society.

Mary Jemison stayed with the Seneca because with them she derived a secure, powerful identity. She loved her Seneca family, particularly her children, whom she feared would not be well regarded by white relatives. She also enjoyed the power of Seneca women over domestic affairs, as her references to "my house" and "my flats" illustrate. Thus, she took pride in her Seneca identity.

SOURCES:

Lenski, Lois. *Indian Captive: The Story of Mary Jemison* (adapted and arranged for Chamber Theater by Gertrude Breen). Chicago, IL: Coach House Press, 1961.

Milliken, Charles F. "A Biographical Sketch of Mary Jemison, the White Woman of the Genessee," in *Researches and Transactions of the New York State Archeological Association.* Vol. IV, no. 3. Rochester, NY: Lewis H. Morgan Chapter, 1924.

Namias, June. *White Captives: Gender and Ethnicity on the American Frontier.* Chapel Hill, NC: University of North Carolina Press, 1993.

Seaver, James. *A Narrative of the Life of Mrs. Mary Jemison.* Syracuse, NY: Syracuse Univ. Press, 1990 (first published, 1824).

Vanderhoof, E.W. *Historical Sketches of Western New York.* NY: AMS Press, 1972.

Wallace, Anthony F.C. *The Death and Rebirth of the Seneca.* NY: Alfred A. Knopf, 1970.

SUGGESTED READING:
Brush, Edward H. *Iroquois Past and Present.* NY: AMS Press, 1975.

Wes Borucki,
doctoral candidate at the department of history of the University of Alabama, Tuscaloosa, and editor (1998–1999) of *Southern Historian,* the University of Alabama's annual journal

Jemmy the Rover (c. 1805–1855).

See Henrys, Catherine.

Jenckes, Virginia Ellis (1877–1975)

American congressional representative, member of the 73rd–75th congresses (1933–39). Born Virginia Ellis on November 6, 1877, in Terre Haute, Indiana; died on January 9, 1975, in Terre Haute, Indiana; daughter of James Ellis and Mary (Oliver) Somes; educated at public schools in Indiana; married Ray Greene Jenckes, on February 22, 1912 (died 1921); children: Virginia Ray Jenckes (died young).

Virginia Ellis Jenckes was born on November 6, 1877, in Terre Haute, Indiana. She attended public schools there and, after her marriage in 1912, helped her husband manage their 1,300-acre farm. Jenckes took full responsibility for the farm's operation after becoming a widow in 1921. She was a founder of the Wabash and Maumee Valley Improvement Association and served as its secretary from 1926 to 1932. In 1932, however, she switched from farming to politics and ran for Congress as a Democrat. Her platform focused on the troubles of the local economy caused by the Depression and addressed the need for federal aid to help with flooding problems. She was also in favor of repealing Prohibition as a stimulus to the economy. With her daughter Virginia serving as her driver, Jenckes campaigned throughout the district during the race, which, due to a recent redrawing of districts, included both Democratic and Republican incumbents. She defeated each of them, in the Democratic primary and in the general election, thus becoming the representative for Indiana's Sixth District.

During her three terms, Jenckes served on both the Committee on Civil Defense and the Committee on the District of Columbia; she also served on the Committee on Mines and Mining in her first two terms. When Franklin Roosevelt's New Deal programs began providing some relief from the Depression, Jenckes turned her focus to supporting the FBI. She was also concerned that children within the Washington, D.C., public school system were being propagandized into an acceptance of Communist doctrine. In 1937, she was a U.S. delegate to the Interparliamentary Union in Paris, France.

Jenckes lost the 1938 election to Republican Noble Johnson but remained in Washington for decades, working for the Red Cross. In 1956, she played a role in helping five priests escape from Hungary during the uprising there. In the early 1970s, Jenckes returned to Terre Haute, Indiana, where she died in 1975 and was laid to rest in Highland Lawn Cemetery.

SOURCES:
Office of the Historian. *Women in Congress 1917–1990.* Commission on the Bicentenary of the U.S. House of Representatives, 1991.

Karina L. Kerr,
M.A., Ypsilanti, Michigan

*Virginia
Ellis
Jenckes*

Jenkins, Carol Heiss (b. 1940).

See Heiss-Jenkins, Carol.

Jenner, Andrea (1891–1985)

Australian actress, journalist, and broadcaster. Name variations: (pseudonym) Andrea. Born Dorothy Gordon in 1891; died in Sydney, Australia, on March 24,

1985; daughter of William A. Gordon (a stockbroker) and Dora (Fosbery) Gordon; attended Ascham and Sydney Church of England Girls' Grammar School, Sydney, Australia; married Murray Eugene McEwen, in 1917 (divorced); married George Onesiphorus Jenner, in 1922 (separated); no children.

Born in Australia in 1891 and educated there, Andrea Jenner began her career in Hollywood, California, performing bit parts and stunts for Paramount. After two short-lived marriages (she divorced her first husband and left the second), she returned to Sydney, where she starred in *The Hills of Hate* (1926) and was a scriptwriter on *For the Term of his Natural Life* (1927). Jenner then left for London and, after a long illness, began writing a column for the *Sydney Sun* under the pseudonym "Andrea." Profiling famous people and fashionable European holiday resorts, the gossip column was a great success, and Jenner remained in London until 1940. She then served as a correspondent during the war in the Pacific and was captured in Hong Kong during the Japanese invasion and imprisoned for four years. Upon her release, she had difficulty reestablishing herself with the *Sun*, which only gave her half-pay for her years as a POW. After a brief stint with the *Mirror*, she moved into Australian broadcasting. During the 1960s, Jenner became nationally known for her pioneering "talk-back" radio show, and her famous greeting "Hullo, mums and dads." The show lasted until 1968, when she was eased out by new management. During her last years, Jenner helped establish the Wayside Chapel and published her memoirs, *Darlings, I've Had a Ball* (1975). Andrea Jenner died in her Sydney apartment on March 24, 1985.

SOURCES:
Radi, Heather, ed. *200 Australian Women*. NSW, Australia: Women's Redress Press, 1988.

Jennings, Frances (d. 1730)

English aristocrat. Name variations: Frances Hamilton. Died in 1730; elder sister of Sarah Jennings Churchill, duchess of Marlborough (1660–1744); daughter of Richard Jennings (Jenyns) and Frances Thornhurst; married Sir George Hamilton.

Frances Jennings, elder sister of *Sarah Jennings Churchill, the duchess of Marlborough, was mentioned by Samuel Pepys in his diary and courted by Richard Talbot, earl and titular duke of Tyrconnel.

Jennings, Sarah (1660–1744).

See Churchill, Sarah Jennings.

Jensen, Elise Ottesen (1886–1973).

See Ottesen-Jensen, Elise.

Jenssen, Elois

American costume designer. Born in Palo Alto, California; attended Westlake School for Girls in Southern California; attended Parson's School of Design, Paris, France; graduated from Chouinard Art Institute (now California Institute of the Arts).

Selected films as costume designer, alone or in collaboration: Dishonored Lady *(1947);* Lured *(1947);* So This Is New York *(1948);* The Pitfall *(1948);* Let's Live a Little *(1948);* Samson and Delilah *(1948);* Outpost in Morocco *(1949);* A Kiss for Corliss *(1949);* Mrs. Mike *(1949);* The Man Who Cheated Himself *(1950);* The Groom Wore Spurs *(1950);* Cry Danger *(1950);* Phone Call from a Stranger *(1951);* Deadline, USA *(1952);* Diplomatic Courier *(1952);* We're Not Married *(1952);* Something for the Birds *(1952);* Forever Darling *(1955);* Tron *(1982).*

The product of the Parson's School of Design, Paris branch, and a four-year course at the Chouinard Art Institute, Elois Jenssen began her career with producer Hunt Stromberg as a sketch artist and assistant to **Natalie Visart**. After Visart left to get married, Jenssen received her first screen credit for the stunningly sophisticated clothes she designed for ***Hedy Lamarr** in *Dishonored Lady* (1947). When Stromberg closed his office, Jenssen freelanced, then was tapped to work with ***Edith Head**, ***Dorothy Jeakins**, Gile Steele, and ***Gwen Wakeling** on the Cecil B. De Mille epic *Samson and Delilah* (1948); for their work, all five designers received the Academy Award for best color costume design in 1950. Jenssen then did a three-year stint with Twentieth Century-Fox before moving into television, where she designed for the series "Private Secretary" (with ***Ann Sothern**), "I Love Lucy" (with ***Lucille Ball**), "My Living Doll" (with ***Julie Newmar**), and "Bracken's World" (with **Evelyn Keyes**). Jenssen returned to film in 1982, winning another Academy Award nomination for her work with **Rosanna Norton** on *Tron*.

Jepson, Helen (1904–1997)

American soprano. Born in Titusville, Pennsylvania, on November 28, 1904; died in Bradenton, Florida, on September 16, 1997; daughter of Charles Henry Jepson and Alice (Williams) Jepson; graduated from West High School, Akron, Ohio; Curtis Institute in Philadelphia, B.A. with honors, 1928; married George Roscoe Possell (also seen as Poselle), on June 3, 1931; children: one daughter Sallie Patricia.

The equal of many of the more prominent European sopranos of her day, American Helen Jepson captured the hearts of opera lovers with her lyric soprano voice and radiant good looks. Born in Titusville, Pennsylvania, to a musical family in 1904, Jepson sang in her church choir and had leading roles in her high school's operettas. The family's modest income, however, precluded music lessons, and after high school Jepson went to work—first in a department store, then in a record shop—to earn money for her training. With enough saved, she took her first vocal lessons with Horatio Connell. She subsequently won a scholarship to the Curtis Institute in Philadelphia, where she studied with *Queena Mario. Graduating with honors, she was engaged by the Philadelphia Civic Opera Company and made her debut in *The Marriage of Figaro*. She then appeared with the Philadelphia Grand Opera Company, singing the role of Nedda in *Pagliacci* to excellent reviews. She remained a leading soprano with the company until it disbanded two years later.

The Depression temporarily interrupted Jepson's burgeoning career, and she had difficulty finding work. When an offer finally came to sing on the radio with the Bamberger Little Symphony Orchestra, she accepted. Her success was such that offers followed to perform with Rudy Vallee as well as Paul Whiteman, who hired her as a permanent singer with his orchestra. As a regular on Whiteman's popular show, she gained national exposure and an opportunity to sing for Gatti-Casazza of the famed New York Metropolitan Opera.

After a successful audition, Jepson made her Metropolitan debut on January 24, 1935, as Helene in Seymour's *In the Pasha's Garden*. She went on to become a featured singer with the Met, performing roles in French, Italian, and German operas. In 1936, she went to Paris to study the roles of Thaïs and Louise with famed singer *Mary Garden, then added them to her already impressive repertoire. In addition to her work with the Met, Jepson also made appearances with the Chicago Civic Opera Company.

In 1931, Jepson had married George Roscoe Possell, with whom she had a daughter. The couple divided their time between homes in New York City and a mountain retreat where Jepson raised rabbits. An avid sportswoman, she engaged in hunting, fishing, and horseback riding. She also enjoyed swing music and frequently entertained friends with renditions of popular songs.

Helen Jepson made numerous recordings of her most popular arias and was the first soprano to record the female lead in Gershwin's *Porgy and Bess*. The singer retired in 1943, after which she taught for many years. She spent her later life in Bradenton, Florida, where she died on September 16, 1997.

SOURCES:

Ewen, David. *Living Musicians*. NY: H.W. Wilson, 1940.

"Obituary," in *The Day* [New London, CT]. September 19, 1997.

Sadie, Stanley, ed. *The New Grove Dictionary of Opera*. Vol. II. NY: Macmillan, 1992.

Slonimsky, Nicolas. *Baker's Biographical Dictionary of Musicians*. 8th ed. NY: Schirmer Books, 1992.

Barbara Morgan,
Melrose, Massachusetts

Jeritza, Maria (1887–1982)

Czech soprano and star of the Metropolitan Opera from 1921 to 1932. Born Marie Jedlitzka or Jedlitska on October 6, 1887, in Brünn, Moravia; died on July 10, 1982, in Orange, New Jersey; studied at the Brünn Musikschule and with Auspitzer; married Baron Leopold von Popper de Podharagn (divorced 1935); married Winfield Sheehan (a motion picture executive), in 1935 (died 1945).

Debuted at Olmütz as Elsa in Lohengrin (1910); debuted at the Vienna Volksoper as Elisabeth in Tannhäuser (1912); debuted at the Hofoper (1913); created the Empress in Die Frau ohne Schatten in Vienna (1919); debuted at the Metropolitan Opera in the American premier of Erich Wolfgang Korngold's opera The Dead City (November 19, 1921); debuted at Covent Garden (1925); received the Austrian Order of Knighthood, first class—one of the highest awards ever bestowed on a civilian by the Austrian government (1935).

From 1921 until 1932, Maria Jeritza sang 290 performances in 20 roles at the Metropolitan Opera. She was the Met's most beautiful and glamorous star since *Geraldine Farrar, who was also greatly beloved by the opera-going public. Jeritza belonged to a category of performers known as "singing actresses" because her performances were more flamboyant than refined. Jeritza arrived in New York as an established fa-

Maria
Jeritza

vorite in Vienna where she sang for two decades. In 1913, she was engaged by the Vienna Hofoper, where she became famous for her interpretations of roles in the operas of Richard Wagner and Giacomo Puccini. The latter considered her the greatest of Toscas. She was the first Ariadne in both versions of Strauss' *Ariadne auf Naxos* in Stuttgart in 1912 and in Vienna in 1916. She also created Marietta in the first Vienna performance of Korngold's *Die tote Stadt* (*The Dead City*). Audiences particularly loved Jeritza's interpretations of Tosca, Minnie, and Turandot.

When she opened at the Met in *The Dead City*, she took America by storm. "Probably not since Calvé has such a vital, happily equipped and quickening personality leaped from European shores to the center of the Metropolitan stage," wrote one critic. "Beauty, stature, magnetism, grace, dramatic liveliness, artistic feeling—she has all these to add to a big radiantly fresh voice." A few days later, she undertook Tosca and was "an incarnation of a woman far greater than the one conceived by the creators of the opera," wrote Henry Krehbiel. She remained with the Metropolitan, appearing in many American premieres including those of Leos Janáček's *Jenufa*, Puccini's *Turandot*, Korngold's *Violanta*, and Richard Strauss' *Ægyptische Helena*. She also appeared as guest artist with other opera companies and gave many concert recitals. Some of her other roles were those of Carmen, Santuzza, Thaïs, and Sieglinde.

Recordings expose Jeritza's faults and genius as a singer. Although taste and technique are sometimes questionable in these recordings, there are also moments of genuine vocal achievement, spotlighting her lustrous, ample voice. After World War II, Maria Jeritza made isolated appearances in Vienna and New York, but had effectively retired after her second marriage in 1935.

In her book, *Coming into the End Zone,* **Doris Grumbach** fondly remembers watching an aging Jeritza, in her customary white fur hat, helped to the front row for a performance of *Der Rosenkavalier.* "She wore dark sunglasses, her body was small and soft. She seemed ageless and frail. . . . She bowed her head from side to side in gentle acknowledgment of the recognition she seemed grateful for." During the performance, when Grumbach would glance her way, Jeritza appeared to be "absorbed in listening." At intermission, Grumbach commented to the man sitting next to her about how wonderful she looked. "'She always does,' he said. 'That floppy hat, that wonderful face. You'd never know she was blind.'"

SOURCES:

Ewen, David. *Living Musicians.* NY: H.W. Wilson, 1940.

Grumbach, Doris. *Coming into the End Zone.* NY: Norton, 1991, pg 64.

Warrack, John, and Ewan West. *Oxford Dictionary of Opera.* Oxford, England: Oxford University Press, 1992.

SUGGESTED READING:

Jeritza, Maria. *Sunlight and Song* (autobiography), 1924.

John Haag,
Associate Professor of History,
University of Georgia, Athens, Georgia

Jermy, Louie (1864–1934)

English country maiden known as "The Maid of the Mill." Name variations: The Maid of the Mill. Born in Sidestrand, Norfolk, England, around 1864; died in 1934; daughter of Alfred Jermy (a miller); never married; no children.

Louie Jermy, or "The Maid of the Mill" as she came to be known, was a lifelong resident of Sidestrand, a small English hamlet on the northeastern coast of Norfolk that became a thriving tourist mecca during the mid-1880s. The small, out-of-the-way village was discovered by Clement Scott, theater critic and travel writer for London's *Daily Telegraph,* who happened upon it while on assignment in Cromer, a coastal resort on the furthest extension of the Great Eastern Railway line. Searching for a peaceful respite from the holiday beach crowd at Cromer, Scott wandered two miles inland where he discovered first a deserted churchyard and tower, and then a windmill and the red-brick farm cottage leased by Alfred Jermy, a widowed miller, and his charming 19-year-old daughter Louie. Scott was so overcome with the peaceful beauty of the place that he took up residence in the cottage for a few days, enjoying Louie's sumptuous country meals and wandering the hillsides and the deserted beach in solitude. He dubbed the place "Poppyland" because of the profusion of red poppies that blanketed its hillsides.

Scott recounted his impressions of Poppyland in his newspaper column for several weeks, attempting to disguise the identity of the village by calling it "Beckhythe." The idyllic setting, however, soon captured the imagination of London's literary and artistic society, and before long many famous names made their way to the Old Mill House of Scott's description. Among the early visitors to enjoy Louie Jermy's cheerful hospitality were the eminent Victorian poet Algernon Charles Swinburne and his fellow writer Theodore Watts-Dunton. Swinburne composed parts of his poem *A Midsummer Holiday* while staying at the cottage, and Watts-Dunton paid homage to the place in his novel *Aylwin,* though he did not refer to it by name. Soon, the area became a fashionable summer destination for London celebrities and the cottage's guests grew to include notables like writer George R. Sims, who made Louie Jermy something of a celebrity by mentioning her in his regular feature "Mustard and Cress," which appeared in the Sunday periodical, *The Referee.* (At one point, Louie was taken to London by some of the society patrons of the cottage, but she felt out of place in the city and could not wait to get home.) Other guests to the cottage included playwright Robert Rees, publisher Andre Chatto, and actors Henry Irving, Herbert Beerbohm-Tree, and *Ellen Terry. As more and more famous names were drawn to the area, other villagers opened their cottages to guests, and many titled people began purchasing land and building grand summer houses. For a while, the place became known as "the village of millionaires."

Poppyland did not attract the general public for some time, mainly because of its obscure location and lack of facilities. Its status as a summer retreat for the rich and famous changed abruptly, however, with a series of events beginning with the publication of Clement Scott's poem "Garden of Sleep," written while standing in the churchyard in 1885 and published in *The Theater*, a periodical he edited. (The poem also appeared in Scott's later book *Poppyland Papers*.) The verse caught the attention of popular songwriter Isidore de Lara, who set it to music and turned it into the popular song "The Hush of the Corn," which captured worldwide attention. Now, everyone clamored for information about Poppyland. The entrepreneurial railways soon capitalized on public curiosity by advertising Poppyland as a destination of choice. Scott himself continued to visit Poppyland regularly—summer and winter—over the course of 15 years, and later published *Blossom Land and Fallen Leaves*, an expanded story of Poppyland and the surrounding Norfolk countryside. Other journalists followed suit, and there was a glut of guide books and articles on the place, as well as postcards, souvenirs, and even a Poppyland perfume, supposedly made from the oil of the poppies.

By 1904, the year of Scott's death, Poppyland had turned into what he termed "Bungalowland," attracting not only the bed-and-breakfast set, but day-trippers as well. During World War I, the area was taken over by the army, and the Jermys hosted military brass in the same homely accommodations that had attracted more select visitors. In 1916, as the war raged, a storm blew in and devastated the old church tower, which collapsed down the cliff's edge into the sea along with many old tombstones. After the war, the cottage attracted a younger, less sedate crowd and in 1919, a year after her father's death, Louie was given notice by her landlord to leave the cottage. George Sims, still writing for *The Referee*, noted her departure in his column: "And now the hospitable reign of the Jermys in Poppyland has come to an end and the Old Mill House will know the joy of Louie's blackberry puddings no more. I stain the paper with a tributary tear."

Rescuing only few treasures from the auction block, Louie Jermy left the pristine cottage of her birth to live out her life in a nearby terrace home. Although she qualified for an old age pension, she refused it because it smacked of charity. For several years, she delighted the locals with poetry readings, wearing the same picture hat framed with poppies that she wore as a girl. When she died in 1934, her coffin was carried by four fishermen from the village and placed in her family plot in the churchyard, the "Garden of Sleep" of Scott's poem.

SOURCES:
Appleyard, Simon. "Poppyland," in *This England*. Autumn 1987, pp. 10–15.

Barbara Morgan,
Melrose, Massachusetts

Jerome, Jennie (1854–1921).
See Churchill, Jennie Jerome.

Jersey, countess of.
See Villiers, Margaret Elizabeth Child- (1849–1945).

Jersey Lily (1853–1929).
See Langtry, Lillie.

Jerusalem, queen of.
See Morphia of Melitene (fl. 1085–1120).
See Maria Comnena (fl. 1100s).
See Melisande (1105–1161).
See Adelaide of Savona (d. 1118).
See Agnes of Courtenay (1136–1186).
See Sibylla (1160–1190).
See Berengaria of Castile (b. around 1199).
See Isabella I of Jerusalem (d. 1205).
See Marie of Montferrat (d. 1212).
See Yolande of Brienne (1212–1228).
See Isabella of Cyprus (fl. 1250s).
See Charlotte of Lusignan (1442–1487).

Jerusha
Biblical woman. Name variations: *Jerushah. Married Uzziah, king of Judah; children: Jotham who succeeded his father.*

Jervey, Caroline Howard (1823–1877).
See Gilman, Caroline Howard for sidebar.

Jesenská, Milena (1896–1945)
Czech journalist and humanist who opposed the Nazis and was entrusted with the diaries of Franz Kafka. Name variations: *Milena Jesenska; Milena Křejcárova or Milena Krejcarova. Born Milena Jesenská in Prague, Czechoslovakia in 1896; died in Ravensbrück concentration camp on May 17, 1945; daughter of Jan Jesensky (a dentist and professor at the Charles University in Prague); attended Minerva School for Girls; married Ernst Polak (a Jewish translator), in 1918 (divorced 1924); married Jaromír Křejcár (an architect), in 1927; children: (second marriage) Honza Křejcár (b. around 1928).*

Milena Jesenská and *Margarete Buber-Neumann first met in the women's concentration camp at Ravensbrück in October 1940. Jesenská, a journalist who had just arrived from Prague, wanted to confirm rumors that the Soviets had handed anti-fascist refugees over to the Nazis, so she sought out the German anti-Stalinist Buber-Neumann. "Her face was prison-gray, marked with suffering," wrote Buber-Neumann in her book *Milena: The Story of a Remarkable Friendship*. "But my impression of illness was dissipated by the light in her eyes and the force of her movements." Hers was an "unbroken spirit, a free woman in the midst of the insulted and injured."

They began to meet daily. While Milena interviewed Margarete about her experiences in the Soviet Union, they discussed their mutual disenchantment with Communism and its failings. They agreed to write a book together when freed, a book about two dictatorships: Germany and Soviet Russia, entitled "The Age of Concentration Camps." At first, Buber-Neumann had laughed; she couldn't write, she said. But Jesenská would have none of it and proceeded to parcel out chapter responsibilities.

There were those in the Czech Communist community of Ravensbrück that found Jesenská's alliance with the German "Trotskyite" Buber-Neumann threatening, and they gave Milena an ultimatum: either drop the friendship or lose membership in their community. Milena

Milena
Jesenská

chose friendship and paid with ostracism. "Deep friendship is always a great gift," wrote Buber-Neumann. "But if such good fortune is experienced in the desolation of a concentration camp, it can become the content of a life. During our time together Milena and I succeeded in defeating the unbearable reality. And because it was so strong, because it filled our whole beings, our friendship became something more, an open protest against the humiliations imposed on us."

By the end of November, they began walking arm-in-arm, a practice strictly forbidden by the SS. "For me nothing existed but Milena's hand on my arm and the wish that this walk might never end." They lived in different barracks. With the constant threat of discovery, they met secretly, climbing out barracks windows, going where they should not go. Milena was audacious. She would wave furtively from the windows of the infirmary where she was working while Buber-Neumann stood at roll call, or she would arrive for a secret meeting whistling softly, "It's a long way to Tipperary."

Born in Prague in 1896, Milena Jesenská lived on the sixth floor of a large house on Wenceslaus Square. Her mother, thought to be artistic, came from a well-to-do Czech family who owned a spa near Náchod named Bad Beloves. Though Milena and her mother often clashed, her mother never spanked her. Her father, however, had no such compunctions; his punishments could be brutal. A dentist and professor at Charles University in Prague, Jan Jesensky was an ultraconservative provincial with a mean temper who was proud of his Spartan virtues: he slept on a hard pallet, took cold baths, dressed impeccably, and did his best to break the spirit of his more than spirited daughter. She lived in terror of him.

For years, while her father dallied with affairs, her mother suffered from pernicious anemia. Milena nursed her until her death when Milena was 13. Within two years, Milena was mentally and physically running loose, defying her father, railing against his "pseudomorality." In the beginning, she was also at odds with her father's sisters, the writers **Marie** and ✤▶ **Ružena Jesenská**. Ružena disliked Milena's ways, while Milena, who had become an ardent reader, disliked Ružena's "sentimental" writing. In later life, after Milena had proved herself as a writer, they became close.

Jesenská attended Minerva School for Girls, a secondary school whose prominent graduates included Dr. ***Alice Garrigue Masaryk**, daughter of Thomas Masaryk, the founder and president of the Czech Republic. Upon her graduation, Jan Jesensky enrolled his daughter in medical school and forced her to aid him in the treatment of soldiers with face wounds during World War I. Milena, who had far too much empathy for that sort of work, promptly dropped out of school. Fraternizing with all strata (she was oblivious to class lines, had great compassion, and could not stand to hurt anyone), Jesenská enjoyed the company of Czech and German intellectuals; she also became enmeshed in the bohemian feminist movement.

> [Milena] has learned time and again from her own experience that she can save another through her own existence and in no other way.
>
> —Franz Kafka, *Briefe an Milena*

Then, she met Ernst Polak at a concert and fell in love. He was ten years older, a Jew, a translator at a bank in Prague, and a mentor to many writers. Polak introduced Jesenská to Franz Kafka, Franz Werfel, Max Brod, Rudolf Fuchs, and Egon Erwin Kisch. She also became friends with **Wilma Lövenbach**, a friendship that would last for 20 years. (Wilma and Milena would compile an anthology of German translations of Czech verse, the first of its kind.) In June 1917, when her father learned of her affair with the Jewish Polak, he had her committed to a mental home at Veleslavin. While there, she wrote Max Brod: "Psychiatry is a terrible thing when misused. Anything can be interpreted as abnormal, and every word can provide the tormentor with a new weapon." Upon her release in March 1918, she married Polak and moved to Vienna. Jan Jesensky disinherited her and severed all connections.

The marriage had problems from the start. Polak believed in free love and indulged in numerous affairs; Milena, who tried to be broadminded, was deeply in love with him but missed Prague. While she gave Czech language lessons to pay the rent, Polak avidly participated in Vi-

---

✤▶ **Jesenská, Ružena** (1863–1940)
*Czech writer. Name variations: Ruzena Jesenska. Born in 1863; died in 1940; sister of Marie Jesenská (a writer); aunt of *Milena Jesenská.*

Ružena Jesenská wrote more than 50 collections of poetry, volumes of short stories, novels, plays and children's books.

ennese café society. Jesenská began writing articles and became the fashion correspondent for the Czech daily *Tribuna*. She also translated the works of Franz Kafka—*The Stoker, The Judgment, Metamorphosis,* and *Contemplation*—from German to Czech, and sent one of the translations to his publisher.

When Jesenská received a reply from Kafka, who was then taking the cure for tuberculosis in Meran, she journeyed there. She would write of their meeting in *The Way to Simplicity* (1926), a book she dedicated to her father, in hopes that he would begin to understand her. To Milena, Franz Kafka was a truly good man, despite his faults. Her father was cruel, despite his virtues. "Rigorously virtuous people are not necessarily the kindest," she observed, "but often on the contrary are dangerous and evil, whereas men with so-called faults are not infrequently far kinder and more tolerant."

The love affair between Kafka and Jesenská began at that meeting in Meran and lasted several years. Though she believed she "belonged" to her husband and could not leave him, Jesenská struck up a lively, intimate correspondence with Kafka, and they met once in Vienna and once in the Austrian town of Gmünd on the Czech border. But Kafka was frightened of love and there was no sexual consummation. The affair was "confined to letters," until Kafka's illness grew worse and, always fearful of life and its offerings, he asked her to stop writing. Jesenská was devastated. Though she stopped writing regularly, she continued to send postcards off and on. For two years, she arrived daily at the general delivery postal window in Vienna, hoping for a letter from him. Meanwhile, Kafka wrote Max Brod:

> You will talk with Milena, I shall never again have that joy. When you talk to her about me, speak as if I were dead. . . . When Ehrenstein came to see me recently, he said more or less that in M. life was holding out a hand to me and I had the choice between life and death, that was a little too high-sounding, not in regard to Milena but to me, but essentially true; the only stupid part was that he seemed to believe that a choice was open to me.

Despite this, Milena began to visit Kafka in later years, especially in 1922, when he was gravely ill, and he eventually entrusted her with his diaries. When he died in 1924, she wrote his obituary for Vienna's *Forum,* then put an end to her sham marriage. The following year, she returned to Prague, partially reconciled with her father, and began writing articles for his party paper, *Národní Listy,* eventually editing the women's page.

Now an established reporter, Jesenská was welcomed into Prague society but still preferred the company of intellectuals and artists. She fell in love with Jaromír Krějcár, a young architect who would go on to earn a worldwide reputation. They were married in 1927. For the next few years, Milena was truly happy, and their house was a gathering of architects, artists, and writers. Between 1926 and 1928, she published three books and edited, with a friend, the illustrated magazine, *Pestrý Týden.* Their tastes were a little too avant-garde, however, and they were replaced the following year.

With her first pregnancy came pain and a visit to a doctor; he assured Milena that there was nothing wrong and advised her not to be a "sissy." But after eight months of the same pain, she came down with chills and fever, was diagnosed with septicemia, and gave birth to a daughter (Honza). As Milena lay near death, her father sat by her bedside, ordering up morphine for his daughter, and never left. After a year of convalescence at a sanatarium, Milena recovered, but her left knee lost its flexibility and she walked with a limp. She had also become a morphine addict. One night, amid pain, sweat, and convulsions as she attempted to withdraw cold turkey, she saw a revolver on the table near her bed. Convinced that it was a not-so-veiled suggestion from Jaromír, who had been involved in numerous affairs, her heart hardened toward him. Much later, she realized that it might have been a hallucination. Feeling her life was meaningless, she stopped writing for her father's paper, joined the staff of a liberal paper, and in 1931 joined the Communist Party. Still fighting the morphine, she twice volunteered for detoxification. By 1936, Jesenská was disillusioned by the party, especially with Stalin's 1936 purges following his Moscow show trials, while the party, just as disillusioned with her unorthodox temperament, had her expelled.

Throughout their marriage, Jesenská and her husband had been in debt. In 1934, invited to design a home for convalescent workers in the Caucasus, Krějcár had gone to Russia, while Milena and Honza stayed behind. While there, he too grew disenchanted with the Soviets but fell in love with a Jewish Latvian named Riva. Two years later (1936), he divorced Milena and married Riva. Even so, he set aside a beautiful apartment for his ex-wife and daughter in one of his buildings in Prague.

In 1937, Ferdinand Peroutka, asked her to contribute to his liberal democratic journal, *Přítomnost (The Present).* A highly respected monthly, it became her salvation. She wrote of the rise in anti-Semitism and the death of Karel Capek; she wrote of Czech spirit and the need to unite; she wrote of Stalin's Great Purge and questioned the Soviets as to the whereabouts of Czech Communist workers who had gone to Russia and had yet to be heard from. She was now denouncing all threats to freedom—national socialism, fascism, and communism. Unlike many of her friends, she saw the handwriting on the wall.

In March 1939, Hitler's minions crossed the border into Czechoslovakia. At daybreak, Jesenská went out on the street to watch the taking of Prague:

> At half-past seven swarms of children were on their way to school as usual. Workers were on their way to their jobs as usual. The streetcars were packed as usual. Only the people were different. They stood there in silence. I have never heard so many people being so profoundly silent. No crowds formed. In the offices no one looked up from his desk. . . . At 9:35 the vanguard of Hitler's army reached the city center, German army trucks rumbled down Narodni Trida, the main street of Old Prague. As usual, the sidewalks were full of people, but no one turned to look. . . . I can't explain how it came about that thousands of people suddenly behaved in exactly the same way, that so many hearts, quite unknown to one another, beat in the same rhythm. . . . The German army was welcomed only by the German population of Prague.

As she watched the Germans invade the city, she said to a friend, "This is nothing. Just wait till the Russians get here."

Peroutka was quickly arrested, and Jesenská took over the editorship of the *Přítomnost*. She wrote cautiously, inserting warnings and subtleties into her articles, determined to keep the journal from being suppressed. She also founded an underground journal, *Vboj!* (*On with the Struggle!*), where her thoughts were less subtle. Her apartment became a hiding place for Jews, Czech officers, and aviators. Soon, it was a central meeting place, sometimes housing as many as ten. Wrote a friend, "Milena, who always wore a blue dress and welcomed every new arrival with a sweeping gesture of hospitality, comforted them all. She did it just by being there. In her presence, people somehow behaved better."

Nevertheless, she was far from careful and a little too defiant to make a good underground agent. When the Jews of Czechoslovakia were told to wear the Star of David, she sewed one on her clothes. In June 1939, she was told to cease publishing, though she continued to edit until August. But she began to worry about little Honza, now a mature 11, who had been distributing underground newspapers, and set about securing a safe haven for her daughter. It was too late. Soon after, while Honza was distributing papers, the Nazis followed her home. They arrested Milena and sent her to Pankrac Prison in Prague. Honza, who went to stay with Milena's father, would visit her mother periodically. A year later, Jesenská was sent to Ravensbrück. She never saw her daughter again.

While sequestered at Ravensbrück, Buber-Neumann and Jesenská kept their eyes open, mentally documenting everything around them, determined they would write their book. They met and talked of freedom. Buber-Neumann "saw a grassy path through the woods, sprinkled with bright spots of light." "What an incurable girl scout you are," cracked Jesenská. "I am an inveterate city slicker. My idea of freedom is a little restaurant somewhere in the Old Town of Prague."

For a breach of camp discipline (she had pushed some bread to the men's side through a crack in the wall), Buber-Neumann lost her job as *Blockälteste* and was transferred to Barracks No. 1, where she "lived under the same roof as Milena and slept in the bed next to hers." In October 1942, Margarete began working as secretary to SS Senior Overseer **Johanna Langefeld** (1900–1974), a decent woman who tried to retain some semblance of humanity. Buber-Neumann became her confidant and began using her position to help other inmates. For this, Langefeld was put under house arrest and separated from her child, while Buber-Neumann was thrown in solitary for 15 weeks and fed every four days.

Meanwhile, Jesenská, who had always suffered from poor health, had her first attack of nephritis. During the winter of 1944 as Buber-Neumann sat in solitary, Milena grew sicker. When one of her kidneys became ulcerated, the infirmary doctor convinced Milena that her only hope was to have it removed. For four months, she was bedridden in the infirmary, while Buber-Neumann, who had been released, broke rule after rule to visit her daily for a quarter hour. In April 1945, Jesenská's other kidney became ulcerated, and she died on May 17. "Life had lost all meaning for me," wrote Buber-Neumann: "I recovered my freedom and carried out Milena's last will by writing *our* book about concentration camps. Shortly before her death she had said to me one day: 'I know that you at least will not forget me. Through you I shall live.'"

SOURCES:

Buber-Neumann, Margarete. *Milena: The Story of a Remarkable Friendship*. Trans. from the German by Ralph Manheim. NY: Seaver Books, 1988.

Glatzer, Nahum N. *The Loves of Franz Kafka*. NY: Schocken Books, 1986.

Kafka, Franz. *Letters to Milena*. Edited by Willi Haas. Trans. by Tania and James Stern. NY: Schocken Books, 1965.

SUGGESTED READING:

Hockaday, Mary. *Kafka, Love and Courage: The Life of Milena Jesenská*. Overlook, 1997.

Jesenska, Ružena (1863–1940).

See Jesenská, Milena for sidebar.

Jesse, Fryniwyd Tennyson
(1888–1958)

Fryniwyd Tennyson Jesse

English playwright and novelist. Name variations: F. Tennyson Jesse; Fryn Jesse. Born Wynifried Margaret Jesse on March 1, 1888, in Chislehurst, Kent, England; died on August 6, 1958, in London, England; the second of three daughters of Reverend Eustace Tennyson d'Eyncourt and Edith Louisa (James) Jesse; attended boarding school in Paris; studied art at the Newlyn School, Cornwell; married Harold Marsh Harwood (a playwright), on September 9, 1918.

Plays: (with H.M. Harwood) The Mask *(1912);* (with Harwood) Billeted *(1917);* (adapted from the French with Harwood) The Hotel Mouse *(1921);* Quarantine *(1922);* (with Harwood) The Pelican *(1924);* Anyhouse *(1925);* (with Harwood) How to be Healthy though Married *(1930);* (with Harwood) A Pin to See the Peepshow *(1948);* Birdcage *(1949).*

Novels: The Milky Way *(1913),* Secret Bread *(1917),* Tom Fool *(1926),* Moonraker *(1927),* The Lacquer Lady *(1929),* A Pin to See the Peepshow *(1934),* Act of God *(1937),* The Alabaster Cup *(1950),* The Dragon in the Heart *(1956); crime novels:* Murder and its Motives *(1924),* Comments on Cain *(1948).*

Nonfiction: The Sword of Deborah: First Hand Impressions of the British Women's Army in France *(1919);* The White Riband *(1921);* Sabi Pas *(1935);* The Saga of San Demetrio *(1942);* The Story of Burma *(1946).*

Short stories: Beggars on Horseback *(1915);* Many Latitudes *(1928);* The Solange Stories *(1931); Poems:* The Happy Bride *(1920);* The Compass *(1951).*

"Notable British trials" series: Madeleine Smith *(1927);* Samuel Herbert Dougal *(1928);* Sidney Harry Fox *(1934);* Rattenbury and Stoner *(1935);* Ley and Smith *(1947);* Evans and Christie *(1957).*

Playwright and author Fryniwyd Jesse was christened Wynifried Margaret Jesse, the second of three daughters of Reverend Eustace Tennyson Jesse and **Edith James Jesse**. Her older sister **Stella** was unofficially adopted by her maternal grandparents and her younger sister Ermyntrude died as a baby, so Fryn grew up virtually an only child. A bout of rickets as a baby left her thin and sickly, and her early life was further complicated by her detached parents, who traveled extensively without her. Jesse arrived at her unusual name (Fryniwyd) by first shortening Wynifried to Fee as a child. That name eventually evolved into Fryn, then, in her late teens, into Fryniwyd. For her pseudonym, Jesse incorporated the family name Tennyson. (Her paternal grandmother was *Emily Tennyson, sister of the poet Alfred, Lord Tennyson.)

Jesse attended boarding school in Paris and then embarked on art studies at the Newlyn School in Cornwell, England, a painters' colony run by Stanhope and **Elizabeth Armstrong Forbes**. Here, for the first time, Jesse lived in the company of people her own age. Here, too, she wrote a modest biography, *The Look Backwards,* and edited a little magazine called *The Paper Chase,* to which she also contributed stories and poetry. When her poetry began to show promise, she decided to trade an artistic career for that of a writer. During her early years, she worked as a reporter for *The Times* and the *Daily Mail* and wrote book reviews for the *English Review,* which also published her first short story "The Mask," the success of which led to the publication of her first novel *The Milky Way* (1913), and a collaboration with playwright Harold Marsh Harwood ("Tottie"), on an adaptation of "The Mask" for the stage.

During World War I, Jesse traveled to the Belgian front as a war correspondent for the *Daily Mail,* one of the first women so assigned. Her stories, commended as well-written and newsworthy, were later picked up by the *Pall Mall Gazette.* She was later assigned by the Ministry of Information to report on the Women's Army, which resulted in the book *The Sword of Deborah: First Hand Impressions of the British Women's Army in France.* The book, published after the war in 1919, provided an honest and unglamorous look at the role of the WAACs (Women's Auxiliary Army Corps), the FANYs (First Aid Nursing Yeomanry), and the VADs (Voluntary Aid Detachment) in the war effort. On the dust jacket, Jesse noted: "It appears to me that people should still be told about the women workers of the war and what they did, even now when we are all struggling back into our chiffons—perhaps more now than ever. For we should not forget, and how should we remember if we have never known." Throughout her life, Jesse continued to speak out for women, particularly as an advocate of divorce and abortion rights.

In September 1918, Jesse had secretly married Harwood in a casual ceremony before he left for a posting in Syria, although she later admitted that she did not love him at the time, but grew into love after the marriage. (The union would suffer periods of intense strain, abetted by Jesse's ill health and bouts of depression caused by her inability to have a child.) By the time of their wedding, the couple had collaborated on several other plays, including *The Pelican* (1916) and *Billeted* (1917), and they would later write *How to be Healthy though Married* (1930). Jesse also wrote two plays on her own: *Quarantine* (1922) and *Anyhouse* (1925), but her greatest success was in collaboration.

Jesse's first mature novel, *The White Riband* (1921), about an illegitimate orphan girl who passionately wants to dance, was extremely well-received. Joseph Conrad called it "this jewel in a casket," and St. John Ervine referred to Jesse as "a genius insufficiently recognized." Among her subsequent novels, *Tom Fool* (1926), a historical novel, *Moonraker; or The French Pirate and her Friends* (1927), a role-reversal adventure about a female pirate, and *The Lacquer Lady* (1929), inspired by a trip to Burma, are notable. Jesse was also interested in criminology and her first crime novel *Murder and its Motives* (1924) was called "an informative, provocative and masterly study" by the *Police Review* and "a fascinating piece of work" by *The Sketch.* Harry Hodge, then editor of the "Notable British Trials" series, was so impressed that he hired Jesse; she worked for him for many years. A later crime novel, *A Pin to See the Peep Show* (1934), was based on the notorious Thompson-Bywaters case of 1922, in which a young wife **Edith Thompson** was convicted for the murder of her husband, a crime which had actually been carried out by her lover Frederick Bywaters. Jesse's body of work also includes a book of poems, *The Happy Bride* (1920), and two collections of short stories, *Beggars on Horseback* (1915) and *Many Latitudes* (1928). She also published a volume of letters, *While London Burns* (1942), and a travel book, *The Story of Burma* (1946). Michael Swan in London's *Sunday Times* called her last novel, *The Dragon in the Heart* (1956), "a tearjerker in an old tradition."

The author was plagued by cataracts during her later life and died in 1958, just as she had begun to dictate the story of her life. In Jesse's obituary for *The Times,* *Rebecca West described her as "a skillful, amusing, clandestine sort of feminist, never tired of getting in an adroit plea for the dignity and independence of womankind."

SOURCES:

Colenbrander, Joanna. *A Portrait of Fryn: A Biography of F. Tennyson Jesse.* London: André Deutsch, 1984.

Shattock, Joanne. *The Oxford Guide to British Women Writers.* Oxford and NY: Oxford University Press, 1993.

Barbara Morgan,
Melrose, Massachusetts

Jessye, Eva (1895–1992)

African-American composer, musician, and choral director. Born on January 20, 1895, in Coffeyville, Kansas; died in 1992; daughter of Al Jessye and Julia (Buckner) Jessye; attended public schools in Kansas, Missouri, and Washington; graduated from Western University, Quindaro, Kansas, 1914; received teach-

ing certificate from Langston University, Langston, Oklahoma, 1916; never married; no children.

Often referred to as "the dean of black female musicians," Eva Jessye was born in 1895 in Coffeyville, Kansas. Her parents separated when she was three, and she was brought up by her mother's family, who encouraged her to develop her natural gifts. At 13, she was accepted early at Western University in Quindaro, Kansas, and after graduation went on to receive a teaching certificate at Langston University in Oklahoma. She directed the music department at Morgan State College in Baltimore and was a newspaper reporter before moving to New York in 1926. There, she joined and later directed the Dixie Jubilee Singers, which eventually became the Eva Jessye Choir and performed regularly at the Capitol Theater. In 1929, Jessye took the choir to Hollywood to perform in King Vidor's film *Hallelujah*, the first African-American musical. "I knew how to put little moans and groans and things that would make it real," she later said about her work on the project.

In 1934, Jessye served as the choral director for the experimental opera *Four Saints in Three Acts* by Virgil Thomson and *Gertrude Stein. Early in 1935, George Gershwin asked Jessye to be choral director for his new folk opera *Porgy and Bess*. Assisting Gershwin in authenticating the score, which she termed "quite white," Jessye and her choir performed on opening night (October 10, 1935), and she later became known as the "Guardian of the Score," having in her possession the original arrangement of the opera with Gershwin's handwritten instructions.

Over the years, Jessye combined teaching with her ongoing choir work, which included a fund-raising Victory Tour during World War II and a 1944 appearance at the American Soviet Friendship Day ceremonies at Madison Square Garden in New York and, later, at the Watergate Theater in Washington, D.C. (for which she also composed the theme music). In 1963, the choir performed for Martin Luther King, Jr.'s March on Washington.

Eva Jessye established music collections in her name at the University of Michigan (Ann Arbor) and Pittsburg State University in Kansas. Kansas was also the place where she did much of her composing, and her best-known compositions *Chronicle of Job* and *Paradise Lost and Regained* were performed there, along with smaller works. Jessye was named one of the six most outstanding women in Kansas history and in 1978 was honored at "Eva Jessye Day." Among her subsequent awards and honors was a tribute to her work held at the Apollo Theater in New York in 1985. Eva Jessye eventually settled in Michigan, remaining healthy and vibrant well into her 90s. In her later years, she wrote poetry and worked on her autobiography and a history of *Porgy and Bess*. She died in 1992, age 97.

SOURCES:

Bailey, Brooke. *The Remarkable Lives of 100 Women Artists*. Holbrook, MA: Bob Adams, 1994.

Smith, Jessie Carney, ed. *Notable Black American Women*. Detroit, MI: Gale Research, 1992.

Barbara Morgan,
Melrose, Massachusetts

Jesús, Carolina Maria de
(c. 1913–1977)

Author of the bestselling work Child of the Dark: The Diary of Carolina Maria de Jesús, *which detailed the misery of life in a Brazilian shanty town. Name variations: Bitita; Carolina de Jesus. Pronunciation: Kah-ro-LEE-nah Mah-REE-ah day HAY-soos. Born Carolina Maria de Jesús in either 1913 or 1914 in Sacramento, Minas Gerais, Brazil; died in Parelheiros of asthma on February 13, 1977; daughter of an unknown father and a mother who was an unmarried farm worker; attended elementary school for two years; never married; children: three illegitimate, João (b. around 1947); José Carlos (b. around 1949); Vera Eunice (b. 1953).*

Very little is known of the childhood of Carolina Maria de Jesús. In general terms, the history of her family, such as it was, probably resembled that of many of Brazil's uprooted rural population that moved from the country into the crowded and fetid shanty towns that migrants built around major cities. Carolina was born in 1913 or 1914—or even 1921 according to one source—to a mother who was an unwed farm worker in Sacramento in the state of Minas Gerais. Carolina, in her diary, claims to have picked cotton. If so, it was likely during this period of her life. Her education was rudimentary, although in her two years of school she did learn to read and write, two skills that would later catapult her into international prominence.

When she was a teenager, de Jesús' mother moved to Franca, near the metropolitan center of São Paulo. There Carolina briefly held a job in a hospital and then ran away. Employment over the next few years was haphazard as she sang in a circus, sold beer, and did housecleaning chores in a hotel. In the late 1930s, perhaps 1937, de Jesús, according to Robert Levine, "followed a migration pattern typical of poor Brazilian women in setting out on her own from Franca to the big city of São Paulo, where she slept under bridges and in doorways until hired by a white family." Her employment was terminated after four months because, in her own words: "I was too independent and didn't like to clean up their messes. Besides, I used to slip out of the house at night and make love."

Levine notes that de Jesús claims to have worked for a brief time for a physician, Euricledes Zerbini, who allowed her access to his library, and a general, Goés Monteiro, an eminent figure in the 1937–45 government of the Estado Novo (New Order). But she seemed unable to hold a job for any lengthy period of time, and employment and dismissals followed one another with regularity. It was in 1947 that she was impregnated by a Portuguese sailor "who got on his ship fast when I told him I was going to have a baby." With the arrival of her first son, Joâo, she was forced to move to a *favela,* or shanty town, because with a baby she could not find regular work. Levine reports that de Jesús selected the *favela* of Canindé because of its proximity to a junkyard. She was aware that junkyards paid cash for scrap paper and salvage and so, "with her son strapped to her back she walked the streets of São Paulo looking for trash." Food was purchased with the small sums of money she earned for her scrap; her rations were supplemented by what could be scavenged from the garbage cans of the rich or in the decaying detritus of a slaughterhouse.

In 1949, de Jesús, who described herself as attractive and attracted to men, became pregnant by a Spaniard "who was white and gave me love and money." He returned to Europe before de Jesús gave birth to her second son, José Carlos. Similar language was used to describe the conception of her third child. It was in 1952 that she "met a rich white man who thought I was pretty. I would visit him and he would give me food and money to buy clothes for my sons. He didn't know for a long time that I bore his daughter." Vera Eunice was born on July 15, 1953.

In her diary, de Jesús consistently sees herself as a "loner" in the *favela,* distrusted by her neighbors and an object of abuse. Set apart by her ability to read and write, de Jesús was accused of putting on "airs." She struck back in her diary and cursed what she saw as the violent, lying behavior of the *favelados.* Those from the northeast were especially disliked by de Jesús because of their violence and unpredictability. She escaped from reality in her writing, "for when I

was writing I was in a golden palace, with crystal windows and silver chandeliers. My dress was finest satin and diamonds sat shining in my black hair." And then reality intruded. "Then I put away my book and the smells came in through the rotting walls and rats ran over my feet. My satin turned to rags and the only things shining in my hair were lice."

> *B*razil needs to be led by a person who has known hunger. Hunger is also a teacher.
> —Carolina Maria de Jesús

Carolina's testimony demands a careful reading of the text, for her written notes on occasion seem to contradict the reality of her life in Canindé. Brazilian scholars cited by Levine note that de Jesús' self-proclaimed antagonistic relationship with her fellow *favelados* was exaggerated. Indeed, even though she felt isolated "she was viewed within the favela as a stable person who could be trusted." Her ability to read and write commanded respect. Homeless or delinquent children discharged from the Fundação Estadual para o Bem-Estar do Menor (State Institution for the Wellbeing of Children) were often released to her care. Also noted by Levine's sources was the fact that it was de Jesús who was expected to call the police to quell a fight, i.e., "she acted as an agent of stability and decency in the sordid world of the favela."

Carolina's world changed dramatically in April 1958 when she came to the attention of Audálio Dantas, a reporter for the *Diário da Noite.* While he was covering the inauguration of a playground, an altercation broke out among men competing for space on the children's seesaw. De Jesús admonished them and threatened to write their names in her book. Intrigued, Dantas asked her about the book. De Jesús took him back to her 4'x12" shack built with boards taken from a construction site and roofed with flattened tin cans and cardboard and showed him her notebooks. He cared little for the stories and poems but focused attention on her diary. With her grudging permission, he took three years' worth of diary notes back to his paper and published excerpts in the next day's issue.

Carolina's insights into the life of the *favela* produced a brief flurry of attention, and Dantas used his coup to good professional advantage. He was offered a position as chief of the São Paulo bureau of *O Cruzeiro,* Brazil's largest circulation weekly newsmagazine. Dantas edited the diaries for the next year when they were published under the title *Quarto de Despejo* (Room of Garbage).

On the first day the diary was in print, de Jesús autographed 600 copies and in less than six months sales exceeded 90,000 copies. Eventually her work was translated into 13 languages and was published in 40 countries. De Jesús was, for a brief time, the focus of the media, politicians, and intellectuals anxious to learn more of the "culture of poverty." The labor minister told the press that the state would give de Jesús and her children the brick house for which she longed. Levine suggests that the diary became a sensation "less because it revealed secrets or truths about slum life in Brazil than because it had been written by a slumdwelling self-taught woman who refused to play by the rules and demanded the right to dream of elevating herself and her children on her own terms."

But intellectuals were quickly disenchanted with de Jesús, for her diary was not the dry tinder needed to ignite revolutions. While she was aware of racism and its impact on poor Brazilian blacks, her attention was consistently drawn to the central issue of hunger and the daily struggle to find enough to eat. The poor were not summoned to confront the system. Historian George Reid Andrews noted: "Food, housing, drinkable water, sewers, personal safety, a job—any of these immediate, concrete concerns ranks higher on poor blacks' lists of priorities than the more elusive, abstract goal of racial equality." Responsibility for the plight of the *favelados* was largely placed in the shanty towns by de Jesús. She cursed their preference for "drunken idleness, cursing and fornication to working or self-improvement." To middle-class Brazilians, she seemed more of a curiosity than a threat.

Carolina's description of what she called reality allowed her to leave the *favela*. The royalties from her book were sufficient for her to move her family into a small brick house in the working-class neighborhood of Imirim. For a few months, de Jesús was invited to speak about life in the *favela* on radio and television. She toured Argentina, Chile, and Uruguay, and in Sâo Paulo, four months after the publication of her diary, she was named an honorary citizen and was presented with the key to the city. Sociology professors in Brazil placed her book on their list of required readings; the Faculty of Law of the University of Sâo Paulo made her an honorary member.

In public, de Jesús proved to be an aggressive and unsettling speaker and refused to reflect the image ascribed to her. She was supposed to offer a testimonial, in keeping with the expectations of a male-dominated society about the role of women in Brazilian society. On the attack, de Jesús soon provoked a counterattack by both journalists and politicians. Levine argues that Brazil's elite and middle class rejected her "because she did not fit their image of how a protester from the slums should behave. . . . Because de Jesús never failed to touch a nerve, she had to be relegated to obscurity quickly." She was treated more kindly by foreign critics. Venezuelan journalist and writer Carlos Rangel explained that for North Americans she fit their expectations of a hero as one who "came from nowhere to achieve glory and fortune."

But de Jesús' glory was fleeting, and she never achieved fortune. Not accepted by her new neighbors and bothered by the incessant surveillance of curiosity seekers, de Jesús was unhappy in her brick home. Her second book, *Casa de Alvenaria: Diário de uma Ex-Favelada* (*The Brick House: Diary of an Ex-Slumdweller*), was published in November 1961 and mirrored her disenchantment. Stung by the rejection of her working-class neighbors, she struck an aggressive tone in the book which, in Levine's terms, "might have been acceptable from a white-skinned radical student or intellectual but was intolerable from a black woman who lacked public manners." Where her first book placed primary blame on the *favelados* for their misery, in *Casa de Alvenaria* she attacked politicians and reformers. Some considered her a communist. It is possible that Audálio Dantas, whom de Jesús accused of trying to manipulate both her life and her writing, may have altered her prose and added an air of stridency through embellishment. While de Jesús' criticism was strong, it was not perceived as threatening by the military dictatorship which had swept into power in 1964. She consistently refused the revolutionary mantle that critics of the military regime offered. When some urged her to attack the regime within a context of social justice, she refused. Indeed, on at least one occasion, she praised General Ernesto Geisel and asserted that people liked his government.

Just as her fame was fleeting so, too, was her fortune. It is likely that she never received a fair share of royalties from her book, for by the late 1960s she was again living on the edge of poverty. One Brazilian newspaper in 1967 printed a photo of her scavenging in the streets of Sâo Paulo. The media were unrelenting in their attack on de Jesús. They mocked her manners and her clothing; they resented the fact that she refused to accommodate the expectations of the public. As Levine wrote: "She refused to conform . . . and paid the price."

Carolina's third book, *Provérbios de Carolina Maria de Jesús*, exhausted what money she had set aside. Publishers were no longer interested in the ex-*favelada*, and she had to subsidize its production. Her last book, *Pedaços da Fome* (*Bits of Hunger*), also published in 1969, attracted little attention. In that year, she moved away from her brick house to Parelheiros, an area of marginal housing on the fringes of the suburban zone. There she tended her garden while her children attended school. One journalist in 1973, as reported by Levine, said that she lived on the level of a "typical poor Brazilian *caboclo*" (an unmannered rustic).

West German television produced a documentary about her life and paid de Jesús $2,500 for the film rights. Over the protests of the Brazilian ambassador, it was broadcast in Europe. The film was censored in Brazil.

On February 13, 1977, Carolina Maria de Jesús died from an acute attack of asthma. A posthumous collection of previously unpublished bits of her diary was published in France and, in 1986, in Brazil. It was entitled *Diário de Bitita*, and its publication passed in virtual silence.

SOURCES:

Andrews, George Reid. *Blacks and Whites in São Paulo, Brazil, 1888–1988.* Madison, WI: University of Wisconsin Press, 1991.

Jesús, Carolina Maria de. *Child of the Dark: The Diary of Carolina Maria de Jesús.* Translated by David St. Clair. NY: Signet, 1962.

Levine, Robert M. "The Cautionary Tale of Carolina Maria de Jesús," in *Latin American Research Review.* Vol. 29, no. 1, 1994, pp. 55–83.

SUGGESTED READING:

Jesús, Carolina Maria de. *I'm Going to Have a Little House: The Second Diary of Carolina Maria de Jesús.* University of Nebraska Press, 1997.

Perlman, Janice E. *The Myth of Marginality: Urban Poverty and Politics in Rio de Janeiro.* Berkeley, CA: University of California Press, 1976.

Salazar, Claudia. "A Third World Woman's Text: Between the Politics of Criticism and Cultural Politics," in *Women's Words: The Feminist Practice of Oral History.* Edited by Sherna Berger Gluck and Daphne Patai. NY: Routledge, 1991, pp. 93–106.

Paul B. Goodwin, Jr.,
Professor of History,
University of Connecticut, Storrs, Connecticut

Jewett, Sarah Orne (1849–1909)

American author who is best known for her depictions of rural life on the coast of Maine. Name variations: First name was Theodora, rarely used. Born Theodora Sarah Orne Jewett in South Berwick, Maine, on September 3, 1849; died on June 24, 1909, at her birthplace; daughter of Theodore Herman Jewett (a rural doctor) and Caroline Frances (Perry) Jewett; graduated from Berwick Academy in 1865; never married; primary relationship was with Annie Adams Fields for approximately 30 years.

Published her first short story at 17; in addition to her short stories, wrote numerous children's books, several popular histories, and three novels; best known for The Country of the Pointed Firs *(1896), a novel hailed by many critics as one of the best in American literature.*

Selected writings: Deephaven *(1877);* Country By-Ways *(1881);* A Country Doctor *(1884);* A White Heron and Other Stories *(1886);* The Story of the Normans, Told Chiefly in Relation to Their Conquest of England *(1887);* The King of Folly Island and Other People *(1888);* Strangers and Wayfarers *(1890);* A Native of Winby and Other Tales *(1893);* The Country of the Pointed Firs *(1896);* The Tory Lover *(1901).*

In the years after the Civil War, America was changing rapidly, lurching forward into a new era of urbanization and industrialization. An old way of life seemed to be dying, a new one was being born, and for those living through this transformation, both experiences could be painful. Just graduating from high school when the war ended, Sarah Orne Jewett was saddened and alarmed by the way these economic changes were affecting life along the coast of Maine. In harbors, wooden clipper ships floated still and empty, rotting on their moorings. In Jewett's home town of Berwick, a few miles from the coast along the tidal Piscataqua River, shipyards that had once turned Maine timber into beautiful four-masted vessels were now abandoned. Maine's golden age of commercial shipping was passing, as wooden sailboats were replaced by more efficient steamships and the railroad.

The town of Berwick was changing with the times, taking advantage of the nation's rapid industrial and commercial growth. New factories were being built, and Jewett's hometown grew into a bustling commercial center for the region. In her mind, this was not progress, but a step in the wrong direction. "Berwick is growing and flourishing," she told a friend, "in a way that breaks my heart."

Jewett was particularly concerned about the way the new industry of tourism was changing life in Maine's beautiful seaport towns. Adapting to the loss of shipbuilding and shipping, Mainers in the late-19th century discovered a new way to make a living from the sea, by catering to wealthy urban visitors who began to flock to the state's rocky coast each summer. These tourists brought much-needed dollars, but with some unwelcome side effects. Working ports were turned into resorts for the rich. Men and women who had once looked out to sea and around the world for their livings, now served the whims of city people who often looked upon them only as ignorant hicks, quaint and simple folk who were part of the scenery.

Jewett had a unique vantage point from which to view this clash of urban and rural cultures. She had grown up in Berwick, spending all her young life among its fishermen, farmers, and townspeople. But she was also the daughter of the local doctor, and granddaughter of one of the town's wealthiest merchants. She had one foot in rural Maine culture and the other in genteel upper-class society. Thus, when she began to write stories at the age of 17, she determined to bridge the gap between these two worlds. She decided to write about the everyday lives of working women and men on the coast of Maine, revealing what urbane visitors from Boston and New York had so often missed: the physical and moral strength, the nobility of soul, that Jewett had found in her neighbors.

Sarah Orne Jewett

In this literary project, Sarah Orne Jewett enjoyed remarkable success. In the late 19th century, she published dozens of stories, sketches, and novels about life on the Maine coast, preserving a rich literary record of a way of life that she knew was passing away. Her contemporaries recognized her as a master of the genre which we now call regionalism, or local color. But modern-day literary critics feel she did much more than compile a nostalgic record of an interesting time and place in America's past. In their view, she not only captured her subject but transcended it, creating works that still have great significance for modern readers. In Jewett's descriptions of the changes occurring along the Maine coast 100 years ago, some critics find an early and eloquent advocate of environmentalism. Other scholars have found, in Jewett's portraits of strong and independent Maine women, an important literary ancestor to the 20th-century feminist movement.

On both sides of her family, Jewett could trace her own ancestry back to some of the earliest founders of colonial New England. In the early 19th century, her grandfather had made a fortune trading Maine timber for West Indies rum and molasses. He settled his family in an impressive mansion in the center of South Berwick, a prosperous shipbuilding town just over the New Hampshire border. When his son Theodore Herman Jewett married **Caroline Frances Perry** and started a family, Grandfather Jewett built them a comfortable Greek Revival house next door. There Sarah was born in 1849, the first of three daughters. The Jewetts were a loving and close-knit family, and their house became a central gathering place for numerous relatives, friends, neighbors and summer visitors.

Though she grew up in the midst of this congenial and bustling household, and played a full role in family activities, Jewett still remembered her childhood as "solitary." She developed an early passion for reading, a habit easily indulged since both of her parents were voracious readers and their house was overflowing with books. But, even more than in the library, Jewett sought solitude in nature. She loved the woods and fields of Berwick and often wandered them alone, observing birds, studying plants, and exploring salt marshes and meadows. As she grew older, she ventured farther away, becoming an excellent rower and horseback rider.

Attending the local Berwick Academy, Jewett proved to be a gifted but undisciplined student. As she later put it, she suffered "instant drooping" when confined in a classroom. Making matters more difficult, she endured severe bouts of rheumatoid arthritis, a painful inflammation of her joints which often kept her out of school and plagued her for the rest of her life. Jewett received her true education, then, from her doctor father. As he made his rounds, Theodore often invited her to come along, glad to have the company and sure that the fresh air would be good for his daughter's health. Traveling country roads in his wagon, Theodore Jewett acquainted his daughter with literature, philosophy, theology, Maine history, local plants and herbs.

Jewett learned even more when they arrived at each destination. While the doctor attended his patients, his daughter was often invited in for a visit. In this way, she got an intimate look at the daily lives of Maine people at all ends of the social spectrum. Without realizing it, she absorbed the language, customs, values, and personal histories of her neighbors, storing up material she would one day use in her writing.

Theodore Jewett encouraged his daughter's independent spirit. While the options available to young women in the late 19th century were usually severely restricted by cultural convention, he seems to have imposed no such limits on her aspirations. Perhaps in part for this reason, Jewett idolized her father, once describing him as "the best and wisest man I ever knew." For a short time, she thought she might follow him into the field of medicine. But, never one for disciplined study, she wavered, still unsure of her true calling.

Jewett had been writing stories throughout her adolescence and, at age 17, she won a small but immediate success by having her first submission accepted for publication. The appearance of "Jenny Garrow's Lovers" in a regional literary magazine gave the young author an important vote of encouragement, but the story, a stock romantic tale set in England, has otherwise been dismissed by critics. Very quickly, Jewett realized that she would do better to write about the world she knew. Following her father's advice, she determined that she would try to "write about things *just as they are.*"

For the next decade, Jewett went through what biographer **Paula Blanchard** has called "a long and silent apprenticeship," working hard at finding her true voice. Most of the stories she drafted in her 20s were moralistic tales, published in children's magazines. But she also wrote some of the first sketches of Maine life which would soon become her trademark. With remarkable confidence, she submitted these to the *Atlantic Monthly,* then the nation's premier literary magazine. Editor William Dean Howells returned most of her earliest efforts, but always included encouraging comments and helpful criticisms. "You've got an uncommon feeling for *talk,*" he praised her. "I *hear* your people." Keep writing about the people and places you know best, he advised, and write from a woman's point of view.

> *I* determined to teach the world that country people were not the awkward, ignorant set [that city people] seemed to think. I wanted the world to know their grand, simple lives.
>
> —**Sarah Orne Jewett**

By the late 1870s, Jewett's hard work paid off. Her "Deephaven Sketches" appeared in the *Atlantic* and were then published in book form in 1877. For the next two decades, she produced a new volume almost every year. Howells continued to serve as one of her most supportive editors and critics, publishing her best pieces and sending back the rest for revision. The two became close friends, and this friendship brought Jewett into the inner circle of Boston's literary elite. She moved to the city and was soon socializing with *Louise Imogen Guiney, *Laura E. Richards, Henry Wadsworth Longfellow, Ralph Waldo Emerson, John Greenleaf Whittier, James Russell Lowell and the rest of Boston's leading writers and artists.

While in Boston, Jewett befriended James and ❦ Annie Adams Fields, the couple who, as publishers and literary critics, had presided over New England's cultural life for decades. When James died in 1881, Sarah grew closer to Annie, a friendship which soon grew into the most important in Jewett's life. For the rest of their days, the two spent many months each year together, sharing Annie's home in Cambridge. In the minds of their friends, they were an inseparable couple, joined in a same-sex partnership that was then known as a "Boston marriage."

This intimate and intense friendship between Sarah and Annie has led biographers to speculate about Jewett's sexuality, some suggesting that she was a lesbian. There is no evidence that she was ever romantically attracted to any man, and she clearly rejected the idea of a traditional marriage, believing that it would end her personal and artistic freedom. Yet there is also no evidence to suggest that her relationship with Fields, or with any of her other close female

❦ *See sidebar on the following page*

❧ Fields, Annie Adams (1834–1915)

American poet, essayist, literary host, and social welfare worker. Born Anne Adams in Boston, Massachusetts, on June 6, 1834; died in 1915; second wife of James Thomas Fields (a partner in the prestigious Boston publishing firm of Ticknor & Fields and publisher and editor of the Atlantic Monthly, *who died in 1881); lived with Sarah Orne Jewett.*

Annie Adams' marriage to James T. Fields, who was 17 years her senior, placed her smack in the center of New England's literary society. Because of her keen critical eye, she was often consulted by her husband in choosing manuscripts for publication. Annie Fields befriended many literary women, including *Celia Thaxter, and most important, *Sarah Orne Jewett. The Fieldses' Beacon Hill home became a hub for writers, including Longfellow, Hawthorne, Lowell, and Emerson. Fields was also a leading figure in charity work, founding the Associated Charities of Boston. After her husband's death, she published a book of poems entitled *Under the Olive* (1881), as well as *The Biography of James T. Fields* (1884), *How to Help the Poor* (1885), *Authors and Their Friends* (1896), *A Shelf of Old Books* (1896), *Life and Letters of *Harriet Beecher Stowe* (1897), and a handbook for charity workers, *The Singing Shepherd* (1896), that sold 22,000 copies in two years.

SUGGESTED READING:

Howe, M.A. DeWolfe. *Memories of a Hostess,* 1922.

friends, was sexual, at least in the 20th-century meaning of that term. Most biographers conclude that, like many other Victorian era middle-class women, Jewett channeled her passion into the creation of intimate, loving, sisterly relationships with a network of female friends. Biographer **Elizabeth Silverthorne** sums up Sarah and Annie's relationship in this way: "In their rich, fulfilling companionship the two women found security and freedom to pursue their independent goals."

Through this friendship with Annie Fields, Jewett was connected to the literary elite on both sides of the Atlantic. The two women traveled to Europe together, visiting great writers and artists, and enjoying the landmarks of European art and culture. Despite these broadening influences in Jewett's life, she never wavered in her artistic purpose and continued to write about the people of rural Maine. Her reputation grew through the 1880s and 1890s. Some critics complained that her stories and novels often lacked effective plots, a "flaw" that Jewett was quick to admit herself. "It seems to me I can furnish the theater," she wrote, "and show you the actors, and the scenery, and the audience, but there never is any play!" She was much more effective at capturing the subtle ebb and flow of ordinary lives, the webs of history and sympathy that bound together the residents of Maine's isolated coastal communities.

And Jewett was always at her best when describing the Maine landscape. Critic Van Wyck Brooks described her sketches as "light as smoke or wisps of sea-fog, charged with the odours of mint, wild roses and balsam." As this comment suggests, one theme which infuses all of Jewett's work is the value of nature. In many of her stories, the noble qualities of her characters are amplified, and their petty evils dwarfed, by the majestic backdrop of their lives—the vast sea, the unyielding granite and the blue-green firs of the Maine coast. Following in the footsteps of Henry David Thoreau, a writer whom she admired, Jewett filled her stories with detailed observations about the plants and animals of her region, the changing moods of New England weather, and the feel of each new season.

Also like Thoreau, she protested against the destructive power of her own society, warning of its tendency to use and waste nature unthinkingly. Perhaps the finest example of her environmental awareness can be found in one of her best-loved stories, *The White Heron.* In this tale, Sylvia, a shy Maine girl living in a remote cabin with her grandmother, encounters a kind young man hiking through the woods. He is a visitor from the city, an ornithologist who is spending his vacation hunting for a rare white heron to add to his collection of stuffed birds. He offers the girl a handsome reward of ten dollars if she can lead him to the heron's hiding place. Tempted by these riches, Sylvia wakes at dawn, climbs to the peak of an ancient pine, and there comes face to face with the exotic and elusive bird, perched on its hidden nest. The ten dollars are within her grasp, but her solitary communion with the heron has taught her that some things are worth more than money. At the climax of the story, Jewett writes: "She remembers how the white heron came flying through the golden air and how they watched the sea and the morning together, and Sylvia cannot speak; she cannot tell the heron's secret and give its life away."

Another facet of Jewett's writing which interests modern readers and critics is her depiction of strong, independent women. In her earliest novel, *The Country Doctor,* Jewett told the semi-autobiographical story of a young woman who decides to defy gender barriers by becoming a physician. To learn her trade, she apprentices with a wise and broad-minded country doctor, a character modeled on Jewett's father. Through the courageous decision of her female heroine, Jewett argues that women should have the right to reject the confines of marriage if they find they are chosen by God to pursue a different calling. According to the story's country doctor, this young woman had to be true to "the law of her nature," pursuing "something else than the business of housekeeping and what is called woman's natural work, for her activity and capacity to spend itself upon."

Many of Jewett's stories depict unmarried women, usually widows or "spinsters," living energetic and independent lives in the small villages of coastal Maine. Through their gossip and their charity, their medicinal wisdom and their maternal common sense, these women weave a sustaining network of social relations, binding together their communities.

Perhaps Jewett's finest creation, in this regard, is the character Elmira Todd, the central figure in her best-known novel, *The Country of the Pointed Firs* (1896). The story is narrated by a young woman writer who has rented a room in the widow Todd's home for the summer, hoping to get some writing done in the quiet village of "Dunnet's Landing." Instead, she gradually gets drawn into Mrs. Todd's world, and the novel traces the two women's growing friendship. In Paula Blanchard's words, the middle-aged Elmira Todd is "earthy and heavy bodied, attuned to the natural cycles of life and death." She is an herbalist, a woman who knows the hidden healing powers of plants. As the residents of the village come to her door, hoping to be healed by her ancient concoctions, her young friend comes to appreciate the bonds of kinship, history, and sisterly affection, and also some of the secret sorrows, that are at the foundation of this community. Many of Jewett's contemporaries recognized *The Country of the Pointed Firs* as her finest work. After finishing it, Rudyard Kipling exclaimed, "It's immense—it's the very life!" Henry James described the book as "Sarah Orne Jewett's beautiful little quantum of achievement."

At the peak of her artistic powers, Jewett's writing career was cut short by an accident. On her 53rd birthday, she was thrown from a wagon and suffered severe head and spinal injuries. For the next six years, she lived on in deep pain, bedridden and unable to write. On June 23, 1909, she died from a cerebral hemorrhage while staying at her family home in South Berwick, Maine.

The year before she died, Jewett was introduced to *Willa Cather, then a young writer just making a name for herself. Cather was deeply impressed by Jewett and turned to her for advice about her fiction. Echoing what Howells had once told her, Jewett advised her young friend to write about the place and people she knew best. "Find your own quiet centre of life," she taught, "and write from that world." Following this advice, Cather turned to her early experiences growing up in Nebraska as a source of inspiration, producing some of her finest works.

Cather returned the favor by becoming an ardent champion of Jewett's work. *The Country of the Pointed Firs,* she once wrote, was one of the three great masterpieces of American fiction, alone in a class with Twain's *Huckleberry Finn* and Hawthorne's *Scarlet Letter*. Yet, for many years, few shared Cather's opinion; Jewett's work was largely ignored by critics, left out of anthologies, and dismissed by some as "regional" literature.

As feminist scholars began to look back through the past to recover and reconsider literature by and about women, there was renewed interest in Sarah Orne Jewett's life and work. Many of her stories and novels were reprinted, new biographies were written, and scholars produced a growing body of appreciative criticism about her writings. A century after she published her last volume, Jewett's stories about the "grand, simple" lives of rural Mainers continue to offer insights which speak to a new generation of readers.

SOURCES:

Blanchard, Paula. *Sarah Orne Jewett: Her World and Her Work*. Reading, MA: Addison-Wesley, 1994.

Matthieson, Francis O. *Sarah Orne Jewett*. Boston, MA: Houghton Mifflin, 1929.

Silverthorne, Elizabeth. *Sarah Orne Jewett: A Writer's Life*. Woodstock: Overlook Press, 1993.

SUGGESTED READING:

Jewett, Sarah Orne. *The Country of the Pointed Firs and Other Stories*. Edited by *Mary Ellen Chase. NY: Norton, 1982.

Ernest Freeberg, Ph.D.
in American History,
Emory University, Atlanta, Georgia

Jewsbury, Geraldine (1812–1880)

English novelist. Born Geraldine Endsor Jewsbury in Measham, Derbyshire, England, on August 22, 1812; died of cancer in London on September 23, 1880; daughter of Thomas Jewsbury (a Manchester merchant and insurance agent) and Maria (Smith) Jewsbury; sister of Maria Jane Jewsbury (1800–1833); never married; no children.

When her mother died in 1819, seven-year-old Geraldine Jewsbury's education and upbringing were taken over by her elder sister *Maria Jane Jewsbury. Both sisters would become writers. Geraldine was strongly influenced by *George Sand, and her first novel *Zoe: The History of Two Lives,* published in 1845, revealed her feminist views as she detailed the drawbacks of marriage. It was followed by *The Half Sisters* (1848), *Marian Withers* (1851), *Constance Herbert* (1855), *The Sorrows of Gentility* (1856), and *Right or Wrong* (1859). In 1850, Geraldine was invited by Charles Dickens to write for *Household Words;* she was also a frequent reviewer of fiction for the *Athenaeum* and *Westminster Review,* as well as other journals and magazines.

In 1841, Jewsbury met the Carlyles. After this first meeting, Thomas described her as "one of the most interesting young women I have seen for years; clear delicate sense and courage looking out of her small sylph-like figure." From this time until *Jane Welsh Carlyle's death in 1866, Geraldine Jewsbury was her closest friend. The selections from Jewsbury's letters to Jane Carlyle (edited by **Annie Ireland**, 1892) define the bond between the two women that continued for a quarter of a century. In 1854, Jewsbury moved from Manchester to Chelsea to be near her friend. When Jane died, Thomas Carlyle asked Jewsbury to write some anecdotes of his wife's childhood and early married life which he incorporated into his essay, "Jane Welsh Carlyle," These same notes were used by J.A. Froude when editing Carlyle's *Reminiscences.*

Consulted by Froude while he was preparing Thomas Carlyle's biography, Jewsbury told him that Jane had at one time thought about having her marriage legally annulled. Thomas Carlyle was "one of those persons who ought never to have married," said Jewsbury, who also maintained that Jane had confided to her on one occasion that Thomas had used physical violence against her. Though there has been a concerted effort to discredit Jewsbury in relation to the domestic violence question, there seems to be little ground for doubting that she accurately repeated the confidences of her friend Jane Carlyle. *Virginia Woolf wrote of their friendship in "Geraldine and Jane" for *The Times Literary Supplement* (February 28, 1929).

Jewsbury, Maria Jane (1800–1833)

English poet and prose writer. Name variations: Mrs. Fletcher. Born Maria Jane Jewsbury in Measham, Derbyshire, England, on October 25, 1800; died in Poona, India, on October 4, 1833; eldest of six children of Thomas Jewsbury (a Manchester merchant and insurance agent) and Maria (Smith) Jewsbury; sister of Geraldine Jewsbury (1812–1880); married Reverend William Kew Fletcher (a chaplain in the East India projects), in 1832.

On her mother's death in 1819, 19-year-old Maria Jane Jewsbury assumed the upbringing of her siblings, despite the fact that she was less than physically hearty. A collection of her verse, *Phantasmagoria,* was published in 1825. Dedicated to William Wordsworth, it allowed her entrée to the poet and his family. During a forced convalescence in 1826, Jewsbury began to write in earnest. Her poetry collection *Lays of Leisure Hours* was published in 1829 and a collection of stories entitled *The Three Histories: The History of an Enthusiast, The History of a Nonchalant, and The History of a Realist,* in 1830. *The History of an Enthusiast* echoed a theme in her sister *Geraldine Jewsbury's book *The Half Sisters.* Both narratives concern two women—one who seeks literary fame, the other who seeks the life of a conventional wife—and both echo *Germaine de Staël's novel *Corinne* (1807). With three printings, *The Histories* established Maria Jane Jewsbury's reputation as a writer. In 1832, she married a chaplain in the East India projects and journeyed with him to Poona, India. Fourteen months later, age 33, she was dead of cholera.

Jex-Blake, Sophia (1840–1912)

British physician and education reformer who was one of the first female physicians in Europe. Name variations: Sophia Jex Blake. Born on January 21, 1840, in Sussex, England; died on January 7, 1912, in Sussex; daughter of Thomas Jex-Blake and Maria (Cubitts) Jex-Blake; never married; no children.

Entered Queen's College (1858); published A Visit to Some American Schools *(1867); started medical studies in Edinburgh (1869); published* Medical Women *(1873); helped establish the London School of Medicine for Women (1874); obtained medical license (1877); opened private practice (1878); founded Edinburgh School of Medicine for Women (1886); retired from practice (1899).*

One of the first female physicians in Europe, Sophia Jex-Blake was a leader in the struggle for higher education for women in Great Britain. She was born in Sussex in 1840, the youngest of three children of **Maria Jex-Blake** and Thomas

Jex-Blake, a prosperous lawyer who gave his off-spring a conservative religious upbringing. Jex-Blake was emotionally close to her parents, a bond which would remain strong throughout their lives. The Jex-Blakes provided an elementary education to Sophia until, at age eight, she was sent to boarding school.

Imaginative and intelligent, Jex-Blake wanted to learn more than her ill-prepared tutors could teach her, even as a child. Throughout the 19th century, boarding schools for girls were designed to provide only a rudimentary education along with the household skills that prepared them for marriage and motherhood. The lack of formal academic study and the strict discipline left Sophia bored, subject to tantrums and misbehavior. Between ages 8 and 16, she had to change schools six times. Nevertheless, by 16, she had managed to secure an education well enough to convince her that she wanted to both advance her own knowledge and to find a vocation other than the expected one of wife and mother.

In the 1850s, teaching in a public school or as a governess was the only professional career open to middle-class women. Having been frustrated in her desire for a formal education such as boys could receive, Jex-Blake saw a career in teaching as a way to perhaps provide such an education to other girls. But she needed to further her own training first. She therefore convinced her disapproving parents to allow her to enter Queen's College in London in 1858. Queen's College was one of the few women's colleges in England, and the only one dedicated to preparing women to be teachers. Jex-Blake thrived in her new academic environment; for the first time, she was in an institution that valued education for women. She took a full load of courses, studying higher mathematics, English, French, natural philosophy, and theology.

Her rapid progress and her natural ability in mathematics led the administration to offer Sophia the position of math tutor for the other students, a rare opportunity for a first-year student. It took some time to persuade her father, who opposed his daughter's plan to work for money, to let her accept the position. Yet instructing other students proved very satisfying to Sophia, further convincing her that teaching was her calling. In July 1859, she passed her first-year examinations; she continued as a math tutor for the next several terms. She also volunteered as an instructor for charitable organizations which provided poor women with the job skills needed to work in retailing, which was safer and better paid than unskilled factory work.

Despite her success, in 1862 Jex-Blake abruptly chose to leave Queen's College to continue her studies with the Edinburgh Ladies' Educational Association in Scotland. Her reason for leaving London appears to have been her broken relationship with another Queen's College student, *Octavia Hill, later a renowned social reformer, with whom Sophia had formed an intimate friendship. When Hill suddenly refused to see Jex-Blake for reasons which remain obscure, Sophia was devastated, as her letters from this period show. Apparently she could not face living in London or attending the same school as Octavia. Yet Jex-Blake did not remain long in Edinburgh. Quickly growing dissatisfied with the level of instruction offered by the Ladies' Educational Association, she began to inquire about educational opportunities abroad.

While she sought a new direction for her studies, Jex-Blake became involved for the first time in the emerging struggle for women to enter the medical profession. *Elizabeth Garrett Anderson, whom Sophia met in Edinburgh, was pe-

Sophia
Jex-Blake

titioning the administration of Edinburgh University for the right to enter its medical program. Jex-Blake tried to help by canvassing the university faculty members for support, making personal calls on the faculty and writing letters to the administrators. Anderson's application was denied, but the experience introduced Jex-Blake to the medical women's cause and to political activism on behalf of women.

In July 1862, she left Edinburgh for Germany to seek a teaching position and broaden her own education. She found a temporary job teaching English at the Grand Ducal Institute for Women in Mannheim, but homesickness brought her back to her parents' home in Sussex in 1863. Less than two years later, Jex-Blake left home again, this time to complete a long-planned tour of American colleges.

She it was, more than anyone else, who compelled the gates of the medical profession to be opened to women; she never lost heart in her Cause.
—*Pall Mall Gazette*

Her first stop was Boston, where among other notables she was introduced to writer and philosopher Ralph Waldo Emerson. She also came to be friends with Dr. *Lucy Sewall, resident physician at the New England Hospital for Women and one of the first American women doctors. Jex-Blake then set off by train across the eastern and central United States, touring universities and public schools and paying particular attention to the opportunities for American women. Following the trip, Sophia, who had sometimes considered a writing career for herself, would turn her detailed notes into a book manuscript of her observations on the functioning of the American educational system. The book was eventually sold to the Macmillan house, which published it to some success in 1867.

On her return to Boston, Jex-Blake's planned departure for England was delayed when the New England Hospital offered her a job as bookkeeper. She readily accepted, and soon became the hospital's *de facto* pharmacist as well when that position fell vacant. Under the doctors' guidance, she made up medicines and accompanied the doctors on their rounds.

Her friendship and admiration of Lucy Sewall and her experience with the often destitute female patients opened Sophia's eyes to the possibility of a medical career. Certainly there was enormous prejudice against female doctors both in the U.S. and England, and she knew that Se-

wall and the few other American women in medicine had fought hard for the right to practice. Even though there were a few female physicians, there was no legal guarantee that women had a right to practice medicine and no guarantee that the few medical colleges which currently admitted women would continue to do so. Indeed, the increasing numbers of women seeking a medical education and fear of competition by women was causing some institutions to revoke inclusive admission policies. Yet Jex-Blake found the science involved exciting and helping the sick rewarding, combining the mental challenges and the sense of usefulness she wanted. She was not yet convinced, though, that medicine could be her calling.

However, during a visit home to England in 1866 she renewed her friendship with Elizabeth Garrett Anderson. Seeing Anderson, who had succeeded in obtaining a pharmacist's license in England and was now developing a thriving private practice, was the inspiration Jex-Blake needed to turn her from her plans for a teaching career to medicine. The unexpected support and encouragement of her parents, who had only a few years before opposed the idea of their daughter working at all, gave Sophia the confidence she needed to return to Boston and begin classes at the New England Female Medical College.

As with most of her previous schools, however, Jex-Blake was not content with the level of instruction she received. Wanting access to the same education men received, she wrote to the president of Harvard University in 1867, requesting admission. Her request was denied, but she did convince several faculty members to give her instruction at Massachusetts General Hospital. In March 1868, she was accepted as a student at the new Women's Medical College of the New York Infirmary. The college and infirmary had been founded by *Elizabeth Blackwell, the first American woman doctor. Jex-Blake was never to actually attend the school, however, for just as classes began she learned of her father's death in England and hastened home to be with her mother.

For the first few months back in England, Jex-Blake distracted herself from her grief by researching and writing an essay on the history of women in medicine in an attempt to refute the arguments of the medical women's opponents. The essay was subsequently published in a collection on women's education in England, edited by the noted feminist *Josephine Butler. Yet when she finished the piece, Jex-Blake found herself restless, unable to give up her desire to become a doctor. There were also the difficulties of living at home after so much time living independently; although they cared about one another deeply, Sophia and her mother had always been too strong-willed to live together peacefully. Realizing that they could not share a residence for long, they both looked for new outlets for Sophia's ambitions.

In March 1869, Jex-Blake applied to Edinburgh University's medical program. Previously, the faculty had voted against the admission of her friend Elizabeth Garrett Anderson, but this time they voted to allow Sophia to enroll, although the decision was overturned when male students protested. Undaunted, Jex-Blake began a vigorous campaign on behalf of herself and four other women who sought admission. After months of effort and much heated public debate over the propriety of female doctors and the suitability of women for work in general, the five women were allowed to enroll in the medical degree course for the winter term of 1870. They were taught in separate classes and subjected to higher fees than male students, but overall Sophia was elated at the opportunity to follow at last, at age 30, the same academic course as men.

Yet soon new problems arose. Some of the faculty stopped teaching separate classes for the women, which they were not required to do. The Royal Infirmary, the teaching hospital which provided the clinical experience required for the medical degree, then announced that it would not instruct the female students. Jex-Blake and the—by then—six other women (*Edith Pechey-Phipson, Mary Anderson, Isabel Thorne, Matilda Chaplin, Helen Evans, and Emily Bovell), referred to as the "Edinburgh Seven," were also subjected to harassment by male students. Matters came to a head in November when several hundred men tried to block the women's entry to their classroom. They were led by a student of Jex-Blake's most influential opponent, the professor and doctor Robert Christison. Sophia, who had emerged as a natural leader among the women, refused to back down and forced her way into the class. The "Riot at Surgeons Hall" brought considerable positive publicity for the plight of the women, who found new allies and sympathizers throughout the city.

Although they received instruction in some courses, the women were confronted with one administrative barrier after another for the next year until under Jex-Blake's leadership they finally filed a lawsuit against the university for its failure to allow them to complete their program. They won the suit, and a campaign fought both

on campus and in the press resulted in their admission to the Royal Infirmary for hospital training. Once again the path to women's educational progress was irregular and its victories temporary, as the university won its appeal against the women and managed to close itself to female students once again. Although Sophia had garnered broad public support, especially following the publication in 1873 of her *Medical Women,* an expanded version of her earlier essay, the university seemed tireless in its efforts to discredit her and hinder her pursuit of a medical license.

Realizing that this series of gains and losses could continue indefinitely, and that the medical degree was to be denied to her by the university, Jex-Blake began to look for another means of finishing her medical studies. In the meantime, she and the other female students received haphazard instruction from several sympathetic medical faculty. Unwilling to take Elizabeth Garrett Anderson's advice and finish her studies in France, Jex-Blake and her supporters turned to Parliament to continue their fight.

A supportive member of Parliament introduced a bill into the House of Commons to allow the Scottish universities the right to admit women. If passed it would remove the legal basis of the university's opposition to teaching women. Again Sophia put herself in the center of a deeply controversial issue which generated an abundance of correspondence and editorials in the London and Edinburgh press. Yet even when her character was attacked, Jex-Blake remained assertive, confident, and firm in her public responses.

In 1874, with the parliamentary bill delayed, Jex-Blake moved to London and led the founding of the London School of Medicine for Women. Physicians friendly to the women's cause agreed to serve as instructors. The school opened in the winter of 1874–75 with 14 students. The bill to allow Scottish universities to admit women was defeated narrowly in 1875; determined to continue their challenge further, Jex-Blake and two other women applied to the Royal College of Surgeons to be examined for the License in Midwifery. The examiners resigned in protest rather than administer the examination to women.

Yet within a few months Jex-Blake's allies in Parliament, encouraged by supporters of the medical women's movement, pushed through a bill allowing all the medical institutions of Great Britain to admit women. Two Irish institutions indicated their willingness to examine female candidates; to prepare for the exams, Jex-Blake spent several months concentrating on her neglected studies in Switzerland, where she passed the exam for the MD degree in the spring of 1877. She then returned to Britain where she passed, along with four other women, the examination at the College of Physicians in Dublin. The goal she had sought for so long was achieved—Sophia Jex-Blake was now a licensed medical practitioner.

To add to her happiness, her beloved London School was finally affiliated with a hospital, so the students could freely obtain clinical experience. This meant that after years of struggle, women students could attend a medical college which provided the necessary academic and clinical instruction and then be allowed to take the exams required for a practitioner's license. It was a stunning accomplishment, and its supporters recognized Jex-Blake for the leading role she had played in its achievement.

With her achievement, however, Jex-Blake suddenly lacked the direction and decisiveness which had characterized her for over a decade. It was not until May 1878 that she opened a private practice, not in London but in Edinburgh, becoming Scotland's only female doctor. She developed a prosperous practice, even though most of her patients were working-class women, and high demand led her to open an outpatient clinic for the very poor. She also found time to remain involved with the London School and with political developments which might concern the status of female medical practitioners.

In 1881, Maria Jex-Blake died, attended by her daughter. Sophia was devastated and withdrew from public life to mourn. Despite their conflicting personalities, they had remained close, and Sophia had often found in her mother the emotional support she needed to continue her political struggles, especially after her father's death. Her mother's passing was followed closely by the death of a young assistant at Jex-Blake's clinic; the combined loss threw Sophia into a deep depression. Her friends had to close her practice and find other physicians to take on her patients, as she became incapacitated and was unable to work. Mentally and physically exhausted, Jex-Blake went to stay at a friend's rural estate to recuperate, but it was almost two years before she practiced medicine again. Late in 1883, having recovered her health and her spirits, she set up a new, larger medical office and soon her practice was again thriving. The outpatient clinic which her friends had kept open to serve the poor was enlarged into a small hospital, the Edinburgh Hospital and Dispensary for Women.

Another period of active political work began in 1885, when several female medical students of Edinburgh University asked for Jex-Blake's aid in arranging for separate classes, since the university still required women to be taught separately from men. For Jex-Blake, this became a call for the establishment of a women's medical school similar to the London School. By 1887, under Jex-Blake's direction, the school was formally founded as the Edinburgh School of Medicine for Women; soon Sophia, as dean, had negotiated with a hospital to provide clinical training to her students, making full instruction in a medical degree program available for the first time to Scottish women.

The school's first year of courses passed peacefully, but in 1888 conflicts erupted between Jex-Blake and some of the students. As dean, Jex-Blake showed the same determination and unyielding personality that had served her well in her years of struggle against powerful institutions. Privately to her friends, Sophia revealed a playful and cheery disposition. However, she felt that strict discipline and strong leadership were necessary to maintain the privileges and reputation of her students in an educational system which still saw them as less capable than men. Several of her students were outspoken in their resentment of her often inflexible rules. When two students were expelled for their rebellious behavior, they filed a successful lawsuit against Jex-Blake for interrupting their education; soon afterwards, several students left Jex-Blake's school to found a new medical college for women. It was a serious blow to Sophia's pride and to the financial security of her school. The rival college's affiliation with the prestigious Edinburgh Royal Infirmary led growing numbers of aspiring women doctors to choose it over Sophia's school.

Through the early 1890s, Jex-Blake was a delegate of the Scottish Universities Commission, speaking at its meetings and providing information to the commissioners on the status of Scottish education. In 1894, she was delighted to learn that the commission had forced the opening of Edinburgh University's medical examinations to women. No longer did women have to go to London or Ireland to complete their exams. She spent the rest of the decade struggling to keep her school solvent, but by 1898 it was forced to close for lack of students. Two years previously, she had tendered her resignation from the governing council of the London School of Medicine for Women due to her disagreements with its dean, Elizabeth Garrett Anderson. Thus Jex-Blake who had been instrumental in founding two medical colleges now found herself, at age 58, outside the educational system altogether.

Although she was disappointed at the failure of the Edinburgh school, in some ways its closing was fortuitous, as her advancing age and years of hard work were taking a toll on her health. She terminated her practice in 1899 after 16 years, and sold the building to the commission directing the flourishing Edinburgh Hospital and Dispensary. The hospital was re-established as Bruntsfield Hospital in the new building, where it remained in operation until 1989.

As for Jex-Blake, she bought a house in Sussex and retired permanently from medicine. She was not alone in retirement, however. A former student at the Edinburgh School, **Margaret Todd** had obtained her medical license in 1894. Yet after only five years in private practice, she gave up her hard-won medical career to share Sophia's home, where they farmed, read, wrote, and entertained visiting family and friends. Jex-Blake had never married, and from her letters and diaries it is clear that she never regretted having giving up the life of marriage and motherhood when she pursued a career. Yet hers was not a lonely life; she had always cultivated intimate and loving relationships with other women, who provided her with emotional closeness and support.

Her relationship with Margaret Todd was perhaps the most meaningful of her personal relationships; despite the 20 years' difference between them, they shared similar political and religious values, and as the years passed they developed a shared past of activism in women's educational reform. In addition to being a doctor, Todd was a fairly successful novelist. Jex-Blake supported Todd's writing career, which continued during their years in Sussex, and Margaret cared for Sophia as her health failed.

Sophia Jex-Blake died on January 7, 1912, at their Sussex home, at age 71. She willed to Margaret all of her possessions, including her extensive collection of a lifetime of correspondence. In 1918, Todd published a biography of Sophia based on her papers and letters, which she apparently then destroyed in accordance with Jex-Blake's wishes. Margaret Todd committed suicide at age 58 only a few months after the publication of *The Life of Sophia Jex-Blake.*

SOURCES:
Roberts, Shirley. *Sophia Jex-Blake: A Woman Pioneer in Nineteenth-century Medical Reform.* NY: Routledge, 1993.

Todd, Margaret G. *The Life of Sophia Jex-Blake.* London: Macmillan, 1918.

SUGGESTED READING:
Bonner, Thomas N. *To the Ends of the Earth: Women's Search for Education in Medicine.* Cambridge, MA: Harvard University Press, 1992.
Kamm, Josephine. *Hope Deferred: Girls' Education in English History.* London: Methuen, 1965.
Levin, Beatrice. *Women and Medicine.* Metuchen, NJ: Scarecrow Press, 1980.

Laura York,
Riverside, California

Jezebel (d. 884 BCE)

Canaanite princess and queen of the nation of Israel, ruling beside her husband King Ahab, whose values and beliefs brought her into violent conflict with those of her adopted country. Name variations: Jezabel. Pronunciation: JEZ-eh-belle. Date of birth unknown, sometime in the late 900s BCE, in Sidon, on the eastern Mediterranean coast; died in 884 BCE in Jezreel, in Israel; daughter of Ethbaal of Sidon (king of Tyre and priest of the goddess Astarte); mother unknown; married Ahab of Israel, date unknown; children: Ahaziah; Jehoram; *Athaliah; perhaps others.

Raised in Sidon and trained for queenship; given in diplomatic marriage to Ahab of Israel; sponsored Canaanite religion in Israel; reigned beside two sons after husband's death; murdered in coup d'état by usurper Jehu.

The name of Jezebel, queen of the nation of Israel in the 9th century BCE, has been so closely identified with the reputation of its owner as the epitome of wickedness that it has come to inspire disgust, and even hatred, while its bearer has at times been perceived more as a symbol than an actual historical character. She was, however, a real woman.

Born a Canaanite princess, the young woman Jezebel was given in diplomatic marriage to King Ahab of Israel, in order to secure an alliance between Israel and Sidon, the Canaanite city-state that was her homeland. The name of Canaan was originally given to the region now covered by the countries of Israel, Jordan, Syria and Lebanon, but dotted in the 10th–9th centuries with city-states that each had its own ruler. Around 1000 BCE, King David had conquered much of southern Canaan for Israel and Judah, but Sidon was one of the cities still held by the Canaanites along the Mediterranean coast.

The significance of the name Jezebel is not entirely clear, but it is thought to be a corruption of a religious phrase, meaning perhaps "Where is the prince?" or "The prince is!" The prince in question is the god Baal, the storm deity of ancient Canaan who was believed to die each year during the dry season, reviving with the rains of winter.

As the daughter of a king, Jezebel was trained for the destiny of queenship, learning the skills and values that were ultimately to get her into trouble with the religious authorities of Israel. For one thing, she grew up under the Canaanite system of laws related to property, in which all the land of the kingdom belonged to the king and queen, who could dole it out as they saw fit. It was a feudal style of government, much like that practiced later in medieval Europe, but conflicted strongly with the beliefs of the people of Israel, for whom all land belonged ultimately to God, who had given it in trust to tribes, clans, and families.

Whatever else tradition has said about Jezebel, and all of it negative, it records a courageous woman, with the dignity to face certain death with no loss of face.

—Peter R. Ackroyd

Jezebel also grew up with an understanding of the role of queen as a royal partner, to be shared with her husband and later, if the king preceded her in death, with a son and further descendants, as long as she lived. In Canaan, a widowed queen ruled, not as queen regent, nor queen mother, but as queen-for-life.

Jezebel was also faithful to her native religion. When she was brought to Israel's royal city of Samaria to marry and rule alongside King Ahab, she kept her childhood faith in the goddess Asherah and the god Baal. Though these deities may well have been worshipped in Israel, she raised them to the status of official deities.

Everything we know about Jezebel comes from a part of the Bible known by scholars as the Elijah-Elisha cycle, a series of narrations found in I Kings 17–II Kings 10, covering the careers of Elijah and Elisha, two important 9th-century prophets. Jezebel and Ahab are supporting players in the drama, mentioned only as they relate to the prophets. Still, there is much to learn about Queen Jezebel, if we remember the nature of the sources. For one thing, the literary composition is not homogeneous, but a piecing together of miracle stories and legends about the prophets, accounts of the wars of King Ahab, and political history that is probably a fairly accurate record of events during the reign of Ahab and Jezebel; and everything included within this editorial framework is meant to illustrate the evil nature, according to the eyes of God, of the northern kingdom of Israel.

In I Kings 18:31 we find the first mention of Jezebel, where text states that, as if everything else about King Ahab was not bad enough, he had married Jezebel; further, he set up an altar in a temple in Samaria for the worship of Baal, along with an image of Asherah, the deity worshipped as the mother of Baal.

It is significant to understand what Jezebel was giving up, moving from her city on the coast to Ahab's capital in the mountains of Samaria. To the cosmopolitan Canaanites of Sidon and Tyre, Israel was probably considered a backwater at the time, and it has been suggested that the marriage was an attempt on Ahab's part to bring Canaanite civilization to his kingdom. Although he supported Jezebel in the worship of her deities, it is also clear that Ahab himself worshipped the God of Israel.

It is clear, as well, that Jezebel participated in the rule of Israel with her husband's consent. While some scholars have held the view that Ahab was either spineless and weak, or so captivated by the sexual charms of his wife that she overcame his better judgment, there is considerable evidence that both Ahab and Jezebel considered her active role in the kingdom as proper behavior. Some confirmation comes from other Canaanite cultures, such as the northern city of Ugarit, where records have survived of a mutually reigning king and queen, although the kingdom was destroyed long before Jezebel's time. Other evidence occurs in the Bible itself, where I Kings 18:19 records that 400 prophets of Baal, and 450 of Asherah, ate at Jezebel's table, meaning that she herself supported them, providing for their daily needs. This is an indication that the queen had her own court with her own agricultural lands and merchants.

Throughout the Biblical account, Jezebel and Ahab are remembered as acting together. Although Jezebel tends to be blamed alone, in the popular imagination, for hunting down and persecuting the prophets of the God of Israel, especially Elijah, Ahab's own manhunt for this prophet is described in I Kings 18:7–14. On the other hand, in places where we might expect Ahab to be mentioned alone, Jezebel is frequently named with him. In I Kings 22:52, describing the ascent of their son Ahaziah to the throne, the verse says that he "walked in the way of his father and mother"; elsewhere in the Bible such formulaic judgments on rulers mention only the king's father. After Ahaziah's brief reign, his brother Jehoram, who succeeded him, is more positively judged, but also in light of both parents as his predecessors. This same king, requesting the help of the prophet Elisha in battle, is told to "go to your father's prophets or to your mother's."

One of the most famous stories about Queen Jezebel involves a contest between Baal and the God of Israel to ascertain who could bring rain in a time of drought. The prophet Elijah proposed the challenge, to see which god could bring fire to consume the sacrifice placed on an altar. According to the story, the 450 prophets of Baal danced around the altar for hours, with Elijah taunting and mocking them by suggesting that the god was away from home, or busy with some other matter, or even asleep. Such insults would have been strongly felt by believers in the deity, since Baal was the god of thunder, storms, and the agricultural fertility that resulted from the rains, and one of his titles was "Rider on the Clouds." Then the Bible records that Elijah, acting alone, pours water around the altar and prays to his God, after which fire, perhaps in the form of lightning, comes down and consumes the sacrifice, followed by rain. Then to complete his performance, Elijah slaughters all the prophets of Baal and thus incurs the exceeding wrath of the queen, who puts out an order for his death, forcing Elijah to flee into the wilderness.

Another story explores the conflict between Israel and Jezebel regarding land ownership. One day, King Ahab expressed a desire to own a vineyard near his palace which belonged to a man named Naboth. Naboth refused to sell it to him, citing his family's commitment to retain the ancestral land. Ahab understood the law but sulked about the matter; it was Jezebel who then schemed to obtain it, since Ahab would not. To do so, she had Naboth falsely accused of blasphemy and treason and sentenced to death, so that Ahab could claim the land. In doing so, she wrote letters in her husband's name and used his seal, involving elders and nobles of the city in the conspiracy that ended with Naboth being stoned to death. For this act, both Jezebel and Ahab were denounced by Elijah.

Two things should be remembered about this story. First, it was written by the queen's detractors, so prejudice is likely to be involved. Second, Jezebel's motives, if not her methods, are understandable in terms of her own cultural background. She may even have considered her actions an appropriate response to insubordination. To her way of thinking, for the king's subject to be unwilling to sell the land to the king for a better vineyard (the generous offer made by

Ahab) could be considered treason. Further, her use of Ahab's seal was probably not a usurpation of the king's authority. As his royal partner, she is likely to have been entrusted with the use of it on official matters.

Jezebel reigned as queen for ten years after the death of her husband, ruling with Ahaziah first, and then with Jehoram. According to II Kings 9, her violent death was brought about indirectly by the prophet Elisha, who commissioned a man named Jehu to avenge the murder of certain prophets of the God of Israel. Jehu's task included cleansing the kingdom of iniquity by slaughtering the royal household and taking over as ruler himself. He assassinated Jehoram and had all the male relatives of the king murdered.

According to the Biblical account, as Jehu arrived at Jezreel, Jezebel greeted him from the window of an upper story, decked out in her royal glory, taunting him as the murderer of his lord the king. She was then pushed from the window by her servants and trampled by the hordes below. There is something amazing in this last act, as she stands regally at the window, taunting the usurper who has slaughtered both her son and her son-in-law, who was king of the neighboring kingdom of Judah. Knowing that all was lost, that all her other male relatives would soon be dead, that all her female relatives would probably become captives of the new king, she may have thought herself better off dead. The story goes on to say that Jehu had his supper before arranging for the burial of the dead queen, and when his servants went to attend to the body, it had been almost entirely eaten by dogs. According to II Kings 9:10, this event fulfilled a prophecy made by Elisha.

Jezebel has often been ridiculed for painting her face and doing her hair before facing certain death. Rather, it is possible to admire her indomitable spirit and dignity; she always remembered that she was queen and went to her death dressed and arrayed accordingly. Further, it has been suggested that she may have hoped still to rally the people against Jehu, and to do so she would have needed to appear in a royal guise.

There are a number of reasons why Jezebel earned such a despicable reputation. One is that a queen who worshipped multiple deities could not be tolerated at a time when Israel was struggling to enforce and popularize the radically new concept of one god. While most nations gladly welcomed the inclusion of foreign gods and goddesses, accepting their worship as an addition to their own native religions, the zealots of Israel would not tolerate such behavior. Jezebel was condemned as an idolater.

Additionally, she did not fit traditional ideas of how a woman should behave. She was indeed violent, and she wielded power openly. However, she was no more violent than her nemesis, the prophet Elijah, who is reported to have killed 450 prophets of Baal on one afternoon, or the usurper Jehu, who took over the throne in a bloody coup and killed all the members of the ruling family. Violence seen as historically acceptable when carried out by male figures can be considered outrageous when carried out by females. In I Kings 21:25, Ahab is the one blamed for doing evil, "urged on by his wife Jezebel." But throughout history, she has carried the weight of the blame.

Also throughout history, women who wield sexual power to their own advantage have typically been called Jezebels. This may be the most far-fetched slander against the queen, but there are a number of reasons for it. First, it is typical to accuse any powerful woman of obtaining her power by sexual influence. The truth, however, was that Jezebel had power because she believed she deserved it as a queen and as a daughter of a king. A misreading of Biblical language may be another cause. In the verse where Jehu greets King Jehoram just before killing him, the usurper declares that there can be no peace "as long as the many whoredoms and sorceries of your mother Jezebel continue." In the Bible, it is common practice for the word "whore" to be used to symbolize idolatry, as opposed to sexual promiscuity; in the case of this queen, history has latched onto the sexual meaning. And finally, because it is recorded that the queen dressed in her finest to face her death, she has been perceived as a "painted lady," or fallen woman.

In short, the record of her life was written by those who saw her as an idolater, a doer of evil, and a killer of true prophets. The editor of that record had a single overweening purpose, which was to show that the kings of ancient Israel were evil one and all, and their kingdom therefore deserved the destruction that would arrive not long after Jezebel's time.

SOURCES:

Ackroyd, Peter R. "Goddesses, Women and Jezebel," in *Images of Women in Antiquity*. Edited by Averil Cameron and Amelie Kuhrt. Detroit, MI: Wayne State University Press, 1983, pp. 245–259.

Avigad, N. "The Seal of Jezebel," in *Israel Exploration Journal*. Vol. 14, 1964, pp. 274–276.

Brenner, Athalya. *The Israelite Woman: Social Role and Literary Type in Biblical Narrative*. Sheffield, England: JSOT Press, 1985, pp. 20–28.

Christensen, Duane L. "Huldah and the Men of Anathoth: Women in Leadership in the Deuteronomic History," in *SBL Seminar Papers*. Vol. 23, 1984, pp. 339–404.

Yee, Gale A. "Jezebel," in *Anchor Bible Dictionary*. Vol. 3. Edited by David Noel Freedman. NY: Doubleday, 1992, pp. 848–849.

SUGGESTED READING:

Camp, Claudia V. "Jezebel (I Kings 16–21; 2 Kings 9)," in *The Woman's Bible Commentary: 1 and 2 Kings*. Edited by Carol A. Newson and Sharon A. Ringe. Louisville, KY: Westminster Press, 1992, pp. 103–104.

Frost, S.B, "Judgment on Jezebel, or a Woman Wronged," in *Theology Today*. Vol. 20. January 1964, pp. 503–517.

Eleanor Amico,
freelance writer with a Ph.D. in Hebrew
and Semitic Studies, has taught Biblical studies

Jhabvala, Ruth Prawer (1927—)

German-born British fiction writer and screenwriter whose works examine the complexities of Eastern and Western mentalities in modern India, and whose status as a "permanent refugee" gave rise to a unique view of cultural traditions. Pronunciation: JAHB-vah-lah. Born Ruth Prawer in Cologne, Germany, on May 7, 1927; daughter of Marcus Prawer and Eleonora (Cohn) Prawer; had two brothers; Queen Mary College, M.A., 1951; married Cyrus S.H. Jhabvala, in 1951; children: three daughters, Renana Jhabvala; Firoza Jhabvala; Ava Jhabvala.

Lived in Germany (1927–39), England (1939–51), India (1951–75), New York (1975—); won the Booker Prize for Heat and Dust (1975); received a MacArthur Foundation grant (1984); won Academy Awards for Best Screenplay Adaptation for A Room With a View (1986) and Howards End (1992); won the Best Screenplay Adaptation award for Mr. and Mrs. Bridge by the New York Film Critics Circle (1990); nominated for an Academy Award for Best Screenplay Adaptation for Remains of the Day (1993); received the Writers Guild of America's Screen Laurel Award, the Guild's highest honor (1994).

Selected writings—novels unless otherwise indicated: To Whom She Will (published in America as Amrita, NY: Norton, 1956); The Nature of Passion (NY: Norton, 1957); Esmond in India (NY: Norton, 1958); The Householder (NY: Norton, 1959); Get Ready for Battle (NY: Norton, 1963); (short stories) Like Birds, Like Fishes, and Other Stories (NY: Norton, 1964); A Backward Place (NY: Norton, 1965); Shakespeare Wallah (NY: Grove Press, 1973); (short stories) A Stronger Climate: Nine Stories (NY: Norton, 1968); (short stories) An Experience of India (NY: Norton, 1972); Travelers (NY: Harper and Row,

Ruth
Prawer
Jhabvala

1973, *published in London as* A New Dominion, *1972);* Autobiography of a Princess, Also Being the Adventures of an American Film Director in the Land of the Maharajas *(NY: Harper and Row, 1975);* Heat and Dust *(NY: Harper and Row, 1974); (short stories)* How I Became a Holy Mother, and Other Stories *(NY: Harper and Row, 1976);* In Search of Love and Beauty *(NY: William Morrow, 1983); (short stories)* Out of India: Selected Stories *(NY: Simon & Schuster, 1987);* Three Continents *(NY: William Morrow, 1987);* Poet and Dancer *(NY: Doubleday, 1994);* Shards of Memory *(NY: Doubleday, 1996); (short stories)* East into Upper East: Plain Tales from New York and New Delhi *(Washington, DC: Counterpoint, 1998).*

Screenplays: (adapted from her novel) The Householder *(1963);* Shakespeare Wallah *(1965); (with James Ivory)* The Guru *(1969);* Bombay Talkie *(1970);* Autobiography of a Princess *(1975);* Roseland *(1977);* Hullabaloo Over Georgie and Bonnie's Pictures *(1978); (with James Ivory, adapted from the novel of Henry James)* The Europeans *(1979);* Jane Austen in Manhattan *(1980); (adapted from the book of *Jean Rhys)* Quartet *(1981);* The Courtesans of Bombay *(documentary, 1982); (adapted from her* novel) Heat and Dust (1983); (adapted from the novel of Henry James) The Bostonians (1984); (adapted from the novel of E.M. Forster) A Room With a View (1986); Madame Sousatzka (1988); (adapted) Slaves of New York (1989); (adapted from the writings of Evan S. Connell) Mr. and Mrs. Bridge (1990); (adapted from the novel of E.M. Forster) Howards End (1992); (adapted from the novel by Kazuo Ishiguro) Remains of the Day (1993); Jefferson in Paris (1995); (adapted from the memoir of Françoise Gilot) Surviving Picasso (1996).

The experience of exile left an indelible mark on the mind and work of fiction and screenwriter Ruth Prawer Jhabvala. She was born in Germany, the daughter of Marcus Prawer and **Eleonora Cohn Prawer**, on May 7, 1927—six years before the emergence of Hitler's Third Reich—and grew up in the overwhelmingly Catholic city of Cologne, whose mayor at the time was Konrad Adenauer. Her father was a successful lawyer, and the family enjoyed its prosperity and social status. Although Marcus had Eastern European Jewish roots (he had escaped from Russian Poland during World War I to avoid military service under the tsar), Ruth's early years were secure and typical of "a well-integrated, solid, assimilated, German-Jewish family." There was little in the way of anti-Semitism to mar these years. Her grandfather, who was the cantor of Cologne's largest synagogue, was a respected member of the community who prided himself on his friendships with Christian pastors and felt himself to be a highly esteemed citizen of Cologne and "a German gentleman." The seemingly idyllic world of the Prawer family was shattered in 1933 with the Nazi seizure of power. Overnight, Germany's Jews became second-class citizens and pariahs.

Ruth began to attend school at age six, during the first years of Nazi rule. As she quickly learned to read and write, a new world opened to her. She would later recall that when instructed by her teacher to write a composition on the subject of *der Hase* (a hare) she was "at once . . . flooded with my destiny; only I didn't know that's what it was. I only remember my entire absorption, delight, in writing about—giving my impression of—*der Hase*. To think that such happiness could be!" Her family's solidarity in the face of adversity and her discovery of the pleasures of self-expression in writing made the ordeal they faced as Jews easier to bear. During the next few years, the not-yet-teenage Ruth Prawer wrote stories and essays, mostly on religious and Jewish topics, and, like her older brother, attended a segregated Jewish school. As

the grim realities of the 1930s bore down on Jews in Germany, members of Prawer's extended family fled Nazi persecution to find refuge in a number of countries. In April 1939, after the horrors of the Kristallnacht pogrom, Ruth and her family emigrated to the United Kingdom.

Settled in London, the young Ruth never looked back, starting to write (and think) in English almost immediately. After graduating from secondary school in 1945, she enrolled at Queen Mary College, London University, and majored in English literature. After earning an M.A. degree in 1951 with a thesis on the short story in English literature, Ruth married an Indian architect, Cyrus S.H. Jhabvala, whom she had met while a student at the University. That same year, she and her husband moved to India, where they lived in one of the older and quieter sections of New Delhi. Although she quickly gave birth to three daughters, Ruth Jhabvala also found the time to continue writing about the variety of human behavior she observed. She had moved to India knowing virtually nothing of the country, having done little more than read novels like *Kim* and *A Passage to India,* and she initially experienced it as a "paradise on earth. Just to look at the place, the huge sky, the light, the colors. I loved the heat, going round with few clothes, the stone floors." Jhabvala was enchanted.

Although her husband was a Parsi, a descendant of Persian Zoroastrians who moved to India more than a millennium ago, the majority of Indians are Hindus and live in households teeming with extended family. In her 1979 Neil Gunn Lecture, entitled "Disinheritance," she explained her experience of being in exile which made it possible for her to write about a culture so different from the German and English ones she had known; she described herself as feeling "disinherited even of my own childhood memories, so that I stand before you as a writer without any ground of being out of which to write: really blown about from country to country, culture to culture till I feel—till I am—nothing. I'm not complaining—this is not a complaint, just a statement of fact. As it happens, I like it that way. It's made me into a cuckoo, forever insinuating myself into other's nests. Or a chameleon hiding myself (if there were anything to hide) in false or borrowed colours."

In 1955, four years after arriving in India, Jhabvala saw her first novel published in London under the title *To Whom She Will* (it appeared the next year in the United States as *Amrita*). In this richly textured book, the young upper-middle-class Hindu woman Amrita falls in love with Hari, a poor Punjabi who works as a part-time radio announcer in New Delhi. By means of complex scheming, both Amrita's and Hari's families keep them from marrying one another, an auspicious outcome as in the end both find happiness with mates chosen in the traditional fashion, by their families. The book was well received both in England and in the U.S. where *Time* praised the work for its depictions of the bustling everyday life of India—"with all the clatter, chatter and haggling delight of an Eastern bazaar"—and noted the book's message as, "Cultural heritage is not a vice but a virtue."

After the critical success of *To Whom She Will*, Jhabvala published several more novels over the next few years. In *The Nature of Passion* (1957), her subject again dealt with the benefits and drawbacks of marriages by arrangement and those based on romantic love. In her review, Indian writer *Santha Rama Rau praised the novel for its presentation of the "richly human texture of life as it is really lived in an Indian city." *Esmond in India,* published in New York in 1958, examines a union between an Englishman and an Indi-

an woman. Jhabvala presents us with Esmond—who is suave, cultured and rotten to the core—and an equally negative character, the Indian Har Dayal, a superficial Babbitt whose life is exposed as being little more than a hollow shell. Jhabvala's next work, *The Householder,* presented the struggles of Prem, a young Hindu man living through a transitional stage in his life. The author was again praised for her skill in painting a subtle and sympathetic portrait of life in contemporary India. Writing in London's *New Statesman,* Maurice Richardson enthusiastically recommended this warm and amusing book to readers, noting that Jhabvala had created several characters that were on the level of "an Indian Dickens."

In 1959, Jhabvala visited England for the first time since her marriage. There she experienced the dramatic differences from life in India. In a 1976 *New York Times* interview, she recalled how shocking it was to compare Europe with an India where "the degradation starts at birth. You have no choice. So after that visit to England, I felt more and more alien in India." Jhabvala's trip to Europe also opened a new

From the movie The Remains of the Day, starring Anthony Hopkins and Emma Thompson, screenplay by Ruth Prawer Jhabvala.

phase of her career with the writing of the screenplay for *The Householder*. Released in 1963, this film was produced by Ismail Merchant, an Indian, and directed by James Ivory, an American. Jhabvala, the German-born "rootless cosmopolitan," completed the collaborative trio. "We're not interested in just making a film, or just making some money," she told an interviewer. "We want to make what we think, what has impressed us, what has touched us."

In the years to come, she would write screenplays for a great variety of films with Merchant-Ivory, including *Shakespeare Wallah* (1965), *The Guru* (with James Ivory, 1969), *Bombay Talkie* (1970), *Autobiography of a Princess* (1975), *Roseland* (1977), *The Europeans* (with James Ivory, based on the novel of Henry James, 1979), *Heat and Dust* (based on her own novel, 1983), *The Bostonians* (based on the novel of Henry James, 1984), *Jefferson in Paris* (1995), and *Surviving Picasso* (based on the memoir by *Françoise Gilot, 1996). She would win Academy Awards for two of her adaptations, *A Room With a View* (based on the novel by E.M. Forster, 1986) and *Howards End* (based on the novel by E.M. Forster, 1992).

After living in India for two decades and raising three daughters to adulthood, Jhabvala began to seek new directions. In an autobiographical essay, "Myself in India" (1966), published in *An Experience of India,* she revealed, "I am no longer interested in India. What I am interested in now is myself in India, which sometimes, in moments of despondency, I tend to think of as my survival in India." In 1974, she published *Heat and Dust,* one of her most memorable and technically innovative novels for which she received the Booker Prize. Clearly influenced by her work in films, the plot moves back and forth between a young Englishwoman in contemporary India and her grandmother in the India of 50 years earlier, when it was the crown jewel of the British Empire. (In the movie, **Julie Christie** plays the Englishwoman; **Greta Scacchi**, the grandmother.) The book's theme presented the notion that India's culture, ancient and brilliant in many ways, was nevertheless profoundly alien to Westerners, and that those individuals who became too deeply enmeshed in it would inevitably come to grief. The novel's dominant image was one of disease, decay, and death. The reader is warned that "India always changes people," but these changes are invariably malevolent, stripping one of one's identity and leaving one to wither and die. This book, with all its technical brilliance, signaled her increasing ambivalence toward India, prompting

the reviewer of *The New York Times* to speculate: "I suspect that she is becoming tired of the literary burden of India she has carried for so many years [and] may be ready, as a novelist, to move on."

By the time Jhabvala's short-story collection *How I Became a Holy Mother* was published in London in 1976, she had become acknowledged by many critics as a major literary figure. Writing in *The Observer* (June 27, 1976), Paul Bailey praised her for a mastery of nuance and detail that built up "a picture of an entire society, [thus raising] large themes by implication." By the mid-1970s, however, she had made the decision to leave the country that had been a base for her creative exploration. Described as "a frail, birdlike woman" standing only 5'1" and weighing no more than 95 pounds, she was increasingly challenged by the physical realities of living there, and contracted jaundice while writing *Heat and Dust.* The poverty and injustices she saw around her became harder for her to deal with emotionally and psychologically. To live in India, she wrote, meant that one existed "on the back of this great animal of poverty and backwardness. It is not possible to pretend otherwise." In a 1980 letter to London's *Sunday Times*, Jhabvala would admit that in the final analysis India had been for her "too strong, too overpowering a place." Having produced eight novels and four books of short stories set in this landscape, she moved to New York City in 1975.

Although her husband remained in India where he headed an architectural firm and taught, their marriage stayed intact. Her daughters were grown and had independent careers. Jhabvala was productive in America, at the same time starting an annual routine of visiting India for several months. By 1976, she was settled in an apartment on Manhattan's East Side in a city where, as she remarked in an interview, "people like myself, displaced Europeans, found a home." In New York, she met other German Jews like herself, who had made a successful transition to a new life. Significantly, after leaving India, she chose to settle in New York rather than London (her older brother Siegbert Salomon Prawer, was a noted professor of German literature at Oxford). As a permanent refugee, Jhabvala felt at home in the quintessential world city which was swarming with a myriad of refugees. She cautiously explored her rootedness in German-Jewish, and Central European, cultural traditions. "I am a central European with an English education and a deplorable tendency to constant self-analysis," wrote Jhabvala in "Myself in India." "I am irritable and have weak nerves."

By 1999, she had lived as many years in New York as she had in India. She produced fewer books in Manhattan, but they were all of substance, earning strong if not unanimous critical acclaim. In her first novel published after leaving India, *In Search of Love and Beauty* (1983), the author investigated the battle-scarred emotional landscape of German- and Austrian-Jewish refugees in Manhattan. The main characters are affluent European-born individuals whose lives are filled with yearnings for yet unachieved love and spiritual meaning. One of the best-drawn characters in the book is Leo Kellerman, a con man, "psychospiritual" guru and lecherous sponger, who attaches himself to a wealthy family in various ways, including persuading their daughter Natasha to work in a menial capacity in his "Academy of Potential Development." A profound emptiness in modern family life is summed up by the lonely Natasha: "There just wasn't enough love to go round and never would be—not here, not now—with everyone needing such an awful lot."

By the end of the 20th century, Jhabvala had published a dozen novels, an impressive collection of short stories, and a large number of screenplays. Although much of her writing was set in India, the human situations she described were universal ones. Some critics have compared the body of her work to the tradition of 19th-century English novelists like Dickens, Thackeray, and Trollope. Her wit and focus on courtship and family life has brought comparisons of her work with that of ***Jane Austen** and Henry James. **Francine du Plessix Gray** noted in *The New York Times Book Review* in 1993 that Jhabvala's writings, particularly those works with an Indian setting, have become for many critics and readers alike "as rich a metaphor for universal experience as Faulkner's Yoknapatawpha County or the czarist Russia of Chekov's fiction."

SOURCES:

Agarwal, Ramlal G. *Ruth Prawer Jhabvala: A Study of Her Fiction*. New Delhi: Sterling Publishers, 1990.

Chakravarti, Aruna. *Ruth Prawer Jhabvala: A Study in Empathy and Exile*. New Delhi: B.R. Publishing, 1998.

Crane, Ralph J. *Passages to Ruth Prawer Jhabvala*. New Delhi: Sterling Publishers, 1991.

———. *Ruth Prawer Jhabvala*. NY: Twayne Publishers, 1992.

———. "Ruth Prawer Jhabvala: A Checklist of Primary and Secondary Sources," in *Journal of Commonwealth Literature*. Vol. 20, no. 1, 1985, pp. 171–203.

Gooneratne, Yasmine. *Silence, Exile and Cunning: The Fiction of Ruth Prawer Jhabvala*. Hyderabad: Orient Longman, 1983.

Gray, Francine du Plessix. "The Cult of the Cousin," in *The New York Times Book Review*. March 28, 1993, pp. 13–14.

Grimes, Paul. "A Passage to U.S. for Writer of India," in *The New York Times*. May 15, 1976, p. 14.

Hamilton, Alex. "The Book of Ruth," in *Guardian*. November 20, 1975, p. 12.

Jack, Ian. "The Foreign Travails of Mrs. Jhabvala," in *Sunday Times Magazine* [London]. July 13, 1980, pp. 32–36.

Jhabvala, Ruth Prawer. "Disinheritance," in *Blackwood's Magazine*. Vol. 326. July 1979, pp. 4–14.

———. "India Overpowered Me," in *Sunday Times* [London]. August 3, 1980, p. 11.

Long, Robert Emmet. *The Films of Merchant Ivory*. NY: Abrams, 1997.

Moorehead, Caroline. "A Solitary Writer's Window on the Heat and Dust of India," in *The Times* [London]. November 20, 1975, p. 16.

Nossiter, Bernard D. "Enjoying the Fruits of Detachment," in *Washington Post*. December 9, 1975, p. C2.

Pym, John. "'Where could I meet other screenwriters?': A Conversation with Ruth Prawer Jhabvala," in *Sight and Sound*. Vol. 48, no. 1. Winter, 1978–79, pp. 15–18.

Shahane, Vasant A. *Ruth Prawer Jhabvala*. New Delhi: Arnold Heinemann, 1976.

———. "Ruth Prawer Jhabvala's *A New Dominion*," in *Journal of Commonwealth Literature*. Vol. 12, no. 1. August 1977, pp. 45–55.

Sucher, Laurie. *The Fiction of Ruth Prawer Jhabvala: The Politics of Passion*. Basingstoke, England: Macmillan, 1989.

Tucker, Martin, ed. *Literary Exile in the Twentieth Century: An Analysis and Biographical Dictionary*. NY: Greenwood Press, 1991.

John Haag,
Associate Professor of History,
University of Georgia, Athens, Georgia

Jhansi, rani of.

See Lakshmibai (c. 1835–1858).

Jiagge, Annie (1918–1996)

Ghanaian lawyer, national and international women's rights activist, and author of the basic draft and introduction to the UN Declaration on Elimination of Discrimination against Women, who was the first Ghanaian woman to become a High Court judge and the first woman judge of the Commonwealth. Name variations: Auntie Annie. Pronunciation: JHEE-aggie. Born Annie Ruth Baeta on October 7, 1918, in Lome, French Togoland; died in Accra, Ghana, on June 12, 1996; one of four surviving children of the Reverend Robert Domingo Baeta (a pastor of the Presbyterian Church) and Henrietta Baeta (a schoolteacher); attended Achimota College, receiving her Teacher's Certificate, 1937; London School of Economics and Political Science, LLB, 1949; married Fred Jiagge, on January 10, 1953; children: Rheinhold (adopted 1959).

Awards: The Grand Medal of Ghana (1969); The Gimbles International Award (1974); LLD, University of Ghana.

Started a career as schoolteacher; was headmistress of Evangelical Presbyterian Girls School (1940–46); gave up teaching to embark on a legal career (1946); admitted to the London School of Economics and Political Science, also to Lincoln's Inn (1946); received LLB (1949); called to the Bar at Lincoln's Inn (1950); returned to Ghana, then known as the Gold Coast (1950) and went into private practice; gave up practice after marriage (1953) and became a magistrate; became a senior magistrate (1956), a Circuit Court judge (1959), a High Court judge (1961), an Appeal Court judge (1969), and president of the Court of Appeal (1980–83); retired (1983).

Member of Executive Committee World YWCA (1955–1960); president of YWCA Ghana (1958–62); vice chair, World YWCA (1962–72); Ghana's representative on the UN Commission on Status of Women (1966); Rapporteur, UN Commission on the Status of Women (1967); authored basic draft of United Nations Declaration on Elimination of Discrimination against Women (1968); president, UN Commission on the Status of Women 21st Session (1968); authored introduction to UN Declaration on Elimination of Discrimination against Women (1966–69); chaired Commission on Investigation of Assets of Senior Public Servants and Named Political Leaders (1975); founded Ghana National Council on Women and Development (1975–82); served as chair, Ghana National Council on Women and Development (1975–83); president, World Council of Churches (1980); leader of Ghana Delegation to International Women's Conference in Mexico (1975) and in Copenhagen (1980); chair, Committee on Churches Participation in Development, Ghana (1984–91); moderator, Program to Combat Racism, World Council of Churches (1985); member, UN Panel to conduct Public Hearings on the Activities of Transnational Corporations in South Africa and Namibia (1991); member, Committee of Experts to make proposals for a Draft Constitution for Ghana (1992); member, the President's Transitional Team (1993–96); member, Council of State, Ghana.

In 1940, in the West African coastal town of Keta, then part of a British colony named British Togoland, the buildings that housed the Evangelical Presbyterian School for Girls were washed away by the sea. When the girls were moved to the nearby Evangelical Presbyterian School for Boys, the new, young head of the girls' school was distressed by the situation. The school was overcrowded, the teaching and learning stressful. Annie Baeta, later known as Annie Jiagge, wanted to see the girls settled in new buildings, but she knew there was little money available for such a project. Instead, she approached the Evangelical Presbyterian Church Choir, convinced it could play a useful role in raising funds. Under her direction, the choir was transformed into a drama group, which performed a highly successful musical by George F. Rool titled "David the Shepherd Boy." The dance rhythms, choreography, and costumes astonished many, and news of the choir's performances spread throughout the country. The group was so successful that it was invited to perform in major cities of the Gold Coast and in neighboring Togo. By December 1945, a new girls' school had been built. The leadership, managerial qualities, and decisiveness which Jiagge displayed in raising funds for her school would be evident throughout her life.

Annie Ruth Baeta was born in 1918 in Lome, French Togoland (Lome would become the capital of the French-speaking West African country of the Republic of Togo in 1960) and grew up during a period of rapid social change. At the time of her birth, many African countries were colonies of European states—France, Britain, Germany, and Portugal. The modern West African states had not yet been created. In the late 1950s, the launching of her career as a judge would coincide with the beginning of the period of decolonization, when several African nations gained political independence from the European colonial powers.

Annie's mother **Henrietta Baeta** was a schoolteacher; her father Robert Domingo Baeta, a minister of the Presbyterian Church, was born into a prominent family, well respected in British and French Togoland as well as in the British Gold Coast. At the time of Annie's birth, Robert Baeta was trying to establish the church in French Togoland. One of eight children, though only four survived to adulthood, Annie and her siblings Christian, William, and Lily were close.

Though Jiagge began her schooling in Lome, her parents were intent on her having an English education. Thus, Annie spent her childhood living with her maternal grandmother in Keta, a coastal town in British Togoland, which in 1956 would merge with the British colony then known as the British Gold Coast. In 1957, the British Gold Coast would become the independent state of Ghana. Jiagge's mother and grandmother both urged the child to think for herself and implanted in her a sense of responsibility, perseverance, and decisiveness.

In 1933, Annie entered Achimota College in Accra, the capital of the British Gold Coast, graduating in 1937 with a teacher's certificate. After working as a schoolteacher and headmistress from 1940 to 1946, Jiagge gave up teaching to embark on a legal career; her stint as a schoolteacher and headmistress, though fulfilling, had left her "restless." While a student at Achimota College, she and a group of students had been taken on a tour of the Law Courts in Accra that had left a strong impression. At the time, however, there were no facilities for the study of law in the Gold Coast. Because her father had died, she turned to her older brother Christian for help. Christian was sympathetic and made enquiries for her to study law at the University of London. Annie's mother also offered her support and secured loans to pay Annie's expenses.

In 1946, Annie was off to London, having been admitted to the London School of Economics and Political Science and also to Lincoln's Inn. In her class, there were only three other

Annie
Jiagge

women: two British and one Indian. Many men from the Gold Coast, who were also students at Lincoln's Inn, thought her goals were unrealistic, since few women were studying law at the time. Convinced that she would not graduate, they urged her to give up her studies, which they thought too difficult for a woman. One of them kindly offered to arrange for her to study dress designing at the Paris Academy in London. Jiagge promised the men that she would pack up and return to the Gold Coast if she failed the first examination. When she passed, these same fellows had no more to say and avoided her. In due course, Annie completed her studies, obtaining a bachelor's degree in Law in 1949. In 1950, she was called to the Bar at Lincoln's Inn.

Injustice eats me internally. I get very restless when I come in touch with it.

—Annie Jiagge

Jiagge's stay in London had not been solely devoted to study; she took on a great deal of social and religious work in her free time, participating in youth camps organized by the Young Women's Christian Association (YWCA) in Britain and on the Continent. Her work with the YWCA and later the World Council of Churches would continue throughout her life. Through these activities, she became aware of the difficulties that women and children face worldwide. In her last years as a student in Britain, she was elected to the Executive Committee of the World YWCA.

On her return to the Gold Coast in 1950, Jiagge went into private practice. In her free time, she led a major public relations drive to establish a national YWCA in the Gold Coast; a documentary film was produced to educate the public on the need for the organization. Annie was president of the YWCA from 1955 to 1960.

In 1961, she spearheaded a campaign to raise funds for the construction of a YWCA hostel for women in Accra, Ghana's capital. By her own account, the need for a hostel for women presented itself when a rape case was brought before her. A young woman had arrived in Accra from the countryside to attend a job interview. At interview's end, it was too late for her to travel back home, and she naively accepted an offer of shelter from a man who then raped and robbed her. Troubled by the young woman's story, Jiagge sought assistance from the government to provide safe, inexpensive accommodations for women who visited the city. Granted an audience with Kwame Nkrumah, president of Ghana, she convinced him of the importance of her project. With support from the government and other sources,

Jiagge raised substantial funds for the YWCA women's hostel, which still stands in Accra.

In January 1953, three years after her return from Britain, Annie married Fred Jiagge, whom she had met when she was a student at Achimota College. The pressure of combining a professional career with domestic responsibilities made her give up the Bar and join the Bench as a magistrate that June. However, she had a brilliant career in the judiciary and progressed steadily up the judicial ladder, becoming a Circuit Court judge in 1959, a High Court judge in 1961, a judge of the Court of Appeal in 1969, and, from 1980 until her retirement in 1993, president of the Court of Appeal. Though most Ghanaians referred to her as Justice Annie Jiagge, those who knew her well tended to call her "Auntie Annie," while to her close nieces, nephews, and cousins, she was "Auntiega," which, in the Ewe language, her mother tongue, means "big aunt."

Perhaps it was her strong commitment to the cause of women that led to Jiagge's appointment in 1962 as Ghana's representative on the UN Commission on the Status of Women. She would represent the country on the commission until 1972, and in 1968 was elected chair of the 21st Session of the Commission. Through her work at the UN, she made her mark internationally as a champion of women's rights. While a member of the UN Commission on the Status of Women, she was exposed, sometimes too much, to the nature of violence against women worldwide. She once recounted how she could not sleep after reading a disturbing report of a man who had killed his sister because of her involvement in an extramarital affair. On another occasion, she was furious to learn that in some countries women were not included in head counts.

History has largely credited Jiagge with authoring the basic draft of the UN Declaration on the Elimination of Discrimination against Women in 1967. According to Jiagge, it all began a year earlier, in 1966, when she was elected rapporteur of the UN Commission on the Status of Women. While meeting in Iran, the commission was charged with the task of preparing a document on the elimination of discrimination against women. After two weeks of studying and discussing reports from different countries, the international team had not yet produced a draft document. As rapporteur, Jiagge was unhappy with the situation. She feared that the group might leave Iran without a document and decided to attempt a basic draft which would serve as a discussion paper. After consulting with other team members, which included Princess *Ashraf

Pahlavi of Persia (Iran), Jiagge sat up from 9 PM to about 7 AM, struggling with the draft. By midmorning, the document was typed and distributed. A decision was taken to send the document to all UN member-states for comment, and it was later adopted. In the following year, 1968, she was asked to write an introduction to the Declaration. Jiagge's Declaration was the forerunner of the International Convention on the Elimination of all Forms of Discrimination against Women (popularly known as CEDAW) which was adopted by the UN General Assembly in 1979. The convention has been ratified by 155 member states of the United Nations. For her work, Jiagge was awarded the Grand Medal of Ghana in 1969, the country's highest honor. That same year, she received the Gimbles International Award for Humanitarian Works.

Back in Ghana, Jiagge's interest and activism on matters regarding women's rights did not flag. In 1975, she founded and served as the first chair of the Ghana National Council on Women and Development, a state-supported organization that promotes the interests and well-being of Ghanaian women. In the same year, she led the Ghanaian delegation to the International Women's Conference in Mexico. In 1980, she was again the leader of Ghana's delegation to the International Women's Conference in Copenhagen. In 1993, she was a member of the UN Secretary-General's advisory group to plan the Fourth World Conference on Women that took place in Beijing in 1995.

Justice Jiagge also played an important role in the establishment of the women's bank which is now known as Women's World Banking. Prior to the 1975 International Women's Conference held in Mexico, Jiagge, as chair of the Ghana National Council on Women and Development, had convened a meeting of a cross-section of women from all over the country. Her aim was to find out the views of Ghanaian women on the theme of the Mexico conference, "Equality, Development and Peace." The broad majority of the women thought that the priority of the conference should be access to credit for women. This point was made in the Country Report on Ghana that Jiagge presented at the NGO Forum during the International Conference. The issue of credit for women was well received, and a few women from various countries caucused with Jiagge and some other members of the delegation from Ghana on how to give credit to women worldwide. They pledged $100 (US) each and presented the forum with a proposal for a bank for women with $1,200 (US) as seed money. The idea was welcomed and supported, and an organization named "Stitching to Promote Women's

World Banking" was set up, with its headquarters in New York. As of 1996, Women's World Banking had affiliates in 50 countries, and Jiagge served on the board of directors of Women's World Banking in Ghana. Members of the Board would refer to her as a "quiet heroine, a woman who understood the pain of women."

It is almost impossible to list all of Annie Jiagge's activities. A devout Christian, she was active not only in the YWCA but participated in the activities of the World Council of Churches, where she was one of the presidents from 1975 to 1983. At the World Council of Churches, she helped mobilize forces against apartheid in South Africa and was the moderator of the Program to Combat Racism from 1984 to 1991.

The government of Ghana called on her expertise several times; in 1966, she was asked to chair a Commission to Investigate the Assets of Senior Public Servants and Named Political Leaders. From 1961 to 1976, she was a member of the Council of the University of Ghana. The university honored her with a Doctor of Laws degree in 1974. In 1979, she served on the Constituent Assembly whose work ushered in Ghana's Third Republic. Even after her retirement from the Bench in 1983, she continued to serve her country and the world. In 1985, she was a member of a UN Panel to conduct Public Hearings on the Activities of Transnational Corporations in South Africa and Namibia. In 1991, she served as a member of a Committee of Experts that drafted Ghana's 1992 Constitution. From 1993 until her death in 1996, Justice Annie Jiagge was a member of Ghana's Council of State.

Justice Annie Jiagge lived a full life and was a woman with a keen sense of justice who did not suffer fools gladly. Though always busy, she found time for her immediate and extended family. She loved gardening, and friends would often find her tending her poultry in her back yard. By the time of her death in Accra, Ghana, at age 78, she was highly respected in Ghana and beyond.

SOURCES:

Personal communication with Justice Annie Ruth Jiagge, May 1995.
Unpublished Order for Memorial, Thanksgiving and Burial Service for the Late Mrs Justice Annie Jiagge, with Tributes. Prepared by the Baeta and Jiagge families. Designed by Orlando Baeta, printed by Buck Press, Accra, Ghana, 1996.

SUGGESTED READING:

Snyder, M., and M. Tadesse. *African Women and Development*. London: Zed Books, 1995 (includes an interview with Jiagge).

Mansah Prah,
Lecturer, Dept. of Sociology, University of Cape Coast, Cape Coast, Ghana, West Africa

Jiang Jieshi, Madame (b. 1898).

See Song Meiling.

Jiang Qing (1914–1991)

One of the most powerful women in China's 4,000-year history, who was, at one point, the most powerful woman in the world. Name variations: Shumeng (1914–c. 1925); Li Yunhe or Li Yun-ho (c. 1925–1934); Lan Ping or P'ing (1934–c. 1940); Jiang Qing (Chiang Ch'ing, c. 1940–1991); Madame Mao. Pronunciation: JEE-yahng CHING (rhymes with ping). Born in March 1914 in Shantung province, China; committed suicide in Beijing on May 14, 1991; daughter of Li Tewen; married a merchant named Fei, in 1930 (divorced 1931); common-law marriage, Yu Qiwei (Yü ch'i-wei, a revolutionary propagandist), in 1931; common-law marriage, Dang Na (also called Tang Na; an arts critic), in 1936 (divorced 1937); common-law marriage, Mao Zedong (Mao Tse-tung), in 1938 (died September 9, 1976); children: (with Mao) daughter Li Na.

On November 20, 1980, a 66-year-old woman in a black trouser suit—her face ivory, her hair black and neatly combed—was escorted into a room by two young soldiers and brought before two clerks who sat at a wooden table. Slim and small-boned, with sloping shoulders, the woman stood calmly, feet planted on a green carpet. Then, she bent over the table, removed her glasses, and signed a paper.

The woman was Jiang Qing, widow of Mao Zedong. The place was the office of the special prosecutor in Beijing, China. The thick document was an indictment for counterrevolution. Six days later, the trial was underway. When the court refused Jiang's conditions for legal representation, she decided to defend herself before 35 judges and 600 guests. The exchanges were stormy. Jiang not only refused to acknowledge any guilt but continually snapped back at her prosecutors. Indeed, she often appeared to be the true master of the situation and several times was removed from the courtroom. Knowing that the tribunal could not well attack the memory of the dead Mao, she boasted of being his willing instrument: "Everything I did, Mao told me to do. I was his dog; what he said to bite, I bit." At one point, a judge felt forced to yell, "Shut up, Jiang Qing." At trial's end, Jiang received the death penalty. The sentence could be altered to life imprisonment, however, if she "repented."

Jiang Qing was born Shumeng ("Pure and Simple") in March 1914 in Zhucheng, a country town of 30,000 on the south bank of the Wei River in northern China. Her father Li Tewen was a carpenter who started a wheel-repair shop, bought a small inn, and later owned farmland. He was also a 60-year-old drunkard. "Because we were poor and had little to eat," Jiang later recalled, "my father was always beating or cursing my mother." Her mother, whose name is unknown, was 30 years younger than Li and his concubine.

When Jiang was about five, her father broke her tooth and her mother's finger while in a rage. Immediately, her mother strapped Jiang to her back and left the house for good. To support herself and her daughter, she took various jobs in the rural areas, working as a transient domestic servant in situations that probably bordered on prostitution. Jiang was often left to fend for herself. At one time, while looking for her mother, Jiang was severely bitten by ravenous dogs.

As a child Jiang's feet were bound, as was customary then, and she wore pigtails. She lived in hand-me-down clothes, often castoffs from her half-brothers. Enrolled in school, she often fought with her fellow students and was expelled after one semester. "I vowed never again to let anyone bully me," she once said.

When Jiang was about ten, her father died of typhus, and her mother took her to her own parents' house in Jinan, a provincial seat. At school, a teacher gave the tall slender girl the name Yunhe ("Crane in the Clouds"). Here again, she fought with classmates and made it clear she abhorred discipline. In 1926 or 1927, she and her mother went north to Tianjin (Tientsin), a major port city, there to live with her half-sister. When Jiang was about 14, her mother abandoned her, possibly to remarry, and she was virtually an orphan.

In 1928, Jiang joined a theatrical troupe in Licheng, a suburb of Jinan, where she played minor roles and did manual labor. "All I knew is that I wanted to feed myself and that I adored drama," she later said. Her grandfather, both furious and humiliated by her behavior, paid an exorbitant sum to the troupe's boss to bring her home. Within a year, however, she joined the Shantung Provincial Experimental Arts Academy, located in Tsinan and housed in an old Confucian temple. The 15-year-old shocked her classmates by entering the innermost chamber of the building, removing the ceremonial headdress of a statue of Confucius, and exhibiting it triumphantly to her classmates.

Late in 1930, a warlord entered the city, and the school closed down. Jiang briefly became an actress in Beijing (Peking) though she was so poor she lacked underclothes. Unsuccessful because of her rustic bearing and speech, she returned to Jinan, where, at age 16, she married a man named Fei, the conventional son of a local merchant. The marriage was stormy, lasting only a few months.

Jiang took the initiative in seeking (and receiving) a divorce, then moved to Qingdao, a major port on the Yellow Sea. There she clerked in the university library, audited classes, and wrote stories, poems, and even a play, "Whose Crime?," about a young leftist. She fell in love with Yu Qiwei, a brilliant upper-class biology student who was secretly chief of propaganda in the university's Communist group. The couple lived together, something accepted within Chinese society as a common-law marriage. Under Yu's tutelage, she joined several Communist societies, including the League of Left-Wing Theater People and the League of Left-Wing Writers in 1931 and the Anti-Imperialist League in 1932. She later told biographer **Roxane Witke** that her political activism was triggered by the Japanese invasion of Manchuria in September

Jiang Qing with Mao Zedong.

1931 and the siege of Shanghai in January 1932. At first, she was so politically naive that she did not know the difference between Nationalists and Communists. Thanks to Yu, however, in 1933 she joined the Communist Party.

That year Yu was imprisoned for political activities, and Jiang sought a fresh start in the Westernized city of Shanghai. She remained involved in radical theater, performing with the city's Work Study Troupe. She also taught at a workers' night school supported in part by the Young Women's Christian Association (YWCA). Because of her underground activities with the Communist Youth League, she was imprisoned. Accounts of prison time vary from three to eight months. Once out of jail, she assumed the name Lan Ping (Blue Apple).

At age 20, Jiang first made her mark as an actress by playing Nora, the protagonist in Henrik Ibsen's *A Doll's House,* a production sponsored by the League of Left-Wing Educators. Though Jiang and others would later downplay her talent, her Nora was acclaimed by critics.

Jiang had many lovers, but it was only when she met Dang Na (Tang Na), a radical and sophisticated art critic, that she felt real attachment. Although the couple lived together, again in a common-law marriage, both Jiang and Dang possessed volatile personalities. Their relationship consisted of abundant tears and many slammed doors interspersed with bursts of romantic passion.

Early in 1937, while still married, Jiang moved in with Zhang Min, a married man who led a theatrical troupe. Dang Na was so distraught that he tried to overdose on sleeping pills; on another occasion, he tossed himself into the Whangpu River. By this time, Jiang was becoming a movie star, playing leading parts in two films: *Blood on Wolf Mountain,* an anti-Japanese allegory, and *Old Bachelor Wang,* the story of a determined young woman married to a much older man.

In the summer of 1937, the Japanese attacked Shanghai, disrupting the city's film industry. Moreover, Jiang was personally unpopular with her fellow actors for trading on her liaison with Zhang Min. Her political radicalism also made her sojourn in the city precarious. Hence, that July, Jiang left the city, bound for Communist headquarters in Yanan, a frontier outpost in northwestern China. Arriving in August, she hoped to resume her acting career amid friendly political circumstances. Conditions in Yanan were indeed primitive, reflecting conditions not

seen in parts of Europe for 500 years. Her biographer Ross Terrill portrays her as an untutored ideologue:

> [Jiang] stood out for willpower but not for political sophistication. Her knowledge of Marxism consisted of phrases, wispy ideas, and militant opinions. When she talked about the issues involved in the revolution and the war, it sounded like a tale of heroes and villains in a Peking opera. "We are right and they are wrong" was all she knew. She felt the passion of it all and the sense of struggle, but history was a closed book for her. Her mind was the wrong shape for social analysis. It was a mind geared for maneuver.

By the summer of 1938, the 22-year-old Jiang had taken two lovers (a propagandist and a film director), enrolled in the prestigious Party School, received military training, and acted and taught at the Lu Xun School of Literature and the Arts. In August 1938, she became secretary of the archives of the party's Military Commission, a post that had the advantage of placing her in close proximity to Mao Zedong. Age 44 and already the unquestioned leader of the Chinese Communist movement, Mao was in the midst of dissolving his marriage to his third wife, ✏➤ He Zizhen, comrade on the Long March and mother of five of his six children. By late 1938, Jiang had become Mao's mistress. When she was eight months pregnant, she entered a high party meeting uninvited and proclaimed "Chairman Mao and I have started living together." Later that night, Mao told the gathering that without her love, "I cannot go on with the revolution."

Top party officials opposed the union, including Zhu De (Chu Te, commander-in-chief of the Red Army and the leading general of the Long March), Zhou Enlai (liaison officer to the Nationalist government), and Liu Shaoqi (party theorist). First, Mao had not yet divorced He Zizhen, whom all greatly admired. Second, Jiang's past was a bit too colorful for a movement devoted to proletarian revolution. Party leaders finally concurred on the marriage provided that Jiang promise to abstain from political activity for 30 years.

Once Jiang married Mao, whom she later claimed to have "worshiped," she took on the name Jiang Qing (River Green). More important, she dropped any theatrical ambitions and played a subservient role. A visiting Russian officer concluded, "Jiang Qing looks after [Mao's] health, daily work, clothes, and food." The couple lived in a three-room cave that lacked electricity and running water. At one point in January 1939, acting under Mao's orders, she joined a labor battalion in Nanniwan, a wasteland 35 miles southeast of Yanan that was supposed to serve as a pilot reclamation project. As she had contracted tuberculosis, the nervous team captain let her fulfill her obligations by knitting ten sweaters.

Yet, beneath the surface, Jiang remained rebellious. Once, in 1942, Li Liuru, Mao's chief of staff, attacked her for making arbitrary judgments, exerting undue influence, and embracing bourgeois habits. (She enjoyed social dancing, horseback riding, and makeshift opera.) Mao rebuked her on the spot. At times, the couple quarreled publicly.

In 1945, when World War II ended, the incipient civil war between the Nationalists and the Communists could no longer be controlled. Jiang left household routines to serve as "political assistant" to Red forces, but the post lacked any concrete tasks and basically served as an excuse for her to travel with Mao. Soon she was on the road, journeying on horse and staying in farmers' caves. Often ill with gastrointestinal ailments, she would eat only string beans. Once, at Wang-Chia-Wang, when their cave was taken over by conferring party officials, she was relegated to a donkey shed infested with lice and flies.

When, in October 1949, Mao proclaimed the People's Republic of China, Jiang had yet to find her own role. That year, she experienced illness and depression. She traveled to Moscow to have her tonsils removed, then recovered for a month at Yalta. Upon return, she realized that her marriage had turned stale, but she refused to be discarded like He Zizhen. Once she commented, "We live together, but he is the silent type; he does not talk much." Later she was more candid: "Sex is engaging in the first rounds, but what sustains interest in the long run is power." Unqualified to do high-level political work, Jiang found low-level activity beneath her and had a short attention span. As Terrill writes, "The impulses of work on the stage were not easy to transfer to the work of bureaucratic bricklaying."

Despite his wife's ambitions, Mao did little to encourage her; to carve out her own place, she engaged in sheer manipulation. From 1949 to 1951, she served on a Film Guidance Committee of the Ministry of Culture, where she engaged in heavy-handed censorship. At the end of 1951, she pushed a land-reform project near Wuhan. It was a curious scene: the wife of the ruler of China, clad in furs while supposedly incognito, exhorting ragged peasants. The incongruity was not lost on party leaders, and the project was

He Zizhen (fl. 1930s)

Chinese Communist and third wife of Mao Zedong. Name variations: Ho Tzu-chen. Flourished in the 1930s; married Mao Zedong (1893–1976, founder of the People's Republic of China), around 1931 (divorced 1937); children: five.

Mao's first wife, whose name is unknown, was chosen by his family when he was 14, but the marriage was not consummated; he married his second wife, Yang Kaihui (Yang K'ai-hui), in 1920; they were divorced in 1930. His third wife, He Zizhen, was with him on the "Long March," the formative event of the Chinese Communist Revolution, which lasted from 1934 to 1935 and covered more than 6,000 miles. The Communists fought constant battles and skirmishes and suffered incredible deprivations and hardships. He Zizhen is said to have suffered 20 shrapnel wounds but survived, though countless numbers died.

soon abandoned. For several weeks in the winter of 1951–52, she headed the secretariat of the General Office of the Party's Central Committee, a strategic slot, but was quickly eased out. In 1954, she attempted to lead a crusade against China's greatest novel, the 18th-century *Dream of the Red Chamber*, though she could not get it purged from China's literary canon.

Frequently ill, Jiang returned to Russia in 1952 and twice in 1955, the latter two times to receive treatment for cervical cancer. By the late '50s, she was spending much of her time outside Beijing, surrounded by nurses and helpers and isolated even from Mao and their daughter Li Na. Unsympathetically Mao said of persons unknown but with an obvious reference to his wife, "I have never heard of so much high blood pressure and liver infection. If a person doesn't exercise but only eats well, dresses well, lives comfortably, and drives wherever he goes, he will be beset by a lot of illnesses."

In the 1960s, however, Mao ceased ignoring Jiang. Indeed, he turned her into a veritable political partner. In 1962, she was given the responsibility for revolutionizing plays and films. In 1964, she was "elected" to the National People's Congress, that is the parliament, representing her native province of Shantung. Mao's Great Leap Forward of 1958, an effort to industrialize his nation with extreme rapidity, had turned sour, causing the death by starvation of 20 million Chinese in the process. After such a costly fiasco, he had to share power with others, including Liu Shaoqi, chair of the People's Republic, and Deng Xiaoping, head of the party secretariat. Furthermore, Mao was suffering from Parkinson's disease. Though his relationship to Jiang had long been shaky at best, he realized that she combined vaulting ambition, native shrewdness, a genius at polarizing situations, and the intensity of one possessed. Hence, she quickly became a significant ally when Mao sorely needed such allies. "Mao knew Jiang's limitations," notes Terrill:

> She was good at lighting fires but not at managing a conflagration or putting one out. She could fire shots from a parapet, but she did not know how to handle troops on a battlefield. It didn't matter; the Cultural Revolution was to be mainly lighting fires and firing shots.

The Great Cultural Revolution, as it was called, lasted from late 1965 to April 1969. It involved a full-scale attack on the party and the bureaucracy, two elements Mao saw as curbing his power. Rallying organized legions of Chinese youth who took the name "Red Guards," Mao's revolution was really a nihilistic upheaval. Among its consequences were the closing of schools and factories, fragmentation of the army, the beating and imprisonment of scholars, and the destruction of priceless art treasures. Under attack were the Four Olds: old ideas, old culture, old customs, old habits. Historian John King Fairbank finds the consequences severe: 400,000 people dead from malnutrition, 60% of the party purged. By mid-1968, the Chinese government itself had disintegrated, although the Red Guards themselves were unable to control the country. At the same time, the Cultural Revolution lacked a political program, much less a coherent ideology.

To be empress is your ambition.

—Anonymous poem, addressing Jiang Qing, seen in Tiananmen Square, 1976

In all this upheaval, Jiang was at the forefront. In fact, biographer Terrill suspects that without her there might not have been a Cultural Revolution at all. She once said, "I am fond of firing cannon shots." She encouraged the smashing of temples, the destruction of ancient books, and the branding as "bourgeois" a host of items, including blue jeans, Beethoven, and sunglasses. Known particularly for her inflammatory speeches to young rebels, she felt that the Red Guards were in some sense personally hers. More directly under her control were thousands of cultural officials and performing artists, who soon felt her wrath if they did not share her vision of "socialist realism." Speaking in general

of the Revolution, she remarked with pride, "We dragged them out and hung them up." She used it to settle scores that went back to the 1930s. Some of her victims died in prison.

Acting first as informal cultural commissar, she wrote and promoted an opera, *Spark Among the Reeds* (later called *Shajiabang*), centering on the exploits of the New Fourth Army in the fight against Japan. Then came her fostering of two ballets, *White-Haired Girl,* dealing with an innocent maiden persecuted by an evil landlord, and *The Red Detachment of Women,* a military saga taking place on Hainan Island. By the winter of 1965, she was brazen enough to tell the Central Philharmonic Society, "The capitalist symphony is dead." In 1966, Lin Biao (Lin Piao), party vice-chair and Mao's heir apparent, appointed her chief adviser to the army on cultural matters, a post that put her squarely in the mainstream of political power.

In September 1967, Jiang, like Mao, found the chaos intolerable. She denounced "ultra-left tendencies" and praised the army and the official government. Yet that very year she backed the Campaign to Purify Class Ranks, a new purge effort.

Jiang's ideology was warmed-over Maoism of the most primitive sort. The world was in constant flux. By continual struggle, light would overcome darkness. China sought only "poor, black, and small friends." The nation must be "Red in quality as well as in name." "Hurricanes of revolution" were imminent everywhere. Unlike many Communists, however, she was extremely xenophobic, seeing foreigners as an unavoidable evil, people simply to be manipulated. Yet, despite her quest for power, she had no real interest in military and economic affairs, much less bureaucratic administration. She was skilled in palace intrigue but did not know how to build a national organization.

In April 1969, Jiang became the first woman ever elected to the 21-member Politbureau. Here she fought incessantly with Lin Biao until 1971, when he was reportedly killed in a plane crash over Outer Mongolia. She started becoming an avid student of the life of Empress *Wu Zetian, a 7th-century ruler who was living proof that a female could reach the pinnacle of power in a male-dominated society. In the 1970s, Jiang again took on lovers, including a pianist, a minister, and a ping-pong champion who was appointed Minister of Sports. At the same time, she became so paranoid over the possibility of assassination that she once lunged at a nurse with scissors.

In her activities, Jiang found close allies in the Shanghai Faction of the Cultural Revolution Group, better known as the Gang of Four: Zhang Chunqiao (Chang Ch'un-ch'iao), chair of the Shanghai Revolution Committee; Yao Wenyuan, a radical polemicist whose article of November 1965 triggered the Cultural Revolution itself; and Wang Hongwen (Wang Hung-wen), a young firebrand who had been a textile worker.

To the degree that the group had a program, it centered on self-sustaining revolutionary development, retention of tight control over all culture, and continuing the communes consolidated in the Great Leap Forward. Working-class youth should be admitted to college without formal examination whereas educated youth must work in the countryside. The "barefoot doctor" system of paramedics must be encouraged. Mao had warned the group in 1974, "You'd better be careful; don't let yourselves become a small faction of four." Be that as it may, Mao kept the faction in power until he died.

As Mao grew progressively weaker, his dependence on Jiang increased. In some ways, he was irritated by her new independent power, saying in private that she harbored "wild ambitions"—including the ultimate post, as party chair. She was "poking her nose into everything" yet "represents only herself." At the same time, Mao did nothing to curb her ambition. When he was away from Beijing for eight months, Jiang appeared to be the very linchpin of the state. She gave out "instructions" that had the power of edicts. As "natural leader," she received in Mao's name such foreign dignitaries as the Philippines' *Imelda Marcos. As Mao grew closer to death, his private remarks on Jiang became more acerbic. "Few people suit her taste. Only one—she herself." He continued, "Come the future, she'll have disputes with everyone. . . . [A]fter I die, she'll make trouble."

When, in January 1976, Premier Zhou Enlai died, a major barrier to Jiang's power was removed. However, at a memorial festival given in Tiananmen Square in Zhou's honor, a poem was hung.

> Lady X, indeed you are insane
> To be empress is your ambition
> Take this mirror
> And see what you are like . . .
> You deceive your superiors
> And delude your subordinates
> Yet, for types like you,
> Good times won't last long.

Jiang ordered all tributes to Zhou removed, causing a riot on April 5 that lasted 14 hours and involved at least 100,000 people. She blamed Deng Xiaoping, the vice premier already in semi-disgrace, for the bitter criticism of her. A panicked Politbureau immediately removed Deng from all posts. Not content with Deng's humiliation, Jiang said publicly, "Deng Xiaoping wants to consign me to hell! He's far worse than even [Nikita] Khrushchev ever was! The man wants to get crowned, to declare himself emperor." She also sought to reinterpret Marxism in light of female power:

> In the sphere of production women are fundamental. For labor is the basic force of production, and all labor is born of woman. Man's contribution to history is nothing more than a drop of sperm. Men should move over and in the future let women take over the management of things.

When Mao died on September 5, 1976, the Gang of Four set out to gain formal control of China. They were backed by 40% of the Politbureau, the city of Shanghai, much of Manchuria, and at least five of China's eleven military regions. Jiang's circle also came up with a document they claimed was Mao's "true will," which—not surprisingly—transferred all power to Jiang.

Marshal Ye Jianying and Hua Guofeng, a Mao protégé who was acting premier, moved quickly. They deployed military units at various stations outside Beijing. The military commander at Canton was on alert in case reinforcements were needed. At a meeting of the Politbureau on October 5, the Gang of Four showed its hand. It proposed Jiang as party chair, Zhang Chunqiao as premier, and Wang Hongwen as head of the National People's Congress. The body adjourned without taking action, agreeing to meet the next day.

When the Politbureau gathered the following evening, Wang, Zhang, and Yao were knocked to the floor by security guards, then arrested. A colonel and two captains drove to Guanyuan Villa, flicked on the light switches of the master bedroom, and unceremoniously told Jiang, "Don't move! You are under arrest." She retorted, "The chairman's body is hardly cold, and yet you have the gall to mount a coup!" Soon the state-controlled press was labeling her the White-Boned Demon. In an effigy of her carried by marchers in Shanghai, a hangman's noose was shown around her neck and calligraphic characters of her name were made to look like bones.

While in prison, Jiang fell into depression. At the end of 1977, she tried to commit suicide by banging her head against the cell wall. Yet by 1980 she was again feisty. "Do you dare release me?" she asked Hua Guofeng. "Just release me and in half a year I'll eliminate the lot of you." Hua replied, "If you were released, people would assail you, and in half an hour you'd be shredded meat."

Ironically, the trial of the Gang of Four was itself a kangaroo court, doing little to reassure foreigners that the rule of law was coming to China. In the words of China historian Jonathan Spence, the Gang was "accused of almost every crime in the political book," ranging from organizing their own military forces to hindering earthquake relief.

After the trial, Jiang and Zhang Chunqiao received a suspended death sentence. Two years later, when Wang Hongwen publicly engaged in massive self-criticism, Jiang wrote on the wall of her cell, "I'm not afraid of having my head chopped off." Four years after her sentence, Deng Xiaoping, by then the controlling force in China, was unrepentant concerning her treatment. Jiang Qing "is a very, very evil woman," he said. "She is so evil that any evil thing you say about her isn't evil enough, and if you ask me to judge her with the grades as we do in China, I answer that this is impossible, there are no grades for Jiang Qing, that Jiang Qing is a thousand times a thousand below zero."

In 1988, Jiang was placed under house arrest, but a year later she was briefly interned again for accusing Deng of being a murderer. Commenting on the events in Tiananmen Square on June 4, 1989, she claimed that neither she nor Mao would have ever massacred crowds. On May 14, 1991, she hanged herself at Beijing's Public Security Hospital. In a four-sentence press release concerning her death, the Chinese government made no mention of the power that she once wielded, or even that she was the widow of Mao Zedong.

SOURCES:

Terrill, Ross. *Madame Mao, The White-Boned Demon: A Biography of Madame Mao Zedong.* Updated ed. NY: Touchstone, 1992.

Witke, Roxane. *Comrade Chiang Ch'ing.* Boston, MA; Little, Brown, 1977.

SUGGESTED READING:

Chi Hsin. *The Case of the Gang of Four.* Hong Kong: Cosmos Books, 1977.

Chin, Steven K. *The Gang of Four.* University of Hong Kong, 1977.

Fairbank, John King. *The Great Chinese Revolution, 1800–1985.* NY: Harper and Row, 1986.

Lotta, Raymond, ed. *And Mao Makes Five.* Chicago, IL: Banner Press, 1978.

Spence, Jonathan D. *The Search for Modern China.* NY: W.W. Norton, 1990.

Zhisue, Li. *The Private Life of Chairman Mao.* NY: Random House, 1994.

Justus D. Doenecke,
Professor of History, New College of the
University of South Florida, Sarasota, Florida

Jimena Munoz (c. 1065–1128).

See Munoz, Jimena.

Jinga (c. 1580s–1663).

See Njinga.

Jingū (c. 201–269)

Legendary empress of Yamato, the ancient kingdom of Japan, who led military campaigns to defeat the Korean kingdoms of Silla and Paekche. Name variations: Jingo; Jingō; Jingo-kogo; Jingu. Pronunciation: gin-GOO. Her historical existence has not been proven; she may have been a composite of several imperial consorts in ancient Japan who were shamanesses. According to the Kojiki *and the* Nihongi, *she was born in 201 in western Japan and died in 269; daughter of Prince Okinaga Sukune and Princess Katsuraki Takanuka; married Emperor Chūai; children: Prince Homuda, later known as Emperor Ōjin.*

Ruled as regent between the reigns of the legendary Emperor Chūai and the Emperor Ōjin when there was no official sovereign; ruled as a shamaness with the assistance of divination and acted as a spiritual medium; during regency, led troops in a number of military campaigns to subdue internal resistance in the Yamato kingdom and defeat neighboring kingdoms, most notably, the Korean kingdoms of Silla and Paekche.

In the ancient kingdom of Yamato, which became the nation of Japan, female and male chieftains ruled in partnership; the female chieftains provided religious protection through spiritual divination, while the male chieftains handled political and economic matters. Female imperial consorts, who at times ruled the kingdom as regents, were given the title *nakatsu-sumera-mikoto*, which meant either "the august medium who transmits the divine word of the heavenly spirits" or "the one who carries on the imperial duties between the death of her husband and the occasion of the next emperor." In the historical chronicles of ancient Japan, these shamaness queens were represented by the portrayal of Empress Jingū, who was depicted as having the capacity to discern the will of heavenly spirits and subdue their malevolent inclinations for the well-being of the kingdom. Jingū was said to have been a sword-wielding military leader who, dressed as a male warrior, used her spiritual powers to lead her troops to victory.

Although archeological evidence supports the existence of shamaness queens, no evidence has yet been found to authenticate the existence of Jingū. The legends of Jingū are found in the *Kojiki* and the *Nihongi,* historical chronicles commissioned in the 8th century by empresses and based on the oral legends that had traditionally been conveyed by women storytellers. While there are chronological discrepancies, modern scholars believe that the legends of Jingū's military exploits represent actual Japanese campaigns in Korea late in the 4th century, and that the figure of Jingū was a composite of several shamaness rulers. The intriguing aspect of the Jingū legend is that the most significant military victories, technological advances, and cultural developments of ancient Japan were attributed to a woman.

According to the chronicles, Jingū was of noble lineage, the daughter of Prince Okinaga Sukune, a descendant of the imperial family, and Princess **Katsuraki Takanuka,** a descendant of a mystical maiden created by the spirits. Jingū's story began, however, with her marriage to the legendary Emperor Chūai. The chronicles depicted Chūai as having been engaged in military campaigns to subdue neighboring warrior families. Jingū accompanied him on these campaigns, frequently performing mystical rites of divination. Her capacity to communicate with the spirits and enlist their support enhanced the imperial couple's popularity with the people.

In the midst of a campaign against the neighboring Kumaso people, the emperor sought the assistance of his consort to divine the outcome of the battle. An imperial minister, a male shaman, strummed a stringed instrument in order to send Jingū into a trance, during which she became a medium used by the spirits to communicate. Through Jingū, spirits conveyed the message that the emperor should cease his battle with the Kumaso and turn his attention, instead, across the sea to a kingdom called Silla, which was rich with gold, silver, and jewels. If the emperor agreed to worship the spirit who spoke through Jingū, with an offering of a ship and a rice field, the spirit promised that the emperor would achieve victory in Silla without the need to draw swords.

Emperor Chūai refused, however, to believe the words that he had heard, first dismissing them as Jingū's own fabrication, later charging that she had been overcome by a treacherous spirit. Jingū again fell into a trance and the spirit repeated the message, angrily declaring that the emperor would never win the riches of Silla. Henceforward, the spirit announced, it would address Jingū as empress, and the child she carried would one day receive the riches of Silla. One source states that the emperor died immediately after rejecting the words of the spirit, while another source states that the emperor pursued the Kumaso and died in battle.

> *M*obilizing troops to make war is a grave decision that affects our state and our future. I wish to assume full responsibility.
>
> **—Empress Jingū**

Jingū initially kept the death of her husband a secret, while she proceeded to obtain the spiritual resources necessary to consolidate her rule. She entered a ceremonial hall to purify herself and the kingdom after the contamination associated with the death of the emperor. Entering into a trance, she sought to identify the spirit whom she should worship. After eight days of supplication, the spirit identified itself and repeated the message it had conveyed to the emperor. Thereafter, Jingū sent envoys to make offerings at the appropriate shrines and named a general to continue the campaigns against the troublesome Kumaso. This time, the Kumaso quickly surrendered. Jingū achieved the goal that had eluded her husband because she divined the will of the spirits, acted in accordance with their words, and enlisted their power for the benefit of the kingdom.

Through divination, Jingū received confirmation that it was the will of the spirits that she clothe herself as a man and lead her troops into battle against the kingdom of Silla and win its riches for the child to whom she would give birth. Summoning the imperial counselors, she sought their approval for a declaration of war. An astute politician, Jingū dressed as a male warrior, informed the counselors that she enjoyed the support of the spirits, and assured them that if victorious, they would receive the credit, and if unsuccessful, she would take the blame. The counselors unanimously supported a declaration of war against the kingdom of Silla.

Thereafter, Jingū sought to recruit and arm troops for the campaign. She invoked divine assistance by making offerings to the spirits, and the recruits arrived in the necessary numbers. Assembling on the beach, three divisions of soldiers cheered Jingū when she appeared dressed as a man, wielding a battle-ax. Addressing them on military tactics, she told them, "You must not engage in atrocities; avoid unnecessary killing and spare those who surrender." She promised to reward those who faithfully followed her instructions and punish those who showed cowardice. Finally, Jingū became a medium, and through her, a spirit promised to attach itself to the person of the empress and protect her, while leading her troops into battle.

After lecturing her troops, Jingū felt her baby move within her. Praying for a sign, she girded her loins with a rock and invoked the spirits to postpone the birth of the child until her successful return from the campaign. The empress and her troops set sail, her ship escorted by large sea creatures and ushered by favorable winds. Under the leadership of Jingū, the Yamato troops landed and, taking the people of Silla by surprise, marched unopposed to the palace of the king. Impressed by her supernatural powers, the king of Silla surrendered and offered Jingū an annual tribute gift of horses (superior continental horses that would prove useful in her future military campaigns) and 100 artisans, both female and male. Some of her troops wished to kill the king, but she reminded them of her earlier admonition and the soldiers acquiesced. Jingū sent her men to local offices throughout the kingdom to confiscate riches, maps, and family registries (which would assist them in levying and collecting taxes). Finally, after her peaceful subjugation of Silla, Jingū planted her spear in front of the Silla king's palace, as a symbol of her victory. Upon her return to Yamato, Jingū gave birth to a son who was to become (the historically verified) Emperor Ōjin. Her prayers had been answered, and the prophecies of the spirits fulfilled.

In the year following her return, Jingū successfully entered battle to protect the eventual succession of her son, and thus, her regency because the sons of an earlier wife of the Emperor Chūai wished to remove her. Consistently, Jingū sought to discern the will of the spirits and offer supplication. As a result, her interests prospered, while those of her enemies failed. The imperial counselors honored Jingū with the title "Empress Dowager." During her life, she ruled, preventing the ascension of her son.

In the 47th year of Jingū's regency, disputes developed between the Korean kingdoms of Silla and Paekche. Envoys from Silla diverted the tribute gifts with which the king of Paekche sought to establish a diplomatic relationship with the kingdom of Yamato. Through divination, Jingū sought an appropriate policy. During the next two years, she punished Silla with an expedi-

tionary force. Yamato troops pacified seven tribal groups and gave their land to the king of Paekche. Thereafter, Paekche sent annual tribute gifts to Jingū's court. In the 52nd year of her reign, the king of Paekche sent a ceremonial sword of steel to Jingū, a sword that is still extant. Jingū died in the 69th year of her regency (there are chronological discrepancies between Korean records and the dates given in Japanese chronicles).

Within the Jingū legends, myth and history were intertwined to represent the political consolidation of the Yamato kingdom and the military exploits on the Korean peninsula which are known to have occurred beginning in the 4th century. The events depicted in the Jingū legends represent a turning point in the ancient Japanese kingdom, when large numbers of Korean and Chinese immigrants poured into Yamato with advanced learning. Many of these immigrants were skilled in metallurgy and rice farming, as well as engineering techniques needed for the construction of irrigation networks. Power struggles for access to the wealth of the Korean peninsula, depicted in the various battle scenes of the Jingū legends, continued in the Korean kingdoms and Yamato in the 6th and 7th centuries. With respect to the historical credibility of the Jingū legends, historian **Michiko Y. Aoki** has concluded, "Jingū is a legendary woman of Japan with a considerable degree of historicity in her way. Not only does she embody certain real-life female leaders in particular, but also testifies to the sincere respect and the honored place commanded by Japanese women in general in ancient time."

SOURCES:

Aoki, Michiko Y. "Empress Jingū: The Shamaness Ruler," in *Heroic with Grace: Legendary Women of Japan*. Edited by Chieko Irie Mulhern. Armonk, NY: M.E. Sharpe, 1991.

Brown, Delmer M. "The Yamato Kingdom," in *The Cambridge History of Japan*. Vol. I. Edited by Delmer M. Brown. Cambridge: Cambridge University Press, 1993.

SUGGESTED READING:

Aston, William George. *Nihongi: Chronicles of Japan from the Earliest Times to A.D. 697*. Rutland, VT: C.E. Tuttle, 1972.

Linda L. Johnson,
Professor of History, Concordia College,
Moorhead, Minnesota

Jinnah, Fatima (1893–1967)

Pakistani politician and sister of Mohammad Ali Jinnah who helped her brother realize his goal of an independent nation for Indian Muslims and stood for the presidency of Pakistan in 1964 as a conservative candidate. Name variations: Mohtarama Fatima Jin-

nah; Fatimah Jinnah; Madar-i-Millat Mohtarama Fatima Jinnah. Pronunciation: FAH-tee-mah JIN-nah. Born in 1893 in Karachi, India; died in 1967 in Pakistan; third daughter of Jinnah Poonja (a merchant) and Mithibai; attended the Bandra Convent school, 1902, and enrolled in Dr. Ahmad Dental College, Calcutta, 1919.

Became the ward of her elder brother Mohammad Ali Jinnah upon the death of her father (c. 1901–18); opened a dental clinic in Bombay (1923); moved in with her brother Mohammad Ali Jinnah upon the death of his wife Ruttenbai (1929); traveled in Europe (1929–35); entered politics (1936), with the express aim of establishing an independent homeland for Indian Muslims; elected delegate to the Bombay Provincial Muslim League Council (March 1947); served as public speaker and politician (1947–67); supported and nursed Mohammad Ali Jinnah during his final illness until his death on September 11, 1948; worked to establish educational institutions, including Fatima Jinnah Medical College for Girls (c. 1949–51); worked to ease the plight of Muslim refugees entering Pakistan by founding Industrial Homes in Karachi, Peshawar, and Quetta (c. 1949–51); assisted in funding and maintaining scholarships, schools, and hospitals in Pakistan (1958–59); unsuccessfully stood for president of Pakistan (1964), challenging Ayub Khan for the leadership of the country.

Fatima Jinnah, the sister of Mohammad Ali Jinnah, was perhaps the biggest supporter of her brother's search for an independent Muslim state in India. She was also a leader in the Pakistani independence movement in her own right. After her brother's early death from cancer, Fatima Jinnah at least partly took his place as a leader for a conservative, Muslim Pakistan. In 1964, she challenged former general Ayub Khan for the presidency of the country, seeing him as antidemocratic and a threat to the freedom of ordinary Pakistanis. Although she lost the election and died only three years later, Fatima Jinnah maintained the loyalty and love of many Islamic Pakistanis. "Whenever Pakistan faced a political crisis," writes Atique Zafar Sheikh, director general of the National Archives of Pakistan, "Fatima Jinnah stood with the people. She always boldly and courageously challenged every action against people, democracy, and Islamic ideology. The people of Pakistan had great faith in her."

In her biography of Mohammad Ali Jinnah entitled *My Brother,* Fatima Jinnah related the history of her family. Her father Jinnah Poonja

was born in the year 1857—the same year as the great Indian Mutiny—in the village of Paneli, in the state of Gondal near the city of Bombay. He established himself in business and married a local girl named **Mithibai**, a native of the village of Datha, in 1874. Jinnah Poonja's business quickly expanded; he taught himself to speak English and relocated to the town of Karachi in the province of Sind. There his children were born, including his eldest son Mohammad Ali and his third daughter, Fatima. "With business contacts established with Grahams Trading Co.," wrote Jinnah, "my father started doing business in isinglass and gumarabic, in addition to his various other business interests." By then, Jinnah Poonja had business connections with a number of countries, in particular with England and Hong Kong. She continued:

> [My] father would collect me and my two sisters at night and teach us to read and write English. He was a strict disciplinarian, and we had to behave in his presence during that tuition hour as if we were at school in our class-room. In our childish eyes father appeared a big man, one who could speak English so well. We envied him for it, and how we wished we could speak English as well as he did. Sometimes when we three sisters met and were in a playful mood, we would imitate father's English. One of us would say to the other, "Ish, Phish, Ish, Phish, Yes"; and the other would reply, "Ish, Phish, Ish, Phish, No." We took this game so seriously, feigning we were at last on the threshold of learning English, if we had not already mastered that language.

This dedication to family was shared by Jinnah Poonja's youngest sister. "Manbai Poofi would gather me, my sisters and my cousins round her after sunset," Fatima Jinnah recalled:

> She was the centre of our eyes and ears, and we listened to her, enraptured by the bewitching way in which she would narrate her stories, night after night. She told tales of fairies and the flying carpet; of jins and dragons; and they seemed to our childish minds to be wonderful tales, stories out of this world.

Fatima Jinnah's devotion to her brother may have had its origins in their close-knit family. She lost her mother when she was very young, in 1894 or 1895. Her father, left with the responsibility of a large family and no wife to help care for them, aged prematurely. His business had collapsed, and he had to rely on his eldest son to help support the family. When Jinnah Poonja also died unexpectedly, Mohammad Ali Jinnah took full responsibility for his younger brothers and sisters. Fatima Jinnah became Mohammad's ward "at the age of eight," she reported, and she lived with him from the death of her father until he married for the second time in 1918. Mohammad oversaw Fatima's education, allowing her to enter the Bandra Convent school in 1902 despite her strict Islamic upbringing. In a time when Indian Muslim women were expected to stay at home and concentrate on raising and tending their families and husbands, he encouraged her plans to enroll in the Dr. Ahmad Dental College in Calcutta.

After the death of Mohammad Ali's second wife **Ruttenbai Petit Jinnah** in 1929, Fatima returned to her brother's household and lived with him until his death in 1948. She also accompanied him on his self-imposed exile in Europe from 1929 to 1935. When he entered politics in 1936 with the express aim of establishing an independent homeland for Indian Muslims, she supported and campaigned to spread his ideas. Her efforts won her a place as a delegate to the Bombay Provincial Muslim League Council in March 1947, a time when independence for all Indians was becoming more and more of a reality. Mohammad recognized the important role his sister played in helping him create his independent Muslim state, noting, "In the days when I was expecting to be taken as a prisoner by the British Government, it was my sister who encouraged me, and said hopeful things when revolution was staring me in the face. Her constant care is about my health."

We worked and fought for Pakistan so that we and the coming generations may live therein freely and in honour, to lead simple, honest and purposeful lives and not to suffocate in an atmosphere laden with fear and reeking with corruption.

—Fatima Jinnah

The greatest strain on Mohammad's health came through his efforts to obtain a separate state for Indian Muslims. Followers of Islam had always been in the minority among native Indians, but they had also for centuries been a ruling elite. From the early 16th century on, the Great Mughuls had ruled all India under an Islamic government centered in Delhi. For the most part, Muslims and Hindus left each other alone, but in the 18th century the Muslim rulers began a massive crackdown on Hindu worshippers. The Mughul ruler Aurangzeb destroyed Hindu temples and places of worship and reinstated special taxes on non-Muslims. The Hindu resistance to this oppression resulted in the breakup of the Mughul empire and the establishment of a number of small semi-independent states, some Mus-

lim, some Hindu, and some neither. The British stepped into the power vacuum left by the end of the Mughul empire and made their own Raj out of the varied pieces left behind. By the mid-20th century, Muslims constituted about 25% of the total Indian population.

Fatima Jinnah and her brother represented only one of many Indian groups that sought self-determination in the breakup of the British Empire. The problem of self-government had plagued the British in India since the late 19th century. In 1885, a retired British official named Allan Octavian Hume assembled native Indians into a Congress for the purpose of promoting Indian unity. At first, the Congress was limited to acting only in an advisory capacity, but as time passed the influential lawyers and wealthy men that made up the Congress sought more and more power. For example, they asked that Civil Service examinations—competitive exams for government posts—be held in India as well as in England.

But the reforms were threatening to the Muslims; more Hindus than Muslims would benefit from moving the Civil Service exams to India. In addition, until 1835 the Indian government had used Persian as its working language—the administrative language of the old Muslim Mughal emperors. "Muslim schools still taught in Persian, so its replacement by English, intended merely as an efficient act of westernisation, had in fact discriminated between one Indian group and another," writes Brian Lapping. "When the Congress won easier access for Indians to the Civil Service, many Muslims feared that the beneficiaries would be Hindus only. They preferred British administrators."

Many Muslims broke with the Congress on the question of minority rights for practitioners of their religion. One of the splinter groups founded to speak to Muslim fears was the Muslim League. By 1937, Mohammad Ali Jinnah had become the leader of the League and was representing its interests in nationwide elections. Though he had originally been a member of the Indian Congress, he had become disillusioned with it. The Congress was dominated by Hindus, but, because it had some Islamic members and Muslims had voted for it, it claimed to represent all Indians. Mohammad rejected the Congress' claim and set out to create a united Islamic state from the scattered Indian Muslims. Between 1939 and 1947, he managed to unite Islamic India behind the idea of Pakistan: a separate Muslim state that would provide political equality and protection for Muslims.

By the end of World War II, the pressure for total independence from both Hindus and Muslims was becoming almost irresistible. "The Hindus believed themselves to be the natural successors to the British as rulers of all India," explains James Morris; "the Muslims believed themselves to be natural rulers *per se*, never subject to Hindu rule and never likely to be; the Sikhs [another religious community with a history of being persecuted by Muslims] believed themselves to be separate from, superior to and irrepressible by any other parties in the dispute; the British thought themselves, *au fond*, indispensable." In addition, there were a number of independent principalities whose rulers owed their allegiance to the Crown, rather than to the Empire.

The key negotiator in the dispute was the last British viceroy of India, Lord Louis Mountbatten, who helped create a division of the subcontinent that was accepted, if not acclaimed, by all sides. Mohandas Gandhi, Jawaharlal Nehru, Mohammad Ali Jinnah, and Mountbatten together devised a partition of British rule into two parts: India, dominated by Hindus, and Pakistan, dominated by Muslims. Each of the individual states was to choose which nation it would join in August of 1947. Most Indian Muslims were concentrated in the states of Punjab, Baluchistan, Sind, Jammu, and Kashmir, and the Northwest Frontier in the river valley of the Indus in the west, and the states of Bengal and Assam in Ganges delta in the east, where Muslims made up 50% or more of the population. Only in a few other states, including Delhi, Bihar and Orissa, Ajmer-Merwara, the Western India States Agency, and Hyderabad, did Muslims make up more than 10% of the total population. Because the Muslims were so widely scattered, the nation of Pakistan came to contain two geographically separate states: West Pakistan around the Indus valley and East Pakistan (now Bangladesh) along the lowest part of the Ganges.

This division was unpopular with many extremists on both sides. On January 30, 1948, Gandhi himself was assassinated by a young Hindu fanatic who felt that the partition was immoral. There was also a massive emigration as people of one faith who lived on the wrong side of the border left home and moved to be with their co-religionists. "Eleven million people abandoned their homes and moved in hordes across the countryside, hastening to the right side of the new communal frontiers," writes Morris.

> The roads were crammed with refugees, people clung to the steps of trains, or crowded upon their roofs, and the old gypsy confusion of India, the crowding and the clutter,

Fatima Jinnah

the always familiar scenes of exhaustion, bewilderment and deprivation, were multiplied a thousand times. Violence erupted on a scale never known in British India before, even in the Mutiny. It was like a gigantic boil bursting, an enormous eruption of frustrations and resentments suppressed for so long by the authority of Empire. Whole communities were massacred. Entire trainloads of refugees died on the tracks, to the last child in arms. In the Punjab gangs of armed men roamed the countryside, slaughtering columns of refugees, and thousands of people died unremarked in the streets of Amritsar.

The other problem facing Mohammad's new government was the question of Kashmir. This state, bordering on the northeast frontier of West Pakistan, was one of the independent states that was supposed to declare allegiance to either Pakistan or India. Mohammad confidently expected that Kashmir, with its majority Islamic population, would enter Pakistan as a Muslim state. In the same year, however, some armed Pakistanis invaded Kashmir to help in a local Muslim revolt. The ruler—who was a Hindu—fled the country and took shelter in New Delhi. While living there, he signed papers turning his country over to the Hindu Indian government. Indian and Pakistani troops fought in India for the next two years, until the United Nations established a cease-fire line in January 1949.

The stress of dealing with the refugee crisis and the problem of Kashmir took its toll on Mohammad Ali Jinnah's health. Recognized almost universally among the new Pakistanis as the father of their country, he had been given the title Quaid-e-Azam (the Great Leader). Mohammad might have been able to hold the nation of Pakistan together by force of personality, but his health broke down completely about a year after the partition. Tuberculosis, made worse by a longtime smoking habit and the fatigue and constant strain of the independence movement, contributed to his death on September 11, 1948. "Only a few months earlier," wrote Fatima Jinnah, "he had said in his address to the students of Islamia College at Peshawar, 'You will learn from your costly experience and the knocks that you shall have received during your life time.' To go his own way and to learn by hard knocks, that had been the dominant keynote of his character throughout his life."

After her brother's death, Fatima Jinnah became the chief focus for his program for the future of Pakistan. Pakistanis perceived her as her brother's political heir, and they believed that she spoke with his voice on affairs of state. In her early speeches, from 1948 to about 1958, she reiterated the themes that had dominated Mohammad's last years: the annexation of Kashmir, the fate of Muslim refugees in Pakistan and India, and the necessity of preserving democratic institutions in Pakistan. She also emphasized three themes of her own: the important place Islam held in the political life of Pakistan, the necessity of developing a feeling of unity and nationhood between East and West Pakistan, and the role Muslim women had played and would continue to play in the future life of the country. These themes continually appear in Fatima Jinnah's writings over the next two decades.

The speech she delivered in 1951 on the third anniversary of her brother's death demonstrates the ways in which she tried to rally support and press for unity between Pakistanis. She reminded the nation of Pakistan that "the problems crying for solution" at the time of her brother's death were still awaiting solution. Besides the Kashmir problem, there was the question of refugees, she continued:

> [I]t should not be forgotten that it is a human problem, and we cannot allow the vast mass of humanity to remain in . . . misery for a long length of time. Let me remind you of the purpose for which Pakistan was established. It was . . . that Muslims may be enabled to lead an independent, honourable and free life according to their own concept of civilization, culture, education and economy. Freedom must be a reality for every individual and he should be able to live in an atmosphere where he can enjoy a peaceful and independent life.

Unfortunately for Fatima Jinnah's hopes, Muslim unity proved less strong than rivalries between East and West Pakistan and rivalries within the government. Liaqat Ali Khan, Mohammad's chosen successor and first prime minister of Pakistan, was assassinated in 1951. Fatima Jinnah continued to speak out on political issues in her annual addresses on Pakistan Day, on the anniversary of her brother's death, and on other occasions when she was invited to speak to the public. In 1953, she attacked Indian prime minister Jawaharlal Nehru for having neglected to hold the promised plebiscite to determine the political future of Kashmir. In 1954, she addressed a public meeting in East Pakistan, urging national unity: "People of East and West Pakistan are one and we shall live together and die together." Later that year in a speech in Karachi, she pleaded for an increased number of women in professional services: "There are many ways in which women can contribute to the growth and strength of the nation. . . . Pakistan requires the services of a number of women social workers, women teachers and above all women doctors and nurses." In a 1957 speech, she warned of the moral and political decline of the country.

By that time, Pakistan had undergone two significant changes. First, it had become a republic, adopting a constitution that gave equal representation in the legislature to East and West Pakistan. Second, its military became an important part of the political process. On October 7, 1958, former General Muhammad Ayub Khan led a coup that overthrew the newly established constitution and established martial law. Ayub Khan introduced another constitution in 1962 and was elected to the presidency of Pakistan later that year.

It was Ayub Khan's military regime that brought Fatima Jinnah thoroughly into politics again. Outraged by his banning of opposition political parties, five parties united and supported Fatima Jinnah to run for president of Pakistan. They believed that only a person with the magic name of Jinnah could overcome the differences between East and West Pakistan and successfully oppose the military regime of Ayub Khan. Fatima Jinnah was simply too well-known and well-loved to be suppressed. In 1964, she announced that she would challenge Ayub Khan for the presidency in the 1965 elections. "Freedom from [a] foreign yoke is worthless unless it results in freedom directly to choose your own Government, Legislature and the Head of the State," she declared in a public speech in October 1964, "the sovereignty in a democratic free country must reside in the people. These elections will decide whether you wish to live in this country as free citizens or that you wish to hand over your ultimate power to others on whom you have no control today. . . . I am afraid another opportunity may not be afforded to you in the future." The elections were held January 2, 1965. Soon after the polls closed, the chief election commissioner declared Muhammad Ayub Khan the winner. Fatima Jinnah asserted later that month that the elections had been irregular: "The recent election campaign has amply demonstrated that in this system the people have no effective means of ensuring that their wishes are reflected and registered in the final results." Fatima Jinnah continued to work for Islamic unity between East and West Pakistan, invoking the name and spirit of her brother, until her death in 1967.

SOURCES:

Ali, Chaudhri Muhammad. *The Emergence of Pakistan.* Columbia, 1967.

Al Mujahid, Sharif. *Jinnah.* Karachi, Pakistan: Quaid-i-Azam Academy, 1981.

Hamdani, Agha Husain. *Fatimah Jinnah: hayat aur khidmat.* Islamabad, Pakistan: Qaumi Kamishan bara'e Tahqiq-i Tarikh o Saqafat, 1978 (in Urdu).

Ispahani, M.A.H. *Qaid-e-Azam Jinnah as I Knew Him.* Karachi, Pakistan: Forward Publications, 1966.

Jinnah, Fatima. *My Brother.* Edited by Sharif Al Mujahid. Karachi, Pakistan: Quaid-e-Azam Academy, 1987.

Khan, Salahuddin, ed. and comp. *Speeches, Messages and Statements of Madar-i-Millat Mohtarama Fatima Jinnah (1948–1967).* Lahore, Pakistan: Research Society of Pakistan, University of the Punjab, 1976.

Lapping, Brian. *End of Empire.* NY: St. Martin's Press, 1985.

Morris, James. *Farewell the Trumpets: An Imperial Retreat.* NY: Harcourt, Brace, Jovanovich, 1978.

National Archives of Pakistan. *Accession List of Mohtarama Fatima Jinnah Papers.* Islamabad, Pakistan: Department of Archives, Ministry of Culture and Tourism, Government of Pakistan, 1987.

Wolpert, Stanley A. *Jinnah of Pakistan.* NY: Oxford University Press, 1984.

Kenneth R. Shepherd,
Adjunct Instructor in History,
Henry Ford Community College, Dearborn, Michigan

Jitō (645–702)

The 41st Japanese sovereign, who completed the centralization of the Japanese state under imperial rule.

Name variations: Princess Uno, Sasara, or Hirono; Empress Jito; Jito-tennō or Jitō Tenno. Pronunciation: jhee-TOE. Born in 645 (some sources cite 625) in the capital, Naniwa; died in 702 (some sources cite 701) in Fujiwara, Japan; daughter of emperor Tenji (also seen as Tenchi) and Oichi; sister of Gemmei (c. 661–721); married Prince Oama who later became Emperor Temmu; children: Prince Kusakabe (r. 690–697).

Jitō was born in 645 in the capital, Naniwa, the daughter of Emperor Tenji and **Oichi**, the sister of Empress *Gemmei. In her youth, Jitō was known for her intelligence; she studied the Chinese classics, which were usually taught only to boys. She was also politically astute, initially assisting her husband, Emperor Temmu, in his ascent to the throne by developing successful military strategies and heroically commanding the troops at Ise (the Ise Shrine, dedicated to the sun goddess, symbolized imperial rule). Jitō educated herself on matters of law and drafted regulations during Temmu's reign. In order to forestall power struggles following Temmu's death, Jitō assumed the throne and moved immediately to consolidate central political authority: she ordered a national census in order to more effectively collect taxes, and she established the army and drafted their training regulations and service codes. In 694, Jitō established a new national capital in Fujiwara.

While these achievements were relatively short-lived, Jitō also made several long-term contributions. First, a government bureaucracy was created (Taika Reforms). The tribal (kingship) system was ended, and the Japanese state was placed under a single sovereign (*tennō*) rather than many chieftains. Second, as a patron of Buddhism, Jitō supervised efforts to proselytize throughout Japan. Finally, a poet herself, she was a patron of the arts. Her poems were included in the imperial anthology, the *Manyōshu.* On the death of her husband, she wrote:

> Sadness I feel at eve,
> And heart-rending grief at morn—
> The sleeves of my coarse-cloth robe
> Are never for a moment dry.

Jitō also recognized local artists and performers, particularly those skilled in the martial arts. She abdicated in 697, installing her grandson, Emperor Mommu, on the throne. She became the first to use the title *dōjo-tennō* (ex-empress), which enabled her to continue wielding power until her death in 702.

SOURCES:

Aoki, Michiko Y. "Jitō Tennō: The Female Sovereign," in *Heroic with Grace: Legendary Women of Japan.* Edited by Chieko Irie Mulhern. Armonk, NY: M.E. Sharpe, 1991, pp. 40–76.

SUGGESTED READING:

Kidder, J. Edward. *Early Buddhist Japan.* NY: Praeger, 1972.

Linda L. Johnson,
Professor of History, Concordia College, Moorhead, Minnesota

Joan.

Variant of Jane, Jeanne, Joanna, Johanna, and Juana.

Joan (d. 858)

Possibly real, possibly fictitious, female pope. Name variations: The She-Pope; Pope Jeanne; John VIII. Reputedly born in Mainz or Ingelheim; sat in the Chair of Peter as pope, 855–58 (some sources cite 853–55); supposedly stoned to death around 858 in Rome; daughter of an Irish father and peasant mother who died soon after her birth.

Pope Joan is one of the most mysterious of all medieval women. To the present day, most historians deny her existence, although a few theorize on why the myth of a female pope proved so lasting and was treated as fact for centuries. However, it remains true that until the early 17th century, the Catholic Church and the people of Europe believed that Pope John VIII was a woman of English birth (or German birth of English parents) who reigned as pope for two years. "Well before the Reformation, Joan was accepted as fact," writes Peter Stanford in his definitive study on the subject, *The Legend of Pope Joan: In Search of the Truth.*

The best discernible facts about her tell us that she traveled to Athens in a monk's habit, pretending to be a man in order to gain a university education. (Another account maintains that after an education at Cologne, she fell in love with a Benedictine monk and fled with him to Athens disguised as a man.) She gained renown for her intelligence and earned a degree in philosophy and theology. Joan then journeyed to Rome, possibly under the name Joannes Anglicus (John of England), and entered the priesthood; her fame and learning led Pope Leo IV (r. 847–855) to make her a cardinal. After his death on July 17, 855, Joan was elected pope as John VIII. (This was not the John VIII, however, who reigned from 872 to 882 before dying of poison.)

Joan ruled for two years, disbanding Leo's concubines, appointing bishops, building churches, and crowning Louis II ruler of the Holy Roman Empire. Giovanni Boccaccio writes that she dallied with Lambert of Saxony, ambassador to Rome, who, "his passion appeased, disappeared courageously and at the right moment." She gained weight, dressed in clerical robes, and confined herself in her apartments, until she had to appear in a Rogation Day procession from St. Peter's to the Lateran Palace. "When the faithful pressed around her to acclaim her," write Mervin and Prunhuber, "she collapsed suddenly, doubled up with pain on the ground—and gave birth." Thus, it was discovered that she was a woman, and she was summarily stoned to death by an angry crowd. The legend that she gave birth to a baby during a papal procession, however, originated centuries after her death.

Pope Joan was listed as a historical pope until around 1601, when Clement VIII officially declared her a myth and ordered all mention of her destroyed. Given the timing of this order, it is feasible that the emerging Reformation and the subsequent weakening of church power led the pope to attempt to improve the church's image by rewriting its history and denying that such an enormous blunder had ever been made. "The Catholic Church's objection to female ordination is based not on scripture but on tradition," writes Stanford, a British journalist and former editor of *The Catholic Herald.* "There have never been women priests so there never can be. That argument might be difficult to sustain if once a woman had sat on Saint Peter's throne." The fact that she impersonated a man would put the lie to the notion that the church ordained a woman, if the church itself did not maintain that the pope is divinely ordained, a vicar of Christ on earth. "For even if Joan fooled the men around her," notes Stanford, "she could not have tricked God. He would have known her real identity and gender. Did God want a female pope? And if he did, where does that leave the current Catholic ban on women at the altar." For whatever reason, the order to obliterate all mention of Joan was put forth, and in some reference works the popes were even renumbered to eradicate John VIII altogether.

Stanford concludes, with qualifiers, that there is truth to the myth: "Weighing all this evidence, I am convinced that Pope Joan was an historical figure, though perhaps not all the details about her that have been passed down through the centuries are true. . . . [S]he achieved the papacy at a time when the office was hopelessly debased and corrupt, [and] was moderately successful, but . . . her triumph was short-lived."

There is a shrine on Rome's Vicus Papissa (which literally means the "street of the woman pope"), writes Stanford, the street where Joan supposedly gave birth. It is believed that the memorial once contained a statue of Joan. On papal orders, it was taken down, and pontiffs avoided that road for future processions. There is a bust of Pope Zachary in the Cathedral of Siena. Writers of the 16th century claim that it was put there in 1601 to replace the bust of Pope Joan by order of Clement. Stanford also uncovered a series of Bernini carvings above the central altar in St. Peter's Basilica that appear to depict a pope giving birth. As well, Stanford found a singular marble throne with a hole in the seat, the *sedia stercoraria,* stored in the Vatican Museum. It was reputedly installed by the College of Cardinals immediately after Joan's death. The Cardinals would file by a newly elected pope, one by one, and each in turn would run a probing hand under the chair, before satisfactorily declaring, "*Testiculos habet et bene pendentes!*"

The Catholic Church maintains that Joan is an invention of Protestant reformers intent on exposing papist corruption, but she was written of long before the advent of Martin Luther. Whether Joan is fact or fiction, Stanford urges the church to be more forthcoming about its past. The Catholic Church, he writes, should "show a little more humility when dictating from on high which episodes of history—usually those that reflect well on it—are worthy of respect and which can be swept under an already lumpy carpet."

Images of Pope Joan can be found in artistic works throughout the Middle Ages and the Renaissance. More than 500 manuscripts between the 13th and 17th centuries address the story, many written by Catholics. Passages about Joan are contained in the pre-Reformation chronicles of the 13-century Dominican priest Martin Polonus. A French Dominican, Steven of Bourbon (d. around 1261), narrates the legend in his *Seven Gifts of the Holy Spirit.* The idea was first seriously addressed by David Blondel, a French Calvinist, in his *Éclaircissement de la question si une femme a été assise au siège papal de Rome* (1647) and *De Joanna Papissa* (1657). The books were refuted by Johann Dollinger in his *Papstfabeln des Mittelalters* (1863, with English translation in 1872). Johannes Duns Scotus writes of her, as well as Boccaccio, Platina, and Petrarch. She also figured prominently in Stendhal's *Voyages en Italie.* As well, Voltaire wrote:

> On credulity, error, and ignorance,
> Priests have skillfully built their power;
> I want to declare and prove today
> That a woman likewise had her hour.

SOURCES:

Gould-Davis. *The First Sex.* NY: Penguin, 1971.

Klapisch-Zuber, Christiane, ed. *A History of Women in the West, vol. II: Silences of the Middle Ages.* Cambridge, MA: Belknap/Harvard, 1992.

Mervin, Sabrina, and Carol Prunhuber. *Women: Around the World and Through the Ages.* DE: Atomium Books, 1990.

Stanford, Peter. *The Legend of Pope Joan: In Search of the Truth.* NY: Holt, 1998.

SUGGESTED READING:

Cross, Donna Woolfolk. *Pope Joan* (a novel). NY: Ballantine Books.

RELATED MEDIA:

Pope Joan (140 min. film), starring *Liv Ullmann, *Olivia de Havilland, Lesley-Anne Down, Keir Dullea, Trevor Howard, and Jeremy Kemp, written and directed by Michael Anderson (an evangelist believes herself to be the reincarnation of Joan), 1972.

Pope Joan, musical by Christopher Moore, produced by Michael Butler, presented by Orlok Productions.

Laura York,
Riverside, California

Joan (fl. 1100)

*Countess of Flanders. Daughter of Rainer, marquess of Montferrat, and *Gisela of Burgundy; half-sister of *Adele of Maurienne (d. 1154); second wife of William III, the Clito, count of Flanders (r. 1101–28).*

Joan (1210–1238)

*Queen of Scotland. Name variations: Joan or Joanna Plantagenet; (nickname) Joan Makepeace. Born in Gloucester, Gloucestershire, England, on December 1210 (some sources cite July 22, 1213); died on March 4, 1238, in London, England; buried at Tarent Nunnery, Dorset; eldest daughter of *Isabella of Angoulême (1186–1246) and John I Lackland, king of England (r. 1199–1216); became first wife of Alexander II (1198–1249), king of Scotland (r. 1214–1249), on June 19, 1221; children: none.*

Though betrothed to Hugh of Lusignan, the younger, 11-year-old Joan was married at York to Alexander II, king of Scotland. Following her death at age 28, Alexander then married **Mary de Coucy** (c. 1220–1260).

Joan (1384–1400)

*English noblewoman. Born in 1384; died on August 16, 1400; buried at Walden Priory, Essex, England; daughter of Thomas of Woodstock, 1st duke of Gloucester, and *Eleanor de Bohun (1366–1399); betrothed to Gilbert, Lord Talbert.*

Joan (c. 1410–1445), queen of Scotland.
See Beaufort, Joan.

Joan I, countess of Artois (c. 1291–1330).
See Jeanne I of Burgundy.

Joan II, countess of Artois (1308–1347).
See Jeanne II of Burgundy.

Joan I of Naples (1326–1382).
See Joanna I of Naples.

Joan II of Naples (1374–1435).

See Joanna II of Naples.

Joan I of Navarre (1273–1305)

*Queen of France and Navarre. Name variations: Jeanne I of Navarre or Jeanne de Navarre; Joan of Champagne and Navarre; Joan of Navarre; Joan de Blois; Jeanne I, countess of Champagne; Juana I, queen of Navarre. Reigned as queen of Navarre (r. 1274–1305) and countess of Champagne (r. 1274–1305); born on January 14, 1273 (some sources cite 1271), in Bar-sur-Seine, France; died on April 2, 1305, in Vincennes, Paris, France; daughter of Henry I, king of Navarre (r. 1270–1274), and Blanche of Artois (c. 1247–1302, daughter of Robert I, count of Artois); married Philip IV the Fair (1268–1314), king of France (r. 1285–1314), in 1284; children: *Isabella of France (1296–1358, who married Edward II of England); Louis X (1289–1316), king of France (r. 1314–1316); Philip V (1293–1322), king of France (1316–1322); Charles IV (1294–1328), king of France (r. 1322–1328), and king of Navarre as Charles I (r. 1322–1328).*

Joan I of Navarre was born in 1273 in Bar-sur-Seine, France, the daughter of Henry I, king of Navarre, and *Blanche of Artois. Joan came to the throne as queen of Navarre on the death of her father in 1274, giving her hegemony over the lands of Navarre, Brie, and Champagne. Though her kingdom was annexed to France by her marriage to the powerful king Philip IV the Fair, she seems to have been allowed to continue free reign over her lands. Wrote *Sarah Josepha Hale in her *Woman's Record; Or, Sketches of all Distinguished Women, from "The Beginning" till A.D. 1850:* "When the Count de Bar attacked Champagne, [Joan I] placed herself at the head of a small army, forced him to surrender, and kept him a long time in prison." Joan I of Navarre founded the College of Navarre in 1304.

Joan II of Navarre (1309–1349)

*Queen of Navarre. Name variations: Jeanne of France, Jeanne of Navarre; Juana II. Born in 1309 in France (some sources cite 1312); died in 1349 in Navarre; daughter of Louis X (1289–1316), king of France (r. 1314–1316), and Margaret of Burgundy (c. 1290–1315); married Philip III (Philip d'Evreux), king of Navarre, in 1317; children: Carlos II also known as Charles II the Bad (1332–1387), king of Navarre; *Blanche of Navarre (1331–1398); Joanna, Agnes, Marie.*

Joan II of Navarre was born in 1309 in France, the daughter of Louis X, king of France, and his queen-consort, *Margaret of Burgundy. When Joan was an infant, her mother was accused of adultery and imprisoned, which put Joan's legitimacy in question and worked against her when her father died without surviving sons. The barons of France did not want to be ruled by a little girl with a suspicious claim to the throne and preferred her uncle Philip as their king. They justified their choice, and her uncle's subsequent succession as Philip V, with the argument that the traditional law of the Franks, called the Salic law, prohibited women from inheriting land, and thus, they argued, by implication from inheriting kingdoms as well. Therefore, Philip displaced his niece. He also usurped her personal inheritance of the county of Champagne.

About 1317, Joan married Philip d'Evreux (Philip III). In 1328, Philip and Joan succeeded to the throne of Navarre, and at age 26, Joan finally wore a crown. Theirs was a double succession, for, as the true heir of the French king, Navarre was Joan's birthright, and her husband was a close relative of the dead French king Philip V. The nobles of Navarre chose this couple to be their rulers while rejecting the new French king, Philip VI. Joan and Philip were competent and well-liked by their new subjects. The queen gave birth to eight children, including Charles II the Bad, future king of Navarre. The born-and-bred French monarchs did not stay in Navarre for many years, however; instead, they left its rule to able governors and returned to their estates in Evreux. Joan was only about 40 when she died.

SOURCES:
Echols, Anne, and Marty Williams. *An Annotated Index of Medieval Women.* NY: Markus Wiener, 1992.
Opfell, Olga. *Queens, Empresses, Grand Duchesses, and Regents.* Jefferson, NC: McFarland, 1989.

Laura York,
Riverside, California

Joan III of Navarre (1528–1572).

See Jeanne d'Albret.

Joan Beaufort.

See Beaufort, Joan (c. 1379–1440).
See Beaufort, Joan (c. 1410–1445).

Joan de Clare (c. 1268–after 1322)

Duchess of Fife. Born around 1268; died after 1322; daughter of Gilbert de Clare (1243–1295), 7th earl of Hertford, 3rd earl of Gloucester (r. 1262–1295) and Alice de Lusignan (d. 1290); married Duncan

(1262–1288), 9th earl of Fife (r. 1270–1288), in 1284 (murdered by Sir Patrick Abernethy); married Gervase Avenel; children: (first marriage) *Isabella of Buchan (fl. 1290–1310); Duncan Fife (1285–1351), 10th earl of Fife. Stepdaughter of *Joan of Acre (1272–1307).

Joan de Quinci (d. 1283)

Countess of Hereford and Essex. Died in 1283; daughter of *Ellen of Wales (d. 1253) and Robert de Quinci; granddaughter of Llywelyn II the Great, Ruler of All Wales; second wife of Humphrey Bohun (d. 1265), 6th earl of Hereford and Essex; children: John Bohun of Haresfield. Humphrey Bohun's first wife was *Eleanor de Braose (fl. 1250s).

Joan de Rouergue (d. 1271).

See Joan of Toulouse.

Joan de Vere (fl. 1280s)

Countess of Warren and Surrey. Daughter of fifth earl of Oxford; married William de Warrenne (d. 1286), 7th earl of Warren and Surrey, in June 1285; children: John de Warrenne (1286–1347), 8th earl of Warren and Surrey (r. 1304–1347); *Alice Fitzalan (d. around 1338).

Joan Holland (fl. 1300s).

See Joanna of Navarre (c. 1370–1437) for sidebar.

Joan Makepeace.

See Joan (1210–1238).
See Joan of the Tower (1321–1362).

Joan of Acre (1272–1307)

Duchess of Hertford and Gloucester. Name variations: Joanna of Acre; Joan Plantagenet. Born in Acre or Akko, Israel, in 1272; died on April 23, 1307, in Clare, Suffolk, England; buried at Clare Priory, Suffolk, England; daughter of Edward I Longshanks, king of England (r. 1272–1307), and Eleanor of Castile (1241–1290); married Gilbert de Clare (1243–1295), 7th earl of Hertford, 3rd of Gloucester, on May 2, 1290, in Westminster Abbey; married Ralph Monthermer (d. 1325), earl of Gloucester and Hertford, in 1297; children: (first marriage) Gilbert de Clare (1291–1314), 8th earl of Hertford and 4th earl of Gloucester; *Eleanor de Clare (1292–1337); *Margaret de Clare (c. 1293–1342); *Elizabeth de Clare (1295–1360); (second marriage) Thomas Monthermer (1301–1340), 2nd baron Monthermer (killed in sea battle against the French in 1340); *Mary de Monthermer (1298–after 1371); Joan de Monthermer, a

nun at Amesbury; Edward de Monthermer (b. 1304), 3rd baron Monthermer.

Born in Acre, Israel, in 1272, Joan of Acre was the daughter of Edward I Longshanks, king of England, and *Eleanor of Castile. After five years in Spain, Joan was betrothed to Hartmann, son of Rudolf of Habsburg in 1279. Instead, 18-year-old Joan married Gilbert de Clare, 7th earl of Hertford, 3rd of Gloucester, on May 2, 1290, in Westminster Abbey. In return, Gilbert had to give up all rights to his castles and manors in England and Wales as a dowry to her father, King Edward. Following the death of Gilbert and without consulting her father, Joan secretly married Ralph de Monthermer, a squire of her deceased husband's, in 1297. Through the intervention of Anthony Beke, bishop of Durham, King Edward I became reconciled with her new husband and eventually "much attached" to him, granting him the titles of her first husband. But in 1306, Ralph warned Robert Bruce of the danger posed by Edward. Later, at the battle of Bannockburn in June 1314, in which Robert Bruce defeated the forces of Joan's brother Edward II, Ralph fought and was captured by the Scots. Robert Bruce repaid his debt to Ralph by releasing him without ransom.

Joan of Arc (c. 1412–1431)

French hero, revered as a national saint, whose achievements can now be seen as a turning point in the Hundred Years' War. Name variations: Jeanne d'Arc; La Pucelle d'Orléans; La Petite Pucelle; The Maid of Orléans or The Maid of Orleans. Born and baptized around 1412 at Domrémy in the duchy of Bar in northern France; burned at the stake on May 30, 1431, at Rouen; daughter of Jacques d'Arc and Isabelle (Romée) d'Arc; never married.

Commanded the French troops who raised the siege of Orléans (April 1429); led Charles VII to his coronation in Rheims cathedral (July 17, 1429); captured by the Burgundians and sold to the English, who imprisoned her before condemning her to death by burning as a relapsed heretic; condemnation revoked by the pope (July 1456); beatified (1909); canonized (1920).

The name of Joan of Arc is renowned throughout the world. Her place in history is assured, her piety celebrated, and her life story a continuous inspiration. From age 13, Joan reported hearing her "voices," as she called them. When she was 17, her "voices" ordered her to free France from the stranglehold of the English occupation and to see the dauphin crowned in Rheims Cathedral, where, by tradition, all French kings were consecrated. At that time, however, Rheims was under the command of the English. These seemingly impossible objectives were successfully achieved in 1429 with the raising of the siege of Orléans in April, which was followed three months later by the coronation of Charles VII as the king of France. In 1430, Joan was captured by the Burgundians and sold to the English, who held her chained and abused in prison for months. When finally she was brought to trial, she was questioned at length without mercy. Despite being an uneducated peasant girl, she answered her inquisitors with a confidence and eloquence that belied her youth. When she was found guilty and condemned to burn at the stake as a relapsed heretic, no one, not even the French king, lifted a finger to save her.

The one pure figure which rises out of the greed, the lust, the selfishness, the unbelief of the time.

—Millicent Garrett Fawcett

Her trials and her execution have inspired numerous books, dramas, and poems by authors as diverse as *Christine de Pisan and George Bernard Shaw. Artists through the centuries have portrayed her as a warrior saint dressed in armor, carrying the banner of God and the standard of France. The unique character of her mission, her faith, her innocence and determination against impossible odds, together with her betrayal and martyrdom, are just some of the ingredients in the extraordinary life of an extraordinary woman. Her victory at Orléans proved to be an important turning point in the fortunes of the French during the Hundred Years' War. Joan of Arc has no resting place since her ashes were thrown into the river Seine to thwart relic seekers. Instead, she lives on in the hearts of every French patriot.

Joan of Arc was born about 1412 in the village of Domrémy, which was situated on the river Meuse between Champagne and Lorraine. Domrémy was in the duchy of Bar and under the jurisdiction of Chaumont in Bassigny. At the time of her birth, all France north of the Loire, and that included Domrémy, had been ravaged by and was in the hands of the English and their allies, the Burgundians. Joan was the youngest child of Jacques d'Arc and **Isabelle d'Arc**, sheep-farmers who were well thought of as leading members of the local community. She had three brothers, Jacquemin, Pierre, and Jean, and one

sister, Catherine. Pierre and Jean would follow her to Chinon and join the French army; Catherine would die young.

Joan's early life was dominated by obedience to her parents and to her religion. She had no formal education and was unable to read or to write. Her mother taught her her faith, prayers and domestic skills such as sewing. Her childhood friends, who would be called to give testimony at the trials of rehabilitation in 1450, would remember her as an exceptionally pious child who spent long hours in the church. Her tasks included leading her father's sheep and the village cattle to pastures for grazing; the hours thus spent supervising them provided her with the time for contemplation of the sorrowful state of France. This otherwise monotonous life was relieved by dancing and singing with other village girls under the "Ladies Tree," sometimes also called the "Fairies Tree."

There is no record of Joan's physical appearance. The only image which survives is a doodle in the margins of the records kept by Clément de Fauquemberghe, clerk to the Parlement of Paris, beside his entry reporting the defeat of the English at Orléans. This depicts a young girl holding a pennon in her right hand with her left hand on the hilt of a sword. Her hair is long and wavy and she is drawn in profile with a stern, small mouth and a Roman nose. It was said that at her trials she answered her inquisitors in a light feminine voice. It is known that medals were struck in her image following her victories but none survive.

The first indications that Joan was more than just a dutiful village girl came in 1425 when, at age 13, she reported hearing voices and seeing visions. There can be little doubt that she was initially frightened, but gradually the voices became familiar to her, her almost constant companions, reminding her of the wretched state of her beloved France and regularly reducing her to tears on its behalf. She later claimed that the voices taught her the self-discipline which guided her through the rest of her life. She was 17 when they became more authoritative, telling her to rise up and rescue France because she alone was to be her country's savior.

The visions were of St. Michael, St. *Margaret of Antioch and St. *Catherine of Alexandria. Much has been made by historians, hagiographers, and psychologists regarding the choice of these particular saints, more especially since doubt now surrounds the existence of the two female saints. (In 1969, their cults were suppressed by the Vatican.) The three were, howev-

Joan of
Arc

er, well-known to Joan and her contemporaries, and in the 15th century their cults flourished. There were statues of them in the parish church of Domrémy. St. Catherine, martyred on a spiked wheel, was particularly popular, and as the patron saint of Maxey, a village adjoining Domrémy, her story was depicted there in paintings and acted out in plays. St. Michael was the emblem of French resistance and patron saint of the Barrois, where Domrémy was situated. All three were depicted carrying arms. St. Michael carried an avenging sword and Sts. Margaret and Catherine bore the swords of their enemies, who beheaded them. All were eminently suitable for the purposes of Joan's mission.

In May 1428, her kin, Durand Laxart, who believed that she had indeed been given a holy mission, took her to the nearest Dauphinist stronghold at Vaucouleurs which was under the command of Captain Robert de Baudricourt. The captain was singularly unimpressed by Joan and her message, and Durand and Joan were forced to retreat to Domrémy which was once again under attack from the Burgundians. In January 1429, Joan returned, and this time Baudricourt gave her permission to visit the dauphin at Chinon. For the dual purposes of safety and comfort during the forthcoming journey, which would mean crossing enemy territory, Joan donned for the first time, or at least the first recorded time, the male attire which was to prove such an anathema to church officialdom. She was escorted by six men, who included Jean de Metz and Betrand de Poulegny. After traveling for 11 days, they reached the castle of Chinon on February 24, 1429, where Joan was kept waiting a further two days before being admitted to the presence of the dauphin.

Charles of Lorraine (the future Charles VII) was the son of Charles VI (1368–1422), king of France (r. 1380–1422), and *Isabeau of Bavaria (1371–1435). As the dauphin, he was not highly regarded, being variously described as "an inglorious leader," "*le bien servi*," and, perhaps more kindly, "enigmatic." Although he had succeeded his father Charles VI in 1422, he had been disinherited by the Treaty of Troyes agreed upon two years earlier on May 21, 1420, by Charles VI, Philip the Good, duke of Burgundy, and Henry V, king of England. By the terms of the treaty, Charles VI was to hold the throne of France during his lifetime, after which it would revert to Henry V of England and his heirs. Henry had become the regent of France immediately and had married *Catherine of Valois, daughter of Charles VI and sister of the dauphin. However, Henry had died on August 31, 1422, followed some seven weeks later by the death of Charles VI. Henry's infant son, Henry VI, was, therefore, now the king of England and France, which were under the control the king's uncles acting as regents; England was ruled by Humphrey, duke of Gloucester and France by John, duke of Bedford. Now, the French countryside was being destroyed by the war waging between the two countries. The French cause seemed to be lost, French morale was at a low ebb, and the country was effectively leaderless.

Arriving at Chinon, Joan went straight to the dauphin, recognizing him immediately although he had sought to deceive her by hiding among his courtiers. "I am come with a mission from God to give aid to you and to the kingdom, and the King of Heaven orders you, through me, to be anointed and crowned at Rheims." His initial doubts as to the authenticity of her mission and her sincerity were apparently dispelled by words she whispered in his ear. She steadfastly refused to repeat these words at her trial since her inquisitors were enemies of Charles. This was a wise decision since it is generally surmised that the words related to the true circumstances of his birth. Strenuous efforts had been made during his youth, encouraged by his mother Isabeau, to illegitimize him.

Charles was a man beset with superstitious fears and lived in a court filled with magicians and satanists, so it would not have been difficult for him to believe that Joan was a sorceress with powers that could drive the English out of France. In fact with the dauphin's cause virtually lost, the French desperately needed help and were more than ready to believe that Joan could do as she said. The English, not unnaturally, disbelieved her but, at the same time, greatly feared her. Joan was claiming divine support at a time when successive English victories had proved to them that God was on the side of the English and approved their actions.

Exhaustive examination by theologians in the presence of Jean, duke of Alençon, and again later at Poitiers, failed to expose Joan as a charlatan; they could find no evidence of heresy or insanity. Charles, advised to make use of her, immediately put the duke of Alençon in charge. On March 22, 1429, Joan dictated letters of defiance to the English, exhorting them to "deliver up to the Maid sent by God, the King of Heaven, the keys of all the towns which you have taken and violated in France." The letter continued, "I have been sent by the King of Heaven to throw you out of all France. Take yourselves off to your own land, for God's sake, or else await tidings from the Maid whom you will soon see."

During April, her transformation into a military leader was effected. Joan was provided with a household and dressed in armor of polished steel, which was unadorned and without any engraved ornamentation; her standard was painted, her personal banner made, and a sword found for her in the church of Ste-Catherine-de-Fierbois. With between 7,000 and 8,000 men under her command, including her brothers, Joan and the army set off for Orléans, which had been under siege by the English forces since

October 12, 1428. A series of strongholds had been established by the English around the town. It was the end of April 1429 when the relief force led by Joan arrived. Since this was a holy war, priests marched at its head chanting psalms, and every soldier made confession and attended Mass. Within days, Joan's troops had overrun the main English earthworks. On May 8, 1429, the English commander John Talbot led the English retreat, and the siege, which had lasted seven months, was at an end. It was a momentous victory. In just eight days, Joan of Arc, despite having been wounded during the attack, had saved the town. The duke of Alençon is reported to have said after the victory that "she was most expert in war both with the lance and in massing an army, and arraying battle, and in the management of artillery. For all men marvelled how far-sighted and prudent she was in war, as if she had been a captain of thirty years standing." The French wanted to press home their advantage by pursuing the retreating English, but since it was a Sunday Joan forbade it. Now that the first part of her mission was complete, Joan was anxious to return to the dauphin and escort him to Rheims.

From the television movie Joan of Arc, *starring LeeLee Sobieski, which aired on CBS, May 1999.*

However, a compromise decision to clear the English from their strongholds along the river Loire was reached. On June 18, 1429, the French and English came face to face at Patay. The French won the day. Victorious, Joan was at the height of her fame, and the Dauphinists believed that the English and Burgundians were powerless against her. By reviving French morale, Joan had revitalized the French army and checked the English advance. How she did it remains beyond the power of historical analysis to determine. But English rule in France was far from being over. French soldiers regarded her as a savior; the English saw her as a witch. Before her advent, God had clearly been with the English in their *just war* and now, suddenly, He had deserted them. The English began to question just how *just* this war was. In such a superstitious age, they saw Joan as one who consorted with devils. She was, they wrote, "a disorderly and disgraced woman wearing the dress of a man." And they were not alone in regarding her with suspicion, for the French court also viewed her influence over Charles VII with hostility.

Again, instead of pressing on, the French army turned back to rejoin the dauphin and reassembled at Gien. On June 25, 1429, invitations to the coronation were sent out, and, on July 16, Joan and the dauphin arrived in Rheims. The consecration of Charles VII took place the following day, July 17, 1429. Joan stood near, holding her banner and, after the ceremony, was the first to kneel before the newly crowned king and call him by his new title. "Gentle king, now is fulfilled the good pleasure of God." Her duty done and her mission successfully completed, she requested permission to return to her home and family. It was refused. When she was asked to name her reward, she asked for Domrémy to be exempt from taxes.

More campaigns followed and in September of the same year Joan was again wounded, this time in an unsuccessful attack on Paris. Her followers were too frightened to be seen rescuing her, so she was left lying in the open until nightfall. The spell of her invincibility had been broken. Charles VII dismissed the army and retired to Gien. Alençon and the other captains went home. The French had no more use for their erstwhile champion. Joan continued to campaign, however, with varying degrees of success and, at times, very little mercy. Then, on May 23, 1430, during a skirmish at Compiègne, she was plucked from her horse and taken prisoner by the Burgundians. She had been betrayed by her own supporters, the "hidden enemy." Since her mission had been completed, her fate was no longer of interest to the French. No help came to her from the king, his nobles or his army.

John of Luxemburg, lieutenant to Philip the Good, duke of Burgundy, sent Joan to his castle at Beaulieu in Vermandois. After she attempted to escape—it was, she said, her duty to do so—he moved her to the castle of Beaurevoir, and then, after a second unsuccessful attempt to regain her freedom, to Arras, a town belonging to the duke of Burgundy. When the University of Paris learned of her capture, it requested the duke, in the interests of the English cause, to hand Joan over to them for judgment either to the chief inquisitor or to the bishop of Beauvais, Pierre Cauchon, in whose diocese she had been captured. The university also wrote in the same vein to John of Luxemburg. On July 14, the bishop of Beauvais presented himself before the duke of Burgundy asking that, on his own behalf and in the name of the English king, Joan be handed over to himself in return for a payment of 10,000 gold francs. The duke passed the request on to John of Luxemburg, who, after hesitating for nearly six months, handed Joan over to the bishop on January 3, 1431. Her trial was to take place in Rouen. Meanwhile she was imprisoned in a tower of the castle of Bouvreuil, occupied by Richard de Beauchamp, earl of Warwick, commander at Rouen. The duke of Bedford, as regent of France, planned to discredit her and counteract her influence by proving that she was a sorceress, the penalty for which was burning at the stake. Beauvais insisted she be tried before his ecclesiastical court, that is one concerned with faith and morals. Her judges were to be Beauvais and Jean le Maistre, the vice-inquisitor of France. At no stage during her imprisonment nor during her subsequent trials did Charles VII do anything to save or protect her. He had valuable hostages with which he could have bargained for her release, but he could not cope with the fact that he possibly owed his crown to a sorceress.

From January 1431 onwards, Joan was never left alone, never had a moment of privacy. There were always two English soldiers at the door of her cell, with three more inside, where she was chained to a wooden block. From February 21 until March 24, she was interrogated more than 12 times by canon lawyers either in the castle chapel or in her prison. Each time, she was requested to swear to tell the truth, but she always made it clear that she would not divulge everything, since they were the enemies of her king and country.

The trial proper, later known as the Trial of Condemnation, began at the end of March

1341, and it took two days for Joan to answer to the 70 charges which had been drawn up against her, and which were based on the contention that her attitude and behavior showed blasphemous presumption. In particular, she had rejected the authority of the church in claiming a personal revelation by God, prophesying, signing her letters in the names of Christ and the Blessed *Mary the Virgin, and in asserting that she was assured of salvation. To these were added the wearing of men's clothing and her insistence that her saints spoke to her in French. As the trial continued, the number of charges was reduced to just 12, which were sent for consideration to many eminent theologians in Paris as well as in Rouen. Joan was not allowed her own counsel or any to witness on her behalf. When she fell ill in prison, she was attended by two doctors, since it did not suit the purposes of the earl of Warwick that she should die with the trial unresolved. Her behavior, her faith and trust in God may have impressed them, but the result was a foregone conclusion. Joan had to be found guilty. The English right to the French throne

was at stake. She proved to be more than a match for her inquisitors, responding to their questioning with an eloquence and confidence unexpected in one so young. However, by misrepresentation, trickery, and downright bullying, the lawyers finally trapped her and obtained the verdict they wanted. Joan was now the responsibility of the secular authorities.

The details of the trial are well known; a record was written in Latin at the time. The glosses added by the scribe, such as "proud reply" and "grand manner," give it a more personal touch. But the trial reports and summaries read more like attempts to justify the ultimate decision rather than the usual court record. Clearly, her prosecutors felt themselves to be in the wrong. Much later, in 1865, the official record was translated into French and, more recently, in 1902 into English.

There was nothing more that could be done. On May 24, she was taken to the cemetery at St. Ouen where the sentence was read out abandoning her to the secular authorities, that is to their

From the movie Joan of Arc, *starring Ingrid Bergman.*

judgment which would be her execution. Faced with this reality, for the first time Joan faltered and with some hesitation signed the form of abjuration, admitting to the charges as laid against her with the following words, "*pourvu que cela plaise a Notre Seigneur*" (on condition that it was pleasing to Our Lord). Her sentence was commuted to life imprisonment, and she was returned to her former prison where she was ordered to dress as a woman. But less than three days later, she was once again wearing men's attire and was declaring that her saints had accused her of "treason" in making the abjuration.

This was seen as a relapse and a violation of the conditions of the abjuration, and so on May 29 she was once again handed over to the secular powers. Her fate was sealed. The following day, May 30, 1431, Cauchon unexpectedly gave permission for her to make her confession and take communion. Both sacraments had previously been denied to her because of the heinous nature of her crimes. Such a privilege was unprecedented for a relapsed heretic. She was then taken to the Place du Viuex-Marché in Rouen accompanied by two Dominicans and escorted by 800 men armed with axes and swords. After a lengthy sermon, sentence was pronounced; Joan was seized by the executioner and marched to the waiting stake. As the fire burned, she was comforted by one of the young Dominicans, Martin Lavenu, who held a crucifix high enough for her to see it and shouted words of salvation over the roar of the flames. An English archer handed her a cross made from twigs. Joan died quickly with the word "Jhesu" on her lips. She was 19 years old.

The execution was a very public affair, and there are therefore many eyewitness accounts. None present was unaffected by the event. All were convinced that they had witnessed the death of a faithful Christian. Many of the clergy felt they were damned for burning a holy woman. An English soldier is reported to have said: "We are lost, we have burned a saint." Her burned body was revealed to all, and her ashes were thrown into the river Seine. There was to be no doubt that she had died, and there were to be no relics.

Joan's death, ordered by a French court acting under English instructions, was almost immediately regarded by all classes in France as a martyrdom. French determination to rid their country of the English crystallized at that moment. After Orléans, the English fortunes had continued to wane as French power grew. In 1435, four years after Joan's execution, Philip the Good, duke of Burgundy, broke with his English allies, and, by the treaty of Arras, joined the party of Charles VII; from about 1438, Charles began at last to act like a true king.

Almost 20 years later, in 1450, Charles ordered an inquiry into the trial and a process of rehabilitation of Joan of Arc was begun. Witnesses were called to give evidence. They included her childhood companions, captains she had fought alongside, women she had lived with, and priests who had heard her confessions and administered the sacraments to her. These testimonies are an important source to any who search for clues to Joan's true character. In 1456, Pope Calixtus III revoked and annulled the condemnation of the court at Rouen and declared Joan of Arc innocent. In 1903, a proposal was made for her canonization. And on May 16, 1920, she was canonized by Pope Benedict XV. In 1922, Joan was declared patron of France. Her feast is celebrated on May 30, and a national festival in her honor is held annually on the second Sunday in May.

There is an overwhelming amount of documentation available for assessing the life of Joan of Arc, including her own letters, the aforementioned witness statements, formal records by contemporary writers and commentators, as well as those who have written with the benefit of hindsight. With this amount of documentation, the difficulties of analyzing and interpreting are equally immense. The trial in particular has been of enduring interest. There are excellent translations of the trial including those by Pierre Champion (Paris, 1921), which is a re-edited work by Jules Quicherat (1861), and by Robert Brasillach (Paris, Gallimard, 1939). There is an English translation by W.P. Barrett entitled *The Trial of Jeanne d'Arc* (1931).

Joan's life and, in particular, her trial, heroism, and martyrdom have been an inspiration for playwrights, poets, and artists. The following works are a small sample: Christine de Pisan's poem, *Ditié Jeanne d'Arc* (1429), Schiller's tragedy, *La Pucelle d'Orléans* (1801), Charles Régny's dramatic trilogy, *Jeanne d'Arc* (1891), G.B. Shaw's *St. Joan* (1923), and Jean Anouilh's *L'Alouette* (1953). In 1928, a film entitled *La Passion de Joan d'Arc,* starring *Renée Falconetti, was made. There are numerous depictions of Joan in paint and in stone but none are contemporary and all reflect the fashions of the age in which they were conceived. After more than 500 years, the tragic, yet triumphant, life of Joan of Arc continues to arouse emotions in the hearts and minds of women and men, and the factual details of her life remain as controversial as they were in the 15th century.

Joan's life story is one of the best established in history, but interpretation of it is a matter for personal conscience. Joan claimed that all she had done she had done at the Lord's command. A believer can accept this, an unbeliever cannot. It is perhaps simpler to admire her as did the people of 15th-century France, rather than try to explain her. "One does not explain greatness," said Robert Bresson, "one tries to attune oneself to it." Assessments of her character are as varied as those who try to define it; some are confident that she was a saint, others are equally certain that she was merely hysterical. There can, however, be no disputing the facts that she succeeded in reviving French fortunes in the Hundred Years' War and that she never, except for a few days at the end, wavered from her appointed path or that her strong personality has defied centuries of alternately sentimentalizing and deprecating her. As Régine Pernoud writes, "Joan is above all the saint of reconciliation, the one whom, whatever our personal convictions, we admire and love because each of us can find in [herself] a reason to love her."

SOURCES:

Buchan, A. *Joan of Arc and the Recovery of France,* 1984.

Fawcett, Millicent Garrett. *Five Famous French Women,* 1905.

Pernoud, Régine. *Joan of Arc: By Herself and Her Witnesses.* NY: 1969.

Seward, D. *The Hundred Years War: The English in France 1337–1453,* 1978.

Thomson, S.H. *Europe in Renaissance and Reformation,* 1963.

Warner, M. *Joan of Arc: The Image of Female Heroism,* 1981.

Wilkinson, B. *The Later Middle Ages in England 1216–1485,* 1969.

SUGGESTED READING:

Hopkins, G. *Joan of Arc.* Translated by L. Fabre, 1954.

Marcantel, Pamela. *An Army of Angels* (fiction). St. Martin's Press, 1996.

Scott, W.S. *Trial of Joan of Arc.* Orléans ms. (1968 reprint).

Wood, C.T. *Joan of Arc and Richard III: Sex, Saints and Government in the Middle Ages,* 1988.

RELATED MEDIA:

Joan at the Stake (Italian-French film), an adaptation of Claudel and Honegger's opera, starring Ingrid Bergman and Tullio Carminati, Produzione Cinematografiche-Franco-London, 1954.

Joan of Arc (145 min. film), based on the play *Joan of Lorraine* by Maxwell Anderson, starring ***Ingrid Bergman**, Jose Ferrer, and **Selena Royle** as Isabelle d'Arc, directed by Victor Fleming, produced by Walter Wanger, RKO, 1948.

La Passion de Jeanne D'Arc (*The Passion of Joan of Arc*), French silent, starring Renée Falconetti, directed by

Carl Dreyer, 1927 (condenses the trial, torture, and execution of the French saint into an intense 24-hour period; based on actual trial records).

The Lark, a play by Jean Anouilh originally titled *L'Alouette,* starring ***Julie Harris**, opened at the Longacre Theater, New York, November 1955.

St. Joan (110 min. film), based on the play by George Bernard Shaw, starring ***Jean Seberg**, Richard Widmark, and John Gielgud, directed by Otto Preminger, screenplay by Graham Greene, United Artists, 1957.

Margaret E. Lynch, M.A.,
Lancaster, England, U.K.

Joan of Beaufort.
> *See Beaufort, Joan (1379–1440).*
> *See Beaufort, Joan (c. 1410–1445).*

Joan of Blois (c. 1320–1384).
> *See Jeanne de Penthièvre.*

Joan of Boulogne (1326–1360).
> *See Blanche of Boulogne.*

Joan of Bourbon (1338–1378).
> *See Jeanne de Bourbon.*

Joan of Bourbon (d. 1493).
> *See Jeanne de Bourbon.*

Joan of Brittany (c. 1370–1437).
> *See Joanna of Navarre.*

Joan of Burgundy.
> *See Jeanne of Burgundy (1293–1348).*
> *See Jeanne of Burgundy (1344–1360).*

Joan of Champagne (1273–1305).
> *See Joan I of Navarre.*

Joan of Constantinople (c. 1200–1244).
> *See Johanna of Flanders.*

Joan of England (d. 1237)

Princess of North Wales. Name variations: Joanna, Anna, or Janet. Died on February 2, 1237, in Aber, Gwynedd, Wales; buried at Llanfaes, Gwynedd, Wales (another source maintains that her stone coffin now resides in Baron Hill Park, Beaumaris); illegitimate daughter of John I Lackland, king of England (r. 1199–1216), and **Agatha Ferrers** *(others suggest her mother was Clementina, wife of Henry Pinel); married Llywelyn II the Great (1173–1240), Ruler of All Wales, in 1205 or 1206; children: David II (c. 1208–1246), Ruler of All Wales; possibly *****Ellen of Wales** *(d. 1253); possibly* **Margaret verch Llywelyn** *(who married Walter Clifford). Llywelyn II the Great also had offspring with his mistress *****Tangwystl**, *and* *there is some confusion between Joan of England and Tangwystl as to who had which children.*

Joan of Evreux (d. 1370)

Queen of France. Name variations: Jeanne d'Evreux; Jeanne of Evreux or Évreux. Born around 1305; died in 1370; daughter of Louis, count of Evreux (son of Philip III, king of France); sister of Philip III, king of Navarre (d. 1343); became third wife of Charles IV the Fair (1294–1328), king of France (r. 1322–1328), king of Navarre (r. 1322–1328), around 1324 or 1325; children: *Blanche of France (1328–1392, who married Philip of Orleans, the brother of John II, king of France). Charles IV's other wives were *Blanche of Burgundy (1296–1326) and *Mary of Luxemburg (1305–1323).

Joan of Flanders (c. 1200–1244).

See Johanna of Flanders.

Joan of Flanders (c. 1310–c. 1376).

See Jeanne de Montfort.

Joan of Hainault (c. 1310–?)

Duchess of Juliers. Name variations: Joan de Juliers. Born around 1310; daughter of *Jeanne of Valois (c. 1294–1342) and William III the Good, count of Hainault and Holland; sister of *Philippa of Hainault (1314–1369) and *Margaret of Holland (d. 1356); married William de Juliers, duke of Juliers; children: Elizabeth de Juliers (d. 1411, who married John, 3rd earl of Kent).

Joan of Kent (1328–1385)

English noblewoman, famous for her beauty, who married Edward, prince of Wales (the Black Prince), was the mother of Richard II, king of England, and left her own her mark on history. Name variations: Princess of Wales; Fair Maid of Kent; Joan, countess of Kent; Joan Plantagenet. Born on September 28, 1328; died on August 7 (or August 14) 1385, of dropsy(?) at Wallingford Castle, Oxfordshire, England; buried in Stamford, Lincolnshire, England; daughter of Edmund of Woodstock (1307–1330), 1st earl of Kent, and Margaret Wake of Liddell (c. 1299–1349); married Sir Thomas Holland, 1st earl of Kent, around 1346 (died, December 28, 1360); married William de Montacute, 2nd earl of Salisbury, around 1348 (annulled by pope Clement VI on November 13, 1349); married Edward, prince of Wales (known as the Black Prince), on October 6, 1361 (died, June 8, 1376);

children (first marriage) five, including Thomas Holland, 2nd earl of Kent (1350–1397); John, duke of Exeter (1352?–1400); Matilda Holland (c. 1359–1391, who married Hugh Courtenay); ◄ Joan Holland (who married John IV, duke of Brittany); (third marriage) Edward (1365–1372, died of the plague at age seven); Richard II (1367–1400), king of England (r. 1377–1399).

Father beheaded (1330) when she was two years old; married Thomas Holland and then contracted to earl of Salisbury; restored to Holland (1349); became countess of Kent (1352); left England for Normandy with Holland (1358); married Edward, prince of Wales (1361), following Holland's death; lived in Aquitaine where another two sons were born (1362–71); following death of husband (1376), her son Richard became heir to the throne of England and succeeded his grandfather (1377); guided her son and played a significant role in English politics until her death (1385).

As the Kentish rebels gathered for the attack on London in June 1381, Princess Joan, returning from a pilgrimage to Canterbury, found herself surrounded. She had become countess of Kent following her father's death some 20 years before and now, as mother of the young King Richard II, might provide either a useful hostage or a symbolic victim for the desperate peasants. However, though she was certainly aware that her life was in the gravest danger, Joan, showing great courage and presence of mind, managed to persuade the rebels to set her free. She then rushed straight to London to be at her son's side throughout the violent and bloody days which were to follow.

The life of Joan of Kent was marked by frequent, sudden change and was full of adventure. Born in 1328, the third child and second daughter of Edmund of Woodstock, earl of Kent, and ***Margaret Wake of Liddell**, she was of royal blood, as her father was the sixth son of Edward I Longshanks. However, Joan was only two years old when the earl was executed for treason. Once her cousin, Edward III, took control of the kingdom, Joan was welcomed into the court and was made the special protégé of the queen, ***Philippa of Hainault** (1314–1369). By her early teens, Joan had become a strikingly attractive woman: to the French author of the *Chronique des Quatre Premiers Valois*, she was "one of the loveliest women in the world." The chronicler Froissart, who came to England in the retinue of Philippa, was overwhelmed by the girl's beauty; it was he who described her as "the

Holland, Joan.
See Joanna of Navarre for sidebar.

most beautiful woman in the whole realm of England and the most amorous." It is difficult to be certain what Froissart meant by the French word *amoureuse*; the word may simply be a synonym for *charming*, but whether or not young Joan fell in and out of love or welcomed the attentions of the many young knights at Edward's court, she certainly inspired devotion and even rivalry. She must have been admired for more than her pleasing appearance, for another court observer called her "a lady of great worth, beautiful, pleasant and wise."

The English court at Westminster in the mid-14th century was cultured and refined; in 1348, Edward founded the Order of the Garter, in conscious emulation of King Arthur's Knights of the Round Table. The French conceit of courtly love had crossed the channel and become the fashionable mode of behavior; ladies were the objects of knightly devotion, and love was as important at the court as courage was on the battlefield. However, Joan inspired more than merely conventional admiration. Perhaps when she was as young as 11, but more likely when she was 15 or 16 years old, she was the subject of a dispute between two prospective husbands, William de Montacute, earl of Salisbury, and his steward of the household, Sir Thomas Holland. Holland seems to have been Joan's own choice; they had made a verbal marriage contract and probably lived together for a short time before he was called away to the war in France. In his absence, the earl of Salisbury seized his chance to enter into a contract of marriage with Joan. Once Holland returned, he appealed to the pope to have Joan restored to him; he won his case, and the return of his wife, in November 1349.

In 1352, Joan inherited the title of countess of Kent in her own right, following the deaths of her two brothers and her older sister *Margaret of Kent, becoming a very wealthy woman as a result, and in 1358 she left England for Normandy where her husband had been appointed governor of the English fort of Creyk. Two years later, Holland died, leaving Joan with five young children. The pattern of her life changed significantly once again within a few months of her husband's death when she agreed to marry the king's eldest son, Edward, prince of Wales, known as the Black Prince (so-called because of the color of his favorite armor). Joan, now aged 33, was two years older than Edward, who was Europe's most eligible bachelor. Rumor has it that the prince had worshipped Joan since they had played as children together and that he had refused to marry anyone else. A French account of their courtship, which compensates in charm

for what it lacks in reliability, has Edward acting as the intermediary for another noble who was eager to marry Joan. She, so the story goes, would have nothing to do with the proposition and only when repeatedly pressed did she admit that she was already in love with someone else. Since marriage to her beloved was impossible, Joan told Edward that she had resolved never to marry. The object of her affection was, of course, ultimately revealed to be the prince of Wales himself.

The match was not made without some difficulty; the king's permission was sought only after the event and, once given, a Papal dispensation had to be obtained, since the two were related and Edward had served as godfather to Joan's sons. The wedding was celebrated in October 1361, and, after spending a few months in England, the couple left for Aquitaine. Recognizing his need for independence now that he was married, King Edward conferred this fertile region of western France upon his eldest son and, as a contemporary observed, "the very noble Prince took his wife with him, for that he loved her greatly." Joan was to remain in Aquitaine for nine years.

> *I*n her time she was the most beautiful woman in all the realm of England and the most amorous.
>
> —Jean Froissart

The prince was a better soldier than administrator; his harsh and unbending rule of the region lead to resentment and revolts, and his love of the battlefield meant that he was frequently away from his capital at Bordeaux, campaigning in French territory and in parts of Spain, leaving Joan alone. Two more sons were born during this period, Edward in 1365 and Richard in 1367, and it was during 1367 that Joan found herself in danger at Bordeaux. With the prince campaigning actively for Peter the Cruel, one of the rival claimants to the throne of Castile, the other contender, Henry II Trastamara (known as the Bastard), assembled his forces for an attack upon Aquitaine. Having received word that Henry was using French territory to assemble his army, Joan sent a series of letters and messages to the king of France "desiring him not to consent that the bastard of Spain should make her any manner of war, saying that her resort was to the court of France, certifying to him that much evil might ensue and many inconveniences fall thereby." The French king was persuaded by Joan's arguments, and Henry, who had already begun his attack, was instructed to withdraw from Aquitaine and leave France.

The embattled period in Aquitaine, for all its dangers, and despite her husband's frequent absences, was probably a happy and fulfilling time for Joan. Joan and Edward continued to be deeply in love, indeed their marriage helped to create a new courtly and literary emphasis on the possibility of love existing within marriage; earlier fashion had regarded marriage among the nobility as a practical necessity, undertaken for reasons which were primarily political and economic, with love confined to extra-marital liaisons. There is ample contemporary evidence of their affection; Edward, in a letter written to Joan in the spring of 1367, after the Battle of Najera, calls her "My dearest and truest sweetheart and beloved companion" and hastens to assure her that he and his companions have secured a victory and survived the encounter unscathed.

Joan was, no doubt, in need of reassurance, for what might well have been an eyewitness account, written by the French herald of Sir John Chandos, describes her grief at the prince's departure in January 1367, a week after the birth of their son Richard:

> Alas! What should I do, God and Love, if I were to lose the very flower of nobleness . . . him who has no peer in the world in valour? Death! thou wouldst be at hand. Now I have neither heart nor blood nor vein, but every member fails me when I call to mind his departure; for all the world says this, that never did any man adventure himself on so perilous an expedition.

The prince was gentle and reassuring in his response: "Lady, we shall meet again in such wise that we shall have joy, we and all our friends, for my heart tells me so."

Once established in Aquitaine, Joan would probably not have often pined for home. England's political interests were so firmly focused on the Continent that their courts at Bordeaux and Angoulême were constantly receiving visitors from home, and the court culture which Joan and Edward developed in Aquitaine was not inferior to that of Westminster; indeed Froissart, who must often have visited the area himself, observed that "the state of the Prince and Princess was so great that in all Christendom was none like." The account of the Chandos Herald is even more impressive:

> [S]ince the birth of God such fair state was never kept as his, nor more honourable, for ever he had at his table more than fourscore knights and full four times as many squires. There were held jousts and feasts in Angoulême and Bordeaux.

Also, the prince's frequent campaigns gave Joan the opportunity to play a role which extended beyond the courtly and domestic spheres to which most medieval women of her class were confined. She was astute and courageous, and life in Aquitaine gave her the chance to demonstrate these qualities. We can only speculate on what kind of a queen of England she would have made, for although her father-in-law was aging rapidly, her husband was never to become king.

Joan's life began another of its many turns when the Black Prince became ill during the summer of 1367. After some brilliant victories, he had been ultimately unsuccessful in his efforts in Castile, and, largely because of the burdensome taxes he imposed, the prince had made himself highly unpopular in Aquitaine. One chronicler suggests that the illness was the result of poisoning. Whatever its cause, all accounts concur that from that time until the day of his death, the prince never again enjoyed good health. The spirits of both parents were further crushed by the death of the prince's favorite elder son, Edward, in 1370, at the age of seven years. In January 1371, the family returned to England. The citizens of London welcomed the prince and princess on April 19 and presented them with a magnificent gift of gold plate to celebrate their return; Joan wrote personally to thank the citizens for their generosity and, as will be seen, she was to call upon their friendship and support in later, more troubled times. However, the return home did nothing to improve the prince's health; he was able to manage one more campaign with his father in the summer of 1372, but, on June 8, 1376, he died at the age of 46. In a truly touching passage, the Chandos Herald describes the prince calling his family and all his men to his bedside and requesting that his father the king, his brother the duke of Lancaster, and his men swear to protect his wife and son:

> [T]he lovely and noble Princess felt such grief at heart that her heart was nigh breaking. Of lamentation and sighing, of crying aloud and sorrowing, there was so great a noise that there was no man living in the world, if he had beheld the grief, but would have had pity at heart.

Less than a year later, the prince's father, King Edward III, died, and Joan's life was to change for the last, and perhaps the most significant time.

Her son Richard had been created prince of Wales four months after the death of the Black Prince, at the age of 9. Joan appears to have had sole charge of her son and was given some early indication of her new powers, even before the death of the old king. In February 1377, while the princess and Richard were staying at the royal manor of Kennington, just outside London, Joan's brother-in-law, John of Gaunt, duke of Lancaster, had provoked the animosity of the citizens of London and, together with Lord Henry Percy, had been forced to flee from the infuriated citizens by taking a boat down the Thames River. They sought refuge at Kennington where Joan received them. She subsequently sent three of her knights to entreat the Londoners, "out of their love for her," to agree to make peace with the duke and to restore order. They responded, the chronicler reports, respectfully (*reverentia*), and agreed to a settlement, provided the duke accepted certain conditions.

A governing council was set up to administer England during Richard's minority. One modern historian, R.H. Jones, has suggested that Joan "lacked the experience and disposition to have been named as regent" but close examination of her life and her demonstrated abilities does not support this view. Rather, given the extreme political tensions and rivalries of the period, the setting up of a council to prevent any one individual or clique from gaining permanent control of policy, seems the obvious solution. Joan's interests were well represented by the appointment of several of her loyal supporters to the council, and Joan herself remained at the center of the court, close to her son in both physical proximity and affection.

Two very different incidents which occurred in 1378, the first full year of the new reign, indicate Joan's powerful position: she was inducted into the Order of the Garter, and she succeeded in stopping heresy proceedings against the reformist preacher John Wycliffe. The question of Joan's religious views is the subject of some speculation. There was certainly sympathy among many at Richard's court, including John of Gaunt, for Wycliffe's criticisms of the Catholic Church, and in particular for his anti-papal theories. A Papal Bull of 1377, instructing the archbishop of Canterbury to warn the king against Wycliffe's heresies, mentioned Joan by name and included several of her household knights in the list of Wycliffe's followers. These same knights were included as executors of Joan's will, but their presence is counterbalanced by two archbishops and by Joan's firm affirmation in the document of her devotion to the Catholic faith.

However, the most dramatic events of Joan's event-filled life were yet to occur. The Peasants' Revolt of June 1381 challenged the way in which the governing classes saw the world; their God-ordained, time-honored position was being violently threatened, and they could neither explain nor control the chaos which ensued. The events, which involved peasants from all over southern, northern, and eastern England, centered upon the attack of the rebels from Kent and Essex upon the city of London and, reflecting the stunned, horrified reaction of the ruling classes, the chronicles of the period describe the events minutely, almost in the equivalent of frame-by-frame slow motion, in order that the reader should miss none of the bloody turmoil of the time. Joan, as might be expected, appears in the central focus of all the accounts, though the incidents happened so quickly and amidst so much confusion that the descriptions of her whereabouts are sometimes contradictory.

Having escaped the clutches of the Kentish rebels, Joan completed the journey from Canterbury to London in one day. She found her 14-year-old son, the king, in the Tower of London, having gathered together with a number of his ministers in fear and bewilderment, apprehensive of the advancing peasant mobs and uncertain that the citizens of London could be relied upon to provide defense. Also in the group were Joan's other two surviving sons, Thomas, earl of Kent, and John Holland. On Thursday, June 13, the rebels entered the city and began burning and looting, one of their first targets being John of Gaunt's palace of the Savoy.

The next day, June 14, Richard, finding only vacillation and indecision among his ministers, agreed to meet with the rebels and discuss their demands outside the city, at Mile End. One source places Joan at the meeting in a carriage (*whirlicote*) but the other chroniclers have her remaining in the Tower which, either during the meeting or shortly afterwards, was invaded by the insurgents. Entering "the chamber of the king and of his mother with their filthy sticks . . . they arrogantly lay and sat on the king's bed while joking; and several asked the king's mother to kiss them." As Froissart describes the scene, the invading peasants broke Joan's bed "whereby she was so sore affrayed that she swooned." Joan was probably still in the Tower when the archbishop of Canterbury and the treasurer of England were dragged out and executed outside the gates on Tower Hill. She was smuggled out of danger by her servants, hidden under some covers on a barge which conveyed her to her London residence, "and there she was all that day and night like a woman half dead, until she was comforted by the king, her son."

The climax of the revolt came on the morning of Saturday, June 15, at Smithfield, just outside the city boundaries. During a second meeting between Richard and the rebels, the rebel leader, Wat Tyler was killed and Richard, showing courage and presence of mind which belied his years, told the peasants that he was now their leader and ordered them to disperse, with the promise that their grievances would be addressed. As quickly as they had come, the rebels departed, and Richard's first concern, on reentering the city, was for his mother. He went straight to her residence and, once again, Froissart gives us a detailed description of the scene:

> [A]nd when she saw the king her son, she was greatly rejoiced and said: "Ah, fair son, what pain and great sorrow have I suffered for you this day." Then the king answered and said: "Certainly, madam, I know it well; but now rejoice yourself and thank God, for now it is time. I have today recovered mine heritage and the realm of England, the which I had near lost."

Joan was now 53 years old, and whether or not the ordeal she had undergone during the revolt had any lasting consequences, we can never be sure. It may be that her role in the center of England's affairs simply diminished as her son grew older. Certainly the chroniclers rarely mention her after 1381. We glimpse her only twice more, both times in 1385, the year of her death. In the early part of the year, she journeyed between Wallingford, where she now lived, close to London, to Pontefract, in the north of England, in a successful attempt to patch up a quarrel between Richard and John of Gaunt. Richard, on his departure for a campaign in Scotland on June 12, assigned five of his trusted knights to remain with his mother for her protection during his absence. However, it was not an external, physical danger which threatened Joan this time. Shortly after the king's departure, word reached her that Richard had decided to punish John Holland, his half-brother and Joan's second son, for the murder of another knight. She sent messengers with a plea for clemency, but her request was refused. Rumor had it that she died of grief. Already in declining health, the princess made her will on August 7, 1385, and died shortly afterwards.

Joan of Kent left orders that she should be buried at Stamford, near the tomb of her first husband. Her funeral seems not to have taken place until January 1386. Richard, unavoidably detained in Scotland, gave instructions that her body was to be wrapped in wax swathings and kept in a lead coffin until his return, no doubt so that he might make his last farewell. The close bond between the king and his mother endured.

Joan's loss was also felt in more than personal terms: during her lifetime, she had been able to reconcile enemies and mediate disputes; after her death, these tensions went unchecked. All three of Joan's surviving sons were dead by 1400, only one of them of natural causes.

SOURCES:

Dictionary of National Biography. Vol. IX. Oxford: Oxford University Press, 1911–1922.

Froissart, Jean. *The Chronicles of Froissart.* Translated from the French by John Bourchier, Lord Berners. NY: AMS Press, 1967.

Herald of Sir John Chandos. *The Life of the Black Prince.* Edited and translated by M.K. Pope and E.C. Lodge. Oxford: Clarendon Press, 1910.

Knighton, Henry. *Chronicon.* Edited by J.R. Lumby. 2 vols. London: Rolls Series, 1889–1895.

Walsingham, Thomas. *Chronicon Angliae, 1328–1388.* Edited by E.M. Thompson. London: Rolls Series, 1874.

———. *Historia Anglicana.* Edited H.T. Riley. 2 vols. London: Rolls Series, 1863–64.

SUGGESTED READING:

Barber, Richard. *Edward, Prince of Wales and Aquitaine.* London: Allen Lane, 1978.

Dobson, R.B. *The Peasants' Revolt of 1381.* London: Macmillan, 1970.

Emerson, Barbara. *The Black Prince.* London: Weidenfeld and Nicholson, 1976.

Jones, R.H. *The Royal Policy of Richard II.* NY: Barnes and Noble, 1968.

McKisack, May. *The Fourteenth Century.* Oxford: Clarendon Press, 1959.

Steel, Anthony. *Richard II.* Cambridge: University Press, 1962.

(Dr.) Kathleen Garay,
Acting Director of the Women's Studies Programme,
McMaster University, Hamilton, Canada

Joan of Kent (d. 1550).

See Bocher, Joan.

Joan of Montferrat (d. 1127)

Countess of Flanders. Died in 1127; daughter of Rainer also spelled Reiner, marquess of Montferrat, and *Gisela of Burgundy; half-sister of *Adelaide of Maurienne (d. 1154); second wife of William III the Clito (1101–1128), count of Flanders (r. 1127–1128). William III's first wife was *Sybilla of Anjou (1112–1165).

Joan of Sicily (1165–1199).

See Berengaria of Navarre (d. 1163–c. 1230) for sidebar on Joanna of Sicily.

Joan of the Tower (1321–1362)

Queen of Scotland. Name variations: Joanna of the Tower; Joan Plantagenet; Joan Makepeace; Johane.

Born in the Tower of London on July 5, 1321; died on August 14, 1362, in Hertford, Hertfordshire, England; interred at Greyfriar's Church, Newgate, London; youngest child of *Isabella of France (1296–1358) and Edward II (1284–1327), king of England (r. 1307–1327); sister of Edward III (1312–1377), king of England (r. 1327–1377); became first wife of David Bruce also known as David II (1323–1370), king of Scotland (r. 1329–1370), on July 17, 1328; no children.

In 1327, the dethronement of Edward II, king of England, by his son Edward III set in motion a series of events that led to a treaty with England, the recognition of Scottish independence, and the acknowledgment of Robert Bruce's kingship. The Scots considered that this nullified a 1323 treaty and again began cross-border raiding. After an abortive expedition against Scotland, in 1328 the English finally recognized both Scotland's independence and Bruce's kingship in the treaty of Edinburgh-Northampton, which was cemented by the marriage of Edward III's sister, seven-year-old Joan of the Tower, to Bruce's four-year-old son David. The treaty and marriage marked the culmination of Robert Bruce's career and represented the fruit of his 20-year struggle against England.

When Robert Bruce died on June 7, 1329, his five-year-old son became king, and in 1331 David was crowned with his queen Joan at Scone. The Scottish cause once again entered trying times. In 1332, Edward Balliol, son of Scotland's king John Balliol and one of those disinherited by Robert Bruce after the battle of Bannockburn, attempted to claim the throne of Scotland for himself. In this effort, he had the covert backing of Edward III who raised a large army in 1333. On July 19, Edward's army crushed the Scots at the battle of Halidon Hill, and within a year David and Joan were forced to flee to France. From 1334 to 1341, they remained in exile. Following the defeat and capture of her husband in England at Neville's Cross in 1346, Joan repeatedly tried to win his release from prison. She was finally successful in 1357, after his 11-year captivity in the Tower of London, when he was ransomed for 100,000 marks to be paid over ten years.

Joan of Toulouse (d. 1271)

Countess of Toulouse. Name variations: Joan de Rouergue. Died in 1271; daughter of Raymond VII, count of Toulouse (r. 1222–1249), and *Margaret le Brun (d. 1283); married Alphonso, count of Poitiers

(Poitou) and Toulouse (r. 1249–1271, son of Louis VIII, king of France, and *Blanche of Castile).

Joan of Valois (c. 1294–1342).

See Jeanne of Valois.

Joan Plantagenet (c. 1312–c. 1345)

Baroness Mowbray. Name variations: Baroness Mowbray. Born around 1312; died around 1345; daughter of Henry, earl of Lancaster (r. 1281–1345), and *Maud Chaworth (1282–c. 1322); married John Mowbray, 3rd baron Mowbray, 1327; children: three, including John Mowbray, 4th baron Mowbray.

Joan the Maid of Sarmaize (fl. 1456).

See Jeanne de Sarmaize.

Joan Valois (1391–1433).

See Joanna of Navarre (c. 1370–1437) for sidebar.

Joana.

Variant of Jeanne, Joan, Joanna, Johanna, or Juana.

Joana de Mendoza (d. 1580)

Duchess of Braganza. Died in 1580; daughter of Diego de Mendoza; married Jaime or James (1479–1532), duke of Braganza, in 1520; children: Jaime (b. 1523, a priest); Constantino (b. 1528, viceroy of India); Fulgencio (b. around 1529, prior of Guimaraes); Teotonio (b. 1530, archbishop of Evora); Isabella of Braganza (c. 1512–1576); Joana of Braganza (1521–1588, who married Bernardo de Cardenas, marquis of Elche); Eugenia of Braganza (c. 1525–1559, who married Francesco de Mello); Maria of Braganza (c. 1527–1586, abbess of Cloisters); Vincenca of Braganza (c. 1532–1603, abbess of Cloisters). The duke of Braganza's first wife was *Eleonore de Guzman (d. 1512).

Joanna.

Variant of Jeanne, Joan, Joanna, Johanna, or Juana.

Joanna

Biblical woman. Married Chuza, the steward of Herod Antipas.

Joanna was married to Chuza, the steward of Herod Antipas and a man of position and wealth. Along with *Mary Magdalene, *Susanna, and others, Joanna provided for Jesus out of her own funds. She was also one of the women who witnessed the empty tomb and announced the Lord's resurrection to the apostles.

Joanna (1333–1348).

See Philippa of Hainault for sidebar.

Joanna (1452–1490)

*Regent of Portugal. Reigned as regent 1471 to 1481; born on February 6, 1452, in Lisbon; died on May 12, 1490, in Aveiro; daughter of *Isabel la Paloma (1432–1455) and Afonso V, king of Portugal (r. 1448–1481).*

Joanna I of Naples (1326–1382)

Queen of Naples from 1343 to 1382. Name variations: Giovanna or Giovanni; Giovanna d'Angiò; Joan I; Joanna of Naples; Joanna of Sicily; Joanna of Provence; also known as Jane. Born in 1326 in Spain; died in 1382 in Naples; daughter of Charles of Calabria and Marie of Valois; sister of Marie of Naples; married Andrew of Hungary, about 1333 (died 1345); married Louis of Taranto; married Jayme of Majorca; married Otto of Brunswick; children: none, except for adoption of Louis I, count of Provence and duke of Anjou (1339–1384), as her successor king.

Joanna I, who reigned as queen-regnant of Naples, was the Spanish-born daughter of Charles of Calabria and *Marie of Valois. In 1343, Joanna inherited Naples and Provence from Robert the Wise of Anjou, her grandfather. She then moved to that state, where she reigned for over 40 years. Her years on the throne were marked by political disruption, warfare, and general turmoil.

Joanna had been married to Andrew of Hungary (son of Charles Robert, king and father of the Anjou line in Hungary) at age seven, and is thought to have murdered him two years after taking the Neapolitan throne in 1343. Her motivation may have been Andrew's desire to rule Naples without her assistance, although in their marriage contract he specifically gave up the right to call himself king. As for her actual guilt, however, Andrew's grasping ambition and arrogance had earned him many enemies, so it is possible that either Joanna had help or that she was not involved at all.

Andrew's death did not solve any of the problems Joanna faced. She was forced by political necessity to marry three more times, although she remained childless. Each subsequent husband—Louis of Taranto, James of Majorca, and Otto of Brunswick—brought to the Neapolitan political scene his own set of power-hungry relatives who schemed to remove Joanna from power. Moreover, each husband lost interest in Naples when Joanna refused to allow them any more authority than a queen-consort would have had.

There were also plots against Joanna's sister and heir, *Marie of Naples. In the meantime, Andrew of Hungary's brother Louis of Hungary was planning an invasion of Naples and hoped ultimately to annex it. None of Joanna's husbands seemed capable of handling these crises, and so Joanna was left to her own devices. Finally, she altered her choice of heir in a last effort to gain a worthy ally. She chose a relative, Louis I of Anjou, brother to the king of France. Louis of Hungary attacked Naples in support of the heir he wanted on the Neapolitan throne, Charles III of Durazzo (who had been married to Joanna's sister Marie of Naples). Unfortunately, Joanna's ally and heir failed to bring his troops to help her soon enough. Joanna was captured, imprisoned, and then murdered, and Charles of Duraz-

Joanna I of Naples

zo became king of Naples. Queen Joanna was 56 years old.

SOURCES:

Anderson, Bonnie S., and Judith P. Zinsser. *A History of Their Own.* Vol. I. NY: Harper and Row, 1988.

Opfell, Olga. *Queens, Empresses, Grand Duchesses, and Regents.* Jefferson, NC: McFarland, 1989.

Uglow, Jennifer, ed. *International Dictionary of Women's Biography.* NY: Continuum, 1989.

Laura York,
Riverside, California

Joanna II of Naples (1374–1435)

*Queen of Naples who reigned from 1414 to 1435. Name variations: Giovanna or Giovanni II; Joan II; Joanna II of Naples; Johanna of Durazzo. Born on June 25, 1374, in Naples; died on February 2, 1435, in Naples; daughter of Charles III of Durazzo, king of Naples (r. 1382–1386), also ruled Hungary as Charles II (r. 1385–1386) and *Margaret of Naples (daughter of *Marie of Naples); sister of Ladislas I, king of Naples (r. 1386–1414); married Wilhelm also known as William (1370–1406), duke of Austria; married James of La Marche (a French count); children: none.*

Joanna II of Naples ruled under the same chaos which had marked the reign of *Joanna I of Naples. She was the daughter of Charles III of Durazzo, king of Naples, who had stolen the throne from Joanna I and had her murdered in 1382. When Charles died in 1385 while trying to take over the throne of *Maria of Hungary (1370–1395), the unstable kingdom of Naples passed to his son Ladislas. When Ladislas died in 1414 without heirs, Naples then accepted his sister Joanna as its queen.

Joanna married more than once but with little success. Her first husband was William of Austria. William died after only a few years, leaving Joanna a childless widow before her succession. After becoming queen in 1414, she wed the French count James of La Marche but refused to make him king. James was thrown out of Naples in 1416 for his arrogance and insistence on giving important political positions to his French relatives. The queen then proceeded to take a long series of lovers, whom she treated as her consorts, provoking the anger of many Neapolitans.

Naples was suffering greatly under the feudal warring and rivalries of its nobility, but Joanna did not seem to care much about its people, concentrating instead on her personal enjoyment. She gave up some of her power to her lovers, which further alienated her people. The barons eventually took up arms against the government which they viewed as corrupt and im-

moral, even by their somewhat lax standards. But because of quarrels between the rebels no one noble was strong enough to take over Naples, and thus Joanna remained on the throne for 20 years.

Joanna was childless, and therefore had to choose an heir. This proved a difficult choice, and for years she would name an heir and soon afterwards change her mind, provoking even more confusion in the city-state as to its future. She was not much mourned when she died about age 61, leaving the question of her successor still undecided.

SOURCES:

Opfell, Olga. *Queens, Empresses, Grand Duchesses, and Regents.* Jefferson, NC: McFarland, 1989.

Laura York,
Riverside, California

Joanna I of Provence (1326–1382).

See Joanna I of Naples.

Joanna I of Sicily (1326–1382).

See Joanna I of Naples.

Joanna Enriquez (1425–1468)

*Queen of Navarre and Aragon. Name variations: Juana Enriquez. Born in 1425; died on February 13, 1468, in Zaragoza; daughter of Fadrique, count of Malgar and Rueda; became second wife of Juan also known as John II (1398–1479), king of Navarre and Aragon (r. 1458–1479), on April 1, 1444; children: Ferdinand II of Aragon (1452–1516) also known as Ferdinand V the Catholic, king of Castile and Leon (r. 1474–1504, who married *Isabella I of Spain); *Joanna of Aragon (1454–1517, who married Ferrante I of Naples); Maria of Aragon (b. 1455, died young).*

Joanna of Aragon (1454–1517)

*Queen of Naples. Name variations: Juana; Giovanna. Born in 1454 in Barcelona; died on January 9, 1517, in Naples; daughter of *Joanna Enriquez (1425–1468) and Juan also known as John II (1398–1479), king of Navarre and Aragon (r. 1458–1479); became second wife of Ferdinand also known as Ferrante I (1423–1494), king of Naples (r. 1458–1494), on September 14, 1476; children: *Joanna of Naples (1478–1518); Carlo of Naples (b. 1480). *Isabel de Clermont (d. 1465) was the first wife of Ferrante I.*

Joanna of Austria (1535–1573)

Habsburg daughter of Charles V who was regent of Spain and the only female Jesuit. Name variations:

Joana or Juana of Austria; Jeanne d'Autriche or Jeanne of Austria; Joanna Hapsburg or Habsburg. Born on June 24 or 27, 1535 (some sources cite 1537), in Madrid; died on September 7, 1573, at Escorial; daughter of Charles V (1500–1558), king of the Romans (r. 1519–1530), Holy Roman emperor (r. 1530–1558) and king of Spain as Charles I (r. 1516–1556), and Isabella of Portugal (1503–1539); sister of Philip II, king of Spain (r. 1556–1598), and king of Portugal as Philip I; sister of **Marie of Austria** *(1528–1603); half-sister of* **Margaret of Parma** *(1522–1586); half-sister of John of Austria; married Portuguese prince Joao or João, the infante, also known as John of Portugal (1537–1554), on January 11, 1552; joined Company of Jesus, 1554; regent of Spain, 1554–1559; children: Sebastiao also known as Sebastian or Sebastián (1554–1578), king of Portugal (r. 1557–1578).*

Birth of Charles V (1500); death of Isabella I of Castile (1504); death of Ferdinand of Aragon (1516); accession of Charles V to Spanish throne (1517); start of Lutheran Reformation (1517); election of Charles V as Holy Roman Emperor (1519); marriage of Charles V and Isabella of Portugal (1526); death of Catherine of Aragon (1535); birth of John, prince of Portugal (1537); death of Isabella of Portugal (1539); Loyola receives papal approval for establishment of Society of Jesus (1540); death of John of Portugal (1554); death of John III of Portugal (1557); death of Mary Tudor, wife of Philip II (1558); death of Charles V (1558); battle of Lepanto (1571); death of Sebastián (1578).

𝒫rincess [Joanna] was perhaps the most interesting woman of the Spanish Habsburgs.

—**Gregorio Marañón**

Of those who survived to adulthood, Joanna of Austria was the youngest of Charles V and *Isabella of Portugal*'s children. She was born on June 24, 1535, in Madrid and passed a healthy childhood. Carefully educated by her mother and royal tutors, by eight years of age, Joanna had learned Latin. She also showed considerable musical ability on the viol and the lute-like vihuela. Her childhood also introduced her to tragedy. She was nearly four when her mother, the Empress Isabella, died from complications of childbirth on April 30, 1539. Like her older brother Philip II, she possessed a solitary personality. Writes historian Geoffrey Parker, "there was something curiously cold about all the children of Charles V."

As was customary for the royal houses of Europe, the marriages of princes and princesses were tools of statecraft rather than personal, romantic unions. Charles V negotiated Joanna's betrothal to Prince John, a nephew of Isabella of Portugal. John was two years younger than she and very sickly. In fact, the Portuguese pressed for an early marriage, hoping to produce an heir to the throne in the event the prince died young. Joanna and John wed on January 11, 1552, in Toro. In the words of Joanna's biographer, Luis Fernández de Retana, "her role was reduced to giving an heir to the Monarchy and retreating to weep her soon-to-be widowhood." Time bore out the Portuguese fears: the marriage was brief. The prince died on January 2, 1554, when she was eight months pregnant. To avoid complications with the impending birth, the court hid his death from Joanna and did not wear mourning. The widow gave birth to Sebastián on January 20. Learning the tragic news of her husband's death, she vowed to dress in mourning the remainder of her life. She also fell into a temporary depression reminiscent of her grandmother, *Juana la Loca (Joanna the Mad).

Charles V wanted her to return to Spain to govern as regent while he was abroad and while her brother Philip was in England for his marriage to *Mary Tudor. Since Sebastián was heir to the throne, the Portuguese would not permit her to take him. On the other hand, perhaps because of her emotionally aloof personality, Joanna seems to have developed little maternal attachment to her son. In the spring of 1554, Joanna returned to Spain, to the displeasure of the Portuguese. Her regency lasted from 1554 to 1559, and she never saw Sebastián again.

Back in Spain, she gave herself over to the political responsibilities of the regency and religious piety. From Valladolid, where she established herself, Joanna penned long reports to her father and brother. She also gave the court an intensely somber, religious air. On January 16, 1556, Charles V abdicated as king of Spain in favor of Philip II, who in turn reappointed Joanna regent while he remained in England and Flanders. She also tried to supervise Philip's son and heir, Charles. The potential spread of Lutheranism in Spain preoccupied her, and she used the Inquisition to defend the kingdom against the protestant heretics. In 1558, she presided at a large auto-de-fe in Valladolid during which 13 heretics were executed and others were punished. In other anti-protestant actions taken on Philip's behalf, she also issued decrees prohibiting the import of foreign books, and in 1559 she ruled that Spaniards could not leave the country to study. Despite her religious scruples, she also dutifully gathered money and other resources for Philip's war against Pope Paul IV over Spain's Italian pretensions.

Meanwhile she used her power to compel the Society of Jesus to secretly make her a member. Ignatius de Loyola had received official papal recognition for his order in 1540, but the Jesuit leadership had decided not to establish an associated group for pious woman. Nonetheless, Joanna was determined to join the Society and had sufficient influence to prevail. Jesuit leaders admitted her under the alias of "Mateo Sánchez," and she remained a member of the Society for the rest of her life. Her political connections served the Jesuits well, but the leaders worried about the consequences should the secret be discovered. Even Philip II did not know of the arrangement. When he returned to Spain in August 1559, Philip was angry that her frequent contact with Francisco de Borja, a prominent Jesuit at court and her spiritual mentor, provoked rumors that she was his mistress.

Joanna of Austria also founded the Las Descalzas convent in Madrid in 1557 and provided it with a rich endowment. After finishing her service as regent in 1559, she began splitting time between the court and the convent. Thanks to her brother Philip, she had her own household at the court. Given her personality, she undoubtedly enjoyed the solitude of Las Descalzas, although she seemed happy and generous in public. Famed for her beauty and still relatively young, she had suitors. *Catherine de Medici tried to negotiate the marriage of her son, Henry of Anjou, to Joanna. At one point there apparently were also suggestions that she marry her nephew Charles, but Joanna remained unwed. Instead she gave herself more and more to religious devotions. Her last months were filled with the pain of cancer. She died on September 8, 1573, in the Escorial Palace and was buried in the convent she had established.

SOURCES:

Carrillo, Juan. *Relación histórica de la real fundación del Monasterio de las Descalzas de S. Clara de la villa de Madrid.* Madrid: Luis Sanchez, 1616.

Fernández de Retana, Luis. *Doña Juana de Austria, gobernadora de España, 1535–1573.* Madrid: El Perpetuo Socorro, 1955.

Lovett, A.W. *Early Habsburg Spain, 1517–1598.* Oxford: Oxford University Press, 1986.

Loyola, Ignatius de. *Letters to Women.* Collected and ed. by Hugo Rahner. NY: Herder and Herder, 1960.

Pierson, Peter. *Philip II of Spain.* London: Thames and Hudson, 1975.

Kendall Brown,
Professor of History,
Brigham Young University, Provo, Utah

Joanna of Austria (1546–1578)

*Grand duchess of Tuscany. Name variations: Giovanna of Austria; Joanna, Archduchess of Austria; Joanna de Medici. Born on January 1, 1546, in Vienna; died on April 11, 1578, in Florence; daughter of Anna of Bohemia and Hungary (1503–1547) and Ferdinand I, Holy Roman emperor (r. 1558–1564); sister of *Elizabeth of Habsburg (d. 1545) and Maximilian II, Holy Roman emperor (1527–1576); married Francesco I also known as Francis I de Medici (1541–1587), grand duke of Tuscany (r. 1574–1587); children: Romola (b. 1566, died young); Eleonora de Medici (1567–1611), duchess of Mantua; Isabella (b. 1567, died young); Caterina also seen as Anna (1569–1584, died young); Marie de Medici (c. 1573–1642); Filippo (b. 1577, died young).*

Joanna of Austria was born in 1546, in Vienna, the daughter of *Anna of Bohemia and Hungary** (1503–1547) and Ferdinand I, Holy Roman emperor. She married Francesco I de Medici, grand duke of Tuscany. Condemned by the Florentines for her Austrian haughtiness, archduchess Joanna was never happy in Florence. She died age 30, in 1578, shortly after giving birth to her sickly son Filippo; he died five years later (1583). She left behind her 11-year-old daughter *Eleonora de Medici** (1567–1611), her nine-year-old daughter Caterina (who would also die young), and her five-year-old daughter, *Marie de Medici**. Francesco's second wife was *Bianca Cappello** (d. 1587).

Joanna of Brabant (1322–1406)

*Duchess of Brabant and countess of Hainault and Holland. Name variations: Johanna, Joan Louvain; Joan of Brabant. Reigned as duchess of Brabant, 1355–1404; abdicated in 1404. Born on June 24, 1322 (some sources cite 1332); died on December 1, 1406; daughter of John III, duke of Brabant (r. 1312–1355), and Marie of Evreux (d. 1335); sister of Margaret of Brabant (1323–1368) and *Marie of Guelders (1325–1399); married William IV (1307–1345), count of Holland and Hainault, before November 1334 (died 1345); married Wenzel of Bohemia also known as Wenceslas (1337–1383), duke of Luxemburg and Brabant (r. 1353–1383), in 1354; no children.*

Joanna of Brabant was born in 1322, the daughter of John III, duke of Brabant, and *Marie of Evreux**. As duchess of Brabant, Joanna succeeded her husband upon his death in 1355; the following year, she offered her subjects a new constitution, known as the *Joyeuse Entrée*, granting much wider liberties. Her successor was Antoine of Burgundy, the grandson of her younger sister *Margaret of Brabant.

Joanna of Castile (1339–1381)

Queen of Castile and Leon. Name variations: Juana Manuela de Castilla; Juana de la Cerda; Joanna de Castilla. Born in 1339; died on March 27, 1381 (some sources cite 1379), in Salamanca, Leon, Spain; daughter of John Manuel also known as Juan Manuel "el Scritor" and *Blanche de la Cerda (c. 1311–1347); married Enrique also known as Henry II Trastamara (1333–1379), king of Castile and Leon (r. 1369–1379), on July 27, 1350; children: John I (b. 1358), king of Castile and Leon (r. 1379–1390); *Eleanor Trastamara (d. 1415); Juana (died young).

Joanna of Castile (1462–1530).

See Juana la Beltraneja.

Joanna of England (1165–1199).

See Berengaria of Navarre for sidebar on Joanna of Sicily.

Joanna of France (1343–1373).

See Jane of France.

Joanna of Naples (1326–1382).

See Joanna I of Naples.

Joanna of Naples (1478–1518)

Queen of Naples. Name variations: Giovanna of Naples. Born in 1478; died on August 27, 1518; daughter of *Joanna of Aragon (1454–1517) and Ferdinand also known as Ferrante I (1423–1494), king of Naples (r. 1458–1494); married her nephew Ferdinand also known as Ferrante II (1469–1496), king of Naples (r. 1495–1496), in 1496.

Joanna of Navarre (c. 1370–1437)

Queen of England by her marriage to Henry IV who was later accused of witchcraft and of plotting the death of her stepson Henry V, imprisoned for three years, and then restored to her former position as dowager queen. Name variations: Joan of Brittany; Joan of Navarre; Joan, Johanne, Juana; Joanna Evreux. Born Joanna around 1370 in Pamplona; died on July 9, 1437, at Havering-atte-Bower, Essex, England; interred at Canterbury Cathedral, Kent; daughter of Charles II d'Albret also known as Charles II the Bad, king of Navarre (r. 1349–1387), and Jane of France (1343–1373, daughter of King John II of France); married John IV de Montfort (1339–1399), 5th duke of Brittany (r. 1364–1399, son of *Jeanne de Montfort), on September 11, 1386, at Saillé, near Guerrand, Navarre (died, November 1, 1399); became second wife of Henry IV (1367–1413), king of England (r. 1399–1413), on February 7, 1403; children: (first marriage) Joanna (1387–1388); daughter (1388–1388); John V (1389–1442), duke of Brittany (r. 1339–1442); Marie of Dreux (1391–1446); Arthur of Brittany (1393–1458), count of Richmond, duke of Brittany (r. 1457–1458); Gilles or Giles (1394–1412), lord of Chantocé; Richard Montfort (1395–1438), count of Étampes; Blanche of Dreux (c. 1396–c. 1418); Margaret de Rohan (1397–1428); (second marriage) none. Henry IV's first wife was *Mary de Bohun (1369–1394).

Betrothed at age ten to John, the heir of Castille (a betrothal which was later broken off); held as a hostage in Paris with her two brothers (1381); became third wife of John IV, duke of Brittany, at age 16; was widowed for four years; married King Henry IV of England (1403); was widowed again after ten years of marriage; imprisoned for three years on charges of witchcraft; remained in England as dowager queen until her death at age 67.

Although Joanna of Navarre was the second wife of King Henry IV of England, and no offspring were produced from this marriage, she has the unique and unforgettable claim of being the only queen of England charged with sorcery and necromancy and imprisoned for treason. Her life leading up to this event, although less well-known, was no less eventful.

Joanna was the second daughter of Charles II d'Albret, king of Navarre, also called Charles the Bad. Her mother was *Jane of France, daughter of King John II of France. In 1380, Joanna was betrothed to John (I), heir of Castile, as her eldest brother Charles (III), heir of Navarre, was married to John's sister ❦➤ Eleanor Trastamara. But upon the death of his father, John I broke his engagement with Joanna and married instead the princess *Eleanor of Aragon (1358–1382).

Charles the Bad's motives and actions centered solely on his desire to regain the disputed throne of his grandfather, King Louis X of France, by any possible means. On one occasion, Joanna and her two older brothers, Charles III and Pierre, were imprisoned in Paris in 1381 and kept as hostages to insure their father's good behavior. While in Paris, the siblings remained under the guardianship of their dead mother's brothers, the dukes of Berri and Burgundy, and consequently were well treated by the French court. John I, now the king of Castille, was responsible for their eventual release from prison.

In 1386, marriage negotiations began between Joanna and another John, John de Montfort IV, duke of Brittany. This was to be his third marriage; neither of his first two marriages with ❧▸ **Mary** (1344–1362), daughter of Edward III of England, and ❧▸ **Joan Holland**, half-sister of Richard II of England, produced children. The dukes of Berri and Burgundy, Joanna's protective uncles, encouraged this union to secure a stronger alliance between Brittany and the French monarchy. Like many marriages of this period, the union was primarily a political one.

After Joanna's father Charles the Bad agreed to give his daughter 120,000 gold francs and to pay 6,000 francs owed to John, duke of Brittany, for the rent of certain lands, the marriage contract was signed at Pampeluna on August 25, 1386. For her dowry, John gave to Joanna the cities of Nantes and Guerrand and three baronies, and the marriage took place in Saillé, on September 11, 1386, before the most noble knights, squires, and ladies of the realm. Many feasts and lavish celebrations followed the wedding ceremony.

By marrying the duke of Brittany, Joanna aligned herself not only with the Bretons, but with the English, for her husband John had developed, during his two marriages with English women, a longstanding relationship with the English in order to resist the influence and powers of the French monarchy. This required, on John's part, ending a lengthy friendship with Oliver de Clisson, who opposed John's political alliances with England. John also formed a strong bond with Charles III, now king of Navarre, Joanna's eldest brother.

At this time, Joanna gave birth to their first child, a girl named Joanna, who lived for only a few months. By the time Joanna was expecting their second child, John had tempered his hostile feelings against the French and went so far as to travel to Paris to perform homage to King Charles VI, although the sincerity of this public service has often been questioned. Despite John's reputation for ruthless political ambitions combined with a violent temper, contemporary sources record that he consistently treated his three wives with kindness and affection.

In 1388, Joanna gave birth to a son, the first heir to the duchy of Brittany. He was baptized Pierre, but afterwards, the duke changed his name to John (V). By the time of Joanna's third child, the princess *Marie of Dreux, rumors had spread that Duke John was secretly renewing treaties with King Richard II of England, causing anger and alarm among the French king and nobles. Joanna urged her husband to put aside his hatred of the French for the sake of herself and their children. Consequently, John met again with the king of France, paid him homage, and together they agreed that the duke's son, John V, would marry the king's third daughter, ❧▸ **Joan Valois**. Once again, the promise of marriage was used to help repair difficult negotiations between political rivals. This reconciliation and marriage agreement were the cause for much celebration and festivity.

The peaceful period which followed proved temporary. Oliver de Clisson and his supporters instigated a civil war in Brittany. Though Duke John was their sovereign, many of the Breton knights and squires refused to fight against de Clisson, so John and Joanna were forced to seek shelter in Vannes while de Clisson won conquest after conquest. Eventually, after realizing his precarious and vulnerable position, John sent a letter to de Clisson proposing reconciliation. De Clisson, not trusting this former friend-turned-adversary, demanded that John's only son be sent to him as a pledge. When John followed through with this request, de Clisson believed

◀❧
*Mary
(1344–1362).*
See Philippa of
Hainault for
sidebar.

❧▸ **Eleanor Trastamara** (d. 1415)
*Queen of Navarre. Name variations: Leonor of Castile. Died in 1415; daughter of Enrique II also known as Henry II, king of Castile and Leon (r. 1369–1379), and *Joanna of Castile (1339–1381); married Charles III, king of Navarre; children: *Blanche of Navarre (1385–1441).*

❧▸ **Joan Holland** (c. 1356–1384)
*Duchess of Brittany. Name variations: Jane. Born around 1356; died in 1384; daughter of *Joan of Kent (1328–1385) and Thomas Holland, 1st earl of Kent; half-sister of Richard II, king of England; second wife of John IV, 5th duke of Brittany.*

❧▸ **Joan Valois** (1391–1433)
*Duchess of Brittany. Name variations: Jeanne, duchess of Bretagne; Joan de France; Joan of France. Born in 1391; died in 1433; third daughter of Charles VI, king of France (r. 1380–1422), and *Isabeau of Bavaria (1371–1435); first wife of John V (1389–1442), duke of Brittany (r. 1339–1442); children: Francis I (b. 1414), duke of Brittany; Peter II, duke of Brittany.*

his sincerity, and a peace treaty was signed on December 28, 1393. In 1396, Joanna's son John, the heir of Brittany, married Joan Valois, further solidifying this political union between the Bretons and the French.

By 1398, Duke John was once again attempting to establish relations with England. This time, he traveled to England, requesting that King Richard return to him the earldom of Richmond. The request was granted and both sovereigns acquitted each other of any debts owed to one another. A year later, John shifted his loyalties by agreeing to assist King Richard's rival, Henry Bolingbroke (the future Henry IV of England), in an assault on England to reclaim his inheritance. Henry's first visit to Brittany, seeking shelter and military assistance, provided Joanna with the chance to meet for the first time the man who would eventually become her second husband.

Duke John died on November 1, 1399, and Joanna assumed the role of regent for their eldest son John V, caring for all his needs and governing in his name. Joanna immediately enacted a public reconciliation with Oliver de Clisson and his supporters, and a treaty between the two sides was signed on January 1, 1400. A little more than a year later, the 12-year-old John V made his solemn entrance into Rennes on March 22, 1401. He was knighted the following day and invested as duke of Brittany. This investiture was a preliminary step in Joanna's eventual marriage to Henry Bolingbroke, now King Henry IV of England. An obstacle to their union was religion, since Joanna was under the jurisdiction of the pope of Avignon, while King Henry held to the authority of the pope in Rome.

Joanna sent a trusted emissary, Antoine de Riczi, to England to finalize her marriage treaty with King Henry IV. After the contract was signed, the marriage took place on April 3, 1402, at the palace of Eltham, with de Riczi standing in as a proxy for Joanna. The French court was highly troubled by this political union, believing that Joanna's children would travel to England with her and eventually form political attachments with that nation. Joanna agreed to leave her older children under the protection of the duke of Burgundy, a powerful figure in the French government who had positioned himself to assume their guardianship as the closest relative of the children and as uncle to Joanna. The young duke, John V, along with his two brothers Gilles and Arthur of Brittany, traveled to Paris with the duke of Burgundy to pay homage to King Charles VI.

Joanna traveled with her two infant daughters, **Blanche of Dreux** and *****Margaret de Rohan**, to Camaret, the port from which she departed for England with a large retinue on January 13, 1403. A violent storm at sea caused the English warship transporting them to land at Falmouth in Cornwall instead of at Southampton. From there, the retinue traveled by land to Winchester to meet with King Henry. The marriage was publicly performed there in the church of St. Swithin on February 7, 1403. Joanna's coronation as queen of England was held in Westminster Cathedral on February 26, 1403, accompanied by great processions and celebrations.

The joyful period following these matrimonial celebrations was shattered by the French fleet's attack on the Isle of Wight and Breton ships assaulting the coast of Cornwall. Suddenly, the new queen fell out of favor with many English people. In February 1404, Arthur of Brittany, Joanna's second son, made a visit to England and, after performing homage to King Henry, was bestowed with the earldom of Richmond. At the same time, Joanna's eldest son John V demanded the return of the princesses Blanche and Margaret, reminding his mother that the children were the property of Brittany, not England. However, it was not until 1406 that both daughters sailed for France, where their brother John was arranging marriages for them.

Subsequent events caused the English populace to be displeased with the situation at the royal court. In 1405, Henry IV pardoned and released Breton prisoners who had been captured during an attack on Dartmouth. In addition, parliamentary records of 1405 state that "great discontents were engendered in the minds of all classes of men, on account of the influx of foreigners, which the king's late marriage had introduced into the realm." The House of Commons then formed a special committee to oversee appointments in the royal household, limiting the presence of foreigners to a small number of the queen's own attendants.

During the summer of 1406, the king and queen stayed at Leeds Castle in Kent, because of terrible plague outbreaks in London that resulted in many deaths. Joanna earnestly encouraged peaceful relations between England and Brittany, between her husband Henry and her son John, which resulted in a truce announced between the two powers on September 13, 1407.

After a period of increasing feebleness and illness, King Henry IV died on March 19, 1413, age 47, and his eldest son from his first marriage assumed the position of monarch as Henry V.

Initially, Henry V maintained good relations with his stepmother, Dowager Queen Joanna. It benefitted both of them to foster amiable feelings towards Joanna's son John V, duke of Brittany; the queen desired her son and stepson to be in accord with one another, while for the new king, an alliance with Brittany could only assist his ambitions to resume the title of king of France. Sources disagree about whether or not Joanna acted as queen regent when Henry V undertook his military campaigns in France. John, duke of Bedford, King Henry V's brother, was appointed lord-lieutenant of England, but the queen continued to command the confidence and respect of her stepson. Before leaving for his expedition on June 16, 1415, Henry V stopped at Westminster to take personal leave of Queen Joanna and granted her a pension of 1,000 marks a year for life. Joanna was permitted, in the king's absence, to reside at any of the royal palaces of Windsor, Wallingford, Berkhamstead, or Hertford.

While Joanna's son John V remained neutral in the contest between England and France, Arthur of Brittany, the queen's second son, led an attack on King Henry V's camp near Agincourt, was wounded in the battle, and imprisoned. When news of the English victory at Agincourt reached London on October 29, 1415, the queen, nobility, and civic leaders of the city marched in procession from St. Paul's to Westminster Abbey for a solemn service of thanksgiving. Joanna's divided loyalties to her former homeland had to remain hidden as she fulfilled the role of queen, even though her brother, Charles III of Navarre, was killed in the battle and her son Arthur of Brittany was held captive.

Arthur was brought before the queen briefly, having not seen his mother for 12 years. Many historians claim that he was unable to recognize his mother from among the ladies of the court, until she identified herself to him, and they fell into each other's arms weeping. After this reunion, Arthur was imprisoned in the Tower of London and later at Fotheringay Castle, since Henry V was unwilling to negotiate for his release or ransom. It was 1417 before Henry would agree to a truce with John V, duke of Brittany, which supposedly resulted from the strong intercession of Joanna.

The situation for Joanna in England changed gravely in October 1419, when she was arrested by the duke of Bedford, the regent of England. According to Walsingham's chronicle, Joanna, "accused by certain persons of an act of witchcraft, which would have tended to the

king's harm, was committed . . . to the custody of sir John Pelham." Charged by her confessor, John Randolf, a Franciscan friar, of resorting to witchcraft to poison Henry V, Joanna was originally detained at the royal manorhouse of Rotherhithe but spent the majority of her confinement at Leeds Castle. Henry ordered that the queen's dowry, rents, and personal property be confiscated. Joanna was imprisoned solely based on allegations and never received the fair treatment of a trial.

Before her accusation and arrest, Henry had attempted to acquire, on loan, monies from the queen's dowry. The king and kingdom were in great need of finances from every quarter to support the ongoing efforts of the military campaign in France, which had left the treasury largely depleted. It has been suggested that the accusation of witchcraft was merely a pretense for securing the queen's resources which, until this time, had been outside of the king's control. Henry returned victorious from France in 1421 with *Catherine of Valois (1401–1437), nearly a

Joanna of
Navarre

relative of Joanna, as his bride. Catherine was the sister of Joan Valois, the duchess of Brittany, Joanna's daughter-in-law.

Joanna was imprisoned for over three years before her stepson had a change of heart and returned to her the property and money that had been confiscated. Realizing that his end was near, he declared on July 13, 1422, to the lords of his council, "that ye make deliverance unto our said mother, the queen, wholly of her said dower, and suffer her to receive it as she did heretofore." Although Henry did not openly declare Joanna's innocence with this injunction, the absence of any mention of the charges seems to imply a recognition of her innocence. After the restoration of her property, Joanna resumed her place of privilege and even favor in the royal court. She was treated with proper consideration by the young Henry VI, who gave her an elaborate gold and jeweled tablet on New Year's Day, 1437.

Joanna of Navarre died on July 9, 1437, while residing at Havering-atte-Bower. "Also the same year died all the lions in the Tower," notes the Chronicle of London, "the which was nought seen in no man's time before out of mind." The queen was buried beside her second husband in Canterbury Cathedral on August 6, 1437.

SOURCES:

Hutchison, Harold F. *King Henry V*. NY: John Day, 1967.

Myers, A.R. "The Captivity of a Royal Witch: The Household Accounts of Queen Joan of Navarre, 1419–21," in *Bulletin of the John Rylands Library*. Vol. 24. October 1940, pp. 263–284.

Strickland, Agnes. *Lives of the Queens of England*. Vol III. Philadelphia, PA: Blanchard and Lea, 1857.

SUGGESTED READING:

Jones, Michael C.E. *Creation of Brittany: A Late Medieval State*. Rio Grande, OH: Hambledon Press, 1988.

Kittredge, George L. *Witchcraft in Old and New England*. Cambridge, MA: Harvard University Press, 1929.

Karen E. Mura,
Associate Professor of English,
Susquehanna University, Selinsgrove, Pennsylvania

Joanna of Ponthieu (d. 1279).

See Eleanor of Castile (1241–1290) for sidebar.

Joanna of Portugal (1439–1475)

Queen of Castile and Leon and mother of Juana la Beltraneja. Name variations: Joana, Juana of Portugal, Juana de Aviz, Juana of Aviz. Born in late March 1439 (some sources cite 1438) in the Portuguese town of Almada; died on June 13, 1475, in Madrid; daughter of Edward also known as Duarte I, king of Portugal (r. 1433–1438), and Leonora of Aragon

*(1405–1445); sister of Alphonso V, king of Portugal (r. 1438–1481), and *Eleanor of Portugal (1434–1467); betrothed to Enrique IV also known as Henry IV of Castile, in 1454; married Henry IV, king of Castile and Leon (r. 1454–1474), on May 21, 1455; children: Juana la Beltraneja (1462–1530).*

Birth of Henry IV (1425); birth of Isabel the Catholic (1451); execution of Alvaro de Luna (1453); death of Juan II and accession of Henry IV (1454); birth of Juana la Beltraneja (1462); death of Alphonso (1468); agreement of Toros de Guisando (1468); marriage of Isabel and Ferdinand of Aragon (1469); revocation of agreement of Toros de Guisando (1470); death of Henry IV (December 11, 1474); Isabella crowned queen of Castile (December 13, 1474).

Joanna of Portugal was born in late March 1439 in the Portuguese town of Almada, the daughter of Duarte I, king of Portugal, and ***Leonora of Aragon**, and the sister of King Alphonso V of Portugal. At age 15, she became betrothed to Henry IV of Castile, who the year before had secured an annulment of his marriage to ✣ Blanche of Navarre (1424–1462). Several factors led Henry to seek the hand of Joanna. As a Portuguese princess, she offered Castile an alliance against the expansionism of John II of Aragon. Furthermore, Henry's marriage to Blanche had proved childless. Rumor held the king to be impotent, the marriage never having been consummated. He undoubtedly saw a new marriage as a way of proving his own virility as well as producing an heir. Joanna's famed beauty probably also led Henry to choose her, even though their mothers were sisters. (Leonora of Aragon and *Maria of Aragon were daughters of *Eleanor of Albuquerque [1374–1435] and Ferdinand I, king of Aragon.)

Magnificent celebrations feted Joanna and Henry in Spain in 1455, but the king initially proved unable to consummate the marriage. Perhaps to cover his failings, he appeared to take **Guiomar de Castro**, a member of Joanna's retinue, as his mistress. A furious Joanna publicly beat her lady-in-waiting. Years passed and Joanna did not become pregnant. Finally, on February 28, 1462, after seven years, she gave birth to a daughter, whom the delighted royal couple named Juana (the future ***Juana la Beltraneja**), after her mother. The monarchs and their subjects seemed genuinely elated about the girl's birth. A brief interval brought another pregnancy, but the son was still-born.

Unfortunately for the queen and her daughter, however, Henry's reign became enveloped in

✣▶

Blanche of Navarre (1424–1462).

See Eleanor of Navarre for sidebar.

controversy, and it harmed their interests. Dissident nobles resented Henry's reliance on Juan Pacheco, the grasping and duplicitous marquis of Villena. Henry found it impossible to quell the rebellious Castilian aristocracy while simultaneously contending with threats from Aragon and Granada. To undercut his authority, the dissidents moved to depose Henry by raising his half-brother Alphonso to the throne. By this time Henry and Joanna had separated and, to appease to rebels, he agreed that Alonso de Fonseca, archbishop of Sevilla, could hold her hostage as a guarantee that Henry would recognize Alphonso as his heir. Frustrated and bored, Joanna waited in Fonseca's castle at Alaejos. In 1468, she became pregnant as the result of an adulterous relationship with the warden's son. When she attempted to escape, her scandalous behavior became public knowledge.

Meanwhile Alphonso died in July 1468, and the dissidents then championed the rights of his sister *Isabella I. Besides brute military power, this strategy also required that Henry and Joanna and their daughter Juana be discredited. In September 1468, the rebellious nobles forced Henry to accept the agreement of Toros de Guisando. By it, Henry renounced his daughter's rights to inherit the throne and instead agreed that Isabella would succeed him. The nobles argued that because Henry and Joanna had not secured a papal dispensation authorizing them to wed as first cousins, they were not legitimately married. Thus, their daughter Juana was illegitimate, eliminating her as a rival to Isabella's claim to the throne.

In 1470, however, Henry abrogated the agreement of Toros de Guisando and named his daughter Juana as his heir once again. By this time, rumors were spreading that Henry was not really the girl's father. Queen Joanna had been close to a courtier, Beltrán de la Cueva, and he was alleged to be Juana's father. Joanna's recent scandalous behavior gave weight to the accusations. Although both Henry and Joanna swore publicly that they were the girl's parents, she became known to the Isabelline faction as *la Beltraneja*.

Henry died in 1474, defeated by rebellion and controversy. Joanna lived in an annex of the Franciscan church of Madrid until she died a few months later on June 13, 1475. Her remains were buried in the church, while her daughter Juana la Beltraneja went into exile in Portugal. It remained for Isabella's propagandists and historians to defame the memory of Henry and Joanna of Portugal to help establish the new monarch's legitimacy.

SOURCES:

Azcona, Tarsicio de. *Isabel de Castilla: Estudio crítico sobre su vida y su reinado*. Madrid: Biblioteca de Autores Cristianos, 1993.

Miller, Townsend. *Henry IV of Castile, 1425–1474*. Philadelphia, PA: Lippincott, 1972.

> [Henry IV]'s adversaries were aided by the increasingly evil reputation of the queen.
>
> —William D. Phillips

Palencia, Alonso de. *Crónica de Enrique IV*. Biblioteca de Autores Españoles 207–208. Madrid: Atlas, 1973, 1975.

Phillips, William D. *Enrique IV and the Crisis of Fifteenth-Century Castile, 1425–1480*. Cambridge, MA: Mediaeval Academy of America, 1978.

Valera, Mosén Diego de. *Memorial de diversas hazañas; chrónica de Enrique IV, ordenada por mos en Diego de Valera*. Madrid: Espasa-Calpe, 1941.

Kendall Brown,
Professor of History,
Brigham Young University, Provo, Utah

Joanna of Portugal (1636–1653)

*Portuguese princess. Name variations: Joana. Born on September 18, 1636; died on November 17, 1653; daughter of *Luisa de Guzman (1613–1666) and John IV the Fortunate, king of Portugal (r. 1640–1656).*

Joanna of Sicily (1165–1199).

See Berengaria of Navarre (d. 1163–c. 1230) for sidebar.

Joanna the Mad (1479–1555).

See Juana la Loca.

Joaquina Carlota (1775–1830).

See Carlota Joaquina.

Jobe, Mary Lee (1878–1966).

See Akeley, Delia J. for sidebar on Mary Jobe Akeley.

Joceline.

Variant of Joscelyn or Josselyn.

Jochebed

Biblical mother of Moses who saved her newborn son from certain death following the nefarious edict of a pharaoh. Name variations: (Hebrew) Yokebed. Pronunciation: JAH-kuh-bed or JOH-kee-buhd. Daughter of Levi; married her nephew Amram; children: Miriam the Prophet; Moses; Aaron.

Noted among the heroes of the faith, Jochebed was the daughter of Levi, the wife of Amram, and the mother of three children,

*Miriam the Prophet, Aaron, and Moses. Moses was born shortly after the pharaoh had issued an edict, part of an ongoing oppression of the Israelites by the Egyptian king, demanding that every newborn male Hebrew child be killed. "The people of Israel are too many and too mighty for us," he said (Exodus 1:9). Following her son's birth, Jochebed hid Moses in her house for three months, hoping to keep his presence secret from the civic authorities. When his concealment became too difficult, she conceived of a plan to bring him to the attention of the daughter of the king (probably *Thermuthis, the daughter of Seti I), with the hope that the princess would take pity on the child.

Constructing a miniature vessel of bulrushes, Jochebed placed Moses inside and set the boat among the reeds on the bank of the Nile, near the spot where the princess came to bathe. She then posted her daughter Miriam the Prophet as a sentinel to watch over him. Indeed, Princess Thermuthis discovered the child and Miriam stepped forth and offered to find a Hebrew woman to nurse him. Miriam then returned with Jochebed, to whom the princess said, "Take this child away, and nurse it for me, and I will give thee thy wages." Thus, Jochebed not only saved Moses from certain death, but had him in her care for a few years.

When he was weaned, he was returned to the palace where he became the adopted son of the princess, although it was believed that Jochebed continued to care for him throughout his formative years. Although Moses grew up in the splendor of the Egyptian court, his mother provided for his religious beliefs and served as the link to his Hebrew roots.

Jochmann, Rosa (1901—)

Leading Austrian official of the underground Social Democratic movement, who spent more than five years in German captivity and was active in Austrian public life after her liberation in 1945. Pronunciation: YOK-mahn or JAHCK-mahn. Born Rosa Jochmann in Vienna, Austria, on July 19, 1901; daughter of Karl Jochmann (a foundry worker) and Josefine Jochmann (a waitress and laundress); self-taught after age 14; never married; no children.

Went to work in a factory that produced chocolate and other confections (1914); transferred to a cable factory and injured her finger in an accident; joined a labor union and began to educate herself; became an official of the Chemical Workers' Union; rising in party leadership in the "Red Vienna" period of socialist reform, concerned with the interests of women, working conditions and environmental hazards to industrial workers (1918–34); arrested and imprisoned by the Austro-Fascist regime of Kurt von Schuschnigg (August 1934); was a leader in the underground Social Democratic movement (1934–38); remained in Austria after the Nazi occupation of March 1938; arrested by the German Gestapo (August 1939); spent more than five years in German captivity, mostly in the notorious Ravensbrück concentration camp, until liberation (1945); remained active in Austrian public life after her liberation.

The childhood of Rosa Jochmann was typical of many who were born in Vienna's industrial working-class district of Brigittenau at the start of the 20th century. Her parents, like many laborers in the Austrian city, were Czech immigrants who had moved there from Moravia in search of jobs. Karl Jochmann worked in an iron foundry while **Josefine Jochmann** labored as a waitress or laundress for a day's wages that were enough to purchase two loaves of bread. Rosa was the fourth of the couple's six children, and soon after her birth the family moved to Simmering, another of the city's industrial districts, where she grew up in a two-room apartment, with only a kitchen and bedroom. To earn a few extra kreuzer (a copper coin valued at one-half of a cent), the Jochmanns rented out two of the family beds to *Bettgeher* (even more impoverished workers) who paid for the right to sleep in the tiny apartment but not to live there. The children were so often hungry that the bread had to be locked up, to prevent them from being tempted to pilfer.

Despite their poverty, the Jochmann family was stable, and Rosa's parents, though their formal educations had ended at the primary level, had a lively interest in the world around them. Although Rosa's father never read a book of Marxist theory, he was an enthusiastic Social Democrat, and sometimes told his young daughter that "when Herr Marx comes, then the situation for us workers will finally begin to improve." Rosa often accompanied her father to Socialist meetings and demonstrations, which sometimes turned violent and were bloodily terminated by police and troops with drawn sabers. On one such occasion, Karl Jochmann was wounded. When he returned home, Josefine scolded him, saying, it was "God's punishment for always going to demonstrations."

Karl Jochmann was often unemployed. Rosa had little choice but to look for work when her primary schooling ended. In 1915, age 14, she got her first job in a factory that manufactured chocolates, confections, and other foods. Spending hours at the backbreaking task of cleaning out large vessels used for mustard, she often broke into tears from exhaustion. But Rosa's misery was somewhat lightened when she was told by her division head that the taking of chocolates from the workplace was strictly forbidden, but she could eat sweets to her heart's content while on her shift. This small act of kindness became one of her first lessons in working-class fellowship.

World War I was raging across Europe at the time, and the wartime job market was volatile. As a young and unskilled female worker, Rosa soon learned the harsh reality of the dictum "last hired, first fired." Her next employment was at a cable factory, where she wrapped cables around drums. It was noisy, dirty, and dangerous work that made extraordinary physical demands on the body of a persistently undernourished 15-year-old. Many workers there had been the victims of serious, often crippling, accidents, and when Rosa caught a finger in one of the machines while working the night shift, the injury proved permanent and remained bothersome and disabling into her old age.

No longer able to work in the cable factory, Jochmann found yet another job at the bottom of the scale in terms of income, safety, and job security, this time with a company that manufactured candles. Her future appeared dreary at best, differing little from that of literally hundreds of thousands of proletarian young girls and women across Austria, when one of her older fellow workers urged her to become a union member. Membership dues were a modest 50 heller, but this was the same small amount Rosa normally spent every so often for her one pleasure, going to see a motion picture. She decided to forego this amusement, however, and joined the union. Almost from the outset, she began to distinguish herself through her direct and outspoken advocacy of the union's weakest and least articulate members. Her first speech at a union meeting was an impassioned plea on behalf of an older fellow worker who had not received the same raise granted everyone else in the factory because her job classification was "servant." From this time on, Jochmann grew increasingly outspoken on issues of immediate importance to her fellow factory workers, and also raised themes relating to the ever-worsening living conditions they faced in wartime.

By the autumn of 1918, when World War I ended, Jochmann and most of her fellow workers lived on the abyss of starvation. They despised the war that had killed so many of their husbands, brothers, and neighbors and ardently desired the creation of a new social order that would guarantee the elimination of the fundamental causes of war and human exploitation by reconstructing society on foundations of working-class power and international harmony.

By this time, Jochmann had undergone a remarkable transformation. At age 17, she was no longer a poorly educated, politically ignorant girl from the very lowest strata of Vienna's working class, but was in the process of becoming a well-read, confident leader. On November 12, 1918, she was part of the jubilant crowd of many thousands outside the Imperial Parliament building on Vienna's elegant Ringstrasse, that stood cheering the birth of the Austrian Republic. For Jochmann and many other workers that cold day, the occasion was bittersweet; the previous day, Dr. Victor Adler, the altruistic Jewish physician who had almost single-handedly founded the Austrian Social Democratic Party many decades before, had died. For years, he had worked in Vienna's slums, tending to the medical needs of indigent workers, yet, after four years of military bloodletting, Rosa and many of her fellow Viennese believed the working class could look forward to a bright era.

By 1919, municipal elections placed Social Democrats in control of Vienna, ushering in a vast experiment in social reform. From 1919 through February 1934, the city was governed by a Social Democratic administration that pursued policies intent on rapidly raising the physical, intellectual, and moral condition of Viennese workers to heights never before seen in a modern society. By raising taxes on the rich and instituting innovative housing and public-health schemes, "Red Vienna," as it was called, brought about impressive and lasting improvements in the lives of the working-class segment of society, who had gone largely ignored in capitalist societies up to that time.

Almost from the outset, Rosa Jochmann was involved in these changes. First as a part-time, then as a full-time functionary of the Social Democratic Party, she ran the factory committee of the Chemical Workers' Union. She also enrolled in virtually every night-school course offered by the educational section of the party. Because of her remarkable intelligence and ability to articulate ideas for both workers and intellectuals, as well her considerable warmth, she soon came to the attention of several leading women within the Viennese organization of the Social

Democratic machine. For many years, Jochmann was nurtured and guided by *Käthe Leichter, a Social Democratic leader about five years her senior, who was from a middle-class Jewish background and profoundly devoted to the cause of Marxist social transformation in Austria.

As a rising star in the Social Democratic Party, Jochmann also came to the attention of its leader, Otto Bauer. Their first encounter was not altogether happy. In the course of an address she was making before a group, her mispronunciation of a word prompted the chair of the meeting, a female functionary from Jochmann's own district of Simmering, to call attention to her error and suggest that she had no right to speak in public if she was going to have such lapses. What could have been a crushing moment psychologically was turned around by the intervention of Bauer, who took the rostrum to praise Jochmann and dismiss her pronunciation for the insignificant thing that it was, while also managing to avoid ruffling the feathers of the meeting's chair. It was a virtuoso performance on the part of Bauer, and the beginning of a fruitful political relationship between the two Socialists, based on mutual respect, that was to last until Bauer was forced to flee Austria in 1934 (he died in exile in Paris in July 1938). On several occasions, Bauer helped Jochmann overcome her stage fright and lack of confidence as she prepared to face large and potentially intimidating audiences.

By the late 1920s, Rosa Jochmann was clearly one of the most gifted younger women in the Austrian Social Democratic Party, when a new generation was needed to carry on the high level of enthusiasm and competence established by the pioneer generation of women Socialists then passing from the scene. By 1930, "Red Vienna" could pride itself on significant achievements in the fields of public housing, health and welfare, but there were dark economic clouds looming. The collapse of the New York stock market in the fall of 1929 was leading to a collapse in world trade and tourism, and the Austrian economy, which had never been strong even in the boom years of the 1920s, now spiraled downward at an alarming rate. Armed units of Fascists and Nazis were prowling the streets of the Austrian provincial towns and even beginning to challenge Vienna's militant workers on their own territory. Essentially an optimist, Jochmann's response was to redouble her efforts at party work and continue to educate herself. On women's issues, she spoke up loud and clear within a party which proclaimed sexual equality but in fact remained as thoroughly male-dominated as the bourgeois political parties. She was strongly in favor of revoking Paragraph 144 of the Austrian Penal Code, which banned abortions, believing that, by upholding this law, conservative Roman Catholic (as well as Nazi) Austrians were denying women a basic human right; she had accumulated a large and tragic collection of stories of women who had died or been permanently injured as a result of undergoing abortions under conditions made dangerous by the illegality of the procedure. The issue was one of many discussed by Jochmann and her cohorts at the Workers' Academy (*Arbeiterhochschule*), an innovative experiment in adult education that lasted from 1929 to 1930. Jochmann also wanted improvements in the working conditions of women exposed on the job site to dangerous substances or extreme heat, dust, and noise. Often her harshest criticisms were reserved not for greedy factory owners but for indifferent and lackadaisical factory inspectors.

In the early 1930s, the impressive achievements and even greater hopes of Viennese municipal socialism began to be eroded by the relentless assaults of Fascism in both Germany and Austria. In Germany, the Nazis became a major electoral force in September 1930, but they did not become a serious threat in Austria until the elections of April 1932. In early 1933, the seizure of power in Germany by Adolf Hitler made the existence of an independent Austria highly questionable, given the strong desire for union of the two countries (*Anschluss*) felt by most Germans and Austrians. Austrian Socialists like Rosa Jochmann believed, as did theorists like Otto Bauer, that a Greater German Socialist Republic should be the ultimate goal of the working class of Central Europe, but this dream came to an end with the triumph of Fascism in Germany. Jochmann often traveled to Germany on party assignments, and, on her last trip to that country before it became a Nazi state, she witnessed the horrors of the emerging Hitler regime firsthand. In Munich, a few days after Hitler was appointed German chancellor, she and a German colleague witnessed the ghastly sight of a father and son in death throes following a beating by Nazi storm troopers.

By the spring of 1933, Austrian Socialism was a political movement on the defensive, struggling desperately to survive. In the bloody civil war of February 1934, Austrian Socialism was crushed and the country brought under the rule of a "moderate" variant of Fascism led by Chancellor Engelbert Dollfuss, who was later to be killed in a botched Nazi coup d'etat. With the Social Democratic Party outlawed, the Vienna municipal government thrown out of office, and Marxist trade unionism toppled, a new "Christian-authoritarian-corporatist" constitution was proclaimed, revoking many of the hard-won rights of workers and women. In the last days of constitutional government, Rosa Jochmann had been elected to the executive board of the Social Democratic Party, but with the onset of the Dollfuss dictatorship, Otto Bauer and most other leaders of the party fled abroad. Jochmann refused to flee and was soon spending her time organizing a new illegal underground party, defiantly and optimistically called Revolutionary Socialists, to lead the opposition to the dictatorship.

The ban on the Social Democratic Party also meant Rosa had no job or income, and life became a desperate struggle. There was a spirit of hope and solidarity among the men and women in the underground work, but the risks were considerable and constant. On July 15, 1934, a secret mass meeting of 3,000 Socialists held in the Vienna Woods was attacked by armed police, resulting in two deaths and many serious injuries. On a mission to distribute illegal leaflets in nearby Wiener Neustadt in August 1934, Jochmann was arrested, found guilty, and sentenced to three months in police confinement and a year in prison. The sentence was pronounced by Alois Osio, an implacable enemy of the Social Democrats, who was to die, ironically, as a Nazi prisoner in the Buchenwald concentration camp in 1939.

In March 1938, a few days before the German annexation of Austria, the Social Democratic leadership, including Jochmann, emerged from hiding to call for a coalition of all anti-Nazi forces to resist the imminent threat to national independence. For a day or two, there was hope that Austria might be able to withstand the tide of Hitlerism, but the illusion soon evaporated, and Europe slid inexorably toward another war. With the Nazis in control of Austria, the fortunate among Jochmann's associates fled abroad to continue their anti-Fascist work. If they were Jewish, as many in the Social Democratic leadership were, they were in double jeopardy in the eyes of the Third Reich, being both a racial threat as Semites, and an ideological enemy as Marxists. In the first months of Nazi control, many thousands of Jews and Socialists, as well as Catholic and conservative foes of the Germans, were arrested in Austria and sent to Dachau and other concentration camps. Jochmann's arrest by the German secret military force, the Gestapo, did not come until August 22, 1939. Held and interrogated for several months in Vienna, she was transferred in March 1940 to the women's concentration camp at Ravensbrück, in a trip that took three weeks.

One of Jochmann's early insights at Ravensbrück was the realization that female officials in the camp were often as cruel and heartless as the SS guards and administrators. In keeping with Nazi racial doctrines, Jewish prisoners were kept segregated from "Aryan" ones, but Rosa soon found that her dear friend from Vienna, Käthe Leichter, was in the camp. She and her colleagues found ways to communicate with the Jewish women, including Leichter, and learned that their work conditions, lodging and nourishment were drastically worse than those of non-Jewish inmates. Despite the degradations, Käthe Leichter's morale remained high. She became an example of courage and dignity to other prisoners, organizing secret celebrations of socialist holidays and writing poetry that was memorized by other prisoners and thus survived to appear in print after the war. In 1942, all the inmates were deeply saddened when she was among 1,500 Jewish women murdered by the Nazis.

By January 1941, Rosa Jochmann had earned the position of a senior leader (*Blockälteste*) among the Aryan political prisoners at Ravensbrück, which presented her with a chance for freedom. In the course of routine tours of inspections by Heinrich Himmler of his concentration camp empire, the Nazis would release a token number of prisoners every so often, for propaganda purposes, as a sign of their generosity and mercy toward enemies of the Reich. Camp officials gave Jochmann the opportunity to make an appeal on these grounds, but when Himmler arrived, she simply read her report as *Blockälteste* without asking for her release. In an interview many years later, Jochmann denied that there was anything heroic in her decision, noting that freedom at that moment would have required her to continue to think of her comrades under terrible conditions; by remaining in Ravensbrück, she was able to do some good and on certain occasions prevent worse evils from taking place.

As the war dragged on, conditions in the camp deteriorated greatly. Jochmann survived months in the notorious "bunker," where prisoners were brought to the edge of death and madness through deprivation of food, light, and adequate clothing. Fearful of being killed by the sadistic SS troops in charge, she summoned up sufficient reserves to respond to their rote demands to identify herself. "Protective Custody Prisoner Jochmann, No. 3014," she would answer.

Rosa Jochmann withstood the terrors at Ravensbrück for five years, while colleagues who were Jewish, Polish, or Russian were sent to their deaths at Auschwitz or died, one by one, of disease and starvation. Some, pushed beyond their psychological limits, committed suicide.

When liberation finally came in April 1945, the surviving women were given food and clothing and treated well by their Soviet liberators. Given the chaos of Germany in defeat, however, getting back home was not a simple matter. In late summer, Jochmann reached her beloved Vienna and found a city in ruins. Immense tasks lay ahead for the Socialist Party and the Austrian population in general, and she was quickly accepted by the new party leadership as a member of the presidium and chair of the women's central committee. Soon she was also serving in Parliament. She did not always agree with the party line, particularly in 1949, when it led to the approval of a new political party reserved essentially for former Nazis.

Zita Johann

Jochmann never forgot the experience of Ravensbrück. She spoke to countless meetings on the evils of Nazism and the dangers of a New Right, particularly those alienated young people who had never been adequately educated about the nature of the regime behind the Holocaust. In March 1965, after being present at a peaceful anti-Fascist demonstration in Vienna that was turned by Neo-Nazis into a bloody riot and resulted in the death of a former concentration camp inmate, she became passionately involved in the work of educating young people about the Nazi era. The Documentation Archive of the Austrian Resistance, with which she was involved, became a model for all resistance archives in Europe; she also appeared on radio and television, and traveled throughout Austria to spread her message of *Niemals wieder!* (Never again).

As a living witness, Rosa Jochmann became a strong voice of conscience in a nation that many felt had developed a disturbing case of national amnesia when it came to National Socialist crimes. In the final years of her life, she bore a strong resemblance to the young working girl from Simmering who possessed an unquenchable thirst for knowledge and justice.

SOURCES:

Buttinger, Joseph. *In the Twilight of Socialism: A History of the Revolutionary Socialists of Austria.* NY: Frederick A. Praeger, 1953.

Gruber, Helmut. *Red Vienna: Experiment in Working-Class Culture 1919–1934.* NY: Oxford University Press, 1991.

Langbein, Hermann. *. . . nicht wie die Schafe zur Schlachtbank: Widerstand in den nationalsozialistischen Konzentrationslagern 1938–1945.* Frankfurt am Main: Fischer Taschenbuch Verlag, 1980.

Pasteur, Paul. "Rosa Jochmann: résistante autrichienne a Ravensbrück," in *Austriaca.* Vol. 9, no. 17, 1983, p. 103–113.

Sporrer, Maria, and Herbert Steiner, eds. *Rosa Jochmann: Zeitzeugin.* 3rd ed. Vienna: Europaverlag, 1987.

Thalmann, Rita. "Les femmes dans la résistance autrichienne," in *Austriaca.* Vol. 9, no. 17, 1983, pp. 89–102.

Waschek, Hans, ed. *Rosa Jochmann: Ein Kampf, der nie zu Ende geht. Reden und Aufsätze.* Vienna: Löcker Verlag, 1994.

John Haag,
Associate Professor of History,
University of Georgia, Athens, Georgia

Johann, Zita (1904–1993)

Hungarian-born stage and film actress. Born near Temesvar, Hungary (now Timisoara, Rumania), on July 14, 1904; died of pneumonia at Nyack Hospital, Nyack, New York, on September 24, 1993; her father had been an officer in the emperor's Hussars; attended Bryant High School on Long Island; married John Houseman; married twice more.

Zita Johann was born in Temesvar, Hungary, in 1904. At age seven, she moved with her family to New York City where she appeared in high school productions. After applying to the Theater Guild for work as an understudy, she immediately won roles in touring productions of *Peer Gynt*, *The Devil's Disciple*, and *He Who Gets Slapped*. She made her Broadway debut in 1924 in the Theater Guild's production of *Man and the Masses*. Other leading roles followed in *Machinal* (1928), *Tomorrow and Tomorrow* (1931) as well as other plays. In 1931, she played the wife of a steelworker who succumbs to drink in *The Struggle*, the last film made by D.W. Griffith. Most memorably, she played Helen Grosvenor in *The Mummy* (1932). After appearing in *Tiger Shark* (1932), *Luxury Liner* (1933), and *Grand Canary* (1934), she returned to the theater, performing in *Panic* (1935), *Flight into China* (1939), *The Burning Deck* (1940) and *The Broken Journey* (1942). During World War II, Johann raised money for war-related charities and organized shows for soldiers bound for overseas. From 1939 on, she lived in a pre-Revolutionary house in West Nyack, New York, where she worked with children and teenagers interested in the theater.

Johanna.

Variant of Joanna or Joan.

Johanna (c. 1410–1445), queen of Scotland.

See Beaufort, Joan.

Johanna Elizabeth of Baden-Durlach (1651–1680)

*Margravine of Ansbach. Name variations: Joanna Elizabeth. Born on November 16, 1651; died on October 8, 1680; daughter of *Christina Casimir and Frederick VI (b. 1617), margrave of Baden-Durlach; became second wife of John Frederick (1654–1686), margrave of Ansbach (r. 1667–1686), on February 5, 1673; children: (stepdaughter) *Caroline of Ansbach (1683–1737), queen of England. John Frederick's first wife was *Eleanor of Saxe-Eisenach (1662–1696).*

Johanna Elizabeth of Holstein-Gottorp (1712–1760)

*Princess of Holstein-Gottorp. Name variations: Joanna Elizabeth. Born on October 24, 1712; died on May 30, 1760; daughter of *Albertina of Baden-Durlach (1682–1755) and Christian Augustus, duke of Hol-*

stein-Gottorp; married Christian August, prince of Anhalt-Zerbst, on November 8, 1727; children: Sophia Augusta Fredericka (1729–1796), princess of Anhalt-Zerbst (who would be known as Catherine II the Great, empress of Russia).*

Johanna Elizabeth's family ruled the Duchy of Holstein. Although she did not control vast land and wealth, her relatives were well-connected with some of the great royal families of Europe. Though small in size, the Duchy of Holstein-Gottorp was strategically placed between Denmark and Germany, on the eastern coast of the Baltic Sea, and thus could exert influence in the region as competing powers wrestled for control of the Baltic and Northern Europe.

Johanna Elizabeth had no particular plans for her daughter Sophia. The girl would later write that her father "saw her very seldom," and her mother "did not bother much about me." In 1744, Joanna and the young Sophia received an invitation to visit the court of Empress *Elizabeth Petrovna of Russia. The purpose of the invitation was to arrange for a marriage between Sophia and Grand Duke Peter Feodorovich (later Tsar Peter III), son of ❧➤ Anne Petrovna (1708–1728) and the duke of Holstein, and heir to the Russian throne. Johanna Elizabeth's intrigues with Frederick the Great, king of Prussia, did not help Sophia win approval in the eyes of Empress Elizabeth, however. When it was discovered that Frederick had asked Johanna Elizabeth to intercede secretly on behalf of Prussian interests at the Russian court, Johanna was promptly banished from Russia in 1745. Mother and daughter never saw each other again. Sophia married Peter and was received into the Orthodox Church as Catherine Alexeievna, later known to the world as *Catherine II the Great.

Johanna of Bavaria (c. 1373–1410)

*Duchess of Austria. Name variations: Johanna Sophia of Bavaria; Johanna Sophia of Bavaria-Straubing. Born around 1373 in Munich; died on October 17, 1410, in Vienna; married Albrecht also known as Albert IV the Patient (1377–1404), duke of Austria (r. 1395–1404); children: Albert V (1397–1439), duke of Austria (r. 1401), king of Hungary (r. 1437), king of Bohemia (r. 1438), and Holy Roman emperor as Albert II (r. 1438–1439); *Margaret (1395–1447), duchess of Bavaria.*

❧❧
Anne Petrovna.
See Elizabeth Petrovna for sidebar.

VOLUME EIGHT   **215**

Johanna of Flanders (c. 1200–1244)

Countess of Flanders and Hainault, as daughter and heir of Baldwin IX. Name variations: Joan of Constantinople; Joan of Flanders; Joanna of Flanders or Jeanne of Flanders; Joanna, Countess of Belgium. Born around 1200; died on December 5, 1244 (some sources cite 1245); daughter of Baudouin also known as Baldwin IX, count of Flanders and Hainault (crowned Baldwin I of Constantinople), and Marie of Champagne (c. 1180–1203); sister of Margaret of Flanders (1202–1280); married Ferdinand of Portugal (1188–1233), on January 1, 1212; married Thomas of Savoy; children: (first marriage) Marie (1224–1236).

Departure of Fourth Crusade (1202); death of Marie of Champagne (1203); death of Baldwin IX (1205); battle of Bouvines (July 27, 1214); death of Philip Augustus (1223); revolt of the "False Baldwin" (1225); release from captivity of Ferdinand (1226); death of Louis VIII (1233); death of Ferdinand (1233); death of Johanna's daughter Marie (1236).

The first child of Baldwin IX, count of Flanders, and *Marie of Champagne, Johanna of Flanders was probably born in 1200; when her father departed on the Fourth Crusade in April 1202, she was reportedly two years old. Johanna's mother left to join Baldwin the following year, but died from an epidemic upon arrival in Acre. Crowned the first Latin emperor of Constantinople on May 9, 1204, Baldwin died a captive of the Bulgars in 1205.

These events not only orphaned Johanna and her sister *Margaret of Flanders (1202–1280), but made Johanna heir to her father's feudal domain, Flanders and Hainault. For several years, the sisters remained under the tutelage of the bishop of Liège, Hugh II of Pierrepont. Meanwhile, Baldwin's brother, Philip of Namur, temporarily governed for Johanna. When his lands were threatened by the duke of Brabant, he sought the protection of his father-in-law, Philip II Augustus, king of France. (Philip of Namur's wife, *Marie of France [1198–c. 1223], was the French king's daughter.) In 1208, Philip of Namur turned Johanna and Margaret over to Philip Augustus' protection.

Ever shrewd and ambitious, the king had less interest in Johanna and Margaret's welfare than he did in controlling Flanders and Hainault, which he had unsuccessfully tried to conquer. To this end, he had Johanna married in January 1212 to Ferdinand of Portugal (1188–1233), who had fled his homeland due to his brother Alphonso II's authoritarian and violent actions. Ferdinand was the nephew of Johanna's tutor, who apparently pressed Philip Augustus to make the union. But the king favored it primarily because he thought it enabled him to control Flanders more easily. Fortuitously possessed of a young bride, the title of count, and the rich county of Flanders, Ferdinand swore fealty to Philip Augustus. In 1213, however, Ferdinand joined forces with the Duke of Brabant and King John I Lackland of England against Philip. The alliance suffered a disastrous defeat in the battle of Bouvines on July 27, 1214, and Ferdinand fell captive to the French.

Philip Augustus allowed Countess Johanna to retain her fiefs, on condition that her fortifications be destroyed and no others built. The king refused, however, to allow Johanna to pay ransom in return for her husband. Ferdinand and Johanna had no children, and Philip Augustus' own daughter, Marie of France, stood to inherit Flanders and Hainault if the countess died childless. The king thus intended to let Ferdinand perish in prison. Meanwhile, Countess Johanna governed an increasingly restive Flanders. The lower classes resented the urban oligarchs who oppressed the cities. Alienation exploded in 1225, when the discontented rallied to the banner of the "False Baldwin," an impostor who claimed to be Johanna's father finally returned from the crusade. Countess Johanna fled for refuge to Tournai, appealing to the new king of France, Louis VIII, for assistance. But the democratic revolt failed, and the countess clung to power.

Even though Philip Augustus had died in 1223, Ferdinand still languished in prison. The Duke of Brittany proposed that Johanna marry him if they could secure from the papacy an annulment of her marriage. This would have strengthened Brittany and Flanders. Consequently Louis VIII agreed to free Ferdinand, upon Johanna's payment of 50,000 livres in ransom. After 12 years, Johanna and Ferdinand were reunited in 1226. His ordeal left him submissive and broken. Before Ferdinand died in 1233, Johanna gave birth to a daughter Marie who was betrothed to Robert d'Artois, brother of Louis IX, but died in 1236. Countess Johanna took a second husband, Thomas, the son of Thomas I of Savoy. No children were born of the new union, and Johanna died on December 5, 1244. Her sister Margaret then became countess of Flanders.

SOURCES:

Pirenna, Henri. *Histoire de Belgique des origines à nos jours.* 4 vols. Brussels: La Renaissance du Livre, 1948.

Kendall W. Brown,
Professor of History,
Brigham Young University, Provo, Utah

Johanna of Pfirt (1300–1351)

Duchess of Austria. Name variations: Johanna von Pfirt; Jeannette de Ferette; Johanna of the Palatinate. Born in 1300 in Basel; died on November 15, 1351, in Vienna; married Albrecht also known as Albert II (1298–1358), duke of Austria (r. 1326–1358), duke of Carinthia (r. 1335); children: Rudolf IV (1339–1365); Albert III (d. 1395), duke of Austria; Catherine (1342–1387); Margaret (1346–1366, who married Meinhold of Tyrol); Frederick III (1347–1362), duke of Austria; Leopold III (1351–1386), duke of Austria.

Johanna of the Palatinate (1300–1351).

> *See Johanna of Pfirt.*

Johanne.

> *Variant of Joanna or Joanne.*

John, Eugenie (1825–1887).

> *See Marlitt, Eugenie.*

John, Gwen (1876–1939)

Welsh painter who lived in Paris for most of her working life and produced a small number of paintings and copious drawings and watercolors, utilizing a narrow range of subject matter, primarily that of her own passionate but somewhat solitary existence. Born Gwendoline Mary John on June 22, 1876, in Haverfordwest, Wales; died on September 18, 1939, in Dieppe, France; daughter of Edwin John (a solicitor) and Augusta (Smith) John; sister of Augustus John (1878–1961) and Winifred John; educated by governesses in Tenby until 1890; attended Miss Wilson's Academy, Tenby, 1890–93, Miss Philpott's Educational Establishment, London, 1893–94, Slade School of Fine Art, London, 1895–98, Académie Carmen, Paris, 1898; never married; no children.

Family moved to Tenby following mother's death when Gwen was eight years old (1884); awarded Melvill Nettleship Prize for figure composition at Slade (1898); lived in London (1899–1903); exhibited periodically at the New English Art Club (1900–11); held joint exhibition with her brother Augustus at the Carfax Gallery, London (1903); settled in France, renting a succession of rooms in Paris (1904–11), then moved to Paris suburb of Meudon, retaining city flat as studio (1911–18); patronized by John Quinn (1910–24); received into Catholic Church (1913); exhibited Girl Reading at a Window *in New York Armory show (1918); exhibited frequently at the Paris Salons (1919–25); had works included in New York exhibition,* Modern English Artists *(1922); had retrospective exhibition of her work held at the New Che-nil Galleries, London (1926); output and exhibition of paintings and drawings diminished (1930s); posthumous exhibitions, organized by Matthiesen Ltd, accelerated the growth of her reputation in England and America (1940, 1946).*

Paintings: The Artist's Sister Winifred *(private collection, c. 1899);* Mrs. Atkinson *(Metropolitan Museum of Art, New York, 1899–1900);* Self-portrait *(Tate Gallery, London, 1902);* The Student *(Manchester City Art Galleries, Manchester, 1903–04); A Corner of the Artist's Room in Paris (Sheffield City Art Galleries, 1907–09);* Nude Girl *(Tate Gallery, London, 1909–11);* Girl Reading at a Window *(Museum of Modern Art, New York, 1910–11);* Mère Poussepin *(versions in private collections, National Museum of Wales, Cardiff, Barber Institute of Fine Art, Birmingham, 1913–21);* Girl in Profile *(National Museum of Wales, Cardiff, c. 1918);* The Convalescent *(Fitzwilliam Museum, Cambridge, c. 1923);* Young Woman Holding a Black Cat *(Tate Gallery, London, c. 1923–28). The largest public collection of her drawings and watercolors, her studio contents, is held in the National Museum of Wales, Cardiff.*

> *A*s to whether I have anything worth expressing that is apart from the question. I may never have anything to express, except this desire for a more interior life.
>
> —Gwen John

By 1923, Gwen John knew Rodin and Rilke well, had met *Maude Gonne, Picasso, and Braque, and had dined with Brancusi and de Segonzac. Though aware of the diversity of artistic experiment in Paris and London, she never attached herself to a group or movement. She chose always to withdraw, preferring to focus her eye on a private world and an "interior life." John created images of extraordinary emotional intensity and formal integrity, drawing upon her own experience and the people and places she knew best. Her greatest paintings achieve a haunting sense of human presence and luminous serenity, in Michael Salaman's words, "so intensely modern in all but their peacefulness."

Little of Gwen John's juvenilia survives, but she painted and drew from early childhood. The Slade School was her first experience in formal art education and provided an escape from the narrowness of home life in Wales. Her younger brother, the flamboyant and prolific Augustus John, who had already attended a Tenby art school, had entered the Slade the previous year.

Gwen (and, in 1897, their sister **Winifred John,** who came to London to study music) joined him in a circle of fellow students which included William Orpen (1878–1931), Ambrose McEvoy (1878–1927), **Ida Nettleship** (1877–1907) who became Gwen's sister-in-law in 1901, **Edna Waugh** (1879–1979), **Ursula Tyrwhitt** (1878–1966) and **Gwen Salmond** (d. 1958), some of whom remained lifelong friends. Under Frederick Brown and Henry Tonks, the Slade's teaching was enlightened and liberal, combining traditional academic methods with a progressive emphasis on the development of individual style. Study in the Antique Room was followed by an early introduction to the life model. The copying of works by the old masters was encouraged. The Slade's celebrated drawing instruction demanded that the use of the line precede the creation of volume with shading. Gwen John's early tendency towards domestic interiors reveals an affinity with the tenor of much British art of the 1890s, such as the work of William Rothenstein, the French intimistes, and Dutch 17th-century genre painters. Her student copy of Metsu's *The Duet* is significant in this context. The self-contained serenity of the greatest of her later images of women recalls Vermeer, whose work she would first have seen in London. Portraits such as *Portrait of the Artist's Sister Winifred* (1899, private collection) reveal how deeply she absorbed the work of artists such as Titian and Rembrandt.

The draughtsmanship John learned at the Slade was complemented by a brief period in 1898 at the Académie Carmen, an art school in Paris founded with the help of Whistler who taught there regularly and insisted on the primacy of color and the "the scientific application of paint and brushes." The school's connection with Whistler and continental *fin de siècle* movements was a great lure for the students who flocked to it. John's rejection of narrative and anecdotal subjects and her interest in the creation of mood through color and formal arrangement owes much to the cult of *l'Art pour l'Art* which she would have found so prevalent on this first trip to Paris. The tonal refinement for which her later work is remarkable is anticipated in Whistler's famous retort to Augustus' praise of his sister's sense of "character": "Character? What's that? It's tone that matters. Your sister has a fine sense of tone."

Gwen John made her debut at the New English Art Club exhibition, London, in 1900 with a self-portrait (probably the painting now in the National Portrait Gallery, London). Like the *Self-Portrait in a Red Blouse* (1902, Tate Gallery, London), its bold color and composition intensi-fy its emotional directness. Frederick Brown owned the latter painting, and, in his own self-portrait (Ferens Art Gallery, Hull), Gwen John's picture is depicted on the wall behind him. The self-portrait was central to John's work.

In 1903, she set out to "walk to Rome" with **Dorelia McNeill**, a magnetically beautiful typist who was studying at the Westminster School of Art, whom Gwen had met in 1902 or 1903 and who subsequently became the second wife of Gwen's brother Augustus. The two women got no further than Toulouse, where Gwen painted a series of portraits of Dorelia which combine a serene monumentality with the warm intimacy of their domestic setting. Settling in Paris in 1904, John supported herself initially by modeling, mainly for women artists, but also for Auguste Rodin. She was the model for *Muse*, Rodin's monument to Whistler (c. 1904–1912, plaster, Musée d'Orsay, Paris) which was never completed. Drawings by Gwen John of classical sculptures in the Louvre (Cardiff, National Museum of Wales) suggest that modeling for Rodin stimulated her own interest in sculpture. She began a long and painful affair with Rodin, the course of which can be followed in surviving correspondence. In contrast with her sometimes ruthless desire for solitariness and independence, especially from Augustus' frequent attempts to organize her life, is a sequence of relationships with both men and women characterized by a desperate and alienating need for love. In the late 1920s, **Vera Oumancoff,** sister-in-law of the philosopher Jacques Maritain and friend of poet Rainer Marie Rilke, felt the need to ration Gwen John's visits to one a week, every Monday, accompanied by the gift of a drawing.

In Paris, Gwen John continued to explore the possibilities of the self-portrait in different media. In 1909, she wrote of one of her early experiments with gouache, "I am doing some drawings in my glass, myself & the room, & I put white in the colour so it is like painting in oil & quicker. I first draw in the thing then trace it on to a clean piece of paper by holding it against the window." Her succession of Paris rooms became increasingly important to her work and emotional equilibrium. She wrote to Rodin: "My room is so delicious after a whole day outside, it seems to me that I am not myself except in my room." She began to paint the room empty. In *A Corner of the Artist's Room, with Open Window* (National Museum of Wales, Cardiff, 1907–09) and *A Corner of the Artist's Room, with Closed Window* (Sheffield City Art Galleries, 1907–09), her possessions and discarded clothes suggest her invisible presence.

*Gwen John
(fragment of her
self-portrait).*

John also painted portraits of friends and fellow artists—particularly women painters, who, like herself, were drawn to the freedom Paris offered. Two paintings of **Chloe Boughton-Leigh** (Tate Gallery, London, 1905–08, and Leeds City Art Gallery, 1910–14) are remark-able for the starkness of their composition and air of intense melancholy. Comparison of the two illustrates the gradual shift in John's style towards a broader handling of paint, monumentality, and an increasing sense of detachment from the individual model. More than ten years later, one sitter recalled, "She takes down my hair and does it like her own. . . . She has me sit as she does and I feel the absorption of her personality as I sit."

Between 1910 and 1924, the patronage of John Quinn (1870–1924), a New York corporate lawyer, helped to sustain Gwen John's artistic independence, and their long epistolary friendship encouraged her. He sought her judgment on other artists' work and passed on to her the praise of the many artists and critics whom he knew. Quinn had collected manuscripts by Joyce, Eliot, Pound, and Conrad before forming one of the earliest collections of modern art in America. In this collection, Gwen John's works were displayed beside those of Brancusi, Epstein, Gaudier-Brzeska, Picasso, Cézanne, Seurat, and Henri Rousseau. Quinn perceived the relationship between John's work and that of her European contemporaries as well as appreciating its deeply personal nature and her aloofness from artistic fashions. He proposed a joint New York exhibition for her and *Marie Laurencin, and, in 1922, having lent his works by Gwen John to an exhibition of British art at the Sculptor's Gallery in New York, he told her that "By right, your work should have belonged with the French paintings . . . the following month, but your things would have been too crowded." Quinn bought everything that he could persuade her to sell and eventually provided her with an annual allowance. Of one of his purchases (*Mère Poussepin*, private collection, c. 1913–20), he wrote: "If I had to make a choice between the painting by you . . . and the Picasso, I should cheerfully sacrifice the Picasso."

In 1911, John wrote Quinn: "I paint a good deal, but don't often get a picture done—that requires, for me, a very long time of a quiet mind, and never to think of exhibition." Despite this, she did think of her work in terms of display, writing in 1918, "I should like to exhibit a lot together. My last drawings look much better if they are seen a lot together." In 1924, she wrote that "it is amusing to have things in [the salons] and to go and see them at the vernissage and to give vernissage cards to friends and make rendez-vous!" Her work was exhibited in London, at the Paris salons, and the New York Armory show alongside some of the most progressive and experimental of her contemporaries and was frequently singled out by critics. In 1909, Laurence Binyon had praised Gwen John for "that intensity . . . which counts for so much more than brilliancy . . . so rare in contemporary art." In 1924, Walter Pach wrote in *Charm* of her "exacting talent . . . as strong as it is delicate" and *Country Life* felt that "Gwen John cannot be called an Impressionist: there is far too much deliberation about her work, far too much monumental design. The last paintings [are] just radiant with a quiet luminosity." In 1928, Alfred Barr, Jr., described three "little pictures" at the Tate for The Arts, "which by their subtlety and colour, make the work of her flashy brother seem awkward and uncertain." However, she became increasingly reluctant to finish and send pictures away, although frequently urged to do so.

New subjects entered Gwen John's work following her conversion to Catholicism in 1913. In the same year, she was asked by the Meudon Chapter of the Order of the Sisters of Charity of the Holy Virgin of Tours to paint a portrait of their founder, *Mére Poussepin* (1653–1744). Between 1913 and 1920, she completed at least six versions of the portrait, derived from a printed prayer card, itself based on an 18th-century oil painting. It appears that the nuns required multiple versions of the image for the convent. This partly reproductive, partly devotional, commission was the starting point for what became her first important series in oil. A tendency to make a series of images had already emerged in her drawing, and her early interest in paired paintings, such as the Chloe Boughton-Leigh portraits and *A Corner of the Artist's Room in Paris* is significant in this context. From the time of the Mére Poussepin commission, the exploration of an image through repetition became the keynote of almost all her work. Although this attraction to repetition recalls Monet's series paintings, particularly when combined with John's quest for luminosity, comparison of the still monumentality of her later work with Cézanne's repeated views of Mont St. Victoire is more telling.

She went on to paint portraits of the nuns living in the convent at Meudon and sometimes posed them like their founder (e.g. *A Young Nun*, Edinburgh, National Galleries of Scotland). John appropriated the features of the individual nuns for the creation of an increasingly archetypal image. The individual ¾-length female figure, seen from the front or turned slightly to one side, hands in lap, dominated her work of the late 1910s and 1920s. She employed local, non-professional models. The sitters are anonymous, the same few faces recurring in paintings throughout the decade. Their settings are increasingly bare and nonspecific; sometimes the woman holds a cat (*Young Woman Holding a Black Cat*, London, Tate Gallery, 1923–28); sometimes a book (*The Convalescent*, Cambridge, Fitzwilliam Museum, c. 1923); some-times she just sits (*The Pilgrim*, Paul Mellon Collection, 1922–25). They share an extraordinary stillness and grandeur of design. Unlike the transparent glazes of her earlier work, the pigment is now thick and opaque, painted directly onto a thinly primed or sometimes chalky canvas, rendering the surface matte and dry. The tonal range is so tight and the surface texture so uniform that in some paintings, such as *Woman with a Coral Necklace* (Cardiff, Welsh Arts Council), the figure appears to merge with the background.

In contrast with the rarity of her finished oils of the period is Gwen John's copious production of watercolor drawings. From 1913, she made hundreds of studies of worshippers in her church at Meudon, usually seen from behind (e.g. versions of *Nuns and Schoolgirls in Church*, National Museum of Wales, Cardiff). She felt unable to pray for long periods, but the drawings themselves have the air of an act of devotion. Sketches in church formed the starting point for sustained experiments with color balance, and the patterns made on the page demonstrate a fascination with the abstract qualities of

A Corner of the Artist's Room in Paris, *c. 1907, painting by Gwen John.*

a motif increasingly detached from the subject itself. She wrote to Ursula Tyrwhitt, "A cat and a man its the same thing—it's an affair of volumes." Both the comic charm and elegant simplicity of many of these Meudon studies are found too in the drawings of children made in Brittany in 1918–19. Many are drawn outside and celebrate a bright seaside spaciousness. Such settings anticipate the tiny landscape drawings upon which John concentrated near the end of her life. The restrained clarity of the lines recalls the artist's comment, "I want my drawings . . . to be definite and clean like Japanese drawings."

After the 1926 London exhibition, the only show devoted entirely to her work held during her lifetime, Gwen John's production of paintings and drawings diminished. During the 1930s, she appears to have painted almost nothing at all. In her last works, she comes nearest to abstraction, particularly in her images of flowers and a favorite view from her window whose landscape was about to disappear under a building. She also produced a seemingly compulsive sequence of drawings based on an old photograph of St. *Thérèse of Lisieux. Most of her last sketches are tiny, sometimes only a few centimeters square. Her health and eyesight were failing.

By 1935, Gwen John's pictures had entered museum collections in Cardiff, London, Manchester, Dublin, Buffalo, and Chicago and were thus becoming more widely known. Her work had been included in an exhibition of modern British painting in Brussels in 1929, and she sent nine paintings to Contemporary Welsh Art at the National Museum of Wales, Cardiff, in 1935. She was increasingly reluctant to sell or exhibit pictures, however, though further exhibitions were planned in New York and gallery representatives sought her out in the chalet-studio which she had had built on land at 8 rue Babie, Meudon. Most of her work remained in her studio at her death.

In these last years of her life, her letters and notebooks reveal an energetic engagement with contemporary art theory and exhaustive analysis of her own method and the "rules and problems of painting." Increasingly interested in Cubism, she attended André Lhote's classes in 1936. She writes of her admiration for the work of artists as diverse as Hogarth, Filippo Lippi, and Chagall, as well as Piero di Cosimo and Ensor. Her writings reveal a preoccupation with methodical preparation and the ordering of visual sensation, most notably in her creation of an elusive system of expressing tonal relationships in terms of numbers. In the preface to the catalogue of her 1926 exhibition she had quoted Maurice Denis: "I have always had the wish to organize my work, my thought, my life and, as Cézanne said, my sensation. The power to suggest connections between ideas and objects has always been the point of art."

SOURCES:

Langdale, Cecily. *Gwen John with a Catalogue Raisonné of the Paintings and a Selection of the Drawings.* New Haven, CT: Yale University Press, 1987.

———, and David Fraser-Jenkins. *Gwen John: An Interior Life.* London: Phaidon Press, 1985.

Taubman, Mary. *Gwen John.* London: Scolar Press, 1985.

SUGGESTED READING:

Fraser-Jenkins, David. *Gwen John at the National Museum of Wales.* Cardiff, 1976.

Holroyd, Michael. *Augustus John: The New Biography.* London: Chatto and Windus, 1996.

Le Normand-Romain, Antoinette and Claudie Judrin. *Exhibition catalogue, Rodin, Whistler et la Muse.* Paris: Musée Rodin, 1995.

Thomas, Alison. *Portraits of Women: Gwen John and Her Forgotten Contemporaries.* Cambridge, England: Polity Press, 1994.

RELATED MEDIA:

Self Portrait, a play by **Sheila Yeger**, directed by **Annie Castledine**, starring **Lucinda Curtis**, first opened at the Derby Playhouse, Derby, England, in September 1990.

COLLECTIONS:

Collections of Gwen John's letters are in the New York Public Library, Musée Rodin, Paris, and the National Library of Wales, Aberystwyth.

Juliet Carey,
Curatorial Assistant, National Museums and
Galleries of Wales, Cardiff, Wales

Johns, Glynis (b. 1923).

See Bergner, Elisabeth for sidebar.

Johnson, Adelaide (1859–1955)

American sculptor and feminist. Born Sarah Adeline Johnson on September 26, 1859, in Plymouth, Illinois; died on November 10, 1955, in Washington, D.C., age 96, of a stroke; daughter of Christopher William Johnson (a farmer) and Margaret Huff (Hendrickson) Johnson; educated in country schools and studied art at St. Louis School of Design; also studied painting in Dresden (1883) and sculpting in the workshop of Giulio Monteverde in Rome (1884); married Alexander Frederick Jenkins (an English businessman) on January 29, 1896 (divorced 1908).

Awarded first and second prizes for her woodcarvings at state exposition (1877); traveled to Europe to study art, first in Dresden, then with Giulio Monteverde in Rome (1883–84); as part of her feminist perspective, exhibited busts of suffragists and a pioneer woman physician at the Woman's Pavilion of the World's Columbian Exposition in Chicago (1893);

differences with Susan B. Anthony prompted her to turn to Alva Belmont, New York suffragist; secured commission for a national monument honoring the women's movement (1904); The Woman Movement, also known as The Portrait Monument (her sculpture containing portrait busts of Susan B. Anthony, Lucretia Mott, and Elizabeth Cady Stanton), was presented to the public at the Capitol building (February 15, 1921); with career in decline and frustrated over her dream of a studio-museum showcasing the women's movement, mutilated many of her works (1939); moved in with friends in Washington, D.C., because of money woes and frail health (1947).

Adelaide Johnson, who is considered the major sculptor of the women's suffrage movement, was born Sarah Adeline Johnson in Plymouth, Illinois, on September 26, 1859, one of three children of Christopher W. Johnson and **Margaret Hendrickson Johnson**. Adelaide's parents also had several children from previous marriages. Educated in country schools, as a teen she studied art at the St. Louis School of Design. In 1877, her artistic skills were recognized when she won both a first and second prize for woodcarving at a state exposition. The following year, she changed her name to Adelaide. Johnson fell down an elevator shaft while studying art in Chicago and injured her hip. With the $15,000 she collected as a result of that injury, she financed her artistic studies in Europe. In 1883, Johnson studied painting in Germany, and the next year moved to Rome to study sculpture with Giulio Monteverde. There she maintained a studio for the next 25 years, as well as at various times studios in Carrara, Italy, London, New York, Chicago and Washington, D.C.

Johnson became a stalwart supporter of the women's movement, perceiving it to be "the mightiest thing in the evolution of humanity," and it became her mission to immortalize its history. She began by exhibiting busts of suffragists *Lucretia Mott, *Elizabeth Cady Stanton and *Susan B. Anthony, as well as pioneer physician Caroline B. Winslow, at the World's Columbian Exposition in Chicago in 1893.

In January 1896, Johnson married English businessman Alexander F. Jenkins, falsifying her age on the marriage certificate so that it appeared she was 24, one year younger than her husband, when she was in reality 36. Both the bride and the groom were vegetarians and embraced spiritualism, which was popular at that time. As a tribute to his wife's genius, Jenkins even adopted her name after their marriage by a

woman minister. In 1908, after many long separations, the couple divorced, with Johnson remaining quite bitter.

Out of Johnson's passionate support for the women's movement was born a dream of creating a gallery and museum to house the movement's history. Lacking funding, she came to think of her own home-studio in Washington, D.C., as this facility. She also wanted the National American Woman Suffrage Association (NAWSA) to fund a woman's monument for the Capitol building, but in 1904, Susan B. Anthony differed with her over the placement of this monument (Anthony preferred the Library of Congress). This caused a split in their friendship as well as in Johnson's relationship with the NAWSA. Johnson then turned to the National Woman's Party and New York suffragist *Alva Belmont, and she eventually was successful in securing a commission for a national monument from *Alice Paul, the militant women's rights activist.

The large sculpture of white Carrara marble, *The Woman Movement,* now referred to as the *Portrait Monument,* was presented to Congress in the rotunda of the Capitol on the anniversary of Anthony's birth, February 15, 1921. Almost immediately the monument—which depicts 19th-century feminist leaders Stanton, Mott, and Anthony—was removed to the basement of the building, called the Crypt. For 75 years, it languished there in obscurity, relegated to a room reserved for storage of broken furniture, despite five attempts since the 1930s to have it brought back to stand in the rotunda among the statues of males.

Finally, in 1995, it looked like the monument would be moved back to a place of honor when a bill designed to do so sailed through the Senate, 100–0. But the bill also required the consent of the House, and a move to thwart the project by five female Republican representatives was successful. First, they said it was too heavy. Then, **Susan Myrick** (North Carolina), **Barbara Vucanovich** (Nevada), **Linda Smith** (Washington), and **Helen Chenowith** (Idaho) denounced the spending of public monies for such a project. **Karen Staser**, a private citizen living in Alexandria, Virginia, countered that she would raise the $75,000 needed to cut the base of the statue and move it upstairs. Then, Republican **Nancy Johnson** (Connecticut) and Myrick suggested the statue of another woman, *Esther Hobart Morris, the first female judge in Wyoming, which was already residing in Statuary Hall, be placed in the rotunda instead. Myrick felt that Morris showed a more "modern" image of women. (The statue of Morris has her standing on a rugged base, holding flowers.) "She gives the appearance of being very strong," said Myrick. "She's doing something, but is feminine at the same time."

It was not until June 1997 that the monument was rededicated in the rotunda, the only sculpture that is a national monument to the women's movement. At the ceremony, Republican senator **Olympia Snowe** (Maine) spoke:

> The bottom line is, the debate should not have been about the weight of the statue, but the weight of an argument, and the worth of a just cause. When Susan B. Anthony said, "What is this little thing we are asking for? It seems so little, yet it is everything," she was talking about a woman's right to vote—but she could have been speaking about the moving of her own statue.
>
> For too long, women in this country had to endure the myth of what—or where—a "woman's place" should be. A woman's place used to be only in the parlor, the kitchen and, I suppose, the crypt. Since then, a lot has changed. Today, a woman's place is in the House, the Senate and, yes, the Rotunda.

Adelaide Johnson supported other women's organizations. She was the founder and a lifelong member of the National and International Councils of Women, and a charter member of the Lyceum Club as well as NAWSA. She also wrote and gave speeches on women's issues.

Johnson's artistic career declined after the 1930s, and she suffered financial problems, relying on support from family and friends. In 1939, frustrated over her plight and failure to realize her dream of a studio-museum, she mutilated many of her sculptures and called the media in to witness the destruction. Efforts to pass a congressional bill granting her $25,000 proved unsuccessful, and finally, in failing health and with little money, Johnson moved in with friends around 1947 in Washington, D.C. She made several attempts to raise money to repurchase her home, even appearing on quiz shows, but to no avail. Realizing that age could also convey special privileges, Johnson reversed her earlier falsification and made herself 12 years older than she really was. She died in Washington in 1955 of a stroke.

SOURCES:

Casey, Maura. Editorials in *The Day* [New London, CT]. August 9, 1995, August 16, 1995, March 24, 1996, June 30, 1997.

James, Edward T., ed. *Notable American Women, 1607–1950*. Cambridge, MA: The Belknap Press of Harvard University Press, 1971.

Newsweek. August 28, 1995.

Jo Anne Meginnes,
freelance writer, Brookfield, Vermont

Johnson, Amy (1903–1941)

British aviator who was the first woman to fly solo to Australia in 1930 and who subsequently broke many records in pioneering flights around the world. Name variations: Amy Mollison. Born Amy Johnson on July 1, 1903, at no. 154, St. George's Road, Hull, England; died on January 5, 1941, after parachuting from a plane she was ferrying for the Air Ministry over the Thames Estuary; eldest daughter of John William Johnson (a herring importer) and Amy (Hodge) Johnson (granddaughter of William Hodge, sometime mayor of Hull); educated at the Boulevard Secondary School, Hull, and at Sheffield University where she graduated in 1925; married Jim Mollison (a fellow pioneer pilot), in July 1932 (divorced 1938); no children.

Intended to become a teacher, instead took a secretarial post in a firm of London solicitors; interest in flying kindled, joined the London Aeroplane Club based at Stag Lane airport (1928); was first woman in Britain to qualify as ground engineer as well as pilot; shot to fame after solo flight to Australia (1930); continued to engage in record-breaking flights until the outbreak of war (1939); joined the Air Transport Auxiliary (1939); killed while on active service with this unit (1941).

Pioneering and record flights: soloed to Australia (May 5–24, 1930); co-piloted, with her engineer and mentor Jack Humphreys, record-breaking flight from England to Tokyo (July 1931); made record-breaking solo flight to Cape Town and back (November 1932); made non-stop flight from London to New York with her husband which narrowly failed (July 1933); made record-breaking flight with her husband from London to Karachi (October 1934); soloed to the Cape and back, beating both records (May 1936).

For the first three days of a solo flight to Australia in her airplane *Jason*, Amy Johnson had encountered minor problems and one bad fright. When dropping through clouds over the Taurus mountains in Eastern Turkey, she found herself heading straight for a mass of rocks; only quick maneuvering saved her from a crash. After spending the night at Aleppo in Syria, Johnson set off to cross 500 miles of featureless desert on May 8, 1930, despite the fact that it was stiflingly hot and visibility was poor. Her destination was Baghdad. Suddenly, she hit a patch of haze much thicker than she had previously encountered—a dust storm. "My machine gave a terrific lurch," she wrote later. "The nose dipped and *Jason* and I dropped a couple of thousand feet. . . . Sand and dust covered my goggles, my eyes smarted, and I couldn't control the machine sufficiently to keep it straight. . . . I have never been so frightened in my life. . . . All at once I felt my wheels touch ground although I could see nothing."

Johnson had no idea where she was, but her first concern was to protect her plane from the swirling dust. Hastily covering the engine as best she could, she was then forced to seat herself on *Jason*'s tail to stop the machine from blowing away altogether. "Once, I heard dogs barking," she wrote, "and my terror broke out afresh as I had heard that these desert dogs wouldn't hesitate to attack and tear their victims to pieces. I therefore pulled out my small revolver and waited." Fortunately, the storm abated, her engine started on first try, and Johnson was able to continue on to Baghdad. Later, however, she remarked casually, "If I had gone in the wrong direction I should have headed into hundreds of miles of trackless desert." Such were the hazards that confronted the pioneer pilot between the World Wars—and Johnson was to encounter many more before she touched down in Australia in just over two weeks' time.

Amy Johnson claimed a happy childhood. She had an affectionate and supportive family and got on well with her three younger sisters, particularly her more outward going sister **Irene Johnson**. Her father was to become her lifelong confidante and adviser; without his unflagging support, none of her later adventures would have materialized. Though rather shy and often put into the shade by Irene, Amy was something of a roughneck in her teens. She revelled in outdoor sports such as swimming and bicycling. Indeed, she would compete with the more daring boys at school, riding her bike full tilt at a brick wall and at the last moment skidding violently sideways, like a speedway rider skids round a cinder track. It was around this time that she was hit full in the face by a cricket ball which smashed her front teeth—a disfigurement she was acutely self-conscious of for the rest of her life, though nobody else seemed to notice.

In 1922, just before enrolling at Sheffield University, 19-year-old Amy fell in love. The young man, a Swiss called Franz, was eight years her senior and accustomed to success with women. For the next six years, the affair would continue on and off, and there is no doubt that Johnson hoped they would eventually marry. It was not to be. When the couple broke up in 1928, Johnson was devastated. Said her closest friend, **Winnie Irving**, Amy "threw herself onto her bed and sobbed as though the storm of tears would never end."

By this time, Johnson, who had graduated from Sheffield, was in London, working as a secretary in a firm of solicitors under Vernon Wood (later to become one of her staunchest supporters in her flying career). The job, however, was humdrum, and not at all suited to someone of Johnson's adventurous temperament. Her unsatisfactory employment situation, combined with her disappointment in love, was one reason why Johnson became smitten with flying. By the late 1920s, flying as a sport, with races and "pageants" and aerobatic contests, was in the news. It appealed to the poetically minded, with its sense of exhilaration and freedom. Flying also seemed to be the transport of the future, and to the early pioneers it became almost a duty to pit their wits, skills, and endurance in opening up routes across the continents and the oceans. On a more mundane level, joining a flying club guaranteed an instant social life—and this is what Johnson felt she desperately needed in 1928.

I admit that I am a woman, and the first one to [fly solo to Australia] . . . but in the future I do not want it to be unusual that women should do things; I want it to be recognized that women can do them.

—Amy Johnson

Amy Johnson's first flying lesson was not a success, and her brusque young instructor did not hesitate to tell her so. Even so, she persevered, and, once she was deemed capable enough to go solo, she flew whenever she could. As the more perceptive of her instructors admitted, however, Johnson was never a natural-born pilot: her landings were often akin to dropping a ton of bricks on the runway. It was her determination and courage that led to her achievements.

Johnson also became fascinated with the mechanics of flying. What keeps an airplane in the air? Why does the engine sometimes falter? How do the compass and instruments work? She was determined to find out. By constantly pestering her club authorities, she managed to get herself apprenticed to the ground engineers. This was not easy, for theirs was very much a masculine world. Arriving on her first morning at the aero workshop, Amy found herself ignored. "At last I asked outright for a job of work," she later recalled. The reply: "You can sweep out the hangar." Within a fortnight, Johnson was "one of the boys" and given the nickname "Johnnie"—a name soon to be famous throughout the world. Her mentor was Jack Humphreys, the kindly chief engineer, who was to give her enormous encouragement and support throughout her flying career. By the end of 1929, she had qualified both as pilot and ground engineer.

Johnson was determined to make aviation her full-time career. She was, however, fully aware of the obstacles that would be set in the way of a woman becoming a professional flyer. As she lamented this fact to an instructor, he cautioned that to be accepted a woman would have to "win her spurs." "How?" asked Johnson. With a laugh, he cracked, "Oh, by flying to Australia for instance." The seed was sown.

By the beginning of 1930, Johnson's plans were beginning to take shape. She had gained the support of Lord Wakefield, an aviation enthusiast; he and her father put up the money for her to buy a second-hand Gypsy Moth airplane. Johnson's aim was to try to beat Australian test pilot Bert Hinkler's record of 15½ days for the flight from London, England, to Darwin, Australia. Meticulous planning was needed to cut through red tape and work out suitable airfields where Amy could refuel. As far as India, this was not too great a problem, but beyond the subcontinent she would be flying over vast stretches of ocean and jungle that had barely been mapped, at a season when the monsoon might well be beginning, and where there was little hope of rescue if things went wrong. Undeterred, Johnson completed her preparations by her deadline of May 5. Witnessed by a small group of friends on a chill, spring morning, the 26-year-old ex-typist, who had never flown farther than from London to Hull, took off for a flight of 11,000 miles to the other side of the world.

Despite a spluttering engine and a gas leak that allowed nauseating fumes to escape into the cockpit, and her hair-raising adventure in the Iraqi desert, Johnson's flight went relatively smoothly as far as British India. She reached Karachi safely and landed in triumph. She had improved on Hinkler's 1928 record for the same distance by two days. The world's press was suddenly interested. THE LONE GIRL FLYER, proclaimed the headlines. THE BRITISH GIRL LINDBERGH. It was only after a cheerful send-off from the Karachi airport that Johnson's troubles began to start "in earnest." Failing to reach her next stop at Allahabad because of a lack of gas, she was forced to set down on the barrack square in Jhansi. An officer who witnessed her landing described it:

> The plane was down. Down on the regimental parade ground, and charging at high speed towards the barracks. It twisted its way round trees, barely missed an iron telegraph pole, scattered a group of men waiting to mount guard, smashed into the name board outside the regimental offices, and then came to rest wedged between two of the barrack buildings. There was a race to reach it. From the cockpit climbed a figure—it was a girl—young, almost a child, fair, wearing only a shirt, an ill-fitting pair of khaki shorts, socks and shoes, and a flying helmet. The skin on her face, arms and legs was burnt and blistered by the sun, and tears were not far from her tired eyes. "I am two days ahead of Bert Hinkler's time so far," she said "and now I'm afraid everything is ruined."

Her pronouncement was premature. As was to happen again and again on this extraordinary journey, Johnson received help from the most unexpected quarters. Skilled workers from among the soldiers soon straightened her bent wing, and, after acceding to the request of a group of Indian women, delighted by her adventure, that "Miss Sahib would just touch them with her hand," Johnson was on her way again.

Flying on over the dense jungle of Burma (now Myanmar), Johnson was due to land at the racecourse at Rangoon but came down with a bang on the playing fields of the Government Technical College instead. "*Jason* ran smoothly past the goal-posts head on for a ditch, into which he buried his head and came to a standstill with a loud noise and a great shudder," wrote Johnson. "This was too much for me. . . . I cried like a baby." The damage proved to be a broken propeller, a ripped tire, a broken undercarriage strut, and a much-damaged wing. Again help was at hand. A local forestry officer was able to make a new strut overnight, and the boys at the college surrendered their shirts with much glee to improvise a covering for the torn wing.

There were several other such incidents. While flying over Thailand on her way to Singapore, Johnson had to make an unscheduled landing at Singora on the coast. Again, her machine needed attention. By this time, exhausted and feeling very weak, she turned to a strong-looking man in the crowd to help her undo the nuts and bolts. "But," as she later wrote, "so soon as he had undone one plug, or nut, or bolt, he ran away as though extremely shy, so that when I wanted something else undone, I had to look round for him and ask for the 'Strong man.' This happened so often that the crowd learned these two words, and so soon as I looked around there was a general outcry for 'Strong man, Strong man,' to everyone's intense amusement. . . . Though I was hot and tired I found myself laughing with them." A new hazard occurred when it was time for Amy to take

Amy
Johnson

off again. The crowd of had become so dense that she only just avoided piling up into them.

Landing in untracked country in Java, *Jason*'s wings were again torn. This time Johnson had to resort to sticking plaster to repair them. On the island of Timor, she landed in a field of ant-heaps miles from anywhere, miraculously hitting none of them. A few minutes later, she wrote, "I was surrounded by a horde of yelling natives, with hair flying in the wind, and knives in their hands or between their red-stained teeth. I pulled out my revolver, but I had no need at all to worry. With a deep salute, the leader came forward and gingerly touched first the machine, then me." It was during these few days that Johnson lost touch with the outside world, and the London placards were shouting, FLYING GIRL MISSING.

Johnson was now on the last lap. Only the Timor strait—500 miles of shark-infested sea—lay between her and her goal. The Shell Company had thoughtfully stationed an oil-tanker halfway across, and it was with great relief that Amy swooped low over its decks. The last few hours seemed interminable. "At last," wrote Johnson, "I saw a dark cloud on the horizon. . . . The cloud slowly assumed shape and after half an hour's flying I made out an island, which I knew to be Melville Island and I was sure of my exact whereabouts. In another half an hour my wheels were touching Australian soil."

Because of bad weather and her various mishaps, Johnson did not beat Hinkler's record, but the world did not seem to care. Despite the fact that there had been no public relations build-up before the flight, the public went wild with spontaneous enthusiasm. The newspapers were ecstatic; the public succumbed to hero-worship: "Amy, wonderful Amy/ How can you blame me for loving you?" went a popular English song. The Australians loved her for her modest gaiety, and she was feted across the continent in verse and song:

> "Johnnie!" There's a shouting goes up and down the land
> "Johnnie's over Darwin!" And millions breathe anew
> There's a plane in the offing and a little waving hand
> Johnnie's making Darwin! Johnnie from the blue!

Johnson was appointed Commander of the British Empire (CBE), the *Daily Mail* newspaper made her a gift of £10,000, the children of Sidney raised a sum of money with which she bought a gold cup, still offered annually at Hull for the most courageous juvenile deed of the year, and when she returned to England she was met on arrival by the secretary of state for air, Lord Thomson. News of her exploit even reached the remote corners of Tibet. On being told of the flight, the Dalai Lama considered the news gravely and then with a puzzled frown asked, "Why was the Honorable Lady in such a hurry?"

After the amazing success of her Australian flight, Johnson's subsequent career may seem something of an anti-climax. However, during the 1930s, she was never far from the news and went on to make some astonishing record-breaking flights. Although at first amazed and thrilled by her fame, Johnson was not always comfortable with it. At times, she came close to having a nervous breakdown. She particularly resented being exploited by the press and publicity firms. In an outburst to her father, she fumed, "I strongly resent interference and efforts to rule my life or control my actions. . . . I've lived my own life for the last seven years and I intend to continue doing so."

But fame brought her financial independence. She could now choose from the best planes available to make her flights, and sponsorship was no longer a problem. After an abortive attempt to fly solo across Siberia in the depths of winter (1930–31), Johnson successfully broke the London to Tokyo record in the summer of 1931, accompanied by her loyal engineering mentor, Jack Humphreys. (He had taught her engineering; she taught him to fly.) Flying across the vast Russian steppes, they found airport facilities primitive, but the Russians in charge—often women—were very friendly. Arriving in Tokyo, she danced with General Nagaoka, the distinguished president of the Imperial Aviation Society, whose whiskers were claimed to be the longest and whitest in the world.

It was at this point that a new love entered Johnson's life. Like Amy, Jim Mollison was a pioneer long-distance pilot. Their paths had crossed briefly when Mollison, as a humble airline pilot, had flown Johnson on one leg of her Australian tour in 1930. They met again in Cape Town in March 1932. Mollison, by now famous, landed at the Cape on March 28, incoherent with exhaustion after making the first lightplane flight across the Sahara to the tip of the African continent. Johnson, in Cape Town to recover from a stomach operation, was at the airport to meet him. Four months later, during which they had only been in each other's company for about 24 hours, they were married.

Jim Mollison had a charming manner and was a brilliant pilot. He was also an inveterate womanizer and a hard drinker. (Indeed, as his flying career progressed, his brandy-influenced performances evoked incredulous surprise at his survival.) These latter two traits were to ruin the marriage in the end, but in the beginning these two "Lovers of the Air," as the press gleefully christened them, were just that—very much in love.

The married couple were soon planning flights they would do together. First, however, Johnson set out on a long-planned solo flight to

South Africa in a new Puss Moth, *Desert Cloud*, to return by the West coast route. "I'm going to try and beat Jim's Cape record—just as a sporting effort," she wrote to her parents. And she did, though she frightened herself badly on the way. "My worst stretch was Douala-Benguela, all by night," she wrote to Mollison. "I must admit it's frightened me of that coastline by night. It took me thirteen hours to fly 800 miles, following the ins and outs of the coast with no forward visibility at all."

After one abortive start when they crashed on take-off, Johnson and Mollison set off on their first attempted record-breaking flight on July 3, 1933. They were determined to fly their black twin-engined de Havilland Dragon, *Seafarer*, around the world. The "Flying Sweethearts" would head first for New York, then on to Baghdad (the record-breaking attempt), and then, with hardly a pause, straight back to London. It was an ambitious, some would say foolhardy, venture.

Taking off from Pendine Sands in South Wales, the couple took 24 hours to reach the coast of Newfoundland. Fuel was now running low and gave out completely over Connecticut. Jim, almost blind with exhaustion, attempted to land at the Bridgeport airport, 50 miles from New York. Unfortunately, he overshot the runway, and *Seafarer* crashed. Rescuers found Johnson moaning over the unconscious body of her husband. By the time the two arrived at a hospital, souvenir hunters had stripped *Seafarer* of every movable part and left it an empty shell.

Neither was seriously hurt, however. Johnson enjoyed recuperating in New York, where she and Mollison were given a ticker-tape welcome, and she soon fell in love with America. As long as "the blonde adventuress of the skylanes" remained in the news, this love affair was reciprocated by the American public. But husband and wife were now moving apart. When they returned to England after seven months, Johnson retreated to the country, leaving Mollison to indulge himself in the bars and nightclubs of London. They were to have one more adventure together: the England to Australia air race in October 1934, for which they acquired a Comet racer—a fast twin-engined monoplane, much likened to a streamlined gas tank and christened *Black Magic*. Jeffrey Quill, an RAF flying officer, recalled seeing the couple take off: "I saw Jim and Amy climb into their Comet. He looked as white as a sheet and as if he had been sloshed for forty-eight hours—which I suspect he was. She looked very nervous and apprehensive and I felt desperately sorry for her having to climb in behind that rather raffish character for such a venture as this."

Nevertheless, the first half of the race was a success. Theirs was the only Comet to reach Baghdad non-stop and on schedule, and their time to Karachi was just 22 hours, halving the existing record. Then things went wrong. Through their own fault in using the wrong kind of fuel, one engine seized up at Allahabad, and the couple were stuck there for three weeks waiting for it to be repaired, while another British twosome, Charles Scott and Tom Campbell, went on to win the race. After this failure, Jim drifted off around the world, leaving Amy very much on her own. Despite a brief reconciliation in 1936, the marriage was now clearly doomed. They were finally divorced in 1938, and Johnson reverted to using her maiden name.

These were difficult times for Johnson, but she was still determined to continue her flying career. After purchasing a Percival Gull machine, she decided to attempt to beat the round-trip London-Cape Town-London records once again—this time by flying over the Sahara. Her first effort in April 1936 failed when the Gull hit a boulder on take-off on the edge of the desert, and the plane collapsed. Undeterred, Amy set off once again a month later. This time her venture was a resounding success, and she beat the records for both flights and the double journey. The *London Times* commented: "Her last flight is no mere flash in the pan but an achievement in keeping with a distinguished aeronautical career."

This was the last of Johnson's long-distance flights. She spent the years up until 1939 alternating between Paris and country cottages in England, taking up gliding, riding, and writing. At one time or other, she was a contributing aviation correspondent to the *Daily Mail*, *Cosmopolitan*, the *Sunday Graphic*, and *Lady Driver*. She also wrote several books—*Myself When Young* and *Sky Roads of the World* being the most widely read.

June 1939 saw her working as a professional pilot for the first time, ferrying passengers to the Isle of Wight. "Folks, you've got the chance of being flown by a world famous pilot for five bob a time!" proclaimed the *Daily Mirror*. With the outbreak of World War II, Johnson and her fellow pilots came under orders of the military, and she was eventually enrolled into the Air Transport Auxiliary (ATA). This meant ferrying military aircraft to different airfields when they were required. Although initially frustrated by the restrictions of military life and the prejudice against women pilots (even famous ones), Johnson was soon enjoying her new role. Indeed, her sister **Molly Jones**, with whom she spent her last evening, recalled that she had never seen her looking so happy and well.

Amy Johnson died in the Thames Estuary on January 5, 1941, after parachuting from a plane she was ferrying for the Air Ministry. The crew on the trawler H.M.S. *Haslemere* desperately tried to rescue her. As they approached the figure in the water, a seaman on board heard a voice shouting, "Hurry, please hurry." "It sounded like a boy's voice at first," he said, "then I realized it was a woman." Life lines were thrown to her, but it appears that Johnson was too numbed by cold to reach them. "The ship was heaving in the swell," said the seaman, "and then the stern came up and dropped on top of the woman. She did not come up again." "Her death was in character with the Amy Johnson legend," wrote her biographer, **Constance Babington-Smith**, "the legend of a woman who, despite every obstacle, not only earned a permanent place in the history of aviation, but also became a world-famous symbol of adventure, tenacity, and courage."

SOURCES:

Babington-Smith, Constance. *Amy Johnson.* London: Thorosons, 1967.

Johnson, Amy. *Skyroads of the World.* London: Chambers, 1939.

Jones, Molly, and Betty Falconer. *Amy Johnson's Letters.* London: British Museum.

SUGGESTED READING:

Cadogan, Mary. *Women with Wings: Female Flyers in Fact and Fiction.* Academy Chicago, 1993.

Mollison, Jim. *Playboy of the Air.* London: Graphic, 1937.

Taylor, Sir George. *The Sky Beyond.* London: Oxford University Press, 1935.

RELATED MEDIA:

They Flew Alone (96 min. film, released in America as *Wings and the Woman*), starring *****Anna Neagle** as Amy Johnson and Robert Newton as Jim Mollison, produced by Imperator/RKO, 1942.

Christopher Gibb,
a scholar of Oxford University, writer and author, London, England

Johnson, Mrs. Andrew (1810–1876).

See Johnson, Eliza McCardle.

Johnson, Celia (1908–1982)

English actress who left behind an enduring reminder of her talent, the movie Brief Encounter, *a classic of British cinema.* Born Celia Elizabeth Johnson on December 18, 1908, in Richmond, Surrey, England; died in Nettlebed, England, on April 23, 1982; daughter of Robert Johnson (a doctor) and Ethel (Griffiths) Johnson; married Peter Fleming (a travel writer, essayist,

and brother of Ian Fleming); children: Nicholas (b. January 3, 1939); Kate Fleming (b. Mary 24, 1946, who wrote her mother's biography); Lucy (b. May 15, 1947, an actress).

Made debut as Sarah Undershaft in Shaw's Major Barbara *at Theatre Royal, Huddersfield, Yorkshire (July 23, 1928); replaced Angela Baddeley in* A Hundred Years Old *at the Lyric, Hammersmith (January 1929); performed in* The Artist and the Shadow *and* Debonair *in West End, and joined West End production of H.M. Harwood and R. Gore-Brown's* Cynara *(1929); played Elizabeth in Somerset Maugham's* The Circle *(1931); performed in* Death Takes a Holiday, *replaced Madeleine Carroll in* After All, *and played Ophelia to Raymond Massey's Hamlet in New York (1931); appeared in* The Man I Killed *by Maurice Rostand (with Emlyn Williams) at the Apollo,* The Vinegar Tree *by Paul Osborn (with Marie Tempest) at the St. James's,* Tomorrow Will Be Friday *at the Haymarket, and* Ten Minute Alibi *by Anthony Armstrong at the Embassy Theatre in Swiss Cottage (1932); appeared in* Another Language *by Rose Franken at the Lyric,* Sometimes Even Now, The Key *by Hardy and Gore-Browne, and Merton Hodge's* The Wind and the Rain *(1933); played Elizabeth Bennet in Jane Austen's* Pride and Prejudice *at the St. James's Theatre, adapted by Helen Jerome (February 1936); appeared in* Old Music *by Keith Winter (1937); performed in* Sixth Floor *(1939); replaced Peggy Ashcroft as Cecily Cardew in* The Importance of Being Earnest *(1940); played Mrs. de Winter in* Rebecca, *adapted by Daphne du Maurier (April 5, 1940) at the Queen's Theater; made short film,* A Letter from Home, *for director Carol Reed and Ministry of Information (1941); made first full-length film* In Which We Serve *(1942); filmed Dodie Smith's* Dear Octopus *(1943) and Noel Coward's* This Happy Breed; *began filming* Brief Encounter *(January 1945); joined the Old Vic, starting with Shaw's* St. Joan *with Alec Guinness as the dauphin; filmed* The Astonished Heart *(1950); filmed* I Believe in You, The Holly and the Ivy, A Kid for Two Farthings, *and J.B. Priestley's* The Good Companions; *replaced Ashcroft in Terence Rattigan's* The Deep Blue Sea *(1952); appeared in* Never Too Late *by Felicity Douglas at the Westminster (1954); played Sheila Broadbent in William Douglas-Home's comedy* The Reluctant Debutante *(1955); performed in Robert Bolt's* The Flowering Cherry *with Sir Ralph Richardson (1957); awarded the CBE (June 1958); appeared in* The Grass is Greener *by Hugh Williams (1958),* The Tulip Tree *by N.C. Hunter (1962),* Out of the Crocodile *by Giles Cooper (1963); replaced Diana Wynyard in Ibsen's* The Master Builder *at the National (1964); played Lady Nelson in "Bequest to the Nation" in Rattigan's teleplay (1964); replaced Edith Evans as Judith Bliss in* Hay Fever *at the National (1965); played Madame Ranevskaya at Chichester in Lindsay Anderson's production of* The Cherry Orchard *(1967); performed in Alan Ayckbourn's* Relatively Speaking *at the Duke of York (1967); played Miss Mackay in film* The Prime of Miss Jean Brodie *(1968); played Gertrude to Alan Bates' Hamlet at Nottingham (1970); played Lady Boothroyde in* Lloyd George Knew My Father *(October 1972); on television, appeared in "Mrs. Palfrey at the Claremont" by Elizabeth Taylor, winning Best Actress at the BAFTA awards (1973); appeared in* The Dame of Sark *by Douglas-Home 1974 and on television in his "The Kingfisher" (1977); played the nurse in* Romeo and Juliet *for the BBC (1978); appeared in* Staying On *with Trevor Howard (March 1980) and nominated for another Best Actress by BAFTA; created a Dame Commander of the British Empire (1981).*

"I won't write my autobiography because I never had an affair with Frank Sinatra," said Celia Johnson, "and if I had had, I wouldn't tell anyone." It was her daughter **Kate Fleming** who published a biography of her mother in 1991. Tall, slim, and easygoing, Celia Johnson was "never very smartly dressed," writes her daughter. "Usually devoid of make-up, and with thick glasses," she was rarely recognized in public. In a hotel in Switzerland, she overheard someone standing nearby say: "I hear Celia Johnson is staying in the hotel—I'm determined not to miss her." Throughout Johnson's 50-year career, says Fleming, "the creative and the conventional" were at "war within her."

Born in 1908, the daughter of Robert Johnson, a doctor, and **Ethel Griffiths Johnson**, Celia spent a happy childhood with her younger brother John (b. 1912) and older sister Pamela (b. 1906). Her forebears owned an outfitters' shop in Cambridge. After World War I, her father became physician to the duke and duchess of York (the future George VI and *Elizabeth Bowes-Lyon). Her mother Ethel, generally nervous, ran a chaotic house. Her father could be teased, her mother could not.

As a child, Celia was all eyes, teeth, and gangly limbs. When she was nine, during the waning days of World War I, both she and her 11-year-old sister Pam had a serious attack of measles for which Celia always blamed her poor eyesight. Short-sighted, she had to wear glasses throughout her life.

In April 1919, Celia entered Miss Fraser's class (Form III) of the elite St. Paul's Girls' School which sent many of its students on to Oxford. Johnson excelled in French and played the oboe in the school orchestra led by Gustav Holst. Competitive, she was also athletic, had a flair for verse, and loved performing in plays. When the family moved to Marshgate House in Richmond, 15-year-old Celia began boarding near school until she left St. Paul's in July 1926 with her general school certificate.

I remember in Paris, being photographed shaking hands with the engine drivers at the Gare du Nord. I got the giggles and they must have thought me rather impolite but I wanted to tell them, as if they didn't know, that they were not shaking hands with a real film star but only with me, and that it was very nice of them to be so kind and pretend so well.

—Celia Johnson

Johnson had no great ambition, but she wanted to act. "I thought I'd rather like it," she said. "It was the only thing I was good at. And I thought it might be rather wicked." Accepted into the Royal Academy of Dramatic Art (RADA) in 1927, she caught the attention of **Alice Gachet**, one of the leading teachers there. Following her final term in 1928, she signed with agent Aubrey Blackburn and spent her first season with **Madge McIntosh**'s Rep. Co. at Theatre Royal, Huddersfield, Yorkshire, debuting as Sarah Undershaft in Shaw's *Major Barbara* on July 23, 1928. Still, Johnson had no drive and absolutely no confidence.

Back in Richmond, in January 1929, she replaced *Angela Baddeley as Currita in *A Hundred Years Old* at the Lyric, Hammersmith. The company also consisted of actors Rupert Hart-Davis and *Peggy Ashcroft. Hart-Davis had taken a shine to Johnson, but his attentions soon turned to his future wife, Ashcroft; he broke the news to Celia following a matinee. When Celia showed some signs of stress, Rupert introduced her to his friend, the brother of Ian Fleming. Peter Fleming, the future author of *Brazilian Adventure* (1933), was at that time assistant literary editor of *The Spectator*.

Johnson then triumphed in two back-to-back flops. In the one-week run of George Dunning Gribble's *The Artist and the Shadow* in the West End, she had a small part in the last act. Critics were of the opinion that, though she could not save the play, she was a smashing success. The second failure was *Debonair,* despite raves for Johnson. Within days, she was joining the prestigious West End production of H.M. Harwood and R. Gore-Brown's *Cynara,* starring *Gladys Cooper and Sir Gerald du Maurier. Johnson had gone from an unknown to someone so well known that one paper headed its review: "Celia Johnson Again." Wrote Kate Fleming:

> These three undistinguished plays . . . all showed aspects of Celia's acting that were to characterise her work throughout her career—a freshness (almost overpowering then), a lack of sentimentality, an absence of technical trickiness, a feeling for comedy, intelligence, sensitivity, and a weakness in the voice; this last was always to be a limitation.

Never comfortable in period costume, Johnson rarely took on the classics during the 1930s, preferring the modern plays and light comedies of the West End. Work came steadily. She played Elizabeth in Somerset Maugham's *The Circle* with Nigel Playfair and *Athene Seyler (1931), and replaced *Madeleine Carroll in *After All,* which also featured *Lilian Braithwaite. Then Johnson sailed for New York to play Ophelia to Raymond Massey's Hamlet (1931). The actors knew they were in trouble when they arrived in New York and producer Norman Bel Geddes met them at the ship with: "I've altered the script a bit." Bel Geddes, having decided that *Hamlet* was a play of action, had cut much of the hero's indecision. The critics were merciless, but Johnson escaped with more plaudits. Even so, that was her last appearance on Broadway.

Back in England, Johnson opened in Merton Hodge's *The Wind and the Rain* with Robert Harris as co-star on October 18, 1933. The play ran for two years. "This actress . . . has brilliantly mastered the art of being adorable on the lines of intelligent sensibility instead of by exploiting glucose charm," wrote Ivor Brown. "It is one of the chief and most commendable differences between the Edwardian theater and our own that the 'ingénue' parts now demand an aspect of intelligence instead of being vehicles for the Lackwit Lovelies who 'dress' a part rather than acting it." In February 1936, Celia scored one of her greatest triumphs as Elizabeth Bennet in *Jane Austen's *Pride and Prejudice* at the St. James's Theatre, adapted by **Helen Jerome**. After a long run, she opened, along with *Greer Garson, in *Old Music* by Keith Winter in 1937.

Though domestically inept, Johnson had married Peter Fleming on December 10, 1935. Both were happy, successful, and enjoyed their friends in their little flat in More's Gardens,

overlooking the Thames, Chelsea. Earlier that year, as a journalist for the *Times,* Peter had joined up with travel writer *Ella Maillart as they traveled through Tibet and had written the book *News from Tartary* about the experience.

In February 1938, he was sent by *The Times* as war correspondent to travel the Burma Road and report on the Sino-Japanese War. Celia went with him. By the time they returned to London at the end of July, she was pregnant. The couple built a spacious brick house, Merrimoles, on his inherited estate in Nettlebed, South Oxfordshire, five miles from Henley-on-Thames. Though Celia hated it, wrote Kate Fleming, "towards the end of her life, when the house in its isolated position was less than ideal for her, nothing would induce her to move from it." In 1940, with Britain at war with Germany, they moved into Merrimoles, along with the family of Peter's other brother, Michael Fleming, who was killed in France. Johnson was now in charge of "a largish, unfinished house . . . [and] a substantial household, as well as a sizeable agricultural estate, with farm workers, foresters, tenants and a gamekeeper," writes Fleming. "Organisation, administration and domestic responsibilities were not where her talents lay. . . . The next five years were for her, as they were for everybody in Britain, emotionally and physically hard."

In 1940, when Peggy Ashcroft took sick with measles, Johnson replaced her as Cecily Cardew in the celebrated production of *The Importance of Being Earnest,* with *Edith Evans as Lady Bracknell, *Margaret Rutherford as Miss Prism, and direction by Sir John Gielgud. Johnson then played Mrs. de Winter while Rutherford played the sinister housekeeper Mrs. Danvers in *Daphne du Maurier's adaption of her book *Rebecca,* which opened at the Queen's Theatre, April 5, 1940. The curtain went up early so that audiences could get home before the blackout. If an air-raid alert was still in effect when the curtain came down, the cast continued to entertain. A popular diversion from the war, *Rebecca* was closed by a bomb shortly after midnight on September 7, 1940—the theater would not reopen until 1959.

In the next five years, Johnson stayed close to home. Because of household responsibilities, she could not commit to the open-end run of a play; instead, she did radio and film with known schedules. In 1941, she made a short film, *A Letter from Home,* directed by Carol Reed, for the Ministry of Information. Peter was wounded while on a mission to organize resistance in Greece when a German bombed his boat. Soon after, he was sent off to India.

From the movie
Brief Encounter,
starring Celia
Johnson and
Trevor Howard.

Next, Noel Coward cast Johnson as his wife in a film he was preparing about the navy. Based on the sinking of the HMS *Kelly*, it would later be titled *In Which We Serve*. There were firsts all round: it was the first full-length film for her and for actor Richard Attenborough, the first movie directed by Coward, and the first co-directed by David Lean. Johnson wrote to Peter:

> My second day's filming consisted of being made up at 8:30 and being used at 6:30. It wasn't improved by seeing the rushes in which I looked like a soused herring and

didn't register anything at all. I don't look nearly as human as I did in the M[inistry] of I[nformation] film and heavens knows I wasn't Lana Turner in that. I don't think I am going to be the V. Leigh of Nettlebed.

As usual, the critics disagreed.

Johnson joined the Henley branch of the Women's Auxiliary Police Corps (WAPC), delivering dispatches and working the switchboard, when available, in the Henley police station. She boasted that she could say, "'Henley Police and Hold the Line' with exactly the right air of boredom and slight malice that all telephone girls affect." The woman who became a film star as the typical English housewife finally learned to cook, dealt with gas rations, made camouflage nets, plowed the acreage on a tractor, and entertained visiting military. She wrote her husband on May 31, 1942: "Tish and I are rather exhausted as we have had a Czech officer for the weekend. He complained that the fault of our race was that of being too polite to our enemies but the strain of being polite to our Allies was so severe that I have none left for even an Italian."

In autumn 1942, *In Which We Serve* was released and took its place in the annals of movie making. Though meant to be a war-propaganda film to boost the morale of the British throughout the world, the movie worked as a story due to the inordinate amount of talent involved. Despite its jingoistic passages, it had a huge impact. One tank driver wrote Celia that he was naming his tank after her. She was thrilled and slightly amused. "I suspect though that he writes similar ones to all film stars and that his tank at the moment is called Greer." In 1943, she filmed *Dodie Smith*'s *Dear Octopus* and the generally praised *This Happy Breed* by Noel Coward. Johnson was rarely happy with what she saw on screen, especially her appearance. As usual, her reviews were upbeat.

The household at Merrimoles took on another family in 1944 when her sister Pam and children returned from India minus a husband who was missing in the war. There were now 15 people in the household. As for her career, Johnson was in great demand, especially by Coward, who sent her a sketch for a new film. Intrigued by it, she was eager to work with the same team: Lean, Coward, and Ronnie Neame behind the camera. Coward's sketch would expand into *Brief Encounter,* a film about a suburban housewife who continually crosses paths with a married doctor in a railway station—friendship turns to love, then loss. Newcomer Trevor Howard was signed to play the doctor. In January 1945, shooting began at a railway station at

Carnforth in Lancashire, in northwest England, far enough away from London to avoid the bombs. Johnson enjoyed being on location and with the tight-knit group. Even so, she still had the jitters before each take, and the film's narration presented acting problems. "You need to be a star of the silent screen really," said Johnson, "because there's such a lot of stuff with commentary over it—it's terribly difficult to do." Celia thought she owed everything to her shortsightedness: "I take off my glasses to do a scene, and I don't see all those terrifying men in sweaters standing about with their hands in their pockets. . . . It's a great advantage."

On May 8, V-E (Victory in Europe) day, she saw a rough cut: "Some bits come off very well and some bits are not so good. But what I can't decide is whether the story itself is strong enough. I'm not bad in some bits, in some I'm rotten." That June, she warned her husband, home on leave and about to see an unfinished version of the film without a soundtrack, that he would be seeing it without Rachmaninoff's Piano Concerto #1 "swishing through it. Perhaps you can hum it to yourself while watching it."

When *Brief Encounter* premiered that October, no one involved with the film had any idea what to expect from the viewing public. Though it won the Critics' Prize at the Cannes Film Festival in 1946, it was the Americans who were bowled over; Johnson was nominated for an Oscar for Best Actress, Lean for Best Director. "The British were the last to appreciate *Brief Encounter*," wrote Kate Fleming, "but over the years they have come to love it and it has become one of the classics of British cinema." David Lean has long given Johnson credit for the success of the film. Fleming continues:

> There is a moment when she had to begin to tell lies . . . she looks at herself in the mirror, and it is clear from that look that she has never told a lie before in her life—a simple point but so difficult to express. On another occasion she decides, just as the train that she is on is pulling out of the station, to keep an assignation with Dr Harvey (Trevor Howard) . . . ; she distractedly jumps from the train, runs down the platform, stops, collects herself, starts walking and then can't stop herself from breaking into a run. . . . David Lean thought it was marvellous; by rushing, trying to walk and starting to run again, she so clearly showed all her fears, hopes, excitement and worries. He congratulated her and asked, "Why did you do that?". . . She just said, "Well, she would, wouldn't she?"

Meanwhile, Peter had returned home, and the families in the extended household began to move out. Kate was born on May 24, 1946. A year later, Celia was 40 when Lucy was born on May 15, 1947. Soon after, Johnson was invited to join the Old Vic, starting with G.B. Shaw's *St. Joan* with Alec Guinness as the dauphin. Most felt her performance "did not quite come off." Her voice did not have enough authority, and, though her performance had clarity, the soldier in *Joan of Arc was missing.

Torn between work and home, filled with guilt when away from her children—as well as the labradors, cats, ponies, owls, fox cubs, and the gray squirrel, who had a predilection for hoarding chocolates—Johnson continued to avoid prolonged engagements. Her husband's life as a nomad had ended, and he was restlessly playing the role of the country gentleman. She and Peter led more separate lives then most. He was taciturn; she was stiff upper lip. There were strains on the marriage.

Johnson made another film for Coward in 1949, *The Astonished Heart,* a sizeable failure which also starred *Margaret Leighton. Two more films followed: the unmemorable *I Believe in You* and, again with Leighton, *The Holly and the Ivy,* now a Christmas television staple. In order to remain home, Johnson was turning down many parts, especially for television, and, after shooting two more films in the 1950s, she would not do another for 11 years.

With her children in school, she began to be drawn back into theater. Major theatrical producer Binkie Beaumont despaired of her commitment: "Oh, Celia will only do it if she wants a pair of new curtains." In 1952, she replaced Ashcroft in Terence Rattigan's *The Deep Blue Sea.* The play and her performance were a *succès d'estime.* She next appeared in *It's Never Too Late* by **Felicity Douglas** at the Westminster in 1954 and took on the part of Sheila Broadbent in William Douglas-Home's comedy *The Reluctant Debutante* in 1955, playing actress **Anna Massey**'s mother. It was Celia who recommended Jack Merivale for the young man. "Is he a good actor," asked the producer. "I wouldn't know about that," she replied, "but he can drop me every night on Henley Bridge on his way home." She had a gift for comedy and in this vehicle could show it off; she stayed for nine months. During rehearsals, the inexperienced Anna Massey was having trouble with the part and was about to be dropped. Celia and character actress **Ambrosine Philpotts** championed the girl, and Massey went on to a distinguished career. In time, Johnson took many young actresses under her wing while performing with them.

With the coming of the British theatrical revolution in 1956, led by John Osborne's *Look Back in Anger,* the theatrical community was split between those who welcomed the changes and those who did not. Johnson was one who was uncomfortable with the new emphasis on working-class speech, attitudes, and anger. Often, she chose plays that belonged to the old guard. Even so, if the script and cast of a new play were good, she would bite. In June 1958, she was awarded the CBE (Commander of the British Empire).

In 1964, Johnson took over for an ailing *Diana Wynyard as Mrs. Solness in Ibsen's *The Master Builder* at the National, starring Sir Michael Redgrave as Solness and **Maggie Smith** as Hilde Wangel. Though Johnson was nervous, she was also honored. Redgrave, however, was on the verge of a nervous breakdown, and the opening did not go well; he was replaced six months later by Laurence Olivier, and the play found its rhythm. Of Johnson, Nicholas de Jongh wrote in the *Guardian*: "Her parched, wrenching performance of the woman was akin to an announcement of her unused powers. She had arrived again." In 1965, she successfully replaced Edith Evans as Judith Bliss in Noel Coward's *Hay Fever* at the National, with Coward directing. That year, Johnson also played Madame Ranevskaya at Chichester in Lindsay Anderson's acclaimed production of *The Cherry Orchard.* She had another comedic triumph in 1967 when she appeared in Alan Ayckbourn's *Relatively Speaking* at the Duke of York. In 1964, she played Lady Nelson in an adaptation of *Bequest to the Nation* by Rattigan for television. Then, in 1968, Maggie Smith requested Johnson for the headmistress Miss Mackay in the film version of *The Prime of Miss Jean Brodie.* So, after a long absence, Johnson returned to the screen.

In July 1971, returning with her sister from a trip to the Greek islands, Johnson was called to the front of the plane and handed a message from a brother-in-law: "Dear Celia, Bad news I fear. Poor Peter dropped dead out shooting today. Absolutely no pain. Making all arrangements." Peter had died of a heart attack at 64. They had been married for 35 years.

In October 1972, with her habit of replacing Ashcroft, Johnson stepped into the part of Lady Boothroyde in *Lloyd George Knew My Father* by William Douglas-Home, opposite Sir Ralph Richardson. It was a welcome diversion after the death of Peter. On television, in 1973, she appeared in *Elizabeth Taylor's "Mrs. Palfrey at the Claremont" for which she won Best Actress at the British Academy of Film and Television Arts (BAFTA) awards. Johnson then took on two more by Douglas-Home, in theater, *The Dame of Sark* (1974), and on television, "The Kingfisher" (1977).

In September 1979, Celia Johnson was abruptly stricken with an odd illness, collapsing for ten days. Abruptly better, she flew to Simla, India, to film Paul Scott's *Staying On* with Trevor Howard in March 1980. That December, she was again nominated for BAFTA's Best Actress. In 1981, while on a promotional tour in America, she was informed she had been made the ninth theatrical Dame Commander of the Order of the British Empire since World War II.

In 1982, during the Falkland War, Celia was set to open in **Angela Huth**'s *The Understanding* with Ralph Richardson at the Strand, Shaftsbury Ave, on April 27. On her Sunday off before opening, she had a stroke while playing bridge at Merrimoles with friends. Two hours later, she was dead. "We can get back the Falklands. We can never replace Celia Johnson," wrote Jean Rook in the *Daily Express*. Celia Johnson once told her son, after a couple of glasses of sherry and 52 years in the theater, "I think I've at last got the hang of it."

SOURCES:

Fleming, Kate. *Celia Johnson*. London: Weidenfeld and Nicholson, 1991.

Morley, Sheridan. *The Great Stage Stars*. London: Angus & Robertson, 1986.

Johnson, Claudia Alta (b. 1912).

See Johnson, Lady Bird.

Johnson, E. Pauline (1861–1913)

Poet and writer, who emphasized her native Indian heritage to become a popular and acclaimed recitalist throughout Canada and England. Name variations: Tekahionwake; Emily Pauline Johnson; The Mohawk Princess. Born Emily Pauline Johnson on March 10, 1861, on the Six Nations Indian Reserve near Brantford, Ontario, Canada; died of cancer on March 7, 1913, in Vancouver, British Columbia, Canada; daughter of George Henry Martin Johnson (a Mohawk chief and Canadian government interpreter) and Emily Susanna (Howells) Johnson; never married; no children.

Attended school in Brantford (1875–77); death of her father (1884); gave first public recital (1892); made trip to England and published first book (1894); death of mother and marriage cancelled (1898);

toured Canada and England as platform entertainer (1892–1909); retired in Vancouver (1909).

Selected publications: The White Wampum *(1894);* Canadian Born *(1903);* Legends of Vancouver *(1911);* The Shaganappi *(1913);* The Mocassin Maker *(1913). Selected poems: "The Song My Paddle Sings," "In the Shadows," "At the Ferry," "Fight On," "Canadian Born," and "Riders of the Plains."*

At the peak of her career as an entertainer, E. Pauline Johnson toured Canada reciting her own poems and other works, wearing the traditional buckskin and beads of a Mohawk and appeared onstage under the names of Tekahionwake and The Mohawk Princess. Biologically, she was in fact less than half Indian; both her mother and her great-grandmother on her father's side were white. By Canadian law, however, she was designated an Indian; more important, she saw herself as Indian and chose throughout her life to emphasize her Mohawk background and to minimize her white ancestry. She took pride in her ancestry, believing the Mohawks to be a distinguished and noble race. As she once wrote:

> There are those who think they pay me a compliment in saying that I am just like a white woman. My aim, my joy, my pride is to sing the glories of my own people. Ours was the race that gave the world its measure of heroism, its standard of physical prowess. Ours was the race that taught the world that avarice veiled by any name is crime. Ours were the people of the blue air and the green woods, and ours the faith that taught men to live without greed and die without fear.

"Singing the glories" of her people to a wide and predominantly white audience, Johnson may have succeeded to some small extent in diminishing the prejudice against the native peoples of Canada at the beginning of the 20th century.

Born on March 10, 1861, on the Six Nations Indian Reserve outside of Brantford, Ontario, Pauline Johnson was the fourth child of George Henry Martin Johnson and **Emily Howells Johnson**. George Johnson came from a prominent Mohawk family, whose members had joined with the British in both the American Revolution and the War of 1812. George's father, John "Smoke" Johnson, was a hero of the War of 1812, who had fought alongside Sir Isaac Brock at Queenston Heights and in other major battles. Through his mother, George Johnson inherited his position as a chieftain and sat on the senate of the Iroquois Confederacy. Fluent in Mohawk and five other languages of the Six Nations, as well as English, French, and German, he held the position of Canadian government interpreter on the reserve. Emily Howells came from Ohio to live with her sister, the wife of an Anglican minister who ran a reserve mission. The young couple's romance brought opposition from both families. George's relatives were particularly opposed because his title to the chieftaincy could not be passed to the sons of a white woman. Nevertheless, the couple persisted and were married in August 1853.

The family was not wealthy but lived comfortably on George's government income. Their home, designated Chiefswood, sat on the outskirts of the reserve, and by the standards of the time, even for the white middle class, it was a stately place. George and Emily entertained many prominent white guests, both government officials and those in the arts. In her early years, Pauline seldom played with other Mohawk children, and she attended school on the reserve only briefly.

From an early age, Pauline was taught to be proud of her native ancestry. From her father, she learned a respect for Mohawk history, legend, and ceremony, which her mother also encouraged. In her childhood, her grandfather spent countless hours telling her stories of his own exploits as well as the history and legends of their people. In later life, many of these legends, as well as her sense of pride in the Mohawk past, were to find their way into her short stories and poetry, including these lines from *The Re-Internment of Red Jacket,* written in 1884:

> And few to-day remain:
> But copper-tinted face, and smoldering fire
> Of wilder life, were left me by my sire
> To be my proudest claim.

In 1865, and again in 1873, George Johnson was brutally beaten, and almost died, because of his efforts to end the illegal traffic in liquor on the reserve. On the whole, however, the peaceful life of his family was rarely disturbed. Pauline was close to her three older siblings and idolized both her parents, perceiving them to be the perfect couple, blessed with an enduring and romantic love. In her early years, she suffered from frequent earaches, colds, and bronchitis, but as she reached her teenage years she grew stronger and began to pursue activities common to Mohawk children. As her siblings left home for schools in other cities, she grew skilled in archery and snowshoeing, and canoeing became her passion. As a young woman, she spent countless hours canoeing on the Grand River, alone or with friends, recognized for her abilities by members of local canoeing clubs.

Poetry became her other passion, evident from an early age. The vast library of the Johnson home was filled with the works of Scott, Longfellow, Byron, and Shakespeare. Emily Howells Johnson loved poetry and valued literature. Thus, Pauline's early education, taught first by her mother and then by a governess, emphasized literature above all else. According to some sources, Pauline was creating poems perhaps even before she could write them down. When, at age 14, she was finally sent to Brantford to attend school, Pauline did well in the literary areas and enjoyed extracurricular activities, such as acting.

My aim, my joy, my pride is to sing the glories of my own people.

—**Pauline Johnson**

In the two years she attended Brantford Collegiate, from 1875 to 1877, it is not clear to what extent Pauline contended with prejudice, but given the prevailing attitudes toward Indians at the time, she must have been affected by it. But as a gregarious, cheerful, and charming girl, she made friends easily and seems to have fit in well, developing a group of friends which lasted beyond the school years.

In 1877, at age 16, Johnson returned to Chiefswood, where her next few years were spent in a happy and idyllic cycle of canoeing, reading, writing, and entertaining friends. But following the death of her father, in February 1884, Emily Johnson could no longer maintain Chiefswood without her husband's income. In the spring of 1885, Pauline moved with her mother and sister Eva into a small home in Brantford; her two brothers were already living away from home.

In 1885, Pauline's poem "My Little Jean" became her first published piece, appearing in a New York magazine called *Gems of Poetry.* Other works followed, in this magazine and others, and her gifts as a poet gained recognition in literary circles.

Why Johnson began to pursue publication at this point is not entirely clear. She loved poetry and had been writing it for some time. Reading and writing verse were acceptable activities for leisured, respectable, middle-class women of the day, and she may have considered herself simply to be passing the time as she waited for marriage. If she hoped to earn support for herself and her mother, it must have been evident that poetry alone would not provide her with a living, regardless of how popular or prolific she became. In January 1892, however, an invitation to recite one of her poems, at a social evening for the Young Liberal Club of Toronto, demonstrated an available means for financial survival.

In the age before television and radio, people often gathered to hear live music, the reading of poetry, and plays. On the night Pauline was first asked to recite, she discovered her talent as an entertainer. Although she lacked training in what was then called "elocution," she had a natural magnetism that carried across the stage lights, and an ability to project the emotion and passion of her work with her body and voice.

The club's organizer, Frank Yeigh, quickly recognized her gifts and arranged a public tour for the young woman across Ontario and eastern Canada. Over the next few months, she made 125 appearances in Ontario and Quebec. In sparsely populated Canada, communities were enormous distances apart; a performer on such a circuit stopped at every small and remote community, performing night after night. But Pauline found the lifestyle compatible; except for brief breaks, she would continue at it until her retirement in 1909.

In the fall of 1892, Johnson teamed up with a fellow entertainer, Owen Smiley. It was common for such shows to have more than one act, providing the entertainers with a break and variety for the audience, and Smiley was an experienced and accomplished platform entertainer whose light-hearted and humorous singing complemented Johnson's poetry readings. In the five years they toured together, their act became one of the most popular in the country.

In 1892, Frank Yeigh coined the stage title of "The Mohawk Princess"; Johnson later supplemented it with the Indian name "Tekahionwake." Understanding what it took to make her act appeal to the average audience, Johnson appreciated the commercial value of her Indian background. By 1894, she was appearing for part of the program in a costume featuring a fringed and beaded buckskin dress with leggings and moccasins, with wampum belts, a hunting knife, and even a Huron scalp as accessories. She also diversified her act. In 1891, she had begun to write short stories incorporating Indian legends, which she later adapted as short plays she and her partner would use onstage, interspersed with crowd-pleasing jokes and bits of doggerel.

From 1892, Johnson justified her tours to her mother by claiming she would perform only as long as it took to earn money to publish a collection of her poems. In turn-of-the-century Canada, stage performers in general, and ac-

Opposite page

E. Pauline Johnson

tresses in particular, were viewed as morally corrupt, following a lifestyle beneath the respectability of the middle class. In April 1894, when Johnson took her act to England, she had earned enough money to arrange for the publication of her poetry. Released late that year by a prestigious British publishing company, *The White Wampum* was well received by the critics and had robust sales in its first edition. The poet, meanwhile, had become a celebrity in the homes of the British upper classes, as guest and performer, before returning to Canada in July 1894; but her life on the stage was not over. Now she justified her career appearances to her mother by arguing that she needed to promote her book.

Johnson's partnership with Smiley ended in 1897, and in February 1898 her touring was interrupted by the death of her mother. It was a devastating event for Johnson, who had been close to her mother throughout her life, and was shortly followed by another. In January 1898, it had been announced that Pauline was to marry Charles Drayton, a socially prominent young man who was an assistant inspector for the Western Canada Savings and Loan Company. Although the newspapers continued to mention the impending marriage for more than a year, the relationship was threatened from the outset by severe opposition from the Drayton family. Pauline was a Mohawk Indian, engaged in a questionable profession, and, at age 37, was 11 years older than Charles; though she maintained a circle of socially and politically prominent friends and there had never been any scandal associated with her, the Drayton family undoubtedly found the marriage unacceptable. Regardless of the cause, the engagement ended sometime in 1898. Throughout her life, Johnson was exceedingly charming, beautiful, and surrounded by an exotic aura; she had always attracted men. For reasons only she knew, Charles Drayton was the only man she considered a suitable partner. With the end of their relationship, she probably knew that she would never marry. In those days, a woman of 37 was considered past the age of marriageability.

Professionally and emotionally, Johnson's next few years remained difficult. Without a partner and inept at handling the business of bookings and promotion, she was in constant financial difficulties until 1901, when she teamed up with J. Walter McRaye. McRaye was one of the innumerable second-rate entertainers who toured Canada and the U.S., never achieving recognition or popularity and barely making a living. However, McRaye was excellent at handling the business and financial aspects of touring. Johnson was by this time a recognized tal-

ent, and many among her family did not understand her choice of McRaye. But what Pauline
did not need was another "star"; she was better
off with someone willing to take second billing,
fill in during her shows, and allow her a break
and time to change. Also, as a business manager
he performed well.

The partnership was perfect for the next
eight years. Johnson and McRaye were on the
road almost constantly, from one end of Canada
to the other. In 1906, they toured England,
where they were also well received. They performed everywhere, from cities and towns to the
smallest and most remote outposts, before audiences of both the elite and the common folk. In
November 1901, they played the prestigious
Orme Hall in Ottawa with the Canadian prime
minister and his wife in attendance; by early
1902, they were in southeastern British Columbia, playing in front of miners in makeshift halls.
Johnson seems to have enjoyed these ventures
into isolated areas. In the summer of 1904, she
toured the remote communities of northern
British Columbia, where travel over 400 miles
was by horse and buggy. Pauline viewed the
booking as an adventurous holiday.

In 1903, Johnson took a break from touring
to prepare for the publication of a second collection of poems, called *Canadian Born*. The book
did not receive the critical praise that had accompanied her first. Most of the material had been
written for performance. Effective when recited
on the stage, these poems lacked the style, emotion, and content to endure. Years as a platform
performer had accustomed her to writing for
commercial ends, and the efforts to sustain her
career on tour no doubt hindered her ability to
mature artistically. Given her earlier show of talent, one can only speculate about the quality of
the work she might have produced had she managed to devote more time to writing in solitude.

The lifestyle of a platform entertainer was
hard, with its endless travel, poor accommodations, and often bad food. In 1909, at age 48,
Johnson was finding it difficult to rally the energy
for her performances and decided to retire. Since
1891, she had been producing articles and short
stories, often about the lives and legends of Native peoples, which had appeared in a number of
magazines. From her years on the road, she could
detail her stories with unusual characters or romantic figures like the Royal Canadian Mounted
Police, and describe the culture and scenery of remote places. As a public figure, she had a following who would be interested in her work, and she
believed she could publish enough work to live

comfortably. Thus, in August, she settled into a small apartment in Vancouver, British Columbia.

For some time, however, Johnson had been ignoring visible signs of illness. In October 1909, she was finally persuaded by a friend to see a doctor, who found her to be in the advanced stages of breast cancer. By then there was little that could be done beyond treating her for pain. Nevertheless, Johnson plunged wholeheartedly into writing stories, which were bought by *The Boys' World* and *Mother's Magazine*. Through her friendship with a chief of the Squamish people of coastal British Columbia, she became interested in preserving the history and legends of the tribe, and wrote several articles which appeared as a series in a Vancouver magazine.

By 1911, however, pain and the effects of morphine injections to counteract it were lessening her ability to work. Unable to bring in income, she was considering a return to her family in Ontario when a group of women friends intervened and arranged for the publication of three collections of her prose works.

Legends of Vancouver was the first of the books, which sold vigorously. Johnson had a wide following, and many people were willing to buy, sometimes at a high price, out of a desire to help. Johnson was able to remain in Vancouver as she wished and received excellent private medical care until her death on March 7, 1913. Because of her popularity, E. Pauline Johnson died knowing that the material of her books would help preserve the heritage of her people for future generations.

SOURCES:

Keller, Betty. *Pauline: A Biography of Pauline Johnson.* Vancouver-Toronto: Douglas and McIntyre, 1981.

Van Steen, Marcus. *Pauline Johnson: Her Life and Work.* Toronto: Musson Books, 1965.

SUGGESTED READING:

Keen, Dorothy, and Martha McKeon, as told to Mollie Gillen. "The Story of Pauline Johnson, Canada's Passionate Poet," in *Chatelaine.* February–March 1966.

Loosely, Elizabeth. "Pauline Johnson," in *The Clear Spirit: Twenty Canadian Women and Their Times.* Edited by Mary Quayle Innis. Toronto: University of Toronto Press, 1966.

COLLECTIONS:

Johnson Collection located in the D.B. Weldon Library, University of Western Ontario, Regional Collections, London, Ontario.

Catherine Briggs, Ph.D. candidate, University of Waterloo, Waterloo, Ontario, Canada

Johnson, Eleanor Murdoch

(1892–1987)

American educator and editor who founded the children's newspaper My Weekly Reader. *Born in Hagerstown, Maryland, in 1892; died in 1987; daughter of Richard Potts Johnson and Emma J. (Shuff) Johnson; attended Colorado College, 1911–12; graduated from the Central State Teachers College, 1913; University of Chicago, Ph.B. cum laude, 1925; Columbia University, M.A., 1932.*

Taught in the public schools of Lawton, Oklahoma (1913–16), Chickasha, Oklahoma (1916–17), Oklahoma City (1917–18); served as superintendent of elementary schools, Drumright, Oklahoma (1918–22), Oklahoma City (1922–26), York, Pennsylvania (1926–30); was assistant superintendent of schools in Lakewood, Ohio (1930–34); co-founded and edited My Weekly Reader *(1934).*

An honors graduate from the University of Chicago (class of 1925), Eleanor Murdoch Johnson was working in Pennsylvania, as an administrator of the elementary school curriculum, when she conceived the idea of a newspaper for children. Taking her idea to American Education Publications, she worked with them in developing the paper's content and format, although she did not join their permanent staff until 1935.

The paper was initially published in 1928, and at the end of its first year boasted a readership of 100,000 schoolchildren. (It is estimated that two-thirds of adults in the 1990s had access to *My Weekly Reader* while in elementary school.) The publication, four-to-eight pages in length, was aimed at improving reading skills and developing responsible citizenship through knowledge of current events. It was also carefully scheduled to reach classrooms on Friday afternoons, when both students and teachers needed a distraction.

Johnson, who received a master's degree from Columbia in 1932, was also involved with the publication of *Current Events* and other newspapers for American Educational Press, and authored a number of educational textbooks. After her retirement in 1965, she served as a consultant to Xerox Educational Publications. She died in 1987, age 94.

Johnson, Eliza McCardle

(1810–1876)

First lady of the U.S. from 1865 to 1869, who taught her husband to read and write and endured separation and hardship to promote his political career. Born on October 4, 1810, in Leesburg, Kentucky; died on January 15, 1876, in Greeneville, Tennessee; only daughter of John McCardle also seen as McArdle or McCardell (a shoemaker and innkeeper) and Sarah (Phillips) Mc-

Cardle; married Andrew Johnson (1808–1875, 17th president of the U.S., 1865–69), on May 17, 1827, in Greene County, Tennessee; children: Martha Johnson Patterson (1828–1901); Mary Johnson Stover (1832–1883); Robert Johnson (1834–1869); Charles Johnson (1830–1863); Andrew Johnson, Jr., called Frank (1852–1879).

Eliza McCardle Johnson was born in Leesburg, Kentucky, in 1810 and grew up in poverty, working alongside her widowed mother to earn enough money for a basic education. She married Andrew Johnson when she was only 17 and set out to teach her illiterate young husband how to read and write in the back room of his small tailor shop in Greeneville, Tennessee. A frugal housewife, Eliza carefully managed her husband's earnings until there was enough for him to begin his political climb, which progressed from local to state legislature, Congress, and eventually the vice presidency.

Johnson's rise to success did not always include Eliza, who during the early years stayed behind with five children and continuing financial woes. Once while Andrew was serving as a border state senator during the Civil War, secessionist sympathizers in Greeneville threw her out of her home with the claim that her husband was a traitor. She and the children wandered around for a month until they were finally reunited with Johnson. The ordeal ruined her health.

By the time Johnson was sworn in as president after the assassination of Abraham Lincoln, Eliza was too ill with tuberculosis to function as first lady. She lived in constant fear that her husband, who was considered by many to be a drunkard, and by a few to be a fellow conspirator in Lincoln's assassination, would also be assassinated. In the White House, she took up residency on the second floor, surrounded by her large family, including five grandchildren. Eliza appeared at only two official functions during her tenure; a reception for Queen *Emma of Hawaii (then called the Sandwich Islands), and one for children honoring her husband's 60th birthday. Most social duties were carried out by her daughters, ☙➤ Martha Johnson Patterson and ☙➤ Mary Johnson Stover. Always feeling inferior about her humble beginnings, Eliza excused herself by explaining, "We are plain people from the mountains of Tennessee, brought here through a national calamity. We trust too much will not be expected of us."

When Johnson's liberal policies for reconstruction in the South, and the subsequent dis-missal of Secretary of War Edwin M. Stanton, resulted in impeachment, Eliza insisted that the White House routine go on as usual. She kept abreast of daily trial proceedings from her upstairs rooms and remained optimistic throughout the ordeal. When her husband won acquittal—by only one vote—she exclaimed, "I knew it."

At the end of Johnson's term, the family returned to Tennessee. Eliza lived to see her husband vindicated by election to the Senate in 1875, but he died that same year. Eliza, who survived him by only six months, died in 1876. She

☙➤ **Patterson, Martha Johnson** (1828–1901)

*White House hostess. Born Martha Johnson in 1828; died in 1901; daughter of *Eliza McCardle Johnson (1810–1876) and Andrew Johnson (1808–1875, 17th president of the U.S., 1865–69); sister of *Mary Johnson Stover (1832–1883); married David Trotter Patterson (1818–1891, a judge of the circuit court of Tennessee and later U.S. senator), in 1885; children: two.*

The eldest of the five Johnson children, Martha Johnson Patterson acted as White House hostess for her ailing mother. She refurbished the White House after the wear and tear of the Civil War years. Martha received guests on Monday afternoons along with her sisters, a tradition that was continued even during Johnson's impeachment trial. It is said that Martha milked the family cow on the White House lawn. In 1885, Martha married David Trotter Patterson, judge of the circuit court of Tennessee, who would later become a senator. They had two children. Martha Patterson died at age 73 and is buried at the Andrew Johnson National Cemetery.

☙➤ **Stover, Mary Johnson** (1832–1883)

*White House hostess. Name variations: Mary Johnson Brown. Born Mary Johnson in 1832; died in 1883; daughter of *Eliza McCardle Johnson (1810–1876) and Andrew Johnson (1808–1875, 17th president of the U.S., 1865–69); sister of Martha Johnson Patterson (1828–1901); married Daniel Stover (1826–1864), a colonel; married William Ramsey Brown (divorced); children: (first marriage) three.*

Four years younger than her sister, Mary Johnson Stover's first husband, Colonel Daniel Stover, was killed in the Civil War, leaving her with three small children. During the Johnson administration, she provided care for her mother *Eliza McCardle Johnson while her sister *Martha Johnson Patterson handled most of the social duties. Mary's second husband William Ramsey Brown was a widower whose first wife was a second cousin of Abraham Lincoln. After seven years of marriage, they divorced. Mary Stover died at age 51 and is buried at the Andrew Johnson National Library.

Eliza McCardle Johnson

is buried with her husband and children at the Andrew Johnson National Cemetery in Greeneville, Tennessee.

SOURCES:

Healy, Diana Dixon. *America's First Ladies: Private Lives of the Presidential Wives.* NY: Atheneum, 1988.

Melick, Arden David. *Wives of the Presidents.* Maplewood, NJ: Hammond, 1977.

Paletta, LuAnn. *The World Almanac of First Ladies.* NY: World Almanac, 1990.

COLLECTIONS:

The Andrew Johnson Papers, Library of Congress.

Barbara Morgan,
Melrose, Massachusetts

Johnson, Ellen Cheney (1829–1899)

American prison reformer. Born Ellen Cheney on December 20, 1829, in Athol, Massachusetts; died on June 28, 1899, in London, England; only child of Nathan Cheney (an agent of a cotton mill) and Rhoda (Holbrook) Cheney; attended public schools in Weare, New Hampshire; attended an academy in Francestown, New Hampshire; married Jesse Crane Johnson (a businessman); no children.

Born in Athol, Massachusetts, and educated in Weare and Francestown, New Hampshire, re-

former Ellen Cheney Johnson taught school before her marriage to Jesse Crane Johnson, a salesman 12 years her senior. Settling in Boston, where her husband later opened a wholesale clothing firm, Johnson became a leading figure in civic affairs and, during the Civil War, was active in the U.S. Sanitary Commission. As a founder of the New England Women's Auxiliary Association, and a member of its executive and financial committees, she traveled to cities and towns across Massachusetts, collecting money and supplies for the war effort. After the war, when it was decided to distribute the surplus funds to veterans' widows and children, Johnson was assigned to the most depressed area of the city, the North End. Her search for dependents often led her to correctional institutions in South Boston, East Cambridge, and Deer Island, in the Boston Harbor. It was during this time that her attention was drawn to the plight of women prisoners, who were often incarcerated under the most deplorable conditions. She began to gather together women within her community (some of whom were her co-workers in the Sanitary Commission), to address the need for a permanent, separate penal institution for women. In 1874, Johnson helped establish the Temporary Asylum for Discharged Female Prisoners in Dedham, Massachusetts, but her years of effort did not come to full fruition until 1877, when legislation was passed authorizing the establishment of the Massachusetts Reformatory Prison for Women in Sherborn, Massachusetts. In January 1884, Johnson, who had served as a member of the state prison commission since 1878, resigned her position to become superintendent of the reformatory.

Ellen Johnson strongly believed in the justness of punishment. She once declared before the National Prison Association that "no lesson is more important than that which teaches respect for law, and dread of its wrath." But she was benevolent in her approach, establishing an institution that incorporated some of the most enlightened practices of her day. Her rehabilitative program for women included work on the institution's independent vegetable and livestock farms, classes in domestic skills and child care, basic schooling for those who needed it, compulsory reading assignments, and both indoor and outdoor recreational activities. She also instituted a program which provided supervised outside domestic employment for women prisoners when feasible. There was even a temperance club for those women reaching the highest level of their rehabilitation. (Johnson had embraced the temperance movement as a girl, and it remained a major interest throughout her life.) In her personal relationships with the inmates, Johnson preferred not to know about a prisoner's history and treated each as an individual with no past, only a hopeful future. The prisoners responded with the utmost respect for her leadership. "No one outside can have more than the remotest conception of . . . her executive ability and her great influence," wrote one prisoner. "Her heart is just overflowing with kindness and charity. She unites mercy with unflinching justice as I believe very few could."

Although Johnson had originally accepted her post for only one year, her tenure stretched to 15 years, during which time the Sherborn facility became a model institution. Ellen Cheney Johnson died on June 28, 1899, while in London for a congress of the International Council of Women. Her replacement at the Massachusetts Reformatory Prison for Women was **Frances A. Morton**. In 1911, Morton's successor, ***Jessie Donaldson Hodder**, had the word "Prison" deleted from the name of the institution.

SOURCES:

James, Edward T., ed. *Notable American Women, 1607–1950.* Cambridge, MA: The Belknap Press of Harvard University Press, 1971.

McHenry, Robert, ed. *Famous American Women.* NY: Dover, 1983.

Barbara Morgan,
Melrose, Massachusetts

Johnson, Esther (1681–1728)

Irish woman immortalized as Jonathan Swift's "Stella." Name variations: Hetty Johnson. Born in 1681; died in Dublin, Ireland, on January 28, 1728; daughter of William Temple's steward; probably secretly married to Jonathan Swift (the satirist), in 1716.

The diplomat, Sir William Temple of Moor Park, in Surrey, England, was related by marriage to Jonathan Swift's mother **Abigail Errick Swift**. For ten years, Jonathan Swift became his amanuensis "for board and twenty pounds per year" (1689–99). About five years into Swift's stay, he "made love to a very pretty dark-eyed young girl who waited on Lady Giffard," wrote Lord Macaulay. Little did Temple "think that the flirtation in his servants' hall, which he perhaps scarcely deigned to make the subject of a jest, was the beginning of a long unprosperous love which was to be as widely famed as the passion of Petrarch or of Abelard. . . . **Lady Giffard**'s waiting-maid was poor Stella."

Stella was in actuality Esther Johnson, who was referred to as Stella in Swift's correspon-

dence and in his *Journal to Stella.* Esther had been only eight when Swift arrived in the household; she was eighteen by the time he left. During those years, Swift devoted himself to study. In 1695, he also undertook the education of Johnson, who grew to be well-read under his direction. At that time, he was about 30, Johnson 14.

He was "perpetually instructing her in the principles of honor and virtue," wrote Swift; "from which she never swerved in any one action or moment of her life. She was sickly from her childhood until about the age of fifteen; but then grew into perfect health and was looked upon as one of the most beautiful, graceful and agreeable young women in London, only a little too fat. Her hair was blacker than a raven, and every feature of her face in perfection."

In 1700, Johnson followed Swift to Ireland, and it is generally supposed that the two were secretly married in the garden of the deanery by the bishop of Clogher in 1716, though in her will, drawn up in December 1727, she refers to herself as Esther Johnson, spinster. Esther Johnson died the following year at age 47 and was buried in St. Patrick's in Dublin. Swift was buried beside her after his death in 1745.

*E*sther
*J*ohnson

Johnson, Georgia Douglas (1877–1966).

See Women of the Harlem Renaissance.

Johnson, Helen Kendrick (1844–1917)

American author, editor, and anti-suffragist. Name variations: Mrs. Rossiter Johnson. Born Helen Louise Kendrick on January 4, 1844, in Hamilton, New York; died on January 3, 1917, in New York City; daughter of Asabel Kendrick and Anne Elizabeth (Hopkins) Kendrick; tutored at home; attended Oread Institute, Worcester, Massachusetts, 1863–1864; married Rossiter Johnson (a newspaper editor), in May 1869; children: two who died young, although she may have had others.

Selected works: Roddy's Romance *(1874);* Tears for the Little Ones: A Collection of Poems and Passages Inspired by the Loss of Children *(edited by Johnson, 1878);* Our Familiar Songs and Those Who Made Them *(1881);* Illustrated Poems and Songs for Young People *(edited by Johnson, 1884);* Raleigh Westgate; or Epimenides in Maine *(a novel, 1889); (with H. P. Smith)* A Dictionary of Terms, Phrases, and Quotations *(1895);* Women and the Republic *(articles and arguments against woman suffrage, 1897); (editor)* Great Essays *(1900);* Mythology and Folk-Lore of the North American Indian *(1908).*

Born in 1844, in Hamilton, New York, and raised there and in Rochester and Clinton, New York, Helen Kendrick Johnson was tutored by her father, a professor of Greek, and spent a year at Oread Institute in Worcester, Massachusetts. She married journalist Rossiter Johnson in 1869, and the couple settled in Concord, New Hampshire, where he edited the *New Hampshire Statesman* until 1873. They then moved to New York City.

Johnson's earliest works were a series of children's stories, the "Roddy" books, followed by *Tears for the Little Ones,* written after the death of her first two children to ease her own grief and to help other parents in a similar situation. Other books for children followed, including *Our Familiar Songs and Those Who Made Them* (1881), a collection of ancient and current ballads that remained in print for a long time, and her six-volume collection of epigrams known as the "Nutshell" series (1884), published under the titles: *Philosophy, Wisdom, Sentiments, Proverbs, Wit and Humor, Epigram and Epitaph.* These were subsequently published in a single volume, *Short Sayings of Famous Men* (1884).

During her tenure as editor of the *American Woman's Journal* from 1894 to 1896, Johnson became active in the suffrage movement. However, she later changed her position and became an outspoken anti-suffragist. A collection of her articles and arguments against suffrage, *Women and the Republic,* published in 1897, was harshly attacked. Johnson rejected the arguments concerning women's equality with men on the grounds that women were already superior. Johnson also contributed to *Appleton's Annual Cyclopaedia,* which her husband edited from 1883 to 1902. Her last work centered on Indian folklore. Helen Kendrick Johnson died in New York City on January 3, 1917.

SOURCES:
Mainiero, Lina, ed. *American Women Writers.* NY: Frederick Ungar, 1980.

McHenry, Robert, ed. *Famous American Women.* NY: Dover, 1983.

Barbara Morgan,
Melrose, Massachusetts

Johnson, Helene (b. 1907).

See Women of the Harlem Renaissance.

Johnson, Lady Bird (1912—)

American first lady from 1963 to 1969, known for her national conservation and beautification campaign. Name variations: Claudia Alta Johnson. Born Claudia Alta Taylor in Karnack, Texas, on December 12, 1912; one of three children and only daughter of Thomas Jefferson Taylor (a merchant and politician) and Minnie Lee (Patillo) Taylor; attended St. Mary's Episcopal School for Girls, Dallas, Texas; University of Texas, B.A. in liberal arts (1933), B.A. in journalism (1934); married Lyndon Baines Johnson (1908–1973, president of the U.S., 1963–1968), on November 17, 1934, in San Antonio, Texas; children: Lynda Bird Johnson Robb (b. 1944); Luci Baines Johnson Nugent Turpin (b. 1947).

Lady Bird Johnson entered the White House in the aftermath of a national tragedy—the assassination of President John F. Kennedy—and had to replace one of the most admired and emulated women of the modern era, ***Jacqueline Bouvier Kennedy.** But Johnson held her own and emerged as a highly respected first lady, compared favorably with ***Eleanor Roosevelt** and ***Abigail Adams.** Throughout the turbulent period of the Vietnam War and racial unrest on the home front, Johnson was both helpmate and foil for her high-spirited and controversial husband. She worked tirelessly in support of the President's War on Poverty, especially in promotion of the Head Start program for underprivileged preschoolers. She is remembered primarily, however, for her own zeal to protect the natural resources of the country, which she accomplished through an ambitious national conservation and beautification campaign. Even when slowed by arthritis and the failing eyesight of advancing age, she still stubbornly advocates the cleaning of the countryside.

Christened Claudia Alta Taylor in 1912, then nicknamed by the family nurse who thought she was "as purty as a Lady Bird," Johnson grew up in an antebellum brick mansion in the remote town of Karnack, Texas, the daughter of a wealthy merchant. Her mother died when she was five, leaving her in the care of

Opposite page

$\mathcal{L}$ady $\mathcal{B}$ird

$\mathcal{J}$ohnson

her maternal Aunt Effie, who traveled from Alabama to help raise her. With her much older brothers away at school most of the time, Johnson endured a lonely childhood and grew into an extremely shy teenager. Bright and well read, however, she graduated third in her high school class and spent two years at St. Mary's Episcopal School for Girls, a junior college in Dallas, before entering the University of Texas in Austin. There, she blossomed, receiving her B.A. in 1933, and staying on to receive a second degree in journalism the following year. Hoping for an adventuresome career as a newspaper reporter, she was instead swept off her feet by Lyndon Johnson, whom she met at the office of a mutual friend. Lyndon, then executive secretary to U.S. Representative Richard M. Kleberg of Texas and often described as a character out of a western movie, proposed the next day. Claiming she had "a moth-and-the-flame" feeling about him, Johnson was only able to hold him at bay for two months. After the wedding, her father was said to have remarked, "Some of the best deals are made in a hurry."

The Johnsons began married life in a small one-bedroom apartment in Washington, where Lyndon continued as a congressional secretary. In 1935, upon his appointment as a state administrator of the National Youth Administration, they moved to Austin, where, in 1937, he ran successfully for a congressional seat. The campaign was financed by Johnson, who borrowed $10,000 against her inheritance from her well-to-do mother. During World War II, while Lyndon served with the navy, Johnson managed his Congressional office in Washington. The experience instilled new confidence in her, and, in 1943, she purchased a small debt-ridden radio station, KTBC, in Austin. Within six months, under her full-time management, the station began to show a profit. Twenty years later, it had grown to a multimillion-dollar radio and television enterprise, the Texas Broadcasting Corporation.

Ten years into her marriage, after suffering several miscarriages (one of which almost killed her), Johnson gave birth to her daughter *Lynda Bird Johnson in 1944; *Luci Baines Johnson was born in 1947. When Lyndon became a candidate for the Senate in 1948, Lady Bird became an integral part of his campaign, recruiting, handling mail, and supervising campaign workers. Although he won by a margin of only 87 votes, he eventually became one of the most powerful men in the history of the Senate. Lady Bird became a popular Washington hostess, celebrated for her Southern charm and self-effacing wit. When Lyndon suffered a serious heart attack in 1955, she

managed his Washington office, keeping her husband informed of events in the capital and the nation. When he became a vice-presidential candidate in 1960, she assumed greater responsibilities in the campaign, traveling over 35,000 miles and prompting Edward Kennedy to proclaim that it was Lady Bird and not Lyndon that carried Texas in the election. As the wife of the vice president, Johnson became an ambassador of good will, making trips to over 30 nations. The couple entertained foreign dignitaries in a luxurious French château in Washington ("The Elms") and at the rambling LBJ ranch near Johnson City, which they bought in 1951.

The assassination of President Kennedy on November 22, 1963, made Johnson's transition to first lady a painful and sorrowful affair. She and Lyndon were in the presidential caravan as it traveled through Dallas the day Kennedy was shot. Hours later, she stood by her husband's side in the cabin of Air Force One, where he was sworn into office as president. Her first days in the White House were marked by a somber surreal feeling, followed by the inevitable comparisons to her predecessor. During the successful 1964 campaign, she undertook a whistle-stop tour of the South aboard "The Lady Bird Special," which covered over 1,600 miles and made 47 stops. By 1965, comfortable as first lady in her own right, she had begun to impress her friendly Texas style on official events, which often took the form of informal barbecues. Social occasions during Johnson's tenure included White House wedding receptions for both of her daughters.

Johnson's chief project—conservation—got under way with the formation of The First Lady's Committee for a More Beautiful Capital and the White House Conference on Natural Beauty. Her Highway Beautification Act of 1965 was dubbed the "Lady Bird Act" and, though generally well-received, was not without its detractors. Her efforts to outlaw billboards along the highways met with some resistance from commercial-interest groups and prompted a cartoon by Bill Mauldin of the *Chicago Sun-Times,* depicting a road heavily lined with signs, one of which read "Impeach Lady Bird."

As an advocate of the Discover America program, Johnson undertook what came to be known as "Lady Bird Safaris," one of which was a four-day trip in a raft down the Saddle River. The first lady's press secretary *Liz Carpenter, who accompanied her on many of her grueling cross-country treks, described her as having "a touch of velvet, with the stamina of steel." This duality often went unseen by biographers. Jan

Jarboe Russell's portrayal of Johnson in *Lady Bird: A Biography of Mrs. Johnson* is remarkably different from the somewhat "pitiable" woman portrayed in Robert Caro's multivolume series on Lyndon Johnson.

By 1968, reaction to the Vietnam War and racial tension at home precluded a run for a second term and had left Lyndon a broken man. In 1969, the couple returned to their Texas ranch, where Johnson continued her beautification and conservation efforts. After Lyndon's death in 1973, she worked on the development of the Lyndon Baines Johnson Library and Museum in Austin. In 1976, she was part of the Salute to America effort and also campaigned for her son-in-law Chuck Robb in his Senate race against Oliver North. (For one fund-raising dinner, she reputedly delivered no less than eight members of her husband's former Cabinet.) She was also appointed to the University of Texas Board of Regents, which she considered her most important accomplishment on her own.

In 1988, Johnson moved to Austin but continued to maintain the LBJ ranch, which in 1972 was deeded, along with 200 acres of ranchland, to the National Park Service, with the provision that the Johnsons be allowed to live there until their death. Her life is rich with longtime friends and grandchildren. In the 1990s, Johnson participated in the dedication of the National Wildflower Research Center, 10 miles outside Austin, the culmination of a dream that began in 1982 with her donation of 60 acres of land and $125,000 to commemorate her 70th birthday. When questioned about her legacy of beauty, she is apt to shrug it off, calling it simply rent for her space in the world.

SOURCES:

Johnson, Marilyn. "In the Bloom of Life," in *Life.* Vol. 19, Issue 4. April 1995, pp. 48–59.

Melick, Arden Davis. *Wives of the Presidents.* Maplewood, NJ: Hammond, 1977.

Moritz, Charles, ed. *Current Biography.* NY: H.W. Wilson, 1964.

Paletta, LuAnn. *The World Almanac of First Ladies.* NY: World Almanac, 1990.

SUGGESTED READING:

Johnson, Lady Bird. *A White House Diary.* NY: Holt, Rinehart and Winston, 1970.

Russell, Jan Jarboe. *Lady Bird: A Biography of Mrs. Johnson.* NY: Scribner, 1999.

Barbara Morgan,
Melrose, Massachusetts

Johnson, Luci Baines (b. 1947)

American first daughter. Name variations: Luci Nugent; Luci Turpin. Born Luci Baines Johnson in 1947;

youngest daughter of *Lady Bird Johnson (b. 1912) and Lyndon Baines Johnson (1908–1973, president of the U.S., 1963–1968); married Patrick Nugent, in 1966 (divorced 1979); married Ian Turpin (a banker), in 1984; children: (first marriage) five.

Following her marriage to Patrick Nugent, Luci Baines Johnson had to drop out of the Georgetown School of Nursing; undergraduates were not allowed to be married. Divorced and remarried, she raised five children and, with her second husband Ian Turpin, managed the Johnson family radio and real estate concerns in Texas. In 1994, Luci Johnson enrolled at St. Edward's University in Austin, determined to have her degree; she graduated with a 4.0 GPA. "These accomplishments," she told *People Weekly* in 1997, "are *mine*. They weren't given to me by inheritance."

Johnson, Lynda Bird (b. 1944)

First daughter of the U.S. Name variations: Lynda Johnson Robb. Born Lynda Bird Johnson in 1944; daughter of Lady Bird Johnson (b. 1912) and Lyndon Baines Johnson (1908–1973, president of the U.S., 1963–1968); married Charles S. Robb (U.S. senator), in 1967; children: three.

Lynda Bird Johnson was born in 1944, the daughter of *Lady Bird Johnson (b. 1912) and President Lyndon Baines Johnson. At that time, her father had been a congressional representative for seven years. "Growing up in politics is a seesaw kind of life," said Robb. "Although I enjoyed some of the privileges of being a congressional child, most of all I remember the separations: Daddy and Mother were always away. Luci and I were raised by other loving people, and our parents called often to remind us we were loved."

Lynda campaigned with her parents and began giving speeches during the 1960 presidential race. When her father became vice president, she felt like a "small fish in a very big pond." Then came her years in the White House where her mail was read, her phone calls were monitored, her anonymity was lost, and her every move analyzed in the press.

In a 1967 White House ceremony, Lynda Bird Johnson married Charles S. Robb, a future U.S. senator. She became a contributor to the *Ladies' Home Journal* and raised her family. An activist like her mother, Lynda Robb campaigned for Reading is Fundamental, a national

organization aimed at motivating children to read, and against high infant mortality rates.

SOURCES:
"Politician's Daughter, Politician's Wife," in *Ladies' Home Journal*. October 1978.

Johnson, Martha (1828–1901).

See Johnson, Eliza for sidebar on Martha Johnson Patterson.

Johnson, Osa (1894–1953)

American explorer, film producer, author, and big game hunter. Born Osa Helen Leighty on March 14, 1894, in Chanute, Kansas; died on January 7, 1953, in New York, New York; daughter of Ruby (Holman) Leighty and William Leighty; attended Chanute High School; married Martin Johnson, on May 15, 1910 (killed, January 13, 1937); married Clark H. Getts, on April 29, 1939 (divorced 1949); children: none.

Met Martin Johnson (1905), who would accompany Jack London on the voyage of the Snark *(1907–09); graduated from Chanute High School (1910); captured by cannibals (1912); produced her first motion picture with Martin (1912); returned to the Solomon Islands (1914); explored Northern Borneo (1917–19); went on first expedition to Africa (1921); discovered Lake Paradise (1921); secured sponsorship from George Eastman and the American Museum of Natural History (1924); began construction of home at Lake Paradise (1924); visited by duke and duchess of York (1925); visited by George Eastman (1925); became a licensed pilot (1929); purchased Sikorsky airplanes (1932); led an expedition through East Africa to obtain footage for film* Stanley and Livingstone *(released, 1939).*

Selected publications: I Married Adventure *(Philadelphia: J.B. Lippincott, 1940);* Four Years in Paradise *(Philadelphia: J.B. Lippincott, 1941).*

Osa Johnson, the well-known explorer and big game hunter, was born Osa Leighty in 1894 and grew up in rural Kansas, the daughter of a railway engineer; her formal education was limited to the local high school in Chanute. At age seven, she asked her father for ten cents, a significant amount of money in 1901, to have a picture of her brother taken by a traveling photographer. Her father hesitated. "All my father earned was a dollar and a quarter a day," Johnson later recalled. "Ten cents would buy a pound of round steak or a gallon of kerosene, or a peck of potatoes, or two yards of calico." At length, Johnson's father agreed, and Osa Johnson had the photograph taken by Martin Johnson, her future husband.

Five years later, Martin Johnson read that author Jack London was planning an expedition to the South Seas aboard the *Snark,* a ship built by London. Managing to secure employment as the cook, Martin sailed out of San Francisco Bay on April 23, 1907. After a voyage of more than 25,000 miles across the Pacific, and visits to Hawaii, the Solomon Islands, Fiji, and Australia, Martin returned to the U.S. with enough money to open three theaters in Independence, Kansas. He also brought with him photographs of the trip, which he showed to theater audiences. As fate would have it, a friend of Osa's worked in one of Martin's theaters. When the friend fell ill, Osa was recruited to take her place as a singer.

Shortly thereafter, 16-year-old Osa Leighty, who had never traveled more than 30 miles from her home in Chanute, Kansas, married the 26-year-old adventurer Martin Johnson. Her expectations of married life soon proved to be wildly different from those of her husband. "I looked forward to a happy, quiet, married life, with children and a cozy home in a small city," she wrote. "Then one day Martin came home and said we were going to sell everything and see the world." For the next two years, the Johnsons roamed America. Martin showed photographs of his *Snark* adventures to vaudeville audiences, while Osa added local color by performing Hawaiian dances and songs taught to her by her husband.

In 1912, the couple journeyed to the Solomon Islands, where the natives still practiced cannibalism. In their luggage, they carried a hand-cranked movie camera, 1,000 feet of film, a rifle, and two revolvers purchased with their life savings. The Johnsons were anxious to photograph the cannibals of Malekula Island but were repeatedly warned against making the attempt. Authorities suggested they visit a less dangerous spot, where they could stage scenes with local inhabitants pretending to be cannibals. The couple refused.

Landing on Malekula, the Johnsons encountered a group of islanders. As Martin filmed the scene, the natives beckoned the couple forward. The crew of their boat refused to follow. In a jungle clearing, the Johnsons were confronted by Nagapate, the local cannibal chief. After attempting to bribe Nagapate with trade goods, Osa was seized. A struggle ensued, in which the couple made a hasty escape, pursued by shrieking warriors. Martin managed to shoot his entire stock of film. Wrote Osa:

> At no time since Martin and I started our adventures together can I remember anything to exceed the anxiety we felt over our exposed film. . . . Light in the tropics offered problems not found in the temperate zones, and what we had—or didn't have—we couldn't possibly know.

The footage was successfully developed in Australia. Upon their return to the United States, the couple presented *Captured by Cannibals* to astonished audiences. The proceeds of the film allowed them to outfit their next expedition.

The Johnsons returned to the Solomon Islands in 1914, intent on producing a complete film record of the cannibals of Malekula. This time they landed on Malekula with a trustworthy party of armed men. Perhaps awed by this display of force, Chief Nagapate was cooperative, not to mention considerably charmed by Osa Johnson. She remembered that "every day he laid gifts of wild fruit, coconuts and yams at the door of the hut. . . . He followed me about . . . and I grew increasingly uneasy." The Johnsons shot thousands of feet of film, then sold the rights to *Cannibals of the South Seas* to the Robertson-Cole Company. The film opened to capacity audiences on Broadway. The company also agreed to finance a film on the head hunters of Borneo.

Between 1917 and 1919, the Johnsons traversed the interior of Borneo, filming the natives. So concerned were British officials with Osa's safety that they insisted a police escort, an interpreter, and a government launch travel with the couple. Martin Johnson began the expedition by filming the indigenous wildlife of Borneo. As occurred on many occasions, animals, this time water buffaloes, took exception to their presence and charged the party. Wrote Osa:

> Frightened at what seemed the certain destruction of our one and only motion picture camera, and with it the end of our expedition . . . I let out a scream that for noise and shrillness must have been startling indeed, for the lead buffalo threw up his head and swerved off, the rest of the herd following him.

The Johnsons also captured the activities of local villagers on film. The inhabitants demonstrated the use of blowguns and the parang, a machete-like weapon upon which hung the scalps of their victims.

During the 1920s, the couple's interests focused increasingly on Africa. When they arrived in Kenya in 1921, Nairobi came as a surprise. Osa remembered their first sight of the Kenyan capital fondly:

> For no reason I can think of I had expected to see a somewhat squalid tropical village

Osa
Johnson

such as we had found in the South Seas, and I was totally unprepared for the clean, white, modern city it proved to be. Our taxi took us smoothly over paved streets flanked by office buildings and department stores and let us out at a hotel.

The Johnsons quickly adapted to life in Africa. Both learned how to hunt. Osa, however, proved the more adept of the two and became a crack shot. She was soon providing security for her husband as he filmed the wildlife of the African plains. On numerous occasions, she saved his life. She also became an accomplished hunter. During their first year in Kenya, Martin perfected the use of blinds for wildlife photography.

At the suggestion of game warden Blaney Percival, the couple set off to explore an uncharted lake in the north. On their journey, they passed Mount Kenya, rising majestically out of the plains, and photographed their first rhinos and lions.

Against all odds, the Johnsons found the lake. Every conceivable animal could be found at the water's edge. "It's paradise," Osa remarked, while standing on a hilltop. And so the lake received its name. After pitching camp, they set to work. The Johnsons stayed at Lake Paradise for three months, during which they shot thousands of feet of film. Their financial resources exhausted, the couple returned to Nairobi.

Martin conceived an ambitious plan to spend the next four years at Lake Paradise, recording the vanishing wildlife of Africa. However, the couple were in no financial position to raise the necessary funds. In 1922, they returned to the U.S. and sought out George Eastman, founder of the Eastman-Kodak Company. After some discussion, the industrialist agreed to invest $10,000 in the scheme. The Johnsons also secured the sponsorship of the American Museum of Natural History.

On December 1, 1923, they set sail for Africa once more. By the spring of 1924, with the help of native labor, the Johnsons began construction on their compound at Lake Paradise, assembling several out-buildings, including a modern photographic laboratory. Osa went to great lengths to make their new home as comfortable as possible; the results were surprisingly pleasant, she recalled:

> Our living room was fourteen by seventeen feet, with a big screened veranda across the front, and our bedroom, fifteen feet square, boasted a large pink stucco bathroom which opened off the end wall. I was delighted to find the clay which gave us this delicate shade. In no time at all, of course, I had put frilled sash curtains at all the windows.

In due course, Osa added a bountiful garden and discovered that asparagus, spinach, black cranberries, coffee, and mushrooms grew wild in the surrounding forest.

The couple settled into a regular routine, completing their documentary record of the area's wildlife. As Osa explained:

> During the rains, when water was available on desert and plain, we could be found there in our blinds, photographing gazelle, ante-lope, giraffe, zebra, wart-hog and lion. During the drier weather, we divided our time among the numerous waterholes and the forests about Lake Paradise where steadily we built up a film record of the buffalo, rhino and, most important of all, the elephant.

The Johnsons were not completely isolated. In 1925, they received a visit from the duke and duchess of York (*Elizabeth Bowes Lyon). The royal couple, having seen several of the Johnsons' films, was anxious to meet them. The duke, later George VI, was especially intrigued by the Johnsons' photographic equipment. Martin attempted to give the future king a crash course in filmmaking; a year later, Osa received a letter from the duke informing her that he had purchased several cameras and was attempting to master them. The royal couple was equally impressed by Osa and Martin Johnson's ambitious project to develop a film library of African wildlife.

No sooner had the duke and duchess taken their leave than a message appeared announcing the imminent arrival of George Eastman and Daniel Pomeroy of the American Museum of Natural Science. Pomeroy, the curator of the African Hall, announced his intention of completing the museum's collection of African animals. As Osa was given the task of filling out the institution's impala collection, her skill as a hunter came in handy. The visit was an unqualified success, with Eastman spending much of his time experimenting with his newly developed 16mm cine camera. The Johnsons then undertook a film study of lions. Deciding that Nairobi was better suited as a base than Lake Paradise, they rented a large house on the outskirts of the city.

On May 16, 1927, the couple arrived in New York City and began to edit their lion footage into separate versions for commercial and institutional release. While there, they were offered several lucrative personal-appearance contracts but declined them all. Instead, the Johnsons decided to return to Africa in the company of Eastman. The 75-year-old industrialist was in failing health, and his fondest wish was to visit the continent once more.

After spending several months with Eastman, the couple traveled to the Serengeti Plains to photograph more lions, using night photography to round out their film record. Osa explained the technique:

> The method followed was to set four flash lamps on firmly planted poles about six feet above the ground, then fasten the cameras securely to solid platforms three feet in front of and below each lamp. These were connected with dry batteries and controlled by a

long "firing" wire. The cameras, especially made for the purpose, took pictures automatically at a speed of one-three-hundredths of a second when the light from the flash was at its maximum.

In 1929, the Johnsons were joined in Africa by a sound crew. Their film *Simba* had just been released in the U.S. to popular acclaim. The first wildlife filmmakers to employ sound in their productions, the Johnsons produced a film on gorillas, *Congorilla,* shot in the Belgian Congo.

Back in the U.S., the couple purchased two Sikorsky monoplanes, which they christened *Osa's Ark* and *Spirit of Africa,* and became licensed pilots. Sailing to Cape Town, South Africa, they landed on January 23, 1933, along with their disassembled aircraft. They then flew *Osa's Ark* and *Spirit of Africa* to Kenya and built an aircraft hangar in Nairobi. The use of airplanes gave Osa Johnson undreamt-of freedom:

> Mountains, jungle, plain, were a vast panorama beneath us; great elephant migrations, herds of thousands, also flocks of white herons and countless giraffe and plains game were spotted one moment from the air and the next moment were being recorded by our cameras. We were able to land in ordinarily inaccessible places where white men had never been, and here saw natives of strange, remote tribes.

Because of Osa's health, the Johnsons' stay in Africa was cut short, and they returned to America. After Osa's release from a hospital, the couple undertook a series of speaking engagements. Disaster struck on January 13, 1937. On a return flight from a speaking engagement in Salt Lake City, Utah, the Western Air Express plane they were traveling on crashed near Los Angeles. Martin was killed and Osa, along with 11 others, was injured.

In later years, Osa Johnson maintained a busy schedule: she designed toy animals for the National Wildlife Federation, published several children's books, and assumed the presidency of Martin Johnson Pictures, the couple's production company. In 1938, she led an expedition through East Africa to obtain footage for 20th Century-Fox's production of *Stanley and Livingstone,* a film that starred Spencer Tracy.

Two years after Martin's death, she married Clark Getts, but the union lasted only a decade. Despite a heart condition, Osa Johnson displayed an irrepressible wanderlust. She considered "everything in the city so artificial" and was planning another expedition to Africa just before she died in New York City on January 7, 1953.

Although the films of Osa and Martin Johnson provided a glimpse into worlds previously unknown to their audience, they betrayed a distinctly eurocentric point of view, which marks them as both quaint and dated. The films she and her husband produced neither sought to seriously interpret the cultures or the animals they recorded, nor did they attempt any profound anthropological or environmental analysis. As Donald Pickens noted, Osa Johnson's contribution to exploration was "explaining exotic places to a mass audience. She did not challenge the cultural and racial assumptions of her day. Guides and porters remained 'black boys,' and her Africa was nearly identical to Hollywood's." The Johnsons were first and foremost popularizers of the nature and travelogue genre of filmmaking. Even so, Osa and Martin Johnson pioneered the use of sound recordings and aerial photography in documentary film production. Many museums screened their films, and the Johnsons were popular staples of the lecture circuit.

SOURCES:

Garraty, John A., ed. *Dictionary of American Biography.* Vol. 5. NY: Scribner, 1957.
Johnson, Osa. *Four Years in Paradise.* Philadelphia, PA: J.B. Lippincott, 1941.
Moritz, Charles, ed. *Current Biography Yearbook.* NY: H.W. Wilson, 1940.
Who Was Who in America. Vol. 3. Chicago, IL: A.N. Marquis, 1966.
Woolf, S.L. "A Quarter Century of Jungle Adventure," in *The New York Times.* April 21, 1940.

SUGGESTED READING:

Imperato, Pascal James, and Eleanor M. Imperato. *They Married Adventure: The Wandering Lives of Martin and Osa Johnson.* NJ: Rutgers University Press, 1992.
Johnson, Osa. *I Married Adventure.* Philadelphia, PA: J.B. Lippincott, 1940.

RELATED MEDIA:

Baboona (78 min.), Martin Johnson Pictures, 1935.
Congorilla (74 min.), Martin Johnson Pictures, 1932.
Stanley and Livingstone (101 min.), starring Spencer Tracy, Cedric Hardwicke, Richard Greene, and *Nancy Kelly, 20th Century-Fox, 1939.

Hugh A. Stewart, M.A.,
University of Guelph, Guelph, Ontario, Canada

Johnson, Pamela Hansford

(1912–1981)

British novelist, dramatist, and critic. Born Pamela Hansford Johnson on May 29, 1912, in Clapham, London, England; died on June 18, 1981, in London, England; daughter of Reginald Kenneth and Amy Clotilda (Howson) Johnson; granddaughter of actor C.E. Howson; educated at Clapham County Secondary School; married Gordon Neil, an Australian journalist, in 1936 (divorced 1949); married C.P.

Snow (a novelist), in 1950; children: (first marriage) a son and a daughter; (second marriage) a son.

Selected writings: This Bed thy Centre *(1935);* Too Dear for My Possessing *(1940);* Winter Quarters *(1943);* An Avenue of Stone *(1947);* A Summer to Decide *(1949);* Catherine Carter *(1952);* An Impossible Marriage *(1954);* The Unspeakable Skipton *(1959);* The Humbler Creation *(1959);* An Error of Judgement *(1962);* Night and Silence—Who is Here? *(1965);* Cork Street, Next to the Hatter's *(1965);* The Honours Board *(1970); (memoirs)* Important to Me *(1974);* A Bonfire *(1981).*

Pamela Hansford Johnson was born on May 29, 1912, in London, England, granddaughter of actor C.E. Howson. She published her first poetry at age 14, and left school after her father died when she was 16. Believing that "a course in [English Literature] has rotted many a promising writer," Johnson claimed never to have regretted the early end to her formal education and credited Aldous Huxley's *Texts and Pretexts* for giving her a solid grounding in English and French literature. After acquiring secretarial skills, she worked in a bank and, in 1934, won a poetry prize for "Symphony for Full Orchestra." Johnson was involved for a time with writer Dylan Thomas, but they decided against marriage and parted as friends. In 1936, she married Australian journalist Gordon Neil and had two children before divorcing him in 1949. A year later, she married novelist C.P. Snow, with whom she had one son.

Johnson's first novel was *This Bed thy Centre* (1935), which received both critical acclaim as well as notoriety for its frank sexuality. Her next few novels did not make much of a mark, but in 1940 she was noticed again for *Too Dear for My Possessing*, the first of a trilogy that also included *An Avenue of Stone* (1947) and *A Summer to Decide* (1949). Besides novels, she wrote seven plays and six radio plays; was a reviewer for *John o' London's*, the *Daily Telegraph*, and the *Sunday Chronicle*; and wrote a pamphlet on novelist *Ivy Compton-Burnett* for the British Council. She also wrote a book about the infamous Moors Murders committed by *Myra Hindley* and Ian Brady, titled *On Iniquity* (1961).

In 1969, Johnson helped found the Migraine Trust, having suffered from migraines for several decades. She was also a fellow of the Royal Society of Literature and was named Commander of the Order of the British Empire in 1975. Her last book, *A Bonfire*, was published two months before she died on June 18, 1981.

SOURCES:

Buck, Claire, ed. *The Bloomsbury Guide to Women's Literature.* NJ: Prentice Hall, 1992.

Shattock, Joanne. *Oxford Guide to British Women Writers.* Oxford University Press, 1993.

Karina L. Kerr, M.A.,
Ypsilanti, Michigan

Johnson, Pauline (1861–1913).

See Johnson, E. Pauline.

Johnson, Virginia E. (1925—)

American psychologist and sociologist. Name variations: Virginia Johnson Masters; Virginia E. Johnson-Masters. Born Virginia Eshelman in Springfield, Missouri, on February 11, 1925; daughter of Hershel Eshelman and Edna (Evans) Eshelman; attended Drury College, Springfield, as a music student, 1940–42; attended University of Missouri, 1944–47; attended Washington University, St. Louis, 1964; honorary D.Sc., University of Louisville, 1978; married George Johnson, on June 13, 1950 (divorced, September 1956); married William Howell Masters (a professor of obstetrics and gynecology and author), on January 7, 1971 (divorced 1992); children: (first marriage) Scott Forstall Johnson; **Lisa Evans Johnson.**

Worked on St. Louis Daily Record *(1947–50); worked at radio station KMOX, St. Louis (1950–51); employed with division of reproductive biology, department of obstetrics and gynecology, Washington University School of Medicine (1957–63), research instructor (1962–64); served as research associate, Masters and Johnson Institute (formerly Reproductive Biology Research Foundation), St. Louis (1964–69), assistant director (1969–73), co-director (1973–94); director of the Virginia Johnson Masters Learning Center, St. Louis (starting 1994); served on advisory board, Homosexual Community Counseling Center.*

Selected writings, all with William H. Masters except as noted: Human Sexual Response *(1966);* Human Sexual Inadequacy *(1970);* The Pleasure Bond *(1975);* Homosexuality in Perspective *(1979);* Textbook of Sexual Medicine *(1979);* Textbook of Human Sexuality for Nurses *(1979);* Sex Therapy and Research *(Vol. 1, 1977, Vol 2., 1980); (with Robert Kolodny)* Crisis: Heterosexual Behavior in the Age of AIDS *(1988).*

Although she possessed no academic credentials, Virginia Johnson wanted to study sociology; in 1957, she became a research assistant to William Masters, a professor of obstetrics and gynecology at Washington University School of

Medicine in St. Louis. Together they researched the physiology and psychology of modern sexual behavior, a subject which had begun to receive serious attention only with the first famous "Reports" of Alfred Kinsey in the late 1940s and early 1950s. At the Reproductive Biology Research Foundation in St. Louis, Masters and Johnson compiled information on human sexuality which both documented the sexual revolution of the 1960s and made their names part of the American lexicon. Although their research was sometimes controversial, it also helped to develop new treatments for sexual dysfunction. Johnson and Masters divorced in 1992 and closed their St. Louis institute in 1994. Together, they had published several works based on their research, including *Human Sexual Response* (1966), *Human Sexual Inadequacy* (1970), *The Pleasure Bond* (1975), and *Crisis: Heterosexual Behavior in the Age of AIDS* (with Robert Kolodny, 1988).

Karina L. Kerr, M.A.,
Ypsilanti, Michigan

Johnson-Masters, Virginia (b. 1925).

See Johnson, Virginia E.

Johnston, Anna (1866–1902).

See MacManus, Anna.

Johnston, Annie Fellows
(1863–1931)

*American writer. Born on May 15, 1863, in Evansville, Indiana; died in Pewee Valley, Kentucky, on October 5, 1931; daughter of Albion Fellows (a Methodist minister) and Mary (Erskine) Fellows; older sister of **Albion Fellows Bacon** (1865–1933); attended University of Iowa for one year (1881–82); married William L. Johnston, in October 1888 (died 1892); children: three stepchildren.*

With the death of her husband Albion Fellows, a Methodist minister, Mary Erskine Fellows took her three daughters, including two-year-old Annie and her baby sister Albion, to live in the tiny country town of McCutchanville, Indiana, where they grew up with their ten cousins. Annie attended the district school, wrote stories and poems, read through the Sunday School library, and became a teacher in the public schools of Evanston.

After traveling in New England and Europe, the 25-year-old Annie married her cousin William L. Johnston, a widower with three children, in a double ceremony with her sister Albion

who married Hilary E. Bacon. Three years later, William Johnston died; Annie Fellows Johnston was now a widow with three stepchildren. Fortunately, throughout the years, Johnston had continued to dabble at writing and had sold stories to *Youth's Companion*. With a household to support, she turned seriously to her hobby. By 1894, she had published *Big Brother*; in 1895, she added *Joel: A Boy of Galilee*.

During a visit to Pewee Valley, near Louisville, Kentucky, where her children had relatives, Johnston chanced upon a small girl who had the temperament of her Confederate colonel grandfather. Enchanted by the antebellum atmosphere of the South at the turn of the century, Annie returned home and wrote the first of her popular 12-volume series of *The Little Colonel* (1896). All told, Johnston would write over 50 books; her output sold over 1 million copies.

From 1901 to 1910, in the hopes of a finding a better climate for an ailing stepson, she moved her brood to Arizona, then to California and Texas. After her stepson's death in 1910, she settled in Pewee Valley and lived there the rest of her life.

SUGGESTED READING:
Johnston, Annie Fellows. *The Land of the Little Colonel: Reminiscence and Autobiography*. 1929.

RELATED MEDIA:
The Little Colonel was filmed by 20th-Century Fox in 1935 and starred *Shirley Temple (Black)*, Lionel Barrymore, *Hattie McDaniel, and Bill "Bojangles" Robinson.

Annie Fellows Johnston

Johnston, Frances Benjamin
(1864–1952)

American photographer who specialized in documentaries, portraits, and architectural and garden photographs. Born Frances Benjamin Johnston on January 15, 1864, in Grafton, West Virginia; died on May 16, 1952, in New Orleans, Louisiana; only child of Anderson Dolophon Johnston (a bookkeeper at the Treasury Department) and Frances Antoinette (Benjamin) Johnston; graduated from Notre Dame Convent, Gov-

anston, Maryland, in 1883; studied drawing and painting at the Julien Academy, Paris, France, 1884–85; studied at the Art Students League, Washington, D.C.; studied photography with Thomas William Smillie, director of the Division of Photography at the Smithsonian Institution; never married; no children.

One of America's earliest documentary photographers, Frances Johnston was born in Grafton, West Virginia, in 1864, but grew up in Rochester, New York, then Washington, D.C., where her father was head bookkeeper at the Treasury Department. Her mother was distantly related to *Frances Folsom Cleveland, which may have accounted for Johnston's later access to the White House. Johnston originally planned to become an artist, and, after graduating from Notre Dame Convent in 1883, she went to Paris to study drawing and painting at the Julien Academy. She returned to Washington in 1885, continuing her studies as a member of the Art Students League. Around that time, she decided to go into journalism. Taking a job with a New York magazine, she illustrated her articles with her own drawings until 1887, when she obtained her first camera. After a brief unsatisfactory apprenticeship with a commercial photographer, she began studying with Thomas William Smillie, who was then director of the Division of Photography at the Smithsonian Institution.

Johnston's first published photographs appeared in *Demorest's Family Magazine* in 1889; they accompanied an article she wrote on the U.S. Mint. She set up her studio in the rose garden behind her father's Washington house, where she produced portraits in addition to her assignments from periodicals and the daily press. During the 1890s, Johnston began photographing the White House, publishing her early interior shots in *The White House* (1893). She continued photographing the executive mansion and celebrities from Washington's political and social circles for the next 15 years, documenting five administrations and earning the title of "Photographer of the American Court." Johnston also created portraits of other distinguished Americans, including Alexander Graham Bell, Mark Twain, Andrew Carnegie, *Jane Cowl, and *Susan B. Anthony.

Once established in her career, Johnston became a champion of women in photography. In 1897, she published an article in the *Ladies' Home Journal,* "What a Woman Can Do with a Camera," urging women to consider photography as a career choice. Later, in 1900, she organized an important exhibition of 142 prints by

26 American women photographers which was presented at the same time as the Exposition Universelle in Paris. The exhibition then traveled to St. Petersburg and Moscow, returning for public exhibition at the Photo Club of Paris in January 1901. Johnston subsequently wrote a series of articles on the exhibition's women photographers for the *Ladies' Home Journal* (1901–02).

Much of Johnston's documentary work focused on industry and education, areas of particular interest to the Progressive reformers of her time, many of whom, like her friend Jacob Riis, were personal acquaintances. In 1891, in conjunction with *Demorest's,* she visited the Kohinoor Mines at Shenandoah City, Pennsylvania, to study the effects of industrialization on the workers. She also photographed an ore-mining operation on Lake Superior and a cigar-box and shoe factory in Massachusetts.

In 1900, Johnston won a gold medal at the Paris Exposition with a series of photographs of the Washington, D.C., school system and the Hampton Normal and Agricultural Institute in Virginia, a school founded during Reconstruction to prepare African-Americans, as well as Native Americans, for vocational jobs. The "Hampton" series, commissioned for marketing purposes, is particularly indicative of Johnston's documentary style and her skill at showing a particular point of view, in this case, the social and economic advantages of industrial education. Her images depicting the educational activities of the Institute, often juxtaposed with photographs of the poor black families of the Virginia countryside, made a vivid statement about the advantages of a Hampton education. (In 1966, the Museum of Modern Art would mount an exhibit of a group of photographs from the Hampton Institute series.) Johnston also produced photographs of the Carlisle (Pennsylvania) Indian School (1900), and the Tuskegee Institute (1902 and 1908), founded by Booker T. Washington, who had actually been educated at Hampton. At Tuskegee, Johnston's goal was to convey the idea that blacks could build and administrate an institution of their own.

Through her documentary and portrait work of the 1890s, Johnston joined the vanguard of artistic photographers of the time. She was chosen, along with her contemporary *Gertrude Käsebier, to sit on the jury for the Philadelphia Photographic Society exhibit of 1899, the first year an all-photographer jury judged a major photographic exhibition. According to Jerald C. Maddox of the Prints and Photographs Division of the Library of Con-

Frances
Benjamin
Johnston

gress, "this was a revolutionary step that not only suggested that photographers might be aesthetically sensitive, but also implied that in this respect they might be the equals of artists in the traditional media." In 1904, Johnston became an associate member of the Photo-Secession, a group organized by Alfred Stieglitz to promote photography as a fine art.

Little is known about Johnston's personal life and relationships; her papers (17,000 pieces of correspondence held by the Manuscript Division of the Library of Congress) reveal little outside of business details or notes concerning her work. Some of her papers suggest that she was often so absorbed in taking pictures that she let business matters slip. She sometimes failed to open her bills and occasionally did not see her assignments through to the end, particularly if another interesting project came up. In a letter dated 1899, her agent expressed some frustration: "You have caused me serious losses by not delivering promptly prints of pictures which I knew had been taken," he wrote.

Devoted to her career, Johnston never married. She had a wide circle of friends, including many actors, poets, and artists from the bohemian set in Washington, who referred to themselves as "The Push." They frequently gathered in her studio for parties, or just good talk and wine. In their biography *A Talent for Detail*, Pete Daniel and Raymond Smock point out that during the 1890s, Johnston really lived two lives, moving between the strict social constraints of official Washington and the freer, less confined world of her friends. That she did so

with ease is testimony to an engaging personality that apparently served her well in both business and social encounters. Another of Johnston's attributes may have been her sense of humor, which is evident in a widely circulated self-portrait dated around 1896, in which she expresses her disdain of Victorian formality. Perched on a box in front of her studio fireplace, Johnston is seen in profile, one leg crossed over the other revealing a ruffled petticoat and a long expanse of stocking, a cigarette in one hand and a beer stein in the other.

Around 1910, Johnston began to move away from photojournalism into garden and architectural photography. From 1913 to 1917, she had a studio in New York with her friend **Mattie Edward Hewitt**. Their first contract to photograph the New Theater in New York led to commissions from architects, businesses, and estates, including those of J. Pierpont Morgan and John Jacob Astor IV. By 1920, Johnston was also in demand as a lecturer on gardens, and that year began an ambitious speaking tour from Cleveland through the Midwest into California.

From "Public School Series," Washington, D.C., 1900, by Frances Benjamin Johnston.

WOMEN IN WORLD HISTORY

The final phase of Johnston's career began in the 1930s, when she received back-to-back Carnegie grants to photograph Southern architecture. Her goal was not to photograph prominent buildings and homes but to seek out "the old farm houses, the mills, the log cabins of the pioneers, the country stores, the taverns and inns, in short those building that had to do with the everyday life of the colonists." The project netted some 7,000 negatives, some of which were published in two books: *The Early Architecture of North Carolina* and *The Early Architecture of Georgia*.

In 1940, Johnston retired to New Orleans, purchasing a house on Bourbon Street and transforming its rundown courtyard into an attractive garden. Only slightly slowed by age, she still lectured occasionally and maintained a small darkroom in an alcove off her bathroom. As a concession to her doctors, she switched from bourbon to cherry wine, which she sipped in establishments along the French Quarter. In 1947, she donated her prints, negatives, and correspondence to the Library of Congress, which held an exhibit of her work. The photographer died on March 16, 1952, at the age of 88.

Although Johnston was a pioneer in photojournalism, and one of only a handful of women in her era to take up photography as a business, she is not credited with any technical or artistic innovations. Daniel and Smock point out that once Johnston found a technique that worked, she tended to stick with it. "Perhaps her genius was in doing the ordinary exceptionally well," they conclude. Whatever the scope of her talent, Johnston maintained consistently high standards as a professional and provided a rich and lasting visual history of the times in which she lived.

SOURCES:

Bailey, Brooke. *The Remarkable Lives of 100 Women Artists.* Holbrook, MA: Bob Adams, 1994.

Daniel, Pete, and Raymond Smock. *A Talent for Detail: The Photographs of Miss Frances Benjamin Johnston 1889–1910.* NY: Harmony Books, 1974.

Rosenblum, Naomi. *A History of Women Photographers.* NY: Abbeville Press, 1994.

Sicherman, Barbara, and Carol Hurd Green, eds. *Notable American Women: The Modern Period.* Cambridge, MA: The Belknap Press of Harvard University Press, 1980.

Barbara Morgan,
Melrose, Massachusetts

Johnston, Harriet Lane (1830–1903).

See Lane, Harriet Rebecca.

Johnston, Henrietta (c. 1670–1728)

Irish-born artist who was possibly the first woman artist in America. Born Henrietta Deering before 1670, probably in Ireland; died in Charleston, South Carolina, on March 7, 1728 (some sources cite 1729); married Gideon Johnston (a cleric of the Church of England), on April 11, 1705; children: several stepchildren.

If ever art was born of necessity, it is the art of Henrietta Johnston, who produced some 40 pastel portraits of distinguished citizens of Charleston, South Carolina, during the early 18th century and, in doing so, provided income for her struggling family. Little is known of her life until her marriage to Reverend Gideon Johnston in Dublin, Ireland, in April 1705. At the time, Gideon, a cleric of the Church of England and a widower with several children, was heavily in debt. In 1707, after Gideon had procured an appointment as rector to a church in Charleston (then Charles Town), the Johnstons sailed for America, hoping for a brighter future.

The voyage, however, was marked by misfortune. Staying ashore too long during a stopover in the Medieras, Gideon missed the ship, and so Henrietta and the children sailed into Charleston without him. While attempting to reach port, he was marooned for 12 days on an offshore island without food or water. When he was finally rescued and brought ashore, half dead from exposure, he found that another cleric had taken over his church. It took several months of negotiations before he regained control of his congregation.

During her husband's prolonged recovery, Johnston acted as his nurse and secretary while also managing the children and household. Charleston, unlike the Eden the Johnstons had imagined, turned out to be a primitive village with muddy roads, legions of ill-mannered inhabitants, and swarms of swamp mosquitoes, from which Henrietta soon contracted malaria. While caring for her husband and tending to her own chronic illness, Johnston somehow managed to supplement the family's income by drawing portraits of the local citizens. Some of her early pictures are of her doctor and his family, and, according to art historian **Margaret S. Middleton**, may have been produced as payment for medical care. Johnston's role as bread-winner is also evident in a letter written by Gideon to Bishop Gilbert Burnet in 1709: "Were it not for the assistance my wife gives me by drawing of pictures (which can last but a little time in a place so ill peopled) I shou'd [sic] not have been able to live." Johnston further assisted her husband by returning to England (1711–12) and obtaining a missionary appointment for him. When Gideon made a trip to England himself (1713–15), Johnston, in his absence, survived two hurricanes and the onset of the Indian wars, during which time she took in some of the throngs of frightened refugees that poured into Charleston.

Johnston's portraits were executed on sheets of 9x12 paper, in pastel chalk that she may have brought from Ireland, as she would have been unable to purchase it in America at the time. Her works are described as crude but competent likenesses, "direct and uncompromising," notes art historian **Anna Wells Rutledge**. Rutledge theorizes that Johnston may have studied with amateur portraitist Simon Digby, bishop of Elphin, her husband's superior in Ireland. Whatever her schooling, Johnston's use of pastels is surprising, as the medium was very new even in Europe, where Italian artist ***Rosalba Carriera** (1675– 1757) had only recently established it as a viable art form.

In 1716, Gideon Johnston was drowned in a boating mishap on Charleston Bay. Little is known of what happened to Henrietta Johnston after that, though there is evidence that at one point she traveled to New York to visit friends. Several pastels attributed to her are signed "New York" and dated 1725. Johnston was back in Charleston by 1727, as the register of the Parish of St. Philip's Church, Charleston, records her burial on March 7, 1928.

Mary Johnston

SOURCES:

James, Edward T., ed. *Notable American Women, 1607–1950.* Cambridge, MA: The Belknap Press of Harvard University Press, 1971.

Rubinstein, Charlotte Streifer. *American Women Artists.* Boston, MA: G.K. Hall, 1982.

Barbara Morgan,
Melrose, Massachusetts

Johnston, Mary

(1870–1936)

American novelist who wrote the bestselling To Have and To Hold. *Born on November 21, 1870, in Buchanan, Virginia; died on May 9, 1936, near Warm Springs, Virginia; eldest of six children of John William Johnston* (a lawyer and major in the Confederate Army) and Elizabeth (Alexander) Johnston; *never married; no children.*

Selected works: Prisoners of Hope *(1898);* To Have and To Hold *(1900);* Audrey *(1902);* Sir Mortimer *(1904);* The Goddess of Reason *(a play, 1907);* Lewis Rand *(1908);* The Long Roll *(1911);* Cease Firing *(1912);* Hagar *(1913);* The Witch *(1914);* The Fortunes of Garin *(1915);* The Wanderers *(1917);* Foes *(1918);* Pioneers of the Old South *(non-fiction, 1918);* Michael Forth *(1919);* Sweet Rocket *(1920);* 1492 *(1922);* Silver Cross *(1922);* Croatan *(1923);* The Slave Ship *(1924);* The Great Valley *(1926);* The Exile *(1927);* Hunting Shirt *(1931);* Miss Delicia Allen *(1933);* Drury Randall *(1934).*

Mary Johnston, the author of 23 historical novels, including her best-known, *To Have and To Hold,* was born in 1870 in Buchanan, Virginia. She grew up in Buchanan, and in New York and Birmingham, Alabama. Due to poor health, she was educated at home by her grandmother and by reading from her father's extensive library. After her mother's death in 1889, Johnston took charge of the household which included five younger siblings. She never married and, following her father's death, settled permanently in Richmond, Virginia. Later, she built a large country estate in Warm Springs, Virginia, where she lived with three of her sisters and her brother, all of whom also remained single.

Johnston began writing stories at an early age, sending them to publishers and often burning them upon their initial rejection. Her first historical novel, *Prisoner of Hope* (1898), achieved moderate notice, but her second, *To Have and To Hold* (1900), about the women of the Jamestown colony, was a phenomenal success. Selling a half-million copies, it was also adapted for the screen several times. Twenty-one additional historical novels followed, which explored such diverse subjects as Henry VII's England, 12th-century feudal France, and Christopher Columbus' voyage to the New World. In addition to her novels, all meticulously researched, Johnston published a volume of history, *Pioneers of the Old South* (1918), and a blank-verse drama, *The Goddess of Reason* (1907), which was produced in New York in 1909, starring ***Julia Marlowe**. She also wrote poetry and magazine stories.

Described as a shy, serious woman, Johnston was an ardent feminist and in 1909, with ***Ellen Glasgow**, founded the Equal Suffrage League in Richmond. She was also involved in a number of other progressive organizations, including the Consumers' League, the National Municipal League, and the Women's International League for Peace and Freedom. Johnston also used her talent as a writer to further the cause of women's rights, producing a number of articles for popular journals, such as the *Atlantic Monthly*. **Dorothy M. Scura**, in *American Women Writers*, points out that female emancipation was also the theme of Johnston's novel *Hagar* (1913), a story about a contemporary Southern writer who goes to New York to work for the rights of women. It was hailed by some critics as "the *Uncle Tom's Cabin* of the women's movement." In a later feminist work, *The Wanderers* (1917), Johnston traces the changing relationships between men and women from early days up until the French Revolution through a series of 19 sketches.

Johnston's earlier works, however, are considered her best, among them two Civil War novels, *The Long Roll* (1911) and *Cease Firing* (1912), which trace two Virginia families through the epic war. Beginning with her sociological novels in 1913, Johnston's readership began to wane, and her later works, some of which ventured into mysticism, confused critics and readers alike. Although criticized for her melodramatic plots and romantic prose style, Johnston, at her best, stands as a consummate historical storyteller. Mary Johnston died of cancer on May 9, 1936, near Warm Springs.

SOURCES:

Contemporary Authors. Vol. 109. Detroit, MI: Gale Research.

Mainiero, Lina, ed. *American Women Writers*. NY: Frederick Ungar, 1980.

Weatherford, Doris. *American Women's History*. NY: Prentice Hall, 1994.

Barbara Morgan,
Melrose, Massachusetts

Johnstone, Anna Hill (1913–1992)

American costume designer in theater, film, and television, who was nominated for Academy Awards for The Godfather *and* Ragtime. *Name variations: Anna Hill Johnstone; Anna Johnstone Robinson. Born in Greenville, South Carolina, in 1913; died in Lennox, Massachusetts, on October 15, 1992; daughter of Albert Sidney Johnstone (a banker) and Anna Hill (Watkins) Johnstone; Barnard College, B.A., 1934; honorary degree from Barnard College in 1974; married Curville Jones Robinson (a mechanical engineer), on May 8, 1937 (died 1989).*

Filmography as costume designer: Portrait of Jennie *(1948);* On the Waterfront *(1954);* East of Eden *(1955);* Baby Doll *(1956);* Edge of the City *(1957);* A Face in the Crowd *(1957);* Odds Against Tomorrow *(1959);* Wild River *(1960);* Splendor in the Grass *(1961);* David and Lisa *(1963);* America, America *(1963);* Ladybug, Ladybug *(1964);* The Pawnbroker *(1964);* Fail Safe *(1964);* The Group *(1966);* Bye Bye Braverman *(1968);* The Night They Raided Minsky's *(1968);* Alice's Restaurant *(1969);* There Was a Crooked Man *(1970);* Cotton Comes to Harlem *(1970);* Who Is Harry Kellerman? *(1971);* The Godfather *(1972);* Play It Again, Sam *(1972);* Come Back, Charleston Blue *(1972);* The Effect of Gamma Rays on Man-in-the-Moon Marigolds *(1973);* Summer Wishes, Winter Dreams *(1973);* Serpico *(1973);* The Taking of Pelham One, Two, Three *(1974);* Gordon's War *(1973);* The Stepford Wives *(1975);* Dog Day Afternoon *(1975);* The Last Tycoon *(1975);* The Next Man *(1976);* The Wiz *(1978);* King of the Gypsies *(1978);* Going in Style *(1979);* Prince of the City *(1980);* Ragtime *(1981);* Daniel *(1983);* Heaven *(1983);* Running on Empty *(1988).*

Anna Johnstone was born in Greenville, South Carolina, in 1913. She began her costume career helping student productions during college and working as a seamstress in summer stock. In 1937, Johnstone received her first full credit for costuming for the Broadway hit *Having Wonderful Time*. Her stage productions included *Bell, Book, and Candle, Lost in the Stars, Tea and Sympathy, The Tender Trap,* and *A Streetcar Named Desire.*

Johnstone began working for films in 1948 with *Portrait of Jennie*, starring *Jennifer Jones. In the next 40 years, Anna Hill Johnstone designed costumes for over 60 films and some television, working frequently with directors Elia Kazan and Sidney Lumet. Besides her Academy Award-nominated films *The Godfather* and *Ragtime*, her film credits include *Serpico, The Wiz, On the Waterfront, East of Eden, America, America, Prince of the City, The Verdict, Running on Empty, Baby Doll, Edge of the City, Dog Day Afternoon, The Group,* and *A Face in the Crowd.* While working on *The Group* in 1965, Johnstone spoke of how she would often find just the right clothes for a period piece by rummaging through the attics and closets of her friends in the Bronx and by scouring thrift shops on the East Side of Manhattan. She also revealed that she sometimes had to change what was scripted for technical reasons, such as substituting satin for taffeta to avoid rustling noises on the soundtrack. Johnstone died at the Kimball Farms nursing home in Lennox, Massachusetts, age 79.

SOURCES:

"Obituary," in *The Day* [New London, CT]. October 19, 1992.

Malinda Mayer,
writer and editor, Falmouth, Massachusetts

Johnstone, Hilda Lorne (b. 1902)

English equestrian. Born in England in 1902.

In 1972, at age 70, Hilda Johnstone was the oldest athlete to compete in the Munich Olympic Games; she placed 12th as a member of the British riding team. Johnstone had also finished 21st in the 1956 Olympics, and 13th in 1968.

Jolande.

Variant of Yolande.

Jolanta.

Variant of Yolande.

Jolanta (fl. 1100s)

*Princess of Hungary. Flourished in 1100s; daughter of *Helena of Serbia* and Bela II, king of Hungary (r. 1131–1141); married Boleslas the Pious, of Kalisz.*

Jolanthe.

Variant of Yolande.

Jolanthe of Lorraine (d. 1500)

*Landgravine of Hesse. Died on May 21, 1500; daughter of *Yolande of Vaudemont* (1428–1483) and Ferrey de Vaudemont also known as Frederick, count of Vaudemont; sister of *Margaret of Lorraine* (1463–1521); married William II, landgrave of Hesse, on November 9, 1497.*

Jolas, Betsy (1926—)

French-American composer, one of France's best-known. Born Elizabeth Jolas in Paris, France, on August 5, 1926; daughter of Maria Jolas (a publisher, editor, and journalist) and Eugene Jolas (who founded transition, *an international literary review, with Maria's help); had one sister, Maria Christina Jolas known as* Tina Jolas; *studied at Bennington College with Karl Weinrich and* Hélène Schnabel *and at the Paris Conservatoire with Darius Milhaud, Olivier Messiaen, and* Simone Plé Caussade; *married a French physician, in 1949; three children.*

Returned to the United States at the outbreak of World War II (1940); served as editor of Ecouter Au-jourd'hui (1955–65); received the French author and composer award (1961); received the prestigious American Academy of Arts and Letters Award (1973); appointed professor of composition at the Paris Conservatoire (1978), replacing Olivier Messiaen; composed numerous orchestral works and made many recordings of these works.

Although she was born in France and has spent much of her composing career in that country, Betsy Jolas is essentially an American artist who was partially educated in the United States. Her mother *Maria Jolas was a musician, as well as a publisher and editor, and so it was not surprising that Jolas followed in her footsteps as a vocalist, pianist, organist, and composer. Betsy composed her first important piece of music at Bennington College, a full-fledged mass which was performed there. Returning to France on her 20th birthday, Jolas studied at the Paris Conservatoire and won second prize at the end of the school year in a competition for writing a fugue. Her full-time career as a composer started slowly, however, as for a while her time was taken up by three young children. From 1955 until 1965, she worked for the French radio-television network editing *Ecouter Au-jourd'hui*, a leading musical periodical. In this role, Jolas kept up with all the new musical compositions. During this time, she met Pierre Boulez and asked him to comment on her work, a turning point in her career. A year later, Boulez premiered her composition *Quatuor II* and within ten years Jolas was recognized as one of France's most important composers. Betsy Jolas' international standing continued to increase outside France and her music has been played frequently worldwide.

SOURCES:

Peyser, Joan. "Betsy Jolas and *Barbara Kolb: Why Can't a Woman Compose Like a Man?" in *The New York Times Biographical Edition*. June 1993, pp. 990–993.

Sadie, Stanley, ed. *New Grove Dictionary of Music and Musicians*. 20 vols. NY: Macmillan, 1980.

John Haag,
Athens, Georgia

Jolas, Maria (1893–1987)

American publisher, editor, translator, critic, and journalist who co-founded with her husband the Paris literary review, transition. *Born Maria McDonald in Louisville, Kentucky, in January 1893; died in Paris, France, on March 4, 1987; studied voice in Berlin, New York, and Paris, 1913–25; married Eugene Jolas in New York, on January 12, 1926; chil-*

dren: Elizabeth Jolas known as *Betsy Jolas (b. 1926, a French composer); Maria Christina Jolas known as Tina Jolas (b. 1929).

Co-founded with husband, transition, in Paris (1927); met James Joyce (December 1926); established the École Bilingue (Franco-American school) in Neuilly, France (1932); moved school to château near Vichy, France (October 1939); left France (August 1940); edited A James Joyce Yearbook (1949); published "Joyce en France 1939–40" published in Mercure de France (1950); Eugene Jolas died in Paris, France (1952).

Maria Jolas was born Maria McDonald in Louisville, Kentucky, in 1893, but lived in France during most of her adult life. "I've never felt that I was an exile, an expatriate," she noted, "and I've never had any of those feelings of being detached either from my own country or from [France]." In 1913, Maria studied voice in Berlin, but left when war broke out in 1914. At the end of hostilities, her teacher went to Paris, and Maria followed. "There was no romanticism, no chestnut trees in bloom, no April in Paris, none of those things," she characteristically recalled. She went there to study, not to escape the provincial, material, philistine culture of America that drove so many expatriates to Paris in the 1920s. Maria was an international woman, fluent in several languages, who could live and work in France without succumbing to the highly charged social life that interfered with the productivity of so many talented expatriates.

When Maria met Eugene Jolas in Paris in 1925, he was city editor of the *Paris Tribune*, "focusing upon intellectual and cultural developments" which allowed him to introduce French writers to Americans and the "real America" to Europeans. Through his articles entitled "Rambles Through Literary Paris," he came in contact with the French and expatriate avant-garde. Maria and Eugene shared an interest in literary experimentation and language. Eugene had been born in the United States, but was brought up in Lorraine, France; like Maria, he was comfortable living in Europe or America. They were married in New York and shortly thereafter moved to New Orleans where Eugene worked for a local newspaper. Their friends included many local artists and writers, and they considered taking over the literary journal *Double Dealing*. However, the Jolases did not want to appeal only to an American audience. Their aim was "to build a bridge between Europe and America, and . . . to make known to America the new aesthetic currents in Europe." This kind of endeavor, they agreed, could be done best in Paris. Thus, *transition* was founded in the fall of 1926, "the most prestigious review in Paris."

Twenty-seven issues of the review appeared from 1927 to 1938. Elliot Paul, who was literary editor for the *Paris Tribune*, served as co-editor for several years. But as Maria Jolas observed, Paul had only a "meager knowledge of French and unfamiliarity with any other foreign language [and] was only superficially aware of what was being written in Europe." Moreover, Paul, unlike the Jolases, was not an admirer of Surrealism, and he often disagreed with them about what should be included in the review—the Jolases' literary taste inevitably won out. Maria was an especially talented translator of both French and German writers; she and Eugene rendered two of Franz Kafka's works into English for the first time. They also prepared a collection of Negro spirituals, translated into French and published in Paris. As well, Maria contributed an article to *transition* in which, writes **Shari Benstock**, "she urges the Negro to fight the forces—political and literary—which had exploited him and to return to his people." Further, she encouraged blacks to "sink their roots even deeper into the rich black loam that is their heritage, lest their inspiration be withered and destroyed by transplanting in soils which are either unfertile or entirely foreign to their genius." This bold call for a genuine black voice in America was considered radical and anomalous in the late 1920s.

Maria had stated that the purpose of *transition* was "to create a meeting place for all those artists on both sides of the Atlantic" who would be given "an opportunity to express themselves freely, to experiment." *Transition* fulfilled this mission. Two writers who were featured in numerous issues were James Joyce and ***Gertrude Stein**, both residents in Paris. The Jolases had approached Joyce through a mutual acquaintance, and on December 21, 1926, Joyce invited the couple to join a few friends at his house where he read the first section of his work in progress (*Finnegans Wake*). Ten fragments of the manuscript were published in *transition*. The Jolases became close friends of James and ***Nora Joyce** and were among James' most devoted advocates, notes Benstock, "giving [Joyce] the unswerving homage of true believers." Joyce's use of language exemplified the "Revolution of the Word" proclaimed by the Jolases in *transition*: "The writer expresses, he does not communicate. The plain reader be damned," they had declared. Among the future famous writers who were introduced to the literate public through *transition* were Ernest Hemingway, Hart Crane, Samuel Beckett, Allen Tate, and Dylan Thomas.

Relations with Gertrude Stein were less amiable. Stein's experimentation with language appealed to the Jolases, and her work, including *Tender Buttons* and her operatic libretto *Four Saints,* appeared in six issues of the review. But a well-publicized falling-out with the Jolases caused a permanent break; according to Samuel Putnam, it "seems to have been due to jealousy on [Stein's] part of the space and advertising given to Joyce." Maria was also critical of Stein's penchant "to play the queen in public," and informed Stein that *transition* had not been established "as a vehicle for the rehabilitation of her own reputation, although it undoubtedly did do this." Stein was one of many women whose work was featured in *transition,* making the Jolases "an exception among literary editors of the period," Benstock writes. *Djuna Barnes, *Kay Boyle, *Laura Riding, *Katherine Anne Porter and other less well-known writers found sincere appreciation of their work from Eugene and Maria.

Maria Jolas displayed her energy and organizational skills in many areas. She was actively engaged in helping the Joyce family, not only in proofreading the numerous revisions of *Finnegans Wake,* but in their personal lives. Their daughter **Lucia Joyce** suffered from severe mental illness, and Maria, over a period of many years, arranged for her care in England and on the Continent, even after James Joyce died in 1941. Maria had arranged for the Joyces to settle near her in Vichy when the Nazis occupied Paris in June 1940, and she constantly solicited funds to aid the family when they finally sought refuge in Switzerland. Later, Joyce's biographer, Richard Ellmann, contacted Maria who shared her memories of his subject, and she read the chapters on Joyce in Paris and suggested changes.

Maria was also interested in education, especially in fostering international communication among the young. In 1932, she started a successful École Bilingue (Bilingual School) in Neuilly, a suburb of Paris. Among her students were *Peggy Guggenheim's daughter **Pegeen Vail** and the Joyces' grandson **Stephen**. In Sep-

Maria
Jolas

tember 1939, war broke out in Europe, and in October, Maria moved her school south to the village of St-Gérand-le-Puy, near Vichy. She encouraged the Joyces to join her there and found accommodations for them. Eugene was in New York, and finally in August 1940, after France fell to the Germans, Maria, her two young daughters, and the grandson of the artist, Henri Matisse, left for America via Madrid and Lisbon. She wanted the Joyces to come to the States, but James did not like America or airplanes, so he remained in Europe.

After the war, the Jolases returned to Europe. Eugene was working for the U.S. Office of War Information in Germany, and Maria settled again in France. In 1948, she sold *transition,* but she continued to do translations. Friend and translator of the writer *Nathalie Sarraute, Maria found a house near her in Chérence, on the fringe of Normandy; the villagers "had an aversion to outsiders," Sarraute's son-in-law, Stanley Karnow notes, but Maria won them over, and when Eugene died in 1952, she paid "a healthy sum" to have him buried there. In the early 1960s, Maria approached Samuel Beckett, who had been close to Joyce, to help her sort through Joyce's increasingly valuable literary estate, but he refused "saying he wanted no part of Joyce's literary remains," Indeed, Beckett had never liked Maria's "domineering manner" and had always resented her influence over the Joyce family. However, she continued to help with the organization and sale of the Joyce estate so that Nora Joyce would benefit financially.

Certainly Maria Jolas contributed to the success of *transition,* was a fervent advocate of the "Modernist movement," a loyal and caring friend, an educator, and a translator. Moreover, she raised her two daughters and worked to further her husband's literary career without sacrificing her own individuality and interests. Benstock notes that living in Paris "wore down some of the expatriates," but not Maria Jolas who, she says, "maintained her joy of living."

SOURCES:

Bair, Deirdre. *Samuel Beckett: A Biography.* NY: Summit Books, 1990.

Benstock, Shari. *Women of the Left Bank, Paris, 1900–1940.* Austin, TX: University of Texas Press, 1986.

Ellmann, Richard. *James Joyce.* NY: Oxford University Press, 1959.

Jolas, Eugene. *Man from Babel.* Edited, annotated and introduced by Andreas Kramer and Rainer Rumold. New Haven, CT: Yale University Press, 1998.

Maddox, Brenda. *Nora: The Real Life of Molly Bloom.* Boston, MA: Houghton Mifflin, 1988.

Putnam, Samuel. *Paris Was Our Mistress: Memoirs of a Lost and Found Generation.* Carbondale, IL: Southern Illinois University Press, 1970.

SUGGESTED READING:

Brennin, John M. *The Third Rose: Gertrude Stein and Her World.* Reading, MA: Addison-Wesley, 1987.

Carpenter, Humphrey. *Geniuses Together: American Writers in Paris in the 1920s.* Boston, MA: Houghton Mifflin, 1988.

Fitch, Noel Riley. *Sylvia Beach and the Lost Generation: A History of Literary Paris in the Twenties and Thirties.* NY: W.W. Norton, 1983.

Karnow, Stanley. *Paris in the Fifties.* NY: Random House, 1997.

Lottman, Herbert. *The Left Bank: Writers, Artists, and Politics from the Popular Front to the Cold War.* San Francisco, CA: Halo Books, 1991.

Paul, Elliot. *The Last Time I Saw Paris.* NY: Random House, 1942.

Jeanne A. Ojala,
Visiting Scholar, Department of History, University of Minnesota, Minneapolis, Minnesota, and Professor Emerita, Department of History, University of Utah, Salt Lake City, Utah

Joleta.

Variant of Yolande.

Joliot-Curie, Irène (1897–1956)

French physicist awarded the Nobel Prize for Chemistry, along with her husband, for the discovery of artificial radium, who was appointed a minister of France before the nation's women were allowed to vote and was dedicated to preserving the use of nuclear energy for peaceful purposes. Name variations: Irène or Irene Curie; Irene Joliot-Curie. Pronunciation: ZHol-yo KÜR-ee. Born Irène Curie in Paris, France, on September 12, 1897; died of leukemia on March 17, 1956, in Paris; daughter of Pierre Curie and Marie (Skolodowska) Curie (both famous physicists); sister of Éve Curie (b. 1904); studied at the University of Paris and worked under her mother's supervision at the Radium Institute in Paris; married Frédéric Joliot, on October 9, 1926; children: Hélène Joliot-Curie Langevin and Pierre (both physicists).

Accompanied mother to battlefield X-ray stations during World War I (1914–18); granted Ph.D. with a thesis on the alpha rays of polonium (1925); assumed joint last name with husband at time of marriage (1926); took increasing responsibility for the Radium Institute and became director (1932); awarded the Nobel Prize for Chemistry with her husband for the discovery of artificial radium (1935); as undersecretary of scientific research, one of three women in cabinet of Léon Blum, helped to establish the National Center for Scientific Research (1936); won the Barnard Gold Medal for Meritorious Service to Sci-

ence, the Henri Wilde Prize, and the Marquet Prize of the Academy of Sciences (1940); driven into hiding in France and Switzerland by husband's active role in the resistance during World War II (1940–45); appointed to the chair of nuclear science at the Sorbonne, previously held by both her father and mother; appointed to the French Atomic Energy Commission (CEA); dismissed with her husband from the CEA for communist sympathies and opposition to the use of atomic energy for nuclear weapons (1950); lobbied successfully for a new Institute of Nuclear Physics, constructed in the 1950s; given a state funeral, befitting one of the pre-eminent scientists of France (1956).

On December 10, 1911, the shy, solemn-faced girl of 14 sat in the auditorium of the Royal Academy of Music in Stockholm, watching as her mother received the Nobel Prize for Physics. Irène Joliot-Curie was already accustomed to the world of high intellectual achievement, as well as to personal tragedy and the everyday labors of science. It was the second Nobel awarded to her mother; her father, who had shared in the first, was now dead. In the past year, Irène had also lost the beloved grandfather who had raised her. Against this background, her future was similarly set along a path of hard work, considerable suffering, dedication, and high achievement.

When Irène Curie was born on September 12, 1897, her parents were still relatively unknown. Her father Pierre Curie worked in the laboratory of the School of Physics and Chemistry at the Sorbonne, developing new equipment that would eventually prove essential to all physics laboratories, and her Polish-born mother *Marie Curie, who had begun her advanced academic career at age 24, was determinedly pursuing her scientific studies at the same school. The couple had been on a bicycling vacation when it was cut short by Irène's birth; she was delivered by her paternal grandfather, Dr. Eugène Curie. It was a fortuitous beginning to the close relationship that was to develop between the French physician and his granddaughter. Widowed soon after Irène's birth, Eugène eventually moved in with his son's family.

Irène was adored by her mother, who called her "my little Queen" and kept track of her growth and the arrival of new teeth in a school notebook. But Marie Curie was also a dedicated, even driven, scientist. Although the Curies held Ph.D.s, Pierre's position at the Sorbonne did not support the family, so Marie lectured in physics at a suburban girls' school and spent hours in the laboratory doing research. Irène's grandfather became the center of her universe. Even so, she did not go to sleep at night until her mother had been to her bedside.

Irène was six the year her mother received her doctorate and both parents were awarded the Nobel Prize for Physics. Their discovery of two radioactive elements, radium and polonium, made the couple famous throughout the world, and the prize money made the family's life somewhat easier. In December 1904, Irène's sister *Éve Curie was born, and the family moved to a larger home. But in April 1906, when Irène was nine, her father Pierre died in a traffic accident.

Despite the loss of her partner, Marie Curie would not accept the offer of a pension. Instead, she accepted her husband's chair in physics and continued her work. The family moved to a house in the Paris suburb of Sceaux where Irène and her mother grew flowers, a shared passion. Her grandfather remained by her side, teaching her botany and natural history; he was "the incomparable friend . . . of that slow, untamed child so profoundly like the child he had lost," wrote Éve. Grandfather Curie died in 1910, four years after his son.

Educated in their early years by governesses who were usually Polish like their mother, the Curie sisters became fluent in French, Polish, and English and were good students in science and mathematics. Madame Curie had high academic standards, but she also believed that women must be physically fit and required that the girls get daily exercise. They often took walks or performed gymnastics on a garden crossbar with a trapeze and flying rings, and both brought home prizes for their gymnastic achievements. They also learned cooking, sewing, and modeling with clay. Although life in the household revolved around Marie's work, the family spent happy holidays cycling through the countryside or visiting the coast. In 1911, after the second Nobel Prize, the sisters visited their maternal Aunt Bronya in Poland, where they learned to ride horseback and took long mountain hikes.

Like her father, Irène was extremely shy, but her gift for mathematics and science was apparent at an early age. As her daughters outgrew the abilities of their governesses, Marie Curie, dissatisfied with available schools, decided to create her own. She set up a teaching cooperative, staffed by Sorbonne professors for their children, where students learned mathematics, chemistry, physics, and art from some of the best minds of the time and were exposed to such famous scientists as Albert Einstein.

With the outbreak of World War I, Irène thought of being a nurse in order to help with the wounded. When her mother's discovery of radium found practical use in X-ray equipment, Irène was trained to operate the equipment and worked closely with Madame Curie in radiological stations set up near the battlefront. By the end of the war, Irène knew that she wanted to be a physicist like her mother. "The fame and the achievement of her parents neither discouraged nor intimidated her," Ève wrote of her sister.

In May 1921, the sisters accompanied Madame Curie on a triumphal tour of the United States. Because their mother found the trip exhausting, Irène often had to assume her mother's social duties despite her shyness; one photograph from the period shows Irène alongside President Warren Harding at the White House as her mother is presented with a symbolic gram of radium. Back in Paris, creature comforts were of little interest to this mother and daughter, whose lives were dominated by their work at the Radium Institute, founded by Madame Curie. Ève describes a typical lunch in the family's charmless apartment on the Ile St. Louis, in which Marie and Irène sat engrossed in scientific dialogue, oblivious to their surroundings, food, or the clothes they wore.

In 1925, Irène was awarded a doctorate for her thesis on the alpha rays of polonium, the element discovered along with radium by her parents. That same year, she met a shy, handsome young man named Frédéric Joliot, regarded as the most brilliant of her mother's assistants. Frédéric idolized the work of Marie and Pierre Curie and kept their pictures in his home laboratory; with him, Irène found someone who could share her passion for science. Frédéric described Irène as "the living replica of what her father had been," and he shared her love of sports and the arts, as well as a dislike for city life. When they married, on October 9, 1926, both changed their names to Joliot-Curie and worked henceforth as equal partners, signing all their scientific papers jointly, as Pierre and Marie Curie had once done.

Because of the pioneering work of the elder Curies, an exciting world of atomic physics had opened up. Other scientists had subsequently discovered the negatively charged particle called the electron, the components of the nucleus, and the existence of various atomic isotopes. The Joliot-Curies, highly skilled in the use of radiation detectors, turned to the study of the atomic by-products created when materials like aluminum

or boron are bombarded by alpha particles, identified as positrons. Using an instrument known as the Wilson cloud chamber, they irradiated samples of boron and aluminum and observed the results. To their surprise, the positrons that they had expected to be emitted continued after the polonium source was removed, demonstrating that portions of the aluminum and boron in their exposed samples had been transmuted into elements which were radioactive and short-lived, but also entirely new and unlike any naturally occurring element. The Joliot-Curies went on to produce a large number of these artificially created radioactive elements and announced their discovery on January 15, 1934.

As a result of prolonged exposure to radioactivity, Madame Curie had meanwhile become severely ill with leukemia, and her responsibilities at the Radium Institute had passed to Irène, who became director in 1932. Before her death in July 1934, Marie Curie fully understood the extent of her daughter's achievement in research, and in 1935 Irène and Frédéric Joliot-

Irène
Joliot-
Curie

Curie shared the Nobel Prize for Chemistry "for their synthesis of new radioactive elements." Thanks to their discoveries, wrote J.W. Palmaer of the Royal Swedish Academy of Sciences, "it has become possible, for the first time, to transform artificially one element into another hitherto unknown. The results of [their] researches are of capital importance for pure science."

By this time, the couple were parents of a daughter and son, Hélène and Pierre, who would one day be physicists like their parents and grandparents. While the work of the Joliot-Curies remained intense, the family enjoyed card games, conversation, tennis, and walks with friends.

Like her mother, Irène Joliot-Curie regretted that women did not have the place in society they deserved and found time for women's issues. In 1936, under France's Popular Front government led by Léon Blum, she was appointed the country's undersecretary of state for scientific research, at a time when the women of France had not yet won the right to vote (denied until 1945). In this role, she helped lay the foundations for the National Center for Scientific Research.

Aware of radiation as the cause of Madame Curie's death, the Joliot-Curies were deeply concerned about the potential for great harm as well as good in the use of atomic energy. In his Nobel lecture, Frédéric had summed up their feelings, saying, "We are entitled to think that scientists . . . will be able to bring about transmutations of an explosive type, true chemical chaining reactions [that liberate vast amounts of usable energy]. But . . . if the contagion spreads to all the elements of our planet, the consequences of unloosing such a cataclysm can only be viewed with apprehension." In fact, the Joliot-Curies demonstrated fission in their laboratory by physical means as early as 1939. Fearful of the consequences and afraid of the growing power of Adolf Hitler in Germany, they stopped publishing papers on their discoveries.

On May 10, 1940, Hitler's German armies invaded France. Shortly before the Nazi troops rolled into Paris, the Joliot-Curies managed to ship a sample of heavy water, vital to nuclear reaction, to Britain. Frédéric had lied to Gestapo agents to get the material out of their hands. Soon after the occupation, Paul Langevin, a longtime friend of the couple, was arrested. (Their daughter Hélène would later marry his grandson, Michael Langevin.) Frédéric, meanwhile, supported by Irène, joined the French Communist Party, believing that it offered the best organized resistance against Nazi repression. "I was impressed by the generosity, courage, and hope for the future that these people in my country had," he said later. "They seemed willing to do the most to give France social reform." On the front lines of the secret resistance, Frédéric directed the manufacture of explosives and radio equipment for the resistance fighters and allowed the publication of an underground newspaper from his lab. Detection in such activities would have meant certain death at the hands of the German Gestapo, and at one point Irène and the children were forced to flee to Switzerland while Frédéric went into hiding.

After the war, many honors were bestowed on the Joliot-Curies. Both were appointed to the French High Commission on Atomic Energy, which developed French nuclear energy and weapons. Like Marie and Pierre Curie before them, they believed that scientific discoveries were worldwide property, and they wanted the work of French scientists communicated to American and Soviet scientists rather than concealed in the interest of national defense. But the Allied bombings of the Japanese cities of Hiroshima and Nagasaki near the end of the war had also reinforced their conviction that nuclear force should be used only for peaceful purposes. "Its use for destruction seemed to [mother] a desecration," said Irène. "In her eyes any political consideration would not have been an excuse to use the atomic bomb."

As the Cold War intensified, the French government grew increasingly afraid of sharing scientific discoveries with Soviet scientists. Irène meanwhile denounced scientific secrecy for its limitations on the free circulation of ideas and discoveries, and she and her husband made several trips to the Soviet Union in the hope of furthering world peace and international cooperation. They became active members of the World Peace Council, and Frédéric became its president. In the Cold War atmosphere of the West, their outlook became increasingly suspect, and in 1949, when Irène visited the United States, she was detained for a day on Ellis Island. Eventually the couple's political beliefs led to their removal from France's High Commission on Atomic Energy.

Meanwhile, the Joliot-Curies began to be dogged by radiation sickness. Irène was the first to show the symptoms but continued to be active in various world peace organizations and drew up a plan for the new nuclear physics laboratories at Orsay, where scientists could work with large particle accelerators. In 1955, the dream of this research center was realized, but by this time Irène was wasting away. "Breathing, eating, all the most elementary functions, are becoming painful," she told a friend. She died of leukemia in the Curie Hospital in Paris on March 17, 1956, followed two years later by Frédéric, who also died of leukemia. Despite the carping of some in the French government, Irène Joliot-Curie was given a state funeral, an honor befitting her scientific achievements.

Though dedicated to family and the consuming work of her lifelong research, Irène Joliot-Curie also understood that the scientific frontier is not enough. Recognizing that humans must be willing to cross new moral and ethical frontiers, she devoted time and energy to the political rights and opportunities of women, and long before there was widespread understanding of this issue, to the cause of eliminating the threat of nuclear destruction. Like many visionaries, she paid a high price for being decades ahead of the rest of the world.

SOURCES:

Curie, Éve. *Madame Curie*. NY: Doubleday, Doran, 1939.
———. "Madame la Secrétaire," in *The Living Age*. Vol. 351, no. 4440. September 1936, pp. 40–42.
Curie, Marie. *Pierre Curie*. NY: Macmillan, 1923.
Goldsmith, Maurice. *Frédéric Joliot-Curie*. London: Lawrence and Wishart, 1976.
Opfell, Olga S. *The Lady Laureates: Women Who Have Won the Nobel Prize*. 2nd ed. Metuchen, NJ: Scarecrow Press, 1986.
Pflaum, Rosalynd. *Grand Obsession: Marie Curie and Her World*. NY: Doubleday, 1989.

Karin Haag,
freelance writer, Athens, Georgia

Jolley, Elizabeth (1923—)

British-born Australian short-story writer and novelist who is considered pre-eminent in Australia and overseas for her innovative and experimental fiction. Pronunciation: JOLL-lee. Born Monica Elizabeth Knight on June 4, 1923, in Gravelly Hill, between Sutton Coalfield and Birmingham, England; daughter of Charles Wilfred Knight (1890–1977, a teacher) and Margarethe Johanna Carolina (von Fehr) Knight (1896–1979); sister of **Madelaine Winifred Knight Blackmore**; attended Bilston Girls' High School until nearly eight; studied at home and then (age 11–17) at Sibford, a Quaker boarding school near the Cotswolds; married Leonard Jolley (1914–1994, a librarian); children: Sarah Jolley; Richard Jolley; Ruth Jolley.

Entered nursing training at 17, leaving to be a housekeeper (1946–50) and, briefly, a school matron (1950); joined Leonard Jolley in Edinburgh, Scotland (1950), moving with him to Glasgow (1956); immigrated with family to Australia (1959); started writing for publication (1960s), having her first book pub-lished and becoming a university lecturer in creative writing (1970s); has produced about a book a year since then, receiving much critical acclaim and many civic, academic, and literary honors.

Awards: *State of Victoria Short Story Award for "A Hedge of Rosemary" (1965); Western Australia Week Award for Fiction and the Age Book of the Year Award for Fiction for* Mr. Scobie's Riddle *(1983); Australia Council-Literature Board grant (1983–85); New South Wales Prize for Fiction for* Milk and Honey *(1985); another Literature Board Fellowship and invitation to the Commonwealth Literary Festival and an Australian Bicentennial grant to write-publish* The Sugar Mother *(1986); honorary Doctorate of Technology from Western Australian Institute of Technology (now Curtin University, 1987); Miles Franklin Award for* The Well *(1987); Western Australian Citizen of the Year (Arts, Culture, Entertainment); Officer of the Order of Australia for Services to the Arts (1988); Canada-Australia Literary Award (1989); Age Book of the Year Award for Fiction, Royal Blind Society-3M Company Talking Book of the Year, both for* My Father's Moon *(1989); Gold Medal of the Association for the Study of Australian Literature for* Cabin Fever *(1991); Alice Award from the Western Australian branch of Society of Women Writers (1992); Western Australia Premier's Book Awards Overall prize for* Central Mischief *(1993); joint winner with* **Françoise Cartano** *of the Inaugural France-Australia Literary Award for* The Sugar Mother *(Tombé du ciel), a book in French translation (1993); Age Book of the Year Fiction Prize (1993) and National Book Council Banjo Award for fiction (1994), both for* The Georges' Wife.

Selected writings: *Five Acre Virgin and Other Stories (Fremantle Arts Centre Press, 1976); Travelling Notebook (Fremantle, 1978 and 1979); Travelling Entertainer and Other Stories (Fremantle, 1979); Palomino (Outback, 1980); Newspaper of Claremont Street (Fremantle, 1981); Miss Peabody's Inheritance (University of Queensland, 1983); Mr. Scobie's Riddle (Penguin, 1983); (stories) Woman in a Lampshade (Penguin, 1983); Milk and Honey (Fremantle, 1984); Stories (including "Self-Portrait: A Child Went Forth," Fremantle, 1984); Foxybaby (University of Queensland, 1985); The Well (Viking, 1986); The Sugar Mother (Fremantle, 1988); My Father's Moon (Viking Penguin, 1989); Cabin Fever (Penguin, 1990); The Georges' Wife (Viking, 1993); Diary of a Weekend Farmer (Fremantle, 1993).*

The dust jacket of Elizabeth Jolley's second novel, *The Newspaper of Claremont Street*, relates that she "was born in the industrial Midlands of England and brought up in a household 'half English and three quarters Viennese,' and later in a Quaker boarding school." Such quirky self-characterization, never self-aggrandizing, encapsulates themes which occur time and again in her work—in this case, working-class desperation, analogous institutions like the household and the school, and intimate situations where the parts do not quite add up.

Jolley's father Charles Knight was a pupil-teacher (someone who went directly from studying to teaching at about 14) who acquired bachelor and master of Science degrees by correspondence courses; he even sat a German examination in London when he was about 80. A Quaker when World War I was declared, he was imprisoned for several years as a conscientious objector; in addition, he was publicly turned out of the family home with only a shilling by his ill-tempered Methodist father, more because of the disgrace of imprisonment than because of his pacifist stance. Later, he went to Europe with other Quakers to distribute food, and in Vienna he met his wife-to-be, **Margarethe von Fehr**, a Montessori teacher passing out British rations to her students. The daughter of an Austrian general, she had come from a privileged background, but the aristocracy had fallen, leaving her to fend for herself. They married in Vienna and again when they returned to England. Margarethe was a lapsed Roman Catholic, obsessive about her household, generous to others but also demanding of them.

When Elizabeth Jolley was born on June 4, 1923 (also her mother's birthday), her parents were living in Sutton Coalfield, her father teaching at the Sir Josiah Mason Orphanage. Her sister Madelaine was also born there on August 20, 1924. At age six, Elizabeth commenced elementary school at the Reddicap Heath School for mixed infants. Her father then received an appointment to the Bilston Boys' Central School, a badly funded school in an area of grinding poverty and depressing sights, such as a coal mine, a brickworks, and a bone-and-glue factory. The family lived first in Wolverhampton, next in Bilston, and then in Wolverhampton again. Jolley went to the Bradmore School for a few weeks and then to the preparatory school of the Bilston Girls' High School for a year or so, Charles driving her in the sidecar of his motorcycle when they lived in Wolverhampton.

Charles helped the boys at school as best he could, for example, by arranging (and paying for) school "dinners," an excuse for seeing that they had some nourishment, and he and his wife practiced Quaker virtues at home; they once took in a miner's child during a coal-miners' strike around 1929. Their domestic life, though materially poor, was culturally rich, if sometimes strained. Charles Knight brought home a small salary as a teacher, making his modest philanthropy possible, and was otherwise didactic; believing that school "spoiled their innocence," he took his two children out of school just before Elizabeth was eight, teaching them at home, for instance, by turning their youthful walking trips into science lessons, examining bricks for what they contained and how they were manufactured. The family spoke German in the household, and there was a series of French, Swiss, and Austrian governesses who instructed the two girls in French and/or German in return for receiving tutoring in English from the Knights, and who, one after the other, quarrelled with Margarethe and were dismissed. Margarethe had her own radio, a gramophone and record collection, introducing the girls to music, and she had them copy four lines of German poetry or prose into a book every morning before breakfast. The Knights often quarrelled, she about their squalid circumstances. Further, Margarethe had a "special friend," Mr. Berrington, a barrister, who would come to dine each Sunday, discuss the father's sermons (by 1938, Charles had returned to Methodism, becoming a lay preacher), then the weather, and next listen to music with Margarethe, or read German with her, or even take her to his own house for the afternoon. Jolley would later write a piece called "Mr. Berrington."

In September of 1934, Elizabeth was sent to board until July 1940 at a Quaker school, Sibford, on the edge of the Cotswolds, an institution which prepared young people for the trades. Though homesick until her sister was sent there in 1939 and though the school was spartan in the extreme, she felt "cherished" by her teachers and was thrilled to continue her education in music, to be introduced to letter-writing and literature (Dickens, Eliot, Shakespeare, and Trollope), to be translating from French and German, and to be reading aloud. The experience left her somewhat ill-socialized (e.g., regarding contemporary dress codes) and quite isolated from world events (e.g, the Depression and the onset of World War II). About the latter she would learn more from visits home between school terms, where the family was housing refugees from Europe, something she and her sister resented because they were displaced from their room. When war was declared, her father fell to his knees praying that "No, nothing so evil would happen again."

In 1938, Elizabeth had had a summer abroad with her mother and Mr. Berrington, an experience which required her to come to terms with this supernumerary family member. (The family had been abroad fairly regularly from about 1930 while Charles studied French and German in Strasbourg.) She was sent again, alone, in 1939, innocently attending a Hitler Maiden's Camp for a two-week holiday (her parents did not believe the rumors of war) and had to hurry home from Hamburg to Hull on a cargo boat. Since boarding school had oriented her toward nursing, Jolley applied to and was accepted by the St. Thomas Hospital in London, but it had been flattened by bombs and evacuated to St. Nicholas and St. Martin's Hospital in Surrey, where she went instead. Previously a home for children crippled by conditions like scoliosis and diseases like tuberculosis, the hospital was then overfilled with injured British soldiers, as well as some injured prisoners of war. Also, just as she arrived, it was even more over-crowded with casualties from an air raid on an airplane factory, some of whom were burned while others were steam-burned. It was, she says, a *rite de passage*, "an experience that I never got over." Nursing experiences figure prominently in her trilogy.

There, Elizabeth met her husband-to-be Leonard Jolley, a patient in his mid-20s hospitalized for over two years with an illness thought to be a "tubercular hip." In fact, he had rheumatoid arthritis. Then, at the beginning of 1943, she moved to the Queen Elizabeth Hospital in Birmingham for general nursing training. In late 1946, she left to be housekeeper to a woman doctor in Edgebaston (Birmingham), and, from May through September of 1950, she was a matron at Pinewood, a progressive school in Amwellbury (Hertfordshire). Despite her title, the position was more devoted to washing, ironing, cooking, and looking after the nursery.

In 1950, Leonard Jolley had taken up a position as librarian to the Royal College of Physicians in Edinburgh, Scotland. Elizabeth joined

Elizabeth Jolley

him there and, though they had few friends, they happily enjoyed housekeeping, gardening, plays and music, but not the Edinburgh Festival which was too expensive for a librarian's salary. In 1956, he became deputy librarian in the University of Glasgow, and they moved to a larger, shabbier house in Jordanhill which their few bits of furniture filled even less than they had the previous one. They joined the East-West Society which welcomed visitors to the university, and she would house some of them, ostensibly for a week or two while they settled in, although some stayed for months, even years. These Chinese, African, Indian, and West Indian people livened up the household considerably, did much to socialize her, and allowed her and her husband to go out while some of the boarders babysat. All this time, she kept diaries; she even drafted a novel which some 30 years later became My Father's Moon.

If the Glasgow position as deputy had been a step down for Leonard Jolley, his next job would be a step up, one involving significant life changes. He was offered the position as head librarian at the University of Western Australia, then one of Australia's newer universities (established in 1911) but ultimately to be one of its wealthiest. Elizabeth's father cautioned that, at his age (45), Leonard would never be able to return to a librarian's post in the United Kingdom, a consideration which did not discourage him. In November of 1959, they arrived by ship in Perth where Leonard commenced a distinguished career: perhaps Australia's first "intellectual" head librarian, he would write an influential book (The Principles of Cataloguing, 1960), recatalogue the university's collection, oversee the construction of its new Reid Library, and nearly quadruple its holdings by the time he retired in 1979.

Both of them were struck by how different Perth was physically and socially—the bright lights, the friendliness of people. In the beginning, Elizabeth spent much time as a faculty wife, first being entertained and then, in turn, entertaining colleagues and visitors from the university. After living more than two years in a house in Parkway, almost on the UWA campus, they moved two or three miles to the suburb of Claremont where Jolley would continue to live for the rest of her life. In 1970, they also purchased five acres with a three-room-plus-verandah cottage on bushland at Wooroloo, some 40 miles east of Perth: the Newspaper dust jacket talks of her "cultivating a small orchard," and the jacket of Foxybaby extends the claim, saying that "she now cultivates a small orchard and goose farm," both genial hyperbolic descrip-

tions. In addition to being a faculty wife, increasingly she was her husband's personal nurse, for his arthritis was a lifelong illness which came more and more to affect the family, requiring his being put into a nursing home in early 1991. Until then, the Wooroloo retreat was a source of enjoyment and refreshment to all of the family members, as documented in Diary of a Weekend Farmer. (Presumably it is the setting for the farm in Palomino and the newly purchased land in Newspaper, and perhaps also the inspiration for the land which figures so prominently in short stories like "Five Acre Virgin," "Bill Sprockett's Land," and "The Jarrah Thieves.")

During the 1960s, Jolley successively held a variety of part-time jobs—the dust jacket continues by saying that "she has worked as a nurse, a door-to-door salesman (failed), real estate salesman (failed), and a flying domestic [house-cleaner]." "I wanted money for typing," wrote Jolley, "and I also wanted the discipline of a job which I could do while the children were not here." (The part-time work at a nursing home no doubt figures in a draft of Mr. Scobie's Riddle from that time, and the cleaning work centrally features in The Newspaper of Claremont Street.)

It was around 1962 that Jolley began to write with publication more consciously in mind: she has said that "I think that fiction writing was for me the creation of a life that could make up for what may be lacking in a life that I wasn't really interested in," namely "the University Wives' Club" on whose executive board she unhappily served in the 1962–68 period. At first, many cruel rejection slips resulted: "Nowhere in Australia is there a market for anything like this or an audience for anything like this," or "This is not US." During that same time, she was also given good advice by "Lucy Walker," the pen-name of *Dorothy Sanders, a popular novelist and wife of the UWA's professor of education, who instructed her on how to rewrite short stories into dramatic material to be sent to the BBC and, if rejected, to the ABC.

In 1965, Jolley had her first short story published ("The Talking Bricks," in *Kylie Tennant, ed., Summer Tales 2). In 1974—by which time Jolley had won a short-story competition and published ten stories and seven poems—Ian Templeman of the Fremantle Arts Centre asked her to teach creative-writing classes there. That was a crucial turning point, and Leonard Jolley acknowledged her new career by saying, "You will go to things there and I won't necessarily come with you. This will be something you will do on your own." After some anxiety about their functioning as separate social units, she became comfortable with the idea and even happy at not always having to prepare or to attend UWA dinners.

Her 1976 book, *Five Acre Virgin and Other Stories* (all previously broadcast by the BBC, some by the ABC), led to her being invited in 1978 to teach fiction classes at the Western Australian Institute of Technology which had started Australia's first B.A. in creative writing, a position she held continually, becoming writer-in-residence when it became Curtin University (1987). Thus from the 1970s, she had two new professions, teacher and writer, and her skill at each has been abundantly acknowledged. In 1990, Curtin University's vice-chancellor gave his foundation's Excel Award to the university's Creative Writing Group, of which Elizabeth Jolley was a key member, and, in 1993, the university named its new 600-seat lecture theater after her. Australian and overseas awards testify to her excellence, as do front-page book reviews in such places as the *Washington Post Book World, The New York Times Book Review,* and the *London Times Literary Supplement.* There are also the final indicators of universal appeal, namely big contracts, healthy sales, and translations of her books into Dutch, French, German, Icelandic, Russian, and Spanish.

A relative latecomer to publishing, Elizabeth Jolley has nonetheless experimented with form and technique from the beginning. The form of the stories and novels range from an effortless lyricism of the 1960s and 1970s (contrasting with the residual Australian impulse to realism), to metafiction in *Peabody,* to Gothic grotesquery in *Milk and Honey,* to fantasy in *Foxybaby,* and to autobiographical in the Vera Wright trilogy. And their overall tone has evolved from being parodic, even manic, to being more sober and meditative. Throughout, however, Jolley's central technique has been the art of juxtaposition, or what she teasingly describes to her students as the "sophisticated space." The technique underlies her compositional style: "I have a manila folder that I open out, and I might make little squares and write little bits in there so that the pages are actually resting on what is like a map of the structure of the book." And that structure is often quite sophisticated. *Mr. Scobie's Riddle* is based on Brahms' *Deutsche Requiem* and *Foxybaby* is informed by Dante's *Inferno.* The result is fiction that invites, in Jolley's words, "the reader . . . to weld the pieces together by the spaces."

The novels are striking, too, for their plethora of bizarre violence and aberrant sexual-

ities. Her topics not infrequently involve murder by omission or commission (*Palomino, Newspaper, Milk and Honey, The Well*). And her novels always imply or depict something of taboo sexual import. For example, promiscuity figures in *Foxybaby, My Father's Moon,* and *Cabin Fever;* bigamy is a feature of *Mr. Scobie's Riddle;* symbolic incest is central to *Palomino, Scobie, The Sugar Mother,* and the Vera Wright trilogy, and there is actual incest in *Palomino, Milk and Honey* and *Foxybaby.* Bisexuality defines two characters in *Scobie,* as does male homosexuality in *Foxybaby* and *My Father's Moon;* lesbianism is imaginable in *Newspaper,* and is foregrounded in *Scobie, Peabody, Foxybaby, My Father's Moon, Palomino, The Well,* and in the Vera Wright trilogy. The lesbian relationships in her work have, not surprisingly, attracted the most attention. The first novel Jolley sent off and had accepted (1976) was *Palomino,* but it did not appear for some years after its acceptance (1980), a half-page reader's report suddenly trailing off: "It is a story about two women."

However, Jolley's provocative topics are never chosen merely for shock value. Rather, she studies institutions for their capacity to facilitate community, and she studies individuals for their ability to attain communion. Institutions *per se* are usually found wanting, because of mindless bureaucratism, or (more frequently) because of their hijacking by desperate people who use and abuse them as a substitute for family. Characters are usually found wanting because they are locked into dysfunctional psychological patterns, some of them being obsessive caretakers who fear abandonment, others being narcissists who fear engulfment, all of them having profound problems with intimacy. Thus, Jolley's work is pessimistic to the extent that it represents social institutions, laws, and mores as restricting human relationships; and such a social institution is as likely to be the family as a school, hospital, or a nursing home. Yet her work is optimistic to the extent that it affirms that communion and love are possible if we can learn the distinction between self and other, be open to choosing and being chosen, and want to cherish and be cherished.

The central ironic premise of Jolley's fiction is that love is essential to human happiness but hardly realizable on a political basis and barely obtainable on a personal one. Her narratives work to define "good" as "love" in all its quintessentially Jolley forms—as community, caring, and communion—and "evil" as its lack—as dependency, fecklessness, and loneliness. Although intimacy is possible in Jolley's world, it is not inevitable nor even likely: you can hope for another person to choose and to cherish you, but you cannot will it. The only thing you can do in the meantime is to practice hope.

SOURCES AND SUGGESTED READING:

Bird, Delys, and Brenda Walker, eds. *Elizabeth Jolley: New Critical Essays.* Collins, Angus and Robertson, 1991.

Ellison, Jennifer. "Interview with Elizabeth Jolley," in *Rooms of Their Own.* Ringwood, NSW: Penguin, 1986, pp. 174–191.

Kavanaugh, Paul, and Peter Kuchs, eds. "This Self the Honey of All Beings," in *Conversations: Interviews with Australian Writers.* Sydney: Angus and Robertson, 1991, pp. 153–176.

Lurie, Caroline, ed. *Central Mischief: Elizabeth Jolley on Writing, Her Past and Herself.* Viking, 1992.

Milech, Barbara, and Brian Dibble. "Aristophanic Love-Dyads: Community, Communion and Cherishing in Elizabeth Jolley's Fiction," in *Antipodes.* Vol. 7, no. 1, 1993, pp. 3-10.

Salzman, Paul. *Helplessly Tangled in Female Arms and Legs: Elizabeth Jolley's Fictions.* University of Queensland, 1993.

Wilbanks, Ray. "A Conversation with Elizabeth Jolley." *Antipodes.* Vol. 3, no. 1, 1989, pp. 27–29.

COLLECTIONS:

The J.S. Battye Library of Western Australian History in Perth has a 97-page transcript of five hours of interviews with Jolley conducted by Stuart Reid in May and June of 1989; and the Mitchell Library in Sydney holds various letters, diaries, and manuscripts.

Dr. Barbara H. Milech,
Director of Graduate Studies, School of Communication and Cultural Studies, Curtin University, Perth, Western Australia, who has written a number of papers on Jolley and produced a bibliography of Jolley's work which appears in the Bird-Walker book

Jonas, Maryla (1911–1959)

Polish pianist who was one of the first artists to record on LP (long-playing records). Born in Warsaw, Poland, on May 31, 1911; died in New York City, on July 3, 1959.

Maryla Jonas was a prodigy who studied with Paderewski, Sauer and Turczynski. Making her official debut in 1926, she had a successful virtuoso career until World War II, when she had to escape to South America. Jonas finally came to the United States, where she made her debut in New York in 1946. She was one of the first pianists to be heard on the newly invented long-playing record. Although she was not a great technician, she played with a profound sensitivity. Her recording of Chopin mazurkas, while controversial as an interpretation, nevertheless displayed a ravishing tone with a gracious sense of rubato. After a long illness that prematurely terminated her career, she died in New York City.

John Haag,
Athens, Georgia

Jonas, Regina (1902–1944)

German-Jewish rabbi, the first woman rabbi in the history of Judaism, who played a key role in maintaining morale at the Theresienstadt-Terezin concentration camp. Born Regina Jonas in Berlin, Germany, on August 3, 1902; murdered in Auschwitz on December 12, 1944; daughter of Wolf Jonas and Sara (Hess) Jonas; brother, Abraham.

Destined to become the first woman rabbi in over three millennia of Jewish history, Regina Jonas was born in Berlin on August 3, 1902, into a religious family. In 1913, her father died, leaving the family in serious financial need. To support herself and her mother and brother, Jonas prepared for a teaching career and was granted her teaching certificate in March 1924. She began teaching in secondary girls' schools and also enrolled as a rabbinical student at Berlin's renowned Hochschule für die Wissenschaft des Judentums (Academy for the Science of Judaism), a seminary for the training of liberal rabbis and educators.

As the only woman enrolled at the Academy, Jonas was fully aware of the prejudices, ancient and modern, against the possibility of a woman becoming a rabbi. Accordingly, in 1930 she wrote a *halakhic* thesis entitled "Can a Woman Hold Rabbinical Office?" which was designed to refute the traditional arguments used to bar women from serving as rabbis. In essence, she argued that the Judeo-Christian tradition was patriarchal, not due to theological truths but rather to social and historical factors that were now clearly outmoded; although traditionally male dominated, androcentric and discriminatory, these elements were separable from Judaism, argued Jonas, and thus not intrinsic to it. To remain a vital faith, Judaism needed to tap the immense spiritual energies of its women.

Early in the 20th century, there were signs of change in Judaism over the question of women's role in religious matters. In Great Britain, the Jewish social worker **Lily Montagu** (1874–1963) had co-founded the Liberal Synagogue of London in 1902. In 1928, Montagu visited Berlin and spoke from the pulpit of a synagogue as part of the meeting in that city of the World Union for Progressive Judaism. Jonas may well have attended this meeting; certainly she heard about it and was very likely inspired by Montagu's example. In a 1939 interview Jonas granted to a Swiss women's magazine, she asserted, "I came to my profession from a religious conviction that God does not oppress any human being, that therefore the man does not rule the woman or occupy a spiritual position of supremacy over her. I came to it from the view of the final and complete spiritual equality between the sexes, which were created by a just and merciful God."

In December 1935, one month after the Nuremberg Laws creating an apartheid regime of official discrimination for German Jews went into effect, Jonas went to liberal Rabbi Max Dienemann in the town of Offenbach to take her oral *halakhic* examination. After she passed, Dienemann wrote (in Hebrew, as required) on her rabbinic diploma: "[H]er heart is with God and Israel and . . . she gives her soul to the purpose which she intends for herself, and that she is God-fearing, and since she passed the examination which I gave her in halakhic matters, I attest that she is capable of answering questions of Halakhah and that she deserves to be appointed to the rabbinical office. And may God support her and stand by her and accompany her on all her ways."

Although a significant number of liberal German rabbis and Jewish community boards sent Jonas letters of congratulation, Rabbi Dienemann's action remained controversial in the minds of many German Jews. Even he initially had warned Jonas not to use the title "Rabbi"; the supportive attitudes of others, however, gave her the courage to present herself in public as "Rabbinerin Jonas." Dienemann retreated over the next months and made the point that his signature on her diploma was only "personal" rather than on behalf of a rabbinic organization, and it was thus no more than a private ordination that had taken place in December 1935. He advised Jonas to be patient, since a majority of German liberal rabbis were not yet ready for a woman to serve a congregation as rabbi. Despite these disappointments, and her inability to function as a rabbi in a synagogue, Jonas continued working as a teacher, first in public schools and, as Nazi persecution of Jews increased after 1935, in segregated Jewish schools. By 1937, she was officially employed by the Berlin Jewish Community to work as an "academically trained teacher of religion." At times, she indicated her frustrations, as in a 1938 interview in a Jewish newspaper, the *C.V.-Zeitung,* in which she acknowledged having experienced a considerable amount of "aggravation and disappointment—even when there are some small successes."

Meanwhile Nazi persecution of Germany's Jews accelerated, reaching a new level of hatred in November 1938 during the infamous Kristallnacht pogrom. As a result of Nazi terrors, organized Jewish religious life in Germany virtually collapsed, not only because most synagogues were desecrated and demolished, but also because a large number of rabbis were in concentration camps or had decided to emigrate. As a result of these cataclysmic changes, great gaps appeared in the rabbinate. Although she was only one individual, and remained controversial because of her gender, Jonas filled in at least a few of these gaps. Never presiding officially over a congregation, she replaced on a temporary basis rabbis in Frankfurt, Bremen, and Stolp. She also gave lectures at three of Berlin's remaining synagogues. In 1941, during its last semester in existence, she re-enrolled at the Hochschule für die Wissenschaft des Judentums and participated in a course on homiletics (sacred rhetoric) with the man universally regarded as the spiritual head of German Jewry, Rabbi Leo Baeck.

By 1942, the Nazi *Endlösung der Judenfrage* (Final Solution of the Jewish Question) was in high gear, and in May of that year Jonas was conscripted as a slave laborer, working in a small packaging firm. In November 1942, she was informed that her property had been confiscated in favor of the German Reich and was told to appear the next day for deportation. Jonas was sent to Theresienstadt-Terezin, a so-called "model concentration camp" near Prague. Mostly German-speaking Jews were sent to this camp, which the Nazis designed to give the outside world the impression that even in wartime Jews were being well treated; a film was produced here with the grotesque title *The Führer Presents the Jews with a City.* In reality, existence in Theresienstadt was relentlessly harsh—with overcrowding, disease and malnutrition universal facts of life and death—and the camp was for many a transit station to Auschwitz.

Jonas spent almost two years in Theresienstadt, which contained many male rabbis including the revered Leo Baeck. Working with Victor Frankl's self-help organization, she volunteered to meet new arrivals to the camp at the train station, part of a welcoming committee that attempted to soften the first shock for trusting Jews who had believed Nazi propaganda that they could reasonably expect humane conditions to be maintained during their "resettlement to the East." Her preaching was meant to provide at least some of these disoriented and despairing individuals with a modicum of hope and a broader perspective in which they could attempt to make some sense of their situation. Although much of the documentation on her life in Terezin has vanished (a handwritten list of 24 lecture topics remains), one set of notes to a sermon she delivered there has survived. It contains evidence of her commitment:

Our Jewish people have been sent by God into history as "blessed." To be blessed by God means, to give wherever one steps, in every life situation blessing, kindness, faithfulness—humility before God, selfless and devoted love to his creatures sustain this world. To erect these fundamental pillars of the world was and is Israel's task. Man and woman, woman and man have taken on this task with the same Jewish devotion. Towards this ideal our grave, trying work in Theresienstadt caters . . . to be servants of God, and as such to be transported from earthly into eternal spheres.

On October 12, 1944, Regina Jonas was transferred as number 722 of Transport Equ 064/328 from Theresienstadt to Auschwitz. She was murdered there on December 12, 1944, at the age of 42. In 1995, **Bea Wyler**, whose rabbinical studies were completed at the Jewish Theological Seminary in New York, continued on the path begun two generations before by Jonas, becoming the first woman rabbi in post-1945 Germany. Wyler presently serves as rabbi to the Jewish community of Oldenburg.

SOURCES:

Erler, Hans, Ernst Ludwig Ehrich, and Ludger Heid, eds. *"Meinetwegen ist die Welt erschaffen": Das intellektuelle Vermächtnis des deutschsprachigen Judentums.* Frankfurt am Main: Campus Verlag, 1997.

Herweg, Rachel Monika. "'Mein Name ist Frau Regina Jonas. Ich bin nicht die Frau eines Rabbiners. Ich bin Rabbinerin. Was kann ich für Sie tun?'. Die Rabbinerin Regina Jonas (Berlin 1902—Auschwitz 1944)," in Elke Kleinau, ed. *Frauen in pädagogischen Berufen—Gestern und Heute. Bd. 1: Auf dem Weg zur Professionalisierung.* Bad Heilbrunn: Julius Klinkhardt Verlagsbuchhandlung, 1996, pp. 152–167.

Jacobson, Jacob. "Bruchstücke 1939–1945" (unpublished manuscript, 1965), Leo Baeck Institute Archives, New York, file C 195.

Kellenbach, Katharina von. "'God Does Not Oppress Any Human Being': The Life and Thought of Rabbi Regina Jonas," in *Leo Baeck Institute Year Book XXXIX.* London: Secker & Warburg, 1994, pp. 213–225.

Regina Jonas Nachlass, Bundesarchiv Potsdam.

Schwarzfuchs, Simon. *A Concise History of the Rabbinate.* Oxford: Blackwell Publishers, 1993.

Schwertfeger, Ruth. *Women of Theresienstadt: Voices from a Concentration Camp.* NY: Berg/St. Martin's Press, 1989.

John Haag,
Associate Professor of History,
University of Georgia, Athens, Georgia

Jone.

Variant of Jane or Joan.

Jones, Barbara (1937—)

African-American sprinter and track star. Born Barbara Pearl Jones in Chicago, Illinois, on March 26, 1937; married Marcellus Slater; children: two daughters.

Was national indoor champion in the 100-yard dash (1954 and 1955); was national outdoor AAU champion in the 100 meters (1953 and 1954); won gold medals in the Olympics in the 4x100 meters (1952 and 1960); was a member of the Tennessee Tigerbelles, a team which produced some of the fastest female runners in the world.

Barbara Jones was born in 1937 and grew up on the South Side of Chicago. At a young age, she demonstrated her abilities on the track. After competing successfully at the national level, she was one of the youngest athletes to qualify for the Olympics at only 15. Jones won a gold medal in the 1952 Olympics in Helsinki where she ran on a 4x100-meter relay team with ***Mae Faggs, Janet Moreau,** and ◀❧ **Catherine Hardy.** The Americans defeated German, British, Soviet, Australian, and Dutch teams with a time of 45.9 seconds. Jones was one of the youngest athletes to win a gold medal. From that time until she was 19, Barbara Jones was a national AAU champion. After graduating from St. Elizabeth High School in 1955, she attended Marquette University. Her freshman year she tried out for the 1956 Olympic games in Melbourne, certain she would make the cut. In the trials, however, Jones could not even reach third place. Three Tennessee State University Tigerbelles beat her in the 100 and 200 meters. Bitterly disappointed, Jones had missed a berth on the 1956 Olympic team.

"The thing for you to do," advised Faggs, "is to come on down to Tennessee State and learn what training is all about." Jones wasted no time in writing Coach Ed Temple who got her a track scholarship at Tennessee. Becoming a Tigerbelle was a new experience for Jones. In Tennessee, she was just another athlete instead of a superstar. Teammates like ***Margaret Matthews** and ***Wilma Rudolph** often warned Jones that they would give her a sound thrashing on the track and they delivered. Temple had the Tigerbelles practice year round, running cross country over open fields and up and down the jagged hills of Tennessee. Temple's goal was to build stamina, as he believed that well-trained athletes did not become injured as easily. They won meets as well.

Jones worked hard as a Tigerbelle, realizing she was in a superior program. From 1956 to 1988, 40 Tigerbelles won places on U.S. Olympic teams. In international competition, Tigerbelles won 13 gold medals, 6 silver medals, and 4 bronze. Temple, however, stressed academic as well as athletic achievement. Of these 40 Olympic team members, 39 received their un-

Hardy, Catherine. See Faggs, Mae for sidebar.

Opposite page

𝒢wyneth
𝒥ones

dergraduate degrees, 28 got master's degrees, and 6 earned their Ph.Ds. Jones worked hard, both in the classroom and on the track.

Tigerbelle training paid off. In 1957, she was AAU 100-yard dash national champion, though Margaret Matthews took this title from her the following year. In 1958, Jones was the 50-meter national AAU champion and shared a 5.7 world record with **Isabel Daniels** in the 50-yard dash. Jones was the first American woman ever to win a race against the Soviets, winning a 100-meter race in 1958, a feat she repeated in 1959.

Coach Temple emphasized two skills at Tennessee—leaning into the tape at the finish and passing the baton. On more than one occasion, the 4x100-meter relay has been lost because a team member dropped the baton. Endless practice built skills, and, when the 1960 Olympics came around, Barbara Jones was a different athlete from the young woman who failed to qualify for the 1956 Olympics. She traveled to Rome with *__Martha B. Hudson__, Wilma Rudolph, and *__Lucinda Williams__. The following day, the Americans defeated the West Germans, Poles, Soviets, and Italians with a time of 44.5 seconds in the 4x100-meter relay, and Jones had won her second Olympic gold medal.

Over her eight-year career, Barbara Jones won 335 medals and 56 trophies. After graduating from Tennessee, she married a fellow student, Marcellus Slater. The couple returned to Chicago where they had two daughters, and Jones became a physical education teacher.

SOURCES:

Davis, Michael D. *Black American Women in Olympic Track and Field*. Jefferson, NC: McFarland, 1992.

Page, James A. *Black Olympian Medalists*. Englewood, CO: Libraries Unlimited, 1991.

Wallechinsky, David. *The Complete Book of the Olympics*. NY: Viking, 1988.

Karin Loewen Haag,
freelance writer, Athens, Georgia

Jones, Beatrix (1872–1959).

See Farrand, Beatrix Jones.

Jones, E.E. Constance (1848–1922).

See Constance Jones, E.E.

Jones, Etta (b. 1928).

See Dandridge, Dorothy for sidebar.

Jones, Gwyneth (1936—)

Welsh soprano. Born on November 7, 1936, in Pont-newyndd, Wales; studied with Ruth Parker at the Royal College of Music at the Accademia Chigiana in

Siena, and with Maria Carpi in Geneva; married Till Haberfeld; children: one daughter.

Made debut in Zurich (1962), in Covent Garden (1963), in Vienna (1966), in Bayreuth (1966), at the Metropolitan Opera (1972).

Gwyneth Jones was born in Pontnewyndd, Wales, in 1936. She studied with **Ruth Parker** at the Royal College of Music at the Accademia Chigiana in Siena, and with **Maria Carpi** in Geneva. Jones went through a severe vocal crisis in the early 1970s at a time when she was involved in recording many complete operas. The result was a series of erratic performances. Although this crisis was eventually surmounted, Jones' performance was never predictable. At times, her singing was thrilling, at other times unpleasant. Despite these problems, Jones, a mesmerizing, supreme singing actress, was in constant demand for a quarter of a century. Her voice was particularly suited for Wagnerian roles, and she performed all three Wagner Brünnhildes at Bayreuth in the internationally televised *Ring* cycle in 1976.

John Haag,
Athens, Georgia

Jones, Jennifer (1919—)

American actress who won an Academy Award for her portrayal of Bernadette of Lourdes in The Song of Bernadette. *Name variations: Jennifer Jones Simon. Born Phylis Lee Isley on March 2, 1919, in Tulsa, Oklahoma; only child of Philip (a vaudeville performer) and Flora Mae (Suber) Isley; attended Edgemere Public School, Oklahoma City; graduated from Monte Cassino, Tulsa, Oklahoma; attended Northwestern University, Evanston, Illinois, 1936; attended American Academy of Dramatic Arts, New York; married Robert Walker (d. 1951, an actor), on January 2, 1939 (divorced 1945); married David O. Selznick (a film producer), on July 18, 1949 (died 1965); married Norton Simon (a businessman), in 1971 (died 1993); children: (first marriage) Michael and Robert; (second marriage) Mary Jennifer Selznick (d. 1976).*

Filmography: (as Phylis Isley) New Frontier (1939); (as Phylis Isley) Dick Tracy's G-Men (serial, 1939); The Song of Bernadette (1943); Since You Went Away (1944); Love Letters (1945); Cluny Brown (1946); Duel in the Sun (1946); Portrait of Jennie (1949); We Were Strangers (1949); Madame Bovary (1949); Gone to Earth (The Wild Heart, UK, 1952); Carrie (1952); Ruby Gentry (1952); Stazione Termini (Indiscretion of an American Wife, It./US, 1954); Beat the Devil (UK/US, 1954); Love Is a Many-Splendored

Thing (1955); Good Morning Miss Dove (1955); The Man in the Gray Flannel Suit (1956); The Barretts of Wimpole Street (1957); A Farewell to Arms (1957); Tender Is the Night (1962); The Idol (1966); Angel Angel Down We Go (Cult of the Dammed, 1969); The Towering Inferno (1974).

A shy, dark-haired beauty, Jennifer Jones fairly burst upon the Hollywood scene in 1943, capturing an Academy Award for her first major movie *The Song of Bernadette*. Her career flourished through the 1940s and 1950s, controlled largely by powerful movie producer David O. Selznick (best remembered for the epic *Gone With the Wind*), whom she married in 1949. Selznick, an inspired filmmaker and one of Hollywood's most notorious womanizers, was obsessed with Jones and determined to make her a star. He selected her scripts, surrounded her with some of the finest directors and co-stars, and saw to it that her day-to-day life was free of distractions. For her part, Jones provided an intense drive and focus that allowed her to rise above her modest talent.

Born Phylis Isley in Tulsa, Oklahoma, in 1919, Jones was an only child who spent her early years on the road with her parents' touring stock company. By age ten, she had already set her sights on a Broadway career. After graduating from Monte Cassino, a convent school in Tulsa, she spent a summer in stock and a semester in the drama department at Northwestern University before entering the American Academy of Dramatic Arts in New York. There, she met Robert Walker, a baby-faced, brooding young actor who had managed to survive a troubled past. The two fell in love and married on January 2, 1939, almost a year to the day that they had first met. Their honeymoon was a trip to Hollywood, where Jones signed a six-month contract with Republic pictures and was immediately cast as "the girl" in a Three Mesquiteers programmer starring John Wayne. Her next assignment was a 15-part serial, *Dick Tracy's G-Men*, but after two months, she grew impatient with her small role and quit her contract. She and Walker, who had landed only a few movie walk-ons himself, returned to New York, hoping they would have better luck on the stage. Jones' career, however, was put on hold by the arrival of two sons: Robert, Jr., born in 1940, and Michael, who came along a year later. While Walker worked as a radio actor, Jones modeled occasionally, but for the most part stayed at home with the children.

Jones' break came when she auditioned for *Kay Brown, David Selznick's renowned New

York representative, for the title role in the film version of the hit Broadway play *Claudia* written by *Rose Franken. On Brown's recommendation, Selznick okayed a screen test for Jones, which subsequently led to her signing a multi-year contract with the Selznick studio. Upon meeting Jones, Selznick, who was married at the time to *Irene Mayer Selznick, was enchanted by the young actress (although the role of Claudia went to *Dorothy McGuire, another of his contract players). Over the next three years, Selznick personally groomed Jones for stardom, providing her with acting lessons and classes in literature and fine arts at Columbia University. He also selected the name Jennifer Jones, which one critic later called "the worst screen name in the business." Selznick found the perfect vehicle for his new discovery in the 20th Century-Fox adaptation of *The Song of Bernadette,* the story of Bernadette Soubirous (*Bernadette of Lourdes), the teenage girl from Lourdes who, in 1858, saw a vision of *Mary the Virgin in a village grotto. Although it was a difficult and pivotal role for a neophyte, Jones managed to pull it off, aided immeasurably by director Henry King and an impressive supporting cast, which including seasoned performers *Gladys Cooper, Vincent Price, Charles Bickford, *Anne Revere, and Lee J. Cobb. The pressure, however, thoroughly exhausted the young actress and took a toll on her marriage, which was already under strain from the weight of Selznick's relentless pursuit and her own growing ambition.

The Song of Bernadette, which had a gala premier in Jones' hometown of Tulsa, as well as in Los Angeles and New York, was an unqualified hit, and Jones received absolutely glowing reviews. *Variety* thought her performance "inspirationally sensitive and arresting," and **Kate Cameron** of the *New York Daily News* gave the picture a four-star ranking and termed Jones a "phenomenon." The young actress went on to receive an Academy Award nomination as Best Actress for her performance, in competition with a prestigious line-up of actresses that included *Greer Garson, ◄❧ Joan Fontaine, *Ingrid Bergman, and *Jean Arthur. When Jones won, she was dumbstruck. "I'd been trying for so long and with such poor luck to get started on a career," she said later, "and then all of a sudden—wham! I had success in my hands. I guess I felt like a starving person sitting down unexpectedly to a sumptuous banquet with no warning."

Selznick, in what some called a sadistic touch of casting, chose Bob Walker to co-star with Jones in her next movie, *Since You Went Away* (1944), the story of star-crossed lovers separated by war, which began shooting before *The Song of Bernadette* was released. The production was barely under way when Jones announced her separation from Walker, making things extremely awkward on the set, particularly since Selznick did not choose to replace Walker, and, though still married himself, was openly courting Jones. The movie somehow survived all the angst to become a box-office hit, and Jones received an Oscar nomination for Best Supporting Actress. She captured a Best Actress nomination the following year (1945) for her role in *Love Letters,* opposite Joseph Cotton, the same year she was divorced from Walker.

Jones' role in the western *Duel in the Sun* (referred to by Edward Epstein in *Portrait of Jennifer* as "the first multimillion-dollar, platinum-edged porn film") was about as far from Bernadette as she could get, and many wondered whether she could make such a transition. Jones' preparation for the gritty part of Pearl Chavez was characteristic of the seriousness with which she approached her work. "Jennifer spent weeks studying how to walk like the Indian girl, until she got it down to perfection," said her longtime friend **Anita Colby**. "She took lessons to acquire that low-pitched, sexy voice she used. She worked hours on end every day to perfect every motion, mannerism, and inflection she could possibly need." The picture endured a number of crises in production, including an industrywide union strike, the walkout of director King Vidor over a dispute with Selznick, and the announcement by Irene Selznick that she was divorcing her husband. Released in 1946, the film sent shock waves throughout the industry. It was panned by reviewers as lewd and exploitative and was banned by the Catholic Church. When the dust settled, however, Jones received yet another Oscar nomination as Best Actress. This time, however, she lost to *Olivia de Havilland.

Jones performed her first comic role in *Cluny Brown* (1946), co-starring matinee idol Charles Boyer. Directed by another top-rated director, Ernst Lubitsch, the actress won accolades for her portrayal of a wide-eyed servant girl. The film was followed by *Portrait of Jennie, We Were Strangers,* and *Madame Bovary,* all of which were released in 1949, the year of Jones' marriage to Selznick. Of the three, only *Madame Bovary,* directed by Vincente Minnelli, served to advance Jones' career to any degree. After their marriage, the Selznicks relocated to Europe, although they commuted frequently to the States. Jones was pregnant during the filming of *Carrie,* a period film with Laurence Olivier, but suffered a miscarriage in her sixth month. William Wyler, who directed the picture, later commented on Jones' professionalism, describing her as "always a little tense on the set and extremely conscientious, yet never quite satisfied with her work." Beset by depression over the loss of her child, Jones was further devastated by the death of her former husband Robert Walker in August 1951. There was much speculation about the troubled actor's death, which occurred under mysterious circumstances. (One rumor put the blame on Walker's doctor who, unaware that Walker had been drinking, administered an in-

❧►
Fontaine, Joan.
See joint entry
under de
Havilland, Olivia.

From the movie
Duel in the Sun,
starring Jennifer
Jones.

jection of sodium Amytal. Another rumor suggested a complicated murder plot actually involving David Selznick.)

Jones' next film was *Ruby Gentry* (1953), in which she played a Carolina mountain girl op-

posite Charlton Heston, who remembered her as possessing a kind of "random instinct" about acting, and was also struck by the fact that she didn't wear make-up in front of the camera. "You could see her coloring change," he said, "you could see her flush or pale during a shot."

Selznick, who feared that his wife's career now rested on the success of this movie, took charge of postproduction, enhancing production values from stock footage, and even selecting the hit theme music. The movie received mixed reviews but was a box-office hit, due in part to Paramount's irresistible promotion of it as the story of "A Siren Who Wrecked a Whole Town—Man by Man—Sin by Sin."

Following the lukewarm reception of her next two films, *Indiscretion of an American Wife* and *Beat the Devil* (both made in Europe, and released in 1954), Jones gave birth to a baby girl, Mary Jennifer, after which she threw herself into preparations for a Broadway play, *Portrait of a Lady,* an adaptation of the Henry James novel that seemed troubled from the start. Although Selznick tried to discourage her, Jones, who was frustrated by her seemingly stalled career (she had recently been passed over for roles in *The Barefoot Contessa* and *The Country Girl*), ignored his pleas. The play, which also starred Robert Fleming and *Cathleen Nesbitt, and was directed by José Quintero, lasted only eight performances. Critics did, however, credit the actress' valiant attempt to save the lackluster adaptation. "Miss Jones does her level best to pump something besides gilly water and lavender flowers into this work," wrote Whitney Bolton in the *New York Morning Telegraph.* "She has life, she has color and warmth and desperation. But the vehicle burdens her." Jones was crushed by the failure, noting that she "bled from every pore." Later, in an interview with Hollywood columnist Joe Hyams, Jones admitted that criticism upset her to the point of tears. "When someone writes unkind things about me I want to go off somewhere and be alone," she told him.

Jones made a strong comeback in her next film, *Han Suyin's *Love is a Many-Splendored Thing* (1955), portraying an Eurasian doctor who falls in love with a British journalist played by William Holden, who was a top box-office attraction at the time and was also known to fall in love with all of his co-stars. (Jones supposedly chewed garlic before their love scenes to keep Holden at bay.) The movie was a box-office smash, and critics, some of whom were lukewarm about the movie, were united about Jones' performance. "Miss Jones is lovely and intense," noted *The New York Times,* "she could be a piece of delicately carved stone." *Variety* praised the film as "one of the best woman's pictures made in some years," and called Jones "pure delight as the beautiful Han. . . . Her love scenes with Holden sizzle without ever being cheap or

awkward." Winning another Oscar nomination for Best Actress, Jones was once again on track with her movie career. This success was followed by an acclaimed performance as a no-nonsense schoolteacher in *Good Morning Miss Dove* (1955). Again on top, Jones won *Photoplay* magazine's "Most Popular Actress of the Year" award in 1955 and received the California Federation of Women's Clubs Motion Picture Award for her performance as Miss Dove. A rematch with Gregory Peck in *The Man in the Gray Flannel Suit* (1956) proved to be another hit with movie-goers, although Jones was discouraged by her reviews, which were mixed at best. She had her fourth consecutive success as *Elizabeth Barrett Browning** in *The Barretts of Wimpole Street* (1957). "Jennifer has the ability to look more like a woman completely in love than almost any other actress I can think of," noted the reviewer for the *Los Angeles Mirror-News.*

Jennifer Jones next embarked on a remake of Ernest Hemingway's famous love story *A Farewell to Arms* (1957), a property that Selznick had dreamed of making for a long time. The picture was doomed from the start. Director John Huston left mid-shoot over differences with Selznick and was replaced by Charles Vidor. Cinematographer Ossie Morris quit after being harassed by Selznick, who accused him of sacrificing Jones' looks in favor of co-star Rock Hudson. (Selznick, who was notorious for his memos, had stated how he wanted his wife photographed in a 20-page, single-spaced directive at the start of filming.) After 30 weeks, filming concluded at $750,000 over budget. The situation only worsened when the critics came down on Jones. "Miss Jones plays the famous Catherine Barkley with bewildering nervous moves and grimaces," wrote *The New York Times*' critic. "Miss Jones as the nurse in love never quite seems to make it," noted *Cue* magazine. William K. Zinsser condemned the entire project in the *New York Herald-Tribune.* "If there were a supreme Bad Taste Award for movies, *A Farewell to Arms* would win it hands down. This smutty version of Ernest Hemingway's novel will set thousands of stomachs to turning."

Both Jones and Selznick were depressed over the notices; he took refuge in an affair with his secretary, she immersed herself in yoga and spiritualism and took "method" acting lessons from Lee Strasberg in New York. Although seriously in debt and beginning to show signs of heart disease, Selznick secured the rights to the F. Scott Fitzgerald novel *Tender Is the Night,* in which Jones would play Nicole, the character based on Fitzgerald's neurotic young wife

*Zelda Fitzgerald. Directed by Henry King, ironically her very first director, and co-starring Jason Robards, Jr., the film began shooting at Fox. To insure that his wife, now 39, looked young and beautiful in the movie, Selznick secured the services of George Masters, then the most sought after and innovative hairstylist and makeup artist on the New York-Hollywood scene. Masters, who was on call 24 hours a day, called the actress "the most beautiful woman I ever worked on," but was quite astonished at Jones' opulent lifestyle and beauty rituals, which included having all her face creams privately tested by top dermatologists and discarding each jar after it had been used once. He was also impressed by Jones' devotion to her husband and his to her. "[David] was completely enslaved by her beauty," he said, "and she was enslaved by sustaining the illusion for him both as an actress and as a wife." (For the Sunday parties hosted by the couple, Jones would often shower and have her hair and make-up redone three times during the day, changing each time into duplicate outfits so that she appeared unchanged to her guests.) Throughout the shooting of *Tender Is the Night,* Jones appeared nervous and insecure and frequently disappeared before she was to go on for a scene. The film opened in February 1962, receiving abominable reviews from which Jones was not spared.

Jones would make no more pictures with her husband. His health began to deteriorate rapidly, and her popularity with movie fans was fading. Selznick's last collaboration with his wife was the short-lived play *The Man with the Perfect Wife,* which had a brief run in Florida. Shortly after the play closed, Selznick suffered a fatal heart attack and died, after which Jones went into seclusion for nearly six months. It was a long adjustment for the actress who, at age 46, was alone for the first time in her life.

Jones returned to films as a replacement for an ailing *Kim Hunter in *The Idol* (1966), which was unmercifully panned and disappeared quickly. In the summer of 1966, Lee Strasberg, remembering that the actress had been the original choice for the film of *The Country Girl,* offered her the lead in a City Center production of the play. Her performance was not well received, and when the run was over, she was once more reclusive. Still wanting desperately to resume her acting career, in 1969 she made another ill-fated attempt at a film comeback, signing on to play a former pornography movie queen in *Angel Angel Down We Go* (retitled *Cult of the Damned*). The film was screened in only a few theaters, mercifully reaching a lim-

ited audience. The *New York Daily News* queried, "Jennifer Jones—how did she ever get mixed up in such a weird production?"

Jones found a renewed sense of purpose in volunteering her time and money to the Los Angeles-based Manhattan Project, a program for emotionally disturbed and drug-addicted youngsters. She solicited funds and invited youngsters into her home for weekends of swimming, tennis, and conversation. Quite unexpectedly, she also found companionship with billionaire industrialist and art collector Norton Simon, whom she met at a party in May 1971 and married a few weeks later. Simon, a large holder of Twentieth Century-Fox stock, may have had a hand in Jones making one last memorable film comeback. Cast in Irwin Allen's disaster film, *The Towering Inferno* (1974), she portrayed a lonely widow who is conned by Fred Astaire. The film was well received and reviewers remarked on the actress' fit appearance and charming scenes with Astaire. As Jones was basking in her success, however, she was jolted by the death of her troubled daughter Mary Jennifer, who at 21 committed suicide by leaping from a building. Devastated and consumed by guilt, the actress went into a deep depression, emerging with a renewed commitment to the cause of mental health. Hoping to provide benefits to the mentally ill that would endure beyond her lifetime, she donated $1 million to establish the Jennifer Jones Simon Foundation for Mental Health and Education.

Jennifer Jones continued to flourish in her role as a society matron and philanthropist, although there were several aborted attempts at another comeback. She took an option on Larry McMurtry's novel *Terms of Endearment,* but eventually abandoned the idea and sold the rights to Paramount. (The picture won the Oscar as Best Picture of 1983, and **Shirley MacLaine,** who played the mother Aurora Greenway, won the award for Best Actress.) Norton Simon subsequently optioned *The Jean Harris Story,* about the schoolmistress who killed her lover, Dr. Herman Tarnower of Scarsdale Diet fame, but that project was also short-lived.

In 1984, Simon was diagnosed with Guillain-Barré syndrome, a progressive nerve disease which results in debilitating muscle weakness. Jones nursed him until his death in 1993, making only occasional public appearances. In the 1990s, Jones served as president of the Norton Simon Museum in Pasadena, California and was also active as a paraprofessional therapist at the Southern California Counseling Center in Beverly Hills. The same ambition that once drove her acting career was now centered on the cause of mental illness.

SOURCES:

Epstein, Edward Z. *Portrait of Jennifer: A Biography of Jennifer Jones.* NY: Simon & Schuster, 1995.

Katz, Ephraim. *The Film Encyclopedia.* NY: Harper-Collins, 1994.

Linet, Beverly. *Star-Crossed: The Story of Robert Walker and Jennifer Jones.* NY: Putnam, 1986.

Rothe, Anna, ed. *Current Biography 1944.* NY: H.W. Wilson, 1944.

Barbara Morgan,
Melrose, Massachusetts

Jones, Lady (1889–1981).

See Bagnold, Enid.

Jones, Linda (1944–1972)

Soul singer. Born in 1944; died in 1972.

Although she has all but been forgotten, Linda Jones was, according to many critics, one of the most dramatic soul singers of all time. Her recording of "Hypnotized" hit the charts in 1967, but it was in her later recordings for Turbo that she displayed the full range of her talent. One critic describes her rendition of "Let It Be Me," as beginning with a climax and working up to a "towering fury" that was pure gospel. Unfortunately, Jones suffered from diabetes and died in 1972, after collapsing during a performance at New York's Apollo Theater. Two later albums showcased the best of her work: *Hypnotized* (CBS, 1989) and *Your Precious Love* (Sequel, 1991).

Jones, Loïs Mailou (1905–1998)

African-American artist and educator. Name variations: Lois Mailou Jones; Madame Vergniaud Pierre-Noël. Born on November 3, 1905, in Boston, Massachusetts; died on June 9, 1998, in Washington, D.C.; second child and only daughter of Thomas Vreeland Jones (a lawyer) and Carolyn Dorinda (Adams) Jones (a hairdresser and hat designer); graduated from the High School of Practical Arts, Boston, 1923; attended Boston Normal Art School (now the Massachusetts College of Art), Boston, 1926; graduated from the School of the Museum of Fine Arts, Boston, 1927; graduate work at the Designers Art School, Boston, 1927–28; attended summer session at Harvard University, 1928; attended summer session at Columbia University, New York, 1934; attended Académie Julian, Paris, France, 1937; Howard University, Wash-

ington, D.C., A.B. in art education (magna cum laude), 1945; married Louis Vergniaud Pierre-Noël (a graphic artist), on August 8, 1954 (died 1982).

Works include: Negro Youth *(1929);* Negro Shack I, Sedalia, North Carolina *(1930);* Mememsha by the Sea *(1930);* Brother Brown, Greensboro, North Carolina *(1931);* Portrait of Hudson *(1932);* The Ascent of Ethiopia *(1932);* Brown Boy *(1935);* Le Petit Déjeuner, Paris *(1937);* Rue St. Michael, Paris *(1938);* Place du Tertre *(1938);* Les Fetiches *(1938);* Les Pommes Vertes *(1938);* La Cuisine dans l'Atelier de L'Artiste, Paris *(1938);* Tête de Nègre *(1939);* Dans un Cafe a Paris *(1939);* Indian Shops, Gay Head, Massachusetts *(1940);* Jennie *(1943);* Mob Victim (Meditation, *1944);* Cockfight *(1960);* Market, Haiti *(1960);* Bazar Du Quai Haiti *(1961);* Marché Haiti *(1963);* Vévé Voudou II *(1963);* Letitia and Patrick, Haiti *(1964);* Vendeuses de Tissues *(1964);* Homage to Oshogbo *(1971);* Dahomey *(1971);* Magic of Nigeria *(1971);* Moon Masque *(1971);* Ubi Girl from Tai Region *(1972);* Street Vendors, Haiti *(1978);* Petite Ballerina *(1982);* Initiation, Liberia *(1983);* Mère Du Senegal *(1985);* The Water Carriers, Haiti *(1985);* Haiti Demain? (Haiti Tomorrow?, *1987);* Le Château Neuf De Grasse *(1989).*

Acknowledged by the art world as one of America's premier painters just two years before her death, black artist Loïs Mailou Jones waited 75 years for the recognition she deserved much earlier. "At 90, I arrived," she gleefully told an interviewer for the *AARP Bulletin* in 1996. Jones, who endured years of racial and sexual discrimination to pursue her goal of becoming an artist, combined painting with a long and distinguished teaching career in the art department at Howard University, an African-American institution in Washington, D.C. To view her work, which encompassed a broad range of styles from the impressionistic landscapes and still lifes of her early works to the political allegories and cubistic canvases of her Haitian and African periods, is to journey through an entire century of American art history, notes **Tritobia Hayes Benjamin**, in her biography of the artist, *The Life and Art of Loïs Mailou Jones.* "Just as American art has unfolded, embracing different styles and different cultures, so too has Jones' career." For Jones, however, process was the ultimate joy. "The wonderful thing about being an artist," she said, "is that there is no end to creative expression. Painting is my life, my life is painting."

Born in Boston, Massachusetts, in 1905, Jones credited her mother **Carolyn Adams Jones**, a hairdresser and hat designer, with inspiring her art career, and said her father Thomas Vreeland Jones, who earned his law degree at age 40, gave her the determination to succeed. The family lived on the top floor of the office building that Thomas Jones managed in downtown Boston, but spent the summers on Martha's Vineyard, Massachusetts, where they owned a house. The island landscapes and the ocean views overwhelmed Jones, even as a young girl. "This beauty affected my life to the extent that I am to this day a great lover of nature," she said. "I think that my experiences on the Vineyard interested me in painting and have motivated me to paint the beauty of the island even to this day." Jones also remembered her mother hanging her paintings on a clothesline and inviting her friends over for punch and a private showing of her daughter's work. "Mother's garden was my gallery," she fondly recalled. At the Vineyard, a haven for artists, Jones also met African-American sculptor ❧➤ **Meta Warrick Fuller** who inspired and encouraged her in her art. One of Jones' earliest works of note, *The Ascent of Ethiopia*, was inspired by Fuller's sculpture *The Awakening of Ethiopia* (1914), one of the first works to present a positive image of a black subject.

Jones' parents steered their talented daughter to the High School of Practical Arts in Boston, where she could pursue her art training within a general secondary course of study. After school and on Saturdays, Jones attended the Boston Museum School of Fine Arts and also apprenticed with costume designer **Grace Ripley** who was a professor at the Rhode Island School of Design. (Jones assisted Ripley in designing costumes and masks for the Ted Shawn School of Dance and a branch of the Bragiotti School located in Boston.) After graduating from high school in 1923, Jones received a scholarship to the Museum School full time. In addition to the design curriculum, she completed elective courses in anatomy, perspective, the history of design, stained glass, book decoration, settings and costumes. In her senior year, she won the prestigious Nathaneil Thayer prize for excellence in design. Upon her graduation in 1927, Jones applied to the Museum School for an assistantship, only to be told by the director that she should go to the South to help her "own people." Undeterred, Jones worked as a textile designer while taking advanced courses at the Designers Art School. There, she studied with Ludwig Frank, an internationally recognized German textile designer, and also worked on a freelance basis for department stores and textile manufacturers, including the F.A. Foster Company in Boston and the Schu-

macher Company in New York. Although Jones was pleased to see her designs on display in interior decorator shops, she was upset by the fact that she was never acknowledged for her work. It was this desire for recognition that changed Jones from a designer into a painter.

In 1930, after a stint heading up the fledgling art department at Palmer Memorial Institute in Sedalia, North Carolina, a private African-American boarding school, Jones joined the staff of the art department at Howard University. During her 47-year tenure there, she touched the lives of some 2,500 art students, grounding them in the fundamentals and urging them to "marry" their art. "Talent is the basis for your career as an artist," she told them, "but hard work determines your success." Jones also involved her students in practical hands-on experience outside the classroom and initiated travel tours to help round out their educational experience. Many of her students went on to notable careers, including painter-historian David Driskell, sculptor-printmaker *Elizabeth Catlett, and painter Robert Freeman.

Jones received her earliest recognition as an artist through the Harmon Foundation of New York, founded in 1922 to "assist in the development of a greater economic security for the Negro race." The foundation held annual competitions for black writers and artists, and it was in the 1930 competition that Jones won honorable mention for the charcoal drawing *Negro Youth* (1929). Benjamin points to this drawing as marking a shift in Jones' work "away from classroom exercises to portraiture as well as compositions predicated on design principles." The paintings of this period, including works like *Negro Shack I, Sedalia, North Carolina* (1930), *Mememsha by the Sea* (1930), *Portrait of Hudson* (1932), and *Brown Boy* (1935), also reflect the renewed interest in African subjects and portrayal of the black experience that sparked the Harlem Renaissance. Benjamin also notes that Jones' breakthrough painting *The Ascent of Ethiopia* (1932), which was exhibited with the Harmon Foundation in 1933, further expresses this move toward cultural identity and "echoes the political tenor of the times."

In 1937, Jones received a Rockefeller grant to study at the Académie Julian in Paris and took a yearlong leave of absence from teaching. The racism and prejudice that had plagued her in America were not evident in Paris, and Jones felt liberated for the first time in her life. Her year abroad was both productive (she produced over 40 works) and influential in the development of

❧➤ ***Fuller, Meta Warrick.*** *See Women of the Harlem Renaissance.*

her artistic personality. "France really was the making of me," she later recalled. "It put my feet firmly on the ground and made me realize that I am talented and I can do it." In Paris, and on the Riviera, Jones moved from the realism of her early period to impressionist landscapes, to Cézannesque portraits and still lifes. She met Symbolist painter Émile Brenard, who let her share his studio and also introduced her to his circle of friends. While in France, she exhibited some of her textile designs for the first time in Asnières, and in 1938 she exhibited two oil paintings (*Les Pommes Vertes* and *La Cuisine dans l'Atelier de L'Artiste, Paris*) in the Salon de Printemps exhibition at the Socièté des Artistes Français. At the end of the year, Jones applied for an extension of her leave from the university but was ordered back to the classroom. However, she returned to France intermittently throughout her life, painting the beautiful French countryside both south and north of Paris.

Back in America, Jones was once again confronted with the racial discrimination she had left behind, particularly when it came to exhibiting her work. Many galleries and museums at the time were simply closed to black artists. In 1941, when Jones submitted her painting *Indian Shops, Gay Head, Massachusetts* (1940) to a competition at Washington's Corcoran Gallery of Art, she was forced to send it via her close friend, **Céline Tabary**, who was visiting her from France at the time. "If I had brought my entry down myself, and the guards had seen me," she recalled, "they would have put it in the reject pile right away. But because Céline took it, it was accepted." When her entry won the prestigious Robert Woods Bliss Prize, Jones had her certificate forwarded in the mail. She did not claim credit for the prize until two years later.

During the 1940s, Jones was encouraged by Alain Locke, poet laureate of the Harlem Renaissance and a colleague at Howard, to address the black experience in her painting. Throughout the 1940s and 1950s, Jones created numerous character studies of blacks, including *The Janitor* (1939), *Jennie* (1943), and the powerful *Mob Victim* (1944), a moving commentary on the fate of victims of the lynching mobs that were prevalent in America during the early decades of the 20th century. Her model had actually witnessed a lynching and imitated in his pose the stance of the victim. "The sympathetic restrained depiction of imminent death is infused with dignity," writes Benjamin in her description of the work. "Jones had originally painted a rope around the subject's neck, but she deemed its inclusion too severe and removed it, relying instead on a sensi-

tive interpretation of the victim's countenance and his contemplative mood."

In 1953, Jones married the distinguished Haitian artist Louis Vergniaud Pierre-Noël, whom she had first met in 1934, during a summer session at Columbia University. The marriage transformed both her life and her art, beginning with her first visit to the Caribbean nation of Haiti in 1954, at the invitation of Haitian president Paul Magloire who commissioned a series of paintings on Haitian life. In conjunction with the commission, she also taught at the Centre d'Art during the absence of its director. At the end of her first visit, Jones had an exhibition of her work sponsored by Haiti's first lady **Madame Magloire**, and was awarded the "Honneur et Mérite au Grade de Chevalier" for outstanding achievement in art. The exhibition was later seen at the Pan-American Union in Washington, D.C., during a visit by President and Madame Magloire to the United States. For more than three decades, Jones and her husband made annual trips to Haiti to paint and relax. (Pierre-Noël died in 1982 and was buried near the couple's Port-au-Prince home.) Inspired by the exuberance of Haitian life, Jones abandoned the formality and restrained palette of her traditional painting for a more aggressive, colorful, and hard-edged style. "The colors, the black people, the drumming and the fire dancers—Haiti was excitement and color," she later remembered. The titles of her Haitian paintings reveal the inspiration she found all around her: *Cockfight* (1960), *Market, Haiti* (1960), *Bazar Du Quai, Haiti* (1961), and the later *Street Vendors, Haiti* (1978) and *The Water Carriers, Haiti* (1985).

Jones' regular visits to Haiti were interrupted in 1986, when Jean-Claude "Baby Doc" Duvalier was ousted from the country. The Haitian boat exodus of 1987, which focused international attention on the problems within that country, was the subject of one of Jones' most exciting and disturbing works, *Haiti Demain?* (*Haiti Tomorrow?*). Produced in her Washington studio and executed in the intense colors that characterized her painting at the time, the work is a political statement indicting the government for its failure to address the social and economic problems of the people. "Haiti is projected as a Kaleidoscope of impending death, wracked with problems of graft, corruption (implied by the floating money in the upper left of the painting), and military control," writes Benjamin. "From afar, Jones composed this heart-wrenching scenario that was so prophetic regarding Haiti's direction."

*L*oïs
*M*ailou
*J*ones

From 1970 to 1971, Jones embarked on a sabbatical year in Africa to research art under a Howard University grant. She toured 11 countries, compiling information on contemporary African artists and photographing works of art for a comprehensive international archive of black artists which is now housed at the university. The African influence on Jones' work was immediate and powerful. Upon her return to Washington in 1971, she completed four pictures—*Homage to Oshogbo, Dahomey, Magic of Nigeria,* and *Moon Masque*—all of which explore the theme of reawakening that she had touched upon in her earlier work *Ascent of Ethiopia*. Utilizing stylized forms of indigenous African art—masks, Dahomean appliques, collage, trompe-d'oeil faces—Jones created canvases that startle the viewer with their power. The painting *Ubi Girl from Tai Region* (1972), described by Benjamin, illustrates how Jones sometimes used a number of different African motifs within a single canvas. "The painting features the head of a young initiated woman from the Ivory Coast, masks from Zaire, and a heddle pulley, also from the Ivory Coast, combining Western portraiture with the geometric patterning of African textiles." Jones liked to point out that much of her African work is closely linked to Haiti, which she believed never severed its ties to Mother Africa. "Some of my most creative compositions for which I researched African icons, patterns, masks, and sculptures were actually done in my Haitian studio."

From 1937 on, Jones exhibited in over 50 shows, including a retrospective of her work at Howard University in 1972 and a 1995 exhibition at Washington's Corcoran, where she had once been forced to hide her identity. Her work hangs in the country's most prestigious galleries, including the Smithsonian's National Museum of American Art in Washington, The Metropolitan Museum of Art in New York, and the Museum of Fine Arts in Boston. In 1962, she was elected a Fellow of the Royal Society of Arts in London. She was honored by foreign heads of state and was one of ten artists commemorated in 1980 by President Jimmy Carter.

In 1989, on her 84th birthday, Jones suffered a massive heart attack, and a week later underwent triple bypass surgery. Her recovery was such that she was able to participate in a solo retrospective exhibition of 76 works, *The World of Loïs Mailou Jones*, held at the Meridian International Center in January 1990. Jones continued to work, albeit on a modified schedule. Among her last commissions was the movie poster for *Cry the Beloved Country*, and a portfolio accompanying the poems of the former president of Senegal, Léopold Stenghor. She also continued to travel to Haiti and to her beloved Martha's Vineyard, where she hosted President Bill Clinton and **Hillary Rodham Clinton** at an exhibit of her work at the Granary Gallery of Art in West Tisbury in August 1993. In her later years, she came full circle, frequently returning to the impressionistic style of her past. Jones, however, remained a forward thinker to the end. "I will be painting until the last day," she said.

The artist died at her home in Washington on June 9, 1998.

SOURCES:

Baker, Beth. "On a Larger Canvas," in *AARP Bulletin*. Vol. 37, no. 9. October 1996.

Benjamin, Tritobia Hayes. *The Life and Art of Loïs Mailou Jones*. San Francisco, CA: Pomegranate Artbooks, 1994.

Cotter, Holland. "Loïs Mailou Jones, 92, Painter and Teacher," in *The New York Times*. June 13, 1998.

Rubinstein, Charlotte Streifer. *American Women Artists*. Boston, MA: G.K. Hall, 1982.

Smith, Jessie Carney, ed. *Notable Black American Women*. Detroit, MI: Gale Research, 1996.

Barbara Morgan,
Melrose, Massachusetts

Jones, Margo (1911–1955).

See Women of the Regional Theater Movement in America.

Jones, Mary (1700–1740).

See Diver, Jenny.

Jones, Mary Harris (1830–1930)

Organizer for the Knights of Labor and United Mine Workers of America who struggled to obtain better working and living conditions for workers and their families. Name variations: Mother Jones. Born Mary Harris on May 1, 1830 (some sources cite 1843) in Cork County, Ireland; died in Silver Spring, Maryland, on November 30, 1930; daughter of Richard and Mary Harris; attended public school in Toronto and one year of normal school; married George Jones (a molder), in 1861; children: four.

Immigrated to Toronto (1841); became private tutor in Maine (1855); taught at St. Mary's Convent, Monroe, Michigan (1859); moved to Memphis, Tennessee (1860); lost husband and children to yellow fever epidemic (1867); moved to Chicago and became first woman organizer for the Knights of Labor (1871); was field organizer for the United Mine Workers of America (1900); led march of mill children (1903); helped found Industrial Workers of the World (1905); participated in strikes nationwide (1877–1923).

Selected publications: magazine articles for International Socialist Review *(beginning 1900);* Autobiography of Mother Jones *(Charles Kerr, 1925).*

During the late 19th and early 20th centuries, Mary Harris Jones traveled thousands of miles throughout the United States, going wherever she was needed in the struggle to obtain decent wages and working conditions for American workers. "My address is like my shoes," she said. "It travels with me. I abide where there is a fight against wrong." Present at a coal mining strike when a mine detective bashed in the skull of a miner, Jones cradled the head of the man as he lay dying. In his delirium, the miner thought that she was his mother; from that time on, the name "Mother" Jones stuck.

Mary Harris was born in Cork County, Ireland, probably on May 1, 1830 (the year is in dispute), the daughter of Richard and **Mary Harris**. Little is known about Mary's childhood. In her autobiography, her first 30 years are relegated to two paragraphs. In 1835, Richard Harris left Ireland to work on railway construction gangs in the U.S. and Canada; six years later, in 1841, he brought his family to America. They settled in Toronto, where Mary attended the Toronto Middle School for one year. The journeys that were to continue for the rest of her life began in 1855, when she left Toronto for a job in Maine as a private tutor. In 1859, she taught school at St. Mary's Convent in Monroe, Michigan, where she earned $8 per month, but she did not like the work of "bossing little children." She moved to Chicago, where she earned a living as a seamstress, until she left there for Memphis, Tennessee, in 1860. The following year, she married George Jones, a molder who also worked as a union organizer. Their first child was born in 1862; three others followed in quick succession.

At times, Mary Jones managed to travel with George on his union organizing trips, until 1867, when tragedy struck. Jones lost her husband and all four children to a yellow fever epidemic that hit Memphis. She remained there, nursing others, until the epidemic abated, then returned to Chicago where she worked again as a seamstress.

Misfortune seemed to follow Mary Harris Jones, however, and the Great Chicago Fire of 1871 destroyed her shop and home. This calamity changed the course of her life. Since her return to Chicago, Jones had learned of the work of the Knights of Labor to help workers, and, even though women were not to gain membership in the union until 1879, she went to work for the group as an organizer in 1871. It was during this time that she made the acquaintance of Terence Powderly, leader of the Knights in 1878; he would remain her lifelong friend.

Thus began Mary Harris Jones' long journey, a journey that would take her wherever workers fought for their rights. She would participate in strikes throughout the country, including the Baltimore and Ohio strike of railroad workers in Pittsburgh (1877); the Pullman

railroad strike in Birmingham, Alabama (1894); the Pennsylvania anthracite coal miners' strike (1902); the Ludlow strike in Colorado (1913); and the nationwide steel strike (1919). In 1886, Jones left the Knights of Labor and became a field organizer for a new union, the United Mine Workers of America (UMWA). By 1904, when she was in her 70s, she would be earning $4 per day for her efforts.

Mother Jones traveled the coal areas—West Virginia, Alabama and Colorado—that were the hardest to organize, so she understood the life of coal miners. She witnessed the terrible conditions in which the majority of miners and their families lived, in towns where everything—houses, stores, even the churches—was owned by the mine owners. She knew the gruesome hazards of the work beneath the ground, and she developed a reputation for fearlessness in the most intense situations, as well as for her use of salty language. She also knew how to keep up the workers' morale, making her words felt by all who heard her. She went underground in the coal mines to convince scabs, who continued to work when others were out on strike, that they should quit and support their brother workers. She also encouraged the miners to improve their minds and their English by reading.

*P*ray for the dead, but fight like hell for the living.

—**Mary Harris Jones**

In her speeches, Jones often made the coal operators and owners the butt of her jokes. She warned the miners repeatedly against trusting the churches in their communities that were supported financially by the coal owners. In one case, when a local justice of the peace upbraided her for holding a union meeting in a "house of God," she retorted, "Oh, that isn't God's house. That is the coal company's house. . . . God almighty never comes around to a place like this." Although she was a lifelong Roman Catholic, Jones never claimed allegiance to the organized church. She believed that the church had abandoned the revolutionary nature espoused by Jesus Christ and that organized religion was being used as a means of keeping people from asking questions about their condition. In her speeches, she portrayed Christ as an organizer of the poor and someone who chose to die rather than to betray the poor.

Mother Jones had great success organizing the southern West Virginia coal fields in the 1890s. On June 20, 1902, she was the featured speaker at a rally near Clarksburg, West Virginia, but at the end of the speech she was arrested and taken to Parkersburg. When it became evident that she was to be held in the local hotel, she demanded to be held in the jail with the other miners who were being detained. When Mother Jones returned to that state during the Cabin Creek and Paint Creek strikes in 1912, she was sentenced to 20 years in prison by a military court and served three months of the sentence in solitary confinement before she was released.

Many times Mother Jones was imprisoned or escorted out of town only to return again and again. During the Ludlow strike in Colorado, she was ordered to leave town or face prison, but the threat of imprisonment did not deter her. After being arrested and held in squalid conditions for one month, she was escorted out of town, but she slipped back into town with the help of men working for the railroad. Many an unsuspecting sheriff found Jones back in his town or county because of the help she received from railway workers.

Mother Jones knew that success in organizing a union often depended on the workers' presenting a united front. One way to accomplish this, often ignored by male organizers, was to get the women of the mining community involved in support of the strike. In 1899–1900, Jones told the miners out on strike in Arnot, Pennsylvania, to "stay home with the children for a change and let the women attend to the scabs." She organized a "mop and broom" brigade that traveled from mine to mine to convince scabs not to come to work, and she employed these tactics successfully at many other strike sites. In August 1907 in Westmoreland, Pennsylvania, Jones urged the wives of strikers to take their children on the picket line; if they were imprisoned, they were encouraged to sing as loud as they could so that the community would be glad to have them released.

Although the majority of Mother Jones' time was spent fighting for her miners in the coal fields, she did not ignore the needs of other workers. She assisted in the formation of a union of domestic servants, and in 1901 she helped the daughters of miners, working as silk weavers, to win their fight for improved work conditions. In order to assess the situation of child employment in southern cotton mills, Jones traveled throughout the South, hiring on and telling the managers that she had several children who would be coming to work with her. She described a scene typical of what she discovered in a cotton mill in Cottondale, Alabama, where she worked in 1904:

> Little girls and boys, barefooted, walked up and down between the endless rows of spin-
> dles, reaching their little hands into the machinery to repair snapped threads. They crawled under machinery to oil it. They replaced spindles all day long, all day long; all night through. Tiny babies six years old with faces of sixty, did an eight hour shift for ten cents a day.

These conditions were not found only in the South. In 1903, in order to bring the plight of the mill children to the attention of the nation, Jones had led a group of the young workers in a march from Kensington, Pennsylvania, to Oyster Bay, New York, where she hoped to meet with President Theodore Roosevelt. Though Roosevelt refused to see them, the march was considered responsible for legislation enacted in various states to introduce the regulation of child labor. In 1909, Mother Jones also came to the aid of striking shirtwaist workers, and in 1910 she helped to organize copper miners in Arizona and women bottlers in Milwaukee breweries; in 1916, streetcar workers on strike in El Paso, Texas, and in New York City found her at their sides.

Her non-stop efforts for the workers did not guarantee that she always got along well with union officials. When she resigned as an organizer for the United Mine Workers of America, it was because of a falling-out with the union's president, John Mitchell, because she believed he had been bought off and was serving the interests of the owners rather than the miners. She had even less respect for John L. Lewis, who became president of the United Mine Workers of America in 1919. She saw Lewis as a self-promoter and described him as "an empty piece of human slime." She carried this conviction to her deathbed, where she contributed $1,000 toward a campaign to oust Lewis from his position.

Her various political stances reveal Jones' single-minded dedication to the issues of workers' rights. She was a great admirer of Abraham Lincoln, John Brown, and Eugene V. Debs (even though she did not vote for him when he ran as the Socialist candidate for the senate in Indiana). In 1895, she had gone to Pittsburgh, Pennsylvania, and Omaha, Nebraska, to sell subscriptions to the socialist newspaper, *Appeal to Reason*. She had attended the founding convention of the Social Democrats of America in June 1897 and had written articles for the *International Socialist Review* beginning in 1900. In 1897, she visited the utopian socialist colony at Pushkin, Tennessee, but decided not to stay; her beliefs and actions regarding workers' rights were borrowed from too many ideologies for her to be comfortably confined to one.

Mary Harris Jones

After her falling-out with Mitchell, Jones became an organizer for the Western Federation of Miners (miners of metals) whose political stance was much more radical than that of the UMWA. The federation sent her as a delegate to participate in founding the new radical industrial union, the Industrial Workers of the World (IWW, or Wobblies). Though she participated at the initial stage, Jones did not continue her affiliation with the IWW.

Jones was concerned about labor conditions affecting Mexican workers who were coming into the United States, and she traveled throughout the U.S. making speeches about the dictatorial policies of President Porfirio Diaz of Mexico. She supported his overthrow and visited his successor, Francisco Madero, but the relationship was short-lived because of Madero's assassination. Nevertheless, in January 1921 she was invited by the Mexican government to speak at the Third Congress of the Pan American Federation of Labor in Mexico City.

Though her political stance was radical, and her economic ideas regarding workers were anti-capitalistic, her labor concerns put her on the conservative side of some issues. For instance, she was adamantly opposed to women's suffrage. Jones was action-oriented and did not believe in politicians or the power of the ballot box. She saw suffrage as supporting inaction, pointing out that women in Colorado had the vote but that had not kept the Ludlow Massacre from occurring. According to Jones, women needed to "realize [that with] what they have in their hands there is no limit to what they could accomplish. The trouble is they let the capitalists make them believe they wouldn't be ladylike." She also opposed the temperance movement, on the grounds that company owners used Prohibition to develop a more efficient work force by taking away one of the only means of escape available to the workers.

Mother Jones continued her work until she was well into her 80s. In 1924, when she could no longer travel, she went to live with her friend Terence Powderly at his home near Washington, D.C.; that same year, she began her autobiography. The book, edited by **Margaret F. Parton**, was published in 1925. The last years of her life were spent with a retired coal miner and his wife, Walter and **Lillie May Burgess**, in Silver Spring, Maryland. On May 1, 1930, although Jones was in poor health, she celebrated her 100th birthday, chatting with friends and appearing in a newsreel. Among the telegrams she received from around the world, her favorite was from John D.

Rockefeller, Jr.: "Please accept my heartiest congratulations on your 100th birthday anniversary. Your loyalty to your ideals, your fearless adherence to your duty as you have seen it is an inspiration to all who have known you."

Mary Harris Jones died on November 30, 1930. A requiem mass was said for her at St. Gabriel's in Washington, D.C., and then her body was sent, at her request, to Mt. Olive, Illinois, for burial at the cemetery that honored the miners killed at the Virden, Illinois, riot of 1898. Survivors of the Virden riot escorted the casket to the Odd Fellows Temple where thousands paid tribute, and the services held at Ascension Church were broadcast over labor radio station WCFL. The Reverend John W.F. Maguire, president of St. Viator's College, in Bourbonnais, Illinois, delivered the memorial address to a crowd of 10,000–15,000: "Wealthy coal operators and capitalists throughout the United States are breathing sighs of relief while toil-worn men and women are weeping tears of bitter grief. The reason for this contrast of relief and sorrow is apparent. Mother Jones is dead." The services were concluded at the cemetery, where a small stone was placed over the grave.

In 1934, the Progressive Miners of America (PMA), owners of the cemetery, began soliciting funds for a monument to mark the grave of Mother Mary Jones. The PMA, along with its women's auxiliaries, collected $16,399.25, and the monument was dedicated on October 11, 1936. The shaft of pink granite stands 22 feet high on a base flanked by bronze statues of two miners. A bas-relief of Jones at the center of the obelisk, and five plaques at the base, commemorate Mother Jones and the four men who died at Virden: General Alexander Bradley, Joseph Getterle, E. Kaemmerer, and E.W. Smith. Other plaques bear the names of the "Martyrs of the Progressive Miners of America."

On the day of the dedication, cars, trucks, chartered buses, and trains brought thousands of miners to Mt. Olive. Senator Rush D. Holt of West Virginia, Congressional Representative William Lemke of North Dakota, and Duncan McDonald, a socialist leader, were among the speakers, all of whom decried the leadership of John L. Lewis as well as the government's handling of the Depression, then in full swing. They spoke with admiration and love about the woman buried there, who had dedicated her life to bettering conditions for workers. The final speaker was Lillie May Burgess, with whom Mother Jones had lived during her last years. Burgess told her listeners that Mother Jones wanted to "live another hundred years in order to fight to the end" so "that there would be no more machine guns and no more sobbing of little children."

SOURCES:

Fetherling, Dale. *Mother Jones: The Miners' Angel.* Carbondale, IL: Southern Illinois University Press, 1974.

Nies, Judith. "Mother Jones" in *Seven Women: Portraits from the American Radical Tradition.* NY: Penguin Books, 1977.

Parton, Mary F., ed. *The Autobiography of Mother Jones.* Chicago, IL: Charles H. Kerr Publishing, 1925.

SUGGESTED READING:

Foner, Philip S., ed. *Mother Jones Speaks.* NY: Monad Press, 1983.

COLLECTIONS:

John Hunter Walker papers, Illinois Historical Survey, University of Illinois Library, Urbana, Illinois.

Mother Jones, Terence V. Powderly, and John P. Mitchell papers, Catholic University of America, Washington, D.C.

Stephane E. Booth,
Assistant Professor of History,
Kent State University, Salem Campus, Salem, Ohio

Jones, Matilda (1868–1933).

See Jones, Sissieretta.

Jones, Mother (1830–1930).

See Jones, Mary Harris.

Jones, Shirley (1934—)

American actress-singer, winner of an Academy Award for her work in Elmer Gantry, *who became the matriarch of television's "The Partridge Family."* Born on March 31, 1934, in Smithton, Pennsylvania; only child of Paul Jones (a brewery owner) and Marjorie (Williams) Jones; graduated from South Huntingdon High School; studied drama at the Pittsburgh Playhouse; married Jack Cassidy (a singer), on August 5, 1956 (divorced); married Marty Ingels (a comedian and actor-agent), in 1978 (separated 1995); children: one son, Shaun Paul Cassidy (a singer); stepson David Cassidy (an actor-singer).

Selected filmography: Oklahoma! *(1955);* Carousel *(1956);* April Love *(1957);* Never Steal Anything Small *(1959);* Bobbikins *(1960);* Elmer Gantry *(1960);* Pepe *(1960);* Two Rode Together *(1961);* The Music Man *(1962);* The Courtship of Eddie's Father *(1963);* A Ticklish Affair *(1963);* Dark Purpose *(1964);* Bedtime Story *(1964);* Fluffy *(1965);* The Secret of My Success *(1965);* The Happy Ending *(1969);* The Cheyenne Social Club *(1970);* Beyond the Poseidon Adventure *(1979);* Tank *(1984). On television, starred in "The Partridge Family" which ran from September 25, 1970, to August 31, 1974, on ABC.*

In a Cinderella story of sorts, Shirley Jones became an overnight star as the sweet-faced, golden-voiced heroine in the film versions of the Rodgers and Hammerstein musicals *Oklahoma!* (1955) and *Carousel* (1956). Refusing from the start to be typecast in good-girl roles, she performed a number of dramatic roles on television, then went on to win an Academy Award for Best Supporting Actress as the prostitute in the powerful *Elmer Gantry* (1960). After a dip in her career during the late 1960s, she came back strong on television as the mother on "The Partridge Family," which ran for four seasons and led to nine hit record albums.

Named after child star ***Shirley Temple (Black)**, Jones was born and raised in Smithton, Pennsylvania, a small town outside of Pittsburgh. An only child, she demonstrated vocal talent at the age of five and received her early training with Pittsburgh vocal coach Ken Welch. At South Huntingdon High School, Jones appeared in numerous school productions and also won a statewide singing contest. Shortly after graduating in 1952, she was selected as Miss Pittsburgh and subsequently was runner-up in the competition to select Miss Pennsylvania for the annual Miss America contest. Jones went on to study drama at the Pittsburgh Playhouse and appeared with the Pittsburgh Civic Light Opera in *Lady in the Dark* and *Call Me Madam*.

In the summer of 1953, while Jones was vacationing in New York prior to entering Centenary Junior College in the fall, Ken Welch arranged an audition for her with the agent Gus Schirmer. Schirmer was so impressed by her talent that he arranged for her to sing for a casting director for Richard Rodgers and Oscar Hammerstein II. On the strength of that audition, Jones was offered a seven-year contract with the Broadway team. As part of the deal, she was provided with further vocal and acting lessons and placed in the chorus of the long-running Rodgers and Hammerstein hit *South Pacific*. Jones was later cast in a small role in *Me and Juliet* but graduated to the starring role when the show went on tour.

Less than a year after her first audition, Jones tested and was cast as Laurey, the wholesome farm girl, in the film version of Rodgers and Hammerstein's *Oklahoma!* (1955), opposite Gordon MacRae as the handsome ranch hand, Curly. Described by Bosley Crowther as "so full of beauty, sweetness and spirit that a better Laurey cannot be dreamed," Jones was a shoo-in for the role of Julie in the follow-up musical film *Carousel* (1956). Once again, she was co-starred

Shirley
Jones

with MacRae, who was brought in to play the hapless Billy Bigelow after Frank Sinatra left the production. The back-to-back musicals catapulted Jones to stardom. *Life* magazine featured her on its cover (February 6, 1956) as "a show business phenomenon." Jones was then off to Paris and Rome as part of a stage tour of *Oklahoma!* for the U.S. State Department.

Returning to the United States, Jones appeared in a stage production of *The Beggar's Opera* in Cambridge, Massachusetts, where she met actor-singer Jack Cassidy. The two were married on August 5, 1956, after which Jones made several appearances on television, includ-

ing her portrayal of an alcoholic in "The Big Slide," an episode of "Playhouse 90." In her third film, *April Love* (1957), she was again cast as a wholesome farm girl, this time helping to reform a juvenile delinquent (Pat Boone). After the birth of her son, Shaun Cassidy, in 1958, Jones, who was by now growing weary of her pristine image, embarked on a nightclub tour with her husband. The couple also cut several LP albums of show tunes for Columbia, including a studio cast version of *Brigadoon*.

Following the mediocre reception of her next two films, Jones was cast against type as the prostitute Lulu Bains in *Elmer Gantry* (1960), a role she won through the efforts of her co-star Burt Lancaster, who played the devious evangelist of the title. It turned out to be a breakthrough role for the young actress, who won the Best Supporting Actress Academy Award for her portrayal. Afterwards, she was reluctant to return to her image as a sweet young thing. "I'm sick of portraying ingénues with sunny dispositions, high necklines and puff-sleeves who are girlishly aggressive about happiness being just around the corner," she told Sidney Skolsky (*New York Post,* July 10, 1960). "I look like what I'm not at all—as wholesome as breakfast food." Despite her protests, she was the personification of sweetness again in the role of Marion, a small town librarian who falls in love with a con man (Robert Preston), in the highly successful musical *The Music Man* (1962).

During the 1960s, Jones' popularity as a film star waned, and a 1962 television series failed to sell. In 1968, she and Cassidy had a moderate run on Broadway in the musical *Maggie Flynn,* and in 1969, a made-for-television movie *Silent Night, Lonely Night* won Jones an Emmy nomination. In 1970, however, Jones' career took a decidedly upward turn with the popular television series "The Partridge Family," a comedy based on the true story of a widowed mother who forms a successful singing act with her children (one of whom was played by her step-son David Cassidy). In addition to the series, which ran for four season, the cast of "The Partridge Family" had several successful single records and albums. Their 1970 single "I Think I Love You" sold over four million copies, and their first of nine albums, *The Partridge Family Album,* was on the charts for 70 weeks. The show also spawned a massive merchandising campaign.

Jones was divorced from Jack Cassidy in the mid-1970s. (He died in a fire in 1976.) She married comic Marty Ingels in 1977, and worked with him on several lucrative business projects. She had a short run in another television series, "Shirley," and also made a trio of feature films: a western, *The Cheyenne Social Club* (1970), a disaster sequel, *Beyond The Poseidon Adventure* (1979), and *Tank* (1984), her last movie.

In 1988, Jones and her husband Marty Ingels received the National Leukemia Council's first Gift of Life Award for their 15 years of volunteer work in fighting the disease. That same year, Jones appeared in the PBS special "In Performance at the White House," and also co-hosted a TV special, "Christmas in D.C." with opera star **Kathleen Battle**. She also had a run-

ning role as Kitty Noland in the comedy television series "The 'Slap' Maxwell Story."

SOURCES:

Katz, Ephraim. *The Film Encyclopedia.* NY: HarperCollins, 1994.

Moritz, Charles, ed. *Current Biography 1961.* NY: H.W. Wilson, 1961.

Parish, James Robert, and Michael R. Pitts. *Hollywood Songsters.* Garland, 1991.

Barbara Morgan,
Melrose, Massachusetts

Jones, Sissieretta (1869–1933)

African-American soprano. Name variations: Matilda Jones; Matilda Joyner. Born Matilda Sissieretta Joyner in Portsmouth, Virginia, on January 5, 1869; died in Providence, Rhode Island, on June 24, 1933; daughter of Jeremiah Malachi Joyner (a minister) and Henrietta Joyner; attended the Meeting Street and Thayer Street schools, Providence, Rhode Island; studied voice at the Providence Academy of Music and the New England Conservatory, Boston, Massachusetts; married David Richard Jones (a newsdealer and bellman), on September 4, 1883 (divorced 1898); no children.

The daughter of a Baptist minister, soprano Sissieretta Jones was born in Portsmouth, Virginia, on January 5, 1869. Around 1879, the family moved to Providence, Rhode Island, where Jones attended grammar school and sang in her father's church. At age 14, she was married to David Richard Jones, a young man from Baltimore who worked variously as a newsdealer and a hotel bellman, and even served as his wife's manager during her early career. However, in 1898, Jones filed for divorce, charging her husband with drunkenness and nonsupport.

Although details of Jones' life and career are obscure, it is generally believed that she received her early voice training at the Providence Academy of Music and may have also attended the New England Conservatory in Boston. She made her New York debut in 1888, followed by a six-month tour of the West Indies as a featured performer with the Jubilee Singers of Fisk University. For the next decade, she appeared with various concert companies and gave some solo concerts. During this period, she reportedly toured Europe, sang at the White House, and gave a command performance for the Prince of Wales. Her most publicized appearances were at the "Grand African Jubilee," held in Madison Square Garden in New York, April 26–28, 1892. Her trained operatic voice was acclaimed by critics as one in a million, and newspapers dubbed her "the Black Patti," a reference to the famous Italian soprano *Adelina Patti. (Jones disclaimed the comparison and always called herself Madame Jones.) Jones generally performed a program combining operatic arias with popular songs like "Old Folks at Home" and "The Last Rose of Summer," although, as time went on, her audiences began to push her toward a more ethnic repertoire.

In 1896, Jones embarked on the second phase of her career, formulating a troupe of jugglers, comedians, dancers, and singers called the Black Patti Troubadours. Combining elements of vaudeville, minstrel, musical review, and grand opera, the troupe enjoyed great success, playing primarily to white audiences in major cities across the country. The second half of the show often included what Jones called an "operatic kaleidoscope," an expanded version of her excerpts, presented with scenery and costume, and including portions of such operas as *Lucia, Il Trovatore, Martha,* and *El Capitan.* The troupe flourished for a decade, but by 1916 audiences for the hybrid productions were growing scarce, and Jones was forced to disband the troupe. The final performance was at the Gibson Theater in New York, and the last payroll checks were said to have bounced.

Sissieretta Jones returned to her home in Providence where she devoted her later years to church work and caring for her ailing mother. She died in obscurity and poverty at the age of 74. Unfortunately, no one ever thought to make a recording of Jones, so her magnificent voice was lost to subsequent generations.

SOURCES:

James, Edward T., ed. *Notable American Women, 1607–1950.* Cambridge, MA: The Belknap Press of Harvard University Press, 1971.

McHenry, Robert, ed. *Famous American Women.* NY: Dover, 1983.

Smith, Jessie Carney, ed. *Notable Black American Women.* Detroit, MI: Gale Research, 1996.

Barbara Morgan,
Melrose, Massachusetts

Jonker, Ingrid (1933–1965)

Afrikaaner poet whose death was regarded by many as a protest against apartheid. Born on September 19, 1933, in Douglas Cape Province, South Africa; drowned herself in the ocean at Green Point, Cape Town, on July 19, 1965; daughter of Abraham Jonker (a writer and editor) and Beatrice (Cilliers) Jonker; attended high school; married Pieter also seen as Peter Venter; children: daughter Simone Venter (b. 1957).

Completed first collection of poetry, Na die Somer *(1949); published first collection,* Ontvlugting *(1956); published* Rook en Oker *(1963); won South Africa's largest literary prize; traveled around Europe; her last collection,* Kantelson, *published from her manuscripts after her death.*

Selected works: Ontvlugting *(Escape, Cape Town: Uitgewery Culemborg, 1956);* Rook en Oker *(Smoke and Ocher, Johannesburg: Afrikaanse Pers-Boekhandel, 1963); "Die Bok" (The Goat, short story published in* London *magazine); (published posthumously)* Kantelson *(Setting Sun, Johannesburg: Afrikaanse Pers-Boekhandel, 1966);* Versamelde Werke *(Complete Works, including the titles listed above, as well as "Enkele vertalings deur Ingrid Jonker" [three poems in English], "Fragmente en opdragte," "Jeugwerk" [poems in Afrikaans], "Prosa," and five short stories, Human & Rousseau, 3rd rev. ed, 1994).*

On July 19, 1965, Ingrid Jonker, an Afrikaaner in her early 30s, took her life, purposefully drowning in the ocean at Green Point, Cape Town. Three decades later, on May 24, 1994, President Nelson Mandela gave his first State of the Nation address to the Houses of Parliament in Cape Town. In his speech, he invoked the memory of a woman whose death many regarded as a tragic protest against the immorality of the South African government during apartheid.

> The time will come when our nation will honour the memory of all the sons, the daughters, the mothers, the fathers, the youth and the children who, by their thoughts and deeds, gave us the right to assert with pride that we are South Africans, that we are Africans and that we are citizens of the world. . . . [A]mong these we shall find an Afrikaaner woman who transcended a particular experience and became a South African, an African and a citizen of the world. Her name is Ingrid Jonker.
>
> She was both a poet and a South African. She was both an Afrikaaner and an African. She was both an artist and a human being. In the midst of despair, she celebrated hope. Confronted with death, she asserted the beauty of life. In the dark days when all seemed hopeless in our country, when many refused to hear her resonant voice, she took her own life. To her and others like her, we owe a debt to life itself. To her and others like her, we owe a commitment to the poor, the oppressed, the wretched and the despised.

Ingrid Jonker was born on September 19, 1933, in Douglas Cape Province, the daughter of Abraham Jonker, a writer and editor, and **Beatrice Cilliers Jonker**. Beatrice had left Abraham before Ingrid was born, and Ingrid's grandfather died when the child was five, leaving three generations of women to eke out an existence. Along with her sister, Ingrid spent her early years accompanying her mother and grandmother, who were relegated to collecting scraps and throwaways. At age six, she began writing poetry, an act she later referred to as "making my own happiness." The rhythms of the Afrikaaner hymn book she used as a guide would later be transformed into free verse.

After the death of their mother around 1943, the Jonker sisters moved to the house of their father who had remarried and had a new family, but the sisters never managed to fit in. It was Abraham Jonker who helped write the laws which censored and silenced dissident voices. At 16, Ingrid completed her first collection of poems, *Na die Somer,* and vainly attempted to get it published, but it would be another seven years before her first book, *Ontvlugting,* appeared in print. Perhaps in response to her difficult childhood, she was often subject to periods of hopelessness, and her poetry is filled with images of despair. Wrote Jonker in "Pregnant Woman":

> I lie under the crust of the night singing,
> curled up in the sewer, singing,
> and my bloodchild lies in the water.

Jonker married Peter Venter and worked as a publisher's reader, a secretary, and a typist while continuing to write. In 1957, she gave birth to a daughter, **Simone Venter**, then, like her mother before her, left her husband soon thereafter. In the same year, a young African lawyer named Nelson Mandela was one of the 156 activists charged in the notorious Treason Trials. The South Africa of Jonker's day was one in which the legislative apparatus of apartheid was being established. Pass laws to control movement of Africans around their country and education laws designed to make sure that Africans learned only how to be menial workers were passed in the early 1950s. In response, anti-apartheid organizations, including the African National Congress (ANC), mobilized people around the country to protest the repression.

In 1960, there were violent clashes in Langa and Sharpeville where the police shot and killed unarmed civilians who were protesting the pass-laws. On March 21 in Sharpeville, 69 people were killed, most of whom died from bullet wounds to the back. In Nyanga, a baby was shot in the head. During a time when the white power minority was repressing the majority African population, Jonker's poetry mirrored the horror. Now the mother of a three-year-old, Jonker wrote "Die Kind wat doodgeskiet is deuv soldate by Nyanga" (The Child Who Was Shot Dead by Soldiers in Nyanga) which tells of a child who, though victim to the violence Jonker was witnessing, lives on in the public conscience. Destined to be invoked as a testament to the evils of apartheid, the poem appeared in her second collection *Rook en Oker,* for which she won South Africa's largest literary prize. With the £1,000 prize, Jonker traveled to England, Holland, France, Spain, and Portugal.

Although she is best known as a poet in the Afrikaans language, Jonker also studied English poetry, especially that of John Keats and Dylan Thomas, and translated some of her own work into English. Her poems have also been translated into 12 other languages including Zulu and Hindi. In addition to her poetry, Jonker published the short story "Die Bok," which appeared in *London* magazine, and completed the play, *A Son after My Heart.*

Ingrid Jonker was unable to come to terms with the despair and sense of foreboding with which she lived. The lines of a poem she had written at age 20—"My body lies in seaweed and in grass/ washed up in every place that we have passed"—foreshadowed her death 12 years later. In a speech delivered at the International Conference on "Children, Repression and the Law in Apartheid South Africa" held in Harare on September 24, 1987, her suicide was called "as powerful an indictment of the apartheid system" as had been her dissident voice. On that occasion, Jonker's poem "Die Kind wat doodgeskiet is deuv soldate by Nyanga" was recited, including the lines:

> The child is not dead
> not at Langa nor at Nyanga
> nor at Orlando nor at Sharpeville
> nor at the police post at Philippi
> where he lies with a bullet through his brain. . . .
> this child who wanted only to play in
> the sun at Nyanga is everywhere

"We share with her," noted the keynote speaker, "the knowledge and confidence that the wanton massacre of the children at Langa and at Nyanga, at Orlando and at Sharpeville, at Soweto, Athlone, Maseru, Gaborone, Harare, Maputo and Kassinga, the knowledge that this succession of massacres will not deny us our journey over the whole world—free at last, at last free, the last to be free but free, at last."

SOURCES:

Ingrid Jonker: Selected Poems. Translated from the Afrikaans by Jack Cope and William Plomer. London: Jonathan Cape, 1968.

In Memoriam: Ingrid Jonker. Kaapstad, Pretoria, South Africa: Human & Rousseau, 1966.

SUGGESTED READING:

A Century of South African Poetry. Introduced and edited by Michael Chapman. Johannesburg: Donker, 1981.

Cope, Jack. *The Adversary Within: Dissident writers in Afrikaans.* Cape Town, South Africa: D. Phillip, 1982 (NJ: Humanities Press).

The Penguin Book of South African verse. Compiled and introduced by Jack Cope and Uys Krige. Harmondsworth: Penguin, 1968.

RELATED MEDIA:

Opdrag: Ingrid Jonker, one-woman play performed by acclaimed South African actor **Jana Cilliers,** written by Ryk Hattingh, directed by Mark Graham.

Muhonjia Khaminwa, freelance writer, Cambridge, Massachusetts

Jönsson, Sara (1880–1974).

See Sandel, Cora.

Joplin, Janis (1943–1970)

American rock and blues singer who found her way into the beatnik and hippie countercultures and became an icon for American youth in the 1960s, leaving an indelible mark on American music as she expressed her own angst through blues. Name variations: (nickname) Pearl. Pronunciation: JOP-lynn. Born Janis Lyn Joplin on January 19, 1943, in Port Arthur, Texas; overdosed and died at the Landmark Hotel, Los Angeles, California, on October 4, 1970; daughter of Seth Ward Joplin (a mechanical engineer) and Dorothy Bonita (East) Joplin (a clerk, registrar); graduated Thomas Jefferson High School; attended Lamar Technological College and the University of Texas to study painting, and Port Arthur Business College; never married; no children.

Absorbed Beat culture during sojourn in Los Angeles and Venice Beach, California (1960); sang in public for first time at Halfway House in Beaumont, Texas (1961); sang at University of Texas hootenannies and Threadgill's in Austin (1962); hitchhiked to San Francisco's Haight-Ashbury, sang in coffeehouses, and began using speed (1963); spent summer in New York City (1964); returned to Port Arthur (1965); went to San Francisco to join Big Brother and the Holding Company, and began using heroin (1966); recorded first album with Mainstream Records (1966); broke out at Monterey Pop Festival (1967); signed with Columbia Records (1968); left Big Brother and formed the Kozmic Blues band (1968); toured Europe (1969); appeared at Woodstock (1969); traveled to Carnival in Brazil (1970); formed the Full Tilt Boogie Band (1970); attended high school reunion (August 1970); while recording Pearl, *died of an overdose of alcohol and heroin (1970); posthumously hon-*

ored by Port Arthur with a bronze statue and permanent exhibit (1988).

Selected albums: Big Brother and the Holding Company *(Mainstream, September 1967);* Cheap Thrills: Big Brother and the Holding Company *(Columbia, September 1968);* I Got Dem Ol' Kozmic Blues Again Mama!: Janis Joplin *(Columbia, November 1969);* Pearl: Janis Joplin/Full Tilt Boogie *(Columbia, January 1971);* Joplin in Concert *(Columbia, July 1972);* Janis Joplin's Greatest Hits *(Columbia, July 1973); (issued to accompany the film)* Janis *(Columbia, 1975);* Farewell Song *(Columbia, January 1982).*

Wrote selected lyrics: "Intruder," "Turtle Blues," "Oh, Sweet Mary," "One Good Man," "Move Over," (with Big Brother and the Holding Company) "Blindman," (with Sam Andrew) "I Need a Man to Love," (with Peter Albin) "Road Block," (with Nick Gravenites) "Ego Rock," (with Gabriel Mekler) "Kozmic Blues," (with Michael McClure) "Mercedes Benz," and (vocal arrangement) "Down on Me."

In the Louisiana border bars that were an easy drive from her hometown of Port Arthur, Texas, Janis Joplin would join her girlfriends in flirting with the Cajun rednecks, trying to get the locals to buy them drinks, until the behavior would grow so outrageous that the Port Arthur visitors would have to flee to escape a fistfight. On one such occasion, Janis and **Patti Denton** had taken the game a bit too far for Patti's boyfriend, Dave McQueen. Ferrying the drunken group of seven home, McQueen furiously pushed his Oldsmobile past 110 miles per hour, lighting matches to check the speedometer on the dark dashboard, and refusing his passengers' pleas to slow down. Inevitably, the car went into a roll, turning over several times, but all seven walked away from the wreck, miraculously untouched, except for the drinks they spilled on themselves. Joplin's companions would later find her remarks about her high school days on a 1970 "Dick Cavett Show" baffling, if not galling. Just before her return to Port Arthur for her Class of 1960 reunion, Joplin told Cavett, "They laughed me out of class, out of town, and out of the state—so I'm going home." Seen together, the two incidents reflect both her need to live life at full tilt and her need to create her own personal mythology.

In fact, Janis Joplin experienced a very moderate middle-class upbringing. Her parents, Seth and **Dorothy Joplin,** brought Janis Lyn home from St. Mary's Hospital to 4048 Procter after her birth on January 19, 1943. When Janis was six and her younger sister **Laura Joplin** was born, the family moved to the Griffing Park area, where her brother Michael was welcomed four years later. The Joplins' backyard served as the neighborhood gathering place, with the standard sandbox and play equipment created by Seth, as well as a puppet playhouse, a homemade Giant Stride, a tightrope, and a circular seesaw. Seth was a mechanical engineer at the Texaco plant, and Dorothy was employed at Sears and Port Arthur Business College, conveying a strong work ethic to Janis and her siblings, who did not lack for attention. Their father talked with them, played classical records for them, and entertained them in imaginative ways, such as taking them to the post office to see "Wanted" posters. Trips to the public library were a highlight of family life, and Joplin remained a voracious reader throughout her life. The family attended the First Christian Church, voted Republican, and subscribed to *Time* magazine. Dorothy, a former radio announcer who played piano and sang until her singing voice was lost from thyroid surgery, encouraged her children to express themselves.

In contrast to her later persona, Joplin did typical childhood things. In elementary school, she joined the Bluebirds, a Girl Scout-like organization, wrote plays for her puppets, took private drawing and painting lessons, and looked after her brother and sister. She showed enough intelligence to skip third grade. Though she performed with the church choir and the junior high glee club, she did not view herself as a singer. In the seventh grade, she was a member of the local bridge club and the Tri Hi Y club.

With the onset of adolescence and high school, her situation changed. "Then the whole world turned!" she once said. "It just turned on me!" Her failure to be accepted into the locally prestigious Red Hussars drum and bugle corps was one early blow. By the ninth grade, in a decidedly conservative and segregated society, she demonstrated her independence of mind by voicing her support for integration, but she was part of the usual school activities, heading the journalism club, illustrating the high school literary magazine, and attending Arthur Murray dance classes. That summer, she appeared in the Port Arthur Little Theater's production of *Sunday Costs Five Pesos* and volunteered at the public library where she drew posters for the children's bulletin board.

The next year, the high school hoodlums caught her eye, but she failed to fit into their clique. Meanwhile, she joined the Future Nurses Association, the Future Teachers Association,

and the Psi Lambda social club. But she also violated the codes of normalcy of most high school kids of the 1950s. Dropping the standard bobby sox and loafers, she took on a less feminine persona. She dressed in shortened skirts, without make-up and declining to act demure, and became "one of the guys." In her junior year, Janis insinuated herself into a group of five boys who viewed themselves as the high school's intelligentsia, listening to jazz instead of the new rock and roll, and reading books not assigned in class. Joplin provided a degree of outrageousness that became a catalyst for their fun, as they climbed the local water tower, held beach parties, sang and drank beer. Embracing exotic philosophies and demonstrating their rejection of established society through unconventional dress, they looked upon themselves as the Port Arthur beatniks. Within this group, Joplin left her former shyness behind, all her awareness of plumpness and poor skin abandoned in the sessions of drinking and talk. Sometimes, she joined them in climbs up the Rainbow Bridge, which spanned the narrow Nueces River at a height that allowed the passage of ocean-going vessels underneath. Once, without her father's permission, she took his car and gathered up the guys for a trip to the bars of the New Orleans French Quarter. On the dawn ride home in the rain, they had an accident, totaling her father's Willis.

> *What* are they going to say about me? . . .
> I think it's going to be that my music was when
> the black and white thing broke down, and black could
> dig what white sang, and white could dig what black
> sang . . . and it was all music.
>
> —Janis Joplin

The accident, and the situation surrounding it, led to gossip and the beginning of Joplin's reputation in Port Arthur as a "slut," a situation not helped after her mother encouraged her to take mechanical drawing in her senior year; as the only girl in the class, she was assumed to be there to "chase" boys. Since many of her gang had graduated by then, she endured the year on her own, reportedly mocked by students who threw pennies at her to signify that she was "cheap." Although the claims later grew about her sexual activity during this time, friends of Joplin have characterized her as a late bloomer, gullible and not even proficient at cussing before her junior or senior year. But in that senior year and the summer after graduation, when she waited tables at the bowling alley, sold theater tickets part time, and also managed to sell a few of her paintings, several of the men who knew her have reported liaisons.

In the fall of 1960, Joplin enrolled at Lamar Technological College in Beaumont to study art. Instead of the freedom she had expected, Lamar replicated the high school scene of Port Arthur; her reputation also preceded her. Home the following spring, she signed up for classes at Port Arthur Business College, at her mother's urging, but missed most classes due to "illness." Joplin began traveling to Houston to soak up the beat culture, along with a great deal of alcohol, at the Purple Onion Coffeeshop. As her dependence on alcohol grew evident, she went to see both a psychiatrist and a psychologist, visits she later played up as a "nervous breakdown."

In the summer of 1961, financed by her parents, Joplin drove to Los Angeles in a Morris Minor convertible to get a job and stay with relatives, in particular her Aunt Barbara. Hired as a keypunch operator for the Los Angeles Telephone Company, she left her aunt's to explore her bisexuality and experience the beatnik scene at Venice Beach, which was by that time in decline. Taking a second job at the Bank of America, Joplin passed her summer in a daze of drug experiments, then returned to Port Arthur.

On New Year's Eve, with little notice, Joplin made her debut as a singer at the Halfway House in Beaumont. A friend allowed her to take the stage for one song, then scooted her off quickly when the performance was poorly received. In 1962, she recorded an advertising jingle for a local bank that went unused and sang in Houston at the Purple Onion, while continuing to wait tables at the bowling alley. Perpetuating her habit of frequenting the Louisiana bars with her cronies, she expanded her drinking tastes from beer to bourbon and Thunderbird wine, while her flirting games grew more dangerous.

That summer, visiting a friend in Austin, Joplin discovered the underground cultural life thriving at the University of Texas. Enrolled shortly afterward as a freshman art major, she drew enough attention with her attitudes and all-black style of dress (taken by some as a sign of her sexual liberation) to be written up by the student newspaper. She became sexually involved with **Juli Paul**, musician Powell St. John, and later underground newspaper editor Bill Killeen, and engaged in recreational one-night stands, while becoming more involved with her singing. Joplin learned to play the autoharp to accompany herself, and later took up the guitar to avoid splitting proceeds with back-up musicians. As she began to experiment with marijuana, peyote, and secobarbital, she now sang weekly with the Waller Creek Boys (Powell St. John on harmonica and Lanny Wiggins on guitar) at campus "hootenannies" and at Threadgill's, a bar that highlighted live folk music, where owner Kenneth Threadgill allowed Joplin to sing one blues song per set.

In 1963, Joplin hitchhiked to San Francisco with Chet Helms, a Beat poet. She later claimed that she had never wanted to be a singer, but only to be a beatnik and have constant fun. Whatever her career goals, she began singing in coffeehouses—Coffee, Confusion, the Coffee Gallery—where she became friends with bartender Howard Hesseman, later a well-known actor, and clothing designer **Linda Gravenites** who became her roommate. Joplin sang at the Monterey Folk Festival and on the KPFA Midnight Special radio show until temporarily halted by a motorcycle accident and a street brawl. In San Francisco's Haight-Ashbury section, soon to become the center of hippie life, Joplin sang for beers and passed the hat, while working part-time jobs and collecting unemployment. Like a number of citizens of the emerging counterculture, she shoplifted for necessary and desirable items, an activity that got her arrested on February 2, 1963. By this time, alcohol and methamphetamine, or "speed," were setting the rhythm of her days.

In the summer of 1964, Joplin found herself in New York City's Greenwich Village without really knowing how she got there. Living on the street and in Washington Square Park, she sang at Slugs and dabbled with everything from marijuana to cocaine, heroin, and speed, and began to deal speed and hashish. Record companies, meanwhile, began to send scouts to see her perform, but drugs ranked higher in her life than her career. In the fall, she returned to San Francisco, where she took a new lover.

The following spring, Joplin committed herself to a hospital in an attempt to get off drugs, but failed to do so. Frightened by her addictions, she returned to Port Arthur, where she sought to conform to the town's expectations, telling her parents that she had come home to prepare to get married. She dressed conservatively, wore makeup, pulled her hair into a neat bun, took up typing and canasta and insisted on being treated like a lady. That summer, she reentered Lamar as a sociology major and saw a therapist. When friends encouraged her to sing at a benefit for a blues singer, she appeared in a business suit.

She was vocalizing again in clubs around southeast and central Texas when she heard of a tryout in California for Big Brother and the Holding Company, a band comprised of bass player Peter Albin, lead guitarist James Gurley, drummer Dave Getz, and guitarist Sam Andrew. The band's manager, her old friend Chet Helms, accompanied Janis to Port Arthur, promising the Joplins that their daughter would return to college in the fall semester if the tryout failed. The duo then hitched rides to San Francisco, becoming lovers along the way; Helms later proposed, but without success. On the journey, Joplin reportedly carried two books, *The Ten Commandments* and *Billie Holiday*'s *Lady Sings the Blues*.

Later in her life, she identified closely with the tragic lives of singers like Holiday, *Bessie Smith, and *Odetta, and with *Zelda Fitzgerald.

Although she had not previously performed their kind of "freak rock," Joplin became the singer for the Big Brother band. Six days after her acceptance, their first performance as a group was at the Avalon Ballroom where they were hired eventually as the house band. Melding into the group, Joplin began an affair with James Gurley, who temporarily left his wife Nancy to live with Janis; according to one

Janis Joplin

source, the affair nearly destroyed the band. In July, however, after the band moved out of the city into a house in Lagunitas, in the San Geronimo Valley, **Nancy Gurley** and Joplin became great friends, and Nancy guided Janis' choices in hippie fashion. The two women also began to share speed. At a time when lysergic acid diethylamide, or LSD, was legally available and the hippie culture's drug of choice, Joplin's preferences remained speed and alcohol; she also experimented with DMT (dimethyltryptamine).

Joplin refused offers from other bands and even turned down a proposal from Elektra Records to go out on her own. In August, the band took a job in Chicago playing at Mother Blues, but did not draw a crowd large enough to cover their pay. Against the advice of their manager, they signed a contract for an album with Mainstream Records, believing they would get enough money to return to San Francisco. The group received so little in pay that they still had to scrounge money to get home, and the album was not released until a year later, when Big Brother had made a name for itself.

In February 1967, Joplin began a live-in romance with Country Joe MacDonald of Country Joe and the Fish, which did not prevent her from taking on several other lovers that year: roadie Mark Brounstein, musicians Jimi Hendrix and Jim Morrison, actors Tom Baker and Howard Hesseman, and disc jockey Milan Melvin. With a gaggle of female friends, dubbed "The Capricorn Ladies," Joplin also liked to ramble down Haight Street, feeling at home, drinking Ripple or Rainer Ale, or taking in an improvisational review by The Committee. LSD joined her stash of pharmaceuticals. In April, she wrote her family that she would soon be the first pin-up for Haight-Ashbury; personality posters were a new fad, and Bob Seligmann had taken a photograph of her posing topless with a cape and strings of beads.

In June 1967, Big Brother and the Holding Company broke out of the pack of California bands at the Monterey International Pop Festival. Originally scheduled for only one performance, the band did two, in order to be included in the film *Monterey Pop*. For the first appearance, Joplin was in her usual funky hip garb, but for the filmed performance she switched to a gold lamé dress that heralded the birth of her honky-tonk, "used-girl" image. In front of an estimated crowd of 72,000, Big Brother and Joplin managed to upstage more established acts like the Mamas and the Papas, Jefferson Airplane, and The Association, rising to the ranks of performers like Jimi Hendrix and the Who. Between the two gigs, the band signed with Albert Grossman, a professional manager from New York, who stipulated that his bands not use heroin. That fall, the band traveled to Seattle, Vancouver, Los Angeles, Boston, and Huntington Beach for shows; Joplin returned to Port Arthur for Christmas, and then traveled to Mexico for an abortion.

In February 1968, Big Brother journeyed to New York for a concert, settled into the Chelsea Hotel and established Max's Kansas City as their hangout. A contract with Columbia Records allowed them to buy their way out of the non-lucrative and damaging contract with Mainstream, and Grossman began shifting their billing from "Big Brother and the Holding Company" to "Big Brother and the Holding Company featuring Janis Joplin," then to "Janis Joplin and Big Brother and the Holding Company."

In February, the band played in Boston, Cambridge, Providence, and Chicago before starting to record their next album, *Cheap Thrills*. During the recording session, Joplin revealed herself to be a hard-working perfectionist, but her drug taking kept her dangerously on the edge. Once during this period, roommate Linda Gravenites had to revive her from an overdose of heroin. Upon release, *Cheap Thrills* reached "gold" by being Number One on the Billboard Charts for eight weeks. Joplin was named Best Female Pop Singer by both the Readers' Poll and the International Critics' Poll of *Jazz and Pop* magazine.

In September 1968, Grossman announced that Joplin and Big Brother had split amicably. To David Dalton, once a reporter for *Rolling Stone*, Joplin would later state that she decided "to sell out" because she wanted "to be rich." She continued to sing with the group through December, a bottle of Southern Comfort by this time accompanying her everywhere. In letters home and to those around her, Joplin began to brag about her growing wealth; she bought a Porsche and struggled with trying to differentiate between her dayself and her stage persona.

Grossman, meanwhile, put together the Kozmic Blues, a band of professional musicians, not friends. The group rehearsed in San Francisco but bombed while debuting at the Memphis Stax-Volt "Yuletide Thing." In early 1969, still lacking cohesion, they opened to four sold-out shows in New York City, where Joplin was still a hot ticket, but the reviews ranged from bad to worse. In March, Joplin appeared on CBS Television's "60 Minutes" and "The Ed Sullivan Show," where Sullivan is reported to have refused to shake her hand. The Kozmic Blues played in San Francisco, again to poor reviews, then traveled through Europe in April and May where they were received with raves. Joplin was named "a hot white soul sister" and "the wildest happening since Elvis" by the British press, but when the time came to return home, Gravenites chose to remain in England, ostensibly to embroider jackets for George Harrison, rather than witness Joplin's further disintegration from alcohol and heroin.

The group traveled to Hollywood to record an album. But as Joplin and her performance deteriorated from the drugs, she began to spend most of her time with the roadies. During the summer of 1969, she appeared on a number of television shows, and at a concert in Atlanta in July she exposed herself to fans. At the Woodstock Festival in August, she gave a markedly bad performance. After a concert in Tampa, Florida, on November 16, she was arrested as she left the stage, charged with two counts of using vulgar and obscene language, a crime for which she later paid a fine of $200 in absentia. On tour, she meanwhile developed a pre-show ritual, spending hours in the dressing room before going onstage, stringing beads and placing each of her many bracelets, one by one, on her arms. Her books were still with her, wherever she traveled, including a biography of Zelda Fitzgerald.

By December, Joplin appeared ready to face her need to kick her addictions when she consulted Dr. Edmund Rothschild, who prescribed methadone and Valium. Returning to California, she purchased a house on Baltimore Avenue in Larkspur, began to adopt dogs, purebred and from the pound, and promised to clean up her act if Gravenites would room with her. In January 1970, Joplin renewed her methadone prescription to help her get off heroin.

Facing the disbanding of the Kozmic Blues Band, she perhaps felt a need to regain control. As a way to get away from the drugs, she and Linda headed for Carnival in Rio de Janiero, Brazil, where Joplin met a young man, David George Niehaus, who was unaware of her celebrity. Reveling in her anonymity, Joplin took a trip into the jungle with Niehaus and made some progress in distancing herself from drugs, then cut the vacation in half and traveled back to Los Angeles where she bought $10,000 worth of heroin before reaching Larkspur. Following her home, Niehaus discovered her in bed, strung out and with a female lover. Gravenites, unwilling to be witness to another overdose, moved out.

Joplin tried to escape the drugs at a Mexican spa but increased her alcohol consumption.

Breaking another gender barrier of the time, she had a bracelet tattooed around her wrist, a bud on her ankle, and a heart over her own. In April 1970, the management company helped her put together a group to match her voice and leadership style, called the Full Tilt Boogie Band. She enjoyed a few reunion gigs with Big Brother, but the performances suffered from her condition. A love affair with singer-songwriter Kris Kristofferson devolved into an alcohol codependency. Her concerts at this point were often performed in an alcoholic blackout, while the ravages of drug use showed in blotchy and bloated skin, bleeding gums, headaches, and a bad stomach. That June, she made her notorious appearance on "The Dick Cavett Show" that included her remarks about Port Arthur and her classmates.

Joplin made her first official appearance with Full Tilt Boogie in Louisville, where the reviews were good. From June 28 through July 4, the band toured Canada on the "Festival Express," a rolling party with free-flowing alcohol, assorted drugs, freewheeling sex, and constant jamming aboard a train carrying their group along with the Grateful Dead. By the end of the tour, the song by Kristofferson that was to be her greatest hit, "Me and Bobby McGee," had become the group's anthem.

In August, Joplin struck up a relationship with Seth Morgan, a drug dealer who made a cocaine delivery to the Larkspur house. Back on "Cavett" the week before her high school reunion, she appeared seriously inebriated. On August 12, Joplin and Full Tilt Boogie performed for the last time, at Harvard Stadium, before traveling the next day with a few friends to Port Arthur for the tenth reunion of the Thomas Jefferson High School Class of 1960. At her parents' home, Joplin slept on a cot in the den while her parents were appalled at the men they found sleeping both in and outside their house. The afternoon before the reunion, the organizers allowed Joplin to hold a press conference. When classmates appeared bemused by Joplin, her companions encouraged her to mingle to stop their stares. She left the reunion early and took her friends partying at Houston's clubs. When she returned to California, Joplin and Morgan announced their engagement, and Joplin commissioned a premarital agreement.

In September, she went to Los Angeles where she moved into the Landmark Hotel, a known drug "shooting gallery," to begin recording a new album with Full Tilt Boogie. Under producer Paul Rothschild, the band worked diligently on the album, commissioning a few new songs at the last minute, including "Buried Alive in the Blues" by Joplin's friend Nick Gravenites. That month, when Jimi Hendrix died, Joplin mused, "Wonder if I'll get as much publicity?" On October 1, she revised her will, excluding her friend Linda, previously a beneficiary, and leaving the bulk of her estate to her family. On October 3, already high on heroin and gulping Ripple wine, Joplin taped "Me and Bobby McGee" and reviewed the instrumental track for the recording of her vocals at the next day's session. Before leaving the studio, the band recorded "Happy Birthday" for John Lennon, which Joplin tagged with "Happy Trails to You," then she retired to Barney's Beanery with some of the musicians for drinks. But in the course of the evening, neither of her planned dates showed up, nor did Linda, who had come to Los Angeles unexpectedly to see her. Around 1 AM, Joplin shot up with heroin before going down to the lobby to buy cigarettes. She chatted with the desk clerk about how well the album seemed to be going, and her plans for another, then returned alone to Room 105.

At the studio the next day, when she did not turn up to record, the producer became worried. Road manager Jim Cooke, noticing her car still at the hotel, entered her room and found Joplin face down on the floor between a chair and the bed. She had died 18 hours earlier of an accidental overdose of heroin combined with alcohol; the coroner found no evidence of suicide. That weekend, a particularly pure, and therefore more lethal, batch of heroin had hit the street. There were eight other deaths by overdose in the area.

Joplin's will provided $2,500 for a wake in her honor at the Lion's Share nightclub in San Anselmo (friends received invitations inscribed, "Drinks are on Pearl"), and her ashes were scattered from a plane over the Marin County coast. Using previously recorded vocal tracks, the band finished the album *Pearl*, released in February 1971, which rose to the top of the Billboard Charts, while "Me and Bobby McGee" became the #1 hit single, and *Rolling Stone* declared Joplin the "premier white blues singer of the 1960s."

In 1988, Janis Joplin was honored with her picture on the cover of *Time*, the magazine favored by her parents. That same year, even Port Arthur began to come around. A former classmate headed an effort to establish the Janis Joplin Permanent Exhibit, and a bronze statue, capturing Joplin in a multitude of poses, was dedicated. Since then, the city, whether out of forgiveness of its prodigal daughter or with an eye toward bolstering its economy through tourism, has hosted an annual Janis Joplin Birthday Bash.

SOURCES:

Amburn, Ellis. *Pearl: The Obsessions and Passions of Janis Joplin.* NY: Warner Books, 1992.

Dalton, David. *Piece of My Heart: The Life, Times and Legend of Janis Joplin.* NY: St. Martin's Press, 1986.

Friedman, Myra. *Buried Alive: The Biography of Janis Joplin.* NY: William Morrow, 1973.

Joplin, Laura. *Love XX Janis.* NY: Villard Books, 1992.

SUGGESTED READING:

Carey, Gary. *Lenny, Janis and Jimi.* NY: Pocket Books, 1975.

Caserta, Peggy as told to Dan Knapp. *Going Down with Janis.* NY: Harcourt, Brace, Jovanovich, 1973.

Echols, Alice. *Scars of Sweet Paradise: The Life and Times of Janis Joplin.* NY: Holt/Metropolitan, 1999.

Landau, Deborah. *Janis Joplin: Her Life and Times.* NY: Paperback Library, 1971.

RELATED MEDIA:

Janis: The Way She Was (1 hr., 36 min., interviews and concert footage), MCA Home Video, 1975.

Janis (musical), written by **Susan Ross**, 1991.

Monterey Pop (film of the 1967 concert), Sony Video, 1969.

The Rose (film), starring **Bette Midler** in a role reminiscent of Joplin's life, CBS/Fox, 1979.

COLLECTIONS:

Janis Joplin Exhibit, Texas Musical Heritage Museum, Gates Memorial Library, Port Arthur, Texas; Janis Joplin files, Lincoln Center Library for the Performing Arts, New York, New York; and Janis Joplin files, Margaret Herrick Library of the Academy of Motion Picture Arts and Sciences, Los Angeles, California.

Laura Anne Wimberley, Ph.D.,
Texas A&M University, College Station, Texas

Jordan, Barbara (1936–1996)

Noted attorney and legal scholar, member of the Texas legislature, and first Southern African-American woman elected to the U.S. House of Representatives, who was a member of the House Judiciary Committee during impeachment hearings on President Richard M. Nixon. Born Barbara Charline Jordan on February 21, 1936, in Houston, Texas; died of pneumonia believed to be a complication of leukemia on January 17, 1996; youngest of three daughters of Benjamin M. Jordan (a Baptist minister and warehouse clerk) and Arlyne Jordan; attended public elementary and secondary schools in Houston; enrolled and graduated magna cum laude from Texas Southern University, an all-black college in Houston, where she was a spellbinding debater, 1956; Boston University, LL.B., 1959; admitted to the bar in both Texas and Massachusetts; never married; no children.

Raised in Houston; after completing law school in Boston, returned to Houston and practiced general civil law; also worked as an administrative assistant to a county judge; became active in Democratic Party politics, and worked to turn out the black vote for the Kennedy-Johnson presidential ticket (1960); ran for the Texas House of Representatives unsuccessfully (1962 and 1964); elected to the Texas State Senate (1966), the first black woman in that body; after a successful career in the Texas Senate, ran for the U.S. House of Representatives (1972), winning handily; pursued many domestic policies to aid the disadvantaged, and was an outspoken critic of increased military expenditures; served on the House Judiciary Committee during the hearings on the impeachment of President Nixon, during which she first came to national prominence for her skilled oratory and fine legal reasoning; was keynote speaker at the 1976 Democratic National Convention, the first African-American woman so honored; retired from the U.S. House (1978), due in part to illness; pursued a distinguished career of public speaking and teaching at the Lyndon B. Johnson School of Public Affairs, at the University of Texas; was recipient of the Presidential Medal of Freedom (1994).

In the first day of public hearings by the House Judiciary Committee into the possible impeachment of President Richard M. Nixon, each member of the committee was allotted time for opening remarks. For weeks, the committee had struggled with the definition and understanding of its own responsibilities in the matter; many members were unsure of the meaning of impeachment, the significance of a vote to impeach, and the constitutionality of a variety of proposals, both about how the committee should proceed and the substance it should review.

In the midst of this uncertainty and confusion, Representative Barbara Jordan, Democrat of Texas, in unprepared remarks, delivered a remarkably moving and clear explanation of the nature of impeachment, the charge of the committee, and the Constitutional meaning of a vote to impeach. Having reviewed these matters, and the behavior of President Nixon which prompted the hearings, Rep. Jordan concluded:

> If the impeachment provision in the Constitution of the United States will not reach the offenses charged here, then perhaps that eighteenth-century Constitution should be abandoned to a twentieth-century paper shredder. Has the President committed offenses and planned and directed and acquiesced in a course of conduct which the Constitution will not tolerate? That is the question. We know that. We know the question. We should now forthwith proceed to answer the question. It is reason and not

passion which must guide our deliberations, guide our debate, and guide our decision.

Biographer Shelby Hearon reports that Jordan's audience that day in Washington sat stunned. This was "the first time she had reached them with no one in between. The first time they had seen and heard her with their own eyes and ears." A Houston resident the next day paid for 25 billboards that said: "Thank you, Barbara Jordan, for explaining the Constitution to us." At this first moment of national prominence, the skills and oratorical ability developed early in her life, and her fine legal training, had served Jordan well indeed, allowing her to do what she had always done—to communicate logically, and yet with deep conviction and passion, complex and significant issues facing the nation.

The story of this African-American leader begins in Houston, Texas, where she would spend much of her life. Born to Benjamin Jordan, a Baptist minister, and **Arlyne Jordan** in 1936, Barbara was the youngest of three daughters. Her father supplemented his income with work as a warehouse clerk. "We were poor," Barbara Jordan told an interviewer in 1972, "but so was everyone around us, so we did not notice it. We were never hungry and we always had a place to stay."

Jordan attended Houston public schools. Reportedly a strict disciplinarian, her father expected her to maintain a straight "A" average in school; she expected the same of herself. She stated later that she always wanted to be something unusual; "I never intended to be a run-of-the-mill person." After hearing *Edith Sampson, a black lawyer from Chicago, speak at a school event, Jordan decided to become a lawyer.

Graduating from *Phillis Wheatley High School in 1952, ranked in the top 5% of her class, Jordan enrolled at Texas Southern University, an all-black college in Houston; while there, she majored in political science and history, traveling back and forth to school on segregated buses, relegated to the seats labeled "colored." Though her first attempt at elected office, a run for the presidency of the Texas Southern student body, failed, she became known as a spellbinding orator, and led the Texas Southern debate team to a series of championships. She graduated in 1956, magna cum laude, and subsequently attended and graduated from law school at Boston University (1959).

Jordan returned to her native Houston, lived with her parents, and conducted a general civil-law practice from their home, using the dining-room table as her office. (Three years later, she finally had sufficient funds to open an office.) In addition to her law practice, she worked for a county judge and became active in the county's Democratic Party organization. During the 1960 presidential campaign, she was in charge of the first black "one-person-per-block" drive to recruit votes for the Kennedy-Johnson Democratic ticket.

Jordan first ran for public office herself in 1962, seeking election to the Texas House of Representatives. She was defeated, but received 6,000 votes, prompting her to conclude that "anybody who could get 6,000 people to vote for them for any office should keep on trying." However, she was again defeated in 1964, so in 1966 she sought a seat in the Texas Senate. In this race, she became the first black woman elected to the state senate as well as the first black elected since 1883. She ran unopposed for the same office in 1968 and was reelected to a four-year term.

I am neither a black politician, nor a woman politician. Just a politician, a professional politician.

—Barbara Jordan

Jordan was extremely effective at legislating in the Texas Senate, and about half of the bills she introduced eventually became law, an extraordinarily high percentage. Her legislation included the establishment of the Texas Fair Employment Practices Commission, an improved workmen's compensation act, and the state's first ever minimum wage law which covered workers not protected by federal minimum wage standards—"the really poor people, laundry workers, domestics and farm workers." She also compelled the state to include non-discriminatory practices as part of its own hiring and contracting procedures. To protect minorities' political rights, she helped to block a restrictive voting rights act.

During her first term, Jordan was voted the outstanding freshman senator. Having earned the respect of her legislative peers, she was also elected president *pro tempore* of the senate in March 1972, the nomination having been seconded by every Texas senator. "I had to get inside of the club," she commented, "not just inside of the chamber." Her service as chair of the Labor and Management Relations Committee, and her outstanding service on that committee, also earned her the recognition and support of organized labor groups.

Late in 1971, Jordan decided to run for the Democratic nomination to the U.S. House of Representatives from the newly drawn 18th Congressional District, located in a heavily populated and ethnically mixed section of Houston. A black man, Curtis Graves, her main Democratic opponent in a contested primary, accused her of "Uncle Tomism," and "selling out to the white establishment," by teaming up with white politicians to create a safe black senate seat for herself. Jordan countered this attack by arguing that she could get things done in Congress, and stressing her legislative achievements in the Texas Senate. She scored an astounding victory in the primary, gaining 80% of the votes cast. "If I got 80 percent of the total votes cast, lots of white people voted for me," she said, "and it was because they felt their interest would be included." In the general election in November 1972, while the Republicans were recording a landslide at the top of the presidential ticket, Jordan trounced her Republican opponent Paul Merritt, with a plurality of 66,000 votes.

Shortly after her election to Congress, she announced that she intended to focus on lawmaking, rather than be a spokesperson for civil rights. "We are legislators, and we ought to remember that is our role," she declared, surprising many. This did not mean abandonment of civil-rights issues, but, rather, using the legislative role to advance those issues. For example, she joined forces with other Democrats and attempted to block the nomination of Gerald Ford as vice president, charging that he lacked commitment to civil rights. (Her attitude softened, however, after hearing Ford's inaugural speech, and she exhorted Americans to give him a chance.) She questioned the reliance on busing to achieve racial integration of schools, but supported the letter and spirit of the 1954 Supreme Court decision in *Brown* v. *the Topeka Board of Education* requiring school integration. When the Voting Rights Act of 1965 came up for renewal, Jordan sponsored an amendment to include Hispanic-Americans, Native Americans, and Asian-Americans. Because of the high number of Mexican-Americans in Texas, Jordan's stance was in direct opposition to the majority of her Texas delegation.

In addition to supporting civil-rights objectives, Congresswoman Jordan also backed many measures designed to raise the standard of living of poor Americans. She supported many of the War on Poverty programs of the mid-1960s, including free legal services to the poor. She voted for increases in the minimum wage and supported a proposal to extend Social Security coverage to American housewives. Committed also to programs designed to promote long-range health planning, she favored measures to create

Barbara
Jordan

federally funded programs for treatment and prevention of cancer, alcoholism, and diabetes. She also supported a variety of programs to assist the aged. In all these areas, she typified the concern of other women legislators of her era for the needs of racial minorities, women, children, and the elderly. Other domestic policies she favored included environmental protection, increased funding for law-enforcement efforts, federal aid to elementary and secondary schools, and urban problems.

In foreign policy, Jordan—again in common with several other prominent congresswomen—was an outspoken critic of increasing military expenditures. She voted to reduce the number of U.S. troops stationed abroad in favor of a ceiling on military aid to South Vietnam, and to override President Nixon's veto of the historic War Powers Act, which limits presidential warmaking authority. Her overall voting record was decidedly liberal; she received a rating of 88% Democratic Party support in her first year in office. The liberal Americans for Democratic Action rated her at 92% in support of their positions, and the conservative Americans for Constitutional Action gave her a 4% approval rating.

In 1974, during the hearings on the impeachment of President Nixon, Americans came to respect Jordan as one of the most knowledgeable and articulate members of the House Judiciary Committee. Her acute understanding of the Constitutional provisions related to impeachment, the appropriate limits and boundaries of presidential action, and her ability to express these matters in a cogent way, earned her wide respect throughout the country. Partly as a result of that respect, she was occasionally mentioned as a potential vice-presidential candidate and was selected as keynote speaker for two Democratic National Conventions, in 1976 and again in 1992. She was the first woman, as well as the first black, so designated. "There is something different and special about this opening night," she said as she addressed the 1976 delegates. "I, Barbara Jordan, am a keynote speaker and, notwithstanding the past, my presence here before you is one additional bit of evidence that the American Dream need not forever be deferred."

As keynote speaker for the Democratic National Convention in 1992, her topic was "Change: From What to What."

> One overdue change already underway is the number of women challenging the councils of political power dominated by white-male policy makers. That horizon is limitless. What we see today is simply a dress rehearsal for the day and time we meet in convention to nominate . . . Madame President. This country can ill afford to continue to function using less than half of its human resources, brain power and kinetic energy. Our 19th century visitor from France, de Tocqueville, observed in his work *Democracy in America,* "If I were asked to what singular substance do I mainly attribute the prosperity and growing strength of the American people, I should reply: To the superiority of their women." The 20th century will not close without our presence being keenly felt.

Jordan left the Congress in 1978, partially due to health considerations, and accepted a position as Professor of Public Service at the Lyndon B. Johnson School of Public Affairs at the University of Texas, a post she held until her death. In 1975, she was voted one of *Time* magazine's ten outstanding women of the year and was also selected as the Democratic Woman of the Year by the Women's National Democratic Club. She received 15 honorary doctoral degrees and was widely respected as an articulate spokesperson for the disadvantaged, a legal scholar, and fine public servant. "When Barbara spoke with that deep, booming voice, it was as though she was speaking in stone," said former Treasury Secretary Lloyd Bentsen. "She had a presence as few people do." For the next several years, she battled multiple sclerosis, using a wheelchair and walker. In 1988, she came close to drowning when she lost consciousness in her swimming pool.

When Jordan died in 1996, age 59, 1,500 attended her memorial service in Houston, including President Bill Clinton. There were eulogies on editorial pages across the nation. Said *Ann Richards, former governor of Texas, "There was simply something about her that made you proud to be a part of the country that produced her."

SOURCES:

Barber, James David, and Barbara Kellerman, eds. *Women Leaders in American Politics.* Englewood Cliffs, NJ: Prentice-Hall, 1986.

Crawford, Ann Fears, and Crystal Sasse Ragsdale. *Women in Texas.* Austin, TX: State House Press, 1992.

Ivins, Molly. *The Washington Post.* October 22, 1972.

Jordan, Barbara, and Shelby Hearon. *Barbara Jordan: A Self-Portrait.* NY: Doubleday, 1979.

SUGGESTED READING:

Bryant, Ira B. *Barbara Charline Jordan—From the Ghetto to the Capitol.* NY: D. Armstrong, 1977.

Rogers, Mary Beth. *Barbara Jordan: American Hero.* NY: Bantam, 1998.

Weddington, Sarah, *et al. Texas Women in Politics.* Austin, TX: Foundation for Women's Resources, 1977.

Jacqueline DeLaat,
McCoy Professor of Political Science,
Marietta College, Marietta, Ohio

Jordan, Dora (1761–1816)

Irish-born British actress. Name variations: Dorothea Bland; Dorothea Ford; Mrs. Jordan; Dorothy Jordan. Born Dorothea Bland near Waterford, Ireland, on November 22, 1761; died possibly in St. Cloud, near Paris, on July 3 (some sources cite August 5), 1816; daughter of Francis Bland (a stagehand) and Grace Phillips (d. 1789, a Welsh actress known as Mrs. Frances); never married; associated with Richard Daly; associated with Richard Ford (a lawyer); associated with William IV (1765–1837), king of England (r. 1830–1837); children: (with Richard Daly) **Fanny** Daly (1782–1821, who married Thomas Alsop); (with Richard Ford) **Dorothea Maria Ford** (b. 1787, later Mrs. Frederick March); son (1788–1788); **Lucy Hester Ford** (1789–1850, later Lady Hawker); (with William IV) ten, including George Fitzclarence (1794–1842), 1st earl of Munster; **Sophia Fitzclarence** (1795–1837, who would marry Philip Sidney, 1st baron d'Lisle and die in childbirth); Henry Fitzclarence (1797–1817); **Mary Fitzclarence** (1798–1864, who married General Charles Richard Fox); Frederick Fitzclarence (1799–1854, a lieutenant general who married Lady Augusta Boyle); **Elizabeth Fitzclarence** (1801–1856,

Dora Jordan

*who married William George Hay, 18th earl of Erroll); Adolphus Fitzclarence (1802–1856); **Augusta Fitzclarence** (1803–1865, who married John Erskine and Lord John Frederick Gordon); Augustus Fitzclarence (1805–1854, who married Sarah Gordon), rector of Mapledurham, Oxfordshire; *__Amelia Fitzclarence__ (1807–1858, who married Lucius Bentinck, 10th Viscount Falkland).*

Dora Jordan was born near Waterford, Ireland, in 1761, the daughter of Francis Bland, a stagehand who claimed to have been a sea captain, and **Grace Phillips**, a Welsh actress who at one time was known as Mrs. Frances. Dora made her debut in Dublin as Phoebe in *As You Like It* when she was 15 and experienced various adventures as a provincial actress in Ireland, Leeds, and others Yorkshire towns. She appeared in 1785 at Drury Lane, London, as Peggy in *The Country Girl.* She quickly won great popularity, exhibiting talent in comedy and musical farce. During a period of 25 years, she was the favorite comedy actress of her time, second only to ***Kitty Clive**.

Jordan's personal life was lively rather than happy. She first took up with the Dublin theater company manager Richard Daly, "a notorious whoremonger who had promptly seduced her, leaving her with child," wrote Charles Carlton. (It was at this point that she adopted the name Mrs. Jordan, a tribute to her escape across the Irish Sea, to her the River Jordan.) She then took up with the theater manager of the Drury Lane, Sir Richard Ford, whose name she co-opted for some years, and with whom she had three more children. Jordan left him when he refused to marry her. In 1790, she became the mistress of the duke of Clarence, the future William IV, king of England. He was 30, she 26, and the successor of **Polly Finch**, a courtesan of some repute.

During her 20-year connection with Clarence, Jordan gave birth to ten children, all of whom took the name of Fitzclarence and were raised to the rank of nobles. "Mrs Jordan is a good creature," said the duke, "very domestic and careful with her children." But ten children put a crimp in his allowance, and he sent her out to engagements between pregnancies. "Some folk audaciously enquire/ If *he* keeps her or *she* keeps *him*," wrote the satirists.

In 1811, "when Mrs. Jordan grew stout and her ability to earn enough to keep him in the manner in which he had become accustomed diminished," writes Carlton, the intimacy was terminated by the duke, who went on to marry the wealthy Princess ***Adelaide of Saxe-Meiningen**. On paper, ample provision was given to Mrs. Jordan and their children. In reality, the amount was inconsequential.

Jordan fled England ahead of her creditors and set down in St. Cloud, near Paris, France. There, it is said, she died in poverty of a broken heart in 1816, "her bed linen being sold off to help pay for the funeral," though there is some suspicion that she lived for seven years more in England under an assumed name. A statue of Jordan, by Sir Francis Chantrey, was erected after the duke's succession to the throne as William IV.

As an actress in comedy, Dora Jordan had few equals, and no woman of the stage was ever more lavishly praised by eminent critics of her time. William Hazlitt spoke of her as "the child of nature whose voice was a cordial to the heart, to hear whose laugh was to drink nectar." Leigh Hunt considered her the first actress of the day, and Charles Lamb's praise was no less elevated. Byron declared her superb, and Charles Mathews the elder called her "an extraordinary and exquisite being, as distinct from any other being in the world as she was superior to all her contemporaries in her particular line of acting." Sir Joshua Reynolds delighted in a creature "who ran upon the stage as a playground, and laughed from sincere wildness of delight," and preferred her to all actresses of his time.

SOURCES:
Carlton, Charles. *Royal Mistresses.* London: Routledge, 1990.

SUGGESTED READING:
Boaden, James. *Life of Mrs. Jordan.* 1831.

Jordan, Elizabeth Garver
(1865–1947)

American editor and author. Born Mary Elizabeth Carver Jordan on May 9, 1865, in Milwaukee, Wisconsin; died on February 24, 1947, in New York City; the eldest of two daughters of William Francis Jordan (a businessman and real-estate broker), and Margaretta (Garver) Jordan; graduated from St. Mary's High School, Milwaukee, 1884; never married; no children.

Selected works: (short stories) Tales of the City Room *(1895); (short stories)* Tales of the Cloister *(1901); (short stories)* Tales of Destiny *(1902);* May Iverson, Her Book *(1904);* Many Kingdoms *(1908);* May Iverson Tackles Life *(1913); (play)* The Lady from Oklahoma *(1913);* Lover's Knots *(1916);* Wings of Youth *(1917);* The Girl in the Mirror *(1919);* The Blue Circle *(1920);* Red Riding Hood *(1924);* Black Butterflies *(1926);* Miss Nobody from Nowhere *(1927); The*

Devil and the Deep Sea *(1928);* The Night Club Mystery *(1929);* The Fourflusher *(1930);* Playboy *(1931);* Young Mr. X *(1932);* Daddy and I *(1934);* The Life of the Party *(1935);* The Trap *(1936); (autobiography)* Three Rousing Cheers *(1938);* First Port of Call *(1940);* Faraway Island *(1941);* Herself *(1943);* Miss Warren's Son *(1944);* The Real Ruth Arnold *(1945).*

Born in 1865 and raised in Milwaukee, Wisconsin, Elizabeth Jordan graduated from Catholic school intent on becoming a nun. Her father, however, encouraged her to write and helped get her a job as the editor of the woman's page at *Peck's Sun,* a paper run by George W. Peck, author of *Peck's Bad Boy.* When she became bored with the work, her father used his influence once again to place her as secretary to the superintendent of the Milwaukee schools. All the while, Jordan was writing stories, several of which were published in the *Chicago Tribune* and the *St. Paul* [Minnesota] *Globe.*

In 1890, Jordan took her career into her own hands and left for New York, where she landed a job on Joseph Pulitzer's *New York World.* One of her early assignments, an interview with America's first lady **Caroline Harrison,* wife of Benjamin Harrison, at the Harrisons' vacation home in Cape May, New Jersey, was so well received that Jordan was made a full reporter. Her talent as an interviewer further led to a series of Sunday features, "True Stories of the News," human interest stories that she obtained in hospitals, jails, and asylums. In addition to her features, Jordan also worked as a reporter, covering events like the ***Lizzie Borden** trial and writing a full-page summation on the murder of **Helen Pott** who was thought to have been poisoned by her fiancé, a medical student. Jordan gained a reputation for her ability to write under the pressure of a difficult deadline. During this period, Jordan also produced short stories, many of which were drawn from her own experiences as a reporter. They were collected under the title *Tales of the City Room,* published in 1895.

In 1900, Jones left the *World* (where she had worked her way up to assistant Sunday editor) to succeed **Margaret Sangster* as editor of *Harper's Bazaar,* a position Jordan held for the next 13 years. She continued to write, producing a series of novels (including *May Iverson, Her Book,* the first of several featuring the popular heroine), short-story collections, and even a play, *The Lady from Oklahoma,* which had a brief run on Broadway in April 1913. She also devised a round-robin novel, *The Whole Family* (1908), to

which authors William James, William Dean Howells, ***Elizabeth Stuart Phelps Ward,** and Henry Van Dyke all contributed a chapter.

When *Harper's* was sold to William Randolph Hearst in 1913, Jordan became a literary adviser for Harper & Brothers. There, she was instrumental in introducing the works of ***Zona Gale,** ***Eleanor Porter,** and ***Dorothy Canfield Fisher,** although her major coup was the discovery of Sinclair Lewis, with whom she worked closely on revisions for his first novel *Our Mr. Wrenn.* In 1915, Jordan collaborated with ***Anna Howard Shaw,** president of the National Women's Suffrage Association, on Shaw's autobiography *The Story of a Pioneer.* Jordan also edited *The Sturdy Oak* (1917), a novel based on the suffrage movement.

Elizabeth Jordan never married, residing in an elegant house in Gramercy Square with her mother **Margaretta Jordan,** two other professional women, a butler, and a secretary. Despite her long work hours, she found time for ice skating,

Elizabeth Garver Jordan

golf, and travel. She was a noted hostess and had a large circle of loyal friends, including authors *Frances Hodgson Burnett and Henry James.

In 1918, Jordan was lured away from Harper & Brothers with the offer of $25,000 per annum to be a script consultant with Goldwyn Pictures at its Fort Lee, New Jersey, studio. As it turned out, the position was an uneasy fit, and she abandoned it when Goldwyn moved its headquarters to California. Turning to her writing in earnest, she produced almost a novel a year for the rest of her life, including an autobiography *Three Rousing Cheers* (1938). In 1922, she began a theater column for the Catholic weekly, *America,* which she continued until her retirement in 1945. Elizabeth Jordan died on February 24, 1947, age 81.

SOURCES:

Belford, Barbara. *Brilliant Bylines.* NY: Columbia University Press, 1986.

McHenry, Robert, ed. *Famous American Women.* NY: Dover, 1983.

Barbara Morgan,
Melrose, Massachusetts

Jordan, Marian (1896–1961)

Radio comedian who co-starred with her husband James Jordan on the popular radio series "Fibber McGee and Molly" (1935–1956). Born Marian Driscoll in Peoria, Illinois, on November 15, 1896; died on April 7, 1961; daughter of Daniel Driscoll and Anna (Carroll) Driscoll; graduated from the Academy of Our Lady, Peoria; married James Edward Jordan (an entertainer); children: James Carroll Jordan; Kathryn Jordan.

On any given Tuesday evening between the years 1935 and 1956, millions of Americans gathered around their radios to listen to "Fibber McGee and Molly," a comedy series created by cartoonist Don Quinn, starring two ex-vaudeville performers from Peoria, Illinois, James and Marian Jordan.

Marian Jordan was born in Peoria in 1896 and had her heart set on a stage career from a young age, despite strong objections from her parents. Educated in parochial schools, she appeared in amateur theatricals and concerts while a student, and later studied voice, violin, and piano at Runnell's School of Music in Peoria. She met James Jordan in the choir of St. John's Church, but marriage was postponed until after the First World War. Though the couple wanted nothing more than to entertain, it took a while for their careers to take off.

While James worked in a machine shop, Marian hatched a scheme to make their dreams a reality. On her initiative, they organized a concert company and embarked on a four-year tour throughout the Middle West, playing schools, churches and opera houses. After they disbanded the company, they were contemplating their next move when they became intrigued by radio. Thinking it might be a perfect outlet for their talent, they auditioned for Chicago station WIBO and were hired to sing for a musical program. Shortly thereafter, they captured the imagination of cartoonist Don Quinn, who saw them more as an acting team and wrote them a sketch featuring a folksy grocer who was always "smack out" of everything. The sketch was expanded into a popular series and the Jordans, in a three-way split with Quinn, were able to make a modest living on radio.

Quinn then developed the amiable braggart Fibber McGee and his down-to-earth wife Molly, the popular characters with which the Jordans realized their full potential. The "Fibber McGee and Molly" show first aired in April 1935 as a daytime series. The program was only moderately successful in the afternoon slot, but when it was changed to 9:30 on Tuesday evenings, its popularity soared. The show was distinguished by sharply-drawn characters, bright, funny dialogue, and a distinctive American small-town spirit. One well-known running gag revolved around Fibber McGee's closet, packed to excess with items squirreled away for future use. Each time the door was opened, all poured forth with appropriate sound effects, thundering, banging, clanging, crashing for an extended period of time, generally ending with one last tiny tinkle. The term "Fibber McGee's closet" became an American idiom.

In addition to Molly, Marian played several other characters, including Grandma, Mrs. Wearybottom, and the exasperating neighbor child Teeny, all with distinctive voice variations. The successful show spawned several movies (the first of which was *This Way Please,* in 1937), in which the couple also starred. In 1938, Marian suffered a nervous breakdown forcing an interruption of the show for two seasons. During her recuperation, the Jordans and their two children made a permanent move to California, where they purchased a parcel of farm land. Marian spent her free time reading mysteries and love stories, and collecting Chinese prints.

In 1959, two years after the show left radio, NBC tried unsuccessfully to adapt the concept to television, with Bob Sweeney and **Cathy Lewis**

in the title roles of Fibber and Molly. The show lasted only one season.

SOURCES:
Brown, Les. *Les Brown's Encyclopedia of Television.* 3rd ed. Detroit, MI: Visible Ink Press, 1992.
Current Biography. NY: H.W. Wilson, 1941.

Barbara Morgan,
Melrose, Massachusetts

Jordan, Mrs. (1761–1816).

See Jordan, Dora.

Jordan, queen of.

See Noor al-Hussein (b. 1951).

Jordan, Sara Murray (1884–1959)

American physician who was co-founder of the Lahey Clinic and director of its gastroenterology department. Born Sara Claudia Murray on October 20, 1884, in Newton, Massachusetts; died on November 21, 1959, in Boston; one of seven children of Patrick Andrew Murray (owner of a carriage and auto body shop) and Maria (Stuart) Murray; attended public schools in Newton, Massachusetts; Radcliffe College, A.B., 1905; University of Munich, Ph.D. in archaeology and classical philology, 1908; Tufts University, Medford, Massachusetts, M.D., 1921; married Sebastian Jordan (a lawyer), on January 14, 1913 (divorced 1921); married Penfield Mower (a broker), on September 26, 1935; children: (first marriage) Mary Jordan.

The second of seven children, Sara Jordan was born in Newton, Massachusetts, in 1884. Jordan became interested in a medical career as a child, but her family would not support her choice until much later. In the meantime, she excelled as a scholar, graduating from Radcliffe in only three years and earning a Ph.D. in archaeology and classical philology from the University of Munich in 1913. Jordan then married a German lawyer she had met at the university and had a daughter. Unfortunately, the marriage was an unhappy one, and the couple parted ways during World War I. (They divorced in 1921, and Jordan would later marry Boston broker Penfield Mower.) Returning with her daughter to her

James and Marian Jordan

family home in Brookline, Massachusetts, Jordan finally obtained her parents' permission to enter Tufts for premed studies. The college, however, would not allow her to matriculate and kept her on "probationary" status until she threatened to appeal to the American Medical Association. In 1921, she was finally awarded her M.D. degree, graduating at the head of her class.

Jordan completed her internship at Worcester Memorial Hospital and received her training in gastroenterology in Chicago. In 1922, she and three other doctors (two surgeons and an anesthesiologist) started the Lahey Clinic in Burlington, Massachusetts, then one of the few independent clinics in the Boston area. Even though she was practicing with two surgeons, Jordan was a proponent of noninvasive treatment when dealing with her gastrointestinal patients, many of them ulcer-prone Boston entrepreneurs. Ahead of her time, she advocated stress reduction, rest, and a regulated diet to treat many stomach problems. She counseled those over 50 to have an afternoon nap and an evening nip to control ulcer attacks. Although ulcers are now routinely treated with antibiotics, her treatment was considered the best at the time.

Jordan served many professional organizations and was the first woman elected to the board of directors of the Boston Chamber of Commerce. She was also the first woman president of the American Gastroenterological Association (1942–44), and was secretary, vice chair, and chair of the AMA Section on Gastroenterology (1941–48). Her numerous awards for medical contributions included the *Elizabeth Blackwell Citation (1951) and the Julius Friedenwald Medal (1952).

Sara Jordan developed a side career as a writer, producing a popular cookbook, *Good Food for Bad Stomachs*, in 1951. After her retirement in 1958, she wrote a syndicated column, "Health and Happiness," providing a simple, common-sense approach to disease prevention. Jordan died of self-diagnosed colon cancer at the age of 75.

SOURCES:

Candee, Marjorie Dent, ed. *Current Biography 1954*. NY: H.W. Wilson, 1954.

Sicherman, Barbara, and Carol Hurd Green, eds. *Notable American Women: The Modern Period*. Cambridge, MA: The Belknap Press of Harvard University Press, 1980.

Barbara Morgan,
Melrose, Massachusetts

Jordan Lloyd, Dorothy (1889–1946).

See Lloyd, Dorothy Jordan.

Jordi, Rosa de Sant (b. 1910).

See Arquimbau, Rosa Maria.

Josaba (fl. 9th c.).

See Athaliah for sidebar on Jehosheba.

Josefa.

Variant of Josepha.

Josefa de Ayala (1630–1684).

See de Ayala, Josefa.

Josefine.

Variant of Josephine.

Joseph, Helen (1905–1992)

Anti-apartheid campaigner, officer of the Federation of South African Women and of the Congress of Democrats, who survived many years of banning and house arrest. Born Helen Beatrice May Fennell in Sussex, England, in 1905; died in Johannesburg, South Africa, on December 25, 1992; attended Roman Catholic convent schools; King's College of the University of London, majoring in English, Bachelor of Arts, 1928; University of London, Diploma of Theology, 1975; married Billie Joseph in Durban, South Africa, in 1931 (divorced 1948); no children.

Moved to India and remained to teach at Mahbubia School for Indian girls in Hyderabad (1928–30); moved to South Africa (1931); joined the South African Air Force as a welfare and information officer (1939–45); supervised National War Memorial Fund community centers for "Coloureds" in the Western Cape (late 1940s); became secretary of the Medical Aid Fund of the Garment Workers' Union in Johannesburg (1951); elected honorary secretary of Transvaal branch of the Federation of South African Women (early 1950s); elected to national executive committee of Congress of Democrats (1953); participated in Congress of the People (1955); was a leader of women's march on Union Buildings, Pretoria (August 9, 1956); charged with high treason (December 1956); banned for five years (April 1957); put under house arrest for five years (1962); put under house arrest for another five years (1967); made national tour of English-speaking white universities of South Africa as honorary national vice-president of National Union of South African Students (NUSAS, 1972); renounced British nationality (1973); jailed for four months for refusing to answer questions which might implicate Winnie Mandela (1977); banned for two years (June 1980).

Publications: If This Be Treason (Andre Deutsch, 1963); Tomorrow's Sin (1966); Side by Side (Zed Books, 1986).

On August 9, 1956, 20,000 South African women of all races, from every region in South Africa, traveled to Pretoria to protest apartheid and the issuing of passes to black women. For a full 30 minutes, they stood in silence in the amphitheater of the government Union Buildings with their fists raised in defiance. Then at 3:30 PM, they sang a new anthem, directed at the prime minister, Johannes Strijdom. "You have struck a rock," they sang, "you have tampered with the women, you shall be destroyed!" The date of August 9, now celebrated annually in South Africa as National Women's Day, is seen as a high point in women's collective participation in the struggle against apartheid. Helen Joseph was 51 when she helped lead the march on the Union Buildings; for the next 30-odd years, she continued her commitment to the eradication of racism and injustice in South Africa.

Helen Beatrice May Fennell was born in Sussex, England, of middle-class parents, in 1905. She learned of faraway places when her father, who was serving in World War I, sent pressed flowers to her and her brother, Frank, while he was stationed in Jerusalem and Bethlehem. Helen felt drawn to the Roman Catholicism of the private convent schools she attended, but her mother insisted that she be confirmed in the Anglican Church. Though Joseph had lost interest in religion by the time she left school, she would begin to attend church regularly during her second term of house arrest in the 1960s.

Helen's father could only afford to send one of his children to university. Since Frank decided to go into business, Helen was able to attend King's College of the University of London, where she obtained a second-class honors degree. Unlike many of her peers, she does not seem to have seen marriage as the immediate goal. Instead, she determined to become a teacher and, because she had no degree, made plans to teach overseas, where she could work without professional qualifications.

In 1928, Joseph arrived in Hyderabad, one of the largest princely states in India, to teach at the Mahbubia School for Indian girls. In retrospect, Helen Joseph came to feel that the princes "ruled tyrannically" in Hyderabad, but at the time, she says, she "absorbed very little of Indian politics" despite the widespread passive resistance movement then being undertaken by Mohandas Gandhi's Indian National Congress. Joseph recalled that in Hyderabad "we were encapsulated in our pleasant social life, but had I wanted to I could then have learnt so much about the Indian fight for freedom and justice, so similar to the struggle which was to absorb me in South Africa later." While in India, she made friends with Indians, however, and this experience possibly helped to raise her consciousness about racial oppression once she arrived in South Africa.

Helen left India in 1931, after a serious horseback riding accident cut short her teaching activities. She headed for Durban, on the lush east coast of South Africa, where she knew an old university friend. Within months, 26-year-old Helen married Billie Joseph, a dentist who was 17 years her senior. For the next eight years, Helen did not work—her husband thought it inappropriate—and spent her days as befitting the white upper-middle class, coming in contact with black South Africans only in their positions as domestic workers and gardeners. According to the *Weekly Mail*, Joseph "was known as beautiful and flighty, leading a life of wining and dining and bridge parties." Later, Helen would acknowledge that both she and Billie had a number of love affairs; by the time World War II broke out in 1939, they were leading separate lives.

I have followed the road "less travelled by," the road of involvement in the liberation struggle. But that road has drawn no sigh from me, as it did from the poet. It draws from me only deep gratitude to know that there was room for me, a white, to walk along that road.

—Helen Joseph

Billie soon joined the South African Dental Corps. Somewhat later, Helen applied to become a lieutenant in the Women's Auxiliary Air Force and moved from Durban to Pretoria, the executive capital of the Union. She joined the ranks of the Information Service whose duty was to "inculcate a liberal, tolerant attitude of mind in the women serving in the forces." This was "truly an astounding mission," recalled Joseph, since the "white women of the WAAF" were "born and bred in a society which denied human rights to others on the grounds of colour and race."

This served as the beginning of Joseph's political education. "That's where I learnt," she said, "because we had to lecture on current affairs and on politics; and in order to be able to lecture I had to learn first. Then I began to see the facts—you know, the facts about bantu education; the facts of the discrimination; the facts of housing—and that began to worry me. I always had a bit of a social worker's conscience . . . that's where I started." She came to see "how black children struggled for education and opportunity" and how black people—the vast majority of the population—had been forced off their land by whites.

At war's end, Helen and Billie Joseph separated, though neither wanted a divorce, and she took a number of jobs directing community health centers, first in Johannesburg and then in Cape Town. While managing the National War Memorial Health Foundation's community centers for the coloured people of Cape Town, Joseph came to feel that "all our social services were only alleviating the existing evils, not eradicating them. . . . Our little islands of concern were not affecting the total situation." When the job of secretary-director of the Medical Aid Fund of the Garment Workers' Union in the Transvaal province became available, she saw it as an opportunity to be more effective and jumped at the chance, starting work in Johannesburg in March 1951. It was in this job, through her professional, then personal, association with Solly Sachs, general secretary of the predominantly female and non-racial Garment Workers' Union, that Helen was introduced into left-wing politics. She campaigned on behalf of Sachs and others when they represented the Labour Party in municipal elections and gradually became more deeply involved in political activity.

In May 1952, the government forced Sachs to step down as head of the union because he was a communist; on May 24, Joseph participated in her first major political demonstration, joining thousands of workers in a march through Johannesburg to protest the government's action. Solly Sachs moved to London, and Joseph went with him, but decided after a while to return to South Africa to be more involved in the fight against apartheid.

When a new radical white organization was launched in October 1953 as the South African Congress of Democrats, Joseph willingly accepted an invitation to serve on the provisional committee. Other outstanding members included *Ruth First and the Reverend Trevor Huddleston of the Anglican Church. The Congress of Democrats became the white branch of the ANC-led anti-apartheid organization called the Congress Alliance, which united the African National Congress, the Indian National Congress, and the South African Coloured People's Organization, and Joseph was soon elected to the National Executive Committee. Her political activism was started in earnest, as the congress participated in most of the big political campaigns of the 1950s, including the Defiance Campaign and the Congress of the People. Joseph told **Beata Lipman**:

> I firmly believe that the Liberal Party would never have got as far as it did, if it hadn't been for us. We were always one step ahead of the Liberal Party. When it came to the Congress of the People they didn't want to come in because they hadn't been consulted at the beginning; we were in—we pushed them into adopting the universal franchise: they couldn't rule it out, because we were there. I think as a ginger group we were very effective . . . and we did have a symbolic value too. Here was one group of whites standing foursquare with the African National Congress, the Indian Congress and the coloureds. The congress alliance itself was tremendously important; and weren't we privileged to be a part of it? I think so.

On April 17, 1954, the multiracial Federation of South African Women (FSAW) was founded as an umbrella organization for affiliated organizations such as the ANC Women's League and trade unions. Joseph helped **Hilda Bernstein** and Ray Alexander, now legendary activists in the struggle against apartheid, to organize the inaugural conference, and she recalled that the gathering "drew over 150 women from all over the country, some wearing brilliantly coloured national dress, all eager to participate in the proceedings. Interpreters were sometimes hard put to accommodate the variety of languages—English, Zulu, Xhosa, Sotho and Afrikaans." Joseph was elected honorary secretary of the Transvaal branch and in 1956 became secretary of the Federation.

Through her leadership roles in the Federation and in the Congress of Democrats, Joseph's life became intertwined with most of the significant political figures and key events in the anti-apartheid struggle within South Africa. She helped organize the Congress of the People held in 1955 at Klipfontein, where the now famous Freedom Charter was read to call "the people of South Africa, black and white, to come together to adopt a people's Freedom Charter." Joseph worked closely with ANC leaders and met Chief Albert Luthuli, who was head of the ANC, and also got to know Nelson Mandela.

In 1955, Joseph traveled to Geneva to attend an organizers' meeting for the World Congress of Mothers, which was to be held later that year in Lausanne. It was at the Geneva gathering that Joseph seems to have come into her own as a public speaker. After discussing apartheid and the South African government's proposed scheme to demolish Sophiatown, a black suburb of Johannesburg and a major cultural center, she ended by declaring to the delegates, "Where you stand today, we shall stand tomorrow!" She said of that moment, "That gathering of women rose to their feet in a standing ovation, not to me as a speaker, but to the women of South Africa whose message I had brought."

The 1950s were a time of dramatic political activity in South Africa, mostly because of the new vibrancy of the ANC and the attempts by the Nationalist government to institute its policies of "grand apartheid." The government targeted members of the Congress Alliance as trai-

tors, and in 1956 Joseph joined Nelson Mandela, Ruth First, and 153 other activists as defendants in what came to be known as the Treason Trial, which dragged on until 1961. The trial inspired Joseph to write her first book, *If This Be Treason,* in which she recounted the events of that period; it was banned in South Africa but published in England in 1963.

While out on bail, Joseph continued in her role as secretary of the Transvaal branch of the FSAW and organized more women's conferences across the Transvaal. The government did not

Helen
Joseph

take kindly to this activity and on April 23, 1957, Joseph was banned for five years: she could not leave Johannesburg and could not attend any political meetings of any kind. While still on trial in 1960 and still banned, she was detained along with thousands of others in the wake of the Sharpeville massacre, when police killed more than 60 peaceful demonstrators who were protesting the pass system. Joseph remained in prison for five months, but the government's intimidation tactics proved useless: on March 29, 1961, the court found the defendants in the Treason Trial not guilty, and all were set free.

Meanwhile, the government had banned the ANC in 1960, leading Mandela and others to believe that they had no option but to go underground and launch an armed struggle against the apartheid government. Though Joseph had always believed fervently in non-violence, she now came to believe that the example set by Gandhi was increasingly of little value in South Africa, where the state was prepared to use "brutal methods, . . . armed force and nationwide intimidation." This view soon proved correct: in 1962, the government banned the Congress of Democrats, passed the General Laws Amendment Act which defined sabotage so broadly that any opposition to the government outside parliamentary circles became illegal, and arrested Nelson Mandela. On October 13, Joseph became the first person to be put under house arrest. Now she had to report to a police station every day and stay at home each night after 6:30 and on weekends. She could not "leave the magisterial area of Johannesburg," she recalled, "or be in any black area, or factory, or communicate with any banned or listed person. Nor could any of my friends visit me in my home, or even walk down my garden path, nor could I attend any gatherings, social or political."

While under her first house arrest, Joseph wrote her second book, *Tomorrow's Sun,* about the hundreds of black activists who had been banished to remote parts of the country because of their political activity. After the book's publication in 1966 in London, the South African government immediately issued banning orders to prevent her from writing another. They also made it illegal for her to enter "any building which housed the offices of a trade union or any organisation which produced a publication," wrote Joseph. "I realised with a sort of sick horror that my office at the Medical Aid Society was in the building which housed the Garment Workers' Union and I could not enter it again."

Joseph found a job in a bookshop: she could be around books as long as she did not write them. In 1967, four days before her house arrest was due to end, the government served an order extending her house arrest for another five years. By 1971, she had served nine years of house arrest, had been the victim of death threats, had had a bomb delivered to her garden gate, and was undergoing treatment for cancer. Under pressure from *Helen Suzman, the single liberal opposition figure in Parliament, and from growing international outrage, the Justice Department finally suspended Joseph's house arrest indefinitely.

In her freedom, Joseph returned to a new political landscape. The FSAW had collapsed under the weight of bannings and imprisonments; the ANC and other organizations had been banned for just over a decade. But the 1970s witnessed a resurgence of anti-apartheid activity within the country, initiated by black students in the Soweto township who led the famous 1976 revolt against inferior education. Joseph found a role as veteran political speaker to a new generation of students. In 1971, she was elected honorary national vice-president of the National Union of South African Students (NUSAS), and, despite being a listed person, she began to speak at student gatherings at the English-speaking white universities across the country. Said Joseph, "It seems to be something that's appealed to everyone—the sight of an old woman saying, 'Bugger the government.'" She again came up against the state, however, when she visited **Winnie Mandela** (Winnie Madikizela) in Brandfort, the rural town to which the black activist had been banished. In 1978, Joseph was ordered to appear before a magistrate in Bloemfontein to answer questions about her visit; on refusing to do so, she was jailed for four months.

In 1980, Joseph embarked on another tour to NUSAS campuses, addressing students about the new education boycott which black and coloured students were undertaking across the country. In June of that year, the government retaliated yet again by banning her for two years from any association with young people or any type of political meeting. "I admit I earned it," said Joseph at the time. "[I] treat it as an accolade anyway, an award of merit. . . . I think they were scared to do it before because they always hoped I wouldn't live that long. And I'm sure that's why it's only two years." But 1980 also witnessed the regeneration of the Federation of South African Women, and on August 9 women activists began anew to formally celebrate National Women's Day. After Joseph's banning order expired, she became part of yet another political era: that of the multiracial United Democratic Front, launched just outside Cape Town in 1983. Joseph was introduced as "mother of the struggle" and was elected an Honorary Patron of the Front, which during the 1980s essentially served as the legal internal wing of the still-banned ANC.

In the last years of her life, Joseph continued to attend significant political events, often in a wheelchair towards the end. Although a foreigner, her commitment to eradicating injustice in that country put most white South Africans to shame. As Nelson Mandela wrote to her on the occasion of her first house arrest: "Courage never failed you in the past. It will not fail you now when all signs point unmistakably to the early defeat of all regimes based on force and violence. You and I and indeed the millions of freedom fighters in this country cannot afford to take this challenge lying down." Helen Joseph's life clearly demonstrated that she was up to the challenge. In 1990, she lived to see the day that the ANC was unbanned and Nelson Mandela walked out of prison a free man. She died in Johannesburg on Christmas Day, December 25, 1992, at age 87, two years before South Africa's general election of Nelson Mandela as its first black president.

SOURCES:
Joseph, Helen. *Side by Side*. London: Zed Books, 1986.
Lipman, Beata. *We Make Freedom: Women in South Africa*. Pandora, 1984.
Lodge, Tom. *Black Politics in South Africa Since 1945*. Johannesburg: Ravan Press, 1985.

SUGGESTED READING:
Bernstein, Hilda. *For Their Triumphs and Their Tears: Women in Apartheid South Africa*. London: International Defence and Aid Fund for Southern Africa, 1985.
Lazerson, Joshua. *Against the Tide: Organized White Resistance to Apartheid, 1940–1964*. Boulder, CO: Westview Press, 1994.
Walker, Cherryl. *Women and Resistance in South Africa*. London: Onyx Press, 1982.

Pamela Scully,
Assistant Professor of History,
Kenyon College, Gambier, Ohio

Joseph, Mother (1823–1902)

Canadian-born American nun who built schools and hospitals across the Pacific Northwest. Born Esther Pariseau in Montréal, Québec, Canada, in 1823; died in 1902.

Referred to by the American Institute of Architects as "the Pacific Northwest's first architect," Mother Joseph was one of four Providence Sisters who journeyed from Montréal, Québec,

to the Washington Territory in 1856. Over the course of the next 46 years, she designed and built hospitals and schools across the region, from Oregon to Alaska, using carpentry skills she had learned from her father. Her institutions were available to all faiths and were financed by funds she raised in "begging tours" through the Army posts and mining camps that dotted the area. In 1977, Mother Joseph was the first American nun honored with a statue in the Capitol's National Statuary Hall in Washington, D.C.

Joseph, Mother Mary (1882–1955).
See Rogers, Mother Mary Joseph.

Josepha.
Variant of Josephine.

Josepha of Bavaria (1739–1767).
See Maria Josepha of Bavaria.

Josephe or Josephé.
Variant of Josephine.

Josephine.
Variant of Josepha or Josephé.

Josephine (1763–1814)

French empress, who married the rising young general Napoleon Bonaparte and became the center of his personal life during the era in which he dominated European history. Name variations: Joséphine Beauharnais; Josephine de Beauharnais; Vicomtesse de Beauharnais; called Yeyette, Marie-Rose, or Rose by her family. Born Marie-Josèphe-Rose Tascher de la Pagerie on her family's sugar plantation on the French Caribbean island of Martinique on June 23, 1763; died at her home at the château of Malmaison outside Paris on May 29, 1814, of diphtheria; daughter of Joseph-Gaspard Tascher de la Pagerie and Rose-Claire des Vergers de Sannois Tascher de la Pagerie; attended convent school in Fort-Royal on Martinique, 1773–77; married Alexandre-François-Marie, vicomte de Beauharnais, in 1779; married Napoleon Bonaparte (1769–1821), emperor of France (r. 1804–1815), in 1796; children: (first marriage) Eugène-Rose de Beauharnais (b. 1781, who married *Amalie Auguste [1788–1851]); Hortense de Beauharnais (1783–1837).

Sailed to France for an arranged marriage (1779); left husband and took up residence in convent (1783); legally separated from husband (1785); returned permanently to France after final visit to Martinique (1790); arrested, then released during the Terror, became mistress to French revolutionary leader, Paul Barras (1794); married Napoleon and started love af-

fair with Captain Hippolyte Charles (1796); Napoleon, campaigning in Egypt, learned of her marital infidelity; Napoleon took dictatorial power upon his return to France (1799); became empress when Napoleon became emperor (1804); Napoleon began love affair with Polish noblewoman Maria Walewska (1807); illegitimate child born to Napoleon and Maria; divorced by Napoleon who then married Princess Marie Louise of Austria (1810); received final letter from Napoleon; had friendship with Tsar Alexander I of Russia (1814).

The quarter century following the outbreak of the French Revolution in 1789 carried millions of Europeans in new and completely unexpected directions. Aristocrats at the top of the social ladder found themselves displaced, impoverished, and often put into deadly peril. Individuals from obscure backgrounds rose to positions of sweeping power and authority. At the same time, the course of war and politics brought countless individuals together in unanticipated personal relationships and often tore them apart. The young daughter of a creole family in Martinique who became the Empress Josephine in 1804 was at the center of such developments. Her life vividly illustrates the personal dimensions of the violent twists and turns in European history over this era.

The Revolution that broke out in France in 1789 began by limiting the power of the French monarchy and ending the privileges of the aristocracy. But the Revolution did not lead to a new period of stability. As social, religious, and political divisions widened at home, and as France began to threaten and to feel threatened by its conservative neighbors like Spain, Austria, and Prussia, the Revolution grew increasingly radical and violent. This culminated in the Reign of Terror in 1793 and 1794, in which leaders of the radical Jacobin Party executed tens of thousands of French men and women, many of them members of the French aristocracy.

The Terror was followed by a period of domestic relaxation under the Directo-

Josephine

ry, a corrupt government that came to depend increasingly on the power of the army. In 1799, after establishing a spectacular military reputation during campaigns in Italy and Egypt, the young general Napoleon Bonaparte pushed the leaders of the Directory aside to become dictator of France. In 1804, in a glittering ceremony at the Cathedral of Notre Dame in Paris, he crowned himself emperor, then placed the crown of empress on the head of his wife, Josephine.

Starting in 1805, Napoleon engaged in almost constant warfare against the other powers of Europe. His campaigns in Central and Eastern Europe produced a series of dazzling military victories. While Josephine languished in Paris, her husband made himself master of much of the Continent. He expanded French territory, established a string of satellite states, and even exerted significant influence over independent countries such as the Austrian Empire and Russia. Nonetheless, the whole structure remained rickety. It was dependent on the continuing success of Napoleon's military forces, which were themselves increasingly comprised of non-French troops. Moreover, without a legitimate heir and faced with the threat of his own death either in battle or at the hands of assassins, Napoleon had no assurance that his empire would outlive him. His divorce from Josephine followed 14 years of marriage in which she had not been able to provide the child he required for political purposes.

The great love of Napoleon's life was born to a family of French sugar planters on the island of Martinique on June 23, 1763. She was the eldest of three daughters of Joseph-Gaspard Tascher de la Pagerie, whose father had come to Martinique in 1726 to make his fortune. The Tascher family were thus "creoles," French who settled in the Caribbean island possessions of their country but who retained close ties to their homeland. The family did not prosper as some sugar planters were able to do, and Joseph-Gaspard, Josephine's father, obtained his own plantation, Trois Islets, through his fortunate marriage to **Rose-Claire des Vergers de Sannois**, the daughter of a more successful clan. The future empress, who adopted the name Josephine at Napoleon's request early in their marriage, was born on this modest family plantation and spent her childhood there. She was the oldest of three daughters. A hurricane destroyed the family home when she was three, and her indolent father chose not to rebuild but instead expanded the plantation's sugar mill into a residence. In her years as empress, Josephine repeated a colorful story from her girlhood. An elderly black woman

Josephine

on this Caribbean island supposedly told the young planter's daughter she would have an unhappy marriage, experience life as a widow, but one day she would be "more than a queen."

Josephine's marriage to a young French aristocrat resulted from a longstanding romantic liaison conducted between her father's sister **Désirée Tascher de la Pagerie** and the governor of Martinique, François de Beauharnais. Although both of them were married to other parties, Désirée followed her lover back to France where their relationship continued. To strength-

en her tie with the Beauharnais family, Désirée promoted a marriage between her lover's son, Alexandre de Beauharnais, and one of the three Tascher girls. Josephine's younger sister **Catherine** was the first choice to become Alexandre's bride, but Catherine's death from tuberculosis gave that role to Josephine.

The future empress left Martinique for the first time in 1779 at the age of 16. Her marriage soon turned into a calamity. Her husband found the young creole girl uncouth and unattractive. He deliberately spent long periods away from her, ostensibly to fulfill his duties as an officer in the French army, but in fact to pursue his own romantic agenda with other women. The birth of a son, Eugène de Beauharnais, in 1781, did nothing to bring the couple together. The birth of a daughter, *Hortense de Beauharnais, in 1783, actually worsened the marriage. During this second pregnancy, Alexandre left, accompanied by his mistress, to campaign against the British in the Caribbean. There, he became convinced that he could not be the father of Hortense, the child Josephine delivered during his long absence; he also claimed to have discovered evidence of her promiscuous conduct in Martinique prior to their marriage. His return to France was followed by the collapse of their relationship.

$\mathcal{S}$he was a woman in every sense of the word, vivid, vivacious, and so tender-hearted.

—Napoleon

The terms of the legal separation were worked out between 1783 and 1785. In November 1784, Josephine took up residence in the convent of Penthémont. Her stay there, which lasted until September 1785, helped make her into a confident and attractive woman. Writes **Evangeline Bruce**, Penthémont was less a convent than "an elegant retreat with separate apartments and communal parlors" for aristocratic women in awkward family situations. Her fellow residents offered her examples of cultivated speech, manners, and poise, all of which she embraced with enthusiastic success. She had always been favored with beautiful chestnut hair, large hazel eyes, and a sweet nature, and French men were intrigued by her creole drawl. Now she learned to carry herself with grace and elegance. Her one great physical flaw, bad teeth that grew worse as she became older, she hid behind a small, mysterious smile.

During the final years before the Revolution, Alexandre de Beauharnais entered circles of liberal reformers, while Josephine lived on a modest annual allowance from her estranged husband. The personal details of her life are uncertain, but she may have become romantically involved with several prominent nobles. Josephine's detractors, ranging from a Beauharnais' mistress in 1782 to political enemies of Napoleon during his reign and after his fall, spread rumors of her promiscuity, which had allegedly started in her girlhood years in Martinique.

Josephine returned to her birthplace in 1788 and the outbreak of Revolution in France in 1789 soon affected this distant tropical island.

In the summer of 1790, Martinique witnessed growing unrest that combined a slave rebellion and a mutiny of the military garrison. Under cannon fire from the insurgents, Josephine and her young daughter Hortense fled the island's capital of Fort-Royal and returned to France.

Between 1790 and 1794, as the Revolution grew more violent, Alexandre de Beauharnais in the role of liberal reformer rose to prominence as a political and military figure, then fell victim to more radical leaders. In March 1794, he was arrested and imprisoned. Josephine had no interest in the politics of the time, but she realized the danger of being identified as an aristocrat. She ceased to refer to herself as the Vicomtesse de Beauharnais, preferring the politically safer name of Citizeness Beauharnais. In her contacts with political authorities, she described herself as "an American," with a "republican household." It did no good. She was the victim of an anonymous denunciation and, in April 1794, joined her husband in the infamous Carmes prison.

Alexandre de Beauharnais went to the guillotine in July 1794. Though the Terror was close to its conclusion with the imminent fall of the radical leader Robespierre and his colleagues on the Committee of Public Safety, Josephine remained in peril. She allegedly survived these final dangerous days due to the favor of a minor employee of the Committee, Delperch de la Bussière, who destroyed the documents pertaining to her case and thus delayed her trial. In 1803, she made a monetary payment to him, explaining it was "in grateful remembrance."

As France relaxed from the era of the Terror, there followed an era of government corruption and open sexual indulgence. Josephine became the mistress of Paul Barras, a former revolutionary leader who had played a prominent role in toppling Robespierre. Meanwhile, the danger of popular unrest remained, and the rising young general Napoleon heightened his reputation and solidified his political contacts by putting down a popular uprising in Paris in October 1795. Later that month, now in a top military position in Paris at the headquarters of the Army of the Interior, Napoleon met his future wife.

The two probably first encountered each other at the home of Barras, but some biographers accept a more romantic version of their first meeting. In this tale, Josephine's son Eugène visited military headquarters in Paris to request permission to keep his deceased father's sword following an order for unauthorized weapons to be handed over to the government. Napoleon granted the teenager this favor; Josephine called on the young general to express her thanks.

The often stormy relationship between the attractive aristocrat, then 31 years of age, and the military hero six years her junior, began in the winter of 1795–96. In its first several years, it was marked by Napoleon's passionate desire for Josephine and her measured response to his devotion. Within four months after their first meeting, the two were married. In the face of objections from Josephine's children and her own cool response to his enthusiastic courtship, Napoleon's enthusiasm carried the day. Most biographers discount the idea that Napoleon had ulterior motives. It was a love match for him, not a desire for marriage to an aristocrat, an effort of currying favor with Barras by relieving him of a now unwanted mistress, nor an attempt to marry someone of financial means.

The marriage ceremony took place in a shabby local official's office in central Paris. Both bride and groom lacked the proper documents, and, in drafting new ones, they fibbed about their ages. Napoleon added a few years, Josephine subtracted a few years, and both claimed to be 28. In less than two days after the wedding, however, Napoleon left to take command of the Army of Italy and to start the string of military successes that opened the way to political power. Away on campaign, he wrote her twice a day—his habit of addressing her as "Josephine" dates from this period—but found her less than eager to reply. She was even less inclined to join him in Italy. In her husband's absence, Josephine began an extended love affair with a handsome and cultivated young army officer, Hippolyte Charles. She also dabbled in shady financial transactions, using her contacts to help military suppliers gain lucrative contracts.

Napoleon completed his victorious campaigns in Italy and left in May 1798 to seek new laurels in Egypt. By then, strains in the marriage were developing. Josephine and the Bonaparte clan were at odds. Napoleon's mother, *Letizia Bonaparte, polite to Josephine in public, privately referred to the older, somewhat disreputable woman her son had married as "the whore." Other members of the family were openly hostile toward her. She spoke of them, in return, as "those monsters." Meanwhile, Napoleon was growing increasingly disappointed at Josephine's failure to get pregnant; and he was jolted by the way she ran up debts. Throughout her adult life, from her marriage to Beauharnais to her death, Josephine lived extravagantly whether or not she had the income to match her expenses. Her most important purchase came in April 1799: the château of Malmaison outside Paris, which she transformed into her favorite residence.

Later that year, when Napoleon returned from Egypt in October 1799, Josephine found her marriage in peril, and their relationship entered a new phase. During the Italian campaign, Napoleon had first expressed jealousy about her tie to Hippolyte Charles. Campaigning in Egypt, however, he had received further and convincing word of her infidelity. Consumed with outrage, the young general had taken a mistress, the wife of one of his subordinates in Egypt. Now, Josephine persuaded him to continue their marriage, but, as Theo Aronson notes, "From this point on, their roles were reversed. Josephine was to become the wooer, and Napoleon the wooed; she the faithful one and he the philanderer."

In November 1799, Napoleon took dictatorial power in a coup backed by the army. In the view of Ernest John Clapton, one of Josephine's biographers, it was "a classic example of how a determined minority, backed by the bayonets of obedient soldiers, can overthrow a spineless regime." In the tense weeks leading up to the coup, Josephine was vaguely aware that momentous events were in progress. She played a small role in aiding her husband, attempting unsuccessfully to cajole Louis Gohier, a member of the Directory, in visiting her on the day of the coup. Gohier refused the invitation and thus avoided falling into the hands of Napoleon's soldiers.

Between in 1799 and 1804, Josephine went from being the wife of the nation's dictator—Napoleon took the successive titles of First Consul and Consul for Life—to becoming France's empress. Resolutely unpolitical, she played the role of gracious host in public and devoted spouse in private. She indulged herself in purchases of clothes and jewelry, and began to create a renowned art collection as well as a garden at Malmaison, featuring exotic plants from throughout the world. Nonetheless, political events intruded. As the dictator's consort, she was deluged with requests from aristocrats who had fled France in earlier years and now wished her help in returning. She responded generously. More ominously, she faced the threat of assassination as she accompanied her husband at public appearances. On Christmas Eve of 1800, her coach was nearly destroyed by a bomb intended to kill the imperial couple on their way to the opera.

Josephine's continuing inability to produce an heir gave her enemies in the Bonaparte family a sharp weapon to use against her. Meanwhile, Napoleon began to indulge himself with mistresses both at home and while on his military campaigns. In 1804, Napoleon's decision to be crowned emperor with Josephine as his empress was a sign he was willing to continue their marriage. In a dramatic and lavish ceremony at the Cathedral of Notre Dame with Pope Pius VII in attendance, the two received their crowns on December 2. Josephine used the occasion to secure her position further by informing the pope that she and Napoleon had been married only in a civil ceremony. The leader of the Catholic Church thereupon informed Napoleon that he would not preside over the coronation unless it was preceded by a marriage within the church. Napoleon agreed, and the religious ceremony took place on the afternoon of December 1, the day before the coronation.

In 1805, Napoleon began a series of military campaigns that lasted until his fall from power in 1814. Away from Josephine for long intervals, he continued to indulge himself in a series of sexual liaisons. In 1807, following his victory over the Prussians at Jena and his advance into Poland, he began a passionate and extended affair with *Maria Walewska, an 18-year-old Polish noblewoman.

The vivacious and still attractive empress found her life darkening. Her beloved grandson and Hortense's eldest son, Napoleon Charles, died suddenly at the age of four and a half. Her requests to join Napoleon in Poland brought firm rejections. "The weather is too bad, the roads are unsure and atrocious, the distances are too great for me to permit you to come here," he wrote. Rumors swirled that the emperor would divorce her: Joseph Fouché, the minister of police, told her bluntly, "The political future of France is compromised by the want of an heir for the emperor." Meanwhile, Josephine occupied herself with the redecorating of Malmaison. There she established a vast collection of flowers and plants as well as a famous gallery of paintings.

The imperial marriage came to end in 1809. During the previous year, Napoleon had begun to contact the ruling houses of Europe to arrange for a suitable bride. His twin goals were to obtain a son and heir and to strengthen his ties with one or another of the great powers of Europe. He began to negotiate with Tsar Alexander I of Russia for the hand of his young sister, Grand Duchess *Anna Pavlovna, while making approaches to the Habsburg dynasty for Princess *Marie Louise of Austria (1791–1847). Two events in late 1809 brought things to a head. In the fall, Napoleon was nearly assassinated in Vienna, and his generals urged him to consider the consequences if he died without a generally accepted heir to inherit his throne. Meanwhile, Napoleon received word that Maria Walewska was pregnant, convincing him that Josephine's childlessness was due to her physical problems rather than his own.

In a brief dinner meeting in Paris on November 30, Napoleon informed Josephine that political factors dictated that their marriage must end. He set his lawyers to work to dissolve their civil marriage and to find cause to annul their religious marriage as well. Both tasks were completed by January 1810. Josephine kept her title of empress-queen, the château at Malmaison, and a generous annual allowance. On March 11, 1810, a ceremony at Vienna attended by Princess Marie Louise and a proxy for Napoleon united the emperor of France and the Habsburg princess in marriage. That same day, Napoleon bestowed a new estate on Josephine and made it clear that she was expected to leave Malmaison for this more remote locale, 60 miles away from Paris.

In the years following, Napoleon and Josephine kept in contact through occasional letters and infrequent visits. The great French empire Napoleon had created began to collapse after his defeat in Russia in 1812. By the spring of 1814, Austrian, Prussian, and Russian armies had pushed into eastern France and occupied Paris. Before leaving for exile on the small island of Elba off the Italian coast, Napoleon told several of his associates that Josephine had provided the greatest happiness in his life, and she remained in his thoughts.

Josephine retired to Malmaison to guard her treasured château. There, in early April 1814, she received a last letter from Napoleon. By that time, she was receiving warm messages from Napoleon's conquerors including Tsar Alexander I. They may have had political motives, since she remained a respected figure among the French population. Possibly, they also wanted to encounter her legendary charm face to face.

This final stage in her adventurous life came to a rapid conclusion. Josephine contracted a chill in late May; it turned into a dangerous inflammation of the trachea. She died on May 29, 1814, probably from diphtheria. Some biographers believe her death was hastened by a cancer on her larynx. She died only a few weeks before her 51st birthday.

SOURCES:

Aronson, Theo. *Napoleon and Josephine: A Love Story*. London: John Murray, 1990.

Bruce, Evangeline. *Napoleon and Josephine: An Improbable Marriage*. NY: Scribner, 1995.

Knapton, Ernest John. *Empress Josephine*. Cambridge, MA: Harvard University Press, 1963.

SUGGESTED READING:

Cole, Hubert. *Joséphine*. NY: Viking Press, 1962.

Cronin, Vincent. *Napoleon: An Intimate Biography*. NY: Morrow, 1972.

Herold, J. Christopher. *Age of Napoleon*. NY: Houghton Mifflin, 1986.

Seward, Desmond. *Napoleon's Family*. London: Weidenfeld and Nicolson, 1986.

Stacton, David. *The Bonapartes*. NY: Simon and Schuster, 1966.

RELATED MEDIA:

Napoleon (various versions range in time from 270 minutes to five hours), directed by Abel Gance and released in 1928, restored by Kevin Brownlow and rereleased with musical score in 1981.

Neil Heyman,
Professor of History, San Diego State University.
San Diego, California

Joséphine (1807–1876).

See Josephine Beauharnais.

Joséphine Beauharnais (1763–1814).

See Josephine.

Josephine Beauharnais (1807–1876)

Queen of Sweden. Name variations: Joséphine; Josephine Beauharnais; Josephine de Beauharnais; Josephine Leuchtenburg. Born on March 14, 1807, in Milan, Italy; died on June 7, 1876, in Stockholm, Sweden; daughter of *Amalie Auguste (1788–1851) and Eugéne de Beauharnais (1781–1824); niece of *Hortense de Beauharnais (1783–1837); granddaughter of *Josephine (1763–1814); married Oscar I (1799–1859), king of Sweden (r. 1844–1859), on June 19, 1823; children: Charles XV (1826–1872), king of Sweden (r. 1859–1872); Gustaf (b. 1827); Oscar II (1829–1907), king of Sweden (r. 1872–1907); *Eugenie (1830–1889); August (1831–1873).

Josephine-Charlotte of Belgium (1927—)

Grand duchess of Luxemburg. Name variations: Josephine Charlotte Saxe-Coburg. Born Josephine Charlotte Ingeborg Saxe-Coburg on October 11, 1927, in Brussels, Belgium; daughter of *Astrid of Sweden (1905–1935) and Leopold III (1901–1951), king of the Belgians (r. 1934–1951); sister of Baudouin I and Albert II, both king of the Belgians; married Jean also known as John (b. 1921), grand duke of Luxemburg (r. 1964—), on April 9, 1953; children: Marie Astrid of Luxemburg (b. 1954); Henri (b. 1955); Jean Felix (b. 1957); Margareta of Luxemburg (b. 1957); Guillaume, prince of Nassau (b. 1963).

Josephine Louise of Savoy (d. 1810).

See Marie Josephine of Savoy.

Josephine of Baden (1813–1900)

Queen-mother of Rumania. Name variations: Josephine Zahringen. Born on October 21, 1813; died on June 19, 1900; daughter of Charles Ludwig, grand duke of Baden, and *Stephanie de Beauharnais (1789–1860); married Charles Anthony I of Hohenzollern-Sigmaringen (1811–1885), prince of Rumania, on October 21, 1834; children: Leopold, prince of Hohenzollern-Sigmaringen (1835–1905); *Stephanie (1837–1859); Carol I (1839–1914), king of Rumania (r. 1881–1914, who married *Elizabeth of Wied (1843–1916); Anthony (1841–1866); Frederick (1843–1904, who married Louise of Thurn and Taxis); *Marie of Hohenzollern-Sigmaringen (1845–1912).

Josephine of Belgium (1872–1958)

Belgian princess. Name variations: Josephine of Hohenzollern-Sigmaringen. Born on October 18, 1872; died in 1958; daughter of *Marie of Hohenzollern-Sigmaringen (1845–1912) and Philip, count of Flanders (d. 1905); sister of Albert I, king of Belgium (r. 1909–1927); married Charles Anthony II (1868–1919), prince of Hohenzollern-Sigmaringen, on May 28, 1894.

Josephine of Lorraine (fl. 1700s)

Princess of Carignan. Flourished in the 1700s; married Victor Amadeus (d. 1780), prince of Carignan or Carignano; children: Charles Emmanuel (1780–1800), duke of Carignan; possibly daughter Gabriela of Savoy-Carignan (1748–1828).

Josiah Allen's wife (1836–1926).

See Holley, Marietta.

Josselyn.

Variant of Joceline or Joscelyn.

Jotuni, Maria (1880–1943)

Finnish author whose realistic depictions of ordinary people paint a group portrait of her country in the first decades of the 20th century, and whose novel A Tottering House remains a powerful statement about the collapse of both a marriage and a civilization.

Name variations: Maria Haggrén or Maria Haggren; Maria Tarkiainen. Born Maria Gustava Haggrén in Kuopio, Finland, on April 9, 1880; died in Helsinki, on September 30, 1943; married Viljo Tarkiainen.

The literature of Finland has a long and rich history. Until the final years of the 19th century, Finland was a bilingual nation in which the Swedish-speaking minority enjoyed elite status. Scholars differ as to whether the literary history of Finland can be seen in terms of two distinct bodies of literature—Finnish-language and Swedish-language—or as a unified but bilingual entity. For almost seven centuries, from around 1150 to 1809, Finland belonged to Sweden and the Swedish language functioned as the vehicle of government, trade and high culture. Held in disdain as the language of illiterate peasants, Finnish was spoken only in the countryside and virtually the only books published in that language were a primer, a translation of the New Testament, and several collections of the Psalms. When Finland became part of Russia in 1809 (enjoying an autonomous status), Swedish remained the language of the urban intelligentsia, while books in Finnish remained almost entirely church books for the use of the peasantry. However, after 1809, inspired by Romanticism and the ideals of cultural nationalism, a growing number of intellectuals began to collect folklore and write poems, novels and plays in Finnish. In 1831, the Finnish Literary Society was founded to collect works of folklore and encourage the publication of periodicals and individual writings. Finnish-language literature came of age with the writings of Aleksis Kivi (1834–1872), a tailor's son who wrote works of lasting merit, including the Romantic tragedy *Kullervo* and *Seven Brothers*, a novel with strongly realistic touches.

Life after all is quite ridiculous if you take it seriously.

—Maria Jotuni

Born into a family of modest means—her father was an artisan—Maria Gustava Haggrén grew up observing the lives of the lower-middle class. After completing her secondary education, she enrolled at the University of Helsinki where she met the man she married, Viljo Tarkiainen (1879–1951), an academic lecturer who went on to become a distinguished literary scholar. In 1905, using her pseudonym for the first time, Jotuni published her first book, *Suhteita* (*Relationships*), a collection of short stories that pleased readers and critics alike by the author's understanding of the subtleties of the speech of ordinary people. Jotuni's comprehension of social mores and aspirations was reflected in this debut work, which announced to the Finnish reading public a significant literary talent.

Her next book, entitled *Rakkautta* (*Love*), appeared in 1907. Because the work also appeared in a Swedish translation, it was read by the influential Danish critic Georg Brandes, who was highly impressed by the "bitter erotic masterpiece." Sharply realistic in her portraits of the Finnish lower-middle class, Jotuni depicted with irony the preoccupation with social climbing and money as well as with other attempts to improve status, particularly through marriage. The women portrayed by Jotuni in these and later writings often reveal themselves in both their words and deeds as greedy, power-seeking, crude, and unpleasant individuals. Critics and audiences alike were shocked and angered by Jotuni's stripping away of Victorian conventions and ideals. The titles of her books, such as *Love* or *Kun on tunteet* (*When There Are Feelings*, a collection of short stories published in 1913), are imbued with irony, given that her characters exhibit a lack of the traits her titles imply.

In her first novel, *Arkielämää* (*Everyday Life*), published in 1909, Jotuni looks at rural life, exploring the strengths and contradictions of its men and women. Set in a remote rural village, the story takes place within a single day. The central character of this short novel (some critics have described it as a long short story) is "Reverend" Nyman, a rootless wanderer who may or may not have once studied theology. He is an acute observer of the human condition in his tour of the village, meeting individuals from all social strata, from domestics and penniless farmhands to the wealthiest farmers. From his observations, Nyman concludes that happiness, social status, and wealth are rarely linked. Whereas a poor farmhand and his beloved, a servant girl, are among the happiest people in the village, an old master of a large farm whose daughter is about to enter into a loveless marriage of convenience knows only miserable loneliness. In *Everyday Life*, Jotuni not only created a sociological cross section of Finnish village life, but also crafted a work of literature that presents attitudes toward life and happiness that can be seen as universal and timeless.

In 1910, Jotuni published her first play, a tragedy entitled *Vanha koti* (*The Old Home*). In this Ibsenesque drama, she portrays a seemingly respectable middle-class family with many skeletons in its closets. By the end of the last act, a death, a suicide and a nervous breakdown have demolished all facades of order and moral stability. At the end, only two impractical dreamers are left, individuals who stubbornly refuse to accept that sometimes life is ugly and painful. Jotuni's 1914 play *Miehen kylkiluu (Man's Rib)* ruffled the theater's board of directors with its frank depiction of man-hunting.

In the several more plays she wrote over the next few years, pessimism coexists with a sharp wit. The ability to see and accept the paradoxes of existence would later be summed up by a character in her 1924 play *Tohvelisankarin rouva (Wife of a Henpecked Husband)*, who states, "Life after all is quite ridiculous if you take it seriously." Jotuni's obvious lack of respect for the sacred cows of society often angered social and cultural conservatives, and when *Wife of a Henpecked Husband* came to the attention of some politicians they started a parliamentary debate on the possibility of cutting off funding to the National Theater because of its showcasing of works with "un-Finnish" sentiments like those found in Jotuni's dramas.

Like so many of Europe's artists and intellectuals, Jotuni was profoundly affected by the carnage of World War I. In the years before 1914, she wrote positively about aspects of the subconscious and instinctive forces of humankind, and in a 1908 essay on the achievements of novelist Knut Hamsun she praised his glorification of the irrational forces that surged uncontrollably within the human psyche and in the world at large. With the onset of the world conflict, however, she began to rethink her earlier position, arguing that "If our social self . . . would not control . . . our instinctive self . . . our world would be full of slavery, violence and disorder, and what would we not be able to do with our present efficient instruments of destruction." Perhaps because she had given up hope of reasoning with adults during the spreading conflict, in 1915 Jotuni published a children's book, *Musta Härkä (The Black Ox)*.

Troubled by the war, which now was raging within Finland itself as a bloody civil conflict between Whites and Reds, Jotuni wrote a play with a contemporary theme, *Kultaine vasikka (The Golden Calf)*. In this drama, first performed in the autumn of 1918, she lays bare one of the ugly by-products of war, namely business profiteering and corruption. Jotuni continued to write plays after the war. Appearing in 1924, *The Wife of a Henpecked Husband*—on the surface a rollicking comedy in which a scheming woman has her plans foiled—had a dark and bitter tone which did not sit well with audiences expecting an intellectually undemanding night's

entertainment. Several other plays from this period were seen by some critics as representing a decline in Jotuni's talent, in that they could be just as easily interpreted as essays in rural sociology as convincing works of dramatic art. Her final plays, *Olen syyllinen (I am Guilty*, 1929), about Saul and David, and *Klaus, Louhikon herra (Klaus, Lord of Louhikko*, published in 1946), a Nietzschean philosophical drama set in the Renaissance, have both been seen as of lesser quality than her earlier dramas.

Although Jotuni wrote a number of works during the last decade of her life, including a comedy and a short novel, much of her time was spent on creating the richly textured novel *Huojuva talo (The Tottering House)*. Not published until 1963, two decades after the author's death, this depiction of a hellish marriage is an epic work of fiction and very likely an autobiographical document. The character of the husband is shown to be one of tyranny incarnate, indicating that even in the most cultured environment the most brutal traits are often only thinly concealed beneath a veneer

Finnish postage stamp issued in April 1980, in honor of Maria Jotuni.

of education and cultivation. By the 1930s, her own marriage to Viljo Tarkiainen was in shreds. Jotuni's real-life alienation from her husband, who was sympathetic to the authoritarian trends of the decade, is mirrored in the novel's husband, whose fascistic personality yearns for totalitarian solutions to the world's woes. Deeply pessimistic in tone, and often written with more passion than stylistic grace, *The Tottering House* has been seen as a powerful work of world literature, a document of one writer's despair and rage against a world devoid of reason and bent on self-destruction. The reputation of this novel has continued to grow since its posthumous publication. It was staged in 1984 at Oslo's Nordic Theater Festival in an adaptation by **Maaria Koskiluoma**. In 1995, a dramatized version of *The Tottering House* was shown on Finnish television. Maria Jotuni died in an age of terror, in the middle of World War II, in Helsinki on September 30, 1943. Finland honored her with a commemorative postage stamp issued on April 9, 1980, the centenary of her birth.

Alice of Jerusalem. See sidebar in Melisande.

SOURCES:

Ahokas, Jaako. *A History of Finnish Literature.* Bloomington: Research Center for the Language Sciences, Indiana University, 1973.

Alho, Olli, ed. *Finland: A Cultural Encyclopedia.* Helsinki: Finnish Literature Society, 1997.

Binham, Philip. "Protest and After in the Finnish Theatre," in *World Literature Today.* Vol. 54, no. 1. Winter 1980, pp. 58–61.

Dasgupta, Gautam. "Nordisk Teaterfestival 1984, Oslo," in *Performing Arts Journal.* Vol. 8, no. 3, 1984, pp. 83–87.

Dauenhauer, Richard, and Philip Binham, eds. *Snow in May: An Anthology of Finnish Writing 1945–1972.* Rutherford, NJ: Fairleigh Dickinson University Press/ Associated University Presses, 1978.

Niemi, Irmeli. "Modern Women Playwrights in Finland," in *World Literature Today.* Vol. 54, no. 1. Winter 1980, pp. 54–58.

———, and Mary Lomas. "Maria Jotuni: Money, Morals and Love," in *Books from Finland.* Vol. 14, 1980, pp. 20–26.

Schoolfield, George C., ed. *A History of Finland's Literature.* Lincoln and London: University of Nebraska Press/The American-Scandinavian Foundation, 1998.

John Haag,
Associate Professor of History,
University of Georgia, Athens, Georgia

Jouarre, abbess of.

See Bertille (d. 705/713).
See Agnes of Jouarre (fl. early 13th c.).

Joveta of Jerusalem (1120–?)

Abbess of Bethany. Name variations: Ivetta; Jovette; Juditta; Yvetta. Born in 1120 in the Frankish principality of Jerusalem; died after 1162; daughter of Baldwin II, count of Edessa, later king of Jerusalem (r. 1118–1131), and Morphia of Melitene (fl. 1085–1120); sister of Hodierna of Jerusalem (c. 1115–after 1162), Melisande (1105–1161), and Alice of Jerusalem (b. 1106); never married; no children.

Joveta was born in 1120, a princess of Jerusalem, the fourth daughter of the powerful king Baldwin II and his Armenian queen, *Morphia of Melitene. Joveta was raised with her three sisters—*Hodierna of Jerusalem, *Melisande, and ◀ Alice of Jerusalem—in the capital city of the Frankish kingdom. At age four, Joveta became an important political pawn in the conflict between her father and his Muslim enemy Timurtash.

Baldwin had been captured by Balak the Ortoqid, a great Muslim military leader. Balak kept the Frankish king in his custody for more than a year, and refused to negotiate for his release; however, on Balak's death his custody passed to Timurtash, who preferred a rich ransom to an idle captive enemy. After a partial ransom was paid, Baldwin was freed, but Timurtash demanded that Baldwin hand over his youngest daughter Joveta as surety for the rest of the money. In June 1124, Joveta was duly given into Timurtash's custody along with several other children of the Frankish nobility. She was housed in one of Timurtash's palaces in Shaizar, in northern Syria. In March 1125, her custody passed to the Muslim *atabeg* (prince) of Mosul, the powerful Aqsonqor il-Bursuqi. Two months later, Joveta's father Baldwin fought a bloody but victorious battle against il-Bursuqi's army. From the booty taken from the Muslim army, he and his knights were able to pay off his ransom, and in June, after one full year as a hostage, Joveta was returned to her family.

Joveta's political importance faded as she matured. Her three older sisters all made significant political alliances when they married. However, Baldwin could not find a husband suitable for his youngest daughter, possibly because of her history with the Turks. As was usual for the younger daughters of the nobility, it was decided that Joveta would enter the religious life. Around 1136, the 16-year-old princess left the family palace to join the convent of St. Anne of Jerusalem. She remained at the convent in relative seclusion until 1138. In that year, her older sister Melisande, who with her husband Fulk of Anjou had succeeded Baldwin II, decided that merely being a nun was not a suitable career for a princess. Melisande therefore found a way to give her sister a position of considerable importance and at the same time contribute to the religious community of Jerusalem.

With her own funds, the queen purchased the village of Bethany and there built a magnificent convent dedicated to Saint Lazarus. Queen Melisande endowed the establishment with a significant amount of arable property, including the rich plains of Jericho. Wanting the abbey to reflect the grandeur and wealth of the royal family, Melisande also took care to furnish it lavishly. After its completion, Joveta, now aged 18, relocated to Bethany to serve as its abbess. Because of her youth, an elderly nun was appointed to serve as abbess until Joveta could take over the responsibilities for herself.

Little information is available about Joveta after she became abbess, but the extent of her duties is known. A royal abbey was very similar to a large manor or estate in terms of administration. An abbess was responsible for the spiritual well-being of all the nuns under her care, as well as for the education of the young girls raised at the convent. She also was the abbey's business manager, directing its agricultural production, scriptorium, and any other industries which members of the abbey community practiced to generate income for the abbey. Joveta would also have been primarily responsible for the day-to-day living conditions of her nuns, overseeing the kitchens and housekeeping duties. It was a demanding job, and she would have delegated many tasks to administrators.

Joveta appears again in the records of Melisande's life in the winter of 1160, when she returned to the royal palaces of her youth to nurse Melisande, who had suffered a stroke. She, along with her sister Hodierna, countess of Tripoli, remained with Melisande until the queen's death in November 1161. Abbess Joveta then returned to Bethany, where she died, a well-respected religious figure, after 1162.

SOURCES:

Hamilton, Bernard. "Women in the Crusader States: Queens of Jerusalem," in *Medieval Women*. Edited by Derek Baker. Oxford: Basil Blackwell, 1978.

Prawer, J. *The Latin Kingdom of Jerusalem*. London: Thames and Hudson, 1972.

Laura York,
Riverside, California

Jovette.

Variant of Joveta.

Joy, Géneviève (1919—)

French pianist, known for her performances of French contemporary music. Born in Bernaville, France, on October 4, 1919; married Henri Dutilleux (a composer).

Géneviève Joy was born in Bernaville, France in 1919. She studied with Yves Nat and went on to receive the first prize of the Paris Conservatory in 1941. Joy has played many contemporary French scores, including the 1948 premiere of her husband Henri Dutilleux's Piano Sonata. In 1970, she premiered his *Figures de resonances* for two pianos.

John Haag,
Athens, Georgia

Joy, Leatrice (1893–1985)

American actress who starred primarily in silent films. Name variations: Mrs. John Gilbert. Born Leatrice Joy Zeidler in New Orleans, Louisiana, on November 7, 1893; died of acute anemia in 1985; married John Gilbert (the actor), in 1922 (divorced 1924); children: Leatrice Gilbert Fountain (who wrote the book Dark Star, *a biography of John Gilbert).*

A leading star of the 1920s, Leatrice Joy began her career as an extra in a *Mary Pickford film in 1915. Three years later, Joy was starring in the comedies of Oliver Hardy and Billy West. The actress, whose bobbed hair set a styling trend, also appeared in many silents directed by Cecil B. De Mille. In 1924, she eloped to Mexico with actor John Gilbert, but the marriage lasted only two years. With the coming of sound, Joy, who was instrumental in fostering the career of *Louise Beavers, her personal maid for 12 years, went into semi-retirement, eventually living in Riverside, Connecticut. Her films include *His Turning Point* (1915), *The Slave* (1917), *City of Tears* (1918), *The Water Lily* (1919), *Blind Youth* (1920), *Smiling All the Way* (1920), *Down Home* (1920), *Manslaughter* (1922), *Java Head* (1923), *The Ten Commandments* (1923), *Triumph* (1924), *The Wedding Song* (1925), *The Angel of Broadway* (1927), *The Blue Danube* (1928), *The Bellamy Trial* (1929), *The Love Trader* (1930), *Of Human Hearts* (1938), *First Love* (1939), and *Love Nest* (1951).

Joyce, Eileen (1912—)

Australian pianist popular in Great Britain and the English-speaking world. Born Eileen Alannah Joyce in Zeehan, Tasmania, on November 21, 1912.

Gave the British premiere performances of Dmitri Shostakovich's two piano concertos; can be heard on the haunting soundtrack for the film Brief Encounter, playing Rachmaninoff's Piano Concerto #1.

Eileen Joyce

A prodigy, Eileen Joyce was born in Zeehan, Tasmania, in 1912, and brought to the attention of Percy Grainger while still young. She went to Europe where she studied with Max Pauer, Tobias Matthay, and Artur Schnabel. From the late 1930s through the 1950s, Joyce was frequently heard and admired in the United Kingdom and several European countries. Giving countless concerts for British commonwealth troops during World War II, she delighted her audiences by changing gowns between selections or concertos, adding a glamorous touch to her stage presence. She gave the British premiere performances of Dmitri Shostakovich's two piano concertos, in 1936 and 1958 respectively. Her recordings reveal a clear and cool musical intellect. Her discs of the Schubert E-flat Impromptu, Grieg's *Brooklet,* and Fauré's F minor Impromptu, gave pleasure because of their musical clarity and balance. At mid-career she began to perform on the harpsichord. In 1981, she was awarded the rank of Companion to the Order of St. Michael and St. George. Joyce has appeared in several films, including one based on her childhood, *Wherever She Goes.*

Opposite page

Joan Joyce

John Haag,
Athens, Georgia

Joyce, Joan (1940—)

American softball player. Born on August 18, 1940, in Waterbury, Connecticut; attended Chapman College in California.

At age 13, joined Raybestos Brakettes, amateur women's fast-pitch softball team in Stratford, Connecticut (1953); launched pitching career during Amateur Softball Association's (ASA) National championships (1958); became a dominant force behind Raybestos Brakettes team with her pitching, hitting and fielding expertise (1970s); led team to World championship, first ever won by Americans (1974); retired from amateur softball and helped found International Women's Professional Softball Association (1975); retired from softball (1978); inducted into National Softball Hall of Fame (1983); inducted into Women's Sports Foundation Hall of Fame (1990); named head coach for women's softball program at Florida Atlantic University (1994).

One of the most successful athletes in the world, Joan Joyce, was born in Waterbury, Connecticut, on August 18, 1940. At age eight, she was taught how to play softball by her father, but girls, at that time, were barred from playing baseball. Joyce also played basketball, volleyball, and in later years, took up golf—all of which led to her often being compared to *Babe Didrikson Zaharias. By her teenage years, Joyce had perfected a fastball which, at the height of her career, was reputedly clocked at over 115 miles an hour. At age 13, in 1953, she joined the Raybestos Brakettes, an amateur women's fast-pitch softball team based in Stratford, Connecticut. Unlike most women's softball teams during those years, the Brakettes were well funded, enjoyed excellent facilities, and were able to acquire exceptional players. In 1958, during the Amateur Softball Association's (ASA) National championship, Joyce's pitching career was launched with the Brakettes when she was called into the game to replace an injured teammate. She pitched a no-hitter for the rest of the game to help win the National championship for her team. With veteran teammate, *Bertha Tickey, Joyce helped the Brakettes win three consecutive Amateur Softball Association National championships.

Joyce attended Chapman College in Orange, California, and joined the school team, known as the Orange Lionettes. While playing for Chapman, she helped the Lionettes defeat her former team, the Brakettes, to win a National championship. Joyce played a total of 20 years as an amateur with the Brakettes and Lionettes. Upon graduation from college, she moved back to Connecticut and opened a travel agency, appropriately named Joan Joyce's All-Star Travel, and rejoined the Brakettes.

Joyce was a major force behind the Brakettes during the early to mid-1970s, leading her team to a World championship in 1974, the first ever won by Americans. In 1975, she decided to retire from amateur softball and turned her attention to help found, along with Dennis Murphy and tennis star *Billie Jean King, the International Women's Professional Softball Association (IWPSA). The IWPSA only lasted for four years, but during that time Joyce again led her team, the Connecticut Falcons, to the first-ever World Series victory in professional softball.

During her softball career, Joyce compiled an impressive list of statistics. During 22 pitching seasons, she had 509 wins and 33 losses; she pitched 105 no-hit games, 33 perfect games, and struck out 6,648 batters in 3,972 innings; she recorded a lifetime Earned Run Average (ERA) of 0.21; she holds or shares the ASA National championship records for most total strikeouts in a National championship tournament (134), most strikeouts in a seven-inning game (19), most innings pitched in one tournament (70), and the most no-hitters in a national tournament (2). Joyce also had considerable talents as a fielder and hitter. Her lifetime batting average was .327, and she knocked in 534 runs, leading the Brakettes in batting six times. She was a member of 15 National championship teams. The ASA named her to All-American teams 18 consecutive years, and she was named MVP eight times. In 1983, she was inducted into the National Softball Hall of Fame, and in 1990, she was named to the Women's Sports Foundation Hall of Fame.

Joan Joyce, women's softball's Babe Ruth, admits that she prefers golf to softball, adding that she was never totally pleased playing women's team sports because "my success wasn't totally my own." She began her golfing career in 1975, and within two years had become a member of the LPGA. She posted a career-low round of 66 at the S&H Golf Classic and tied her career-best finish, a tie for sixth. Joyce also earned AAU All-American basketball honors three times while at college, compiled a 180 average in bowling, and starred on a leading amateur volleyball team. In 1994, she accepted a position as head women's softball coach at Florida Atlantic University.

SOURCES:

Johnson, Anne Janette. *Great Women in Sports*. Detroit, MI: Visible Ink Press, 1998.

Jordan, Pat. *Broken Patterns*. NY: Dodd, Mead, 1977.

Markel, Robert, Nancy Brooks, and Susan Markel. *For the Record: Women in Sports.* NY: World Almanac, 1985.

Woolum, Janet. *Outstanding Women Athletes.* Phoenix, AZ: The Oryx Press, 1992.

SUGGESTED READING:

Joyce, Joan, and Anquillare, John. *Winning Softball.* Chicago, IL: Henry Regnery, 1975.

Jo Anne Meginnes,
freelance writer, Brookfield, Vermont

Joyce, Nora (1884–1951)

Wife of Irish novelist James Joyce and the inspiration for many of the female characters in his works. Name variations: Nora Joseph Barnacle; Norah Barnacle. Born on March 22 (or 23), 1884, in Galway, Ireland; died on April 10, 1951, in Zurich, Switzerland; daughter of Thomas Barnacle (a baker) and Honoraria "Annie" (Healy) Barnacle (a dressmaker); married James Joyce (d. 1941, the writer), in 1931; children: Giorgio Joyce (b. 1905); Lucia Joyce (1907–1982).

Ran away with James Joyce (1904); birth of first child (1905); settled in Paris (1920); fled to Switzerland (1940); widowed (1941).

Nora Barnacle Joyce is one of modern literature's most intriguing real-life personalities, though she wrote no more words than those within a meager amount of letters to her husband, James Joyce. As the lifelong companion to a man whom some scholars deem the 20th century's most masterful and influential writer in the English language, Nora Joyce gambled and sacrificed a great deal for her husband's art, fleeing a harsh, repressive Ireland with him in 1904 and living for years in poverty on the Continent. Moreover, James Joyce was blessed with a less-than-easygoing personality, and drank prodigiously; Nora Joyce seemed to deal effortlessly with these traits and also became a lifeline to him when his eyesight failed. In turn, James Joyce was passionately devoted to his wife—whom he only formally wed after their children were adults—and scholars and their contemporaries note that her voice—which teased, hectored, and assailed him—is clearly echoed in that of his similarly frank and memorable female characters.

Nora Barnacle was born in Galway in 1884 into a relatively prosperous family. Her father was a baker, but her mother **Annie Healy Barnacle**, a dressmaker by profession, believed she had married "beneath" her, for Tom Barnacle was fond of drink, and the family moved often, never owning their own quarters. When her mother gave birth to another daughter and then twin girls not long after, Nora was sent to live with her prosperous grandmother in a home near the Galway docks. At age five, she was sent to the nearby Convent of Mercy for her education. She did well enough until she completed the curriculum at the age of 12, but few women in her day in Ireland went on to higher education. To pursue a university degree was even rarer. The sisters of the convent found Nora a job as a "porteress" at another convent, which was a cloistered nunnery. Around this time, her mother, exasperated by her husband's drinking, left him. Both this event and the death of two of her first boyfriends made an indelible impression on Nora during her teen years. Later, in James Joyce's story "The Dead" in *Dubliners*, Gretta Conroy cries as she tells her paramour about the death of her 17-year-old beau years before, and her belief that he died from lovesickness.

Barnacle was a headstrong teenager, tall, and often described as striking in appearance. She probably worked as a laundress in Galway, and may have been employed in a bookbindery for a period. Her voice was also memorable to those who knew her, described as low in register and resonant, and with the lilt of western Ireland. She used this voice freely, and as a young woman was known for her strong opinions and sharp wit. Yet Barnacle's behavior sometimes exceeded the bounds of conservative Catholic Galway. She and a friend liked to dress in men's clothes to explore the city at night (in an era when young women were usually not allowed out after dark without an escort), and her strict uncles found her a challenge. When one of them beat her after she was found to be dating a Protestant, she ran away to Dublin.

There, Barnacle worked as a chambermaid at Finn's Hotel, and she received room and board in addition to a small wage. On Nassau Street on June 10, 1904, she met James Joyce. He was a young Irish writer with a degree from University College, recently returned from Paris. He asked her out, but she stood him up. He sent a letter to her at Finn's, and she accepted a second invitation. That day may have been June 16, 1904, a day immortalized in Joyce's later fiction as the day in which the entirety of his novel *Ulysses* takes place. (Nearly a century later, lovers of Joyce's fiction celebrate June 16 around the world as "Bloomsday.") Over the next few months, they wrote innumerable letters to one another on a daily basis; at that time, there were five postal deliveries a day in Dublin. They talked of running off together, and he began inquiring about English-teaching positions abroad. On October 8, 1904, they sailed from

Dublin, a great act of daring, especially for the 20-year-old Barnacle (Joyce was 22). Her family could have forcibly brought her back, had they heard of her plan; more ominously, unmarried women had very little protection or means to support themselves in this era. His friends assumed he would soon abandon her, and leave her penniless in a foreign country whose language she did not understand. Without the benefit of matrimony, she had no protection whatsoever. Had she become pregnant, her situation would have been even more dire.

But James Joyce did not leave her. By most accounts, he was deeply devoted to her all his life and found it difficult to write or even function without her nearby. All of his fiction was intensely Irish in flavor, and since he returned to Ireland only once more in his lifetime, it has been said that her purpose in his life was to remind him of his native land every time she opened her mouth. James Joyce was, however, fervently anti-Catholic, and would not make their union legal. They settled in Trieste, an Ital-

ian-speaking port on the Adriatic that was then part of Austria. There their first child Giorgio was born in 1905. Because they were unmarried, they were forced out of their lodgings. Two years later a daughter, **Lucia Joyce**, was born. For several of these early years, James Joyce spent his day teaching English and working on his fiction. They often lived in cramped rooms, and both were notoriously poor at managing their meager finances: they dined out every night and dressed well, and he was known to be a stupendous drinker. For many years, they were supported by James Joyce's devoted brother Stanislaus, who later moved to Trieste. In 1914, James Joyce's autobiographical *A Portrait of the Artist as a Young Man* was published in serial form. The 15 short stories that made up his next book, *Dubliners*, was also issued that same year, though not in Ireland where it was pilloried for its unflattering portrayal of the Irish and their Catholic faith. Both caused a literary sensation for the writer's innovative use of the English language, usually expressed through the dialogue or interior monologues of his garrulous characters.

*Nora
Joyce*

His works also made use of psychological insight, and he was hailed as a modernist writer of the first order.

In 1915, the family departed from Trieste because of World War I. For much of his adult life, James Joyce was plagued by eye problems, and he underwent the first of many surgeries to correct glaucoma, ilitis, and conjunctivitis in 1917. In 1920, the family moved to Paris, where the writer befriended *Sylvia Beach, an American expatriate who owned a book store called Shakespeare and Company. She printed and issued his next novel, *Ulysses,* in 1922 after his numerous attempts to find a publisher in England had failed; few would touch it for fear of facing prosecution for obscenity. The work was considered extremely shocking in its day for Joyce's intense themes and ribald language. In all of these works as well as his last, *Finnegans Wake,* the spirited, headstrong female characters were clearly modeled on Nora Barnacle Joyce. In the 1918 play *Exiles,* she is Bertha; in *Ulysses,* the memorable Molly Bloom. Contemporaries of the Joyces called their union one of great passion and interdependence. He read his work aloud to her nightly, usually before heading off to a cafe to imbibe several bottles of wine, and she both assisted him in his writing when his eyesight grew poor and bundled him into taxicabs when she found him too drunk to find his own way home. Sometimes she tried to leave him, and when their children were young she would threaten to have them baptized to anger him.

The Joyces spent very little time apart after sailing that October day from Dublin in 1904, except for one period when he returned to Ireland to try to find a publisher for *Dubliners* in 1909. Their correspondence during this 1909 interval was quite lascivious, and in his later characters like Molly Bloom there are clear echoes of Nora Barnacle's expressions and unabashed sexuality. Reportedly she never read *Ulysses,* however; she may have considered many of Molly's thoughts and utterances far too close for comfort.

Barnacle herself returned to Ireland only twice, once in 1912 and again in 1922 during a period of political turmoil. Their 17-year-old son Giorgio faced danger of being conscripted right off the street as Ireland battled for independence from England. Civilians in Galway were in great danger, and James Joyce, knowing of the peril from news reports, was understandably agitated. Their children, however, came away with a great deal of contempt for the country. They were far more comfortable in Paris, where the Joyces belonged to an impressive circle of writers and expatriates, among them Ernest Hemingway, who often drank with James Joyce. For years, the family had been supported financially by *Harriet Shaw Weaver, a wealthy English woman who was a fervent believer in James Joyce's literary genius. But the couple were usually unable to manage whatever largesse came their way, and quickly squandered it on clothes and vacations that made good use of the grandest hotels in Europe.

Among their Parisian circle were two wealthy Americans, Leon Fleischmann, who was in the publishing business, and his glamorous American heiress wife, **Helen Kastor**. Though they had a young son, Kastor scandalously left her husband for Giorgio, several years her junior. The Joyces, who had actually grown rather strait-laced in their middle age, were extremely dismayed, but came to accept the union by the time of the couple's marriage in 1930. Furthermore, Kastor's brother was a friend of Bennett Cerf, who would become instrumental in getting *Ulysses* finally published in America after several years of official censorship. Cerf's company, Random House, took the book and made it into a test case for obscenity; a federal district judge ruled in the book's favor in late 1933. *Time* magazine then put James Joyce on its cover and hailed the novel as a great literary achievement.

Nora Barnacle and James Joyce formally wed in 1931. The reason for the civil service, held in London and widely reported in the popular press, was to solidify the rights of inheritance of their two children. Though it was widely known back in Galway that an unmarried Nora Barnacle had run off with a writer back in 1904, the couple apparently claimed for years that they had wed in Trieste. Later, however, their grown children were shocked to learn that they were illegitimate. The strain may have exacerbated daughter Lucia's mental illness, and her behavior grew increasingly erratic after this point. On one occasion she suddenly threw a chair at her mother, and began to disappear for days at a time.

Over the next several years Lucia was hospitalized at some of Europe's most luxurious sanitariums, often at great expense. She was even treated at one by eminent psychoanalyst Carl Jung, and it became clear that she suffered from schizophrenia. The ongoing crisis was extremely difficult for Nora Joyce. She blamed her husband for the problems, the way in which he had constantly uprooted the family for years, forcing a nomadic existence upon the children, and for the cramped living quarters, which meant that Lucia had to share a bedroom with her parents until far into her adolescence. When Lucia's mental illness became known, there were rumors that she had been the victim of incest, and though some of her father's fiction does touch upon this as a literary theme, his biographers discount any actual capacity to carry such thoughts out in reality. Only in 1936 did James Joyce finally relent and commit her permanently to a hospital in Northampton, England; Nora Joyce never saw her daughter again, since her daughter was so hostile to her the doctors strongly advised against it.

The Joyces continued to live in Paris through the late 1930s, and celebrated the publication and positive critical reception of his last book, *Finnegans Wake*, in 1939. It had taken him 17 years to write and, during that period, was referred to in his correspondence as "Work in Progress"; only Nora Joyce knew of its title and kept it a secret, for her husband attached great significance to names. The book concludes with the words "Is there one who understands me?"—the same phrase he had uttered to her in persuading her to run off with him to the Continent in 1904.

With the outbreak of World War II, the family's situation deteriorated. Failing health added to their problems: James Joyce had suffered from a stomach ulcer for years, and believed his pain to be psychosomatic. Nora Joyce was afflicted with arthritis. Giorgio's wife, Helen, grew increasingly erratic and was eventually locked up by the Paris police; her American family rescued her not long before the Nazis occupied France. Her fate as a Jewish woman, and a mentally ill person as well, would not have been kind. After this, the Joyces assumed responsibility for their grandson, Stephen, as well as for Giorgio, who had never worked. In December of 1940, they all moved to Switzerland under great duress; they also tried to remove Lucia from a sanitarium in Brittany, but the occupying Germans would not grant her an exit visa. James Joyce died the following January in Zurich. Nora honored his wishes and, though she herself had resumed practicing her religion in her middle age, did not give her husband the Catholic burial that some assumed he should have, instead allowing him to have his final act of defiance.

Nora Joyce survived the next ten years under great strain at times. The war had cut off her access to her late husband's resources, and she could not pay for Lucia's hospital bills; Giorgio had no income or inclination toward much of a career outside of singing. Furthermore, many of the intellectuals who had adored James Joyce for his literary talents had never been as taken with her as her husband had been, and privately derided her as uneducated and vulgar. Many shunned her socially after she was widowed; others demanded repayment for money they had lent the Joyces, though it was clear she was in dire financial straits until his will emerged from probate. Her son reported that she spent a great deal of time visiting Joyce's grave in Zurich's Fluntern cemetery during these years. Harriet Weaver, the executor of James Joyce's personal and literary estate, managed to send Nora some funds, though it was illegal to send money abroad from England during the war. Some urged Nora Joyce to return to Ireland—an idea she found abhorrent. She was also loathe to leave his grave behind with no family to visit. After his will was settled and the war had ended in 1945, her elder years were further saddened when her grandson, whom she had virtually raised and whose company she greatly enjoyed, decided to join his recovered mother, Helen Kastor, in America. Furthermore, Giorgio had inherited his father's alcoholic tendencies.

Nora Joyce, who had suffered from cancer in the late 1920s and had undergone a hysterectomy, died on April 10, 1951. She was buried in the same cemetery as James Joyce, but only in 1966 did officials at Fluntern inter them in plots next to one another; there had been no space near his at the time of her death. Giorgio Joyce lived in Germany until his death in 1976. Lucia Joyce died, still institutionalized, in 1982.

SOURCES:

Maddox, Brenda. *Nora: A Biography of Nora Joyce*. NY: Fawcett Columbine, 1988.

Carol Brennan,
Grosse Pointe, Michigan

Joyeuse, duchess of.

See Marguerite of Lorraine (c. 1561–?).

Joyner, Florence Griffith

(1959–1998)

Gold medal-winning African-American Olympic sprinter known as "the fastest woman alive." Name variations: Flo-Jo. Born Delorez Florence Griffith on December 21, 1959, in Los Angeles, California; died of heart seizure on September 21, 1998; grew up in Watts section of L.A.; seventh of eleven children of Florence Griffith and Robert Griffith; attended California State University at Northridge; attended University of California at Los Angeles; married Alfred Joyner (her trainer), on October 10, 1987; sister-in-

*law of Jackie Joyner-Kersee (b. 1962); children: **Mary Ruth Joyner** (b. 1990).*

Began running track at age seven, eventually qualifying for the Olympics (1984) after supporting her training by working as, among other things, a waitress and a hairstylist; won a silver medal in the 200-meter sprint at the Olympic Games in Los Angeles (1984); medaled at the World Outdoor Championships, taking second in the 200-meter and running on the winning 4x100 relay team; returned to the Olympic arena for the Olympic Games in Seoul, South Korea, in which she won three gold medals (100, 200, 4x100) and one silver (4x400), becoming the most decorated female sprinter in Olympic history (1988); named U.S. Olympic Committee's Sportswoman of the Year, Track and Field magazine's Athlete of the Year, Associated Press Sportswoman of the Year, United Press International's Sportswoman of the Year, and Tass News Agency's Sports Personality of the Year (1988); given the Jessie Owens Award as most outstanding track-and-field athlete, as well as being named co-chair of the President's Council on Physical Fitness (1988); won the Sullivan Trophy (1988); announced her retirement from professional track and founded the Florence Griffith Joyner Youth Foundation (1989); inducted into the USATF Hall of Fame (1995); chosen by President Bill Clinton, along with basketball player Tom McMillen, to co-chair the President's Council on Physical Fitness (1997).

You ou never fail until you stop trying.

—**Florence Griffith Joyner**

It was not the best weather for a track-and-field meet. The thousands of spectators, crowded into Indiana University's stadium one sweltering July day in 1988, shielded themselves from the 98° heat with umbrellas, or mingled in the shade of the stands between events. It was worse down on the track, where a reading of well over 100° rippled off the running surface. Given the lethargic heat of a Midwest summer, an unusual amount of excited energy filled the stadium when a tall, strikingly beautiful runner assumed her assigned position at the blocks for a preliminary heat of the women's 100-meter dash—the first salvo in the fierce competition for a berth on the U.S. Olympic team which would travel to Seoul, South Korea, in two months' time. Her long, dark hair flowed freely onto her shoulders; she wore eye makeup and lipstick, had long, brightly painted nails; even more eye-catching, she wore an iridescent, emerald green body suit. But the crowd completely forgot about these outward attractions as soon as the starting gun

fired, watching Florence Griffith Joyner set a new world's record in little more than ten-and-a-half seconds. Sports reporters and commentators raced for the phones to report that "Flo-Jo" was back in the game.

No one who knew Joyner was surprised at the attention, for she had been deliberately courting notice since her childhood days as one of eleven children. Her mother Florence, after whom she was named, had moved to Los Angeles from North Carolina as a young woman with hopes of becoming a model, but had settled for seamstress work before marrying Robert Griffith, an airline electronics technician. Their seventh child, Delorez Florence, nicknamed "Dee Dee," was born on December 21, 1959. Not long after the birth, the Griffiths moved to a small town in the Mojave Desert, where four more children were born before **Florence Griffith**, deciding the desert was no place to raise a family, divorced her husband and moved back to Los Angeles and a housing project in the city's Watts section. Despite being a single mother of 11, Florence was convinced that opportunities for her youngsters were more plentiful in the city. "I explained to the children that life was like a baby," she said. "A baby comes into the world without anything. Then it starts crawling, then it stands up. Then it takes its first step and starts walking. When we moved into the housing project, I told them 'Start walking.'"

Dee Dee ran instead. On visits to her father, who had remained in the desert, she attracted attention by chasing jackrabbits; at home in Los Angeles, she could outrun her six brothers and was entering races by the time she was seven, under the auspices of the Sugar Ray Robinson Youth Foundation. Running, Joyner later remembered, was "just another thing to do," a legitimate way to channel the energy pent up by a decidedly strict upbringing. Her mother allowed no television during the week and made sure lights were out by ten at night. She taught her daughter crocheting, knitting, and hairstyling. Once a week, she conducted a Bible study class with her children, during which they were required to reveal what they'd done wrong since the last such meeting. Dee Dee would admit many years later that her independent spirit and discipline came from her mother. "She taught us all that nothing is going to be handed to you," she said. "You have to make things happen." As if to underscore her mother's lessons, Joyner made sure she stood out at school by twisting her hair into a single braid and training it to stand straight up; and she was once evicted from a mall

Florence
Griffith
Joyner

for strolling the corridors with her pet boa constrictor, Brandy, wrapped around her neck.

When she was 14, Florence (who had by now abandoned her childhood nickname) was named the top athlete at the Jessie Owens National Youth Games in Los Angeles, winning a trip to San Francisco; by the time she graduated from Jordan High School in 1978, she had broken several records for sprinting and for the long jump. Even so, running remained a part-time activity when Joyner enrolled the next year at California State University in Northridge (CSUN), majoring in business administration. When money ran out after her first year, she was forced to leave school and take a job as a bank teller; but if Florence did not see her future in running, one of her acquaintances at CSUN did.

Bob Kersee, the school's track coach at the time, quickly recognized Joyner's talent and helped her find financial aid, allowing her to return to school, where he advised her to concentrate on the 200-meter dash. The next year, when Bob Kersee moved to the University of California at Los Angeles (UCLA) to become that school's women's track coach, Florence followed. Bolstered by Bob Kersee's coaching, Florence entered the trials for the 1980 Olympics, to be held in Moscow, but missed qualifying for the team by a few hundredths of a second, trailing *Valerie Brisco-Hooks, who was also from Watts and whom she had known since childhood. Florence's disappointment may have been tempered somewhat when the United States joined several Western nations in boycotting that

Florence Griffith Joyner

year's games in protest over the Soviet Union's military intervention in Afghanistan.

Now setting her sights on the 1984 Games to be held in Los Angeles, Florence began training in earnest with Bob Kersee, becoming an active member of his World Class Track Club and meeting two other athletes who would figure as prominently in her life as Bob Kersee himself— *Jackie Joyner (Kersee), who was in training for the heptathlon to be offered for the first time at the '84 Games, and her brother Al Joyner, who was also intent on competing in the triple jump. Under Bob Kersee's rigorous eye, Florence's remarkable athletic gifts blossomed. After two years with Bob Kersee, Florence won the 200-meter at the 1982 NCAA championships with a time of 22:39. Returning to the championships the next year, she won the 400-meter and placed second in the 200-meter. By early 1984, Bob Kersee felt she was ready for Olympic competition and was proved right when Florence qualified for the 200-meter dash.

It was at the Los Angeles Games that Florence's skill came to world attention, along with the expected comments about her flamboyant running outfits, elegant makeup, and her red, white, and blue fingernails. Only nine of them were so patriotically colored, for Joyner chose to paint the tenth a sparkling gold to symbolize her hopes for a gold medal. But she was to be disappointed once more, even though she came away with the silver medal for the 200-meter after once again trailing Valerie Brisco-Hooks. Despite an impressive time for the race of 22:04, Joyner decided to quit serious running, over Bob Kersee's vehement protests. Instead, she worked as a customer service representative by day and supplemented her income by braiding hair at night; she also relaxed her training and gained 15 pounds.

Added to Bob Kersee's blandishments were those from Al Joyner, who had won his gold medal for the triple jump at Los Angeles. Al had told his sister Jackie that he thought Florence was "the most beautiful woman in the world"; Florence would later admit that it was Al's encouragement that brought her back to Bob Kersee's gym and a new training regimen for the 1988 Games in South Korea. Unable to afford quitting her jobs, Florence trained in her spare time, sometimes going without sleep for two days at a stretch. She ran up to four miles a day, despite the ruling wisdom that sprinters should avoid running long distances; and on the advice of runner Ben Johnson, she began a weight-lifting program. "If you want to run like a man, you have to train like a man," she said, working her way up to pressing 320 pounds. But by early 1987, Florence's independent streak took hold. She began to chafe under Bob Kersee's system, which laid great emphasis on emulating other, more successful, runners—in Florence's case, *Evelyn Ashford and *Marita Koch, both triumphant rivals. Early in 1987, Florence announced she was breaking with Bob Kersee and would be training instead with Al Joyner.

Her relationship with Al had progressed far beyond athletics, however. Al's traditional proposal during the summer of 1987, hand to heart and knee to floor, was no doubt enhanced by the fact that, at the time, the two of them were in the back seat of a limousine he had rented for the occasion; Florence's delayed answer was given at a pizza parlor some nights later, when she took a yellow charm in the shape of the word "yes" that her nephew had won at Skee-Ball and passed it under the table to Al. Their marriage in Las Vegas on October 10, 1987, completed what would come to be called the Royal Family of track, for Bob Kersee had, the year before, married Al's sister, Jackie. All four denied rumors of frictions and hard feelings following Florence's decision to leave Bob Kersee's gym. "I hold no personal contract with any athlete," Bob Kersee said. "[Florence] was free to do what she thought best. We have to not let gold medals . . . interfere with the family." And Florence pointed out to a press conference that "no matter what we say, we love each other. I hope Bobby knows it's good for me to move on, like a child leaving the nest."

For her new training regimen with Al Joyner, Florence increased the intensity of her weight training and made use of a simple observation she had made about other runners—that stress and tension affected an athlete's performance on the track, preventing muscles and mind from working together harmoniously. Instead, Joyner realized that what was needed was a relaxed attitude (she especially pointed to Carl Lewis as an example) which would allow for greater concentration at the starting block. By the time she arrived at the World championships in Rome shortly after her marriage to Al Joyner, she was ready to put her theories to the test. The result was a silver medal in the 200-meter dash and the decision to focus on the upcoming 1988 Olympic Games. "When you've been second best for so long," Florence said, "you can either accept it or try to become the best. I made the decision to try and be the best in 1988."

By the spring of 1988, most commentators gave Florence a good prognosis for the 200-meter, but both Bob Kersee and Al Joyner knew that Florence was in peak condition and ready for more than one event. Al remembered going for an early evening run with Florence, during which he reminded her to slow down after the first 50 yards only to watch her increase her pace with no apparent effort; and Bob Kersee had clocked her at 10:89 in a 100-meter dash in San Diego—little more than a tenth of a second behind the current world record—only to have Florence complain afterward about what a bad day she was having. In July of 1988, Florence headed to Indianapolis for the summer trials, the first stage in her quest for Olympic gold, hoping for a spot on the women's track team going to the autumn games in Seoul. Her suitcase contained 14 running outfits she had designed herself.

Her first time out of the starting block at Indianapolis, in her emerald green suit for the 100-meter, Joyner electrified the spectators by breaking Evelyn Ashford's world record with a time of 10:60, even though the record was not officially accepted because of tail winds which were clocked some three and half miles stronger than allowed by Olympic rules. Advancing to the quarterfinals, Florence sported a turquoise-and-purple running suit, with one leg covered and one leg exposed, along with nails painted in orange and black stripes, as she streaked down the track in 10:49, breaking her own record. "When I saw the time," Joyner later recalled, "I couldn't believe it. It made me realize that if I kept concentrating, I could go faster." Now that she had flummoxed the sports press by winning an event for which they had not given her much of a chance, she went on to set a U.S. record for the 200-meter, with a time of 21:77, only six-hundredths of a second slower than the world record then held by two German runners, Marita Koch and ❧ Heike Drechsler, and turning the tables on Valerie Brisco-Hooks, who came in second. "Now, I'm ready for my final goal, some

---

❧ **Drechsler, Heike** (1964—)

German track-and-field champion. Born on December 16, 1964.

In 1988, Heike Drechsler took the silver in the long jump in the Seoul Olympics, along with bronze medals in the 200-meters and the 100 meters. In the Barcelona Olympics in 1992, she won the gold medal in the long jump with a 7.14 effort. **Inessa Kravets** of the Soviet Union came in second while *Jackie Joyner-Kersee took the bronze.

Olympic gold," she told the admiring press conference which immediately dubbed her "Flo-Jo."

Her arrival in Seoul two months later got off to a worrisome start when, at the airport, Al's baggage cart toppled over onto her ankle, injuring her Achilles' tendon and forcing her to miss several days of training. Although the press seized on the incident as a bad omen, Joyner begged to differ and proved it when she stepped to the block for the 100-meter, in which she outran Drechsler in the semifinals by little more than two-tenths of a second. Joyner faced Drechsler again in the finals, along with Evelyn Ashford, who then held the world record for the event. Track fans still remember the huge smile that flashed across Flo-Jo's elegant features at the 90-meter mark and the arms raised in victory ten meters later as she obliterated Ashford's world record with a time of 10:54. Ashford placed a distant second, at 10:83. "That smile came from within," Florence later said. "I was finally seeing myself on the Olympic team, as a gold medalist." The only disappointment was the judges' decision not to enter the time as a world record, again because of high tail winds.

Three days later, Florence sported a white lace running suit (her "athletic negligée," as she called it) as she swept to another gold in the 200-meter, after breaking the world record twice—once in the semifinals, and then surpassing herself in the finals with a time of 21:34. She broke the tape four meters ahead of Jamaica's *Grace Jackson, while Drechsler placed a distant third. As Joyner knelt on the field in thanks and then opened her arms to hug an ebullient Al, cameras focused on her long, scimitar-like nails which would, oddly, become an issue in Florence's next event, the 4x100 relay.

Judges had actually disqualified her from the relay in 1984 because of the six-inch nails, claiming they would interfere with passing the baton in the exchange zone. The same argument was raised in Seoul, but Al and American Olympic officials prevailed, and Joyner was assigned the third, 100-meter leg, in which she led her competitors by three feet by the time she reached a waiting Evelyn Ashford, who would run the final leg. Although Florence did, indeed, bobble the baton in the pass, Ashford managed to get a grip and completed the race in first place. Florence now had her third gold medal. Any athlete would have been proud of such a stunning, three-event Olympic record, but Joyner eagerly accepted a last-minute offer to run the 4x400-meter relay with its allure of an unprecedented fourth gold medal. Thus, just 40 minutes

after running the 4x100, she streaked off on the final leg of the 4x400-meter and arrived at the finish line in 48:10, setting another record for the fastest time over her assigned distance. Even though she placed second behind a Soviet runner, whose team took the gold while the Americans captured the silver, Florence beamed with pride at the finish line. "I felt that the silver was the special one, because of the team's trust in giving me the chance," she said. "That silver is gold to me."

Along with every other track-and-field competitor at the 1988 Games, including her sister-in-law Jackie Joyner-Kersee, Florence suffered from the controversy generated by her friend Ben Johnson's disqualification for competing while using steroids; and along with Jackie, she vehemently and repeatedly denied using any such substances at any time during her career, becoming particularly incensed when Carl Lewis implied at a press conference that Bob Kersee had routinely made steroids part of his training regimen. Al was quick to come to his wife's defense. "Florence runs 10:49 in the Olympic trials," Al bitterly complained, "and it's wind. She does 21:34 here, and they say it's drugs." But no one could take away Joyner's stunning performance in Seoul and her newfound stature as the most decorated female sprinter in Olympic history. She had become the first American woman since *Wilma Rudolph in 1960 to win more than two gold medals in one Olympics for track and field; she had nearly equaled the four-medal record set by Holland's *Fanny Blankers-Koen in 1948 and could claim responsibility, in combination with Jackie, for five-sixths of the U.S. women's track-and-field gold medals that year (Jackie Joyner-Kersee had won the gold for the high jump and the heptathlon).

More practically, the financial rewards of sports stardom finally put an end to the economic tightrope that had been such a part of Florence's years in training. Although she had been approached even before the trials in Indianapolis, the multimillion-dollar offers for endorsements, story rights, and public appearances began to mount to such affluent proportions that some wags in the press began to refer to her as "Cash Flo." Starting with advertisements for everything from pharmaceutical companies to running shoes, Joyner's glamorous image became associated with copying machines, nail and hair products, a "Flo-Jo Doll," and a line of sporting apparel that Florence designed herself. Amid all the activity and demands for her time, suggestions from both her parents and from Al that her peak running years were over began to make sense. In February of 1989, at 30 years of age, Joyner announced her formal retirement from running after receiving the Jessie Owens Award as 1988's most outstanding athlete. "I was denying reality," she said. "I cried about it, but I decided."

But her retirement was not easy. Only a few months after her announcement, Joyner admitted that she missed running more than she'd ever imagined and swore that she'd be running in a marathon within five years. She began competing in celebrity races and fund-raising events, but an attempt to qualify for the 400 meters at the 1996 Games in Atlanta had to be abandoned because of an injury to the same Achilles' tendon that plagued her just before the games in Seoul. Joyner sought other outlets for her energies by serving on the President's Council on Physical Fitness and lending her name to programs designed to help disadvantaged children; helping Jackie Joyner-Kersee train for her third Olympic heptathlon gold at the 1992 Games in Barcelona; writing a series of children's books and a novel; and accepting guest appearances on television chat shows and sitcoms.

Precisely because Joyner's boundless energy had spilled over into so many areas outside of sports, news of her untimely death on September 21, 1998, was all the more shocking. She was only 38 when an apparent heart seizure claimed her life as she slept. Al Joyner revealed that two years earlier, Florence had suffered a similar incident which required hospitalization but had insisted at the time that the episode not be publicized. "We were dazzled by her speed, humbled by her talent, and captivated by her style," President Bill Clinton told reporters in Washington; while Jackie Joyner-Kersee told the media, "A great athlete passed away today, but more importantly" she was "a great human being."

Taking her mother's lesson of self-reliance to heart, Florence proved that sheer determination was enough to break through any obstacle, and that feminine sensibilities had a place in a world normally infused with masculine standards. "For a long time, we've been thought of as jocks," Wilma Rudolph pointed out after watching Joyner's colorful performance in Seoul. "Florence brings in the glamour." Florence Griffith Joyner, with a flash of gold, a streak of bright color, and a stream of flowing dark hair became "the fastest woman alive."

SOURCES:

Aaseng, Nathan. *Florence Griffith Joyner: Dazzling Olympian.* Minneapolis, MN: Lerner Publications, 1989.

Koral, April. *Florence Griffith Joyner: Track and Field Star.* NY: Franklin Watts, 1992.
Moore, Kenny. "A Special Fire," in *Sports Illustrated.* Vol. 69, no. 16. October 10, 1988.
———. "The Spoils of Victory," in *Sports Illustrated.* Vol. 70, no. 16. April 10, 1989.
Salem, Dorothy C., ed. *African-American Women: A Biographical Dictionary.* NY: Garland, 1993.

Norman Powers,
writer-producer, Chelsea Lane Productions, New York

Joyner, Marjorie Stewart (1896–1994).
See Inventors.

Joyner, Matilda Sissieretta (1869–1933).
See Jones, Sissieretta.

Joyner-Kersee, Jackie (1962—)

African-American Olympic track-and-field athlete who won three Olympic gold medals in the heptathlon, making her the greatest multi-event champion ever, man or woman. Name variations: Jackie Joyner. Born on March 3, 1962, in East St. Louis, Illinois; one of four children of Mary and Albert Joyner; sister-in-law of Florence Griffith Joyner; attended University of California at Los Angeles; married Robert Kersee (her coach), on January 11, 1986.

Began competing in local track-and-field events at age nine (1971); won first of four AAU Junior Olympics pentathlon titles (1977); won a basketball scholarship to UCLA; became a star performer on that school's women's basketball and track teams; competed in first Olympic Games in Los Angeles (1984), winning the silver medal in the heptathlon; broke the world high-jump record at the Goodwill Games in Moscow, and became the first woman to score more than 7,000 points (1986); won two gold medals in the high jump and heptathlon at the Olympics in Seoul, South Korea (1988); won a bronze in the long jump and a gold in the heptathlon at the Olympic Games in Barcelona, Spain (1992); won a bronze in the long jump at the Olympic Games in Atlanta, Georgia (1996); won a gold medal in the heptathlon in the Goodwill Games in New York (1998). Also active in self-development programs for inner city youth, especially in her hometown, where she has organized and funded the Jackie Joyner-Kersee Community Foundation using the proceeds of her various commercial endorsement contracts.

On most afternoons during the school year in the late 1960s, students streaming out of a grade school in East St. Louis, Illinois, could be seen buying a few pieces of candy from a tall, graceful schoolmate to sweeten the trip home. The pennies and nickels they handed over to Jackie Joyner were the first contributions toward an athletic career that would make her the most famous woman athlete of the century since *Mildred "Babe" Didrickson Zaharias, and would lead an admiring Bill Cosby to call her "the best athlete in the world, period." Joyner-Kersee carefully saved the money to finance her travel with the school track club, of which she had been a star performer since the age of nine. It was an early sign of the remarkable spirit that would bring her such success in later years, a spirit based on what she once described as her "three D's": desire, dedication, and determination. "If you want to be successful in anything," Joyner-Kersee has pointed out, "you must have discipline. You have to set goals and then accomplish them."

$\mathcal{O}$ne day, I'm going to go to the Olympics.

—Jackie Joyner, at 14, to her brother.

Jackie was the second of four children of Alfred and **Mary Joyner**, who had married in their teens and were barely in their twenties when their first daughter was born on March 3, 1962. By the time of Jackie's birth, East St. Louis—a once prosperous, mostly African-American community on the eastern bank of the Mississippi River, opposite St. Louis, Missouri—had become a symbol of the deteriorating urban conditions that still plague so many American cities. The family lived in a ramshackle house on Piggot Street once described as little more than a few sticks with wallpaper attached; Joyner-Kersee still remembers sleeping in the kitchen during the winters, the stove providing the only warmth in a house where the pipes routinely burst from the cold. Jackie's father, who had been a record-setting hurdler and footballer in high school, was forced to spend days away from his family because of his job as a railroad switcher in distant Springfield, Illinois. Mary supplemented her husband's income by working as a nurse's assistant at a nearby nursing home. But the Joyners envisioned a better life for their children and instilled in them the value of hard work and education. "We didn't think we were poor," Jackie once said. "We didn't have a lot, but we knew our mother and father were doing their best."

It was Jackie's maternal grandmother, **Ollie Mae Johnson**, who named her new granddaughter after then-First Lady *Jacqueline Kennedy because, she said, "Some day this girl will be the first lady of *something*." As the Joyner family grew, Albert and Mary looked to Jackie as a role model for her sisters and brother. "I felt I was the one who was supposed to set an example," Jackie says, recalling the pressure she always felt to perform well in school and keep away from bad influences. She quickly discovered that sports was a legitimate means to let off steam, especially the running and jumping in track-and-field competitions held at East St. Louis' Mary E. Brown Community Center, just around the corner from her house. "I think she uses athletics to let out energy and emotion," sister Angela says. "If she's in a bad mood or something like that, she'll definitely go to the field." More dangerous outlets, like the alcoholism and drug abuse that often afflict urban centers, were never an option for Jackie. She still remembers her father's difficult, eventually successful, battle with alcoholism, and the time she was looking forward, when she was 11 years old, to a visit from Ollie Mae, only to learn that her grandmother had been killed by her second husband, who returned home one night in a drunken rage carrying a shotgun. "I never got into drugs or drank any type of alcohol," she has said, "because . . . I saw how it was destroying my family."

Nino Fennoy, Joyner-Kersee's coach at the Mary E. Brown Center, long felt that she was a gifted athlete, even though she trailed the rest of the field in her first race. "When I'm speaking of gifted," he later said, "it's not just the athletic portion. She had the mental attitude . . . to weather the ups and downs." By the time Jackie began attending Lincoln High School, it was plain to everyone that her future lay with sports. She had won the first of three National Junior Pentathlon championships at 14 and had set a state record for the long jump by the time she graduated from Lincoln in the top 10% of her class. Her sports and academic performance brought several offers of full scholarships from colleges throughout the country, and Jackie finally settled on a basketball scholarship offered by the University of California at Los Angeles, which she entered in 1980 as a history major. Away from home for the first time in her life and living in a one-room apartment, she was once again rescued by sports as her extraordinary athletic prowess enhanced UCLA's track and basketball teams.

It was her competition schedule that prevented her from returning to East St. Louis for the Christmas holidays during her freshman year, despite pleas from her mother. Not long after Christmas, Mary Joyner was stricken by spinal meningitis. By the time Jackie and her brother Al Joyner (who was attending school in Tennessee) arrived back in East St. Louis, Mary had lapsed into a coma, kept alive by machines. Doctors advised the family that there had been severe brain damage from the disease. With the remaining Joyners looking to her for a decision, Jackie knew her mother would have wanted to die peacefully and asked that she be disconnected from her life support. It was Jackie who was the strong one at the funeral, stoically comforting her more outwardly distraught relatives, and it was Jackie who bottled her emotions up for months before a dinner with her teammates in Los Angeles reminded her of the last Christmas dinner with her mother that she had missed. Only then did her grief spill out, and Jackie came to realize how much her mother had contributed to her sports career. "Today I feel that my success is also her success," she says. "I'd never have been able to come this far without her guidance."

During her first year at UCLA, Joyner-Kersee successfully competed in her first Olympic trials, becoming one of three women track-and-field competitors on the American team for the 1980 Games in Moscow. Her hopes were crushed, however, when the U.S. joined several other Western countries in withdrawing from the Games to protest the Soviet Union's invasion of Afghanistan. Jackie redoubled her efforts in collegiate sports so that, by 1984, her record on the basketball court with the UCLA Lady Bruins averaged 9.6 points and 6.2 rebounds per game, earning her a berth on the school's NCAA all-conference team. More significantly, she met during her college years the coach who would bring her to the peak of her sports career.

Bob Kersee had joined the UCLA faculty in 1980 and was the assistant coach of the women's track-and-field team when he learned of Jackie's mother's death. Having recently lost his own mother, Kersee offered a sympathetic ear while encouraging Jackie not to lose faith in her own abilities. Kersee, with an eye on the 1984 summer Olympic Games scheduled for Los Angeles, recognized Jackie's potential for the grueling two-day heptathlon, a seven-event com-

Jackie Joyner-Kersee

petition which had been developed from the five-event pentathlon by adding the javelin throw and the 800-meter run to the long jump, high jump, shot put, 100-meter hurdle, and 200-meter dash. It was to be offered for the first time at the '84 Games. Kersee became Jackie's personal coach in 1982 and prepared her for the World Track and Field Championships in Helsinki, Finland, to which Jackie traveled in 1983 full of enthusiasm and determination. But she was forced to withdraw from competition because of a pulled hamstring, the first of several such injuries that would plague her career. It was the first time, Jackie later said, that she realized she wasn't an invincible competitor.

Bob Kersee refused to let such negative thinking ruin her chances for the Olympics and adjusted her training to minimize stress on her hamstrings. By the time the summer of 1984 arrived, Jackie was back in top form. She stunned spectators around the globe by winning the silver medal in the heptathlon, missing a gold by only five points. Jackie's brother Al, also coached by Kersee, won a gold medal in the triple high jump, making the 1984 Games the first in which a brother and sister had placed in the medals on the same day. More important, it was the first time an American woman had won a multi-event medal. Fans were even more astonished at her performance when it was revealed that Jackie suffered from asthma, a childhood ailment that had been professionally diagnosed only two years previously and which in her case was triggered, ironically, only by physical exertion. "I try not to use it as an excuse," Jackie told reporters, but admitted that it sometimes prevented her from running her usual four miles a day. "I'll only be up to two miles and I'll get this burning sensation in my chest which makes me feel as if I'm going to die," she said. Jackie knew her asthma would be exacerbated by the Olympic Committee's ban on certain drugs, many of which contained the same ingredients found in Jackie's medication and which would thus disqualify her if found in her bloodstream during random testing. Forced to avoid her medication at a time when she most needed it, Jackie relied on diet and breathing exercises while in competition and was, in fact, hospitalized several times during her Olympic career after collapsing, gasping for air, after a race.

With Bob Kersee's intuition about her abilities amply confirmed at the 1984 Games, Jackie undertook an even more rigorous training schedule under his direction. At the same time, their relationship began to grow beyond the merely professional, and the two began dating shortly after the Los Angeles Games. Kersee and Joyner had discovered a mutual spirituality, with Bob training in his spare time for the ministry and Jackie publicly acknowledging the deep religious faith instilled in her at home by joining a Baptist congregation in 1985. "She always had faith," Bob Kersee has said, "and I think there's where her strength came from." Jackie has observed that her willpower stems from "trying to hear that quiet voice within and to know God is with you." One night, in between pitches at a Houston Astros game in 1985, Kersee turned to her and said, "You know, we get along so well, we might as well be married."

In 1986, just before Jackie traveled to Moscow for the Goodwill Games, she and Bob were wed at the Los Angeles church at which Kersee was an assistant minister, amid predictions that either Jackie's career or the marriage itself would crumble. But the critics were proved wrong in Moscow, where Jackie broke the world record for the heptathlon by gathering 7,148 points, and set a new record for a single high jump, clearing 23 feet. Two years later, in July of 1988, she qualified for the 1988 Olympics by breaking her own heptathlon record at the trials, scooping up 7,215 points. As for her marriage, Jackie pointed out that any disagreements she and Kersee had were strictly sports related and had nothing to do with being husband and wife.

Arriving in Seoul in September, Bob told reporters he was expecting two gold medals and two world records for Jackie, a prediction some thought overly optimistic after the first day of the heptathlon. Although Jackie led her nearest competitor by 181 points, she had hurt her knee in the long jump and had to spend the night with a mild electric current running through her leg to try to relieve the strain. Bob shrugged off the media's low opinion of Jackie's chances of recovery. "They were people who didn't know Jackie," he later said. Complicating matters was the controversy over the use of steroids that plagued that year's summer games after Canadian runner Ben Johnson tested positive for the drug and was disqualified from competition. Jackie bristled when she, too, was forced to submit to testing. "They began lumping the innocent with the guilty," she later said. "They were looking in my direction, and they were looking in the wrong direction, because they were not going to find any positive tests from *this* young lady."

The next day, Joyner-Kersee set a new world high-jump record at 23'10¾" and won the gold medal for that event, fulfilling half of Bob Kersee's prediction. She met the other half later in the day, when her time in the 800-meter set another world record and put her total points for the heptathlon at 7,291, earning Jackie her second gold medal and making her the first woman to win back-to-back heptathlon medals in two consecutive Olympics.

As with the '84 Games, the name Joyner was a prominent one in Seoul that year. Brother Al's wife, runner *Florence Griffith Joyner (also coached by Bob), found gold on the track as well. Jackie and Florence, in fact, won or shared five-sixths of America's gold medals in woman's track and field at Seoul, and each of them broke at least one world record. But Jackie firmly denied rumors of friction between herself and her more flamboyant sister-in-law, whose alluring outfits and long, bright-red nails attracted a good deal of media attention and comment. Florence's stylishness, she said, was good for the sport, attracting viewers who would otherwise bypass track-and-field events; and Jackie credited Florence with helping her overcome her asthma by serving as her training partner. "We're not competitive," Jackie said. "The media try and make it look that way, partly because we're family."

Now firmly established as a world-famous sports celebrity, Joyner-Kersee found herself spending six days out of every week on the road, speaking to school groups and civic gatherings and appearing on television chat shows and on the front covers of national magazines. She signed several lucrative product endorsement contracts, using a large portion of her earnings to fund programs to alleviate what she called "my two causes"—poverty and homelessness. In her hometown of East St. Louis, she opened the Jackie Joyner-Kersee Community Foundation as a center for sports, recreation, and self-development programs for poor children, and contributed $40,000 to help reopen the Mary E. Brown Community Center, which had been closed for lack of money in 1982. In Santa Monica, California, she funded an anti-drug program called New Start; and on being named one of several winners of the Essence Award for outstanding achievement in 1988, Jackie donated her $1,000 in prize money to a fellow winner to help with his educational expenses. In 1989, with the financial support of two of her commercial sponsors, Jackie and Bob took a group of children from East St. Louis to New York City for the Macy's Thanksgiving Day parade. For many of the youngsters, it was the first time they had ever left East St. Louis. "There were people, when I was little, reaching into their pockets trying . . . to make things possible for me," Jackie says. "I feel that in return I can do

that for the next generation. I hope I can inspire someone to take the right path and be successful." Her generosity can be of a more personal nature, too. "She was there when I needed her," remembers runner *Valerie Brisco-Hooks, herself a three-time gold medalist whom Jackie helped through a particularly painful divorce; and Fred Thompson, Jackie's assistant coach at the 1988 Games, once told an interviewer, "I don't know a person in the world who has a negative thing to say about her. She's a lady. And it's not just on her lips—she goes out there and does things." Bob Kersee puts it more simply. "She's just good," he says.

Despite her demanding public-speaking schedule, Joyner-Kersee kept to her training regime and announced her intention of going to her third Olympic Games in Barcelona in 1992. But at the World Track championships in Tokyo in 1991, she was seized by a painful cramp at the turn in the 200-meter dash and fell. As with her experience in Helsinki in 1983, it took Bob Kersee months to rebuild Jackie's confidence and toughen her up for Barcelona, especially since the two of them knew Jackie would be facing stiff competition in the heptathlon from Germany's ❧▸ Sabine Braun and the Russian track star ❧▸ Irina Belova. After the 100-meter hurdle and the high jump, Jackie seemed poised to top her own world record set in Seoul. But she faltered at the shot put, falling some five feet short of her expected distance, and at the end of the 200-meter dash, found herself trailing Braun and Belova in overall points.

On the eve of the heptathlon's second day, Bob reminded Jackie of something she'd once told reporters after her 1988 triumph. "I have a lot of fun," she had said at the time. "I'm not out there to break any records. When you focus

❧▸ **Braun, Sabine** (1965—)
German heptathlon champion. Born in Germany on June 19, 1965.

Sabine Braun won the Olympic bronze medal in the heptathlon in Barcelona, Spain, in 1992.

❧▸ **Belova, Irina** (1968—)
Russian heptathlon champion. Born in the Soviet Union on March 27, 1968.

In 1992, Irina Belova won the Olympic silver medal in the heptathlon in Barcelona, Spain.

on breaking records, you put pressure on yourself, and that can spoil your performance." The next day, Jackie held her placing of the previous day by clearing 23 feet in the high jump, and edged ahead of Braun and Belova in the long jump with a distance that won her the bronze medal for that event. Then, in an impressive show of strength late in the competition, Jackie surged to the top with a 147'7" javelin throw and a time of 2:11:78 in the 800-meter, giving her a total of 7,044 points. Although it was below the record she had set in Seoul, it was enough to defeat Braun and Belova and win a third Olympic heptathlon gold medal. Statisticians noted that Joyner-Kersee was now responsible for six of the seven times the women's heptathlon had broken the 7,000 point mark. Former Olympic decathlon champion Bruce Jenner caught up with Jackie during her victory lap and spoke for many by calling her "the greatest multi-event athlete ever, man or woman."

Not content with three Olympic victories, Joyner-Kersee decided to aim for one final stretch, the 1996 summer games in Atlanta. Against the advice of friends who tried to convince her she had earned the right to set more modest goals, Jackie appeared in full force at the 1994 U.S. Olympic Festival in Illinois in July. Her performance let the world know she was intent on at least one more Olympic medal. Jackie's time in the 400-meter sprint and the 1600-meter relay earned her team a bronze medal at the Festival, while she broke the American women's record in the 100-meter hurdle with a time of 12:69—all this despite an asthma attack just before the relay, when Jackie confessed she had been "wheezing pretty hard" but decided to run anyway.

But when the Atlanta Games began, it seemed that Joyner-Kersee's friends had been at least partially right. Jackie—now 34 years old and competing against much younger athletes—was forced out of the heptathlon by another severely strained hamstring, and she and Bob gave serious thought to withdrawing completely from competition. But the idea was soon dismissed. "I knew the pain she was feeling in her leg," Bob said. "I knew she could quit anytime. But I knew she had a seven-meter jump in her." Once again, Bob's prediction proved true, although it took all of Jackie's willpower and determination to walk out on the field for the long jump. She jumped exactly seven meters and won her sixth Olympic medal, a bronze, for her effort. "This was a really tough Olympics," she told a press conference just after the Atlanta Games ended. Formally announcing her retirement from Olympic competition, Joyner-Kersee admitted her own surprise at the difficulty she experienced. "I never dreamed it would be like this," she said. "The bronze medal meant a lot to me."

Although universally acknowledged as the finest American track-and-field athlete of her generation and as a pioneer in women's sports, Jackie Joyner-Kersee's retirement by no means indicates she intends to live off those accolades. She continues to compete professionally in long jump competitions around the country; and in September of 1996, she announced that she would be returning to the basketball court by signing a one-year contract with the Richmond Rage in the new, all-women's American Basketball League. Her schedule of public appearances and charity work is as busy as ever, and in 1998 she attended the groundbreaking ceremony for the Jackie Joyner-Kersee Youth Center in East St. Louis. Most important, her marriage to Bob Kersee remains a strong and rewarding one. "I think it's really great for me to have someone like Bobby, who understands and doesn't interfere with what I'm trying to do," she says. Her husband, now a minister with his own congregation, is equally complimentary. "There's no period at the end of her sentence," Kersee says. "Jackie is just to be continued."

SOURCES:

Cain, Joy Duckett. "The Jackie Nobody Knows," in *Essence*. Vol. 20, no. 4. August 1989.

"Can World's Greatest Woman Athlete Cash in on Olympic Gold?," in *Ebony*. Vol. 44, no. 6. April 1989.

Gardner, Ralph Jr. "Cosmo Talks to Jackie Joyner Kersee," in *Cosmopolitan*. Vol. 206, no. 6. June 1989.

Harrington, Geri. *Jackie Joyner-Kersee: Champion Athlete*. NY: Chelsea House Publishing, 1995.

Hine, Darlene Clark, ed. *Black Women in America*. Brooklyn, NY: Carlson, 1993.

Moore, Kenny. "Dash to Glory," in *Sports Illustrated*. Vol. 77, no. 6. August 10, 1992.

———. "Proving Her Point," in *Sports Illustrated*. Vol. 69, no. 15. October 3, 1988.

———. "A Special Fire," in *Sports Illustrated*. Vol. 69, no. 16. October 10, 1988.

———. "Our Woman in Moscow," in *Sports Illustrated*. Vol. 65. July 21, 1986.

Smith, Jessie Carney, ed. *Notable Black American Women*. Detroit, MI: Gale Research, 1996.

SUGGESTED READING:

Joyner-Kersee, Jackie, with Sonja Steptoe. *A Kind of Grace: The Autobiography of the World's Greatest Female Athlete*. NY: Warner, 1997.

Norman Powers,
writer-producer, Chelsea Lane Productions, New York

Juana.

Variant of Joan or Joanna.

Juana, Sor or Sister (1651–1695).
See Juana Inés de la Cruz.

Juana I of Navarre (1273–1305).
See Joan I of Navarre.

Juana II of Navarre (1309–1349).
See Joan II of Navarre.

Juana de Asbaje y Ramirez de Santillana (1651–1695).
See Juana Inés de la Cruz.

Juana de Aviz (1439–1475).
See Joanna of Portugal.

Juana de la Cerda (1339–1381).
See Joanna of Castile.

Juana Inés de la Cruz (1651–1695)

Mexican poet and playwright who was recognized in her own time for her genius but who nonetheless struggled against great odds to achieve the freedom to devote herself to scholarship and creative activity. Name variations: Sor (Sister) Juana Ines de la Cruz; the Tenth Muse; the Mexican Nun. Pronunciation: HWAH-na ee-NEYSS they la KROOTH. Born Juana Ramírez de Asuaje, frequently spelled Asbaje, near San Miguel de Nepantla, Mexico, on November 12, 1651 (some writers, citing plausible but inconclusive evidence, have argued that it was actually three years earlier, in 1648); died on April 17, 1695, in Mexico City; daughter of Isabel Ramírez de Santillana and Pedro Manuel de Asuaje y Vargas Machuca; never married; no children.

Entered Hieronymite convent, Mexico City (1668); had earliest known work published in Mexico (1676); had first collection of works published in Spain (1689); engaged in polemic on women's rights (1691); withdrew from literary life (1693).

Selected works: long poem Primero sueño *(First Dream), numerous sonnets and* villancicos, *religious and secular plays, and an important autobiographical essay entitled* Respuesta a Sor Filotea *(Reply to Sister Filotea).*

During the 17th century, Spanish colonial Mexico was known as New Spain. A male-dominated society, it afforded few options to women, but Sor Juana Inés de la Cruz defied the limits imposed by Hispanic tradition and the Roman Catholic Church to become one of the most significant writers in the history of Spanish literature. For more than 20 years, Sor Juana maintained a brilliant literary career, but, shortly before her death, she was finally forced into si-

lence. Her admirers in her own day called Sor Juana the "Tenth Muse," a name also applied to her approximate contemporary, the early Massachusetts poet *Anne Bradstreet (1612–1672). In the early 20th century, because of her outspoken defense of the equality of the sexes in matters of intellect, **Dorothy Schons** labeled Juana "the first feminist of America."

The future nun, poet, playwright, and essayist was born Juana Ramírez de Asuaje (frequently spelled Asbaje) at San Miguel de Nepantla, approximately 45 miles southeast of Mexico City. The date traditionally accepted for her birth is November 12, 1651, but some writers, citing plausible but inconclusive evidence, have argued that it was actually three years earlier, in 1648. Sor Juana's mother, **Isabel Ramírez de Santillana**, a creole, as Mexican-born Spaniards were called, was an independent-minded woman who had at least six children with two different men, neither of whom she ever married. The father in Sor Juana's case was a Basque military officer who may or may not have been at home during his daughter's early years.

Defensive about her illegitimacy, Sor Juana almost never mentioned her father in her writings. The principal male influence during her childhood was her maternal grandfather Pedro Ramírez. A local landowner, Ramírez was an enthusiastic reader with an impressive private library. It was in his house that young Juana first cultivated her remarkable appetite for learning. In her important 1691 autobiographical essay known as the *Respuesta a Sor Filotea* (Reply to Sister Filotea), Sor Juana tells us that she learned to read at the age of three. By the time she was six or seven, she was pestering her mother to send her to live with relatives in Mexico City, where she proposed to dress as a boy and attend classes at the university, which accepted only male students. Barred from formal education beyond the rudiments of literacy available at a local grammar school for girls, Juana sought consolation by immersing herself in her grandfather's books. She later recalled that "there were not enough punishments, nor reprimands, to prevent me from reading," a reminder that, even in her apparently somewhat unconventional family, intellectual pursuits were not considered altogether suitable for female children.

When she was about eight years old, Juana produced her first known literary composition, now lost, a *loa,* or prologue, to a sacred play to be performed at the church at nearby Amecameca. About the same time, she got her wish to leave her grandfather's farm for Mexico City, where she lived at first with her mother's sister **María de Mata**, who was married to an influential man named Juan de Mata. In the Mata household, Juana was able to continue her studies, mastering Latin grammar, she tells us, in "no more than twenty lessons." Not only brilliant and talented, but also physically attractive, Juana was a remarkable prodigy who could not long escape notice in the glamorous circles of Mexico City society. Among her chief admirers were the Spanish viceroy of New Spain, Antonio Sebastián de Toledo, marquis of Mancera (r. 1664–1673), and his wife, the vicereine, Leonor Carreto (**Leonor de Mancera**). The Manceras were patrons of art and learning, and they brought Juana to the viceregal court as lady-in-waiting to the marquise. In this capacity, she became something of an official poet, producing verses for all occasions on commissions from both civil and ecclesiastical authorities.

*H*ad Aristotle done the cooking, he would have had a great deal more to write about.

—Sor Juana Inés de la Cruz

At court, Juana grew close to the vicereine, to whom, as "Laura," she later addressed poems of loving friendship. Sharing his wife's pride in her protégée's attainments, on one occasion the marquis arranged an unusual show in which Juana submitted herself to a public oral examination by some 40 of the city's most learned men. As Mancera later told Sor Juana's earliest biographer, the Spanish Jesuit Diego Callejas, the learned teenager from the provinces performed brilliantly in every area of specialization, fielding the examiners' questions "like a royal galleon might repel an assault by a handful of sloops."

In 1667, despite her triumphs in secular society, Juana decided to leave the court and become a nun. With the viceregal couple's support, she entered the Mexico City convent of the Barefoot Carmelites, where she remained only three months. The discipline of this reformed order may have proved too rigorous, or there may have been other problems. Whatever the cause, Juana left the sisters and returned briefly to live with the Manceras. Early in 1669, she tried again, choosing this time the convent of San Jerónimo, which belonged to the Hieronymite order, whose rule was less demanding than that of the Carmelites. Juana would spend the rest of her life at San Jerónimo. When she took her vows as a Hieronymite nun, she adopted the religious name by which she ultimately became fa-

mous—Sor Juana Inés de la Cruz, that is, Sister Juana Inés of the Cross.

In recent times, Juana's reasons for taking the veil have been the subject of scholarly debate. Despite the claims of her traditional Catholic biographers, she does not appear to have had any particular religious vocation. Some writers have claimed that she was fleeing a painful love affair, but there is little evidence for this assertion, either. More likely, Juana acted on a rational assessment of the options open to her as a young woman in late 17th-century Mexico. Essentially, there were only two such options, marriage or a convent. Matrimony would mean dependence upon a husband, as well as the constant demands of childbearing and domestic responsibilities, and, in any case, her status as the illegitimate daughter of an absent father might have prevented her from making an advantageous match. Sor Juana herself tells us that it was "the total antipathy [she] felt for marriage" that led her to choose the convent as "the least unsuitable and most honorable" way of life.

Only in a convent could a woman hope to enjoy the leisure time and the peace and quiet necessary to pursue scholarly and literary activities. Once Sor Juana joined the Hieronymites, she turned her cell, which was actually a spacious apartment, into a study and surrounded herself with musical and mathematical instruments, as well as an extensive personal library. Some writers claim that she possessed as many as 4,000 books, but this figure is almost certainly an exaggeration.

Any time not occupied by her duties as a member of the community Sor Juana spent in reading, writing, and visiting with her friends. The fact that she had taken religious vows did not mean that she was isolated from outside human contact. Sor Juana's literary works were widely admired in the Spanish-speaking world, and she maintained an active correspondence with kindred spirits, both male and female, not only in Mexico, but also in Spain and in the viceroyalty of Peru. Also, the 17th-century cloister was less secluded than is generally supposed. The rules of Sor Juana's order prohibited her from leaving the convent, but they did not prevent the world from coming to her. The scholarly nun turned the locutory, or reception hall, at San Jerónimo into a kind of literary salon that came to be frequented by some of the most learned, powerful, and influential men and women in the colony.

Among the many admirers who called on Sor Juana were fellow scholars, such as the poet,

scientist, and mathematician Carlos de Sigüenza y Góngora (1645–1700), as well as high-ranking ecclesiastics, such as the archbishop of Mexico City, Payo Enríquez de Rivera, who also served for several years as viceroy (r. 1673–1680). Particularly close to Sor Juana was another viceroy, Tomás Antonio de la Cerda, marquis of La Laguna (r. 1680–1686), who with his wife, **María Luisa Manrique de Lara**, countess of Paredes, came to play a role in the poet's life similar to that played by the marquis and marquise of Mancera some years before. Sor Juana became close friends with the vicereine, whom she addressed in poems as "Filis," "Lysi," and "Lísida." In 1689, following the couple's return to Spain, the countess arranged the first edition in Madrid of Sor Juana's collected poetry, a volume bearing the imposingly baroque title *Inundación castálida* (A Muse-Fed Flood). The poet and her friend kept in touch, and Sor Juana continued to send manuscripts to Spain for publication. A second collection appeared in Seville in 1692, and a third was published posthumously in Madrid in 1700. Altogether, these three volumes of works by Sor Juana Inés de la Cruz went through some 20 editions by 1725.

The support and protection of powerful admirers, such as viceroys and their wives and high-ranking ecclesiastics, enabled Sor Juana to get away with things which might not otherwise have been tolerated in a woman, and especially not in a nun. Although much of her literary output was religious in nature, a great deal of it was not. She tried her hand at virtually every genre and meter currently in vogue and excelled at them all. Her style was exemplary of the best of the Spanish baroque, and reflected the influence, among others, of the poet Luis de Góngora y Argote (1561–1627), whom some critics believe she surpassed in quality. Sor Juana's secular works included cloak-and-dagger comedies which were performed in Mexico City during her lifetime, love poems which even to modern ears sound erotic, and unabashedly bawdy burlesque sonnets. More than once, the nun poet turned her attention to the condition of women in colonial Mexican society, as in the famous poem addressed to

> Thick-headed men who, so unfair,
> Bemoan the faults of women,
> Not seeing as you do that they're
> Exactly what you've made them.

In the opinion of many writers, Sor Juana's most important work was a long poem she called *Primero sueño* (First Dream). Written probably in the mid-1680s and published for the first time in 1692, this difficult composition recounts a voyage of the soul, momentarily freed from its sleeping body, in a quest for comprehension of the created universe. In the end, the seeker realizes that such an understanding is impossible, and, disappointed, the dreamer awakes. The Mexican poet and critic Octavio Paz has noted that Sor Juana's *Sueño* is unique in Spanish letters in its attempt to synthesize science and poetry. It is also a peculiar bridge between the Middle Ages and the modern era. Although the scholarly nun takes creation as her topic, she makes little

reference to the Creator himself, and none to the redemptive mission of his son Jesus Christ. The universe as Sor Juana describes it is no longer the limited geocentric cosmos of medieval thought; instead, it is a vast space with no center and no fixed limits. It is unlikely that Sor Juana was familiar with the revolutionary theories of the German astronomer Johannes Kepler (1571–1630), but the vision she presents is clearly reminiscent of ideas for which the Italian Giordano Bruno (d. 1600) was burned at the stake.

There are many places in the work of Sor Juana Inés de la Cruz where it appears that she came perilously close to heresy and blasphemy, offenses against orthodoxy which could have brought her under the scrutiny of the Mexico City tribunal of the Holy Office of the Inquisition. Intellectually adventurous, she was not afraid to take risks in order to increase her knowledge and understanding; in fact, a favorite theme of hers was the story of Phaëthon from Greek mythology, who, although considered unqualified to do so, had defiantly driven the chariot of the sun. But Sor Juana was not a fool. She was cautious about what she wrote and how she wrote it, and she was always careful to cultivate powerful allies who could protect her against her detractors.

Critics and detractors Sor Juana Inés de la Cruz certainly had. It was not particularly unusual for nuns to write. In fact, there was a long tradition of them, going back to the early Middle Ages. Before the modern era, the only woman, other than Sor Juana, who achieved a secure place in the canon of Spanish literature was also a nun, Saint *Teresa of Avila (1515–1582); but Teresa, and the many other religious women of more modest talent who also wrote, restricted themselves to works of devotion and edification. What set Sor Juana apart from her sisters was the large amount of her literary output that was secular in nature. Also, it did not help her case that her work, being of extremely high quality, attracted admirers on both sides of the Atlantic. Worldly fame was bad enough; what was worse was that Sor Juana appeared both to court it and to enjoy it.

In her autobiography, Sor Juana tells us that she suffered throughout her life from the jealousy and resentment of others. Some of her critics resented her talent and fame, while others held against her the fact that she was a woman. There were also well-intentioned meddlers, such as the prioress who once forbade Sor Juana to write for three months, who sought to discourage her literary activities out of concern for her own spiritual welfare. In general, the poet could count on her powerful and influential friends to protect her against those who, for whatever reason, might have wished to silence her. The network of personal alliances she actively developed and maintained kept her free to do pretty much as she pleased for more than 20 years. In the end, however, it failed her.

Toward the last years of her life, the protective little environment Sor Juana Inés de la Cruz had managed to build around her began to come apart. In 1681, her friend Payo Enríquez de Rivera was replaced as archbishop of Mexico City by Francisco de Aguiar y Seijas, a neurotic and misogynistic ascetic who condemned public spectacles such as bullfights and theater productions, and who complained of lax discipline in the city's convents. In his mind, the worldly nun who wrote plays and secular poetry was symbolic of both evils. A close ally of the Society of Jesus, the archbishop worked through the Jesuit Antonio Núñez de Miranda, who had been Sor Juana's confessor and spiritual director since before she had entered the convent, in an attempt to bring her activities under tighter church supervision. The poet resisted all such efforts, however, and as a result she and Núñez de Miranda became estranged.

Sor Juana had nothing to fear from the archbishop and Núñez de Miranda as long as she enjoyed the protection of the marquis of La Laguna and the countess of Paredes, who, even after they returned to Spain, continued to defend her and to promote her career. The marquis' successor as viceroy, Gaspar de Sandoval, count of Galve (r. 1688–1696), was also friendly to the poet nun, and she enjoyed another important ally in Aguiar y Seijas' rival prelate, the powerful bishop of Puebla Manuel Fernández de Santa Cruz. In addition to admiring Sor Juana and her work, it appears that Bishop Santa Cruz had a personal grudge against the archbishop and his Jesuit friends.

In 1690, Bishop Santa Cruz asked Sor Juana to put in writing some critical thoughts she had expressed to him regarding a sermon by the famous Portuguese Jesuit António Vieira (1608–1697), of whom the archbishop happened to be particularly fond. Acting ostensibly without her permission, Santa Cruz then published the essay under the fawning title *Carta atenagórica* (A Letter Worthy of the Wisdom of Athena), preceded by a prologue which he supplied himself under the pseudonym "Sor Filotea de la Cruz." In a peculiar twist, although the fictitious Sor Filotea opened her remarks with praise for the poet nun, she went on to parrot Aguiar y Seijas and Núñez de Miranda by admonishing Sor Juana not to waste her time with vain pursuits, such as secular learning. Warning her sister that "learning that engenders pride God does not want in a woman," Sor Filotea urged her instead to study "the book of Jesus Christ."

Some scholars claim that Bishop Santa Cruz genuinely intended to counsel his old friend to abandon her secular studies, while others disagree, saying that Sor Filotea's challenge was only a clever ruse to provide Sor Juana an opening to justify herself in writing. Octavio Paz subscribes to the latter view and argues further that the whole affair was a carefully calculated insult to the archbishop, meant to humiliate him and his allies by attacking them through a woman. Whatever the intent, the scholarly nun rose to the occasion in magnificent fashion and the result was her justly famous *Respuesta a Sor Filotea* (1691), which is both her intellectual autobiography and a manifesto in support of the right of all women to study and to express themselves. A favorite theme of Sor Juana's throughout her career was that neither the soul nor the intellect had gender. Although she accepted certain customary restrictions, such as that women should neither preach in churches nor teach in the universities, she rejected most other limits on feminine intellectual expression. In recounting her own scholarly development, Sor Juana noted that some traditionally female experiences might afford insights ordinarily denied to men. "Had Aristotle done the cooking," she declared, "he would have had a great deal more to write about."

In itself, Vieira's sermon was unimportant, and Sor Juana's criticisms of it were not particularly provocative. Even so, the publication of her essay placed the scholarly nun in the middle of a local political dispute. She found herself the object of an angry controversy which involved, among other things, the question of a nun's obligation of obedience and of the appropriate behavior for women in general. Unfortunately for Sor Juana, about the same time, for reasons completely outside of her control, her protective network of personal friendships began to disintegrate. Flooding and famine in central Mexico during 1691 and 1692 led to political difficulties for the count of Galve, whose ineffective response to rioting which broke out in the capital in June 1692 left his leadership discredited and provided an opening for Archbishop Aguiar y Seijas to emerge as the real power in the colony. Recognizing the dramatic shift in political fortunes, Bishop Santa Cruz withdrew from the fray, abandoning his protégée to her enemies.

Sor Juana still had friends in Spain. In fact, she was at the height of her fame and acceptance there, and, in 1692, the countess of Paredes brought out the second volume of her collected works, complete with multiple testimonials in the nun's favor by prominent theologians, including some Jesuits. But the death of the marquis of La Laguna the same year diverted the countess' attention from Sor Juana's problems, and, at any rate, Spain was a long way from Mexico and political realities there. To the archbishop and his crowd, the arrival of Sor Juana's new book looked more like a provocation than a vindication.

In her *Respuesta a Sor Filotea*, Sor Juana had made it clear that she had no intention of giving up studying or writing, but two years later, in 1693, she did precisely that, renewing her nun's vows and giving up her books and other possessions to be sold for charity. Traditional writers have portrayed this sudden reversal as a genuine religious conversion, but others, including Octavio Paz, have argued instead that Aguiar y Seijas and his allies simply succeeded in intimidating Sor Juana into silence.

While it is impossible to know what was going through Sor Juana's mind at this time of personal crisis, it is likely that she felt alone and defenseless. Because she was a believing Catholic, even if she was never a particularly enthusiastic nun, it is also possible that she experienced inner conflict between her desire for autonomy as an intellectual and writer, and the obligations imposed upon her by her vows. She may even have allowed herself to sense some personal responsibility for the natural and social calamities occurring around her. Prior to her submission, Sor Juana had accepted back as her confessor the Jesuit Núñez de Miranda, who would have encouraged her to turn her back on what he would have called her pride and willful nature. Whatever her reasons, after 1693 Sor Juana wrote nothing else. Instead, she devoted herself entirely to the life of the convent and died two years later, having fallen ill while nursing her fellow nuns during an epidemic.

Some critics complain that it diminishes Sor Juana's importance to describe her as a woman poet, because her work is of universal significance and better than that of many of her male contemporaries. It remains true, however, that the fact that she was a woman determined the conditions under which Sor Juana had to live and work, and in many cases the themes which she addressed in her writings. Certainly, in her day a life devoted to secular letters would not have been thought inappropriate in any male writer, not even a member of the clergy, and no man would have been silenced the way she was, for no other cause than having insisted upon his right to learn and express himself.

SOURCES:

[Calleja, Diego.] "Vida de la madre Juana Inés de la Cruz, religiosa profesa en el convento de San Jerónimo, de la ciudad imperial de México" (c. 1700), in *Juana de Asbaje*, by Amado Nervo. Madrid: Biblioteca Nueva, 1920.

Juana Inés de la Cruz, Sor. *A Woman of Genius: The Intellectual Autobiography of Sor Juana Inés de la Cruz* [Respuesta a Sor Filotea]. Trans. and ed. by Margaret Sayers Peden. Salisbury, CT: Lime Rock Press, 1982.

Paz, Octavio. *Sor Juana: Or, the Traps of Faith*. Trans. by Margaret Sayers Peden. Cambridge, MA: Harvard University Press, 1988.

Sabat-Rivers, Georgina. "Sor Juana Inés de la Cruz (1651–1695)," in *Latin American Writers*. Ed. by Carlos A. Solé and María Isabel Abreu. NY: Scribner, 1989.

Schons, Dorothy. "Some Obscure Points in the Life of Sor Juana Inés de la Cruz," in *Modern Philology*. Vol. 24, 1926, pp. 141–162.

SUGGESTED READING:

Arenal, Electa, and Amanda Powell. *The Answer/La Respuesta: The Restored Text and Selected Poems of Juana Inés de la Cruz*. Feminist Press, 1993.

Flynn, Gerard C. *Sor Juana Inés de la Cruz*. NY: Twayne Publishers, 1971.

Juana Inés de la Cruz, Sor. *A Sor Juana Anthology*. Trans. by Alan S. Trueblood. Cambridge, MA: Harvard University Press, 1988.

———. *Sor Juana's Dream* [Primero sueño]. Trans. and ed. by Luis Harss. NY: Lumen Books, 1986.

Leonard, Irving A. *Baroque Times in Old Mexico: Seventeenth-Century Persons, Places, and Practices*. Ann Arbor, MI: University of Michigan Press, 1959.

Merrim, Stephanie, ed. *Feminist Perspectives on Sor Juana Inés de la Cruz*. Detroit, MI: Wayne State University Press, 1991.

Stephen Webre,
Professor of History, Louisiana Tech University, Ruston, Louisiana

Juana la Beltraneja (1462–1530)

Heir of Henry IV of Castile and rival of Isabella I for the crown of Castile. Name variations: Infanta of Castile; Joanna of Castile. Born in Madrid, Spain, on February 28, 1462; died in Lisbon, Portugal, in 1530; only child of Enrique also known as Henry IV, king of Castile (r. 1454–1474), and Joanna of Portugal (1439–1475, sister of Afonso also known as Alphonso V of Portugal); never married; no children.

When *Joanna of Portugal, queen of Castile, went into labor on February 28, 1462, she gave birth to a daughter destined to symbolize the turmoil of late medieval Spain, torn apart by weak monarchs and rapacious, feuding nobles. Henry and his queen named the baby Juana (Joanna), after her mother. To history, however, the girl became known derisively as *la Beltraneja,* meaning that she was the bastard offspring of an adulterous relationship between the queen and a royal favorite Beltrán de la Cueva. But in 1462 these rumors lay in the future. The girl was the delighted monarchs' sole child, even though Henry and Joanna had married in 1454. A few weeks after the girl's birth, the king convened the cortes (a feudal assembly of aristocratic and municipal representatives) in Madrid and had it recognize young Juana as his heir to the Castilian crown. Unlike France or Aragon, Castile had no traditions which prevented a woman from ruling. But civil war would soon engulf Castile. Many nobles would disregard Juana's claims to the throne and support Juana's aunt *Isabella I, who was 11 years older than Juana and Henry's half-sister.

Juana's life is murky, often visible only through the documents which victorious Isabella and Ferdinand II of Aragon, the Catholic kings, permitted to survive. Most of those reinforce the victors' propaganda, which buttressed Isabella's claim to the throne by discrediting Juana's legitimacy and her father's competence. The Isabeline faction confiscated and destroyed documents held by Juana which supported her right to rule Castile.

Henry did what he could to ensure Juana's right to the throne. He had her baptized at eight days of age in the royal palace of Madrid by the archbishop of Toledo. Standing as the infant's godparents, the French count of Armagnac, the 11-year-old Princess Isabella, Juan Pacheco, marquis of Villena, and his wife promised to assist Juana and protect her interests. To strengthen his own position against dissident Castilian nobles, Henry also formed alliances with the kings of Granada and Portugal, and tried to win aristocratic supporters by granting them estates and honors. On the surface, the kingdom seemed happy in the knowledge that the royal heir would lend stability to the monarchy and nation.

Yet Juana's position was precarious. Prior to her birth, powerful nobles had forced Henry to name his half-brother Alphonso (1453–1468) as his successor. The aristocrats' intent was murky. They obviously believed Castile needed to have a clearly defined heir to the monarchy. But their partisanship on young Alphonso's behalf also reflected their belief that they could manipulate him into granting them lands and other favors. Some historians have also argued that by supporting Alphonso the nobility hoped to weaken Henry's political centralization. Juana's birth upset their plans and strengthened Henry's position.

To make matters worse for Juana, her father's allies included nobles whose behavior discredited her. Pacheco, for example, was Henry's long-time companion and possibly the king's homosexual lover. Treacherous by nature, Pacheco's greed for wealth and power threatened other nobles, who bitterly hated him. Also controversial was Beltrán de la Cueva, a newcomer to the court upon whom the king bestowed surprising favors. The Sunday following Juana's birth, Henry made Beltrán count of Ledesma. He later raised him to duke of Albuquerque and made him the highly coveted Master of the Order of Santiago. Other nobles resented his connections and good fortune. Perhaps it was inevitable that rumors would surface that Beltrán was Queen Joanna of Portugal's lover. After all, Henry had been married to ❧▶ **Blanche of Navarre** from 1440 to 1453 without producing any children and had divorced her on the grounds that the marriage had never been consummated. Six years of his marriage to Joanna of Portugal passed without offspring, and only after Beltrán arrived at court was Juana born in 1462.

Information about Juana's childhood is scarce. She moved from place to place with her father's court, learning feminine arts, such as embroidery, and acquiring some ability to read and write. The only surviving portrait of her shows Juana to have been an attractive young woman, with a dark complexion and hair. Quiet and introverted, she lacked her aunt Isabella's aggressive drive. How soon Juana became aware of the contention surrounding her claim to the throne is not known. But it erupted in 1464, when she was only two and too young to have any idea of the stakes at play. In that year, dissident nobles—buttressed by the conniving Pacheco—issued a proclamation which criticized Henry for esteeming Muslims and Jews over Christians and showing undue favoritism to Beltrán de la Cueva. It said nothing, however, about the latter being Juana's real father, an allegation which arose later. Seeking as usual to avoid confrontation, Henry negotiated with the troublemakers. He eventually agreed to reinstate Alphonso as his heir, but on the condition that the boy marry Juana when she came of age. To placate the nobles further, Henry forced Beltrán to renounce the mastership of Santiago and sent him into exile for six months.

By the end of 1464, allegations about Juana's paternity had begun circulating. It was then that the dissidents claimed that Beltrán de la Cueva was the princess' father and dubbed her *la Beltraneja.* To add weight to their propa-

◀❧
Blanche of Navarre (1424–1462).
See Eleanor of Navarre for sidebar.

ganda, they asserted that Henry was impotent, unable to father a child. Thus, Juana could not be his daughter. Centuries later, it is impossible to unravel the rumors enough to arrive at the truth. Henry certainly behaved as if the child were his own daughter. She bore no physical resemblance to Beltrán. Furthermore, the rumors apparently did not start immediately after Juana's birth but nearly three years later when it served the nobles' interests.

Not content with the king's concessions, the rebels staged a mock dethronement of Henry and crowned Alphonso in 1465, thinking the boy could be easily persuaded to grant their desires and enhance their power. Both king and anti-king doled out lands, titles, and favors to attract allies. When Alphonso died unexpectedly in July 1468 (some suspected poisoning), the rebels marshalled themselves behind Isabella. In September, the leaders of the warring factions met near Avila at Toros de Guisando to negotiate a peace. Isabella's supporters claimed that Henry and Joanna of Portugal were not legally espoused because they had not secured a papal dispensation for marriage between close relatives. This, they implied, made Juana illegitimate; they said nothing about Beltrán. Under pressure, the king recognized Isabella as his successor. He also agreed that Juana be removed from the custody of the queen, who during the previous year had lived openly with Pedro de Castilla and had a son with him. The princess was to remain under the tutelage of both Henry and Isabella, giving the latter opportunity to forestall any claims Juana might make regarding

the crown. To strengthen its position, each faction sought a suitable husband for each princess. Acting on her own and without Henry's permission, Isabella chose Ferdinand II of Aragon and married him on October 18, 1469. He soon played a vital role in protecting her claim to the Castilian crown.

Meanwhile, at age five Juana was too young to defend her own interests; but after the peace negotiations at Toros de Guisando, her father showed new determination. In October 1470, he overturned his concessions and reinstated Juana as heir to Castile. He also sought a husband who could assist in protecting the young girl's inheritance. She was betrothed and married by proxy to Charles, duke of Berry and Guienne, and brother of Louis XI. But the Frenchman died in 1472, perhaps poisoned by Louis XI, before claiming his child bride. Hurried negotiations to marry Juana to Alphonso V of Portugal, her uncle, failed in 1472. Complicating Juana's situation was Henry's attitude toward Isabella: he still retained cordial feelings for his half-sister and was reluctant to plunge Castile into war over the question of succession. For Juana's protection and care, he placed her under the tutelage of Pacheco, who had returned to Henry's side.

On December 11, 1474, Henry died, but not before swearing on his deathbed that Juana was his daughter and legitimate heir to his kingdoms. But Isabella wasted no time and had herself crowned queen of Castile two days later. Most of the nobility found it advantageous to support her, including Beltrán de la Cueva. Juana's coterie was smaller and weaker. Isabella shrewdly offered to grant Diego López Pacheco, whose father had died the previous October, the mastership of Santiago if he turned Juana over. Pacheco insisted that he receive the honor before surrendering the princess, and negotiations deadlocked. Meanwhile, the 12-year-old Juana performed what was possibly her first public act: she swore that she was "the certain and legitimate heir and successor in the kingdoms of Castile." She did not declare herself queen but possibly waited for her nobles to acclaim her. They in turned appealed to Alphonso that he marry Juana and defend her throne. With a changed heart and fearful of the union between Castile and Aragon implicit in Isabella and Ferdinand's marriage, Alphonso decided to aid his niece.

Although 30 years her senior, he offered to wed Juana and began gathering an army to invade Castile. In May 1475, Alphonso crossed the border with a force of 20,000 men and met Pacheco and Juana at Plasencia. There they were betrothed on May 25 and acclaimed king and queen of Castile. As close relatives, however, they dared not celebrate the marriage without a papal dispensation, which Isabella's partisans blocked. In the end, Juana and Alphonso never married. On May 30, Juana issued a *Manifiesto,* in which she energetically laid out her claim to the throne and even accused the Isabeline faction of poisoning Henry IV. Juana's army dealt her rival some indecisive defeats that summer. The following year, Ferdinand defeated Alphonso at Toro, causing the Portuguese monarch and Juana to retreat westward across the border.

The war of succession dragged on, with Juana's prospects dimming. While more Spanish nobles went over to Isabella, Juana and Alphonso tried unsuccessfully to secure the aid of Louis XI. Alphonso invaded again in 1479, but defeat at Albuera caused him to negotiate a peace settlement. Juana showed continued determination, despite "her difficult situation of queen without a kingdom, and of symbolic wife." Nonetheless in the Treaty of Tercerías signed in September, Alphonso renounced his claim to the Castilian crown and to Juana's hand.

Although he tried to defend her prerogatives as best he could, neither Alphonso nor the Catholic kings permitted Juana to participate in the treaty negotiations which decided her fate. The treaty forced upon Juana a disagreeable choice: within six months, she could enter a convent; or she could become betrothed to Isabella's eldest son John of Spain, born the previous year, and marry him when he reached 14, if he agreed. If Isabella really believed Juana to be Beltrán's bastard, it is curious that she would have offered *la Beltraneja* her son. Isabella also carefully stipulated that Juana must surrender all her papers and documents related to her legitimacy and rights to the throne. Unwilling to accept the marriage offer, especially because it included no guarantee that the union would ever occur, Juana had no alternative but the cloister. Eager to restore peace between Portugal and Castile, Alphonso and his son John (II) of Portugal carried out the treaty's provisions.

Juana spent a year as a novice, first in the convent of Santa Clara of Santarem and later in its sister house in Coimbra. In an act of kindness, Alphonso granted her the title and honors of a princess (*infanta*) of the Portuguese royal house. Then, on November 15, 1480, and in the presence of emissaries from Isabella's court, Juana, with her hair shorn, took vows as a nun. Those present reported her pale and tearful yet dignified. Juana faced a miserable future, al-though her fate was similar to that of thousands of other medieval women consigned against their wills to convents. She either needed to dedicate herself sincerely to a life of prayer and meditation, even if she felt little religious vocation, or at the young age of 18 resign herself to "vegetating without remedy nor compensation."

> *S*he was the queen's daughter, she was born in the royal household and her birth was welcomed by the king, the kingdom recognized her as the legal heir, and international opinion saw her as the king's daughter. For his part, [Henry] never—not even under the pressure of the meeting at Toros de Guisando—denied her as his daughter.
>
> —William D. Phillips, Jr.

Relations between Castile and Portugal soon led to a slight improvement in her situation. By 1482, John, who had succeeded Alphonso the previous year, defied the Spanish monarchs and allowed Juana to leave the convent. He even approached the king of Navarre, Francisco Febo, about marrying Juana, but Febo died before negotiations could be completed. Meanwhile Juana enjoyed limited freedom of movement, to the dismay of Isabella and Ferdinand, who secured several bulls from popes Sixtus IV and Innocent VIII demanding that she return immediately to the cloister. As a small sign of defiance, Juana signed her correspondence "I the Queen" (*Yo la reyna*), and the Portuguese called her the Excellent Lady (*a Excelente Senhora*).

The years passed, with Juana refusing to relinquish her claim to Castile. The Portuguese rulers treated her with respect, and she lived ostentatiously but judiciously, doing nothing to provoke scandal or Castilian outrage. Isabella's death in 1504 led to the most ironic event of Juana's life: Ferdinand reportedly proposed that she marry him. He opposed the union of Aragon and Castile under his daughter *Juana la Loca and her Habsburg husband, Philip the Fair of Burgundy. Ferdinand thus wanted to leave another child to inherit Aragon independently. By now in her early 40s, Juana la Beltraneja firmly and wisely rejected her old nemesis. Ferdinand soon married ❧ Germaine de Foix but failed to produce his desired heir. On July 20, 1522, Juana formally abdicated as monarch of Castile in favor of John III of Portugal. Now age 60, she considered herself too old to rule and besides had no way of leaving a direct heir. By that time

See sidebar on the following page

no one paid any attention. Juana died in 1530, having long outlived Isabella, her rival for the crown of Castile.

SOURCES:

Artaud de Silva, Julia. *Juana la Beltraneja.* Barcelona: Los Amigos de la Historia, 1975.

Bermejo de la Rica, A. *El triste destino de Enrique IV y la Beltraneja.* Madrid: Editorial Lepanto, [1943?].

Phillips, William D., Jr. *Enrique IV and the Crisis of Fifteenth-Century Castile 1425–1480.* Cambridge, MA: The Medieval Academy of America, 1978.

Sarasola, Modesto. *Isabel la Católica y el destino de Doña Juana, la Beltraneja.* Valladolid: Tip. Casa Martín, 1955.

Sitges, J. B. *Enrique IV y la Excelente Señora, llamada vulgarmente Doña Juana la Beltraneja.* Madrid: Sucesores de Rivadeneyra, 1912.

SUGGESTED READING:

Liss, Peggy K. *Isabel the Queen: Life and Times.* NY: Oxford University Press, 1992.

Miller, Townsend. *Henry IV of Castile 1425–1474.* Philadelphia, PA: J.B. Lippincott, 1972.

Kendall W. Brown,
Professor of History, Brigham Young University, Provo, Utah

Juana la Loca (1479–1555)

Queen of Castile from 1504 to 1555, during which time Spain became a world power, who never actually ruled due to her own mental instability and the greed for power of her father, husband, and son. Name variations: Juana or Joanna the Mad; Juana of Castile; Juana of Spain; Joanna of Spain. Born on November 6, 1479, in Toledo, Spain; died in Tordesillas on April 11 or 12, 1555; second daughter and third child of Isabella I (1451–1504), queen of Castile (r. 1474–1504), and Ferdinand II, king of Aragon (r. 1479–1516); sister of Catherine of Aragon (1485–1536); married Philip I the Fair also known as Philip the Handsome (1478–1506, son of the Holy Roman Emperor Maximilian I), archduke of Austria, king of Castile and Leon (r. 1506), on October 19, 1496; children: Eleanor of Portugal (1498–1558); Carlos also known as Charles V (1500–1558), king of Spain (r. 1516–1556), Holy Roman Emperor (r. 1519–1558); ◀❧ Elisabeth of Habsburg (1501–1526); Fernando also known as Ferdinand I (1502 or 1503–1564), king of Bohemia (r.

1526–1564), king of Hungary (r. 1526–1564), Holy Roman Emperor (1558–1564); *Mary of Hungary (1505–1558); Catherine (1507–1578, who married John III, king of Portugal).

Marriage of Isabella I of Castile and Ferdinand of Aragon (1469); death of Juana's brother John of Spain (1497); death of Juana's elder sister Isabella of Asturias (1498); death of Miguel, Juana's nephew, making Juana heir to the throne (1500); Juana and Philip are acclaimed crown princess and prince (1501); Juana proclaimed queen of Castile upon the death of her mother (1504); Cortes of Toro recognized regency of Ferdinand (1505); Juana and Philip arrived in Spain from Flanders and were acclaimed monarchs of Castile (1506); Juana confined to palace in Tordesillas by Ferdinand, where she remained for rest of life (1509–1555); death of Ferdinand (1516); arrival of Charles in Spain to rule (1517); election of Charles as Holy Roman emperor (1519); Comunero Revolt temporarily frees Juana from seclusion (1520); abdication of Charles I (1555); death of Charles I (1558).

Early on the morning of November 6, 1479, Queen *Isabella I of Castile gave birth to her third child, a daughter named Juana in honor of King Ferdinand II of Aragon's mother, ***Joanna Enriquez**. Although Juana was a princess, destiny seemed to hold little of importance for the infant girl, whose brother John of Spain, born the preceding year, stood to inherit the Spanish kingdoms. Should he die, the monarchs' eldest child, *Isabella of Asturias (1471–1498), would rule. Yet with ironic twists, destiny brought Juana to the throne of Castile and Aragon, although misfortune denied her the chance to rule in her own right. Instead, she spent most of her adult life under forced seclusion, isolated for more than four decades within the dreary walls of Tordesillas castle.

Little is known of Juana's childhood. She apparently bore a striking resemblance to Ferdinand's mother, so much so that Isabella I sometimes jokingly called the girl "mother-in-law." A slender brunette with an elongated face, Juana was "the beauty of the family," according to eminent historian Garrett Mattingly, who added that she also was "high-strung, ill-balanced, excessively responsive to affection or ill-treatment." Her parents trained Juana in more than the domestic arts and religious piety appropriate to a princess. They intended to marry her to one of Western Europe's royal families, creating a useful political alliance for Spain. Thus, Juana learned about politics and studied foreign languages. For the latter, she showed real talent, mastering both Latin and

❧▶
Elisabeth of Habsburg (1501–1526).
See Willums, Sigbrit for sidebar.

French. Juana also displayed passion for music and was an accomplished musician, playing the clavichord, organ, and guitar.

As a youth, Juana observed her parents' maneuvers to build their combined kingdoms into a great power. In 1490, she bid farewell to her sister Isabella of Asturias, who departed to marry Prince Alphonso, heir to the Portuguese throne. When Alphonso died from a riding accident shortly after the marriage and Isabella of Asturias returned home, Juana learned how fleeting marital happiness could be. She was present for the siege of Granada, culminating in its formal capitulation to the Catholic kings on January 2, 1492. The Moors' surrender of their last stronghold on Iberian soil must have seemed far more important to the princess than her mother's support of Columbus' voyage later that year. Meanwhile, to enhance Aragon's interests in Italy and to strengthen Spain's position against France, Ferdinand and Isabella had opened negotiations with Maximilian I, the Austrian emperor, regarding marital alliances between the two families.

When concluded in 1495, the negotiations provided for two royal marriages: Juana's to Philip the Fair, Maximilian's heir; and the Spanish crown prince John's to *Margaret of Austria (1480–1530), Maximilian's other child. These marriages joined Spanish geo-political interests to those of the Austrian Habsburgs and strengthened Spain's ties to Flanders, the principal market for Iberian wool. After months of preparation, a fleet of over 100 ships sailed from Laredo on August 22, 1496, to carry Juana to Flanders. Accompanying her was a large retinue of nobles and servants, intended by Isabella to guide the 16-year-old through the political shoals of continental politics. Beset by storms, the fleet arrived late and without forewarning. As a result, neither Maximilian nor the bridegroom was on hand to welcome Juana.

> $\mathcal{S}$he is under guard in a fortress so that no one may see her or talk with her. She is the most unfortunate woman ever born and would be far better off as the wife of a laborer.
>
> —Miguel Pérez de Almazán to the Castilian ambassador in Rome

Messengers relayed the news to Philip in Austria, while Juana's entourage made its way to Lierre, feted everywhere along the way by the Flemish. When Philip and Juana met for the first time on October 19, the wedding had been scheduled for the following day. Philip already had a reputation for philandering, and Juana was perhaps glad to be free of her mother's pious control. Driven by passion, the two ordered a priest in the entourage to marry them on the spot, whereupon they retired to a hastily prepared bedroom. Juana gave herself ardently to her husband, described by the Venetian ambassador as "handsome, skillful, and vigorous." For a while, he reciprocated her love and passion. Juana soon gave up her sober Spanish clothes in favor of more daring, luxurious Flemish dresses for the continual round of parties and dances in Brussels.

But the insecure girl, unprotected in a foreign land, soon discovered the vagaries of fortune. Rumors of her husband's affairs provoked Juana to "brief hysterical outbursts and of weeping or anger, alternating with long periods of silent melancholy." Philip failed to support his wife and her retinue as the marriage contract stipulated, causing her further chagrin. Back in Spain, her sickly brother John succumbed to fever on October 4, 1497, although rumor had him dying of sexual excess. His wife Margaret of Austria was pregnant but miscarried, leaving Juana's older sister Isabella of Asturias to inherit the crown. Again fate intervened. Married to Manuel I of Portugal, Isabella of Asturias died in childbirth in 1498. Her surviving infant son Miguel died two years later, and Juana became heir to the thrones of Castile and Aragon. Meanwhile, back in Flanders, Juana had given birth to Princess *Eleanor of Portugal in 1498 and the future Charles V in 1500.

With the death of Prince Miguel, Ferdinand and Isabella insisted that Juana and Philip come to Spain to live. Isabella worried about reports of the skeptical Juana's irreligiosity and the public scandal of her marital disputes. Both Ferdinand and Isabella feared that Spaniards would not accept a foreign monarch. Philip was also heir to his father's realms and, from the viewpoint of his parents-in-law, acted too friendly to France. He tried to dominate his wife politically, although Juana refused to sanction anything without consulting first with her parents. Thus, it was important that Juana, along with her husband and children, return home to prepare for eventual ascension to power.

After many delays, the young couple left for Spain in 1501, journeying overland through France. His Flemish possessions made Philip a nominal vassal of the French monarch, and, to cement an alliance with France, he negotiated the marriage of their son Charles (V) to Louis XII's daughter, *Renée of France. Juana refused to pay obeisance to her parents' French foe, however, and dismayed her husband and the French court with her air of independence. Lingering overlong, they traversed the Pyrenees in winter, and in early 1502 Juana was again in her homeland, following an absence of seven years. In Toledo, her parents convoked the cortes, an assembly representing the towns and nobility of Castile, which recognized Juana as Isabella's successor and Philip as her consort. A few months later, on August 4, 1502, she received the oath of the Aragonese cortes in Saragossa.

Thereupon, Philip determined to return to Flanders, despite Juana's "tenacious resistance" to his departure. Pregnant with her son Ferdinand (I), who was born two months later, Juana felt intensely Philip's lack of love. She tried to join him, but her mother refused to let her leave Spain. In response, the princess resorted to a tactic she had employed in Flanders against Philip's abuse: passive resistance. She refused to eat or sleep, and soon doctors began to worry about her health. In Flanders, Philip was anxious to wrest Juana from Isabella and Ferdinand's control. Using emotional blackmail, he had young Charles write a plaintive letter asking her to return home. Visited by her mother at La Mota castle in Medina del Campo, Juana berated Isabella, who later confided that her outburst "was in no way proper to her station." Although Isabella worried about her daughter's mental stability, the queen's chief concern was political: would xenophobic Castile allow Juana to wear the crown should she return to Flanders and try to rule from there?

Yet Juana's melancholy was so intense that Isabella finally relented and in 1504 allowed the princess to join Philip. Their separation had done nothing to make Philip more attentive or Juana less jealous. Her public rages scandalized Flanders. Philip openly berated and even struck her. In a desperate attempt to win his affection, she lavished care on her toilette, assisted by Moorish slaves. But the more extreme her emotions, the more disgusted Philip became. He finally locked her in her apartments. Historians have ascribed her affliction to "erotic obsession," echoing her contemporaries who concluded: "She only sees in the archduke the man and not the husband and governor." In reality, she suffered from manic depression.

Despite Philip's callous neglect, he needed Juana as his only claim to power south of the Pyrenees. A few months after she reached Flanders, on November 26, 1504, her mother Isabella died, making Juana and Philip monarchs of Castile. The great queen's will clearly stated that Juana was to exercise power and Philip was merely to act as her consort unless she proved unfit to rule. In that case, Ferdinand should govern as regent until young Charles was old enough to reign. Isabella had no intention of turning her kingdom over to the foreigner Philip. Thus, Juana was Philip's key to power in Castile, if he could dominate her completely. But he could not put her aside as incompetent because that would give power to Ferdinand as regent.

More dangerous to Juana's claim was the attitude of her father Ferdinand, who was, according to historian Townsend Miller, "quite as greedy and unprincipled as his son-in-law." As king of Aragon, Ferdinand had no right to rule Castile, and in fact many Castilian nobles hated him. But he needed the military might of Castile to back his forays into Italy. Thus, he could not permit his daughter to rule, out of fear that her francophile husband would thwart Aragon's Italian policies. Betraying Juana at the cortes of Toro, Ferdinand announced that he would rule as regent because of his daughter's "illness and passion." For political motives, he had declared her incompetent. Meanwhile, recognizing the threat Ferdinand posed, Philip became more attentive to Juana. In early 1506, Philip and Juana departed for Castile, where they hoped the anti-Ferdinand aristocrats would enable her to take the throne.

A storm beset the fleet on the voyage home and forced Juana's ship to put in at Weymouth, where they were received by Henry VII. Juana briefly met her widowed sister ❧ **Catherine of Aragon,** soon to be forced into her tragic marriage with the future Henry VIII. In Spain, Ferdinand married ❧ **Germaine de Foix** in the futile hope of begetting an heir rather than leaving Aragon to Philip and Juana. Departing England, they proceeded on to Castile, making landfall at La Coruña on April 26, 1506. Powerful nobles rallied to their cause, chiefly out of enmity for Ferdinand. In June, Ferdinand and Philip met secretly at Villafáfila without consulting Juana. Her father agreed to surrender Castile to them, in exchange for certain monetary concessions, but the two men also declared the queen unfit to rule. Ferdinand thus acknowledged Philip's right to rule, although it remained to be seen if Castile would submit to the foreigner. Though Philip intended to imprison her in a castle and rule in her name, visitors to Juana found her responsive and lucid. Philip needed to prepare carefully before casting her aside.

He never had the chance. In Burgos, he fell ill (probably of a fever, although some claimed poison). Juana set aside her anger at him and assiduously nursed him for six days to no avail. When he died on September 25, 1506, she shed no tears but "fell as though petrified. She passed days and nights there, disconcerted, melancholy, and defenseless." Chroniclers later reported that she constantly had his coffin reopened to gaze on Philip's decaying remains. But such stories of necrophilia are greatly exaggerated and reflect the political need of Ferdinand and later of Charles to discredit her. Juana made hesitating attempts to rule Castile, revoking concessions Philip had made to win aristocratic support and expelling his Flemish courtiers from positions of

Catherine of Aragon. See Six Wives of Henry VIII.

Foix, Germaine de. See Juana la Beltraneja for sidebar.

power. But she had no court or financial resources nor any real ambition to reign.

Ferdinand returned, and father and daughter met on August 29, 1507, in Tórtales, where she turned the government over to him. He brutally suppressed the dissident nobles, who called for a rising in Juana's name. To protect his hold on Castile, he sequestered her in Tordesillas castle in 1509. She rebelled by raging against her jailer, Luis Ferrer, or by refusing to eat or sleep. Manic depression afflicted her more frequently, and as months and years passed, she paid less attention to hygiene and clothing. Imprisoned with Juana was her youngest child ❧ **Catherine**, upon whom the queen lavished affection. In seven years, her father visited Juana only twice.

Then, on January 23, 1516, Ferdinand died, and the populace of Tordesillas rebelled against Ferrer's treatment of the queen. In Flanders, Charles claimed the throne, but Castilian authorities informed him that as long as Juana was alive, she was the monarch. When he arrived in Spain in September 1517 and went to Tordesillas, he had not seen his mother for 12 years. Out of compassion for Catherine, he secretly had the 11-year-old taken from her mother. But the queen rebelled, refusing to eat, drink or sleep, and Charles finally returned Catherine. He also improved his mother's physical conditions, but his grasp on power was too precarious to allow him to free her. Instead, he secluded her even more, even preventing her from going to mass at

the convent of Santa Clara where Philip's remains were. She resorted to passive resistance again, including a refusal to attend mass which led to accusations of heresy. Her warden, Bernardo de Sandoval y Rojas, marquis of Denia, even tried to isolate her servants from the outside world. On Charles' orders, no one told her Ferdinand had died, and they blamed him for her imprisonment. The marquis warned Charles: "It cannot be permitted that she speak with anybody because she would convince anyone." In other words, she suffered isolation because of the political threat she represented rather than disabling mental illness.

Juana had one last chance to escape her prison. In 1519, Charles was elected Holy Roman emperor and the following year departed for Central Europe. Tired of being ruled by a Flemish king, Castile erupted in the Comunero Revolt. The rebels besieged Tordesillas and freed Juana. Despite their appeals, however, she refused to sign decrees legitimizing the rebels. Instead, she told them: "Don't try to make me quarrel with my son, for I have nothing that is not his." She enjoyed eight months of relative freedom and showed a renewed interest in the outside world. But when Charles succeeded in defeating the rebels, he isolated her once again, with the detested marquis of Denia as her jailer. In 1525, Charles returned to Tordesillas and took her remaining jewels, to which she retorted: "It's not enough that I let you reign but you sack my house." Worse still for Juana, he took Catherine away from her, to marry the girl to the king of Portugal. As her daughter left, Juana reportedly watched stone-like and tearless from a window. She remained there motionless for two nights.

For the next 30 years, Juana's isolation shrouded the horrible mystery of her life. In such bleak conditions, her obsessive behavior and depression intensified, yet no one cared. Matters of state dictated that she remain imprisoned even though she had never shown interest in wielding power. When death approached, her grandson Philip wanted her to convert to Catholic orthodoxy. He sent Jesuit Francisco de Borja to minister to the queen, but she remained largely indifferent to religion. In February 1555, she suffered burns from a hot bath. These developed into gangrene which claimed her life on Good Friday, April 12, 1555.

Queen Juana's life was a tragedy provoked by mental illness and others' greed for political power. Abusive treatment undoubtedly heightened her manic depression. Yet her illness probably would not have disqualified her from gov-

❧➤ **Catherine** (1507–1578)

Queen of Portugal. Name variations: Catalina; Katherine; Katherina Habsburg. Born on January 14, 1507, in Torquemada; died on February 12, 1578 (some sources cite 1577), in Lisbon; daughter of Philip I the Fair also known as Philip the Handsome, king of Castile and Leon (r. 1506), and *Juana la Loca (1479–1555); sister of *Eleanor of Portugal (1498–1558), *Mary of Hungary (1505–1558), Charles V, Holy Roman emperor (r. 1519–1558), Ferdinand I, Holy Roman emperor (r. 1558–1564), and *Elisabeth of Habsburg (1501–1526); married Joao also known as John III (b. 1502), king of Portugal (r. 1521–1557), in 1525; children: Alfonso (1526–1526); *Mary of Portugal (1527–1545, first wife of Philip II of Spain); Isabella (1529–1530); Manuel (1531–1537); Filippe (1533–1539); Diniz (1535–1539); John of Portugal (1537–1554, who married *Joanna of Austria [1535–1573]); Antonio (1539–1540); Isabella (1529–1530); Beatriz (1530–1530).

erning had she been a man. After all, Philip V suffered long and severe bouts of depression yet remained king of Spain for nearly half of the 18th century. On the other hand, Juana's father, husband, and son all brutally sacrificed her to their own ambition, despite the fact that Juana showed little inclination to reign.

SOURCES:

Altayó, Isabel, and Paloma Nogués. *Juana I: La reina cautiva*. Madrid: Silex, 1985.

Dennis, Amarie. *Seek the Darkness: The Story of Juana la Loca*. Madrid: Sucesores de Rivadeneyra, 1956.

Liss, Peggy K. *Isabel the Queen: Life and Times*. NY: Oxford University Press, 1992.

Mattingly, Garrett. *Catherine of Aragon*. Boston, MA: Little, Brown, 1941.

Miller, Townsend. *The Castles and the Crown; Spain: 1451–1555*. NY: Coward-McCann, 1963.

SUGGESTED READING:

Pfandal, Ludwig. *Juana la Loca*. Madrid: Espasa-Calpe, S. A., 1969.

Prawdin, Michael. *The Mad Queen of Spain*. Boston, MA: Houghton Mifflin, 1939.

Kendall W. Brown,
Professor of History, Brigham Young University, Provo, Utah

Juana of Austria (1535–1573).

See Joanna of Austria.

Juana of Castile (r. 1366–1374).

See Jeanne de Castile.

Juana of Castile (1479–1555).

See Juana la Loca.

Juana of Portugal (1439–1475).

See Joanna of Portugal.

Juana of Spain (1479–1555).

See Juana la Loca.

Juana the Mad (1479–1555).

See Juana la Loca.

Juchacz, Marie (1879–1956)

German Social Democratic leader who was chosen to replace Clara Zetkin as women's leader of the party when it split over the issue of World War I and the Bolshevik Revolution. Born Marie Gohlke in Landsberg-Warthe, Germany, on March 15, 1879; died in Bonn on January 28, 1956; daughter of Friedrich Theodor Gohlke and Henriette (Heinrich) Gohlke; married Bernhard Juchacz, 1904; children: two.

Founded the social welfare organization Arbeiterwohlfahrt (1919); was a member of the Reichstag (1920–33); fled Nazi Germany (1933) and became a member of the German Social Democratic Party in exile; found refuge in the United States (1941); returned to (West) Germany (1949).

Among the few positive achievements amidst the chaos that accompanied the defeat of Germany in November 1918 was the accomplishment of women's suffrage. A woman with impeccable proletarian credentials, Marie Juchacz was among a handful of women elected to the German National Assembly in January 1919. In February of that year, she had the distinction of being the first woman in the history of Germany to address a national parliamentary body:

> Through political equality my sex has now been given the possibility to develop fully its potential. Only now may one justifiably speak of a new Germany and of the sovereignty of the whole people. . . . I would like to say here that in the present climate in Germany the woman question no longer exists in its old form, that it is solved. We will no longer need to fight for our rights with demonstrations, resolutions and petitions. From now on the political struggle will take different forms. Henceforth we women have the opportunity to use our powers within the framework of freely chosen party groups sharing a similar philosophy of life.
>
> But with this we do not give up the right to be different, to be female persons. It is far from our aim to deny our womanhood merely because we have stepped into the political arena.

Although women enjoyed legal political equality in Germany after 1918, there remained immense barriers to the achievement of genuine social and personal equality, obstacles which have yet to be totally removed. A true "child of the people," Juchacz dedicated her long life to realizing these goals. She was born Marie Gohlke in Landsberg, a provincial village in Brandenburg, and grew up in poverty. Her father was a skilled laborer who lost his job for participating in a strike, thus throwing his family into the ranks of the proletariat. Marie's formal education ended when she was 14, and she found work at the local factory. Here she experienced the pains of working-class life ("I still remember with horror, the misery of this night work") made worse when she married Bernhard Juchacz in 1904, soon giving birth to two children. The marriage was not a happy one, and within a few years Marie left both Landsberg and her husband behind, moving to Berlin in 1906 with her children. There she lived with her sister **Elisabeth Gohlke** and her brother Otto. While Elisabeth remained at home caring for Marie's children, Marie worked as a seamstress. In the evenings, the sisters organized reading clubs for working-class women. During this time, Juchacz was drawn to the ideals of socialism, particularly after having read August

Bebel's classic *Die Frau und der Sozialismus* (*Woman and Socialism*)—a stirring manifesto of gender equality that had an equally powerful inspirational impact on countless thousands of women, including *Rosa Luxemburg and *Clara Zetkin. The collapse of her marriage created a personal crisis for Juchacz which she was able to resolve at least partially by devoting her energies to the cause of socialism.

After joining the Social Democratic Party (SPD), Juchacz moved up in its ranks, gaining respect from the almost exclusively male leadership for her reliability, willingness to work long hours, and discretion in never taking a controversial stand. In contrast to Clara Zetkin, who was well educated, personally self-confident, and a fiery Marxist zealot, Juchacz was reticent, deferential to the SPD hierarchy, and, because of her impoverished background, deficient in formal education. She received a major promotion in 1913 with her first paid position in the SPD as party secretary of Upper Rhine Province, headquartered in Cologne. The outbreak of World War I in 1914, in which the German government was surprisingly supported by the SPD leadership—and which resulted in soul-searching among many Social Democrats—brought no public statements from Marie Juchacz, who maintained that it was simply not her place to reveal her opinion on matters not directly related to her party tasks.

By 1916, dissatisfaction with the war had brought the SPD to the brink of open revolt. That year, party head Friedrich Ebert called Juchacz to Berlin, asking her to replace **Luise Zietz** as secretary for women's affairs in the party executive. At first, Juchacz declined, claiming she was not prepared to take the place of a seasoned veteran like Zietz, but at Ebert's urging she finally accepted. The situation she found after arriving in Berlin was catastrophic, with morale low and many female members having abandoned the party for the more radical new Independent Social Democratic Party (USPD). Day and night, she worked to restore the shattered organization. In 1917, she was asked to take over editorial duties at the women's journal *Die Gleichheit* (*Equality*), whose former editor, the legendary Clara Zetkin, was removed by Ebert's executive board because of her increasingly radical views.

German democracy was born under less than optimal circumstances, in an atmosphere of national defeat and humiliation and a bloody civil war that split the working class between moderate Social Democrats and revolutionary

Communists. Juchacz hoped to salvage as much from this grim world as possible. Reticent and very much a private person, she was much more "female" from a conservative male point of view than such brilliant militants as Luxemburg and Zetkin. Writing in the SPD flagship newspaper *Vorwärts*, Friedrich Stampfer confirmed that a new era had dawned in German Social Democracy: "With Marie Juchacz, we have a new and totally different kind of woman. Gone is the era when the activists of the women's movement believed that they had to prove their equality by taking on male characteristics." Although she received much public praise from the SPD leadership, she was never accepted in the party's inner circle, the executive board, and her policy-making influence remained extremely limited.

The one arena in which Juchacz wielded significant power was in the area of SPD social welfare activities. In 1919, she declared that because of the collapse of the monarchy and the creation of the Weimar Republic, German women had become "the freest in the world." In December of that year she was instrumental in founding what would become the party's permanent institution for proletarian social welfare work, the Arbeiterwohlfahrt (AW). The founding of this organization represented the overcoming of major obstacles, since many SPD leaders looked upon welfare as essentially a bourgeois activity—of "the rich giving to the poor." Juchacz, on the other hand, saw social welfare activity as a rich field for recruiting new members for the party as well as an area for making an immediate impact on society. Above all, the working class was to be encouraged to be less passive, taking welfare work out of the hands of the well-meaning daughters of the upper classes.

In the view of historian Jean H. Quataert, the creation of the AW as a welfare bureau within the SPD bureaucracy "irrevocably welded women to municipal reform activity," setting aside a sphere of activity primarily for socialist women. As early as 1917, Juchacz had advanced a body of ideas that as a package amounted to an alternative to the theory of women's emancipation formulated by Zetkin. Rejecting the orthodox Marxist concept of class struggle, Juchacz substituted the notion of "practical activity in the service of socialism." Over the next years, this reformist ideal would serve to infuriate Marxist purists like Zetkin, now a leader of the German Communist Party, who dismissed it as being little more than a capitulation to capitalism.

By 1930, Juchacz's efforts were yielding impressive results. Over 2,000 AW local organizations across Germany provided many kinds of social services, including child-care centers, homes for teenage girls, children's camps, soup kitchens, care for pregnant women, and household assistance for women who were ill, pregnant or had recently given birth. Juchacz worked tirelessly to keep alive the varied activities of the organization, which assisted "children and young people in their development, [supported] mature people in their struggle for existence, and [gave] the old and invalid economic help and a little sunshine." Looking ahead, she also hoped that AW training courses for its female staff would make women more confident in their skills. By preparing them to break down traditional barriers and inhibitions, such training could help women to be more effective leaders in the nation's public life. Always a realist, Juchacz had no illusions about the ultimate strengths of the AW organization in the face of the nation's immense and growing social ills. The onset of the world depression and rapidly growing unemployment made it clear to her that only the German state itself could bring about a lasting change: "other powers have to work on changing economic and social conditions."

Despite its good intentions and noble ideals, by 1930 the SPD found itself to be more and more out of touch with conditions in Germany. The party executive, increasingly middle class in its attitudes, presided over a mass but aging organization with only 18.1% of members in 1930 under the age of 30, compared with 31.8% for the Communists. More ominous still was the fact that many Social Democrats, including Juchacz, grossly underestimated the threat of Nazism. During the crucial election campaign of 1930, she gave speeches in which, remarkably, the Nazi threat was not mentioned even once.

Too late, the Social Democrats tried to reform themselves on the eve of the Nazi takeover in 1933. Even then, many hoped that they could remain within Nazi Germany as a passive "loyal opposition," but in June 1933 the SPD was banned by the Hitler regime. Juchacz was not invited to join the SPD executive when it fled to Prague—an omission she would remember with bitterness for the rest of her life, even though she chose never to raise the subject in public. She fled instead to the Saar District, still under French administration, where she worked with refugees from Nazism. Then in January 1935, when the region reverted to Germany after a plebiscite, she had to flee into France. Working with other anti-Nazi refugees in Mulhouse, Alsace, over the next few years, Juchacz organized resistance groups within Nazi Germany. By the late 1930s, however, most of these organizations had been infiltrated and destroyed by the Gestapo.

With the invasion and occupation of France by Nazi Germany in 1940, Juchacz's life was in danger. She was able to flee to the unoccupied zone of southern France and from there went to the United States on an emergency visa in May 1941. At first supported by American Quakers, living in the town of Scattergood, Iowa, by the autumn of 1942 she moved to New York City. Here she quickly became active in the passionate world of German exile politics, often disagreeing with the SPD leadership on policy issues. Sympathetic to the left-wing group calling itself *Neu Beginnen* (New Beginnings), she also became an active member of the Council for a Democratic Germany, among whose members was the theologian Paul Tillich. Now over 60, Juchacz learned English and became involved in welfare work. She was particularly active in both the Workmen's Circle and the Jewish Labor Committee, eventually being elected chair of the latter organization despite the fact that she was not of Jewish origin.

After the defeat of Nazism in May 1945, Juchacz made plans to return to Germany. While waiting for a visa, she became a leading personality in relief efforts for German Social Democrats who had been persecuted during the Nazi period, and she set up a U.S branch of the Arbeiterwohlfahrt to raise funds as well as collect food and clothing for these often destitute individuals and their families. In early 1949, she returned to a Germany still in ruins. Juchacz was received with great respect as one of the veterans of the SPD and was elected honorary chair of the reconstituted Arbeiterwohlfahrt organization. In her final years, she wrote a book entitled *Sie lebten für eine bessere Welt* (*They Lived for a Better World*), a biographical study of 29 women who had fought for social betterment and justice. As a legacy for the next generation, Juchacz hoped with this work to leave behind "a treasure of tradition, which lies hidden away. . . . We should bring that tradition to life, we should find the spirit which moved the socialists of the past to their great accomplishments. We must attempt to understand and learn from them. Especially we women in our present need and distress should know that before us, bold women fought gladly and fearlessly for their human rights and women's rights." Marie Juchacz died in Bonn, Federal Republic of Germany, on January 28, 1956. The Federal Republic honored her with a commemorative postage stamp issued on August 11, 1969.

SOURCES:

Buchholz, Marlis, and Bernd Rother, eds. *Der Parteivorstand der SPD im Exil: Protokolle der Sopade 1933–1940*. Bonn: Verlag J. H. W. Dietz Nachfolger, 1995.

Eifert, Christiane. "Coming to Terms with the State: Maternalist Politics and the Development of the Welfare State in Weimar Germany," in *Central European History*. Vol. 30, no. 1, 1997, pp. 25–47.

Gruber, Helmut, and Pamela Graves, eds. *Women and Socialism, Socialism and Women: Europe Between the Two World Wars*. New York and Oxford: Berghahn Books, 1998.

Harsch, Donna. *German Social Democracy and the Rise of Nazism*. Chapel Hill, NC: University of North Carolina Press, 1993.

Hunt, Richard N. *German Social Democracy 1918–1933*. New Haven, CT: Yale University Press, 1964.

Pore, Renate. *A Conflict of Interest: Women in German Social Democracy, 1919–1933*. Westport, CT: Greenwood Press, 1981.

Quataert, Jean H. *Reluctant Feminists in German Social Democracy, 1885–1917*. Princeton, NJ: Princeton University Press, 1979.

Schröder, Wilhelm Heinz. *Sozialdemokratische Parlamentarier in den Deutschen Reichs- und Landtagen 1867–1933: Biographien, Chronik, Wahldokumentation: Ein Handbuch*. Düsseldorf: Droste Verlag, 1995.

Schumacher, Martin, ed. *M. d. R. Die Reichstagsabgeordneten der Weimarer Republik in der Zeit des Nationalsozialismus—Politische Verfolgung, Emigration und Ausbürgerung: Ein biographische Dokumentation*. Düsseldorf: Droste Verlag, 1991.

Thönnessen, Werner. *The Emancipation of Women: The Rise and Decline of the Women's Movement in German Social Democracy 1863–1933*. Translated by Joris de Bres. London: Pluto Press Limited, 1973.

John Haag,
Associate Professor of History,
University of Georgia, Athens, Georgia

Judd, Winnie Ruth (1905–1998)

American known as the "trunk murderess." Name variations: Marian Lane. Born Winnie Ruth McKinnell on January 29, 1905, in Oxford, Indiana; died in Phoenix, Arizona, in October 1998; one of two children of a minister and a schoolteacher; married William C. Judd (a physician), on April 18, 1924; no children.

Winnie Ruth Judd was to Arizona what *Lizzie Bordon was to Massachusetts. In one of the most notorious murder cases of the 1930s, the frail, sickly medical secretary, who had been born in Indiana but had moved to Phoenix for her health, was accused of killing two women, dismembering one of the bodies, and shipping all the remains (in two trunks and a suitcase) to Los Angeles via the Southern Pacific railroad. A baggage handler at Union Station noticed blood dripping from one of the trunks as Judd disembarked from the train on October 18, 1931. Asked to open the trunk, Judd instead climbed into the waiting automobile of her brother Burton McKinnell and fled. Apprehended by the police after several days on the run, Judd was indicted and went on trial in January 1932, with her husband at her side.

Through her lawyer (she never testified in her own defense), Judd alleged that she had argued with her former roommates, **Hedvig "Sammy" Samuelson** and **Anne LeRoi**, over Jack Halloran, a prominent Phoenix businessman with whom Judd was having an affair. As the argument grew bitter and escalated, Judd claimed that Samuelson had tried to shoot her, wounding her in the hand. Judd grabbed the gun, fired at Samuelson, then turned the weapon on LeRoi to fend off an attack with an ironing board. Judd further claimed that she was not present when Samuelson was dismembered and both bodies were placed in trunks, although she did admit to transporting them. Even at the time of her trial, many doubted that Judd could have acted alone; doctors reported that the hacked-up corpse had been dismembered with a surgical skill Judd did not possess. Even so, Judd was found guilty and

Winnie Ruth Judd

sentenced to hang but was spared when her lawyer persuaded her to plead insanity.

Winnie Ruth Judd was committed to the Arizona State Hospital for the Insane in Phoenix from which she escaped seven times (once for a period of six years, 1962–68, during which she worked as a maid and companion for a wealthy blind woman in a mansion in Piedmont, California), only to be captured and returned again. In 1971, after 38 years, she was paroled by the state of Arizona and took up residence in California under the assumed name of Marian Lane, working for the same family that had previously employed her. She later lived in Stockton then moved back to Phoenix.

In her book, *The Trunk Murderess: Winnie Ruth Judd*, Phoenix-based journalist **Jana Bommersbach** revisited the case in depth, and even conducted a three-day interview with Judd, the first Judd had ever granted. Bommersbach's investigation revealed a massive cover-up, including suppression of evidence, an inept courtroom defense, and a biased juror. Perhaps the most unsettling aspect of the cover-up involved Jack Halloran, whose identity was kept out of the trial and the local papers because of his prominence, although he was indicted as an accessory to the crime. Evidence points to Halloran as having arranged to have Samuelson dismembered and then bullying Judd into transporting the bodies. "The whole criminal justice system was subverted to protect him," claims Howard Sauter, a private detective who has studied the evidence in the case. "The movers and shakers allowed all this to happen to her to protect the image, reputation, and marriage of Jack Halloran. Winnie was the sacrificial goat."

SOURCES:

Bommersbach, Jana. *The Trunk Murderess: Winnie Ruth Judd*. NY: Simon & Schuster, 1992.
"Winnie R. Judd, 93, Infamous as 1930's 'Trunk Murderess,'" in *The New York Times*. October 27, 1998.

SUGGESTED READING:

Dobkins, J. Dwight, and Robert Hendricks. *Winnie Ruth Judd: The Trunk Murders*, 1973.

Barbara Morgan,
Melrose, Massachusetts

Judith

Biblical woman, one of the six wives of Esau. Name variations: Aholibamah. Daughter of Beeri (also known as Anah), the Hittite; married Esau; children: three sons.

Judith, the daughter of Beeri, was one of the six wives of Esau. A district in the mountains of Edom (probably near Mt. Hor) was named after her. Her three sons founded the three tribes of Edomites.

Judith (fl. early 6th c. BCE)

Hebrew heroine-slayer and Biblical widow of Bethulia who, through insistence on absolute fidelity to Mosaic Law, saved Judea from the Assyrians by decapitating their commander, Holofernes. Name variations: Judith of Bethulia; Judith of Bethulin. In the Biblical account, Judith was born in Bethulia (near Jerusalem) after the Jews returned from exile in Babylonia (537 BCE); died in Bethulia at 105 years of age; married Manasses (died); no children.

Lived in devout seclusion until Judea was threatened by an Assyrian army, at which time Judith saved her people by a feigned defection to the enemy which allowed her the opportunity to decapitate their general, Holofernes. The Book of Judith is contained in the Apocrypha. There is no evidence, however, that the incident related in the book of Judith corresponds to a single historical event, and we should not think of Judith as a real person, but as a composite or a symbol of Judaism generally.

According to the Book of Judith, in the 12th year of his reign Nebuchadnezzar, the Assyrian king, commanded the peoples of the Fertile Crescent to join him in war. When his summons was disregarded, the king sought to punish the inhabitants of the land: he sacked cities, massacred townspeople, routed armies, collected booty, and forced into submission the region from Egypt to Persia. General Holofernes, second in command to the king, was sent with an army 132,000 strong to subdue the western cities, to fill the valleys with their dead, make their mountains drunk with blood, choke the rivers with their corpses, and send survivors into captivity. Holofernes followed orders well. He devastated Put and Lud, plundered Rasses, and ravaged all the towns along the Euphrates River, destroying crops and animals, throwing down shrines and putting the inhabitants to the sword. Town after town, fearing destruction, sent envoys to Holofernes suing for peace.

Only the Israelites of Judea held strong within their fortified hill towns, for submission to the Assyrians would result in violation of their sanctuaries and desecration of the newly restored temple in Jerusalem. Holofernes was enraged at the resistance he encountered from the hill-country. He summoned Achior, leader of the Amonites, and questioned him about these people who dared defy him. Achior assured the Assyrian that as long as the Israelites were faithful to their God no enemy could prevail against them; they would remain unmolested. This was unwelcome news to Holofernes. He had Achior seized and turned over to the elders of the small Jewish town of Bethulia with the threat that—when the town fell to the Assyrians—Achior would share the fate of the Israelites whose God he so revered.

The Assyrian host marched to Bethulia and encamped at the foot of the hill-country, thinking to bring the citizens to submission by cutting off their water supply. The plan was well laid. The Bethulians became so weakened by thirst that they decided it was better to come to terms with Holofernes than to perish for want of water. They resolved that if no deliverance came in five days they would surrender.

*L*ook," she said. "The head of Holofernes, the Assyrian commander-in-chief! The Lord has struck him down by the hand of a woman!"

—Judith (13.15)

News of these deliberations reached Judith, the pious widow of Manasses. She summoned the magistrates of Bethulia and chided them for testing God by placing Him under a five-day constraint. She assured the elders that if they remained faithful, God would deliver the Israelites by her hand. That night, after prayer, Judith took off her widow's weeds, donned her gayest clothes, anointed herself with perfume, put on her bracelets and rings and, with her maid, left Bethulia. When the two women were apprehended by the Assyrian outpost, they declared that they had deserted their town because the Hebrews had offended God and would, indeed, fall to Holofernes. She claimed that the citizens, in their hunger, had decided to eat the meat and first-fruits reserved for the tithe and dedicated to God. The guards took her to the general's tent where Holofernes reclined under a purple net interwoven with gold, emeralds and precious stones. All were struck by Judith's beauty and convinced by her story. It was agreed that each night she and her maid would go alone to the plains outside the camp to carry out rituals of prayer and bathing, and when God revealed to Judith that the Bethulians had sinned, the Assyrians would begin their sortie.

On the fourth night of her stay, Holofernes gave a banquet to which only his personal servants and Judith were invited. The general hoped to allure the Hebrew woman whom he had desired since she first entered camp. In anxious anticipation of the seduction, he ate and drank immoderately. It grew late and the servants retired. Judith and her maid were left alone in the tent with Holofernes who had, by this time, passed out with drink. The devout widow now steeled herself to carry out the plan which would deliver her people from the Assyrians. She seized Holofernes' sword and, grasping the hair of his head, struck twice at the neck of the great general. The maid stashed the severed head in a bag while Judith rolled the body off the bed. She quickly grabbed the jeweled net and, with the general's head in her food bag, she and her maid left camp, as usual (thought the guards), to pray and bathe.

Judith quickly crossed the valley and climbed the hill to Bethulia, announcing her triumph. The citizens rejoiced and sang her praises as Judith displayed the head of the enemy. Achior, the alien Ammonite, was brought to identify the head. In his admiration of Judith's faith, he had himself circumcised and became a Jew. The next morning, the Israelites, on Judith's advice, hung the head of Holofernes on the battlements of the wall and took the offensive against the encamped army. The Assyrians, thrown into confusion by the unexpected attack, rushed to waken their general, only to find his headless body on the floor of his tent. So flummoxed were the Assyrians that they fled the plain of the hill-country in panic and disarray, closely pursued by the Bethulian host which swelled as the men of all the neighboring towns joined in the rout.

The Assyrian army was defeated; the Hebrews celebrated. All sang praises of the heroine, Judith, who struck up a hymn of thanksgiving as she led the women of Bethulia in a triumphal dance. The high priest of Jerusalem came to Bethulia to thank Judith. She was awarded the spoils from the tent of Holofernes which she dedicated to God and gave to the temple of Jerusalem. Now that her homeland was safe, Judith retired once more to her estates and resumed the life of a pious widow until her death at the age of 105. Judith's brave deed not only averted the imminent onslaught of the Assyrians, but assured peace in Judea for many years to come.

This story of Judith slaying Holofernes is preserved as one of the books of the Jewish, and subsequently Christian, Apocrypha. Although the earliest extant copy of the work is written in Greek, the book was almost certainly composed in Hebrew. It is not known definitively when the

Judith and
Maidservant
with the Head
of Holofernes,
*by Artemisia
Gentileschi.*

work was written or by whom. There is no evidence, however, that the incident related in the book of Judith corresponds to a single historical event, and we should not think of Judith as a real person, but as a composite or a symbol of Judaism generally.

Most scholars agree that the book of Judith, as we know it, was composed in the mid-2nd century BCE—possibly based on an earlier version. Although the author hoped to give his (or her) narrative some appearance of historicity, many of the people and places named cannot be identified. Also, the author has conflated known historical circumstances which actually occurred centuries apart. For instance, Nebuchadnezzar was king of the Babylonians (not the Assyrians) from 605 to 561 BCE. The Assyrians were enemies of the Hebrews in the 8th century BCE. Further, the story is set soon after the Hebrews returned from their exile in Babylonia (537 BCE), by which time Nebuchadnezzar was dead. The author may have chosen to make Nebuchadnezzar king of the Assyrians in an effort to evoke from his readers a potent image of Israel's archenemy. Some scholars guess that the oppressive general, Holofernes, may be an oblique reference to Artaxerxes Ochus who was campaigning in Syria about 350 BCE. More important to the author, however, than historical exactitude was the moral lesson the story teaches. The author may have employed vague and contradictory historical information to indicate the fictional nature and timeless quality of the work. It was probably written at a time of trial and persecution and was meant to encourage and edify the people by providing a model of pious resistance. The story is an example of God's fidelity to his covenant people and a reminder that the power of Israel hinges on observance of the Law.

Judith, whose name means "Judean woman," is an allegory for the Jewish people themselves. Her city, Bethulia (which has not been identified), is a variant of a Hebrew term meaning "House of God." Throughout the Old Testament, Israel is characterized as a female: virgin, bride, whore, or widow. The 40 months of Judith's mourning for the death of her husband recalls the 40 years of Israel's wandering in the wilderness. Modeling the strict observance of righteous Israel, Judith is fastidious in prayer, fasting, and conformity to Mosaic dietary laws. Like a priest of Israel slaying a sacrificial lamb, the killing of Holofernes, whose goods are eventually dedicated to the temple, requires two strokes. Also, despite the fact that Judith does not correspond exactly to any historical character, she represents a type which recurs in Biblical literature. She is an analogue to *Deborah, *Miriam the Prophet, the wise women of Tekoa and Abel-beth-Maacah, *Esther, and ◄ Jael. Both Jael and Judith slay an enemy by attacking his head; Jael, Deborah and Judith all act when their husbands are absent for one reason or another, and all three are childless; Deborah and Judith are steadfast in obedience to the will of Yahweh (a name of God) when the magistrates waver; both Jael and Judith use deceit and their physical appeal as weapons; neither Jael nor Judith are specifically commissioned to their deeds by God; and, finally, the vic-

tory song of Judith is reminiscent of the Song of Miriam and that of Deborah.

It is likely that the author of the book chose Judith as his messenger because of her gender. The notion that God uses the weak to manifest his strength is common in Biblical narratives. The fact that Holofernes was brought down by the "hand of a woman" is meant to provide evidence that it is Yahweh who is responsible for the defeat of Israel's enemies, and not his human agent, even one who represents Israel at its most devout. In her prayer, Judith praises God: "For your power stands not in multitude, nor your might in strong men. . . . [M]ake every nation . . . know that . . . you are the God of all power and might, and that there is none other that protects the race of Israel but you" (Judith 9.14).

The story of Judith, the Jewish heroine, has provided moral and didactic inspiration in both the Jewish and Christian traditions. The Book of Judith, a Hebrew text which circulated among Jewish communities in Greco-Roman times, was not included in the Hebrew Bible after about 200 CE. It is, however, canonical in early Christian and Greek old Testaments. As early as the 2nd century CE, it was thought that the Apocrypha were omitted from the Hebrew Scriptures because they were written in Greek. We now know this is not true; the Apocrypha were originally composed in Hebrew. Although the term *apocryphal* can denote spurious, heretical works, or those of inferior sacred standing, it need not. In its earliest Hebraic usage, the term referred to books which were more valuable than the canon because they carried mysterious or esoteric wisdom meant only for the select. Augustine and other Church Fathers held that the Apocrypha were useful as allegory, profitably read in church, but should not be interpreted literally. In the Vulgate (the Latin version of the Bible), Jerome (following the Greek Bible) interspersed the Apocrypha among the books of the Old Testament, thus giving them an official standing as inspired works. Protestant reformers of the 16th century rejected the Apocrypha as divine works and Martin Luther excised and placed them at the end of the Bible as a sort of addendum (1534). Puritans rejected the Apocrypha altogether. The 16th-century Catholic reform Council of Trent upheld Jerome's acceptance of the Apocrypha as orthodox and adopted most of them (including Judith) as authoritative and declared, "If any one receive not, as sacred and canonical, the said books . . . let him be anathema."

The drama of Judith and Holofernes has provided grist for artistic interpretation from the

Jael. See Deborah for sidebar.

early Middle Ages to the present. The subject has been treated in medieval manuscript illuminations, miracle books, sculptures and frescoes. It appears in a 12th-century Jewish Piyyutim (liturgical poems included in the services on holidays and special Sabbaths in addition to the established prayers) and Latin church hymns. It is the basis of an Old English epic and two High German poems. Throughout the early modern era, painters, sculptors, printmakers, poets, and playwrights made use of the story. In the 17th century, Judith was repeatedly dramatized (including a puppet play); in the 18th century, oratorios (extended musical compositions usually based upon religious themes) and operas were derived from the story, as were poems and romantic fiction in the 19th century, and plays by Arnold Bennett and Jean Girardoux, and operas by Arthur Honegger and Mordechai Seter, in the 20th century. The varieties of interpretation of this simple Biblical chronicle are legion and allow scholars to chart social and artistic trends based on the way the themes are treated and which aspects of the narrative are emphasized.

The story of Judith is told in an Old English epic poem, of which only a fragment is extant. The work was likely produced between 950 and 1000 in Wessex. Although there have been efforts to connect the composition of the poem with the lives of heroic Anglo-Saxon women (such as *Ethelflaed, Lady of the Mercians, daughter of Alfred the Great, and *Judith Martel, stepmother of Alfred), it is more likely that the poem was inspired by the Viking invasions of England. The Judith of the poem is a holy warrior and a female saint. The existing fragments concentrate on the killing of Holofernes, and the only characters mentioned by name are Judith and the antagonist. The plot moves quickly to the poet's major alteration of the Biblical narrative—the addition of a protracted battle between the Assyrians and the galvanized Hebrews. Nothing is said of Judith's later life or the peace she secured for Israel. The trappings of this religious epic are true to their period. The feast, battle, kenning of the warriors, and armor are all Germanic.

In medieval pictorial interpretations, Judith's exploit is generally represented as a public expression of religious right-thinking and heroic devotion. In this context, artists tended to portray an enlarged version of the narrative, including as many scenes as possible. Because Judith stood for the entire community, it was important to show her emanating from the besieged city and returning to it having subdued the enemy. The 13th-century Arsenal Bible illustrates six scenes: the army of Holofernes, the council of Jewish magistrates, Judith excoriating the elders, Judith deceiving the Assyrians, the murder of Holofernes, and the jubilant Bethulians praising their deliverer as she stands in the orans position (arms outstretched in prayer) holding the head of Holofernes in her left hand. A 12th-century illustration by *Herrad of Hohenberg, abbess of St. Ottile or Odile, telescopes the events of the narrative into two scenes: the decapitation and the return of Judith and her maid to the expectant city. This is an interesting piece because it demonstrates that even when the narrative must be abbreviated, the public consequences of Judith's deed are paramount. French liturgical celebrations of *Joan of Arc included verses from the Book of Judith.

In some medieval Jewish prayer books, the story is stripped to the minimum. Even the character of Holofernes is missing. Judith stands in the tent—scene of God's triumph—sword in one hand and severed head in the other. Here, the audience is to associate the heroine with Judas Maccabaeus, another deliverer of the Jewish people. As in the prayer books, there are ample early examples from Byzantine and Christian sources of one symbolic scene isolated from the narrative. On the right portal of the north transept of the Cathedral of Chartres, Judith is sculpted kneeling in prayer. Marginalia often concentrate on the moment of decapitation. For Christians, Judith represented the Church militant. In this context, she is sometimes portrayed trampling Satan underfoot (in the form of Holofernes' head), forming a parallel to Christ and *Mary the Virgin, who are often engaged in this same activity.

The inclination to emphasize a defining moment in the narrative was continued by Renaissance and Baroque artists. For them, Judith's private instant of crisis was often more interesting than an extended presentation of Bethulia's communal response to her accomplishment. The meaning of the decapitation scene, although presented in a private, even secretive setting, often had public significance. Judith became a symbol of civic virtue and patriotic rebellion, especially in the bellicose city-states of Renaissance Italy. The decapitation was depicted by Ghiberti, Donatello, Botticelli, Mantegna, Giorgione, Tintoretto, Michelangelo, *Artemisia Gentileschi and others. On the podium of Donatello's statue of the triumphant Judith was engraved: "Kingdoms fall through Luxury; Cities rise through Virtue: Behold the Neck of Pride severed by the hand of Humility." Wolfgang Schmeltzl's play, *Judith* (1542), emphasizes the dangers of Turkish attack and exhorts the people of Vienna to take courage from the story. Jewish nationalists of the period used images of Judith in the same way. She became a popular figure on Italian Hanukkah candelabra, sometimes supplanting the crown of the Torah over the Ark. Baroque artists and literati of both Protestant and Catholic reform movements appropriated Judith to their cause. In the Catholic tradition, she was a favorite theme for Jesuit scholastic drama, and, for the Protestant dramatist Joachim Greff, Judith afforded a symbol of God's protection against papal tyranny.

The facility of the Judith story to express the sensibilities of whichever culture tells it continues to be evident in the 17th century. At this time, the association of Judith with communal interests waned in favor of her connection to triumph-of-love motifs. Although in the Biblical tale Judith's love was for her people, by 1600 she and Holofernes were correlated in art with other great male/female couples of which the females were women who betrayed the men who trusted them: Adam and *Eve, Samson and *Delilah, David and *Bathsheba. Judith's deed came gradually to be seen as the act of a single woman dominating a man—clandestinely, viciously, and in a virile fashion, therefore unbecoming a woman. In the work of Caravaggio, Goltzius, and several *caravaggisti,* Holofernes, far from being the belligerent oppressor of the Israelites, becomes an innocent victim of feminine duplicity. These artists play upon a Western tradition in which nakedness represents honesty and simplicity while sumptuous clothing connotes falsehood and deception. The cunning Judith, who decked herself lavishly "to beguile the eyes of all men" (Judith 10.5), achieved her ends only through deceit. She is cold and unyielding—remorseless. Often entitled "The Tragedy of Holofernes," 16th and 17th-century dramas were devoted to Judith and Holofernes. In Christofano Allori's 1609 painting of the moment after decapitation, Judith is a portrait of a local beauty who scorned the artist, while the countenance of the severed head is that of Allori.

Judith, then, is a woman for all seasons. Her story has been molded to suit the ideologies and biases of each generation that portrayed her. That is no less true of the past than of the 20th century, when the Book of Judith came under the scrutiny of feminist scholarship. Some analyses point out that the character of Judith has not historically been treated differently than other female personages, like Athena and Mary the Virgin. She is an allegory, not a human woman, and for this reason it was possible for her to accom-

plish her heroic mission. For some feminists, the narrative makes clear that Judith is unusual and that her subjugation of the man, Holofernes, by a thinly masked castration (for decapitation is often analogous to castration in ancient literature) is not meant to be normative. Judith is set apart in many ways. She lives at the edge of town alone on her estates. She is childless and devout beyond the requirements of the Law. She bests the magistrates through her faith, the Assyrian soldiers through her cunning, and acts the part of priest in sacrificing the life of Holofernes to the good of her people. The actual deed, however, transpires outside the Jewish community. Her accomplishment is grisly and requires manly verve. (The 1536 drama, *Judith,* includes a scene in which the women of Bethulia congregate at the well and comment on the *mannligkeyt*—manliness—of Judith.) When Judith returns to Bethulia, she gives up her share of the plunder and retires to private life. This woman is thus a useful and safe vehicle for the author's purpose. She is a symbol for Jewish virtue without being a model for Jewish women. Because of her gender she embodies that weakness through which God displays his strength. Because she never fully interacts with quotidian village life she does not upset established gender roles.

Another line of feminist analysis has concentrated on unveiling and critiquing the dynamic of Judith's portrayal through Western history. Although praised and admired in both religious and secular exegeses, Judith has also been criticized because she realized her ends by guile and the promise of sexual favors. Her act of heroism is tainted because it was carried out covertly and against an unarmed adversary. In short, although courageous, it was not honorable, and therefore not truly manly. Some contemporary scholars argue that this condemnation of Judith, of which there are strains throughout Jewish and Christian history, reveals the uneasiness of male commentators and interpreters with the notion of a woman subduing a man. The chief argument in the 16th century by those who wished to remove Donatello's *Judith* from the public square in Florence was that it is not appropriate for a woman to kill a man. *Judith* was replaced by Giambologna's statue, *Rape of a Sabine Woman.*

Seldom does a figure as provocative as Judith belong to one period or one people. Although the pious widow never lived, never slew her Assyrian foe, and never delivered the citizens of Bethulia, for centuries she has fired the imagination of readers, writers, poets, artists and scholars and has lent her name to a multitude of ideologies and interpretations.

SOURCES:

Charles, R.H, ed. *The Book of Judith* in *The Apocrypha and Pseudepigrapha of the Old Testament.* Oxford: Clarendon Press, 1913.

Dancy, J.C., ed. *The Shorter Books of the Apocrypha.* Cambridge: Cambridge University Press, 1972.

Dobbie, Elliott Van Kirk, ed. *Beowulf and Judith.* NY: Columbia University Press, 1953.

Dubarle, A.M. *Judith: Formes et Sens des Diverses Traditions.* Rome: Institut Biblique Pontifical, 1966.

Garrard, Mary D. *Artemisia Gentileschi: The Image of the Female Hero in Italian Baroque Art.* NJ: Princeton University Press, 1989.

Moore, Carey A. *Judith.* Garden City, NY: Doubleday, 1985.

Purdie, Edna. *The Story of Judith in German and English Literature.* Paris: Librairie Ancienne Honoré Champion, 1927.

Timmer, B.J., ed. *Judith.* Exeter: University of Exeter Press, 1978.

Tkacik, Arnold J., ed. *The Book of Judith* in *The New English Bible with the Apocrypha.* NY: Oxford University Press, 1976.

Vanderkam, James C., ed. *"No One Spoke Ill of Her": Essays on Judith.* Atlanta, GA: Scholar's Press, 1992.

SUGGESTED READING:

Craven, Toni. *Artistry and Faith in the Book of Judith.* Chico: Scholar's Press, 1983.

Enslin, Morton, and Solomon Zeitlin. *The Book of Judith.* Leiden: E.J. Brill, 1972.

Williams, James G. *Women Recounted: Narrative Thinking and the God of Israel.* Sheffield: Almond, 1982.

Martha Rampton,
Assistant Professor of History,
Pacific University, Forest Grove, Oregon

Judith (fl. 10th c.)

Queen of the Falashas. Name variations: Esther; Esato; Yehudit. Flourished in Ethiopia in the 10th century.

According to tradition, Judith was a Jewish queen of the Falashas, who fought the Christian persecutors of her people. The Falashas are a population of Black Jews who trace their origins to Menelik, the legendary son of Solomon and *Sheba. Although this claim is of dubious historicity, Judaism in Ethiopia is of great antiquity and a testament to the degree of social and economic contacts with both southern Egypt (where Jews settled in significant numbers, especially under the Ptolemies) and with that part of Arabia lying directly across the Red Sea from Ethiopia. In fact, northern Ethiopia was ruled by a dynasty claiming descent from Menelik, from the 2nd to the 4th century. By the 4th century, however, the Christianization of Ethiopia had begun, and those who remained faithful to their, by that time, ancestral faith fled south into the mountainous interior of their country. There they long existed in rugged isolation, until the press of northern conquest drove Christianization southward, especially in the form of monastic communities: they themselves establishing a control of land, traditionally pastoral, which was essential to the maintenance of the herds upon which the Falashas depended.

In part inspired by Queen Judith in the 10th century, the Falashas fought back against Christian encroachment and forced conversion. Although little concrete is known about her career, it is clear from the fact that there remains a considerable population of Falashas today to the south of Lake Tana, and from the fact that this region constituted an independent Jewish province of the kingdom of Ethiopia until the 17th century, that her counter-offensive—aimed primarily at the churches and monasteries which intended first to convert her people before politically incorporating them—was successful in checking the religious and cultural absorption of her people.

William Greenwalt,
Associate Professor of Classical History,
Santa Clara University, Santa Clara, California

Judith (1271–1297)

*Queen of Bohemia. Name variations: Jutta; Guta or Gutta. Born on March 13, 1271; died on June 18, 1297; daughter of Rudolph or Rudolf I Habsburg, Holy Roman emperor (r. 1273–1291), and *Anna of Hohenberg (c. 1230–1281); sister of Albert I, duke of Austria and Holy Roman emperor (r. 1298–1308); first wife of Wenceslas II (1271–1305), king of Bohemia (r. 1278–1305). Wenceslas II's third wife was *Elizabeth of Poland (fl. 1298–1305); his second was *Ryksa of Poland (1288–1335).*

Judith (1876–1930).

See Zauditu.

Judith Martel (c. 844–?).

See Martel, Judith.

Judith of Bavaria (802–843)

*Holy Roman Empress. Born 802 in Bavaria; died in 843 in France; daughter of Welf of Bavaria and Heilwig; sister of *Emma of Bavaria (d. 876); became second wife of Louis I the Pious (778–840), king of Aquitaine (r. 781–814), king of France (r. 814–840), and Holy Roman emperor (r. 814–840), in 819; chil-*

dren: *Charles I the Bald (823–877), king of France (r. 843–877), known also as Charles II, Holy Roman emperor (r. 875–877); *Gisela (c. 819–c. 874, who married Eberhard of Friuli). Louis I the Pious' first wife was Ermengarde (c. 778–818).*

Born into a powerful family of Germany, Judith of Bavaria became Holy Roman empress when she married Louis I the Pious, who had succeeded his father Charlemagne and kept intact the empire Charlemagne had built. Judith and Louis were joint rulers of the expansive Frankish kingdom; she was crowned empress in a formal ceremony which spoke of the important place the queen would hold in Louis' administration. Judith was involved in political negotiations, issued decrees in her own name, and presided over the royal court at Aachen.

In 823, she gave birth to a son, Charles (I the Bald), whom Louis proclaimed would succeed him; however, Louis had already promised the imperial throne to Lothair, the eldest child of his first wife, *Ermengarde. Conflict ensued and for the remainder of their reign, Judith and Louis were in constant struggle with the older sons over the inheritance. Twice Judith's enemies managed to have her banished from court on false charges of adultery and witchcraft, but each time she persuaded Louis to take her back and was reinstalled in her position of power. The empress died in 843 with the issue of Louis' succession still unresolved; Louis died soon afterwards. Judith's son Charles did eventually become emperor, but he continued to fight his half-brothers in a bloody civil war for several years, until it was decided for the sake of peace that Charlemagne's empire would be split up to accommodate all the contenders.

SOURCES:
Anderson, Bonnie S., and Judith P. Zinsser. *A History of Their Own.* Vol. I. NY: Harper & Row, 1988.
Holmes, George, ed. *Oxford Illustrated History of Medieval Europe.* NY: Oxford University Press, 1988.

Laura York,
Riverside, California

Judith of Bavaria (c. 925–987)

Duchess of Bavaria. Born around 925; died on June 28, 987; daughter of Arnulf the Bad, duke of Bavaria, and *Judith of Fiuli; married Henry I the Quarrelsome (918–955), duke of Bavaria (r. 947–955), in 938; children: *Gerberga, abbess of Hildesheim (r. 959–1001); Henry II (b. 951), duke of Bavaria; Hedwig (d. 994, who married Burckhardt, duke of Swabia); Brunon I (d. 972), count of Brunswick.

Judith of Bavaria (fl. 1120s)

Duchess of Swabia. Flourished in the 1120s; daughter of Henry the Black (d. 1126), duke of Bavaria, and *Wolfida of Saxony (c. 1075–1126); sister of Welf also known as Guelph VI (d. 1191) and Henry the Proud (d. 1139), duke of Bavaria and Saxony; married Frederick II (c. 1100–1139), duke of Swabia; children: Frederick I Barbarossa (1123–1190), first of the Hohenstaufen kings of Germany and Holy Roman emperor (r. 1152–1190).

The marriage of Judith of Bavaria and Frederick II, duke of Swabia, united the Guelph (Welf) and Hohenstaufen families.

Judith of Bavaria (fl. 1390s–1400)

Bavarian princess. Name variations: Joanna of Bavaria. Flourished from the 1390s to 1400; first wife of Wenceslas IV the Drunkard (1361–1419), duke of Luxemburg (r. 1383–1419), king of Bohemia (r. 1378–1419), and Holy Roman emperor (r. 1378–1400) as just Wenceslas.

Judith of Bethulia or Bethulin

(fl. early 6th c. BCE).
See Judith.

Judith of Brittany (c. 982–1018).
See Judith of Rennes.

Judith of Fiuli (fl. 910–925)

Duchess of Bavaria. Flourished between 910 and 925; daughter of Eberhard, count of Friuli, and *Gisela (c. 819–c. 874); sister of Berengar, Holy Roman emperor (r. 905–924); married Arnulf the Bad, duke of Bavaria (r. 907–937), around 910; children: Eberhard, duke of Bavaria (r. 937–938); *Judith of Bavaria (c. 925–987); Arnulf, platzgraf of Bavaria; Hermann; Berthold, margrave of Bavaria; Luitpold, margrave of East Mark; Ludwig.

Judith of Flanders (1032–1094)

Duchess of Bavaria. Name variations: Fausta. Born in 1032 in Flanders; died on March 5, 1094, at Weingarten Abbey in Bavaria; daughter of Baldwin V, count of Flanders (r. 1035–1067), and Adela Capet (c. 1010–1079); sister of Matilda of Flanders (c. 1031–1083); married Tostig Godwinson (an English knight and brother of King Harold II), earl of Northumberland, in October 1051 (died 1066); married Guelf or Guelph also known as Welf IV (c.

1035–1101), duke of Bavaria, in 1071; children: (first marriage) Skuli Tostisson; Ketil Tostisson; (second marriage) Guelph also known as Welf V the Fat (c. 1073–1120), duke of Bavaria; Henry III the Black (b. around 1074–1126), duke of Bavaria.

Judith of Flanders was a Flemish noblewoman widely recognized for her artistic patronage. Her parents were Baldwin V, count of Flanders, and ❧➤ Adela Capet; her sister was *Matilda of Flanders. At about 18 years old, Judith was married to the Anglo-Saxon knight Tostig Godwinson and moved to England. The couple seem to have become deeply devoted to one another and shared an intense piety. In 1061, Judith and Tostig went on a pilgrimage to Rome and returned more devout than ever.

Judith spent much of her time patronizing artists of religious works and commissioning numerous books to be copied for her as well. The most magnificent in her collection was a Book of Gospels which was commissioned in celebration of her marriage to Tostig. It was encased in an ornate leather and metal cover worked in gold and decorated with precious stones.

Tostig died in 1066. In 1071, Judith married Welf IV, duke of Bavaria, who had previously been married to Ethelinde of Northeim. Judith took her books with her when she moved to Germany. She is thus credited with bringing the first examples of the magnificent Anglo-Saxon illuminated manuscripts to the Continent, where their artistic and calligraphic techniques were studied and emulated by numerous scribes and painters. Welf IV went on the first crusade about 1096 and died returning from the Holy Land. Judith of Flanders retired to a Bavarian abbey, where she died about age 62.

SOURCES:

Anderson, Bonnie S., and Judith P. Zinsser. A History of Their Own. Vol. I. NY: Harper & Row, 1988.

Klapisch-Zuber, Christiane, ed. A History of Women in the West, vol. II: Silences of the Middle Ages. Cambridge: Belknap/Harvard, 1992.

Laura York,
Riverside, California

Judith of Hungary (fl. late 900s)

Queen of Poland. Flourished in the late 900s; daughter of Geza, prince of Hungary (r. 970–997), and *Sarolta (fl. 900s); became second wife of Boleslaw Chobry also known as Boleslaus the Brave (967–1025), king of Poland, in 988 (divorced); children: possibly Regelinda; Mieszko II (990–1034), king of Poland (r. 1025–1034).

Judith of Normandy
(c. 1054–after 1086)

Countess of Huntingdon and Northampton. Born around 1054; died after 1086; daughter of Lambert II, count of Ponthieu, Lenz, and Champagne, and *Adelicia (1029–1090, half-sister of William the Conqueror); niece of William the Conqueror; married Waltheof (d. 1076), earl of Huntingdon and Northampton, in 1070; children: *Matilda of Northumberland (c. 1074–1131, who married David I, king of Scotland); Judith of Huntingdon (who possibly married Ralph II de Toni); and another daughter who died young.

Judith of Rennes (c. 982–1018)

Duchess of Normandy. Name variations: Judith of Brittany. Born around 982; died in 1018; daughter of Conan I the Crooked, duke of Brittany (r. 990–992); married Richard II the Good (d. 1027), duke of Normandy (r. 996–1027), around 1000; children: Richard III (c. 1008–1027), duke of Normandy (r. 1027–1028); Robert I the Devil (1010–1035), duke of Normandy (r. 1028–1035); Nicholas of Normandy (d. 1025, also referred to as William), a monk at Féchamp; *Alice of Normandy (fl. 1017–1037); Eleanor of Normandy.

Juditta.

Variant of Joveta or Jovita.

Judson, Ann Hasseltine
(1789–1826)

American Baptist missionary to Burma and first American woman missionary to the East. Name variations: Nancy Judson. Born Nancy Ann Hasseltine on December 22, 1789, in Bradford, Massachusetts; died on October 24, 1826, in Amherst, near Rangoon, Burma (now Myanmar), from a jungle fever; daughter of John Hasseltine (a deacon in the Congregationalist church) and Rebecca Hasseltine; attended Bradford Academy; married Adoniram Judson (a Congregationalist minister), on February 5, 1812; children: Roger Williams Hasseltine (1815–1816); Marie Elizabeth Butterworth (1825–1827).

Left for missionary work in India (February 6, 1812); landed in Calcutta (June 18, 1812); baptized as a Baptist (September 6, 1812); arrived in Rangoon, Burma (1813); returned to United States weakened from fever (1822); returned to Burma (late 1823); moved to Ava, Burma (February 1824); husband Adoniram Judson taken prisoner by Burmese nation-

Adela Capet.
See Matilda of Flanders for sidebar.

als during British-Burma war (June 1824); husband released and the Judsons return to Rangoon (February 21, 1826); moved to Amherst in Burma with the British (July 5, 1826).

Ann Hasseltine was born in 1789, in Bradford, Massachusetts, the daughter of **Rebecca Hasseltine** and John Hasseltine, a deacon in the Congregationalist church. After attending Bradford Academy, she married Adoniram Judson, a Congregationalist minister, on February 5, 1812. The Judsons left for missionary work in India the following day.

Upon their arrival in Calcutta, the Judsons and their fellow missionaries were ordered back to the United States by the East India Company. Following their baptism as Baptists and unwilling to return, the Judsons moved on to Burma, settling in Rangoon. The formation of the Baptist General Convention in Philadelphia in 1814 and the subsequent appointment of the Judsons as Baptist missionaries provided them with support to continue this mission. The primary focus of the Judsons during their first nine years was the translation of the New Testament into Burmese and educating the Burmese in Christianity. Ann Judson established a school for Burmese girls and ran this while helping her husband in his translation and evangelizing work.

Severely weakened by a series of fevers, Ann journeyed to America in 1822 and spent her time preparing her account of *The American Baptist Mission in Burma* which was published in March 1823. She returned to Burma in the late summer of 1823. During her absence, her husband completed the translation of the New Testament and prepared a 12-section summary of the Old Testament. Upon her return, the Judsons went upriver to Ava, then the capital of Burma, intending to establish a mission there. They entered into the tensions between the English and Burmese and soon after the outbreak of war Adoniram was imprisoned, and Ann remained under all but house arrest. Giving birth to a daughter Marie and suffering from small pox, tropical fever, and spotted fever during Adoniram's captivity, Ann's health was severely jeopardized. Throughout his captivity, Ann kept his work hidden from the authorities; it would be published following her death.

Following Adoniram's release on February 21, 1826, the Judsons returned to Rangoon and soon moved on to Amherst in lower Burma to establish a new mission. Shortly after their arrival, Adoniram was called back to Ava to assist as a translator in the peace negotiations. A final jungle fever ended Ann's life on October 24, 1826. (In 1834, Adoniram would marry *Sarah Boardman Judson.)

Ann Judson's assistance in the translation of the Bible into Burmese, a work that served as the cornerstone of the Christianization of the East, and her status as the first woman missionary to the East, is regarded as incomparable in the history of the Christian mission to the East.

SOURCES:

Deen, Edith. *Great Women of the Christian Faith*. NY: Harper & Brothers, 1959.

Hartley, Cecil B. *The Three Mrs. Judsons, the Celebrated Female Missionaries*. NY: United States Book Company, 1863.

Knowles, James Davis. *Life of Mrs. Ann H. Judson, Late Missionary to Burma with an Account of the American Baptist Mission to that Empire*. Philadelphia, PA: American Sunday School Union, 1830.

SUGGESTED READING:

Simmons, Dawn Langley. *Golden Boats from Burma: The Life of Ann Hasseltine Judson, The First American Woman in Burma*. Philadelphia, PA: Macrae Smith, 1961.

COLLECTIONS:

Some papers pertaining to the Burma mission and the Judsons are located at Harvard University. The remaining papers of Ann H. Judson (she destroyed most of her letters and diaries during the war) are held at the Baptist Board of Missions. Other documents and a memorial read at the presentation of a portrait of Judson to the academy are housed at Bradford Academy.

Amanda Carson Banks,
Vanderbilt Divinity School

Ann Hasseltine Judson

Judson, Nancy (1789–1826).

See Judson, Ann Hasseltine.

Judson, Sarah Boardman

(1803–1845)

American missionary. Name variations: Sarah Hall Judson. Born Sarah Hall on November 4, 1803, in Alstead, New Hampshire; died on September 1, 1845, anchored just off the island of St. Helena; daughter of Ralph Hall and Abiah (Hall) Hall; briefly attended local female seminary; largely self-educated; married George Dana Boardman, on July 3, 1825 (died 1831); married Adoniram Judson, on April 10, 1834; children: (first marriage) Sarah Ann Boardman (1826–1829); George Dana Boardman (b. 1828, later a well-known Baptist minister); Judson Wade Boardman (b. 1830, lived only nine months); (second marriage) Abigail Ann Judson; Adoniram Brown Judson (later an orthopedic surgeon); Elnathan Judson; Henry Hall Judson; Edward Judson (later a minister); and three others who did not survive infancy.

With husband George Boardman moved to Burma (now Myanmar) to be a missionary; set up schools and church for the Karen, an indigenous tribe; translated the New Testament, various religious tracts, and Adoniram Judson's Life of Christ *into the language of the Peguans; translated the first part of* Pilgrim's Progress *into Burmese and put together a Burmese hymn book.*

Sarah Judson was born Sarah Hall in New Hampshire on November 4, 1803, the oldest of Ralph and **Abiah Hall**'s 13 children. The family soon moved to Massachusetts, and Sarah grew up in Danvers and in Salem. In 1820, she joined the First Baptist Church. Unable to continue her studies at a local female seminary because of family finances, she helped care for her siblings and educated herself at home. Sarah taught school for a short while and wrote poems which appeared in the *Christian Watchman* and the *American Baptist Magazine*; she was introduced to the idea of missionary work by her pastor and by a meeting in 1823 with ***Ann Hasseltine Judson**, the wife of pioneer Baptist missionary to Burma Adoniram Judson.

Sarah's poem on the death of Burmese missionary James Colman caught the attention of George Boardman, a seminary student who himself planned to be a missionary to Burma, and led to their meeting. Two weeks after the couple married in 1825, they set off for Burma. In early December, they reached Calcutta and were forced to remain there for over a year due to the Anglo-Burmese war; Sarah spent the time learning the Burmese language and giving birth to her

first child. Finally, in the spring of 1827, the family arrived in Burma.

The Boardmans lived in Amherst, a hub for missionaries near Rangoon, and then in Moulmein. Early in 1828 they moved to Tavoy on the Bay of Bengal, where they began evangelizing the Karen tribe. Their second child, George Dana, was born that year.

From 1829 to 1831, the Boardmans experienced great hardships. Their daughter died in July of 1829 and the anti-British revolt that year made it necessary for them to quit the area in fear for their lives. In January of 1830 their third child was born but lived only nine months. The whole family suffered from dysentery, and by April of 1830 they had moved back to Moulmein to recuperate. A few months later they were back in Tavoy to baptize the numerous Christian converts, despite the fact that George was still sick. His health continued to decline, and he died on February 11, 1831.

Sarah carried on her work as a missionary after George's death. For three years, she continued working in Tavoy, reestablishing the schools they had built earlier and traveling through the jungle to preach. Adoniram Judson, who had been widowed in 1826 and to whom many Baptist missionaries looked for advice and assistance, remained in contact with Sarah during this time. They were married on April 10, 1834, and worked in Moulmein for eleven years. Together they had eight children, although only five lived past infancy. Adoniram encouraged Judson to study the language of the Peguan peoples of southwestern Burma, and she eventually translated the New Testament, Adoniram's *Life of Christ,* and several religious tracts into the Peguan language.

After the birth of her last child in December of 1844, Judson suffered a recurrence of dysentery. In May of 1845, she was forced to sail for America, along with her husband and three oldest children, in hopes of recovering. Sarah died during the voyage, scarcely a month before her 42nd birthday, and was buried on the island of St. Helena where Napoleon had spent his last days in exile. Adoniram Judson's third wife, writer **Emily Chubbuck (Judson)**, published an account of Sarah Boardman Judson's 21-year missionary service in 1848.

SOURCES:

James, Edward T., ed. *Notable American Women, 1607–1950.* Cambridge, MA: The Belknap Press of Harvard University Press, 1971.

McHenry, Robert, ed. *Famous American Women.* NY: Dover, 1983.

Karina L. Kerr, M.A.,
Ypsilanti, Michigan

Judy, Aunt (1809–1873).

See Gatty, Margaret.

Julia (d. 68 BCE)

*Roman noblewoman and aunt of Julius Caesar. Died in 68 BCE (some sources cite 69 BCE); daughter of *Marcia (fl. 100 BCE) and Gaius Julius Caesar; sister of C. Julius Caesar (praetor, 85 BCE, father of Julius Caesar) and Sextus Julius Caesar (consul, 91 BCE); aunt of Julius Caesar, Roman emperor; married Gaius Marius (consul, d. 86 BCE).*

It was the marriage of Julia, aunt of Julius Caesar, to dictator Gaius Marius that propelled the young Caesar into politics. As a result of Julia's efforts, Marius planned to name Caesar the *flamen Dialis* (priest of Jupiter). Despite Caesar's previous plans to marry the daughter of a wealthy *equestrian* (business-class) family, he married *Cornelia, daughter of the consul Lucius Cornelius Cinna, to fulfill the requirement that the *flamen* marry a patrician. Because of Marius' changing political fortunes, however, Caesar was never appointed *flamen*.

Caesar eventually triumphed, nonetheless. In 73 BCE, the Romans elected him one of the 24 military tribunes, his first elected office. Elected *quaestor* (junior magistrate) in 69, he gave public funeral orations honoring his recently deceased aunt Julia and his wife Cornelia. According to Suetonius, Caesar took the opportunity in his oration to glorify his family:

> The family of my aunt Julia is descended by her mother from the kings, and on her father's side is akin to the immortal Gods. . . . Our stock therefore has at once the sanctity of kings, and the claim to reverence which attaches to the Gods.

Julia (d. 54 BCE)

*Daughter of Julius Caesar. Born around 83 BCE; died in 54 BCE; daughter of Roman emperor Julius Caesar (c. 100–44 BCE) and *Cornelia (c. 100–68 BCE); married Pompey (106–48 BCE), the Roman general, in 59 BCE.*

In 60 BCE, the Roman general Pompey formed a coalition, the First Triumvirate, with Crassus and Julius Caesar. To cement the bond between the leading men, Pompey married Caesar's daughter, Julia. But events would move toward an inevitable break between Pompey and Caesar. Julia died in 54 BCE, dissolving the marriage bond between them, and Pompey refused to negotiate a new one.

Julia (39 BCE–14 CE)

Only daughter of Augustus, first emperor of Rome, who was a favorite and politically useful child—until her love affairs brought him disgrace and he banished her from Rome forever. Born in Rome in 39 BCE; died in Rhegium near the end of 14 CE of malnutrition and despair; daughter of Gaius Julius Caesar Octavianus also known as Octavian or Augustus (63 BCE–14 CE), first emperor of Rome, and Scribonia (c. 75 BCE–after 16 CE), a Roman noblewoman; educated at home in spinning and weaving, also in literature; married Marcus Marcellus (a son of Augustus' sister Octavia, and thus Augustus' nephew), in 25 BCE (died, autumn 23 BCE); married Marcus Vipsanius Agrippa, in 21 BCE (died 12 BCE); married Tiberius Claudius Nero (emperor), in 11 BCE; children: (second marriage) Gaius Caesar (20 BCE–4 CE); Julia (b. 19 or 18 BCE); Lucius Caesar (17 BCE–2 CE); Agrippina the Elder (c. 14 BCE–33 CE); Marcus Vipsanius Agrippa Postumus (born after March, 12 BCE); (third marriage) one son (b. 10 BCE) who died in infancy. Prosecuted for adultery and banished from Rome, 2 BCE.

In the year 39 BCE, when Julia was born to *Scribonia and Gaius Octavius (Augustus), Rome was in the midst of one of the most turbulent points in its history. The Republican government that had sustained it for centuries was buckling under the responsibility of administering an empire that fairly spanned the known world. Powerful and ambitious men of the great families were asserting themselves as much for the sake of personal power as civil stability; civil war was the frequent result of this rivalry. At one point in the 1st century, the strife looked as if it might cease through the efforts of one Julius Caesar, who with the extraordinary but constitutional office of dictator sought to bring the disparate interests of the powerful under his own domination. But when he began to flirt with kingship, a notion abhorrent to Roman citizens since they had abolished their own centuries earlier, a conspiracy of well-born senators assassinated him.

It was left to Julius Caesar's young great-nephew, Gaius Octavius, who was posthumously adopted as his heir in 44 BCE, to set Rome on a new course. Known from the time of his adoption as Gaius Julius Caesar Octavianus (and to modern historians as Octavian or Augustus), he first allied himself with, and then defeated various of his compatriots from the Roman nobility. The Battle of Actium (31 BCE) marked the beginning of his second transformation. In this decisive sea-battle, Octavian and his trusted lieutenant Marcus Agrippa decisively triumphed over Mark Antony, the last of his Roman rivals, who was fighting with the aid of Egyptian forces under his paramour, *Cleopatra (VII). Gradually, and by means that had the superficial appearance of constitutional sanction, Octavian consolidated for himself supreme monarchical power: in 27 BCE, he was given the name "Augustus" ("venerable," "magnificent") by the Senate, and in 2 was named "Pater Patriae" ("father of his country").

Julia was born at a pivotal point in her ambitious young father's public career. Throughout the history of pagan Rome, marriages, like adoptions, were rather freely taken up and broken for political purposes; they were used to seal the alliance of powerful families and individuals. Thus, Augustus divorced Julia's mother Scribonia only a few months after Julia's birth in order to marry *Livia Drusilla, a noblewoman of excellent family and exceptional character. It was not long at all before Augustus tried to exploit the marriage value of his tiny daughter. His sister *Octavia had been married to Mark Antony, and in order to shore up their precarious alliance the two-year-old Julia was betrothed in 37 BCE to Antony's son (by a previous wife) Marcus Antonius Antyllus. The marriage never took place, for after Antony's estrangement and defeat, such a union was worse than useless in Augustus' eyes. Foreseeing a potential danger in the living heir of his greatest enemy, he had Antyllus executed soon after the battle of Actium. It was also circulated in the scandalous literature of Antony's party that Augustus betrothed Julia to Cotiso, king of the Getae, a tribe in the Roman province of Thrace. But such a marriage between a freeborn Roman and a barbarian would have been all but unthinkable at the time, and there cannot be much truth in the claim.

Julia's upbringing took place in a home presided over by her stepmother Livia Drusilla and Augustus. From her earliest youth, Julia would have felt the effects of Augustus' program for the regeneration of Rome. In order to guarantee the fresh imposition of order that he had accomplished, Augustus and his ministers engineered a return to the "Republican morals" of the imagined past: to the customs of a simple and upright people as yet unperverted by luxuries of body and spirit imported from the East. By means of sumptuary laws and artful (indeed, much artistic) propaganda, he sought to purify his people. But as *princeps* or "first citizen," he also had to provide them with a worthy example. Julia was reared strictly and under Augustus' direct supervision. She was taught traditional spinning and weaving because the wealthy *princeps* preferred homemade clothing, and her exposure to young men was very closely monitored. Yet this austere household did not despise learning. Augustus was a patron of the arts, and Julia would have had ample instruction in literature at home.

When she reached the age of 14, Julia was old enough by Roman standards to be married, and Augustus' arrangements for her engagement reflect not only his acute sense of political expediency, but also a personal problem that afflicted him and Livia Drusilla. Having been married for 11 years in 25 BCE with no children of their own, it began to seem likely that no direct male heirs would be forthcoming. Augustus accordingly fixed his hopes on his 16-year-old nephew, Marcus Claudius Marcellus, much as the sonless Julius Caesar had looked to the teen-aged Gaius Octavius. Marcellus was the son of Augustus' sister Octavia and her first husband. Marcellus and Julia were married in a splendid ceremony in Rome in 25 to great popular acclaim. Augustus, who was at the time afflicted by one of his frequent spells of grave illness, was unable to attend and entrusted Agrippa to take his place at the nuptials.

> *Thus it was that [Augustus] once observed, when talking among some friends, that he had two spoiled daughters to put up with—Rome and Julia.*
>
> —Macrobius

The few contemporary testimonia of this marriage certify that it was a happy union, and this should not surprise us, despite the modern aversion to marriage between close blood relations. In fact, it is likely that as first cousins, Julia and Marcellus probably knew each other quite well at the time of their engagement, and were not, as so often must have been the case with political marriages, complete strangers.

Contented or not, Julia's first marriage did not last long. In the fall of 23, having already advanced far in public life for one so young, Marcellus died suddenly of a fever. Augustus had lost his heir and had no fresh candidates in view, given that his daughter and his nephew produced no children. Augustus himself had been gravely ill again earlier in the year, and the need to marry Julia off to a suitable heir (or to a man worthy to beget an heir with her) was paramount. After some debate, and the rejection of Augustus' friend Gaius Proculeius on the grounds that he did not possess adequate political standing, the *princeps* was persuaded by his trusted advisor Gnaeus Maecenas that Julia should be married to his right-hand-man Agrippa. At this point in the story, the convolution of Augustan politics, friendships, and family life becomes extreme, and it is useful, if not indispensable, to have at hand a genealogical table of the family of Augustus. (*See genealogical chart "The Julian Line," p. cxxxiii in Volume I of this encyclopedia.*)

It is difficult to say if the marriage of Julia and Agrippa, which was planned to take place in 21 BCE, was an entirely satisfactory arrangement for either of them. It must have been strange for Julia to look for the first time at her father's old bosom friend as husband. Agrippa, after all, had stood in for her father to give Julia away at her first wedding. Moreover, he was nearly twice Julia's age and already married at the time. Nevertheless, both parties apparently played the part well; Julia as Augustus' obedient daughter, and Agrippa as his best friend and son-in-law. In order to marry his new bride, he was compelled to dissolve his marriage to *Marcella the Elder, a daughter of Augustus' sister Octavia, and sister to Julia's first husband Marcellus. From the date of this marriage, Agrippa began to be rewarded with high offices and honors both ordinary and extraordinary and, though never officially named as Augustus' heir, was held second in dignity and power only to him.

In about 20 BCE, Julia proved to Augustus that he had made a good decision in her second marriage. In that year, the first of her five children with Agrippa was born. At the tender age of three, the child, called Gaius Caesar, was officially adopted by his grandfather—a clear sign of Augustus' dynastic intentions. Following the birth of Gaius, a daughter, *Julia, was born in either 18 or 19 BCE. (Her life would play out, even to its sad end, like a faint echo of her mother's.) In 17 BCE, a second son, Lucius Caesar, was born and immediately adopted by Augustus to share his older brother's distinction. A second daughter, Agrippina (sometimes called *Agrippina the Elder), was born in about 14 BCE. Finally, in 12 BCE, just a few months after his father's death, another son was born. Given the circumstances of his birth, he was called Agrippa Postumus.

Inscriptional data suggests that Julia accompanied Agrippa on parts of his Eastern diplomatic missions beginning in the year 16 BCE; this might have taken her to the Bosporus and as far as the Levant, where Agrippa visited Beirut and contracted a friendly alliance with Herod the Great, king of the Jews. It is uncertain whether Julia preceded Agrippa back to Rome in 13 BCE.

Early in 12 BCE, Agrippa was called to the province of Pannonia (overlapping parts of present-day Austria, Hungary, Slovenia, and Croatia) in order to redress an incipient rebellion. Shortly after his return to Rome in March of 12 BCE, he died suddenly. At 27 years of age, Julia was twice a widow.

Once again, the question of whom she should marry engaged Augustus and his advisors. With Gaius and Lucius thriving in his own house, the problem of succession was certainly not acute, as it had been before. But as a young woman Julia could still be a great asset to Augustus if she married the right man. This time around, the name of Tiberius came to the fore. Tiberius Claudius Nero was the eldest son of Augustus' wife and Julia's stepmother Livia Drusilla, and it is possible, but not likely, that he was chosen at her instigation. In fact, it seems probable that Tiberius' name had been broached in deliberations over Julia's first and second marriages, but the complications of allegiance and personal preference had prevented his being chosen. At the time of Julia's first marriage, Augustus had already campaigned in Spain with both Marcellus and Tiberius. Though both young men had served well, Augustus always showed greater favor to Marcellus, who was of cheerful disposition, in contrast to the sometimes sullen and moody Tiberius. Also complicating the prospects of a union between Tiberius and Julia in 25 BCE was the fact that he had been previously engaged to Agrippa's daughter (*Vipsania Agrippina), and Augustus would not risk offending him.

The unforeseen result of the latter calculation was that by 11 BCE, when it was decreed that Tiberius and Julia should wed, Tiberius had been very happily married to Vipsania for some dozen years. He was nevertheless compelled to divorce and remarry. Despite the pain Tiberius felt at the loss of Vipsania (he once met her later by chance and was seen to break down), his marriage with Julia was at first satisfactory. What was to follow, however, has led prominent modern historian J.P.V.D. Balsdon to remark on Augustus' "consummate folly" in deciding to pair the two in the first place.

The initial cause for the estrangement of Tiberius and Julia is not clear, but speculation informed by historical reports does expose some possibilities. At bottom, it will not seem farfetched to suppose that whatever the stumbling blocks to marital bliss in the following years, the naturally morose and depressive Tiberius might weigh them against his years of happiness with his first wife, thus causing an uncomfortable situation to worsen. In any case, the couple did experience an almost immediate calamity when in 10 BCE their only child, a son, died soon after birth. Moreover, as an exceptionally successful and by this point indispensable general, Tiberius was often campaigning near the borders of the empire to block barbarian incursions or to quell disturbances. His time away from Julia might have made her feel abandoned, and since the responsibilities of bringing up her own children had been largely undertaken by Augustus, she must have felt especially alone when her husband was gone. But several ancient authorities report that it was Tiberius who refused to sleep with Julia in the years following 10 BCE. Mention of sex leads the story inevitably to an account of what Julia, justly or unjustly, is best remembered for.

It is unfortunate that the majority of the ancient sources that make reference to Julia's life, and especially those of near contemporaneity, are prone to reproduce gossip and party propaganda. The sheer weight of testimonia alleging extramarital affairs, however, makes the mere fact impossible to disbelieve. Allusions to adultery during her first two marriages exist, though without much substantiation. Surprising as it may seem, the imperial biographer Suetonius reports the popular belief that Julia had harbored a passion for Tiberius, which he perceived and disapproved of, even while Agrippa was still alive. Only one reputed partner in adultery is named for the period of Julia's marriage with Agrippa, the eloquent noble Sempronius Gracchus. Since Tacitus, a generally reliable historian, is among those who report his name, we can have some confidence in the truth of the allegation. Tacitus also tells us that it was actually this Gracchus, a "persistent adulterer," who wrote the insulting letter about Tiberius that Julia sent to Augustus under her own name, apparently hoping that her father would punish her husband for neglecting her.

As his marriage deteriorated, Tiberius' public station increased. Already Augustus' choice general with significant victories in Dalmatia and Pannonia (9 BCE), Tiberius was granted special powers of command and immunity in 6 BCE. He was at this point indisputably the second man in Rome, yet his position in the line to ultimate authority was blocked by Gaius and Lucius Caesar, Julia's sons by Agrippa, whom Augustus was grooming to succeed him. We cannot know for certain whether it was jealousy of these boys or outrage at the behavior of their mother that prompted Tiberius suddenly to withdraw from public life in 6 BCE. In that year, he was reluc-

tantly given permission to relocate to Rhodes in order to study philosophy.

Velleius Paterculus, a minor but significant historian for the period, sums up Julia's behavior after Tiberius' departure thus: "she was in the habit of measuring the magnitude of her fortune only in the terms of license to sin, setting up her own caprice as a law unto itself." At this point, the accounts of her deeds become both lurid and fanciful. Still, there must be a core of truth in them. Readers of the fine historical novel *I Claudius* by Robert Graves (or viewers of the television series based upon it) are amply familiar with most of the allegations. The 1st-century CE philosopher and courtier Seneca has the most concisely comprehensive account of them, claiming:

Julia
(39 BCE–14 CE)

> that she had been accessible to scores of paramours, that in nocturnal revels she had roamed about the city, that the very forum and the rostrum [speaking platform] from which her father had proposed a law against adultery, had been chosen by the daughter for her debaucheries, that she had daily resorted to the statue of Marsyas [a place of business for prostitutes in the forum], and, laying aside the role of adulteress, there sold her favours, and sought the right to every indulgence with even an unknown paramour (*De Beneficia* 6.32.1).

If Julia's dalliances had been only a fraction of those reported, it is hard to see how they could have escaped Augustus' notice, given the grip that he held over Roman society. But for at least four years, from Tiberius' departure in 6 until 2 BCE, when the scandal broke, Augustus was apparently silent about the matter. Perhaps, having always been an indulgent father to Julia, he allowed some early allegations to slide. We have no record of his private remonstrations with her. But the 2nd-century CE historian Cassius Dio says that it was Augustus himself who uncovered the extent of the scandal, made a speech to the senate denouncing Julia (the quotation from Seneca above purports to outline the content of this speech), and then began legal proceedings against her.

Augustus was enraged, and in one sense we can understand why. As part of his program for the inculcation of old-time morals, he had passed strong marriage legislation in 19–18 BCE. These laws were aimed at increasing the birthrate, regulating marriage between the social classes, and maintaining the stability and sanctity of the marriage bond by stipulating specific rules for the prosecution and punishment of adultery. Previously, punishment for adultery had been the sole responsibility of the family; the new law allowed for prosecution by the public at large if a husband refused to act first. The various terms and penalties of the law are well outlined; it is interesting to note, however, that there was no provision for a wife to initiate prosecution against a guilty husband, and that adultery for him included only liaisons with free married or unmarried women. Trysts or casual relations with slaves or registered prostitutes were legal. The regular punishment for a wife, unless the adultery took place in the husband's house or if the lovers were caught by him *in flagrante delicto* (in which case he was permitted to kill them), was exile to a remote corner of the empire.

Augustus' harshness in dealing with Julia perhaps exceeded the letter of his own law. Suetonius says that he at first considered killing her, but at last decided to exile her to Pandateria (present-day Ventotene), a tiny wind-swept island some 31 miles west of the Bay of Naples. Augustus straightaway divorced her from the absent Tiberius and confiscated her personal property. In her rough island villa, she had only the bare necessities of life and was forbidden wine. For company, there were only her guards and a few slaves, and, by a touching act of kindness, her mother Scribonia, who accompanied her voluntarily. Visitors were very strictly screened, and only unattractive, politically loyal men were allowed to set foot on the island.

Personal humiliation may be the best explanation for the depth of Augustus' anger and the extent of the punishments he imposed on his daughter, but there are hints in the ancient sources that there may be other, hidden, causes. How else, several scholars have asked, can we explain so sudden and final an about-face in a previously doting father? Certainly it is remarkable that even Tiberius wrote to Augustus from Rhodes to request some leniency for his detested ex-wife. The list of Julia's lovers furnished by Velleius may offer a clue. The five names he provides (along with a parenthesis claiming that there were many others) all indicate well-placed men from the senatorial and equestrian social

orders, and include not only the ambitious Sempronius Gracchus, but also Iullus Antonius, a surviving son of Augustus' old arch-rival, Mark Antony. It is just possible, as some ancient authors claim and as several modern historians argue, that this young man and his associates may have formed a conspiracy to do away with Augustus and his autocratic regime, and that Julia, either wittingly or unwittingly, was implicated in the plot through her lovers. Following Julia's relegation to her island, four of her named lovers were also exiled, and Iullus Antonius was either executed like his brother before him, or driven to suicide like his father. Further, Augustus soon passed legislation that made male association with Julia or any of the women of his house subject to the charge of high treason. We cannot know for certain if Julia was involved in such parricidal plans; indeed, several recent works of scholarship have strenuously denied it.

Despite her scandal, Julia was very popular with the people of Rome, and there were demonstrations in her favor. Later, there were even rumors of a scheme to rescue her from her island prison. Augustus was at first unrelenting, but subsequently softened somewhat and allowed Julia to move to house arrest in Rhegium, in the south of the Italian peninsula (4 CE). When Augustus died in 14 CE, Tiberius succeeded him as *princeps*, and this was the sad end of Julia. The meager allowance that Augustus had provided her was cut off, and she died of malnutrition, at 53 years of age, later in the same year. Her shamed husband had had his revenge. Finally, an item in the will of Augustus forbade her burial in the family tomb, extending her exile beyond the grave.

For all that we know of Julia's life through her membership in Augustus' family, more than one modern historian has complained about our lack of insight into her character. The 5th-century CE writer Macrobius offers a small collection of her witty sayings, which purportedly come from a source contemporaneous with her life. Some show evidence of her learning, some of her vanity, almost all of her cleverness. A particularly memorable one combines elegant wit with a surprising vulgarity and could emblemize neatly the received opinion of her morality. When asked by certain intimates who knew about her affairs how it was that her children resembled Agrippa so closely, she replied, "passengers are never allowed on board until the hold is full."

Whatever the element of personal culpability in Julia's downfall, her life represents a facet of the history of the Augustan house which, in its quick ascendancy to a previously uninhabited peak on the Roman landscape, saw much suffering and even tragedy amongst its individual members. Even the legacy of children that Julia left behind after her disgrace, those boys and girls in whom Augustus had placed so much hope, came to abrupt, sorrowful, and even disgraceful ends. As Velleius says, "Her many children were to be blessing neither to herself nor to the state." Lucius Caesar died of a fever in 2 CE, Gaius after being wounded in battle in 4 CE. The young Julia followed in her mother's doomed footsteps and was banished twice for adultery, the second time, in 8 CE, for life. The youngest, Agrippa Postumus, grew into such a vicious and troubled character that his grandfather hated and feared him. Soon after Augustus' death, and apparently on his orders, Agrippa Postumus was executed in his place of exile. Finally, Agrippina the Elder, mother of the deranged and detested emperor Caligula, though upright throughout her life, came into conflict with Tiberius and was banished to Pandateria, where she starved to death in 33 CE.

SOURCES:

Balsdon, J.P.V.D. *Roman Women: Their History and Habits*. London: Bodley Head, 1962 (reprint ed., Westport, CT: Greenwood Press, 1975).

Cassius Dio. *Dio's Roman History*. Edited and translated by Earnest Cary. Vols. 6 and 7. Cambridge, MA: Harvard University Press, 1992.

Macrobius. *The Saturnalia*. Translated with an introduction by Percival Vaughan Davies. The Records of Civilization: Sources and Studies 79. NY: Columbia University Press, 1969.

The Oxford Classical Dictionary. 3rd ed. Edited by Simon Hornblower and Antony Spawforth. Oxford: Oxford University Press, 1996.

Paulys Real-Encyclopädie der Classischen Alterumswissenschaft. 2nd ed. Edited by Georg Wissowa, *et al.* S.v. "Julia 550," "Julia 551." Stuttgart: J.B. Metzlersche Buchhandlung, 1894–1980.

Suetonius. *Suetonius: Lives of the Caesars*. Translated by J.C. Rolfe. The Loeb Classical Library. Cambridge, MA: Harvard University Press, 1960.

Syme, Ronald. *The Roman Revolution*. Oxford: Clarendon Press, 1939.

Tacitus. *The Annals of Imperial Rome*. Translated with an introduction by Michael Grant. Hammondsworth: Penguin, 1956.

Velleius Paterculus. *Compendium of Roman History and the Res Gestae Divi Augusti*. Edited and translated by Frederick W. Shipley. The Loeb Classical Library. Cambridge, MA: Harvard University Press, 1979.

Wells, Colin. *The Roman Empire*. 2nd ed. Cambridge, MA: Harvard University Press, 1992.

SUGGESTED READING:

Ferrero, Guglielmo. *The Women of the Caesars*. Translated by Christian Gauss. NY: Knickerbocker, 1925.

Serviez, Jaques Boergas de. *Lives of the Roman Empresses: The History of the Lives and Secret Intrigues of the Wives, Sisters and Mothers of the Caesars*. Introduction by Robert Graves. NY: Wise, 1935.

NOVELS:

Graves, Robert. *I Claudius*. NY: Knopf, 1934.

Massie, Allan. *Augustus: A Novel*. London: Bodley Head, 1986.

———. *Tiberius: A Novel*. London: Bodley Head, 1990.

SUGGESTED READING:

Giacosa, Giorgio. *Women of the Caesars: Their Lives and Portraits on Coins*. Translated by Ross R. Holloway. Milan: Edizioni Arte e Moneta, n.d. (contains ancient contemporary coin portraits).

RELATED MEDIA:

I, Claudius. (13 episodes), adapted for television from the book by Robert Graves, London: BBC/London Films, 1976, available on videocassette from the *Library Video Classics Project* of the John D. and Catherine T. MacArthur Foundation.

Peter H. O'Brien,
Boston University, Boston, Massachusetts

Julia (c. 18 BCE–28 CE)

Roman noblewoman. Name variations: Vipsania Julia. Born around 18 or 19 BCE; died in 28 CE; daughter of *Julia (39 BCE–14 CE) and Marcus Agrippa; granddaughter of Octavian also known as Augustus (Roman emperor); sister of *Agrippina the Elder; married Lucius Aemilius Paullus; children: M. Aemilius Paullus; Aemilia.

In 8 CE, the 26-year-old Julia was banished by Augustus into perpetual exile to the island of Tremerus for adultery. Her stepgrandmother *Livia Drusilla, her main support, kept her alive until 28 CE.

Julia, Sister (1827–1901).

See McGroarty, Sister Julia.

Julia Agrippina (15–59 CE).

See Agrippina the Younger.

Julia Berenice (28 CE–after 80 CE).

See Berenice (28 CE–after 80 CE).

Julia Domna (c. 170–217 CE)

Empress of Rome. Name variations: Julia Domna Augusta. Born around 170 CE; died in 217 CE: daughter of Julius Bassianus (the high priest of Elagabalus at Emesa); sister of Julia Maesa (c. 170–224 CE); became second wife of Lucius Septimius Severus (who subsequent to their marriage became emperor of Rome), in 187; children: Septimius Bassianus (b. 188), later known as Marcus Aurelius Severus Antoninus or "Caracalla"; Publius Septimius Geta (b. 189).

Julia Domna was born in Emesa, a city of Arab foundation in the rich Orontes River valley of Roman Syria. Emesa was strategically situated near Rome's frontier with the Parthian Empire, Rome's single strongest foreign rival in the second century. Emesa's importance, however, pre-dated the strategic value it possessed in Domna's day, for it had long stood as a regional crossroads where different peoples (including especially Phoenicians and Greeks) interacted commercially with its Arabic founders. A cosmopolitan city, Emesa's population was too intermixed to determine Domna's ethnicity beyond a doubt: likely, she was of mixed ancestry, although *Domna* itself was of Semitic origin (meaning "black"). Nevertheless, her family's legal name was "Julius" (which Domna bore in the feminine form, "Julia"), and held Roman citizenship. Although a Roman citizen, Domna's father was also a priest of the god, Elagabalus, an important regional deity who by the time of Domna's birth encompassed two originally distinct gods: El of the mountain (worshiped in the form of a black conical stone), and Heliogabal (a Phoenician sun god also known as Sol Invictus, in which form he would later be associated with Mithras). When Emesa had been an independent city, the priesthood of Elagabalus had been in the possession of its ruling house, a right which probably was retained by its non-royal descendants under Roman rule. Thus, however mixed her ancestry might have been, it is likely that Domna could trace her line directly back to the olden kings of Emesa.

Septimius Severus undoubtedly met Julius Bassianus for the first time when he commanded the IV Scythian legion in Syria during the early 180s. Whether or not he also met Domna at this time is unknown, but he seems then to have learned that Domna's horoscope promised that she would one day marry a king—a fact which the very superstitious and astrologically addicted Septimius seems to have kept in the back of his mind. (Perhaps this prediction was validated by the name *Domna* itself, which, to a speaker of Latin, could have been mistaken for a contraction of *Domina,* meaning Sovereign Mistress.) As a result, when **Paccia Marciana** (Septimius' first wife) died in Gallia Lugdunensis several years after his Syrian command, Septimius married Domna. (It should be noted that Septimius and Paccia were from the African city of Lepcis Magna. Their ancestries were north-African and Phoenician. Throughout Septimius' entire life, wags made fun of his provincially accented Latin.) Septimius married Domna in 187, he being 41 and childless, while she was about 17 years old. Their union soon proved fruitful: Caracalla (as he is best known) was born April 4, 188, with Geta following on March 7, 189.

The birth of two sons to Septimius after a barren marriage anchored Domna in his affections. Of course, Domna's beauty (her comely portraits yet exist) and manifest shrewdness in his interests undoubtedly helped to secure the undying affection of her husband.

Whether the stars played a role in their subsequent fates or not (both principals thought that they did), Septimius' career advanced rapidly after his marriage to Domna. After Gaul, Septimius served as proconsul in Sicily, where he was fortunate to have been acquitted of the charge of having taken the Emperor Commodus' horoscope, though he quite likely was guilty. If he had been convicted of this crime, Septimius would have been in serious trouble, for it was a capital offense to consult the emperor's horoscope, it being assumed that if one did so, one had treasonous intentions. Despite the suspicion Septimius generated in Sicily, the emperor Commodus named him as one of Rome's consuls for the year 190—a lofty honor, even though Septimius had a record 24 consular colleagues that year. Then Commodus again displayed his confidence in Septimius by giving him a very prestigious military command along the strategic Pannonian (Danubian) frontier. Septimius remained there from 191 to 193 and as such was removed from the political blood-letting which Rome knew during that period. Julia Domna and sons accompanied Septimius from Gaul, to Sicily, to Rome and to Pannonia, and it was during these years Domna established herself as Septimius' confidante, whose mind was more valuable to his career than were her physical charms.

Septimius' Pannonian command not only removed him from Rome through a rough period, it also placed him in a very auspicious position when the heirless Commodus was assassinated on the last day of 192. Although a successional crisis followed that act, Septimius initially remained out of the running for the imperial throne. In fact, he initially supported the imperial claims of one Pertinax, an old friend and benefactor. Pertinax was of humble birth but was popular among Rome's political elite and recognized as a man of talent. His established reputation, however, did him little good when a financial crisis forced him to impose austerity measures on Rome's Praetorian Guard, the only military corps stationed near Rome. As a result, elements of this less-than-pleased military unit mutinied and murdered Pertinax after a reign of only about two months.

After this treachery, the Praetorian Guard compounded its crime by literally putting the imperial office up for auction. For a princely sum, one Didius Julianus briefly possessed the throne, but when the armies on the frontier heard about the disgraceful behavior of the Guard, they reacted violently. Three armies hailed their respective commanders as emperors: the Pannonian legions supported Septimius; the British, Clodius Septimius Albinus; and the Syrian, Pescennius Niger. Septimius, however, was the closest of these three to Rome, giving him a leg up in the civil wars which followed. He quickly marched on Rome where Julianus' support evaporated in the face of Septimius' superior force and speed. Before Septimius even reached Rome, Julianus was murdered, in the hopes of mitigating the expected slaughter. Once in Rome, Septimius saw his elevation confirmed by the Senate and the People: henceforth he was an Augustus (senior emperor). Domna reigned at his side as an official Augusta (empress). The Praetorian Guard as it had existed was disbanded by Septimius and subsequently reformed.

Septimius' official recognition in Rome did not forestall civil war, for neither Albinus nor Niger yet recognized his imperial legitimacy. Septimius, however, acted nimbly so as to avoid fighting both of his rivals simultaneously. This was accomplished by the brokering of a deal whereby Septimius appointed Albinus as his Caesar (junior emperor and imperial heir) in return for Albinus' acknowledgment of his own status as Augustus. This agreement secured Septimius' northern flank, allowing him to focus his attention on Niger and the East. The conflict which followed was not overly protracted: in fact, Septimius' victory there was completed militarily in the spring of 194 at Issus (the site of one of Alexander the Great's battles, which both Septimius and Domna took as a very good omen).

At her husband's side throughout this campaign, Domna's connections helped Septimius secure the loyalty of Niger's Syrian base quickly and thoroughly. Domna's family ties, however, were not her only contributions to her husband's enterprise, for Septimius exploited both her propaganda value and her intellect in the process of securing his imperial position. As far as propaganda was concerned, in 193 coins were struck with Domna's portrait, hailing her as "Venus Victrix, Venus Genetrix"—titles which simultaneously portended victory and the foundation of a new order, and which also linked Septimius' house to that of the house of Julius Caesar (whose heirs established Rome's first imperial dynasty), because the great Caesar had claimed descent from Venus. Thus did Septimius begin to assert his imperial legitimacy.

Julia Domna

Another link to the legitimate past was forged in April of 195 when Domna was honored with the title "Mater Castrorum" ("Mother of the Camp"), a title which had first been granted by the emperor Marcus Aurelius to his wife *Faustina II, some 20 years before. Aurelius had been Rome's last universally popular emperor (although he *did* father Commodus), so that by the resurrection of this honorific, Septimius began the policy of defining himself as the legitimate heir to Aurelius' authority. This policy was soon taken a step further by Septimius' adoption of the long dead Aurelius as his father. In addition, "Mater Castrorum" did something more for Domna: it publicly recognized her role in devising the political and military strategy which culminated in Septimius' unrivaled mastery of the Roman Empire.

After Septimius' consolidation of the East, it was time for a showdown with Albinus. This was precipitated soon after the announcement of Domna's new title, when Septimius officially renamed Caracalla as Marcus Aurelius Antoninus (the legal name of Septimius' new "father"), and then recognized this seven-year-old as his Caesar. Albinus knew the significance of these moves and rebelled, only to be finally defeated by Septimius in battle near Lyon (France) in February of 197. Thereafter, a vicious purge of all supporters of one-time competitors cemented Septimius' authority as Rome's unrivaled master.

After these events, Domna remained at Septimius' side when he invaded the Parthian Empire in 197–98 (where, with victory, he proclaimed Caracalla an Augustus and Geta a Caesar). She was also with him when he visited Syria in 198–99 and Egypt in 199–200; when he returned to Syria in 200–202; when he called on Rome in 202; when he revisited his hometown and points west in Africa in 203; when he sojourned in Italy from 203 to 208; and when he campaigned in Britain between 208 and 211. Domna's influence over her husband, however, was not without challenge. In particular, one Gaius Fulvius Plautianus for a time gained Septimius' trust, and having it, did his best to undermine Domna's influence over Septimius. Plautianus' reasons for so behaving seem to have been a combination of professional ambition and personal hatred, for the sources make it clear that he and Domna were bitter enemies. For some while, Septimius tolerated Plautianus' abuse of Domna, undoubtedly because Plautianus was a competent administrator. While this state of affairs was current, Domna took solace in the company of sophists and philosophers, and in the process got a reputation for promiscuity, probably as a result of Plautianus' slanders. Among those who frequented Domna's salon during this time was Philostratus, who wrote for her a biography of Apollonius of Tyana, and Cassius Dio, who was a historian as well as a politician. Even with an enemy at court, Domna continued to function as Septimius' Augusta, presiding over court ceremonies, religious rituals and sporting contests. Plautianus' ascendancy, however, collapsed in 205 amid suspicions that his competence was fueling disloyalty to Septimius. Thereafter, Septimius reinstated Domna as his intimate confidante.

In such favor Domna remained until Septimius died at York (Britain) in February of 211. Just prior to his death, Septimius made every attempt to insure that his sons would cooperate as imperial colleagues, and clearly he relied on Domna to oversee their continued collaboration. Caracalla, however, would accept no imperial peer, and for their parts, neither Geta nor the faction which supported him at court would even consider the surrender of the imperial status which Septimius had granted to his second son. Thus, the relationship of the brothers deteriorated, and both sought safety in bodyguards. After months of high tension, Domna's efforts at reconciliation finally seemed to bear fruit in December of 211: Caracalla asked her to arrange a meeting where only she, he and Geta would be present, so that they could arrange a peaceful solution to the existing rivalry. Domna did so, and for secrecy's sake planned an auspicious session to meet in her private apartments. Trusting in his mother's neutrality, Geta arrived without a guard. Arbitration, however, was not what Caracalla had in mind. Without Domna's knowledge he planned an ambush for his brother, so that when Geta came to greet his mother, he was simultaneously attacked by assassins. Geta died in his mother's blood-soaked arms. Other bloodshed quickly ensued, and Geta's faction was eradicated.

Whatever Domna might have thought about Caracalla's callous abuse of her trust, she demonstrated no intention of severing ties with him. As events unfolded, Caracalla needed Domna's talents and connections, and so bought her continued support with more honors and real power. Domna thus became the "Mother of the Senate" and the "Mother of the Fatherland." Even more significantly, Caracalla employed her as the manager of his copious official correspondence, in which capacity Domna determined which petitions should be brought to the emperor's attention and which should not. As a gatekeeper controlling access to Caracalla, Domna was in a position to influence imperial policy. As such, those who wished their business to come to the eyes of the new emperor did well to stay on Domna's good side.

Domna also advised her son about financial matters, and, in this capacity, often chastised him for squandering imperial revenues, and even more so about the unpopular measures which by necessity had to follow so that financial solvency could be maintained. The fact that Domna could do so and retain her place in the court of her thin-skinned and suspicious son is a testimony to how valuable she was to Caracalla's reign. Apparently her competence in her duties more than out-weighed whatever annoyance Caracalla had to endure to tap that competence. Thus did Domna serve Caracalla for several years, reigning as the most influential woman of the empire. (Caracalla was not then married. His first wife was the daughter of Domna's hated rival, Plautianus, forced upon him against his will. However, when Plautianus fell from grace, Caracalla rid himself of his unwanted spouse.)

A political force to be reckoned with at her son's court, during his reign Domna also maintained her interest in intellectual and cultural matters. Nevertheless, things began rapidly to change in 217, when Caracalla began his own Parthian war over the rejection of his proposal to marry a Parthian princess. Domna accompanied Caracalla to Antioch, where she established her chancery while he advanced to the frontier. In retrospect, Caracalla should have retained Domna at his side, for although he may (as is attested) have inherited her cleverness, he clearly inherited neither his father's military ability nor his good fortune. Caracalla's campaign bogged down, and without success the morale of the army flagged. As the army's mood soured, Caracalla sought scapegoats for his lack of success. A prime candidate for the role of victim was the Praetorian prefect, Macrinus, an equestrian, who, despite his middling status, had political ambitions. Whatever these might have been, however, he had little opportunity to exploit Caracalla's failures. When the time came to act decisively, Macrinus probably did so more out of self-preservation than out of ambition. In a court rife with suspicion and finger pointing, two letters about Macrinus' "disloyalty" to the emperor apparently surfaced. One went to Domna in Antioch, while the other was apparently intended for Caracalla himself. Here Domna's distance from her son mattered, for when her copy arrived, she forwarded information about a purported plot involving Macrinus as quickly as she could. This warning, however, failed to reach Caracalla in time, for a similar letter was misdirected through Macrinus' office where it became a self-fulling prophecy: preferring Caracalla's death and an uncertain future to his own extermination, Macrinus murdered Caracalla before the latter could himself strike.

Her husband and sons now all dead, Domna languished for a short while in Antioch, but she did not relish the prospect of surrendering the political influence she had so long wielded. Rather than retire, Domna began plotting Macrinus' overthrow and his replacement, obviously hoping to retain her political influence. (Although not in her direct line and very young, Domna had living male relatives—see ***Julia Maesa** and ***Julia Mamaea**.) When Macrinus learned of her political maneuvering, however, he ordered Domna out of Antioch and into exile. Her plans as yet underdeveloped and her health failing (she was then stricken with a cancer), Domna held on for a time, but when reports from Rome made it known that news of Caracalla's death there had been greeted with jubilation, she surrendered to despair. Suicide became her alternative of choice: her preferred method—self-imposed starvation (before the end of 217).

Her remains were returned to Rome where they were temporarily deposited in the Tomb of Gaius and Lucius Caesar. Later, she was re-interred in the mausoleum of Hadrian, an Antonine, next to the remains of her husband. Septimius Severus' adoption of Marcus Aurelius as a father had won for himself and Domna an eternal association with the Antonine line of emperors.

William S. Greenwalt,
Associate Professor of Classical History,
Santa Clara University, Santa Clara, California

Julia Livilla (c. 16 CE–after 38 CE)

*Roman noblewoman. Name variations: Livilla. Born around 16 CE; daughter of Germanicus Caesar (15 BCE–19 CE) and *Agrippina the Elder (c. 14 BCE–33 CE); sister of *Agrippina the Younger (15–59), Caligula (12–41), and *Drusilla (14–38); exiled in 38.*

Julia Maesa (c. 170–224 CE)

Empress of Rome. Name variations: Julia Varia; Julia Maesa Augusta. Pronunciation: sound the "æ" dipthong as a long "i." Born around 170; died in 224 CE; daughter of Julius Bassianus, the high priest of Elagabalus at Emesa; sister of Julia Domna (c. 170–217 CE); married Gaius Julius Avitus Alexianus also known as Julius Avitus (a Roman senator); children: Julia Soaemias Bassiana and Julia Avita Mamaea, whose respective sons, Elagabalus and Severus Alexander, both became Roman emperors.

Julia Maesa was the daughter of a priest of the god Elagabalus, whose cult flourished at Emesa in Roman Syria (see ***Julia Domna**). Her historical prominence, however, was due to the fact that her sister, Julia Domna, married Septimius Severus in 187, who thereafter reigned as Rome's emperor (193–211). Since Domna's connections promised greater things than Emesa could ever offer, Maesa followed her sister to the heart of the empire. With her came Gaius Julius Avitus Alexianus, an Emesan of equestrian birth (and thus a member of the empire's lesser nobility) who either was, or was soon to become, Maesa's husband. We do not know who was older, Maesa or Domna, nor do we know when Maesa married.

Avitus' career began well, if conventionally, for one of his class: he held several military commands in the imperial *auxilia* (non-citizen military units) and the procuratorship which oversaw the arrival at Ostia of the city of Rome's grain supply. His prospects, however, improved dramatically after the imperial accession of his brother-in-law, beginning with Avitus' promotion to senatorial rank. Thereafter, Avitus commanded a legion in Raetia (the Alpine region of what is now southern Germany, Switzerland and Austria), governed the same province, served as a consul in Rome, and accompanied Septimius as a political and military advisor when the latter campaigned in Britain. Under Septimius' son and successor, Caracalla (r. 211–217), Avitus served as an imperial prefect of the *alimenta* (an allowance for the feeding of underprivileged children), was appointed imperial legate to Dalmatia, and governed as proconsul the province of Asia, a very prestigious post. Avitus died of natural causes (that is, of disease in old age) sometime before the death of Caracalla, having served two emperors loyally and competently.

Important as she was to her husband's career, Maesa's historical significance multiplied many-fold after his death. Not long after Avitus died, Caracalla was assassinated (217) at the instigation of his Praetorian prefect, Macrinus, in the context of a sputtering war Caracalla had commenced against Rome's eastern neighbor, the Parthian Empire. The motivation behind Macrinus' action may have included ambition, but self-preservation probably incited him more than a lust for power, for at the time of Caracalla's murder the emperor was seeking a scapegoat upon whom he could lay the blame for the military debacle he himself had launched. Regardless of his primary incentive, having brought about Caracalla's death Macrinus could do little else but declare himself emperor. His was a stormy regime from the start, however, largely because he was the first Roman of equestrian (that is, less-than-senatorial) status to claim imperial authority. Compounding his difficulties were his own lack of military success against the Parthians (he concluded an unpopular peace), and a lack of diplomatic tact which quickly alienated those under his command. Another obstacle confronting Macrinus was Julia Domna, who naturally hated the murderer of her son and worked for his deposition. Within a year of Caracalla's death, however, Domna fell prey to illness and despair, and starved herself to death.

Unlike Domna at the end of 217, Maesa relished neither death nor the loss of the imperial influence she had been able to exert at her sister's side for close to 30 years. Having no sons of her own, Maesa's hope to remain politically prominent rested initially in the person of her oldest grandchild, Varius Avitus Bassianus, the son of Maesa's daughter, ✒➤ **Julia Soaemias** Bassiana and one Sextus Varius Marcellus. This child was commonly referred to as Elagabalus because, although only about 14 years of age, he was al-

ready the priest of Elagabalus at Emesa, to whom he was fanatically devoted. Elagabalus physically resembled Caracalla, and the idea was floated by Eutychianus (or Gannys, the sources are not in agreement), a member of Maesa's household (which after Domna's death was temporarily re-established in Emesa), suggesting that the young priest should pose as the dead emperor's illegitimate son, dressed in the clothes of his "father." Although (or perhaps because) Eutychianus had been both Elagabalus' tutor and the lover of her daughter Soaemias, Maesa embraced the idea.

Elagabalus was presented to one of the many disgruntled Roman legions near Emesa, which immediately, and not knowing anything about him other than whom he resembled, hailed him emperor and renamed him "Marcus Aurelius Antoninus," to link him more directly to Septimius Severus (who had once enhanced his own popularity by posthumously adopting Marcus Aurelius as his "father"). With Elagabalus emerging as an imperial candidate, a broader revolt against Macrinus erupted to restore the newly discovered "son" of Caracalla to his proper imperial status. After a campaign prominently influenced by Maesa and Soaemias, Macrinus was unseated, having reigned about 14 months. Thus, Elagabalus became Rome's emperor, while Maesa was appointed an "Augusta" in reward for her role in his accession. Unfortunately for Maesa, her desire to become the power behind the throne never quite panned out as she hoped, for she had considered neither the ambitions of her daughter nor the character of her grandson as she fought for his enthronement. Little did Rome know what it was in for.

By the fall of 219, Elagabalus was in Rome, with mother and grandmother in his entourage. Although Maesa attempted to guide and manipulate her imperial grandson, Elagabalus quickly came to relish the perquisites of imperial rule and was urged to do so to an outrageous degree by Soaemias. Soaemias abetted Elagabalus' irresponsible search for pleasure so as to undermine whatever influence either Maesa or Eutychianus had over Elagabalus. Clearly, Soaemias aspired to the public role which Maesa held, and was mostly successful in undermining her mother's temperate influence over Elagabalus. Eutychianus' efforts to abet Maesa's control of Elagabalus was even less successful: Elagabalus and some of his friends, tired of his old tutor's puritanical perorations, simply decided to murder him. Those with artistically "liberated" tastes had little tolerance for one advising respect for traditional Roman values or the necessity of public responsibility.

Elagabalus was perhaps Rome's most irresponsible emperor ever, itself a kind of achievement. Still a teenager and addicted to the fast life of chariot racing and exotic entertainment, he was a cross-dresser who relished playing the role of a woman (he requested of his doctors that they perform a sex-change operation) in the presence of his chosen "husband," a Carian freedman named Hierocles. Whatever his sexual orientation, Elagabalus seemed determined to outrage Roman popular opinion, for—by Roman standards, certainly—he was not only a sexual outlaw, but was also a religious fanatic who proselytized on behalf of his god to the exclusion of Rome's traditional deities. Even more outrageous to his contemporaries, he once mandated that one of Rome's serving Vestal Virgins legally consummate a marriage with him (one of three marriages to women officially contracted while he was in Rome), even though he clearly preferred men as sexual partners. The Vestals constituted one of Rome's oldest and most hallowed religious orders, with virginity being an absolute requirement imposed on all who so served throughout the entirety of their 30-year tenure in office.

In such ways, Elagabalus outraged Roman sensibilities. The problem for four years, however, was how to remove Elagabalus (who was without a heir) without thrusting Rome into another debilitating civil war. This problem was overcome when Elagabalus was convinced (probably with Maesa's connivance) to adopt as his heir, his cousin, Severus Alexander in 221. This son of *Julia Mamaea (Maesa's second daughter) had been kept far away from Elagabalus before the adoption was finalized. The two cousins were very different, and Alexander had no intention of mixing with Elagabalus' crowd. This attitude quickly made him a very popular "anti-Elagabalus" throughout Rome, which naturally both angered and made Elagabalus jealous. As a result, less than a year after Alexander's adoption, Elagabalus began to plan his murder. However, when news of his intentions leaked to the Praetorian Guard (again, probably through Maesa's machinations), it ran amok and executed Elagabalus instead, in a latrine where he had taken refuge with his mother, who was also murdered. Elagabalus was only 18 years old at the time of his death; his body was deposited in the Tiber River.

Thus, Severus Alexander became emperor. Undoubtedly, Maesa expected at last to become the unfettered Augusta her sister had once been, and which she had expected to become when Elagabalus was originally put forward. For a short while, things went as planned, but fate cut

short her impact. In 224, Maesa died, apparently of natural causes.

William Greenwalt,
Associate Professor of Classical History,
Santa Clara University, Santa Clara, California

Julia Soaemias (d. 222)

*Empress of Rome. Name variations: Julia Soaemias Bassiana; Julia Soaemias Augusta; Julia Soemias; Julia Symiamira. Birthdate unknown; died in 222; daughter of *Julia Maesa (c. 170–224 CE) and Gaius Julius Avitus Alexianus also known as Julius Avitus (a Roman senator); married Sextus Varius Marcellus; children: Elagabalus (Roman emperor, with whom she was assassinated).*

Julia Maior

*Sister of Julius Caesar. Name variations: Julia the Elder. Born before 100 BCE; daughter of Gaius Julius Caesar (a patrician who had attained relatively modest political offices) and *Aurelia (c. 120–54 BCE, of the Cotta family); sister of Julius Caesar (100–44 BCE) and Julia Minor (c. 100–51 BCE).*

Julia Mamaea (c. 190–235)

Empress of Rome. Name variations: Julia Avita Mamaea; Julia Mammaea; Julia Mamaea Augusta. Born around 190; died in 235; daughter of Gaius Julius Avitus Alexianus and Julia Maesa (c. 170–224 CE); married twice, the first time to an unknown, the second time to Gessius Marcianus; children: Gessius Bassianus Alexiaus known later as Marcus Aurelius Severus Alexander or Severus Alexander (a Roman emperor); daughter Theocleia.

Julia Mamaea's family rose to prominence with the marriage of her aunt *Julia Domna to Septimius Severus, who subsequently reigned as Rome's emperor. Mamaea's mother, *Julia Maesa, was the sister of Domna. Mamaea's father, Julius Avitus, knew a distinguished career under two emperors but owed most of his success to Maesa's imperial connection. However significant Maesa was to her husband's career, her own historical significance soared after his death because she was to be the reason that Caracalla's murderer, Macrinus, was overthrown and replaced by her grandson, Elagabalus. In power, however, Elagabalus governed irresponsibly and decadently, squandering his initial popularity to the point where even Maesa came to hate him. As a result, Maesa joined forces with her second daughter, Mamaea, to work first for Elagabalus' adoption of his cousin, Mamaea's son Severus Alexander, and then for Elagabalus' deposition. Both of these goals had been accomplished by 222, bringing the 14-year-old Severus Alexander to the throne.

Alexander's father, Gessius Marcianus, from the Syrian town of Arca, was Mamaea's second husband, her first being an unknown of consular rank. Marcianus, too, came to hold high rank but influenced his son's reign almost not at all, for Maesa and Mamaea were to be the powers behind Alexander's throne. It was Mamaea who kept Alexander as far away from Elagabalus as she could before his adoption, permitting him to come to court only once it was clear that Maesa was plotting to replace her older grandson Elagabalus with her younger grandson Alexander. In Rome, Mamaea rigorously chaperoned Alexander to prevent him from falling under Elagabalus' influence. Alexander's distance from his cousin quickly made him popular with the already alienated majority, even as it angered Elagabalus himself. The latter's anger prompted him to conspire Alexander's murder, but when his plot was revealed to the Praetorian Guard (Maesa and Mamaea found it expedient to have

Julia Mamaea

the Guard so informed), the 18-year-old Elagabalus became the Guard's victim, not Alexander.

Alexander thus became emperor in 222, officially as a bastard of Caracalla, a status also once claimed for Elagabalus. Soon after, Mamaea became an "Augusta," thus assuming the status already held by Maesa. For a little over a year, the two women collaborated and together ran the Roman Empire with Alexander as its figurehead, but with Maesa's death in 224, Mamaea began to run the show by herself. Not satisfied with the title of Augusta, Mamaea saw to it that her prominence was broadcast with the addition of such honorifics as: "Mother of the Camp," "Mother of the Senate," "Mother of the Fatherland," and "Mother of the Whole Human Race." Mamaea's hold over Alexander throughout his reign was almost complete, a fact which may have irked him once in a while, but which definitely upset the army and its commanders simply because she was a woman. As long as military affairs were not critical, however, Mamaea's regency was both efficient and enlightened. Certainly, for a time she won over large segments of the civil administration by extensively seeking counsel before pursuing any public policy, and by seeing to it that Rome's traditional gods (the neglect of which had cost Elagabalus dearly) were revered. She also initially won favor by appointing such respected figures as the famous jurist, Ulpian, to the post of Praetorian prefect, and the historian, Cassius Dio, to a variety of consular and proconsular commands. Unfortunately, these nominations eventually backfired, for when such officials tried to impose discipline upon the military units under their command, they ran into more than the usual resistance from the ranks mostly because they were known confidants of the empress (not the emperor), who was truly running the show. Ulpian would be assassinated by his own troops, probably in 224, while Dio would go into exile in 229 to avoid a similar fate.

Tension also developed within the civil administration as a result of Mamaea's ambition to dominate her son completely. For example, not long after she appropriately betrothed Alexander to the daughter of a Roman patrician, namely Gnaea Seia Herennia Sallustia Orba Barbia Orbiana, in 225, Mamaea became jealous of the joint elevations of her daughter-in-law to the status of Augusta and her daughter-in-law's father to the status of Caesar. As a result, Mamaea eventually had Alexander's wife expelled from court and his father-in-law executed (227), actions which both created a substantial civilian opposition to Mamaea's influence and publicized the "effeminacy" of Alexander, now 19 and still under the rule of his mother.

Events began to spin out of Mamaea's control when Ardashir, a Persian underling to the Parthian king Artabanus, overthrew his lord in 224. The Parthians had long been Rome's primary adversaries in the East, but had seen their authority eroded over time, not the least by the military campaigns of Septimius Severus. Thus the time was right for Ardashir to launch his coup, which, having been accomplished, was ratified by his assumption of royal authority in 226, as the king of a revived Persian Empire. The new (Sassanid) dynasty knew a dynamism long lacking in its Parthian predecessors, and as such, its threat to Rome was greater than had been experienced in some time. Once assured of his domestic following, Ardashir turned his attention to his west and in 230 overran the Roman province of Mesopotamia, which had been won by Septimius Severus. Alexander, accompanied by Mamaea, launched a counter-offensive in 231, augmenting the size of his eastern army by stripping his northern frontier of many of its troops. Alexander's military competency was under question, so that when he arrived in the East he first found grumbling and then open opposition to his rule. This initial unrest was stifled, but the mood of Alexander's campaign had been set. There was planned for 232 a three-prong assault upon the newly re-founded Persian Empire, with Alexander supposedly commanding the central force. Although the northern wing of the army saw some success, Alexander was reluctant to proceed into enemy territory and his hesitation cost his southern army large numbers of casualties. Both sides suffered significant losses before Alexander retreated to Antioch. The Persians may have been temporarily checked, but Alexander's reputation suffered irreparable damage: the army now saw him as a coward who did not even possess the backbone of his unpopular mother.

Compounding Alexander's problems was a subsequent German breakthrough along the Rhine frontier for which he readied another campaign, this time by transferring eastern troops to the new breaches. His army thus raised, Alexander assumed his northern command in 234, but, under the influence of Mamaea, he preferred diplomacy to military action. This alone confirmed for the army its estimation of his "manhood," but when it came out that Alexander's diplomacy was constituted of nothing more than an attempt to bribe the German chieftains arrayed before him to go away, his troops became irate, demanding both battle and the money that Alexander was prepared to pay the Germans. Conspiracies abounded, and in 235 an imperial rival, Julius Verus Maximinus, was acclaimed near Mainz. When Alexander heard the news, he handled it in the wrong way: instead of acting decisively, he broke down emotionally before the troops under his immediate command as he reminded them of past favors and accused Maximinus of gross disloyalty. The sight of the sobbing emperor won from his army a short-lived oath of loyalty, but when Maximinus with his following approached the imperial camp, both Alexander and Mamaea were murdered by their own troops. It is said that Alexander died weeping, clutching Mamaea and berating her as the source of all his sorrow. Whatever condemnation might be made of Mamaea's domination of her son's reign, clearly without her Alexander would not have lasted a day. And, although her administration may not have been the most successful, it nevertheless was much better than what the empire was in for: between 235 and 284, the Roman world would face its greatest crisis in half a millennium.

William Greenwalt,
Associate Professor of Classical History,
Santa Clara University, Santa Clara, California

Julia Minor (c. 100–51 BCE)

Younger sister of Julius Caesar and grandmother of the emperor Augustus. Name variations: Julia; Julia the Younger. Born in Rome some time after 100 BCE, the date of her elder brother Julius Caesar's birth; died in Rome in 51 BCE; daughter of Gaius Julius Caesar (a patrician who had attained relatively modest political offices), and Aurelia (c. 120–54 BCE, of the Cotta family); received the education of Roman noble woman; sister of Julia Maior; married Marcus Atius Balbus; children: two daughters, Atia the Elder (c. 80 BCE–?) and Atia the Younger.

Possible witness in the Bona Dea trial of Publius Clodius Pulcher (61 BCE); supervised the upbringing and education of her grandson, the future emperor Augustus (c. 58–51 BCE); at time of death, was lauded in a funeral oration by her grandson (51 BCE).

The Roman system of nomenclature is not the most daunting obstacle to researching the lives of women in Republican times, but it is a frequent source of confusion for moderns. Julia Minor, younger sister of Gaius Julius Caesar the dictator, is only one of dozens of Julias who have come down to us in written record, and it will be helpful to say a few words about women's names in Rome before discussing her life. Every man from a free Roman family possessed at least two names: the *praenomen*, or given name, and the family name, the *nomen*. Frequently a third (or even fourth) name, the *cognomen*, was added to the other two to further distinguish the individual who bore it. Thus Gaius (*praenomen*) Julius (*nomen*) Caesar (*cognomen*). Women, however, usually bore only the feminine form of the family name. Thus the Gaius Julius Caesar under discussion had two sisters, an elder and a younger, both called Julia. To avoid inevitable confusion in such situations, the Romans distinguished their daughters either by adding the word for "older" (*maior*) or "younger" (*minor*) to the family name or, in the case of multiple daughters, by adding an ordinal number to the *nomen*. It is for this reason that Caesar's younger sister is sometimes called Julia Minor, and not because she was of any less importance than his elder sister, about whom we in fact know much less.

Although we have no explicit date, Julia Minor was probably born in the early years of the 1st century BCE, since we know that she was younger than her famous brother and that he was born in the year 100. The Julii were an ancient, and therefore an especially distinguished, family of the first (patrician) rank, and in their own mythology they claimed descent through Iulus, son of Aeneas, the founder of the Roman people, and grandson of the goddess Venus. By the time that Julia Minor's father, also named Gaius Julius Caesar, had entered public life, however, the family's prominence was much diminished: the senior Julius Caesar never attained the consulship, the highest office in the Republic, and his wife *Aurelia came from the Cotta family, which was patrician indeed, but of a much more recent elevation than his own.

We may assume that Julia Minor received the typical education of a Roman noble girl, which might have included spinning and weaving along with Latin and Greek grammar and literature. We do not know the exact date of her marriage to Marcus Atius Balbus, but matrimonial custom in the Republic often saw women married as early as 12; she would most certainly have been married before she had completed her teens. The Balbi were an old patrician family that originated in Aricia, a Latin town just south of Rome. Julia's husband attained the judicial office of praetor before 59 BCE and was a commissioner in an important agrarian law passed by Julius Caesar in the same year. The 1st-century CE biographer Suetonius reports that in factional propaganda directed against Octavian, Balbus' grandson, the family is derided as having stemmed from an African emigrant who owned a perfume shop, bakery, or operated a money-lending business. None of these "charges" is confirmed.

We know Julia principally for her involvement in the upbringing of her grandson between the years 58 and 51. However, she (or less likely, her sister *Julia Maior) is mentioned by Suetonius for her involvement in an infamous event in the chaotic final years of the Roman Republic. The cult of the Bona Dea (the "Good Goddess") was confined solely to women; her yearly celebrations were held in the house of a high civil magistrate in Rome. In 61 BCE, Julia's brother, Julius Caesar, was praetor (as well as Pontifex Maximus, or Chief Priest), and the celebrations were held in his house, under the direction of his second wife *Pompeia. During the celebrations, which included the drinking of wine and culminated in the sacrifice of a sow, it was brought to the attention of Caesar's mother Aurelia that a man disguised as a female harp-player had entered the house. She immediately found the man and ordered him to leave. Later she claimed to have recognized him as Publius Clodius Pulcher, a patrician who was rumored to be having an affair with Pompeia; his imputed purpose for infiltrating the female celebrations was his desire to debauch her in the midst of the activities.

It is no wonder that to the religiously conservative Roman public of the day this rather lurid episode was a shock and provoked great interest. It is chiefly remembered, however, because of the political repercussions it caused during a very unsettled time. A debate ensued among various factions about whether or not Clodius could be tried for his crime, for which there was no recorded precedent, and hence no governing law. Eventually Clodius was tried but found not guilty, despite the fact that both Aurelia and "Caesar's sister Julia" (Suetonius does not specify the elder or the younger) provided the jurors "a faithful account of the whole affair." The wily Caesar, it should be noted, refused to give testimony against Clodius, though as Pontifex Maximus he almost surely had a hand in bringing him to trial. And despite the not-guilty verdict, he still divorced Pompeia, claiming that because he was Supreme Pontiff the members of his family should be free of both accusation and suspicion.

If there is some shadow of doubt as to Julia Minor's participation in the Clodius trial, we can be more certain of her involvement in the upbringing of her grandson. Out of her marriage with Marcus Atius Balbus came two daughters (both, naturally, called Atia), the elder of whom married Gaius Octavius, a wealthy member of the middle social rank, the equestrians (or "knights"), from Velitrae, another ancient Latin town south of Rome. ◄❖ **Atia the Elder** gave Octavius a son, also called Gaius Octavius, on Sep-

❖► *Atia the Elder.* *See Octavia for sidebar.*

tember 23, 63 BCE. After the elder Octavius' death in 59 BCE, Atia married Lucius Marcius Philippus in the following year, and her mother Julia Minor undertook the supervision of her young grandson's education until her death six years later. Her own importance in Roman circles and in the life of her grandson is borne out by the fact that the 12-year-old boy was allowed to deliver her funeral oration before an assembly. This performance is strikingly similar to one of Octavius' uncle Julius Caesar, who had lauded his aunt (yet another *Julia [d. 68 BCE]) at her burial in 68 BCE. Julius Caesar's oration is often seen as an important stepping-stone in his advancing public career; Octavius' may also have marked his entry into public life. Coincidence or not, Octavius' connection with the political goals of his uncle Julius did not stop with the funeral oration of a beloved Julia. Julius Caesar's will both named Octavius his heir and formally adopted him: from this point, Gaius Octavius became Gaius Julius Caesar Octavianus, later to be known simply as "Augustus," the first emperor of the Roman World.

SOURCES AND SUGGESTED READING:

Balsdon, J.P.V.D. *Roman Women: Their History and Habits*. London: Bodley Head, 1962 (reprint ed., Westport, CT: Greenwood, 1975).

Bonner, Stanley F. *Education in Ancient Rome: From the elder Cato to the younger Pliny*. Berkeley, CA: University of California Press, 1977.

Deutsch, Monroe E. "The Women of Caesar's Family," in *Classical Journal*. Vol. 13, 1918, pp. 502–514.

Gelzer, Matthias. *Caesar: Politician and Statesman*. Translated by Peter Needham. Cambridge, MA: Harvard University Press, 1968.

The Oxford Classical Dictionary. 3rd ed. Edited by Simon Hornblower and Antony Spawforth. S.v. "Augustus," "Balbus (1)," "Bona Dea," "Caesar (1)." Oxford: Oxford University Press, 1996.

Paulys Real-Encyclopädie der Classischen Alterumswissenschaft. Edited by Georg Wissowa, *et al.* S.v. "Julia 546." Stuttgart: J.B. Metzlersche Buchhandlung, 1894–1980.

Suetonius: Lives of the Caesars. Translated by J.C. Rolfe. The Loeb Classical Library. Cambridge, MA: Harvard University Press, 1960.

Peter H. O'Brien
teaches English and Classics at Boston University Academy, Boston, Massachusetts

Julia Paula (fl. 220 CE)

Roman empress. Born Julia Cornelia Paula; married Varius Avitus Bassianus Marcus Aurelius Antoninus, known as Elagabalus, Roman emperor (r. 218–222), in 219 (divorced 220/221).

Julia Paula was the first of Roman emperor Elagabalus' three wives (he was also married to Aquilia Severa and Annia Faustina). Julia Paula married him in 219 and was divorced between 220 and 221.

Julia Soaemias (d. 222).

See Julia Maesa for sidebar.

Julia the Elder.

See Julia Maior.

Julia the Younger (c. 100–51 BCE).

See Julia Minor.

Julian of Norwich (c. 1342–c. 1416)

English Christian mystic and theologian best known for her Revelations of Divine Love. Name variations: St. Juliane in Norwice. Pronunciation: JEW-lee-an of NOR-which. Born around December 1342, probably near Norwich, England; died around 1416 (although some have speculated as late as 1423), in an anchorhold attached to the church of St. Julian in Norwich; parents and education unknown; never married; no children.

As a girl, wished for three gifts from God, including an illness, which she endured at age 30; received a series of 16 revelations of God's love when thought to be at the point of death; shortly after, wrote an account of her experience; in an expanded version of her recollections, written 20 years later, included her understanding of their meaning; became an anchoress at the church of St. Julian in Conisford at Norwich and adopted the name of the church as her own, which is all we know of her given name; apparently remained in her cell until her death.

Selected writings: Revelations of Divine Love, also referred to as Showings (the work exists in two versions, the early account known as the "Short Text" and the longer and later version known as the "Long Text").

In May 1373, the woman who became known as Julian of Norwich lay gravely ill, gradually losing feeling throughout her body until she could no longer speak. On the third day, expected to die, she received the last rites of the church; on the fifth day, May 13, at four o'clock in the morning, her mother and her parish priest stood at her bedside, in anticipation of her death. When she showed signs of reviving a little, the priest set a cross before her face and told her to look at it. Suddenly, Julian felt the departure of all pain. As a child, she had asked for three graces from God—a longing for God, an experience of feeling Christ's suffering, and an illness to test her commitment to God. Now recognizing her illness as the first of the gifts, she prayed that her body might be "completely filled with the recollection and feeling of His blessed Passion," so that she might show her love for God by suffering with Christ.

Then, she experienced a vision of Christ's suffering so authentic that she exclaimed, "Blessed be the Lord." The moment was the beginning of a succession of 15 visions lasting over the next five hours, followed a day later by her 16th and final vision, amounting to an experience so profoundly astonishing that she was to puzzle over its meaning for the next 20 years. It also secured Julian's place in history, through the two accounts that she wrote, which are lauded not only as a fascinating look at the life of a medieval woman, but as an amazingly original and insightful understanding of the doctrines of Christianity.

Everything that we know about Julian of Norwich is based on her book *Revelations of Divine Love*. It mentions nothing about her family and makes only two references to her youth. We assume that she was born in late 1342 or early 1343 because she writes that she was 30½ at the time of her revelatory experience. Besides telling us that she prayed as a girl for three graces or gifts from God, she mentions that during one of her visions Christ thanked her for her service and labor as a youth. The meaning of this is not entirely clear since she makes no further reference to her service, and, at the time of her writing, an adult under 30 might still be described as a "youth." Although we know nothing about her educational background, some have speculated that she was educated in a nearby nunnery or might have received education as a nun, based on the amazing depth of knowledge about Christianity evident in her book; all of these theories, however, have been disputed.

The strongest clue to Julian's history comes from a preface to the short version of her book, which refers to the author as: "Julian, who is a recluse at Norwich and still alive, A.D. 1413." Thus we know not only that Julian is from Norwich, a town in England, but that she lived the life of a recluse, or anchoress. Four wills from this same period mention an anchoress named Julian of Norwich as a beneficiary, suggesting that Julian lived with a maidservant in a room adjoining the parish church of St. Julian in Conisford at Norwich, probably named for Julian the Hospitaller, patron saint of ferryworkers.

An anchoress, sometimes referred to as a recluse, was a woman who lived an enclosed life dedicated to prayer. A man in this role was called an anchorite, and the plural for both is anchorites. The word comes from the Greek, mean-

ing "I withdraw" or "retire," and the lifestyle has its roots in the "desert fathers," early Christians who retreated from the distractions of community life to concentrate on meditation and devotion to God. An anchoress could be a maiden or widow who chose this form of religious devotion as an alternative to becoming a nun, or a nun who wanted a more advanced form of monasticism. Like hermits, anchorites lived alone, but unlike hermits they did not roam around the countryside. Instead, an anchoress was locked into a room, sometimes called a "cell," which she could not leave for the rest of her life.

In order to become an anchoress, a woman had to receive the approval of a bishop, who rigorously investigated the sincerity of her desire to live a solitary life of prayer as well as her ability to pay for the necessary food and clothing during her confinement. This concern was crucial since the bishop was ultimately responsible for the support of all anchorites. If the candidate was approved, a service of enclosure was performed in which she publicly proclaimed her desire to be enclosed, was sprinkled with holy water, and marched to her room along with the bishop and members of the congregation. The bishop declared her dead to the world and alive unto God and walked out of the room, closing the door behind him; the penalty for violating her vows was excommunication.

While this choice of such a solitary life may be hard for modern readers to imagine, it was not considered extreme in its day. The anchoress might spend her days teaching girls, counseling women and men, and doing needlework which could be sold for food and clothing. It is generally believed that the enclosure at Norwich was a room comfortable in size, built against the side of the church of St. Julian, with a window pierced through the interior wall so that the anchoress could follow the daily service. Through a window to the outside, Julian could talk to people who came to her for counsel, and a third window opened to another room which housed the personal servant responsible for her cooking, cleaning, and other household tasks. From bequests in wills of the time, we know two of Julian's servants were named Sara and Alice.

A book entitled *The Ancrene Rule* suggests that anchorites were not asked to starve or required to wear a particular type of dress. In all things they were expected to practice moderation, so that they could focus on their real task, development of love for God through prayer. An anchoress was to be like the sisters *Martha and Mary of Bethany*. Mary sat and listened to Jesus while Martha, like the servant to the anchoress, prepared supper. "And Mary's part is quietness and rest from all the world's din, that nothing may hinder her from hearing the voice of God." To increase the likelihood of hearing a divine voice, the rule suggested that an anchoress follow a schedule of prayer seven times a day and limit the time spent counseling and talking with her servant.

Grace Jantzen observes that the greatest temptation for an anchoress was impatience or boredom with her life of prayer which could lead to other temptations, the largest of which was gossip through her window with passersby. Thus, the Ancrene Rule advises women to be as silent as possible, following *Mary the Virgin, mother of Jesus, rather than *Eve, who chatted with the serpent. "Now my dear sisters, keep your eyes far from all evil speech that is of this threefold kind, idle, foul and poisonous. . . . Christ knows this is a sorry saying! that an anchorhouse, which should be the loneliest place of all, can be compared to these three places that are most full of gossip." Such warnings had the effect of reminding an anchoress of her human weaknesses and correcting any misconception that enclosure alone would keep her safe from temptation.

As an anchoress, Julian would have received respect from local people. The 14th century has been called "The Golden Age of the English Recluse." There is evidence that at least 28 women and 47 men lived in anchorholds in Norfolk during the 14th and 15th centuries. Towns such as Norwich valued anchorites for their spiritual guidance and prayers. Since this was also the time of the plague which decimated the population of England, and the Hundred Years' War that greatly increased economic hardship, people had much for which to pray. Norwich was a wealthy city, second only to London in size, and home to a thriving wool trade, as well as many churches and schools, but also deeply affected in Julian's time by social upheaval. In 1369, it was looted during a violent peasant revolt, which was put down by the equally brutal reprisals carried out by the local bishop. In 1397, a pit for burning religious radicals belonging to a group called Lollards was built within sight of Julian's cell. During these trying times, it is likely that people sought out Julian for prayers and support.

The solitary life of the anchoress would have given Julian the privilege of privacy, independence, and economic stability needed for writing. Many scholars explain the existence of the two versions of the *Revelations of Divine Love* by arguing that Julian became an anchoress after writing the Short Text and wrote the Long Text after contemplating its meaning for 20 years. This the-

ory cannot be proven since the first reference we have to Julian as an anchoress is in 1393, 20 years after the publication of the long text, but the fact that the other three best known 14th century mystic writers—Richard Rolle, Walter Hilton, and the anonymous author of *The Cloud of Unknowing*—all lived solitary lives is taken as evidence in its support.

> *Because I am a woman should I therefore believe that I ought not to tell you about the goodness of God since I saw at the same time that it is his will that it be known?*
>
> —Julian of Norwich

If Julian wrote while enclosed, her writing gives us an interesting perspective on the self-understanding of an anchoress. Living such a specialized life, Julian might be expected to write for the benefit of those like herself, yet she states that her concern is for the common Christian. "Everything I say about myself," she writes, "I intend to apply toward all my fellow Christians, for I am instructed that this is what our Lord intended in this spiritual revelation. . . . I am not trying to tell the wise something they know already, but I am seeking to tell the uninstructed, for their peace and comfort." She is careful in her insistence that her writing will not lead common people astray: "In everything I believe as Holy Church preaches and teaches. For the faith of Holy Church, which I had before I had understanding . . . I intend to preserve whole." It may be to insure the orthodoxy of her ideas for her readers that she pondered over the meaning of her experience for 20 years.

The most important independent witness to the life of Julian is another English mystic, *Margery Kempe, whose biography includes a description of her meeting in 1413 with an anchoress named "Dame Julian." Margery had also experienced some strange spiritual revelations and went to Julian for advice and council, because she was "well known to be an expert in spiritual guidance." Julian's advice to Margery confirms our image of Julian as compassionate and concerned for others. She accepted the validity of Margery's experience and advised her to trust in it. Margery wrote that Julian advised her: "set all your trust in God and fear not the language of the world. . . . Patience is necessary to you, for in that you shall keep your soul." **Joan Nuth** observes that this confirmation of Margery was "the comfort that Margery needed, voiced by an authority that Margery's world was compelled to acknowledge." Wrote Margery: "Much was the holy dalliance that the anchoress and this creature [Margery] had by communing in the love of Our Lord Jesus Christ the many days that they were together."

For her part, Julian does not mention Margery or anything else about her life as an anchoress. Neither does she make reference to the social turmoils of her day. She does not even tell us her real name, but rather adopts the name of the church in which she resides, a common practice of anchorites. Instead, her writing focuses on what she considers to be the only really important part of her history, the 16 revelations. While some of her visions are visual, others are aural and still others are moments of intellectual insight; all, however, center on understanding the suffering of Christ. In her first vision, it is the sight of blood running down from Christ's head as the crown of thorns is placed on his brow that fills her with a new awareness of how Christ, and therefore God, suffers for her. She states that she is astonished by this "wonder and marvel" which indicates to her the nearness of God.

Modern scholars have struggled with understanding these visions. Some have speculated that Julian was delirious or mentally ill, but in 1958 Paul Molinari argued for the validity of her experience, and his arguments have been generally accepted. In her own day, such visions would be considered highly unusual but not fabrications. The three gifts or graces for which Julian prayed are typical of the piety of the time, which stressed awareness of the passion of Christ as the means towards spiritual growth. Art of the time also emphasized the theme of pity for Christ's suffering, often depicting the thinness of Christ's body and the agony on Mary's face as she looks at the cross.

Julian writes that the desire for three graces was inspired by the story of *St. Cecilia, who received three physical wounds and died. Her desire for an illness is suggested in the *Ancrene Rule,* which urges aspiring anchorites to cultivate an awareness of Christ's physical sufferings and the healing effects of illness sent by God in order to feel confidence that their own sins were forgiven. **Caroline Bynum** has outlined the frequency of visions among women mystics of the Middle Ages and **Elizabeth Petroff** has argued that for women, who had little access to education, visions served as the primary texts of their religious understanding. States Julian: "What is truly important is not the fact of these experiences themselves, but the deepened love of God which results from them and insights communicated with them." In the Long Text, she admits that after struggling with the meaning of her revelations

she realized the key: "I knew it well, love was His meaning. Who shows it to you? Love. What did He show you? Love. Why did He show it to you? For love. In this love we have our beginning and in all this we shall see God eternally."

The main theme of her book is understanding the nature of divine love as it relates to the church's teaching about the pervasiveness of sin. How can a loving God condemn humanity for their sin? And, given the reality of sin, how can Christians ever hope that "all shall be well" in eternity? Julian answers such questions through exploring the meaning of one of her visions. Commonly referred to as the parable of the Lord and Servant, this vision describes how the mystery of God's love surpasses the logic of human reason. To describe the quality of that love, Julian describes Christ as our Mother: "And so in our making, God almighty is our loving Father, and God all wisdom is our loving Mother, with the love and goodness of the Holy Spirit, which is all one God, one Lord." The result is an overwhelming confidence in the ultimate mercy of God's love to grant humans life everlasting.

While Julian is not unique in exploring the theme of the motherhood of God (Anselm also refers to this theme), she develops this idea more thoroughly than any other theologian of her time. In doing so, she deviates from the bulk of theological writing of her day, which focused on divine judgment. By comparing the two versions of her text, we catch a glimpse of the difficulty of claiming her own ideas, as well as her growing confidence as a thinker and writer. In the sixth chapter of the Short Text, she urges her readers not to think of her as a teacher, "for I am a woman, ignorant, weak, and frail," yet she speculates that at the same time it was God's will that she tell others about the goodness of God. She suggests that her readers will understand this better as they read, that is, if her writing is "well and truly accepted." The chapter ends with an assertion that Jesus is the true teacher, and that the teaching revealed to her did not lead her astray from "the true doctrine of the holy Church."

In the Long Text, this entire section is replaced by a simple statement that the revelation was given to her to teach "our souls wisely to adhere to the goodness of God." The deletion is in stark contrast to the rest of the Long Text, which generally amplifies the earlier version. Unique to the Long Text, which expands 25 chapters of the Short Text to 86, are two of the author's most important theological themes, explored in the parable of the Lord and Servant (chapters 51–57) and the motherhood of Christ (chapters 58–61). Throughout the Long Text, also, are assertions of the orthodoxy of the writer's ideas especially in regard to sin, salvation, and the nature of God, which seem to be included more to comfort the reader than to defend herself against critics.

Few copies of Julian's work have survived, suggesting that it had limited appeal in her time. Some copies may have been destroyed during the English reformation and the dissolution of monasteries in the 16th century, or the work may have been judged heretical. Readers are warned in notes added to the end of the Long Text to accept and understand it all as in agreement with scripture, rather than take sections out of context, which is the downfall of heretics. In any case, there are only three complete manuscripts of the Long Text, and one known copy of the Short Text, included in an anthology of short spiritual texts. The earliest copy of the Long Text, found in Paris, is probably from the 17th century and was most likely brought to France by monks and nuns who had fled from England.

Julian remained a little-known figure until this century which has seen revived interest in her work, especially her ideas about the motherhood of God, as a source of mystical and theological insight. One indication that she has achieved status as a significant Christian mystic and writer is the fact that Julian's book was published as the first volume of the acclaimed series *Classics of Western Spirituality.*

In May 1973, an ecumenical celebration was held in Norwich to commemorate the 600th anniversary of Julian's revelations. One can still find evidence of her influence at the Julian shrine, where prayer and spiritual counsel continue in a chapel built where her cell once stood. As her popularity grows, Julian's message of God's love may indeed become well known.

SOURCES:

Jantzen, Grace. *Julian of Norwich: Mystic and Theologian.* NY: Paulist Press, 1988.

Jones, Catherine. "The English Mystic: Julian of Norwich," in *Medieval Women Writers.* Edited by Katharina M. Wilson. Athens, GA: University of Georgia Press, 1984, pp. 269–296.

Julian of Norwich. *Showings.* Translated by Edmund Colledge and James Walsh. NY: Paulist Press, 1978.

Nuth, Joan. *Wisdom's Daughter: The Theology of Julian of Norwich.* NY: Crossroad, 1991.

Wolters, Clifton. Introduction to *Revelations of Divine Love* by Julian of Norwich. NY: Penguin Books, 1966.

SUGGESTED READING:

Bynum, Caroline Walker. *Jesus as Mother: Studies in the Spirituality of the High Middle Ages.* Berkeley, CA: University of California Press, 1982.

Petroff, Elizabeth Alvilda. *Medieval Women's Visionary Literature.* NY: Oxford University Press, 1986.

Jane McAvoy,
Associate Professor of Theology,
Lexington Theological Seminary, Kentucky

Juliana (1729–1796).

See Caroline Matilda for sidebar on Maria Juliana of Brunswick, queen of Denmark and Norway.

Juliana, queen of the Netherlands (b. 1909).

See Queen Wilhelmina for sidebar.

Juliana Falconieri (1270–1341).

See Falconieri, Juliana.

Juliana Marie (1729–1796).

See Caroline Matilda for sidebar on Maria Juliana of Brunswick, queen of Denmark and Norway.

Juliana of Cornillon (1192–1258)

Saint. Born in Rhétines in 1192; died in Fosses in 1258.

A nun at Liége, Juliana of Cornillon was instrumental in establishing the feast of Corpus Christi. Her feast day is April 5.

Juliana of Nicomedia (d. about 305)

Saint. Died around 305; daughter of Africanus.

Legend surrounds the story of Juliana of Nicomedia. Supposedly, her father Africanus betrothed her to a young noble named Evilase (Evilatius). Juliana, it is said, informed her intended that she would not marry him until he became prefect of Nicomedia. He did so. She then reneged, demanding that he become a Christian before their marriage. Evilase refused. Africanus inflicted "every kind of ill treatment" on his daughter before he gave up and handed her over to Evilase. After subjecting her to torture, including casting her into a furnace only to have the fire go out, Evilase had her beheaded. In all this, the only certainty is that Juliana was put to death for her faith under the rule of either Maximian or Galerius in 305. Her feast day is February 16.

Juliana of Norwich (c. 1342–c. 1416).

See Julian of Norwich.

Juliane of Nassau-Dillenburg (1546–1588)

*Countess Rudolstadt. Born on February 11, 1546; died on August 31, 1588; daughter of *Juliane of Stolberg-Wernigrode (1506–1580) and William (1487– 1559), count of Nassau-Dillenburg (r. 1516–1559); sister of William I the Silent (1533–1584), prince of Orange, and stadholder of Holland, Zealand, and Utrecht (r. 1572–1584); married Albert VII (1537–1605), count Rudolstadt, on June 14,*

*1575; children: **Anna Sibylle** (1584–1623, who married Christian Gunther, count Sonderhausen).*

Juliane of Norwice (c. 1342–c. 1416).

See Julian of Norwich.

Juliane of Stolberg-Wernigrode (1506–1580)

*Countess of Nassau-Dillenburg. Name variations: Juliana of Stolberg-Wernigerode; Juliane von Stolberg-Wernigerode. Born on February 27, 1506; died on June 18, 1580; daughter of Botho III, count of Stolberg-Wernigrode, and **Anna von Eppenstein**; became second wife of William (1487–1559), count of Nassau-Dillenburg (r. 1516–1559), on September 20, 1531; children: William I the Silent (1533–1584), prince of Orange, and stadholder of Holland, Zealand, and Utrecht (r. 1572–1584); John (b. 1536), count of Nassau-Dillenburg; *Juliane of Nassau-Dillenburg (1546–1588). William, count of Nassau-Dillenburg, was first married to **Walpurgis von Egmont** (1505–1529).*

Julianna du Guesdin (fl. 1370)

French nun. Name variations: Julienne du Guesdin. Flourished in 1370 in Brittany; never married; no children.

Julianna du Guesdin played a small but unusual role in protecting France from English aggression during the Hundred Years' War. In 1370, a small English war troop tried to take the Breton convent where she was a cloistered nun, but found that the nuns, under Julianna's leadership, would not give it up easily. The warriors tried storming over the walls but Julianna rallied her sisters to stay firm, and eventually the Englishmen were forced to give up in defeat.

Laura York,
Riverside, California

Julianna of Ruthenia (fl. 1377)

*Grand princess of Lithuania and mother of the king of Poland. Flourished around 1377; married Olgierd, grand prince of Lithuania (died 1377); children: Jagiello, grand duke of Lithuania (1377–1434, who became Ladislas or Vladislav II [or V] Jagello, king of Poland and married *Jadwiga (1374–1399]).*

Julie, Chévalier de Maupin (c. 1670–1707).

See Maupin, d'Aubigny.

Juliers, duchess of.

See Joan of Hainault (c. 1310–?).

See Mary of Guelders (d. 1405).
See Mary (1531–1581).

Julitta of Caesarea (d. about 305)

Saint. Died around 305; lived in Caesarea, Cappadocia. Her feast day is July 30.

From a homily of St. Basil, it is known that Julitta was a wealthy widow who lived in Caesarea, Cappadocia. Taken advantage of by a unscrupulous townsman who sought to rob her of her property, she brought suit against him. Just as it looked as if the judge would rule in her favor, the man made one last impassioned plea before the forum. "This woman," he proclaimed, "ought not to appear in court, for she is a Christian; and those who refuse to adore the gods of the emperors enjoy no civil right." Indeed, the imperial edict of 303 did place Christians outside the law, and the president of the tribunal had an altar and incense brought in and requested that Julitta sacrifice to the idols. "May my body perish rather than deny God, my Creator!," she cried. Further professing to be Christ's servant, she not only lost her property, but was condemned to the stake. Accepting her fate calmly, Julitta smiled to her friends in consolation and urged them to also suffer for Christ should it become necessary, then flung herself on the pyre. Reputedly, the fire choked her without destroying her body. It was also said that at the place of her torture, a spring arose which sometimes healed the sick.

Jumel, Eliza Bowen (1775–1865)

Infamous American beauty and second wife of former vice-president Aaron Burr. Name variations: Betsy Bowen; Eliza Brown. Born in 1775 in Providence, Rhode Island; died on July 16, 1865; daughter of John Bowen and Phebe Kelley; married Stephen Jumel, on April 9, 1804 (died 1832); married former vice-president Aaron Burr, on July 1, 1833 (divorced 1836); children: (illegitimate) George Washington Bowen (b. October 9, 1794); (adopted) Mary Eliza (the illegitimate daughter of Eliza Jumel's half-sister Polly Clarke).

Although Eliza Jumel claimed that her family name was Capet and that her mother died in childbirth while on a ship traveling to the West Indies, she was in fact born to one **Phebe Kelley** in Rhode Island in 1775. Her father John Bowen was a sailor, and it is unclear if her parents were married. Bowen was also the father of Eliza's older sister, although probably not of her two younger siblings; he was not around much and had drowned in Newport harbor by the time

Eliza was 11. Her mother supported the family mainly through prostitution until she married, or remarried, in 1790. Eliza, known as Betsy, was at that time living on her own and most likely supporting herself as a prostitute. She had an illegitimate son, George Washington Bowen, in October of 1794 and gave him to foster parents when she moved to New York City a few weeks later.

Information about the next five years of her life is sketchy, although she may have been the wife or mistress of Jacques de la Croix, a French sea captain. However, by 1800 she was living under the name of Eliza Brown in a mansion at Whitehall and Pearl streets as the mistress of Stephen Jumel, a wealthy French wine merchant who had moved to New York five years previously. Although Stephen was popular with New York society, Eliza was ostracized even after the couple married in 1804.

By 1810, the Jumels had moved into a 19-room mansion in Washington Heights. The house was renowned in the city and had been one of George Washington's headquarters during the Revolutionary War; however, neither this fact nor the couple's extravagant entertainments were enough to win them acceptance into society.

The Jumels left for France with an adopted daughter, Mary Eliza (the illegitimate daughter of Eliza's half sister **Polly Clarke**), on June 1, 1815. In France the couple found the acceptance they longed for among Parisian aristocrats. Stephen also learned more about his wife's scandalous early life, however, and in 1816 she returned to New York without him. Jumel lived in the New York mansion with her daughter for five years before returning to Stephen in France. Once again she took up her social role, but by that time her husband's money had begun to run out. In 1826, he sent her back to New York with instructions to sell the property there and send him the money. Jumel did sell the property for a large sum, but kept the money herself. Nearly broke, Stephen came to New York in 1828 and on May 22, 1832, fell from a haycart and died.

The following July, Eliza Jumel married 77-year old Aaron Burr. The former vice-president, notorious both for the 1804 duel in which he had killed founding father Alexander Hamilton and for an unrelated trial on treason charges (at which he was acquitted), was sorely in need of funds. The marriage appears to have been based on Jumel's desire for social acceptance and Burr's desire for money, and was never a happy one; she began divorce proceedings just a year after the wedding. The divorce was granted on September 14, 1836, the day Burr died.

Jumel spent the next 28 years moving around the New York area, chasing after and being rebuffed by society until gradually she grew more reclusive. In 1843, her daughter died, and Jumel's son-in-law, Nelson Chase, and two grandchildren were virtually her only visitors until a permanent falling-out deprived her even of them. Her last years were spent in the deteriorating mansion in Washington Heights, "half-insane" and seeing no one but her servants. She died on July 16, 1865, around the age of 90, and was buried in Trinity Cemetery.

Eliza Jumel left most of her estate to charity, but the courts set aside her will on the basis of mental incompetence; her illegitimate son made an unsuccessful claim for the estate, and it was eventually awarded to Nelson Chase and his children. The Jumel mansion, bought in 1903 by the City of New York, is one of Manhattan's historical landmarks.

SOURCES:

James, Edward T., ed. *Notable American Women, 1607–1950*. Cambridge, MA: The Belknap Press of Harvard University Press, 1971.

Karina L. Kerr, M.A.,
Ypsilanti, Michigan

June (1829–1901).

See Croly, Jane Cunningham.

Junia (fl. 1st c. BCE)

Roman noblewoman. Flourished in the 1st century BCE; daughter of Servilia (c. 100–after 42 BCE) and D. Junius Silanus (a consul); married M. Aemilius Lepidus.

Junia (fl. 1st c. BCE)

Roman noblewoman. Flourished in the 1st century BCE; daughter of Servilia (c. 100–after 42 BCE) and D. Junius Silanus (a consul); married P. Servilius Isauricus.

Junia (fl. 1st c. BCE)

Roman noblewoman. Flourished in the 1st century BCE; daughter of Servilia (c. 100–after 42 BCE) and D. Junius Silanus (a consul); married C. Cassius Longinus, better known as Cassius (an assassin of Julius Caesar).

Junia Claudilla (fl. 32 CE)

Roman noblewoman. Flourished around 32 CE; first wife of Caligula (12–41), Roman emperor (r. 37–41).

Sometime between 32 and 37 CE, Junia Claudilla became the first wife of Caligula on the island of Capri, at the urging of Tiberius.

Following Junia Claudilla's death, Caligula married **Livia Orestilla**.

Junkin, Margaret (1820–1897).

See Preston, Margaret Junkin.

Junko Tabei (b. 1939).

See Tabei, Junko.

Junot, Madame (1784–1838).

See Abrantès, Laure d'.

Jurado, Katy (b. 1927).

See Del Rio, Dolores for sidebar.

Jurca, Branca (1914—)

Slovenian writer, best known for her autobiography You're Only Born Once. *Name variations: Branka Jurca. Born near Sezana, Slovenia, in 1914; educated in Maribor.*

Worked as a teacher, editor and freelance author; was a member of the anti-Nazi resistance during World War II; survived concentration camps to complete her education and embark on a writing career.

Although Slovenia was, along with Croatia, the most prosperous region of Yugoslavia before the country's breakup, a literary culture developed relatively late in this part of Europe. The first full-length novel written in the Slovenian language, Josip Jurcic's *Deseti brat* (*The Tenth Brother*), was not published until 1866. By 1918, however, a rich intellectual culture had developed in Slovenia, and different schools of writing were experimenting with the newest trends as well as continuing to build on older, more traditional forms of expression.

Branca Jurca was born near Sezana in 1914. Her life was disrupted by World War II, which resulted in occupation of Yugoslavia by Italian and German forces and led to the emergence of a national anti-Fascist resistance movement. Jurca was active in the resistance as a partisan. She was captured and sent to two concentration camps, first to Gonars and then to Ravensbrück, the notorious camp for women in Germany. Jurca survived the camps and in 1945 returned to Yugoslavia, which was now a Communist republic led by war hero Marshal Josip Broz Tito. Trained as a teacher, she taught for a number of years. In addition, she wrote and published several books and articles, eventually becoming a full-time editor and freelance writer who concentrated on books for young readers. In her autobiographical 1972 volume *Rodis se samo enkrat* (*You're Only Born Once*), Jurca won critical praise for depicting with clarity and wisdom a childhood that was marred by war and social upheaval.

In her well-received 1974 novel *Ko zorijo jagode* (*When the Berries Bloom*), the bittersweet joys and crises of adolescence are depicted with sensitivity and insight. The novel tells the story of a romantic triangle between two girls, Jagoda and Nejc, who both are interested in Dragi, a teenager in turmoil because of his unstable family life. The story was filmed in Slovenia under the title *Strawberry Time*, with Rajko Ranfl directing, and was produced by Viba Films with support from the Slovenian Film Fund. Jurca's books have been popular in Slovenia for a generation.

SOURCES:

Davison, Milena. "The Waste Land in a State of Siege: Comments on the Contemporary Slovene Novel," in *Slovene Studies: Journal of the Society for Slovene Studies*. Vol. 3, no. 2, 1981, pp. 72–86.

Jurca, Branca. *Ko zorijo jagode*. Ljubljana: Mladinska knjiga, 1980.

——. *Pod Bicem: podobe iz taborise*. Ljubljana: Izdala zalozba Nasa zena, 1945.

——. *Rodis se samo enkrat*. Ljubljana: Mladinska knjiga, 1984.

Pynsent, Robert B., and S.I. Kanikova, eds. *Reader's Encyclopedia of Eastern European Literature*. NY: HarperCollins, 1993.

John Haag,
Associate Professor of History,
University of Georgia, Athens, Georgia

Juric, Maria (1873–1957).

See Zagorka, Maria.

Jurinac, Sena (1921—)

Bosnian soprano. Born Srebrenka Jurinac on October 24, 1921, in Travnik, Yugoslavia; married Sesto Bruscantini (a baritone), in 1953 (divorced 1957); married Josef Lederle, in 1975; studied with Milka Kostrencic in Zagreb.

Made debut at Zagreb (1942), Vienna Staatsoper (1945), Salzburg (1957), Teatro all Scala (1948), Glyndebourne (1949), Chicago (1963).

Born in Yugoslavia in 1921, Sena Jurinac was one of many fine sopranos championed by Herbert von Karajan who also brought *Elisabeth Schwarzkopf*, *Lisa Della Casa* and *Hilde Gueden* to international attention. Sena Jurinac had one of the most beautiful voices of her time, and she specialized in Mozart and Strauss whose styles suited that voice. She was also a naturally gifted, charismatic actress, popular with operatic audiences. Known for her Butterfly, Tosca, and Donna Anna, Jurinac excelled in tragedy, though she sang a number of comic roles with great success. Less impassioned than some of her contemporary sopranos, Jurinac was involving nonetheless. Unfortunately, she made few recordings, probably because of competition from *Maria Callas and *Renata Tebaldi. Those that do exist preserve her poised attack and incandescent tone.

SUGGESTED READING:

Tamussino, U. *Sena Jurinac*. Augsburg, 1971.

John Haag,
Athens, Georgia

Justin, Enid (1894–1990)

American boot manufacturer who became a leader in the industry. Name variation: Miss Enid. Born Enid Justin in Nocona, Texas, near the Red River, on April 8, 1894; died on October 14, 1990, in Nocona; daughter of Herman Joseph Justin and Anna (Allen) Justin (pioneer Texas bootmakers); completed the seventh grade in the Nocona public school system; married Julius L. Stelzer, on August 6, 1915 (divorced 1935); married Harry Whitman, on November 9, 1940 (divorced 1945); children: (first marriage) Anna Jo (1916–1918).

Left Nocona school at 13 to work in father's boot factory (1907); only child died and father died (1918); brothers moved boot company to Fort Worth (1925); opened Nocona Boot Company (1925); built larger boot factory and relocated it away from downtown area in Nocona (1948); after several expansions, plant reached its greatest size (1981); following controversial legal action, Nocona Boot Company merged with Justin Industries, and Justin effectively retired (1981).

During the 1970s and 1980s, when Western wear temporarily became *haute couture* for the chic, Nocona boots were often the footwear of choice. Not many of the would-be ranch hands realized that they were wearing boots bearing the name of a small Texas town near the Red River. Fewer still knew that their boots were the product of determination and hard work by a Texas woman, known affectionately in the area as "Miss Enid." Enid Justin had started the Nocona Boot Company in 1925, becoming in the process the first woman in what was truly the male-dominated world of bootmaking.

She was born into a family of bootmakers. Her father Herman Joseph Justin, the son of German immigrants, began making boots in Spanish Fort, Texas, soon after migrating there from Indiana in 1878. He had been a cobbler in nearby Gainesville but moved to Spanish Fort, where the Chisholm Trail crossed the Red River, and where the herds' drovers congregated. When the Missouri, Kansas and Texas Railroad was built through Nocona in 1889, Herman Justin moved there and opened his first boot factory. He called his enterprise, "H.J. Justin and Sons," and made Justin Boots.

Sena Jurinac

Enid Justin learned the business from the bottom up. While still a child in 1907, she quit school and was given a job in the plant. Just 13, she had been suspended by the school principal for dancing at her brother's birthday party. Angry because of the injustice, she received permission to end her few years of formal education. The Justins were a close-knit family. As a consequence, Enid had few contacts with males outside her home. In a day when women married young, Justin was 21 before dating and marrying Julius L. Stelzer, a telegrapher for Western Union.

After the marriage, she and Stelzer moved to Hollister, Oklahoma, where he became depot master for a few weeks. Homesick, Enid convinced Julius to return to Nocona and work for her father. She too resumed work, but became pregnant and decided to quit. She gave birth to her only child, Anna Jo, on December 26, 1916. A year and a month later, on January 27, 1918, the baby died during an epidemic of whooping cough and measles. Although Enid and Julius remained married until 1934, family life was never the same. Still, Justin did not return to work until after her brothers decided to move the boot company to Fort Worth in 1925.

John and Earl Justin had operated Justin Boots for seven years after their father's death in 1918. The Fort Worth Chamber of Commerce, interested in having the company come to their city, offered the brothers a building site and tax abatement for several years. Convinced that relocation would help sales and make diversification possible, they moved to Fort Worth despite Enid Justin's opposition. When she told them that she intended to stay in Nocona and start her own boot company, brother Earl warned her that cowboy boots wouldn't be around much longer.

I've always been accused of having a pretty big ego, of being strong-willed, aggressive and a staunch businesswoman. I plead guilty to all of the above.

—Enid Justin

Even though Enid decided to stay in Nocona, she kept her stock in the family concern, claiming that "nobody wanted to buy it." She then borrowed $5,000 from the local bank and began operation of her own company. Her husband became the first president, since "ranchers and cowhands wanted a man in charge," but Enid Justin ran the business. She rented a small building (1,000 square feet) that had been one of her father's early plants and leased the machinery necessary for bootmaking from United Machine Company in St. Louis. Most of the skilled workers had gone to Fort Worth, but five remained. With this nucleus, the Nocona Boot Company opened its doors for business on September 1, 1925. It was chartered by the state during the next year, having ten stockholders and a five-member board of directors by 1926.

During the first year of operation, Justin divided the production line into various departments, including those for cutting, fitting, and lasting. To meet expenses at the plant, she was forced to turn her "home into a rooming house." She also "cooked for boarders, sewed and ironed for people, peddled coal . . . and sold washing machines," to make financial accounts balance. Her wages were $3 a week; Julius received $15. Justin worked night and day acting as shipping clerk, stenographer, and anything else that was needed. She was the company's first traveling salesperson and, with her sister as a companion, drove the dusty and occasionally muddy roads of north Texas in a Model-T Ford. At first, Justin sold more laced boots to oil field workers than traditional Western boots to cattle

drivers. Despite her husband's presidency, cowboys were averse "to buying their footwear from a lady." The quality of the exclusively cowhide boots changed their minds, as did Enid's persuasiveness. Still, at the end of the first year, Nocona Boots was $267.61 in the red.

In that year, she increased the company's stock from $10,000 to $40,000, a figure maintained until the firm merged with Justin Industries in 1981. Justin kept slightly more than 50% of the stock, a "working majority." She also established the principle and practice that made the business a success. Nocona Boots produced what the customers wanted: a correct style of high-quality boots at a reasonable price. Cowboys demanded high-heeled, thin-soled boots of good leather with an 18" top to protect them against rattlesnake strikes. They also liked the decorative stitching which she added to keep the boots from folding at the ankle. Silk thread was waxed for the sewing and a solid leather heel, instead of the more common hollow one, was used. Enid Justin did most of the design patterns on the tops and toes of the boot. She borrowed her ideas from unusual sources and gave them names fitting the occasion. For example, the design called "brocade" came from a brocade couch in her home. The design called "neck" from the wrinkled neck of an old man who sat in front of her at a funeral.

Business improved rapidly. By 1934, she was sure that "Nocona Boots were headed for the top." She had enlarged the building, which had been purchased after a few years of operation. She also bought the company's machinery and added a sales force. But when she caught her husband with another woman and divorced him, the breach made her feel inferior. Julius went to Oklahoma and started the Olsen-Stelzer Boot Company, which made a "pretty good" boot but failed. The divorce caused Enid to "work even harder," if that was possible. In 1940, she met and married Harry Whitman.

This marriage was less satisfactory than the first. She believed that Harry married her for position and money. When he left in 1945, he cautioned her to get an attorney because "I came here broke, and I am not leaving that way." Harry got about $11,000 and used it to start a short-lived boot factory in Wichita Falls, Texas—"Whitbern Boots." The only good Enid realized from this episode was the opportunity to buy lasts for Nocona Boots. Harry's firm had purchased most of her supplier's inventory. Now, she bought them at a discount.

The Great Depression did not hurt Nocona Boots particularly. No one was laid off and wages were not cut. In 1935, sales were given a boost by Paramount Pictures, which featured Enid and the firm in its series on "Unusual Occupations." World War II was more of a problem. The difficulty of getting leather from northeastern tanneries, which she considered the best, meant temporary lay-offs for some of the work force. After the war, the business moved from its factory in downtown Nocona to a new building east of the business district on Highway 82, near where the Chisholm Trail had crossed. By the 1950s, her typical day began at 5:00 AM when she arose and ate. She then went to the post office to pick up mail, read it, and answered most of it by 8:00 AM. She was at the plant meeting dealers, suppliers, and employees until well into the evening.

Because of increased demand for her boots, Justin kept expanding the plant, especially during the 1970s when the Western fashion craze hit. Modifications were made to the original Nocona boot. She had good steel shanks put under the sole and hardwood pegs, not nails, in the insteps. The first boot tops had been eighteen inches and the heels three. These both were shortened. The new style was called "PeeWees." The older fashion had to be special ordered by the 1970s. She also produced boots called "Mule Ears," with straps that flapped down the side. The use of names for designs gave way to numbers, and many different types of leather began to be used—python, kangaroo, lizard, rattlesnake, and elephant, to name a few.

The Nocona plant was briefly unionized in the mid-'70s. "That just burned me. That just killed me," she said. "I felt like . . . we were family, you know. That is the way I felt towards my employees. They were people that we trained and that we knew and knew their families." She did approach her work force as a family, and some stayed for over 50 years. She planned parties, picnics, festivals, and other galas. She took family and individual problems into consideration when making judgments on workers. She kept informed about them and was genuinely concerned for their welfare. Her benevolence was effective. The labor union failed after one year, either because of her opposition or because of its inability to convince the workers that they were better off with it than with Miss Enid.

The plant on Highway 82 that went into operation in 1948 was 33,000 square feet and employed about 100 workers. In 1972, 26,000 square feet were added and 250 laborers employed. In 1981, the Nocona plant had 89,000 square feet and 500 employees, while another plant that had been built in Vernon, Texas, dur-

Enid Justin

ing 1977, had 26,000 square feet and 150 workers. As plant size increased, output rose. Four hundred and fifty boots were produced daily in 1948, 1,200 in 1972, and 1,700 in 1981. By this time, Nocona boots were sold at thousands of outlets in every state in the Union and overseas. Justin had begun introducing computerized production into the plant in 1980. In 1948, her sales were about $1 million, in 1972, approximately $8 million, and by 1981 roughly $27 million.

By 1981, Enid Justin was 87 years old and in bad health. She had suffered a stroke and was confined to a wheelchair. Whether she voluntarily decided to merge with Justin Industries or was tricked into it became a question to be settled by the Texas court system. According to Enid's version, her nephew, John Justin, Jr., chief executive officer of Justin Industries, recommended an attorney to her, and during one of the attorney's visits he had her sign a paper that he assured her was "an agreement not to sell Nocona Boot Co. to anyone for a year." In fact, she had signed a call option agreement granting Justin Industries the right to purchase her controlling shares of Nocona Boot's common stock. Justin Industries was then able to negotiate to acquire all of Nocona's stock through exchanges for Justin Industries' stock.

Enid Justin claimed that her interest in selling, which preceded the signing of the call option, was triggered by her inability to go to the plant daily, and the result of a confrontation she had with another nephew, Joe Justin, who was running the boot company in her absence. She subsequently believed she had been wrong to fire Joe and rehired him. Justin Industries' interest in the Nocona enterprise stemmed from a desire to be the largest bootmaker in the United States. At the time, Tony Lama Boots of El Paso was first, Justin second, and Nocona third in Western boot production. During the 1970s, Enid Justin had refused offers made by Charles Tandy of the Tandy Corporation and Tom Florsheim, the shoe manufacturer.

The point of contention among the Justin family appears to have been the amount of money needed to complete the merger. Apparently, the option sum was several million dollars, and Enid and Joe believed their company was worth at least $10 million. Ultimately, the merger was realized with Enid continuing as president and chair of the board of Nocona Boots for a short time before becoming a "consultant." She later maintained that the merger resulted from her desire to keep the factory in the family, and that she received $3 million in stock from Justin Industries, a conglomerate that owned the boot companies, coal mines, real estate, Acme Brick, and several other enterprises. Of her nephew John, Jr.'s desire to own Nocona Boots, she said: "He told my sister, 'I intend to own that Nocona Boot Company in its entirety someday.' But he doesn't own it, it is in a conglomerate."

Enid Justin died in the Nocona hospital and was buried in the city's cemetery; she never left the town she loved. During her active years, she was constantly engaged in advertising her product. She met movie stars, politicians, financiers, sports figures, bandleaders, monarchs, opera performers, and even tried to secure an audience with Pope Pius XII to give him a pair of her boots. She had a red pair made for the pontiff, but the American ambassador to the Vatican refused to let her give them to him. She spent millions in magazines, newspapers, and other media to spread the name of her boot company, and sponsored a 1939 "Pony Express Race" from Nocona, Texas, to San Francisco for publicity. The winner received a wheelbarrow full of silver dollars. She made sure the name Nocona and her boots were known across the country and overseas.

Throughout her long life, she received honors from social groups, business organizations, governmental bodies, and historical societies. For her pioneering contribution to Western heritage, she was made a member of the National Cowboy Hall of Fame in Oklahoma City and the National Cowgirl Hall of Fame in Hereford, Texas. Ironically, although she "loved boots like her family," she did not care to wear them. She saw boots as objects of beauty, but was too old-fashioned to wear them as footwear except on promotional or special occasions. As a woman in what was once the man's world of bootmaking, she was a pioneer and became a success regardless of gender.

SOURCES:

Dallas Morning News. Sec. B. August 28, 1980, p. 5.

"Interview with Enid Justin by Floyd Jenkins, November 13, 1981," in North Texas State University Oral History Collection (Business Archives Project). No. 63, Denton.

Justin, Enid, as told to Dale Terry. *"Miss Enid," The Texas Lady Bootmaker: An Informal Story of the Life of the Founder of Nocona Boot Company.* Austin: Nortex Press, 1985.

"Obituary," in *Fort Worth Star-Telegram.* Sec. 1. October 16, 1990, p. 11.

"Pony Express—1939 Version," in *Boot and Shoe Recorder.* March 25, 1939.

Taliaferro, Paul. "Her Boots Built the Town," in *Independent Woman: Official Publication of the National Federation of Business and Professional Women's Clubs.* Vol. XXVII. November 1948, p. 331.

Who's Who of American Women. 5th ed., 1968–1969.

SUGGESTED READING:

"Bootmaker Chooses NCR Century," in *NCR News.* Vol. XL. August 30, 1972, p. 2.

"Enid Justin—The World's Only Lady Bootmaker," in *Leather and Shoes: The International Weekly.* Vol CLVIII. August 16, 1969, p. 12.

"The Legend of Miss Enid," in *Ranch and Rodeo.* 1976 Annual.

"Lifelong Ambition Realized in Making of Nocona Boots," in *Southwestern Retailer.* December 1937, p. 23.

COLLECTIONS:

Enid Justin Collection, Archives, Willis Library, University of North Texas, Denton.

Robert S. La Forte,
Professor of History, University of North Texas, Denton, Texas

Justina (d. 64)

Saint and patron of Padua. Name variations: Justina of Lombardy. Died around 64 CE; her martyrdom is placed by most under the reign of Nero (54–68 CE).

Justina is said to have been a native of Padua and to have suffered martyrdom in that city in 64 CE, during the reign of Nero. Her supposed relics, said to have been recovered in 1177, are preserved at Padua in a church which bears her name. Known as a patron of Padua and, with St. Mark the Evangelist, of Venice, Justina is commemorated by the Roman Catholic Church on October 7.

Justina (d. 304)

Saint. Name variations: Justina of Damascus. Died in 304. Her martyrdom is placed by some under the reign of Diocletian (284–305); others have her living during the reign of Claudius II (268–270).

The story of Justina, who shared her martyrdom with St. Cyprian, has been accepted by Prudentius and St. Gregory of Nazianzus. The East Roman empress *Eudocia (c. 401–460) recorded the story in verse during the 5th century.

Cyprian was a famous magician who had studied every aspect of his art and settled into a life of sin and evil-doing, since no one was able to resist his powers. However, one day when he attempted to seduce a young Christian woman called Justina, she successfully resisted him. Believing that he had encountered divine grace, Cyprian burned his magic books and embraced Christianity. After many years of penance, he became a priest and then a bishop. Following the persecution edict of 304, however, he and Justina were condemned and tortured. Cast into a caldron of boiling oil, they reportedly felt no pain and survived their ordeal unscathed, only to be beheaded afterwards. According to custom, the bodies were left without burial, but it was believed that some Christian soldiers transported them to Italy. St. Justina's emblem is the unicorn, because it is believed that the unicorn can only be brought under control by a sinless woman. Her feast day is on September 26.

Justina (fl. 350–370)

*Roman empress. Flourished between 350 and 370; second wife of Valentinian I, Roman emperor (r. 364–375); children: Valentinian II, Western emperor of Rome (fl. 375–392); *Galla (c. 365–394); Justa; Grata. Valentinian I's first wife was Marina Severa.*

Jutta.

Variant of Judith.

Jutta (d. 1284)

*Prioress of Roskilde. Name variations: Jutta Eriksdottir or Ericsdottir. Died in 1284; daughter of Erik or Eric IV Ploughpenny (1216–1250), king of Denmark (r. 1241–1250) and *Jutta of Saxony (d. around 1267).*

Jutta of Huy (1158–1228).

See Ivetta of Huy.

Jutta of Mecklenburg-Strelitz (1880–1946)

*Nominal queen of Montenegro. Name variations: known as Militza following her marriage. Born Augusta Charlotte Jutta Alexandra Georgina Adolpine on January 24, 1880; died on February 17, 1946; daughter of Adolphus Frederick V, grand duke of Mecklenburg-Strelitz, and *Elizabeth of Anhalt-Dessau (1857–1933); married Daniel or Danilo Petrovitch-Njegos (son of Nicholas, king of Montenegro), on July 15, 1899.*

Jutta of Saxony (d. around 1267)

*Margravine of Brandenburg. Died before February 2, 1267; daughter of Albert I, duke of Saxony, and Agnes of Thuringia; married Erik or Eric IV Ploughpenny (1216–1250), king of Denmark (r. 1241–1250), on November 17, 1239; became second wife of John I, margrave of Brandenburg, on May 7, 1255; children: (first marriage) *Ingeborg of Denmark (d. 1287); *Sophie of Denmark (d. 1286); *Jutta (d. 1284, prioress of Roskilde); Agnes (a nun at Roskilde); Christof; Knut; (second marriage) *Agnes of Brandenburg (d. 1304). John I's first wife was *Sophia of Denmark.*

Jutta of Sponheim (d. 1136)

German mystic. Flourished between 1100–1136; died in 1136 at the convent of Disibodenberg in Germany; sister of Count Meginhard of Sponheim; never married; no children.

Jutta of Sponheim was a German noble and holy woman who felt a religious calling even as a child, and grew up receiving mystical visions which she shared with others. As a young woman, Jutta felt she needed to confine herself to truly reach God, and thus became a recluse at the small establishment of Disibodenberg. However, a woman whom so many people viewed as being especially blessed could not remain isolated for long. Within a few years, a large community of women had established itself near her cell. Among those who came to Disibodenberg was a young girl (c. 1106), *Hildegard of Bingen, who also received visions and whom Jutta raised to understand the calling of the mystic. Although Jutta did not take an official position in the community, she acted as a spiritual director of the nuns. Hildegard took over this role on Jutta's death in 1136, eventually surpassing even Jutta in her fame as a blessed woman with special gifts of prophecy.

SOURCES:

Anderson, Bonnie S., and Judith P. Zinsser. *A History of Their Own.* Vol. I. NY: Harper & Row, 1988.

Gies, Frances, and Joseph Gies. *Women in the Middle Ages.* NY: Harper and Row, 1978.

Laura York,
Riverside, California

Kaahumanu (1777–1832)

Chief wife of Kamehameha I and, as co-regent of Kamehameha II and Kamehameha III, the driving force behind the abolition of the kapu *system in the Hawaiian Islands and the architect of the first code of secular law. Name variations: Ka'ahumanu. Pronunciation: Kah-ah-HEW-mon-ew. Born in 1777 (some sources cite 1768) in the village of Hana on the island of Maui, Hawaii; died on June 5, 1832, at her Manoa home, Oahu, Hawaii; daughter of Keeaumoku (a chief of the island of Hawaii) and Namahana (daughter of a chief of Maui); at age five, given to Kamehameha I the Great (1758–1819), king of Hawaii (r. 1810–1819), to live in his household until old enough to become his wife, around 1782; no children.*

Took her father's place in the chiefs' council (1794); received from Kamehameha the power to be a puuhonua *or sanctuary (1795); named* kahu *(sacred guardian) of the heir of Kamehameha I (1804); served as* kuhina nui *(reigned as regent, co-ruler, 1819–1832); influenced Kamehameha II to abandon the* kapu *system (1819); adopted Christianity (1824); established a code of law for the Hawaiians based on Christian teachings (1827).*

When Kaahumanu died on the evening of June 5, 1832, she left behind a Hawaii that was vastly different from the relatively isolated islands she had known as a girl. Intertribal warfare had given way to diplomatic shuffling with consuls and trade delegations from Europe and North America. The old gods had been replaced with the god of the Christian missionaries, Hawaiians were being taught to read and write, and women were no longer barred from the religious and secular councils of power. The moving force behind most of the changes was a woman the missionaries referred to as "her who had been the reformer of her nation," the queen regent of the Hawaiian Islands, Kaahumanu.

Born to Keeaumoku, a chief of the island of Hawaii, and **Namahana**, a daughter of a chief of Maui, Kaahumanu came into the world armed with a powerful network of family ties that were being pulled apart by interisland warfare. The Hawaiian Islands were made up of many small islands and seven principal islands, each with its own ruling family of chiefs: Maui, Hawaii, Oahu, Lanai, Molokai, Kauai, and Niihau. Kahekili, the ruling chief of Maui, looked upon the marriage of Namahana and Keeaumoku, a rival chief, as an act of treason. He forced the couple to flee to the island of Hawaii and join political forces with Kamehameha I, a high-ranking chief from Hawaii who had distinguished himself in battle and was determined to unite the islands under his sole leadership. In a definitive act of unification with Kamehameha, Namahana and Keeaumoku sent their five-year-old daughter, Kaahumanu, to live in the 30-year-old Kamehameha's home until she was old enough to become one of his wives.

Doted upon and sequestered, Kaahumanu was said to have become a skilled surfer to escape the tedium of the seclusion imposed on her as she grew up. As Kamehameha's wife, she was protected and sheltered from everyday life. Because she was his favorite wife, her actions were carefully monitored, but she was also allowed more freedom to do as she wished.

While Kaahumanu was still a girl, Kamehameha conquered the island of Maui. *Keopuolani, a woman of the purest bloodlines and holding the most powerful *mana* (supernatural force) in all the islands, became Kamehameha's sacred wife and, according to custom, the future mother of the heirs to his kingdom. Kamehameha had at least 16 wives, but Kaahumanu remained his special wife. According to Europeans who came to the islands for fresh water, whales, and recreation, she visibly shared his power and was his primary confidante. Perhaps because they had no children, and Kaahumanu was, therefore, committed to no one in the succession of power, Kamehameha was comfortable sharing his power and knowledge with her.

As a woman chief in her own right, Kaahumanu's life traditionally lay in being part of her husband's household and enhancing their shared role and status, but this did not mean that she remained in his shadow. Like most Polynesians, Hawaiian women were subject to a system of *kapus* (religious restraints) that regulated much of their lives. They could not ride in boats, catch fish, or speak to the gods except through male intermediaries. They could not eat many local foods, including pork, bananas, and certain fish, and they were barred from eating with men or from cooking their food in the same oven as the men. However, while women were banned from attending the councils of religious and political power and were subject to many other constraints stemming from the *kapu* system, they still had a great deal of personal autonomy and relative sexual egalitarianism. Hawaiian women often acted in opposition to the interests of their men if it suited them. They controlled their own property and engaged in commerce on their own ground. It has been postulated that the independence of Polynesian women was at the heart of the creation of the *kapu* system, since it was the only way Polynesian men could exert any control. The *kapu* system began to crack as foreign sailors reached the islands.

When George Vancouver, commander of a British exploring expedition, first stopped at Kaahumanu's village, her mother Namahana insisted on going out to the boat to see Vancouver in violation of a *kapu* that prevented her, as it did all women, from going on the ocean. Namahana reasoned, however, that the *kapu* which prevented her from going out in a Hawaiian canoe could not apply to foreign boats belonging to foreigners who did not come under her people's restrictions. Vancouver says this "ingenious mode of reasoning" persuaded her husband to let her go. Namahana was conveyed to the *Discovery* in one of its own boats, and her way of using the presence and practices of foreign visitors to shape new freedoms for herself was adopted with great success by her daughter, Kaahumanu. When a ship's officer came to call on Kaahumanu, she offered him fruit and had coconuts brought. This was a clear violation of the *kapu* against women eating with or preparing food for men. Kaahumanu reasoned, however, that the village women who visited the ships ate there with the men and suffered no ill effects, so she was only bringing the foreign ships' custom to the land.

Size was important to the Polynesians; great height and weight conveyed prosperity and health and commanded respect. Kaahumanu was about 15 years old, stood over 6' tall, and weighed close to 300 pounds when Vancouver first met her in 1793. She was the only woman Vancouver ever mentioned as being present at formal ceremonies between Kamehameha and British representatives. He described her as "one of the finest women he had yet seen on any of the islands." Another young officer wrote in his journal that she was "plump, jolly, very lively and good humored." Jacques Arago, an artist aboard a French ship, was less kind, describing her as very fat but with elegant tattoos on her legs, left palm, and tongue. Samuel Kamakau, a Hawaiian historian, noted that Kaahumanu had a lively enjoyment of men and loved to flirt.

Vancouver's journal indicates that there was true affection between Kaahumanu and her husband; however, when he returned to the islands the following year, he found Kaahumanu estranged from Kamehameha. Rumors that she had been intimate with Kaiana—a young, good looking and, according to his detractors, sly chief of Kauai—had reached Kamehameha's ears, and she had fled to her family for protection. Adultery was not a serious offense, however; Kaiana was one of Kamehameha's political rivals, and Kamehameha relied on the high rank of his Maui wives, specifically Kaahumanu and Keopuolani to support his ascendancy over the other chiefs. If Kaahumanu's father and several of the other chiefs threw their support to Ka-

Kaahumanu

iana, it could lead to Kamehameha's downfall. Vancouver, realizing that such a turn of events could jeopardize the investment he had already made in his relationship with Kamehameha, offered to help afford a reconciliation between Kamehameha and Kaahumanu. Kamehameha accepted on the condition that their meeting look like an accident. Vancouver did this by inviting them on board the *Discovery* at the same time. According to Vancouver, both parties were happy to see each other and were relieved to end the estrangement. Before they went ashore, however, Kaahumanu asked what she termed an important favor of Vancouver: that he secure Kamehameha's promise that he would not beat her when she got back to the house. Vancouver complied and obtained Kamehameha's assurance.

She prefers to go before, rather than follow others, and consequently, whenever she acts, she acts in such a manner to distinguish herself from others.

—William Richards, missionary

Kamehameha, a pragmatist, used the *kapu* system to regulate trade with foreigners, a purpose unconnected to religion, and to consolidate his power over the other chiefs. After he won control of the island of Oahu in battle around the summer of 1795, he abolished the old *puuhonua* (sanctuary) of Oahu and designated sanctuaries of his own. In so doing, Kamehameha cut the people's ties with their traditional Oahu gods. Conversely, he gave Kaahumanu the god-like power to be a *puuhonua*, in effect granting her the power to protect life and designate places of refuge. Following the conflict, many of the chiefs of Oahu who had been taken prisoner came to Kaahumanu to beg for their lives. Cleverly, she gave their lives back to them, incurring their lifelong indebtedness and loyalty. She also designated areas where women and children fleeing wars and other internal strife could find sanctuary. Kamehameha's actions lessened the religious significance of the concept of sanctuary and made it part of government and, as the *kapu* system was used more and more for secular purposes, it was weakened and the power of the priests diminished.

In 1804, Kaahumanu was named the *kahu* (sacred guardian) of the baby boy Liholiho (the future Kamehameha II). Liholiho was the first of Kamehameha and Keopuolani's children and the heir to his kingdom. Kaahumanu had no innate *mana* or sacred power, her authority was purely secular, enhanced by what personality, intelligence, beauty, and strength of will she possessed. She used the position of *kahu*, and the great power it conferred, to create her own path to the center of control.

In May of 1819, nine years after he succeeded in uniting the seven major Hawaiian Islands under his leadership, Kamehameha died. Kaahumanu was named *kuhina nui* (regent) and was chosen to convey the last commands of Kamehameha to Liholiho. This great honor meant that it was Kaahumanu who installed Liholiho as *alii nui* (ruling chief). In her first public bid for power, Kaahumanu stood alone before the Hawaiian people with Kamehameha's cloak of office on her shoulders, his helmet on her head, and his spear in her hand. The message was clear: as long as Kaahumanu and her family stood with him, Liholiho had the strength to hold his kingdom. Without her consent, none of his orders or actions would be decisive. Kaahumanu now effectively held the reigns of government, usurping the power of the throne not by killing the prior *alii nui*, but by engulfing and overwhelming the heir and gathering his power into her own hands.

Barely six months later, Kaahumanu moved to abandon the restrictive *kapu* system for good. She told Liholiho, in front of the Hawaiian people, that if he wanted to continue to observe the laws that had come down from Kamehameha he could do so, but "As for me and my people, we intend to be free from the kapu." Food for men and women would be cooked in the same oven, and they would eat out of the same bowl. She meant to eat pork, bananas, coconuts and to live as the *haole* (foreigners) did. In a speech which exhibited a strong flair for diplomacy, she told the Hawaiians, "If you think differently, you are at liberty to do so; but as for me and my people we are resolved to be free." At that moment, Kaahumanu abolished the old laws for herself and her followers. In giving the Hawaiian people a choice, she broke both the mind set and the power of the autocracy. She also removed power from the hands of the *kahunas* (priests) and began a social revolution.

Liholiho, afraid that if he crossed the *kapu* he would shorten his reign and his life, continued to observe it. Liholiho's mother Keopuolani, recognizing the political danger of a divided stand on the issue, stood with Kaahumanu against her own son. When Keopuolani asked Liholiho to send his five-year-old son to eat with her, he complied and by doing so gave tacit, if not actual, approval to his family's support of Kaahumanu.

As Liholiho's vacillation continued, political instability grew out of the chiefs' disagreement over whether or not to abolish the Hawaiian gods and the *kapu*. When it threatened to pull apart Kamehameha's unified nation, Kaahumanu took matters into her own hands. She commanded that a feast be set for all the chiefs at Kailua, Hawaii. Then, she sent a figurative message to Liholiho, "The ti leaf *kapu* is to be declared to your God upon arrival at Kailua." In essence, she was saying that, upon his arrival at the feast, the gods were to take back the *kapu* and leave men free.

Liholiho was drunk when he arrived and had to be escorted to the banquet. Still in observance of the *kapu*, the men were sitting separately from the women. Accounts say that Liholiho, expecting to be struck dead by the gods, timidly circled the gathering and then sat down with the women and began to eat. When he finished, he realized that he was still alive and, with Kaahumanu, issued an order that the local *heiau* (place of worship) be destroyed along with the gods. The *kapu* system was still not quite dead. A cousin of Liholiho gathered support from those who still clung to the old gods and the *kapus*. But a naval force, assembled under the command of Kaahumanu, attacked and subdued him and his followers. Her victory convinced the common people that it was safe to give up the old ways.

Six months later, a new brand of foreigner arrived from America: the first Christian missionaries. Prior to this time, the only outsiders the Hawaiians had contact with were sailors and explorers. The islands were favorite rest stops with whalers and Yankee traders who exchanged Chinese tea, silk, and other luxury items for Hawaiian sandalwood. The Hawaiian port cities of Honolulu and Lahaina were riotous places filled with shops, saloons, and women who were unencumbered by the moral rectitude of Europe and North America.

Kaahumanu had little time for the missionaries and had to be persuaded to grant permission for them to stay in the islands for a year on a trial basis. The missionary, Hiram Bingham, upon hearing of Kaahumanu's work in suppressing the old gods, recognized that she would be a great asset to the growth of Christianity and took it upon himself to win her over. He had little success. Kaahumanu turned down his offer to teach her to read and write and persisted in treating the missionaries with what they described as great haughtiness.

Kaahumanu continued to show little interest, if not contempt, for the missionaries until she fell ill in 1821 and was nursed back to health by missionary wives. One of these, **Mercey Whitney**, astutely wrote home in one of her letters, "Kaahumanu has more influence in political affairs than any other person in this nation." It was during Kaahumanu's convalescence that ❧▶ **Sybil Bingham**, visiting Kaahumanu daily, finally convinced her to learn the alphabet.

❧▶
See sidebar on the following page

Through Bingham's efforts, Kaahumanu became a Christian, if only for pragmatic reasons, and allied herself with the missionaries' interests. She began to lay down rules for her people based on the moral teachings of the Bible and took on herself the role of *kahuna*. Over time, she issued edicts that controlled aspects of people's lives that had never concerned the chiefs before. By so doing, Kaahumanu created a role for herself that would not have been permitted within either the American or Hawaiian culture, but because Hawaii now existed somewhere between the two, it worked.

Finally recovered from her illness, Kaahumanu had a New England style, two-story frame house built for her at the harbor in Honolulu and shortly thereafter married Kaumualii (chief of Kauai). The marriage cemented the blood lines of Kauai to those of Maui and Hawaii and secured the allegiance of the last semi-independent islands for Kamehameha's kingdom. It also guaranteed Kaahumanu's place at the center of Hawaiian power. There were rumors that Kaahumanu and Kaumualii planned to depose Liholiho and take over rule of the islands, but they were never substantiated. The marriage appears to have been purely for political purposes for, according to a Yankee trader, Kaumualii is said to have confessed that "he was miserable, and wished the devil had Kaahumanu."

In 1824, when news came that Liholiho and his wife *Kamamalu died of measles while on a trip to London, England, the chiefs chose Liholiho's 12-year-old son, Kauikeaouli, to succeed him as Kamehameha III. Kaahumanu, continuing as regent, began the work that would later prompt one missionary to describe her as "the reformer of her nation." She began with education. In a speech given on December 20, 1825, she told her people, "I want you to learn what is right in order that you may acquire righteousness and that our hearts may be of one mind." By 1831, the number of Hawaiians attending

❧▶ Bingham, Sybil Moseley (1792–1848)

American missionary who helped found the first Christian mission established in the Hawaiian islands by New England Congregationalists. Born in Westfield, Massachusetts, on September 14, 1792; died in Easthampton, Massachusetts, on February 27, 1848; eldest of four daughters of Pliny and Sophia (Pomeroy) Moseley; married Hiram Bingham (a missionary), on October 11, 1819; children: **Sophia Bingham** *(1820–1887, who married William Augustus Moseley); Levi Parsons (1822–1823); Jeremiah Evarts (1824–1825);* **Lucy Whiting Bingham** *(1826–1890, who married Charles Olmstead Reynolds);* **Elizabeth Kaahumanu Bingham** *(1829–1899); Hiram II (1831–1908); Lydia Bingham (1834–1915).*

Sybil Moseley was a teacher when she met and married the young minister Hiram Bingham. Almost immediately, they set sail from Boston for Hawaii, where Hiram was posted to lead a mission. With five other missionary families, the Binghams endured the five-month journey, landing in the Port of Honolulu on April 19, 1820.

The Binghams settled into a one-room thatched cottage, which, in addition to their residence, served as a Sunday meeting house and, during the week, a schoolhouse. In 1821, with materials sent from Boston, a permanent home for the missionaries was built. It also housed several separate families, fellow missionaries, and visiting guests. For their entire stay in Hawaii, the Binghams lived in the "common stock system," with all supplies, including gifts from relatives and friends, divided between the missionary families according to need. The only piece of furniture Bingham ever owned was a rocking chair Hiram made for her from Koa wood.

Although the missionaries' goal was to save souls, during her 21-years of service Sybil Bingham used her talent as a teacher to establish the first school on the islands. Her work began in 1820 with a class of 12 to 14 students in her home, thus establishing the first school for native Hawaiian girls. Within two months, the class grew to 40, including both children and adults. Bingham planned, supervised, and participated with her students in the construction of an adobe brick schoolhouse which was completed in 1835. Soon, 52,000 students flocked to the many schools springing up on the islands.

In addition to her teaching duties and caring for her own five children, Bingham often made the treacherous journey to missionary posts on neighboring islands to assist with childbirth or other medical emergencies. She wrote numerous letters to fellow missionaries and friends in New England. One, written in 1839, describes a single day: "Last Wednesday I rode to Waikiki; had a meeting with a house full of mothers and children. After this visited eleven families, called at the doors of two or three more, rode back to Punahou, attended to matters there then got myself and family to the Mission House."

Understanding the importance of teaching the Hawaiians in their own language, Bingham worked with the other missionaries to turn the islanders' vocal sounds into written words through the formation of an alphabet. In 1822, the earliest English-Hawaiian speller was prepared, which was also the first ever printed in Hawaiian. The book was instrumental in winning support from the highest chiefs for the missionaries and their teaching. Bingham established a weekly prayer meeting, known as the *Poalima*, for the 1,500 women of Kawaiahao Church. For over 15 years, she led them in prayer and discussions of the scripture, and her efforts helped win over the powerful *alii* (members of the chiefly class), who, after embracing Christianity, protected and aided the missionaries. A strong and lasting bond of mutual respect developed between the Hawaiian *alii* women and the missionaries, thanks to Bingham's work.

In 1840, when her health began to fail, the Bingham family returned to Massachusetts. It soon became apparent that Sybil would not be able to continue missionary service, and the Binghams were released from their duties. In 1847, Sybil Bingham died of tuberculosis, while sitting in the rocking chair her husband had made for her. She was buried in Massachusetts but later reburied beside her husband and his second wife, **Naomi Emma (Morse) Bingham**, in the New Haven, Connecticut, city burial ground. The two youngest Bingham children followed in their parents' footsteps. Hiram II served as a missionary to the Gilbert Islands in Micronesia from 1857 to 1863. **Lydia Bingham**, a teacher like her mother, returned to Honolulu in 1867 to establish the Kawaiahao Female Seminary, where she served as principal for six years.

SOURCES:

Peterson, Barbara Bennett. *Notable Women of Hawaii.* Honolulu, HI: University of Hawaii Press, 1984.

COLLECTIONS:

Bingham family papers located at Yale University Sterling Memorial Library, New Haven, Connecticut.

school had jumped from some 2,000 in 1824 to over 52,000.

Concerned about the effect of foreign intervention on her nation, she determined that the council decide upon a national code of laws. The council agreed on six laws based on what they had been taught by the missionaries. The British consul, anticipating a problem with these new constraints, put pressure on Kaahumanu to send the laws to England for approval before they were put into effect. Kaahumanu vehemently disagreed and stood her ground. Recognizing that the consul had his own agenda, she said that he was undependable, and "calls good evil and turns and whirls about every way." Kuakini, her brother, supported her, saying that if they sent the laws to England for approval, "We shall forever be their servants, we shall no more do as we please." Kaahumanu agreed. The first three laws were put into effect on December 14, 1827. The first law was against murder—especially the killing of newborn babies—and decreed punishment by hanging. Other laws forbade theft, adultery, drunkenness and brawling, punishable by confinement in irons. She also required the people to observe the sabbath and reiterated her command that, as soon as schoolhouses could be built, they must go to school to learn.

Kaahumanu's strength of purpose was noted by the foreigners with some curiosity and misgivings, as they were unused to dealing with women in such total control of power. The missionary Asa Thurston defined the situation while describing Kaahumanu's executive officer and commander of the military forces, "unquestionably the great man, the greatest . . . in the nation at the time. But then there was a woman above him; & she could have called him to order at any time."

Not all of Kaahumanu's reforms were looked upon with approval. A law against prostitution was strenuously objected to by the foreigners and temporarily put aside. Still, she forbade the women from swimming out to the ships, prompting Ferdinand Vrangel, a Russian naval officer, to comment angrily, "One senile old woman, of distinguished and eminent origin, the days of her frivolous youth long forgotten, now oversees with tireless vigilance the preservation of the purity of the young women of the island."

In 1829, she strengthened the chief's rule in relation to foreigners by preventing the British consul from taking the law into his own hands over a property dispute. Laws against distilling

liquor, prostitution, and gambling were now enforced, despite the objections of certain Europeans. In a subsequent murder case, Kaahumanu set up a 12-man jury and sat, herself, as judge. "She has exhibited a singular union of moderation and decision in the case," said Hiram Bingham, "vigilant lest the guilty should escape and cautious lest the power of punishing should be abused."

In 1832, at age 55, Kaahumanu was taken ill once more and retreated to her home in the Manoa valley overlooking Honolulu. She died on June 5 and was greatly mourned as the protector of her people.

SOURCES:

Grimshaw, Patricia. *Paths of Duty*. Honolulu, HI: University of Hawaii Press, 1989.

Kamakau, Samuel. *Ruling Chiefs of Hawaii*. Rev. ed. Honolulu, HI: Kamehameha Schools Press, 1992.

Silverman, Jane L. *Kaahumanu, Molder of Change*. Honolulu, HI: Friends of the Judiciary History Center of Hawaii, 1987.

Vancouver, George. *A Voyage of Discovery to the North Pacific Ocean and Round the World*. 3 vols. London: G.G.and J. Robinson and J. Edwards, 1798.

SUGGESTED READING:

Joesting, Edward. *Hawaii: An Uncommon History*. NY: W.W. Norton, 1972.

Linnekin, Jocelyn. *Sacred Queens and Women of Consequence*. Ann Arbor, MI: University of Michigan Press, 1990.

Lyman, Sarah Joiner. *Sarah Joiner Lyman of Hawaii: Her Own Story*. Compiled by Margaret Greer Martin. Hilo, HI: University Press, 1970.

Menton, Linda K., and Eileen Tamura. *A History of Hawaii*. Honolulu, HI: University of Hawaii Press, 1987.

Paula A. Steib,
freelance writer, Kaneohe, Hawaii

Kabos, Ilona (1893–1973)

Hungarian musician who specialized in performing works for two pianos. Born in Budapest, Hungary, on December 7, 1893; died in London, on May 28, 1973; married Louis Kentner.

Ilona Kabos was born in Budapest in 1893 and studied in her native country. After teaching at the Royal Budapest Academy of Music from 1930 through 1936, she became a resident of London in the late 1930s. Kabos specialized in duo-piano music, often performing the works of Béla Bartok with her husband Louis Kentner. Settling in the United States in 1965, she taught for a number of years at the Juilliard School of Music in New York, where she was highly regarded. Her recordings, especially of Bartok, excited considerable critical interest.

John Haag,
Athens, Georgia

Kadijah (c. 555–619 CE).

See Khadijah.

Kael, Pauline (1919—)

American film critic. Born on June 19, 1919, in Petaluma, Sonoma County, California; daughter of Isaac Paul Kael (a farmer) and Judith (Friedman) Kael; graduated from the University of California at Berkeley, 1940; Georgetown University, LL.D., 1972; divorced (three times according to some published sources; four according to others); children: one daughter, Gina James.

Selected writings: I Lost It at the Movies *(1965);* Kiss Kiss Bang Bang *(1968);* Going Steady *(1970);* The Citizen Kane Book *(1971);* Deeper Into Movies *(1973);* Reeling *(1976);* When the Lights Go Down *(1980);* Taking It All In *(1984);* State of the Art *(1985);* Hooked *(1989);* 5001 Nights at the Movies *(1991);* For Keeps *(1994).*

Probably the most influential movie critic from the 1960s to the 1980s, Pauline Kael retired in 1991, age 71, because of increasing problems with Parkinson's disease. "It started to really give me trouble in 1990," she said. "You can't go shaking to screenings. I also froze in line a few times." Kael left behind a lengthy and distinguished career that included 24 years with *The New Yorker*. William Shawn, the longtime editor of the magazine, dubbed Kael "the quintessential movie lover" and noted that there was probably no one else in the world who had reviewed more movies or knew more about the film industry. "In herself, she is the international history, library, archive, encyclopedia of film—the cinemathèque," he wrote in the foreword of her 1991 book, *5001 Nights at the Movies*.

Pauline Kael was born in Sonoma County, California, in 1919, the youngest child in a large family. She grew up on a sizeable farm, 30 miles north of San Francisco, until the family moved to the city when she was eight. "I remember my father taking me along when he visited our local widow," Kael wrote in her review of *Hud*. "At six or seven, I was very proud of my father for being a protector of widows. . . . My father, who was adulterous, and a Republican who, like Hud, was opposed to any government interference, was in no sense and in no one's eyes a social predator. He was generous and kind, and democratic in the western way that Easterners still don't understand." Kael was even closer to her mother.

In 1940, Kael graduated from the University of California at Berkeley with a degree in philosophy and a passion for the arts and literature. After college, she tried her hand at writing (films, plays, and essays), while working at odd jobs to support herself and her daughter, **Gina James**. Kael would marry several times. She worked as a seamstress and had some success as a copy writer—too much success, she recalls. "The *day* they were putting up the partition and putting my name on the door I went in and quit in tears because I suddenly saw myself behind that partition for years. And I didn't want that, I wanted to write."

Kael's first piece of film criticism was written for *City Lights* magazine in San Francisco and was followed by articles in *Partisan Review, Sight and Sound, Moviegoing, Kulchur,* and the *Film Quarterly,* which ran her pieces on a regular basis. From 1955 through the early 1960s, she also managed two art film houses (Berkeley Cinema Theaters) and reviewed films on a radio show carried by several Pacific network stations. Her reputation grew steadily and a widely acclaimed collection of her articles in book form, *I Lost It at the Movies* (1965), led to assignments from mainstream journals such as *Life, Holiday,* and *Mademoiselle*. She was also the regular film critic for *McCall's* (1965–66) and *The New Republic* (1966–67).

In 1968, Kael joined *The New Yorker,* where she shared reviewing duties with **Penelope Gilliatt** for the next 11 years. In this somewhat unconventional arrangement, the two women split the year, each writing for a six-month period. Although Kael called her assignment with *The New Yorker* "the best job in the world," she sometimes had to fight to retain her edgy style. "The editors tried to turn me into just what I'd been struggling not to be: a genteel, fuddy-duddy stylist," she explained. "Sometimes almost every sentence was rearranged." As regards content, however, she would not be pressured. When her much-respected New Yorker editor, Wallace Shawn, referred to her pan of Terrence Malick's *Badlands* with, "I guess you didn't know that Terry is like a son to me," Kael replied, "Tough shit, Bill."

Over the years, her reviews were collected regularly in such volumes as *Kiss Kiss Bang Bang, Going Steady,* and *When the Lights Go Down*. In 1974, Kael received the National Book Award for *Deeper into Movies,* the first book on film to receive the honor, but many point to *The Citizen Kane Book* (1971) as her crowning achievement. It grew out of a

50,000-word essay, entitled "Raising Kane," which was first published in two successive issues of *The New Yorker,* and was praised by one critic as "a mixture of journalism, biography, autobiography, gossip, and criticism, carried along by a style so exhilarating that one seems to be reading a new, loose kind of critical biography."

In the middle of 1979, Kael took a leave of absence from *The New Yorker* to work in the movie industry. Originally hired to assist Warren Beatty on a film, she wound up as an executive consultant of film projects for Paramount. "I was dying to leave after a few months," she said; "I missed writing terribly. Also, you see all the arrogance and the money- and honor-chasing. You find part of what makes someone a director is an amalgam of qualities not desirable in the home." She returned to *The New Yorker* in 1980 as the magazine's year-round film reviewer. Her Hollywood experience was valuable, however, because it allowed her to see the obstacles in movie making more clearly. "You have more sympathy for bad pictures when you see what people have to go through before they can get *any* picture under way."

Although many question Kael's opinions, most agree that she was a captivating writer. "Kael's reviews are a total turn-on," wrote Gary Carey in *Library Journal,* "a combination of uncanny perceptions and an idiosyncratic prose style that takes its rhythms and patterns from the movies themselves." Jack Kroll of *Newsweek,* called Kael "the literary intellectuals' favorite movie critic, a liaison woman between the sacred groves of academe and the plebeian, popcorn-redolent movie houses."

Kael viewed movies as a kind of sociological barometer of the times. In her introduction to *Deeper into Movies* (1973), she writes that the collection of reviews represent "a record of the interaction of movies and our national life. . . . I try to use my initial responses (which I think are probably my deepest and most honest ones) to explore not only what a movie means to me, but what it may mean to others, to get at the many ways in which movies, by affecting us on sensual and primitive levels, are a supremely pleasurable—and dangerous—art form."

"What's so dangerous?," asked an interviewer. "At a movie house, you feel alone with the image and you're affected deeply," replied Kael. "The different elements that go into movies—music, cinematography, actors, design—get to you very strongly. That's why so

Pauline Kael

many educated people disapprove of movies; they're not used to giving themselves over to that much emotion. They feel more at home with foreign films full of humane little lessons." She found screen violence objectionable only when the audience is manipulated into identifying with the killer. "There's a lot of violence at the beginning of *Grand Illusion,* but you're appalled by it," she noted. "Bonnie and Clyde suffered for their indifference and casualness about using weapons. Whereas in a Clint Eastwood movie, you identify with the guy with the biggest gun, not the victim. That's a big difference emotionally. *Natural Born Killers* is a horrible movie—the victims are purposely made ludicrous and pathetic, so you're supposed to cheer the killers on."

In 1994, three years into retirement, Kael came out with another collection, *For Keeps,* her largest and perhaps her best volume yet. Richard Corliss of *Time* found it intoxicating. "Reading *For Keeps* is like going on a toot with *Mary McCarthy, Belle Barth* and *Billie Holiday,*" he wrote. "It's movie analysis with a serrated edge; film criticism as stand-up bawdry; intellectual improvisation that soars into the highest form of word jazz."

SOURCES:

Corliss, Richard. "That Wild Old Woman," in *Time*. November 7, 1994.

Evory, Ann, ed. *Contemporary Authors*. New Revision Series, Vol. 6. Detroit, MI: Gale Research, 1982.

Goodman, Susan. "She Lost It at the Movies," in *Modern Maturity*. March–April 1998.

Green, Carol Hurd, and Mary Grimley Mason, eds. *American Women Writers*. NY: Continuum, 1994.

Kael, Pauline. *5001 Nights at the Movies*. NY: Holt, 1991.

Katz, Ephraim. *The Film Encyclopedia*. NY: Harper-Collins, 1994.

Malko, George. "Pauline Kael Wants People to Go to the Movies," in *Audience*. Vol. 2, no. 1. January–February 1972.

McHenry, Robert. *Famous American Women*. NY: Dover, 1983.

Barbara Morgan,
Melrose, Massachusetts

Kaffka, Margit (1880–1918)

Hungarian poet and novelist, generally regarded as Hungary's first major woman writer. Born in Nagykároly, Hungary (now Carei, Rumania), on June 10, 1880; died of influenza in Budapest, Hungary, on December 1, 1918; daughter of Gyula Kaffka; married Bruno Fröhlich, in 1905; married Ervin Bauer, in 1914; children: (first marriage) son, László.

In novels and short stories, probed two pressing issues of her day in Hungary, the decline of the gentry class and the problems faced by women in an era of major social changes; having earned a reputation as a major writer, died of influenza during her late 30s (1918), her son László dying the next day.

Margit Kaffka was born in Hungary in 1880 in the provincial town of Nagykároly (now Carei, Rumania) in the Eastern Lowlands region. The daughter of a Hungarian mother and a father of Czech ancestry, in later years she would trace her restless temperament to her ethnically mixed parentage. The family on her mother's side was typical of the impoverished rural gentry, in that it claimed among its ancestors a member of Árpád's train, that is, with the very first Magyar invaders. Margit's father died when she was only six, leaving the family destitute. Her mother married again, but Margit was unhappy at home and was sent to board in a local convent, a horrifying three-year experience that she would describe years later in a short story entitled "Letters from a Convent." Determined to escape from Nagykároly, Kaffka aspired to a teaching career and was even willing to endure an additional year as a student teacher at the school run by the Sisters of Mercy, in whose convent she had gone through unpleasant experiences.

In 1899, her dreams were realized when she received a scholarship to study in Budapest for her higher diploma to qualify to teach on the secondary school level. After three years at the prestigious Erzsébet Training College for Women, Kaffka received her diploma in 1902 and began teaching.

In 1905, she married a forestry engineer, Bruno Fröhlich, and gave birth to a son László in 1906. The marriage, however, was dissolved within a few years. Supporting herself and László in Budapest by teaching, the single mother used every spare moment to write short stories and poems, the latter being published in the journals *Hét* and *Magyar Geniusz*. Kaffka enjoyed motherhood. Her poem *Petike Jár* ("Peter's First Steps"), an observation of a toddler's first steps, looks ahead in the last stanza to the day when the child, now a young man, pays a visit to a still-anxious mother who hobbles out to greet him. This poem remains a favorite in Hungarian anthologies.

Resuming her maiden name, Kaffka increasingly was to be seen in Budapest's most advanced literary and intellectual circles that met in opulent bourgeois homes and smoky coffee houses, including the avant-garde Sunday Society whose leading lights were Béla Balázs and Georg Lukács. She was one of the few women in this and other similar artistic cliques. Sometimes the writers and artists were invited to her small apartment on Márvány Street, where they would sit in a circle with an oil light flickering, "tracking the flow of ideas."

The most progressive writers among them, including Kaffka, published their poetry and short stories in the journal *Nyugat* (The West). The writers of the *Nyugat* circle, which also included such brilliant poets as Endre Ady and Árpád Tóth, were radical modernists who saw themselves as part of a new European generation seeking truth in all areas of life and art. In prosperous Budapest, which had a large, mostly Jewish middle class which was willing to support new ideas, *Nyugat* found many subscribers from a sympathetic audience who could afford to buy impressionist canvases, regularly attend the theater and concerts, and collect the novels of unknown young writers with bold ideas. From the start, conservative elements attacked the *Nyugat* circle for its alleged subversion of traditional Hungarian values, with one journalist charging:

It is treason and slander, what they do in *Nyugat* under the pretext of civilizing the barbarian Magyars. They want to ruin our morals, they want to disillusion us of our faith, and they want to crush to pieces our national pride. A storm of outrage should sweep away all those who commit such deep offenses against the nation.

Leading political figures like István Tisza, soon to be prime minister, entered the fray by labeling the new literature as "incomprehensible bombast [that] is nothing more than the chaotic exterior of spiritual anarchy and an emptiness of mind and heart." Uncowed, Kaffka and her contemporaries continued to write and publish in *Nyugat,* and by 1912 an editorial in that journal could proclaim with satisfaction: "We have our new literature, and a new audience for it."

After she published a significant body of poetry and short stories in this journal, Kaffka's reputation as a major writer was further enhanced with the publication of four volumes of short stories as well as two volumes of verse, *Tallózó évek* (Years of Search, 1911) and *Utolszor a lyrán* (For the Last Time on the Lyre, 1912). In her first novel *Szinek és évek* (Colors and Years, 1912), she presents an emotionally stark and technically sophisticated study of a miserable widow of 50 who remembers her happier days in a world of the rural gentry, now doomed and crumbling. With its polished prose, this work gave proof that Kaffka had mastered one of modern literature's most challenging forms of expression, and she won near-unanimous critical praise for the novel. By 1914, she was recognized as Hungary's most gifted and popular woman writer. Amid the satisfactions derived from her achievements, Kaffka found gratification in her personal life during these years. In the summer of 1914, after a whirlwind courtship, she married Ervin Bauer, a young physician ten years her junior. The marriage was happy, despite the couple's separation almost immediately following their honeymoon: World War I broke out and Bauer was drafted to work in a military hospital.

In her next novel, *Mária évei* (The Years of Mária, 1913), Kaffka probed the psychology of a so-called "New Woman" of the day who chooses a career and personal independence rather than taking the traditional path of marriage, motherhood, and domesticity. In what is doubtless a self-portrait of the author during one stage in her life (as is the case in all of her novels), the protagonist Mária is shown as supremely optimistic while enrolled at teacher-training college in Budapest, with a romantic

spirit fueled by the literature she loves. Life's realities, however, soon hit her like a sledgehammer when she starts her career as a schoolteacher in a suffocating provincial town. Correspondence with a famous writer in Budapest does little to assuage her growing misery, which is only made worse with the possibility of marriage to an uninspiring teaching colleague. A final, desperate attempt to find fulfillment in Budapest also crumbles. Eventually, the conflict between Mária's literary fantasies and the wretched world of reality reaches a breaking point, and she ends her life by jumping from a bridge into the Danube. This difficult, melancholy novel sold well, continuing to attract buyers even during World War I (it sold 372 copies between December 1915 and May 1917, making it the second most popular book sold during that period by the *Nyugat* publishing house). Many Hungarian critics regard *Mária évei* as Kaffka's most artistically successful novel, with György Király hailing the portraiture of its heroine as representing nothing less than "a feminine Werther."

Kaffka's third novel, *Állomások* (Stations, 1914, final revised version, 1917), is a *roman-à-*

Hungarian postage stamp honoring Margit Kaffka, issued June 1980.

clef that presents thinly disguised portraits of the men and women of the intellectual circles she frequented. Budapest's literary life is portrayed in sharp detail, showing the great variety of backgrounds and personality types that made up this brilliant generation of artists. By now a master novelist, Kaffka captured the voice of the mostly Jewish individuals, preserving for posterity the idiom of their speech which gave occasional hints of German and Yiddish linguistic lineage. Unlike many non-Jewish intellectuals of the day who were infected by a growing spirit of anti-Semitism, Kaffka was strongly philosemitic in her views. In 1917, she wrote to a literary friend, "I must argue with my husband . . . and I must defend his own sect against him." In addition to her husband Ervin Bauer, most of her friends and literary colleagues were of Jewish origin. Increasingly attracted by the internationalist ideals of socialist doctrine, Kaffka went considerably beyond defending Jews against anti-Semitism, showing a growing sympathy for the aspirations of other ethnic groups that had been discriminated against within the Hungarian half of the Habsburg Monarchy, including the oppressed Croatians. Returning from Zagreb, she deplored the fact that even in wartime most Hungarians managed to know so much more about the literary and artistic life of Paris, London, or even New York than they did about the Croatian capital, a city with a vibrant intellectual life that was an integral part of the Kingdom of Hungary.

The immense suffering caused by World War I made an almost immediate impact on Margit Kaffka and her contemporaries. Alone one Christmas, she wrote a poem, "I Tried to Pray," to release some of her despair; in this work, she asked God to take pity on the suffering of the women whose lives were being irrevocably transformed by the war. Regarding support of the conflict as virtually a crime against humanity, Kaffka was horrified by the attitudes of some writers, including her *Nyugat* colleague, poet **Sarolta Lányi**, who hailed the coming of war in 1914 with jingoistic verse. Kaffka was radicalized by the constant barrage of official propaganda, which neither she nor her fellow intellectuals believed to be true, as well as by stories, relayed by her husband and others, of the carnage and suffering of the war.

She gave voice to her antiwar sentiments in the 1916 short novel *Két nyár* (Two Summers). In this work, her anger surfaces in a reflection on woman's fate, that of giving birth to a new life in pools of blood:

. . . and so a surplus of tiny bundles of steaming bodies; in order that some lives from the womb might always survive all those destined to be exterminated with most terrible weapons, in an infinite variety of bloody ways after twenty, a hundred, a thousand years to come. Thus there will always be an endless multitude of murderers and the accumulating dust of individual souls born to be destroyed in unimaginable numbers.

Increasingly radicalized by the utter lack of meaning of the war and the oppressive nature of the existing social order, Kaffka was more than a despairing pacifist. She empathized with the lowest of the low on the social order in Budapest, the women servants, and wrote with eloquence about the plight of illiterate workers. Kaffka became convinced that only a revolutionary upheaval could create a new order in which the subjugation of women was no longer central to the functioning of the system. These radical sentiments were expressed in a poem she published in *Nyugat* in 1912, "Sunrise Rhythms: 23 May 1912," after having been an eyewitness to the brutal suppression by the authorities of a peaceful socialist workers' demonstration:

"Men," I said quietly, and looked into their handsome bright eyes
"If anything should happen, don't forget to send for us too!" . . .
If only for a short while, you might untie the chains binding us. . . .
And, as in previous revolutions, thrust us onto your barricades again.

In 1917, Kaffka published what would turn out to be her last novel. Entitled *Hangyaboly* (The Ant Heap), it is clearly autobiographical and set in a convent school similar to the one in which she had been enrolled during her youth. The novel was written in 1916, while visiting her husband at his field hospital in Temesvár (now Rumania), with a motive as practical as it was artistic—she hoped to earn enough money from its sales to buy her husband a Zeiss microscope for his medical work. The themes in the novel include sexual awareness (taken as common knowledge in the school), as well as the temptations of the priests for their pupils and the nuns' passions for each other. Whereas some readers and critics have declared *The Ant Heap* to be a dogmatically anti-clerical and bitterly pessimistic work in which the dissection of religion and sexuality is little better than blasphemous and pornographic, others have come to regard the novel as essentially a work of considerable nostalgic charm, containing much that is affectionate and humorous. **Charlotte Franklin**, whose translation-adaptation of the novel into English appeared in print in 1995, suggests that through Kaffka's literary artistry the convent has become "a microcosm of life, portrayed refreshingly without sentimentality or vulgarity."

By early November 1918, four years of bloodletting ceased. Like many of her fellow intellectuals, Kaffka was optimistic about the future. She signed an appeal to the Hungarian intelligentsia which appeared in the Budapest newspaper *Világ* (World) on November 3rd urging support of a federation of all nations of the old monarchy—each an independent, equal nation, democratic and autonomous—based on the principles enunciated in Woodrow Wilson's Fourteen Points. In her personal life, too, there was much to look forward to. Her husband was released from his medical duties and returned to Budapest. But news of the ominous "Spanish influenza" was a dark cloud on the horizon, and Margit worried about Ervin, whose work at the hospital included performing autopsies on flu victims. She was also worried about her son László and the risks of contagion he was facing at his boarding school. In a letter, she voiced these concerns: "If we can survive the war none of us should succumb to a silly epidemic. . . . No more army, hospital, rural isolation, bug infested messy rooms, constant journeys in overcrowded trains. There will be peace and order. And work."

In late November 1918, Kaffka began to plan the research and writing of her next major work, a historical novel set in Biblical times. While discussing terms, advances and deadlines with her publisher, she began to suffer from headaches. Soon she was gravely ill with the dreaded influenza. Margit Kaffka died on December 1, 1918; her son László died the next day. Like one of the unexpected endings in the author's stories, her death was a profound blow for her husband, friends and literary colleagues. Mother and son were interred in a joint burial and the elite of Hungary's intellectual life appeared to pay tribute.

Margit Kaffka continues to be read by young and old in Hungary more than two generations after her death. Only in the 1990s, with the publication of a translation into English of *The Ant Heap*, has her work begun to be made accessible to the English-speaking world. Her powerful novel *Colors and Years* remains unknown to us, despite the fact that it has been translated into Czech, German, and Polish. Perhaps Kaffka summed up her life's work best in this novel, when the heroine turns to her suitor and says: "The word is the greatest human gift."

SOURCES:

Brunauer, Dalma H. "A Woman's Self-Liberation: The Story of Margit Kaffka (1880–1918)," in *Canadian-American Review of Hungarian Studies*. Vol. 5, no. 2. Fall, 1978, pp. 31–42.

Czigány, Lóránt. *The Oxford History of Hungarian Literature: From the Earliest Times to the Present*. Oxford: Clarendon Press, 1984.

Fenyo, Mario D. *Literature and Political Change: Budapest, 1908–1918*. Philadelphia, PA: The American Philosophical Society, 1987 (transactions of the American Philosophical Society, Vol. 77, part 6).

Gluck, Mary. *Georg Lukács and His Generation 1900–1918*. Cambridge, MA: Harvard University Press, 1985.

Kadarkay, Arpad. *Georg Lukács: Life, Thought, and Politics*. Oxford: Basil Blackwell, 1991.

Kaffka, Margit. *Az élet utján; versek, cikkek, naplójegyzetek* (Along the Road of Life: Poems, Articles, Diary Notes). Budapest: Szépirodalmi, 1972.

———. *The Ant Heap: A Novel*. Translated by Charlotte Franklin. London and NY: Marion Boyars, 1995.

Konnyu, Leslie. "Modern Magyar Literature: A Literary Survey and Anthology of the XXth Century Hungarian Authors," in *The American Hungarian Review*. Vol. 2, no. 3–4, 1964, pp. 1–124.

Lukács, Georg. *Gelebtes Denken: Eine Autobiographie im Dialog*. Edited by István Eörso, translated by Hans-Henning Paetzke. Frankfurt am Main: Suhrkamp Verlag, 1981.

Makkai, Adam, ed. *In Quest of the "Miracle Stag": The Poetry of Hungary*. Chicago and Budapest: Atlantis-Centaur/ M. Szivárvány/ Corvina, 1996.

Marcus, Judith, and Zoltán Tar, eds. *Georg Lukács: Selected Correspondence 1902–1920*. Budapest: Corvina Kiadó, 1986.

Reményi, Joseph. *Hungarian Writers and Literature: Modern Novelists, Critics, and Poets*. Edited by August J. Molnar. New Brunswick, NJ: Rutgers University Press, 1964.

Tezla, Albert. *Hungarian Authors: A Bibliographical Handbook*. Cambridge, MA: The Belknap Press of Harvard University Press, 1970.

Wittmann, Livia Käthe. "Desire in Feminist Narration: Reading Margit Kaffka and Dorothy Richardson," in *Canadian Review of Comparative Literature/Revue Canadienne de Littérature Comparée*. Vol. 21, no. 3. September, 1994, pp. 399–415.

Wittmann, Livia Z. "The New Woman as a European Phenomenon," in *Neohelicon*. Vol. 19, no. 2, 1992, pp. 49–68.

Zsuffa, Joseph. *Béla Balázs, The Man and the Artist*. Berkeley, CA: University of California Press, 1987.

John Haag,
Associate Professor of History,
University of Georgia, Athens, Georgia

Kafka, Helene (1894–1943).

See Restituta, Sister.

Kagan, Elsa (1896–1970).

See Triolet, Elsa.

Kahina (r. 695–703 CE)

Priestess and queen of Carthage who was a powerful and ruthless ruler of the Berber tribes of northern Africa. Name variations: Cahina; Dhabba the Kahina; Dahiyah Kahinah; Dahia-al Kahina; Kahiyah. Reigned between 695 and 703 CE.

Around the time of the capture of Carthage by the Arabs (695 CE), the normally pastoral Berber tribes of the Atlas Mountains of North Africa rallied under the leadership of Queen Kahina, a powerful black Jew known variously as Dahiyah Kahinah or Kahiyah, who was also said to be a prophet. Gathering Christians as well as Jews into a powerful army, Kahina led her tribes in an attack against the Arabs who were lead by Hassan ibn al-Nu'man, an Arab prince of Egypt. Successful in driving the Arabs back to Egypt, Kahina remained queen over a large region of North Africa for the next five years, while Prince Hassan planned his revenge. Hoping to ward off another attack, Kahina laid waste to her lands, ordering all the Berber cities destroyed, the gold and silver buried, and even the fruit trees cut down, leaving a desert. Unfortunately, her tactic succeeded only in impoverishing her people and did nothing to dissuade Hassan. Around 705 CE, when the Arabs attacked again, Queen Kahina was either killed in battle or beheaded, and the Berbers ultimately became allies of the Arabs.

Barbara Morgan,
Melrose, Massachusetts

Kahlo, Frida (1907–1954)

Mexican painter whose singular self-images, unconventional in style and startling in content, distinguished her from her peers. Name variations: Frida Rivera. Born Magdalena Carmen Frida Kahlo y Calderón in Coyoacan, Mexico, on July 6, 1907; died in Coyoacan on July 13, 1954; daughter of Guillermo Kahlo (a photographer) and Matilde Calderón; married Diego Rivera, in 1929 (divorced 1939, remarried 1940).

Injured in a bus accident (1925); painted first self-portrait (1926); held first solo exhibition, New York (1938); selected as a member of the Seminario de Cultura Mexicana (1942); held first Mexican solo exhibition (1953).

While many art historians believe that a painting, like any manufactured product, can be examined with scant attention to its creator, there remain artists whose work is so reliant upon personal experience that an understanding of their lives becomes essential. Frida Kahlo is such an artist.

Magdalena Carmen Frida Kahlo y Calderón was born on July 6, 1907, the third of four daughters of Guillermo Kahlo (born Wilhelm Kahl), a successful photographer of German-Jewish origins, and his second wife, **Matilde Calderón**. This frail quiet man, prone to epileptic seizures, was closer to Frida than was her mother, a woman who had placed two children from Guillermo's first marriage in an orphanage. In later life, Frida recalled, "My childhood was marvelous because although my father was a sick man (he had vertigos every month and a half) he was an immense example to me of tenderness, of work (photographer and also painter) and above all, of understanding for all my problems."

Polio at the age of six marked the beginning of a life of physical suffering for Frida and left her with an atrophied and shortened right leg. Early photographs of the family reveal Kahlo's attempts at concealing her difference, posing with her withered leg behind the healthy one. Losing a year of schooling to illness had no effect on her intellectual abilities, however, and in 1922 she was admitted to the National Preparatory School in Mexico City, one of just 35 girls in the best school in the country. There Kahlo embarked upon a five-year program leading to medical school. On entering the "Prepa," she immediately established the eccentricity of dress which was to become her trademark: she set off to school in her navy pleated dress, white shirt, black boots and stockings, looking for all the world like a German schoolgirl—although the school had no uniform. (Family photographs some years later show Kahlo with cropped hair, wearing a man's suit.) Frida, as a member of the elite gang of *Cachuchas* (named for the red hats they wore to distinguish themselves from other students) and girlfriend of its leader, Alejandro Gomez Ariaz, became part of the school intelligentsia and major pranksters. When an act of mischief led to her expulsion, the young girl took her case straight to the top—to the minister of education, José Vasconcelos. He berated the principal, saying, "If you can't manage a little girl like that, you are not fit to be a director of such an institution," and Kahlo was reinstated.

Vasconcelos' influence stretched far beyond his involvement with the preparatory school. As a key philosophical influence in the creation of a new Mexico following the revolution of 1910 against the dictator, Porfirio Díaz, he had initiated a movement of programs based, he said, upon "our blood, our language and our people." Rejecting the European influences of the previous decades, Mexicans had begun to look with new national pride at their native culture. Harnessing this wave of "Mexicanization," the minister of education launched a massive literacy campaign; promoted education for the masses; and contracted with the great Mexican artists of the day to create inspirational murals extolling Mexican culture.

As part of this initiative, Diego Rivera, one of the most famous Mexican painters of the time, returned from Paris in 1922 to work upon a mural at Kahlo's school. In spite of his obesity and frog-like features, Frida was entranced by him, spending long hours watching him work on the scaffold, oblivious to the glares of his current lover. She later confessed, to the disgust of a friend, that her ambition was to have a child by Rivera—an ambition which would never be realized.

In 1925, an accident befell the 18-year-old Kahlo which would alter her life forever. The bus upon which she was traveling home from school was crushed by a runaway trolley car, leaving Frida impaled upon a handrail. Ariaz described a surreal scene: "Something strange had happened. Frida was totally nude. The collision had unfastened her clothes. Someone in the bus, probably a house painter, had been carrying a packet of powdered gold. This package broke, and the gold fell all over the bleeding body of Frida. When people saw her they cried, 'La bailarina, la bailarina!' With the gold on her red, bloody body, they thought she was a dancer."

The injuries were horrific: a broken pelvis, shattered right leg and foot, dislocated shoulder, broken collarbone, broken ribs, and a spinal column broken in three places. The steel rod had exited her body through her vagina, in the process destroying, as Kahlo later noted, her virginity.

Throughout her recuperation, Kahlo read avidly, focusing her attention on anything related to art. Although her only artistic experience had been in helping her father to touch up photographs in his studio, she demonstrated natural drawing skills. Just one year after the accident, she produced her first serious painting, a self-portrait, the first of over 55 works she would make representing her own image.

By 1927, Kahlo had almost recovered and soon became involved in the circle of revolutionaries, artists, and intellectuals which included Diego Rivera. Determined to win his attention, she presented him with three of her paintings, asking for his comments. Diego was intrigued by this forthright young woman, agreed to visit her home to view her other works, and their romance began. In 1929, they were married in a civil ceremony, Kahlo, petite and strikingly attractive, dressed in a traditional Mexican costume borrowed from a maid, contrasting sharply with her fat, 42-year-old husband in his European-style suit.

Frida's early paintings are distinguished by a naiveté and primitivism most likely adopted to mask her lack of formal training. But her use of color, redolent of the Mexican landscape, set her apart from her European-influenced contemporaries. The confinement of her illness had led her to select subjects close to home—friends, family, animals, and, naturally, herself.

I never painted dreams. . . . I painted my reality.

—**Frida Kahlo**

Kahlo was devoted to her new groom, visiting him as he worked obsessively on his murals, bringing his lunch in a little basket decorated with flowers, as peasant women would have done. But their early married years were anything but rosy: Diego was an unreconstructed philanderer who continued his affairs, while Frida, in 1930, underwent an abortion due to fetal difficulties.

Both were committed communists, and, although they left the Mexican Communist Party in 1929 following factional disagreements, they retained a lifelong commitment to socialism. The late 1920s marked the beginning of a period of political repression and anti-communism in Mexico, forcing the couple to leave for the United States where Diego had received a commission to paint a mural in a most unlikely setting—given his political affiliations—the San Francisco Stock Exchange.

While Diego worked, Kahlo explored "Gringolandia," as she called it in letters to her friends. In San Francisco, she met the famous photographer, Edward Weston, who described her: "a little doll alongside Diego, but a doll in size only, for she is strong and quite beautiful, shows very little of her father's German blood. Dressed in native costume even to *huaraches* (sandals), she causes much excitement in the streets of San Francisco. People stop in their tracks to look in wonder." It was here that, in 1931, she painted a portrait of Luther Burbank, a California horticulturalist, in a style marking the advent of a more fantastical Frida Kahlo: in the painting, Burbank becomes a man-tree, his legs ending in roots in the earth into which he is planted.

After a brief visit to Mexico, Frida returned to the United States with Diego where a highly acclaimed show of his works was held in the New York Museum of Modern Art in 1932. A further mural commission led them to Detroit where Kahlo suffered the miscarriage which effected another stylistic change in her painting, evidenced in her work *Henry Ford Hospital* (1932), "the first of the series of bloody and terrifying self-portraits that were to make Frida Kahlo one of the most original painters of her time." In this work, she is lying, dishevelled and naked, on a hospital bed which appears to float above the ground. She is hemorrhaging and holds the ties to six symbols, then representative of herself and her emotions. Kahlo's grief in her inability to produce a much longed-for child displayed itself in many other paintings and drawings. It was also manifested in the way in which she collected and mended dolls, and lavished affection on other peoples' children and on her menage of animals.

Kahlo and Diego returned to Mexico in 1933 and moved into their newly built houses. Connected only by a bridge, the separate homes allowed each party the freedom to work in their own way: Kahlo, in quiet solitude; Diego, surrounded constantly by a noisy group of friends. Although she had been desperate to go back to her homeland, Frida's initial thrill at being there was marred when her husband began an affair with her sister, **Cristina Kahlo**. This dual betrayal affected Kahlo much more than had Diego's previous alliances, leading to the first of many separations, though the couple continued to see each other frequently. Frida's emotional anguish was compounded by physical suffering; in 1934, she underwent an operation on her injured foot, had her appendix removed, and suffered another abortion. But from all of these trials, Kahlo gathered new strength. The realization that her husband would never change but that she would need and love him nonetheless, coupled with a drive towards greater independence, resulted in a Frida Kahlo who was no longer "Mrs. Rivera," an ornament on the arm of the great man. A reconciliation with Diego took place, his affair with Cristina ended, but from now on Kahlo was to become less reliant upon her husband. Increasingly, she had affairs with other men (incurring the wrath of Diego) and women, bisexuality causing no scandal in the bohemian art circles of the day.

In 1937, Kahlo became actively involved with politics again when she and Diego played hosts to the Bolshevik revolutionaries, Leon Trotsky and his wife *Natalia Trotsky, who had been offered asylum in Mexico after their exile from the Soviet Union. Leon Trotsky's intelligence and, no doubt, his idolization by Diego, attracted Kahlo, and they progressed from public flirtation to an illicit love affair. After she had tired of him and broken off the relationship, Frida presented him with a seductive self-portrait but remained unswayed by his continued infatuation with her.

Kahlo began to develop, in her work, the portrayal of her inner self, as well as the sense of loss at her inability to have a child. *My Nurse and I* (1937) depicts Frida as a child being suckled by a native Indian nurse. With references to pre-Columbian idols, the painting combines the recurrent themes of childlessness and Mexican heritage. Kahlo later described it: "I appear with the face of an adult woman and the body of a baby girl, in the arms of my nana. From her nipples falls milk as from the sky. . . . I came out looking like such a little girl and she so strong and so saturated with providence, that it made me long to sleep."

Championed by the famous surrealist, André Breton, Kahlo held her first one-woman show in New York in 1938, receiving favorable reviews from the critics. From there, she exhibited in Paris where the Louvre purchased one of her self-portraits and where she was embraced as a true Surrealist(e). The fear of imminent war and the disorganization of the artists in charge of the exhibition did not make Kahlo's stay in France a happy one. Nevertheless, her show brought acclaim from the major figures in the art world. Duchamp, Miró, Tanguy, Kandinsky, and Picasso (who was reputedly entranced by Frida) attended and praised her work.

By the end of the following year, Kahlo and Diego were divorced for reasons which neither ever made explicit. Now living back in her family home in Coyoacan but unwilling to accept any money from her ex-husband, she painted at a furious pace in an attempt to become financially independent but refused to compromise her style. *The Two Fridas,* completed in 1939, depicts the Frida her husband had loved seated alongside, and holding the hand of, the Frida he had rejected. The hearts of both women are visible. A vein carries the blood from the loved Frida to the unloved Frida, who tries to stem its flow with surgical pincers as it drips onto her white dress and forms a pool on the ground. Kahlo presents herself, despite her distress at the divorce, as necessarily self-reliant, nurturing her wounded self with the other, stronger side of her personality.

In late 1940, the couple were married again, in San Francisco, after Kahlo had set terms stip-

Frida
Kahlo

ulating financial independence and no sexual relations. They returned to live together in the house in Coyoacan, their union this time on a happier and more placid basis. Frida worked on further self-portraits, decorated her home, tended to Diego, and amassed a veritable zoo, including monkeys, parrots, dogs, and an eagle, which all lived in the grounds of the house.

Although recognized in the United States, Kahlo's art was not formally acknowledged in Mexico until the early 1940s. Her selection, in

1942, as a member of the Seminario de Cultura Mexicana, whose aim was to promote Mexican culture, showed her growing reputation, as did a later government award of 5,000 pesos—a substantial amount at the time. Financial problems resulting from the difficulty of selling her unconventional works were slightly alleviated when Kahlo was invited to join a prominent group of artists as a teacher at La Esmeralda—an art school for working-class children. An inspiring if unstructured teacher, Frida attracted a group of students, known as *los Fridos,* who, when illness prevented her from traveling to the school, received their lesson in her home and often at her bedside. Beyond her specified role, Kahlo became mentor, confidant, and comrade to these students who, with her help, successfully established a group of painters with left-wing ideals to take art to the people.

By the mid-1940s, Kahlo's health had deteriorated, and she suffered increasing pain in her spine and damaged foot. Treatment to straighten her spine required her to wear surgical corsets made of steel, leather, or, most frequently, plaster. On one occasion, the plaster contracted so much as it dried that she was unable to breathe, and she was saved by a friend who sliced it open with a razor. Without the support of a corset, Frida resorted to tying herself upright against a chair-back so that she could continue her work. The paintings of this period depict her suffering: in *The Little Deer,* Frida is pierced by arrows; in *The Broken Column,* her torso is split in two to reveal a crumbling ionic column; in *Without Hope,* a weeping Frida vomits a funnel of gore onto her easel. An operation to fuse her spine proved unsuccessful, and in 1950 she entered a hospital for further surgery.

Kahlo was to spend a year in hospital after the incisions on her back proved resistant to healing. She decorated her room, as she had done her home, with puppets, paper doves, and candy skulls. She invited the stream of visitors to decorate her plaster corsets with feathers, photographs, and pebbles, and, when she was feeling well enough, she painted, lying on her back, on an easel suspended above her bed. She continued to adorn her hair with flowers and decorations and flirted with the hospital staff.

Returning to her home, she lived as an invalid, tended by Diego and nurses and, as a result of her physical restrictions, used the available subject matter in a series of still-life paintings. The pain she now suffered was made bearable only by massive doses of drugs which caused violent mood swings. In 1953, prompted by fears among friends that she was close to death, the first Mexican solo exhibition of her works was held in the gallery of **Lola Alvarez Bravo**. In an appropriately theatrical scene, a drugged and wide-eyed Frida was carried into the gallery on a stretcher to receive congratulations from her decorated bed in the center of the room. The exhibition attracted international attention, and Kahlo was revered for her heroism in attending.

Later that year, her right leg was amputated. The gangrene which had already cost her two toes had spread. Though publicly making light of the matter, Kahlo was deeply affected, writing in her diary "I am DISINTEGRATION." For the first time, she was unable to muster the reserves of strength and determination which had pulled her through previous crises: the ravaging of her body and, as she believed, of her beauty—the source of so many of her images—left her inconsolably depressed. She was increasingly dependent upon drugs and alcohol, and her relationship with Diego became even more tempestuous. For a full year, she did not paint. Her final paintings are testimony to her diminishing abilities.

In early July 1954, Kahlo made her last public appearance at a Communist rally, sitting for hours in the rain which led to her contracting pneumonia. For almost two weeks, her condition deteriorated; entries in her diary and her behavior towards friends indicate that she was aware that death was close. On July 13, 1954, Kahlo died, and, although the cause of death was cited as "pulmonary embolism," the possibility exists that she committed suicide. Her last painting, a still-life of watermelons, is inscribed vividly with the words "VIVA LA VIDA."

Even in death, drama surrounded Frida Kahlo. As she was slid into the oven for cremation, the intensity of the heat caused her body to sit up, her hair blazing around her face, and made her appear, according to an onlooker, as though she was smiling from the center of a sunflower.

The uniqueness of Frida Kahlo's work emanates from her ability to portray, in an original form, the singularity of her life, her suffering and her experience. Defying the limitations of a definable style, the inventiveness of her work places her in the vanguard of women artists of the 20th century for whom existing modes of representation were insufficient.

SOURCES:

Drucker, Malka. *Frida Kahlo: Torment and Triumph in her Life and Art.* NY: Bantam Books, 1991.

Herrera, Hayden. *Frida: A Biography of Frida Kahlo.* NY: Harper & Row, 1983.

———. *Frida Kahlo: The Paintings.* NY: HarperCollins, 1991.

Lowe, Sarah M. *Frida Kahlo.* Universe Series on Women Artists, Universe, 1991.

SUGGESTED READING:

The Diary of Frida Kahlo: An Intimate Self-Portrait. Foreword by Sarah M. Lowe. Mexico: Al Vaca Independiente, 1995 (printed in America by Harry N. Abrams).

The Letters of Frida Kahlo: Cartas Apasionadas. Selected and edited by Martha Zamora. Chronicle, 1995.

Tibol, Raquel. *Frida Kahlo: An Open Life.* Translated by Elinor Randall. University of New Mexico, 1993.

Diane Moody,
freelance writer, London, England

Kahn, Florence Prag (1866–1948)

American Republican congressional representative from Utah (1925–37). Born in Salt Lake City, Utah, on November 9, 1866; died in San Francisco, California, on November 16, 1948; daughter of Conrad Prag and Mary (Goldsmith) Prag; University of California at Berkeley, A.B. 1887; married Julius Kahn (a politician), in March 19, 1899 (died 1924); children: Julius Kahn; Conrad P. Kahn.

The daughter of Polish immigrants, Florence Prag Kahn was born in Salt Lake City, Utah, in 1866, but grew up in San Francisco, California, where her family moved in 1869. After graduating from the University of California in 1887, she aspired to a career in law, but the family's modest income precluding any further education. Instead, she became a schoolteacher, working for 12 years before her marriage to Julius Kahn, an actor turned politician who had just been elected the Republican congressman from California's Fourth District. With the exception of one term, Julius served for the next 25 years, during which time Florence supported his career, working particularly closely with him during the final years of his tenure when illness prevented him from fully carrying out his duties. Upon his death in 1924, she decided to run for his vacated seat. Elected in a special election held in February 1925, Kahn was reelected to five succeeding Congresses. Not only did she effectively advance her husband's legislative agenda, particularly in the area of military preparedness, but she became an effective member of the House in her own right. From her earliest days, she was known for her wit, especially during floor debates.

Kahn was somewhat dismayed over her early committee assignments, which included the Committee on the Census, the Committee on Coinage, Weights, and Measures, and the Committee on Indian Affairs, about which she bristled, "The only Indians in my district are in front of cigar stores." Later she served on the Committee on Military Affairs and on the Appropriations Committee. She was credited with securing expanded military installations in her district and was instrumental in gaining congressional approval for the San Francisco Bay Bridge, linking San Francisco and Oakland. She was also a staunch supporter of the FBI, and was friendly with its head J. Edgar Hoover, who referred to her as the "mother of the bureau."

Despite her popularity, Kahn lost her bid for a sixth term during the Democratic landslide of 1936. She retired to California and died there on November 16, 1948.

SOURCES:

McHenry, Robert, ed. *Famous American Women.* NY: Dover, 1980.

Office of the Historian. *Women in Congress, 1917–1990.* Commission on the Bicentenary of the U.S. House of Representatives, 1991.

Barbara Morgan,
Melrose, Massachusetts

Florence Prag Kahn

Kahn, Madeline (1942–1999)

American actress and comedian, best known for her ditzy characters in the films of Mel Brooks. Born Madeline Gail Kahn on September 29, 1942, in Boston, Massachusetts; died of ovarian cancer on December 3, 1999, in New York, New York; daughter of Bernard B. Wolfson (a dress manufacturer) and Paula (Wolfson) Kahn; graduated from Martin Van Buren High School, Queens; Hofstra University, Hempstead, Long Island, B.A., 1964; married John Hansbury (an attorney), on October 6, 1999.

Selected theater: Made Broadway debut in New Faces of 1968; *appeared as Goldie in* Two by Two *(1970), Chrissy in* Boom Boom Room *(1973), the shopgirl in* She Loves Me *(1977); appeared in* On the Twentieth Century *(1978), as Billie Dawn in* Born Yesterday *(1988), as Gorgeous Teitelbaum in* The Sisters Rosensweig *(1992).*

Selected filmography: What's Up Doc? *(1972);* Paper Moon *(1973); From the Mixed-up Files of Mrs. Basil E. Frankweiler *(1973);* Blazing Saddles *(1974); Young Frankenstein *(1974); At Long Last Love *(1975); The Adventure of Sherlock Holmes's Smarter Brother *(1975); Won Ton Ton—The Dog Who Saved Hollywood *(1976); High Anxiety *(1977); The Cheap Detective *(1978); (cameo)* The Muppet Movie *(1979); Simon *(1980); Happy Birthday, Gemini *(1980); Wholly Moses! *(1980); First Family *(1980); History of the World: Part I *(1981); Yellowbeard *(1983); Slapstick of Another Kind *(1984); City Heat *(1984); Clue *(1985); (voice only)* My Little Pony *(1986); (voice only)* An American Tail *(1986); Betsy's Wedding *(1990).*

A zany presence on stage, screen, and television, Madeline Kahn reached her zenith as the tired saloon singer Lili von Shtupp in Mel Brooks' western spoof *Blazing Saddles* (1974), a performance that Frank Rich termed "falling-down-on-the-floor funny." Brooks, who went on to cast Kahn in several of his subsequent movies, called the actress "one of the most talented people that ever lived." Kahn viewed acting as a compulsion. "I need to do it for some reason, and I love doing it," she once explained in interview for the *Christian Science Monitor* (January 29, 1976). "I suppose it's a way of reaching out to other people. . . . If I didn't love to do it, I wouldn't do it. . . . It isn't easy, and sometimes it's scary."

Madeline Gail Kahn was born in Boston and raised in New York City, primarily by her mother, who divorced Kahn's father when Madeline was very young and then remarried when she was 11. Shy and insecure as a child, she was en-couraged by her mother to "flower creatively" and was given piano, dance, and voice lessons to expedite the process. She slipped through high school unnoticed and won a scholarship to Hofstra University, where she majored in drama, then switched to music, and finally graduated as a speech therapist. Meanwhile, she kept up with her singing and following college decided to pursue an acting career. After waiting tables and making the rounds, in 1965 she snagged a role in the chorus of a City Center revival of *Kiss Me Kate*. She then spent two years performing opera and light opera roles with the Green Mansions repertory company in upstate New York. She got her first break with a role in *New Faces of 1968*, in which she delighted the critics with a Brecht-Weill parody, "Das Chicago Song." She won additional raves and her first Tony nomination for her portrayal of Chrissy, an ambitious go-go dancer, in David Rabe's *Boom Boom Room* (1973), performed at Lincoln Center. "She is extraordinary in the quality of her emotion, her evocation of a fighting vulnerability, her struggle to seize the sweetness of her humanity," wrote Jack Kroll in *Newsweek* (November 19, 1973).

The actress made her film debut in Peter Bogdanovich's *What's Up Doc?* (1972), stealing several scenes from superstar **Barbra Streisand.** "Miss Kahn, who has a voice that sounds as if it had been filtered through a ceramic nose, just about takes off with the movie," exclaimed Vincent Canby in *The New York Times* (March 10, 1972). Bogdanovich cast her again in *Paper Moon* (1973), this time as Trixie Delight, a Depression stripper who takes up with a con artist (Ryan O'Neal) and his equally crafty young daughter (**Tatum O'Neal**). Kahn's performance, described by **Judith Crist** as "sheer delight," earned her an Oscar nomination as Best Supporting Actress.

Kahn was in peak form in *Blazing Saddles*. Her portrayal of Lili von Shtupp, a spoof of *Marlene Dietrich's spoof in *Destry Rides Again*, brought her a second Oscar nomination for Best Supporting Actress. "Gartered, ruffled, a heaving sea of bosom and thigh, she sneers, sulks, lisps, and pouts her audience into a state of frenzied lust," wrote Robert Berkvist, describing Lili for *The New York Times*' readers (March 24, 1974). "Lili, Lili, Lili, they roar. Phooey, she yawns, go away. Later in her dressing room, she disarms the town's admiring sheriff by accepting the gift of a single flower with the immortal words, 'Oh, one wed wose, how wovely.'"

With Brooks directing her again, Kahn joined Gene Wilder and Marty Feldman in

Young Frankenstein (1974), a black-and-white parody of both *Mary Shelley*'s book and the 1931 movie based on the novel. In one of the film's more notorious scenes, Kahn, as Elizabeth, the fiancée of Dr. Frankenstein (Gene Wilder), the grandson of the original baron, responds to a moment of sexual ecstasy with a full-throated operatic rendition of "Sweet Mystery of Life," an episode termed sexist but hilarious by William Wolf in *Cue* (December 23, 1974). Kahn was teamed with Wilder and Feldman again in *The Adventure of Sherlock Holmes's Smarter Brother* (1975), which was

also written by Wilder and served as his directorial debut. In the role of Jenny, a music-hall singer and a woman of mystery, the actress was once again right on the mark. "Kahn contributes another wonderful impersonation of a sex tease with a weird combination of airiness and the pouts," reported Richard Schickel in *Time* (December 2, 1975). "Within that well-formed woman lurks the soul of a perpetual adolescent." Kahn also worked with Mel Brooks once more in *History of the World: Part I* (1981), but it proved to be a less successful venture for both of them.

Madeline Kahn

Kahn was on stage again in 1977, portraying an unfaithful wife in *Marco Polo Sings a Solo,* a comedy produced at the New York Public Theater, and—a month later—in the role of the shopgirl who finds love in the concert version of the musical *She Loves Me,* at Town Hall. Kahn's later stage appearances included a romp as Billie Dawn in a 1989 revival of *Born Yesterday* with Ed Asner, and a Tony-winning performance as the yearning sister Gorgeous in **Wendy Wasserstein**'s *The Sisters Rosensweig* (1992). That same year, Kahn made a one-time-only appearance in a Carnegie Hall tribute to Stephen Sondheim, giving a definitive performance of the fast-paced tongue-twister "Getting Married Today" from *Company* (1970).

Throughout her career, Madeline Kahn frequently performed on television, making the rounds of the late-night shows and appearing in three television series, "Oh Madeline" (1983–84), "Mr. President" (1989), and "Cosby" as the ditzy neighbor Pauline.

Kahn lived a quiet, unassuming life, eschewing the social scene and relishing her privacy. The actress was diagnosed with ovarian cancer in 1998, but did not make her illness public for almost a year. She even kept working, shooting four episodes of the Cosby show between chemotherapy treatments. On October 6, 1999, just two months before she died, she and her long-time companion, attorney John Hansbury, were married in a hospital ceremony. Following her death on December 3, Hansbury called the actress a "performer of brilliance and a loyal and trusted friend to everyone she encountered."

SOURCES:

Hodgman, George. "Farewell, Funny Lady," in *Entertainment Weekly.* December 17, 1999, p. 26.

Katz, Ephraim. *The Film Encyclopedia.* NY: HarperCollins, 1994.

Moritz, Charles, ed. *Current Biography 1977.* NY: H.W. Wilson, 1977.

Obituary in *The Boston Globe.* December 4, 1999.

Barbara Morgan,
Melrose, Massachusetts

Kairi, Evanthia (1797–1866)

Greek educator who was a leading feminist following the liberation of Greece from Turkish rule. Born in 1797 (some sources cite 1799) on the island of Andros; died in 1866; sister of Theophilos Kairis (a well-known philosopher).

Having received her education from her scholarly brother Theophilos Kairis, Evanthia Kairi was particularly concerned about the education of young girls and for many years headed up a famous girls' school in Kydonies (Greek Asia Minor, now Turkey), where she also taught history and the Classics. As well, she translated into Greek many French works concerning the education of young women.

Starting in 1821, during the Greek War of Independence against the Turks, Kairi solicited help from women's organizations in Europe and, through her contacts, influenced the development of a strong philhellenistic movement in Europe and the United States among women intellectuals. In 1826, with the fall of the garrison at Missolonghi to the Turks after years of brave defiance, she wrote the play *Nikiratos,* about the Greek women who had given their lives during the siege. Kairi's final years were spent on her native island of Andros, where she ran a home for war orphans.

Kaiser, Louisa (c. 1835–1925).

See Dat So La Lee.

Kaiulani (1875–1899)

Hawaiian princess who was named heir to the throne by Queen Liliuokalani. Born Victoria Kawekiu Lunalilo Kalaninuiahilapalapa Kaiulani Cleghorn on October 16, 1875, in Honolulu, Hawaii; died on March 6, 1899; only child of Archibald Scott (a businessman) and Princess Miriam Likelike; attended Great Harrowden Hall, Northhamptonshire, England; tutored privately in Brighton; never married; no children.

Saddened by the events of her young life, the beautiful Hawaiian princess, Kaiulani, once wrote: "I must have been born under an unlucky star." She began life in 1875 as the cherished daughter of Princess **Miriam Likelike** and her Scottish businessman husband Archibald Cleghorn. When Kaiulani was three, her family moved from their downtown Honolulu home to a Waikiki estate ("Ainahau"), deeded to Kaiulani on her christening day by her godmother Princess **Ruth Keelikolani**. There, the princess was educated by tutors and spent her spare time horseback riding, swimming, and surfing. At age 11, Kaiulani's idyllic world was shattered by the death of her mother, who was then in line to succeed Queen *Liliuokalani to the throne. The princess was further devastated by the decision to send her to England to prepare her for the royal succession that might now fall to her. Her only consolation at the time was a farewell poem written to her by Robert Louis Stevenson, who had frequently visited Ainahau and had befriended the young princess. ("Forth from her land to mine she goes,/ The Island maid, the Island rose.") In England, Kaiulani studied at Great Harrowden Hall in Northhamptonshire, and later in Brighton under a private tutor.

In 1891, upon the death of King Kalakaua and the succession to the throne of his sister Queen Liliuokalani, the 15-year-old princess was named heir presumptive. Liliuokalani's succession, however, was not well received by a growing faction who favored annexation of Hawaii to the United States and attempted to overthrow the monarchy. In January 1893, word reached Kaiulani that the queen had been forced to yield her authority to a provisional government. The princess, accompanied by her guardian, immediately traveled to Washington, D.C., where she petitioned President Grover Cleveland to help restore the monarchy in her struggling country. Although Cleveland did not sign the congressional bill authorizing annexation of Hawaii to the United States, he could do nothing to unseat the provisional government, and Kaiulani returned to England to resume her studies. (At one point, there was a movement in Hawaii to place the princess on the throne under a regency, but it was rejected by the provisional government.) In 1897, President William McKinley, who succeeded Cleveland, submitted to the Senate the Annexation Treaty that, if approved, would make Hawaii part of the United States, and Kaiulani returned to Honolulu, heir to a nonexistent throne. (Hawaii officially became a territory of the United States on August 12, 1898.)

Kaiulani, now a charming, beautiful woman, took up residence again at Ainahau, serving as a hostess to her father and performing a number of ceremonial functions. Although she was active in charity work and was pursued romantically by several eligible men, her spirit was broken. "I shan't be much of a Princess, shall I?," she reportedly told a friend. "They haven't left me much to live for. I think my heart is broken." In January 1899, Kaiulani became ill with what appeared to be a cold. She seemed to be recuperating on schedule when she died suddenly on March 6, 1899, age 24. The official causes of death were listed as "cardiac rheumatism and exophthalmic goiter," but many believed that the princess had simply succumbed to her broken heart. Thousands attended her funeral, after which she was laid to rest at the Royal Mausoleum at Nuuanu.

SOURCES:
Peterson, Barbara Bennett. *Notable Women of Hawaii.* Honolulu, HI: University of Hawaii Press, 1984.

Barbara Morgan,
Melrose, Massachusetts

Kaiulani

Kalama (c. 1820–1870)

Hawaiian queen who was the wife of Kamehameha III. Name variations: also known as Hakaleleponi Kapakuhaili. Born at Kaelehuluhulu, near Kailua, in the district of Kona, Hawaii, around 1829; died on September 20, 1870; daughter of a naval officer known as Captain Jack the Pilot; married Kauikeaouli (1814–1854), later known as Kamehameha III, king of Hawaii (r. 1824–1854), in February 1837; children: Keaweaweula I and Keaweaweula II, both of whom died in infancy; (adopted son) Alexander Liholiho (1834–1863), later known as Kamehameha IV, king of Hawaii (r. 1855–1863).

The daughter of a naval officer, known only as Captain Jack the Pilot, who was in the small navy of Kamehameha I, Queen Kalama had a decidedly humble background. Little is known of her life before her marriage to Kamehameha III in February 1837, which was recorded by **Laura Fish Judd**, a missionary's wife who was a friend of court. "The King is married to his favorite Kalama, a very sprightly young girl," Judd wrote in her memoirs. The royal couple had two children, both of whom died in infancy, but they later adopted a son, Alexander Liholiho, who became Kamehameha IV. According to Judd, the young queen "had few advantages of improvement" and needed assistance in managing her household. Judd also noted that there was some friction in court over Kalama's lack of aristocratic blood. "The old premier, **Kekauluohi** [1794–1845], was a little jealous of the Queen, being her superior by birth, and when I made purchases for them, I was

Kalama

the valley of Khidistavi in the Gurian region of western Georgia; daughter of a scientist (father) and a
teacher (mother).

Published six volumes of poetry (1953–85); active during the Soviet era in both literary and political
organizations.

always obliged to allow the old lady her first
choice. She always wanted her sash a little longer
and her bows a little larger than the Queen's."
Kalama, who was praised for her beauty and ladylike demeanor, also possessed a charitable nature. Steen Bille, a royal visitor, found her "a most
excellent, pious and benevolent lady, passing the
greater part of her time in preparing feather ornaments or sewing dresses for the poor; she is said
to be an expert with her needle."

When the king died in 1854, Kalama retired
from court and divided her time between her residence "Haimoeipo," near the State Capitol, and
another home in Nuuanu Valley. Having attained
considerable business acumen through the years,
she established a sugar plantation on several
hundreds of acres of land she owned at Kaneohe
and skillfully turned the venture into a successful
operation. Through careful management of her
assets, she became a wealthy woman and, at the
time of her death in 1870, owned over 22,000
acres of land on Oahu. She was laid to rest beside
her husband in the Royal Mausoleum.

SOURCES:
Peterson, Barbara Bennett. *Notable Women of Hawaii.*
Honolulu, HI: University of Hawaii Press, 1984.

Barbara Morgan,
Melrose, Massachusetts

K'alandadze, Ana (1924—)

*Georgian poet whose first poems, melodious and im-
pressionistic, were published in 1945 and reflected a
people's yearning for peace after many years of war.
Name variations: Ana Kalandadze. Born in 1924 in*

Located south of the Caucasus mountains
and east of the Black Sea, Georgia has a long and
proud history. A high level of civilization had already been achieved when St. Nino introduced
Christianity in the 4th century. The earliest
known texts in the Old Georgian language date
back to the 5th century. One of the more striking
aspects of Georgian culture has been its capacity
for absorbing the influence of the powerful civi-
lizations on its borders, and then transforming
these traditions into something distinctly Georgian. Throughout the history of Georgia, poets
have always played an important role in national
life. Many of the nation's great writers were also
public figures, and even such renowned kings as
David IV (known as David the Builder,
1089–1125), Temuraz (late 1600s) and
Vakhtang VI (1700s) were often as respected for
the quality of their writings as for their courage
in battle or wisdom in dispensing justice.

Ana K'alandadze was born in the Georgian
region of Guria where she was influenced as a
child by the area's natural beauties and cultural
traditions, including the Gurian folk dialect. In
1941, she moved to Georgia's capital, Tbilisi, to
study at the university. By the time she graduated
in 1946 with a degree in Caucasian languages,
she had already become a literary sensation.
While still a student, K'alandadze had been discovered by the poet Simon Cikovani, who insisted that she give a reading of her verse at a meeting of the Writers' Union. By 1945, her poems
were appearing in newspapers and magazines.

The years immediately following the Soviet
victory over fascism in 1945 were a period of
hope for the future as a war-weary nation
looked forward to a time of peaceful reconstruction. K'alandadze's lyrical poems appealed to
young and old, presenting simple, eternal images
of snow-capped mountain peaks, puppies sway-
ing on their wobbly legs, and a shy girl holding a
bunch of violets in her hand. To a public which
was daily inundated with propaganda, these
poems were refreshing in their lack of message
about the triumphs of Socialism or other elements of indoctrination. The poet's deep love of
nature was evident in her lyrics, which were not
intended, however, to provide literal descriptions of landscapes or vistas; instead, her poetry

helped readers experience a general, sensual perception of reality. Nature in K'alandadze's literary universe has its own animate personality:

> The wood has thrown off its shroud,
> Birches slowly step along the road.
> Somewhere wild puppies wake up
> And set off along quiet paths.

After achieving great literary success in her early 20s, K'alandadze continued to write poems over the next decades, publishing her first collection of verse in book form in 1953. Five more volumes, all of them simply entitled *Poems,* would appear in print over the next three decades. She became an active member of the Georgian Writers' Union in 1946, serving on its important organizing committee, and also became a member of the editorial board of the union's journal, *Literary Georgia.* Not only a literary personality but also public figure, K'alandadze was active in the political life of Georgia's capital, being elected twice to the Tbilisi City Council, and three times to the Tbilisi Workers' Council. She was also a scholar and devoted much of her time to working as a lexicographer on the ongoing publication of the Georgian National Dictionary, a project of the Linguistics Institute of the Georgian Academy of Sciences.

In a 1985 interview, K'alandadze stated that the inspiration that sparked her poetry remained essentially a mysterious force:

> I don't know how it comes or what makes it come. . . . Sometimes I'm just walking in the street, and a poem will strike me. It always comes very suddenly. And I walk along and memorize the images and the lines that come to me, and when all the lines and possible variations are clearly in my mind, then and only then do I begin to write it down. . . . We're lucky we don't know how we write poems, I think.

SOURCES:

Gvetadze, Manana. "Anna Kalandadze, 'Poems'," in *Soviet Literature.* No. 4, 1985, pp. 181–182.

Osborne, Karen Lee. "Ana K'alanddze and Lia St'urua: Two Contemporary Georgian Poets," in *The Literary Review: An International Journal of Contemporary Writing.* Vol. 30, no. 1. Fall 1986, pp. 5–16, 21–23.

Pynsent, Robert B., and S.I. Kanikova, eds. *Reader's Encyclopedia of Eastern European Literature.* NY: HarperCollins, 1993.

John Haag,
Associate Professor of History,
University of Georgia, Athens, Georgia

Kaleleokalani or Kaleleonalani
(1836–1885).

See Emma.

Kalich, Bertha (1874–1939)

Famed Yiddish actress. Name variations: also seen as Kalish. Born in Lemberg, Galicia (Austrian Poland), on May 17, 1874 (also cited as 1872); died in New York City, on April 18, 1939; the only child of Solomon Kalich (a brush manufacturer) and Babette (Halber) Kalich; attended the Chatsky School, Lemberg; studied voice at the Lemberg Conservatory; married Leopold Spachner, around 1890; children: Arthur (died in childhood); **Lillian Spachner.**

Referred to variously as "the Jewish Bernhardt" and "the Yiddish Duse," Bertha Kalich was a leading dramatic actress of New York's Yiddish theater during the late 19th and early 20th century. After a stunning English-speaking debut in 1905, she also played successfully on Broadway for several years. Strikingly tall, with a deep, resonant voice and expressive face, the actress, by her own count, took on 125 different roles in seven languages during the course of her career.

The events of Kalich's early life are sketchy. Born and raised in Lemberg, the capital of the Austrian province of Galicia (Poland), she apparently studied music and voice as a child and made her stage debut in 1887, age 13, at the Skarbeck Theater in her native city. She subsequently became a leading singer in the newly established Yiddish Theater in Lemberg and also made appearances in Budapest, Hungary, and Bucharest, Rumania. Around 1890, she married Leopold Spachner, whom she had met during her conservatory days. The couple had two children, a son who died in early childhood, and a daughter.

In 1894, amid the rising tide of anti-Semitism, the family immigrated to the United States and settled in New York, where Kalich first appeared at the Thalia Theater in a Yiddish version of *La Belle Hélène,* a comic opera adaptation that was typical fare in the early Yiddish theater. The following year, she made a transition from musicals to drama, performing with great success in Abraham Goldfaden's *The Ironmaster.* As the Yiddish theater began to produce the more serious plays of Jacob Gordin and others, as well as translations of Shakespeare and modern European dramatists, Kalich's career flourished. One of her more outstanding performances was in Gordin's *The Yiddish King Lear,* but she was equally as effective in realistic plays depicting ghetto life, such as *The East Side Ghetto, The Kreutzer Sonata, The Truth,* and *God, Man, and the Devil.* Over the course of ten years, Kalich reigned as the leading dramatic actress of the Yiddish theater.

The actress could not help but attract the attention of Broadway producers, who, in spite of the language barrier, were eager to exploit her extraordinary talent. After working hard to overcome her Polish accent, Kalich made her first English-speaking appearance in the title role of Victorien Sardou's *Fedora*, on May 22, 1905, at the American Theater. The performance apparently caught everyone by surprise. "Here was a Yiddish actress from the Bowery precincts," wrote one incredulous critic, "wearing Paris gowns as though to the manner born, and as regal and distinguished looking as Duse or Rejane!" Manager Harrison Grey Fiske, who later recalled Kalich's Broadway debut as a "wholly unexpected revelation," signed the actress to a five-year contract. After further tutoring in English by *Minnie Maddern Fiske, Kalich appeared in such plays as *Monna Vanna* (1905), an English version of Gordin's *The Kreutzer Sonata* (1906), *Therese Raquin* (1906), *Marta of the Lowlands* (1907), *Sappho and Phaon* (1907), *The Unbroken Road* (1908), and *Cora* (1908).

Bertha Kalich's appeal, however, was somewhat limited, her ethnicity and accent presenting too great a challenge for more conventional audiences. "In nothing but an exotic part, where she is either a woman of foreign birth or a strange creature doing strange things can the American public accept her," commented the *Boston Transcript*. Eventually, even Fiske found it difficult to find roles suited to Kalich's unique talent, and the two parted ways in 1910. Kalich subsequently acted for producers Lee Shubert and Arthur Hopkins, among others, and made several movies between 1916 and 1918. Her later stage roles included performances in *Jitta's Atonement* (1923), adapted from German by George Bernard Shaw, *Magda* (1926), and *The Soul of a Woman* (1928). While performing in the latter, she caught a cold which affected her eyesight. Despite three operations, she became increasingly blind and officially retired from the stage in 1931. She made occasional benefit and testimonial appearances, the last of which was a performance at the Jolson Theater on February 23, 1939. Bertha Kalich died on April 18, 1939, following several weeks of treatment for a stomach ailment.

SOURCES:

James, Edward T., ed. *Notable American Women, 1607–1950*. Cambridge, MA: The Belknap Press of Harvard University Press, 1971.

McHenry, Robert, ed. *Famous American Women*. NY: Dover, 1980.

Wilmeth, Don B., and Tice L. Miller, eds. *Cambridge Guide to American Theater*. London and NY: Cambridge University Press, 1993.

Barbara Morgan,
Melrose, Massachusetts

Bertha Kalich

Kallen, Kitty (1922—)

American pop vocalist. Born in Philadelphia, Pennsylvania, in 1922 (some sources cite 1923).

A popular singer during the 1940s and 1950s, Kitty Kallen was born in Philadelphia in 1922 and as a child performed on the local "Children's Hour." During her teen years, she sang on the radio with Jan Savitt, then, in 1939, joined Jack Teagarden's band. She subsequently sang with some of the biggest bands of the era, under the batons of Jimmy Dorsey, Harry James, and Artie Shaw. During the 1940s, Kallen was a frequent headliner on the popular radio shows hosted by Danny Kaye, David Rose, and Alec Templeton. When the swing era ended, she went out on her own, but her career waned until 1954, when she finally hit the charts with "Little Things Mean a Lot." In gear again, she had hits with "In The Chapel in The Moonlight" (in the top five) and "I Want You All To Myself" (in the top 30). Kitty Kallen retired in 1957 but came back with another blockbuster, "If I Give My

Heart To You," in 1959. She recorded a popular LP for RCA in 1962, *My Coloring Book.*

Kallir, Lilian (1931—)

Austrian pianist, known for her chamber-music recitals and recordings. Born in Prague, Czechoslovakia, on May 6, 1931; daughter of Rudolf F. Kallir and Moina M. (Rademacher) Kallir; graduated from Gardner School, New York City, 1948; studied at Mannes College of Music, 1946–49; studied at Berkshire Music Center, 1947–49; attended Sarah Lawrence College, 1948–50; studied piano with Hermande Grab and Isabelle Vengerova; married Claude Frank (a pianist), on August 29, 1959; became a naturalized citizen of U.S. (1947).

Lilian Kallir and her Austrian parents fled Nazism in 1939. She studied at New York's Mannes School of Music and later with *Isabelle Vengerova. Her New York debut in 1949 was with Dimitri Mitropoulos conducting the New York Philharmonic-Symphony Orchestra. Kallir married Claude Frank and appeared with him in duo-piano recitals. Her recording of the Mozart Concerto No. 17, K. 453, received high praise, and her chamber-music work did much to enhance her reputation.

John Haag,
Athens, Georgia

Kalmus, Natalie (1892–1965)

American entrepreneur who, with her husband, perfected the process of Technicolor for movies. Born Natalie Dunfee in 1892; died in 1965; graduated from Boston Art School and the Curry School of Expression; married Herbert T. Kalmus (an inventor and film pioneer), around 1912 (divorced).

Natalie Kalmus, who alluded to herself as "ringmaster to the rainbow," was instrumental in perfecting and marketing the film process known as Technicolor, which was initially invented by her husband Herbert T. Kalmus. The couple met and married around 1912, when Natalie was a young art student and Herbert was a college professor just starting to experiment with film color processing. Later he joined with Daniel Comstock and W.B. Westcott to develop an additive color motion-picture process which was eventually refined into the three-color process that is now used. In 1915, in order to exploit their invention, Herbert and his associates founded the Technicolor Motion Picture Corporation, for which Natalie Kalmus served as color consultant.

Kitty Kallen

In 1917, the company produced the first Technicolor film, *The Gulf Between,* a one-reeler made by superimposing red and green colored images on the screen at the same time through a special projector. Although most reviewers agreed that it was the finest natural color ever produced on film, the process was far from ideal. It was also highly expensive and was initially used only in selected sequences rather than in an entire film. The process was eventually improved into a true two-process color technique that was successfully used in *The Black Prince* (1926), starring Douglas Fairbanks. Rouben Mamoulian's *Becky Sharp* (1935) was the first feature film to use the more sophisticated three-color printing process.

While Technicolor was still in its infancy, Natalie Kalmus recognized its potential and took it upon herself to spread the word. She traveled extensively in the United States and Europe, conducting courses for art directors and technicians interested in learning the new color process. In 1932, she put together the first business package designed to "sell" color to the Hollywood studios. The package was intended to take the studio from pre- to post-production and included everything from equipment to personnel, all overseen by Kalmus on site. After laying out the color plan for a movie, she then provided an entire color consulting service, including the camera designed to handle the color process, a trained camera operator, set and wardrobe designers, makeup artists, lighting designers, and lab processing. "Until 1948," writes Marc Wanamaker, "her name was required to appear as 'Color Consultant' on every motion picture made by the company."

Kalmus also developed several techniques to make Technicolor seem more realistic. "Natural colors and lights do not tax the eye nearly as much as man-made colors and artificial lights," she explained. "Even when nature indulges in a riot of beautiful colors, there are subtle harmonies which justify these colors." To achieve this natural blend, Kalmus perfected a method of "color separation," in which differences in hues would be separated out from one another photographically. She also discovered that under the strong Technicolor lights the color white tended to reflect surrounding colors and become muddy, while a neutral gray always appeared white on the film.

During her career, Kalmus supervised the Technicolor process on some of the great film classics, including *Robin Hood* (1938), *The Wizard of Oz* (1939), and *Gone With the Wind* (1939). In her heyday, she commanded a salary of $65,000 a year, an almost unheard of sum for a woman in those days. As color became a more standard procedure, however, Kalmus' presence on the set was unnecessary and became intrusive. In 1950, now divorced from Herbert but retaining her position as a prime stockholder of the company, Kalmus formed her own television production company. She returned to film in 1956 to consult on *The Ten Commandments*.

SOURCES:

Aker, Ally. *Reel Women: Pioneers of the Cinema 1896 to the Present.* NY: Continuum 1991.

Katz, Ephraim. *The Film Encyclopedia.* NY: Harper-Collins, 1994.

Barbara Morgan,
Melrose, Massachusetts

Kalsoum, Oum (c. 1898–1975).

See Um Kalthum.

Kalthum, Um (c. 1898–1975).

See Um Kalthum.

Kalypso (fl. 200 BCE).

See Calypso.

Kamal, Sufia (1911–1999)

Bangladeshi poet, political activist and feminist. Born in 1911 in Barisal, southern district of what is now Bangladesh; died on November 20, 1999; only daughter of eminent lawyer; self-educated; married cousin Syed Nehal Hossai, in 1922 (died 1932); married Kamaluddin Ahmed, in 1937; children: (first marriage) daughter, Amena Kahnar; (second marriage) two daughters, Sultana Kamal and Saida Kamal, and two sons, Shahed Kamal and Sazid Kamal.

Published first story at age 14; began activism and involvement in socio-economic issues (1952); during early 1970s, aided women hurt by war of independence between Pakistan and Bangladesh; denounced fundamentalists' treatment of women and Islamic fundamentalist group called for her execution (1993); was first Bangladeshi woman to be buried with full state honors (1999).

Sufia Kamal was born in 1911, in what is now Bangladesh, the only daughter of an eminent lawyer. Denied a formal education because of her gender, Kamal educated herself, with her mother's encouragement, in the library of an uncle. At age 11, she married a cousin, Syed Nehal Hossain, who was then a law student, and had a daughter, **Amena Kahnar**. Hossain died in 1932. Sufia remarried five years later. With her second husband, Kamaluddin Ahmed, she had two more daughters, **Sultana Kamal** and **Saida Kamal**, and two sons, Shahed Kamal and Sazid Kamal.

Kamal had her first poem published at the age of 14. Her prose and poetry were well received, and some of her works were translated into English and Russian. Her writings and activism promoted democracy and women's emancipation while decrying religious communalism, fundamentalism, and superstition. In an interview on her 88th birthday, she lamented the lack of "wise men" and "honest politicians" in her native land and was critical of the overwhelming corruption she felt existed in Bangladesh.

As a woman, Kamal was allowed to learn Arabic and some Persian, but not Bengali. Violating tradition, she mastered Bengali from people working in her household and used the language for her writing. Kamal's political activism began in 1952 and continued through the 1960s. During the Bangladeshi war of independence from Pakistan in 1971, she began working for war-affected women. She also tried to bring Pakistani officials, whom the Bangladeshis considered war criminals, to justice. In her last decades, she focused her energies on women's rights and headed Bangladesh's largest women's organization for many years. She felt that all women in her native country were discriminated against, and that it was not a class issue. A deeply religious woman,

Kamal opposed religious extremism and, in 1993, was placed on a hit list by Harkatul Jihad, an Islamic extremist group.

Toward the end of her life, Kamal was hospitalized for age-related illnesses. She died, age 88, on November 20, 1999. Despite her request for a simple funeral, more than 10,000 paid their respects to Kamal, as she was accorded state honors at her interment, held in Dhaka, Bangladesh. She was the first woman in her country to receive that recognition.

Jo Anne Meginnes,
freelance writer, Brookfield, Vermont

Kamamalu (c. 1803–1824)

*Hawaiian queen who was the wife of Kamehameha II. Born around 1803; died in London, England, on July 8, 1824; daughter of Kamehameha I the Great (1758–1819), king of Hawaii (r. 1810–1819), and Kaheiheimalie; sister of *Kinau (c. 1805–1839); as a teenager, married half-brother Liholiho known as Kamehameha II (1797–1824), king of Hawaii (r. 1819–1824); no children.*

Born around 1803 and educated by missionaries, Kamamalu married her half-brother Kamehameha II (Liholiho), when she was a teenager. Noted for her intelligence and beauty, the young queen was described as "Amazonian" by the Reverend Hiram Bingham, a member of the first company of missionaries arriving in Hawaii in 1820, "tall and portly, of queenlike air, yet affectionate, filial, courteous, patriotic and friendly to the missionary cause."

Kamamalu, who read and wrote both in English and Hawaiian, was also characterized as "a woman of business," who oversaw the vast collection of gifts brought to the king as taxes, and corresponded daily with missionaries and those chiefs who could read and write. She was known as a gracious host and was particularly solicitous of the queen mother *Keopuolani, whom she nursed through her final illness.

On November 27, 1823, the queen accompanied her husband to England aboard the English whaleship *L'Aigle*. After a stopover in Rio de Janeiro, the royal party arrived in England on May 18, 1824, where they were entertained by King George IV. They were put up in the Caledonian Hotel near Charing Cross and attended service at Westminster Abbey and performances at the Covent Garden and Drury Lane theaters. The trip, however, had a particularly tragic outcome. One of the chiefs in the royal party contracted measles, a disease for which the Hawaiians had no immu-

Kamamalu

nity. Soon, almost all in the party became ill, including Kamamalu and Kamehameha. The young queen died on July 8; the devastated king died a short time later, on July 14. Both laid in state at the hotel before their bodies were removed to a vault in St. Martin's Church. They were taken home aboard the British frigate HMS *Blonde*, arriving in Honolulu on May 6, 1825. The bodies remained buried on the Iolani Palace grounds until 1867, when they were removed to the Royal Mausoleum in Nuuanu Valley.

SOURCES:
Peterson, Barbara Bennett. *Notable Women of Hawaii.* Honolulu, HI: University of Hawaii Press, 1984.

Barbara Morgan,
Melrose, Massachusetts

Kamamalu, Victoria (1838–1866)

Hawaiian princess who was kuhina nui (co-ruler) of the kingdom and heir to the throne. Born on November 1, 1838; died on May 29, 1866, in Honolulu; only daughter and youngest of five children of Kekuanaoa (governor of the island of Oahu) and Kinau (kuhina nui); sister of Alexander Liholiho (1834–1863), later known as Kamehameha IV, king of Hawaii (r. 1855–1863), and sister of Lot Kamehameha (1830–1872), later known as Kamehameha V, king of Hawaii (r. 1863–1872); granddaughter of Kamehameha I the Great (1758–1819), king of Hawaii (r. 1810–1819); never married; no children.

Born in a fort overlooking Honolulu Harbor in 1838, Victoria Kamamalu was named for

Queen *Kamamalu, a wife of Kamehameha II who died in 1824. She was the only daughter of Kekuanaoa, the governor of Oahu, and his wife *Kinau, a *kuhina nui* (co-ruler), and as a child was given to John Papa Ii and his wife Sarai, who, according to custom, acted as the child's royal guardians. Kinau, died when Kamamalu was five months old, but before her death she requested that her daughter receive a proper education. Her dying wish led to the establishment of the Chiefs' Children School, in which Kamamalu was enrolled in 1840, along with the children of other chiefs.

In April 1850, Kamamalu was officially elected the heir of her aunt *Kaahumanu, the first *kuhina nui* of the kingdom, and received title to large areas of land throughout the islands. It later became necessary for her to sell and lease some of her holdings in order to support herself. (The princess never married; her planned marriage to Prince William Lunalilo did not work out, and she turned down a later proposal.)

In 1854, when Kamehameha III died and Kamamalu's brother, Alexander Liholiho, succeeded to the throne as Kamehameha IV, Kamamalu, now 16, was named an heir to the throne (to follow Lot Kamehameha, another brother), and also given the title *kuhina nui*. She retained the title until 1863, when her brother Lot ascended the throne as Kamehameha V and appointed their father as *kuhina nui*. Kamamalu, who adopted the official name Victoria Kamamalu Kaahumanu, took her duties as co-ruler of the kingdom seriously and was considered a worthy successor of her aunt and her mother. She was a member of the Kawaiahao Church and the founder and lifetime president of the Kaahumanu Society, an organization concerned with the ill and elderly. In 1861, Sophia Cracroft, an English visitor to Hawaii, described Kamamalu as "tall and large," with "a good deal of stateliness about her." Cracroft also noted that Kamamalu set a good Christian example. "Victoria is doing very much with her people to counteract evil influence," she said. Seemingly, the only controversy in Kamamalu's life was a love affair with an American merchant.

Victoria Kamamalu took ill at a party in Honolulu in February 1866 and died on May 29 of that year, at age 27. Her body lay in state for four weeks before her funeral service. She was buried at the Royal Mausoleum in Nuuanu Valley.

SOURCES:
Peterson, Barbara Bennett. *Notable Women of Hawaii.* Honolulu, HI: University of Hawaii Press, 1984.

Barbara Morgan,
Melrose, Massachusetts

Kamenshek, Dorothy (1925—)

American athlete who played first base for the Rockford Peaches (1943–52) and was considered the best player in the history of the All-American Girls Baseball League. Name variations: Kammie Kamenshek; Dottie Kamenshek. Born on December 21, 1925, in Cincinnati, Ohio; attended the University of Cincinnati; graduated from Marquette University, Milwaukee, Wisconsin, 1958.

Considered the best player in the history of the All-American Girls Baseball League (AAGBL), Dorothy "Kammie" Kamenshek was born in Cincinnati, Ohio, on December 21, 1925. Coming from a poor family (her father died when she was nine), she wanted to join the army to learn a skill, but her mother would not hear of it. Instead, Kamenshek was allowed to take a bus to Chicago and try out for the new all-girl baseball league. (Her mother was convinced that her daughter would fail and soon be on the bus home.) Out of 250 hopefuls, however, Kamenshek was one of two Cincinnati women who made the final cut of 60 (the other was Betsy Jochum).

Kamenshek, standing 5'6" and weighing 135 pounds, started in the outfield with the Rockford (Illinois) Peaches, having played that position during her years on an industrial softball team. After a dozen games, she switched to first base and remained there for the rest of her

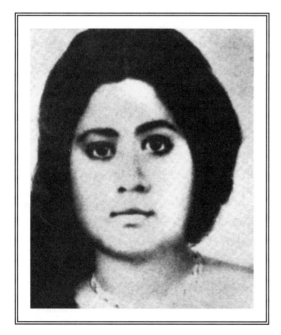

Victoria
Kamamalu

career. Her fielding set her apart from other first-base players, particularly her ability to stretch in every direction while keeping her foot on the bag. "Kammie was ahead of her time," said Peaches teammate *Rose Gacioch. "She used to make a split at first base the way they do in the majors now. It's like they learned from her." Though blessed with natural ability, Kamenshek never stopped working to better herself. "I practiced my footwork in winter on a pillow," she explained. "I threw it on the floor in front of a full-length mirror and pretended the pillow was first base. You try to make yourself as long as possible. I practiced shifting my feet. I stayed flexible year round."

As good as she was at first base, Kamenshek could also swing a powerful bat. In 1946, she won the AAGBL batting title with a .316 average, and she triumphed again the following year, hitting .306. In 1948, when the smaller 10⅜" ball was introduced, her averages went up. She hit .334 in 1950 and .345 in 1951. She could both drop a bunt in place when necessary, or drive the ball to the outfield. "She was a great hitter," said South Bend Blue Sox hurler *Jean Faut. "The free wingers were not too bad for me to handle, but she was a punch hitter and she gave me a lot of trouble." Indeed, Kamenshek was the bane of many pitchers, garnering a lifetime batting average of .292, the highest of any long-time league player. In 3,736 at-bats, she struck out only 81 times.

Kamenshek's talent was such that at one point the Fort Lauderdale club of the Florida International League tried to lure her to the minor league, but the AAGBL would not release her. Kamenshek was also dubious about the offer, thinking that it may have been designed "to draw in an audience," rather than to advance women in baseball. "I didn't want to be a guinea pig, so I turned the offer down."

In 1950, the Peaches fans held a "Kamenshek Night" in Beyer Stadium to honor her. Friends, family, teammates, and fans showered her with so many gifts that a truck had to be brought in to cart them away. Manager Bill Allington told reporters that Kamenshek "had a good cry and three hits." In spite of a back injury, she finished out that season and another, retiring from baseball in 1952 and pursuing a second career in physical therapy. After graduating from Marquette University in 1958, age 32, she worked for several years in Michigan as a physical therapist before moving to California in 1961. There she became chief of the Los Angeles Crippled Children's Services Department. "I

Dorothy Kamenshek

ended up in the *Orange County Who's Who* for work in physical therapy," she said. "I'm just as proud of that as I am of my baseball."

SOURCES:
Gregorich, Barbara. *Women at Play: The Story of Women in Baseball.* NY: Harcourt Brace, 1993.

Barbara Morgan,
Melrose, Massachusetts

Kaminska, Ida (1899–1980)

Russian actress, best known in America for her performance in The Shop on Main Street, *who was also manager and director of the Jewish State Theater of Poland. Name variations: Ida Kaminski. Born Ida Kaminska on September 4, 1899, in Odessa, Russia; died on May 21, 1980, in New York City; sixth child and only surviving daughter of Abraham Isaac Kaminski (an actor, playwright, director, and producer) and Esther Rachel (Halpern) Kaminska (an actor); graduated from the Gymnasium Francke, Warsaw, 1916; married Zygmunt Turkow (an actor and director), on June 16, 1918 (divorced 1932); married Marian Melman (a lawyer and journalist), in July 1936; children: (first marriage) Ruth Turkow; (second marriage) Victor Melman.*

Theater: made professional debut as Itzik in Akejdas Itzchok (Kaminski Theater, Warsaw, 1916); performed in Jewish and classical repertory (Kaminski Theater, Warsaw, 1916–17); performed in similar repertory (E. R. Kaminska Theater, Warsaw, 1917–19); toured the Soviet Union in repertory (1919–21); co-founded the Warsaw Jewish Art Theater (1922); was founder and producing director of the Ida

Kaminska Theater (1928–39); toured Russia (1939–45); was founder and artistic director of the Jewish State Theater of Poland (1945–68); made London debut in title role of Glikl fun Hameln *(Aleksander Theater, 1948); made New York debut with Jewish State Theater of Poland in title role of* Mirele Efros, *which she also adapted into Yiddish and directed (Billy Rose Theater, October 1967); adapted, directed and played title role in* Mother Courage *(Billy Rose Theater, November 1967); adapted, directed, and played the Grandmother in* The Trees Die Standing *(Roosevelt Theater, date unknown); again performed in* Mirele Efros *(Roosevelt Theater, December 1969).*

Selected filmography: A Vilna Legend *(Pol., 1924);* Without a Home *(Pol., 1936);* The Shop on Main Street *(Czech., 1965);* The Angel Levine *(US, 1970).*

Although remembered for her moving performance as the aging and deaf button-shop proprietor in the award-winning Czech film *The Shop on Main Street* (released in the United States by Paramount in 1966), Ida Kaminska was primarily associated with the Polish stage, as an eminent actress and as the manager and director of the Jewish State Theater of Poland. She once proclaimed that her life work was "the cultivation of a truly artistic Jewish theater."

A child of the theater, Kaminska was born in Odessa, in the Ukraine, while her parents were on tour. Her father Abraham Isaac Kaminski was a noted actor, playwright, director, and producer and the founder of the Yiddish Theater in Moscow. Her mother **Esther Kaminska**, known as the "mother of the Jewish stage," was a leading Yiddish actress until her death in 1925. Kaminska made her stage debut at five in her father's company, and as a child appeared regularly on the stage. Her earliest ambition, however, was to be a psychiatrist. After graduating from the Gymnasium Francke in Warsaw, she had already applied to the university when her parents cast her in a leading role in an operetta. She was so well received by the audience that she changed her mind and decided to remain in the theater. "I can't say I'm sorry," she later told an interviewer for the New York *World-Telegram and Sun* (April 22, 1966). "But it has been a hard life."

By the age of 18, still with her father's company, Kaminska was directing plays as well as acting in both comedies and tragedies. In 1918, she married Zygmunt Turkow, a member of the troupe, and after a three-year tour of the Soviet Union from 1919 to 1921, the couple returned to Warsaw where they established the Warsaw Jewish Art Theater, for which Kaminska was a principal actress and also directed many of the productions. Although the theater flourished, the marriage did not, and in 1932, following a divorce from Turkow, Kaminska organized her own company, the Drama Theater of Ida Kaminska, which she directed until 1939.

During World War II, Kaminska spent time in the Ukraine and in Moscow, where in addition to acting in Yiddish productions, she worked with the United Polish Patriotic League and did radio propaganda work for the Soviet government. Returning to Warsaw after the war, she found the Polish Jewish community almost entirely wiped out. Wanting to honor the Jews who had lost their lives, Kaminska and her second husband Marian Melman (whom she married in 1936), decided to try and reestablish the Jewish theater. "There was no good reason to do it," she said in an interview with Anthony Mancini of the *New York Post* (December 7, 1968), "for most of the Jews were gone. But we had the wish to make a monument to the murdered Jews. And the government helped us." The Yiddish theater in Warsaw reopened in November 1946, an event that Kaminska later remembered as the most profound and moving of her life. In 1949, the government granted the theater full subsidy as the Jewish State Theater of Poland. Kaminska served as artistic director of the theater, starred in numerous productions, and translated much of the company's repertory. The theater, which during its time was the only Yiddish permanent repertory theater in the world, gave 150 performances a year, half in Warsaw and half in the provinces. To accommodate the 60 or 70% of the audience who were non-Jewish, earphone translations into Polish were made available. The company also toured other Eastern European capitals and, with the easing of travel restrictions over the years, was able to play in additional capitals around the world. By 1967, the Polish government was providing the theater with $180,000 a year and was also constructing a new modern facility to house the company.

In addition to her stage work, Kaminska had also appeared sporadically in films from 1924 to 1936, but it was her performance in *The Shop on Main Street*, opposite Czech actor Josef Kroner, that brought her international fame. Her portrayal of Rosalie Lautmann, the 80-year-old widowed shopkeeper whose deafness and senility prevent her from fully comprehending what is happening to her and her fellow Jews during the Nazi occupation of Czechoslovakia, was described by critics as "brilliant" and "extraordinary." "It manages to translate the apocalyptic tragedy of our century into human terms and to do so with laughter and tears, with scorn and compassion, and with the simple beauty of truth," wrote **Judith Crist** in the *New York Herald Tribune* (January 25, 1966). For her performance, Kaminska won an acting award from the Cannes Film Festival, and an Oscar nomination for Best Actress (1966). The film received the 1966 Oscar as the Best Foreign Film and the 1966 New York Film Critics Award.

With Kaminska's emergence as an international star, Polish officials finally made funds available for the Jewish State Theater to travel to the United States. The company debuted at New York's Billy Rose Theater on October 19, 1967 (under the auspices of Harold Leventhal and **Marie Desmarais**). They chose for their first production Jacob Gordon's *Mirele Efros,* in which Kaminska's mother had starred during her New York engagement in 1911. The company was well received, and *Variety* (October 25, 1957) thought Kaminska's performance in the title role was "an eloquent characterization in a rich but economical style of playing." In November, the company performed Bertolt Brecht's *Mother Courage and her Children,* in which Kaminska again performed the title role. Richard Shepard, of *The New York Times* (November 17, 1979), who did not think Brecht was well suited to the Yiddish theater, nonetheless found Kaminska brilliant. "Brecht's lines roll off her tongue witheringly," he wrote. "There is no quavering little old lady here. She dominates the stage."

While in the United States, the company came under sharp attack from the Polish government following the defection of Henryk Grynberg, a novelist and member of the troupe. Called upon to denounce what the government called a "worldwide Zionist campaign slandering Poland," Kaminska refused to yield to pressure. Taking advantage of the regime's relaxation of exit rules for Jews, she resigned as director of the State Theater and, on August 23, 1968, with her husband and daughter **Ruth Turkow** and her family, left for Vienna where she was later joined by her son Victor. In November 1968, the family returned to the United States under a special State Department rule allowing immigration of

From the movie The Shop on Main Street, *starring Ida Kaminska.*

"involuntary" Communists. In March 1969, Kaminska and her troupe had just embarked on a tour of the United States and Canada when she suffered a serious heart attack.

Following her recovery, Kaminska concentrated her efforts on establishing a permanent Yiddish repertory in the United States, but found it difficult to obtain sponsorship. With the help of Harold Leventhal and the Association of Friends of Ida Kaminska, she established the Ida Kaminska Ensemble, which briefly performed at the Roosevelt Theater in Union Square, but failed to gain a foothold. Kaminska also starred in the film *Angel Levine*, which was filmed in the United States in 1969.

In addition to her countless translations, Kaminska was the author of two plays, *Once There Was a King* (1928) and *Close the Bunkers* (1964), both of which were successfully produced in Poland. She also wrote two autobiographies, one in 1936 and another in 1967. She was the recipient of numerous awards, including the Polish National Prize and the Czechoslovakian price for acting. She also received the Polish National Flag of Labor, First and Second Class, the Officer's Cross of Polish Liberation, and the Polish Cross of Merit. Ida Kaminska died in New York City on May 21, 1980.

SOURCES:

Katz, Ephraim. *The Film Encyclopedia*. NY: Harper-Collins, 1994.

Moritz, Charles, ed. *Current Biography 1969*. NY: H.W. Wilson, 1969.

———, ed. *Current Biography 1980*. NY: H.W. Wilson, 1980.

Barbara Morgan,
Melrose, Massachusetts

Kanaga, Consuelo (1894–1978)

African-American photographer who worked with portraits, still lifes, documentation, and news photography. Born in Astoria, Oregon, in 1894; died in Yorktown Heights, New York, in 1978; married Evans Davidson (a mining engineer), in 1919 (divorced 1926); married briefly for a second time during the early 1930s; married Wallace Putnam (a painter), in 1936.

Important in the study of both women and African-Americans in the history of American photography, Consuelo Kanaga produced portraits and cityscapes of New York which are outstanding examples of early 20th-century photography. Unfortunately, after her death in 1978, Kanaga's work did not become available to galleries or to individual collectors for years, and, therefore, was seldom seen. The 2,500 negatives and 375 prints that comprise the photographer's archive remained with her third husband, artist Wallace Putnam, but after his death were given to the Brooklyn Museum, which held a retrospective of her work in 1992. On the occasion of the exhibit, **Barbara Head Millstein**, associate curator of painting and sculpture at the Brooklyn Museum, and **Sarah M. Lowe**, guest curator of the exhibit, published *Consuelo Kanaga: An American Photographer*, which provides a rare look at the photographer's life and work.

Consuelo Kanaga was born in Astoria, Oregon, in 1894, and grew up around San Francisco, California. Little is known about her mother; her father was a lawyer who also published a magazine on farming and irrigation. Kanaga's first job was as a writer-reporter for the *San Francisco Chronicle*, whose editor encouraged her to also become the newspaper's photographer. She worked for the paper from 1915 to 1922, during which time she also became involved in portrait photography. In 1918, she joined the California Camera Club and discovered Alfred Stieglitz' *Camera Work*, which by her own account "changed her life." Viewing Stieglitz' prints as "the most beautiful things that had ever been done in photography," Kanaga was inspired to become an art photographer.

Kanaga married mining engineer Evans Davidson in 1919, but left him in 1922 and moved to New York, working as a news photographer for the *New York American* until 1924, then opening a portrait studio in San Francisco. After divorcing Davidson in 1926, she spent a year in Europe, returning to San Francisco with a new husband. (The marriage, difficult from the start, was relatively short-lived.) By the early 1930s, Kanaga's work had become widely respected, and she was included in the historic exhibit of Group f/64 in 1932, along with photographers *Imogen Cunningham and Edward Weston, who were also her friends.

In 1935, Kanaga moved to New York, where she worked on assignment for Index of American Design, a WPA project, and aligned herself with the political left, photographing for such publications as *New Masses, Labor Defender,* and *Sunday Worker*. She married painter Wallace Putnam in 1936, after which she lectured at the New York Photo League and continued to maintain a successful portrait business. Throughout the decade of the 1940s, she and Putnam lived and worked in Manhattan and were part of an artistic circle that included Adolph Gottlieb, Mark Rothko, and other luminaries of the period. In 1948, Kanaga's work was included in three important shows at the Museum of Modern Art.

In 1952, at Putnam's insistence, Kanaga moved permanently to the couple's modest vacation home in Yorktown Heights, New York (the Icehouse), an event which pretty much halted her career. "Connie herself was dispossessed—that is to say, she was in the wrong place," said William Maxwell, her neighbor in Yorktown Heights. "The people she wanted to be photographing were in the city, in black neighborhoods, or in the deep South." Although she continued her portrait business, which provided most of the couple's income, Kanaga lost interest in promoting her career. In the late 1950s, **Helen Gee**, who owned the Limelight Gallery in Manhattan, visited the photographer with a friend, hoping to arrange a show. Upon their arrival, Kanaga's only interest was in providing a meal for her guests. After they ate, Gee asked to see some of Kanaga's photographs. "She proceeded to wander around the house looking for them in an aimless fashion," Gee recalled. "She couldn't seem to focus at all. She couldn't find the photographs. The conclusion was that Wally began to show us his canvases of two birds. . . . There must have been two hundred canvases. . . . I didn't see one photograph and it didn't seem to bother her at all." The last solo exhibition of Kanaga's work while she was alive was at the Brooklyn Museum in 1976–77.

Although Kanaga produced landscapes, interiors, still-lifes and cityscapes, her portraits comprise the soul of her work. In attempting to capture the essence of her subjects, she found much of herself. "The great alchemy is your attitude, who you are, what you are," she said about portrait-making. "When you make a photograph, it is very much a picture of your own self. That is the important thing. Most people try to be striking to catch the eye. I think the thing is not to catch the eye but the spirit." Most outstanding among Kanaga's portraits are those of children. Millstein points out that her images are unsmiling and contemplative, and are examples of portraits that do not focus on making children cute. Also outstanding are her portraits of African Americans: one of Langston Hughes draped on a couch is notable, as is an image of a young African-American mother with her baby girl.

Elsa Dorfman, who reviewed the Millstein-Lowe book for *The Women's Review of Books,* suggests that although it is the first and probably only study that will be devoted to Kanaga's work, it raises as many questions about the photographer as it answers. Most pressing: Why, given her talent and opportunity, did Consuelo Kanaga produce such a modest body of work?

SOURCES:

Dorfman, Elsa. "An interrupted career," in *The Women's Review of Books.* Vol. X, no. 7. April 1993.

Millstein, Barbara Head, and Sarah M. Lowe. *Consuelo Kanaga: An American Photographer.* Seattle, WA: University of Washington Press, 1992.

Rosenblum, Naomi. *A History of Women Photographers.* NY: Abbeville Press, 1994.

Barbara Morgan,
Melrose, Massachusetts

Kanahele, Helen Lake (1916–1976)

American labor leader. Born on May 26, 1916, in Kona, Hawaii; died on June 12, 1976, in Honolulu, Hawaii; educated up to the eighth grade at Central Intermediate School in Honolulu; married Alfred Kanahele; children: Mary Jane Kanahele; Helen Kanahele.

Helen Lake was born in Kona, Hawaii, in 1916. Her English father died when she was five and her Hawaiian mother one year later, so Helen was adopted by **Irene West**. At a young age, she gained fame as a singer and dancer—performing three world tours—but her interest in politics proved to be the stronger ambition. Helen's first introduction to politics occurred at age 12 when she assisted Democratic candidates in their political campaigns.

Not much is known about Helen's life from the mid-1930s to the mid-1940s; during this period, she married Alfred Kanahele and had two daughters, Mary Jane and Helen. Three years after their marriage, Alfred walked away from the marriage and disappeared from their lives, leaving Helen to support her two children. In 1948, she was employed by the City and County of Honolulu as a laundry worker at Maluhia Hospital. While there, she started to assemble the workers into a division of the United Public Workers (UPW). When the chief administrator of the hospital, Dr. Thomas Mossman, discovered her union activities, he transferred Kanahele to the morgue to assist in autopsy work. She filed a grievance against Mossman, which led eventually to her work as custodian at the Kalakaua Intermediate School. In the spring of 1949, Kanahele joined the Hawaiian Homesteaders Improvement Club, leading campaigns to benefit the homesteaders. She held several offices in the club, including vice chair and director, as well as corresponding secretary.

The International Longshoremen and Warehousemen's Union (ILWU) strike in early May of 1949, to gain wage parity with the West Coast longshoremen, proved to be a turning point in Helen Kanahele's public life. The community divided into two camps over the strike: one supported the strikers, the other was angered by the interruption. When the ILWU's Women's Auxiliary formed a counter-picket line in response to the May 31 protest by 200 women sympathetic to the employers' side in the strike, Kanahele became so impassioned that she marched all day alongside the ILWU picketers. She also joined the ILWU Women's Auxiliary and became an active and enthusiastic member.

Kanahele was an active member of the Democratic Party. In 1950, she ran unsuccessfully as a delegate to the Constitutional Convention on a seven-point platform that included equal rights for women, guarantees of individual and minority rights, and the right to a job and a decent wage. Throughout the 1950s, she continued to be a strong advocate of women's political rights. In 1951, Kanahele was elected president of the ILWU Women's Auxiliary.

Helen Kanahele was also an advocate of human rights. Perhaps her most public cause was her campaign to save two Hawaiian youths, James E. Majors and John Palakiko, from being hanged in March of 1948 for the murder of **Therese Wilder**. With just three days to spare before the execution, she visited Governor Oren E. Long to commute Majors' and Palakiko's sentences to life imprisonment; however, he offered no support. Kanahele remained undeterred and obtained the aid of labor attorney **Harriet Bouslog**. She also initiated an island-wide petition

campaign, gathered thousand of signatures for clemency, and raised money to pay the youths' legal defense fees. Kanahele's and Bouslog's efforts would pay off in 1961 when the new governor, John A. Burns, commuted the sentence.

Kanahele remained active in union organization activities throughout the Majors-Palakiko campaign. She recruited new members into the UPW, worked as a lobbyist, and served on grievance committees. From 1954 on, she held numerous offices, including Oahu division vice president, territorial secretary-treasurer, and secretary and board member of the political action committee. Her courage and charisma as a labor leader were legendary. For example, in April of 1954, she was subpoenaed to appear before the Territorial Committee on Subversive Activities. The committee questioned her beliefs on capital punishment, world peace, activities in the UPW, and leadership in the ILWU Women's Auxiliary, attempting to elicit a confession that she was a Communist. Despite the pressure, Kanahele held her ground and testified that she took full responsibility for her political actions and statements.

Helen had so severely injured her arm during her janitorial duties at Kalakaua Intermediate School that she retired on a disability pension; her influence in the union, however, remained strong. Helen Kanahele died in Honolulu in 1976 and was buried in Oahu Cemetery. She was a controversial figure in Hawaiian public life. Although some regarded her as an enemy, she was much admired by union loyalists and others in the Hawaiian community. At a time when women were not involved as leaders in union and other organizational activities, her authority and power were accepted.

SOURCES:

Peterson, Barbara Bennett. *Notable Women of Hawaii.* Honolulu, HI: University of Hawaii Press, 1984.

Kim L. Messeri,
freelance writer, Austin, Texas

Helen
Lake
Kanahele

Kanakaole, Edith K. (1913–1979)

Hawaiian composer, chanter, dancer, teacher, and entertainer. Name variations: Aunt Edith; Kanaka'ole. Born Edith Ke'kuhikuhi-i-pu'u-one-o-na-ali'i-o-kohala Kenao on October 30, 1913, in Honomu, Puna district, Hawaii; died on October 3, 1979; daughter of John Kanaele Kenao and Mary Keliikuewa Ahiena; married Luka Kanakaole on January 21, 1933; children: six, including daughters **Nalani Kanakaole** *and* **Pualani Kanakaole**, *who studied and then danced with her.*

Instructor at Hawaii Community College (1971–79) and University of Hawaii at Hilo (1973–79); pio-

neered courses and seminars in ethnobotany, chant, mythology, genealogy, land ownership, and ohana *(extended Hawaiian family)*, *Polynesian history, and the Hawaiian oral arts; trained in* oli *chanting, choreographed hulas for many of her chants.*

Edith Kanakaole believed that the *oli* chant (the unaccompanied chant) formed the basis of Hawaiian culture and history. She learned this art first from her mother **Mary Keliikuewa Ahiena** and then from **Akoni Mika**, the well-known dancer and chanter. In order to better understand this ancient art, Edith Kanakaole became fluent in Hawaiian so that she could ascertain the hidden meaning of a chant or its *kaona*. Her compositions encompassed all the major styles of delivery. She performed in many places, often choreographing hulas for many of the chants, and founded her own *halau* (hula school) Halau O Kekuhi in 1953. Kanakaole received the Distinction of Cultural Leadership award in 1979. She represents women throughout the world who for millennia have handed down history and culture through oral story and song.

Her record albums *Haakui Pele I Hawaii* ("Pele Prevails in Hawaii," a selection of traditional and original chants) and *Hiipoi I Ka Aiina Aloha* ("Cherish the Beloved Land") won the Na Hoku Hanohano (Stars of Distinction) award for best traditional albums in 1978 and 1979.

SOURCES:

Cohen, Aaron I. *International Encyclopedia of Women Composers*. 2 vols. NY: Books & Music (USA), 1987.

Peterson, Barbara Bennett, ed. *Notable Women of Hawaii*. Honolulu: University of Hawaii Press, 1984.

John Haag,
Athens, Georgia

𝓔dith 𝓚. 𝓚anakaole

Kander, Lizzie Black (1858–1940)

American welfare worker and author. Born on May 28, 1858, in Milwaukee, Wisconsin; died on July 24, 1940, in Milwaukee, Wisconsin; second daughter and one of five children of John Black (the operator of a dry goods shop) and Mary (Pereles) Black; sister of Herman Black, publisher of the Chicago American *(1913–33); attended the Fifth Ward School, Milwaukee; graduated from Milwaukee High School, 1878; married Simon Kander (a businessman and politician), on May 17, 1881 (died 1931): no children.*

A lifelong resident of Milwaukee, Wisconsin, Lizzie Kander attended both grammar and high school in that city and, as a young girl, helped out in her father's dry goods store. A graduate of Milwaukee High School, she was married in May 1881 to Simon Kander, a businessman and local politician. As a young matron, Lizzie Kander became involved in welfare work and remained committed to volunteerism for the rest of her life. (She rose at five o'clock, completing her housework early in the day so she could devote her afternoons to her welfare activities.) In her 20s, she was a member of the Ladies Relief Sewing Society of Milwaukee, a group that collected, repaired, and distributed discarded clothing to poor immigrant families. In 1896, after serving as president of the society for a year, she was selected to be president of the newly organized Milwaukee Jewish Mission, whose purpose was to provide vocational and domestic training to children age 5 to 14. In 1900, under Kander's leadership, the mission joined with another Jewish charitable group, the Sisterhood of Personal Service, to form the city's first social settlement house. With financial backing from the Federated Jewish Charities of Milwaukee, the Settlement, as it was called, expanded its educational program to include classes in English, American history, and music. It also served as a community center, providing a gymnasium and public bath, as well as boys' and girls' clubs, and even a club for mothers.

Kander was particularly interested in the Settlement's cooking classes, which she taught with several other women. To facilitate the distribution of recipes to class members, she prepared a collection of them in book form, *The Settlement Cook Book: The Way to a Man's Heart* (1901). Financed by selling advertising space, the cookbook became immensely popular outside the Settlement. Kander continued to collect recipes from friends and cooks around the world in preparation for a second edition which came out in 1903 and sold 1,500 copies, earning a modest profit. Kander continued to help edit subsequent editions and from 1914 took over sole responsibility for editing each new revision. Revised and expanded through the years, the book went through 40 editions and sold well over a million copies.

Lizzie
Black
Kander

Under Kander's leadership, the Settlement outgrew its original facilities and in 1911 moved into new and larger quarters, the Abraham Lincoln House; Kander remained president until 1918. (In 1931, the Abraham Lincoln House became the Jewish Community Center.) Kander was also active in other community activities, particularly those involving education. She served as a member of the Board of School Directors of Milwaukee (1907–19), and was instrumental in the creation of a vocational high school for girls. Lizzie Kander died of coronary thrombosis at the age of 82, having survived her husband by nine years. She is buried in Milwaukee's Greenwood Cemetery.

SOURCES:
James, Edward T., ed. *Notable American Women, 1607–1950*. Cambridge, MA: The Belknap Press of Harvard University Press, 1971.
McHenry, Robert, ed. *Famous American Women*. NY: Dover, 1983.

Barbara Morgan,
Melrose, Massachusetts

Kane, Helen (1904–1966)

American actress and singer. Born Helen Schroeder in the Bronx, New York, on August 4, 1904; died in 1966.

Filmography: Nothing but the Truth *(1929);* Sweetie *(1929);* Pointed Heels *(1929);* Paramount on Parade *(1930);* Dangerous Nan McGrew *(1930);* Heads Up *(1930).*

A vaudeville performer from the age of 17, Helen Kane made her Broadway debut in the musical *A Night in Spain* (1927). In 1928, her squeaky "boop-boop-a-doop" rendition of the song "I Wanna Be Loved by You," in the musical *Good Boy*, catapulted her to a short-lived career in early talkies. Kane was portrayed by **Debbie Reynolds** in the 1950 film *Three Little Words* (about the songwriting team of Kalmar and Ruby), in which Kane provided the off-screen singing.

Kane, Margaret Fox.

See joint entry on Fox, Kate and Margaret.

Kane, Sarah (1971–1999)

Provocative British playwright. Born around 1971 in Brentwood, Essex County, east of London, England; died on February 20, 1999, at King's College Hospital in London, England, of an apparent suicide; daughter of a journalist; graduated from Bristol University, honors in drama; graduated from Birmingham University, master's degree in playwriting.

Selected writings: (plays) Blasted, Phaedra's Love, Cleansed, *and* Crave.

Sarah Kane, born the daughter of a journalist around 1971, grew up in a home that "went through an obsessive Christian redemption process during her youth," writes Warren Hoge. At age 17, she denounced her family's beliefs, claiming they were "a spirit-filled, born-again lunacy." Kane was interested in the theater as a teenager and directed school productions, including Chekhov's *The Bear* and ***Joan Littlewood**'s *Oh, What a Lovely War.* After graduating with honors in drama at Bristol University and earning a master's degree in playwriting at Birmingham University, she became a writer-in-residence at Paines Plough, an experimental company. She also ran workshops for the Royal Court International in Bulgaria and Spain.

When she was 23, Sarah Kane's first play was performed in London. In her *New York Times* obituary, Hoge wrote of *Blasted*: "No play or playwright had caused such outrage since Edward Bond . . . 30 years earlier on the same Royal Court stage." The Royal Court has a reputation of working with frank writers, and three of Kane's four plays were presented there.

Although she was quite popular in continental Europe, Kane and her plays were the subject of controversy in Britain. She was criticized for the amount of explicit sexual and violent content in her work. Said Kane: "The reading I did in my formative years was the incredible violence of the Bible. It was full of rape, mutilation, war and pestilence." Her plays include the cannibalization of a dead baby, savage amputations, rape, and eye gouging. Many critics and viewers described her work as depraved and "a disgusting feast of filth." However, other critics praised her work for its honesty. Writes Benedict Nightingale, in *The London Times*: "She is not the gloating opportunist that some reviewers of 'Blasted' thought. She has no less integrity than Pinter or Bond, but, God knows, I would hate to live in her head." Kane, upset by all the negative publicity, used a pseudonym during the early run of her last play, *Crave*.

Sarah Kane lived alone in Brixton in South London and wrote during the early morning hours when most people were sleeping. Friends said that she talked so much about suicide that it became a joke, and her play, *Crave*, ends with a suicide. On February 20, 1999, while in King's College Hospital being treated for depression, she was found hanged in her room.

SOURCES:

Hoge, Warren. "Sarah Kane, 28, Bleak, Explosive Playwright," in *The New York Times*. February 25, 1999.

Karina L. Kerr, M.A.,
Ypsilanti, Michigan

Kanga (fl. 1220)

*Queen of Norway. Flourished in 1220; first wife of Haakon IV the Elder (1204–1263), king of Norway (r. 1217–1263); children: Sigurd; Cecilie (d. 1248, who married Gregor Anderson and Harold, king of Man). Haakon's second wife was *Margaret (d. 1270).*

Kang Ke-ching (1911–1992).

See Kang Keqing.

Kang Keqing (1911–1992)

Chinese revolutionary veteran who survived the rigors of the Long March, participated in the Communist Revolution, and emerged as an eminent woman leader in the People's Republic of China. Name variations: Kang Ke-ching; K'ang K'o-ching. Pronunciation: KAHNG ke-CHING. Born Kang Guixiu in autumn 1911 (some sources cite 1910 or 1912 but 1911 is documented), in Wanan, Jiangxi, China; died in Beijing, China, on April 22, 1992; daughter of Kang Nianxiao (a fisherman) and Huang Niangu; attended the Red Military Academy at Ruijin, Jiangxi; attended the Kangda (Anti-Japanese Political and Military Academy) at Yanan, Shaanxi; married Zhu De (Chu Teh, a general), in 1929 (died July 6, 1976); children: (stepson) Zhu Qi; (stepdaughter) Zhu Min.

Adopted by peasant Luo Qiqing (1911); served as chair of the Women's Union at Luotangwan, Jiangxi, and was a member of the Communist Youth (1927); joined the Red Army (1928); married General Zhu De (1929); was a member of the Chinese Communist Party (1931); served as commander of the Women Volunteers, Ruijin (1932); participated in the Long March (1934–36); was vice-chair of the Committee for the Protection of Children in the Liberated Areas (1946); was a member of the Preparatory Committee for the Foundation of the Democratic Women's Federation (1948); was a member of the Standing Committee of the Democratic Women's Federation (1949–55); served as secretary of the Democratic Women's Federation (1955); was a member of the Chinese People's Political Consultative Conference (1949–75); was a deputy for Henan Province to the First National People's Congress (1954) and reelected to the Second NPC (1959); was a vice-chair of the Federation of Women (1957–77); was deputy for Jiangxi to the Third NPC (1965); was a member of the Standing Committee of the Fourth NPC (1975), reelected to the Fifth NPC (1978), reelected to the Sixth NPC (1986); was a member of the Standing Committee of the Chinese People's Political Consultative Conference (1975–78); was a member of the Central Committee of the Chinese Communist Party (1977–85); was chair of the Federation of Women (1977–88); was a vice-chair of the Chinese People's Political Consultative Conference (1978–92); was honorary chair of the Federation of Women (1988–92).

On October 16, 1934, the Chinese Communists broke through the Nationalist stranglehold outside Ruijin, Jiangxi, and undertook one of history's longest retreats. Savaged by skirmishes, forbidding terrain, harsh weather, shortage of supplies, and illness, they trekked over 6,000 miles before establishing a foothold in north China by October 1935. Rumors about the "Red-bandits," ranging from Communist brutalities to its dissolution, were then flying around. Not until the visit of Western reporters to the Communist headquarters was the epic march known to the outside world.

Among the first visitors was Edgar Snow, the American journalist. On the heels of his visit came his wife *Helen Foster Snow, writing under the pseudonym Nym Wales, who ventured to Yanan, Shaanxi, with an enthusiasm to collect research materials on the Communist struggle. It was evident that the Long March had taken its toll on the Communists. Among other things, Helen Snow noticed that most of the women in the veteran Communist ranks were ill from tuberculosis or the aftereffects of pregnancies. The only exception was the "girl commander" who was in glowing health.

"During the Long March," wrote Helen Snow, "she carried her own rifle and knapsack, and once or twice she carried wounded soldiers on her back. . . . She had become famous for being one of the best sharpshooters in the whole army, and for having the ability to use a pistol with either hand. . . . Except for her liking for soldiering, she lacked masculine characteristics and looked like a maternal peasant woman." *Agnes Smedley, biographer of General Zhu De, described her as a "grave, disciplined and hard-working veteran." The American writer found in her the "extraordinary independence of the new revolutionary women of China."

The driving force in her life seemed to be to prove . . . that women are not by nature inferior to men in any field.

—Helen Foster Snow

This strong and energetic woman warrior was Kang Keqing, wife of General Zhu De. As "father" of the Chinese Red Army, the general was proud of his life companion's achievements. Together they made the Long March, fought for the same goal, and celebrated the Communist victory in 1949. After the establishment of the People's Republic of China, Kang served the party and the government in a different capacity. For several decades, she was one of the important leaders of the Federation of Women in China.

At the time of Kang's birth in Wanan, Jiangxi, in 1911, China was in political turmoil. The 1911 Revolution, which eventually brought down the decadent Manchu regime, opened the way to warlordism. While warlord rivalries plunged the country into a state of anarchy, the revolutionaries continued their struggle in the south.

Kang Keqing was one of the daughters of Kang Nianxiao and **Huang Niangu**. In order to support his three sons, Kang Nianxiao, a poor fisherman, gave away the daughters to become maids, farmhands, and kitchen slaves. Keqing was adopted by Luo Qiqing, a childless peasant, one month after her birth. As hired laborers, the Luos lived a hand-to-mouth existence. Keqing learned to take care of herself at an early age. Like other poor peasant children, she soon worked in the fields and made strings for sale.

Kang's life took a dramatic turn at the age of 15. By chance, she was drawn into the revolutionary current. In 1926, the Nationalists, having formed a United Front with the Communists, launched the Northern Expedition against the warlords to unify China. Communist cadets were sent to Jiangxi to mobilize the peasants. Luo Qiqing became chair of the village Peasant Union, while Kang joined the Communist Youth and was made captain of the Youth Pioneers. But the tide changed abruptly the next year. In 1927, the Nationalists turned the table and ruthlessly suppressed the Communists. To evade persecution, Kang and her foster father went into hiding in the mountains. Fortunately, through the help of their neighbors and friends, they were allowed to return to their village.

No sooner had one trouble gone than another appeared. "Although my foster father was a Communist," Kang told Snow, "he still had a feudal mind. He had previously arranged a marriage for me with a shop clerk whom I did not even know, and the marriage was scheduled to take place. I tried to escape, and my foster father locked me in a small room." At that juncture, a detachment of the Red Army passed by the village. Kang escaped from the house in which she was confined and joined the army the next day. She became a member of the Fourth Front Army in 1928. Under the leadership of Zhu De and Mao Zedong, the army formed the core of Communist power in the late 1920s and early 1930s.

In 1929, at age 17, Kang married Zhu De who was then 42. It was General Zhu's fourth marriage. His first two marriages had ended in divorce; the third wife ✿➤ **Wu Lanying**, a radical intellectual, was arrested and executed by the Nationalists in 1929. Kang later confided to Helen Snow that she did not fall in love with Zhu at the first encounter, though she liked him for his personality and integrity. The marriage was built on mutual respect. "Neither of us orders the other around," Kang said. Smedley observed that in terms of social background and character, the couple appeared remarkably well matched.

Shortly after their marriage, the Fourth Front Army evacuated the Jinggangshan base under Nationalist military pressure. In 1930, Mao and Zhu set up a new base at Ruijin in southwest Jiangxi. In mid-1930, Li Lisan, president of the Chinese Communist Party, ordered all the Communist forces to attack the key cities of central China to pave the way for a Communist revolution. When Li Lisan's policy went bankrupt, Mao and Zhu's base emerged as the sole Communist stronghold in China. Between 1930 and 1934, the Nationalists launched four successive campaigns to destroy the Ruijin base, but the Communists successfully thwarted all the Nationalist attempts.

During her first two years in the army, Kang was mainly responsible for organizational and propaganda work. Aware of her handicap as an illiterate, she lost no time in educating herself. Within two years, she was able to read a newspaper. "I had no special teacher, but learned by myself from slogans and the like," she told Snow. Starting from 1930, Kang began to occupy more important positions in the army. She was director of the Youth School for a short while. Afterwards, she headed the Headquarter Guard Regiment. Kang formally joined the Chinese Communist Party in 1931 and attended the first Soviet Congress at Ruijin in the same year.

In 1932, Kang was made commander of the Women Volunteers. After six months' training in the Red Military Academy, she was awarded a lectureship in the institution in 1933. Later, she was in charge of field medical services. While she always wore a gun, she never fought in battle. There was, however, one short engagement with Nationalist troops in 1934. When Kang went with a team of Communists to western Jiangxi on a mission, they met an unknown number of Nationalist soldiers by chance. In the confusion, she led the Communists and exchanged fire with their enemies for two hours. Thereafter, she was known as the "girl commander" in the Red Army.

Late in 1934, the Nationalists started the fifth extermination campaign. By the fall of 1935, the situation at Ruijin had reached crisis proportions. That October, the famous Long March began. Mao regained control of the Chinese Communist Party at the meeting of Xunyi, Guizhou, in January 1935. In July, Zhu's army rendezvoused with the forces of Zhang Guotao in Sichuan. After a meeting on plans and goals, the Communist forces split. Zhang Guotao and Zhu De moved westward to Xikang, while Mao Zedong marched north and reached Shaanxi in the fall of 1935. Communist historians often assert that Zhu had been held under duress by Zhang and was thus forcibly separated from Mao. In June 1936, another Communist force from Hunan reached Xikang. After the meeting of the two Communist armies, Zhu and Zhang decided to go north. They rejoined Mao in Shaanxi in October 1936.

Kang Keqing stayed with General Zhu throughout the course of the Long March. She walked with the others and carried all her belongings, sometimes helping those who were weaker. Three years later, she told Snow that it was as easy as taking a stroll every day. Accord-

Wu Lanying (d. 1929)

Chinese revolutionary. Name variations: Wu Lan-ying. Executed in 1929; became third wife of Zhu De (Chu Teh, a general), in 1928.

All four of Zhu De's wives were involved in reform. In 1912, he married the daughter of a Yunanese reformer. She gave birth to a son in 1916, and died shortly thereafter. In 1917, he married **Chen Yüzhen** (Ch'en Yu-chen), who came from a small town near Luchou. A Sichuan woman, Chen Yüzhen was active in the revolution and had been involved in the opposition to block Yüan Shikai's 1916 takeover bid. Zhu De and Chen Yüzhen later separated. In 1928, Zhu married Wu Lanying, an educated Hunanese woman whom he had met when his forces occupied her home province. In 1929, Wu Lanying was captured by the governor of Hunan and executed.

ing to Kang, the most difficult spot was in northern Sichuan where they found no food and subsisted on a diet of grass, bark, and barley. Despite the difficulties, they marched on and held mass meetings along the way to recruit new members.

In Yanan, Shaanxi, Kang studied at the party school. Later, she enrolled in the Kangda, the Anti-Japanese Political and Military Academy. By this time, the Nationalists and Communists had reached an agreement to form a United Front against the Japanese. The Red Army, which was renamed the Eighth Route Army under the command of General Zhu, coordinated with Nationalist forces in the defense of the northwest.

On July 7, 1937, when the war with Japan broke out, Zhu's army began to conduct frontal as well as guerilla warfare against the Japanese in northern China. Kang at this time served in the Political Department of the Eighth Route Army. As the Sino-Japanese War continued, Chinese Nationalist-Communist differences were exacerbated. Negotiations were held to resolve their differences. In August 1940, General Zhu and Kang represented the Communists to meet with Nationalist generals at Luoyang and Xian, but the effort was futile. Conflicts between the two sides eventually led to the New Fourth Army Incident when Nationalist forces openly attacked the Communists' New Fourth Army in central China in January 1941. By then, the United Front had virtually fallen apart. The civil war resumed after the surrender of the Japanese in August 1945.

In 1946, Kang was elected vice-chair of the newly formed Committee for the Protection of

Children in the Liberated Areas. One of the responsibilities was the management of the well-known Los Angeles Nursery, which was founded in 1938 with funds raised by Madame Sun Yat-sen (◄❧ **Song Qingling**) in Hong Kong and the United States. When the Nationalists occupied Yanan in mid-March 1947, Kang moved with General Zhu to the Communist controlled areas in Shaanxi and Hebei.

In 1948, the Nationalists were decisively defeated. With final victory in sight, the Communists were busy planning for a new government, and Kang was appointed a member of the Preparatory Committee for the foundation of the Democratic Women's Federation. With the establishment of the Federation in 1949, Kang was elected a member of the Standing Committee. Her role in the People's Republic of China was clear: she would coordinate with other women veterans to guide the Chinese women in the building of a socialist China.

In 1950, the new Marriage Law was passed as one of the steps to liberate women from the restrictions of the feudal order. Mass campaigns were launched to publicize the concepts of freedom of marriage and women's rights. As a result, there was a significant improvement in the status of women. Between 1955 and 1957, Kang was the secretary of the Democratic Women's Federation. In 1957, she became one of the vice-chairs of the Federation of Women, a successor of the former Democratic Federation. In accordance with party policies, the new goal for Kang and the women leaders was to mobilize the Chinese women for economic production.

In the People's Republic of China, Kang was one of the more active women leaders. From 1949 to 1975, she served on the National Committee of the Chinese People's Political Consultative Conference. She was elected deputy for Henan Province to the First National People's Congress in 1954 and was reelected in the Second National People's Congress in 1959. As political leader, Kang went on various cultural missions abroad. She attended the World Peace Council in Warsaw in 1950 and visited North Korea in 1953.

When the ultra-leftists were in power during the Cultural Revolution, both Zhu De and Kang Keqing became the targets of Red Guards. In January 1967, large character posters appeared in the streets of Beijing, condemning Zhu as the "black general," and his house was ransacked by Red Guards. The next month, Kang was under attack. She was branded a member of the "revisionists" and paraded in the streets.

As the tide of extremism receded after the fall of Lin Biao, China gradually opened its door to the West. In 1972, Zhu and Kang appeared in reception parties held in honor of Western guests, among whom was Helen Snow, their American friend. Zhu was then in his 80s. He passed away on July 6, 1976.

The deaths of Zhou Enlai, Zhu De, and Mao Zedong in 1976 opened the way for the reemergence of Deng Xiaoping. As one of the senior veterans, Kang assumed greater responsibilities in the government. In 1977, she was elected a member of the Central Committee of the Chinese Communist Party and held the position for eight years. The year 1977 also saw the beginning of her ten-year tenure as chair of the Federation of Women. In her inaugural speech, "Women's Movement in China: Guiding Concepts and New Ideals," Kang urged the Chinese women to contribute towards the fulfillment of the "four modernizations," a goal set by Deng Xiaoping for the reconstruction of the country. In 1978, Kang was elected vice-chair of the Chinese People's Political Consultative Conference. At the same time, she served on the Standing Committee of the Fifth National People's Congress. Busy as she was, she also headed delegations to North Korea, Japan, Rumania, Yugoslavia, and Denmark.

In 1985, Kang stepped down from her post as a member of the Central Committee of the Chinese Communist Party. Two years later, her term as chair of the Federation of Women ended, and she was elected honorary chair instead. After the Sixth National People's Congress (1986), she was not reelected to the Standing Committee. In her last few years, she appeared on occasions to greet foreign guests and congratulate the Federation of Women for various achievements. Her role in state and party affairs was essentially ceremonial. On April 22, 1992, she died in Beijing, at the age of 80.

Yang Shangkun, then president of the People's Republic of China, summarized Kang's career:

> She is the epitome of the common people of the old society who courageously fight for social liberation. She is the representative of the ordinary women who unfailingly forge onward in their revolutionary pursuits. Fearless on the battlefield, she was once a young military commander. Skilled at mobilizing the mass, she was an outstanding party organizer. Realistic yet judicious, she would not blindly join other factions. She is a good Communist. She has made remarkable contributions to the women's movement.

❧► ***Sun Yat-sen, Mme.*** *See Song Qingling in entry on The Song Sisters.*

Opposite page

𝒦arin 𝒦ania-ℰnke

SOURCES:

Kang Keqing. "Women Revolutionaries I Have Known," in *China Reconstructs*. Vol. 27, 1978, pp. 2–8.

———. "Women's Movement in China: Guiding Concepts and New Ideals," in *Peking Review*. September 29, 1978, pp. 5–11.

Li, Tesheng, ed. *Jiang-shuai furen zhuan (Biographies of the Wives of Marshalls and Generals)*. Vol. 1. Jilin: Beifang funu ertong chuban she, 1996.

Smedley, Agnes. *The Great Road: The Life and Times of Chu Teh*. NY: Monthly Review Press, 1956.

Snow, Helen Foster. *The Chinese Communists: Sketches and Autobiographies of the Old Guard*. CT: Greenwood Press, 1972.

SUGGESTED READING:

Bartke, Wolfgang. *Who's Who in the People's Republic of China*. NY: M.E. Sharpe, 1981.

Henry Y.S. Chan,
Associate Professor of History,
Moorhead State University, Moorhead, Minnesota

Kania-Enke, Karin (1961—)

East German speed skater. Name variations: skated as Karin Enke and Karin Kania; Karin Enke Kania. Born in Dresden, East Germany, on June 20, 1961; attended Dresden Technical University; married second husband Rudolf Kania (a school sports instructor); children: son Sasha (b. 1985).

Winner of nine Olympic medals: gold (1980), silver (1984), and bronze (1988) in the women's 500 meters; gold (1984) and silver in the women's 1,500 meters (1988); gold (1984) and silver in the 1,000 meters (1988); silver (1984) and bronze (1988) in the 3,000 meters; holder of six World sprint titles (1980, 1981, 1983, 1984, 1986, 1987) and two World all-around championships (1986, 1987).

In the beginning, East German Karin Kania-Enke was a figure skater. In 1975, at 14, she placed 4th in the junior national championships; two years later, she placed 9th. But injury and illness plagued her career, along with her considerable growth. At 5'9¼" and 158 pounds, the mature Kania-Enke was a large woman. Switching from figure to speed skating, she learned the crouched stance and the knack of changing lanes in a matter of weeks. "All that smiling when it hurt in figure skating . . . was not for me," Kania-Enke said, delighted that she no longer had to please judges.

From the first, it was apparent that Kania-Enke was a natural. In West Allis, Wisconsin, in 1980, she won the World sprint championship (*Leah Poulos Mueller of the U.S. came in second). In the 500-meters at the 1980 Lake Placid Olympic Games held a week later, Kania-Enke won the gold medal and set an Olympic record

at 41.78, despite the fact that she was only an alternate on the team. She then came in 4th in the 1,000-meters. In 1981 in Grenoble, she repeated her win in the World sprint championships, winning again in 1983 and 1984 after losing to *Natalia Petruseva of the Soviet Union in 1982. Kania-Enke would pick up two more gold medals in the World sprint championships in 1986 and 1987.

At the 1984 Sarajevo Olympics, Kania-Enke led a record-shattering sweep of the four gold medals in women's speedskating for the German Democratic Republic. Nicknamed "Monster Woman" by awe-struck American rivals, she won the gold in the 1,000- (in which she set an Olympic record of 1:21.61) and 1,500-meters (in which she set a world record of 2:03.42, topping the 2:04.4 record set by Petruseva in 1983). Kania-Enke also won the silver in the 500 meters while her East German teammate *Christa Rothenburger won the gold at a time of 41:02. When Kania-Enke won the silver in the 3,000-meters, another teammate, longtime friend *Andrea Mitscherlich Schöne, took the gold at 4:24.79. The GDR women bettered the Olympic record in all four events.

In Calgary, in 1988, *Bonnie Blair came in 1st in the 500, while Kania-Enke placed 3rd; and Christa Rothenburger placed 1st in the 1,000, while Kania-Enke took another silver. Kania-Enke also picked up a silver in the 1,500 meters. One of the best-liked athletes on the winter circuit, Kania-Enke retired in 1988, intent on opening a beauty salon in her hometown of Dresden.

SOURCES:

Markel, Robert, Nancy Brooks, and Susan Markel. *For the Record: Women in Sports.* NY: World Almanac, 1985.

Karin Loewen Haag,
Athens, Georgia

Kanin, Fay (1917—)

American screenwriter, playwright, and actress who was the second woman to become president of the Motion Picture Academy of Arts and Science. Born Fay Mitchell on May 9, 1917, in New York City; daughter of David Mitchell (a department store manager) and Bessie (Kaiser) Mitchell; attended Elmira College, Elmira, New York, 1933–36; University of Southern California, Los Angeles, B.A., 1937; married Michael Kanin (a screenwriter), in April 1940; children: Joel (deceased); Josh.

Screenplays—with Michael Kanin: Sunday Punch *(1947);* My Pal Gus *(1952);* Rhapsody *(1954);* The Opposite Sex *(1956);* Teacher's Pet *(1958);* The Right Approach *(1961);* The Swordsman of Siena *(1967).*

Plays: Good-bye, My Fancy *(1948); (with Michael Kanin)* His and Hers *(1954); (with M. Kanin)* Rashomon *(1959); (with M. Kanin)* The Gay Life *(book only, 1961).*

Television: "Heat of Anger" *(1972);* "Tell Me Where It Hurts" *(1974);* "Hustling" *(1975);* "Friendly Fire" *(1979);* "Fun and Games" *(1980).*

Fay Kanin was born in New York City in 1917, the daughter of **Bessie Kaiser Mitchell** and David Mitchell, a department store manager. Fay wanted to write for movies from the age of 12. "No one ever told me I couldn't become anything I wanted to be," she recalled. She grew up in Elmira, New York, where she attended Elmira College, the first college in the country to offer women a degree equivalent to the one they awarded to men. After three years, however, Kanin wanted to finish college in Los Angeles where the movie industry was centered. In an overwhelming display of support, her parents decided to make the move with her. David went to California ahead of Bessie and Fay to see if he could find a job, and when he was successful, the family relocated. "It was the ultimate kind of approval," Kanin said. "Whatever self-confidence I mustered came from them."

After graduating from the University of Southern California in 1937, Kanin started making the rounds, beginning at Goldwyn Productions, where she was turned away because of her lack of experience. RKO's story editor, Robert Sparks, was more receptive and hired her as a writer, although three weeks later, when the head of the studio left and the personnel were shifted, she was demoted to script reader. Over the next two years, Kanin made it her business to learn everything she could about the movies. "I invaded cutting rooms, snooped in the music department, made friends in publicity, learned about shooting scripts and how they were turned into movies," she recalled. She also met Michael Kanin, a talented young screenwriter (and brother of Garson Kanin), who had recently arrived at RKO from New York. In 1940, a year after meeting, the two married and began a successful writing collaboration as well. During this period, Kanin also did a bit of acting, appearing in stock in Hollywood and in *Petticoat Fever* at the RKO Studios in 1948. She would later play the lead in a production of her own play *Goodbye My Fancy* at the Pasadena Playhouse.

During the 1950s and 1960s, the Kanins wrote a number of hit movies together, including *Rhapsody* (1954), and *Teacher's Pet* (1958), starring *Doris Day and Clark Gable, which won an Academy Award and a Writers Guild nomination. The Kanins also wrote two successful plays together, *His and Hers* (1954) and *Rashomon* (1959), based on stories by Ryunosuke Akutagawa, and created the book for the musical *The Gay Life* (1961). There came a time, however, when the collaboration began to strain the marriage, and the two decided to pursue separate screenwriting careers.

Fay had already had a solo success with her play *Goodbye My Fancy* (1948), which ran for two years on Broadway, and she later found a creative outlet in television. Her first television movie, "Heat of Anger" (1971), won the Gavel Award from the American Bar Association as "the best movie of 1972 devoted to the law," and her second, "Tell Me Where it Hurts" (1974), garnered Emmy and Christopher Awards for its stars, *Maureen Stapleton and Paul Sorvino. Kanin's script for the television movie "Hustling" (1975), which starred *Lee Remick, received a Writers Guild Award and an Emmy nomination. In 1980, she teamed with Lillian Gallo to create the script for *Fun and Games* (1980), one of the first movies to address the problem of sexual harassment in the workplace. Kanin's most controversial script, however, was *Friendly Fire* (1979), which starred Carol Burnett, and dealt with the aftermath of the Vietnam War.

In addition to her outstanding career as a writer, Kanin served the film industry as the president of the Motion Picture Academy of Arts and Science for four terms. She was only the second woman to serve in that post, the first being *Bette Davis, who left after a month in office to do war work. Kanin also served a long stint as president of the Writers Guild of America and was a board member of the American Film Institute.

SOURCES:

Aker, Ally. *Reel Women: Pioneers of the Cinema 1896 to the Present.* NY: Continuum 1991.

McGill, Raymond D., ed. *Notable Names in the American Theater.* Clifton, NJ: James T. White, 1976.

Barbara Morgan,
Melrose, Massachusetts

Kanner-Rosenthal, Hedwig

(1882–1959)

Hungarian pianist and teacher. Born Hedwig Kanner in Budapest, Hungary, on June 3, 1882; died in Asheville, North Carolina, on September 5, 1959; studied in Vienna with Theodor Leschetizky and Moriz Rosenthal; married Moriz Rosenthal.

Hedwig Kanner-Rosenthal was born in Budapest in 1882 and studied in Vienna with Theodor Leschetizky and Moriz Rosenthal, whom she married. After her Vienna debut, she taught in that city for five years. Her musical activities were varied, as a concert artist, accompanist, chamber-music pianist and duo-piano partner. She often performed with her husband. Starting in 1939, she worked alongside her husband at his piano school in New York City. Her students included Robert Goldsand and Charles Rosen.

John Haag,
Athens, Georgia

Kanwar, Roop (c. 1969–1987)

Young Indian woman whose death incited national controversy over the religious tradition of sati. Name variations: Roopwati Kunwar. Pronunciation: Kun-WAR. Born around 1969 (most sources cite her age upon death as 18) in the city of Jaipur in Rajasthan, India; burned to death on her husband's funeral pyre on September 4, 1987; passed India's tenth standard; married Maal Singh in February of 1987; no children.

Roop Kanwar had been married to her husband Maal Singh for eight months prior to his death from gastroenteritis. During the time of their marriage, she lived primarily with her parents in Jaipur, reportedly spending a total of 20 days with Singh as his wife. On September 4, 1987, in the village of Deorala in Rajasthan, the 18-year-old Kanwar mounted Singh's funeral pyre and burned to death in its flames. Thirteen days later, at the traditional *chunari* ceremony, a crowd of at least 250,000 gathered at the site of her death to worship her as a goddess. "Sati mata ki jai" was the oft-repeated cry; it is an invocation of the goddess, or "devi," that Kanwar was said to have become. Despite official warnings against such a ceremony, the small village was crowded with devotees bent on witnessing the miraculous disappearance of the *chunari*, or bridal finery, into heaven, and the spontaneous reignition of the funeral pyre. Some wished simply to pray to the blessed "sati."

Kanwar's death was considered by many to be a miracle, a blessing upon the village and its inhabitants, and especially upon her in-laws, whose family would, according to legend, "be blessed for seven generations before and after." To many others, her death was seen as a tragedy born of a culture in which a woman's life had no meaning after the death of her husband. Finally, there were those who believed that she had been coerced into the practice of sati by her in-laws, that she had been opiated before the ritual, and that upon trying to flee the flames she was repeatedly pushed back into the fire.

Although it remains unconfirmed whether Kanwar was forced to immolate herself or if the 18-year-old willingly accepted her fate by burning, the controversy around her death prompted strong outcry from sati supporters and from anti-sati activists, and debates still rage over the cultural and legal implications raised by her death and the deaths of other widows like her.

The practice of sati, or self-immolation of a widow upon her husband's funeral pyre, has had somewhat of a revival in a newly independent India. Although instances of sati have been only sporadically documented throughout India's history, at the height of the custom it was estimated that one widow among one thousand became a sati. At certain historical periods and in certain regions sati was deemed the custom of the regal and scores of women burned with one husband. At other times, the practice was seen as an outmoded custom of the poor, backward, rural illiterate to rid the dead husband's family of an economic liability. But whatever the circumstances sati has historically been defended as a sanctified religious ideal.

The word "sati" derives from the root "sat," or truth. The original sati was **Dakshayani**, wife of Lord Siva, in Hindu legend. When Dakshayani's father insulted Dakshayani and her husband in the sacrificial site in front of a crowd, she resolved to give up her body as protest. According to the Hindu text Bhagavata, she sat in deep meditation and burned her body to ashes in *yognagni,* the fire generated by yogic meditation. Sati as a practice of burning on a husband's funeral pyre, however, is explicitly enjoined in none of the Hindu scriptures with the exception of the Vishnu Dharma Sutras, according to Swami Harshananda in an article in *The Hindu* (October 1987). The most authoritative of the Hindu texts, the Vedas, makes no outright mention of widow-immolation. Yet the practice is forcefully argued for as a sacred Hindu religious rite by its supporters, who insist that Roop Kanwar's death was a miracle born of courage and supreme loyalty, which makes it worthy of celebration.

An account of the burning made by a member of her husband's family to a reporter for the *Indian Express* on September 17, 1987, recalled Kanwar's last moments in the following terms:

> The girl spent time with her husband's body, without shedding a tear. . . . [S]he dressed herself in her bridal finery, helped by close relatives, and got on to the pyre where she sat serenely with her husband's head in her lap. Even after the pyre was lit she sat still, a beatific smile on her face. More than 2,000 revering people watched her burn herself.

Two days later, a reporter for the same newspaper said otherwise:

> Roop Kanwar had been buried under a heavy load of firewood so that she could not escape. The fire was lit once and died out. Partially burnt, Roop Kanwar screamed and begged for mercy and help. Out of the 90 odd people who had gathered for Maal Singh's funeral, most did not know that they were going to witness a "sati." Those who could neither bear to see the pain of Roop Kanwar nor had the courage to help her quietly moved away in shame as the fire was cruelly relit by those determined to murder her.

Another purported eyewitness claimed that Kanwar tried three times to escape the flames and each time was pushed back. A fact-finding team of the Women and Media Cell of the Bombay Union of Journalists found that Kanwar had hidden in a barn when she heard of the sati preparations, and others found that she had been opiated prior to being "pushed onto the sacrificial altar." An article in the *Times of India* on September 13, 1987, reported that it was unlikely that Kanwar had been forcibly burned or coerced because she had brought with her into marriage a "sizable dowry of 25 tolas of gold, TV, radio, fans and a refrigerator." Kanwar's brother told the *Sunday Observer* that she had always been very religious and may actually have suggested the sati herself.

Roop Kanwar was neither poor, illiterate, nor on bad terms with her husband's family. She was an educated woman from an affluent family that owned a transport business in the city. Her in-laws too were well-educated, and her husband had planned to attend medical school. These factors led to many questions about the motivations behind her burning, regardless if the act was voluntary or coerced. Women's organizations argued that her death was forced—if not physically than through societal indoctrination that subordinates a woman's existence to that of a man's. Increased instances of infanticide and dowry-deaths in India during recent years also point to a larger cultural bias against women. "She had no life to look forward to. . . . The society treats a widow as a 'kulachani' (an evil omen). . . . She has to remain barefoot, sleep on the floor and not venture out of the house. She is slandered if seen talking to any male. It was better that she died, than lead such a life," said a teacher in Deorala to a reporter for the *Times of India* at Kanwar's *chunari* ceremony. "We are not like Western women who dance when their husbands die. Our lives are over when we are widowed," was the sentiment expressed by a group of women to Shiraz Sidhva of the *Sunday Observer* at the same ceremony.

The practice of sati has been outlawed in India since 1829, and in 1958 the Rajasthan High Court ruled that even those participating in a sati procession would be considered abettors to suicide. Yet the custom persisted, and Rajasthan alone has had at least 30 sati incidents since independence, with no ensuing convictions. Roop Kanwar's death in 1987 sparked the controversy that would call into question the meaning for such a trend.

On September 6, two days after her death, women activists demanding prosecution were turned down in their attempt to meet with Chief Minister Harideo Joshi. On September 9, Maal Singh's 15-year-old brother, Pushpendra Singh, who had lit the pyre, was arrested. While women's groups continued to exert pressure, young girls in Deorala looked at Roop Kanwar as a heroine, and photos of her wearing a glowing expression while sitting on the funeral pyre were sold to eager customers. Sumer Singh, Kanwar's father-in-law, was arrested on September 19, as was the priest who had performed the last rites, Babu Lall. The arrests came only in the wake of highly publicized protests by scores of Indian women's groups condemning the government's complacency in the matter. Another result of this furor was the inception of the Rajasthan Sati (Prevention) Ordinance in October of 1987, under which an attempted sati could be punished with one to five years of imprisonment and a fine. Those convicted of abetting a sati, either directly, or indirectly (through glorification of sati), could face the death penalty. The ordinance received criticism by many of the same women's groups for punishing the widow through imprisonment, as well as legislating a distinction between sati and murder, in effect glorifying it once again. These protests went unheeded.

Writing in *Manushi* (November–December 1994), Madhu Kishwar remarked on the conflict: "Instead of a dialogue, there was only a confrontation between the villagers and the activists, leading to a hardening of positions on both the sides, thus defeating the very purpose for which the campaign was launched. While the progressive outsiders continued to condemn sati, Rajput women joined their men in sati's defence."

In 1996, nearly ten years after Roop Kanwar's immolation, all 32 people eventually accused as abettors to her death were acquitted by the Supreme Court due to a lack of evidence. Bystanders had refused to depose against the accused. Religious ceremonies are still regularly held inside the temple erected for this "Sati Mata," or Mother Sati.

SOURCES:

Kishwar, Madhu. "A Code for Self: Some Thoughts on Activism," in *Manushi*. November–December 1994.

Mangalwadi, Vishal. "Making a Carnival of Murder," in *Indian Express*. September 19, 1987.

Narasimhan, Sakuntala, *Sati: Widow Burning in India*. NY: Doubleday, 1990.

Sidhva, Shiraz. "Sati: Who's Guilty?" in *Sunday Observer*. September 20, 1987.

Swami Harshananda, "A formidable challenge that can be met," in *The Hindu*. October 27, 1987.

Kathy Rubino,
freelance writer, Boston, Massachusetts

Kapiolani (c. 1781–1841)

Hawaiian high priestess, famed for her defiance of the fire goddess Pele and her role in introducing Christianity to the islands. Born in Hilo, on the island of Hawaii, around 1781; died on May 5, 1841; daughter of Keawemauhili (half-brother of Kalaniopuu), king of the island of Hawaii, and Kekikipaa (former wife of Kamehameha I the Great); tutored by missionaries; discarded all her husbands except Naihe (chief, orator, and councilor of King Kamehameha).

Hawaiian priestess Kapiolani, the daughter of highly ranked parents, was born around 1781 and as a child was presented to her aunt **Akahi**, in keeping with the custom among Hawaiian chiefs of giving children to relatives as an expression of good will. Her lifetime covered the period following Captain James Cook's discovery of the islands and the subsequent arrival of the New England missionaries, who brought Christianity and basic education to Hawaiian shores. Kapiolani was one of the chiefesses who greeted the first missionaries upon their arrival aboard the brig *Thaddeus* in March 1820. She eagerly embraced their teachings and was quick to adopt Western dress and decorum. In keeping with Christian doctrine, she abandoned all her husbands except Naihe, chief, orator, and a councilor of King Kamehameha I. Kapiolani often made the journey from her home at Kealakekua to study with the missionaries some 12 miles away, traveling by horse or double canoe with a train of attendants. In 1896, a missionary's daughter shared her childhood memories of Kapiolani with the Woman's Board of

Missions: "On public occasions or when visiting away from home she wore a tight fitting dress, not even adopting the *holoku* (or 'Mother Hubbard') which afterwards became the national style. Silk and satin of the gayest colors were the chosen dress of the chiefs, but she preferred grave and quiet shades."

Kapiolani also adopted the missionaries' evangelical zeal and was a leading force in spreading Christianity, although she first had to break down beliefs in the old idols. In the fall of 1824, determined to challenge the hold of the fire goddess Pele on her people, she made a 100-mile pilgrimage to the crater of Mount Kilauea, one of the most active volcanoes on the island. "If I perish by the anger of Pele, then fear Pele," she told her followers. "If Jehovah protects me, then fear Jehovah!" After enduring the journey on foot, much of it over cindery desert and rough lava, she actually entered the mouth of the crater, positioning herself on the edge of the firepit and proclaiming that her faith and belief in God would save her from Pele's wrath. This dramatic act inspired the poem by Alfred, Lord Tennyson entitled *Kapiolani*, which brought the priestess worldwide attention. Kapiolani made similar tours in the cause of Christianity and was also generous in her support of the missions and in building schools and churches.

Kapiolani's husband Naihe died in 1831, after which she succeeded him as magistrate over the districts of Ka'u and South Kona on the island of Hawaii. In 1841, diagnosed with breast cancer, she displayed her remarkable courage again by undergoing a mastectomy without anesthetic, which was not yet available. She survived the operation only to die of a massive infection a few weeks later. Her body was placed in the royal tomb on the palace grounds in Honolulu, but her name was absent from the list of those moved to the Royal Mausoleum when the palace tomb was abandoned. In the 1930s, during an extensive landscaping project on the palace grounds, an elaborate coffin was discovered that may have been Kapiolani's.

*K*apiolani
(1834–1899)

SOURCES:

James, Edward T., ed. *Notable American Women, 1607–1950*. Cambridge, MA: The Belknap Press of Harvard University Press, 1971.

Peterson, Barbara Bennett. *Notable Women of Hawaii*. Honolulu, HI: University of Hawaii Press, 1984.

Barbara Morgan,
Melrose, Massachusetts

Kapiolani (1834–1899)

Hawaiian queen and philanthropist. Born on December 31, 1834, in Hilo; died on June 24, 1899, at her home in Waikiki; daughter of Kuhio (high chief of Hilo) and Kinoiki (daughter of Kaumualii, last king of Kauai); married Bennett Namakeha, a high chief (died 1860); married David Kalakaua (1836–1891), a high chief and later king of Hawaii (r. 1874–1891), on December 19, 1863; no children.

Came to Honolulu and married High Chief Namakeha (c. 1855); three years after first husband's death, married High Chief David Kalakaua (1863), who later became king; presided over opening ceremonies of Kapiolani Home for Girls in Kakaako (1885); visited U.S. and also attended Queen Victoria's Silver Jubilee in England (1887); raised funds for and opened maternity home for Hawaiian women (1890); second husband died (1891); led quiet life in Waikiki.

Kapiolani was the niece and namesake of *Kapiolani (c. 1781–1841) who defied the goddess Pele. She was born in Hilo on December 31, 1834, the daughter of Kuhio, high chief of Hilo, and **Kinoiki**, a daughter of Kaumualii, the last king of Kauai. Kapiolani had two sisters, **Victoria Kalanikuikapooloku Kalaninuiamamao Poomaikelani** and **Mary Kinoiki Kekaulike**, who were both given the title of princess after Kapiolani became queen. Kapiolani spent her childhood in Hilo and Kona, then went to Honolulu around 1855, where she was married to Namakeha, a high chief. In 1857, she traveled with Namakeha to the Gilbert Islands aboard a missionary packet, in an unsuccessful attempt to improve her husband's health. Three years later, he died in Honolulu.

On December 19, 1863, Kapiolani was quietly married to High Chief David Kalakaua, who was later to be named king (1874). It is reported they were very close, and as queen Kapiolani chose to remain in her husband's shadow. She is portrayed as friendly, even bearing no malice toward her husband's political enemies. Both she and her husband were concerned over the rapid decrease in numbers of the Hawaiian race, and they adopted the motto *Hooulu Lahui* (To Increase and Preserve the Nation). For more than ten years, they worked toward the establishment of a maternity home for Hawaiian women, and in June 1890 the Kapiolani Maternity Home (forerunner of the present Kapiolani Children's Medical Center) was opened. Kapiolani was also responsible for the Kapiolani Home for Girls in Kakaak and presided over its opening ceremonies in 1885. This institution took care of and educated the non-leprous children of leprous parents. In 1887, with her sister-in-law, Princess *Liliuokalani, Kapiolani visited the United States and met President Grover Cleveland; she also attended Queen *Victoria's Silver Jubilee in England.

When informed of her husband's death in January 1891 while he was in San Francisco, Kapiolani tried to throw herself from the balcony of the palace but was restrained by companions. For the rest of her years, she lived a quiet life at her modest home in Waikiki and continued to devote herself to the welfare of women. Kapiolani was a wealthy woman and shortly before her death on June 24, 1899, after several strokes, she transferred her assets to two nephews. She was accorded a lavish Hawaiian funeral. A hospital, community college, boulevard, park and many businesses in Honolulu bear her name.

SOURCES:
Peterson, Barbara Bennett. *Notable Women of Hawaii.* Honolulu, HI: University of Hawaii, 1984.

Jo Anne Meginnes,
freelance writer, Brookfield, Vermont

Kapralova, Vitezslava (1915–1940)

Czech composer. Born in Brünn, Moravia (later Brno, Czechoslovakia, now Czech Republic), on January 24, 1915; died in Montpellier, France, on June 16, 1940; received first musical instruction from her father Vaclav Kapral (1889–1947), a gifted composer and teacher; studied composition and conducting at the Brno Conservatory with Zdenek Chalabala from 1930 to 1935; studied at the Prague Conservatory with Vitezslav Novakl (composition) and Vaclav Talich (conducting).

Received a scholarship for study in France (1937), enabling her to study conducting with Charles Münch and composition with Bohuslav Martinu; appeared as a guest conductor of the BBC Symphony Orchestra at the Festival of the International Society of Contemporary Music in London (1938); returned to France after the Nazi occupation of Bohemia and Moravia (1939); had to flee Paris from the advancing German armies; the stress of evacuation and tuberculosis resulted in her death.

One of the great tragedies of Central European music in the 20th century was the immense destruction of human capabilities and the incalculable loss of future achievements brought about by Fascism and war in the 1930s and 1940s. Many musicians fled, never to return to their homelands, while others died at the front or were killed in Nazi death camps in the Holocaust. A poignant "might-have-been" was the profoundly talented Czech composer Vitezslava Kapralova, whose death in France on the very eve of the Nazi triumphal march into a prostrate Paris in June 1940 is one of the most emblematic of these many losses. Daughter of a highly gifted composer father, Kapralova astonished her teachers with her extraordinary talents as both a performer (her greatest abilities lay in the art of conducting) and her amazing composing skills. By the time she was 20, her Piano Concerto had been performed in her hometown of Brno. In November 1937, her *Military Sinfonietta* was performed in Prague. By the time Kapralova went to France as a refugee in 1939, her health had become precarious and even life-threatening, but she continued to compose to the end of her brief life. A *Concertino for Violin, Clarinet and Orchestra* remained unfinished at her death in June 1940, when she succumbed to the physical and emotional stresses accompanying the military defeat of France by Nazi Germany. The tragic death of Vitezslava Kapralova may well have deprived Czech and European music of the female counterpart of Antonin Dvorak, Leos Janacek or Bohuslav Martinu.

SOURCES:
Cohen, Aaron I. *International Encyclopedia of Women Composers.* 2 vols. NY: Books & Music (USA), 1987.

John Haag,
Athens, Georgia

Kapule, Deborah (c. 1798–1853)

Queen and favorite wife of Kaumualii, believed to be the last king of Kauai and Niihau. Name variations: also known as Haakulou. Born in Waimea, Kauai, Hawaii, around 1798; died in Waimea, Kauai, Hawaii, on August 26, 1853; daughter of Kahekili, sometimes called Haupu (chief of Waimea, Kauai) and Hawea; married King Kaumualii, around 1815 (died 1824); married Kealiiahonui (a son of Kaumualii), around 1822 (ordered to Honolulu to become the husband of Kaahumanu); married Simeon Kaiu (a judge), in April 1824.

The daughter of **Hawea** and Kahekili, the chief of Waimea, Deborah Kapule was married in 1815 to Kaumualii, the last king of Kauai and Niihau. Tragedy befell her, however, in 1821, when her husband was kidnapped by King Kamehameha II (Liholiho) and taken to Oahu, where he was forced to become the husband of *Kaahumanu, the powerful widow of Kamehameha I. In her husband's absence, the imposing Kapule, who was 6' tall and weighed 300 pounds, became a leading local personality. She married the king's son Kealiiahonui and maintained a school in Waimea that served 50 students. Her new marriage, however, was once more disrupted when Kaahumanu ordered Kealiiahonui to Honolulu to also become her husband. Kapule was married yet a third time in April 1824, to Simeon Kaiu, a devout man who was also a judge.

King Kaumualii's death in 1824 caused great turmoil among the people of Kauai, who were divided into two camps: those who wanted Hawaii to remain part of a united kingdom and a splinter group of rebels who did not. Kapule raised her sword to help defend an attack by the rebels at a fort near Waimea and swayed many to remain loyal to a united Hawaii. Returning to Kauai, she became a Christian and gave birth to a son, Josiah Kaumualii. When her husband Simeon died, she experienced a period of grief and confusion and became involved with a young man who was married to a daughter of Kaumualii by another wife. Her behavior caused her to be excommunicated from the church and dispossessed of her property. For a time, she lived in poverty on the island of Oahu, but with the help of the Reverend William Richards, she was returned to Wailua and some of her property was restored.

By 1847, Kapule was back in the good graces of the missionaries. She built a church at Wailua and helped raise money for the construction of a church at Koloa. The final tragedy of her life was the death of her only child Josiah in 1850. Deborah Kapule died on August 26, 1853, at the age of 55. Her obituary noted that she had been a great influence for good among her people.

SOURCES:
Peterson, Barbara Bennett. *Notable Women of Hawaii.* Honolulu, HI: University of Hawaii Press, 1984.

Barbara Morgan,
Melrose, Massachusetts

Kar, Ida (1908–1970)

Russian-born Surrealist photographer who also did portraits and documentary work. Born Ida Karamian in Tambov, Russia, in 1908; died in London, England, in 1970; educated in Paris; married Edmond Belali (a photographer), in the late 1930s (divorced); married Victor Musgrave, in 1944 (separated 1979); no children.

Born Ida Karamian in Tambov, Russia, in 1908, photographer Ida Kar spent her early years in Russia, Iran, and Egypt, although her family eventually settled in Alexandria. In 1928, her father sent her to Paris to study medicine, but Kar chose instead to study music and take up with the avant-garde. She returned to Alexandria in 1933 and worked as an assistant in a photography studio. In the late 1930s, she married photographer Edmond Belali and moved with him to Cairo, where they opened a photography studio called Idabel. They also exhibited in two Surrealist exhibitions in Cairo in 1943 and 1944. Kar subsequently divorced Belali and married Englishman Victor Musgrave, moving with him to London in 1945. There, she began photographing artists and writers, including Marc Chagall, T.S. Eliot, Eugene Ionesco, *Doris Lessing, and Henry Moore. During the late 1950s, she worked as a photojournalist, creating picture stories around London for the *Tatler* and *Observer* and taking photographic junkets to Armenia, Moscow, East Germany, and Sweden. From 1963 to 1964, Kar worked exclusively for *Animals* magazine. In 1964, as the result of a solo exhibition at the House of Friendship in Moscow, Kar was invited to photograph the Celebration of the Cuban Revolution. Always considered somewhat eccentric, Kar reportedly grew mentally unstable during her later years. She died in London in 1970.

SOURCES:
Rosenblum, Naomi. *A History of Women Photographers.* NY: Abbeville Press, 1994.

Barbara Morgan,
Melrose, Massachusetts

Karadjordjevic, Helen (1884–1962)

*Grand duchess of Russia. Born on November 4, 1884 (some sources cite 1881); died in 1962; daughter of *Zorka of Montenegro (1864–1890) and Peter I (1844–1921), king of Serbia (r. 1903–1921); married Ivan Constantinovich, grand duke and prince of Russia, on September 3, 1911; children: Vselevod Ivanovich Romanov, prince (b. 1914); Ikaterina or Catherine Ivanovna Romanov, princess (b. July 12, 1915, who married Rugero Farace di Villaforesta in 1937, divorced in 1945).*

Karatza, Rallou (1778–?)

Greek theater producer and freedom fighter. Born in 1778 in Walachia, Rumania; the daughter of a Greek prince.

Opposite page

Anna
Karina

Born in 1778 to a Greek prince living in Walachia, Rumania (belonging to the Ottoman Empire of which Greece was a part), Rallou Karatza was educated in the arts and culture of Europe. She became particularly interested in the theater and was the first Greek woman to organize her own theater group, recruiting her actors from the Greek School in Bucharest. When Karatza became a member of the secret society "Philiki Etaireia" which organized the Greeks to fight against the Turks, she began to use her theater group for propaganda purposes. Presenting revolutionary plays espousing freedom, she did much to raise the political fervor among the Greeks that led to the uprising of 1821. Karatza presented an international repertory of didactic dramas which she translated herself, and she also directed many of her productions. She even provided scholarships for her actors to go to Paris and study. In 1829, after Greece had won its independence, Karatza moved to Athens, where she resided until her death.

Karina.

Variant of Catherine or Katherine.

Karina, Anna (1940—)

Danish actress. Born Hanne Karin Blarke Bayer on September 22, 1940, in Copenhagen, Denmark; married Jean-Luc Godard (a film director), in 1961 (divorced 1964 or 1967); married Daniel-Georges Duval (a film director), in 1978.

Selected films: Le Petit Soldat *(release delayed until 1976);* Ce Soir ou jamais *(1960);* Une Femme est une Femme *(A Woman Is a Woman, 1961);* She'll Have to Go *(Maid for Murder, UK, 1962);* Vivre sa Vie *(My Life to Live, 1962);* Les Quatre Vérités *(Three Fables of Love, 1962); (title role)* Shéherazade *(Scheherazade, 1963);* Dragées au Poivre *(Sweet and Sour, 1963);* Bande à Part *(Band of Outsiders, 1964);* La Ronde *(Circle of Love, 1964);* De l'Amour *(1965);* Alphaville *(1965);* Pierrot le Fou *(1965);* La Religieuse *(The Nun, 1965);* Made in USA *(1966);* Lo Straniero *(The Stranger, Italy-France-Algeria, 1967);* Le plus Vieux Métier du Monde *(The Oldest Profession, 1967);* The Magus *(UK, 1968);* Before Winter Comes *(UK, 1969);* Laughter in the Dark *(UK/France, 1969);* Justine *(US, 1969);* Rendez-Vous à Bray *(1971);* The Salzburg Connection *(US/Germany, 1972); (also wrote and directed)* Vivre Ensemble *(1973);* Pane e Cioccolata *(Bread and Chocolate, It., 1973);* L'Invenzione di Morel *(It., 1974);* Les Oeufs brouilles *(1976);* Chinesisches Roulett *(Chinese Roulette, Ger., 1976);*

Also es war so *(Germany-Austria, 1977)*; Just Like at Home *(Hungary, 1978)*; Chaussette Surprise *(1978)*; The Story of a Mother *(Denmark, 1979)*; L'Ami de Vincent *(1983)*; Ave Maria *(1984)*; Dernier Eté à Tanger *(1987)*; Cayenne Palace *(1987)*; The Man Who Would Be Guilty *(Denmark-France, 1990)*.

A successful model before breaking into movies, actress Anna Karina first appeared in a Danish short that won a prize at the Cannes Festival. She was launched into French films by New Wave director Jean-Luc Godard, who starred her in *Le Petit Soldat*, a disturbing, graphic film about the Algerian conflict that was not released until 1976. Karina married Godard in 1961 and that year also played the lead in the director's most charming film, *Une Femme est une Femme* (*A Woman is a Woman*, 1961), about a stripper who wants to settle down and have a baby. Karina also appeared in Godard's *Vivre sa Vie* (*My Life to Live*), a gloomy Brechtian film in which she portrayed a Paris prostitute. By the time the couple divorced (in either 1964 or 1967), Karina's career was well established. She made other French New Wave films and, in 1973, wrote, directed and starred in *Vivre Ensemble*. Karina later married director Daniel-Georges Duval.

Karin of Sweden (c. 1330–1381).

See Catherine of Sweden.

Karioka, Tahiya (c. 1921–1999)

Arab actress and belly dancer. Born Badawiya Mohammed Karim around 1921; died in Cairo, Egypt, on September 20, 1999; married 14 times.

Acclaimed as the "Queen of Oriental Dancing," actress and belly dancer Tahiya Karioka began dancing as a young girl and starred on Cairo's equivalent of the Broadway stage during the 1930s and 1940s. Her first film, *Doctor Farahat* (1935), was followed by some 300 films, plays, and television soap operas. Notable among her movies was *Youth of a Woman*, in which she portrayed a landlady who seduces a naive peasant student. The film was an entry in the 1956 Cannes Film Festival and won an international prize for directing in 1958. Karioka's beauty and elegance attracted some of Egypt's most prominent personalities, including the late King Farouk. Karioka died of a heart attack on September 20, 1999, and was buried later that same day. Her funeral procession was led by Egyptian Culture Minister Farouk Hosni.

Karlovna, Anna (1718–1746).

See Anna Ivanovna for sidebar on Anna Leopoldovna.

Karlstadt, Liesl (1892–1960).

See Jacobi, Lotte for sidebar.

Kärnten, Margarete von (1318–1369).

See Margaret Maultasch.

Karolina or Karline.

Variant of Carolina or Caroline.

Karsavina, Tamara (1885–1978)

Outstanding dancer of her generation who helped introduce Russian ballet to Western audiences before World War I and, in later years, continued to exercise a major influence on the development of European ballet through her teaching and writing. Name variations: Tamara Karsavin; Tata. Pronunciation: Ta-ma-ra Kar-SA-vina. Born Tamara Platonovna Karsavina in St. Petersburg, Russia, on March 9, 1885; died in her sleep in London, England, on May 26, 1978, at age 93; daughter of Platon Karsavin (a ballet dancer and instructor); her mother was a housewife (name unknown); received her academic education as well as her early dance training at the St. Petersburg Theater School, graduated in 1902; married Vasili Moukhin (divorced); married Henry J. Bruce, in 1915 (died 1950); children: (second marriage) son Nikita (b. 1916).

Became a junior member of the Marinskii Theater Ballet of St. Petersburg (1902); promoted to rank of prima ballerina (1912); was the leading dancer with Serge Diaghilev's Ballets Russes in Paris and partner to Vaclav Nijinsky (1909–14, and irregularly, 1919–20); returned to Russia at beginning of WWI and resumed her dancing career with the Marinskii until the 1917 revolution; escaped to England (1918), which became her permanent home until her death; continued to dance in Europe and toured U.S. (1924); after retiring from dancing (1933), established herself as a ballet teacher, writer on the art of the dance, and choreographic consultant; was vice-president of the Royal Academy of Dance in London (1930–55).

Selected publications: wrote the autobiographical Theatre Street (London, 1930) and two volumes of reprints from previously written articles for Dancing Times: Ballet Technique (London, 1956), and Classical Ballet: The Flow of Movement (London, 1962).

Beginning in 1902 at the Marinskii Theater, danced in Giselle, the Nutcracker, La Bayadere, Swan Lake, and other ballets; created the leading female roles for many of Diaghilev's Ballets Russes produc-

tions such as Michel Fokine's Les Sylphides *(1908),* Cleopatre *(1909),* Firebird *(1910),* Narcisse *(1911),* Petrushka *(1911),* Le Dieu Bleu *(1912),* Tamar *(1911),* Daphnis and Chloe *(1912),* Pappillion *(1914), as well as Nijinsky's* Jeux *(1913), and Leonid Massine's* Le Tricorne *and* Pulcinella *(1920).*

Tamara Karsavina's ascent to the position of prima ballerina of Diaghilev's epoch-making Ballets Russes, and the important role she played in transforming the 19th-century classical ballet traditions, was achieved through a combination of talent, intense self-discipline acquired over the many years of her schooling at the St. Petersburg Theater School, a single-minded dedication to her chosen art form, and exceptional intelligence.

As Karsavina recounted in her autobiography, she was born into the needy household of a moderately talented ballet dancer with the Marinskii Theater, and a mother whose gentry family had become impoverished during the previous generation. After Platon Karsavin had to retire from dancing earlier than he had expected, he managed to eke out only a very modest living for his family by giving ballet lessons. Karsavina remembers that at a very early age—before she was five—she was already interested in the theater, and began to take dancing lessons with her father. A few years later, with the strong support of her mother, young Tamara applied to, and was accepted at the Theater School, after undergoing a rigid selection process during which all but eight of the numerous applicants were eliminated. The Theater School was free, being wholly subsidized by of the imperial treasury. It provided both a standard academic curriculum and instruction in various aspects of the theater arts, including a separate ballet department. In the first year, the students attended only during the day; thereafter, however, and until graduation, they were required to live on the premises during the school year and were allowed to visit their families only on Sundays and holidays.

It was in this environment, totally dedicated to the ballet, that Karsavina learned to overcome her timidity and initial lack of physical stamina. The atmosphere of the establishment, as she recalled, was one of intense discipline and complete absence of frivolity. Heavy emphasis was placed on modesty, proper deportment, and dedication to the art of the dance. The hours were long, the physical demands on the young dancer's bodies strenuous, and there were no other recreational activities available besides that of reading classical literature. It is to this Spartan and monastic upbringing that Karsavina attributed her later ability to meet the daunting challenge of achieving the pinnacle of success in her art.

Despite this severe regimen, Karsavina experienced a great deal of happiness at the Theater School. Close and often lifelong friendships were formed between the girls of the same age. As they indulged in romantic fantasies about future ballet careers, they also had intense but passing infatuations with some of their male teachers. From the very beginning classes the future ballerinas were included in the Marinskii Theater ballet productions, first as flower-girls and other "extras" on the stage, and later, as they grew older, in bit parts. Some of these performances were given in front of gala audiences. Karsavina recalled the thrill of being on the stage during a performance given by Tsar Nicholas II for his cousin, the German Kaiser Wilhelm II. At another time, she was one of the youthful dancers who took part in the annual presentation in front of the imperial family, including *Alexandra Feodorovna, and was personally addressed by Tsar Nicholas.

On her graduation in 1902, Karsavina was invited to become a junior ballerina with the Marinskii Theater, where she would remain until her flight from Soviet Russia. While there, she had to learn much that had not been taught her at school: how to survive in the highly competitive world of the professional theater, how to get along and win the favor of choreographers, impresarios, critics, and the public. Karsavina especially recalled the group of affluent balletomanes, as she called them, who were regular and highly demanding attendants at all ballet performances.

As a dedicated pupil and lifelong friend of the choreographer Michel Fokine, whose innovative ideas Karsavina helped bring to the attention of the public, she was instrumental in transforming the rigid traditions of the Russian ballet, as it moved away from the fixed forms of Marius Petipa's classicism and towards Fokine's more expressive forms. While she never had any difficulty in finding praise from the younger audiences for her romantic and innovative style, at first she had great difficulty in finding favor with the highly conservative and tradition-oriented older ballet aficionados and with critics.

It was not until she began dancing in Paris with a new troupe formed by the brilliant impresario Serge Diaghilev, that Karsavina came into her own, attaining worldwide prominence. Before the First World War, Paris was the artistic capital of the world, and it was there that Diaghilev chose to present the flower of Russian artistic talent. Having plucked for his company the most gifted artists, such as the choreographer Fokine, composer Igor Stravinsky, the great basso Fedor Shaliapin, and dancers like Nijinsky, Diaghilev opened the 1909 Paris season to the astonished and enthusiastic acclaim of refined Paris.

Diaghilev's intentions to mount a Russian season of ballet and opera in France had been known for some time to the artists of St. Petersburg, and had caused a good deal of excitement in the Marinskii Theater and the Theater Street circles. Karsavina was one of the young up-and-coming dancers whom Diaghilev recruited. Initially, she was scheduled to dance only in secondary parts. She had met the dynamic impresario several years earlier, had been very impressed by him, and on hearing about his plans for Paris, had eagerly sought his invitation to join his newly formed Ballets Russes company.

She traveled to Paris in an odd mood of expectancy and dismal foreboding.

> Paris was for me a city of eternal pleasure, dissipation and sin. So exaggerated had been my ideas of its inconceivable elegance that in my heart of hearts I expected the streets to be like ballroom floors and to be peopled exclusively with smart ladies, walking along with a frou-frou of silk petticoats. . . . Above all, I dreaded that I should be too provincial for Paris.

Karsavina claimed that the two months of 1909 that she spent in Paris were unforgettable. The fortnight preceding her performances, everything seemed to her to be hysterical. "[I]n a cataclysm of squabbles between artists, musicians, and producers, we approached the day of the dress rehearsal." On the first night, she danced in Fokine's *Pavillion d'Armide,* with scenery by Alexander Benois. On ensuing evenings, she performed in *Prince Igor* and *Firebird.* The leading female role in this ballet had been originally assigned to ***Matilda Kshesinskaia**, Diaghilev's prima ballerina and former mistress of the young Tsarevich Nicholas, before his ascension to the imperial Russian throne. Wrote Karsavina:

> Firebird, the ballet, had come to me through a stroke of luck. In Petersburg I had wistfully considered that the best chances had been given to elder and more accomplished dancers than I. Firebird had been intended for Matilda, but she changed her mind and refused to come to Paris.

After this performance, Karsavina became "La Karsavina" to her Paris audience, and an object of almost unimaginable adoration. On subsequent nights, she danced the leading female parts in *Firebird, Petrushka,* and *Rite of Spring,* set to music by Igor Stravinsky and choreographed by Michel Fokine. These performances first brought the superlative level of Russian musical, artistic, and dancing art to the attention of Western European audiences. At the end of this period of triumph, wrote Karsavina: "The Russian season, like a gust of fresh wind, passed over the stale convention of the French stage."

Beginning with her leading role in 1909 in the *Firebird,* Karsavina, together with her renowned dance partner, Nijinsky, astounded the ballet world with her creations in *Les Sylphides, Carnival, Petrushka, Specter of the Rose, Thamar,* and *Sheherizade* (music by Rimsky-Korsakov). Following the brilliant season in Paris, Karsavina returned in triumph to St. Petersburg and the Marinskii Theater. In 1912, she was formally given the rank of prima ballerina by the company, to take her place along with ***Anna Pavlova** and Kshesinskaia as one of the three leading Russian women dancers. She continued performing in St. Petersburg through the war period. After the Bolshevik overthrow of the Provisional government in October 1917, Karsavina fled to the northern port of Murmansk, together with her infant son Nikita and English-diplomat husband Henry J. Bruce, and escaped Soviet Russia by sailing to England.

She never returned to her native land but spent the rest of her long life in Western Europe, primarily in England. In 1919, she worked with choreographer Leonid Massine, portraying the Miller's Wife in Manuel de Falla's *The Three-Cornered Hat,* with sets designed by Pablo Picasso. Except for one brief and unsuccessful American tour in 1924, Karsavina continued dancing in Western Europe, and occasionally with Diaghilev's Ballets Russes until the impresario's death in 1929. When her husband found himself frequently without work, Karsavina was compelled to dance more often than her health permitted. Nevertheless, she continued to expand the limits of classical ballet by performing in numerous modern pieces. After Nijinsky was institutionalized for mental illness, her frequent partner became Vladimirov, with whom she toured the United States, and who also danced with Pavlova.

After her final appearance with the Ballet Rambert early in the 1930s, Tamara Karsavina devoted her time to teaching, writing about her life and ballet techniques, as well as serving as a consultant for revivals of the most famous of Diaghilev's ballets. She taught ***Margot Fonteyn** her former roles in *Firebird* and *Giselle,* and coached Sir Frederick Ashton through the mime scenes from *La Fille mal Guardee.* She also served for many years as the vice-president of the Royal Ballet and assisted the Western Theater Ballet (now the Scottish Ballet). Admired for her superb dancing, beauty, and intelligence, and universally loved by her public, Tamara Karsavina celebrated her 90th birthday at a party where Ashton and Sir John Gielgud toasted her for her accomplishments and service to the art of the dance.

SOURCES:

Bruce, H.J. *Silken Dalliance.* London, 1946.
———. *Thirty Dozen Moons.* London, 1949.

Chujoy, Anatole, and P.W. Manchester. *The Dance Encyclopedia*. NY: Simon and Schuster, 1967.

Clark, Mary, and David Vaughan. *The Encyclopedia of Dance and Ballet*. London: Peerage Books, 1977.

Cohen-Stratner, Barbara Naomi. *Bibliographical Dictionary of Dance*. London: Collier Macmillan, 1982.

Koegler, Horst. *The Concise Oxford Dictionary of Ballet*. 2nd ed. London: Oxford University Press, 1982.

Vronskaya, Jeanne. *Bibliographical Dictionary of the Soviet Union, 1917–1988*. London: K.G. Saur, 1989.

Dr. Boris Raymond,
Adjunct Professor in the Department of Sociology and Anthropology,
Dalhousie University, Halifax, Nova Scotia, Canada

Karsch, Anna Luise (1722–1791)

German poet. Name variations: Anna Louisa Karsch or Karschin. Born Anna Louisa Dürbach in Silesia, Germany, in 1722; died in 1791; schooled by an uncle at home; married twice; three children, including daughter **Karoline Luise von Klencke** *(1754–1812) who was also a poet.*

Works include: Auserlesene Gedichte *(Selected Poems, 1764);* Einige Oden über verschiedene hohe Gegenstände *(Odes on Various Subjects, 1764);* Poetische Einfälle, Erste Sammllung *(Poetical Ideas, 1764);* Kleinigkeite *(Little Nothings, 1765);* Neue Gedichte *(New Poems, 1772).*

Poet Anna Karsch was the first woman writer in Germany to support herself and her children by writing. Her fame, however, was born of struggle, beginning with her childhood in Silesia. Born in 1722, she was the daughter of a innkeeper who died when she was six. She was then sent to live with her uncle who fortunately taught her to read and write before sending her back to her mother who had remarried. At 16, Karsch married a weaver who abused her and then left her when she was pregnant with their third child. Her second marriage was to a tailor named Karsch, an alcoholic who had difficulty holding down a job. With her family on the brink of poverty, Karsch began writing poetry to celebrate patriotic and family occasions. Her talent soon captured the attention of literary figures such as Gotthold, Mendelssohn, Herder, and even Goethe, who extolled her as "Sappho Resurrected." In recognition of her long poem inspired by the Seven Years' War, she was granted an audience by Frederick II, king of Prussia. Karsch fell in love with the poet Johann Wilhelm Gleim (1719–1803), who arranged for the first publication of her poetry in 1764, but did not return her affection. She later moved to Berlin, establishing herself there as a writer of note and a woman of independence. The poet died in 1791.

Kartini (1879–1904)

Indonesian feminist and nationalist whose youthful writings, chiefly letters, led to the liberation and education of the women of Indonesia. Name variations: R.A. Kartini; honorary titles "Raden Adjeng or Ajeng" and "Ibu" are sometimes added, though she preferred to use only her one name. Born Kartini on April 21, 1879, in the town of Mayong on the island of Java; died on September 17, 1904, at age 25, soon after childbirth; daughter of Raden Adipati Sosroningrat (an Indonesian civil servant of high rank) and Ngasirah (one of his two wives); educated in Dutch schools, at elementary level, and after age 16; married Raden Adiati Djojo Adiningrat, November 8, 1903; children: one son, Raden Mas Singgih (b. 1904).

At age 12, as prescribed by Islamic law, was sequestered in preparation for marriage (1891); resisted the practice, leading to increased freedom (beginning 1896); was permitted to enroll in a Dutch school in Japara (1898); founded a school for women (1903); accepted an arranged marriage (November 3, 1903); died four days after birth of her son (1904).

At the end of the 20th century, few were aware of the radical effect that the simple act of reading or attending school had on a female child born a century earlier into a traditional Eastern culture. But these are the influences that placed a young Indonesian woman, known as Kartini, at a cultural crossroads that was to help virtually every woman of her country to break away from the rigid rules of their traditional society.

Born on April 21, 1879, in the town of Mayong on the Indonesian island of Java, Kartini was the daughter of wealthy native aristocrats who had prospered under Dutch rule. At the time, Java was the most important and the most heavily settled of the Netherlands' overseas possessions, where spices, rubber, and tobacco were grown for export. The largest in the string of Indonesian islands, Java lies between the Indian Ocean and the South China Sea. The year after Kartini's birth her father, Raden Adipati Sosroningrat, became regent of the area, having worked his way up through the Indonesian ranks of the colonial civil service. Her paternal grandfather, Pangeran Tjondronegoro, had been a famous regent of Central Java, and the first Javanese aristocrat to have his children educated by a Dutch tutor. His son inherited many of Tjondronegoro's liberal notions but maintained a traditional Indonesian household. Polygamy was an integral part of the old Hindu-Javanese social system, and some members of the aristocracy maintained large retinues of women, though Muslims rarely had more than four wives and sometimes fewer.

Kartini's mother **Ngasirah** was her father's first, but not his chief, wife. The name of Ngasirah's father included the title *haji,* which denotes a pilgrim to Mecca and suggests a family of devout Muslims as well as persons of means. Ngasirah was married to Kartini's father at age 14 and gave birth to eight children. According to the traditional family hierarchy, however, the person Kartini referred to as "mother" was her father's second wife, Raden Ayu Sosroningrat, a descendant of another aristocratic house, whose superior status made her the feminine head of the household. She had three children.

Kartini's status came from her father, rather than her mother, and was enhanced by her position as an older child. Rules of etiquette dominated daily life. Younger brothers or sisters, for example, had to pass by Kartini crawling on the ground with heads bowed and could only address her in formal terms while making a *sembah* (putting both hands together and bringing them below the nose) after every sentence. They also had to offer her the best foods at meals.

Despite these traditions, Kartini had an unusual opportunity for a girl of her class. Her father allowed her to attend a European-style school up to the age of 12. There, she learned the Dutch language and became an avid reader of European literature. But as she approached puberty, her world was completely changed. Islamic law, known as *Adat,* required that Muslim girls be isolated and trained in the skills and traditions of a wife, and Kartini was confined to the home in preparation for a marriage expected to occur around age 15 or 16. For daughters of the wealthy during this period of seclusion, every material desire was met: they ate rich foods, wore beautiful clothes, and were waited on by servants, but they were denied all personal freedom. Wrote Kartini:

> I was locked up at home, and cut off from all communication with the outside world, whereto I would never be allowed to return except at the side of a husband, a stranger, chosen for us by our parents, and to whom we are married without really knowing about it. European friends—this I heard later—had tried every possible way to dissuade my parents from this cruel course for me, a young and spirited child, but they were unable to do anything. My parents were inexorable; I went to my prison. I spent four long years between four thick walls, without once seeing the outside world.

Kartini's early educational experience had given her both cultural insight and fluency in Dutch.

She loved school and was a brilliant student, although she became painfully aware that Europeans regarded Indonesians as inferior. Later she wrote, "It was hard for many teachers to give a Javanese child the highest mark, no matter how well deserved."

Although Kartini's brothers attended secondary school in Semarang, and her outstanding abilities led several Europeans to encourage her father to allow her to pursue a secondary education, the liberal leanings of Adipati Sosroningrat did not go far enough for him to allow his daughters to escape the traditional period of seclusion before marriage. From age 12 to 16, Kartini lived entirely within the family's large walled compound, learning the skills which would be required of her as a wife—household duties, preparation for festivals and ceremonies, and the Indonesian art of batiking, or painting and dyeing waxed cloth. Along with the practical lessons came restrictions in physical movement and emotions, meant to curtail youthful exuberance and prepare the young girl for submission to the will of her future husband, creating a certain type of woman Kartini later described:

> The ideal Javanese girl is quiet, as immobile as a wooden doll; speaking only when it's

Kartini

absolutely necessary in a tiny, whispering voice which can't be heard by ants; she walks step by step like a snail; laughs noiselessly without opening her mouth.

Forced to confront inequalities sanctified by tradition, Kartini rejected those she could. Denying the idea of her own superior status among her siblings and others, she insisted that she be approached equally by everyone, just as she expected to approach others equally. She also perceived that women themselves often perpetuated many inequities by teaching young boys to hold women in contempt. Hearing the way older women spoke of young girls, she longed for the chance to prove that women were human beings just the same as men.

It will be a tremendous satisfaction to me when the parents of other young women who also want to fend for themselves will no longer be able to say, "no one of our community has done that yet."

—Kartini

Although Adipati Sosroningrat insisted on his daughter's seclusion, he was a loving father, and no bully. He allowed her to continue reading the books she loved and continued to reach for a compromise between the Western influences that had invaded his personal life and the only culture he knew. Kartini maintained a tender affection for him and wrote, "Father has borne so patiently with all my caprices; I have never heard a harsh or bitter word from his lips. He is always loving, always gentle."

Kartini read the works of Dutch feminists as well as standard texts on a wide variety of topics, and felt strongly influenced by *Hilda van Suylenburg*, published in 1897, a novel by the Dutch feminist **Cécile Goekoop**. The book involves a love story that culminates in a marriage seen as a partnership between two equals, in which the protagonist becomes a lawyer to prevent social injustice and marries an engineer with radical social notions.

Among her siblings, Kartini remained envious of her younger sisters who were still allowed to go to school, and felt at odds with those siblings who found her notions strange. She was supplied books by her brother Kartono, and formed a close-knit circle with her sisters **Roekmini** and **Kardinah**, who joined her in seclusion and helped her to define her struggle against the larger culture.

Kartini reached the outside world through her letters. She corresponded with **Stella Zeehandelaar**, a pen pal in Amsterdam. She also wrote to **Marie Ovink-Soer**, wife of the Assistant Resident, living in Japara. Ovink-Soer wrote children's books and contributed to the major feminist journal of the day, *The Dutch Lily*. Kartini also wrote the members of the Abendanon family, and it was J.A. Abendanon, who would collect and the publish the letters which are her chief literary legacy. **Hilda de Booy-Boissevain**, Dr. N. Adriani, Professor G.K. Anton, and **Nellie van Kol-Porrey** were others who participated in the correspondence that dealt with, among other topics, polygamy, relations between men and women in marriage, education, women in relation to the law, and the cruelties imposed by the colonial caste system.

In 1896, Kartini was 16 when her prison doors gradually began to open. Her father, persuaded by Marie Ovink-Soer, allowed his daughters to leave seclusion for visits to Ovink-Soer's home, ostensibly for lessons in handicrafts and painting. Kartini and her sisters traveled to and from her house in a closed carriage. They were also allowed to visit a village of woodcarvers producing traditional Indonesian art. When their travels were extended to the cities of Semarang and Batavia, their activities did not go unnoticed among the local Dutch and Indonesian elites. Knowledge of Kartini's letters had begun to spread, and newspapers began to refer to her as "the well-known Raden Ajeng Kartini," although her father refused to allow publication of the articles she had begun to write.

In 1898, she and her sisters were "officially" granted their freedom when they were allowed to go to the capital and participate in festivities held in honor of Queen *Wilhelmina's investiture which was taking place in the Netherlands. The governor-general gave a ball in Semarang to mark the occasion. As regent, Kartini's father was invited, but the governor-general's special invitation also included his daughters. It was usual for the colonial government to invite representatives of the Indonesian upper class, but this was the first time an invisible element of Indonesian culture had been recognized—single women. Writing about the ball, Kartini showed an increasingly nationalistic outlook: "We have long ceased to believe that the European civilization is the only true one, the most superior and unsurpassed."

That same year, Kartini began to attend a Dutch school in Japara, one of the first Indonesian women ever to attend a European school. In a classroom with only 11 European girls, she discovered more attitudes foreign to her: their free relations with their brothers and sisters,

RADEN ADJENG KARTINI
1879 — 1904

1 00

REPUBLIK
INDONESIA

Indonesian postage stamp honoring Kartini, issued in 1961.

their dreams of careers, and their notions of possessing certain rights. At the same time, Kartini believed that European-style education was not enough. She valued the traditional Indonesian attachment to family and home, and emphasized the influence of mothers in the shaping of personality and character. Since women instilled thrift, industry, and honesty in children, she felt their role should be elevated. Wrote Kartini:

> Can anyone deny that the woman has a great role to play in shaping society morally? She is precisely the person for it. . . . Never will the uplifting and development of the Javanese people proceed vigorously so long as the woman is left behind with no role to play.

In mid-September 1900, Kartini traveled with her parents and sisters to Batavia, to meet with the principal of a girls' school. It was her dream by then to establish a boarding school for Javanese girls of the upper class, where she hoped to study. In 1901, the plan was rejected by the island's regents, saying that the time was not ripe for such a venture. When a marriage was arranged for her younger sister, Kardinah, Kartini and Roekmini remained united in their opposition to marriage for themselves, and their father continued to respect their wishes. Determined to be recognized as a full human being outside the bounds of marriage, Kartini wrote, "We must declare ourselves adults and force the world to recognize our majority."

In April 1902, Kartini had a case brought before the States General, the lower house of the national legislature, pleading for her to be allowed to take teacher training in the Netherlands. A scholarship was awarded, but Kartini's family and friends, including many Europeans, urged her to stay in Indonesia and begin teaching there. In July 1903, Kartini was 24 when she and Roekmini opened a school for upper-class girls, with ten pupils. She was an unmarried woman, with an outlook that had earned her an international reputation, and she was at the start of a teaching career. Then, unexpectedly came a request for her hand in marriage. Raden Adiati Djojo Adiningrat was a widower many years Kartini's senior, who had lived for some years in the Netherlands and was considered a progressive leader in his region. Like Kartini, he was interested in traditional Indonesian arts.

Caught between radical principle and real practice, Kartini's family pressured her to accept the proposal. Finally she accepted, on the condition that Djojo Adiningrat would allow her to continue her school. Shocked by her decision to marry, Stella Zeehandelaar ceased her correspondence with Kartini. There is evidence, however, that Kartini had gained a new perspective in a letter to Abendanon-Mandri: "Didn't I say to you that we gave up all personal happiness long ago? Now life has come to claim that promise from me. Nothing will be too bitter, too hard, too difficult for us if we are able through it to contribute even one drop of sand to the building of that beautiful monument: the people's happiness."

Determined that her marriage would set a new standard, Kartini met with her future husband before their marriage, which took place on November 8, 1903. In her school she had begun to educate aristocratic young women who were brought to live in her house, and she had plans to build a place for training apprentice woodcarvers in Rembang. When she became pregnant, she continued to teach, and one of her last letters discussed the problems of combining teaching and motherhood. On September 13, 1904, Kartini gave birth to a son, Raden Mas Singgih, and seemed to be recovering, but she died four days later, at age 25.

By every standard of measurement, Kartini led a sheltered life. Still she managed to escape the narrow confines of her time and her culture, addressing questions that continue to confront women. Her plea for women's equality struck a timely chord, and her determination that her people be treated equally with Europeans enhanced her legacy. In 1911, a number of Kartini's letters were published by J.H. Abendanon, under the title *From Darkness into Light*. The collection was highly censored; for example, it is thought that Abendanon deleted sections critical to Dutch colonial rule. A more complete version appeared in English in 1920, titled *Letters of a Javanese Princess* and edited by **Agnes Symmers**, but the translation was poor and the title misleading, since Kartini was an aristocrat but never a princess. Translated into regional languages spoken by 90 million Indonesians, however, the letters have exerted a powerful influence in her homeland, and proceeds from their publication have been used to found "Kartini schools" for women throughout Indonesia. Regarded as a pioneer for women's liberation and national liberation, Kartini holds the honorary titles "Raden Ajeng" and "Ibu," and her birthday, April 21, has become a national holiday.

SOURCES:

Beekman, E.M. "Kartini," in *Fugitive Dreams: An Anthology of Dutch Colonial Literature*. Amherst, MA: University of Massachusetts Press, 1988, pp. 235–283.

———, trans. and ed. "Letters from a Javanese Feminist, 1899–1902," in *Massachusetts Review*. Vol. 25, no. 4. Winter 1984, pp. 579–616.

Berninghausen, Jutta, and Birgit Kerstan. *Forging New Paths: Feminist Social Methodology and Rural Women in Java*. London: Zed Books, 1992.

Cribb, Robert. *Historical Dictionary of Indonesia*. London: Scarecrow Press, 1992.

De Iongh, R.C., ed. *Indonesia: Yesterday and Today*. Sydney: Ian Novak, 1973.

Kartini, Raden Adjeng. *Letters of a Javanese Princess*. Translated by Agnes Louise Symmers. Foreword by Eleanor Roosevelt. NY: W.W. Norton, 1964 (reprint of 1920 edition).

———. "Javanese Letters," in *Atlantic Monthly*. Vol. 124. November 1919, pp. 591–602; Vol 124. December 1919, pp. 749–759; Vol. 125. January 1920, pp. 56–65.

Nieuwenhuys, Rob. *Mirror of the Indies: A History of Dutch Colonial Literature*, Amherst, MA: University of Massachusetts Press, 1982.

Penders, Christiaan L.M. *Indonesia: Selected Documents on Colonialism and Nationalism, 1830–1942*. St. Lucia, Queensland, Australia: University of Queensland Press, 1977.

Ricklefs, M.C. *A History of Modern Indonesia*, Bloomington: Indiana University Press, 1981.

Shiraishi, Takashi. *An Age in Motion: Popular Radicalism in Java, 1912–1926*. Ithaca, NY: Cornell University Press, 1990.

Taylor, Jean Stewart. "Raden Ajeng Kartini," in *Signs: Journal of Women in Culture and Society*. Vol. 1, no. 3, part 1. Spring 1976, pp. 639–661.

Zainu'ddin, Ailsa G. Thompson. "'What Should a Girl Become?' Further Reflections on the Letters of R.A. Kartini," in *Nineteenth and Twentieth Century Indonesia: Essays in honour of Professor J.D. Legge*. Edited by David P. Chandler and M.C. Ricklefs. Clayton, Victoria, Australia: Southeast Asian Studies, Monash University, 1986, pp. 243–279.

Karin Loewen Haag,
freelance writer, Athens, Georgia

Kaschnitz, Marie Luise

(1901–1974)

German poet and writer. Born in 1901 in Karlsruhe, Germany; died in 1974; married Guido von Kaschnitz-Weinberg (a Viennese archaeologist), in 1925.

Selected writings: Liebe beginnt *(Love Begins, novel, 1933);* Griechische Mythen *(retellings of Greek myths, 1943);* Menschen und Dinge *(Men and Things, essays, 1945);* Gedichte *(Poems, 1947);* Totentanz und Gedichte zur Zeit *(Danse Macabre and Poems for the Times, 1947);* Zukunftsmusik *(Music of the Future, 1950);* Das dicke Kind und andere Erzählungen *(The Fat Kid and Other Tales, 1951);* Ewige Stadt *(Eternal City, 1952);* Das Haus der Kindheit *(The House of Childhood, 1956);* Neue Gedichte *(New Poems, 1957);* Lange Schatten *(Long Shadows, 1960);* Dein Schweigen—meine Stimme *(Your Silence—My Voice, 1962);* "Zoon Politikon" *("Political Zone," 1962);* Wohin denn ich? *(Where Am I To Go?, 1963);* Ein Wort weiter *(One More Word, 1965);* Gespräche im All *(Conversations in Space, 1971);* Kein Zauberspruch *(No Magic Formula, 1972).*

Marie Luise Kaschnitz was born in 1901 into the aristocratic von Holzing-Berstett family in Karlsruhe, Germany. She enjoyed writing from a young age and used it both as a release from and a means of understanding the world around her. Her observation of and reflections on that world remained the basis for her work throughout her life, although her writing became less bound by tradition and absolute realism as she matured. She was also influenced by Georg Trakl, Friedrich Hölderlin, Franz Kafka, Hermann Hesse, and Samuel Beckett. Kaschnitz's protagonists are often children or young adults experiencing the difficulties of growing up and coming to a self-realization, as well as adults attempting to come to terms with their pasts. As for many artists, World War II and its profound implications also influenced her later work. *Men and Things,* a collection of essays published in 1945, describes the devastation of war-torn Germany, and much of her postwar poetry is informed by an understanding of how conditions in the world impact upon even the most personal of emotions and events. Her early poetry has been described as "grandiloquent and elegiac" as well as poignant, and her short stories are said to "have a haunting quality."

In 1925, Kaschnitz married Guido von Kaschnitz-Weinberg, a Viennese archaeologist. The couple lived in Königsberg, Marburg, Frankfurt, and Rome, where he died in either 1958 or 1962. After her husband's death, Marie Luise Kaschnitz moved to Frankfurt am Main and then back to Rome, where she died in 1974.

Karina L. Kerr, M.A.,
Ypsilanti, Michigan

Käsebier, Gertrude (1852–1934)

Turn-of-the-century American photographer who gained renown as one of the finest pictorialists in the country. Name variations: Gertrude Kasebier. Born Gertrude Stanton in Fort Des Moines, Iowa, on May 18, 1852; died in New York City, on October 13, 1934; daughter of John W. Stanton (an entrepreneur) and Gertrude Muncy (Shaw) Stanton (a homemaker); completed a four-year art course at the Pratt Institute, Brooklyn, New York, 1889–93; married Eduard Käsebier, on May 18, 1874; children: Frederick William (b. 1875); **Gertrude Elizabeth O'Malley** *(b. 1878); Hermine Mathilde Turner (b. 1880).*

Opened a professional portrait studio, Brooklyn, New York (1896); established reputation at the first Philadelphia Photographic Salon (1898); was one of the first two women admitted to The Linked Ring (1900); had photographs included in "The New School of American Photography" exhibition at the Royal Photographic Society, London (1900); was *founding member of the Photo-Secession Group (1902); joined the Professional Photographers of New York (1906); resigned from the Photo-Secession Group (1912); named honorary vice-president of the Pictorial Photographers of America (1916); had last major exhibit of her work during her lifetime at Brooklyn Institute of Arts and Science (1929).*

The history of photography in the late 19th and early 20th centuries is one of a nascent artistic form struggling for recognition alongside painting and poetry. Among the earliest photographic pioneers who sought to explore the new medium's artistic possibilities was the pictorialist and portrait photographer Gertrude Käsebier. In her portraits of high-profile personalities and well-known artists such as Auguste Rodin and Alfred Stieglitz, she elevated the role of the portrait photographer from technician to artist. As a founding member of the Photo-Secession Group, her allegorical pictorial photographs of women and children remain among the most arresting and recognizable photographs hanging in modern-day museums.

The key to artistic photography is to work out your own thoughts by yourself. Imitation leads to disaster.

—Gertrude Käsebier

Born Gertrude Stanton in Fort Des Moines, Iowa, on May 18, 1852, she was the first of two children of John W. and **Muncy Stanton**. During the 1859 Gold Rush, when Gertrude was eight, the family moved to the Colorado Territory and settled there for the next five years. The Stantons were not a typical pioneer family. Her father, an entrepreneur who owned and operated a saw mill, prospered greatly from a building boom and by expanding his mill to extract gold from ore. He was also the first mayor elected in the town of Golden, then the capital of the Colorado Territory. Her mother Muncy, Käsebier later recalled, "hadn't an atom of artistry in her whole being," but she was resourceful and adventuresome and passed on those traits to her daughter. She encouraged Gertrude to be self-reliant and express herself, and even entertained hopes that her daughter would one day become a musician. But music did not interest Gertrude; instead, from the time she was old enough to hold a pencil, she was interested in art. As one of the first white children to arrive in the area, she occasionally played with the nearby Native American children, but most of her time was spent alone drawing pictures.

In 1864, the family moved to Brooklyn, New York. From 1868 to 1870, Gertrude lived in Bethlehem, Pennsylvania, with her maternal grandmother and attended the Moravian Seminary for Women, one of the first and best women's schools in the United States. She later described her grandmother as "an artist with a loom" who "was a model to me in many ways, and . . . what I have accomplished in art came to me through her."

On her 22nd birthday in 1874, Gertrude married Eduard Käsebier, a 28-year-old German businessman who had been living as a boarder in her mother's house. Eduard was a hard-working, ambitious shellac importer who came from a well-to-do family, and her parents appeared to have been pleased with the match. The young couple spent the next ten years in Brooklyn and then moved to a farmhouse in New Jersey. Together they raised three children: Frederick William (b. 1875), Gertrude Elizabeth (b. 1878), and Hermine Mathilde (b. 1880). The marriage, however, was largely unhappy. Käsebier's viva-

Gertrude Käsebier (right) preparing to photograph her studio assistant, Harriet Hibbard, 1903.

cious, artistic temperament was not suited to the steady, reliable disposition of her husband. She later claimed to have married impulsively following a broken romance with another man. It is clear that although they continued to share the same house, they were living largely separate lives by 1889, when Gertrude, then aged 37, convinced her husband to move back to Brooklyn so that she could enroll in the newly founded Pratt Institute of Art. By this time, the youngest of her children was nearing adolescence, and her ambitions to be an artist resurfaced with renewed vigor. Käsebier completed the four-year art program in 1893 and spent the next year abroad studying art and chaperoning a group of young American women enrolled in a summer program in France. It was during her time abroad in 1894 that she appears to have developed a serious interest in photography. She wrote and photographed two articles on French village life that appeared in *The Monthly Illustrator* and won a photo contest sponsored by the magazine. She also spent time in Germany where she apprenticed herself to a chemist so as to improve her un-

derstanding of the technical aspects of the medium. Though Pratt had not offered any courses in photography, Käsebier had become an avid amateur photographer. She had begun taking pictures of her family in the late 1880s when the photographic process was simplified and cameras became portable. Of her earliest efforts, only *First Photograph* (c. 1885) remains.

Upon her return to the U.S. in 1895, she apprenticed herself to Samuel H. Lifshey, a Brooklyn portrait photographer. A year later, she set up her own dark room at her home and began a portrait business. Shortly after she opened her studio, her mother came to live with the family and assumed all housekeeping duties, leaving Käsebier free to concentrate on her work. In late 1897 or early 1898, Käsebier moved her studio to New York City and immediately distinguished herself. She was affable and went to great pains to relax her subjects before she photographed them, often keeping the camera out of sight until she was ready to take their picture. Unlike other portrait photographers of the time, she resisted using backdrops, props, or furniture. Instead, she focused her attention entirely on capturing the essence of the individual. Käsebier once explained that in producing a portrait she sought "to bring out in each photograph the essential personality that is variously called temperament, soul, humanity." Indeed, she was so attentive to character that some of her earliest portraits resemble Old Masters' paintings. In 1899, Alfred Stieglitz called her "beyond dispute the leading portrait photographer in the country." By 1901, her celebrity portraits were being reproduced in such magazines as the *Ladies' Home Journal* and *Everybody's Magazine*. She was also regularly commissioned by *The World's Week*, a well-respected arts and public affairs magazine, to photograph American notables, such as Mark Twain and Booker T. Washington. In his 1901 book *Photography as a Fine Art*, art critic Charles Caffin wrote: "Mrs. Kasebier will tell you that she is a commercial photographer; unquestionably she is an artist."

In addition to well-known personalities and well-to-do New Yorkers, Käsebier turned her camera on Native Americans; from about 1898 until 1912, she regularly invited Sioux Indians from Buffalo Bill's troupe to pose for her. Her most famous image from this photographic series is *The Red Man* (1902). She also created a series of portraits of the famous Indian musician, writer and teacher Zitkala-Sa (*Gertrude Simmons Bonnin**).

During this time, Gertrude Käsebier was gaining renown as one of the finest pictorialist photographers in the country. Following European trends in photography, the American pictorialists regarded photography as a fine art, much like paintings or poetry. Her own reputation as an artistic photographer was established at the groundbreaking First Philadelphia Photographic Salon in the fall of 1898. Based on the model of the then-fashionable European photographic salon, the exhibition was organized by Stieglitz and sponsored jointly by the Photographic Society of Philadelphia and the Pennsylvania Academy of Fine Arts. Ten of Käsebier's photographs were exhibited and were roundly praised. One of the judges, the distinguished painter William Merritt Chase called Käsebier's work "as fine as anything Van Dyck has ever done."

Her photograph entitled *The Manger* was the sensation of the Second Philadelphia Photographic Salon the following year. The photograph was taken in a whitewashed stable in Newport, Rhode Island, and depicted a woman dressed in white, a long veil flowing from her head to the floor, holding what appears to be an infant swaddled in white. A print of that photograph sold for $100, more than had ever been previously paid for a pictorial photograph.

Motherhood, a subject Käsebier understood well enough from her own experience, was often explored in her photographs, and she frequently photographed her daughters together with their children. Her images raised motherhood to almost mythic heights, yet she avoided sentimentality. "Children are an awful bother," she wrote. "But a woman never reaches her fullest development until she's a mother. You have to pay the price." She once remarked that she saw photography as a medium of light, and her dramatic photographs beautifully expressed the complications, sorrows and joys of the mother-child relationship in contrasting tones of light and shadow. Käsebier's work was also influenced by the revolutionary theories of motherhood espoused by Friedrich Froebel, who emphasized the mother's role as teacher and liberator. One photograph, *Mother and Child* (1899), shows a mother coaxing a reluctant child through a doorway, ostensibly guiding the child toward independence; another, among her most famous images, entitled *Blessed Art Thou Among Women* (1899), depicts a mother standing in a doorway turned toward her daughter (who in turn, is looking directly into the camera), one hand protectively resting on the child's shoulders. On the wall behind the two figures hangs a print of The Annunciation. The woman in the photograph was poet and children's book author Agnes Lee ✎▶ **Agnes Rand Freer**); the

See sidebar on the following page

❧▶ Freer, Agnes Rand (1878–1972)

American poet. Name variations: (pseudonym) Agnes Lee; Mrs. Otto T. Freer. Born Agnes Rand on May 19, 1878, in Chicago, Illinois; died in Ashtabula, Ohio, in December 1972; daughter of William Henry Rand and Harriet Husted (Robinson) Rand; educated mainly in Switzerland; married second husband Otto Freer, in May 1911 (died 1932); children: Peggy (d. around 1900).

Agnes Rand Freer's books, written under the pseudonym of Agnes Lee, include *Verses for Children* (1901), *The Border of the Lake* (1910), *The Sharing* (1914), *Faces and Open Doors* (1922), *New Lyrics and a Few Old Ones* (1930). She also translated from the French Théophile Gautier's *Enamels and Cameos* and Fernand Gregh's *The House of Childhood* and contributed to many anthologies and magazines. *Poetry* magazine awarded Freer a prize for high achievement in the art of poetry.

child was Lee's daughter Peggy. Shortly after the picture was taken, Peggy took ill and died. Five years later in 1904, Käsebier took a haunting photograph of Agnes Lee, *The Heritage of Motherhood*, a powerful statement on motherhood's darker side. In the murky picture, Lee is sitting by the water's edge. She wears a dark cloak over a white dress, her hands are folded, her head tilted back in grief.

In 1899, Gertrude Käsebier joined the influential New York Camera Club which operated under the leadership of Alfred Stieglitz. Stieglitz mounted a solo exhibition of her photographs, and the two quickly became close friends and fans of each other's work. Käsebier certainly owed much of her growing reputation as an artist to Stieglitz, but there is some evidence that her feelings for him may have gone beyond that of friendship and gratitude. On the back of a personal print of a portrait she had made of him was written "the only man I ever loved." Whatever the true nature of her feelings, her friendship with Stieglitz would remain her most important professional relationship for the next decade.

In 1900, she became one of two women admitted to the exclusive Linked Ring, a British pictorialists organization. That same year, her photographs were included in a large exhibition, "The New School of American Photography," organized at the Royal Photographic Society in London. During a trip abroad in 1901, she met Edward Steichen with whom she began a lifelong friendship.

In 1902, Gertrude Käsebier, along with Stieglitz, Steichen, Clarence White and others, formed the "Photo-Secession," an organization devoted to promote further recognition of photography as a fine art. Stieglitz started a new publication, the influential *Camera Work* (1903–17), and opened a gallery in New York, The Little Galleries of the Photo-Secession (soon nicknamed "291"). The first issue of *Camera Work* featured six reproductions of Käsebier's photographs, and for the next few years she exhibited regularly at 291. In 1905, she traveled to Paris and there embarked upon an extended photographic study of the artist Auguste Rodin, with whom she maintained a friendship until his death in 1915.

Throughout this time, Käsebier maintained her lucrative portrait business. This commercial activity increasingly put her at odds with Stieglitz, who believed her interest in professional photography compromised the artistic aims of the Photo-Secessionists. Käsebier did not share his view, as she found portrait photography artistically challenging as well. The need for money may have also been a motive in her continuing interest in commercial photography. Though she was, for all intents and purposes, estranged from her husband, Eduard Käsebier's protracted illness during this time (he died in December of 1909) seems to have prompted financial worries. At any rate, she was spending more time with professional portrait photographers than with the pictorialists. When she joined the Professional Photographers of New York in 1906, Stieglitz was furious. The final breach between Käsebier and Stieglitz occurred over a dispute about money for prints sold at a 1910 Photo-Secession exhibit in Buffalo. On January 1, 1912, Käsebier officially resigned from the Photo-Secession Group, a move which permanently severed her personal and professional relationship with Stieglitz, though she remained friends with White and Steichen.

Finally freed from her disappointing marriage with Eduard and the artistic struggles with Stieglitz, Käsebier pursued an unconstrained life of traveling and socializing. Though her later photographs never received the acclaim of her earlier ones, she remained dedicated and active. In 1912, she undertook an ambitious photographic study of Newfoundland; the following year, she began teaching at Clarence White's School of Photography in Maine and in New York. Four years later, in 1916, when White formed The Pictorial Photographers of America, he made Käsebier honorary vice-president in recognition of her "contribution to the art of photography."

By the early 1920s, Käsebier had moved her studio to Greenwich Village and was increasingly dependent on her daughter, **Hermine Mathilde Turner**, and granddaughter, to care for her and run the business. Käsebier was now completely deaf (a bout of scarlet fever as a young child had affected her hearing), increasingly lame and housebound. In 1925, at age 73, her sight began to fail. In spite of this physical deterioration, her professional reputation remained unaffected. Novice photographers like *Imogen Cunningham and Paul Strand flocked to her studio to meet her. In 1929, the Brooklyn Institute of Arts and Sciences (now the Brooklyn Museum) honored her with a retrospective of her work. It was the last major exhibit of her photographs during her lifetime. Gertrude Käsebier died on October 13, 1934, at the age of 82.

SOURCES AND SUGGESTED READING:

Green, Nancy E. "Likenesses That Are Biographies," in *Belles Lettres*. Vol. 9, no. 3, p. 23.

Henisch, Heinz K., and Bridget A. Henisch. *The Photographic Experience 1839–1914: Images and Attitudes.* University Park, PA: The Pennsylvania State University Press, 1994

Michaels, Barbara L. *Gertrude Käsebier: The Photographer and Her Photographs.* NY: Harry Abrams, 1992.

Newhall, Beaumont. *The History of Photography.* NY: The Museum Of Modern Art, 1982.

The Picture Book *by Gertrude Käsebier, 1903.*

Whelan, Richard. *Alfred Stieglitz: A Biography*. Boston, MA: Little, Brown, 1995.

Suzanne Smith,
freelance writer and editor, Decatur, Georgia

Kasia (c. 800/810–before 867).

See Kassia.

Kasilag, Lucrecia R. (1918—)

Philippine composer, pianist, professor and writer. Born in La Union, the Philippines, on August 31, 1918; Philippine Women's University, B.A. cum laude, in 1936; St. Scholastica College, a music teacher's diploma, 1939; Philippine Women's University, Bachelor of Music, 1949; a Master's of Music from the Eastman School of Music, University of Rochester, Master's of Music, in 1950; Centro Escolar University, Doctorate of Music, in 1975; held degrees in law as well.

Chair of the League of Philippine composers; wrote almost 100 works, including a violin concerto recorded in the 1980s.

Lucrecia Kasilag earned many academic credentials including a B.A. cum laude from the Philippine Women's University in 1936, a music teacher's diploma from St. Scholastica College in 1939; a Bachelor of Music in 1949 from the Philippine Women's University; a Master's of Music from the Eastman School of Music, University of Rochester in 1950, a Doctorate of Music from the Centro Escolar University in 1975, a Doctorate of Law from the Philippine Women's University in 1980, and a Doctor of Fine Arts from St. John's University in 1981.

From 1953 to 1977, while she was pursuing her education, Kasilag served as dean of the College of Music and Fine Arts at the Philippine Women's University as well as professor of music. In addition, she directed the Theater for Performing Arts and presided over the National Music Council of the Philippines. Kasilag headed cultural delegations to the United Nations and presided over international music conferences. The Fulbright Scholar Commission, John D. Rockefeller III Fund, Colombo Plan, Asia Foundation, and the Federal Republic of Germany all supported her work. She also received numerous awards. Kasilag was interested in occidental and oriental instruments, a theme reflected in her compositions and in her writing. Her compositions range from European to Philippine folksongs. A prolific composer, Lucrecia Kasilag pioneered the concept of East-West compositions.

John Haag,
Athens, Georgia

Kassebaum, Nancy Landon

(1932—)

U.S. senator (R-Kansas), noted for both independence and consensus-building, who worked on legislation in foreign affairs, aviation, labor, welfare and health-care reform. Name variations: Nancy Baker. Born Nancy Josephine Landon on July 29, 1932, in Topeka, Kansas; daughter of Alfred Mossman (an entrepreneur and politician) and Theo (Cobb) Landon; University of Kansas, B.A. 1954; University of Michigan, M.A. 1956; married Philip Kassebaum, on June 8, 1955 (divorced 1979); married Howard Baker (former U.S. senator from Tennessee), on December 7, 1996; children: (first marriage) John Philip Kassebaum, Jr.; **Linda Josephine Kassebaum***; Richard Landon Kassebaum; William Alfred Kassebaum.*

Civic and community work in Wichita, Kansas (1955–75), including the Maize school board (1973–75); served as vice-president of the family-owned Kassebaum Communications; worked as aide to U.S. senator James Pearson (R-Kansas) and was a member of Executive Committee of Kansas Republican Party (1975); elected to U.S. Senate (1976); re-elected (1984 and 1990); announced retirement from Senate (1996).

Nancy Landon Kassebaum's first campaign gave ample evidence that hers would be an unpredictable political career. First, she hesitated between running for the Senate and opening a restaurant, then decided to run for the Senate despite the fact that her only previous elected position had been two years on the rural Maize school board. She then proceeded to tell striking farmers that although she favored higher grain prices, she did not support government parity prices. She announced to the state teachers' union that she opposed the creation of a Department of Education. She informed her fellow Republicans that she admired President Jimmy Carter's Panama Canal Treaty and that she disagreed with a Republican plan to cut federal income taxes by 33% in three years. The woman candidate surprised the Kansas Women's Political Caucus (KWPC) with the news that although she supported the Equal Rights amendment, she was against extending the deadline for ratification (the KWPC endorsed her male opponent). But she proved able to turn liabilities into assets: when the Democratic candidate, Dr. Bill Roy, criticized her lack of experience, she campaigned in a simple print housedress, saying she wanted to "bring government back to the people." She won, becoming the only woman in the Senate, the first elected since the defeat of Senator *Margaret Chase Smith (R-Maine) in 1972.

Nancy Landon had been born into a political family near the height of her father's career. Alf Landon, who had earned a comfortable living in the oil business he had learned from his father, was campaigning for governor the year Nancy Jo was born. Alf had been something of a maverick himself, bolting the Republican Party in 1912 to support Theodore Roosevelt's Progressive "Bull Moose" Party, and supporting progressive stands on civil rights and environmental protection in the conservative 1920s. Left a widower with an infant child in 1918, he had married Theo Cobb a decade later. Their daughter, born a few days before the 1932 Republican primary, became the focus of considerable media attention, an asset to the 45-year-old Landon.

Alf Landon cut his own salary by 25%, as part of a state-wide austerity program during the Depression, and won a national reputation for balancing the budget. Toward the end of his second term, he was nominated by the Republicans to challenge Franklin D. Roosevelt for the presidency in 1936; once again Nancy Jo, by then a fetching four-year-old, received considerable coverage in the press. Although Landon lost spectacularly, failing to carry even his own state, he remained an important figure in the party; politicians and journalists continued to congregate at the Landons' Topeka house for consultation. Her mother and siblings were uninvolved, but Nancy, intrigued by political discussions, eavesdropped on the conversations until sent to her room, where she would listen through the heating vents. Her reading tended toward biography and news magazines.

Nancy Landon was studying political science at the University of Kansas when she met Philip Kassebaum during her sophomore year. After graduating in 1954, she studied for an M.A. in diplomatic history at the University of Michigan while Philip earned a law degree. They were married at the Landon home on June 8, 1955, and returned to Michigan to finish their studies, graduating in 1956. The couple had four children in the next six years, and Nancy Kassebaum shelved plans for a career in the U.S. Foreign Service to rear her family on a farm in the Wichita suburb of Maize. She was active in community organizations such as the United Fund, the Kansas Governmental Ethics Commission, and the Kansas Committee for the Humanities. She was president of the Women's Association, president of a drug-prevention program, and active in her children's 4-H programs. She also took part in local Republican election campaigns, stuffing envelopes and writing position papers. Her husband, in addition to his career in law, founded Kassebaum Communications, publishing a newspaper and operating radio stations; Nancy Kassebaum served as the company's vice-president. From 1973 to 1975, she also served on the Maize school board.

> *Politics is nothing more or less than the working out of our competing interests and priorities as a nation.*
>
> —Nancy Landon Kassebaum

When the Kassebaums separated in 1975, Nancy Kassebaum joined the Washington, D.C., staff of Senator James Pearson of Kansas, working on constituent problems with governmental agencies. Her oldest son was by then in college, and the three younger children went with her. When Pearson decided not to run for reelection in 1978, Kassebaum debated whether to try for his seat. As Pearson's legislative aide, she had been appointed to the Executive Committee of the Kansas Republican Party. Although they were willing to support her, they were not particularly encouraging. Most of Kassebaum's family thought she should run, including Philip, to whom she remained close, and even her mother, who had never taken much part in politics. Alf Landon, however, was doubtful, believing that politics was not a field for women. He even tried to enlist President Gerald Ford to help convince his daughter not to run.

Nancy Landon Kassebaum ran against eight other contenders for the Republican nomination, including another woman who was serving in the state senate. Her famous middle name probably helped Kassebaum stand out in the crowded field, and she won the nomination, to face former congressional representative and physician William Roy, who had nearly beaten Bob Dole in the Senate race of 1974. When Roy tried to make an issue of her lack of experience, Kassebaum made a virtue of the outsider image that had worked for Jimmy Carter in 1976; her campaign slogan was "A Fresh Face, a Trusted Kansas Name." When he criticized her for riding on her father's coattails, she smilingly replied that she couldn't think of better ones. He also tried to make an issue over her income taxes, but although she finally disclosed what she had paid, she steadfastly refused to release her tax statements, even when polls showed she was losing support. Nevertheless, she won comfortably with 54% of the vote.

Nancy Landon Kassebaum was only the fourth woman in U.S. history to be elected to a full six-year Senate term. More significantly, she was the first who had not followed a husband into politics. Her path-breaking election was all the more remarkable because, as the *London Daily Mail* observed, she came, not from "a trendy East Coast or West Coast state but from conservative Kansas, where a man's a man and a woman's his cook."

Kassebaum was assigned to the Senate committees on Commerce, Science and Transportation, on Banking Housing and Urban Affairs, on the Budget, and on the Special Committee on Aging, as well as to six subcommittees. In her maiden speech, she advocated term limits: two terms (12 years) for senators. Although she preferred to call herself a "humanist" rather than a "feminist," she recognized that she had two constituencies, Kansas and women. She opposed the Carter administration's embargo on grain sales to the Soviet Union, which she contended hurt the American farmer most, and she advocated tax reform to enable widows to keep family businesses or farms. She stated repeatedly her belief that "abortion is seldom, if ever, the right moral choice, but it should nevertheless be a choice" which should not be addressed in any legislative forum.

In the 97th Congress, Kassebaum was appointed to the Committee on Foreign Relations, and began a career of active involvement in Central American and African affairs, often at odds with the Republican president Ronald Reagan. She wrote the committee restrictions on foreign aid to El Salvador, was one of a group of relatively conservative legislators on Capitol Hill challenging military expenditures, and spoke of the need to keep the Administration's "feet to the fire" on the issue of arms control, concerned that the Republican stance on the "war and peace issue" was costing support among female voters. Later, she would also oppose the MX missile in 1985 and vote against the Strategic Defense Initiative known as the "Star Wars" program. She demonstrated her Republican roots, however, by drafting the Kassebaum amendment to withhold part of the United States' dues until the United Nations overhauled its budget process. This was the first of her continuing efforts to force the UN to streamline its bureaucracy.

By the time she was up for reelection in 1984, Kassebaum had won a reputation both for compromise—she helped shape the allocation of military aid compared to economic aid which Congress would permit Reagan to apportion to Central America—and for principled stands, as when she successfully challenged her Senate Commerce Committee chair Bob Packwood on a significant procedural issue, after building a coalition to support her position. Although women did not fare particularly well in the 1984 election, which saw the Democratic ticket with *Geraldine Ferraro as its vice-presidential nominee decisively defeated, Kassebaum garnered 76% of the vote in her state.

Senator Kassebaum served on the Foreign Relations Subcommittee on African Affairs, and although in 1985 she argued that Congress should not attempt to legislate American policy toward South Africa, during the following year she sponsored legislation to impose phased economic sanctions on the white-minority government, warning Reagan that Congress would act if he would not. In 1989, she joined Democratic committee members to vote for a cap on aid to Zaire (now Republic of Congo) after hearing reports of political repression by the government. She also parted ways from Republicans in 1990 to vote in support of economic sanctions against Iraq at a time when the U.S. was supporting the brutal regime of Saddam Hussein, believing he provided a bulwark against Iran's domination of the Middle East. Her vote was especially courageous because of its potential to hurt Kansas farmers. However, starting with legislation introduced in 1987, she worked to consolidate all U.S. foreign aid programs.

After the 1986 election, Kassebaum was joined by a second woman senator, **Barbara Mikulski** (D-Maryland) who had previously served in Congress. They planned jointly to introduce legislation to ease the burden on spouses and children by controlling health-care costs for the elderly.

When Nancy Kassebaum's second Senate term ended, fellow Kansas Senator Bob Dole and others persuaded her to reverse her original plan to retire after two terms, and run for a third. She agreed, noting that she had been unsuccessful in getting Congress to pass term limits. Again she won in a landslide; *Congressional Quarterly*, in the 1996 edition of *Politics in America*, noted that "By the end of her second term, Kassebaum had established a more lasting political legacy than her father." She was consistently on the short list of potential presidential or vice-presidential candidates.

A *Chicago Tribune* article which ran shortly after the beginning of her second term noted that she refused to use the auto-pen machines that most members of Congress employed. She personally reviewed and hand-signed 1,000 to 1,500 answers sent out from her office each week. Her press secretary conceded that this

Nancy
Landon
Kassebaum

might not be efficient, but noted that Senator Kassebaum felt it was important to stay in touch with her 2.5 million constituents and to know what they were thinking. Despite her success, she occasionally appeared to be shy in her public role. "Someday I'm going to hit someone over the head for calling me diminutive and soft-spoken," she promised, "but I am." Although annoyed by comparisons to Dorothy in *The Wizard of Oz*, she could still laugh at her staff when they included a reference to the movie in a patchwork quilt they made for her.

Nancy Kassebaum continued to define herself as thoughtful and independent. She had been a member of the Budget Committee since her arrival in the Senate, and was an early proponent of the need to balance the budget, one of the first senators to propose a one-year across-the-board budget freeze. She argued against worthwhile but costly programs like the 1989 Act for Better Child Care Services and the National and Community Service Act of 1990. Never a token where women's issues were concerned, she believed that the Civil Rights Act of 1990 only encouraged litigation without addressing effectively the issue of workplace discrimination. She also expressed doubts about the economic feasibility of the Family and Medical Leave Act, supporting President George Bush's veto. "I always feel like the skunk at the picnic on this issue," she was quoted as saying in *Congressional Quarterly*, "but I feel it is wrong for us to mandate benefits."

On the other hand, she frequently opposed the majority of her party when feminist principles were at stake: she was the only Republican to vote against John Tower for secretary of defense in 1989, citing concern about his relationships with defense contractors. Although she voted to confirm Clarence Thomas as a Supreme Court Justice in 1991, she criticized the Senate Judiciary Committee for subjecting **Anita Hill**, who had accused Thomas of sexual harassment, to an "intellectual witch hunt." Later, she admitted she regretted her vote, disappointed with Thomas' opinions. She called for Senator Bob Packwood's resignation in 1993 after he not only was accused of sexual harassment but also of obstructing the investigation. In 1994, she joined other women in the Senate (who by then totaled seven) to vote against giving the Navy's top admiral a four-star retirement rank because of his connection to the Tailhook sex scandal.

She also broke ranks with the Republican Party over the 1994 crime bill, despite pressure from her state's senior senator, GOP leader Bob Dole, and joined six other Republicans to vote against ending the arms embargo against the Bosnian Muslims.

After Republicans gained control of both houses of Congress in the 1994 elections, Senator Nancy Landon Kassebaum became the chair of the Labor and Human Resources Committee, replacing Senator Edward Kennedy (D-Massachusetts). She was the first woman to chair a full committee. (In 1931, Senator *Hattie Caraway [D-Arkansas] chaired the Senate Enrolled Bills Committee, which did not deliberate on legisla-

tion.) The committee dealt with many vital issues such as job training, student loans, affirmative action, arts funding, and the minimum wage, which, like many Republicans, Kassebaum opposed on the grounds that it would eliminate jobs. She also favored welfare reform, and as early as 1994 proposed a plan to turn three major welfare programs over to the states, in exchange for the federal government assuming Medicaid funding for the elderly and disabled. However, she differed from the House Republicans who wanted to limit benefits to welfare recipients after two years.

She was part of a small coterie of moderate Republicans who often deviated from their party line, especially on social issues. Although she opposed the nomination of Dr. Henry Foster as surgeon general in June 1995, she voted in favor of ending a Republican-led Senate filibuster on his nomination. She joined several other moderate Republicans to sign a letter opposing tax cuts, which many Republicans were demanding, before budget cuts were complete. Together with Senator Richard Lugar (R-Indiana), she fought her party's call for deep reductions in foreign aid, urging, "We cannot abdicate out leadership in world affairs." *Congressional Quarterly* observed that "her views often help define where the middle ground lies."

In 1996, Kassebaum capped her career in the Senate by authoring health-care legislation guaranteeing that working Americans would have access to health insurance when they changed or lost jobs even if they or their family members had preexisting health conditions. Although *Meg Greenfield, writing in *Newsweek* on March 27, 1995, remarked that "Kassebaum, who has become more authoritative and sure-footed with the passage of time, is a good argument against term limits," Nancy Landon Kassebaum, citing personal reasons, announced late in 1995 that she would not run for a fourth term in 1996. On December 7, 1996, she married Republican colleague, Howard Baker, U.S. senator from Tennessee for 18 years, who had also served as senate majority leader in 1985 and Reagan's White House chief-of-staff.

SOURCES:

Barone, Michael, and Grant Ujifusa, with Richard E. Cohen. *The Almanac of American Politics 1996: The Senators, the Representatives and the Governors: Their Records and Election Results, Their States and Districts.* Washington, DC: Times Mirror, 1996.

Duncan, Philip D., and Christine C. Lawrence. *Congressional Quarterly's Politics in America 1996: The 104th Congress.* Washington DC: Congressional Quarterly, 1995.

LaTeef, Nelda. *Working Women for the 21st Century: 50 Women Reveal Their Pathways to Career Success.* Charlotte VT: Williamson, 1992.

Morin, Isobel V. *Women of the U.S. Congress.* Minneapolis, MN: Oliver Press, 1994.

Kristie Miller,
author of *Ruth Hanna McCormick:
A Life in Politics 1880–1944* (University of New Mexico Press, 1992)

Kassi (1241–?)

Empress of Mali. Born in 1241; chief wife and paternal cousin of Emperor Suleyman who governed Mali; children: son Kassa.

Born in 1241, Empress Kassi was very popular with the Malian royal court, which included some of her relatives. When her husband Emperor Suleyman divorced her to marry a commoner, **Bendjou**, a feud developed. Kassi assembled the aid of the noblewomen of the court who were unwilling to pay reverence to Empress Bendjou. The noblewomen, still regarding Kassi as the empress of Mali, continued to pay homage to her by tossing soil on their heads and revealed their contempt for Bendjou by casting earth on their hands. The defiant behavior of the royal court's women vexed the emperor and empress, and compelled Kassi to seek refuge in the mosque.

From her sanctuary, Kassi influenced the nobles, particularly her cousins, to rebel against Emperor Suleyman; however, the revolt was just one part of a much larger fight for control of the Malian empire. One sect supported Emperor Suleyman, while the other party backed the sons of former ruler, Mansa Maghan I, who was Suleyman's nephew. The group who identified with the sons of Mansa Maghan I also encouraged Kassi. In order to discredit Kassi, the emperor proved that she was plotting with her cousin Djathal, who had been banished for treason. Kassi's son, Kassa, governed Mali after Suleyman for only nine months before being deposed by his cousin, Mari Diata.

Kim L. Messeri,
freelance writer, Austin, Texas

Kassia (c. 800/810–before 867)

Byzantine author of liturgical hymns. Name variations: Kasia; Kasiane; Elkasia. Born (probably in Constantinople) between 800 and 810 CE; died before 867 CE, perhaps much before.

Kassia was famous throughout the Byzantine Empire as the author of liturgical hymns, dedicated to the ethical and moral strengths and weaknesses of women. Not above addressing issues of the flesh, Kassia wrote verse about lust and physical vanity, and about the need for atonement after women had fallen prey to physical weaknesses. Kassia is reported to have participated in the "Bride Show" of Theophilus, which she, however, lost to a rival named *Theodora the Blessed. This Byzantine institution saw a commission crisscross the empire in search of feminine "talent" which thereafter would be brought to the imperial court where those selected by the commission would compete in a kind of beauty pageant. The winner would then become the wife and queen of the reigning emperor or his heir. If the tradition that Kassia participated in such a competition is true, she almost certainly knew at firsthand the temptations associated with beauty.

Whether physically attractive or not, Kassia became a nun in a convent in Constantinople at a time when a religious controversy split Byzantium in two. The issue which proved to be so divisive involved the use of icons in a religious context: many thought that artistic portrayals of religious subjects were justified to bring the word of God to the illiterate, while others thought all such artistic portrayals should be destroyed, for they encouraged the ignorant to worship—not the ideal behind the depiction—but rather, the physical object itself. Hence, the iconoclasts (those who would destroy all icons) believed that religious art encouraged a kind of heathenism. In this controversy, Kassia appears to have sided with those who thought icons not only acceptable, but beneficial.

William Greenwalt,
Associate Professor of Classical History,
Santa Clara University, Santa Clara, California

Kasten, Barbara

American experimental photographer. Born in Chicago, Illinois; University of Arizona, Tucson, B.F.A., 1959; California College of Arts and Crafts, Oakland, California, M.F.A., 1970.

Barbara Kasten came to photography by way of her interest in traditional Native American arts and fiber sculpture. After receiving a B.F.A. from the University of Arizona, and an M.F.A. from the California College of Arts and Crafts, Kasten was granted a Fulbright scholarship to study for a year with fiber sculptor *Magdalena Abakanowicz, in Poland. Upon returning to California, Kasten began to work in photography, making abstract photograms of folded mesh and large-scale Polacolor prints of sculptural arrangements. She was the recipient of a National Endowment for the Arts fellowship in 1977 and, in 1980, received a NEA service-to-the-field grant to create videotape documentaries of women photographers.

Based in New York since 1982, Kasten has been involved in a number of varied and interesting projects, including designing stage settings for the Margaret Jenkins Dance Company in San Francisco, photographing existing modern architecture for an architectural series, and creating a series of photographs based on the 19th-century (Jackson) Pollock-(*Lee) **Krasner** House and Study Center in East Hampton. In 1988, Kasten worked on a site series in New Mexico.

In 1991, Kasten was awarded both the Pont-Aven Artist-in-Residency from the Musée de Pont-Aven in France and an Apple photographic grant. She has had solo exhibitions at the John Weber Gallery, New York (1990 and 1992), the Ehlers/Caudill Gallery, Chicago (1990), the Gallery RBI at Orbi, Paris (1991), the Parco Exposure Gallery, Tokyo (1991), Place Sazaby, Los Angeles (1992), and Tinglado Dos, Tarragona, Spain (1992).

SOURCES:
Rosenblum, Naomi. *A History of Women Photographers.* NY: Abbeville Press, 1994.

Barbara Morgan,
Melrose, Massachusetts

Katarina.

Variant of Catharine or Catherine.

Katarina of Saxe-Lüneburg
(1513–1535)

Queen of Sweden. Name variations: Catherine of Saxe-Luneberg, Luneburg, or Lauenburg. Born in 1513; died on September 23, 1535; daughter of Magnus, duke of Saxe-Luneburg, and Catherine of Brunswick-Wolfenbuttel (1488–1563); became first wife of Gustavus I Adolphus Vasa (1496–1560), king of Sweden (r. 1523–1560), on September 24, 1531; children: Eric XIV (1533–1577), king of Sweden (r. 1560–1568).

Katarina of Saxe-Lüneburg was born in 1513, the daughter of Magnus, duke of Saxe-Luneburg, and *Catherine of Brunswick-Wolfenbuttel. Katarina married Gustavus I Adolphus, king of Sweden, in September 1531. According to an unconfirmed rumor, Gustavus killed Katarina with a hammer.

Katarina Stenbock (1536–1621)

Queen of Sweden. Born on July 22, 1536; died on December 13, 1621; daughter of Gustav Stenbock; became third wife of Gustavus I Adolphus Vasa (1496–1560), king of Sweden (r. 1523–1560), on August 22, 1552; no children.

Katarzyna.

Variant of Catharine or Catherine.

Kate, Dirty (1751–c. 1800).

See Margaret Corbin in entry titled "Two Mollies."

Katerin.

Variant of Catharine or Catherine.

Katharine.

Variant of Catharine or Catherine.

Katherine.

Variant of Catharine or Catherine.

Katherine (fl. 13th c.)

English physician. Flourished in the 13th century in London.

Katherine represents the many medieval women who broke through clerical stereotypes yet about whom we have little information. Katherine was a highly skilled physician who lived and worked in London. She specialized in surgery and gained widespread respect for her healing abilities. Her father was also a surgeon of London; Katherine probably studied under him before taking on her own patients. Although women as a rule were expected to act as healers, medieval ideology disapproved of the numerous women like Katherine who healed those outside their immediate families, and who performed surgery and other hands-on medical procedures.

SOURCES:
LaBarge, Margaret. *A Small Sound of the Trumpet: Women in Medieval Life.* Boston, MA: Beacon Press, 1986.

Laura York,
Riverside, California

Katherine Howard (1520/22–1542).

See Howard, Catherine in Six Wives of Henry VIII.

Katherine of Aragon (1485–1536).

See Catherine of Aragon in Six Wives of Henry VIII.

Katherine of France (1401–1437).

See Catherine of Valois.

Katherine of Holland (d. 1401)

Countess of Guelders. Died in 1401; daughter of Albert I (b. 1336), count of Hainault and Holland (r. 1353–1404); sister of *Margaret of Bavaria (d. 1424); married Edward, count of Guelders.

Katherine of Portugal (1540–1614).

See Catherine of Portugal.

Katherine Plantagenet (1479–1527).

See Woodville, Elizabeth for sidebar.

Katinka.

Variant of Catherine or Katherine.

Katren, Katrein, or Katrin.

Variant of Catherine or Katherine.

Katznelson, Shulamit (1919–1999)

Israeli professor who brought Jews and Arabs together through language studies. Born in Geneva, Switzerland, in 1919; died on August 6, 1999, of a heart attack at her home in Netanya, Israel; daughter of Bat-Sheva Katznelson (legislator in Israel's Parliament); niece of *Rachel Katznelson-Shazar (1888–1975); attended high school and teacher's college in Jerusalem and master's program at University of Michigan.

At age two, immigrated to Palestine with her family (1921); founded Ulpan Akiva, an independent, residential language school in Netanya, Israel (1951); received Israel Prize for Life Achievement for bringing Arabs and Jews together through study of each other's language (1986); nominated for Nobel Peace Prize for helping to reconcile Jews and Arabs (1993); retired as head of Ulpan Akiva (1997).

Born in Geneva, Switzerland, in 1919, Shulamit Katznelson immigrated with her family to Palestine in 1921. Her mother **Bat-Sheva Katznelson** served in Israel's Parliament; her brother, Shmuel Tamir, was a justice minister; and her uncle, Zalman Shazar, was Israel's third president. She attended high school and teacher's college in Jerusalem, and then pursued her master's degree at the University of Michigan at Ann Arbor.

In 1951, Katznelson founded Ulpan Akiva, an independent, residential language school in Netanya, Israel. For almost 50 years, she focused her energies at the school on reconciling Jews and Arabs through person-to-person contacts and learning to speak each other's language. Katznelson also believed that one's language and culture were inseparable. As a result, students were asked to intersperse language lessons while learning about each other's history and culture. Many of the Jews and Arabs who attended the school became friends and continued their friendships. Approximately 100,000 people from 148 countries have studied at the school. Two branch offices were set up in the Gaza Strip towns of Gaza City and Khan Yunis. Following Katznelson's retirement in 1997, Ephraim Lapid, a former Israeli military officer, took over as her successor. For her efforts to achieve reconciliation between the Arabs and the Jews, Katznelson received her country's highest honor in 1986, the Israel Prize for Life Achievement; in 1993, she was nominated for the Nobel Peace Prize. Shulamit Katznelson died of a heart attack on August 6, 1999, at age 80, at her home in Netanya, near Tel Aviv, Israel.

SOURCES:
Obituary, in *The New York Times*. August 7, 1999.

Jo Anne Meginnes,
freelance writer, Brookfield, Vermont

Katznelson-Rubashov, Rachel (1888–1975).

See Katznelson-Shazar, Rachel.

Katznelson-Shazar, Rachel (1888–1975)

Russian-born Israeli editor, teacher, and labor union activist who was first lady of Israel (1963–73) as the wife of Zalman Shazar, third president of Israel. Name variations: Rachel Shazar; Rachel Katznelson-Rubashov; Rachel Katznelson-Rubachov. Born Rachel Katznelson in Bobroisk, Russia, in 1888; died as a Zionist pioneer in Israel on August 11, 1975; daughter of Nissan Katznelson and Selde (Rosowski) Katznelson; aunt of *Shulamit Katznelson (d. 1999); married Schneor Zalman Rubashov (1889–1974), who, as third president of the Jewish State, was known as Zalman Shazar; children: daughter, Roda Shazar.

Like **Vera Weizmann** and *Rachel Ben Zvi, the two Israeli first ladies before her, Rachel Katznelson-Shazar played a notable part in the foundation and development of the Jewish State. She was born in 1888 in Bobroisk, Russia, into an affluent family, and attended a women's college in St. Petersburg, before going to Germany to study at the Academy of Jewish Studies in Berlin. Committed to the ideals of Socialist Zionism, in 1912 she moved to Palestine, then a province of the decaying Ottoman Empire. Palestine was overwhelmingly Arab in population, economically primitive, and disease-ridden, and life there, even for a healthy young idealist, required overcoming immense physical and psychological challenges. At first appointed to a teaching post at the kibbutz Kvztzat Kinneret, she soon decided that manual labor would bring her closer to the pioneering spirit of Palestine's Jewish settlers.

Katznelson and many of her contemporary female Zionists saw two problems inherent in the institution of the family: its potential threat to the collectivity and its inevitable role in isolating women at home to raise children, thus keeping them from participating in the public life of the community. Many women in the early kibbutzim decided not to get married and not to have children. Writing in her diary in July 1918, Katznelson reflected: "We are group beings not family beings. . . . No, we will not have children."

In 1920, she married Schneor Zalman Rubashov, also a Russian-born Zionist. He had visited Palestine as early as 1911, returned to Russia to report for his military service, and immigrated to Palestine after the Russian Revolution. Years later, when Hebrew-sounding names became the norm with high officials of the new State of Israel, he would choose the name Shazar which was made up of the initials of his full name.

Both Rachel Katznelson-Shazar and her husband had busy careers in journalism, politics and other spheres of Palestinian-Israeli public life. Devoted to improving the position of working women in the emerging Zionist community, she was one of the first women to join the Mapai Party which grew out of the original Achdut Avoda labor organization. From 1924 through 1927, she was a member of the central cultural committee of the Histadrut, the General Federation of Jewish Labor. In the years after 1925, when her husband was a co-founder and member of the editorial board of the labor daily newspaper *Davar*, she became increasingly active in labor politics, eventually serving on the executive committee of the Mapai Party. Katznelson-Shazar was also active in the labor movement from the first days of her arrival in Palestine. A member of the presidium of the Zionist Actions Committee, she was a familiar face as a delegate to Zionist Congresses for almost four decades, as was her husband.

Writing in flawless Hebrew, a skill not all early Zionists mastered, Katznelson-Shazar was a respected journalist and editor who won several literary prizes. These included an Israel Prize in 1958 for her book *Masot Urshimot* (Essays and Articles), which was taken from her journalistic contributions over the decades to the labor

journal *Dvar Hapoelet*. She founded this journal in 1934 and served as editor until 1963. That year, she became chair of the journal's editorial board, thus guaranteeing her broad guidance of the journal. Some of the other awards Katznelson-Shazar received for her literary work and public service included the Brenner Prize in 1947, the Chaim Greenberg Prize, and the Prize of the Pioneer Women in the United States.

As one of the most influential members of the Women's Workers Council from 1930 to 1963, Katznelson-Shazar both participated and witnessed significant changes in the status of Jewish women, first in British-administered Palestine and later in the State of Israel. In theory at least, the Zionist ideology that justified the creation of a Jewish State in Palestine was based on ideas of gender equality. Although this was the Zionist ideal, from the start Zionist reality was very different. As **Rachel Elboim-Dror** has noted, in the Zionist movement's formative years as well as in Zionist literary utopias, women figure mainly as sex objects. There were no women delegates to the first Zionist Congress (held in Basel, Switzerland, in 1897), and nothing had changed a decade later when in 1907 Shalom Aleichem reported on the eighth Zionist Congress, commenting on the beauty of the lovely women "whom God created to make our life pleasant, pretty and enchanting. . . . It is a pity that no one of them is willing, or is able, to take part in the debates on the platform."

The inequalities seen in the Zionist movement in Europe continued when Jewish women immigrated to Palestine to help in the creation of a Jewish State. One of them, **Zipora Bar-Daroma**, writing in an anthology edited in Hebrew by Katznelson-Shazar (1930), gave voice to her grievances: "A feeling of inequality came over us with the first breath of air in *Eretz Israel*. We came together with the men but were divided into two camps: 'builders,' and 'servants' who nursed and served them." Writing in the same anthology, an anonymous woman revealed her sense of anger and betrayal: "You see the commune and the fate of women in it—the fate of a domestic servant as always, only instead of a small cooking-pot—a big one, instead of 'my child'—'our children,' and the same endless laundry." Another anonymous woman spoke at the time of feeling injured and insulted because her existence was secondary to that of men: "her life a narrow spring beside the main flow of life—his."

Writing in 1955, **Ada Maimon-Fishman**, one of the most militant activists in the Women Workers' Movement wrote, "Even in Erets Israel, within the revolutionary and innovative Labor Movement, the woman was pushed into her *traditional* occupation, into housework and primarily into kitchen work." The same theme is repeated by Rachel Katznelson-Shazar in her 1989 book of notes and diaries, *The Person as She Was,* where she speaks candidly of the disappointments experienced by that pioneer generation of Zionist women, who saw themselves again and again relegated to the roles of being "an observer, a sister, a servant, but never in the front row."

The Jewish labor movement in Palestine and later Israel was theoretically committed to full equality of men and women. Established in 1920, the General Federation of Jewish Labor (Histadrut) was the all-encompassing organization for Jewish wage earners, skilled and unskilled, men and women. The beginning of urban development and the prosperity that accompanied new waves of immigration in the 1920s did not lead to significant improvements for women, in view of the fact that the building trades were almost totally male dominated and would remain that way. Although women proved that they were qualified to do the work, by 1926 there were only 51 women tile layers, 19 women painters and 13 women masons. Most female workers were associated with the Women Worker's Movement, founded in 1911, which was an integral part of the Histadrut. In 1921, this organization elected a smaller operative body—the Women Workers' Council (WWC)—which met annually, as well as a secretariat of four to deal with day-to-day matters. Katznelson-Shazar was a member of the WWC; witnessing vast social and intellectual changes over the decades, she participated in its deliberations.

In 1963, her husband Zalman Shazar was elected to the ceremonial post of president of Israel. As the third president of the Jewish State, Shazar continued his career as a writer, as did his wife, now the first lady of Israel. During her years as president's wife, she published two books. Born and raised in a very different pre-Holocaust world, the two elderly intellectuals and Zionist pioneers were respected in Israel, but the younger Sabra generation had little in common with them. The Shazars' world was now one of distant, faded ideals, long-forgotten debates, and personal animosities that lived only in the yellowed pages of old books and newspapers. But in these writings, read by a select circle of scholars, much of interest can still be found. Rachel Katznelson-Shazar examined difficult problems that would remain unresolved after her death. Of one such concern, she

wrote: "The Women's Movement is full of contradictions, like nature which created the human being in two images, distinguishing these biologically as well as spiritually; and like civilization which both frees and enslaves." In another context, she noted in 1937: "If we ask ourselves, 'What is it to be a mother?' and if we remember that it is the wife of the worker who has to educate the children, keep house, decorate and design it, come into contact with doctors and teachers, then once again we may say: 'This is enough for one person. We have no more strength.'"

Zalman Shazar retired after two terms as president of Israel in 1973. He died on October 5, 1974, one day before his 85th birthday. By now a frail invalid, Rachel Katznelson-Shazar died less than a year later, on August 11, 1975.

SOURCES:

Bernstein, Deborah. "The Plough Woman Who Cried into the Pots: The Position of Women in the Labor Force in the Pre-State Israeli Society," in *Jewish Social Studies.* Vol. 45, no. 1. Winter 1983, pp. 43–56.

———. *The Struggle for Equality: Urban Women Workers in Prestate Israeli Society.* NY: Praeger, 1987.

———. "The Women Workers' Movement in Pre-State Israel, 1919–1939," in *Signs: Journal of Women in Culture and Society.* Vol. 12, no. 3. Spring 1987, pp. 454–470.

———, ed. *Pioneers and Homemakers: Jewish Women in Pre-State Israel.* Albany, NY: State University of New York Press, 1992.

Brilliant, Moshe. "Zalman Shazar Is Dead at 84; President of Israel for 10 Years," in *The New York Times Biographical Edition.* October 1974, p. 1498.

Daniel, Clifton. "Christians Submit Aims in Palestine," in *The New York Times.* July 12, 1947, p. 5.

Elboim-Dror, Rachel. "Gender in Utopianism: the Zionist Case," in *History Workshop Journal.* Issue 37. Spring 1994, pp. 99–116.

Izraeli, Dafna. "The Zionist Women's Movement in Palestine, 1911–1927: A Sociological Analysis," in *Signs: Journal of Women in Culture and Society.* Vol. 7, no. 1. Autumn 1981, pp. 87–114.

Katznelson-Shazar, Rachel. *Adam kemo she-hu: pirke yomanim u-reshimot* (The Person as She Was). Edited by Michal Hagiti. Tel Aviv: Am Oved, 1989.

———, ed. *The Plough Woman: Records of the Pioneer Women of Palestine.* Rendered into English by Maurice Samuel. Reprint of 1932 ed. Westport, CT: Hyperion Press, 1976.

———, oral history file, Department for Oral Communication, Institute for Contemporary Jewry, Hebrew University, Jerusalem.

"Rachel Shazar," in *Jewish Chronicle* [London]. August 15, 1975, p. 27.

John Haag,
Associate Professor of History,
University of Georgia, Athens, Georgia

Kauai, queen of.

See Kapule, Deborah (c. 1798–1853).

Kauffmann, Angelica (1741–1807)

Swiss artist who achieved fame and fortune in portraiture and the hitherto male domain of history painting. Name variations: *Angelika Kauffman; Maria Angelica Kauffmann; Kauffmann-Zucchi; Kauffman-Z; K.-Z.; A.K.Z. Born Marie Anne Angelica Catherine Kauffmann on October 30, 1741, in Chur (or Coire), capital of Graubünden canton, Switzerland; died on November 5, 1807, in Rome; daughter of Johann Josef Kauffmann (an itinerant painter) and Cléofa Lucin (or Lucci, or Luz) Kauffmann; married "Count Frederick de Horn," in fact an impersonator by the name of Brandt, on November 22, 1767 (legally separated on February 10, 1768); married Antonio Zucchi, on September 8, 1781; children: none.*

Began commissioned portraiture in Como, Italy, at age 11 (1752); traveled with father in Italy and France, studying and painting; elected to the Academy of Fine Arts, Florence, and the Academy of St. Clement, Bologna (1762), and the Academy of St. Luke, Rome (1765); accompanied Lady Wentworth to England (1765 or 66); selected as a founding member of The Royal Academy of Art, London (1768); left England (1781), traveled in Europe and elected to the Academy of Fine Arts, Venice; established her last studio in Rome by December 1782.

Paintings: The Family of the Earl of Gower *(National Museum of Women in the Arts, Washington, D.C., 1772);* Zeuxis choosing his Models for the Painting of Helen of Troy *(Brown University, Providence, R.I., late 1770s);* Cornelia, Mother of the Gracchi *(Virginia Museum of Fine Arts, Richmond, 1785);* The Sadness of Telemachus *(Metropolitan Museum of Art, New York, 1788);* Angelica Kauffmann hesitating between the Arts of Music and Painting *(Nostell Priory, Yorkshire, c. 1794–96); and many more. Signed work:* Angelica Kauffmann (or Kauffman) Pinx.

In casting about for an explanation of Angelica Kauffmann's lasting renown, Lady **Victoria Manners** and Dr. G.C. Williamson, her English biographers of the early 20th century, ultimately conclude that it is due to the exceptional complementarity between the artist, her works, and the sensibility of her time. Kauffmann was a central figure in the neoclassical movement in art which began in mid-18th-century Europe, and it was she who introduced history painting in the neoclassical style to England. Moreover, Kauffmann's own "prudish prejudices" were in complete accord with those of 18th-century England's middle and upper classes, whose patronage was so important to her early career. "Not one of her works contained anything that could bring the slightest blush to the cheek of a young girl," report Manners and Williamson, and most important, she "never forgot the fact of her own femininity and she never allows us to forget it when we look at her works." So profound was her influence that English artists held to the standards of "ultra-refinement and delicacy" established by Kauffmann for 100 years after her death.

At the same time, Kauffmann's life was in many ways a contradiction of the social prescriptions for 18th-century womanhood. Perhaps because she married painter Antonio Zucchi well after her reputation was established, she retained her maiden name for professional purposes, signing her paintings "Angelica Kauffmann Pinx" all of her life. For personal correspondence, she employed another strategy more common to our time than hers, that of hyphenating her husband's surname or initial to her own.

Furthermore, Kauffmann's relationships with key men in her life were role reversals. From an early age, she supported the households she was a member of, the first including her father and a female cousin, the second her husband and a male cousin. Each man in turn—father, husband, cousin—managed the households and much of the business side of her career. In another "modern" touch, Kauffmann and her husband signed a nuptial agreement protecting each's modest savings and investments from the other. In a time when motherhood as well as domesticity was the destiny of women, she did not have children. Rather, Angelica painted.

She began painting as a child and painted until the final months of her life. From this long and prolific career came hundreds of canvases, dozens of roundels and ovals decorating the homes and furnishings of aristocratic England, and a handful of engravings by her own hand (many of her paintings were engraved by others). She was elected to many of the important art academies of Europe, and was one of two female founding members of the Royal Academy of Art in London. Her work is preserved in nearly all of Europe's important national galleries, and many major U.S. museums hold representative canvases.

Her biographers mark the beginning of Kauffmann's professional career with her 1752 portrait in pastel of Nevroni Cappucino, bishop of Como, Italy. The artist was 11 years old; her sitter a powerful elder whose satisfaction with the likeness generated a flood of commissions for the young portraitist. A German biographer,

Frances Gerard, reports that by the age of eight Kauffmann had already taken portraits of "several beautiful ladies and pretty children," but these are not generally viewed as part of her professional work. In any case, the historical evidence is clear that Angelica's painter father, Johann Josef Kauffmann, had recognized and cultivated his daughter's interest and talent from the time she was able to take chalk and crayon in hand, and that before demand for her own work occupied her full time, she assisted her father in his primary vocation—church decoration.

Johann Josef's work had brought the Kauffmann family to Como and in contact with the bishop; Angelica's need for advanced training took them next to Milan. There, by virtue of being the rare female artist in the galleries studying and copying the works of the masters, she attracted the attention of the duke and duchess of Modena (*Charlotte-Aglae). As in Como, a portrait was taken, this one of the duchess, who was delighted with it, and again the elite of the city lined up to be painted by the young artist. For two years, the Kauffmann family mingled with the Milanese nobility and enjoyed their patronage and favors.

Then Angelica's mother **Cléofa Kauffmann** died, just as Angelica turned 16. Cléofa had been a moderating influence in Angelica's life, to some extent protecting the child prodigy from her father's proud and enthusiastic promotion. Her death initiated a period in which father and daughter traveled widely, cultivating contacts with the rich and powerful. But first they returned to Johann Josef's native village of Schwartzenberg, Germany, which Angelica had never seen. There, daughter assisted father in completing a commission to decorate the parish church. The cardinal bishop, being pleased with their work, invited them to Morsburg where he sat for Angelica for his portrait. Again, other notables in the vicinity followed suit, and soon Kauffmann had earned enough to return with her father to the arts-rich environment of northern Italy.

From then on, Angelica's reputation and earning power increasingly guided their moves. During a second stay in Milan, she painted portraits of many of the family and friends of their host, the Count de Montfort. Here, too, she seriously considered giving up painting for a career in music, for she played clavichord and zither, and had an excellent voice and singing ability. Both a musician suitor and her father urged her toward music, the latter reportedly because he believed the financial rewards would be quicker and greater. Angelica was a popular portraitist, but her commissions were small. However, the Kauffmanns were devout Catholics, and Angelica also sought the counsel of a priest and family friend who advised her that the opera stage was no place for a virtuous young woman. After much indecision, she chose painting, and years later commemorated the moment with one of her best-known canvases, *Angelica Kauffmann hesitating between the Arts of Music and Painting* (c. 1794–96).

In October 1765, Angelica and her father arrived in Venice, having spent time in Parma, Bologna, Florence, Naples, and Rome. In each city, she studied, painted, and charmed the arts community and its aristocratic patrons. She met the celebrated German art critic Abbé Winckelmann in Rome, won his admiration, secured his portrait in one of her more critically acclaimed efforts, and was deeply influenced by him. Winckelmann was a powerful proponent of the neoclassical style, and he urged Kauffmann toward the allegorical and mythological subjects in classical compositions which she explored in her major canvases.

But in Venice she met **Lady Wentworth**, wife of the British diplomatic representative, whose influence was more dramatic if less intellectual. Lady Wentworth was engaged in a favorite 18th-century entertainment of the British nobility: doing "the grand tour" of Europe and patronizing artists. She took a liking to and urged Kauffmann to return to London with her, no doubt expecting to enhance her own popularity and reputation by introducing a rising young artist to London society. Angelica accepted, eager to see a new country and to enjoy the patronage of the English who, she had already learned, would pay her more generously for their portraits than the Italians.

Thus Angelica Kauffmann came to introduce history painting in the neoclassical manner to England. But though it might have been history painting which won her selection as a founding member of the Royal Academy of Art, it was primarily portraiture and house decoration which enabled her to bring her father and cousin to England within a few years, and to return to Rome after 16 years with a modest fortune.

Two events during her tenure in England require special attention: her first marriage and her election to the Royal Academy. It is ironic that a woman perceived by so many to be the professional equal of men, who held mutually respectful relationships with so many notable men of her day (Winckelmann, Goethe, Sir Joshua Reynolds, to name a few), and whose relationships with her father and second husband were so clearly role reversals, should also have been so thoroughly deceived and used by a man. But such was, in fact, the case, the man being "Count Frederick de Horn," actually a child-out-of-wedlock and former employee of the real count, using the count's money, jewels and clothing (perhaps stolen, perhaps gifts or pay-offs) to present himself convincingly to London society as the count. How an intelligent, accomplished, cosmopolitan woman should have been susceptible to the poseur is something of a mystery. Certainly many did not immediately question "the count's" identity, but Kauffmann abandoned her usually careful consideration of important decisions. For the first time in her life, she failed to consult her father; indeed, she hid the engagement and marriage from him for a time. Moreover, she was far from inexperienced in matters of romance, for she had had several serious suitors, each of whom she had encouraged for a time without committing herself. In fact, the English painter Nathaniel Dance, who met Kauffmann in Rome, followed her back to England thinking they were engaged. By then, Angelica was apparently involved in a flirtation with England's most celebrated painter of the time, Sir Joshua Reynolds, and she gave Dance the cold shoulder.

Perhaps, indeed, there is a theme that connects Angelica's romantic history with her susceptibility to the pseudo-count and even her success as an artist. That theme is her ambition, for just as she set her professional goals high, she had decided that when she married, she would marry well, into wealth and position. Thus the handsome, seemingly wealthy pseudo-count, who entered her life just as it was becoming clear that the flirtation with Sir Joshua would not lead to marriage, must have appeared to Angelica to be the opportunity of a lifetime. In any case, she succumbed to his mysterious stories of enemies and court intrigues in his homeland (Sweden) that only she could save him from by marrying him quickly and secretly.

Within a month, the deception began to unravel; the "Count de Horn" not only was not a count but, Kauffmann eventually learned, he was already married to a young German girl whom he had abandoned to poverty. Much of the historical record of this incident is incomplete or unclear. Some sources say that the imposter was arrested and released for unknown reasons, others that Angelica was too humiliated to press charges. Whichever, on February 10, 1768, after several months of negotiations, Angelica Kauffmann signed a deed of separation to which his signature (in the name of Brandt) was already affixed, and paid him 300 English pounds to be rid of him. And though the marriage had been bigamous and therefore theologically invalid from the beginning, Kauffmann declined to appeal to Rome for an annulment, apparently out of embarrassment and desire to have the incident forgotten. Thus she did not marry again until 1781, just a few months after Brandt's death.

After Kauffmann's disastrous first marriage, she threw herself into painting as never before, and her friends supplied her with many commissions which helped her recover her lost savings and legal expenses. Later in the same year of her separation from Brandt, she received one of her greatest honors as an artist: selection as a founding member of the Royal Academy of Art. She was one of two women nominated and chosen, the other being *Mary Moser (whose career faltered and faded thereafter). And though these two were founding members, the Academy's charter did not in fact allow for the election of women. Thus it was not until the charter was amended almost 200 years later that another woman, *Laura Knight, was elected to full membership in 1936.

The Academy's records inform us that from the beginning, Kauffmann was a prolific member, commonly submitting six or more canvases to the annual members exhibition. These were mostly history paintings, many large in scale, which she viewed as her most important work. Some of her most loyal patrons, who continued to commission paintings long after she returned to Italy in 1781, apparently first encountered her work at Academy exhibitions. The value Kauffmann placed on her Academy membership is indicated by the shipments of paintings for the annual membership exhibit which continued to make the journey from Rome to London for many years.

The anachronistic quality of Kauffmann's and Moser's position in the Academy is revealed in a famous painting by Zoffany, *The Academicians of the Royal Academy* (1772). In the painting, the academicians are assembled for a life-class; the model is a nude male. Zoffany's choice of this scenario highlights the importance of studying the nude to 18th-century art, but women were excluded from the life-class to protect their feminine virtue and sensibility. (It is particularly ironic that one of the most common criticisms leveled by her contemporaries was that Kauffmann's drawing—especially of male figures—was weak.) Thus, while the male academicians study, discuss and sketch from the model, the two female members, Kauffmann and Moser, are represented in the painting only by their framed portraits hanging on the studio wall, interestingly enough, along with other decorative objects.

Art historian **Angela Rosenthal** argues that Kauffmann responded to Zoffany's painting, rejecting her passive positioning on the wall, in a painting of her own: *Zeuxis choosing his Models for the Painting of Helen of Troy* (late 1770s). In the painting, Kauffmann placed herself as one of four beautiful women the artist Zeuxis is examining. But while three are arrayed in front of Zeuxis as the objects of his gaze, Angelica the model has stepped past the artist, seized his brushes, and herself gazes back toward him and the model he seems transfixed by. It is a "life-class" in which the woman painter knowingly trespasses and asserts her claim to the profession and all of its tools. As if to underscore this meaning, Zeuxis' waiting canvas within the canvas is signed "Angelica Kauffmann Pinx."

Kauffmann's second marriage, to Antonio Zucchi on the eve of her departure from England, seems to have been one of comfort and stability rather than romance. The demand for Angelica's work completely occupied her time by then, and her aging father was deeply concerned that he be replaced as advisor and manager of her household and career by a respectable husband. With her permission, Johann Josef let it be known that Zucchi's interest in Angelica was welcome and that a request for her hand would be favorably received. So it was done, and in the most proper manner. Zucchi largely set aside his own moderately successful career to support and manage his wife's. One of his lasting contributions was to begin keeping a record of Kauffmann's paintings—subjects, patrons, commissions and gifts—upon their return to Italy in 1781. This *Memorandum of Paintings,* discovered in the archives of the Academy early in this century, has greatly assisted historians in locating, identifying, and dating her works from mid-career onward. Angelica's personal correspondence suggests that a deep affection developed between them, and that she suffered his

Virgil Writing His Own Epitaph at Brundisium, *painting by Angelica Kauffmann.*

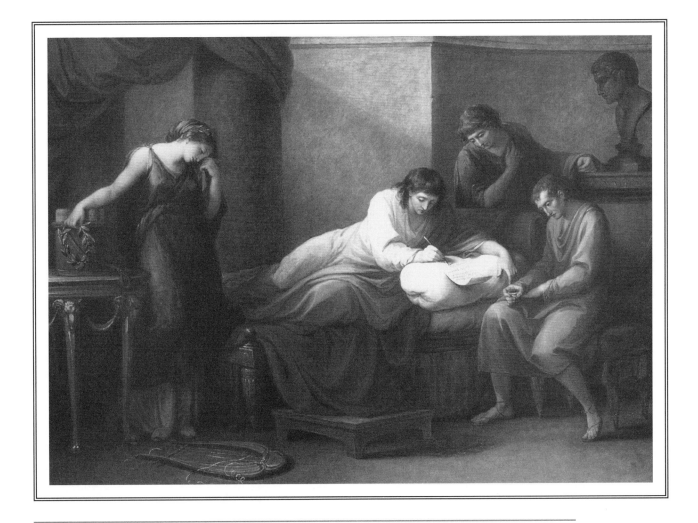

death in 1795 greatly. (He was 15 years her senior.) Like her father, who died within months after Angelica's marriage to Zucchi and their return to Italy, Zucchi had provided for his own successor. About two years before his death, he called Angelica's young cousin, Anton Josef Kauffmann, from Schwartzenberg to Rome and installed him as manager of her household and business affairs.

Angelica Kauffmann's fame and fortune continued to grow and reached their apex in the years following her return to Rome. Commissions from England continued apace, a few of her patrons there ordering pictures regularly once or more per year. The royal family of Naples placed heavy demands upon her time, Queen *Maria Carolina (1752–1814, wife of Ferdinand IV, king of Naples) in fact offering her a permanent post as court painter. This Angelica declined, always preferring to preserve her independence, but she was a royally treated guest in Naples for two periods of several months each. During these times, she tutored the royal children and made preliminary sketches for a huge, composite family portrait which she completed, along with several smaller, individual portraits, at her studio in Rome.

Kauffmann's studio became a necessary stop for visiting royalty and nobility from all over Europe. Few left without sitting for sketches for a portrait or ordering a painting on some historical or mythological subject; some waited up to two years for their canvases. In addition, her home was a mecca for the European artists' community. Not only painters visiting Rome, but poets as well, became Angelica's admirers and friends, among them the German poets Goethe and his less well-known peer, Herder.

When Angelica Kauffmann died in 1807, at the age of 66, the local art community, led by the sculptor Canova, organized a huge and glorious funeral for her. According to Gerard, the procession through the streets was "swelled by every one of rank and distinction then in Rome." Two of her paintings with religious subjects flanked the altar of the Church of Sant' Andrea delle Fratte, while a bust of her in Carrara marble by Canova, finished just a month before her death, occupied the center. By her own request, her body was laid next to Zucchi's in a side chapel.

By all accounts, Angelica Kauffmann was not only a skilled painter but an exceedingly charming woman. Her biographers comment repeatedly on her sweetness, her graciousness, her modesty, and provide numerous supporting comments from references to her in published works (poems, reviews, etc.) as well as in the personal correspondence of her friends. Gerard, for example, quotes an unnamed German writer on the friendship between Goethe and Kauffmann: "It was natural that he, the favourite of the Graces, should be, so soon as he came within her spell, attracted by this sweet impersonation of womanly grace." This notion of her presence as a kind of spell, an irresistible paradigm of femininity, is virtually a theme of her life.

To set the stage for her analysis of Kauffmann's *Zeuxis choosing his Models . . .*, Angela Rosenthal quotes Angelica Kauffmann's contemporary, the popular novelist *Eliza Haywood, from the *Female Spectator* (1774–76): "and I again repeat it as the most infallible maxim, that whenever we would truly conquer, we must seem to yield." Rosenthal calls Haywood's maxim "masking," the art employed by women intellectuals of presenting challenges to the status quo so thoroughly cloaked in precisely the trappings most pleasing so as to disarm critics and ensure reception of the works. Angelica Kauffmann's life as well as her art would appear to be an example.

SOURCES:

Gerard, Frances A. *Angelica Kauffmann: A Biography*. 2nd ed. NY: Macmillan, 1893.

Manners, Lady Victoria, and Dr. G.C. Williamson. *Angelica Kauffmann, R.A.: Her Life and Her Works*. London: The Bodley Head, 1924.

National Museum of Women in the Arts. Catalog of the permanent collection. NY: Harry N. Abrams, 1987.

Rosenthal, Angela. "Angelica Kauffman Ma(s)king Claims," in *Art History*. Vol 15. March 1992, pp. 38–59.

SUGGESTED READING:

Adam, Malise Forbes, and Mary Mauchline. "Ut pictura poesis: Angelica Kauffmann's literary sources," in *Apollo*. Vol. 135. June 1992, pp. 345–349.

Bachmann, Donna G., and Sherry Piland. *Women Artists: An Historical, Contemporary and Feminist Bibliography*. Metuchen, NJ: Scarecrow Press, 1978.

Harris, Ann Sutherland, and Linda Nochlin. *Women Artists, 1550-1950*. NY: Alfred A. Knopf, 1976.

Rice, Louise, and Ruth Eisenberg. "Angelica Kauffmann's Uffizi Self-Portrait," in *Gazette des Beaux-Arts*. Vol. 117. March 1991, pp. 123–126.

Roworth, Wendy Wassyng. "Angelica Kauffman's Memorandum of Paintings," in *The Burlington Magazine*. Vol. 126. October 1984, pp. 629–630.

COLLECTIONS:

The Royal Academy of Art, London, holds some documents, including her *Memorandum of Paintings* and catalogues of exhibitions she participated in as a member.

Bette J. Kauffman,
Associate Professor of Mass Communication at Northeast Louisiana University, Monroe, Louisiana

Kauffmann, Maria A. (1741–1807).

See Kauffmann, Angelica.

Kautsky, Luise (1864–1944)

Austrian Social Democratic activist and author. Born in Vienna, Austria, on August 11, 1864; arrested in the Netherlands, where she and her husband had fled in 1938 to escape the Nazis, and sent to the Auschwitz-Birkenau; died in Auschwitz-Birkenau concentration camp in early December 1944; married Karl Kautsky (1854–1938, a noted Marxist theoretician and son of writer **Minna Kautsky** *[1837–1912]); children: Benedikt Kautsky (1894–1960).*

Married to Karl Kautsky, one of the major personalities of the heroic period of European Socialism, Luise Kautsky was a significant figure in her own right. Born into a bourgeois Jewish family in Vienna on August 11, 1864, she quickly found her way to the nascent Socialist movement, where she became an important voice for women's rights. Her journalistic skills enabled her to make a strong case for every issue she championed. Karl had spent much of his political career in Berlin, but in 1920 he and Luise settled in Vienna, where despite his advancing years he remained productive as a historian and polemicist. Luise Kautsky, too, was active in Vienna, her articles appearing in many Socialist newspapers and journals. In 1932, for example, she published a finely crafted article on "Russian Women of Yesterday and Today" to the proceedings of that year's Socialist women's organization.

With the Nazi annexation of Austria in March 1938, the physical safety of Karl and Luise Kautsky could not be guaranteed, and they fled to the Netherlands. Profoundly shaken by the events of recent months, Karl died on October 17 of that year in Amsterdam. Luise determined to live on, particularly since her son Benedikt Kautsky (1894–1960) had been arrested by the Nazis soon after the Anschluss and was being held captive in Dachau concentration camp. A Social Democratic activist, Benedikt had worked for many years at Vienna's *Arbeiterkammer* and was regarded by the Nazis as a dangerous Marxist intellectual. Thus he could not gain his freedom to emigrate, and his mother, being abroad, often had little reliable information on his condition or whether he was in fact still alive.

The Nazi occupation of the Netherlands put Luise Kautsky's life at risk, but bureaucratic confusions and delays kept her free until the fall of 1944, when Nazi occupation authorities deported her to the dreaded Auschwitz-Birkenau death camp. Although old and feeble, she was saved from the gas chambers because Dr. *Ella Lingens-Reiner, a brave, resourceful Austrian prisoner whose work as a physician saved countless lives, took note of her presence and was able to have her placed in the camp infirmary. Though this action temporarily saved Luise Kautsky's life, her condition continued to deteriorate and after six weeks she died, in early December 1944. Ironically, her son Benedikt, who was imprisoned at one of the other Auschwitz camps about three miles away, knew about his mother's presence in the area through the camp grapevine, but could do nothing to either see her in her final days or alleviate her suffering. Benedikt Kautsky survived his imprisonment, returning to Vienna where he wrote his memoirs about his camp experiences and went on to become an important leader of the postwar Austrian Social Democratic Party.

Luise Kautsky

SOURCES:

Institut für Wissenschaft und Kunst, Vienna, "Biografisches Lexikon der österreichischen Frau," n.d.

Kammer für Arbeiter und Angestellte für Wien, *Handbuch der Frauenarbeit in Österreich.* Vienna: Kammer für Arbeiter und Angestellte, 1930.

Sporrer, Maria, and Herbert Steiner, eds. *Rosa Jochmann: Zeitzeugin.* 3rd ed. Vienna: Europaverlag, 1987.

COLLECTIONS:

Luise Kautsky Papers, International Institute for Social History, Amsterdam.

John Haag,
Associate Professor of History,
University of Georgia, Athens, Georgia

Kavan, Anna (1901–1968)

French writer whose work continues to receive considerable attention. Name variations: original name Helen Woods changed by deed poll to Anna Kavan; Helen Ferguson; Helen Woods Edmonds. Born Helen Woods in Cannes, France, in 1901; died in London England, on December 5, 1968; daughter of C.C.E. Woods and Helen (Bright) Woods; attended church school and was privately tutored; married Donald Ferguson; married Stuart Edmonds (a painter); children: (first marriage) one son (deceased).

Selected novels, all under the name Anna Kavan, except as noted: (as Helen Ferguson) A Charmed Cir-

cle *(1929); (as Helen Ferguson)* The Dark Sisters *(1930); (as Helen Ferguson)* Let Me Alone *(1930, reprinted under Anna Kavan, 1979); (as Helen Ferguson)* A Stranger Still *(1935); (as Helen Ferguson)* Goose Cross *(1936); (as Helen Ferguson)* Rich Get Rich *(1937);* Change the Name *(1941);* The House of Sleep *(1947, published in England as* Sleep Has His House, *1948);* A Scarcity of Love *(1956);* Eagles' Nest *(1957);* Who Are You? *(1963);* Ice *(1967).*

Short stories as Anna Kavan: Asylum Piece and Other Stories *(1940);* I Am Lazarus *(1945);* A Bright Green Field and Other Stories *(1958);* Julia and the Bazooka and Other Stories *(1970);* My Soul in China: A Novella and Stories *(1975).*

Writer Anna Kavan was born Helen Woods in 1901, the daughter of C.C.E. Woods and **Helen Bright Woods**. Initially, she would write under the name Helen Ferguson, reflecting her first marriage to Donald Ferguson. By 1940, she would be writing under the name Anna Kavan, borrowed from a central character in her novel, *A Stranger Still* (1935). She had an identity and past that she longed to put behind her.

Kavan was born in Cannes, France, but grew up in California, in a well-to-do but troubled environment. Her father committed suicide when she was 14, and her emotionally distant mother generated a rage in her that frequently surfaced in her work. "What could have been done to make me afraid to grow up out of such a childhood?," she wrote in the short story, "A World of Heroes." "Later on, I saw things in proportion. I was always afraid of falling back into that ghastly black isolation of an uncomprehending, solitary, oversensitive child."

Kavan wrote conventional romantic novels during the 1920s and 1930s, reflecting aspects of her first two marriages, both of which ended in divorce. Her first marriage to produced a son who died in World War II. After her second marriage to painter Stuart Edmonds failed, Kavan entered a Swiss clinic for treatment of acute depression, a mental illness that would plague her for the rest of her life and lead to a dependence on daily doses of heroin. She initially wrote about her experiences with mental illness in *Asylum Piece* (1940), a collection of short stories and her first work under the name Anna Kavan. It was viewed as "extraordinarily moving and original," by Rhys Davies, a critic for *Books and Bookmen* and a friend of Kavan's from her Ferguson days. Davies, who lost track of Kavan for three or four years and knew nothing of her mental problems or her drug addiction, scarcely

recognized his friend when they reunited. "This spectral woman, attenuated of body and face, a former abundance of auburn hair shorn and changed to metallic gold, thinned hands restless, was so different that my own need to readjust to her was a strain."

The conventional novels of Kavan's early period are strongly biographical and foreshadow her later development. Her first novel, *A Charmed Circle* (1929), concerns a family living in an isolated British house near an ugly manufacturing town and examines the struggle of the children to escape the forces of their environment. The themes of isolation and retreat from a threatening world turn up again and again in Kavan's work. The later novel, *A Stranger Still* (1935), is also rich in autobiographical elements from her fear-filled childhood. *Change the Name* (1941) is considered by some to be Kavan's best early novel, although it is also something of a transitional work. The story, again autobiographical, traces Celia Henzell's development from a privileged but neglected child to a successful writer who pursues her ambition while destroying the lives around her. Although a growing disillusionment is evident in its pages, Davies refers to this novel as part of Kavan's "metamorphosis," as it still contains traces of the Ferguson style.

Despite her addiction and a number of stays in mental institutions, Kavan managed to carry on the activities of a normal life. She traveled extensively and purchased and renovated several houses at Campden Hill, in England. She also designed and supervised the building of a modernistic house in which she resided for the last 12 years of her life. In addition to writing novels and numerous short stories, she did editorial work for a literary magazine. However, her mental instability did shape her work into its later surrealistic form. Both *House of Sleep* (1947) and *Ice* (1967) fall into the science-fiction genre, which Kavan explained as the way she "sees the world now."

Kavan committed suicide in 1968, after two unsuccessful attempts during her lifetime. Since her death, her work has received worldwide recognition and has been translated into seven major European languages. Re-releases of her books bring accolades from the critics and a new generation of readers. "Kavan's prose is like pollen, frail yet enduring," commented science-fiction writer Brian Aldiss, "She is de Quincey's heir, Kafka's sister and a true writer." Kavan's appeal is perhaps best explained by **Jill Robinson** in an article in *The New York Times Book*

Review: "The facts of one's difficult existence do not guarantee literature," she writes. "Anna Kavan is not interesting because she was a woman, an addict or had silver blond hair. She is interesting because her work comes through with a powerful androgynous individuality and because the stories are luminous and rich with a fresh kind of peril. She knows how to pull us into her world, her dreams and nightmares—how to have all of it become ours."

SOURCES:

Evory, Ann, ed. *Contemporary Authors*. New Rev. Series. Vol 6. Detroit, MI: Gale, 1982.

Harris, Gale. "Reprints," in *Belles Lettres*. Vol. 9, no. 3, pp. 65–66.

Yntema, Sharon. *More Than 100 Women Science Fiction Writers*. Freedom, CA: Crossing Press, 1988.

SUGGESTED READING:

Callard, David. *The Case of Anna Kavan: A Biography*, 1994.

Barbara Morgan,
Melrose, Massachusetts

Kavanagh, Julia (1824–1877)

British novelist, historian and biographer. Born at Thurles, County Tipperary, Ireland, in 1824; died in Nice, France, on October 28, 1877; daughter of Morgan Peter Kavanagh (1800–1874, a writer); educated at home; never married; no children.

Selected writings: Three Paths *(1847);* Madeleine: A Tale of Auvergne *(1848);* Woman in France during the 18th Century *(1850);* Nathalie *(1851);* Women of Christianity *(1852);* Daisy Burns *(1853);* Grace Lee *(1855);* Adéle *(1857);* A Summer and Winter in the Two Sicilies *(1858);* French Women of Letters *(1862);* English Women of Letters *(1862);* Queen Mab *(1863);* Beatrice *(1865);* Dora *(1868);* John Dorrien *(1875);* The Pearl Fountain *(1876).*

The only child of would-be poet, novelist and philologist Morgan Peter Kavanagh, Julia Kavanagh was born in 1824 and would become estranged from her father in 1857, when he credited his second-rate novel *The Hobbies* to their joint authorship. Kavanagh spent her early life in Normandy and Paris, returning with her family to London in 1844. Thereafter, much of her time was spent caring for her invalid mother, with whom she would publish a book of fairy tales, *The Pearl Fountain* (1876). Her writing career began with magazine stories and a series of children's books, the first of which was *Three Paths* (1847). Her years in France provided the inspiration for many of her subsequent novels, including *Madeleine* (1848) and *Nathalie* (1851); the latter is said to have influenced

Charlotte Brontë's Villette. Most popular among her novels were *Adéle* (1857), *Queen Mab* (1863), and *John Dorrien* (1875).

Although her style was considered graceful rather than striking, and her characters interesting rather than strongly individualized, she was cited for her poetic feeling and her keen insights into French modes of thought. Kavanagh was perhaps better known for her nonfiction, particularly her biographical volumes about women: *Woman in France in the 18th Century* (1850), *Women of Christianity* (1852), *French Women of Letters* (1862) and *English Women of Letters* (1863). At the onset of the Franco-German War, the author moved with her mother to Rouen. Following her mother's death, Kavanagh went to live in Nice where she died suddenly in October 1877, at age 53. Her last work, *Forget-me-nots*, a collection of short stories, was published a year later.

Kavanagh, Spencer (d. 1910).

See Cook, Edith Maud.

Kawashima Yoshiko (1906–1948).

See Yoshiko Kawashima.

Kaye, Nora (1920–1987)

American ballerina who achieved the rank of prima ballerina following her portrayal of Hagar in Pillar of Fire. *Born Nora Koreff in New York, New York, on January 17, 1920; died in Los Angeles, California, on April 30, 1987; daughter of Gregory Koreff (an actor) and Lisa Koreff; studied at the Metropolitan Opera Ballet School, New York City, and under Russian dancer and choreographer Michel Fokine; studied at the School of American Ballet, New York City; married Michael Van Buren, on January 2, 1943 (divorced); married Isaac Stern (a violinist), on November 10, 1948 (divorced); married Herbert Ross (a director and choreographer), in 1959.*

Of Russian parentage, Nora Kaye was born in Manhattan in 1920, named after the heroine of Ibsen's play *A Doll's House*. She changed her surname (Koreff) early in her career because she thought "an American dancer should have an American name." It was her mother **Lisa Koreff's** wish that she become a dancer, and at age four she had her first dance lesson. At eight, Nora was enrolled at the Metropolitan Opera Ballet School where she studied for seven years, graduating to the Metropolitan's corps de ballet at the age of 15. Kaye joined George Balanchine's American

Ballet in 1935, when it became the resident company of the Metropolitan. Meanwhile, she continued to study, taking two lessons a week with choreographer, Michel Fokine.

During the late 1930s, Kaye abandoned the ballet for Broadway, wanting to be part of what she considered to be a more exciting medium. She began to view ballet as "something dragged up from three hundred years ago that didn't make any sense and wasn't going any place," she told an interviewer for *Time* (May 2, 1949). Kaye danced in the musical productions *Virginia*

(1937), *Great Lady* (1938), and *Stars in Your Eyes* (1939), and spent nine months in the corps de ballet of the Radio City Music Hall. Her period of rebellion also included a job dancing at the International Casino and an unsuccessful attempt at a night-club act.

It was choreographer and teacher Anthony Tudor who brought Kaye back into the fold. In the fall of 1939, she accompanied her roommate to an audition with the newly formed Ballet Theater (later American Ballet Theater) and was accepted into the company's corps de ballet. "I

Nora
Kaye

WOMEN IN WORLD HISTORY

joined only because most of my friends were joining," she explained. But her experience working with Tudor changed her outlook and made ballet exciting for her once again. Her first important character role with the company was as the haughty Russian ballerina in Tudor's *Gala Performance* (February 1941), after which she performed small roles in a number of other works, including *Peter and the Wolf, Pas de Quatre, Giselle,* and *Princess Aurora.* Kaye achieved the rank of prima ballerina following her portrayal of the tortured heroine Hagar in *Pillar of Fire* (1942), a role Tudor choreographed especially for her. John Martin of *The New York Times,* called the work's premiere a "distinguished event," and Kaye's characterization among "the great examples of tragic acting of its generation." Kaye subsequently danced new and classic roles in a variety of ballets, including Tudor's *Dark Elegies, Lilac Garden,* and *Dim Lustre,* Fokine's *Bluebeard* and *Apollo,* Massine's *Mademoiselle Angot* and *Romeo and Juliet,* Balachine's *Waltz Academy* (premiere, October 1944), Kidd's *On Stage!* (premiere, October 1945), Semenoff's *Gift of the Magi* (premiere, October 1945), Taras' *Graziana* (premiere, October 1945), and Jerome Robbins' *Facsimile* (premiere, October 1946). In the spring of 1948, Kaye scored a great success as the Accused in *Agnes de Mille's *Fall River Legend* (based on the story of *Lizzie Borden), although she missed the world premiere due to illness and assumed the role later in the engagement. In 1950, during the tenth anniversary season of the Ballet Theater, Kaye danced the leading roles in Tudor's *Nimbus* and William Dollar's version of *Jeux,* prompting the critic of *Dancing Times* to hail her as "the greatest actress of the dance today." During her period with the Ballet Theater, the term "dramatic ballerina" came into popular use.

In 1951, Kaye left the Ballet Theater to join the New York City Ballet, where she performed in Robbins' *The Cage* (premiere, June 1951), and Tudor's *La Gloire* (premiere, February 1952), among other works. In 1952, she appeared as the principal dancer in the *Bette Davis revue, *Two's Company,* choreographed by Jerome Robbins. Ultimately, the style of the New York City Ballet proved unsuited to Kaye's talents, and she returned to the Ballet Theater in 1954, creating the role of Blanche in *Valerie Bettis' *A Streetcar Named Desire* in her first season back. She subsequently danced in *Winter's Eve, Journey,* and in *Paean,* choreographed by Herbert Ross, who would become the dancer's third husband. (Kaye was previously married and divorced from Michael Van Buren and the noted violinist Isaac Stern. She was also briefly engaged to Jerome Robbins in 1951.)

In August of 1959, shortly after their marriage, Kaye and Ross formed the Ballet of Two Worlds, a group which performed at the Spoleto Festival in 1959 and 1960, and subsequently toured for a season in Europe. The troupe presented Ross' *Angel Head,* and *The Dybbuk,* as well as *Within the Grove,* based on the play *Rashomon.*

Nora Kaye, described as "sad-eyed and mobile-faced," retired from performing in 1961, after which she worked with her husband on several musicals he choreographed. In 1964, she was named assistant to the director of the American Ballet Theater, and in 1977, she became associate director. Kaye was also the executive producer of the movie *The Turning Point* (1977), the story of an aging ballerina which starred **Anne Bancroft** and **Shirley MacLaine** and was directed by her husband. Kaye, who died in April 1987, once spoke to an interviewer for *Cue* magazine about the total commitment required of a dancer. "Unless you feel that ballet is a religion with you," she said, "nothing could compensate for the enormous amount of time and work put in it."

SOURCES:

Candee, Marjorie Dent, ed. *Current Biography 1953.* NY: H.W. Wilson, 1953.

McHenry, Robert, ed. *Famous American Women.* NY: Dover, 1980.

Moritz, Charles, ed. *Current Biography 1987.* NY: H.W. Wilson, 1987.

Teachout, Terry. "A 'Made in the U.S.A.' Genius," in *Time.* August 10, 1998, p. 82.

Barbara Morgan,
Melrose, Massachusetts

Kaye-Smith, Sheila (1887–1956)

English novelist and poet known for her Sussex tales.
Name variations: Mrs. Penrose Fry. Born in St. Leonard's-on-Sea, Sussex, England, on February 4, 1887; died near Rye, Sussex, England, on January 14, 1956; daughter of Edward Kaye-Smith (a physician and surgeon); her mother, whose maiden name was de la Condamine, was his second wife; attended Hastings and St. Leonard's Ladies' College; married Theodore Penrose Fry, later known as Sir Penrose Fry (a minister turned farmer); no children.

Selected works—novels: The Tramping Methodist *(1908);* Starbrace *(1909);* Spell Land *(1911);* Isle of Thorns *(1913);* Three Against the World *(1913);* Sussex Gorse *(1916);* The Challenge to Sirius *(1917);* Little England *(1918);* Tamarisk Town *(1919);* Green Apple Harvest *(1920);* Joanna Godden *(1921);* The

End of the House of Alard *(1923)*; The George and the Crown *(1925)*; Joanna Godden Married *(1927)*; Iron and Smoke *(1928)*; The Village Doctor *(1929)*; Shepherds in Sackcloth *(1930)*; The History of Susan Spray *(1931)*; Gallybird *(1932)*; The Ploughman's Progress *(1933)*; The Children's Summer *(1933)*; Superstition Corner *(1934)*; Selina is Older *(1935)*; Rose Deeprose *(1936)*; Faithful Stranger *(1937)*; The Valiant Woman *(1938)*; Gipsy Waggon *(1939)*; Ember Lane *(1940)*; Tambourine, Trumpet and Drum *(1943)*; Summer Holiday *(1947)*; The Lardners and the Laurelwoods *(1948)*; Treasures of the Snow *(1950)*; The Hidden Son *(1952)*; Mrs. Gailey *(1953)*; The View from the Parsonage *(1954)*.

Nonfiction: John Galsworthy *(1915)*; Mirror of the Months *(1925)*; Anglo-Catholicism *(1926)*; Three Ways Home *(1937)*; *(with G.B. Stern)* Talking of Jane Austen *(1944)*; Kitchen Fugue *(1945)*; *(with G.B. Stern)* More Talk of Jane Austen *(1950)*; Quartet in Heaven *(1952)*; The Weald of Sussex and Kent *(1953)*; All the Books of My Life *(1956)*. *Poetry and plays:* Willow's Forge *(1914)*; Saints in Sussex *(1926)*; Songs, Late and Early *(1931)*.

English writer Sheila Kaye-Smith was born in St. Leonard's-on-Sea in 1887 and raised in the beautiful countryside of Sussex, which later became the setting of most of her novels. The daughter of a prominent physician, she was well educated at home and also attended Hastings and St. Leonard's Ladies' College. In 1924, she married T. Penrose Fry, who was then vicar of St. Leonard's but later served churches in Norland and in London, where the couple lived for a short time. In 1929, however, they converted to Roman Catholicism, and Fry resigned his ordination and went to work on a farm that the couple purchased in Northiam, Sussex ("Little Doucegrove"). Kaye-Smith combined her prolific writing career with her duties as a farmer's wife. The author had no children but doted on her friends and relatives, as well a series of pet cats. Upon her death in 1956, Kaye-Smith was

buried near the little chapel she had built on the grounds of the farm.

Kaye-Smith's first work of fiction, *The Tramping Methodist,* was published in 1908, when she was 21. Several novels followed as well as a book of verse, but it was her novel *Sussex Gorse* (1916), that established her as a writer. Considered by some to be her best work, it concerns an ambitious landowner who exploits the people around him to expand his landholdings. Love of the land is also the dominant theme in all of the 31 novels that followed, and all have strong religious overtones. Those of note include *Little England* (1918), *Green Apple Harvest* (1920), and *Joanna Godden* (1921), which was later made into a film starring *Googie Withers** and Jean Kent. In addition to her poetry and novels, Kaye-Smith was known for two studies of *Jane Austen** written in collaboration with novelist *G.B. Stern**: *Talking of Jane Austen* (1943) and *More Talk about Jane Austen* (1950). Kaye-Smith also wrote a three-volume autobiography, *Three Ways Home* (1937), an informal cookbook-autobiography, *Kitchen-Fugue* (1945), and a memoir describing her reading at important junctures of her life, *All the Books of My Life* (1956).

As a novelist, Kaye-Smith may have offered her readers too much of a good thing. On the one hand, she was praised for her realistic depiction of the rural countryside and its people, as well as her handling of rustic speech; on the other, she was criticized as repetitive and overly regional. An appraisal by Mary Stack reflects the often ambiguous feelings among the critics. "In spite of brilliance in characterization, she is not a novelist of character, any more than she is a novelist of local color. She is, rather, a novelist with a deep understanding of life and love, with a rich feeling for the land. . . . She has the power of presenting all this in prose that is often beautiful and sometimes masterly. And yet. . . she has all gifts in abundance but greatness is excepted."

SOURCES:
Kunitz, Stanley, ed. *Twentieth Century Authors.* NY: H.W. Wilson, 1955.
Shattock, Joanne. *The Oxford Guide to British Women Writers.* Oxford and NY: Oxford University Press, 1993.
Walthew, Betty. "My Famous Aunt Sheila," in *This England.* Spring 1987, pp. 50–51.

Barbara Morgan,
Melrose, Massachusetts

Kayser, Louisa (c. 1835–1925).

See Dat So La Lee.

Kazankina, Tatyana (1951—)

Soviet runner who won two Olympic gold medals in the 1,500 meters. Born on December 17, 1951; married; children.

Won the gold medal in the 800 meters and 1,500 meters in Montreal Olympics (1976); won the gold medal in the 1,500 meters in Moscow Olympics (1980).

With an impressive leap over her previous performances, Tatyana Kazankina set a world record for the 1,500-meters in 1976 with a time of 3:56.0. That same year, she won the gold medal in 1,500 meters in the Montreal Olympics with a time of 4:05.5; she also won a gold medal in the 800 meters with a world record time of 1:54.94. In the Moscow Olympics in 1980, two years after the birth of her daughter, Kazankina repeated her conquest of the 1,500 meters (3:56.6) with another gold. In the 3,000 meters at the Helsinki World championships in 1983, she came in third behind *Mary Decker (Slaney) and **Brigita Kraus**. But Kazankina's greatest success had come at Zurich Letzigrund on August 13, 1980, when she ran the 1,500 in 3:52.47, faster than the men's record set by Paavo Nurmi in 1924.

Kazem, Tahia (b. 1923).

See Nasser, Tahia.

Kcshessinskaya, Matilde (1872–1971).

See Kshesinskaia, Matilda.

Kean, Mrs. Charles (1805–1880).

See Kean, Ellen.

Kean, Ellen (1805–1880)

English actress. Name variations: Ellen Tree; Mrs. Kean. Born Ellen Tree in 1805; died in London, England, on August 21, 1880; sister of singer-actress Maria Bradshaw (Mrs. Bradshaw); sister of a Mrs. Quin, a dancer at the Drury Lane; married Charles John Kean (c. 1811–1868, an actor and second son of Edmund Kean), in January 1842, in Dublin.

Ellen Kean made her debut as Ellen Tree during the 1822–23 season at Covent Garden, playing Olivia to her sister ❧ **Maria Bradshaw**'s Viola in *Twelfth Night.* Ellen's performance was regarded by the critics as merely promising, forcing the young actress to spend the next four years in the provinces. From 1826 to 1828, Ellen was at the Drury Lane meeting with a more conspicuous success performing in

❧ Bradshaw, Maria (1801–1862)

English singer and actress. Name variations: Mrs. Bradshaw. Born Ann Maria Bradshaw in 1801; died in 1862; sister of *Ellen Kean (1805–1880).

Maria Bradshaw often appeared in the roles of Shakespeare's women: Ophelia, Rosalind, Viola, Imogen, and Julia in *Two Gentleman of Verona.* She retired in 1825.

comedies—appearing as Lady Teazle and *Jane Shore. She returned to Covent Garden in 1829, where she originated several parts until 1836. While there, she played Romeo to *Fanny Kemble's Juliet. From 1836 to 1839, Kean toured America, becoming famous there under the name Ellen Tree. In 1842, she married Charles Kean, with whom she played leading parts at the Princess Theater in London, and whose success she helped to further. Ellen Kean's greatest successes were in the roles of Viola, Rosalind, Gertrude in *Hamlet,* and Mrs. Beverley.

Keane, Constance.

See Lake, Veronica.

Keane, Molly (1904–1996)

Irish novelist and playwright whose Good Behaviour, *published when she was 77, won the Booker Prize.* Name variations: Mary Nesta Skrine; (pseudonym) M.J. Farrell. Born Mary Nesta (Molly) Skrine in County Kildare, Ireland, on July 20, 1904; died at Ardmore, County Waterford, on April 22, 1996; third of five children of Walter Clermont Skrine and Agnes Shakespeare Higginson Skrine (who wrote under the pseudonym Moira O'Neill); educated privately and at French School, Bray, County Wicklow; married Robert Lumley Keane, in October 1938 (died, October 7, 1946); children: Sally Keane; Virginia Keane.

Awards: honorary doctorates from the National University of Ireland and the University of Ulster; elected member of Aosdána (1981); Booker Prize (1981).

Selected writings: Devoted Ladies (1934, new ed., Virago, 1984); Two Days in Aragon (1941, new ed., Virago, 1985); Good Behaviour (Deutsch, 1981); Time after Time (Deutsch, 1983); Loving and Giving (Deutsch, 1988).

Molly Keane came from a landed, wealthy Anglo-Irish gentry family and lived through a turbulent period between 1914 and 1923 when the comfortable world of the Anglo-Irish Big House was drawing to a close with the establishment of the new Irish state in 1922. It was a world of paradox, as her writings were to illustrate with their portraits of an Anglo-Irish society insulated within its gracious 18th-century houses, obsessed with horses and hunting and, for the most part, cheerfully philistine. Her father Walter Skrine cared only for his horses while her mother *Agnes Skrine, a poet and literary reviewer who wrote under the pseudonym Moira O'Neill, preferred to live in her own 19th-century world. "You can't think how neglected we were by our parents," Molly later observed. "I mean, they didn't do anything with us at all, they simply didn't bother. They were utterly reclusive. . . . My father was a very remote figure to me as a child. He just didn't enter my life very much and when he did it was a dreadful chore." Although she later confessed that she fought constant battles with her mother, nonetheless she was very fond of her: "She had a sort of 'star quality' even though I didn't see a great deal of her." Horses and riding were very important to the young Molly, "It was the only thing that counted." But in the society she moved in, literature was quite a different matter as she later recounted. "For a woman to read a book, let alone write one was viewed with alarm. I would have been banned from every respectable house."

This was the main reason Molly and her mother used pseudonyms. Molly wrote under the name M.J. Farrell (adopted from a public

Molly
Keane

house sign) when she eventually started to write at the end of the 1920s. She said she wrote because she needed pin-money to finance her social life, but she had also been profoundly influenced by her friendship with the Perry family who lived at Woodrooff in County Tipperary and with whom she stayed for long periods. The Perrys were cultured and well-read and the son of the house, John Perry, had close connections with the London theater. Molly sold her first novel, *The Knight of Cheerful Countenance* (1928), for $350. Her second book, *Young Entry,* was bought for $500 and published in 1928. Her early novels, as **Ann Owens Weekes** observed, "combine wit, alert intelligence, and willingness to broach controversial subjects." In *Devoted Ladies* (1934) she dealt with lesbianism in fashionable London. However, despite the seriousness of the theme, Keane enjoyed poking fun at herself when her character Jessica scolds the heroine Jane for reading *Young Entry*: "It's full of the lowing of hounds and everyone stuffing themselves with buttermilk scones dripping with butter. Plenty of picturesque discomfort and cold bath water and those *incredible* Irish mountains *always* in the distance."

In 1938, the year of her marriage to Robert Keane, Molly embarked on the first of a successful playwriting collaboration with her old friend John Perry. *Spring Meeting* ran successfully in London and New York and was followed by *Ducks and Drakes* (1941), *Guardian Angel* (1944), *Treasure Hunt* (1949) and *Dazzling Prospects* (1961); with the exception of *Guardian Angel* (which was produced in Dublin), each of these plays was directed by John Gielgud, a close friend. After the late 1930s, Molly wrote comparatively few novels of which *Two Days in Aragon* (1941) was the most important and which prefigured the darker themes of her last three great novels of the 1980s.

The years after the Second World War were more uncertain for Keane. Her husband died suddenly, leaving her with two small daughters to bring up. Her postwar plays and novels were less successful and the hostile reaction to her last play with Perry, *Dazzling Prospects,* prompted her to give up writing in 1961. She retired to Ireland. The appearance of *Good Behaviour* in 1981, published under her own name when she was 77 and which won the Booker Prize, caused considerable surprise (many people thought she was dead). In her study of the last three novels, *Good Behaviour, Time After Time* (1983) and *Loving and Giving* (1988), **Vera Kreilkamp** calls them "darkly comic explorations of individual delusion" which "represent a new and corrosive dissection of the [Anglo-Irish] society she had previously evoked with occasional nostalgia." Keane's Anglo-Irish gentry were now portrayed as insulated from history; their exquisite good manners disguised the vacuity of their lives; and the men—fathers, brothers and husbands—have become ciphers in the dynamics of family power which have now shifted decisively to the women—Aroon St Charles in *Good Behaviour,* the Swift sisters in *Time after Time* and Nicandra in *Loving and Giving*—who were expected to sacrifice themselves on the altar of the Big House and family interests.

Recognition for Keane came in 1981 when she was one of the first writers elected to Aosdána, an affiliation of Irish artists who receive state subsidies. This ensured her an income for the rest of her life. There were successful television adaptations of *Good Behaviour* and *Time after Time* in 1983 and 1986. The exclusion of Keane from the *Field Day Anthology of Irish Writing* (1991), supposedly because of hostility to her Big House theme, aroused some controversy and, as Kreilkamp points out, ignored the way Keane had subverted the genre. Keane, one suspects, was quietly amused.

SOURCES:

Devlin, Polly. Introduction to *Devoted Ladies.* London: Virago, 1984.

Kreilkamp, Vera. *The Anglo-Irish Novel and the Big House.* Syracuse, NY: Syracuse University Press, 1998.

Profile in *The New Yorker.* October 13, 1988.

Quinn, John, ed. "Mollie Keane," in *A Portrait of the Artist as a Young Girl.* London: Methuen, 1986.

Weekes, Ann Owens. *Irish Women Writers: An Uncharted Tradition.* Lexington: University Press of Kentucky, 1990.

Deirdre McMahon,
lecturer in history at
Mary Immaculate College, University of Limerick

Ke-ching, Kang (1911–1992).

See Kang Keqing.

Keckley, Elizabeth (c. 1824–1907)

African-American writer, dressmaker, and White House modiste. Born Elizabeth Hobbs in Dinwiddie, Virginia, around 1824; died in Washington, D.C., on May 26, 1907; daughter of slaves, Agnes and George Pleasant; married George Keckley (separated); children: one son, George, who died in battle as a young man.

Elizabeth Keckley was born into slavery around 1824 in Dinwiddie, Virginia. Her mother Agnes belonged to the Burwell family; her father George Pleasant was owned by a man named Hobbs. The family was separated permanently when Hobbs moved west, taking Keckley's father with him. Like many slaves, Keckley suffered physical and psychological abuse at the hands of her owners. At age 14, she was raped and had a child whom she named George. Soon after her son's birth, Keckley was given to the Burwells' married daughter **Anne Burwell Garland**. Anne took Elizabeth and George to St. Louis, Missouri, where Elizabeth worked as a seamstress to help support the Garlands and their five children.

While there, Elizabeth married James Keckley, a man she had first met back in Virginia. The union began happily enough, but began to disintegrate when Keckley learned that James was a slave, not a free man as he had claimed. "With the simple explanation that I lived with him eight years, let charity draw around him the mantle of silence" was all she ever said about her marriage.

After leaving her husband, Keckley set her sights on purchasing freedom for herself and her son, which she was eventually able to do in 1855, with the help of some patrons. She lived in Baltimore for six months before settling in Washington, D.C., where she began a modest dress-making business. Having attracted a prominent clientele, including Mrs. Jefferson Davis (*****Varina Howell Davis**), and Mrs. Stephen A. Douglas (**Adele Cutts Douglas**), Keckley set her sights on sewing for the women of the White House and, with this goal in mind, worked even harder to expand her business. By 1861, she was well established, operating out of rented rooms on 12th Street and employing 20 young women as seamstresses.

Keckley was recommended to *****Mary Todd Lincoln** by a friend of the first lady and was chosen over four other applicants. Through her skill as a seamstress and her trustworthiness, Keckley developed a close relationship with the first lady and in due course became her personal maid, traveling companion, and confidante. Keckley's services often extended to President Abraham Lincoln, who credited her with taming his unruly hair. She also nursed the Lincolns' young son Willie during his final illness, helped prepare him for burial, and tended to Mary Lincoln through her inconsolable grief. After Abraham Lincoln's assassination in 1865, Keckley cared once again for the grieving widow and helped her pack up her belongings in preparation to leave the official residence. After attending Mary Lincoln for some time in Chicago, Keckley returned to Washington and re-established her dressmaking business.

*E*lizabeth
*K*eckley

In March 1867, against her better judgment, Keckley joined Lincoln in a project to market some of Mary's elaborate wardrobe. At the time, Mary Lincoln harbored the irrational belief that she was destitute and had to do something to raise money. The venture was a disaster. It not only lost money but invited unfavorable publicity; newspapers labeled it the "Old Clothes Speculation." Thinking she could help present Mary Lincoln in a better light, Keckley then enlisted a ghost writer and prepared a book, *Behind the Scenes; or, Thirty Years a Slave, and Four Years in the White House.* Sadly, this project only served to tarnish the former first lady's reputation further and also brought Keckley under attack for its revelations. Apparently, Keckley gave her collaborator a number of Mary Lincoln's letters with instructions to exclude all personal material and to quote from them with discretion. The personal documents were printed in full, however, revealing Mary Lincoln's emotional instability and humiliating the family. Although the book was not widely read, it destroyed the bond between the two women. Keckley, who attempted to apologize on several occasions, was turned away and only heard from Mary Lincoln "in a roundabout way."

Keckley's sewing business gradually declined, and she abandoned it in 1892. For a brief period (1892–93), she taught domestic art at Wilberforce University in Xenia, Ohio, after which she returned to Washington. She lived for some time on a small pension she received as the mother of a Union soldier—her son George had been killed on August 10, 1861, at Wilson's Creek, Missouri—but spent her final years in the Home for Destitute Women and Children in Washington, where she died of a paralytic stroke on May 26, 1907. To the end, Keckley would not speak of her controversial book, referring to it only as a "sad memory."

Over the years, the authorship of Keckley's book has been called into question. In a November 11, 1935, article in the *Washington Star,* David Barbee attributed *Behind the Scenes* to *Jane Swisshelm and went so far as to question the existence of Elizabeth Keckley. John Washington countered in his book *They Knew Lincoln* (1942) that Keckley had collaborated with James Redpath. In yet another publication, *Mary Lincoln, Biography of Marriage* (1953), **Ruth Randall** states that the Keckley book is certainly of value to the scholar, but should be checked carefully for inaccuracies.

SOURCES:

James, Edward T., ed. *Notable American Women, 1607–1950.* Cambridge, MA: The Belknap Press of Harvard University Press, 1971.

Smith, Jessie Carney, ed. *Notable Black American Women.* Detroit, MI: Gale Research, 1992.

Wefer, Marion. "Another assassination, another widow, another embattled book," in *American Heritage.* Vol. XVIII, no. 5. August 1967.

COLLECTIONS:

Papers relating to Elizabeth Keckley are housed at the National Archives, the Library of Congress, and the Moorland-Spingarn Research Center at Howard University.

Barbara Morgan,
Melrose, Massachusetts

Kedrova, Lila (1918–2000)

Russian-born actress. Born in Leningrad, Russia, in 1918; died in Sault Ste. Marie, Ontario, Canada, in April 2000.

Selected films: Weg ohne Umkehr *(No Way Back, Ger., 1953);* Le Defroqué *(Fr., 1954);* Razzia sur la Chnouff *(Razzia, Fr., 1955);* Des Gens sans Importance *(Fr., 1956);* Calle Mayor *(The Lovemaker, Sp., 1956);* Montparnasse 19 *(Modigliani of Montparnasse, Fr., 1958);* La Femme et la Pantin *(The Female, Fr.-It., 1959);* Zorba the Greek *(US-Greek, 1964);* A High Wind in Jamaica *(US/UK, 1965);* Torn Curtain *(US, 1966);* Penelope *(US, 1966);* Tenderly *(The Girl Who Couldn't Say No, It., 1968);* The Kremlin Letter *(US, 1970);* Escape to the Sun *(Israel-Fr.-Ger., 1972);* Soft Beds Hard Battles *(Undercovers Hero, UK, 1974);* Perchè?! *(It., 1975);* Eliza's Horoscope *(Canadian, 1975);* Le Locataire *(The Tenant, Fr., 1976);* Moi Fleur bleue *(Fr., 1977);* Widows' Nest *(US-Sp., 1977);* Le Cavaleur *(Practice Makes Perfect, Fr.,*

1979); Clair de Femme (Fr.-Ger.-It., 1979); Tell Me a Riddle (US, 1980); Sword of the Valiant (UK, 1984); Some Girls (US, 1988).

A flamboyant character actress of European and American films, Lila Kedrova was born in Russia, but lived in France from 1928. She won an Academy Award as Best Supporting Actress for her portrayal of an aging French prostitute in *Zorba the Greek* (1964) and received the Golden Mask at Taormina for *Tell Me a Riddle* (1980).

Kee, Elizabeth (1895–1975)

Democratic congressional representative from West Virginia (82nd–88th Congresses, July 17, 1951–January 3, 1965). Name variations: Maude Elizabeth Kee. Born Maude Elizabeth Simpkins in Radford, Virginia, on June 7, 1895; died in Bluefield, Virginia, on February 15, 1975; attended public and private schools in Montgomery County and Roanoke, Virginia, Washington, D.C., and Bluefield, West Virginia; graduated from Roanoke Business College; married John Kee (an attorney and politician), in September 1926 (died May 1951); children: James Kee; Frances Kee.

Not only was Elizabeth Kee the only woman representative from West Virginia, but her congressional seat was very much a family affair. Her husband served as a Democratic representative from 1932 until his death in 1951, after which Kee won a special election held to fill his vacant seat. Kee served for six terms and was then succeeded by her son James Kee, who had acted as her administrative assistant during her congressional tenure.

Born in Radford, Virginia, in 1895, Kee was raised in Roanoke and graduated from the Roanoke Business College. She worked as a secretary for the *Roanoke Times* and as a court reporter for a law firm before marrying attorney John Kee in 1926. During the early years of her marriage, Kee wrote a weekly column, "Washington Tidbits," which was syndicated to West Virginia newspapers. When her husband was elected to Congress in 1932, Kee became his executive secretary, a position she held until 1949, when he became chair of the Committee on Foreign Affairs.

Throughout her years in House service, Kee was a member of the Committee on Governmental Operations and chaired a Veterans' Affairs subcommittee on veterans' hospitals. A liberal like her husband and ardently pro-labor, she was a proponent of many of the domestic policies of the Kennedy and Johnson administrations. Her

Elizabeth Kee

tenure was marked by her support of economic aid to Europe, consumer price and federal rent controls, and higher Social Security benefits. She also launched a campaign to obtain books for the Woodrow Wilson Rehabilitation Center in Fisherville, Virginia. Ill health forced Kee into retirement, and she did not seek an eighth term in 1964. Elizabeth Kee lived in Bluefield until her death in 1975.

SOURCES:

Office of the Historian. *Women in Congress, 1917–1990.* Commission on the Bicentenary of the U.S. House of Representatives, 1991.

Barbara Morgan,
Melrose, Massachusetts

Keeble, Lillah, Lady (1875–1960).

See McCarthy, Lillah.

Keeler, Christine (1942—)

British call girl of the 1960s involved in the infamous Profumo Affair. Born in Wraysbury, England, in

1942; married James Levermore (divorced); remarried; children: (first marriage) son Jimmy.

Christine Keeler was the "tainted woman" of the notorious "Profumo Affair," the scandal that brought England's Tory Party to the brink of disaster in 1963. She was born in 1942 in the

working-class suburb of Wraysbury, England, and was raised in a converted railway carriage by her mother and stepfather. After a troubled adolescence, Keeler left school at 15 and went to work in Soho, first as a sales clerk in a gown shop and then as a waitress. For a short time, she shared a flat with ◄✿ **Mandy Rice-Davies**, another attractive young waitress who would also become embroiled in the government scandal. In 1959, Keeler left waitressing and took a job in a seedy West End cabaret as a showwoman. It was there that she was introduced to Stephen Ward, a charming, successful osteopathic doctor who was also an amateur artist and a staunch supporter of the Communist Party. A darker side of Ward's personality was his attraction to young, down-and-out girls, whom he groomed as prostitutes for his rich and often distinguished friends. Keeler was soon lured in by Ward and moved into his flat in the upscale Wimpole Mews. Although her relationship with her benefactor was termed "brotherly," she had numerous other liaisons with rich and powerful men, including simultaneous affairs with Captain Eugene "Honey Bear" Ivanov, naval attaché at the Soviet Embassy in London, and British War Minister, John Profumo, who was married at the time to actress *Valerie Hobson. A troubling aspect of Profumo's association with Keeler, aside from the obvious moral questions it raised, was the risk of blackmail because of Keeler's association with Ivanov.

Profumo's affair was conducted with the utmost discretion, and his relationship with Keeler cooled within a year. Although the British Secret Service had Dr. Ward under surveillance because of his Soviet sympathies, the sexual link between Ivanov, Profumo, and Keeler might have remained under wraps had it not been for a subsequent affair Keeler had with John Edgecombe, a West Indian who was overcome with jealousy when the relationship ended. On the afternoon of December 14, 1962, Edgecombe arrived outside Ward's flat, armed with a gun, and fired seven shots into the front door. He was arrested, and Keeler was later called as chief witness at his trial. In the interim, the British press, which had since gained access to Keeler's background but was prevented from printing anything by England's libel laws, began hinting at improprieties involving the call girl and a number of other celebrities. Keeler, flattered by the limelight, also began talking indiscreetly to friends, mentioning Ward, Ivanov, and Profumo, and providing additional grist for the rumor mill. By March 1962, part of the truth began to leak out and the corridors of the House of Commons as well as

✤► **Rice-Davies, Mandy** (1944—)

Involved in Profumo scandal. Born in Birmingham, England, in 1944; married Rafael Shaul (an airline pilot), in 1966; children: one daughter.

Mandy Rice-Davies also quit school at age 15 and worked as a shopgirl before moving to London where she befriended *Christine Keeler. The two girls shared a flat before Keeler moved in with Stephen Ward. Although Rice-Davies continued to live independently, she later testified to being one of Ward's "girls" and entertaining a number of clients at his residence. When the scandal broke, her descriptions of Ward's parties and mirrored bedrooms made her excellent copy for the tabloids, and she apparently reveled in the publicity. After the scandal died down, Rice-Davies moved to Munich where she headlined in a nightclub. Her side of the affair was published in magazine format as *The Mandy Report*, but attracted little attention. In 1966, at age 26, Rice-Davies converted to Judaism and married Rafael Shaul, an Israeli airline steward who later became a pilot. The couple settled in Tel Aviv and had a daughter.

SOURCES:
Lamparski, Richard. *Whatever Became of . . . ?* 3rd series. NY: Crown, 1970.

the bars on Fleet Street were abuzz with the story of "a Minister and a call-girl ring." When Keeler failed to appear in court for Edgecombe's trial (she apparently forgot to return from a holiday in Spain), a deliberate cover-up was suspected, and Profumo was called into question concerning his relationship with Keeler.

In a statement before the House of Commons on March 22, 1963, Profumo denied any improprieties, claiming that he and Keeler were merely friends. By the end of June, however, he had been undone by his own lies and was forced to resign. (Steadfastly supported by his wife, he would go on to do a great deal of charitable work in the East End.) In the meantime, the handsome Soviet attaché, Ivanov, was hustled back to Russia. While Prime Minister Harold Macmillan attempted to rally his party and the government from the backlash of the scandal, Dr. Stephen Ward was arrested on morals charges. At the end of his trial, just as the jury was to start deliberations, he took an overdose of drugs. While he lay in a coma, he was found guilty on two charges, but he died before sentencing.

As for Keeler, in the course of a year, she had testified in three criminal trials: the case of John Edgecombe, the ex-lover who had tried to shoot her; the case of Aloysius Gordon, another ex-paramour whom she accused of beating her; and of course, the Ward trial, where both she and her friend Mandy Rice-Davies took the stand. Keeler testified that Ward had a hypnotic hold on her, and encouraged her to have sex with his friends so she could repay loans he had made to her. After serving a nine-month prison sentence for morals offenses, Keeler slipped into obscurity, as did the whole sordid affair (although the Conservative Party's loss of majority in the next general election was attributed to the affair). Keeler moved the Chelsea, dyed her hair blonde, and married a handsome engineer by the name of James Levermore with whom she had a son. They later divorced, and Keeler subsequently married and divorced a second time. Although the tabloid *News of the World* paid her £20,000 for her memoirs, a book deal never materialized.

SOURCES:
Crimes and Punishment. Vol. 9. London: BPC Publishing, 1974.
Lamparski, Richard. *Whatever Became of . . . ?* 3rd series. NY: Crown, 1970.

Barbara Morgan,
Melrose, Massachusetts

Keeler, Ruby (1909–1993)

*American actress, dancer, and singer, best known for her energetic hoofing in films of the 1930s. Name variations: Ruby Keeler Jolson. Born Ethel Hilda Keeler on August 25, 1909, in Halifax, Nova Scotia, Canada; died on February 28, 1993, in Palm Springs, California; one of six children (five girls and a boy) of Ralph Keeler (a truck driver) and Elnora (Lehy) Keeler; attended parochial school and Professional Children's School, New York; married Al Jolson (a singer-actor), on September 21, 1928 (divorced 1940); married John Lowe (a real estate broker), on October 29, 1941 (died 1969); children: (adopted with Jolson) son, Al (whose name was later changed to Peter); (second marriage) John Lowe; **Christine Lowe**; **Theresa Lowe**; **Kathleen Lowe**.*

Selected theater: made professional appearances in cabaret as a buck-dancer; made theater debut in the chorus of The Rise of Rosie O'Reilly *(Liberty Theater, New York, December 1923); appeared as Ruby in* Bye Bye Bonnie *(Ritz Theater, January 1927), Mazie Maxwell in* Lucky Knickerbocker *(New Amsterdam Theater, March 1927), Mamie and Ruby in* Sidewalks of New York *(Knickerbocker Theater, October 1927); appeared in* Whoopee *(New Amsterdam Theater, December 1928); appeared in the revue* Show Girl *(Ziegfeld Theater, July 1929); appeared as Shirley in* Hold Onto Your Hats *(Grand Opera House, Chicago, Illinois, July 1940), Sue Smith in* No, No, Nanette *(46th St. Theater, January 1971).*

Filmography: (bit part) Show Girl in Hollywood *(1930);* 42nd Street *(1933);* Gold Diggers of 1933 *(1933);* Footlight Parade *(1933);* Dames *(1934);* Flirtation Walk *(1934);* Go Into Your Dance *(1935);* Shipmates Forever *(1935);* Colleen *(1936);* Ready, Willing and Able *(1937);* Mother Carey's Chickens *(1938);* Sweetheart of the Campus *(1941); (cameo)* The Phynx *(1970).*

Ruby Keeler will forever be associated with a series of lavish Warner Bros. movie musicals of the late Depression era, many of which became classics because of their colossal dance numbers staged by Busby Berkeley. Frequently cast as the sweet-natured chorine who fills in for the ailing star at the last minute, and usually paired with Dick Powell, Keeler retired from films in 1941, but made a phenomenal comeback in the 1971 stage revival of *No, No Nanette*. No one was more surprised by her successful return to the stage than the actress herself, as she had never been overly confident about her looks or her talent and had always viewed her career with some amazement. "I couldn't act," she said in 1966. "I had that terrible singing voice, and now I can see I wasn't the greatest tap dancer in the world, either."

Ruby Keeler was born in Halifax, Nova Scotia, in 1909, but the family moved to New York when she was three, settling in a tenement between First and Second Avenue. There were five other children (four girls and a boy), and her father's salary as a driver for the Knickerbocker Ice Company was stretched thin. From the age of five, Keeler took dance lessons from a woman named **Helen Guest**. "We were very poor," said Keeler, "and I think she gave me the lessons for nothing." From age 11, she was enrolled in Jack Blue's Dance Studio, where one of her classmates was *Patsy Kelly who would also appear with Keeler in No, No, Nanette. At 14, lying about her age, Keeler landed a role in the chorus of George M. Cohan's The Rise of Rosie O'Reilly (1923). Later she worked in the chorus line at a number of speakeasies, including the El Fey Club, where *Texas Guinan was the hostess. While employed at The Silver Slipper, Keeler was signed for a featured role in the Broadway show Bye, Bye Bonnie (1927). Her tap number, "Tampico Tap," was favorably reviewed by the critics, as was her performance in the subsequent The Sidewalks of New York (1927), starring newcomer Bob Hope. The latter performance also caught the eye of producer Flo Ziegfeld, who offered her a part in his upcoming production of Whoopee, starring Eddie Cantor. Before rehearsals began, however, Keeler went off to the West Coast for a stage engagement and a part in a Fox short. It was there that she met singer-actor Al Jolson, who was so smitten with the pretty brunette that he followed her back to New York. The two were secretly married on September 21, 1928, and after a brief honeymoon, Keeler joined the cast of Whoopie, only to leave during the out-of-town tryout. A year later, billed as Ruby Keeler Jolson, she appeared in the George Gershwin revue Show Girl (1929), but left the cast after four weeks to join her husband in California.

In 1933, Keeler launched her film career at Warner Bros., as the ingenue in the backstage musical 42nd Street, co-starring established star Dick Powell and featuring the choreography of Busby Berkeley, whose lavish, geometrically patterned dance routines (often filmed from overhead) would soon become legendary. One film critic later described a Berkeley routine as "kaleidoscopic patterns of female flesh, dissolving into artichokes, exploding stars, snowflakes, and the expanding leaves of water lilies." Keeler's film debut was such a success that Warner Bros. immediately recast her with Powell in Gold Diggers of 1933. A star after only two pictures, Keeler could not have cared less. "I had no

ambition and being a movie star truly didn't interest me," she said later. "You've got to have the drive. I never did. I always felt there was more to life than show biz. The idea of an early retirement appealed to me no end."

In spite of her ambivalence, Keeler honored her contract, Her third film with Powell, Footlight Parade (1933), which also starred James Cagney, contained one of Berkeley's most spectacular numbers, an aqua-ballet to "By a Waterfall" for which Keeler had to learn to swim. The film also had its subtler moments, among them a memorable dance with Cagney and Keeler to "Shanghai Lil." Keeler's fourth and fifth films with Powell were less successful. In Dames (1934), she had only one number, and in Flirtation Walk (1934), she did not dance at all. Abandoning co-star Powell temporarily, Keeler made one movie with her husband Al Jolson, Go into Your Dance (1935), in which she danced in two of the numbers Jolson sang: "Latin from Manhattan" and "A Quarter to Nine." Keeler was back with Powell for Shipmates Forever (1935) and Colleen (1936), both unsuccessful. "My screen musicals didn't get better, they merely got bigger," she said. Keeler did one more movie for Warner Bros., Ready, Willing and Able (1937), before leaving because of a quarrel Jolson had with the front office. Signing with RKO, she made one cheery programmer, Mother Carey's Chickens (1938), about a widow and her daughters who run a boarding house, based on a play by *Rachel Crothers and *Kate Douglas Wiggin.

In the meantime, Keeler's marriage was failing, and in 1939, she filed for divorce, alleging that Jolson never agreed with her about anything and ridiculed her in public. The actress, who gained custody of the couple's adopted son, had no further comment about her marriage, except to say, "It was a mistake—a long mistake." In 1946, when Sidney Skolsky produced the biopic The Jolson Story, Keeler would refuse to permit the use of her name. Her character, portrayed by **Evelyn Keyes**, was called Julie. Keeler made one more movie, Sweetheart of the Campus (1941), before her marriage to John Lowe, a successful real estate broker whom she met through friends. She promptly left Hollywood without a backward glance and took up residence in Newport Beach, California, where she raised her son and the four additional children she had with Lowe. She seldom made public appearances, aside from a few television shows and some "film festivals" in the 1960s that honored Busby Berkeley. In 1968, she appeared in a summer-stock production of Bell, Book and Candle, and in 1970, she made a cameo appearance, along with other

Ruby Keeler with Dick Powell.

celebrities, in the movie *The Phynx*.

In 1970, a year after Lowe's death of a heart attack, Keeler agreed to play the lead in a Broadway revival of the 1925 musical *No, No, Nanette,* though she was initially terrified. After being told that her old friend Patsy Kelly would be in the cast and that 75-year-old Busby Berkeley would supervise the dancing, she was considerably more at ease. (Her son John was also assistant stage manager, and her sister **Gertrude Keeler** stepped in as her business manager.) At the opening performance in January 1971, Keeler's initial entrance down a long staircase was greeted by thunderous applause and her two dance numbers, "I Want to Be Happy" and "Take a Little One Step," were praised by audiences and critics alike. "[S]he dances like a trouper and wears indomitability shyly like a badge of service," wrote critic Clive Barnes. "She is just enormously likable." For her comeback appearance, Keeler received the George M. Cohan Award from the Catholic Actors Guild in May 1971, presented to the actress by actor Cyril Ritchard, president of the guild. In her acceptance speech, Keeler expressed gratitude for her life both on and off the stage. "For some reason the good Lord has chosen to bless me, because in addition to an awful lot of happiness, I've been given something no one else gets. In a sense, I've had two lives."

SOURCES:

Barnes, Clive. "Stage: 'No, No, Nanette' is Back Alive," in *The New York Times.* January 20, 1971.

Bowers, Ronald L. "Ruby Keeler," in *Films in Review.* Vol. XXII, no. 7. August–September 1971, pp. 405–414.

Lamparski, Richard. *Whatever Became of . . . ?* 1st and 2nd series. NY: Crown, 1967.

O'Malley, Wini Shaw, as told to Don Koll. "Ruby Came Back," in *Film Fan Monthly.* July–August 1971, pp. 3–6.

Barbara Morgan,
Melrose, Massachusetts

Keeley, Mary Anne (c. 1806–1899)

Irish-born English actress. Name variations: Miss Goward. Born Mary Anne Goward in Dublin, Ireland, on November 22, 1806 (some sources cite 1805); died on March 12, 1899; daughter of a brazier and tinman; married Robert Keeley (1793–1869, a comedian), in 1829.

Born in Dublin around 1806, Mary Anne Keeley moved to London in 1825 and became a member of the Covent Garden Company. In June 1829, she married the comedian Robert Keeley with whom she had often appeared. Between 1832 and 1842, the couple acted at Covent Garden, at the Adelphi with John Buckstone, at the Olympic with Charles Mathews, and at Drury Lane with William Macready. In 1836, they toured America.

In 1838, Keeley had her first major success in the role of Nydia, the blind girl, in a dramatization of Bulwer-Lytton's *The Last Days of Pompeii*; she followed this with an equally striking portrayal of Smike in *Nicholas Nickleby.* The following year, she was triumphant with her charming and lively acting as the hero of a play based on Harrison Ainsworth's *Jack Sheppard.* With its glorification of an escaped convict, the play's popularity was considered so threatening that the Lord Chamberlain ultimately forbade future performances of any plays of a similar nature.

From 1844 to 1847, Keeley and her husband managed the Lyceum, where their production of *Cricket on the Hearth* ran for over a year. She then returned for five years to the Adelphi; she made her last regular public appearance at the Lyceum in 1859. The final 40 years of her life were spent in retirement, though Keeley occasionally appeared at benefits. On her 90th birthday, a public reception was given for her at the Lyceum. In spite of her age, it was said that she "preserved an altogether exceptional vigor and youthfulness of disposition."

SUGGESTED READING:

Goodman, Walter. *The Keeleys on the Stage and Off.* London, 1895.

Keen, Dora (b. 1871)

American traveler, mountain climber, and writer. Born in Philadelphia, Pennsylvania, in 1871.

Following her graduation from Bryn Mawr College in 1896, Dora Keen held consequential positions in Philadelphia, helping to bring about reforms. After traveling in various parts of the world, she made eight ascents of first-class peaks in the Alps in 1909–10. In 1911, her underequipped expedition failed to make the ascent of Mount Blackburn (16,523 feet) in Alaska. But returning early in 1912, she battled snowstorms to accomplish in 33 days the first ascent of this sub-Arctic peak without Swiss guides, and the first by way of the avalanche-prone southeast face via a direct route on the Kennicott glacier. One storm forced her eight-person team to shelter in a cave for 13 days. This expedition was followed by a journey of 300 miles on foot and by open, camp-built boat over the Alaskan wilderness to the Yukon River, by way of Skolai Pass, which Keen was the first woman to ever cross. In 1914, with three men, she made scientific observations of various glaciers in Alaska, contributed numerous articles to popular and geographical magazines, and lectured on her experiences. She became a fellow of the Royal Geographical Society, London, the same year.

Keene, Carolyn.

*See Adams, Harriet Stratemeyer (c. 1893–1982).
See Benson, Mildred (b. 1905).*

Keene, Constance (1921—)

American pianist and teacher. Born in New York, New York, on February 9, 1921; married Abram Chasins, in 1949.

Constance Keene became a student of Abram Chasins (whom she married in 1949). A winner of the Naumburg Award, Keene has played hundreds of solo recitals and appeared with such orchestras as the Boston Symphony and Berlin Philharmonic. She has had a long career as a teacher and served on the faculty of the Manhattan School of Music. Her recordings offer an interesting variety of repertoire. Among the high points are the three Mendelssohn études, Dussek and Hummel sonatas, a convincing interpretation of the problematical Charles Tomlinson Griffes Sonata, a very stylish record of Chopin's 24 Preludes, and the 24 Rachmaninoff Preludes, played with vibrancy and a fastidious musicality.

John Haag,
Athens, Georgia

Keene, Laura (c. 1826–1873)

British-born American actress and theatrical manager. Born possibly Mary Moss around 1826 in London, England; died on November 4, 1873, in Montclair, New Jersey; married John Taylor, around 1846 (died around 1860); married John Lutz, in 1860 (died 1869); children: (first marriage) Emma Taylor; Clara Marie Cecilia Stella Taylor.

One of first two American female theatrical managers; introduced America to Our American Cousin; *first to produce Dion Boucicault's* The Colleen Bawn *(March 1860); was present at Abraham Lincoln's assassination and identified John Wilkes Booth as his killer.*

Not much is known about Laura Keene's early life, although there is speculation that her name may have been Mary Moss. Born around 1820 in London, she met her first husband, John Taylor, while working as a barmaid. After the couple married around 1846, Taylor opened a tavern but was later sent to a penal colony in Australia after being convicted of a felony. Left with sole responsibility for their two daughters, and described as a beautiful woman, Keene became an actress. She made her London debut in October of 1851, playing Pauline in *The Lady of Lyons*; some six months later, she became a member of *Lucia Vestris' company at the Royal Lyceum Theater. While working at this theater, Keene caught the attention of James W. Wallack, an American actor and manager scouting for new talent, who offered her a job in America.

Keene's American debut, on September 20, 1852, at Wallack's Lyceum in New York City, was enthusiastically received by both the press and the public. The New York *Mirror* described her as having a "natural and unstagy style, . . . admirable articulation . . . [and a] winning voice." In November of 1853 she left Wallack and went to Baltimore with John Lutz, who became her business manager and, eventually, her husband after the death of her first husband around 1860. In Baltimore, she took over as theatrical manager for the Charles Street Theater and opened on December 24, 1853, making her managerial debut. That same day, **Catherine Sinclair** opened a play as manager in San Francisco, making them the first women theater managers in America; Keene appeared briefly in Sinclair's company in San Francisco the following March.

Over the next couple years, Keene toured in Australia with Edwin Booth and spent a season in San Francisco. The opening of Laura Keene's Theater in New York in November of 1856 initiated the greatest successes of her career. For seven years, she produced well-received comedies and extravaganzas, playing all the lead female roles and involving herself in scenery, costumes, writing, and publicity. Members of her company included such well-known actors as Joseph Jefferson, E.A. Sothern, Dion Boucicault, John T. Raymond, and William J. Florence. Keene excelled in high comedy and melodrama; *Our American Cousin*, in which she played Florence Trenchard, became her most famous production, running steadily for five months from its opening on October 18, 1858. At the time, this was an unprecedented run in New York theater. In May of 1863, Keene tired of being a manager, and *Matilda Wood** took over. Although she did go back to managing for a brief period from 1869 to 1870 at the Chestnut Street Theater in Philadelphia, Keene spent most of the following years in touring. Revivals of *Our*

$\mathcal{L}$aura
$\mathcal{K}$eene

American Cousin were included in some of these tours, and on April 14, 1865, President Abraham Lincoln attended that play at Ford's Theater in Washington, D.C., sitting in a private box near the stage. During the third act, John Wilkes Booth shot and mortally wounded the president; Keene recognized the actor as he escaped over the stage. *Mary Todd Lincoln being distraught, Keene held the president's head in her lap until he was carried from the theater.

Laura Keene did much to promote quality theater in America and to make New York City the theater capitol of the country, including establishing the matinee as a standard feature, initiating the long run for a specific play, and encouraging American playwrights. However, middle age and her husband's death in 1869 brought personal and financial struggles to Keene's life. She continued to act on occasion and gave public lectures for a few years before dying of consumption on November 4, 1873.

SOURCES:
James, Edward T., ed. *Notable American Women, 1607–1950.* Cambridge, MA: The Belknap Press of Harvard University Press, 1971.
Weatherford, Doris. *American Women's History.* NY: Prentice Hall, 1994.

SUGGESTED READING:
Creahan, John. *Life of Laura Keene,* 1897.

Karina L. Kerr, M.A.,
Ypsilanti, Michigan

Kegendorf, Madame (1777–1848).

See Jagemann, Karoline.

Kehajia, Kalliopi (1839–1905)

Greek educator and feminist. Born in Greece in 1839; died in 1905; educated as a teacher in London.

Kalliopi Kehajia devoted her life to improving the social and intellectual status of the women of her country. Educated as a teacher in London, Kehajia then returned to Athens, where for many years she was the headmistress of the Hill School for girls. Over the course of two years, she also offered an innovative series of 80 open lectures on classical literature and social problems, many of them dealing with women's issues. In 1872, she founded the Society for Promoting Women's Education, an organization which provided both practical training in various crafts and classes in academic subjects. In 1875, by invitation, she went to Constantinople (now Istanbul) to organize the Zappeion School for Girls, of which she was head mistress for 15 years. She traveled to the United States in 1888,

visiting schools, orphanages, and women's organizations. Upon her return, she published a series of newspaper articles about women in the United States, hoping to alert people in her own country to the inferior status of women in Greek society.

Kehew, Mary Morton (1859–1918)

American labor and social reformer. Name variations: Mary Kimball Kehew. Born Mary Morton Kimball in Boston, Massachusetts, on September 8, 1859; died in Boston of nephritis on February 14, 1918; fourth of eight children of Susan Tillinghast (Morton) Kimball and Moses Day Kimball; educated privately in Boston and in Europe; married William Brown Kehew, on January 8, 1880; no children.

Served as president, Women's Educational and Industrial Union of Boston (WEIU, 1892–1913 and 1914–18); was trustee, Simmons College (1902); served as president, National Women's Trade Union League (WTUL, 1903).

As the daughter of a banker, the granddaughter of a Massachusetts governor, and the wife of a wealthy oil merchant, Mary Morton Kehew was a member of Boston's social, economic and political elite. Like so many women of her class, Kehew devoted herself to volunteer activities. However, those causes she espoused—especially labor reform—were not the most popular. Secure in her standing as a Boston Brahmin, Kehew sought to use her social position, her political connections, and even her own economic resources on behalf of the working class.

Mary Morton Kehew joined the Women's Educational and Industrial Union (WEIU) in 1886. Within four years, she became a director and in 1892 she became president, an office she would hold for 25 years. Founded in 1877, the WEIU was an organization of middle- and upper-class women interested in the plight of working women. Kehew transformed the WEIU from a charity group to a more pro-active agency interested in educating and organizing women workers. In 1892, through her sister **Hannah P. Kimball**, Kehew brought *Mary Kenney O'Sullivan to Boston. Two years later, Kehew, the Boston socialite, and O'Sullivan, the Irish-American AFL organizer, founded the Union for Industrial Progress, an adjunct of the WEIU devoted to trade unionism for women. In 1903, Kehew became the first president of the National Women's Trade Union League, a cross-class alliance formed by O'Sullivan and various other reformers.

Uncomfortable in a public role, Kehew was most effective behind the scenes, lobbying legislators, meeting with political bosses, and raising money among her wealthy friends. She served on numerous legislative committees investigating Massachusetts labor conditions and played a leading role in several social-reform organizations, including the Boston settlement, Denison House, the Tyler Street Day Nursery, and the Milk and Baby Hygiene Association. As president of the WEIU, she encouraged that organization to pursue vocational training, some of which it turned over to Simmons College after its founding in 1902. On the first board of trustees of this Boston college was Mary Morton Kehew. Struck down by kidney disease at the age of 58, Kehew would be remembered by her friend and fellow reformer, *Emily Greene Balch, as "the never failing fairy godmother" of Boston social and labor reform during the Progressive era.

SOURCES:

James, Edward T., ed. *Notable American Women, 1607–1950.* Cambridge, MA: Belknap Press of Harvard University Press, 1971, pp. 313–314.

Randall, Mercedes M. *Improper Bostonian: Emily Greene Balch.* NY: Twayne, 1964.

Kathleen Banks Nutter,
Manuscripts Processor at the Sophia Smith Collection,
Smith College, Northampton, Massachusetts

Kéita, Aoua (1912–1979)

Politician and stateswoman in the struggle for independence in the former French Sudan, now the Republic of Mali, who came to her feminist outlook through the practice of midwifery, established an agenda for women's participation in the political life of her country, and became the first woman elected to the Mali National Assembly. Name variations: Aoua Keita. Born Aoua Kéita in Bamako, the French Sudan, in 1912; died in Bamako in 1979; daughter of a French-educated laboratory worker (member of the influential Kéita family) and one of his several wives who came from the village of Kadjouga on the Ivory Coast; educated at the École des filles, the Orpheliat des Métisses, and the School of Midwifery in Dakar; married M. Diawara (a physician), in 1935 (divorced 1949); married Mahamane Alassane Haidara (a senator representing the Sudan in the French National Assembly 1942–59); children: none.

Began practice of midwifery, one of few professional women in her country (1931); joined the USDRA, the main nationalist party, and became politically active after her first marriage (1935); campaigned vigorously in the first elections in which women were allowed to vote (1946); founded the Union of Salaried Women of Bamako (1957); participated in the creation of the Federation of Black African Workers, or UGTAN (Union Générale de Travailleurs de l'Afrique Noir); served as representative to the World Federation of Trade Unions, or FSM (Fédération des Syndicats du Monde); helped draft a constitution for the new Mali Federation (1958); was the first woman elected to the Mali National Assembly (1959); retired from politics (1968); wrote her autobiography, Femme d'Afrique, in retirement.

In 1935, Aoua Kéita was a 23-year-old professional woman, skilled in midwifery, when she married M. Diawara, a medical doctor with whom she had shared work at a number of medical posts throughout the French Sudan. As educated and politically sophisticated young Africans of the French West African territories, the couple had every intention of basing their marital relationship on social and professional equality. In their country, however, it was still customary for an older female to witness the first intercourse of newlyweds and to assist the groom in case the bride resisted. When **Dagnouma**, a female relative, showed up on their wedding night to do her duty, Kéita's husband put the woman out the door, creating a scandal that exposed the young couple to severe criticism. While this personal event might seem a relatively minor and amusing episode, it also demonstrates the kind of social upheavals inevitable in African countries that have made the transition from colonial status to independent republics in the 20th century, and the redefinition of the political and economic roles in those societies that African women have undergone.

Aoua Kéita was born in 1912 in Bamako, a small town of some 8,000 inhabitants that was the capital of the French West African territory of French Sudan. Her highly respected and well-to-do family was believed to be descended from Sundiata Kéita, one of the founders of the 13th-century Malian Empire, and her father was a native of Kouroussa, in Guinea, who fought for the French in World War I. On his return to Mali during her childhood, he took a job in Bamako as an educated laboratory worker.

Like many Africans of the time, Aoua's father was polygamous, and she grew up in a large household, containing 25 apartments, with many half-brothers and half-sisters. Aoua's mother came from the village of Kadjouga on the Ivory Coast, spoke the Dioula dialect, and held a traditional view of women's role in society, believing that men were superior and should be in charge of all political, social, and economic decisions. She taught Aoua that the only political role a woman should exercise was to pass along advice to a brother, husband, or son in confidence, and then only if she were asked.

Emotional self-mastery was highly valued in Mali culture, and children learned at an early age to keep their feelings under control. Self-discipline was especially important among people of prominence like the Kéitas, who served as models to the rest of their community. Although Mali society had undergone some changes since the advent of French colonialism and the abolition of slavery in 1906, a strong caste system still existed. As a Kéita, Aoua had a position at the top of the social hierarchy, but as a woman, she was expected to be submissive to men.

The mass of people were beginning to become conscious of their condition as slaves. . . . Local unions have been organized. I undertook my administrative and political activities with these encouraging impressions.

—Aoua Kéita

As the patriarch, Aoua's father exercised unquestioned authority over all the members of his household and observed the tradition of taking several wives. He was, however, socially progressive regarding the education of his sons and daughters. Aoua first attended the École des filles, and later the Orpheliat des Métisses, where she received her Certificat des études primaires (CEP) in 1928, at age 16. Even more remarkable, she was encouraged by her father to seek higher education, and in 1928 she moved to the coastal city of Dakar to obtain training at the School of Midwifery, which was then the only form of education available for women in the French West African territories who had completed high school. Admittance was extremely competitive, with only 15–30 students accepted annually, but Aoua was always a bright and gifted student and successfully passed her qualifying exams.

In 1931, Aoua graduated, becoming one of the few Mali women to receive a professional degree. As a member of an upper-class family, as well as a professional woman trained in the latest European medical techniques, she was soon recognized as a member of the Franco-African elite, who would shape the future of their country in years to come. Like other educated Sudanese, Aoua was proud of her heritage and did not abandon the African oral culture in which she had grown up, but she did join with other bright

young people in charting a different path for their personal lives, embracing French secular culture, and choosing to reject some Mali traditions.

Since the French worked diligently to obliterate class and gender oppression, one of the main forms of rebellion among the French colonials revolved around the youthful rejection of parental authority in choosing a spouse. Like most of her educated contemporaries, Aoua planned to marry for love rather than to please her parents.

After three years of study, Kéita took a position in Gao, a small administrative outpost and trading center with an ethnically mixed population, where French colonial policy had made few inroads and most of the inhabitants were Muslim. Kéita learned to speak Songhai, the local dialect, but found many of the townspeople suspicious of her emancipated outlook. Women there were accustomed to giving birth with the help of a traditional midwife who brought an amalgam of folk wisdom and acquired skill to the process. They knew nothing, however, about the reasons behind sterile techniques, and the death rate was often high.

In order to gain the confidence of the local women, Kéita took up sewing, reasoning that women would be interested in new clothes whether they were pregnant or not. "Thanks to this secondary activity," she later wrote, "I was able to come into contact with women of every age and of every condition." Kéita was gradually asked to attend at several births, and her skill in handling difficult deliveries eventually became widely known. Her goal was to synthesize modern medical practice with traditional cultural custom, and she learned a great deal about indigenous beliefs and procedures surrounding childbirth, although some women continued to reject sterile techniques, considering them unnecessary. Kéita described the social delicacy of the situation when she wrote, "How can we act to combat and eliminate certain customs and manners without being criticized by the people whose support we so badly need to reach our . . . objectives?"

Kéita's position of leadership grew in the community. "All the young people paid me assiduous and continual court," she wrote. "[M]y house became a pole of attraction. . . . Every day after dinner during the cold season young civil servants, merchants and nobles gathered in my living room." Her ability to bring people together would prove valuable in the coming years.

After her marriage to Dr. Diawara in 1935, Kéita grew increasingly interested in politics.

Her husband was deeply concerned about their country's future, and current events were raising the levels of political passion to new highs. Twice during the late-19th century, Italy had tried and failed to control a part of the African continent by colonizing Ethiopia (then Abyssinia). In 1935, Benito Mussolini, the Italian dictator, made a third attempt, and in the face of the Europeans' introduction of airplanes and machine guns, Ethiopian resistance was doomed. As the fascist dictator had his way, young Africans like Kéita and her husband began to view Italian fascism as another form of bankrupt European rule. Europeans, they decided, must be ousted from the continent.

The couple joined the USRDA (Union Sudanaise du Rassemblement Démocratique Africain), and their days became filled with political meetings. Kéita's work as a midwife proved crucial in spreading the political word: women who gathered in her home now learned not only about birth and delivery, but about voting and national independence; her position was strengthened by the fact that the mothers and families of babies she had safely delivered became extremely loyal to her. It was comparatively easy for her to garner considerable support for the USRDA among a large segment of the population that might otherwise have been apathetic.

The USRDA was in the avant-garde of the African liberation movement. In 1946, years of effort culminated in the first elections in which women of the Sudan were allowed to vote. Although Kéita campaigned vigorously for the USRDA, the party did not win on June 2, but its organizing skills were soon to be felt at a national level.

In the 13 years of their marriage, Kéita and her husband found their life as a couple beset with many contradictions. Although her husband treated her as an equal in private, the couple found this a luxury they could not afford to demonstrate in public. Many political topics were considered taboo for Mali women to discuss outside the home, and when Kéita's husband felt it best not to defy social convention, she bowed to his wishes and kept silent, apparently accepting the public submissiveness as the means required to accomplish larger goals. Eventually, it was the force of traditional attitudes that destroyed the couple's marriage.

Despite several surgical interventions, Kéita proved unable to have children. Since Kéita was unwilling to live in a polygamous relationship, her husband intended at first to stay with his childless wife, until the couple was threatened by his mother's curse. Finally, in compliance with his mother's wishes, he divorced Aoua, then refused for a long time to take another wife, angering his family even more. Despite the divorce, Kéita maintained amicable relations with her husband's extended family and raised two of his nieces. Later, she married Mahamane Alassane Haidara who represented the Sudan as a senator in the French National Assembly from 1942 to 1959.

Politically and personally, the end of Kéita's first marriage proved liberating, as she no longer stood in her husband's shadow. By then in her late 30s, she assumed a greater public role, becoming an advocate for a number of issues, especially health reform, which she viewed as critical to the improvement of welfare for women in her country. In 1957, along with **Aissata Sow**, she founded the Union of Salaried Women of Bamako, which gave professional women a voice in the political sphere. She helped establish the Federation of Black African Workers, or UGTAN (Union Générale de Travailleurs de l'Afrique Noir), which represented African workers of both sexes, and became a representative to the World Federation of Trade Unions, or FSM (Fédération des Syndicats du Monde). As the French Sudan moved toward independence, Kéita, at the center of political events, was asked to help draft a constitution for the Mali Federation in the fall of 1958.

In her attempts to organize women, Kéita still faced cultural obstacles emanating from the women of traditional Mali society. In setting up the Federation of Salaried Women, for example, some members resisted the election of a president, because the office represented a European approach that challenged their accepted social norms. To provide the party with the officer required by the USDRA, while retaining the egalitarian spirit demanded by the group, Kéita exercised her considerable skill and diplomacy.

In 1958, she organized the Bamako Women's Bureau, which became another political vehicle for presenting the interests of women to the USRDA Party. Through its efforts, the following goals were recognized as part of the USRDA Party platform:

1. Women should participate in the struggle for their country's liberation.
2. Women should participate in Mali's economic development.
3. Women should be given improved educational opportunities.
4. Women should have access to improved health services.

A women's bureau was organized within the USDRA to implement these goals as policies.

In 1959, Aoua Kéita ran as a USRDA candidate from the region of Sikasso and won, becoming the first woman deputy elected to the national assembly of the nascent Republic of Mali. After its constitution was adopted in 1962, the government faced many problems. Its newly elected president was Modibo Kéita, a strong anti-colonialist whose attitudes scared off Western governments, which had never been attracted to investing much capital in the area in any case. Some Communist aid was available during these Cold War years, but not enough to sustain the new government. In 1968, the first president was overthrown and imprisoned in a coup, and the administration of Moussa Traoré which followed proved very corrupt. Aoua Kéita left the government and returned to Bamako, where she wrote her autobiography, *Femme d'Afrique* (African Woman).

In 1979, Aoua Kéita died, at a time when Mali remained poor and weak. Not long afterwards, however, a series of massive public demonstrations occurred, in which large numbers of Malian women of all ages participated, and a number died when government troops opened fire on the crowds. The corrupt government of Traoré was eventually brought down, by which time it was clear that women in the country had long since abandoned a passive role in national affairs.

Never a militant by nature, Aoua Kéita nevertheless became a radical feminist in promoting the rights of women in the French Sudan. Her moderate approach allowed her to reach large numbers of people who might not otherwise have felt women's liberation as an especially important issue. In both her public and private life, she was determined, as she said, not to "overturn our traditions, because it is on these traditions that our African society is based." Her ability to fuse tradition with new ideas proved a potent political combination. As a USRDA Party member, a representative to the national assembly, and a national leader, she became a founder of the Republic of Mali.

SOURCES:

Denzer, LaRay. "Towards a Study of the History of West African Women's Participation in Nationalist Politics: The Early Phase, 1935–1950," in *Africana Research Bulletin*. Vol. 6, no. 4, 1976, pp. 20–32.

Hay, Margaret Jean, and Sharon Stichter, eds. *African Women South of the Sahara*. London: Longman, 1984.

Imperato, Pascal James. *Historical Dictionary of Mali*. 2nd ed. London: Scarecrow Press, 1986.

Jayawardene, Kumari. *Feminism and Nationalism in the Third World*. London: Zed Books, 1986.

Kéita, Aoua. *Femme d'Afrique: la vie d'Aoua Kéita racontée par elle-même*. Paris: Présence Africaine, 1975.

Mohanty, Chandra Talpade, Anne Russo and Lourdes Torres, eds. *Third World Women and the Politics of Feminism*. Bloomington, IN: Indiana University Press, 1991.

Morgenthau, Ruth Schachter. *Political Parties in French West Africa*. Oxford: Clarendon Press, 1964.

Turrittin, Jane. "Aoua Kéita and the Nascent Women's Movement in the French Soudan," in *African Studies Review*. Vol. 36, no. 1. April 1993, pp. 59–89.

Karin Loewen Haag,
freelance writer, Athens, Georgia

Keith, Agnes Newton (b. 1901).

See Colbert, Claudette for sidebar.

Keith, Marcia (1859–1950)

American physicist. Born in Brockton, Massachusetts, in 1859; died in Braintree, Massachusetts, in 1950; daughter of Arza Keith and Mary Ann (Cary) Keith; Mount Holyoke, B.S., 1882; attended Worcester Polytechnic Institute as a special student, 1887 and 1889; attended the University of Berlin, 1897–1898; attended the University of Chicago, summer, 1901.

A noted teacher of physics, Marcia Keith received her B.S. from Mount Holyoke College in 1882. She was a science instructor at the Michigan Seminary from 1883 to 1885, then returned to her alma mater, Mount Holyoke, as a mathematics instructor. In 1889, Keith became the first full-time instructor in the physics department at Mount Holyoke and also chaired the department from 1889 to 1903. In this position, she had both the opportunity to instruct young women in physics and to serve as a role model where few existed.

In 1899, along with one other woman, **Isabelle Stone** of Vassar, Keith was among the 36 founders of the American Physical Society. The group met in Fayerweather Hall at Columbia, the home of the APS for the next 60 years. Keith later left education to become an engineer with the firm Herbert Keith in New York City.

Keith, Margaret (fl. 1395)

Noblewoman of Scotland. Name variations: Lady Lindsay: Margaret Lindsay. Flourished 1395 in Scotland; possibly married Sir James Lindsay, 9th Baron Crawford, of Lanarkshire (d. 1396).

Margaret Keith was a Scottish noble, one of many medieval women who organized the defense of their castle-estates during wartime. In Margaret's case, the enemy was her own nephew Robert Keith.

Macy, Anne Sullivan (1866–1936)

American teacher and activist for the blind. Name variations: Anne or Annie Sullivan; Anne Mansfield Sullivan. Born Joanna Sullivan in Feeding Hill, Massachusetts, on April 14 (some sources cite April 13), 1866; died in Forest Hills, New York, on October 20, 1936; daughter of Thomas (an Irish immigrant farmer) and Alice (Cloesy) Sullivan; married John Macy (a writer, Harvard professor, and Helen Keller's literary agent), on May 2, 1905 (separated 1914); no children.

Anne Sullivan Macy is best known as the lifelong teacher and companion of Helen Keller, the deaf and blind woman who became one of the 20th century's most celebrated Americans. Born into extreme poverty in 1866, Annie Sullivan was the daughter of Thomas Sullivan and **Alice Cloesy Sullivan**, immigrants who had settled in Massachusetts after fleeing Ireland during the potato famine. It was an unhappy family; her mother suffered from tuberculosis, and her father was an abusive alcoholic. When her eyesight began to fail during an early childhood illness, Annie learned the manual alphabet. When she was eight, her mother died; two years later, her father deserted her and her two siblings. Annie and her lame brother were sent to the state poorhouse in Tewksbury where her brother died soon after. The unsanitary conditions there exacerbated the degenerative eye disease called trachoma which Annie had contracted earlier; her eyesight was to fail gradually over the next few decades.

In 1880, after four years at Tewksbury, Annie was fortunate to be allowed to enter the Perkins School for the Blind in Boston. Although at first temperamental and hostile towards her teacher, Annie matured at Perkins into an insightful young woman eager to serve others. During her stay there, a series of operations helped regain much of her sight, and she graduated in 1886 at the head of her class. The following year, fascinated by the case of *Laura Bridgman, Annie Sullivan traveled to Tuscumbria, Alabama, hired as governess to the unruly seven-year-old girl known as *Helen Keller, who had been stricken blind and deaf in infancy. Undisciplined, lacking the ability to hear or see, Helen was a formidable challenge. But Annie was determined to break through to Helen's sealed-off mind using a manual alphabet by which words were spelled out into Helen's hand; after many weeks, she was successful in teaching Helen that the movements she felt in her hand were the names of objects. Annie's pupil then progressed rapidly under her dedicated efforts; soon the wild, angry child was transformed into a sweet, intelligent girl who was as devoted to her "Teacher" as her teacher was to her. Publicity about Annie's unprecedented success in teaching a deaf-blind child soon led to national fame for the two. However, throughout their lives, Helen would always garner more attention than Annie, a situation which both women resented, for both believed theirs was an equal partnership.

Although Annie married John Macy, a Harvard professor and editor of several journals, in 1905, the marriage was doomed because Annie's primary commitment was always to Helen. Teacher and student together formed, as Samuel Clemens commented, "a complete and perfect whole," making it impossible for others to share fully in that bond, especially as Annie and Helen always shared a home. John and Annie separated in 1914, though the women continued to support him out of their income from Helen's books and from the lectures they gave.

In 1919, Helen and Annie began performing a successful vaudeville act, reenacting Annie's education of Helen, which took them across the country. In 1924, they agreed to work for the American Foundation for the Blind, holding meetings to solicit donations and public support for the foundation's work. However, Annie was almost completely blind by this time (she was nearly 60 years old), and she suffered from numerous other physical ailments. Despite spending several years traveling abroad with Helen and their assistant **Polly Thomson** in an effort to get well, her health continued to fail rapidly. Anne Sullivan Macy died in 1936. In death, she received more recognition for her life's accomplishments than she had in life, for her ashes were placed in a special vault at the National Cathedral in Washington, D.C., an exceptional honor which was also granted to Helen Keller, whose ashes were placed, as she wished, next to Annie's.

SOURCES:

Braddy, Nella. *Anne Sullivan Macy.* NY: Doubleday, 1933.
Keller, Helen. *Teacher.* NY: Doubleday, 1955.
Lash, Joseph P. *Helen and Teacher.* NY: Delacorte Press, 1980.

COLLECTIONS:

Papers of Anne Sullivan Macy, located at the Perkins Institution, Watertown, Massachusetts.
Letters of Anne Sullivan Macy, located at the American Antiquarian Society, Worcester, Massachusetts

Laura York,
Riverside, California

her pupil French, Greek, and some Latin. Keller impressed others as a sweet, sympathetic girl, very affectionate and eager to please, traits which she would not outgrow.

Sullivan continued to teach Keller at her home in Alabama until the autumn of 1889, when they returned to Perkins for Helen to study as a regular student. Since Keller could not hear the lectures as could most of the students, Sullivan had to sit with Keller and translate every lecture into the manual alphabet. The next year, Helen began speech lessons in addition to her studies. The two remained at Perkins through the 1890–91 school year, after which they returned to Alabama because the Kellers could no longer afford to keep Helen in school. In January 1893, Captain Keller, Annie, and Helen traveled to Washington, D.C., once more, where they attended the second inauguration of Grover Cleveland, after which they continued to Chicago for the World's Fair. Keller attracted much attention in Chicago even though she was only a visitor to the fair; her written account was published in December 1893 by the youth magazine *St. Nicholas*. The enthusiastic response of the public to her article made Keller, now 13, decide to become a writer. In September of that year, the philanthropist William Wade, who was interested in helping the disabled, made it possible for Keller, accompanied by Sullivan as always, to study in Pennsylvania under the classicist John Irons.

> *I* have often tried to analyze what it is in Helen Keller that so awakens the better part of our natures. . . . It is not pity—not emotion—it must be the great soul within her.
>
> —**Moses Charles Migel**

The next fall, Keller and Sullivan moved to New York City, where Helen enrolled as a student at the new Wright-Humason School for deaf children. Though she was the only student who was also blind and sometimes felt isolated because of it, she remained there for two school years and recalled her time there as a pleasant one. While in New York, she met the celebrated writer Samuel Clemens (Mark Twain), who was very impressed with her; afterwards, the two began a correspondence which lasted many years. In 1896, Keller entered the Gilman School for Young Ladies, a college preparatory school, in Cambridge, Massachusetts. Her intent was to prepare to enter Radcliffe College, the women's school attached to the all-male Harvard University. Her expenses and Sullivan's were covered by donations from a group of philanthropists,

including Alexander Graham Bell and Mrs. J. Pierpont Morgan (***Frances Louisa Morgan**). Although Keller proved an apt student and progressed rapidly in her studies, Sullivan came into conflict with the school's dean in 1897.

Through her special connection and history with Helen, Annie Sullivan had become Helen's surrogate mother. Keller always referred to her as "Teacher." Because Annie was unwilling to let school administrators decide how best to teach Helen, the Gilman dean eventually acted to have Sullivan removed from the school. Keller, feeling betrayed, withdrew from Gilman permanently. Instead, she finished her preparatory work with private tutors paid for by philanthropic friends. During this period, Helen showed her first interest in world politics when she became absorbed in the Spanish-American War and issues of American imperialism. By the fall of 1900, Keller had passed all her entrance examinations and was admitted to Radcliffe College. As always, Annie made her studies possible by translating lectures as well as books into the manual language. Keller's benefactors provided some of her required books in Braille, but most had to be "read" to her manually, a very lengthy process. She continued to develop increasingly more liberal attitudes towards the issues of racial and sexual equality as well as to pacifism. She excelled in her courses, but despite this she suffered from feelings of unworthiness and low self-esteem.

In her junior year at Radcliffe, Keller finished her first full-length book, an autobiography published as *The Story of My Life*, which was simultaneously published in the U.S. and Britain, and found a wide audience in both countries. Later in 1903, a small collection of Keller's essays entitled *Optimism* was also published to positive reviews and strong sales. Keller, despite her heavy courseload and the manuscripts which demanded most of her time, still made an effort to work as an advocate for the education of the deaf and blind through her writing and correspondence; she also let agencies use her now well-known name in their fundraising. In June 1904, Keller received her Bachelor of Arts degree, awarded with honors, from Radcliffe. She and Annie purchased a house in Wrentham, Massachusetts, with Keller's book royalties. The inseparable pair continued to live together even after Sullivan married Keller's literary agent, John Macy, in 1905 (the couple would separate in 1914, partly due to Sullivan's primary commitment to serving Keller's needs).

Keller continued writing after graduation; her book of essays *The World I Live In*, pub-

lished in 1908, explained how Helen "viewed" the world, how her remaining senses compensated for the two she had lost. Reviewers praised the book for offering rare psychological insights into the world of the blind and deaf. Keller also wrote poetry and kept up a steady correspondence with admirers, family members, and philanthropists. In 1908 and 1909, her articles on the need for work opportunities for the blind appeared in *Ladies' Home Journal*, which had also serialized *The Story of My Life*. Keller was instrumental in establishing the Massachusetts

Commission for the Blind in 1908 and served as its representative.

The year 1909 saw another step in Keller's development, when, influenced by John Macy, she joined the American Socialist Party. Through her advocacy for government to aid the disabled, she had come to believe that the state was the key to helping all citizens improve their lives. (At this time, the Socialist Party was an important American political party, boasting millions of members from all walks of life and social classes, and running its own candidates for major offices.) She also came out for women's suffrage. (Annie Sullivan, more conservative by nature, declined to follow Keller's political lead.) The next year, Keller began writing and speaking on behalf of the Socialists and related economic issues.

As royalties from Keller's books began to decrease, she and Sullivan went on lucrative lecture tours; they traveled across the U.S. and Canada for several years relating the story of Helen's remarkable education. Audiences were awestruck by Keller's accomplishments, and her fame spread even wider. Some of the most notable figures of the time came to hear her, including former President William Howard Taft, Thomas Edison, *Maria Montessori, and Henry Ford. During these years, however, Sullivan's primary contribution as Keller's teacher was often overlooked by listeners; this neglect was to become a trend in their career, one which Sullivan deeply resented and which Keller tried desperately to amend.

In 1913, *Out of the Dark,* a collection of previously published material on social issues, was published. It did not find a wide audience, evidence that Keller's personal history was more agreeable to her readers than her political positions. Throughout Keller's life, book and lecture audiences preferred to hear her own story rather than her political arguments; Keller was often criticized by the conservative media when she chose to speak on social issues. This criticism was often cast in patronizing tones, implying that Keller, despite her accomplishments, could not possibly have the awareness and knowledge needed to form political opinions due to her handicaps. However, she did find acceptance among American liberals, suffragists, and other Socialists. She joined the Industrial Workers of the World (IWW), a militant union which eventually split off from the Socialist Party, because they advocated "direct action" over the more moderate political methods of the mainstream Socialists. Her affiliation with the IWW cost Keller some of her admirers; many could not rec-

oncile their image of the sweet, affectionate blind and deaf girl with the radical socialist woman she had become. During this period, she embraced a myriad of liberal causes, including anti-child labor legislation, birth-control advocacy, and anti-capital punishment legislation in addition to her pro-suffrage stance.

In the fall of 1916, Keller and Sullivan experienced their first major separation since 1887. Now 50 years old and diagnosed with consumption (tuberculosis), Annie traveled to Puerto Rico to recover her health under the care of **Polly Thomson** (a Scottish woman who had become an aide and companion to both Sullivan and Keller). Annie and Helen were separated for five months, a time in which Keller, who had returned to her family home in Alabama, came to realize just how much she depended on Sullivan to take care of her. Annie was a surrogate mother and caretaker, but she was also Helen's primary contact with the outside world, a constant daily companion for more than 25 years. However, Keller did not cease her political involvement. She wrote in support of equal rights for black Americans and donated money to the National Association for the Advancement of Colored People (NAACP), despite her conservative Southern family's shock and disapproval.

Reunited in 1917, Annie, Polly, and Helen moved to a new home in Forest Hills, New York. Due to U.S. involvement in World War I, the opportunities to make money on the lecture circuit dwindled dramatically. Needing new sources of income, Keller and Sullivan sold the movie rights for their life story to a Hollywood filmmaker and traveled to California to participate in the production. Though a commercial failure, the film *Deliverance* opened in 1918 to enthusiastic reviews. The movie, in which Helen, Annie, and members of Helen's family appeared as themselves, was directed as a series of tableaux with symbolic, often mythical scenes. Used to the standard narrative film, audiences found *Deliverance* too unusual to enjoy, and box-office sales fell quickly. Disappointed, Keller and Sullivan returned to New York.

They did not stay long. In 1919, the two women and Thomson set out on another commercial venture. For the next year, they appeared in vaudeville halls across the country. Their act, unusual for the vaudeville circuit, consisted of the same material they had given during lectures, only in a more theatrical style. They told the story of Keller's education, reenacting scenes such as the famous "W-A-T-E-R" episode, and closed with Keller answering questions from the audience (through Sullivan's translation). The act became very popular. Though Sullivan found road tours stressful, they returned to the lecture circuit in 1921 and 1922.

Between 1923 and 1926, Helen and Annie traveled widely speaking on behalf of the American Foundation for the Blind (AFB). They had a contract to speak at fundraising events, soliciting donations to the newly formed Helen Keller Endowment. Keller's name proved a successful fundraising tool, and they gathered thousands of dollars in gifts. In 1927, *My Religion* was published. In the book, Helen explained the principles of Swedenborgism, a sect of Christianity emphasizing a view of the world as a battle between good and evil which Keller had embraced years earlier. It went through several editions and sold quite well. The next year, another autobiographical work, *Midstream: My Later Life,* was published, another commercial and critical success.

Keller's newfound prosperity was marred by Sullivan's failing health and vision. Sullivan had been partially blind since childhood, but, as she neared old age, her eyesight began to fail altogether. By the late 1920s, Polly Thomson had taken over most of Sullivan's former duties in caring for Keller and had to care for Annie now as well. In 1930, the three enjoyed their first trip together abroad when they visited Great Britain. They returned to Europe twice in the next two years, the first year to Britain, the second year traveling to France, Germany, and Yugoslavia. Each country received them enthusiastically and treated them as "official guests" of the government. Also in 1931, Keller was a major organizer of an international conference of workers for the blind in Washington, D.C., in the course of which she dined at the White House as the special guest of President Herbert Hoover and *Lou Henry Hoover.

Helen, Annie, and Polly took another trip to Europe, in 1933, to escape from the pressures of advocating for the blind on behalf of the AFB, which they had taken up again in 1932. The trio returned to the United States in fall 1933 but did not remain at home long; Sullivan was more ill than ever, and her doctors recommended that

From the movie The Miracle Worker, *starring Anne Bancroft and Patty Duke.*

she travel to get the rest she needed. Accordingly, her committed student and assistant spent the next three years of their lives traveling with her, from as far north as New York state to as far south as Jamaica. Unfortunately, their efforts were in vain, for Sullivan died after their return to the United States in October 1936. Her ashes were placed in a vault at the National Cathedral in Washington, D.C., a privilege offered only to those who had made a significant contribution to the country. Thus in death, Sullivan finally received the recognition she and Keller had sought for her in life. Polly and Helen, both bereft, continued to travel after Sullivan's death to escape the painful memories of their home in Forest Hills. At the end of 1936, they once again visited England and Scotland. The next year, they traveled to Japan for the first time, to promote Japanese-American goodwill and to speak on education issues and on the need for peace; Keller was popular with the Japanese, and the trip was considered a success.

In 1938, Keller's sixth book, *A Journal,* was published, an edited collection of her diary entries for the previous few years; reviewers praised its style and its intimacy, preferring it over her earlier publications, and it sold well. Helen immediately began work on her next book, a biography of "Teacher." During the late 1930s and throughout World War II, she also occupied herself with more work on behalf of the blind and deaf. Her efforts were in part responsible for the inclusion of the blind as recipients of federal aid in the Social Security Act of 1935, after which she came to be on intimate terms with President Franklin D. Roosevelt and First Lady *Eleanor Roosevelt. Among other projects, Helen lobbied Congress to include aid for diagnosis and treatment for the blind in the bill known as Title X, and she pressured the president into authorizing funds for recorded books to be made by the Library of Congress for the blind. Also during the war, Keller fulfilled a self-described need by visiting wounded soldiers at military hospitals. Her victory over her own handicaps was an inspiration, and she was a popular figure in the hospital wards. After the war, Keller and Thomson returned to Europe, visiting the sick in military hospitals across the Continent and doing fundraising events for the American Foundation for the Overseas Blind (AFOB). Each country she visited treated her as a visiting dignitary; among other highlights, in Italy, she had an interview with Pope Pius XII, and in England she met privately with Queen *Elizabeth II. Helen and Polly returned home briefly in 1947 but spent the better part of the next four years overseas, despite Keller's advancing age (she was 67 in 1947). Their world tour included Australia, New Zealand, Japan, South Africa, Egypt, Lebanon, Syria, Jordan, France, and Israel (where they were guests of *Golda Meir, later prime minister).

In 1952, *The Unconquered,* another film based on Keller's life opened. Though it failed commercially, the documentary received positive reviews and spurred Keller to finish her biography *Teacher,* which was published in 1955. Keller's biography of Annie Sullivan seems almost protective in what was covered and not covered; even after Sullivan's death, Keller felt it important to defend Annie from those who had criticized her control of Helen's life. That year, Keller was awarded an honorary doctorate from Harvard University. Two years later, 77-year-old Keller and Polly Thomson took their last trip abroad, visiting Iceland and Scandinavia. Also in 1957, Keller's last book appeared. Called *The Open Door,* it was a collection of previously published essays which enjoyed moderate sales.

The year 1959 saw the opening on Broadway of William Gibson's *The Miracle Worker,* starring **Anne Bancroft** and **Patty Duke,** which was based on that early battle of wills between Sullivan and a six-year-old Keller. The play received rave reviews, played across the country to packed houses, and saw scores of revivals and regional productions. Keller was pleased with the work, which she considered a tribute to Sullivan's life. In March 1960, Keller suffered a second great loss when her longtime companion and assistant Polly Thomson died after enduring poor health for many years. "Our sweet Polly has left me," Keller wrote a friend. "I thank God that [her] years of anguish are over." Yet despite her love for Thomson and her gratitude for Polly's years of selfless service, Keller tried to stop plans for Polly's ashes to be placed with Annie's at the National Cathedral, where Helen's own ashes would be placed. Why Helen refused to honor Polly in this way is unclear, though biographer Joseph Lash speculates in *Helen and Teacher* that "so far as the world was concerned, Helen wanted it to realize that she and Teacher were bound to each other in a way that admitted no others."

Although Keller of necessity had caretakers for the remaining few years of her life, she never formed a close relationship with anyone else after the deaths of her two companions. In October 1961, age 81, Keller suffered a stroke, after which she retired from public life. She remained at her home in Westport, Connecticut, seeing very few visitors and venturing forth only rarely.

Helen Keller died at her home on June 1, 1968, at the age of 88. As planned, her ashes were deposited next to those of her beloved "Teacher," Annie Sullivan, after a memorial service at the National Cathedral.

SOURCES:

Keller, Helen. *Midstream: My Later Life*. Garden City, NY: Doubleday, 1930.

———. *The Story of My Life*. NY: Andor Press, 1976.

Lash, Joseph P. *Helen and Teacher: The Story of Helen Keller and Anne Sullivan Macy*. NY: Delacorte Press, 1980.

SUGGESTED READING:

Gibson, William. *The Miracle Worker: A Play for Television*. NY: Alfred A. Knopf, 1957.

Herrmann, Dorothy. *Helen Keller: A Life*. NY: Alfred A. Knopf, 1998.

Keller, Helen. *Teacher: Anne Sullivan Macy*. NY: Doubleday, 1955.

———. *A Journal*. NY: Doubleday, 1938.

RELATED MEDIA:

The Miracle Worker opened in Broadway at The Playhouse on October 19, 1959, starring Anne Bancroft, Patty Duke, *Patricia Neal, and *Beah Richards, produced by Fred Coe, directed by Arthur Penn.

The Miracle Worker (107 min. film), starring Anne Bancroft and Patty Duke, and **Inga Swenson**, directed by Arthur Penn, produced by Playfilms/United Artists, 1962.

COLLECTIONS:

Helen Keller Scrapbooks located at the Perkins Institution, Watertown, Massachusetts; Helen Keller Archives located at the American Foundation for the Blind, New York City, New York; Helen Keller Archives located at the Alexander Graham Bell Association for the Deaf, Washington, D.C.

Laura York,
freelance writer in medieval history and women's history,
Riverside, California

Kellerman, Annette (1886–1975)

Australian-born athlete, swimming star, and actress, both on stage and screen, who played a significant role in the popularization of swimming as a sport, especially for women. Name variations: Kellerman or Kellermann (both spellings are found, but Kellerman was in the information provided to the press at the time of her death and is found in Australian sources); known as "The Diving Venus," "The American Venus," "The Million Dollar Mermaid," and "The Form Divine." Born Annette Marie Sarah Kellerman in Sydney, Australia, on July 6, 1886 (and not in 1887, as is sometimes found); died in Southport, Queensland, Australia, on November 6, 1975; married James R. Sullivan (her manager), in 1912.

Began competing in swimming meets while still a teenager; went to England as an athlete and performer (1904); with her brother as manager, came to U.S. and made first public appearance (1907); made first film, a kind of documentary, *as early as 1909, and her last just before the end of the silent era; a champion swimmer, recognized health authority, and exponent of physical culture, was the first woman swimmer to achieve acclaim; is said to have devised the idea of formation swimming as an art, is credited with having introduced the single-piece swimsuit, and did much to facilitate the entry of women into the aquatic sports by gradually making acceptable the kind of minimal swimwear necessary to allow freedom of movement and speed in the water; retired to her native Australia (1935). Awards: Holder of the world record for the two-, five- and ten-minute swimming championships.*

Filmography: Miss Annette Kellerman Fancy Swimming and Diving Displays (both reportage, 1909); Neptune's Daughter (1914); Isle of Love (1916); A Daughter of the Gods (1916); The Honor System (1917); Queen of the Sea (1918); (reportage) The Art of Diving (1920); What Women Love (1920); Venus of the South Seas (1924).

Born on July 6, 1886, in Sydney, Australia, Annette Kellerman is said to have suffered from bowleggedness as a child, supposedly as a result of having been encouraged to walk too early. By age nine, she had been taught to swim as a therapeutic means of overcoming this condition. It now appears from Australian sources that her childhood ailment was actually a case of Poliomyelitis that had left her partially crippled, and that the braces she wore and the swimming lessons she took were designed to correct the results of this disease. On the other hand, there is no truth to the exaggerated stories that occasionally appeared in the press, that she was declared "a hopeless cripple" as a child, that she was forced to wear "an iron brace up to her hips," that the calisthenics required of her were "pure torture," or that at the age of five she was forced to swim by her father even though she was "deathly afraid of the water." Whatever the exact degree of her condition, her legs were normal by the time she was 13, and she was soon swimming first one, then two, then ten miles at a stretch.

As early as the 1880s, Australians were extraordinarily devoted to outdoor sports, especially cricket, hockey, archery, skating, and swimming. Women participated in these activities in almost as great a proportion as the men, a custom attributed to the fact that until 1840, male immigrants to the continent outnumbered women ten to one, so that the entire culture was said to have been thoroughly "masculinized" from an early date. Whatever the case, turning to athletics as a cure for childhood deformity was a natural recourse for Australian parents in those days. By age 15, Annette Kellerman had won her first contest, swimming 100 yards in the New South Wales swimming championships in 1902, an achievement quickly followed by similar triumphs, one after the other.

From her youthful swimming successes in Australia, Annette Kellerman journeyed with her father to England in 1904, where she quickly attracted attention by appearing in the water in a daring, one-piece, cotton bathing suit of her own design, consisting of an ankle-length leotard over which she wore a snug fitting, hip-length tunic. In England, she won a 26-mile race on the Thames and, sponsored by the London newspaper, the *Daily Mirror*, three times attempted to swim the English Channel before she gave it up after covering three-quarters of the distance in a record-breaking 10½ hours. Already aware of a public image, her words at the time were a fuzzy "I had the strength but not the endurance," but the truth was that while she was a good swimmer, notable for her stamina and endurance, she simply wasn't that good. Nevertheless, the record she set on her last attempt stood for 17 years.

Decency is a question of common sense.
—Annette Kellerman

Having developed an "aquatic act" consisting of swimming and diving, however, Kellerman attempted to present it in public but, at first, she had some difficulty in getting her act across, particularly because the women in the audience were shocked—or feigned shock. Swimming was still a novelty in the early years of the 20th century. Bathing suits for men, and especially for women, were bulky and unsuited for speed, and many women, usually unable to swim at all, simply waded, while attempting to look modest and fetching at one and the same time. All the while, they carefully avoided the sun, which was then thought to be bad for the complexion—a fear justified, of course, by findings after World War II. Young as she was, however, Annette Kellerman already had an entrepreneur's instinct. After appearing at the Bath Club for charity, an event attended by the duke and duchess of Connaught (*Louise Margaret of Prussia), who thereby put their stamp of approval on her art, she found herself able to secure engagements, in particular, one at the London Hippodrome that was followed by a successful tour of the Continent. In 1906, she competed as the only woman in a 12-kilometer (7½ mile) swimming race on the Seine in which she defeated all but two of the men.

In 1907, Kellerman brought her show to the United States in the company of her brother, who managed the act. Their first engagement was at White City Amusement Park in Chicago, where she was required to do 55 shows per week. From there, she went on to Revere Beach in Boston, where her performance was seen by the impresario B.F. Keith, who gave her a contract for an engagement in New York at Keith and Proctor's Fifth Avenue Theater. There, she received top billing, packing the house for seven weeks. In the course of her act, which included both swimming and diving, Kellerman both shocked and delighted audiences with her remarkable one-piece bathing suits, especially designed to provide unhampered movement in the water, and which, in short order, came to be known as "Annette Kellermans." Her engagement at Keith's was followed by vaudeville tours culminating in her arrest the same year at a Boston beach for appearing in public with her unconventional swimsuit. "I was wearing a very modest one-piece suit," she recalled 25 years later, "and didn't remove my robe until I got to the edge of the water. I was in training for long distance swims and I had to have something practical. There were some other women on the beach—how funny they would look today. They wore long skirts, blouses with sleeves and ruffles on the shoulders, and stockings. Of course, they didn't go in the water much, and they couldn't swim. Very few women could in those days." Undoubtedly an unpleasant experience at the time, the arrest was worth a million dollars in free publicity, and Kellerman found herself famous at 21.

Thereafter, Annette Kellerman continued to tour both in the U.S. and abroad, dancing, demonstrating her skills in the water, lecturing on health and exercise, and varying her act with acrobatics and highwire walking. In 1911, she made her Broadway debut with an aquatic act in the musical review *Vera Violetta*, which starred the French soubrette *Gaby Deslys but which also launched the careers of a number of newcomers including Al Jolson, *Mae West, and, of course, Kellerman. In time, she became world famous as a health authority, exponent of physical culture, advocate of physical exercise for women, and supporter of universal military training. An astute showwoman, Kellerman knew well the uses of publicity. The "hype" generated by her performances and public statements, as well as by the various lawsuits undertaken by promoters vying for the opportunity to present her on the stage, helped keep her in the public eye. A Harvard professor pronounced her "the most perfectly formed woman in the

Annette
Kellerman

world," after which she was much sought after by women, who flocked to hear her lecture on health as well as on her beauty secrets.

Much had been written about exercise as a means of maintaining good health, but it was only in the 1870s that swimming was seen as an important means of providing this, and that the idea arose that women should exercise as well. This notion emerged among medical specialists who were troubled by the fact that women died far too often in childbirth—a supposed "natural" process—but that lower-class women, more use to physical work on the farm, in the home, or in the factory, were less inclined to do so. At first, women's exercises were limited to girls swinging narrow-necked clubs or ladies genteelly tapping croquet balls through a little hoop, but gradually, the positive results of regular exercise became clearer and more widely known. By the end of the century, tennis, bicycle riding, and other more strenuous activities had begun to be included in the regime, especially at women's colleges.

Swimming, too, became popular, but the development of the sport was long handicapped by Victorian prudishness. If a respectable woman was not to reveal her ankle (and proper young ladies were taught how to get on and off a streetcar without doing so), how was it possible to appear in a swimsuit unless the garment was as modest as everyday wear. Fortunately, the changing times, the emergence of the "new woman," and the positive benefits attached to swimming wore down the opposition. Annette Kellerman was not only a pioneer in fully active swimming for women, but, as a strikingly beautiful woman with a superb figure, became the world's first "bathing beauty." Billed as "The Diving Venus," "The Form Divine," and, oddly enough since she was an Australian, "The American Venus," she not only did much to publicize and popularize swimming, and to generate a steady reduction in the amount of yardage required for women's bathing suits, but also contributed to a changing taste in feminine beauty. In 1900, the large-framed, well-rounded, even heavy woman, so popular since the 1870s, was still the ideal, but within a decade the trend turned towards a slimmer, more lithe figure, culminating in the tall, wisp-like slenderness of the 1930s and the decades which followed. Careful to nurture her youthful image, Kellerman kept it a secret when she married her manager, James R. Sullivan, in Danbury, Connecticut, in 1912.

As a theatrical attraction, Kellerman probably reached the height of her career when she appeared in *The Big Show* at the Hippodrome in New York City. The very nature of her act made it difficult for her to find theaters with stages sufficiently large to accommodate a swimming pool so that her appearances tended to be relatively far between—geographically if not in time. The New York Hippodrome, however, was a vast venue, especially suited to spectacles, and in this production, billed as "The Diving Venus, Annette Kellerman (herself)," she appeared in an on-stage water extravaganza together with a company of 200 "water nymphs," concluding

her act with a high dive into a massive tank of water. Her last appearance at the Hippodrome—and her first in New York in five years—took place in 1925, when she was 38. Fourteen years later, the Hippodrome was demolished.

Annette Kellerman was especially proud of what she called her "swimologies," actually short films with minimal plots designed to demonstrate her skills as diver and swimmer. The first of these, *Fancy Swimming* and *Diving Displays*, were filmed as early as 1909, the underwater scenes being shot by her manager (and future husband) from within a diving bell submerged for the purpose. The last, *The Art of Diving*, was made in 1920. In between and afterwards, Kellerman appeared in several full-length features, the first of which, entitled *Neptune's Daughter*, was filmed on location in Jamaica. In this production, filmed before the advent of process or "trick" photography, Kellerman not only set a world record for women by diving off a cliff some 90 feet above the water, but also allowed herself to be hurled from a cliff while bound hand and foot. Her later films included *Isle of Love* and *A Daughter of the Gods* (both 1916), *The Honor System* (1917), *Queen of the Sea* (1918), *What Women Love* (1920), and *Venus of the South Seas* (1924). Reviewing *A Daughter of the Gods*, directed by Herbert Brenon, a bemused film critic for *The New York Times* described the opus:

> The beautiful figure of Miss Annette Kellermann [*sic*] and her matchless skill as an amphibienne [*sic*] are made the most of in "A Daughter of the Gods," an elaborate, spectacular and somewhat monotonous photofable which was unfolded for the first time at the Lyric Theater. On tropic strands, in vine-hung pools, on coral reefs, through dismaying rapids and in the marble harem plunge, the diving Venus disports herself. . . .
>
> The result is a photoplay carefully cultivated to shock the late Anthony Comstock [a New York guardian of the morals at the turn of the century] and certain to please many others. There are long passages when Kellerman wanders disconsolately through the film all undressed with nowhere to go. **Audrey Munson**, as exhibited in the short-lived "Purity," has nothing on Kellerman. And as it has been observed elsewhere, neither has Kellerman. . . .
>
> But the submersible star is unrivaled in diving and swimming, and this photoplay, taken amid settings as fantastic and Arabic as are to be found anywhere in the Caribbean, must leap from a hundred-foot tower, plunge into a pool full of crocodiles, be dashed against forbidding rocks, and fall down a waterfall, till the life amid the break-

ing china and falling pies of the comic studios seems serene by comparison.

Four years later, *The Times* reviewed a later Kellerman film, *Queen of the Sea,* in less glowing terms:

> At the Academy of Music the new Annette Kellerman film, "Queen of the Sea" was shown for the first time in New York yesterday afternoon. It is not so impressive as Miss Kellerman's previous picture, "Daughter of the Gods," mainly because that film largely exhausted Miss Kellerman's film possibilities, and the present picture can do little more than duplicate the tricks of the other.

Annette Kellerman, lively and enthusiastic, retained her figure and firmness of muscle tone until well into middle age. When she appeared swimming in public, as she often did, onlookers were astonished that this was the same woman they had thrilled to in their youth. A well-educated woman, she spoke French and German fluently and, when lecturing in countries like Denmark, Sweden, or the Netherlands, had her lectures translated into the local languages and learned their pronunciation and accent sufficiently well to present them herself. Although she earned a good living with her performances, dancing, lectures, and demonstrations of swimming and diving, she was not above augmenting her income through endorsements and, in 1917, was seen in advertisements for Black Jack gum. She also worked in the rehabilitation of crippled children through aquatic exercise and undertook to give physical therapy to those willing to pay for it. The silent film actress, *Blanche Sweet, was said to have been under her care for a year. Kellerman's own health was excellent, and in her later years her heart, arteries, and blood pressure remained normal, remarkably so for a woman of her advancing years. Apart from her exploits on stage, on screen, and in the swimming pool, Kellerman was also a successful author, her books include such titles as *How to Swim* (1919), *Physical Beauty: How to Keep It* (1919), and *Fairy Tales of the South Seas* (1926).

Annette Kellerman valued her privacy, maintaining her permanent home in Australia, where she lived quietly with her husband, described as "a small, methodical man." Together, they purchased a small atoll in the Barrier Reef off the northeast coast of Australia known as Pindarus Island, where they spent their weekends whenever they were in Sydney. However, because she was deeply committed to physical fitness, Kellerman was a good interview, ever open to a medium for propagating her views. Speaking in 1932, she was quoted as saying:

> Bathing suits are now more sensible than ever before. I am all for abbreviated bathing suits; the more abbreviated the better. Decency is a question of common sense. Complete nudism, no. . . . The trouble with women today is that so many of them are trying to get too thin. A woman should find out what her normal weight should be. An exaggeration to thinness causes all sorts of nervous complaints and the process is devastating to the health.

Annette Kellerman died on November 6, 1975, at age 87. At the time, she was living as a widow with her sister in Southport, in the Gold Coast resort area of Queensland, Australia. In the last decades of her life, she made it her business to keep out of the public eye and tended to be forgotten. She wrote no autobiography, nor were any books written about her, even in her native land. Her name rarely appears in books on swimming as a sport, and she has generally been overlooked. Although she was the first woman swimmer ever to achieve fame, in summing up her life's work, she always claimed that her greatest achievement was the role she played in liberating women from uncomfortable and impractical bathing wear and thus freeing them for exercise in the water.

In 1952, *Million Dollar Mermaid,* a fictionalized screen biography of Kellerman, was filmed with *Esther Williams in the title role, a logical choice since Williams was the only other female swimming champion to take to the screen and, in this way, not only followed up on what Kellerman had achieved, but may be considered to have been the Annette Kellerman of the talking pictures.

SOURCES:

"Million Dollar Mermaid Dies," in *The New York Times.* November 6, 1975.

"Kellerman, Annette Marie Sarah," in *The Australian Encyclopaedia.* 3rd rev. ed. New York, 1979.

The Free Library of Philadelphia, Theater Collection.

SUGGESTED READING:

"Annette Kellerman, First 'New Woman' of the Modern Age," in *Chicago Sunday Tribune.* April 28, 1938.

"Annette Kellerman," in *People* (Australia). May 23, 1951.

Robert Hewsen,
Professor of History, Rowan University,
Glassboro, New Jersey

Kelley, Abby (1810–1887)

American abolitionist and woman's rights lecturer.
Name variations: Abigail Kelley; Abigail Kelley Foster.
Born Abigail Kelley in Pelham, Massachusetts, on January 15, 1810; died in Worcester, Massachusetts, on January 14, 1887; daughter and fifth of seven children of Wing Kelley (a farmer) and his second wife Diana

*(Daniels) Kelley; attended Quaker schools, including several years at the Friends School, Providence, Rhode Island; married Stephen Symonds Foster (also an abolitionist lecturer), in December 1845 (died 1881); children: one daughter, **Pauline Wright Foster**.*

Abby Kelley was born in Pelham, Massachusetts, in 1810, the daughter of Wing Kelley, a Quaker farmer, and his second wife **Diana Daniels Kelley**. Raised in rural Massachusetts, Abby Kelley was teaching in a Quaker School in Lynn, when she became a follower of abolitionist William Lloyd Garrison. From 1835 to 1837, as secretary of the Lynn Female Anti-Slavery Society, she was involved in door-to-door canvassing, petition collection, and fundraising. In 1838, she joined Garrison in founding the New England Non-Resistant Society, and also participated in the first and second woman's national antislavery conventions in New York and Philadelphia, where she made her first public speech. Kelley was so well received that abolitionist leaders urged her to continue as a lecturer for the cause, and in 1839, she resigned her teaching job. The decision did not come without a price, for traveling the country speaking out publicly was a precarious career for a woman at the time. Not only did Kelley endure the wrath of those opposing her view, but she was denounced as a fallen woman for even daring to mount a public platform.

Abby Kelley

She also became the target of controversy within the movement. During the convention of the American Anti-Slavery Society in 1840, when Kelley was appointed to the business committee, it so angered the male delegates that almost half of them, led by Arthur and Lewis Tappan, left to form the American and Foreign Anti-Slavery Society. Enduring continuing hardships and personal attacks, Kelley continued lecturing, traveling as far west as Indiana and Michigan. During the 1840s, she found an ally in a fellow lecturer, Stephen Symonds Foster, who was even more radical in his views than she. After a four-year courtship on the road, the couple married in 1845 and continued to travel together as a lecture team until 1861. After the birth of her daughter Pauline in 1847, 37-year-old Kelley began to spend more time at the couple's Worcester farm, which also became a haven for fugitive slaves. She was careful, however, to not let domestic duties end her career, and often left her daughter with her husband or relatives while she was on the road.

Abby Kelley was described as a woman of considerable charm, tall, blue-eyed, and quite attractive in her younger days. Because she was totally committed to reform, quite willing, if necessary, to risk health, reputation, and physical safety for the cause, she could also be dogmatic and humorless. Kelley was attracted to various fads of the day, including novelty diets, homeopathy, phrenology, and spiritualism, although they did not distract her from the job at hand. For many, her extreme views represented an unwelcome challenge to the status quo. Summing up the feelings of many of her opponents was an Oberlin professor, who dismissed her as one of those "women of masculine minds and aggressive tendencies . . . who cannot be satisfied in domestic life."

During the 1850s, Abby Kelley also began to address temperance and feminist meetings, including the fourth national woman's rights convention in Cleveland in 1853. By now, she had become so zealous and radical in political philosophy that even her sympathizers began to turn away. Late in the decade, convinced that the abolitionists must organize into a third political party so that the Republicans would not win over their supporters, Kelley and her husband broke with Garrison.

After the Civil War, Kelley was slowed by age and ill health, and generally limited her activities to local affairs. On several occasions during the 1870s, she and her husband, following the example of *Abby and *Julia Smith, refused to pay taxes on their farm, arguing that she, being unable to vote, was taxed without representation. (Each time, friends bought back the farm at auction and returned it to them.) One of Kelley's last speeches was in 1880, at the 30th anniversary of the first national woman's rights convention, in which she denounced the Massachusetts law giving women the franchise in school elections on the grounds that half a vote was worse than none. She died in 1887, several months after attending an abolitionists' reunion organized by *Lucy Stone, who, in a later tribute, called her a heroine. Abby Kelley, "for more than thirty years, stood in the thick of the fight for the

slaves," she wrote, "and at the same time, she hewed out that path over which women are now walking toward their equal political rights."

SOURCES:

"Abby Kelley Foster, Abolitionist," in *A Bright Spot in the City—Abby's House.* Vol 1, no. 4. April 1996.

James, Edward T., ed. *Notable American Women.* Cambridge, MA: The Belknap Press of Harvard University Press, 1971.

McHenry, Robert, *Famous American Women.* NY: Dover, 1981.

Weatherford, Doris. *American Women's History.* NY: Prentice Hall, 1994.

SUGGESTED READING:

Sterling, Dorothy. *Ahead of Her Time: Abby Kelley and the Politics of Anti-Slavery.* NY: W.W. Norton, 1991.

COLLECTIONS:

The Foster-Kelley Family Papers are located at the American Antiquarian Society and the Worcester Historical Society, both at Worcester, Massachusetts.

Barbara Morgan,
Melrose, Massachusetts

Kelley, Florence (1859–1932)

First factory inspector in Illinois and general secretary of the National Consumers' League, who fought against child labor and promoted safer working conditions for all laborers. Name variations: Florence Kelley Wischnewetzky. Often confused with *Florence Finch Kelly (1858–1939). Born Florence Molthrop Kelley on September 12, 1859, in Philadelphia, Pennsylvania; died in Philadelphia on February 17, 1932; daughter of Caroline Bantram (Bonsall) Kelley (a homemaker) and William Darrah Kelley (a lawyer, judge, and congressional representative); schooled at home and at Quaker schools in Philadelphia; received bachelor's degree from Cornell University in 1882; began graduate study in Zurich in 1883; received law degree from Northwestern University in 1894; married Lazare Wischnewetzky, in 1884 (divorced 1892); children: Nicholas Wischnewetzky (b. 1885); Margaret Wischnewetzky (1886–1905); John Bartram Wischnewetzky (b. 1888).

Following graduation from Cornell, traveled to Europe; returned to U.S. (1886); expelled from Socialist Labor Party (1887); was a resident of Hull House (1891); served as investigator for Illinois Bureau of Labor (1892); was chief factory inspector, State of Illinois (1893); dismissed (1897); served as general secretary, National Consumers' League (1899); was an organizer, New York Child Labor Committee (1902); was an organizer, National Child Labor Committee (1904); was an organizer, National Association for the Advancement of Colored People (1909); was a founding member, Women's International League for Peace and Freedom (1919).

Selected publications: four chapters of a projected autobiography appeared in Survey *(October 1, 1926, February 1, April 1, and June 1, 1927); contributed articles to* International Law Review, Survey, American Journal of Sociology, Journal of Political Economy, Annals of the American Academy of Political Economy, Outlook, *and* Century, *as well as other magazines.*

As a seven-year-old, Florence Kelley was taught to read by her father, using what she called a "terrible little book," illustrated with pictures of children no older than herself toiling in the brickyards of England. In the book's woodcuts, sadly disfigured children labored under burdens too heavy for their small frames to bear. It was a deliberate choice on her father's part, showing her the plight of children less fortunate than she. Her early years were filled with such lessons, as her father wished to create in her a social conscience, and to impress upon her the duty to fight against economic injustice. Florence Kelley was a willing pupil. She dedicated the majority of her adult years to a crusade against child labor and for better working conditions for all.

> *E*verybody was brave from the moment she came in the room.
>
> —Newton D. Baker

Born in Philadelphia, Pennsylvania, on September 12, 1859, Florence Kelley entered into a family with long-standing concerns about social issues. She was one of eight children (only three survived childhood) born to **Caroline Bantram Kelley**, a Quaker homemaker, and William Darrah Kelley, an abolitionist and a crusading congressional representative. Kelley noted in her autobiography that her father was a formidable opponent of *laissez-faire* economics of the day, believing in "forty acres and a mule for freedmen, homesteads for immigrants, and tariffs for American manufacture." William Darrah Kelley was the greatest influence in Florence Kelley's early life, and her education consisted of reading his library, top to bottom, before entering Cornell University at the age of 17.

Kelley began her studies at Cornell University in 1876, determined to achieve the education that was unavailable to women at the University of Pennsylvania, in her hometown of Philadelphia. Cornell was very much a leader in coeducation, allowing women relatively equal access to intellectual pursuits, although the college provided no athletics for women. There, she plunged into her studies, remedying her deficiencies in classical languages and mathematics. The thesis she wrote for her bachelor's degree foreshadowed a lifelong interest in the plight of children. She wrote a study of the legal status of children, based not only on statutes, but on labor reports as well. Her work was evidently well received, because she graduated from Cornell in 1882 and was elected to Phi Beta Kappa. *The International Law Review* published her thesis in the same year.

After her graduation, she was to discover that not all institutions of higher learning were as receptive to women as Cornell had been. Kelley wished to study law and applied to the University of Pennsylvania in order to prepare for further study. After a long delay, her application was refused. Instead, she founded an evening school for young working women. She also accompanied her brother on a trip to Europe, and while abroad discovered that the University of Zurich had opened its doors to women. In September of 1883, she began her studies there.

While in Zurich, Florence Kelley was enlisted to translate into English Friedrich Engels' volume, *The Condition of the Working Classes in England in 1844,* and the translation coincided with her conversion to socialism. On June 1, 1884, she also married Lazare Wischnewetzky, a Russian socialist, who was a medical student. Their first child, Nicholas, was born in Zurich on July 12, 1885.

In 1886, Florence Kelley returned to the United States with her husband and young son, settling in New York City just before the birth of her daughter, Margaret. She intended to be an active member of the Socialist Labor Party but soon found herself expelled. The Socialist Labor Party was a German enclave, and Florence Kelley, with her impeccable credentials as a native-born American, was almost immediately in conflict with the group. Kelley had assumed that her personal relationship with Engels entitled her to a special position within the party, an assertion with which the other members did not agree.

Little is known about her family life in this period. There is no information about her husband's practice of medicine, or how the family supported itself during its time in New York. Kelley's third child, John, was born in January of 1888, and, sometime in the first half of that year, her husband experienced a serious bout of rheumatic fever. Kelley also began a work, never completed, on child labor in the United States. She believed that the problem of child labor was far more widespread and appalling than most people knew, and proposed that minimum wage laws and compulsory school attendance were the solution to the problem. She advocated government intervention in the form of factory inspectors, truant officers, and financial support for orphans. Although she never wrote the book she had planned, her pamphlet "Our Toiling Children," brought attention to the subject and to Kelley. In articles and speeches, she continued to attack the problem.

In 1891, Kelley's life took a dramatic turn, as she packed her bags and took her children with her to Illinois. Her marriage to Wischnewetzky had dissolved, for reasons unknown, and she wished a divorce on the grounds of non-support. Under New York law, she would have only been allowed a separation; Illinois law provided for divorce. The children remained for a time with the family of Henry Demarest Lloyd, while she established herself at Hull House, in Chicago. All around her, she found opportunities to fight the evil of child labor. In the multiethnic neighborhoods surrounding Hull House, the families were uniformly poor and forced to put their children to work at an early age. In her autobiography, Kelley claimed that even children as young as 18 months were not immune from the shared labor of piecework in their parents' homes.

In 1892, Kelley suggested that the Illinois Bureau of Labor Statistics investigate the sweatshops of Chicago, and the Bureau named her as the agent to conduct the investigation. The U.S. Bureau of Labor also asked Kelley to conduct an intensive study of an area near Hull House as a part of a national examination of city slums. The resulting reports led the state legislature to pass the Factories and Workshops Act, which required a number of reforms, such as cleanliness in the workplace, a minimum age of 16 for all workers, and limitations on the numbers of hours of work for women. Enforcement of the law was to be insured by state factory inspectors. Kelley, under the Illinois law, became the first woman in the United States to be appointed a state's chief factory inspector.

Kelley used her position as chief factory inspector to promote her concerns about the welfare of children. Her inspectors ferreted out more than 8,000 underage children in Illinois factories and pushed for public and private relief for families whose children worked out of financial necessity. She also fought with local school boards, trying to force them to abide by compulsory attendance laws. Concerned about the plight of women workers as well, she attempted to enforce the state's eight-hour law for women in industry, but the Illinois Supreme Court overturned restrictions on women's hours of work in 1895. Perhaps as a result of her vigorous pursuit of the law, a new governor, John R. Tanner, replaced Kelley with a less forceful factory inspector in 1897. She remained in Illinois only two more years. In 1898, she helped to organize the Illinois Consumers' League and, a year later, returned to New York as the general secretary of the National Consumers' League.

In her position with the National Consumers' League, Kelley continued to promote those issues she held most dear, such as child-labor laws, factory safety laws, and regulation of the labor of women. The National Consumers' League sought to reform the behavior of manufacturers through the purchasing power of the American woman. The League encouraged women, who made the majority of purchases for their families, to buy only those products adorned with the League's "white label," showing that they had been produced by responsible manufacturers.

Kelley's work for the National Consumers' League was not her only concern. On her return to New York, she had moved with her children to *Lillian Wald's Henry Street Settlement house. There, she helped organize the New York Child Labor Committee in 1902 and the National Child Labor Committee in 1904. Her daughter's death in 1905 may have pushed her to even greater efforts on behalf of children in the workplace. In 1907, the U.S. Supreme Court heard the case of *Muller* v. *Oregon,* deciding the constitutionality of an Oregon law restricting women to a ten-hour work day. Kelley and her colleague *Josephine Goldmark were instrumental in persuading Louis D. Brandeis to prepare his famous brief in favor of the protection of women in the workplace. Following the success of the case, Kelley continued to promote maximum hours and minimum wages for women in industry.

A great believer in racial equality, Kelley was also one of the organizers of the National Association for the Advancement of Colored People (NAACP) in 1909. As a pacifist, she was a founding member of the Women's International League for Peace and Freedom in 1919. She was also a member of the National Woman Suffrage Association, but, unlike many of her fellow suffragists, did not support the Equal Rights Amendment. As a promoter of protective legislation for women, she did not wish to see an amendment passed that might endanger her work.

The 1920s were a difficult decade for Kelley. After the reform enthusiasm that the nation had experienced during the Progressive Era, the '20s were a grave disappointment. Many of the laws for which she had fought succumbed to the decade's commitment to cooperation between government and business. The Supreme Court struck down minimum-wage and maximum-hour legislation, as well as child-labor laws. The only bright spot was the passage of the Sheppard-Towner Maternity and Infancy Act in 1921. The act provided for public health nurses to teach maternal and child welfare; unfortunately, it was discontinued by the decade's end. Kelley's frustrations were enormous. Knowing that the courts would not support child-labor legislation, Kelley began a struggle for an amendment to the U.S. Constitution, barring child labor. For her troubles, she was castigated by many organizations as an unpatriotic radical. Her proposal made little headway.

One of Kelley's last crusades was against industrial poisoning in the dial-painting industry. In 1924, it came to her attention that a number of women workers at the U.S. Radium Corporation in Newark, New Jersey, were either ill or dying. The women placed glowing paint, containing radium, on the dials of clocks. In the painting process, they repeatedly placed the brushes in their mouths, and some had developed horrific jaw diseases. No amount of treatment could save them. Kelley believed that the Consumers' League would have to take action.

Studies undertaken by scientists soon proved that radium poisoning existed and was responsible for the women's injuries and deaths. Researchers found that the bones of the women who had died from radium poisoning were so saturated by the material that even four or five years after their deaths they glowed with the element. The women of the Consumers' League determined that they would ask the surgeon general for an investigation of the problem, and the development of a means to protect industrial workers from the effects of radium. The result was regulation of the manufacture of products using the substance. Workers would no longer "point" brushes with their lips, or inhale radium vapors.

When Florence Kelley died in Philadelphia on February 17, 1932, she was 73 years old. For more than 30 years, she had vigorously pursued reform issues. Her confrontational style had won her enemies as well as admirers. Although not as well known as her contemporaries *Jane Addams and *Julia Lathrop, she was instrumental in promoting the idea that childhood was a time for learning, rather than toil, and that all laborers had the right to humane working conditions. Florence Kelley was a powerful woman who refused to sit on the sidelines; instead, she sought to create her own opportunities.

SOURCES:

Blumberg, Dorothy Rose. *Florence Kelley: The Making of a Social Pioneer*. NY: Augustus M. Kelley, 1966.

Goldmark, Josephine. *Impatient Crusader*. Urbana, IL: University of Illinois, 1953.

Harmon, Sandra D. "Florence Kelley in Illinois," in *Journal of the Illinois State Historical Society*. Vol. LXXIV, no. 3. Autumn 1981, pp. 163–178.

Kelley, Florence. *Notes of Sixty Years: The Autobiography of Florence Kelley*. Chicago, IL: Charles H. Kerr, 1986.

SUGGESTED READING:

Muncy, Robyn. *Creating a Female Dominion in American Reform, 1890–1935*. NY: Oxford University Press, 1991.

COLLECTIONS:

Kelley Family Papers, Columbia University; papers of the National Consumers' League, Library of Congress.

Pamela Riney-Kehrberg,
Associate Professor of History,
Illinois State University, Normal, Illinois

Kellogg, Clara Louise (1842–1916)

American soprano, impresario, and first American-born prima donna to achieve a solid reputation in Europe who organized her own opera company. Born Clara Louise Kellogg in Sumterville (now Sumter), South Carolina, on July 9, 1842; died of cancer at her home Elpstone, in New Hartford, Connecticut, on May 13, 1916; interred in nearby Town Hill Cemetery; daughter of George Kellogg (an inventor, schoolteacher, and graduate of Wesleyan University) and Jane Elizabeth (Crosby) Kellogg (a schoolteacher who was considered an excellent musician); studied with Achille Errani and Emanuele Muzio; married Carl Strakosch (nephew of her former manager Max Strakosch), on November 9, 1887.

Clara Louise Kellogg

America's first prima donna and one of the first female impresarios, Clara Louise Kellogg was born in Sumterville, South Carolina in 1842. Throughout her career, she worked to bring opera to the American stage. Kellogg learned music from her parents who took her to New York in 1856 for further study with Achille Errani and Emanuele Muzio. On February 27, 1861, she debuted as Gilda in Verdi's *Rigoletto* at the Academy of Music. On November 23, 1863, she sang Marguerite in the first New York performance of Gounod's *Faust* which became the most popular opera in America for the next three decades. For half of that period, Kellogg was closely identified with this opera. French composer Hector Berlioz, who was in the United States at the time, was astonished at her skill in interpreting the subtler shadings of the poet, which he believed were beyond the reach of lyric art. In 1867, she made her London debut in the same role at Her Majesty's Theater and was again triumphant. She also sang in the Handel Festival held in the great Crystal Palace, a great honor for an American.

Clara Kellogg began a successful four-year tour of the United States in 1868 and was met throughout by crowded houses. At tour's end, she decided to form her own opera company with *Pauline Lucca (1872). Following that, she directed the English Opera Company (1873–76). In her role as impresario, Kellogg guided translations, helped construct stage sets, and supervised rehearsals. Extremely energetic, she managed to sing 125 performances in the 1874–75 season alone. This pioneer effort in presenting grand opera in English took a great deal of energy, as Americans had little experience with opera. In 1887, she married Carl Strakosch, the nephew of her former manager Max Strakosch, and retired from the stage. Kellogg had sung more than 40 roles including Aïda, Carmen, and Lucia in Donizetti's *Linda de Chamounix*. In youth, her voice was a high soprano with a range from C to E flat; with age, it lost some of the highest notes but gained in power and richness. Her memoirs contain "acute observations" on contemporary artists, including *Adelina Patti and *Lillian Nordica.

SOURCES:

Sadie, Stanley, ed. *New Grove Dictionary of Music and Musicians*. 20 vols. NY: Macmillan, 1980.

Warrack, John, and Ewan West. *Oxford Dictionary of Opera*. Oxford University Press, 1992.

SUGGESTED READING:

Kellogg, Clara Louise. *Memoirs of an American Prima Donna*. New York, 1913 (revised 1978).

John Haag,
Athens, Georgia

Kellogg, Louise Phelps (1862–1942)

American historian. Born Eva Louise Phelps Kellogg in Milwaukee, Wisconsin, on May 12, 1862; died in Madison, Wisconsin, on July 11, 1942; one of two

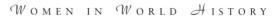

daughters (her younger sister died in infancy) of Amherst Willoughby Kellogg (an insurance executive) and Mary Isabella (Phelps) Kellogg; attended school in Evanston, Illinois; attended Dearborn Seminary, Chicago; graduated from Milwaukee College, 1882; University of Wisconsin, B.L., 1897; attended the Sorbonne and the London School of History and Economics, 1898–99; University of Wisconsin, Ph.D., 1901; never married; no children.

Born in Milwaukee, Wisconsin, in 1862, historian Louise Kellogg, who dropped her given name Eva, grew up there and in Evanston, Illinois. After attending Dearborn Seminary in Chicago and graduating from Milwaukee College (later Milwaukee-Downer), Kellogg taught in private schools for 13 years before entering the University of Wisconsin in 1895, as a junior. Upon receiving her B.L. degree in 1897, she embarked on graduate work in American history. Awarded a travel fellowship from the Woman's Education Association of Boston, she spent a year studying at the Sorbonne and at the London School of History and Economics. She returned to the University of Wisconsin to continue her graduate studies under Frederick Jackson Turner, receiving her Ph.D. in 1901. (Her thesis, *The American Colonial Charter,* was later awarded the American Historical Association's Justin Winsor Prize.) After receiving her advanced degree, Kellogg was appointed research and editorial assistant to Reuben Gold Thwaites, executive director of the State Historical Society of Wisconsin.

Until his death in 1913, Kellogg assisted Thwaites in editing and publishing some 40 volumes of documents from the Society's collection. She then continued the work they had begun together, editing three volumes on her own: *Frontier Advance on the Upper Ohio* (1916), *Frontier Retreat on the Upper Ohio* (1917), and *Early Narratives of the Northwest, 1634–1699* (1917). During this time, she also edited a Caxton Club edition of *Charlevoix's Journal of a Voyage to North America* (two volumes, 1923). Kellogg then began to write her most successful and highly regarded work, *The French Régime in Wisconsin and the Northwest,* published in 1925. Over the next decade, while contributing numerous articles to scholarly journals, she wrote a companion volume, *The British Régime in Wisconsin and the Northwest* (1935). As an established authority on the history of the region, Kellogg was also in demand as a lecturer and radio speaker and held memberships in numerous professional organizations and honorary

societies. As she gained notoriety, she was awarded a number of honorary degrees and was made a fellow of the British Royal Historical Society. In 1930, she was the first woman to be elected president of the Mississippi Valley Historical Association (later the Organization of American Historians), and, in 1935, she received the prestigious Lapham Medal from the Wisconsin Archaeological Society.

During her 40-year tenure at the State Historical Society, Kellogg became an invaluable source of information and encouragement to countless students and scholars. Described by one young associate as "wearing her scholarship easily," she had a constant stream of drop-ins to her first floor office. As she aged and grew quite deaf, she carried with her a large, unwieldy hearing machine which she would nonchalantly place between herself and her visitor so as not to miss a word. A staunch Methodist, until her later years when she became an Episcopalian, she also carried her hearing device to church each Sunday, placing it midway between her seat in the front pew and the pulpit.

Kellogg, who never married, lived with her father until his death in 1923. Age apparently did not dim her mind or her enthusiasm for new adventures. In her 70s, she purchased a car, hired a chauffeur, and embarked with her cousin on a trip to California. At the age of 79, she traveled to historic Vincennes, Indiana, then continued on to Lexington, Kentucky, to attend a meeting of the Mississippi Valley Historical Association. Clara Kellogg died of an embolism in 1942 and was buried in the family plot in Forest Home Cemetery in Milwaukee. A portrait of the historian, commissioned by her friends, hangs in the editorial offices of the State Historical Society of Wisconsin.

SOURCES:
James, Edward T., ed. *Notable American Women, 1607–1950.* Cambridge, MA: The Belknap Press of Harvard University Press, 1971.
McHenry, Robert. *Famous American Women.* NY: Dover, 1983.

Barbara Morgan,
Melrose, Massachusetts

Kellor, Frances Alice (1873–1952).
See Dreier Sisters for sidebar.

Kelly, Edna Flannery (1906–1997)
Democratic congressional representative from New York (1949–69). Born Edna Patricia Kathleen Flannery on August 20, 1906, in East Hampton, Long Island, New York; died in Alexandria, Virginia, on December

14, 1997; one of seven daughters (two of whom were adopted) of Patrick Joseph Flannery (a horticulturist) and Mary Ellen (McCarthy) Flannery; graduated from East Hampton (New York) High School; Hunter College, New York, B.A., in 1928; married Edward Leo Kelly (a lawyer), in June 1928 (died); children: William Edward Kelly; Maura Patricia Kelly.

The longest serving congresswoman from New York (20 years beginning in 1949), Edna Flannery Kelly was one of seven daughters of Patrick Joseph Flannery, a horticulturist, and **Mary Ellen Flannery**, and the only one who did not become a schoolteacher. Born and raised in East Hampton, Long Island, Edna graduated from Hunter College in 1928, and that same year married Brooklyn attorney Edward Kelly. While her husband enjoyed an active political life, Kelly's life centered mainly on her home and family, which soon included two children.

Following her husband's death in an automobile accident in 1942, life changed for the young housewife, who became active in politics "to carry on in the Kelly family tradition." Put in charge of the women's auxiliary of the Madison Democratic Club by district leader Irwin Steingut, Kelly proceeded to work in a succession of party offices beginning with her election in 1944 to the Democratic executive committee of Kings County, New York. Reelected to three consecutive terms on the committee, Kelly also served as research director for the Democratic Party in the New York State legislature from 1943 to 1949.

In 1949, Kelly was chosen as the Democratic candidate to fill the vacancy caused by the death of Representative Andrew L. Somers. She was probably selected because of her experience in Albany, she surmised. "Perhaps, too," she was quick to add, "the leaders may have decided that it would be a sound thing for the Democratic Party in Brooklyn to express its confidence in women by nominating one to run in an election that looked like a sure thing." Indeed, Kelly defeated her Republican and Liberal rivals handily, becoming the fourth woman from New York State to serve in the House of Representatives At the onset, she vowed to fly home each weekend so that she could be available to her constituents and to her children who remained in Brooklyn.

Edna Kelly's tenure was marked by her support of federal social and economic programs and her concern for U.S. interests in defense and foreign aid. She served on the Committee on Foreign Affairs and chaired its Subcommittee on Europe, as well as a special Subcommittee on the Canada-United States Inter-Parliamentary group. She proposed legislation to extend rent control, to provide working mothers with tax cuts, and to require the Post Office to cancel mail with the postmark reading, "In God We Trust." She also introduced a number of bills to provide equal pay for women. As a foe of communism, she sponsored a successful amendment to President Truman's 1952 foreign aid request which suspended aid to Yugoslavia. Her amendment to the Agricultural Trade Development and Assistance Act of 1954, outlawing the sale of farm surplus commodities to the Soviet Union, was also successful. She later supported a higher minimum wage and lower retirement age requirements for beneficiaries of old age and survivors' insurance benefits.

In 1968, the New York Legislature divided Kelly's district between the Twelfth District and the Tenth District of long-time Representative Emanuel Celler. In a bid to unseat Celler, who had not been challenged since he entered Con-

Edna Flannery Kelly

gress in 1923, Kelly lost the June primary, receiving only 32% of the vote in a three-way race. In later years, she made her home in Alexandria, Virginia.

SOURCES:
Office of the Historian. *Women in Congress, 1917–1990.* Commission on the Bicentenary of the U.S. House of Representatives, 1991.

Barbara Morgan,
Melrose, Massachusetts

Kelly, Emily "Pat" (?–1922)

British mountain and rock climber. Birth date unknown; died in 1922, following a fall on Tryfan; married Harry Kelly (a rock climber).

Primarily a rock climber, Pat Kelly, who loved solo climbing, helped found the Pinnacle Club in 1921 and was its first honorary secretary. It was the earliest rock climbing club founded by and for women. "Perhaps we got tired of being taken in hand by men climbers, kind and helpful though they may be," said Kelly, "perhaps we sympathised with the would-be climbing woman who had no man friend to take her in tow; what would then become of her latent climbing powers, if she were never to be able to exercise them, except by favour? As in other walks of life, women wanted to find their own feet."

SOURCES:
Birkett, Bill, and Bill Peascod. *Women Climbing: 200 Years of Achievement.* London: A. & C. Black, 1989.

Kelly, Ethel (1875–1949)

Canadian-born Australian actress and author. Name variations: Ethel Mollison. Born Ethel Knight Mollison on January 28, 1875, in St. John, New Brunswick, Canada; died on September 22, 1949, in Sidney, Australia; elder daughter of William Knight Mollison (a merchant) and Margaret (Millen) Mollison; educated in St. John; married a man named Moore around 1893 (died around 1894); married Thomas Herbert Kelly (a metal merchant), on August 29, 1903; children; two sons and two daughters.

Ethel Kelly was born in 1875 in St. John, New Brunswick, Canada, and was educated there and in Britain. She enjoyed reading and dramatics as a child and, in 1893, made her stage debut in the play *A Mischievous Miss,* produced in St. John. Around this time, she married a man named Moore and moved to New York. Widowed within a year, she remained in the

United States, where for the next eight years she was associated with a number of major stage companies. Acting under her maiden name, she appeared in such classics in *Cyrano de Bergerac* and *The Taming of the Shrew.* In 1903, while on tour on tour in Australia, Kelly married metal merchant Thomas Kelly, after which she left the professional stage. The couple settled in Melbourne, where Kelly raised a family (two sons and two daughters), and pursued a number of charitable activities. A visit to India inspired her first book, *Frivolous Peeps at India,* which was published in 1911.

During World War I, Kelly used her theatrical experience to stage a number of fund-raising events. From 1922 to 1923, she served as the woman's page editor of *Smith's Weekly.* One of her assignments took her to Tutankhamun's tomb in Egypt, which inspired a second novel, *Why the Sphinx Smiles* (1925). Another novel, *Zara* (1927), and her memoirs, *Twelve Milestones* (1929), were completed in Italy while she was supervising her daughters' education. Returning to Australia in 1934, she and her husband built an Italian villa at Darling Point, near Sydney. In 1937, she served as the president of the Pageant of Nations advisory committee for the 150th Anniversary Celebration.

During World War II, Kelly was involved in numerous charitable organizations including the French-Australian League of Help, the Victoria League, the St. John Ambulance Association, and the French Red Cross Societies. She subsequently raised money for St. Vincent's hospitals, the Kindergarten Union of New South Wales, and the Actors' Benevolent Fund. In private life, she shared her husband's love of music and enjoyed collecting antiques. Kelly died in September 1949.

SOURCES:
Radi, Heather, ed. *200 Australian Women.* NSW, Australia: Women's Redress Press, 1988.

Barbara Morgan,
Melrose, Massachusetts

Kelly, Eva Mary (1826–1910).
See O'Doherty, Mary Anne.

Kelly, Florence Finch (1858–1939)

American journalist and author who worked at The New York Times Book Review *for three decades beginning in 1905. Often confused with *Florence Kelley (1859–1932). Born in Girard, Illinois, on March 27, 1858; died in New Hartford, Connecticut, on December 17, 1939; youngest of six sons and two daugh-*

ters of James Gardner Finch (a farmer) and Mary Ann (Purdom) Finch; briefly attended a county high school, Miami County, Kansas; graduated from the University of Kansas, 1881; married Allen P. Kelly (newspaper publisher), on December 9, 1884: children: son who died in childhood; Sherwin Kelly, a geophysicist.

Selected writings: With Hoops of Steel (1900); The Delafield Affair (1909); What America Did: An Everyman's Story of the War (1919); Flowing Stream (1939).

One of eight children of **Mary Ann Finch** and James Finch, a farmer, Florence Finch Kelly was born in 1858 in Girard, Illinois, but spent much of her girlhood in Miami County, Kansas, where her family moved when she was 11. Kelly aspired to a writing career from an early age, but found it necessary to work as a teacher for two years before she could properly educate herself. Graduating from the University of Kansas in 1881, she worked briefly in Chicago before settling in Boston, where she worked as a reporter and columnist for the *Globe* for three years. She left the *Globe*, dissatisfied with the low pay and lack of recognition, and worked on a paper in Troy, New York, before joining *Globe* colleague Allen P. Kelly in his attempt to established a newspaper in Lowell, Massachusetts (*The Lowell Bell*). The paper failed, but Florence's relationship with Allen flourished, and the couple married in 1884. They had two sons; the first died before he was five, and the second, Sherwin, grew up to become a geophysicist. For many years, the couple criss-crossed the country, working on newspapers in San Francisco, New Mexico, Los Angeles, and Philadelphia. In addition to her newspaper writing, Kelly wrote three novels during the 1890s, publishing them anonymously or under a pseudonym.

Widowed at the age of 47, Florence Kelly moved with her ten-year-old son to New York, where she secured a job reviewing books for *The New York Times*. She stayed there for three decades, eventually earning her own byline. In support of publisher Adolph Ochs' goal of "democratizing" literature, she turned out hundreds of reviews a year, mostly of nonfiction. In addition to reviews, she contributed feature stories, interviews, and syndicated articles to the paper. On her own time, she published another half-dozen books of fiction and nonfiction. In 1916, she took a leave of absence from the paper to campaign for the reelection of Woodrow Wilson. Kelly retired at the age of 78 and died in

1939, shortly after completing her autobiography *Flowing Stream.*

SOURCES:

Edgerly, Lois Stiles. *Give Her This Day.* Gardiner, ME: Tilbury House, 1990.

James, Edward T., ed. *Notable American Women, 1607–1950.* Cambridge, MA: The Belknap Press of Harvard University, 1971.

Weatherford, Doris. *American Women's History.* NY: Prentice Hall, 1994.

Barbara Morgan,
Melrose, Massachusetts

Kelly, Grace (1928–1982)

American stage and film actress who won an Academy Award, then walked away from Hollywood to marry the prince of Monaco. Name variations: Princess Grace of Monaco; Grace Grimaldi. Born on November 12, 1928, in Philadelphia, Pennsylvania; died in an automobile crash, age 52, on September 14, 1982; third of four children of Jack Kelly (a self-made millionaire) and Margaret (Majer) Kelly; married Prince Rainier III of Monaco, on April 18, 1956; children: Princess Caroline Grimaldi (b. 1957); Prince Albert Grimaldi (b. 1958); Princess Stephanie Grimaldi (b. 1965).

Attended private schools before moving to New York and studying acting; won her first Broadway role (1949), attracting the attention of Hollywood with her sophisticated manner and classic beauty; was cast in her first major film role, opposite Gary Cooper in High Noon *(1952); won an Oscar as Best Actress for her work in* The Country Girl *(1954); starred in three of Alfred Hitchcock's most successful films; announced her retirement from show business on her marriage to Prince Rainier III of Monaco (1956), becoming known to the world from then on as Her Serene Highness Grace, princess of Monaco, a glamorous addition to the world's royal families; never returned to the screen, although there were persistent rumors that she might until her death in an automobile crash at age 52.*

Filmography: Fourteen Hours *(1951);* High Noon *(1952);* Mogambo *(1953);* Dial M for Murder *(1954);* Rear Window *(1954);* The Country Girl *(1954);* Green Fire *(1954);* The Bridges at Toko-Ri *(1955);* To Catch a Thief *(1955);* The Swan *(1956);* High Society *(1956).*

The studio was small and dingy, clods of dust floating down from the lighting grid and grimy dirt coating the concrete walls. It was noisy, too, that August day in 1951 as the set crew banged and rattled, lighting grips shouted out to one another from overhead and prop carts wheeled to and fro with the paraphernalia needed to create an Old West interior. Director Fred Zinnemann thought the blonde, blue-eyed, elegantly dressed young woman who walked uncertainly into the chaos had taken a wrong turn on her way to somewhere more suited to her white gloves, tailored suit, and high-heeled shoes. The woman was, in fact, his leading lady in the Western to begin shooting in a few days. "She was beautiful in a prim sort of way," Zinnemann later described his first sight of Grace Kelly. It was exactly the impression that he wanted for the character of Amy Kane in *High Noon*, and it was exactly what Grace would need for the real-life role she would play in the future as Her Serene Highness Grace, princess of Monaco.

"I was terribly shy when I was young," Princess Grace once said. "I was so bland, they kept having to introduce me again and again before people noticed me." The competition, it must be said, had been tough in the rambunctious Kelly household. Grace was the third of Jack and **Margaret Kelly**'s four children, all born in the grand brick house on a hill overlooking Philadelphia's East Falls section. Jack, an Irish Catholic and one of ten children, had been a mere bricklayer before borrowing money to start his own construction business, turning it into one of the biggest contracting firms on the East Coast, and marrying Margaret Majer in 1924. He was the horror of Philadelphia's stodgy Main Line, a self-made millionaire. Margaret was from a comfortably genteel background. She was also beautiful, with lustrous blonde hair and the kind of square, regular features that were the blue-blooded emblems of good breeding and taste in those days. Grace was born on November 12, 1928, three years after her older sister **Peggy Kelly**, always her father's favorite, and her handsome brother Jack, Jr. A younger sister, **Lizette Kelly**, arrived two years after Grace.

Throughout childhood, Grace was known as the quietest of the four Kelly children, even after she began attending the Catholic girls' school Margaret had chosen for her three daughters, Ravenhill. It was someone outside the immediate Kelly household who would draw Grace out of her shell. Uncle George Kelly, one of Jack's numerous siblings, had built his living out of words rather than bricks. He was an actor turned playwright who had enjoyed several successes on Broadway stages of the early 20th century. One of his plays, *Craig's Wife,* had won a Pulitzer Prize in 1926, and several had been made into films in the early 1930s with stars like

Spencer Tracy and ***Joan Crawford**. Grace's visits to his home around the corner from Jack's brick mansion were filled with stories of her uncle's adventures in the theater, the dapper George acting out all the parts of his tales. By the time George began spending considerable amounts of time in Hollywood, where he had been hired by MGM as a script doctor, his magic had done its work. Shy Grace Patricia began appearing in school plays, and could send her schoolmates into fits of giggles with her parodies of her sisters. At 12, she had made her stage debut with the Old Academy Players, a local amateur group that included one of her mother's brothers. She told her father that she intended to be an actress, a statement that Jack shrugged off as adolescent fantasy.

When do I get to be just a person?
—Grace Kelly, 1956

At 14, Grace was sent off to the Stevens School, a finishing school for young ladies of quality. Grace learned deportment, household management, proper teatime etiquette and all the other skills required of a genteel young woman, all the while continuing to appear in amateur theatrical productions. With her parents' approval, she began dating toward the end of her time at Stevens and was a popular companion, putting everyone at their ease with a certain bonhomie that boys found attractive. "She was attentive to her dates," one of them remembered years later. "She made each escort think he was King Bee." She did not resist displays of physical attraction, either, remembering in particular the blue roadster of one of her most ardent suitors. "I hope it's safely in the scrapyard," Her Serene Highness impishly told an interviewer nearly 20 years later. "Just think of the tales that back seat could tell."

Graduating from Stevens in 1947, Kelly won admission to the American Academy of Dramatic Arts in New York. The enrollment list that year was full, but her Uncle George's name still carried enough weight in New York theatrical circles for room to be made for her. Her parents made sure she was securely installed at the venerable, women-only Barbizon Hotel on Lexington Avenue, where the vulnerable tenants were guarded by a platoon of lobby security guards. Grace supplemented her Academy education with voice lessons; she supplemented her income with modeling jobs after a friend showed a snapshot of her to an advertising agency. Shorn of her glasses and ten pounds lighter, Kelly's all-American good looks now sold cigarettes, handcreams and toothpastes, and adorned the covers of *Redbook* and *Cosmopolitan.* Her earnings were dutifully sent home to Jack to pay for her tuition and her hotel room.

Grace was, in fact, spending less and less time at the Barbizon, for men were fascinated by her. She had a certain cool, aloof manner that intrigued them, and a passionate response to their advances that surprised them. Kelly had discovered the pleasures of sex not long after her arrival in New York after finding herself alone with the husband of a friend. "We were just talking," she claimed afterward, "and the next thing I knew we were in bed." It was the only such encounter with the errant husband, and the succession of men whom Grace dated had no inkling of her enthusiasm for sex until the suggestion was made. "She was always shy, that's why I liked her so much," one of them recalled many years later. "She didn't dress as the sort of girl that would jump into bed with you." But when he reached out and touched her knee one evening in the back of a taxi, he went on, "she just jumped right into my arms. I could not believe it. She was the very opposite of how she seemed." Her first serious relationship was with one of her acting teachers at the Academy, a liaison quickly cut short when her rigorously Catholic parents discovered her paramour was in the midst of a divorce and was Jewish. Both discoveries were made by Margaret, who secretly inspected the contents of the young man's suitcase during a weekend visit to Philadelphia with Grace and found legal papers relating to the pending divorce. Her mission was accomplished while the lover was downstairs telling Jack that his daughter would one day be a movie star. "Don't worry, she'll soon get over *that!*" Jack guffawed.

As if to prove her father wrong, Kelly was one of only two American Academy students to be chosen at graduation for the Bucks County Playhouse's 1949 summer season, during which she was cast as the ingenue in a play of her Uncle George's, *The Torch Bearers.* She enchanted a local reviewer, who wrote: "For a young lady whose previous experience was slim, Miss Kelly came through this footlight baptism of fire splendidly." Jack was impressed enough to bring friends to see his daughter perform, and allowed her to return to New York for her Broadway debut in August Strindberg's *The Father,* playing Raymond Massey's daughter. Jack installed Grace in a sprawling complex on 66th Street for which he had been a principal contractor, where Kelly promptly resumed her affair with the acting teacher, inviting threatening phone calls to

her lover from her brother and an attempt to buy him off with a Jaguar from her father. Neither was effective, although the affair gradually faded as Grace's play opened in November of 1949 and Broadway sat up and took notice. "Grace Kelly gives a charming, pliable performance," Brooks Atkinson told his *New York Times* readers; while George Jean Nathan, who rarely liked anything he saw, thought that "only the novice Grace Kelly . . . relieves the stage from the air of a minor hinterland stock company on one of its off days." *The Father* had a respectable two-month run, after which hopes for a successful theatrical future quickly faded. "People were confused about my type," Kelly later said, "but they agreed on one thing. I was in the 'too' category— too tall, too leggy, too chinny."

Television came to the rescue. She first appeared in January of 1950 in a network adaptation of a Sinclair Lewis novel, the first of some 60 television roles that taught her more about her craft than she had learned in any classroom. Kelly quickly established a reputation for taking a part on short notice and learning it in just a few days, a valuable talent in an era before videotaped performances. Some years later, after she had graduated to feature films, an amazed Cary Grant asked how she learned dialogue so quickly. "Dozens of soaps," replied Kelly.

She continued to enjoy the company of men, including the banqueting manager of the Waldorf who invited her to attend a reception at the venerable hotel for the visiting Shah of Iran, touring the United States on his first diplomatic mission to America. The shah, then one of the world's most eligible bachelors, was so taken with Kelly that the two seemed inseparable during his week-long stay. It was Grace's first experience with royalty, and she never forgot how the entire house at the Metropolitan Opera rose to its feet in applause to mark the shah's appearance in the box reserved for him and his demurely beautiful companion. By week's end, the shah had proposed marriage. Grace politely refused, still determined on an acting career and telling her mother later that, in any event, she did not love the man. Margaret insisted she give back the opulent jewelry which the shah had bestowed on her, but Kelly stubbornly refused. Nor did she return the bracelet known to be the standard gift of the wealthy playboy Aly Khan for beautiful young ladies whom he had taken to bed. Grace sported the bracelet for another lover as a signal that she was not his alone. "She had become a career carnivore," the lover bitterly claimed later. "She was rapacious about getting famous and being important."

Grace
Kelly

Kelly's combination of cool professionalism and high-profile love affairs was making her very famous, indeed. She was offered her first movie role in 1950 in an unusual film released by Fox called *Fourteen Hours,* an experiment in gritty storytelling in which Grace was one of a number of characters whose lives are examined as a man threatens, over the time period of the film's title, to jump to his death from a building ledge. Kelly's screentime was short, and she was identified only as "lady in lawyer's office," the office being across from the building where the main drama is unfolding. She refused Fox's offer of the standard seven-year contract after she completed work on the picture, having no intention of becoming one of a stable of young hopefuls.

That same year, independent producer Stanley Kramer was searching for the female lead in *High Noon*. The film's budget was such that Kramer could only afford one star, and that was to be Gary Cooper. Kelly's alert agent sent pictures. "I couldn't afford anybody else, so I signed her," Kramer later said of his decision to hire Grace to play Amy Kane, the prim Quaker wife to Cooper's sheriff. For Kelly, it was another opportunity to act in a film while avoiding, because of Kramer's independent status, a long-term contract. There was the added benefit of playing opposite Cooper, ruggedly handsome, talented, 25 years her senior, and separated from his wife. "Grace was very serious about her work," Cooper remembered years later, "and she had her eyes and ears open. She was trying to learn, you could see that." Cooper could apparently see something else, too, for not far into *High Noon*'s 28-day shooting schedule in the Sonoma Mountains, and despite the fact that she was being chaperoned by her younger sister Lizette, Grace and her leading man became lovers. Margaret quickly flew to California and chaperoned Grace through the final days of the shoot.

Although *High Noon* became one of the most famous Westerns ever made, mythical in its stark confrontation between good and evil, Kelly hated her work in it. She was mortified that while Cooper's great talent silently communicated every emotion, she had no such gift. "I thought, 'God! This girl may not make it unless she does something very quickly.' I was horrified," she said, "I was miserable." Classes at New York's Neighborhood Playhouse with Sanford Meisner helped Kelly put more emotion into her acting, although her next role was as another inhibited woman, Linda Nordley, in MGM's *Mogambo*. Instead of the Sonoma Mountains with Gary Cooper, it was Africa with Clark Gable, 30 years her senior and between wives.

Kelly had carefully arranged her own terms before signing the studio contract she had been avoiding, making sure that clauses were inserted that allowed her to live in New York between pictures, limited her to three pictures a year, and allowed her to appear in the legitimate theater as her schedule permitted. For *Mogambo*, her first picture for MGM, Grace was cast in the second lead, behind *Ava Gardner (then Mrs. Frank Sinatra) as the proper married Englishwoman whose hidden passions are aroused by Gable's

big game hunter. It was a remake of 1932's *Red Dust*, in which Gable had starred with *Jean Harlow. Soon, Grace was skinny-dipping with Gable in Lake Victoria and writing home to a friend, "What else is there to do if you're alone in a tent in Africa with Clark Gable?" In London, where some of the film's interiors were shot on the crew's return from Africa, the two lovers kept a low profile until Margaret swooped in once again and began primly chaperoning the pair in an effort to scotch all the scandalous talk. Gable pitched in by answering a telephone query from gossip queen *Hedda Hopper with, "Good God, no! I'm old enough to be her father!"; but when it came time for Kelly to return to America, leaving Gable behind, her tearful goodbyes at the airport appeared on the covers of gossip sheets and tabloids throughout the United States. All was forgotten on *Mogambo*'s release in 1953. Kelly was nominated for an Oscar that year and was hailed as the new *Ingrid Bergman, who had been hounded from Hollywood for her adulterous affair with Italian director Roberto Rossellini. *Look* named Kelly Best Actress of the year, a refreshing replacement to the "sweater queens" of the day. "Grace Kelly is all the more exciting for her quality of restraint," one reviewer wrote.

Among the many captivated by Kelly's performance in *Mogambo* was Alfred Hitchcock, the director who would elevate her to the ranks of international stardom. Hitchcock had a well-known penchant for blonde leading ladies, beginning in England with *Madeleine Carroll in the 1930s and extending through the now-disgraced Bergman. He delighted in presenting audiences with a heroine whose carefully controlled emotions are unleashed in threatening circumstances by a handsome leading man, and Grace's work in *Mogambo* convinced him that he had found, as he called her, a "snow-covered volcano." Their collaboration resulted in three films that are still considered the best work of each, all produced within a two-year period starting in 1954—*Dial M for Murder, Rear Window,* and *To Catch a Thief.*

The first starred Grace as a wife whose husband plots to kill her but who instead kills her intended assassin with a pair of scissors in the film's most famous scene. The scandal and cruel gossip surrounding Kelly's affair with leading man Ray Milland nearly broke up Milland's marriage, caused endless anxieties for MGM's publicity department, and made Kelly feel, as she later said, "like a street walker. As an unmarried woman, I was thought to be a danger," she went on. "Other women looked on me as a rival, and it pained me a great deal." Particularly hurtful were Hedda Hopper's description of her as "a nymphomaniac," and Hopper's unsuccessful efforts to convince producers and directors not to hire her.

For her second Hitchcock film, *Rear Window*, Hitchcock set off Grace's beauty with stunning costuming by *Edith Head and the performance that made her career, as the uninhibited girlfriend of Jimmy Stewart and the only one who believes he has witnessed a murder. *To Catch a Thief*, the third picture and the most romantically inspired film Hitchcock ever made, set Kelly against the glamorous French Riviera as a wealthy American who falls for Cary Grant's raffish jewel thief. The film became famous for its playful sexual innuendo and its final, passionate embrace with fireworks exploding in the background, broadly hinting at what lay ahead for the lovers after the fadeout. The fact was that Grace at the time was considering a marriage proposal from couturier Oleg Cassini, with whom she appeared at dinner engagements during the shoot to form a threesome with the Hitchcocks and the Grants (Grant was then married to his third wife, actress **Betsy Drake**). Because Cassini was twice divorced, Margaret was adamantly opposed to any such union but had so far been unable to break up the relationship.

By the time Kelly had arrived in France to begin production on the film in the spring of 1954, she had shot five pictures in eight months. In addition to her previous two pictures with Hitchcock, she had taken a small but significant role as William Holden's wife in the Korean War saga *The Bridges at Toko-Ri* and played opposite Stewart Granger in a lurid tale involving emeralds and misplaced passion which she had shot in Colombia, *Green Fire*. She found Granger conceited and boorish, but Holden was more to her liking. The affair they began during *The Bridges at Toko-Ri* had continued into a second picture, *The Country Girl*, in which Kelly had won the part fought over by every leading lady in Hollywood.

Based on the Clifford Odets play of the same name, the story of a quietly strong-willed woman who saves the career of her actor-husband from alcoholic oblivion cast both Grace and her leading man against type, for Bing Crosby abandoned his debonair crooning to play a helpless drunk and Kelly forsook her glamorous gowns and high heels for frayed sweaters and pumps. (Holden played the director trying to coax Crosby back to the stage.) Hollywood gossips claimed that Holden had graciously stepped aside when Crosby,

whose first wife had recently died, was as unable as any other man to resist Kelly's beauty and charm. His proposal of marriage, however, was gently refused. Despite these off-screen dramas, or perhaps because of them, Kelly's performance as Georgie Elgin brought her a second Oscar nomination for Best Actress. "As close to theatrical perfection as we are likely to see onscreen in our time," *Cue* magazine claimed, while *The New York Post* wondered at how "Miss Kelly extends her range down to the bottoms of un-glamour and dead-faced discouragement."

The competition for the Oscar that year was stiff, with *Audrey Hepburn (for *Sabrina*) and *Judy Garland (for *A Star Is Born*) among the competitors. The Oscar, however, went to Grace Kelly. After the accolades and post-award parties, Grace returned to her house in the wee hours of the morning, alone with the diminutive golden statue. "There we were, just the two of us," she remembered later. "It was terrible. It was the loneliest moment of my life." Her father's telephoned congratulations earlier in the evening had been lukewarm, for he remained the one man whose admiration for her accomplishments eluded her. Kelly once told a friend that she would do anything for her father, but claimed her love was never returned. Indeed, when once asked by a reporter what he thought of his daughter's success, Jack had merely shrugged and said, "I'm glad she's making a living."

After that triumphant 1954, Kelly had achieved the kind of international celebrity reserved for only a handful of stars. Her appearances at the 1955 Cannes Film Festival drew hordes of photographers and journalists, and an exhausted Grace confessed to her old friend, French actor Jean-Pierre Aumont, that she was thinking of refusing an appearance arranged by *Paris Match* with Prince Rainier, the scion of the ancient House of Grimaldi that had ruled the tiny principality of Monaco for six centuries. Convinced by a horrified Aumont that one did not stand up a reigning prince, Kelly impatiently sat through the hour that Rainier kept her waiting, then obligingly smiled as she walked with him in the royal gardens of the castle in Monte Carlo long enough to satisfy the photographers. Kelly wrote a polite thank-you note on her return to the United States, then began work on her next picture. It was *The Swan*, a film adaptation of Molnar's play about a beautiful young princess who cannot choose between her love for her tutor and her duty to marry a prince.

Rainier, meanwhile, was making discreet inquiries. He found himself in a peculiar position,

V OLUME EIGHT   **531**

for under the centuries-old terms under which Monaco had become a principality independent of France, Monaco's subjects would become French citizens if the ruling prince did not produce an heir to the throne. Among the many liberties enjoyed by Monaco's population was the lack of an income tax; the revenues produced by the famous casino in Monte Carlo could support what Somerset Maugham had called "a sunny place for shady people." The possibility of having to pay French income tax made the prince's marriage of intense interest. Rainier, 31 years old at the time he met Grace, had dallied for some years with a French actress, and had been prepared to marry her until fertility tests indicated she would be unable to bear children. Kelly, child-bearing abilities aside, had fascinated him with her beauty and regal bearing, something he had not expected to find in a movie actress. The fact that she was Catholic was a great advantage, too, for the intensely Catholic Grimaldis had been close to the Vatican since seizing Monaco from rebellious papal subjects in the 13th century. Rainier's Catholic adviser, Father Francis Tucker, carefully checked Grace's credentials and spent hours grilling hapless friends of the Kelly family who had come to Monaco on vacation. By autumn of 1955, Prince Rainier's first visit to the United States had been arranged, ostensibly diplomatic in nature; but as Grace finished work on *The Swan* in early December, she learned that Rainier would be spending Christmas Day with her family in Philadelphia. On the journey from Monaco, Rainier described his ideal woman to reporters as having "long hair floating in the wind, the color of autumn leaves. Her eyes are blue, or violet, with flecks of gold."

Suddenly, Kelly found herself in the position of having to choose between her career and marriage to a man she had met only once. She had told Aumont before leaving France earlier that year that she had found Rainier charming, and she gushed to her old friend, actress **Rita Gam**, "I love his eyes. I could look into them for hours"; but to many of her friends, these hardly seemed reasons to cut short a brilliant career which as yet showed no signs of fading. Kelly said nothing about her plans, the press reporting on her dates in Hollywood with Frank Sinatra, David Niven, and Spencer Tracy. A friend later reported that Kelly had seemed distracted during a dinner engagement early in December 1955, as she was finishing work on *The Swan*. Grace's explanation was that she was trying to decide whether to go home to Philadelphia for the holidays, but she said nothing about why she was so concerned about the visit.

In New York shortly after the New Year, Kelly called Oleg Cassini and asked him to take the ferry with her to Staten Island and back. Cassini believed he and Grace had a future together, but with the towers of lower Manhattan gleaming behind her in the sharp winter light, Kelly told him that Rainier had proposed to her at her parents' home on Christmas Day, and that she had accepted. To Cassini's objection that she hardly knew the man, Grace replied firmly, "I will learn to love him." She offered no other explanation for her decision, but later wrote that she acted on instinct. "But then, I always have," she said. "We happened to meet each other at a time when each of us was ready for marriage. There comes a time in life when you have to choose." The announcement was made public a few days later, Rainier finding the publicity distasteful but bearing the press' onslaught with as much royal reserve as he could maintain. Kelly had to withstand her father's embarrassing wheedling during the negotiations over the dowry his daughter was required to provide; worse, Margaret wrote and published a series of detailed articles in the *Los Angeles Herald Examiner* called "My Daughter Grace Kelly: Her Life And Romances." Kelly was publicly humiliated by her mother's exposé of her *amours*, despite Margaret's protests that she was donating all her royalties from the articles to charity. "First I had to fight the studio to avoid being a commodity, and now my own family trades me on the open market!" Grace exploded. "Why couldn't she just bake some cookies or organize some damn benefit!" Kelly cut off all communication with her mother for weeks as she began work on her last picture, *High Society*.

There was a certain irony in Grace's acceptance of the role of Tracy Lord, a wealthy socialite who nearly marries the wrong man. Although MGM had hired a singer to dub Grace's voice for its musical version of Phillip Barrie's stage play *Philadelphia Story*, Grace insisted on doing her own singing—to particularly good effect with Cole Porter's lyrics in the drunken "You're Sensational," where Grace sang "I don't care/ If I am called/ The Fair Miss Fridigaire." The shoot, Kelly's last time before the camera, was a bittersweet experience. The film, directed by veteran Charles Walters, co-starred two old friends, Bing Crosby and Frank Sinatra, as the two men Grace must choose between; and the studio, which had only a year before placed Kelly on temporary suspension for refusing roles offered to her, now generously donated all the dresses she wore in the picture for her trousseau. As if to declare her pending freedom from Holly-

Princess
Grace of
Monaco

wood stardom, Kelly sported in the film the huge white diamond Rainier had given her for their engagement. When the picture wrapped in February of 1956, Grace left the MGM lot for the last time.

Within weeks, doctors had confidentially reported to Rainier that his intended was fully capable of bearing children, while at the same time delicately sidestepping the issue of Kelly's virginity. On April 18, 1956, Grace Patricia Kelly was metamorphosed into Her Serene Highness, Grace, princess of Monaco, the royal consort of a kingdom that was, at less than 400 acres, smaller than one of MGM's back lots. It took three ceremonies to complete the transformation—the civil wedding required by Monaco law, a second one performed strictly for the press of reporters and whirring cameras that had descended on Monte Carlo, and a full-blown royal wedding by strict Catholic rite in the Cathedral of Monte Carlo. Show business royalty, including Cary Grant, Ava Gardner, Frank Sinatra, and Alfred Hitchcock, rubbed elbows in the cathedral with minor potentates and jet setters, all eager to be seen at the media event of the decade. As gifts to her bridesmaids, Kelly handed out the jewelry she had been given by the shah of Iran so many years before.

Precisely nine months and six days later, Princess **Caroline** was born to the royal couple, the only one expressing disappointment at the infant's sex being Grace's father. "Aw, shucks," Jack told reporters, "I was hoping for a boy." Two more children followed over the next eight years, Rainier obtaining his heir and keeping his kingdom with the birth of Prince Albert in 1958. By 1962, Kelly was taking such an active role in state affairs that she was generally credited with averting a potential French blockade of the border and seizure of Monaco's assets in France after Rainier fired a meddlesome foreign minister who, as it turned out, was an agent of Charles de Gaulle's. "Grace is the best ambassador I have," he said. His wife was widely admired, too, for her charitable activities, particularly on behalf of the elderly, and for sponsoring the construction of Monaco's first state theater at the bottom of the royal palace's hill.

But by the birth of her third child, Princess **Stephanie**, in 1965, the rigid order of palace life was having its effect on Kelly. A palace gossip reported that when Rainier asked his wife in 1966 what she wanted for their tenth anniversary, Grace snapped, "A year off!" Rainier apparently granted her wish, for Kelly took her own apartment in Paris and spent considerable time there,

and later that same year arranged to be named to the board of directors of 20th Century-Fox, which required her to be in Hollywood for quarterly meetings. Back on the studio party circuit, Her Serene Highness sometimes belied her title with liberal helpings of martinis and became, as Ava Gardner reported, "just another one of the girls dishing the dirt." She referred to Rainier as "The Dodo" but insisted that her marriage and position were all that she could have hoped for. Nevertheless, Kelly jumped at her first offer of film work in over a decade—Alfred Hitchcock's plea to return to the screen in the title role of his upcoming film, *Marnie*, again opposite Cary Grant.

Rainier did not object at first, even going so far as to arrange the rental of a house in Los Angeles for the production period; but his subjects thought otherwise. They had been disturbed by the way Kelly had broken state protocol by meeting Grant alone at the airport in Monaco when he came visiting and, worse, had kissed him as cameras flashed. Grace had, in fact, been carrying on an affair for some time with her former leading man, who had just divorced his fourth wife, actress **Dyan Cannon**. She told a confidante that Grant was the only man who understood her and wondered if she should have married him instead of Rainier. Besides her overfamiliarity in public with a film actor, the role Grace had accepted was problematical for a reigning princess, too, the character being a kleptomaniac with a sexually explosive secret. In the end, Kelly was forced to refuse the role, writing Hitchcock that she was heartbroken at the decision. (The title role went instead to Hitchcock's new blonde leading lady, **Tippi Hedren**.)

Denied her return to the screen and the freewheeling Hollywood *milieu*, the 1970s became Kelly's loneliest decade. Her affair with Cary Grant ended when Grant remarried, while her own marriage to Rainier became little more than a formal friendship. The couple had long ago taken to occupying separate quarters in the palace on the hill. "If I had a choice," Kelly confided to a friend, "I'd divorce him. But I have no choice. He'd keep my children." In 1981, she received permission to appear, as herself, in a television film being made by an Austrian director whom she had been seeing in Paris. *Rearranged* was a social farce about a gardening club in Monaco, and Kelly's presence in the film had drawn the interest of American television networks. Completing her work on the picture in Paris, Kelly and her youngest daughter, Stephanie, broke their drive back to Monaco by spending the night at a villa the family owned near St. Tropez, on the Côte d'Azur not far from

Monaco. Grace wanted to use the time alone with her daughter to try and convince Stephanie to end her much-publicized affair with Paul Belmondo, the son of French actor Jean-Paul Belmondo, which had been causing considerable embarrassment to the royal dignity. The next morning, September 13, 1982, Grace and Stephanie set off in their Land Rover for Monaco, less than an hour's drive along the winding Corniche—the same stretch of road, in fact, along which Grace Kelly had recklessly driven Cary Grant 30 years before in *To Catch a Thief*. Now Kelly was once again at the wheel, although she had often said that she disliked driving.

Less than a mile from the Monaco border, as a truckdriver following behind later reported, the Land Rover swerved, seemed to straighten, then failed to make a sharp curve and plunged off the road, tumbling 50 feet down an embankment and rolling on its roof before coming to rest. Both women were pulled unconscious from the wreckage. Stephanie later revived at the hospital and was treated for relatively minor injuries, but Grace never regained consciousness. On the evening of September 14, after being informed by doctors that there was no hope, the family agreed to disconnect the life-support equipment that had been maintaining Grace's vital functions. She died peacefully at 10:15.

The world would never learn what had happened in the Land Rover that sunny September morning, for the royal family has maintained a strict secrecy ever since Kelly's death. It is known that Grace suffered a stroke, but doctors were unable to say whether it had struck her while driving or whether it was a consequence of her fatal injuries and subsequent trauma; nor will there ever be proof for rumors that Grace's attention had wandered from the twisting road during a heated argument with Stephanie over the disputed affair with Belmondo.

The same illustrious guests that had attended Kelly's wedding nearly 30 years before now saw her to her rest in the royal tomb in the Cathedral of Monte Carlo four days after her death. A grieving Cary Grant was so distraught that he had to be helped to and from his car, while Rainier himself, for the first time in public memory, was unable to maintain his regal demeanor and sobbed uncontrollably. "Can there be any doubt that he loved Grace with all his heart?" Grant later said.

Rainier has never remarried and appears in public only when protocol demands it. Grace's picture is still lovingly displayed throughout Monaco and her name adorns public buildings, monuments, and streets dedicated to her memory. But it is her films, particularly her radiant work for Hitchcock, that are the true keepsakes of a life marked by both notoriety and regal splendor, by passionate spontaneity and cool logic. In the weeks after her death, friends would often recall Kelly's favorite bit of poetry, from Kahlil Gibran. "When love beckons to you," the line went, "follow him, though his voice may shatter your dreams."

SOURCES:

"Grace Kelly and Prince Rainier" as part of "The Greatest Love Stories of the Century," in *People Weekly*. Vol. 45, no. 6. February 12, 1996.

Lacey, Robert. *Grace*. London: Sidgwick & Jackson, 1994.

Spoto, Donald. *The Dark Side of Genius: The Life of Alfred Hitchcock*. NY: Little Brown, 1983.

Wayne, Jane Ellen. "Grace Kelly's Men" (book excerpt), in *Cosmopolitan*. Vol. 210, no. 4. April 1991.

Norman Powers, writer-producer, Chelsea Lane Productions, New York

Kelly, Kate (1862–1898)

Sister of bushranger Ned Kelly, and a supporter of the Kelly gang. Born in 1862; daughter of John (an Irish ex-convict) and Ellen (Quinn) Kelly; married, in 1888; no children.

Kate Kelly gained her place in Australian folklore more by association than by deed. Her brothers, Dan and Ned Kelly, along with two other men outside the Kelly family, formed one of the last of Australia's notorious bushranging gangs.

In 1866, following the death of the Kelly patriarch John "Red" Kelly (an outlaw in his own right), the family became residents of northeastern Victoria, between Greta and Glenrowan, where they joined the ranks of the rural poor. The Kelly boys, suspected at the time of stealing cattle and other minor crimes, were also frequently persecuted by the police. In April 1878, an officer by the name of Fitzpatrick (later dismissed from the police force) went to the Kelly shanty to arrest Dan for stealing horses. Although what really happened that day was never determined, Fitzpatrick claimed he had been shot by Ned, who reportedly was not even home at the time. Dan escaped to a hideout where he was later joined by Ned, so it was the boys' mother **Ellen Kelly** who was arrested and sentenced to three years of hard labor for taking part in the alleged murder attempt.

In retaliation for the conviction of their mother, the Kelly brothers, with accomplices Joe Byrne, Steve Hart, and Tom Lloyd, Jr. (who was never identified as a member of the Kelly gang), raided a police camp at Stringybark Creek and killed three policemen. A third officer escaped and would later testify at Ned's trial. The gang avoided capture for close to two years, largely due to a "bush telegraph" operated by sympathizers. During that time, they committed bank robberies in Euroa and in Jerilderie, New South Wales. The climax of their activities occurred in June 1880, when the Kellys, Hart, and Byrne, ensconced in a hotel in Glenrowan, planned to derail a special police train from Melbourne. The train crew, however, was warned in advance of the attack by the local schoolmaster. In the ensuing battle, the police killed Dan Kelly, Hart, and Byrne in the hotel, and Ned Kelly, dressed in metal armor, was wounded and captured. In October 1880, he was tried and convicted for one of the Stringybark Creek murders. Sentenced to death, he was executed on November 11, 1880, ending what to the minds of many was a reign of terror. However, 32,000 people petitioned to spare Kelly's life, and since his execution the Kelly legend in Australian folklore has grown in song, verse, prose, and film.

Kate Kelly never participated in any criminal activities, although she was a staunch defender of the Kelly gang, particularly her brother Ned. She was present at the siege of Glenrowan and subsequently pleaded Ned's case before the governor of Victoria and before a theater audience in Melbourne on the night of his execution. After the release of her mother in 1881 and before her marriage in 1888, Kate toured as an equestrian and worked on a central western station in north South Wales. She drowned in 1898. With the rest of the Kelly gang, Kate lives on in Australian folklore. She is the subject of Frank Hatherley's play *Ned Kelly's Sister's Travelling Circus* (later titled *Kate Kelly's Roadshow*), first performed in 1980, and **Jean Bedford**'s novel, *Sister Kate*, published in 1982.

SOURCES:

Wilde, William H., Joy Hooton, and Barry Andrews. *The Oxford Companion to Australian Literature.* Melbourne: Oxford University Press Australia, 1985.

SUGGESTED READING:

Brown, Max. *Australian Son*, 1948.
Clune, Frank. *The Kelly Hunters*, 1954.
Farwell, George. *Ned Kelly, What a Life!* 1970.
McQuilton, John. *The Kelly Outbreak 1879–1880*, 1979.
Seal, Graham. *Ned Kelly in Popular Tradition*, 1980.

Barbara Morgan,
Melrose, Massachusetts

Kelly, Kathryn Thorne (1904–1998?)

American kidnapper who allegedly advanced the career of her husband, Machine Gun Kelly. Name variations: Cleo Brooks; Cleo Coleman; Cleo Frye, Kathryn Frye; Kathryn Thorne. Born Cleo Brooks (some sources cite Cleo Coleman) in Saltillo, Mississippi, in 1904; possibly died on July 27, 1998, in St. Paul, Minnesota; daughter of James Emery Brooks and Ora Brooks (who would later marry Robert K.G. "Boss" Shannon and take the name Ora Shannon); married Lonnie Frye (a laborer), in 1919 (divorced soon after); possibly married Allie Brewer (briefly); married Charles Thorne (a bootlegger), in 1924 (died 1927); married George Kelly Barnes also known as George R. Kelly also known as Machine Gun Kelly (1895–1954, a bootlegger, robber, and kidnapper), in September 1930; children: (first marriage) **Pauline Frye.**

Associated with the crime wave that swept the United States during the 1930s, Kathryn Kelly was headed for trouble from a young age. Born Cleo Brooks in 1904 in Saltillo, Mississippi, she was married, had a daughter, and divorced by her early teens. She then changed her name to the more glamorous Kathryn and joined her mother **Ora Shannon**'s bootlegging operation at age 17. In 1924, Kathryn married a local bootlegger Charles Thorne who was found shot to death three years later. Though the coroner's jury called it suicide, Kathryn had allegedly told a gas station attendant the day before he died, "I'm bound to Coleman, Texas, to kill that goddamned Charlie Thorne."

By this time, Kathryn had developed into an outwardly sophisticated, gracious woman and was ready to involve herself in more lucrative criminal endeavors. She also had a record. She had been arrested in Fort Worth in 1929, working under the alias of Dolores Whitney, and charged with shoplifting. She had been convicted in Oklahoma City, then using the name Mrs. J.E. Burnell, of robbery, but the conviction was reversed on appeal. When she met bootlegger George Kelly, who had served a stint at Leavenworth for smuggling liquor, she felt that he was the kind of man she could mold into her ideal outlaw. They married in Minneapolis in 1930. Legend has it that she then set out to market her husband into a criminal superstar.

Under Kathryn's direction, George Kelly, along with several cohorts, carried out a series of bank robberies in Texas, Oklahoma, and Washington state. She is said to have bought Kelly his first Thompson submachine gun and made him practice with it. She also gave out the spent cartridges to family and friends as souvenirs from "Machine Gun" Kelly, boasting he was a desperate criminal wanted in three states for murder and bank robbery. Possibly, it was Kathryn who spread the stories that he had been a machine gunner during World War I (though George was a college student at that time) and was so proficient with the "chopper" that he could write his name in lead and knock walnuts off a fence. The stories held. The wanted poster dispersed by the FBI on August 14, 1933, would describe George as an "Expert machine gunner."

Kathryn used the ill-gotten money to purchase cars, jewelry, and furs, but soon grew anxious to move into "the big time." Reading about the increasing number of kidnappings across the country, she convinced George into upgrading their criminal activities. Her first kidnap victim, found in the phone book, was Howard Woolverton, a manufacturer and banker's son from South Bend, Indiana. After holding Woolverton hostage for several days in 1932, the Kellys discovered that his family had no money to pay for his release, so they let him go.

Kathryn was more selective in choosing her second victim, millionaire oilman Charles F. Urschel, whom George and his henchman Albert Bates snatched from the front porch of Urschel's mansion in Oklahoma City on the night of July 22, 1933. Urschel was taken to the remote Texas ranch owned by Kathryn's mother Ora Shannon and Ora's second husband Robert K.B. "Boss" Shannon, a Democratic political boss in Wise County, Texas. Urschel was held until a substantial $200,000 ransom was paid through a family intermediary in Kansas City.

Upon his release, Urschel provided clues to FBI agents who subsequently apprehended Kathryn's parents and half-brother at the Texas ranch and carted them off to jail. Meanwhile, the Kellys traveled in Kathryn's 16-cylinder Cadillac to St. Paul, Minnesota, then a haven for outlaws who were tolerated by the corrupt local government for a price, where they began spending the ransom. From there, they traveled around, from Chicago to Texas, from Kansas City to St. Louis, staying on the move, now panicked as the law closed in. While spending her newfound wealth, Kathryn schemed to get her family released from federal custody. At one point, she offered to trade her husband for their release, but the FBI turned her down. Law enforcement also received the following letter from Kathryn:

> The entire Urschel family and friends, and all of you will be exterminated soon. There is no way I can prevent it. I will gladly put George Kelly on the spot for you if you will save my mother, who is innocent of any wrong doing. If you do not comply with this request, there is no way in which I can pre-vent the most awful tragedy. If you refuse my offer I shall commit some minor offense and be placed in jail so that you will know that I have no connection with the terrible slaughter that will take place in Oklahoma City within the next few days.

A more threatening letter would arrive at the Urschels'.

On September 27, 1933, while the Kellys were hiding out in a Memphis boardinghouse, the local police, accompanied by a few FBI agents, captured the pair in a raid. When found, Kelly was in his pajamas and Kathryn was asleep. Both were so hungover from consuming six quarts of gin the previous night that they did not put up a fight. The FBI spread the myth that George cried, "Don't shoot, G-men!" Rather, George dropped the gun on his foot and mumbled, "I've been waiting for you all night."

The Kellys were tried, convicted, and sent to prison for life. Said Kathryn, "My Pekingese dog would have got a life sentence in that court." During the trial, it became obvious that George was not the gun-toting, brazen killer depicted in the media, though he may not have been the Casper Milquetoast now put forth by crime buffs either. Kathryn claimed to be an innocent victim of her "marriage to a gangster."

Kathryn was incarcerated at a federal prison in Cincinnati and later transferred to Milan, Michigan. Before imprisonment, she deeded her Fort Worth home (owned by husband Charles Thorne) to her 14-year-old daughter Pauline Frye who was then sent to live with an aunt. George Kelly was confined in Leavenworth, transferred to Alcatraz in 1934, where he became a Bible student and wrote contrite notes to Urschel, then returned to Leavenworth where he died of a heart attack on July 18, 1954.

In prison, Kathryn began to write and became assistant editor of a prison newspaper, the "Terminal Island Gull." In December of 1940, she wrote:

> We realize that every "feminine fluff" beneath our roof carries within her heart a full quota of loneliness, grief and mental suffering. None of us like to do "time." It isn't play, it is sapping three hundred and sixty-five days filled with golden opportunities slipping away year by year, each day gone forever from the span of life. The drabness, the necessary discipline attached to an institution pulls at the vital organs of living twenty four hours each day. The Government can never fashion from steel and stone a prison that will mean "home" to any of its inmates.

Kathryn Kelly served time until June 1958, when she was released from prison, along with her mother, on $10,000 bond, pending an appeal. Her lawyer maintained that the government's case was based on a handwriting expert who testified that she had written the letters to the FBI and Urschel family. This, he said, might have been disputed by another expert. The judge granted a new trial and ordered the FBI to produce its files. Rather than produce files, the FBI let the case lapse, and Kathryn Kelly went free. Her mother was institutionalized at the Oklahoma County Home and Hospital in Oklahoma City, and Kathryn took a job there as bookkeeper. In 1970, she was still working there and living on the premises as a virtual recluse. She may have died in 1998. In 1970, a suppressed report among the FBI files was revealed. It contained an affidavit from another FBI handwriting expert who claimed that the letters might have been written by George.

SOURCES:

Cooper, Courtney Ryley. *Ten Thousand Public Enemies.* Boston, MA: Little, Brown, 1935.

Finnegan, James. "Machine Gun Kelly," in *Master Detective.* April 1970.

Moreland, Harrison. "The Untold Mystery Behind the Urschel Abduction Horror," in *True Detective Mysteries.* March–May 1934.

Scheneck, Stephen, and William W. Turner. "Mrs. Machine Gun Kelly," in *Scanlan's Monthly.* May 1970.

Whitehead, Don. *The FBI Story.* NY: Random House, 1956.

Barbara Morgan,
Melrose, Massachusetts

Kelly, Mary Anne (1826–1910).

See O'Doherty, Mary Anne.

Kelly, Nancy (1921–1995)

American actress, best known for her role as the mother of a murderous little girl in The Bad Seed, *which won her a Tony Award and an Academy Award nomination in 1956. Born on March 25, 1921, in Lowell, Massachusetts; died in Bel Air, California, on January 2, 1995; eldest of four children of John A. Kelly (a theater ticket broker) and Ann Mary (Walsh) Kelly (an artist's and commercial model); sister of actor Jack Kelly (1927–1992); attended the Immaculate Conception Academy, New York City; attended St. Lawrence Academy, Long Island; attended the Bentley School for Girls; married Edmond O'Brien (an actor), in 1941 (divorced 1942); married Fred Jackman, Jr. (a cinematographer, divorced); married Warren Caro (an executive director of the Theater Guild), on November 25, 1955.*

Selected theater: Broadway debut as Buteuse Maiden in Give Me Yesterday *(Charles Hopkins Theater, March 1931); Blossom Trexel in* Susan and God *(Plymouth Theater, October 1937); toured as Evelyn Heath in* Guest in the House *(1942); Patricia Graham in* Flare Path *(Henry Miller Theater, December 1943); Marion Castle in* The Big Knife *(National Theater, February 1949); Emily Crane in* Season in the Sun *(Cort Theater, September 1950, and subsequent tour, 1951); Kate Scott in* Twilight Walk *(Fulton Theater, September 1951); toured as Georgie Elgin in* The Country Girl *(1953); Christine Penmark in* The Bad Seed *(46th Street Theater, December 1954, and subsequent tour, 1955–56); Katy Maartens in* The Genius and the Goddess *(Henry Miller's Theater, December 1957); Adele Douglas in* The Rivalry *(Bijou Theater, February 1959); Barbara Smith in* A Mighty Man Is He *(Cort Theater, January 1960); Jane McLeod in* A Whiff of Melancholy *(New Hope, Pennsylvania, August 1961); Myra Brisset in* Giants, Sons of Giants *(Alvin Theater, January 1962); Ellen Hurlbird in* Step on a Crack *(Royal Alexandra Theater, Toronto, September 1962); for some performances played Martha in* Who's Afraid of Virginia Woolf *(Billy Rose Theater, July 1963. and tour 1963–64); The Long-Winded Lady in* Quotation from Chairman Mao Tse-Tung *(Billy Rose Theater, September 1968).*

Selected films: Untamed Lady *(1926);* Mismates *(1926);* The Girl on the Barge *(1929);* Convention Girl *(1935);* Submarine Patrol *(1938);* Jesse James *(1939);* Tail Spin *(1939);* Frontier Marshal *(1939);* Stanley and Livingstone *(1939);* He Married His Wife *(1940);* Sailor's Lady *(1940);* One Night in the Tropics *(1940);* Scotland Yard *(1941);* Parachute Battalion *(1941);* To the Shores of Tripoli *(1942);* Friendly Enemies *(1942);* Tarzan's Desert Mystery *(1943);* Show Business *(1944);* Double Exposure *(1944);* Betrayal From the East *(1945);* Song of the Sarong *(1945);* Follow That Woman *(1945);* Murder in the Music Hall *(1946);* Crowded Paradise *(1956);* The Bad Seed *(1956).*

The daughter of a theater ticket agent, actress Nancy Kelly was born in 1921 in Lowell, Massachusetts, but grew up in New York City, where the family moved when she was a child. Her mother was a model for the artist James Montgomery Flagg, which may explain why Kelly became a child model, making her professional debut in a Flagg magazine illustration. At age five, she was named America's Most Healthy Child by a group of professional photographers. Modeling led to films, and by age eight Kelly was the veteran of 50 movies. She "retired" from film in 1929, after completing *Girl on the Barge.*

Back in New York, she made her Broadway debut in A.A. Milne's *Give Me Yesterday* (1931), a story about the imaginary lives of three children. Entering her teenage years, Kelly also began appearing on the radio, on such programs as "Forty-Five Minutes from Hollywood," "Cavalcade of America," "Gangbusters," and "The Shadow," among others.

Kelly caught the attention of the critics with her portrayal of the lonely adolescent Blossom in *Rachel Crothers' play *Susan and God* (1937), which starred *Gertrude Lawrence. Brooks Atkinson called her performance one of "poignant simplicity and unstudied charm," while Joseph Wood Krutch thought she was probably the best thing in the play. Her success on Broadway prompted a call-back to Hollywood, and Kelly embarked on an intense period of movie-making beginning with *Submarine Patrol* (1938), and including *Stanley and Livingstone* (1939), *Jesse James* (1939), *He Married His Wife* (1940), *A Very Young Lady* (1941), and *To the Shores of Tripoli* (1942). Included in a 1942 "Stars of Tomorrow" poll, Kelly later reflected on that period of her life with a hint of regret. "I wish young actors wouldn't feel compelled to rush off to Hollywood as soon as they make good," she told a reporter for *Pictorial Review* in 1951. "They don't give themselves a chance to learn their trade honestly by scuttling the stage and scurrying West."

As her film career burgeoned, Kelly occasional returned to Broadway, notably as the wife of a disillusioned magazine writer in Wolcott Gibbs' comedy *Season in the Sun* (1950), which critic William Hawkins called "a sophisticated uproar." After a disappointing run in A.B. Shiffrin's *Twilight Walk* (1951), Kelly hit upon the most memorable role of her career, that of Christine Penmark, the tortured mother in Maxwell Anderson's unsettling drama *The Bad Seed* (1954), based on the William March novel. Walter Kerr's glowing review in the New York *Herald Tribune* was one of many the actress received. "Though Miss Kelly has done attractive work on Broadway before she has never really prepared us for the brilliance of the present portrait," he wrote (December 19, 1954). "The role is an almost unbearable, certainly an unrelieved, series of crises: the woman is simultaneously discovering that her daughter [*Patty McCormack] is a criminal and that it is she herself who has passed on the taint." Kelly won a Tony Award as Best Actress for her performance and recreated the role for the screen version, which earned her an Academy Award nomination.

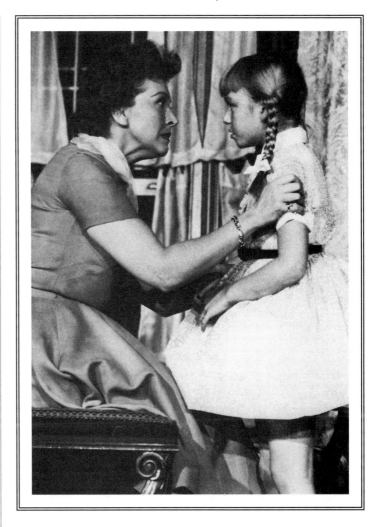

Nancy Kelly was married three times; her first two marriages, to actor Edmond O'Brien and cinematographer Fred Jackman, Jr., ended in divorce, after which she wed Warren Caro, the executive director of the Theater Guild. She continued to play character roles on Broadway throughout the 1960s and made frequent television appearances on such shows as "Climax" and "Alfred Hitchcock Presents." In 1956, she won an Emmy for "The Pilot," an episode of "Studio One." The actress, who died at the age of 73, never took her career for granted, particularly the high points. "All of us should realize," she said, "that when we are successful we should thank our lucky stars."

From the movie The Bad Seed, *starring Nancy Kelly and Patty McCormack.*

SOURCES:

Candee, Marjorie Dent, ed. *Current Biography 1955*. NY: H.W. Wilson, 1955.

Katz, Ephraim. *The Film Encyclopedia*. NY: HarperCollins, 1994.

"Obituary," in *The Day* [New London, CT] . January 16, 1995.

Barbara Morgan,
Melrose, Massachusetts

Kelly, Patsy (1910–1981)

American actress-comedian. Born Sarah Kelly on January 12, 1910, in Brooklyn, New York; died on September 24, 1981, following a stroke in Woodland Hills, California; never married; no children.

Selected theater: New York debut in Harry Delmar's Revels *(1927);* Earl Carroll's Vanities *(1930);* The Wonder Bar *(1931);* Flying Colors *(1932); Pauline in revival of* No, No, Nanette *(1970); Mrs. O'Dare in revival of* Irene *(1973).*

Filmography: Going Hollywood *(1933);* Countess of Monte Cristo *(1934);* The Party's Over *(1934);* The Girl from Missouri *(1934);* Transatlantic Merry-Go-Round *(1934);* Go Into Your Dance *(1935);* Every Night at Eight *(1935);* Page Miss Glory *(1935);* Thanks a Million *(1935);* Kelly the Second *(1936);* Private Number *(1936);* Sing Baby Sing *(1936);* Pigskin Parade *(1936);* Nobody's Baby *(1937);* Pick a Star *(1937);* Wake Up and Live *(1937);* Ever Since Eve *(1937);* Merrily We Live *(1938);* There Goes My Heart *(1938);* The Cowboy and the Lady *(1938);* The Gorilla *(1939);* The Hit Parade of 1941 *(1940);* Road Show *(1941);* Topper Returns *(1941);* Broadway Limited *(1941);* Playmates *(1941);* Sing Your Worries Away *(1942);* In Old California *(1942);* My Son, The Hero *(1943);* Ladies' Day *(1943);* Danger! Women at Work *(1943);* Please Don't Eat the Daisies *(1960);* The Crowded Sky *(1960);* The Naked Kiss *(1964);* The Ghost in the Invisible Bikini *(1966);* C'mon, Let's Live a Little *(1967);* Rosemary's Baby *(1968); (cameo)* The Phynx *(1970);* Freaky Friday *(1977);* North Avenue Irregulars *(1979).*

Usually cast as a dumpy, wisecracking maid or the friend of the heroine, talented comedian Patsy Kelly endeared herself to Broadway and movie audiences during the 1930s. Retiring from films during the 1940s, she returned in the 1960s, playing mostly minor roles. In 1971, with her childhood friend *Ruby Keeler, Kelly made a stunning comeback to the Broadway stage in the hit revival of *No, No, Nanette,* winning a Tony for her role as Pauline the maid.

Patsy Kelly was born in 1910 in Brooklyn, New York, and started her career as a dancer in the Broadway musicals of the early 1930s. Roles in *Earl Carroll's Vanities* (1930) and *Wonder Bar* (1931), with Al Jolson, paved the way to Hollywood and a series of 21 memorable comedy shorts paired with *Thelma Todd. After Todd's mysterious death of carbon monoxide poisoning in 1935, Kelly was briefly teamed with **Lyda Roberti**, who also died at an early age. Her first feature film was *Going Hollywood* (1933), with *Marion Davies, one of several movies she made with the star, who was also the mistress of newspaper tycoon William Randolph Hearst. (In a 1971 interview in *Film Fan Monthly,* Kelly recalled meeting Hearst and being absolutely stunned by his high-pitched voice. "You'd see this tremendous man, he looked seven or eight feet, with a big Stetson hat, and he'd say 'Hello, Patsy, how are you?' and it would be shocking.") Kelly made three memorable feature films in 1936: *Every Night at Eight* (which introduced the song "I'm in the Mood for Love"), *Thanks a Million,* with Dick Powell and **Ann Dvorak**, and *Page Miss Glory,* her second movie with Davies.

Following *Ladies' Day* (1943), Kelly had difficulty getting movie roles. During the War, she had a radio show with Barry Wood, and afterwards had a nightclub act. In 1955, she toured the country with *Tallulah Bankhead in the farce *Dear Charles,* in which she made the most of a mere 15 minutes on stage. Kelly returned to films in 1960, with roles in *Please Don't Eat the Daisies* and *The Crowded Sky.* She was a reluctant witch in Roman Polanski's 1968 thriller *Rosemary's Baby.* "I threw Holy Water on that set all the time I was on it," she

𝒫atsy 𝒦elly

said. "But that was a great experience." Later films included *The Ghost in the Invisible Bikini* (1966) and *North Avenue Irregulars* (1979).

Kelly was thrilled to be part of the revival of *No, No, Nanette,* in which she sparkled as the maid, Pauline. "Doesn't Patsy Kelly mug?" began critic Walter Kerr's review in *The New York Times* (January 31, 1971). "Uh huh. That's what maids did in those days. And it has been arranged for her to do it all at once, in a sequence in which she can slap everything within reach, her own face, the nearest balustrade, a couple of suitcases that must be hustled upstairs. Given the opportunity, she gives it the works: the result is a graduate course, short but exhaustive, in all the slow-burn, flat-palm possibilities developed in two-reel comedies by the masters and mistresses, herself included, of the form. She is grand." Winning a Tony for her performance, Kelly went on to play a featured role of in the 1973 revival of *Irene* (1973), starring **Debbie Reynolds**. Kelly, who never married, died in September 1981.

SOURCES:

Katz, Ephraim. *The Film Encyclopedia.* NY: Harper-Collins, 1994.

Kerr, Walter. "A Door Opens, Miss Keeler Enters," in *The New York Times.* January 31, 1971.

Lamparski, Richard. *Whatever Became of . . . ?* 1st and 2nd series. NY: Crown, 1967.

Maltin, Leonard. "FFM Interviews Patsy Kelly," in *Film Fan Monthly.* March 1971.

Wilmeth, Don B., and Tice L. Miller, eds. *Cambridge Guide to American Theater.* Cambridge and NY: Cambridge University Press, 1993.

Barbara Morgan,
Melrose, Massachusetts

Kelly, Pearl (1894–1983)

Australian harness driver. Born Pearl O'Brien at Koo-wee-rup, Victoria, in 1894; died in 1983; married Charles Kelly.

Pearl Kelly was a pioneer in the esoteric sport of harness racing, riding and driving harness horses from the age of 16. During the First World War, she married and moved to Melbourne where she continued her unusual career. During the early 1920s, in addition to her own horses, she drove for leading trainer Percy Shipp and finished third on the Melbourne Drivers' Premiership. Despite her talent and success, Kelly had a running feud with the Victorian Trotting and Racing Association who declared the sport unsafe and banned the issuance of driving permits to females in the late '20s. Kelly was forced to give up driving, but continued to train horses until 1961. By the time of her death in 1983, the attitudes of the 1920s had been reversed and a new generation of women was free to pursue the sport.

Barbara Morgan,
Melrose, Massachusetts

Kelly, Petra (1947–1992)

German political activist, feminist, and two-term representative to German Parliament who was a founding member of the German Green Party and the European Green Peace movement. Born Petra Karin Lehmann on November 27, 1947, in Günzburg, Bavaria, West Germany; killed by her companion at her home in Bonn, Germany, in October 1992; daughter of Richard Siegfried Lehmann and Margarete-Marianne (Birle) Lehmann (who divorced Richard Lehmann in 1954 and married U.S. Army Lt. Col. John Edward Kelly in 1958); attended Englisches Institut for Catholic girls in Günzburg (1954–59); U.S. Army base schools at Nellingen, Germany, and Fort Benning, Georgia (1959–60); Baker Junior High at Fort Benning (1960–63); graduated with honors from Hampton High, Virginia (1966); School of International Service at American University, Washington, D.C. (1966–70), B.A. cum laude in International Relations (1970); Diploma in European Integration from Europa Institute, University of Amsterdam (1971); registered for doctorate with the Institute of Political Studies at the University of Heidelberg (1972) but later abandoned doctoral research for political activism; never married; lived with Gert Bastian; no children.

Awards: awarded scholarship and nominated Most Outstanding Foreign Woman Student at American University (1967); Alan M. Bronner Memorial Award, Bruce Howard Award, and Woodrow Wilson Scholarship (1970); Alternative Nobel Prize, Stockholm (1992); Peace Woman of the Year Award (1993).

Raised by mother and grandmother in Günzburg, Germany, until mother remarried (1958); her half-sister Grace Patricia Kelly was born (1959); family moved to U.S. and half-brother John Lee Kelly born (1960); sister Grace diagnosed with cancer of the eye (1970); while family moved to Würzburg, Germany, stayed in the U.S. to attend university; worked with Hubert Humphrey election campaign (1968); sister Grace died (1970); moved to Amsterdam, while family moved to Newport News, Virginia (1970); accorded internship with the European Commission in Brussels and research grant by the Christian Democrat Press and Information Office (1971); transferred to cabinet of Sicco Mansholt, president of European

KELLY, PETRA

Commission, administrator to the Health and Social Policy Section of the Economic and Social Committee of the European Commission (1972–83); established Grace P. Kelly Foundation (1973); elected to board of Bundesverband Bürgerinitiativen Umweltschutz, an umbrella organization for citizens environmental action groups in Germany (1977); was co-founder of Sonstige Politische Vereinigung—Die Grünen in Frankfurt (1979); at founding conference of Die Grünen, the German Green Party, elected one of three speakers (1980); was co-organizer of International War Crimes Tribunal for possession of weapons of mass destruction (1983); elected member of German Bundestag (Parliament), member of Foreign Relations Committee (1983–87); was a representative at Western European Union (1985–87); was re-elected to Parliament (1987); served as chair of German Association for Social Defence (1988–90); organized first International and Non-Partisan Hearing on Tibet and Human Rights in Bonn (1989); lost seat in Parliament (1990); profiled as one of the 1,000 makers of the 20th century by The Sunday Times, London (1991).

Selected publications: Fighting for Hope (London: Chatto & Windus, 1984); Hiroshima (Bornheim: Lamuv, 1986); (with Gert Bastian and Pat Aiello) The Anguish of Tibet (Berkeley, CA: Parallax Press, 1991); Thinking Green! Essays on Environmentalism, Feminism, and Nonviolence (Berkeley, CA: Parallax Press, 1995). Published and edited numerous books, collections of essays, book chapters, articles, and speeches.

Alarmed by the fact that friends and family had not heard from Petra Kelly and her companion Gert Bastian for more than three weeks, **Charlotte Bastian**, Gert's estranged wife, called and asked neighbors on the evening of October 18, 1992, to check the couple's residence in a suburb of Bonn. Detecting a strong odor and an entrance hall filled with yards of fax paper, the neighbors called police, who found the decomposed bodies of Gert Bastian, a former major general of the German army, and Petra Kelly, Germany's most prominent and influential advocate of peace, environmental protection, human rights, and nonviolence. Beside Bastian's body on the second floor landing of the staircase lay a gun, and in the study the electric typewriter, with an unfinished letter in it, was still humming. Bastian had broken off the letter to his lawyer, which mentions nothing about his or Kelly's impending death, in the middle of the word müs[sen] (must). Kelly's body was found in her bed; she had been shot at close range. Beside Kelly's body were her reading glasses and an

open book. After a brief investigation, police concluded that Bastian had shot Kelly—probably in her sleep—and then shot himself. Police found no indication of a third-party involvement, and there was no note or letter from either Bastian or Kelly explaining their deaths.

Friends and family were stunned, and when the news was reported throughout the world the next morning, rumors began to circulate. There was talk of a double suicide and a suicide pact; however, family and friends asserted that Kelly had no inclination and no reason to commit suicide, and that it would be entirely out of character for her to agree to a suicide pact. There was no indication that Kelly had agreed to being killed. Other reports and rumors promoted conspiracy theories and suspected an assassination by the Chinese, the KGB, neo-Nazis, international gun-runners, and pro-nuclear power groups. To this day the circumstances surrounding Kelly's and Bastian's death remain a mystery, and Kelly, the charismatic environmentalist and feminist committed to nonviolent action, will be remembered not only for her unswerving dedication to peace, justice, and the environment, but also for her sudden and violent death, probably at the hands of the man she loved.

Born two years after the end of World War II in the Bavarian town of Günzburg, Petra Kelly was part of the postwar generation which grew up in the lingering shadow of Germany's past. While witnessing the so-called economic miracle, this generation—the protest generation of the '60s—began to question postwar Germany's focus upon economic growth and fought against the collective repression of the past by the German people and of past deeds by individual Germans. Kelly, who left Germany at age 11, claimed that it was only through her studies in the United States that she learned about the full extent of the Nazi crimes.

Kelly's grandmother **Kunigunde Birle**, a war widow, had opposed the Nazi regime and had forbidden her daughter **Marianne (Kelly)**, Kelly's mother, to take part in the Nazi organization for young girls. After the war, Kunigunde Birle and Marianne took in a young Pole from Dresden, Richard Siegfried Lehmann, who first worked as a journalist with the local Günzburg paper and later worked for the American occupational forces. Marianne and Richard married in May 1947, and in November Petra was born. When Petra was six years old, Lehmann left, and Petra's parents divorced in 1954. Lehmann, who played no further role in Petra's life, wrote his daughter only one letter, in 1985. By this time

Kelly had become famous, and apparently Lehmann felt that he was being portrayed unfairly in articles and television shows about Kelly. Despite Kelly's willingness to meet him, an encounter did not take place and nothing further was heard from Lehmann.

After her husband left in 1953, Marianne Lehmann supported herself and her daughter by working for the Americans. Raising Petra was left mainly to the grandmother, a strong and energetic woman, who nurtured Petra emotionally, spiritually, and intellectually. By the time Petra started school in 1954, she could read and write and had discovered the profound pleasure in learning that stayed with her. Despite her illness caused by painful episodes of urinary tract infections and kidney stones and the first of three kidney operations, Petra was an exceptional student at the Catholic girls' school, where she learned the importance of discipline and hard work. Kelly wanted to become a nun and live and work in Günzburg where she could stay close to *Omi,* as she lovingly called her grandmother. Kunigunde Birle remained a central

force in Petra's life; she supported Kelly's political endeavors, traveled with her to rallies, and allowed her apartment to be turned into Kelly's first campaign office. In the 1980s, Birle was well-known in Germany as the "green granny."

Petra, however, could not stay in Günzburg. Her departure was imminent when her mother married John Edward Kelly, an American lieutenant-colonel in the Engineering Corps in 1958. Although John Kelly never formally adopted Petra, because Petra wanted to keep her German citizenship, he became a good stepfather and friend, and Petra took his name. The family moved to a base in Nellingen near Stuttgart where Kelly's half sister, **Grace Patricia Kelly,** was born in May of 1959. In December, the family moved to Fort Benning, Georgia, and in 1960, Petra's half-brother, John Lee Kelly, was born. Petra quickly learned English and was once again at the head of her class at Baker Junior High School. She was "top scholar" in her final year, sat on junior class councils and organizing committees, wrote for the school newspaper, and was a cheerleader for the football team. She contin-

Petra Kelly

ued with similar activities at Hampton High, Virginia, where she graduated with honors in 1966. Kelly won oratory contests, was nominated class poet, and Most Likely to Succeed.

In autumn 1966, Kelly began her studies at the School of International Service at American University in Washington, D.C. She continued to have close ties to her family, who often attended her class presentations. In 1967, Grace was diagnosed with eye cancer. At her sister's request, Petra wrote to the Vatican asking for an audience with the pope, and the Kelly family traveled to Rome in 1968 to fulfill Grace's wish. That same summer, Kelly took a trip to Prague with her grandmother and experienced first hand the invasion of Czechoslovakia by Soviet forces while under house arrest in their hotel. From the hotel window, Petra and Kunigunde witnessed the end of the so-called "Prague Spring," the Czech attempt of democratization and emancipation from the Soviet Union. After five days, they were allowed to leave Czechoslovakia, and Kelly was deeply impressed by the passive, non-violent resistance of the Czechs.

In 1970, Grace died after four operations and radiation treatments that had left her disfigured. Her suffering and courage throughout her illness had a profound influence upon Kelly's life and work. Petra later labored tirelessly on behalf of children with cancer: she collaborated on a report on children and cancer for the European Commission, established in 1973 the Grace P. Kelly Foundation—a charity to support cancer research and adequate care for children with cancer. She wrote a book about children and cancer entitled *Viel Liebe gegen Schmerz: Krebs bei Kindern* (Love can Conquer Sorrow: Cancer in Children) published in 1986, the same year in which she pushed through a bill in German Parliament allocating two million marks for research into facilities for children with cancer. In 1971, Kelly began sponsoring a Tibetan refugee orphan, a girl of Grace's age.

In 1970, Petra had graduated from American University cum laude with a Bachelor's of Arts in International Relations. While there, she organized International Week, was on the student senate, and met and corresponded with Robert F. Kennedy and Vice President Hubert Humphrey. In 1968, she coordinated the Students for Kennedy group and, after John F. Kennedy's assassination, joined Humphrey's campaign. Apparently Humphrey appreciated Kelly's honesty and directness; she was able to provide him with a more European view of the United States while acting as a sounding board

for his attempt to appeal to the younger generation. Humphrey won the Democratic nomination but failed in the presidential race against Richard Nixon. The failed campaign gave Petra insight into both the cruelty and exhilaration of political campaigning.

In autumn 1970, Kelly enrolled at the Europa Institute at the University of Amsterdam and began a research project entitled "The Development and Influence of Private European Organizations which have Promoted European Integration and Unity." In 1971, she was awarded a diploma in European Integration by the Institute. At this time, she became increasingly critical about the teachings of the Roman Catholic Church but did not formally leave the church until 1980. Despite her doubts, Kelly never lost interest in questions of faith and remained deeply spiritual. For Kelly, politics needed spirituality. The profound political changes essential to healing the planet, wrote Kelly, would not come about through fragmented problem solving or intellectual analysis, but rather through a holistic vision based upon mature values, deep intuitions, and a regard for spiritual concerns and wisdom. Kelly's models were Martin Luther King, Jr. and Mahatma Gandhi. She was interested in Buddhism and befriended the Dalai Lama, with whom she traveled and appeared in public on several occasions. Her female model of a revolutionary was *Rosa Luxemburg.

In October 1971, Kelly began a six-month internship at the General Secretariat of the European Commission in Brussels, where she was assigned to the cabinet of Altiero Spinelli, the commissioner for industrial, technological, and scientific policy. Kelly received a stipend from the conservative Christian Democrat Press and Information Office which was to fund her research for one year. In 1972, she registered her doctoral thesis at the Institute of Political Studies at the University of Heidelberg and returned to Brussels to take up a new post at the male-dominated European Commission as administrator to the Economic and Social Committee, where she began to adopt strong feminist positions. Petra wanted to make women's rights one of the priorities of European institutions and insisted that "women's issues" should be dealt with by both men and women. Kelly saw a relationship between militarism, environmental degradation, and sexism, and advocated non-violent resistance to male dominance. For Kelly, it was not a question of overthrowing patriarchy and replacing it with a system of female dominance; she called for the cooperation of men and women in the transformation of patriarchal patterns.

In her research, Kelly discovered that the European Community tended to favor, with its financial support, conservative organizations of industry and finance while largely ignoring action-minded, more left-oriented groups. Kelly's findings prompted the Christian Democratic Press and Information Office to suspend support for her research. Nevertheless, she continued traveling throughout Europe to speak to organizations concerned with European integration. She was interested in finding ways to engage ordinary citizens in the process of Europeanization.

Having lost the funding for her research, Kelly moved in late 1972 to the cabinet of 64-year-old Sicco Mansholt, president of the commission, with whom she had a brief affair. "Lover lets beloved be free," Kelly noted after the affair ended. She no longer pursued her doctoral dissertation and became increasingly involved in politics. She was active in the German Social Democratic Party, the Young European Federalists, and the developing citizen's movements in Germany, especially the anti-nuclear movement. In close contact with the anti-nuclear movement in the United States, she worked with numerous organizations advocating non-violence, ecology, feminism, and a new kind of grass-roots European federalism. She was involved with the Irish anti-nuclear movement and befriended the Irish trade unionist John Carroll, with whom she coedited *A Nuclear Ireland?*

In 1977, Kelly traveled to Australia, where she attended a Hiroshima Day Rally and visited several Aboriginal groups. Toward the end of the 1970s, she lead two busy lives: one in Brussels at her full-time job at the European Commission and one in Germany campaigning for her political causes. She organized rallies, wrote countless articles, gave innumerable speeches, and attempted to forge associations between the grass-roots, anti-nuclear, and environmental groups in Germany. This was achieved in 1972 with the formation of the Bundesverband Bürgerinitiativen Umweltschutz, an umbrella organization for citizens' environmental action groups; Kelly became one of its first board members.

Disillusioned by the unwillingness of the German government to take seriously the demands of these grass-roots organizations and dismayed by the disarray of the movement, several activists—among them famous artists and writers such as Joseph Beuys and Heinrich Böll—began considering the formation of a new political party. In March 1979, the Sonstige Politische Vereinigung-Die Grünen (Alternative Political Alliance—the Greens) was founded, and

Petra was elected to be one of the candidates running for the first direct elections to the European Parliament. The Alliance failed to win seats but had become a formidable political entity with seats in the regional governments. On January 12–13, 1980, the informal Alliance turned into a formal political party, Die Grünen (the Greens). Its new members agreed upon the "four pillars" of the Green Party: ecology, social responsibility, grassroots-democracy, and non-violence. From March 1980 to November 1982, Kelly was one of three speakers of the Green Party. In the 1983 federal elections, the Green Party received 5.4% of the votes and won 27 seats in the German Parliament. Elected a member of Parliament, Petra was finally able to give up her job in Brussels. She became a member of the Foreign Relations Committee and one of three speakers of the Green Party's parliamentary group. During her first two years in Parliament, Kelly continued to organize and participate in anti-nuclear protests, won the Peace Woman of the Year Award, served as representative on the board of the Western European Union, met with East German dissidents and with Erich Honecker, the former head of state of East Germany, and tried unsuccessfully to block the Parliament's vote to accept U.S. nuclear missiles on German ground. During this time, the Green Party became increasingly influential in German politics and succeeded in their 1984 run for the European Parliament.

> *Patriarchal power has brought us acid rain, global warming, military states, and countless cases of private suffering.*
>
> —Petra Kelly

The estrangement between Kelly and the Green Party began when, according to party rules, Kelly was to hand over her parliamentary seat to her successor in 1985. Although Members of Parliament are elected to a four-year term, the Green Party had decided to rotate its members every two years. Kelly refused to give up her seat, and the party abolished the two-year rotation principle in 1986. However, because of her refusal to rotate, Kelly became isolated within her own party and turned for support more than ever to Gert Bastian, whom she had first met in 1980, shortly after Bastian, a major general, had resigned from the German army in protest against the deployment of nuclear missiles in Germany. Bastian had become Kelly's companion in 1982; he also became a member of the Green Party and a fellow member of Parliament, from which he resigned in 1984 before the end of his term. Kelly and Bastian were inseparable, appearing everywhere together, and became in the eyes of their friends and acquaintances, as one writer noted, "Petraandgert."

In 1987, Kelly was re-elected to Parliament and continued advocating her causes. She also continued publishing books and articles and successfully drafted a bill on human rights in Tibet, which Parliament supported unanimously. In 1987, she participated in the Moscow Peace Forum, where she met with the Soviet dissident Andrei Sakharov and the Soviet head of state, Mikhail Gorbachev. From 1988 to 1990, she served as chair of the German Association of Social Defense, and in 1989 she organized the first International and Non-Partisan Hearing on Tibet and Human Rights.

In the first federal elections after German unification in 1990, the Green Party (West) won no seats in Parliament. Because of her opposition to forming coalitions with other parties, Kelly became even more isolated within her own party, and it was a shock to many when she received only 39 out of 646 votes in the 1991 election for party speaker. Having lost the resources available to Members of Parliament, Kelly began searching for opportunities to continue her work. In 1992, she began moderating a series of environmental programs for a German cable television station. The series was not successful and disputes between Kelly and the producers led to its cancellation. Kelly's last public appearances were in September 1992 at the World Uranium Hearing in Salzburg and the Global Radiation Victims' Conference in Berlin. On September 26, 1992, Kelly and Bastian met with a publisher and a Buddhist teacher and writer. Neither these two men nor the people who had attended the Salzburg and Berlin conferences had detected anything strange or amiss with either Kelly or Bastian. Their presence, they stated, was overwhelmingly forward looking, courageous and life-affirming, and nobody could believe that a few days later the nice elderly gentleman would kill Petra Kelly.

SOURCES:

Kolinsky, Eva, ed. *The Greens in West Germany.* Oxford: Berg, 1989.

Parkin, Sara. *The Life and Death of Petra Kelly.* London: Pandora, 1994.

SUGGESTED READING:

Kelly, Petra K. *Thinking Green: Essays on Environmentalism, Feminism, and Nonviolence.* Berkeley, CA: Parallax Press, 1994.

COLLECTIONS:

Correspondence, manuscripts, and memorabilia are located at the Petra Kelly Archiv at Archiv Grünes Gedächtnis, Romerstrasse 71, 53332 Bornheim-Widdig, Germany.

Karin Bauer,
Assistant Professor of German Studies,
McGill University, Montreal, Canada

Kemble, Adelaide (1814–1879)

English soprano and author. Name variations: Adelaide Sartoris; Mrs. Edward Sartoris. Born in London in 1814; died in Warsash on August 4, 1879; daughter of Charles Kemble (an actor) and Maria Theresa (De Camp) Kemble (1774–1838, an actress); younger sister of Fanny Kemble (1809–1893); studied in London with Braham, in Italy with Pasta; married Edward Sartoris (a wealthy Italian), in 1843; children: Algernon Charles Sartoris (married Ellen "Nellie" Grant [1855–1922], the daughter of Ulysses S. Grant).

Born in 1814 in London into a famous dramatic family, Adelaide Kemble was the daughter of actor Charles Kemble and actress *Maria Theresa Kemble, the niece of *Sarah Siddons, and the younger sister of *Fanny Kemble. Adelaide chose to pursue, instead, musical studies, making her operatic debut as Norma in Venice in 1838. After much success in Italy, she also sang Norma at London's Covent Garden in 1841. She then appeared in *Figaro, Sonnambula,* and *Semiramide.* After a short though brilliant career, she married Edward Sartoris, an Italian of wealth, and retired to his estate in Italy in 1843. In 1874, her son Algernon Charles Sartoris married **Ellen "Nellie" Grant**, one of *Julia Grant and President Ulysses S. Grant's daughters. An account of Adelaide Kemble's career can be found in Fanny Kemble's *Record of a Girlhood* (London, 1878). Adelaide is the author of *A Week in a French Country House.*

Kemble, Mrs. Charles (1774–1838).

See Kemble, Maria Theresa.

Kemble, Eliza (1761–1836)

*English actress. Name variations: Mrs. Whitlock. Born Elizabeth Kemble in 1761; died in 1836; daughter of Roger Kemble (an actor-manager) and Sarah (Ward) Kemble; sister of *Sarah Siddons (1755–1831); aunt of *Fanny Kemble (1809–1893); married Charles Edward Whitlock, in 1785.*

In 1783, Eliza Kemble appeared in *The Merchant of Venice* with her sister *Sarah Siddons at the Drury Lane. Following her marriage in 1785, Eliza accompanied her husband actor

Charles Edward Whitlock to America and would make one other journey to that country before she retired in 1807, subsequent to her appearance as Elwina in *Percy* at the Drury Lane.

Kemble, Elizabeth (c. 1763–1841)

English actress. Name variations: Elizabeth Satchell; Mrs. Stephen Kemble. Born Elizabeth Satchell around 1763; died in 1841; married Stephen Kemble (1758–1822, an actor manager and brother of *Sarah Siddons), in 1783; aunt of *Fanny Kemble (1809–1893); children: Henry Stephen Kemble (1789–1836, an actor who played leading parts at Drury Lane).

Elizabeth Satchell performed at Covent Garden as Polly Peachum in *The Beggar's Opera* in 1780; the following season, she appeared as Juliet in *Romeo and Juliet*. Continuing her Shakespearean roles, she played Desdemona to Stephen Kemble's Othello in 1783 and married him that same year. Elizabeth Kemble's career would go on to surpass that of her husband, whose "chief distinction," groused one of his rivals, "was his ability to play Falstaff without stuffing."

Kemble, Fanny (1809–1893)

English Shakespearean actress who divorced a prominent American slave-owner and condemned slavery in her best-known book, Journal of a Residence on a Georgia Plantation. *Name variations: Frances Anne Kemble or Fanny Kemble (1809–1834, and in print); Frances Butler (1834–1849); Mrs. Fanny Kemble (1849–1893). Born Frances Anne Kemble in London, England, on November 27, 1809; died in London on January 15, 1893; daughter of Charles Kemble (an actor and theatrical impresario) and Maria Theresa (De Camp) Kemble (an actress and dancer); sister of Adelaide Kemble (1814–1879); fraternal niece of Sarah Siddons (1755–1831); married Pierce Butler, in 1834 (divorced 1849); children: Sarah Butler Wister (1835–1908); Frances Butler Leigh (1838–1910).*

Appeared as an actress (1829–34, 1847–49); toured as a public dramatic reader (1849–70); was a lifelong writer and poet.

Selected writings: Journal *(1935);* Year of Consolation *(1847);* Journal of a Residence on a Georgia Plantation *(1863);* Records of a Girlhood *(1878);* Records of a Later Life *(1882);* Further Records *(1884);* Far Away and Long Ago *(1889).*

Fanny Kemble was one of the first trans-Atlantic celebrities—she crossed the Atlantic 30 times and remained popular in British and American high society from almost the beginning to the end of her life. Famous in her youth as a beautiful Shakespearean actress, she fell passionately in love with and married a rich American slave-owner, reacted violently against him and his way of life, and wrote a superb anti-slavery tract in the form of a journal at his Georgia Sea-Island plantation.

She was born in London in 1809 into a leading theatrical family, and in 1823, when she was 14, her father Charles Kemble became head of the Theatre Royal in Covent Garden. Her mother *Maria Theresa Kemble had been a dancer, but Fanny herself was educated in the ladylike arts, learned singing, French, German, and Italian, and went to a French finishing school. She was saturated in the romanticism of the era and was very proud to have met Sir Walter Scott, the most popular novelist of the day. An attack of smallpox in her teen years marred her complexion, but she remained strikingly attractive.

> *The death I should prefer would be to break my neck off the back of a good horse at full gallop on a fine day.*
>
> —Fanny Kemble

Her father was a good actor but a bad businessman, and his company was on the brink of bankruptcy in 1829, facing heavy debts and litigation. Fearing its collapse, he asked his beautiful 20-year-old daughter to play the heroine's role in a new production of Shakespeare's *Romeo and Juliet*. It was only because her own aunt, *Sarah Siddons, had demonstrated in the previous generation that a woman could be an actress without losing her high moral character that Fanny agreed (at that time most actresses had a social reputation as "loose women"). Untrained but highly intelligent and gifted, she was an instant success, and the company, after its triumphs in London, capitalized on it in a provincial tour. By the time she was 21, Kemble was famous throughout Britain. As the sensation of the moment, she was invited in 1829 to ride on the locomotive during the historic inauguration of the Liverpool and Manchester Railway, the world's first public railroad. She found the iron horse, which ran at 30 miles per hour, wildly exciting and said she worshipped the dour, 50-year-old George Stephenson, the project's designer and builder.

Fanny also contributed to the family's fortunes by writing a historical drama, *Francis I*, and playing the leading female role. The profits enabled the family to buy an army commission for her brother. Despite her success on stage, she regarded herself more as a writer than as an actress. In fact, she disparaged the stage as an inferior career, and often wrote that she would rather abandon it and take up writing as her real vocation. In 1832, unfortunately, money troubles recurred and the Kembles decided to visit America on an acting and fund-raising venture. There, too, they enjoyed critical acclaim, with many critics arguing that Kemble was the best actress ever to appear in the United States. One young Philadelphia law student, after watching her perform, wrote: "It would be hard to depict the wild intoxication that overtook me. I forgot everything else, law included. I did nothing but frequent the theater and abandon myself to the fascination of this bewitching actress." He added that "to the sorcery of the stage [she] added rare charms of person, brilliant accomplishments and high culture."

Fanny, however, was appalled by many aspects of American life and kept a diary expressing her displeasure at American manners and customs. She compared the roads, the servants,

Fanny
Kemble

the horses, the food, and everything else with its British counterpart and always found the American version inferior. She was shocked that store clerks tried to chat with her and did not call her "Ma'am." She found many of her hosts and hostesses vulgar and boring, lacking elements of the refinement she had come to enjoy in her years of English celebrity. As **Elizabeth Fox-Genovese** comments of this journal: "Above all she is English. From first to last, England affords the standards by which she judges everything American. From first to last England figures as the sign of everything she values." She relented a little as she became familiar with American manners, and she was impressed by the drama of Niagara Falls and the beauties of the Hudson River valley.

Pierce Butler, the heir to extensive plantations in the Sea Islands off the Georgia coast, had seen her performing in Philadelphia. He fell in love with her at once and began to follow the touring company, making himself useful as a guide and helper, and, before long, pleading with Fanny to marry him. At first, she rebuffed him, anticipating that she would soon be returning to England with her father, who expected her to continue her brilliant stage career, and telling Butler that she planned a literary career and had no intention of marrying. Butler, however, was rich, attractive and, on the face of it, highly eligible, having better manners than most of the Americans she had met, and easing the Kembles' problems as they moved from town to town. Eventually she succumbed and accepted his proposal, handing over the profits of the American tour to her father before he went home alone. The couple married in Philadelphia in 1834. She fainted during the ceremony and the next day, on a steamer to New York, wept all the way, which was an augury of difficulties to come.

Butler soon found that his new wife was anything but the Victorian ideal of female docility. She was neurotic, moody, and extremely stubborn—traits which some of her American hosts had already discovered—and she was bored by domestic confinement after her five years in the spotlight. She was determined to publish her American journals, even though he opposed the idea. Many people Butler knew were lampooned or openly criticized in its pages. She had at first hoped that by publishing them as a book she might raise money to pay the medical bills of her aunt who, traveling with them, had been badly injured in a carriage accident. Before long the project took on a life of its own. She pressed on with publication plans even after her aunt's death had made the original plan unnecessary. She compromised with her husband by

deleting most of the names (circumstantial evidence still made their identities evident in many cases) but then, against his wishes, saw the book into print. It was an immediate success, capitalizing on the author's dramatic fame. Educated Americans were feeling particularly bruised in the 1830s as a succession of critical British commentaries on American life appeared, most notably those by *Harriet Martineau, *Frances Trollope, and Charles Dickens. This one rubbed salt into the raw wound but thousands read it anyway while English audiences were delighted.

The newly married couple argued violently, about his leisurely way of life, his gambling, and her book. She gave birth to a daughter, ⬥ **Sarah Butler (Wister)**, within a year, but showed little interest in being a mother, and her letters from the time show her struggling against perpetual boredom, homesickness, and a sense of unwelcome confinement. The couple undertook the first of several trial separations in 1837 and Fanny, to her intense pleasure, returned to England and to her role there as a high-society celebrity. She saw the new queen, *Victoria, opening Parliament, and resumed her visits to the aristocratic salons that had welcomed her in the early days of her success. Butler, however, came to fetch her back, and during a brief reconciliation she conceived her second child, ⬥ **Frances Butler (Leigh)**. Her difficulty, then and later, was that she was passionately attracted to Butler though disgusted by many aspects of his way of life. She later wrote that he expected her to be content with being the mother of the two girls; that his attitude was: "What need of intellectual converse, have you not an affectionate husband and two sweet babies?" to which she retorted: "You might as well say to a man who has no arms, 'Oh! no, but you have two legs.'"

So long as she was in the north with Butler, she could make the most of his worldly wealth without reflecting on its origins, but once she went south to the rice and cotton plantations he had now inherited she was brought face to face with the fact that it came from slavery. Merely getting to the plantations, on the Georgia coast, was a difficult task, and her description of travel on early railroads, "corduroy" log roads, shoddy steamboats, disgusting food and filthy hotels, has become a minor classic in its own right. She spent 1838 and 1839 on the plantation and wrote another journal, mainly in the form of letters to her friend **Elizabeth Sedgwick**. She was already, as an evangelical Protestant, opposed to slavery in general but she was ready, she wrote in one of the first letters, "to find many mitigations . . . much kindness on the part of the mas-

⬥
See sidebar
on the
following page

⬥
See sidebar
on the
following page

✧➤ Wister, Sarah Butler (1835–1908)

American socialite. Born in 1835; died in 1908; daughter of Pierce Butler (d. 1867, a plantation owner) and Fanny Kemble (1809–1893); married Owen Jones Wister (a Philadelphia physician); children: Owen Wister (1860–1938, a novelist who wrote The Virginian*).*

Socialite Sarah Butler Wister, who married a prominent physician, was very close to her novelist son Owen Wister. When he was still quite young, the two began a correspondence that continued until Sarah's death in 1908. Early on, while on a trip out West, Wister shared with his mother his growing desire to write. "The only thing I do is to jot down all shreds of local colour and all conversations and anecdotes decent or otherwise that strike me as native wild flowers. After a while I shall write a great fat book about the whole thing." Like his grandmother *Fanny Kemble, Owen had learned the importance of getting it all down. "Former experience has taught that you can hardly make a journal too full," he wrote his mother. "I hope I shall be able to keep it up and get down in notes, anyhow, all the things that are peculiar to this life and country." Always eager for her opinion, Wister sent his mother a copy of his newly finished epic, *The Virginian*, in 1902. She did not like it and told him so.

Owen Wister's daughter **Fanny Kemble Wister** (Stokes) wrote *My Father, Owen Wister* (Laramie, Wyoming, 1952) and edited *Owen Wister Out West: His Journals and Letters* (University of Chicago Press, 1958), *That I May Tell You: Journals and Letters of the Owen Wister Family* (Haveford House, 1979), and *Fanny, the American Kemble: Her Journals and Unpublished Letters* (Tallahassee: South Pass Press, 1972).

✧➤ Leigh, Frances Butler (1838–1910)

*American Reconstruction-era plantation manager. Name variations: Fanny Butler. Born in 1838; died in 1910; daughter of Pierce Butler (a Georgia plantation owner) and *Fanny Kemble (English-born actress, author, abolitionist); married Reverend James Wentworth Leigh, in 1871.*

Parents divorced (1849); returned to plantation with father from North (1866); father died (1867); worked to convert plantation to pay-basis (1867–71); moved to England with husband (1871); returned to plantation and repaired it to prosperity (1873).

ters, much content on that of the slaves." In fact, however, she found the slave system far *worse* than she had anticipated, and her book became a slashing indictment of slavery, both because of the cruelty inflicted on the slaves, and because of the way the system turned slave-masters into tyrants. She described the distinction between house-slaves and field-slaves, the use of trusted slaves as "drivers," and the system of punishing all signs of disobedience with the lash. To avoid punishments, she added, slaves became servile, flattering, and deceitful.

It was not that she befriended the slaves: she described those who served her in the house as "perfectly filthy in their persons and clothes," and the maid she had been given, known only as Mary, as "so intolerably offensive in her person that it is impossible to endure her proximity." Like many abolitionists of her era, she hated slavery without feeling any particular affection for the enslaved. Nevertheless, she tried to improve conditions, especially of the female slaves. These women lived in insanitary huts full of ducks and chickens, and gave birth to their children in a bare-earth infirmary. They were forced back to work in the fields just three or four weeks after giving birth, while the babies were put into the care of slightly older children, and they suffered—especially those who worked on the Butler Island rice plantation—from rheumatism, malaria, and other afflictions. Kemble surreptitiously taught a young slave, Aleck, to read, in contravention of the Georgia slave-code, and encouraged slaves with grievances to tell her their problems, so that she might intercede on their behalf with the master. Butler was furious, and forbade her to do it. Despite her indignation and her growing disillusionment with her husband, however, she soon recognized that there was no possibility of him freeing the slaves. She could see, indeed, that he was part of an entrenched system that would regard him as a lunatic if he voluntarily surrendered his livelihood.

In the early 1840s, Butler and Kemble visited England again. She was still a celebrity at home, feted by the aristocracy and introduced to Queen Victoria at court. A publisher, having heard about her Georgia journal, asked to publish it, but this time Butler strictly refused his permission. He was enraged when he discovered that she had instead given the publisher her diary of the difficult journey, by sea and land, from Philadelphia to Georgia, an act which he saw as a breach of their family privacy and a violation of his rights as a husband. He retaliated by intercepting and reading all her correspondence, to which she reacted by leaving him altogether. She had frequently threatened to leave him, if necessary by selling her jewelry to raise the money, but their stormy scenes had usually been followed by tearful reconciliations. Unlike most men and women of the era, she was totally opposed to the idea that a woman's freedom should be limited and controlled by her husband and that she must, as the wedding service then specified, "love, honor, and obey" him. In one letter, he wrote: "If you will govern your irritable temper, and if you can consent to submit your will to mine, we will be reconciled and may be happy. I firmly believe that husband and wife cannot live happily on any other terms and it would be vain for us to be reunited unless upon a clear understanding of the conditions I propose, and a full determination to abide by them."

Back in America and living in a boarding house (much humbler than their London splendor, which had run them into debt), Butler tried to enforce these rules on his wife with unbending strictness. He restricted Fanny's opportunities to talk with their two daughters, and ordered the governess, Miss Hall, to keep the girls out of their mother's orbit as much as possible. He even sold Fanny's horse, which she liked to ride every day, without warning her beforehand. She suspected that he was having (or had previously had) an affair with another woman—possibly Miss Hall herself. Unable to speak to each other without getting into furious arguments, she and Butler bombarded each other with letters (even though they were in the same house), each accusing the other of unreasonable conduct.

In the end Fanny separated from him for the last time and returned to England in 1845, now aged 36. Her sister *Adelaide Kemble, who had made a successful career as a singer and then married happily, invited her to recuperate from her psychological trials by spending a year with them in Italy. After this vacation, being short of money and reluctant to depend on Butler, who had informally agreed to send her $1,000 per year, Fanny resumed her acting career in 1847, going on stage for the first time since 1834. She was a stout, middle-aged woman by then but still an accomplished actress, able to command high fees and playing to enthusiastic audiences. Back in America to finalize her divorce settlement in 1849, she gave a dramatic reading from Shakespeare to a Boston audience. It was a success and led to reading tours in Britain and America in which she gave passionate renderings of entire Shakespeare plays, reading every part with broad gestures, exaggerated expressions, and the maximum of sentiment. Critical opinions varied. Her friend Henry Greville wrote: "It is wonderful the effect she produces; it is like seeing the whole play admirably acted, and delightful to hear the beautiful poetry, which is usually so murdered on the stage, spoken by her melodious voice, and with her subtle expression." Charles Dickens and Henry Wadsworth Longfellow, on the other hand, both thought the performances pretty awful, following, as they did, her father's early 19th-century convention of deliberate over-enunciation.

Kemble herself found it hard work as she was constantly on the move during these tours, staying in hotels all over Britain and America, usually accompanied by a maid. But the span of her lifetime witnessed a great change in transportation. When she began her acting career, she had to travel by stagecoach and cross the ocean by sail. By the time of her retirement, she enjoyed rail travel, throughout both countries, and steamers for her numerous Atlantic crossings. Using the proceeds from her readings, she built a house in Lenox, Massachusetts, close to the homes of Herman Melville and Nathaniel Hawthorne, with whom she was friendly, and near her long time friends and confidantes Elizabeth and *Catherine Sedgwick. Kemble became a familiar figure among the transcendentalists, though her own religious views were always more evangelical—earlier she had fired her daughters' best nurse out of fear that she was trying to turn the girls into Roman Catholics.

Elizabeth Sedgwick, the original recipient of her Georgia plantation letters, had urged her not to publish them even after her divorce, and she kept the book to herself until 1863. By then the American Civil War was at its crisis, and her ex-husband was fighting for the Confederacy, even though debt had forced him to sell most of his slaves. Some Britons favored supporting the Confederacy—it was the source of raw cotton for Britain's manufacturing cities of Liverpool and Manchester. But humanitarian feeling in Britain favored the anti-slavery cause of the Union. Kemble finally decided to publish the *Journal* near the end of 1862 and by the time it came out, just after the Battle of Gettysburg the following year, Lincoln's Emancipation Proclamation had in effect brought slavery to an end. Even so, the book helped sway popular opinion in England against aiding the Confederacy, and contributed to the British government's decision to remain neutral throughout the war. Union reviewers in America, meanwhile, were as delighted by this book as they had been angry at her earlier journal. *Harper's Monthly* described it as "the most powerful anti-slavery book yet written." Kemble aided the Union cause by reading dramatic antislavery passages from the book aloud on her tours, and was delighted to see the Union prevail.

Of her two daughters, the elder, Sarah, was loyal to her mother and to the American north while the younger, Frances, stood beside her father, and tried to keep his much-depleted plantation going after his death in 1867. Kemble herself began writing a long memoir of her early life, *Records of a Girlhood,* in 1875 (her memoirs later grew to five volumes). She wrote it on one of the world's first typewriters, which she quickly mastered, and first published it in the *Atlantic Monthly* in installments, under the heading "Old Woman's Gossip." Fanny returned to Britain in 1877 to live out her later years there (partly in Stratford on Avon, partly in London) and on annual visits to southern Europe. She was a friend of the American anglophile novelist Henry James, whom she met in 1872 and with whom she remained on close terms until her death in London in 1893, at age 84. Her daughter Sarah, married to Dr. Owen Wister of Philadelphia, passed on Fanny's literary vocation to her son, Owen Wister, whose novel *The Virginian* (1902), was the first great cowboy adventure story.

SOURCES AND SUGGESTED READING:

Furnas, J.C. *Fanny Kemble: Leading Lady of the Nineteenth Century Stage.* NY: Dial Press, 1982.

Gough, Monica, ed. *Fanny Kemble: Journal of a Young Actress.* With a foreword by Elizabeth Fox-Genovese. NY: Columbia University Press, 1990.

Marshall, Dorothy. *Fanny Kemble.* London: Weidenfeld and Nicolson, 1977.

Mavor, Elizabeth, ed. *Fanny Kemble: The American Journals.* London: Weidenfeld and Nicolson, 1990.

Wister, Fanny Kemble, ed. *Fanny, the American Kemble: Her Journals and Unpublished Letters.* Tallahassee, FL: South Pass Press, 1972.

COLLECTIONS:

Fanny Kemble Collection, Columbia University Library; Massachusetts Historical Society; Bodleian Library, Oxford, United Kingdom.

Patrick Allitt,
Professor of History, Emory University, Atlanta, Georgia

Kemble, Frances Anne (1809–1893).

See Kemble, Fanny.

Kemble, Mrs. John Philip (1756–1845).

See Kemble, Priscilla.

Kemble, Maria Theresa

(1774–1838)

English actress. Name variations: Marie Thérèse De Camp, Mrs. Charles Kemble, Miss De Camp. Born Maria Theresa De Camp in Vienna, Austria, on May 13, 1774; died in 1838; the daughter of a French captain father and a Swiss mother; sister of Adelaide De Camp (Aunt Dall); married Charles Kemble (1775–1854, an actor and theatrical impresario), in 1806; children: John Mitchell Campbell (1807–1857, a philologist and historian); *Fanny Kemble (1809–1893); *Adelaide Kemble Sartoris (1814–1879).

Victorian writers tended to summarize Maria Theresa De Camp's origins as "vulgar" (meaning plain); there was no theatrical dynasty in her background. Her parents met while her father was a captain in the French army then invading Switzerland. Newly married and penniless, the De Camps arrived in London hoping for a new life, but Captain De Camp soon died of tuberculosis. The widow De Camp and her five children had to fend.

Maria Theresa Kemble, born in Vienna on the same month and day as that of Empress ***Maria Theresa of Austria,** first appeared under her maiden name at the Drury Lane in 1786, age 12; she was the sole support of her family. Six years later, she scored a hit as Macheath in *The Beggar's Opera.* She went on to create the role of Judith in *The Iron Chest,* Caroline Dormer in *The Heir at Law* (1797), and Madge Wildfire in *Heart of the Midlothian;* she also portrayed Shakespeare's women: Portia, Desdemona, and Katherine. From 1806 to 1819, she appeared at Covent Garden, having married actor-manager Charles Kemble that first year; Charles would become manager of Covent Garden in 1822. Maria Theresa Kemble also wrote and appeared in *First Faults* (1799), *The Day after the Wedding* (1808) and *Smiles and Tears* (1815).

Kemble, Priscilla (1756–1845)

English actress. Name variations: Mrs. Brereton; Mrs. John Philip Kemble. Born Priscilla Hopkins in 1756; died in 1845; married John Philip Kemble (1757–1823, brother of *Sarah Siddons), in 1787.

Priscilla Hopkins performed with the Garrick company at the Drury Lane in 1775. She went on to create the roles of Harriet in *The Runaway,* Eliza in *Spleen, or Islington Spa,* and Maria in Richard Brinsley Sheridan's *School for Scandal* (1777). She continued her career in secondary parts as Mrs. Brereton until she married John Philip Kemble in 1787. Priscilla Kemble retired eight years later and, upon the death of her husband in 1823, lived out her days at her country place, Heath Farm, in Hertfordshire, lent to her by Lord Essex.

Kemble, Sarah (1755–1831).

See Siddons, Sarah.

Kemble, Mrs. Stephen (c. 1763–1841).

See Kemble, Elizabeth.

Kempe, Anna Eliza (1790–1883).

See Bray, Anna Eliza.

Kempe, Margery (c. 1373–after 1438)

Religious pilgrim, mystic, and author of the oldest extant autobiography in the English language, a document known only in a severely excerpted form until the discovery of the full manuscript in 1934 which led to a reassessment of her controversial spiritual life and her position in the Western mystical tradition.

Name variations: *Margery Burnham Kempe; Margerie Kempe.* Pronunciation: *Kemp.* Born Margery Burnham around 1373 at King's Lynn (then Bishop's Lynn) in the county of Norfolk, England; died in King's Lynn sometime after 1438; daughter of John Burnham, or de Brunham (five times mayor, alderman of the merchant guild, six times member of Parliament, coroner, and justice of the peace); nothing is known of her mother; married John Kempe (a tax-collector, miller, and brewer), around 1393; children: 14, about whom little is known; wrote with the aid of two scribes *The Book of Margery Kempe* between 1431 and her death.

Margery Kempe's prevailing concern was her own personal relationship to Christ. In her late years, when she was moved to record it, she made no reference to such monumental events of her time as the Hundred Years' War, the Peasants' Revolt of 1381, the spread of plague across Europe known as the Black Death, or the period of the "Babylonian Captivity" during which more than one pope reigned in the Catholic Church; Chaucer and Froissart, the great secular authors of her day, also receive no mention. What Margery Kempe gave to history was her highly personal and detailed account of the spiritual life of a woman of the merchant class living at the end of the Middle Ages, including her religious transformation. Periodically subjected to ostracism and persecution by those who found her emotional displays hypocritical and downright annoying, Kempe believed in the necessity of her suffering for the sake of maintaining her close mystical communication with Christ. She saw herself as a mirror reflecting the Passion, Christ's suffering and death on the cross. By becoming such a mirror, Kempe thought she could lead others to feel deeply the love and devotion she herself felt for her Lord.

Margery Burnham Kempe was born into a family of local prominence at Bishop's Lynn, in the county of Norfolk, England, around the year 1373. Her father was John Burnham, or de Brunham, who was alderman of the merchant guild and five times mayor, as well as coroner, justice of the peace, and a member of Parliament; nothing is known of her mother. At about age 21, Margaret married John Kempe, also a man of good social standing, as a miller, brewer and tax-collector. Kempe's own story begins with her first pregnancy, a dangerous time for any woman in a period when many did not survive childbirth. When the birth became extremely difficult, Kempe grew terrified, her fright compounded by the memory of an old sin she had never confessed to a priest, causing her to fear a death that would cause her to go straight to hell. A priest who had been called in showed her no compassion, and Kempe again neglected to confess the unnamed sin, then fell into an intense hallucinatory state, scratching and biting herself as she felt the threat and punishment of demons. As her torture reached the crisis point, she had to be tied to her bed to protect her from suicide.

In the mystical tradition, such deep spiritual suffering can be viewed as a "dark night of the soul." Passing through this difficult phase, the mystic can reach an "illumination" which allows a kind of direct communication, or union, with the absolute divinity that the mystic recognizes as God. Such *via negativa* mysticism, exemplified by Saint John of the Cross and the anonymous author of *The Cloud of Unknowing,* a medieval work, has traditionally been regarded more highly than more emotional, affective mysticism. Biographer **Clarissa W. Atkinson** warns against seeing the experience of Margery Kempe as closely allied to this type of spiritual approach which emphasizes the emptying of mind and senses to allow the soul to receive the divine. According to Atkinson, Kempe's form of mysticism preserved her own will and individual self in a way that meant she "was never very far from God, but neither was her soul 'merged' with the divine." Kempe's visions, which extended from this early period throughout her life, took the form of conversations with Christ, while her emotions helped her "to participate in divine experience through the humanity she shared with Christ."

What is particularly significant about Kempe's place in the mystical tradition is that her record of her spiritual life, *The Book of Margery Kempe,* was lost for five centuries, except for a severely excerpted portion, including some prayers, which was brought into print in 1501 by Wynkyn de Worde. As Karma Lochrie, another scholar interested in Kempe has noted, the absence of her full manuscript "meant that scholars constructed the story of medieval mysticism without her."

In any case, the full autobiographical work reveals that Jesus Christ appeared to Kempe, when she had reached her lowest point, bringing her safety, joy, forgiveness, peace and love. Her dramatic recovery from "madness" that followed had the appearance of a miracle, in which the young woman's formerly bizarre behavior gave way to a seemingly balanced, lucid and controlled normalcy. At this stage in the narrative, her account reveals a little of the social context of Kempe's life, when she began to show a returned interest in spending money for stylish clothes, resuming a satisfying physical relationship with her husband, and even to chide her husband as one who was beneath her socially. The impact of her salvation experience was meanwhile not forgotten. When Kempe became involved in two business ventures, as a brewer and later as a miller, she took her failures as a sign of punishment from God for her vanity and voluptuousness in seeking profitable means to support her extravagant material desires. Then, after several years, she began to take up the idea of being specially chosen by Christ and wanting to dedicate herself to loving him.

Our Lord would say [to me] . . . daughter, I have ordained thee to be a mirror amongst them, to have great sorrow, so that they should take example by thee, and have some little sorrow in their hearts for their sins, so that they might there-through be saved.

—Margery Kempe

Margery Kempe never took up the cloistered life, and in her marriage to John Kempe she gave birth to 14 children. At some point during these years, she had an experience of music that she found so spiritual, she thought she was hearing the sounds of paradise. Moved by this, she approached her husband about her desire to live a more spiritual life, proposing that they live together in chastity. John Kempe at first refused to agree, while Margery took up a regimen of penance, fasting, and prayer that became a disruption to the family, and persisted in weeping whenever she heard music that recalled the sounds of her heavenly vision. At her parish church of St. Margaret's, she took to crying out, weeping and throwing herself onto the floor, displaying passionate, almost erotic, behavior common to the ecstatic mystical tradition known at that time on the European Continent. In Bishop's Lynn, Kempe's behavior made her an outlandish spectacle, subjected to gossip and avoided by many, while John Kempe continued to insist on his marital rights, and the family grew.

Kempe's book, written years later, includes almost nothing, however, about the family.

In the 15th century, eccentric behavior like Kempe's could be dangerous, attracting charges of religious heresy. In 1417, after her theatrical outbursts had begun to include the chiding of parishioners and priests for their spiritual failings, she was arrested twice and tried for Lollardy. The Lollards were followers of John Wycliffe, active during the late 14th and early-15th centuries, who were denounced as heretics, and burned, primarily for their denial of the orthodoxy of transubstantiation (the communion wafer and wine offered during Mass were believed to become the actual body and blood of Christ). Lollards also denounced the clergy as corrupt and accepted lay people in the reading and interpreting of scripture, preaching, and administering the sacraments. Kempe's behavior was not found to be heretical, but socially it remained extreme. Still eager to declare herself spiritually wedded to Christ by observing marital chastity, she prayed to the Lord for a miracle to change her circumstances. When one was not forthcoming, she succumbed to temptation, finding herself attracted to a young man she saw outside her church. Coldly rebuffed when she offered to spend the night with him, she attributed the pain she felt to punishment for her presumptuousness in expecting a miracle.

Taking a more conventional approach, Kempe next sought the advice of the saintly vicar of St. Stephen's of Norwich and attained an audience with the famous anchoress *Julian of Norwich, renowned for her piety and intellect. Julian spent her days mostly in prayer and silence, living the more traditional spiritual life of a religious recluse, never leaving her cell. It was a contemplative existence that allowed a woman to express religious enthusiasm in a hidden, and therefore acceptable, way. In Julian, Kempe found considerable support for her claim to grace, and began to undertake a number of spiritual pilgrimages, first in England, and then to Jerusalem, Rome, Germany, and Spain.

In England, Kempe was accompanied on her travels by her husband John, who still resisted the idea of ending their physical relation. But by 1413, when they had been married 20 years, and Margery Kempe was probably 40, the couple had struck a bargain: if Margery, who had come into an inheritance from her father, would pay her husband's debts and agree to join him for dinner on Fridays instead of observing her regular fasts on that day, John would live with her in chasteness. That year, the couple took their vow of chastity before the bishop of Lincoln, and in 1414 Kempe departed on a pilgrimage to the Holy Land.

Visiting Jerusalem and the sites where Jesus had been born, lived and died, Kempe drew startled attention with her public tears and bellowing cries. Moving on to Rome, she earned further derision when she declared her chastity and espousal to Christ by wearing white clothes—a practice at the time considered unthinkable for a married woman—and a ring signifying her love for Jesus.

Abroad, Kempe aroused the same suspicions of hypocrisy, or worse, that neighbors in Lynn had ascribed to her. In the Middle Ages, many pilgrims undertook their excursions for more than the spiritual benefits that would accrue. All would receive a plenary indulgence from the Church meant to guarantee a swift passage to heaven at the time of their death, without a sojourn in purgatory. Besides this spiritual insurance policy, pilgrims could see the world and gain the admiration of their acquaintances. Among those who made the trip with Kempe, there were those who were comfortably devout but had come to expect some leisure away from constant prayer and self-edification. Such companions objected to Kempe's insistence on injecting her devotions into dinner conversation, or found her extravagant expressions of emotion irritating at every holy stop. Expelled from the group more than once, she was always taken back into their company, since even her worst critics were not sure of the weight carried by her devoutness. Once, when she decided to wait for another ship, they even delayed their sea passage to accompany her. Given the precariousness of medieval travel, it was not wise to flaunt a possible messenger of God, who might embody their protection against disaster.

Around 1431, Kempe ended her travels, returning home to stay after a fall left her husband paralyzed and in need of her care. Approaching the age of 60, she now considered making a record of her spiritual life, and, in one of her exchanges with Christ, she believed she received assurance that the time spent nursing John Kempe was equal in grace to the time she would otherwise have spent in meditation and prayer. Such work takes on what **Susan Dickman** refers to as "'active' versions of the quasi-religious life." In this path to holiness that she pursued, as opposed to the more widely accepted contemplative ideal, Kempe's life lends witness to the growing change from the medieval approach, separating the secular from the clerical, to a new spiritual culture which included those laity who wished to lead lives imbued with pious observance.

The dictation of Margery Kempe's autobiography began in 1432, the year after the martyrdom of another religious eccentric, ***Joan of Arc**, in France. Kempe lived until the book was finished, in 1438, but nothing beyond that date is known. In 1501, she had probably been dead a half-century, when some of Kempe's prayers were printed by Wynkyn de Worde, demonstrating not only the spread of devotional reading among the laity, but their profitability for printers. In one sense, Kempe's life, from early on, represents the Renaissance spirit of the Reformation, in its emphasis on a personal relationship with Christ, bypassing the interpretative powers of the clergy. At another level, however, Kempe clearly remained a medieval woman, staunchly orthodox and firmly entrenched in affective piety, a tradition inspired in large part by Saint Francis of Assisi and marked by an intense emotional emphasis on the human aspects of the life of Jesus. Despite the lack of sympathy she often received from acquaintances, she always had the clear support of the mainstream clergy, who were happy to support her brand of devotion, and especially the pain of humiliation she was willing to welcome as penance that brought her closer to Christ. Traveling on the Continent, however, where the seeds of sophisticated Renaissance thinking were already sown, her outward displays of devotion must often have seemed a bit anachronistic and quaint. And since the discovery of her complete work, in 1934, critics have had difficulty trying to fit her strongly individualistic brand of spirituality into the traditional canon of medieval mysticism.

Influenced by holy women of her times, such as ***Catherine of Siena**, ***Bridget of Sweden**, ***Mary of Oignies** and Julian of Norwich, Margery Kempe probably did not differ from many lay women who were attracted both to pursuing a pious life and remaining in the world. What distinguishes her, and also makes her controversial, is the intimate portrait of her spiritual life that is offered by her autobiographical work, with its clearly delineated attributes of a particularly proud and egotistical, overachieving, frenzied, and even schizophrenic woman. The document itself presents scholars with further difficulties. Like most women of her time, Margery Kempe was apparently illiterate, but also well-to-do enough to engage two scribes, who were most likely priests, to provide the autobiographical portrait of her as a specially chosen daughter of Christ. The fact of dictation, however, also blurs the convenient distinctions between biography and autobiography, hagiography, and mystical treatise. Recent feminist readings, including the one initiated by **Hope Emily Allen**, have begun to evaluate Margery Kempe anew. Past views of her, as primarily a misfit, have now been broadened for a more generous reading of her qualities, as a strong and ambitious individual, deeply spiritual but complex, whose fully assessed nature is likely to stimulate reappraisal, and even historic revision, of the Western mystical tradition and European medieval bourgeois culture.

SOURCES:

Atkinson, Clarissa W. *Mystic and Pilgrim: The Book and World of Margery Kempe.* Ithaca, NY: Cornell University Press, 1983.

Kempe, Margery. *The Book of Margery Kempe.* Edited and translated by William Butler-Bowden. NY: Devin-Adair, 1944.

———. *The Book of Margery Kempe.* Edited by Sanford B. Meech and Hope Emily Allen. London: Oxford University Press, 1940 (reprinted, 1961).

Cholmeley, Katharine. *Margery Kempe: Genius and Mystic.* NY: Longmans, Green, 1947.

Dickman, Susan. "Margery Kempe and the Continental Tradition of the Pious Woman," in *The Medieval Mystical Tradition in England: Papers Read at Dartington Hall, July 1984.* Edited by Marion Glasscoe. London: D.S. Brewer, 1984.

———. "Margery Kempe and the English Devotional Tradition," in *The Medieval Mystical Tradition in England: Papers Read at The Exeter Symposium, July 1980.* Edited by Marion Glasscoe. *Exeter Medieval English Texts and Studies.* General editor M.J. Swanton. University of Exeter, 1980.

Holbrook, Sue Ellen. "Margery Kempe and Wynkyn de Worde," in *The Medieval Mystical Tradition in England: Papers read at Dartington Hall, July 1987.* Exeter Symposium IV. Edited by Marion Glasscoe. London: D.S. Brewer, 1987.

Lochrie, Karma. *Margery Kempe and Translations of the Flesh.* Philadelphia, PA: University of Pennsylvania Press, 1991.

Riehle, Wolfgang. *The Middle English Mystics.* Translated by Bernard Standring. London: Routledge and Kegan Paul, 1981.

Stone, Robert Karl. *Middle English Prose Style: Margery Kempe and Julian of Norwich.* The Hague: Mouton, 1970.

Watkin, E.I. "On Julian of Norwich and In Defence of Margery Kempe," in *Exeter Medieval English Texts and Studies.* General Editor M.J. Swanton. University of Exeter, 1979.

SUGGESTED READING:

Collis, Louise. *Memoirs of a Medieval Woman: The Life and Times of Margery Kempe.* NY: Harper & Row, 1983.

Claudia Marie Kovach,
Professor of English and French,
Neumann College, Aston, Pennsylvania

Kempson, Rachel (1910—)

British actress and matriarch of the family Redgrave.

Born in Dartmouth, Devon, England, on May 28, 1910; daughter of Eric William Edward (a headmaster) and Beatrice Hamilton (Ashwell) Kempson; attended St. Agnes School, East Grinstead, and Oaklea Buckhurst Hill; studied for the stage at the Royal Academy of Dramatic Art; married (Sir) Michael Redgrave (an actor), in 1935 (died 1985); children: Vanessa Redgrave (b. 1937); Corin Redgrave (b. 1939); Lynn Redgrave (b. 1942).

Selected theater: made stage debut as Hero in Much Ado About Nothing *(Memorial Theater, Stratford-on-Avon, April 17, 1933); subsequently played Juliet in* Romeo and Juliet *and Ophelia in* Hamlet; *London debut as Bianca in* The Lady from Albuquerque *(Westminster, November 8, 1933); Ariel in* A Midsummer Night's Dream, *Olivia in* Twelfth Night, *Princess in* Love's Labour's Lost *(Stratford-on-Avon, 1934); Christina in* Two Kingdoms *(Savoy, October 1934); Anne in* The Witch *and Stella in* The Sacred Flame *(Playhouse, Oxford, February 1935); Naomi in* Flowers of the Forest *(Liverpool Repertory Company, March 1935); during the 1935–36 season appeared as Yvonne in* Youth at the Helm, *Eulalia in* A Hundred Years Old, *Anna of Bohemia in* Richard of Bordeaux, *Anne in* The Wind and the Rain, *Viola in* Twelfth Night, *Agnes Boyd in* Boyd's Shop, *Victoria in* A Storm in a Teacup; *Princess of France in* Love's Labour's Lost *(Old Vic, September 1936); Celia in* Volpone *(Westminster, January 1937); Maria in* The School for Scandal *(Queen's, November 1937); Jane in* The Shoemaker's Holiday *(Playhouse, November 1938); Jean Howard in* Under One Roof *(Richmond, March 1940); toured as Naomi in* Family Portrait, *Naomi in* Noah, *and Mrs. Bradman in* Blithe Spirit *(June 1940–February 1942); Faith Ingalls in* The Wingless Victory *(Phoenix, September 1943); Lucy Forrest in* Uncle Harry *(Garrick, March 1944); Marianne in* Jacobowsky and the Colonel *(Piccadilly, June 1945); Charlotte in* Fatal Curiosity *(Arts, December 1946); Chris Forbes in* Happy as Kings *("Q," January 1947); Dr. Rosamond Long in* The Sparks Fly Upwards *("Q," October 1947); Joan in* The Paragon *(Fortune, May 1948); Violet Jackson in* The Return of the Prodigal *(Globe, November 1948); title role in* Candida *(Playhouse, Oxford, May 1949); Queen Margaret in* The Saxon Saint *(Dunfermline Abbey, August 1949); Hilda Taylor-Snell in* Venus Observed *(St. James's, January 1950); Katie in* Top of the Ladder *(St. James's, October 1950); Maman in* The Happy Time *(St. James's, January 1952); joined the Shakespeare Memorial Theater Company, 1953, and during the season appeared as Queen Elizabeth in* Richard III, *Octavia in* Antony and Cleopatra, *and Regan in* King Lear; *Mrs. Thea Elvsted in* Hedda Gabler *(Lyric,*

Hammersmith, September 1954, and tour of Holland, Denmark, and Norway, 1955); with Dublin Gate Theater Company, appeared as Theodora in Not for Children *(Belfast, April 1955); joined the English Stage Company at the Royal Court, April 1956, and appeared as Cora Fellowes in* The Mulberry Bush, *Mrs. Ann Putnam in* The Crucible, *Evelyn in* The Death of Satan, *Miss Black Panorbis in* Cards of Identity, *and Mrs. Mi Tzu in* The Good Woman of Setzuan; *with the Shakespeare Memorial Theater Company, Stratford-on-Avon, 1958 season, appeared as Lady Capulet in* Romeo and Juliet, *Dionyza in* Pericles, *and Ursula in* Much Ado About Nothing; *toured with company in Moscow and Leningrad as Lady Capulet (December 1958); Mary in* Teresa of Avila *(Vaudeville, October 1961); Polina Andreyevna in* The Seagull *(Queen's, March 1964); Martha in* Saint Joan of the Stockyards *(Queen's, June 1964); Chorus in* Samson Agonizes, *and Lady Mary in* Lionel and Clarissa *(Yvonne Arnaud Theater, Guildford, June 1965).*

Selected filmography: The Captive Heart *(1946);* A Woman's Vengeance *(US, 1948);* Georgy Girl *(1966);* The Jokers *(1966);* Out of Africa *(1985);* Stealing Heaven *(1988);* Déjà Vu *(1998).*

The name Rachel Kempson is sometimes lost among the more recognizable names of the famous theatrical family Redgrave: Sir Michael Redgrave (1908–1985), Kempson's husband, and the three children, **Vanessa Redgrave**, Corin Redgrave, and **Lynn Redgrave**. Kempson was born in 1910, the daughter of Eric Kempson, a schoolmaster who taught science at Rugby and later became headmaster at the Royal Naval College at Dartmouth, and **Beatrice Ashwell Kempson**, a beautiful, difficult woman who suffered bouts of melancholia throughout her life. Rachel studied for the stage at the Royal Academy of Dramatic Art and made her stage debut in 1933 at the Memorial Theater, Stratford-on-Avon, as Hero in *Much Ado About Nothing*. That season, she also turned in admirable portrayals of Juliet in *Romeo and Juliet* and Ophelia in *Hamlet*. In 1935, as her career was on the upswing, she met and fell in love with Michael Redgrave, with whom she was performing in a season of repertory in Liverpool. Michael, who had worked as a journalist and a schoolmaster, was just getting started in the theater at the time. At Rachel's suggestion, they married a year later and joined the Old Vic Theater Company in London, where they appeared together in *Love's Labour's Lost* during the 1936 season.

Like many actresses, Kempson's career was interrupted for the birth of each of her three

Rachel Kempson

children, and she may have also been eclipsed by her husband's growing popularity. In her autobiography, Vanessa Redgrave writes that although her mother was always in demand, "she did not really come into her own until television in the 1960s brought her a range of parts that no theatrical producer has ever had the foresight to offer her." Kempson, however, did enjoy a respectable career, playing numerous supporting roles in major London productions and on tour. From 1945, she also appeared in occasional films, including *Georgy Girl* (1966), which starred her daughter Lynn, who was nominated for an Oscar and won the New York Film Critics Best Actress award for her touching performance of the plump ugly duckling of the title. Kempson's television credits include roles in "Conflict," "Man and Superman," "Howards End," and "Uncle Vanya."

Vanessa Redgrave characterizes her mother as a modest woman who never believed she was beautiful or a very good actress. However, she cites Kempson's performance in a small production of Shaw's *Saint Joan* (1954), as particularly memorable, calling it "brave, eager, direct, and very moving." In Vanessa's eyes, Rachel Kempson remained magical even as an old woman. "I saw her early this year," she writes toward the end of her autobiography, "using her cane to get onto the platform for a recital. She laid the cane down, that gentle profile lifted, and the years vanished from her face and body. Fourteen-year-old Juliet stood before us." In 1998, mother and daughter co-starred in an independent movie, *Déjà Vu*, directed by Henry Jaglom.

SOURCES:

Hartnoll, Phyllis, and Peter Found. *The Concise Oxford Companion to the Theater*. Oxford and NY: Oxford University Press, 1993.

Redgrave, Vanessa. *Vanessa Redgrave: An Autobiography*. NY: Random House, 1994.

SUGGESTED READING:

Kempson, Rachel. *Life Among the Redgraves* (autobiography). NY: Dutton, 1986.

Barbara Morgan,
Melrose, Massachusetts

Kemp-Welch, Joan (1906—)

British actress and director who was responsible for over 450 television and stage productions. Born Joan Kemp-Welch Green in Wimbledon, England, on September 23, 1906; daughter of Vincent Green and Helen (Kemp-Welch) Green; attended Roedean; married Ben H. Wright (divorced); married Peter Moffatt.

Selected acting credits: made stage debut in Maya *(Gate Theater, 1927); appeared in* Ghosts *(Wyndham's Theater, 1929),* John Gabriel Borkman *(Arts Theater, 1929),* Silent Witness *(Comedy Theater, 1930),* Traffic *(Lyceum Theater, 1930); toured in* Baa Baa Black Sheep, Cynara, *and* Admirals All *(1931); appeared as Miss Macadam in* Lovely Lady *(Phoenix Theater, February 1932); played in repertory (Q Theater, 1932–33); appeared as Clara in* Finished Abroad *(Savoy Theater, March 1934), Tondeleyo in* White Cargo, *Portia in* The Merchant of Venice, *Maria in* Twelfth Night *(repertory at Northampton), Bessie in* Glory Be *(Phoenix Theater, 1935), Charlotte in* Nina *(Criterion Theater, 1935); toured in title role in* Nina *(1936); toured in* Late Night Final *and* Boy Meets Girl *(South Africa, 1936); with Baxter-Somerville Company (Royal Brighton Theater, 1937);* The Melody That Got Lost *(Phoenix Theater, January 1938); appeared as Ellen in* A Doll's House *(Duke of York's Theater, February 1939), Diana in* Lady Fanny *(Duke of York's Theater, March 1939), Lucy Gillham in* Ladies in Retirement *(St. James's Theater, December 1939, and St. Martin's Theater, August 1941), Mrs. Thompson in* It Happened in September *(St. James's Theater, December 1942); appeared in* Damaged Goods *(Whitehall Theater, May 1943).*

Selected films as actress: Once a Thief *(1935);* The Girl in the Taxi *(1937);* Busman's Honeymoon *(1940);* Pimpernel Smith *(1941);* Jeannie *(1941).*

Selected director credits—theater: director at the Buxton Repertory Theater (1944), at Colchester Repertory (1945–48), at Wilson Barrett Company in Scotland (1948–51), at New Theater Bromley (1953–54), at the Pitlochry Festival (1968–69); directed over 250 plays including: Hedda Gabler, The Cher-

ry Orchard, Winterset, A Streetcar Named Desire, Desire Under the Elms, An Ideal Husband, Miss Hargreaves *(Court Theater, 1952);* Vicious Circle *(New Watergate Theater, 1955);* Dead on Nine *and* Albertine by Moonlight *(Westminster Theater, 1956); also directed revues and pantomimes.*

Selected television credits: A Midsummer Night's Dream *(BBC live in the 1960s, starring Patrick Allen,* **Jill Bennett, Anna Massey**, *Peter Wyngarde, and Benny Hill);* The Bonegrinder *(by Dennis Potter, aired on May 13, 1968, on ITV Playhouse);* Uldridge *(1968); episodes 4–7 of "Upstairs, Downstairs" (1971–72); episodes of "Life with the Lyons," starring* ***Bebe Daniels**; *also* Cool for Cats, Free and Easy, Rush Hour, Woman of no Importance, Birthday Party, Night School, The Problem of Girl Friends, A View From the Bridge, *and* Electra.

Primarily cited today for her television work, Joan Kemp-Welch began her career as a character actress, playing shy girls and spinsters on stage and in occasional films. She went on to direct over 250 productions for the theater, including such classics as *Hedda Gabler, The Cherry Orchard, Winterset, A Streetcar Named Desire,* and *Desire Under the Elms.* Entering television in the 1950s, Kemp-Welch directed over 200 programs, including features, dramas, and light entertainments. She won numerous awards for her work, including a television Oscar for "Cool for Cats" (1958), a *Prix Italia* for "The Lover" (1963), the Desmond Davis Award for service to television (1963), and the Wilkie Baird award for creative work on television.

Kendal, duchess of.

See Schulenburg, Ehrengard Melusina von der (1667–1743).

Kendal, Madge (1849–1935)

English actress who was enormously famous in her day. Name variations: Dame Madge Kendal; Mrs. Kendal; Margaret Brunton Robertson. Born Margaret Shafto (also seen as Sholto) Robertson on March 15, 1849 (some sources cite 1848) in Grimsby, Lincolnshire, England; died on September 14, 1935, in Hertfordshire, England; the 22nd child and last daughter of William Robertson (an actor and theatrical manager) and Margherita (also seen as Margaretta) Elisabetta (Marinus) Robertson (an actress-comedian); sister of dramatist T(homas) W(illiam) Robertson (1829–71); married W(illiam) H(unter) Kendal (an actor), on August 7, 1869 (died 1917); four children.

Selected theater: made stage debut as Marie in The Orphan of the Frozen Sea (Marylebone Theater, February 20, 1854); made adult London debut as Ophelia in Hamlet (Haymarket Theater, July 29, 1865); appeared as Blanche of Spain in King John, Desdemona in Othello, Cupid in Exion, Jessica in The Merchant of Venice (all at Haymarket Theater, 1865); Anne Carew in A Sheep in Wolf's Clothing, Julie in Richelieu, Lady Macbeth in Macbeth (all at Theater Royal, 1866); toured as Juliet in Romeo and Juliet, Peg Woffington in Masks and Faces, and Pauline Deschappelles in The Lady of Lyons (1866); Edith Fairlam in The Great City (Drury Lane Theater, 1867); Georgina in Our American Cousin (Haymarket Theater, 1867); Alice in Brother Sam, Ada Ingor in David Garrick, Blanche Dumont in A Hero of Romance, Marguerite in A Wife Well Won, Hippolyta in She Would and She Would Not (all at Haymarket, 1887); Florence in On the Cards and Lady Clara Vere de Vere in Dreams (both at Gaiety Theater, 1868); toured in As You Like It, Twelfth Night, She Stoops to Conquer, The School for Scandal, The Rivals, The Heir-in-Law, and The Country Girl (with Haymarket Company, 1868); appeared as Charlotte in The Hypocrite, Lilian Vavasour in New Men and Old Acres, Florence Marigold in Uncle's Will, Princess Zeolida in The Palace of Truth, Queen Selene in The Wicked World, Mrs. Van Brugh in Charity, Ellen Petworth in Barwise's Book, Lydia Languish in The Rivals, Lady Teazle in The School for Scandal, Rosalind in As You Like It, Kate Hardcastle in She Stoops to Conquer, Miranda in The Busy Body, Ada in Faded Flowers, Ethel in A Little Change, Mrs. Whymper in His Own Enemy, Mrs. Sebright in The Overland Route, Lady Gay Spanker in London Assurance, Jessie Meadows in Single Life, Elinor Vane in A Madcap Prince, and Mrs. Honeyton in A Happy Pair (all with the Haymarket Company, 1869–74); title role in Lady Flora, Mrs. Fitzroy in A Nine Days' Wonder, Lady Hilda in Broken Hearts, Susan Hartley in A Scrap of Paper (all at Court Theater, 1875); Lady Ormond in Peril, Clara Douglas in Money, Dora in Diplomacy (all at Prince of Wales Theater, 1876); Countess d'Autreval in The Ladies' Battle and Kate Greville in The Queen's Shilling (both at the Court Theater, 1879); Lady Giocanna in The Falcon, Mrs. Sternhold in Still Waters Run Deep, Isobel Ransome in Good Fortune, Millicent Boycott in The Money Spinner, Anne Carew in A Sheep in Wolf's Clothing, Mrs. Pinchbeck in Home, Mrs. Frank Preston in The Cape Mail, Kate Verity in The Squire, Mrs. Beresford in Impulse, Nora Desmond in Young Folks' Ways, Clair de Beaupre in The Iron Master, Lilian Selkirk in The Castaways,

Agnes Roydant in Mayfair, title role in Antoinette Rigaud, Countess in The Wife's Sacrifice, Mrs. Spencer Jermyn in The Hobby Horse, title role in Lady Clancarty, Lady Amyot in The Wife's Secret (all at the St. James Theater, 1879–87); Lady Vivash in The Weaker Sex, Kate Desmond in A White Lie (Court Theater, 1889); American debut as Susan in A Scrap of Paper (Fifth Avenue Theater, New York City, October 7, 1889), followed by four American tours 1890–92; toured as Paula in The Second Mrs. Tanqueray (Provincial tour, England, 1893); fifth tour of America, 1894–95; Mrs. Armitage in The Greatest of These (Garrick Theater, London, 1896); Sara Leaster in A Flash in the Pan, Dorothy Blossom in The Elder Miss Blossom, and Mrs. Grantham in Not Wisely But Too Well (tour of the Provinces, 1896–98); Margaret Hulestone in The Poverty of Riches, Mildred Archerson in The Likeness of the Night, and the Duchess of Cluny in The Secret Orchard (tour, 1899); Mistress Ford in The Merry Wives of Windsor (His Majesty's Theater, June 1902); Anne McLeod in One People (tour, and Coronet Theater, London, May 1903);

Marjorie Lyall in Dick Hope *(tour and Coronet Theater, December 1903); Audrey Whitby in* The Housekeeper *and Nora in* The Bird at the Neck *(both at the St. James Theater, fall 1905); Mrs. Hyacinth in* A Tight Corner, *Constance Livingstone in* The Whirlpool, *Madame Armières in* The House of Clay *(all at Coronet Theater, 1907–08).*

Born into one of England's oldest theatrical families in 1848, Madge Kendal was the daughter of William Robertson, an actor and theater manager, and **Margherita Marinus Robertson**, a Scandinavian-born actress who also distinguished herself by giving birth to 22 children, Madge being the last. Others of the Robertson clan (E. Shafto Robertson and **Fanny Robertson**) also aspired to the stage, although only brother T.W. Robertson, a playwright and creator of the "cup-and-saucer dramas" (so called because of their realistic domestic settings), achieved any notoriety. Kendal's father, in partnership with J.W. Wallack, managed the Marylebone Theater in London, and it was there that young Madge made her acting debut just short of her sixth birthday, playing Marie in *The Orphan of the Frozen Sea* (1854). She made her adult London debut at age 17, playing Ophelia to Walter Montgomery's Hamlet. By the time of her marriage to actor William Hunter Kendal, known as W.H. Kendal, at age 21, she was the veteran of over 50 parts. On her wedding night, she appeared with her new husband in *As You Like It*, and from then on their careers were inseparable.

Although Mrs. Kendal always professed that William was the superior actor (often citing his remarkable ability to turn pale at will), it was she who was the box-office draw. Indeed, Madge Kendal was considered the greatest comedian of her generation. "I defy any other actress, living or dead, to get a laugh out of some of the poor lines with which Mrs. Kendal simply rocked the house," said **Mary Jerrold**, who acted with the Kendals for over three years. "And what control she had! One moment she would have her audience roaring with laughter and in a flash she could have them quiet as mice." Kendal was also adept at playing darker emotions. As one critic noted: "Nor is she much less at home in the more pathetic portions of her part."

The Kendals performed with the Haymarket Company until 1874, during which time Madge played in all the classics as well as new plays. Her biographer, T. Edgar Pemberton, vividly remembered her early triumph as Charlotte in *The Hypocrite*: "I can conscientiously say that I have never seen anything so perfect on the stage. The

sweet, vivacious, graceful and altogether winsome Charlotte of that evening will ever linger in the memories of those who were fortunate enough to witness the impersonation." After the Haymarket Company broke up, the Kendals toured on their own, then joined John Hare at the Court Theater in 1875, where Madge was first seen as Susan Hartley in an adaptation of a Sardou comedy, *A Scrap of Paper*, a role she would repeat many times. In 1879, William Kendal went into partnership with John Hare at the St. James's Theater. The Kendals remained at the St. James's until 1888, playing leading roles in numerous productions, although many of the plays of their later years did not survive. In February 1887, they gave a command performance of the comedy *Sweethearts* for Queen *Victoria at Osborne House, after which Madge received a brooch shaped like a royal crown and encrusted with precious stones.

In the autumn of 1889, the Kendals set out for their first American tour, making their New York debut at the Fifth Avenue Theater on October 7 in *A Scrap of Paper*. The *New York Dramatic Mirror* reported that Mrs. Kendal's "skills as a comedienne were not exaggerated. Her art is as fine as old point lace, and yet it is laid upon a temperament so genuinely sympathetic and so pliant and transitional that there is no sign of effort, no direct exhibition of method in anything she does." The Kendals would make four subsequent tours of America, the last one covering 40 cities. Upon Kendal's return to the London stage in June 1896, in the role of Mrs. Armitage in *The Greatest of These*, George Bernard Shaw wrote: "Mrs. Kendal, forgetting that London Playgoers have been starved for years in the matter of acting, inconsiderately gave them more in the first ten minutes than they have had in the last five years, with the result that the poor wretches became hysterical and vented their applause in sobs and shrieks."

Kendal was highly disciplined about her art and demanded the same from others. "The actor must give his best performance and the public value for their money," she contended. According to Jerrold, she ruled her company with an iron hand, instructing young women to part their hair in the middle, wash daily without fail, and avoid even a hint of flirtation in the workplace. Kendal could hardly be faulted for taking the moral high ground, for in her day women of the theater came under close scrutiny. Kendal also set the standard for respectable "stage business." An actor never touched an actress above the elbow. "Never let an actor take you by the upper arm," she advised a young actress. "It looks so ugly."

The Kendals had their own special technique for playing love scenes. She would stand with her arms crossed and he would lean against her, giving the feeling of intimacy without breaching the code of conduct. In light of today's unrestrained acting, it is hard to imagine that intimate "lean," but the Kendals maintained a particularly high degree of respectability; many who went to see them wouldn't think of going to see any other actors. Mrs. Kendal's reputation, in fact, was called into question only once, during her American tour in *The Second Mrs. Tanqueray*. One critic called her portrayal of Paula "crude, noisy, and vulgar," and another queried, "Why should she pain her admirers, and risk her popularity after all these good years, by devoting her talents to the exemplification of how an abandoned woman would behave under certain distasteful circumstances?" The very mention of impropriety, of course, drew Americans to the theater in record numbers.

The Kendals continued to play in London and tour the provinces, consistently playing to full houses. "I am always called a lucky woman," Mrs. Kendal wrote later in her career, "but I don't think it's all luck. I am vain enough to think that some of it is hard work—very hard work—constant and everlasting work. You must never cease to study. As you get older, you must fill up the wrinkles with intelligence." The Kendals retired in 1908 with little fanfare. Their last performance was in *The House of Clay* at the Coronet Theater in London in October of that year. "Like the Arab," said Mrs. Kendal, "we folded our tents and stole away."

The lack of fuss attending the Kendals' retirement was not surprising, as their stage popularity did not spill over into their private life. By some accounts, they were insufferable snobs and had few friends. Even the couple's four children, two of whom went on the stage, were alienated from them. Madge Kendal attributed her husband's death in 1917 to a broken heart caused by the loss of his children's affection. In retirement, she grew formidable in appearance and denunciatory in her statements to the press. Eric John, author of *Dames of the Theatre*, describes his first sighting of Kendal at the lounge at Claridges, when she was well into her 80s. "Dressed in funereal black from head to foot, she might have been a despotic dowager Empress in Exile. With a forbidding and hostile expression on her face she looked, as Queen Victoria so often did, as if she had never laughed in her life." Kendal became harsh in her opinions of the young, criticizing them for their lack of morals and manners. She denounced the increasing use of make-up, on and off-stage, and what she referred to as "curtailed clothing." She decried the ingratitude of young actors. "I have taught many actors and actresses the early part of their business—what is called the ground work—but I have never been thanked by anyone except Seymour Hicks." She also dismissed critics as simply criticizing what they could not do themselves. "I maintain that a man must have some practical and not merely a theoretical knowledge of an art before he can write understandingly of it and its technique," she said.

Given her immense talent and her contribution to the theater, Kendal can probably be forgiven the crankiness of her later years. Perhaps she simply felt bereft, having lost the profession that had been her life for over 50 years and the man who had shared most of it with her. Most who saw her perform describe her as simply the best of her time. *Marie Lohr, who worked with the Kendal company for two years as a teenager, called the actress "the greatest of them all. No other artist, not even Duse, could so firmly hold an audience in the hollow of her hand. She could break your heart in her tragic roles, not with a display of flamboyant histrionics, but by the sheer depth and sincerity of her acting." Dame Madge, who was awarded the DBE in 1926 and the Grand Cross of the Order the following year, died on September 14, 1935, at the age of 87.

SOURCES:

Hartnoll, Phyllis, and Peter Found, eds. *The Concise Oxford Companion to the Theater*. Oxford and NY: Oxford University Press, 1993.

John, Eric. *Dames of the Theatre*. New Rochelle, NY: Arlington House, 1974.

Morley, Sheridan. *The Great Stage Stars*. London: Angus & Robertson, 1986.

Barbara Morgan,
Melrose, Massachusetts

Kendal, Mrs. (1849–1935).

See Kendal, Madge.

Kendall, Kay (1926–1959)

English actress of sophistication whose drunken trumpet solo in Genevieve *launched her career. Born Justine Kay Kendall McCarthy on May 21, 1926, in Withernsea, near Hull, England; died in London, England, of leukemia on September 6, 1959; buried in St. John's Parish Churchyard, London, between Sir Herbert Beerbohm Tree, actor, and George Du Maurier, author and artist; daughter of professional dancers; married Rex Harrison (an actor), in 1957.*

Selected filmography: Fiddlers Three *(UK, 1944);* Champagne Charlie *(UK, 1944);* Dreaming *(UK,*

1944); Waltz Time (UK, 1945); Caesar and Cleopatra (UK, 1945); Spring Song (Spring Time, UK, 1946); London Town (My Heart Goes Crazy, UK, 1946); Night and the City (UK, 1950); Dance Hall (UK, 1950); Happy Go Lovely (UK, 1951); Lady Godiva Rides Again (UK, 1951); Wings of Danger (Dead on Course, UK, 1952); Curtain Up (UK, 1952); It Started in Paradise (UK, 1952); Mantrap (also known as Man in Hiding, UK, 1953); Street of Shadows (Shadow Man, UK, 1953); The Square Ring (UK, 1953); Genevieve (UK, 1953); Meet Mr. Lucifer (UK, 1953); Fast and Loose (UK, 1954); Doctor in the House (UK, 1954); The Constant Husband (UK, 1955); Simon and Laura (UK, 1955); The Adventures of Quentin Durward (also known as Quentin Durward, 1955); Abdullah the Great (Abdullah's Harem, Egypt, 1956); Les Girls (U.S., 1957); The Reluctant Debutante (U.S., 1958); Once More with Feeling (U.S., 1960).

Kay Kendall was born in Withernsea, near Hull, England, in 1926, the daughter of professional dancers. This stylish English actress joined the chorus line at the London Palladium at age 13, then toured with her sister Kim in a music-hall act. A sophisticated comedian, Kay Kendall played minor roles in film early in her career, before turning to stage repertory. Seventeen forgotten movies later, she burst forth with a showy role and a drunken trumpet solo in the engaging comedy Genevieve with **Dinah Sheridan** and Kenneth More; it was chosen as Best British Film of 1953.

In 1955, during the filming of the aptly titled The Constant Husband, Kendall met and fell in love with Rex Harrison, while his wife *Lilli Palmer was in Munich making her first German film. This was not the first extramarital indulgence of Harrison's but certainly the most serious. When a doctor told Harrison that Kendall had leukemia and only three years to live, he divorced Palmer and married her. Kendall was not informed of the seriousness of her illness.

In her first U.S. picture in 1957, Kendall teamed up with Gene Kelly, *Mitzi Gaynor and

𝒦ay
𝒦endall

Taina Elg for MGM's *Les Girls* and was a rollicking success with both the critics and the public. She then played wife to husband Harrison in the film *The Reluctant Debutante*. Wrote Jay Nash and Stanley Ross: "Let's all say a prayer for the immortal soul of Kay Kendall, who died a year after this film was released, and whose few performances captured on screen continue to be a delight for anyone who sees them. . . . It's Kendall's film from start to end as she is charming, loveable, bubbly, and funny in what was to be her penultimate motion picture. If there is such a thing as reincarnation, let Kendall come back soon." Kay Kendall's life was cut short by myeloid leukemia in 1959; she was 32.

SOURCES:
Nash, Jay, and Stanley Ross. *Motion Picture Guide*. Chicago, IL: Cinebooks, 1986.

Kendall, Marie Hartig (1854–1943)

French-born American photographer who specialized in portraits, landscapes, and documentation. Born in Mulhouse, France, in 1854; died in Norfolk, Connecticut, in 1943; trained as a nurse at Bellevue Hospital, New York, and Charity Hospital on Blackwell's Island; married John Kendall (a physician), in the late 1870s; children: three.

Marie Hartig Kendall, a nurse by training, was 30 years old when she discovered photography as a way to create portraits of her three children. She was talented and in demand, but photography always remained just one of her many interests and activities.

Born in Mulhouse, France, in 1854, where her parents owned cotton and shoe factories, Kendall immigrated to the United States with her family following France's defeat in the Franco-Prussian War. She and her sister began nurses training at Bellevue Hospital, in New York, but Marie was forced to leave when she became engaged to John Kendall, a resident physician there. She completed her training at Charity Hospital on Blackwell's Island and married John late in the 1870s. The couple had three children and moved to Norfolk, Connecticut, in 1884. Unable to afford professional portraits of her children, Kendall saved her money and purchased her own equipment. She was soon selling portraits to her neighbors and friends, and entering camera club competitions. In 1893, she won a bronze medal for her entry in the World's Columbian Exposition in Chicago, and in 1904 she exhibited at the Louisiana Purchase Exposition in St. Louis. One of her landscape shots was used by the New Haven Railroad in an advertising campaign. Kendall was also a teacher of anatomy and nutrition and was active in temperance and women's suffrage campaigns. Unfortunately, before her death in 1943, Kendall destroyed some 30,000 of her glass negatives; the remaining 250 images, including shots of the 1888 blizzard, are held at the Norfolk Connecticut Historical Society.

SOURCES:
Rosenblum, Naomi. *A History of Women Photographers*. NY: Abbeville Press, 1994.

Barbara Morgan,
Melrose, Massachusetts

Kennedy, Caroline (b. 1957).

See Schlossberg, Caroline Kennedy.

Kennedy, Ethel (1928—)

American philanthropist and wife of Senator Robert F. Kennedy. Born Ethel Skakel in Chicago, Illinois, on April 11, 1928; sixth of seven children of George Skakel (a coal magnate) and Ann (Brannack) Skakel; attended the Dominican Day School, Larchmont, New York; attended the Greenwich Academy, Greenwich, Connecticut; graduated from the Convent of the Sacred Heart, Maplehurst, the Bronx, New York, 1945; Manhattanville College of the Sacred Heart, New York, B.A., 1949; married Robert F. Kennedy (b. 1925, a U.S. senator), on June 17, 1950 (assassinated on June 5, 1968); children: Kathleen Kennedy Townsend (b. 1951, lieutenant governor of Maryland); Joseph Patrick Kennedy II (b. 1952, spent six terms in Congress); Robert F. Kennedy, Jr. (b. 1954, is an environmental lawyer with Riverkeeper, a conservation group based in New York's Hudson River Valley); David Kennedy (1955–1984, died of drug overdose); (Mary) Courtney Kennedy Hill (b. 1956, a human-rights activist); Michael Kennedy (1958–1998); (Mary) Kerry Kennedy Cuomo (b. 1959, who works for Amnesty International and the R.F.K. Center for Human Rights); Christopher Kennedy (b. 1963, a businessman); Matthew Maxwell T. Kennedy known as Max Kennedy (b. 1965, was assistant district attorney in Philadelphia); Douglas Harriman Kennedy (b. 1967, a reporter for Fox News Channel); Rory Kennedy (b. 1968, an award-winning documentary filmmaker).

Ethel Skakel Kennedy was the sixth of seven children of George Skakel, head of the Great Lakes Carbon Corporation, one of the largest privately owned businesses in the country, and

Ann Brannack Skakel, a massive woman (over 200 pounds), whose world revolved around her social activities and the Catholic Church. When Ethel was five, George Skakel decided to move the executive offices of his company East, and the family lived in Larchmont and Rye, New York, for several years before purchasing the 30-room furnished mansion on Lake Avenue in Greenwich, Connecticut, that had previously been owned by Frances Simmons, the widow of the heir to the Simmons' mattress fortune. While the largely Protestant residents of Greenwich did not particularly welcome the boisterous Skakel family, Ethel seemed to be an exception. Sent by her mother to the prestigious Greenwich Academy, she assimilated quickly and made friends easily. "Ethel was so open and so honest that everybody adored her," said classmate Pan Jacob, "She was successful because she was so natural about herself." Though Ethel was only an average student, she was good at sports and an excellent equestrian. She owned several horses and rode at Greenwich's exclusive Round Hill Club, where she won most of the competitions, but she was also known to break Club rules and do anything on a dare.

Aside from their strict religious training, the Skakel children, by most accounts, were indulged and undisciplined. "They had money but they didn't have anything else," said Jacob. "There was no structure. . . . It was an abstract painting as opposed to a formal painting, more surreal than Rembrandt; a Jackson Pollock world where everything was exploding; where there was no cohesiveness." In her exuberance and love of pranks, Ethel most resembled her brothers, Jim and George, who apparently held the neighborhood hostage with their antics. "Those Skakel kids would get up to ninety miles an hour in nothing flat and tear all over the place, very likely shooting large-caliber pistols out of the widow at the same time," recalled Ken McDonnell, a friend of the boys at the time. "They were always looking for trouble." Ethel, when she was old enough, also drove her red convertible recklessly and at high speed, sometimes turning off the lights at night and driving around in the dark.

For her final two years in high school, Ethel attended the Convent of the Sacred Heart, Maplehurst, in the Bronx, where she was the first to flaunt the rules and lead the after-dinner high jinks. Despite her reputation as a troublemaker, Ethel seriously embraced the spiritual training she received as part of the convent's curriculum. Active in the school's Christopher Club, a social-action and missionary group, she was

even interested in religious life at one point. "Ethel was certainly not religious in the pious sense," recalled Mother Elizabeth Farley. "She was too lively. But she had a lot of faith, and inherited a lot of faith, and influenced others with her faith."

When she entered Manhattanville College of the Sacred Heart in September 1945, Ethel quickly became part of the "in" crowd, the girls with money who filled their free time with shopping and club hopping in New York City. Given an unlimited amount of spending money, Ethel became a world-class shopper, filling her closet with the finest apparel from swanky Fifth Avenue shops and sometimes spending thousands of dollars on a single dress. Ethel's college roommate was ◄❧ Jean Kennedy (Smith), and it was through Jean that Ethel met and began dating Robert F. Kennedy. Ethel hardly seemed a likely match for the shy, introspective Bobby Kennedy, but, according to Jean, he adored her. "He needed her because he was much less out-going—more thoughtful and serious," she said.

Following her graduation in 1949, Ethel had serious doubts about a future with Bobby, and went through a brief period of intense introspection. By Thanksgiving, however, her confidence was restored, and she never again wavered in her devotion to Bobby, even though the Skakel and Kennedy families were never close. The couple married in a splendid ceremony on June 17, 1950, and following a three-month honeymoon, set up housekeeping in a small house in Charlottesville, Virginia, their home while Bobby finished his law degree at the University of Virginia. Ethel, who at the time of her marriage had vowed to have more children than her mother-in-law, the late *Rose Fitzgerald Kennedy, gave birth to her first child, Kathleen Kennedy (Townsend), in July 1951, and had a child on the average of every 15 months thereafter, until her last, daughter Rory Kennedy (number 11), in 1968. During the early 1950s, the Kennedys lived in Georgetown, in close proximity to Bobby's work in Washington. The first of the tragedies that would come to dominate Ethel's life occurred on October 3, 1955, when both her parents were killed in a plane crash on their way to Los Angeles. Dazed, but possessing a stoicism that would become a trademark, Ethel flew to Connecticut with Bobby for the enormous funeral which was attended by hundreds of friends and business associates.

By the end of the Eisenhower era, Bobby Kennedy had obtained the high-profile post of chief counsel of the Senate Permanent Subcom-

Smith, Jean Kennedy. See Kennedy, Rose Fitzgerald for sidebar.

Opposite page

Ethel Kennedy

mittee on Investigations (the Senate Rackets Committee), and Ethel had come into her own as the chic and energetic wife of the young crime buster. The constantly expanding family finally settled into their own home, a McLean, Virginia, estate (Hickory Hill), the former residence of *Jacqueline Kennedy and John Fitzgerald Kennedy, Bobby's brother. Around the same time, Bobby's father Joseph P. Kennedy made them a gift of a summer home near his own at Hyannis Port, Massachusetts. Ethel, by all accounts, ran her household the same way that her mother had run hers, with no discipline and no controls. Boston *Globe* writer Tom Oliphant, a long-time family friend and a frequent visitor at Hickory Hill, recalls that just walking into the house could be a life-altering experience. "You could be tripped by a kid or a dog or hit by anything from a football to a glass of lemonade." According to Jerry Oppenheimer, author of *The Other Mrs. Kennedy,* Ethel had a laissez-faire approach with the children. "I just don't believe a child's world should be entirely full of 'don'ts,'" she said. "We think it's possible to have discipline and still give the children independence without spoiling them." Ethel's life, however, was so full that she had little time to spend with the children, and they were most often left in the care of hired help.

In September 1959, Bobby resigned as chief counsel of the Senate Rackets Committee to join his brother Jack's campaign for the presidency. Ethel turned out to be a first-rate campaigner herself, criss-crossing the country on her brother-in-law's behalf and winning the admiration of the press corps who dubbed her "Miss Perpetual Animation." Upon winning the election, Jack rewarded his brother with the Cabinet post of attorney general. Over the next eight years, Ethel would become the most visible and popular woman in Washington next to First Lady Jacqueline, and, except for the White House, Hickory Hill would become the most famous residence of the Camelot years.

According to Peter Collier and David Horowitz, Hickory Hill was where the "New Frontiersmen" met for serious intellectual seminars and was also the scene of exuberant parties, over which Ethel presided as mistress of ceremonies. "She imported the Lester Lanin orchestra for dances and brought in Harry Belafonte to teach them all the twist. She used live bullfrogs as a centerpiece for a St. Patrick's Day dinner; she put distinguished Cabinet members in closets with attractive secretaries during impassioned games of hide-and-seek; invited Robert Frost to dinner and gave out paper and pencils

to guests for a poetry-writing contest." Perhaps the most notorious of the Kennedys' soirees were the "people-dunking" parties, during which some of the best and brightest of the Administration—presidential adviser Arthur Schlesinger, for one—found themselves in the Kennedy swimming pool fully clothed. While Schlesinger was a great fan of Ethel and viewed the dunkings as great fun, others were less enthusiastic, including Schlesinger's then wife, **Marian Cannon Schlesinger**. "Ethel was childish and self-indulgent," she wrote years later. "She created a certain atmosphere of fun and games as it were, and everything was done on a lavish scale. It was like a great big party all the time, extravagant and excessive, too much of everything. Everyone was attracted to Ethel, but that was because of Bob's p-o-w-e-r."

By 1963, Jack's brother Edward "Ted" Kennedy had been elected to the U.S. Senate, and Bobby appeared to be headed for a governorship of his own and then the presidency. Ethel was at the height of her popularity; women throughout the country copied her chic little dresses and read her advice on motherhood and healthy living that she regularly dispensed in the popular magazines and Sunday supplements. But life was about to change drastically for the Kennedys, and for the entire nation.

On November 22, 1963, John F. Kennedy was assassinated as he rode in a motorcade through the streets of Dallas, Texas, an event of such magnitude that every American who was alive at the time remembers exactly where they were when they received the tragic news. Ethel and Bobby Kennedy were having lunch near the pool at Hickory Hill with two of Bobby's associates when the call came through from FBI director, J. Edgar Hoover that the president had been mortally wounded. The death of the 46-year-old president plunged the country into a deep despair that was mirrored through his brother Robert. Ethel, resolute in her faith, held up stoically. "He's in heaven looking down on us," she told her sister after the funeral. "Bobby and I will be with him one day ourselves. We will all be together." Bobby, however, was completely shattered. A journalist friend who saw him a few weeks after the assassination described him as "crushed beyond hope, mentally, spiritually, and physically." It was Ethel who pushed Bobby back from a dark depression, and friends generally agreed that without her he might have been lost forever in his grief. By 1964, he had resumed normal activities and had announced his candidacy for the U.S. Senate seat from New York. Though pregnant with her ninth child, Ethel

threw herself into his campaign, becoming more self-assured with each speech and enjoying a new-found power. During the nine weeks before election day, she appeared at more than a dozen rallies and hosted nine "at-homes." Bobby won the election overwhelmingly, and six days after his swearing in ceremony, January 10, 1965, Ethel gave birth to another son, Max Kennedy.

Although the Kennedys purchased an apartment in the United Nations Towers, Ethel continued to spend most of her time at Hickory Hill, where she hosted huge parties for friends and galas for charity. Oppenheimer notes that during this period, Ethel began making headlines by showing up at official functions in trendy fashions of the 1960s known as "Mod"—short, short skirts, vinyl shifts, and Courrèges boots. While most found her behavior characteristic, her close friends apparently viewed it as something more. "They had started to interpret her growing flamboyance as a shield for what they saw as insecurity and resentment—," he wrote, "insecurity about her abilities, resentment at the limitation of her role as a Kennedy wife."

In July 1966, Ethel received the happy news that she was pregnant with number ten, the number that would push her over Rose's record. Beginning in September, however, she experienced a round of tragedies that dominated her existence for 20 months. Two months into her pregnancy, her brother George Skakel was killed in a plane crash. His widow **Pat Skakel** and her four children were just putting their lives back together when the older daughter was involved in an automobile accident that took the life of a young friend. Shortly after Ethel gave birth to Douglas Kennedy in May 1967, Pat Skakel died of asphyxiation cause by a piece of meat lodging in her larynx. A month following Pat's funeral, in what many viewed as poor timing, Ethel threw her largest party yet at Hickory Hill to celebrate her 17th wedding anniversary. Three-hundred guests—including a Hollywood contingent comprised of Andy Williams, *Carol Channing, Jack Paar, and Kirk Douglas—attended the affair, at which Peter Duchin's orchestra provided the dance music. The party, which lasted until dawn, was the last wedding anniversary Ethel and Bobby would celebrate.

While Bobby agonized over his historic decision to run for President, Ethel encouraged him and did her best to squelch any naysayers. During his campaign, which lasted 85 days, Ethel, once again pregnant, hit the trail, supported by a retine of personal assistants to help with her clothes and hair, and to care for the unruly brood on the home front. On June 4, 1968, Bobby Kennedy had just won the California primary, and Ethel was in a jubilant mood when she left with him for the downtown Los Angeles Ambassador Hotel, where he would make his victory speech. Following his speech, Bobby was being escorted through a pantry area to the Colonial Room, where he was to meet with a journalist. Ethel had just stopped to talk with some of the kitchen help, when 24-year-old Sirhan Bishara Sirhan stepped around a tray rack shouting and wielding a revolver. Before anyone could register what was happening, he shot eight bullets into Robert F. Kennedy's head. In the pandemonium that followed, Ethel, dazed and shocked, attempted to comfort her fallen husband who was immediately transported to Good Samaritan Hospital, where shortly after midnight on June 6, he was pronounced dead.

"From the moment Bobby was shot until he was buried, Ethel rarely left his side," wrote Oppenheimer. "In his death, as in his life, her sole wish was to be with him." On the flight back to New York, Ethel sat near his coffin, falling into a fitful sleep against it at one point. Many who were present at the time, marveled at her composure, including her obstetrician who said it was almost impossible to tell that she had just survived a trauma. Ethel also remained strong and controlled throughout the ordeal that followed. In arranging the funeral mass, held at St. Patrick's Cathedral, she insisted that it be uplifting rather than grim. "If there's one thing about our faith," she told one of the priests, "it's our belief that this is the beginning of eternal life and not the end of life. I want this Mass to be as joyous as it possibly can be." On the 21-car funeral train which carried Bobby back to Washington for burial, Ethel made her way up and down the aisles, greeting friends and joking on occasion. Most of the time, however, she sat next to the casket with a rosary in her hand. An accident in Elizabeth, New Jersey, during which two mourners who were on the northbound tracks to get a better view of the Kennedy train were killed by an oncoming New York-bound express train, delayed the train's arrival in Washington by five hours. It was close to midnight before the final graveside ceremony for Robert Kennedy at Arlington National Cemetery was over.

In much the same manner as her mother-in-law Rose Kennedy, Ethel endured the assassination of her husband with a stoicism born of deep religious faith. Friends, who rallied around to ward off the depression they were sure would overcome her, were surprised by her calm demeanor, although some noted sudden mood swings and an edge to her voice that had not been there before. Ethel spent the summer at Hyannis then returned to Hickory Hill to await the birth of her last child, who arrived slightly past her due date on December 12, 1968. Ted Kennedy, upon whom Ethel now relied as a surrogate father to her children, was with her at the hospital and helped her name the child Rory. Back home following the birth, Ethel's problems with the children grew. Many felt that without Bobby's influence, she completely lost control of them. "They ran rampant," said **Barbara Gibson**, Rose Kennedy's longtime secretary. "It was nothing to see the little ones, like Max and Rory, up on the roof. You'd worry that someone was going to fall and kill himself."

The older children, who felt the impact of their father's death more keenly, dealt with their pain in more complex and destructive ways. In 1970, Robert F. Kennedy, Jr., was charged with possession of marijuana but escaped conviction because it was a first offense. Ethel threw him out of the house, an act of anger and frustration that would become habitual. (Bobby, Jr., eventually licked his drug problem and became an attorney for the Natural Resources Defense Council; he also teaches law at Pace University.) In 1973, future congressional representative Joseph P. Kennedy II, then 20, was charged with reckless driving when the jeep he was driving overturned, leaving **Pamela Kelley**, a longtime friend of the Kennedys, paralyzed below the chest. Though found guilty of negligent driving, Joe was let off with a $100 fine and a scolding from the judge. (For many, it was a replay of the Chappaquiddick incident in the summer of 1969, when Ted Kennedy pleaded guilty to leaving the scene of the accident that killed **Mary Jo Kopechne** and received a suspended two-month jail sentence and a year on probation.) David Kennedy, who had always been the most sensitive and troubled of the brood, turned to drugs to quiet his pain, quickly graduating from marijuana to heroin. Over the years, Ethel sent him to countless rehab centers and even employed a live-in detox expert, but nothing helped. On April 24, 1984, just shy of his 29th birthday, David was found dead in a Palm Springs hotel room, apparently the victim of a cocaine overdose. Once again Ethel displayed remarkable strength, telling friends that she believed her son had joined his father in heaven. There was a private funeral service for David at Hickory Hill, after which he was buried alongside his grandfather, Joseph P. Kennedy, at the family plot at Holyhood Cemetery in Brookline, Massachusetts.

Through the years, Ethel's name has been linked romantically with a number of men, but she never remarried. In the early 1970s, the gossip columns linked her to singer Andy Williams, who, with his first wife **Claudine Longet**, had been pals with the Kennedys during the 1960s. Although the couple dated for a time, a romantic relationship was evidently more a media invention than a reality. Ethel subsequently dated *Look* magazine's Warren Rogers, also an old friend, and New York attorney William vanden Heuvel, a longtime aide of Bobby's. Other supposed suitors included New York governor Hugh Carey, ABC news and sports executive Roone Arledge, and sportscaster Frank Gifford. But Oppenheimer believes that it was all a game, that Ethel was devoted to Bobby's memory. "She talked to him constantly, and she never removed her wedding rings. At a hockey match to benefit retarded children in Madison Square Garden in 1974, six years after Bobby's death, Ethel shook hands with a blind child. When he asked her whether she was Rose Kennedy, Ethel answered, 'No, I'm Ethel, Bobby's wife.'" Ethel also turned Hickory Hill into something of a shrine, keeping numerous pictures of Bobby on the walls and tabletops. "The ghost of Bobby haunted Hickory Hill," commented one friend. "How in the world any man ever thought they could win her and compete with Bobby Kennedy's spirit, I'll never know."

Though the periods of tranquillity in Ethel's life continued to be overshadowed by calamity in either her Skakel family, or that of the Kennedys, she was generally there when the call went out to circle the wagons. "She's more a Kennedy than the Kennedys," writes author Dominick Dunne, who covered William Kennedy Smith's 1991 rape trial, at which Ethel was in frequent attendance. But there are good times, too, and much to be proud of. The majority of Ethel's children are happily settled in productive careers, and many are married with children of their own, providing Ethel with a slew of grandchildren.

In later years, Ethel devoted more time to charitable causes, which included overseeing the $10 million Robert F. Kennedy Memorial Foundation, established shortly after her husband's death to fund journalistic and humanitarian endeavors. In the years immediately following Bobby's death, she became active in some of his causes, including the grape pickers' movement of *Dolores Huerta and Cesar Chávez in California, the Bedford-Stuyvesant Restoration Corporation, and the political campaigns of John Glenn in Ohio and John Lindsay in New York.

For years, Ethel has also supported the Special Olympics, the Kennedy family's favorite charity. Since the early 1990s, through the auspices of the RFK Center for Human Rights in Boston, founded by Ethel's daughter **Kerry Kennedy (Cuomo)**, she has also been associated with various human-rights and humanitarian causes. In 1992, with her son Michael and her daughter **Courtney Kennedy Hill**, she toured Eastern Europe, where they donated medical equipment, and in late 1997, she traveled to Kenya to promote democratic reforms. On the occasion of Chinese President Jiang Zemin's state visit in the fall of 1998, she joined a mass rally across from the White House protesting human-rights abuses in Tibet and China. Closer to home, she supports Washington's Mount Carmel House shelter for homeless women and the St. Ann's Home for orphaned and abandoned children. She also assisted her son Max in preparing *Make Gentle the Life of This World: The Vision of Robert F. Kennedy,* a volume containing Robert Kennedy's journal entries, selected speeches, and favorite sayings. Max, who was three when his father was slain, still misses his father. "Obviously I've had a life of enormous privilege and opportunity," he says. "But the essential fact of that life is the absence of this man. There's not a single day that any member of my family wouldn't trade all that privilege and opportunity to have our father back."

In January 1998, Ethel lost yet another son, Michael, through a tragic accident. In the middle of a scandal—an alleged affair with his children's teenage babysitter, he careened into a tree while skiing in Aspen. In light of her overwhelming losses, Ethel's resilience and strength almost mystifies those who know her. Former New York governor Mario Cuomo, whose son is married to Kerry Kennedy, attended Michael's funeral and found himself recalling Robert's funeral 30 years earlier. "It was the same Ethel Kennedy, apparently impassive, controlled," he said. "She must have been terribly wounded, but she showed no evidence of it. I suspect when she's at mass and alone in a pew that she allows herself a tear. But she won't allow herself a tear with you. She doesn't make her problem your problem. It's probably harder in her life than anyone else's to find the evidence that God is good. Yet she believes it."

SOURCES:

Collier, Peter, and David Horowitz. *The Kennedys: An American Drama.* NY: Warner Books, 1984.

Jerome, Richard. "Tale of Two Women: Guardian of the Flame," in *People Weekly.* Vol. 49, no. 24. June 22, 1998, pp. 44–55.

Oppenheimer, Jerry. *The Other Mrs. Kennedy.* NY: St. Martin's Press, 1994.

SUGGESTED READING:

Taraborrelli, J. Randy. *Jackie, Ethel, Joan: Women of Camelot*. NY: Warner, 2000.

Barbara Morgan,
Melrose, Massachusetts

Kennedy, Eunice (b. 1921).

See Shriver, Eunice Kennedy.

Kennedy, Florynce (1916—)

African-American lawyer who fought for civil and women's rights. Name variations: Flo Kennedy. Born on February 11, 1916, in Kansas City, Missouri; second of five daughters of Wiley Kennedy and Zella Kennedy; graduated from Lincoln High School, Kansas City; bachelor's degree from Columbia University, New York City; law degree from Columbia Law School, 1951; married Charles Dudley Dye (a writer), in 1957 (divorced); no children.

Described variously as outrageous, outspoken, aggressive, profane, and shocking, lawyer and activist Florynce "Flo" Kennedy made a name for herself during the turbulent 1960s and 1970s as a civil and women's rights activist and as a spokesperson for other diverse groups as well. "I'm just a loud-mouthed middle-aged colored lady with a fused spine and three feet of intestines missing and a lot of people think I'm crazy," she wrote in her autobiography *Color Me Flo: My Hard Life and Good Times* (1976). "Maybe you do too, but I never stop to wonder why I'm not like other people. The mystery to me is why more people aren't like me."

Born in 1916 in Kansas City, Missouri, Kennedy described her family as part of the "Pooristocrats" of the black community, and she attributed her outspoken, aggressive nature to an upbringing in which she was taught to question authority and to trust in herself. "Our parents had us so convinced we were precious," she writes, "that by the time I found out I was nothing, it was already too late—I knew I was something." Even before high school, Kennedy knew she wanted to be a lawyer, but she was 28 before she was able in enter college. She graduated Columbia pre-law with an "A" average, but was initially turned down when she applied to Columbia Law School. When she alleged that she was rejected because of race and threatened a fight, the university reversed its decision and accepted her. She graduated in 1951 and, by 1954, had established her own private practice. Although she was never keen on the institution of marriage, in 1957 Kennedy wed Charles Dudley

Dye, whom she later described as a "Welsh science-fiction writer and a drunk." The union was short-lived, and Kennedy never married again.

Flo Kennedy was briefly in partnership with Don Wilkes, with whom she defended *Billie Holiday against government charges that the singer failed to register before leaving the country on her last European tour. Holiday's agent neglected to advise her of the federal statute requiring persons convicted on narcotics charges to inform the government each time they left the country, so Holiday embarked on her tour without doing so. Wilkes persuaded the U.S. attorney not to indict the singer, but Holiday died shortly after winning the case. Kennedy later represented Holiday's estate, and that of the late Charlie Parker, in efforts to recoup monies in royalties and sales denied the performers. She also represented the activist H. Rap Brown on several occasions, although by this time she was beginning to grow disenchanted with what she saw as a racist and bigoted court system in which no justice could be found.

During the 1960s and 1970s, Kennedy was an active and outspoken leader in the civil rights and feminist movements, although her fight for equality embraced, as she put it, "all aspects of our oppressive society." In 1966, she founded the Media Workshop, designed to "deal with racism in media and advertising," and she was also an original member of the National Organization for Women (NOW), but left when it "got to be so boring and scared." Believing that racism is the most blatant form of oppression in the country, Kennedy attended all four Black Power Conferences (1967, 1968, 1969, and 1970) and also formed the Feminist Party, which worked to support *Shirley Chisholm as a presidential candidate. Kennedy also spoke at numerous colleges and universities and at rallies across the country.

In 1972, Flo Kennedy moved from New York to California. That same year, she filed a complaint against the Catholic Church with the Internal Revenue Service, alleging that the church violated the tax-exempt requirement by spending money to influence political decisions, particularly those dealing with abortion. She also co-authored, with **Diane Schulter**, one of the first books on abortion, *Abortion Rap*.

In 1975, on the occasion of her 70th birthday, Kennedy was roasted by friends and colleagues at an affair in New York City. In attendance were comic activist Dick Gregory, civil rights lawyer William Kunstler, and television talk show host Phil Donahue. After the celebration, she was back on the speaking circuit, bringing yet another cause to the public's attention.

SOURCES:

Smith, Jessie Carney, ed. *Notable Black American Women*. Detroit, MI: Gale Research, 1992.

Barbara Morgan,
Melrose, Massachusetts.

Kennedy, Jacqueline (1929–1994)

One of America's most popular first ladies who was much admired for her artistic sensibility, sophisticated beauty, and patronage of the arts. Name variations: Jacqueline Bouvier; Jacqueline Kennedy Onassis; Jackie O. Born on July 28, 1929, in Southampton, New York; died from cancer on May 19, 1994, in New York City; buried in Arlington National Cemetery; daughter of John "Black Jack" Bouvier (a wealthy stockbroker) and Janet (Lee) Bouvier (a socialite), later known as Janet Auchincloss; educated at Vassar, Smith College, George Washington University and the Sorbonne; married John Fitzgerald Kennedy (35th president of the United States), on September 12, 1953 (assassinated November 22, 1963); married Aristotle Onassis (a Greek industrialist), in 1968 (died 1975); children: (first marriage) Caroline Kennedy Schlossberg (b. 1957, a lawyer and writer); John F. Kennedy, Jr. (1960–1999); Patrick (1963–1963); (second marriage) stepchildren, Alexander and Christina Onassis.

Met John F. Kennedy, who at the time was beginning his campaign for U.S. senator from Massachusetts (1952); married during John Kennedy's first year in the Senate (September 1953); became first lady on her husband's election to the presidency (1960); was riding next to her husband in a Dallas motorcade when an assassin's bullet took his life (November 1963); married Greek industrialist Aristotle Onassis (1968), spending much of her time abroad until his death (1975), after which she moved back to New York; became an editor for Doubleday (1978), remaining by choice out of the public eye and living quietly until her death from cancer (May 1994), in New York City; buried in Arlington National Cemetery next to John F. Kennedy.

January 20, 1961, dawned in Washington, D.C., with bright blue skies, thin winter sunshine and freezing temperatures. There had been a paralyzing snowstorm the night before, but it was of no consequence to the handsome young couple hurrying to dress for ceremonies scheduled to begin later that morning, although as usual he was ready before she was and complained loudly of the delay. But Jacqueline Bouvier Kennedy would not be hurried, even if she

was keeping the president-elect of the United States and all of Capitol Hill waiting. Later, walking onto the inaugural platform at her husband's side, a gust of wind attempted to sweep away her pillbox hat. Jackie's last minute grab saved the hat but unfortunately left a dent in its thick wool fabric; nevertheless, as Chief Justice Earl Warren administered the oath of office to her husband John, and Jackie stood serenely in a fawn wool coat with sable trim designed by Oleg Cassini, fashion-conscious eyes fixed on the matching hat. Soon, women throughout the nation were carefully denting their own hats and designers were manufacturing hats with dents already in them. Jackie had turned near-disaster into triumph with her usual effortless sophistication and, more important, had begun the process that would transform her into a national legend.

She had learned early on to deal with upsetting surprises, growing up with the privileges of wealth in a household ruled by a charming philanderer of a father and a socially rigid mother. John Bouvier had long earned the sobriquet "Black Jack" by the time of Jackie's birth on July 28, 1929. Bouvier's reputation as a hard drinker, devoted gambler, and inveterate womanizer had long been established when his pending marriage to socialite Janet Lee (later known as **Janet Auchincloss**) had been announced early the previous year. One rumor on the weekend house party circuit was that Bouvier needed the Lee family's money, having gambled and drunk away most of his own family's fortune earned several generations earlier in the banking business by ancestors made of sturdier stuff. Old-line New York families scoffed at the pending union, considering the Lees, who had earned their money in the real estate business within the past two generations, too *nouveau* for the more blue-blooded Bouviers. The truth was that both families relied on manufactured genealogies. The Bouviers, who claimed descent from French Catholic nobility, were actually descended from a cabinetmaker who had fled France after Napoleon's defeat at Waterloo. The Lee family's ancestry, meanwhile, bore no relation to the famous first family of Southern aristocracy, as was claimed, but stemmed from a poor Irish immigrant who settled in New York in the 1840s.

Janet's father James Lee considered Jack Bouvier a libertine and a spendthrift, and attempted to talk his daughter out of the marriage, but the wedding took place as planned in the summer of 1928 in East Hampton, Long Island, and was the social highlight of the season. In later years, Jack would boast to his daughter of his sexual conquests while on his honeymoon with Janet aboard the ship carrying them to England, notably a passionate assignation with tobacco heiress **Doris Duke**. Everyone hoped the birth of Jacqueline a year later would help save a marriage in trouble almost as soon as it began. But the stock-market crash three months after Jackie's birth destroyed what was left of her father's money, forcing him into the embarrassing position of borrowing from his father-in-law and living in an 11-room apartment paid for by James Lee; and it was Lee money that paid for young Jacqueline's private tutors and the ponies she was riding at age five, when she won her first blue ribbon—the beginning of a lifelong attachment to equestrian pursuits. The death of a beloved brother seemed to plunge Jack Bouvier into even deeper despair relieved by endless romances and drinking so severe that Jacqueline would remember all her life putting Jack to bed after he had collapsed in a stupor. Even the birth of a second daughter, Caroline Lee (**Lee Radziwell**), in 1931 failed to bring Jack back to his senses. It was obvious to Janet that her older daughter adored her father and had inherited some of his wildness, as evidenced by the kindergarten teachers who wrote notes home calling Jackie a "problem child," prone to mischief like smearing the school's toilet bowls with hand cream. "I know you love horses and you yourself are very much like a beautiful Thoroughbred," one exasperated headmistress told the young Bouvier girl. "But if you're not properly broken and trained, you'll be good for nothing."

By 1936, when Jackie was eight and her sister Lee just five, Janet left her husband for a trial separation. After several attempts to resuscitate the marriage, Janet took her two girls to Reno, Nevada, to obtain a divorce in the state where it was easy to get one. Jack offered no opposition, especially after Janet leaked a private investigator's findings to the press, to the horror of New York's elite. The divorce was granted during the summer of 1940.

Two years later, Janet married Hugh Auchincloss, a prim investment banker and lawyer with everything Janet was looking for in a husband—a love of home, family, and money. "The word 'swashbuckling' has never been applied to an Auchincloss," as one of their number once drily noted. Auchincloss himself had recently divorced **Nina Auchincloss**, who vacated the premises with a son from her first marriage—then called Eugene but soon to take his father's name and make his way as Gore Vidal. Vidal later described Jackie and Lee as the "two frizzy-haired step-daughters who took my place in [Hugh's] ample heart." Now it was Jackie and Lee who spent their winters at their new family's Merrywood Farm in Virginia, with its 46 acres, swimming pool, badminton court, and stables, and their summers at Hammersmith Farm in Newport, Rhode Island, with its 28 rooms set on 83 acres. The girls liked their "Uncle Hughdie" well enough, but Jackie especially missed her father, who never remarried.

Perhaps under the influence of the more staid Auchincloss household, Jackie was known to Miss Porter's boarding school in Farmington, Connecticut, where she was sent in 1944, as a rather quiet, studious girl who chose her friends carefully and never dated. "I just know no one will ever marry me," she confided to a classmate, "and I'll end up as a housemother at Farmington." Her favorite times were her father's weekend visits, during which Jack would openly and with great gusto describe his latest sexual exploits, which grew to such numbers that Jackie would often point to a visiting mother and gleefully ask, "That one, Daddy?," followed by a vigorous nod from her father. She found it all tremendously amusing.

> *Throughout the world, people love fairy tales, and especially those related to the lives of the rich.*
>
> —Jacqueline Kennedy

Three years later, Jackie had been formally introduced to New York society in the ritual "coming out." She made her first appearance at a summer party arranged at Hammersmith Farm by Janet, who decided to use the occasion to also introduce Jackie's new half-brother, "Master James Lee Auchincloss," as the invitation presented the baby which had arrived in late spring. Fall brought the usual round of debutante balls, crowned by society columnist Igor Cassini's choice of Jackie as "Debutante of the Year." Jackie expressed genuine surprise at the title, for despite her slim figure and classic features, she had never considered herself a great beauty and was, in fact, particularly self-conscious about her large hands and feet. Then there were her eyes which, she once wrote, were "so unfortunately far apart that it takes me three weeks to have a pair of glasses made with a bridge wide enough to fit over my nose." But for Cassini, who wrote his society column under the name of "Cholly Knickerbocker" and was Oleg's elder brother, Jackie's attractions were other than physical. "I felt something very special in her, an understated elegance," Cassini later said. "Although shy and extremely private, she stood out in a crowd. She had that certain something."

Fresh from her social triumphs, Jackie entered Vassar that same autumn, keeping to herself most of the time, earning good grades and only occasionally taking weekend trips to Boston to date admirers from Harvard. She chose her dates carefully and heeded her father's advice to guard her reputation by playing hard to get—an ironic suggestion from a man who revealed in the same breath that he only slept with women who made him work for his seduction. After only a year at Vassar, Jackie convinced her mother to let her continue her education in Europe. She had been particularly enamored of French culture during a chaperoned summer vacation in Paris, which made Vassar and its surrounding town of Poughkeepsie, New York, seem depressingly provincial. October of 1948 found Jackie at the Sorbonne and living with a French family in the 12th *arrondissement,* with whose six members she shared one bathroom and no central heating. She had purposely chosen not to live in the dormitory usually reserved for American women at the Sorbonne and stood in line with other Frenchwomen to buy food and supplies with a postwar ration card. She immersed herself in Left Bank culture, read Hemingway and Baudelaire at Les Deux Magots and the Café des Fleurs, and dated American writers then living in Paris, including George Plimpton, who was working for the *Paris Review,* and novelist John Phillip Marquand, Jr., whose father had won the Pulitzer Prize for his novel *The Late George Apley.* Much to her mother's alarm, there were rumors that Jackie and Marquand were discussing marriage and, even more disturbing, that Jackie had been sleeping with him. The former was proven false, and Marquand insisted that the latter was equally untrue. After a year, Janet insisted that her 20-year-old daughter, with no prospects for marriage, return home and consider her future. But Jackie's year in Paris would have a profound influence on every aspect of that future, from the clothes she wore to the ease with which she would manage state dinners with glittering international guest lists.

No sooner had she arrived back in New York than Jackie learned she had won *Vogue* magazine's Prix de Paris essay contest, offering the chance of working for six months as a junior editor at *Vogue's* Paris bureau. She had been one of some 1,200 young women to enter the contest, writing in a style that was at once amusing, charming, and practical. Janet pleaded with her to refuse the award and find a husband; Hugh offered to pay for a summer vacation in Paris and to find her a newspaper job when she returned. After working for only a week at *Vogue's*

New York office, also part of the prize, Jackie politely declined a career that the quality of her writing indicated would have been a successful one. "I guess I was too scared to go to Paris again," she later wrote. "I felt then that if I went back, I'd live there forever."

In 1951, Jackie graduated from George Washington University with a degree in French literature. True to his word, Hugh Auchincloss sent her off to Paris with her sister Lee for the summer, after which the two sisters self-published a book of their experiences, *One Special Summer,* in which Jackie assured a worried "Uncle Hughdie" in the book's preface that they had been careful to do nothing to embarrass him. "I know you are right about us representing our country and that we must never do anything that would call attention to us and make people shocked at Americans," she wrote in an oddly succinct statement of her future responsibilities.

Also true to his promise, Auchincloss found Jackie a newspaper job by calling on his old friend Arthur Krock, who was then the Washington correspondent for *The New York Times.* Krock in turn called the editor of the old *Washington Times-Herald* to ask, "Are you still hiring little girls?" The *Times-Herald,* as it turned out, was looking for an "inquiring photographer"—someone who could stop passersby with an interesting question, report their response, and take their photograph. Jackie was told she could have the job, at $42.50 a week, if she could learn to handle a clumsy Speed Graphic camera by the next day. She managed to learn the camera's intricacies (although a six-foot reporter had to lay down on the floor to give her an idea of how far to stand from her subjects) and hit the streets of Washington to ask questions of her own invention. "What would you serve someone for his last meal?" was her query to a chef at one of the city's top restaurants (a vodka martini, turtle soup, and Chateaubriand, the chef said). When willing interview subjects proved sparse, Jackie merely turned to her friends, dressing them appropriately and suggesting interesting answers to her questions. Most of the newspaper's reporters were unimpressed with her journalistic abilities and sniped around the water fountain that she only had the job because of her family connections. But the paper's editor tried to be more fair. "She worked hard at the paper," he said, "never whined or ratted. . . . She's a good example of a youngster who takes advantage of her opportunities."

More than a few of Jackie's invented questions had to do with marriage—whether wives

Jacqueline
Kennedy

should pretend their husbands were smarter; whether men are as anxious to get married as women; what was the perfect age for a girl to find a husband. As it turned out, there was something more than journalistic creativity behind the questions, for in January of 1952 Jackie announced her engagement to a young investment banker named John Husted, Jr. Husted came from the requisite good family, comfortably situated but not so comfortably as to prevent Jackie's mother from feeling her daughter could do better. "You must realize that [the importance of money] was the one thing that Janet Auchincloss pounded into the heads of her daughters," Gore Vidal told an interviewer years later. Novelist Louis Auchincloss, Jackie's cousin, put it more bluntly. "The major motivation in her life was money." The fact was that Jackie had very little financial security of her own, particularly after old John Bouvier, Jackie's paternal grandfather, wrote his spendthrift son out of his will and thus deprived his granddaughter of an inheritance of her own. Jackie relied almost entirely on Hugh Auchincloss' largesse for support. Janet's remonstrances must have had an effect on her elder daughter, for friends who saw Jackie and Husted together felt there was a certain coolness in the relationship, and Husted might have wondered about Jackie's intentions when she arrived three hours late for the arranged meeting at which Jackie accepted his offer.

Planning began for a June wedding, while Jackie shuttled between her job in Washington and weekends with Husted in New York during the winter and early spring of that year; but rumors grew that the marriage would never happen, especially when Jackie began dating other men. Finally, she invited Husted down to Merrywood one April weekend and gently broke the news. "I may not be the most appropriate person for you," she told him. "I'm thinking of you, John, not me." What she was also thinking of was the man she had met at a cocktail party almost a year earlier and who was now actively pursuing her. He was handsome, ambitious, charming, and from a very wealthy family, indeed. His name was John Fitzgerald Kennedy.

Mutual friends had introduced her to Jack Kennedy before her engagement, and had arranged for Jack to escort her to one of their dinner parties as soon as news that Jackie was once again a free woman began circulating. Jack was 12 years Jackie's senior and was just beginning a political career promoted by his father Joseph P. Kennedy, who had begun as an Irish political boss in Boston, smuggled bootleg liquor during Prohibition, had been a Hollywood movie executive, and had ended up as ambassador to Britain under Franklin Roosevelt. When his eldest and favorite son Joseph Kennedy, Jr., died in World War II, Joe senior had turned to his next oldest son, one of his ten children with the equally formidable *Rose Fitzgerald Kennedy, to glorify the family name in the halls of Washington. Jack was already a U.S. congressional representative from Massachusetts' 11th district when he first met Jackie Bouvier, and was mounting his successful campaign for Henry Cabot Lodge's Senate seat by the time their relationship grew more serious.

Janet Bouvier Auchincloss may have thought the Kennedys vulgar *nouveau,* but even she had to be impressed by the family's fortune, then estimated at some $400 million. Jack himself had been assigned a trust fund of some $10 million by his father. For her part, Jackie may have seen something of her beloved father in Jack's considerable charms and somewhat raffish manner, although she chose to overlook Jack's reputation as an enthusiastic womanizer and his almost childlike vanity. "If we go out to a party or reception or something where nobody recognizes him," she told her cousin John Davis, "he sulks afterward for *hours.*" More of a challenge was the Kennedy clan itself, a tight-knit group of boisterous, relentlessly athletic and caustically witted Irish Catholics ruled by two parents who believed winning was everything. Jack's sisters *Eunice Kennedy (Shriver), ◄ Jean Kennedy (Smith), and ◄ Patricia Kennedy (Lawford) guffawed at Jackie's genteel manners, calling her "The Deb" and mocking Jackie's insistence that her given name be pronounced "Jac-CLEAN" ("rhymes with 'the Queen'," Pat wisecracked). Equally difficult was the Kennedys' enthusiasm for contact sports of all kinds, Jackie suffering various bruises, cuts and twisted ankles in her efforts to join in. "They'll kill me before I ever get to marry him," Jackie wrote to a friend in desperation. Rose Kennedy shared her daughters' disdain for Jackie's aristocratic airs, but it was precisely her gentility that won Joseph P. Kennedy to her side. Joe Kennedy had never been able to convince Boston society's elite that he was one of them, and Jackie's sophistication and classic bearing convinced the old man that his son would be advancing the family's social standing by marrying her. "Jackie's got more class than any girl we've seen around here," he told one of his cronies. Besides, he said, "a politician's got to have a wife, and a Catholic politician's got to have a Catholic wife." Amid all this family drama, there could have been no better symbol of the differences between them than what the Kennedys packed for lunch for a cruise on the family yacht, and what Jackie brought along for herself. The Kennedys consumed quantities of peanut butter and jelly sandwiches with lemonade; Jackie brought pâté, quiche, and white wine.

Not long after Jackie's sister Lee married for the first time, Jack Kennedy finally proposed in the spring of 1953. It was a sign of Jack's priorities, however, that he asked his fiancée to delay announcing the engagement until the summer so that a planned *Saturday Evening Post* article

---

Smith, Jean Kennedy. See Kennedy, Rose Fitzgerald for sidebar.

Lawford, Patricia Kennedy. See Kennedy, Rose Fitzgerald for sidebar.

---

called "The Senate's Gay Young Bachelor" could appear as scheduled. It was, he explained, an important public relations tool for his career. While the announcement was under wraps, Jackie accepted an invitation to accompany a friend to the coronation of Queen *Elizabeth II in London, which she covered for the *Times-Herald* to meet her expenses for the trip. She was away from Jack for a month and must have been thinking of the implications of her decision to marry a man whose roving eye was common knowledge. "How can you live with a husband who is bound to be unfaithful, but whom one loves?," she asked a friend. She might also have paused when, arriving for a weekend visit at Hyannis Port after the engagement was finally announced, she was met by a *Look* photographer assigned to shoot an article to be called "Senator Kennedy Goes A'Courtin'." Her protests that nobody had asked for her permission fell on deaf ears. She had to do it, Joe Kennedy told her, for the good of Jack's career.

More conflict arose over the Auchincloss' preference for a small, private wedding and the Kennedys' demand for a large, very public affair that would give Jack maximum exposure. The guest list for the ceremony at St. Mary's Church in Newport on September 12, 1953, numbered nearly 800, joined by 500 more at the reception held on the lawns of Hammersmith Farm. "Black Jack" Bouvier, however, was not among them, for Janet had barred him from the wedding ceremony and the reception as well. (Rumors that Janet had arranged for someone to go to Bouvier's room and make sure he got drunk have never been substantiated.) Jackie was bitterly disappointed that her father was unable to give her away, but as usual hid her emotions under a serene smile as Hugh Auchincloss led her to the altar and her waiting husband, who joked to throngs of reporters that he was marrying Jackie to reduce the press corps' number by one.

The couple's first years together were not promising, especially to a woman who had told her boarding-school friends a mere ten years earlier that her ambition in life was "not to be a housewife." Married to an ambitious politician, there was little else Jackie could be. "Housekeeping is a joy to me," she dutifully told a reporter after she and Jack had moved into their first home, a rented townhouse in Georgetown. "When it all runs smoothly, when the food is good and the flowers fresh, I have much satisfaction." But as she acted the smiling, invisible host to Jack's political cronies, attended Capitol Hill cocktail parties and joined women's charitable committees, and turned a blind eye to her husband's philandering, she struggled to keep depression at bay. "Jackie was wandering around looking like a survivor from an airplane crash," one friend remembered of these years. Still, some deep-seated bond kept the marriage intact, especially after Jack nearly died from complications of surgery intended to relieve the agonizing back pain of a slipped disc. It was an ailment that had tortured him for years and might well have put him in a wheelchair for life. Even so, doctors warned that an operation could prove fatal because of Addison's Disease, a disorder of the immune system that Jack had been able to control with cortisone but which made any post-operative infection potentially disastrous.

Even Joe Kennedy failed to dissuade his son from taking the risk. The operation was performed in October of 1954, but as had been feared, an infection followed. Jack sank into a coma and was so near death that a priest was hastily called to administer the last rites of the Catholic Church. For days, Jackie sat at her husband's bedside holding his unresponsive hand, reading poetry to him softly and, for her dedication and strength, finally earning the respect of Rose Kennedy and her daughters. Jack ultimately regained consciousness and began a slow recovery, during which he relied on Jackie to answer his mail, screen visitors, and help him with research for his landmark study of political integrity, *Profiles in Courage*. "This book would not have been possible without the encouragement, assistance and criticisms offered from the very beginning by my wife, Jacqueline, whose help during all the days of my convalescence I cannot adequately acknowledge," Jack wrote in his introduction.

In March of 1955, Jack walked for the first time in over a year without crutches; and by July, Jackie traveled with her husband to Rome, where the couple met Pope Pius XII, and to Paris for a state dinner with the French prime minister, who was much impressed with Jackie's knowledge of French language and culture. During their seven weeks abroad, the Kennedys also attended a party in honor of Winston Churchill aboard the yacht of Greek shipping magnate Aristotle Onassis, one of the world's wealthiest men, during which Churchill paid more attention to Jackie than to her husband.

On their return home, Jackie discovered she was pregnant and convinced Jack that it was time for a permanent home. She chose a small estate called Holly Hill in McLean, Virginia, not far from Merrywood. The couple had hardly moved in, however, when Jackie miscarried early in her first trimester. Four months later, she was pregnant again. This time she carried the baby nearly to term, although the strains of accompanying Jack to the 1956 Democratic Convention and campaigning with him for his near-victory as Adlai Stevenson's running mate proved too much for her. She collapsed at Hammersmith Farm soon after returning from the Convention with severe stomach cramps and hemorrhaging; her stillborn daughter was born just hours later at a nearby hospital. It was not Jack, however, who came to comfort her as she lay weak from loss of blood. It took three days to contact Jack, on a Mediterranean cruise at the time with friends, and it was his younger brother Robert F. Kennedy that offered Jackie comfort and who tried to shield her from the Washington gossip that Jack only agreed to return to her after being told that not doing so might hurt his political aspirations. By now, the three-year-old marriage had reached its lowest point, and there were rumors a divorce was imminent. But once again political necessity intervened.

Over Thanksgiving at Hyannis Port that year, Jack and Bobby spent long hours in discussions with their father about Jack's possible presidential candidacy. Joe Kennedy felt that the political climate was right but urged Jack not to let his wife seek a divorce. Electing a Catholic to the White House would be hard enough, he said, let alone a divorced one, although the family would later deny rumors that Joe had offered his daughter-in-law $1 million to stay in the family. Even if it was a false report, the existence of such gossip indicated the enormous power Jackie now wielded over her husband's future. Further intricacies arose when Jackie announced in the spring of 1957 that she was once again pregnant. After two unsuccessful pregnancies, apprehension mounted about a third one when Jackie's beloved father died of liver cancer in August of that year. Happily, the fears proved groundless. The couple's first child, *Caroline Kennedy (Schlossberg), was born in New York on November 27. But even a baby was not immune from the Kennedys' political juggernaut. Over Jackie's objections, little Caroline was photographed with her father for national publication during his successful campaign for re-election to the Senate when she was barely a month old. The election, which Jack won by a wide margin, was seen as a final test of his chances for the White House.

Jackie did not travel with her husband to the Democratic Convention in Los Angeles a year and a half later, for by then she was carrying a second child and refused to subject herself and her baby to the strain. She remained in the background after Jack's nomination, in contrast to *Patricia Nixon, who appeared with her husband at almost all his campaign appearances. The Nixon campaign, sensing that Jackie might be perceived as a high society snob in designer clothes, recalled to voters Nixon's famous "Checkers" speech of 1952 about his humble origins and his wife's "Republican cloth coat"; but Jackie, very obviously pregnant in her few interviews with reporters, turned her condition to advantage, emphasizing her dedication to home and family. "I feel I should be with Jack when he's engaged in such a struggle," she told them, "and if it weren't for the baby, I'd campaign even more vigorously than Mrs. Nixon." On the occasions when she did take the stump for Jack, however, Jackie seemed to reach her audience with a combination of sincerity and a wry sense of humor. She once marched up to the manager's office in a crowded supermarket, asked for the microphone, and announced "Just keep on with your shopping while I tell you why you should vote for my husband, John F. Kennedy"; and during the primaries, she told the press that among Caroline's first words had been "New Hampshire, Wisconsin, and West Virginia." She predicted that by the end of the primaries, "we would have a daughter with the greatest vocabulary of any two-year-old in the country." In November of 1960, Jack Kennedy was elected the 35th president of the United States, narrowly defeating Richard Nixon in the popular ballot by less than 120,000 votes. While the rest of the Kennedys celebrated at Hyannis Port, Jackie walked alone on the beach.

She was alone, too, when her second child, John F. Kennedy, Jr., arrived nearly two months early on November 26, 1960, just weeks after the election. Jack was on a plane to the family's Palm Beach estate, but this time ordered the pilot to return to Washington. "John-John," as he would be called, was only six pounds at birth and placed in an incubator, but he was otherwise healthy. With the safety of her son assured, Jackie put her attention on the inauguration and turned to Oleg Cassini, a longtime supporter of the Kennedys, to design the wardrobe that would catch the nation's eye that cold January day. Assembling the staff that would assist her at the White House, Jackie was persuaded to hire a press secretary, becoming the first first lady to do so. Her predecessors, most recently *Mamie Eisenhower and *Eleanor Roosevelt, had always managed the small amount of letter-writing and public scheduling the position required, but television had come of age during the Kennedy-

Nixon contest, it being generally agreed that the small screen now found in nearly every American living room had emphasized Jack's youth and charisma at Nixon's expense. The Kennedy Administration would make masterful use of the new electronic media and of what later generations would call "spin," and it would be television that would help create the phenomenon known as "Jackie fever."

It began when Mamie Eisenhower invited Jackie to the White House for the traditional tour given by an outgoing first lady to her successor. The place, Jackie later confided to her social secretary, looked like a "hotel that had been decorated by a wholesale furniture store during a January clearance." Her redecoration of the White House during her three years there is her lasting gift to the nation, launched by her now-famous live television tour of the executive mansion on CBS during prime time. Her television presence, it was generally conceded, was less than commanding, described by her CBS co-host Charles Collingwood as "that deer-caught-in-the-headlights look," while her mastery of un-scripted repartee was sadly lacking. As they entered the Blue Room, for example, Collingwood casually remarked that it had a very different feeling from the Red Room they had just left. "Yes," Jackie replied after some hesitation, "it's blue." Nonetheless, the broadcast watched by 56 million viewers was the first time the country had really had a chance to see her, and it seemed they were suitably impressed. Some $2 million in private donations, much of it in small bills from the household cookie jar, poured into the mail after the broadcast, not to mention the money from 14 countries that bought rights to air the program abroad.

Jackie's influence on her imposing surroundings was more than physical, however. She brought a new, contemporary sensibility to state dinners, for one thing, by substituting the traditional long, U-shaped tables with smaller, round ones, lending a more informal atmosphere to even the weightiest occasion of state. Her sponsorship of the arts injected a cultural excitement into a town long used to dull concerts and road tours of plays, an excitement she brought directly into the White House by inviting the likes of Leonard Bernstein, Jerome Robbins, and Pablo Casals to perform there. She called for the creation of a formal government structure to fund the arts, long the standard in most European countries, leading to the eventual creation of the National Endowment for the Arts and the National Endowment for the Humanities. Her major achievement, though, was the creation of the Washington National Cultural Center, now called The Kennedy Center, as Capitol Hill's answer to New York's Lincoln Center.

A year into the Kennedy Administration, despite civil-rights violence in the South and political fiascos like the disastrous Bay of Pigs invasion, the First Family was the focus of intense national interest, and the "Jackie Look" a national obsession, from her bouffant hairdo to her strapless evening gowns. The craze was just as intense overseas, so much so that Jack Kennedy once joked to a French audience, "I am the man who accompanied Jacqueline Kennedy to Paris, and I have enjoyed it." Even Charles de Gaulle was not immune, insisting that Jackie sit next to him at a state dinner and later telling Jack, "I now have more confidence in your country."

As Jackie's political stock grew, so did her husband's regard for her. By October of 1962, while the world's two major powers stared each other down during the Cuban Missile Crisis, Jack insisted that his wife be nearby, and Jackie refused to be evacuated to a bomb-proof retreat as long as Jack remained in Washington. Jack loved the humorous notes she would leave on his desk, often bursting out in laughter during staff meetings in the Oval Office; and he refused to let even the most serious national crisis interrupt the two hours set aside in the afternoon for he and Jackie to be alone. When a third son, named Patrick, was born prematurely in August of 1963, Jack was this time at his wife's side, where he remained until the child died of respiratory failure six days later. Both parents did not try to hide their grief from the press and wept openly at the loss. When Jackie began to slip into depression, Jack insisted she take time off after the tragedy and encouraged her to accept an invitation from a sympathetic Aristotle Onassis to spend a few weeks aboard his yacht *Cristina* with her sister Lee. Onassis tactfully kept a low profile during the Bouvier sisters' visit, partly out of respect for Jackie's emotional state and partly because his notorious affair with opera diva *Maria Callas* could prove a political weapon for her husband's opposition. Like everyone else, Aristotle was charmed by his famous guest and offered a diamond and ruby necklace as a parting gift.

Back in Washington, Jackie resumed her normal activities under the watchful eye of the press, a presence that was making her increasingly uncomfortable. Her family's constant public exposure, she said, made them "like sitting ducks in a shooting gallery" despite the constant presence of Secret Service officers, for whom she was code-named "Lace." There had already been one instance of a Florida drifter arrested outside the Kennedy compound in Palm Beach with a carload of firearms and ammunition with which he later confessed he intended to shoot the president. But as Jack began laying the groundwork in 1963 for his re-election campaign, Jackie agreed to accompany him to a particularly troublesome state where internal party bickering threatened his chances of victory. On November 21, the Kennedys and their entourage boarded Air Force One for the flight to Texas.

It was obvious from the moment the First Couple stepped off the plane in Fort Worth, where they spent their first night, that it was Jackie the crowd wanted to see. "Mrs. Kennedy is organizing herself," the president felt pressed to explain the next morning, November 22, when he appeared without her outside their hotel. "It takes a little longer, but of course she looks better than us when she does it." Rounds of applause greeted Jackie's arrival a few moments later in a pink wool suit, her trademark pillbox hat, and white gloves, the wardrobe she had chosen to wear for that day's activities in Dallas, the next stop on the tour.

The president was scheduled to deliver a luncheon address downtown, traveling to the site in an open-topped convertible from Dallas' Love Field. At 12:30, as the motorcade wound its way through Dallas' Dealey Plaza with the nation's favorite couple waving and smiling, Lee Harvey Oswald fired from the top floor of the Texas Book Exchange building. "My God, they've killed Jack; they've killed my husband!" Jackie screamed. The president's skull had been hit with such force that it was as if he had been rudely shoved down onto her lap, his blood staining the pink wool of her suit. Terrified, Jackie tried to scramble over the back of the car to safety but was pushed back by a Secret Service agent as the car screeched away toward Parkland Memorial Hospital, where John F. Kennedy died during emergency surgery. Throughout the nightmare of the next hours—in the limousine bearing Jack's bronze coffin back to Love Field, aboard Air Force One while Vice-President Lyndon Johnson was hurriedly sworn into office on the flight back to Washington, then during a hastily arranged autopsy at Bethesda Naval Hospital—Jackie refused to change out of her blood-soaked wool dress. "Let them see what they've done," she was heard to mutter. "I want them to see."

John F. Kennedy was laid to rest on November 25 at Arlington National Cemetery. It was Jackie who convinced the Kennedys that Jack should be buried in nationally consecrated ground and not in the family's private plot in Boston, as they wanted; and it was Jackie who saw to every detail of the state funeral, using protocols she studied from the records of another victim of an assassin's bullet, Abraham Lincoln; and it was Jackie's steady hand that lit the eternal flame that still watches over her husband's final resting place. As the mournful procession bearing his father's coffin to Arlington passed by, little John-John, waving his tiny American flag in one hand and saluting with the other, etched an unforgettable image on the nation's memory. Eleven days later, Jackie and her children left the White House. She remained out of sight for the next two months, finally appearing on national television in January of 1964 to publicly thank the nation for its support. "The knowledge and affection in which my husband was held by all of you has sustained me," she said, "and the warmth of these tributes is something that I shall never forget."

A year later, Jackie told an interviewer that Jack's status as a myth, rather than a man, is what had finally killed him. The public was unaware, however, that Jackie had spent the last 12 months creating that myth and making sure it would remain stainless, with no hint of her husband's sexual escapades with women ranging from his personal secretaries to *Marilyn Monroe. Jackie was, for example, the source for the long-lived comparison between Jack's years in Washington and the legend of King Arthur and his mythical Camelot, planting the idea in journalist Teddy White's mind during a long evening at Hyannis Port two months after the assassination. She began by describing Jack's murder in gruesome detail, then outlined what he might have accomplished for his country had he lived, and explained how Jack had drawn inspiration from the legendary kingdom where virtue and gallantry prevailed. On nights when his back ailment was particularly painful and robbed him of sleep, she said, she would play him the recording of the Rodgers and Hammerstein musical and its concluding lament for "the one brief, shining moment" of Camelot and its bright hope for the future. "At that moment," White later said, "she could have sold me anything from an Edsel to the Brooklyn Bridge." White's influential article in *Life* magazine appeared just a few weeks later. Another journalist did not fare so well. Jackie considered his reporting ethics too dangerous and blocked his work on a book about the assassination while promoting one which she considered more favorable, William Manchester's *Death of a*

President. Household employees, meanwhile, were required to sign a contract in which they pledged not to speak to the press. Infractions were met with instant dismissal. So effective were Jackie's efforts to preserve her husband's image that it was not for another 20 years that anyone dared to openly discuss Jack's sexual voracity or the Kennedy men's proclivities for, as Jackie once confided, "going after anything in skirts."

After a year living in a rented townhouse in Washington, it became clear to Jackie that it was no longer the place for her. She disliked the Johnsons and their back-slapping Southern ways, privately calling the new First Couple "Colonel Cornpone and his little pork chop," and refused LBJ's offers of an honorary White House position; and with the public now adding treacled sympathy to its continued fascination with her, she longed to escape the Washington fishbowl. Bobby Kennedy was an important source of comfort for her, as he had been all during her involvement with his tumultuous family, and their frequent appearances together inevitably led to the widely held opinion they had

become lovers. The rumors gained even more strength when both Jackie and Bobby moved to New York—he, to mount a successful campaign for one of that state's U.S. Senate seats, and she, to move herself and her two children into a 14-room apartment on Park Avenue in Manhattan, bought with some of the considerable funds assigned to her from her late husband's trust.

The two were often observed at restaurants and cultural events around town, often holding hands, and at a country home in Glen Cove, Long Island, that Jackie had taken. "There was always something oddly intense in her voice when she mentioned [Bobby] to me," Gore Vidal later said, and it was generally accepted that the grief they both shared at Jack's death had grown into something more. Jackie's emotional state on the first anniversary of Jack's murder was so perilous, in fact, that she confided to a friend that she had considered taking an overdose of sleeping pills. "Everyone who loved her was very concerned about her state of mind," the friend revealed years later. "All the terrible memories had flooded back, and Bobby was the only one who

Shortly after her husband's assassination, a stunned Jacqueline Kennedy witnessed the swearing-in of Lyndon Johnson.

could pull her out of her depression." But as the years passed and those terrible memories lost some of their power, Jackie began to regain her balance in a city where she had spent some of her happiest years, appearing more often at public events and on the streets she had known so well. "Taking you anyplace is like going out with a national monument," one of her frequent escorts, director Mike Nichols, complained one afternoon in 1967 after the two were swamped by admirers outside of Bergdorf Goodman's. "Yes," Jackie sighed, "but isn't it fun?"

She seemed determined to carry on with her new life free of politics, but she found it a more difficult task than she expected. Bobby announced his presidential candidacy in March of 1968, and it went without saying that Jackie would be expected to appear on his behalf. She found her brother-in-law's intentions worrisome, especially after Martin Luther King, Jr.'s assassination just a month later and Bobby's much-publicized efforts as attorney general during his brother's administration to crack down on organized crime. "There's too much hate in this country," she told Arthur Schlesinger, "and more people hate Bobby than hated Jack." The Kennedys, for their part, were fearful that Jackie's involvement with Aristotle Onassis, who had begun paying her court some months earlier, would hurt Bobby's campaign. Onassis was Greek Orthodox, not Catholic, and had divorced **Tina Onassis**, his wife of many years, to openly carry on his affair with Maria Callas, even while he was pursuing Jackie. The public would hardly view such a match for their beloved Jackie with favor, the Kennedys knew, and might register their unhappiness at the ballot box. Onassis' generous contribution to Bobby's campaign eased matters somewhat, but Jackie agreed to delay any marriage announcement until after the November elections. With her promise secure and the encouraging news that he had just won the important California primary by a landslide, Bobby left for Los Angeles to deliver his victory speech. On June 6, 1968, a Palestinian dissident named Sirhan Sirhan fired at near point-blank range as Bobby shook hands with kitchen workers at the hotel where the celebration was held. He died the next day. "I hate this country," Jackie bluntly stated after Bobby's funeral. "If they're killing Kennedys, my kids are number one targets." Four months later, on October 20, 1968, Jackie married Onassis in a sparsely attended ceremony on the Greek island of Skorpios after receiving permission from Richard Cardinal Cushing to wed not only a divorced man, but a non-Catholic.

"HOW COULD YOU?" moaned one tabloid when the news became public knowledge, echoing the nearly universal condemnation of the union of the world's favorite tragic princess to a short, ostentatiously vulgar international playboy. When a friend commented that the marriage had succeeded in knocking her off her pedestal, Jackie quickly replied, "It's better than freezing there." Another paper printed the more shrewd headline "JACKIE MARRIES BLANK CHECK," for Onassis' largesse toward beautiful women was well known and Ted Kennedy had brokered a highly favorable prenuptial agreement for his sister-in-law, which included a $3 million outright gift, another $1 million placed in a trust fund for John, Jr., and Caroline, and $200,000 a year for Jackie's support in case of Onassis' death or their divorce. Although Onassis was genuinely fond of his new bride and his new daughter and son, the marriage was seen only in terms of its monetary value and Jackie, now universally called "Jackie O," as a spendthrift jet-setter. There was much reporting, too, on the frictions between Jackie and Onassis' own two children, Alexander and *Christina Onassis, both of whom had begged their father not to marry the woman they called "the American geisha," whom they claimed was only after his money. Christina, a deeply troubled young woman struggling with clinically diagnosed depression, was particularly resentful of Jackie's suggestions about losing weight, changing her wardrobe and a host of other bits of advice Jackie no doubt thought helpful.

Nevertheless, the marriage was a relatively happy one at first. Onassis, with business interests throughout the world, allowed Jackie the freedom of his many homes and his credit cards. But even Onassis became alarmed after two years when Jackie's expenses sometimes amounted to $20,000 a month. Tragedy struck, too, when Onassis' son Alexander was killed in an airplane crash. With Jackie spending more time in the United States, where Caroline and John, Jr., were attending school, Onassis turned to Callas for comfort, then to his ex-wife Tina before she died in the autumn of 1974, less than two years after his son. Christina began to call Jackie "the Black Widow," who killed everyone close to her.

By now Onassis had become so upset with Jackie's aloof manner that he hired an investigative reporter to publicly document Jackie's expensive lifestyle, including a bill for $60,000 for 100 pairs of shoes, and began to plan divorce proceedings. But early in 1975, Onassis collapsed in Paris from an apparent stroke. Jackie visited him several times as his condition worsened, but was in New York when Onassis died in March. She and Teddy Kennedy attended the funeral a week later in Greece with a distraught Christina, who wept bitterly as Jackie knelt and kissed her second husband's bronze coffin. Unlike her stepdaughter, Jackie showed little emotion.

Anticipating the press scrutiny of her relations with Christina, Jackie issued a statement after the funeral claiming that Onassis had "rescued me at a time when my life was engulfed in shadows" and asserting her continued love and care for Christina. Christina herself issued a brief announcement that she and Jackie were on the most affectionate terms, but the long, ugly lawsuit that erupted over the disposition of Onassis' $1 billion fortune indicated otherwise. It dragged on for a year and half as Jackie's lawyers tried to prove that Onassis' will, in which he left nearly everything to his daughter, was invalid. Finally, Jackie accepted Christina's offer of $26 million to settle out of court. It has been estimated that in her six-year marriage to Onassis, Jackie had received from him and his estate a total of $42 million.

Her marriage to Onassis would be her last, and his death the end of her controversial lifestyle, but even her harshest critics were unprepared for the next chapter in her life. Jacqueline Kennedy Onassis, international celebrity and one of the world's wealthiest women, went to work. The inspiration may have had something to do with President Gerald Ford's designation of 1975 as International Women's Year, or the fact that John, Jr., and Caroline were now well-adjusted teenagers developing lives of their own, or perhaps it was simply Jackie's wish to polish her press-battered image. Eager potential employers, from TV networks to department store chains, courted her by the score, but it was the more modest position as an editor with Viking Press that appealed to her. "She knew literally everyone," Viking's president Thomas Guinzberg later said, "and in publishing it's not so much what but whom you know." Guinzberg was proof of his own statement, for he had long known Jackie through his friendship with her sister, Lee Radziwell (Lee had married Prince Stanislaus Radziwell after divorcing her first husband). Jackie accepted Guinzberg's offer of an entry level position at $10,000 a year.

At the outset, Jackie had about as much knowledge of book editing and publishing as of the camera of her inquiring photographer days 25 years before; but, as one of Viking's staff later recalled, "she was willing to roll up her sleeves and learn." There were conflicts, however. There was constant public debate among Jackie-watchers about how much she actually contributed to the books on which she worked and whether Viking had hired her only as a draw to attract authors from other houses. The situation did not improve when Viking published a suspense novel by British author Jeffrey Archer called *Shall We Tell the President?*, the president of Archer's fictional Washington being Teddy Kennedy, who is nearly killed in an assassination attempt. With both Jack's and Bobby's deaths little more than a decade old, the novel was considered by some in extremely bad taste. Jackie, in fact, had nothing to do with the book's acquisition and editing, but the press refused to believe it. "Anybody associated with its publication should be ashamed of herself," *The New York Times* stated pointedly. Stung by the accusations, Jackie resigned from Viking in 1977 and was immediately hired by Doubleday as an associate editor. By 1982, she had been promoted to a full editor and worked on such varied projects as Michael Jackson's 1984 *Moonwalk* and on a number of books for the equestrian market, all of which profited from her sense of style and elegant presentation.

Outside her office, Jackie generally kept out of the public eye—not an easy task, given the relentless throng of papparazzi that followed her everywhere, one of the most persistent of whom she successfully sued twice. She stayed away from politics and from the Kennedys, although she remained close to Teddy and took part in many commemorative observances to both Jack's and Bobby's memory, as well as serving as an advisor to the John F. Kennedy Library in Cambridge. She was an active and generous supporter of women's causes, particularly the plight of working women in the 1970s. "What has been sad for many women of my generation," she wrote in *Ms.,* "is that they weren't supposed to work if they had families. There they were, with the highest education, and what were they supposed to do when the children were grown— watch the raindrops coming down the windowpane?" In her private life, she saw to it that her mother was well provided for when Hugh Auchincloss died in 1976 and left Janet in straitened circumstances because of a series of bad real estate investments. Janet herself died in 1989. (The developers who bought Hammersmith Farm renamed it "Camelot Gardens.") Jackie never spoke of her years with Jack or their time together in the White House and prevailed upon her children to do the same. Both complied, John once telling an insistent reporter, "My mother would kill me."

Although she had several discreet, genteel relationships during these final New York years, Jackie's greatest comfort came from financier Maurice Templesman who, with his businessman's knowledge of African affairs, had been an occasional adviser to Jack on African policy and had attended several state functions at the White House with his wife **Lily Templesman**, who separated from him on learning of his relationship with Jackie. Templesman was the ideal companion. Like her, he loathed public scrutiny and never publicized the relationship, choosing quietly elegant and secure restaurants for their rare public outings together and firmly guiding Jackie's familiar figure, complete with her trademark head scarf and dark glasses, past sidewalk gawkers. His financial expertise, meanwhile, made the most of Jackie's fortune inherited from Onassis, increasing the worth of her portfolio over the years by nearly four-fold. At his suggestion, Jackie had bought a parcel of land on Martha's Vineyard in the late 1970s on which she was able to build a $4 million, 19-room house. In 1993, Bill Clinton, just elected in a campaign that had emphasized his affinities with Jack Kennedy, visited her on Martha's Vineyard and was much photographed with Jackie and **Hillary Rodham Clinton** aboard Templesman's yacht.

It was in the Clintons' company, too, that Jackie made her final public appearance, in a rededication of the newly renovated JFK Library in October of 1993. Three months later, she was diagnosed with non-Hodgkins lymphoma, a deadly cancer of the lymph nodes. Doctors announced that with the early diagnosis, a course of chemotherapy might give Jackie a fighting chance, but by April the disease had spread beyond treatment. On May 19, 1994, at 10:15 in the evening, Jacqueline Bouvier Kennedy Onassis died quietly at home, her children and Maurice Templesman at her side to the end. She was buried next to Jack at Arlington National Cemetery.

Even after she was gone, however, controversy continued. Early in 1996, when John and Caroline announced that much of the contents of their mother's estate would be auctioned at Sotheby's, the outcry was almost as fervent as the anticipation of seeing Jackie's carefully guarded life on display. It was, complained *The New Yorker*, "viscerally cruel . . . for Caroline and John to auction off their mom as Home Shopping Network fodder." But it was Jackie herself who had suggested the idea by inserting it into her will as a practical and sensible method of dispersing her accumulated treasures and giving her children a comfortably assured future. The 5,000 items put up for bid in April of 1996 brought nearly $35 million, wildly over the most conservative estimates. Sotheby's later admitted that it had deliberately placed low estimates on most of the articles to attract the largest number of buyers, 5,000 of them, one of whom, for example, paid some $33,000 for a small stool with a torn seat that Sotheby's catalogue had estimated at no more than $150.

Jackie had, in fact, suffered the same historical fate as Jack. Her humanity had been overpowered by her own myth, her life picked over by the historians she once called "bitter old men," and her personality transformed into caricature in the media. Her efforts to preserve her version of history finally succumbed to the demands of a new American public eager for titilating revelations about the private lives of public figures. But it was a fate she had all along suspected. "The trouble with me is that I am an outsider," she once wrote to a friend. "And that's a very hard thing to be in American life."

SOURCES:

Anderson, Christopher. *Jackie After Jack: Portrait of the Lady.* NY: Morrow, 1998.

Davis, John H. *Jacqueline Bouvier: An Intimate Memoir.* NY: John Wiley & Sons, 1996.

Ladowsky, Ellen. *Jacqueline Kennedy Onassis.* NY: Park Lane Press, 1997.

SUGGESTED READING:

Klein, Edward. *All Too Human: The Love Story of Jack and Jackie Kennedy.* Pocket Books, 1996.

Leamer, Laurence. *The Kennedy Women.* Villard, 1994.

Taraborrelli, J. Randy. *Jackie, Ethel, Joan: Women of Camelot.* NY: Warner, 2000.

Norman Powers,
writer-producer, Chelsea Lane Productions, New York

Kennedy, Jean (b. 1928).

See Kennedy, Rose Fitzgerald for sidebar on Jean Kennedy Smith.

Kennedy, Joan (1936—)

*American socialite and former wife of Edward "Ted" Kennedy. Born Virginia Joan Bennett on September 5, 1936, in Riverdale, New York; eldest of two daughters of Harry Wiggin (an advertising executive) and Virginia Joan "Ginny" (Stead) Bennett; graduated from Bronxville (New York) High School, 1954; graduated from Manhattanville College of the Sacred Heart, New York, 1958; married Edward "Ted" Kennedy (b. 1932, a lawyer and U.S. senator), on November 29, 1958 (divorced 1982); children: **Kara Anne Kennedy** (b. 1960, a homemaker who married architect Michael Allen); Edward "Teddy" Moore Kennedy, Jr. (b. 1961, a lawyer); Patrick Joseph Kennedy (b. 1967, a congressional representative). Ted Kennedy married **Victoria Reggie** in 1992.*

The daughter of a successful advertising executive, Joan Bennett Kennedy was born in 1936 and grew up in the upper-middle-class community of Bronxville, New York, just blocks from where her future husband spent his early childhood. A stunning blonde, Joan was an accomplished pianist and also modeled briefly while attending Manhattanville College of the Sacred Heart, where she met Edward "Ted" Kennedy during a campus dedication ceremony of the Kennedy Physical Education Building in 1957. The couple had their first date in New York City during Thanksgiving break and were married a year later. Very early in the marriage, Ted devoted himself to his brother John F. Kennedy's presidential candidacy, and Joan vowed "to be ready to go anywhere and to accommodate myself to my husband's schedule." She held to that promise through Jack's election and Ted's own campaign for the Senate in 1962. Arriving in Washington in 1963, she embarked on a glamorous life as the wife of a senator and the sister-in-law of the president.

It was not long, however, before Joan began feeling like an outsider among the highly competitive Kennedy clan. Although she struck out on her own to successfully narrate "Peter and the Wolf" with the National Symphony Washington and several other orchestras, it was not enough to compensate for her feelings of inferiority. She began to wear attention-seeking clothes to Capitol functions—mini-skirts, see-through blouses, and shiny knee-high black boots—that set tongues wagging and made national headlines.

Then, there were the ceaseless tragedies during the 1960s and 1970s: the assassinations of John and then Robert F. Kennedy; Ted's own brush with death in an airplane crash; the incident at Chappaquiddick which resulted in the death of Ted's campaign aide **Mary Jo Kopechne**; and, finally, son Teddy's bout with cancer in 1973, which resulted in the amputation of his lower right leg. These events, coupled with Ted's philandering and Joan's growing dependence on alcohol, put further strains on the already shaky marriage. After several separations and reconciliations, one in 1979, when Ted attempted a presidential run, the Kennedys divorced in 1982. Joan eventually overcame much of her insecurity, though she still considers herself a recovering alcoholic. She remains joined to the Kennedy clan only through her three children.

SOURCES:

Collier, Peter, and David Horowitz. *The Kennedys: An American Drama*. NY: Warner Books, 1984.

Lester, David. *Joan: The Reluctant Kennedy*. NY: Funk & Wagnalls, 1974.

SUGGESTED READING:

Taraborrelli, J. Randy. *Jackie, Ethel, Joan: Women of Camelot*. NY: Warner, 2000.

Kennedy, Kathleen (1920–1948)

American socialite and sister of President John Fitzgerald Kennedy. Name variations: Kick; Marchioness of Hartington. Born Kathleen Agnes Kennedy in 1920; died in a plane crash in Belgium on May 13, 1948; daughter of Joseph P. Kennedy (1888–1969, a financier, diplomat, and head of several government commissions) and Rose Fitzgerald Kennedy (1890–1995); attended Sacred Heart Convent, Roehampton, England; attended Fitch Junior College; married William "Billy" Cavendish (1917–1944), marquess of Hartington and future duke of Devonshire, in May 1944 (shot by a German sniper on September 9, 1944).

Kathleen Kennedy was born in 1920, the daughter of Joseph P. Kennedy and *Rose Fitzgerald Kennedy. Blonde and petite, Kathleen, nicknamed "Kick" by her father, was the most lively and vivacious of the Kennedy girls. Her father's favorite, she was also particularly close to her brothers Joseph Kennedy, Jr. and John Fitzgerald Kennedy. "Those three—Joe Junior, Jack, and Kick—were like a family within the family, a charmed triangle," said a friend. "They were the pick of the litter, the ones the old man thought would write the story of the next generation."

After her debut in London in 1938, while her father was U.S. ambassador to Great Britain, Kathleen became popular with World War II English society and began dating William Cavendish (Billy to his friends), the eldest son of the duke of Devonshire and heir to an enormous estate. The Irish-Catholic Kennedys were strongly opposed to the match because Cavendish was Protestant, and when the two married in a civil ceremony on May 6, 1944, only Kathleen's brother, Joe Junior, was present to represent the Kennedys. Following the honeymoon, Cavendish, who was serving with the Coldstream Guards in France, returned to his unit, while Kathleen went home to try and patch things up with her family. Tragically, Cavendish was killed by a German sniper just a month after Kathleen's brother Joe Junior, a Navy pilot, lost his life in a plane crash. Mourning both her husband and her brother, Kathleen took up residence in England where she worked with the Red Cross until the end of the war. Gradually, she eased back into society, dating a number of prominent young men and turning her house in Smith Square into something of a salon for such luminaries as Anthony Eden, George Bernard Shaw, and Evelyn Waugh.

When Kathleen fell in love again, her choice was Peter Fitzwilliam, an elegant and wealthy aristocrat who was not only Protestant, but married. Described as older, charming, something of a rake, Fitzwilliam was said to have many of the same qualities as Joe Kennedy, Jr. Early in 1948, Kathleen came home to tell her family that she planned to wed Fitzwilliam after he divorced his wife. Her mother Rose, the one most shaken by the announcement, threatened to disown Kathleen if she went through with the marriage. Joseph Kennedy was more open to compromise and planned to ask for some sort of dispensation from the pope that might allow Kathleen to marry without losing her standing as a Catholic. Before he had a chance to do anything, Kathleen and Fitzwilliam were killed in a private plane crash over Belgium on their way to a holiday weekend getaway. Joseph Kennedy was the only family member to attend Kathleen's funeral and burial, which took place in England at the request of the Cavendish family. At Joe's request, the Boston papers related that the couple were only casual acquaintants, and that Kathleen had accepted the plane ride only because she had a pressing appointment in Paris.

SOURCES:

Collier, Peter, and David Horowitz. *The Kennedys: An American Drama.* NY: Warner Books, 1984.

SUGGESTED READING:

McTaggart, Lynne. *Kathleen Kennedy: Her Life and Times.* NY: Dial Press, 1983.

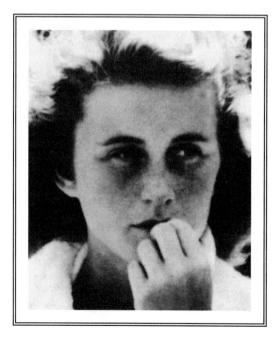

Kathleen Kennedy

Kennedy, Madge (1890–1987)

American actress. Born in Chicago, Illinois, in 1890; died in Woodland Hills, California, on June 9, 1987; daughter of Gordon Kennedy and Carolyn (Warner) Kennedy; married Harold Bolster; married William B. Hanley, Jr. (a radio producer), in 1934 (died 1959); no children.

Selected theater: made professional debut in The Genius *(1910); succeeded* **Margaret Lawrence** *as Elsie Darling in* Over Night *(1911); appeared in the title role in* Little Miss Brown *(Forty-eighth Street Theater, New York, 1912), as Anne Grey in* The Co-respondent *(Poughkeepsie, New York, May 1913), as Blanche Hawkins in* Twin Beds *(Fulton Theater, New York, August 1914), as Blanche Wheeler in* Fair and Warmer *(Eltinge Theater, New York, November 1915), in the dual role of Mary Brennan and Margaret Waring in* Cornered *(Astor Theater, New York, December, 1920), as Elizabeth Dean in* Spite Corner *(Little Theater, New York, September 1922), as Poppy McGargle in* Poppy *(Apollo Theater, New York, September 1923), as Miriam Holt in* Badges *(49th Street Theater, New York, December 1924), as Joyce Bragdon in* Beware of Widows *(Elliott Theater, New York, December 1925), as Diana Wynne in* Love in a Mist *(Gaiety Theater, New York, April 1926), as Mary McVittey in* The Springboard *(Mansfield Theater, New York, October 1927), as Mary Hutton in* Paris Bound *(Music Box Theater, New York, December, 1927); toured as Susan in* The Perfect Alibi *and as Mary in* Michael and Mary *(1930); succeeded* ***Gertrude Lawrence** *as Amada Prynne in* Private Lives *(Times Square Theater, May 1931); appeared as Joyce Burroughs in* Bridal Wise *(Cort Theater, New York, May 1932), as Fanny Grey in* Autumn Crocus *(Studebaker Theater, Chicago, January 1934).*

Selected filmography: Baby Mine *(1917);* Nearly Married *(1917);* The Danger Game *(1918);* The Fair Pretender *(1918);* The Service Star *(1918);* Friendly Husband *(1918);* The Kingdom of Youth *(1918);* A Perfect Lady *(1918);* Day Dreams *(1919);* Leave It to Susan *(1919);* Through the Wrong Door *(1919);* Strictly Confidential *(1919);* The Blooming Angel *(1920);* Dollars and Sense *(1920);* The Truth *(1920);* Oh Mary, Be Careful *(1921);* The Girl With a Jazz Heart *(1921);* The Highest Bidder *(1921);* The Purple Highway *(1923);* Three Miles Out *(1924);* Scandal Street *(1925);* Bad Company *(1925);* Lying Wives *(1925);* Oh Baby! *(1926);* The Marrying Kind *(1952);* The Rains of Ranchipur *(1955);* Three Bad Sisters *(1956);* The Catered Affair *(1956);* Lust for Life *(1956);* Let's Make Love *(1960);* They Shoot Horses,

WOMEN IN WORLD HISTORY

Don't They? *(1969)*; The Baby Maker *(1970)*; The Day of the Locust *(1975)*; The Marathon Man *(1976)*.

Madge Kennedy was recruited from the Broadway stage by Sam Goldwyn in 1917 and played successfully in silent movies through the 1920s, mainly in demure lady-like roles. While her screen career flourished, she also made occasional appearances on Broadway, notably in *Poppy* (1923) with W.C. Fields. Kennedy disappeared from films during the 1930s and 1940s, but made a strong comeback in the early 1950s as a character actress. Her later films include *The Marrying Kind* (1952), *The Rains of Ranchipur* (1955), *Lust for Life* (1956), *They Shoot Horses, Don't They?* (1969), *The Day of the Locust* (1975), and *Marathon Man* (1976). She also appeared on Broadway in *A Very Rich Woman* in 1965. Most critics believe that Kennedy's talents were better realized during her later film career, and often cite her portrayal of the elderly tenant of a shabby boarding house in *The Day of the Locust* as one of her best.

Kennedy married radio producer William B. Hanley, Jr., in 1934, and after his death in 1959, lived alone in Woodland Hills, California. She died at the age of 96.

Kennedy, Margaret (1896–1967)

British novelist, playwright, and critic. Born Margaret Moore Kennedy in London, England, on April 23, 1896; died in Adderbury, Oxfordshire, England, on July 31, 1967; eldest of four children of Charles Moore Kennedy (a barrister) and Elinor (Marwood) Kennedy; attended Cheltenham Ladies' College; received honors degree from Somerville College, Oxford, 1919; married David Davies (a barrister and county court judge), in 1925; children: one son, and two daughters, including Julia Birley (a novelist).

Selected writings—novels: The Ladies of Lyndon *(1923)*; The Constant Nymph *(1924)*; The Game and the Candle *(1926)*; Red Sky at Morning *(1927, not to be confused with the 1971 movie of the same name)*; The Fool of the Family *(1930)*; The Feast *(1950)*; Lucy Carmichael *(1951)*; Troy Chimneys *(1953)*; The Oracles *(1955)*.

Plays: (with Basil Dean) The Constant Nymph *(adapted from her novel, 1926)*; Escape Me Never! *(1933)*; *(with Gregory Ratoff)* Autumn *(1937)*.

Nonfiction: A Century of Revolution *(1922)*; The Mechanized Muse *(1942)*; The Outlaws on Parnassus *(1958)*; *(autobiography)* Where Stands a Winged Sentry.

Margaret Kennedy was born in London, England, in 1896, the daughter of Charles Moore Kennedy, a barrister, and **Elinor Marwood Kennedy**. Margaret began her creative life before she could read or write, composing a "play," which was frequently performed by cousins and playmates. By the time she entered Somerville College, at Oxford, she had written five novels and three plays and had destroyed them all. As it turned out, her first published book was neither a play nor a novel, but a historical study on the French Revolution, *A Century of Revolution* (1922). Her first novel, *The Ladies of Lyndon*, was published in 1923. Her second book *The Constant Nymph*, loosely based on a bohemian circle that surrounded the painter Augustus John, was a huge success in 1924. In 1926, she collaborated with Basil Dean on a stage dramatization of *The Constant Nymph* that starred Noel Coward (and later John Gielgud). There were four film versions, including the 1933 production by Gaumont-Fox which starred **Tess Sanger** and Brian Aherne, with screenplay by Kennedy and Basil Dean, and a 1943 Warner Bros. remake, which starred *Joan Fontaine, Charles Boyer, *Alexis Smith, and Dame *May Whitty, with screenplay by Katheryn Scola.

Kennedy's 1933 stage play *Escape Me Never*, starring *Elisabeth Bergner, also enjoyed enormous success. Filmed in England in 1935, it again starred Bergner and Hugh Sinclair, while the 1947 Warner Bros. remake starred *Ida Lupino, Errol Flynn, and *Eleanor Parker (the second version was based on both the novel *The Fool of the Family* and the play *Escape Me Never*).

Unconventionality versus respectability was a recurring theme in Kennedy's work, as was the deterioration of family relationships. Her books were popular book club selections in both England and the United States, and the novel *Troy Chimneys* (1953) won the James Tait Black Memorial Prize. In addition to novels and plays, Kennedy produced several nonfiction works, including *The Outlaws on Parnassus* (1958), on the art of the novel, and *The Mechanized Muse* (1942), about screen-writing.

Kennedy was married to a barrister David Davies and had three children; her daughter **Julia Birley** is also a novelist. Although Kennedy suffered from Bell's palsy from 1939, she continued to write, producing much of her work from a desk in her bedroom. She also produced an autobiography, *Where Stands a Winged Sentry*. Margaret Kennedy died on July 31, 1967.

SOURCES:

Buck, Claire. *The Bloomsbury Guide to Women's Literature*. NY: Prentice Hall, 1992.

Kunitz, Stanley, and Howard Haycraft. *Twentieth Century Authors*. NY: H.W. Wilson, 1942.

Shattock, Joanne. *The Oxford Guide to British Women Writers*. Oxford: Oxford University Press, 1993.

Barbara Morgan,
Melrose, Massachusetts

Kennedy, Patricia (b. 1924).

See Kennedy, Rose Fitzgerald for sidebar on Patricia Kennedy Lawford.

Kennedy, Rose Fitzgerald

(1890–1995)

American matriarch of the Kennedy dynasty, a family with traditions rooted in public service. Born in Boston, Massachusetts, on July 22, 1890; died in Hyannis Port, Massachusetts, on January 22, 1995; eldest of the six children of John Francis "Honey Fitz" (a politician) and Mary Josephine (Hannon) Fitzgerald; graduated from Dorchester High School, Dorch- *ester, Massachusetts, 1906; attended the Convent of the Sacred Heart, Boston; attended the Manhattanville College of the Sacred Heart, Purchase, New York; attended Blumenthal Academy, Valls, the Netherlands; married Joseph Patrick Kennedy (1888–1969, a financier, diplomat, and head of several government commissions), on October 7, 1914 (died November 18, 1969); children: Joseph Kennedy, Jr. (1914–1944); John Fitzgerald Kennedy (1917–1963, 35th president of the United States, assassinated in Dallas, Texas); Rosemary Kennedy (b. 1918); Kathleen Kennedy (1920–1948); Eunice Kennedy Shriver (b. 1921, who married Robert Sargent Shriver); Patricia Kennedy Lawford (b. 1924, who married actor Peter Lawford); Robert Francis Kennedy (1925–1968, U.S. senator, assassinated in Los Angeles, California, who married *Ethel Skakel Kennedy); Jean Kennedy Smith (b. 1928, who married Stephen Smith); Edward "Ted" Kennedy (b. 1932).*

The matriarch of America's media-dubbed "royal" family, Rose Fitzgerald Kennedy lived through the kind of political triumph and numbing tragedy that is usually reserved for classical drama. During a remarkable life span of 104 years, she witnessed three of her nine children elected to the U.S. Senate and one become the country's first Catholic president. She endured the death of her first-born son Joseph Kennedy, Jr., and her daughter *Kathleen Kennedy in plane crashes and saw her sons John F. Kennedy and Robert F. Kennedy gunned down by assassins. In her twilight years, she lost her grandson David Kennedy, Robert's son, to a drug overdose at the age of 28. Possessed with an unshakable faith and an iron will, she persevered through it all. "I just made up my mind that I wasn't going to be vanquished by anything," she once said. "If I collapsed, then it would have a very bad effect on the other members of the family. . . . I refuse to be daunted."

The eldest of six children born to John "Honey Fitz" Fitzgerald and **Mary Josephine Hannon**, Rose Kennedy acquired her deep religious faith from her mother and her flair for politics from her father who was the first Irish-American congressional representative from Boston, and later became mayor of that city. Standing in for her mother who shied away from the limelight, Rose frequently accompanied her father on official duties around town and abroad. After graduating from Dorchester High School, where she was voted prettiest girl in her class, she wanted to attend Wellesley College, but her father sent her to a series of convent

Rose
Fitzgerald
Kennedy

schools instead. "It was a real turning point," says **Doris Kearns Goodwin**, who interviewed Rose Kennedy for her 1987 biography *The Fitzgeralds and the Kennedys*. "When I asked what her greatest regret was, I expected it would be the death of her sons. Instead it was that she didn't get a chance to go to Wellesley."

At 20, Rose returned to Boston, where she had a coming out party attended by 400 people, among them the city council which declared the day a holiday in her honor. However, as Peter Collier and David Horowitz point out, Rose was excluded from the fashionable women's clubs of "proper (and Protestant) Boston, and was not on the visiting list of the better families." Among a string of eligible suitors, Rose fell in love with Joseph P. Kennedy, the cocky young son of a saloon-keeper, whom she had first encountered years earlier on a family vacation at Old Orchard Beach, Maine. Despite Honey Fitz's protestations, which included barring young Kennedy from the Fitzgerald home, the couple married in October 1914 and settled in their first home on Beals Street in Brookline, Massachusetts, now a national historic site as the birthplace of President John F. Kennedy. They would later live in Riverdale and Bronxville, New York, and also acquire homes in Hyannis Port, Massachusetts, and Palm Beach, Florida. When the couple married, Joe was already the country's youngest bank president, and his career advanced steadily, culminating in his appointment by President Franklin D. Roosevelt as U.S. ambassador to Great Britain in 1937. Along the way, Joe amassed a fortune in banking, real estate, movies, and, it was rumored, bootlegging. While he built his empire, Rose ran the house and tended to the couple's nine children—Joseph Kennedy, Jr. (1914–1944), John Fitzgerald Kennedy (1917–1963), *Rosemary Kennedy (b. 1918), Kathleen Kennedy (1920–1948), *Eunice Kennedy Shriver (b. 1921), ✥➤ Patricia Kennedy Lawford (1924—); Robert F. Kennedy (1925–1968), ✥➤ Jean Kennedy Smith (1928—), Edward "Ted" Kennedy (b. 1932)—all born within the first 18 years of her marriage.

Rose Kennedy, who could be a stern disciplinarian, instilled in the children her deep sense of faith and her love of history, frequently taking them on outings to numerous points of interest in and around Boston. "Children should be stimulated by their parents to see, touch, know, understand and appreciate," she said. At mealtimes, she encouraged lively discussions about religion, literature, and current events, and she also devised competitive programs in swimming, tennis, skiing, and other sports. The intense rivalries between the Kennedy siblings began at early age and continued through adulthood. To solve the more practical problems of her growing brood, Rose hired an army of nursemaids and governesses, and even employed a traveling orthodontist who visited the children at their various boarding schools to keep the notorious Kennedy teeth in line. She also kept careful records of the children on index cards which listed such things as weight, shoe size, and medical and dental information.

The greater challenge for Rose Kennedy may have been her husband. A notorious philanderer, Joe alternately pampered and humiliated his wife. Of his many mistresses, the most widely known was *Gloria Swanson, who was a guest at Hyannis Port several times. "If she resented me," Swanson wrote about Rose in her memoirs, "she never gave any indication." According to author Charles Higham, who wrote the biography *Rose,* the Kennedy marriage was successful in spite of Joe's dalliances. "[Rose] enjoyed everything that went with being with Joe Kennedy," he wrote. "She relished the parties, the galas, the politics and all that went with it." Another biographer, Nigel Hamilton, agreed that Rose enjoyed the trappings of wealth, commenting that she "blew a fortune on the latest fashions and jewelry." Indeed, during the 1930s, Rose Kennedy was named the best-dressed woman in public life by a poll of fashion designers.

There were sorrows, however, that defied compromise. The eldest Kennedy daughter, Rosemary, was mentally retarded and in 1941, when her usually docile nature turned violent, it was arranged for her to have a lobotomy, an operation then frequently performed to control behavior. Rosemary, who was 23 at the time of the surgery, was never able to function on her own again and was placed in a convent in Wisconsin where she remains. (In 1946, Joe Kennedy established the Joseph P. Kennedy, Jr. Foundation to help the retarded and later made a will leaving the bulk of his estate to that foundation.) Then there was the unfortunate situation with Kathleen "Kick" Kennedy, the golden girl of the family until she fell in love and married William Cavendish, marquess of Hartington, the non-Catholic heir to one of the great titles of England. Rose was so outraged that her daughter was marrying outside the faith that she did not attend the wedding and, according to one biographer, checked herself into a Boston hospital for minor surgery two weeks before the ceremony so she would not have to face the press. While still reeling from Kathleen's marriage, the Kennedys lost their eldest son Joe Junior, a Navy

❧▶ Lawford, Patricia Kennedy (1924—)

American socialite and daughter of Rose Fitzgerald Kennedy. Born in 1924; sixth child and fourth daughter of Joseph P. Kennedy (1888–1969, a financier, diplomat, and head of several government commissions) and Rose Fitzgerald Kennedy (1890–1995); graduated from Manhattanville College of the Sacred Heart, New York; married Peter Lawford (an actor), in June 1954 (divorced 1966, died 1984); children: Christopher Kennedy Lawford (b. 1955, an independent film producer and actor); **Sydney Maleia Lawford** *(b. 1956, a former model and homemaker who married Peter McKelvy);* **Victoria Lawford** *(b. 1958, a homemaker who married Robert Beebe Pender); Robin Lawford (b. 1961, a marine biologist).*

Patricia Kennedy Lawford was born in 1925, the sixth child and fourth daughter of Joseph P. Kennedy and *****Rose Fitzgerald Kennedy**. Auburn-haired and similar to her mother in personality, Pat was star-struck from her childhood. After college, she worked for a time for NBC in New York then, in 1951, left to become a production assistant for the "*****Kate Smith** Hour." Pat first met actor Peter Lawford on a trip to Hollywood in 1949 and ran into him again at the Republican Convention in 1952, which she was attending with her father. Their courtship was threatened by the fact that Lawford was a Protestant and an actor, but in 1954, after he converted to Catholicism, the two were married. (Before the wedding, Joseph P. Kennedy supposedly told Lawford: "If there's anything I think I'd hate worse than an actor as a son-in-law, it's an English actor.") The couple moved into the former Louis B. Mayer house in Malibu and formed the Kenlaw Production Company, through which they channeled Lawford's series, "Dear Phoebe" (1954–55), and "The Thin Man" (1957–59). Lawford, a member of Hollywood's notorious "rat pack," was instrumental in introducing John F. Kennedy to Sinatra and *****Marilyn Monroe**, but for the most part he remained something of an outsider. The marriage produced four children, but began to come apart with Lawford's philandering and drinking. Pat left him following the assassination of her brother in 1963 (they were formally divorced in 1966) and moved back East. After a difficult period during the 1960s, she returned to an active life, concentrating much of her energy on charitable organizations.

SOURCES:

Collier, Peter, and David Horowitz. *The Kennedys: An American Drama.* NY: Warner Books, 1984.

❧▶ Smith, Jean Kennedy (1928—)

*U.S. Ambassador to Ireland. Born Jean Ann Kennedy in St. Margaret's Hospital, Boston, Massachusetts, in 1928; daughter of Joseph P. Kennedy (1888–1969, a financier, diplomat, who was head of several government commissions) and *****Rose Fitzgerald Kennedy** *(1890–1995); sister of *****Patricia Kennedy Lawford***,* *****Eunice Kennedy Shriver***, John Fitgerald Kennedy (president of the U.S.), and Robert F. Kennedy (a U.S. senator); graduated from the Manhattanville College of the Sacred Heart, New York; married Stephen Smith (an attorney), in 1956 (died 1990); children: Stephen Edward Smith, Jr. (b. 1957, a conflict-resolution consultant); William Kennedy Smith (b. 1960, a doctor);* **Amanda Mary Smith** *(b. 1967, a writer);* **Kym Maria Smith** *(b. 1972, a homemaker).*

The youngest of the Kennedy sisters, Jean Ann Kennedy was born in 1928 and graduated from Manhattanville College of the Sacred Heart, but with no clear-cut goal for her future. She went to Chicago to work in public relations for the Mart, then returned to New York to work as an aide for Father John Keller, founder of the Christophers, an organization dedicated to fighting communism. In New York, Jean met Stephen ("Steve") Smith, an executive for a New York transportation firm founded by his grandfather. An Irish-Catholic, Steve was readily accepted into the Kennedy clan, and he and Jean married in 1956. The Smiths settled in New York, but also had a house in Hyannis, Massachusetts, a stone's throw from the senior Kennedys' compound. Steve became a valuable asset to all the Kennedy campaigns, and Jean, a behind-the-scenes supporter, also did her part. In addition, she devoted a great deal of time to charitable work, including Very Special Arts, an organization which attempts to bring experiences with the arts to the disabled. The Smith marriage encountered some difficult periods during the 1960s, but survived until Steve's death in 1990, one year before their son William Kennedy Smith was put on trial for rape, then acquitted. In 1993, Jean Smith was appointed ambassador to Ireland by the newly elected president, William Clinton.

SOURCES:

Collier, Peter, and David Horowitz. *The Kennedys: An American Drama.* NY: Warner Books, 1984.

Kennedy, Rose Fitzgerald. *Times to Remember.* Garden City, NY: Doubleday, 1974.

Smith, Jean Kennedy. "'Faith Above All' (a talk delivered as the commencement address at Fairfield University in Connecticut, May 21, 1995)," in *America.* June 17, 1995.

pilot, when his plane exploded over the English Channel. A month later, William Cavendish, serving as an officer in the Coldstream Guards, lost his life to a German sniper's bullet. Kathleen remained in England and subsequently fell in love with Peter Fitzwilliam, who was not only Protestant but married, though he planned to divorce his wife to marry Kathleen. Rose was so affronted by the affair that she threatened to disown Kathleen completely if she carried out her plans to marry Fitzwilliam. Weeks later, Kathleen and Fitzwilliam were killed in the crash of a private plane in France. Purportedly, Rose, who did not attend her daughter's funeral, regarded the tragedy as divine intervention to keep the couple from marrying.

In a foreword to Rose Kennedy's 1974 autobiography, *Times to Remember*, the Kennedy children call their mother "the best politician in our family." Certainly, Rose's contribution to both her husband's and children's political careers was substantial. "It was only natural that [some of the children] should choose a political career," she said. "We always told them that their time and their talents were not be devoted to self-aggrandizement or self-amusement, but to the service of others." Rose campaigned for all three of her sons, with zeal and effectiveness. During John's 1960 presidential campaign, she was particularly active. "For six weeks," said Dave Powers, a longtime friend of the family, "every night I'd pick her up and we'd go to meetings. Maybe the first place would be an abandoned North End garage, and she'd put on a babushka and talk to the women about children. And the next stop might be West Roxbury, so in the car she'd change her shoes and maybe put on a mink jacket." Sometimes, however, Rose Kennedy's frankness got her into hot water and embarrassed the family. During Robert Kennedy's presidential campaign in 1968, when she was questioned about the large sums of money her family was spending on his behalf, Rose told a reporter: "It's our money and we're free to spend it any way we please. It's part of this campaign business. If you have the money you spend it to win."

Rose Kennedy often recalled that one of the greatest thrills of her life was standing by her son and his wife, *Jacqueline Kennedy, on January 20, 1961, when Jack was sworn in as the 35th president of the United States. Earlier in the day, she had followed Jack into a Georgetown church. "No one, including my son, knew I was there," she wrote years later. "I was infinitely pleased and thanked God for the grace which had prompted Jack to start his Administration

with a prayer on his lips and in his heart." Other high points in Rose Kennedy's life were linked to her religion. In the late 1930s, while her husband was serving as U.S. ambassador to Great Britain, the Kennedy family had attended the coronation of Pope Paul XII and had also enjoyed a private audience with the pontiff. Another special honor from the church came in 1951, when she was honored by the Vatican with the title of papal countess, in recognition of her "exemplary motherhood and many charitable works." Only the sixth woman from the United States to be so honored by the Roman Catholic Church, Rose was thrilled.

The decade of the 1960s tested Rose Kennedy's faith and resilience. Shortly after John's inauguration in 1961, Joe suffered a massive stroke which left him partially paralyzed and completely unable to speak until his death in 1968. There followed Jack's assassination in Dallas on November 22, 1963, and Robert's assassination five years later in June 1968, while campaigning in Los Angeles. The decade ended with a scandal involving her sole surviving son Senator Ted Kennedy, who had his own brush with death in the crash of a chartered plane in 1964, in which the pilot and his close friend Ed Moss were killed. On July 19, 1969, he was involved in a car accident on Chappaquiddick Island in Massachusetts, in which a young political aide, **Mary Jo Kopechne**, was killed. Admitting that he left the scene of the accident, he ended his chances for the White House, and many believed at the time that he should not even run again for Senate. Rose, however, not only encouraged her son to run, but campaigned vigorously and successfully on his behalf.

During her later years, Rose Kennedy proudly watched a second generation of Kennedys enter politics. Two of her grandsons, Robert's son, Joseph P. Kennedy II, and Ted's son, Patrick Kennedy, were elected to Congress and her granddaughter, **Kathleen Kennedy Townsend**, Robert's oldest child, was elected lieutenant governor of Maryland in 1994, becoming the first woman in the Kennedy clan to be elected to public office. In addition to tracking the accomplishments of her grandchildren, Rose also spent a great deal of time enlightening the public about mental retardation and overseeing the work of the Joseph P. Kennedy, Jr. Foundation. Remaining physically active into old age, she swam, played golf regularly, and attended daily Mass. After a stroke in 1984, however, Rose withdrew to the family compound in Hyannis Port, which had become the backdrop for both family celebration and family loss. She died there on January 22, 1995, from complications of pneumonia. After a Mass at St. Stephen's Church in Boston's North End, where she was baptized in 1890, Rose Kennedy was buried in Holyhood Cemetery in Brookline, next to her late husband. In his eulogy, Ted Kennedy said that his mother accepted death not as leaving, but as returning. "She has gone to God," he said. "And at this moment she is happily presiding at a heavenly table with both of her Joes, with Jack and Kathleen, with Bobby and David. She is home."

SOURCES:

Beck, Joan. "The Stormy Times of Rose Kennedy," in *The Day* [New London, Connecticut]. January 28, 1995.

Collier, Peter, and David Horowitz. *The Kennedys: An American Drama.* NY: Warner Books, 1984.

Gleick, Elizabeth. "Death of a Matriarch," in *Time.* February 6, 1995, p. 77.

Goodman, Mark, with Jennifer Longley and Avery Brown. "The Last Matriarch," in *People Weekly.* February 6, 1995.

Kennedy, Rose Fitzgerald. *Times to Remember.* Garden City, NY: Doubleday, 1974.

Krebs, Albin. "Rose Kennedy dead at 104," in *The Day* [New London, Connecticut]. January 23, 1995.

McLaughlin, Jeff, and Tom Coakley. "Kennedys Prepare for Last Goodbye," in *The Boston Globe.* January 24, 1995.

Moritz, Charles, ed. *Current Biography 1970.* NY: H.W. Wilson, 1970.

Richwine, David. "Rose Kennedy dies at 104," in *The Boston Globe.* January 23, 1995.

Barbara Morgan,
Melrose, Massachusetts

Kennedy, Rosemary (1918—)

American daughter of Rose Fitzgerald Kennedy. Born in 1918; third child and eldest daughter of Joseph P. Kennedy (1888–1969, a financier, diplomat, and head of several government commissions) and Rose Fitzgerald Kennedy (1890–1995); briefly attended public school in Brookline, Massachusetts; also attended private schools; never married; no children.

Born during the 1918 flu epidemic, Rosemary Kennedy was the third child and eldest daughter of Joseph P. Kennedy and *Rose Fitzgerald Kennedy. Rose noted that she was a sweet, peaceful baby, her pride and joy after the birth of two sons. Although healthy, Rosemary was slow in developing and by the end of first grade was diagnosed as mentally disabled. Rose Kennedy chose to keep Rosemary at home rather than send her away, and she carefully supervised her education and saw to it that she was involved in all family activities. In 1941, however, Rosemary began to display disquieting symptoms; she

regressed in mental skills and her good nature gave way to frequent tantrums and convulsive episodes. At the suggestion of medical specialists, she was lobotomized, a common procedure at the time for controlling behavior. The operation left her in a childlike state. Rosemary never recovered her ability to function on her own and has spent her adult life, over 50 years, at the St. Coletta School in Jefferson, Wisconsin.

SOURCES:

Kennedy, Rose Fitzgerald. *Times to Remember.* Garden City NY: Doubleday, 1974.

Leamer, Laurence. *The Kennedy Women.* Villard, 1994.

Kennelly, Barbara (1936—)

American politician who was a Democratic congressional representative from Connecticut (1982–1998). Born Barbara Bailey in Hartford, Connecticut, on July 10, 1936; daughter of John Bailey (a politician) and Barbara (Leary) Bailey; Trinity College, Washington, D.C., B.A. in Economics, 1958; graduated from Harvard-Radcliffe School of Business Administration, 1959; Trinity College, Hartford, Connecticut, M.A., 1973; married James J. Kennelly (a lawyer and Connecticut legislator), on September 26, 1959; children: Eleanor Bride Kennelly; Barbara Leary Kennelly; Louise Moran Kennelly; John Bailey Kennelly.

The daughter of **Barbara Leary Bailey** and legendary party boss John Bailey, who served as chair of the Democratic National Committee under presidents John F. Kennedy and Lyndon B. Johnson, Barbara Kennelly entered the political arena in 1975, when she became a member of the Hartford Court of Common Council. Serving as secretary of state for Connecticut (1979–81) and elected to Congress in 1982, Kennelly was a congressional representative until 1998, distinguishing herself by becoming the third woman ever appointed to the prestigious Ways and Means Committee. She later became the first woman ever to serve on the Select Committee on Intelligence, and the first to be appointed Chief Deputy Majority Whip. Early in the 105th Congress, she was reelected for a second term as vice chair of the Democratic Caucus, making her the highest ranking woman and the fourth ranking Democrat in the House.

Barbara Kennelly was born and raised in Hartford, Connecticut, and graduated from Trinity College in Washington, D.C., in 1958; in 1973, she would receive a master's in government from Trinity College in Hartford. Married to lawyer and politician James J. Kennelly in 1959, Kennelly had four children and worked in social service before joining the Hartford City Council in 1975, after which she won a full term on her own. In 1978, when **Gloria Schaffer**, the Democratic secretary of state, resigned her post, Kennelly made a successful run for the office, drawing inspiration from her mentor, the late former Connecticut Governor *Ella T. Grasso. "She was a great strength to me," she said. "She proved a woman could do it."

Kennelly served in state office until 1981, when she announced her candidacy for the congressional seat vacated by the death of Representative William R. Cotter. Nominated by acclamation, she easily won the special election against Republican **Ann P. Uccello**, a former mayor of Hartford. Kennelly was subsequently reelected six times, never receiving less than 60% of the vote.

Characterized by Democratic Senator Joseph I. Lieberman as "a work horse and not a show horse," Kennelly's congressional tenure was marked by her quiet presence and her ability to create strong alliances from diverse groups. "Barbara's very good at trying to piece together a consensus out of conflicting viewpoints," said House Minority Leader Richard A. Gephardt. "That's what leadership is: the ability to bring diverse opinions together for a consensus and then fight for that consensus." Kennelly was committed to insurance issues—a prime employment sector in Hartford—and made enormous strides in the area of child support; her first bill to become law established a tougher mechanism for enforcing court-ordered child support payments across state lines. Later, she was instrumental in the landmark 1996 welfare-reform bill, which included a provision for denying driver's and professional licenses to parents who refused to pay child support. From her seat on the Ways and Means Committee, Kennelly also fought for the survival of the social security system and was a leading advocate for pension reform. In the area of health care, she championed long-term care reform and increased access to mammograms and other health screening. She also lead the fight to secure increased health coverage for children.

Addressing the plight of working families, Kennelly helped secure the Earned Income Tax Credit, allowing low-income employees to keep more of their earnings. She also sponsored legislation to let terminally ill patients collect life insurance benefits early, and tax free, to help eliminate devastating family debt. She additionally authored the 1996 legislation that reduced vesting periods for multi-employer pension plans.

Kennelly, who credits her three daughters with getting her up to speed on feminist issues, was extremely vocal in her outrage concerning the Senate's desire to vote on the Clarence Thomas nomination to the Supreme Court before hearing **Anita Hill**'s allegations of sexual harassment. She petitioned for female representation at Bill Clinton's Inauguration Day luncheon in 1993, arguing that it might be prudent for a president who campaigned on diversity to have a woman present at the event. Kennelly has also served as an inspiration to the many young democratic congresswomen she mentored and guided during her years in Congress. "She set goals for us," said Representative **Karen Thurman** (Dem.-Florida), whom Kennelly helped get appointed to the House Ways and Means Committee. "She led and gave us an example in which to follow. I don't know many people who can say that." In a further tribute to her efforts in promoting women and women's issues, Kennelly received the Women's Research and Education Initiative's 10th annual American Woman Award (1998). Past recipients include Kennelly's own mentor, *Lindy Boggs, who was instrumental in urging her to pursue her appointment to Ways and Means.

During her congressional career, Kennelly occasionally expressed an interest in moving up to a statewide office. She was discussed as a possible gubernatorial candidate in 1990, when Democrat William O'Neill retired, and again in 1993, when independent Lowell P. Weicker, Jr. announced he was stepping down. She chose not to enter those races, however, opting to remain a behind-the-scenes force in the House. In 1997, however, Kennelly decided to forgo a ninth term in Congress and to enter the Connecticut gubernatorial race against first-term Republican Governor John G. Rowland. Plagued early on in her campaign by financial woes and difficulty getting her message out to voters, she was ultimately unsuccessful in her bid. But Kennelly has never been one to dwell in the past. "You've got to go on," she said, in answer to those who questioned her decision to run for governor in the first place. "I've tried to tell my children that all the time. Go on, don't look back."

SOURCES:

Duncan, Philip D., and Christine C. Lawrence. *Congressional Quarterly's Politics in America 1996: The 104th Congress.*

Haigh, Susan. "From House to Home." *The (New London, Connecticut) Day,* September 20. 1998.

Peter, Jennifer. "Kennelly crafting a separate political legacy." *The [New London, Connecticut] Day,* October 18, 1997.

Women in Congress 1917–1990.

Barbara Morgan,
Melrose, Massachusetts

Barbara
Kennelly

Kenney, Annie (1879–1953)

English trade unionist and militant suffragist. Born in Springhead, near Oldham, Lancashire, England, on September 13, 1879; died in 1953; fifth of twelve children of Nelson Horatio Kenney and Anne (Wood) Kenney; sister of Jessie Kenney (also a militant suffragist); attended village school; took correspondence courses at Ruskin College; married James Taylor, in 1921.

Annie Kenney was born in Springhead, near Oldham, Lancashire, England, in 1879, the fifth of twelve children of Nelson Horatio Kenney and **Anne Wood Kenney**. Her parents worked in the Oldham textile industry. By age ten, Annie was working part-time in the same mill. Three years later, at 13, she joined the "great masses," she wrote, of those "whose lives were spent spinning and weaving cotton. I was a full-time. I rose at five o'clock in the morning. I had to be in the factory just before six, and I left at five-thirty at night." It wasn't long before she formed a union and organized other unions as well in other mills. In 1905, after meeting *Christabel Pankhurst, Kenney began speaking for the Women's Social and Political Union (WSPU) and became a dependable lieutenant to Christabel, especially when the Pankhursts were in exile in Paris. Kenney also campaigned for the election of Keir Hardie for prime minister.

Like the others, Annie Kenney was arrested and imprisoned numerous times. During one arrest, in 1913, she was found guilty of making an inflammatory speech which she did not deny. But, she told the magistrate, she had filched her speech from Sir Edward Carson, a respectable lawyer and leader of Irish resistance in Ulster, and had only replaced the word *Irish* every time it was used with the word *women*. Thus, she suggested that they arrest Carson for the speech, "the alterations alone being mine." Kenney retired from activism when she married in 1921. Her memoirs were published in 1924 as *Memories of a Militant*.

RELATED MEDIA:

"Shoulder to Shoulder," produced by the British Broadcasting Company, based on the documentary book of the same name compiled and edited by **Midge MacKenzie**, was shown in the United States as a six-part series on "Masterpiece Theater" in 1988. The episodes are titled, "The Pankhurst Family," "Annie Kenney," "Lady Constance Lytton," "Christabel Pankhurst," "Outrage," and "Sylvia Pankhurst."

Kenny, Elizabeth (1880–1952)

Australian-born nurse, without formal medical training, who became known as "Sister" Kenny in World War I and later made a name for herself through her new therapy for polio victims. Name variations: Sister Kenny. Born Elizabeth Kenny on September 20, 1880, in the village of Warialda, in northwestern Australia; died in Brisbane on November 30, 1952; daughter of Michael Kenny and Mary (Moore) Kenny; learned to read and write and took a three-year training course to become a certified nurse; never married, no children.

Completed training course as a certified nurse (1911); volunteered for the Australian Nursing Service (1915); promoted, despite lack of formal nursing training, to rank of "sister," the title used for the rest of her life (1916); after a worldwide outbreak of polio, opened a clinic in Brisbane, using her unorthodox form of treatment (1934); moved to U.S., where she first introduced her therapy in Minneapolis (1940); named "Woman of the Year" by a New York City newspaper (1942); ranked second after Eleanor Roosevelt in a Gallup poll for "Most Admired Woman in America," a position she continued to hold for the next nine years (1943); movie of her life, starring Rosalind Russell, released (1946).

Selected writings: And They Shall Walk: The Life Story of Sister Elizabeth Kenny *(written in collaboration with* **Martha Ostenso**, *Dodd, Mead, 1943);* The Kenny Concept of Infantile Paralysis and its Treatment *(written in collaboration with John F. Pohl, Bruce, 1943);* Treatment of Infantile Paralysis in the Acute State *(Bruce Press, 1941).*

Elizabeth Kenny was born on September 20, 1880, in the village of Warialda, meaning "place of wild honey," in northwestern Australia. Her parents' families had immigrated to the wild new country a couple of decades earlier, and in 1872, Michael Kenny, aged 37, had married **Mary Moore**, aged 28. Elizabeth, a strong, healthy child, was the fourth of many children born to the couple, though few lived through infancy and childhood.

In the harsh conditions of the Australian outback, as her restless father searched for both security and freedom, Elizabeth soon came to share responsibility for the care and nurture of her younger siblings. Because of her family's nomadic ways, reinforced by the general lack of interest in teaching girls in this frontier society, she received little formal education beyond learning to read and write. Otherwise, she learned mostly from observing nature and human interactions with nature. Her parents were Anglican and Catholic, with her Protestant father exerting more influence by his absence than her Catholic mother did by her presence.

In her adolescent years, a broken wrist led to Elizabeth's first brief acquaintance with "civilization," when she stayed in town with the family of a well-to-do physician, Dr. Aeneas John McDonnell, while he treated her. In McDonnell's home, she became acquainted with his medical anatomy books and also decided to become a missionary. McDonnell advised her that she could be more effective in missionary work if she became a certified nurse. In 1911, having spent most of her life helping her mother and nursing sick neighbors or delivering babies, Kenny completed the three-year training course for becoming a full-fledged certified nurse. She was 31.

As far as can be guessed from her own incomplete autobiographies, Elizabeth Kenny had only one serious romance. She nearly married a man named Dan, or possibly named David and known as Dan because of his fondness for singing the Irish ballad "Danny Boy." According to her, she broke a date to attend an annual picnic with him in order to help deliver a premature baby, causing Dan to demand that she choose between him and her vocation. What Dan lost, the world won.

Poliomyelitis, also known as "polio" and infantile paralysis, was one of the world's most dreaded diseases when Kenny experienced her first exposure to it in the Australian bush. The name comes from the Greek words, *polio* (gray), *myelos* (marrow), and *itis* (inflammation), and its victims are most often children. Oblivious to the conventional medical opinion about treatment, Kenny first applied heat "fomentations" (strips of woolen cloth boiled in a basin) to the tortured, paralyzed limbs, and then prescribed a regimen of exercise to regain mobility. Most of her slightly paralyzed patients recovered completely, and many who were more severely paralyzed regained some use of their limbs. When McDonnell, who had become chief surgeon at a regional hospital in Toowoomba, learned of Elizabeth's successes, he apprised her of the treatment methods of mainstream medical doctors, who prescribed casts and splints to immobilize the limbs. Kenny's response was, "My method works and theirs doesn't."

World War I began in August of 1914, and Australia, as a member of the British Empire, went to war in support of the mother country. Early in 1915, Elizabeth volunteered to serve in the Australian Nursing Service. Informed that she lacked the proper nursing credentials, she went anyway. Thanks partly to the many letters

Elizabeth Kenny

of recommendation written by McDonnell, and even more to the flood of Australian casualties pouring in from the disastrous British campaign in Turkey at Gallipoli, Kenny was accepted as an army nurse in the field. In 1916, despite her lack of formal nursing training, she was promoted to the rank of "sister," giving her two insignia decorations, or "pips," and the title she was to use the rest of her life.

While her general war experience reinvigorated Sister Kenny's nascent Roman Catholic faith, her more particular medical experience reinforced her conviction that heat packs and exercise cured disease. She treated wartime meningitis patients with exercise, along with splints and crutches retrieved from the shrine to *Mary the Virgin at Lourdes. Kenny did not concern herself too much about whether cures came from supernatural or natural sources, so long as they worked.

The war ended in 1918, only to be followed by a massive influenza epidemic that killed more people than had died in combat. Exhausted and sick from overwork and the flu, Elizabeth was mustered out of the military and off the government payroll. In fact, it was her old friend and patron, McDonnell, now a colonel in the Australian army, who pronounced her as suffering acute myocarditis (inflammation of the muscular wall of the heart), rendering her both unfit for further service and ineligible for a government pension.

At age 39, with her morale at its lowest point, Kenny told herself, "If I have only six months to live, I'd better get busy." Back in the Australian bush, she resumed her medical work. After observing that patients were sometimes literally shaken to death during transport to hospitals over terribly bumpy back roads, she perfected a stretcher used to strap patients while they were moved. It was called the "Sylvia Stretcher," for a family friend whose life had been saved by its use.

At age 50, Kenny had recovered her health, but she was still an unknown nurse toiling in the Australian outback when polio swept through the Western world along with the Great Depression. By November 1933, when Americans elected Franklin D. Roosevelt, a polio victim, as president, it was apparent that traditional medicine

Poster from the movie Sister Kenny, *starring Rosalind Russell.*

could not cope with the disease, and people were seeking help wherever it could be found. Early in 1934, Sister Kenny moved to the city of Brisbane, where she established a clinic using her therapeutic techniques, and by 1935, patients were pouring into Brisbane from the all over the world. A headline in Australia's leading newspaper, *The Sydney Morning Herald,* read: "PARALYSIS. A New System of Treatment Presented to Nation. Doctors' Praise." By the end of 1936, Sister Kenny was treating 600 patients in clinics throughout Australia, with 600 more on waiting lists.

What was this magic treatment? Sister Kenny's diagnosis focused on the muscles and mind, not cells and bones. According to her interpretation, the symptoms of polio were caused by the "spasm" of the muscles. In her terminology, this "spasm" caused the patient involuntarily to do three bad things. The disease caused the patient to pull the opposite muscles from their normal position and distorted the skeleton; the resulting tenseness, tenderness, and pain caused the second symptom, of "mental alienation," in which the patient was unwilling and eventually unable, i.e. would actually "forget," how to move the muscles even though the nerve paths were intact. This situation led to the third condition, the jerky grotesque body movements Kenny called "incoordination." Here the patient used the wrong muscles in jerky and grotesque motion. According to her prognosis, if muscles "in spasm" were left untreated, their alienated opposites eventually atrophied, while the ones in spasm became hard, fibrous, and inelastic, pulling the skeleton into permanent deformities.

Sister Kenny's prescribed treatment was to exercise and arouse the live but dormant muscles. Stripping away casts, splints, and all the other devices immobilizing her patients, she forced them into various stretching motions. On the psychological level, she commanded the patient to learn the names of the muscles and to exercise will-power in relearning to move them.

Criticism of such a radical approach soon emerged. In the area of traditional medicine, doctors and nurses were not impressed by Sister Kenny's theoretical explanations of what she was doing. Distrusting and even resenting her lack of scientific education, they ridiculed her use of vague terms and seized upon the fact that she was not conversant enough with prevailing medical language to be able to articulate her theories in a clear and convincing way. Moreover, she did not cure everybody. There were many

The Wedding Gown that Waited...

RKO PROUDLY PRESENTS

ROSALIND ALEXANDER
RUSSELL · KNOX
in
"SISTER KENNY"
with DEAN JAGGER
PHILIP MERIVALE · BEULAH BONDI · CHARLES DINGLE
Produced and Directed by DUDLEY NICHOLS
Screen Play by DUDLEY NICHOLS, ALEXANDER KNOX & MARY McCARTHY

patients in her care who were not relieved of their tragic paralysis, and some who died.

In the second place, the effectiveness of Sister Kenny's treatment was oversold, and she allowed her success to go to her head. Never shy or smooth, and not even especially likeable, she lacked the temperament to cope with the extremes of adulation and criticism. As is the case with many people of humble origin who find themselves pushed into the public spotlight, she was not equipped with the social graces to disguise her own weaknesses. As her fame soared, she became less tolerant of criticism and more inclined to claim that her treatment was the only viable one. When she met medical resistance, she resorted to promoting her convictions through media campaigns. Just as the medical profession resented her zealous self-promotion, so disillusioned patients and their loved ones, and even potential supporters were offended by her brusque behavior.

Nevertheless, her therapy did work better than anybody else's, and her fame did soar. On April 16, 1940, Sister Kenny arrived in San Francisco and was greeted by polio-conscious Americans as a messiah. Touring across the United States, she visited hospital after hospital, where she jeered at the sight of patients plastered up in casts and splints, and promised to revolutionize the situation. Initially attracted to the famous Mayo Clinic in Rochester, Minnesota, she settled in Minneapolis, 90 miles to the northwest, because there were many polio patients in the Twin Cities hospitals.

One case converted many Minnesota physicians to her methods. Dr. John Pohl, at age 36, was a rising star in the Minnesota medical establishment, and he remained skeptical as he presented Henry Haverstock, Jr., 18-year-old son of a prominent attorney, for treatment by Sister Kenny. After Henry was struck by polio in 1939, he had been sent to Warm Springs, Georgia, for the standard treatment, which involved being fitted with two steel leg braces, a steel-and-canvas body corset, and an arm splint. A year later, Henry had a curved spine, a paralyzed right leg, a paralyzed left leg that was all but useless, a weak arm, and weak muscles of the chest, back, and abdomen. Told he would never walk again, he was confined to a bed where he could not even sit up.

Discarding the corset and braces, Sister Kenny proceeded with her heat treatment and began teaching Henry to use the muscles that the real paralysis had not rendered useless. Within a week, he could straighten one contracted leg; before the end of the year, he walked out of his room using hand crutches. He continued his treatment for more than a year, and by the spring of 1942, he started attending the University of Minnesota. Although his movement never became normal, he was able with the aid of hand sticks to walk up 21 flights of steps every day. He became a lawyer and lived a productive life, and Dr. Pohl became Sister Kenny's most active supporter.

Although the conversion of Minnesota doctors was accomplished, the leaders of the American Medical Association remained suspicious and vigilant against the exaggeration of Sister Kenny's success. In fact, however, she had initiated a revolution in polio treatment that conquered the United States. For example, the demand for splints and frames which numbered nearly 15,000 in the Manhattan area of New York City in 1941 had dropped by 1943 to only three.

> *S*he was no scientist; she was a crusader. . . . Her concept of polio and therefore the kind of treatment that was needed was new and different and made [the medical profession] focus on how the neuromuscular system really functions.
>
> —Victor Cohn

In 1942, less than two years after her departure from Australia, Sister Kenny was named "Woman of the Year" by a New York newspaper; in 1943, she was ranked second after *Eleanor Roosevelt as the "Most Admired Woman in America" by the Gallup poll, a ranking she kept for nine consecutive years. With this kind of fame, Hollywood came next. On September 27, 1946, the movie *Sister Kenny* opened in New York, with *Rosalind Russell in the starring role for which she received an Oscar nomination. Kenny's life now seemed cast in Hollywood terms. In the film, she was characterized as a saint who had rejected love for medicine; Kenny clinics opened around the world, becoming shrines that seemed to replicate the healing powers of the religious shrine at Lourdes in France; and medical doctors in Australia and America, with few exceptions, were portrayed as medieval clerics, either bone-headed skeptics or cruel inquisitors. All this intensified both the adulation of Sister Kenny, which was not good for her on the personal level, and the criticism of her, which was not good for her professional work.

Just as President Roosevelt became the prime mover in the National Foundation for Infantile Paralysis and its March of Dimes campaign, Sister

Kenny herself became an institution dedicated to raising money and promoting medical research and public education. Together, the most famous victim of polio and the most famous crusader for its treatment laid the foundation for funding medical research in the disease for the second half of the 20th century. The Sister Elizabeth Kenny Foundation marked both the highest and lowest points in the life of its founder.

Unfortunately, the independent-minded Australian bush nurse was neither a good administrator, nor a good judge of character. As the symbolic leader of the national organization, she allowed her name to be used in raising vast amounts of money to finance what was being advertised as a medical miracle. With the massive publicity campaigns came enormous amounts of charitable donations and huge opportunities for corruption. Kenny became the organizational figurehead, a stalking-horse for people using her name to line their own pockets. Fortunately for her peace of mind, the fund-raising scandal that wrecked the Kenny Foundation was not uncovered until after her death back home in Brisbane, on November 30, 1952.

Trimmed back and reorganized, the Kenny Foundation is now a respectable supporter of training for rehabilitation workers, while the "institutionalization of Sister Kenny," meaning the transformation of a crusader into a corporation to raise money for charity, has entered the language as a cautionary tale against the danger of corruption lurking in every charitable enterprise. Nevertheless, it is impossible to imagine the subsequent conquest of polio through the vaccines of Drs. Jonas Salk and Albert Sabine without appreciating the massive financial support provided by the organizations created by the president and the nurse. And just as it is probably better to remember the personal courage of Franklin Roosevelt in living a rich life after he was crippled by polio, it is certainly better for us to remember the personal courage of the outback nurse without even the training of a Registered Nurse (R.N.), whose convictions about a therapy that worked helped to open the way for the transformation of medical and nursing approaches throughout the world, especially the rigorous use of exercise in recovery from assorted forms of disease and surgery.

SOURCES:

Cohn, Victor. *Sister Kenny: The Woman Who Challenged the Doctors.* University of Minnesota Press, 1975. [There have been an enormous number of pamphlet and magazine articles written about Kenny; they are divided between the popular culture magazines which with few exceptions glorify her and the medical association journals which with few exceptions vilify her. Cohn's biography is the best, and in fact the only reasonably objective study which covers her personal life and career and attempts to evaluate her professional achievement; it also contains an excellent bibliography.]

Crofford, Emily. *Healing Warrior: A Story About Sister Elizabeth Kenny.* Carolrohda Books, 1989.

Fritz, Karen Kay. "A History of the Concept of Creativity in Western Nursing: A Cultural Feminist Perspective," D.N.Sc. dissertation, University of San Diego, 1995.

O'Kiersey, Niamh. "Muscle Woman . . . Elizabeth Kenny," in *Nursing Times.* Vol. 92, no. 2, 1996, pp. 38–39.

Wilson, J. "The Sister Kenny Clinics: What Endures?," in *Australian Journal of Advanced Nursing.* Vol. 3, no. 2. December, 1985–February, 1986, pp. 13–21.

RELATED MEDIA:

Sister Kenny, film based on the book *And They Shall Walk,* with screenplay by Dudley Nichols, Alexander Knox, and *Mary McCarthy, was produced by RKO and starred Rosalind Russell, 1946.

David R. Stevenson,
Professor of History, University of Nebraska at Kearney, Nebraska

Kent, Allegra (1938—)

American ballerina. Born Iris Margo Cohen in Santa Monica, California, on August 11, 1938; youngest of two children of Harry Herschel Cohen and Shirley (Weissman) Cohen; attended the Ojai Valley Boarding School in Southern California; attended Berkley Hall, a private Christian Science school in Los Angeles; attended Beverly Hills High School, Los Angeles; attended the Professional Children's School, New York; briefly attended the University of California, Los Angeles, and the University of Utah; studied ballet at the School of American Ballet; married Bert Stern (a photographer) on February 28, 1959 (divorced 1975); married Bob Gurney; children: (first marriage) Trista, Susannah, and Bret.

Considered one of the most faithful exponents of famed choreographer George Balanchine, Allegra Kent achieved ballerina status with the New York City Ballet at the age of 18 and remained a principal in the company for three decades. Her extraordinary career, however, was accompanied by a somewhat disastrous personal life. "In real life," she once said, "I was a sleepwalker—dance my only light."

Born Iris Margo Cohen in Santa Monica, California, Allegra was two when her mother Shirley changed the family surname to Kent in hopes of escaping her Jewish identity. Later, **Shirley Kent** would further distance herself by embracing the Christian Science religion. Kent's parents divorced when she was young, and she and her brother Gary shuttled back and forth between them, attending schools in Miami and California. Her half-sister **Barbara Kent**, the product of her mother's earlier marriage and substantially older, left home when Kent was still young to pursue an acting career. Kent discovered music and dance at the age of 7, but she was 11 before she took her first ballet lesson. That year, she began calling herself Allegra, a name her sister had discarded from a list of possible stage names. Kent began what was to be a trial period of six months of ballet lessons in California, where she lived with her mother and attended Berkley Hall, a private Christian Science school. Proving to be an eager and talented student, she went on to study with a variety of outstanding teachers, including *Bronislava Nijinska, *Carmelita Maracci, and **Maria Befeke**. At 13, Kent and her mother moved to New York, where she entered the School of American Ballet (the training school for the New York City Ballet) on a scholarship.

Kent quickly captured the attention of New York City Ballet's director George Balanchine, who offered her an apprenticeship in the company's corps de ballet. In 1953, she became a permanent member of the company and gained her first public notice with a performance of the Viola *pas des deux* in *Fanfare* (1954). Later that year, she danced "The Unanswered Question," a segment from *Ivesiana* choreographed especially for her by Balanchine. While Kent gained stature in the company, her mother kept careful watch, being both wary of Balanchine's libidinous reputation and anxious for her daughter to succeed. She also decided that the time was right for Allegra to undergo plastic surgery to alter her nose and chin. "Then you would be beautiful," she told her daughter, setting aside the Christian Science tenet forbidding surgery. Despite nagging misgivings and her own religious objections, Allegra agreed. The operation was unfortunately botched by a less than competent doctor, and Kent, hating her new face, lapsed into a serious depression, the first of many to come. "For thirty years after this, I struggled with depression and my inability to handle it," Kent wrote in her autobiography *Once a Dancer*. "I'd fall into the same trap over and over again. Raspberries, whipped cream, ice cream. Exercise would end. I would be embarrassed about my weight, so I'd stop going to class. Sleeping would become a problem. . . ."

In 1955, for unknown reasons, Shirley Kent had a serious change of heart concerning her daughter's career and convinced Allegra to leave dancing and enter college. After brief stays at the University of California, Los Angeles (UCLA),

and the University of Utah, Allegra followed her heart back to the New York City Ballet and, in May 1956, danced a leading role in *Divertimento No. 15* at the Mozart Festival in Stratford, Connecticut. During the company's 1956 European tour, she helped to fill the void left when *Tanaquil LeClercq, Balanchine's young wife, was stricken with polio. Despite Balanchine's pleas, Kent refused to take polio vaccine to protect her from the disease, claiming that it was against her religion. Gaining status as a full-fledged ballerina, Kent danced solo roles in *Serenade, Souvenirs,* and *Western Symphone.* John Martin of *The New York Times* (January 1, 1957) praised both the newcomer's dancing and personality. "She has a lissome, well-placed body, an innate gift for movement and a warm and simple personal appeal," he wrote. During the 1956–57 season, she also performed in *Valse Fantasy, Interplay, Concerto Barocco,* and *Symphony in C.* At the end of the season, she created the role of a woman who comes to the emotional aid of a blind man in Francisco Moncion's *Pastorale.*

After a break in the spring of 1957 to appear in the Broadway musical *Shinbone Alley,* Kent returned to the New York Ballet, dancing memorably as the Countess in Menotti's *The Unicorn, the Dragon and the Manticore,* and in a number of new roles, including Jerome Robbins' *Afternoon of a Faun.* Her repertoire continued to expand with performances as the Swan Queen in *Swan Lake* (which John Martin praised as "a disarmingly simple and altogether genuine work of art"), the novice in *The Cage,* leader of the Bacchantes in *Orpheus,* Terpsichore in *Appolo,* and the *pas de deux* in *Agon.* Kent reached the zenith of her career in January 1959, when she danced the part of Annie II in the Kurt Weill-Bertolt Brecht ballet *The Seven Deadly Sins,* choreographed by Balanchine. The role brought Kent new respect as both a dancer and an actress, and made her a national celebrity, although she had little time to bask in the trappings of success. Maintaining a grueling schedule of eight or nine classes a week and half-day practices, her life remained disciplined and controlled by her art. Her dedication paid off. Early in 1960, she created another memorable portrayal as the Sleepwalker in the restaging of *The Night Shadow,* later titled *La Sonnambula.* Walter Terry, of the New York *Herald Tribune* (January 7, 1960), called the dancer "utterly lovely, moving as if she were a disembodied spirit floating across the ground."

Preceding her triumph in *La Sonnambula,* Kent was to marry photographer Bert Stern, with whom she had endured an erratic two-year courtship that left her, at 21, doubtful about the possibilities of their long-term relationship. Urged on by her mother, who was still concerned about her relationship with Balanchine, Allegra went ahead with the wedding. The marriage proved a disaster from the start, and Kent left her husband after less than six months. This established a pattern of separations and reconciliations that lasted until the two finally divorced in 1974. In the meantime, Kent continued with the New York City Ballet, taking maternity leaves for the birth of three children: Trista (b. 1960), Susannah (b. 1964), and Bret (b. 1967). To overcome her weight gains from pregnancy and bouts of overeating caused by depression, Kent discovered the restorative power of water exercises. She eventually wrote a book about it, *Allegra Kent's Water Beauty Book*, published in 1976.

In 1962, the New York City Ballet made a historic eight-week tour of the Soviet Union, where Kent became an immediate favorite, especially for her dancing in *Agon*. In 1963, the dancer won acclaim in two somewhat exotic creations: *Bugaku*, a Balanchine work in which she danced with Edward Villella, and *The Chase*, in which she portrayed a man-chasing vixen that is transformed into an appealing young woman. Kent made a European tour with the company in 1965, and the following year captivated audiences with her performance in the *Sylvia Divertissement*. "Miss Kent swept through the complexities of Balanchine's choreography . . . with a swift and sweet efficiency," raved Clive Barnes in *The New York Times* (April 6, 1966). "More dancers should dance like this. Here is Balanchine as Balanchine should be danced—and throughout the entire dance world there is nothing better."

During the 1970s, on advice from a new psychiatrist, Kent sought to supplement her dancing income by opening a school in Scarsdale, New York, where she had moved to facilitate her children's education. At that time, she entered into an agreement with Balanchine to limit her performances with the New York City ballet while continuing to draw a salary. The school eventually became a burden, and Kent returned to her career, though her position with the company had been seriously jeopardized by her absence. She remained with the New York City Ballet until 1982, but in her final years with the company, she only danced on an average of once a season. Just one week after the company let her go, George Balanchine died, marking the end of her career with even greater sadness. "For me, ballet—the continuation of my childhood dreams and the way I chose to rebel against my

mother, visually but soundlessly—was over," Kent wrote in her autobiography.

After leaving the company, Kent, desperate for income, held a variety of temporary teaching positions. While in Los Angeles auditioning for a teaching job at the University of California, she met John Clifford, an old friend from the New York City Ballet who was teaching and arranging Balanchine's ballets for various dance companies around the world. Clifford cajoled her into dancing in a performance of *Apollo* at a benefit in Red Bank, New Jersey, and into joining him for later tours. Dancing in Clifford's *Notturno*, Kent proved that at 50, she had lost none of her personal charisma. "Kent's very special quality, still very much intact, was always an emotional abandon mysteriously and implausibly registered within a classical line of breathtaking perfection," wrote a reviewer for the *Washington Post*. "*Gelsey Kirkland was the only other dancer I've ever seen who could work this particular magic."

Allegra Kent finally found regular work as the director of a ballet school in Stamford, Connecticut. A flexible contract allowed her to take on other projects, among them dancing assignments and the role of Cousin Ophelia in the motion picture *The Addams Family*. By the time she had completed her autobiography, which was published in 1997, Kent was happily remarried and apparently at peace with herself. "What I regret is that it took so long for me to emerge into a somewhat normal person who could handle everyday life with easy grace," she writes. "But it did happen."

SOURCES:

Kent, Allegra. *Once a Dancer. . . .* NY: St. Martin's Press, 1997.

Moritz, Charles, ed. *Current Biography* 1970. NY: H.W. Wilson, 1970.

Barbara Morgan,
Melrose, Massachusetts

Kent, Constance (1844–?)

English murderer. Born in 1844; the ninth of ten children of Samuel Kent (a carpet manufacturer) and Mary Ann (Windus) Kent.

One of the most shocking murders of the Victorian era took place on the night of June 29, 1860, in a quiet village five miles from the town of Trowbridge in Somerset, England. In the early morning hours of June 30, the body of three-year-old Francis Savile Kent was discovered in a detached privy on the family property. The little boy's throat had been slashed with such violence that the head was nearly severed from the body and there was a congealing stab wound in the child's chest which was believed to have been made after his death in an attempt to force the body further down the privy cavity. Almost as shocking was the fact that the murderer was not some crazed stranger, but the victim's half-sister, an intelligent, demure schoolgirl of sixteen who covered up her crime for a period of four years. She unexpectedly confessed in 1864, although her declaration of guilt raised more questions than it answered.

Constance Kent grew up in a more-than-typically repressive Victorian family. She was the ninth of ten children (five of whom died in infancy) of Samuel Kent, a rug manufacturer and later inspector of factories for the West of England, and his first wife **Mary Ann Windus**, the daughter of a respected merchant. Samuel was said to be a pompous, ostentatious man, who was not particularly well liked by his neighbors. At home, he was a tyrant. He spent his salary lavishly on entertainment, clothes, and horses, and left his wife with little to run the household and care for her children. Mary Ann, burdened with a frail constitution, lost ground with each of her ten pregnancies, and by the time Constance was born in 1844, was deemed mentally disturbed and unable to care for the infant. After the birth of another son, William, the following year, Samuel hired a well-educated young governess for the children and removed himself to another bedroom in the house. "Mrs. Kent was left by her husband to live in the seclusion of her own room," reported a friend at the time, "while the management of the household was taken over" by **Mary Pratt**, "a high-spirited governess." When the older Kent children went away to boarding school, it was general knowledge among the townsfolk that Mary Pratt had become mistress of the house in every respect.

Mary Ann Kent died in 1852, and, after the customary year of mourning, Samuel married Mary Pratt. Constance, then nine, served with her older sisters as a bridesmaid at the ceremony, which was apparently her last moment in the spotlight. The couple immediately started a new family on which they lavished their attention. By the accounts of the servants and others, Constance was neglected and harshly disciplined, although it was also acknowledged by friends that she was a difficult, willful child. In the summer of 1856, after some particularly harsh treatment by her stepmother, Constance convinced her brother William to run away to sea with her. The pair made it to Bath before they were apprehended by the police and returned home. They

were both beaten, and Constance was locked in the cellar for two days.

By 1860, Mary Pratt had given birth to three more children: five-year-old Amelia, three-and-a-half-year-old Francis Savile, and a baby daughter Eveline. A nurse, **Elizabeth Gough**, was hired to care for the smaller children. On the morning of June 30, 1860, when baby Francis was acknowledged as missing, Samuel Kent immediately took off for Trowbridge, to alert the police. In his absence, nearby villagers began searching the grounds, where they eventually found the murdered boy.

*C*onstance *K*ent

Adding to the horror of the crime was the ineptitude of the local investigation. After a bumbled investigation and testimony before the coroner's jury, it was determined that the murderer was an outsider. When official inquiries did not produce any formal indictments, Scotland Yard sent famous Chief Inspector Jonathan Whicher to take over the case, a move that rankled the local police who refused to cooperate further in the investigation. Whicher quickly fingered Constance as the most likely suspect, but he had little proof. He began to probe deeper, questioning former servants and acquaintances of the family. He learned that Constance resented her father's new family, and that in school she referred to her family as "different." In searching Constance's room one day, Whicher found some three-year-old copies of the London *Times*, containing stories of the trial of **Madeleine Smith** of Glasgow, Scotland, who was accused of murdering her lover but acquitted. The detective concluded that Constance's interest in the Smith case was highly abnormal, and that perhaps she had a touch of her mother's mental instability. Whicher's only solid evidence, however, was the fact that a nightdress belonging to Constance, presumably the one she had been wearing the night of the murder, was missing.

On July 20, 1860, 16-year-old Constance was arrested and charged with the murder, causing a fury of protest from the locals. Knowing his case was shaky, Whicher hoped that Constance would break down under close interrogation and confess, but he was wrong. After a week's imprisonment, Constance emerged calm and resolute, telling the magistrates at her hearing—yet again—that she had been in her room the night of the murder and knew nothing about it. In the end, the judgment of the original coroner's jury, death by "person or persons unknown," was allowed to stand. Constance was released on £200 bail in order to guarantee her reappearance should she be called upon in the future.

To escape notoriety, Constance was sent to a convent school in France. She was allowed to return to England three years later, and enrolled under an assumed name at a High Church establishment affiliated with a hospital in Brighton, where she planned to train as a children's nurse. A year-and-a-half into her studies, she returned to England for a religious retreat, staying at St. Mary's Home in Brighton. Sometime over the next 12 months, Constance underwent a spiritual epiphany that moved her to bare her soul. On April 25, 1864, she appeared at the office of the magistrate in London and confessed to the murder of her half-brother. Her declaration was later printed in the London *Times* in the form of a letter to the editor from Dr. John C. Bucknill, who had examined her and declared her sane. She had told Bucknill that on the night in question, she took the child from his bed and into the privy, which she lighted with a candle. While the child slept, she inflicted the wound to the throat with a razor she had stolen from her father. She further confessed to burning the stained nightdress in her bedroom after discovering that the two blood stains on it did not wash out completely. Although she denied that "cruel treatment" had prompted her actions, she failed to offer any other motive for the murder. She further declared that she harbored no ill will against the boy except that he was one of the children of her stepmother. She also said that her father and stepmother had always been kind to her.

On July 21, 1865, Constance Kent was condemned to death by a tearful judge and jury. The sentence was subsequently commuted to life imprisonment, and she was imprisoned at Millbrook. In 1885, after serving 20 years, she was released. Following a brief period with an Anglican sisterhood, she immigrated to Canada, where she was believed to have become a nurse. The date of her death is unknown.

SOURCES:
Hartman, Mary S. *Victorian Murderesses*. NY: Schocken, 1977.

Barbara Morgan,
Melrose, Massachusetts

Kent, countess of.
See Gytha (fl. 1022–1042).
See Joan of Kent (1328–1385).
See Fitzalan, Alice (1352–1416).
See Percy, Katherine (b. 1423).
See Grey, Elizabeth (1581–1651).

Kent, duchess of.
See Margaret de Burgh (c. 1193–1259).
See Margaret Wake of Liddell (c. 1299–1349).
See Constance (c. 1374–1416).
See Victoria of Coburg (1786–1861).
See Marina of Greece (1906–1968).
See Worsley, Katherine (b. 1933).

Kent, Fair Maid of.
See Joan of Kent (1328–1385).

Kent, maid of.
See Joan of Kent (1328–1385).
See Barton, Elizabeth (c. 1506–1534).
See Marchant, Bessie (1862–1941).

Kent, nun of.
See Barton, Elizabeth (c. 1506–1534).

Kent, queen of.
See Bertha of Kent (c. 565–c. 616).
See Redburga (fl. 825).
See Sexburga, Saint (d. 699?).

Kent, Victoria (1898–1987)
Spanish lawyer and politician during the 1930s. Name variations: Victoria Kent y Siano. Born in Málaga, Spain, in 1898; died in New York City on September 27, 1987; studied law at the University of Madrid.

Victoria Kent was born in Málaga, Spain, in 1897. She studied law at the University of Madrid and first gained national prominence when she acted as defense lawyer for one of the accused officers who had led the Jaca military uprising against the Spanish monarchy in late 1930. This made her the first woman to argue before the Spanish Royal Tribunal of Law. Following the abdication of Alphonso XIII and proclamation of the Second Republic in 1931, Kent stood as a candidate of the Radical Socialist Party and was elected to the Cortes (national assembly) to represent Madrid. She introduced several initiatives to make Spanish prisons more humane.

When the Spanish Civil War erupted in 1936, Kent was still a member of the Cortes and sided with the Republican government against the Nationalists and Francisco Franco. She spent part of the war in Paris, aiding Republican refugees who fled Spain. When the Germans invaded France, Kent took refuge in the Mexican embassy. She recounted her experiences there in *Cuatro años en París, 1940–1944* (1947). After the war ended, Kent moved to Mexico and taught law there. In 1950, she emigrated to the United States. She worked for the United Nations and founded an anti-Franco political journal, *Ibérica,* which she edited for two decades. Following Franco's death in 1975, she returned temporarily to Spain. She died in 1987 in New York City. The same year King Juan Carlos of Spain had awarded her the Grand Cross of the Order of San Raimundo of Peñafort.

SOURCES:

Kent, Victoria. *Cuatro años de mi vida.* Barcelona: Bruguera, 1978.

The New York Times. September 28, 1987.

Kendall W. Brown,
Professor of History, Brigham Young University, Provo, Utah

Kenyatta, Margaret (1928—)

*Kenyan activist and politician. Born Margaret Wambui Kenyatta in Nairobi, Kenya, in 1928; only daughter and one of two children of Jomo Kenyatta (1891–1978, nationalist, politician, and first president of Kenya) and his first wife, **Nyokabi**; attended Ruthimitu Primary School; attended Church of Scotland Mission School, Kikuyu; attended the Alliance High School; never married; no children.*

The daughter of Jomo Kenyatta, the controversial nationalist who was the driving force in the liberation of Kenya from British rule and the country's first president, Margaret Kenyatta inherited her father's toughness and charisma and followed him into politics. She was born in 1928 and raised in the Dagoretti area of Nairobi, the capital of Kenya, and has vivid memories of her famous father: "I can remember the crowds of people who used to visit him at home, and I often used to make him play with me and he held me up in front of the people and they all laughed." After high school, Margaret took a teaching post at Githunguri College, where her father was principal. In 1952, when he was arrested for his involvement with the Mau Mau and others protesting white suppression, the college was closed by government order. At the time, Margaret was also arrested and detained for a week.

While her father served a seven-year prison term, Margaret held various odd jobs and became active in the Peoples Congress Party, which worked for African rights and the release of political prisoners. She also joined a number of social welfare organizations, including Maendeleo ya Wanawake, one of Kenya's most important women's organizations. In 1959, when Jomo Kenyatta was released from prison and became head of the Kenya African National Union (KANU), a political party formed to work for African liberation, Margaret also joined the party, serving as assistant secretary and later as secretary of the KANU branch at Kiambu.

The KANU was finally victorious in the general election of May 1963, and Kenya won independence that same year, after which Jomo Kenyatta became prime minister and then president. Margaret joined her father's efforts to build a unified nation, working particularly to interest women in political activism. Although Jomo had promised to give the women of Kenya "every encouragement to involve themselves in the exciting task of Nation building," it proved difficult to break old patterns. Not a single woman was elected to the house of representatives, and women achieved only small victories at other levels. In 1963, **Grace Onyango** was elected chair of the education committee of Kisumu. Onyango would later become Kenya's first African woman mayor and a member of Parliament. That same

Victoria Kent

year, Margaret was elected a councilor for Dagoretti in the city council of Nairobi. Reelected for four subsequent terms, she continued her efforts to unify women in a quest for equality, utilizing her contacts with international movements like Countrywomen of the World, International Council of Women, Women Presbyterians of Canada, and the YWCA. In 1964, she became president of the National Council of Women of Kenya and began to travel widely, addressing conferences and seminars throughout the world on women's roles in nation-building. Speaking to groups in Europe, Asia, America, the U.S.S.R., the People's Republic of China, and India, her message always emphasized the importance of the home and children, and the place of education in building a solid future. In 1964, in recognition of her efforts, she was awarded the Order of the Queen of Sheba by Emperor Haile Selassie of Ethiopia.

Surprisingly, Kenyatta passed up a run for Parliament in May 1966, when some seats were vacated and prospects for her election seemed ideal. She offered no explanation at the time, but did reiterate her belief that woman should be given every opportunity to advance in politics. In 1969, however, Kenyatta was elected deputy

mayor of Nairobi, and in 1971 was elected mayor, thus becoming the first African woman to become mayor of Kenya's capital city and the second African woman mayor in the country. Her tenure in office was marked by many developmental programs, including expansion of the subways, the building of low-cost housing and sewerage, and the expansion of public health facilities. Kenyatta's first priorities, however, remained women, children, and education, which she viewed as the hope for Kenya's future.

Margaret Kenyatta, who never married, was once described by a long-time friend as "a mature woman with large sad eyes and a rare but infectious laugh." Although she defied tradition in a country where women were expected to marry, raise children, and tend to domestic matters, she remained modest about her personal victories, preferring to focus on the future of her country.

SOURCES:
Crane, Louise. *Ms. Africa*. Philadelphia, PA: Lippincott, 1973.

Barbara Morgan,
Melrose, Massachusetts

Kenyon, Doris (1897–1979)

*American actress. Born in Syracuse, New York, on September 5, 1897; died in 1979; daughter of a cleric-poet; spent two years in Europe studying with *Yvette Guilbert; married Milton Sills (an actor), in 1926 (died); married twice more and divorced; married Bronislaw Mylnarski (a music expert who died in 1971); children: (first marriage) Kenyon Sills (1927–1971).*

Born in Syracuse, New York, in 1897, Doris Kenyon made her stage debut at age 18. She moved on to silent films, starring as a flighty ingenue, then made a successful transition to more mature parts in talkies; along the way, she also continued her Broadway career. Kenyon's films include *The Rack* (1915), *The Inn of the Blue Moon* (1918), *The Bandbox* (1919), *Shadows of the Sea* (1922), *Bright Lights of Broadway* (1923), *Men of Steel* (1925), *The Valley of the Giants* (1927), *Road to Singapore* (1931), *Whom the God's Destroy* (1934), and *Girls' School* (1938). One reviewer noted that the screen "fairly sizzles during her love scenes with Rudolph Valentino" in 1924's *Monsieur Beaucaire*. With her cultured voice and aristocratic demeanor, Kenyon also took on biographical roles, appearing as Betsey Hamilton (*Elizabeth Schuyler Hamilton) opposite George Arliss in *Alexander Hamilton* (1931), *Madame Pompadour, once again opposite Arliss, in *Voltaire* (1933) and Queen *Anne in *The Man in the

Doris Kenyon

Iron Mask (1939). Following her retirement from films, she sang and toured for the USO during World War II. Her fourth husband, music expert Bronislaw Mylnarski, and her son, Kenyon Sills, died in the same year, 1971.

Kenyon, Dorothy (1888–1972)

American lawyer, feminist, judge, and civil libertarian. Born on February 17, 1888, in New York City; died on February 11, 1972 (some sources erroneously cite February 12), in New York City; daughter of William Houston Kenyon, a lawyer, and Maria Wellington (Stanwood) Kenyon; educated at Horace Mann High School in New York City; graduated from Smith College, A.B. in economics, 1908; graduated from New York University Law School, 1917.

Dorothy Kenyon was born on February 17, 1888, and grew up with her two younger brothers on Manhattan's Upper West Side and at a summer house in Connecticut; her father was a patent lawyer, and her mother a descendant of Massachusetts Bay colonists. Kenyon graduated from high school in 1904 and from Smith College in 1908 with a degree in economics and history. After witnessing social injustices during a trip to Mexico, she entered law school, graduating and passing the New York Bar in 1917. Kenyon rejected the opportunity to join her brothers at their father's law firm and, other than a partnership in the 1930s with **Dorothy Straus** and a few short stints at other firms, spent the majority of her 54-year career in independent practice. In 1937, she was one of the first women admitted to the New York City Bar Association.

Dorothy Kenyon was an ardent advocate of liberal causes. In the 1920s and 1930s, she supported the suffragist and birth-control movements, and during the Depression opposed discrimination of married women workers (whom many believed should be forced to quit their jobs so that unemployed men could be hired instead). From 1930 until her death, she sat on the national board of directors of the American Civil Liberties Union, and she was one of the few who opposed the dismissal of *Elizabeth Gurley Flynn, a member of the Communist Party, in 1940. Active in the liberal wing of New York City politics in the 1930s as well as later, Kenyon served on committees for the American Labor Party, worked against the Tammany Hall political machine, and was appointed first deputy commissioner of licenses in 1936 and a municipal court judge in 1939, both by Mayor Fiorello La Guardia. She served on several public commissions, including

ones that dealt with issues of relief, minimum wage, public housing, and court procedures for women, as well as being a founder and director of numerous consumer corporations and serving as legal counsel for the Cooperative League of the United States. In 1938, Kenyon was appointed by the council of the League of Nations to be one of seven jurists forming a committee to study the legal status of women throughout the world. During World War II, she supported the cause of women physicians who sought military commissions. She was also the U.S. delegate to the U.N. Commission on the Status of Women from 1946 to 1950, and in those years was granted four honorary degrees.

Kenyon's career, like that of so many others, was damaged when she was accused by Senator Joseph McCarthy in 1950 of membership in Communist-front organizations. She became the first person to appear before the investigators on the Senate Foreign Relations Subcommittee, strongly denying either membership in the Communist Party, being a fifth-columnist, or disloyalty to her country, while concurring that she had worked with liberal organizations. Despite the support Kenyon received from the liberal press and many respected public figures, McCarthy's accusation marked the end of her public appointments. She continued practicing law, and from the 1950s became involved in challenging the country's draconian abortion laws. She did not receive another honorary degree for nearly two decades.

During the 1960s, Kenyon was active in both the feminist movement and the civil-rights movement. She promoted integration of New York City public schools, prepared briefs for the NAACP Legal Defense Fund, and, after the assassination of Martin Luther King, Jr. in 1968, marched with sanitation workers. She also joined in feminist marches and used her position on the ACLU board of directors to push that institution to fight for women's rights. Initially perceiving the Equal Rights Amendment as a menace to protective legislation, Kenyon opposed it until her disappointment over the Supreme Court's lack of commitment in striking down legal differentiations based on sex caused her to join the pro-ERA side in 1970. Before her death from cancer in New York City on February 11, 1972, Dorothy Kenyon also participated in the antiwar movement, helped to organize a women's coalition seeking to divert federal money from the defense budget to social purposes, and was instrumental in establishing the first legal services for the poor on the Lower West Side of Manhattan.

SOURCES:

Sicherman, Barbara, and Carol Hurd Green, eds. *Notable American Women: The Modern Period.* Cambridge, MA: The Belknap Press of Harvard University Press, 1980.

Karina L. Kerr, M.A.,
Ypsilanti, Michigan

Kenyon, Kathleen (1906–1978)

One of the most productive and controversial British archaeologists of the 20th-century, who pioneered modern field methodology and contributed to the understanding of the role of the city in the growth of civilization. Name variations: Dame Kathleen Kenyon. Born Kathleen Mary Kenyon on January 5, 1906, in London, England; died on August 24, 1978, in Erbistock, Wales; daughter of Sir Frederic George Kenyon (director and principal librarian of the British Museum) and Amy (Hunt) Kenyon; graduated from Somerville College, Oxford, in 1928; awarded M.A., D.Litt, D.Lit, L.H.D.; never married; no children.

Began career as an archaeologist by joining the British Association's expedition to Southern Rhodesia (1929); excavated at Verulamium as part of Sir Mortimer and Tessa Wheeler's team (1930–35); participated in the Crowfoot expedition to Samaria (1931–34); helped found the University of London Institute of Archaeology (1937); was acting director of same (1942–46); served as secretary of Council for British Archaeology (1944–49); excavated the Roman town of Sabratha (1948, 1949, and 1951); was director of the British School of Archaeology in Jerusalem (1951–66); excavated at Jericho (1952–58); created CBE (1954); excavated at Jerusalem (1961–67); served as principal of St. Hugh's College, Oxford (1962–73); served as chair of the Council of the British School of Archaeology in Jerusalem (1967–78); created Dame of the British Empire (1973); was a fellow of the British Academy and Fellow of the Society of Antiquaries.

Principal general publications: Beginning in Archaeology (1952); Digging Up Jericho (1957); Archaeology in the Holy Land (1960); Excavations at Jericho (vol. 1, 1960, vol. 2, 1965); Amorites and Canaanites (1966); Royal Cities of the Old Testament (1970); Digging up Jerusalem (1974); The Bible and Recent Archaeology (1978).

In 1952, Kathleen Kenyon arrived at the site of Jericho, in the Jordanian desert, to follow up on previous excavations which had linked the site to the Biblical story of Joshua. Instead, her application of new methods to Near Eastern archaeology revealed that virtually no traces of the Biblical era city remained. Soon, however, the papers would be full of the most significant revelation concerning Jericho, the fact that it had been occupied by about 6800 BCE; it appeared to be, in fact, the oldest city in the world.

Kathleen Mary Kenyon was born on January 5, 1906, the first child of Sir Frederic and **Amy Kenyon**, both of Shropshire. Sir Frederic George Kenyon was director and principal librarian of the British Museum, as well as the president of the Society of Antiquaries, and the secretary of the British Academy until 1949, when he was succeeded by Mortimer Wheeler. He was a distinguished Biblical scholar, but Kathleen Kenyon considered her interest in Palestine to be a matter more of chance than of his influence. The title of her book *The Bible and Recent Archaeology* (1978), however, was chosen to echo his *The Bible and Archaeology* (1940). She attended St. Paul's Girls' School, where she became head girl, and Somerville College, Oxford. While reading modern history, she was also the president of the Oxford University Archaeological Society and a hockey blue. By the time of her graduation in 1928, she was determined to pursue a career in archaeology.

But Kenyon was entering a field which was largely male; while she was not the first to do so, she was one of only a few women who were able to rise to the top of the profession, which was somewhat zealously guarded. The most notable pioneer in this respect was ***Margaret Murray**, the first female Egyptologist, who was able to overcome the bias in the field only with great perseverance. Murray was told at a 1913 meeting of the British Association that anthropology was not a fit subject for women, because there were many things women ought not to know, and she frequently had difficulty finding journals to publish her articles, if they were on matters not considered suitable for women. Another woman who helped break down, to some extent, the barrier in archaeology was ***Harriet Boyd Hawes**, an American. Hawes was one of the first female excavators, and among the first generation of archaeologists to dig on Crete, where she excavated Gournia in 1901. ***Amelia B. Edwards**, author and archaeologist, had an enormous impact on the field; she was among the first to recognize the need for dating sites by means of the objects found at them, and not only by written records. To encourage this, she founded a chair for the study of Egyptian archaeology at University College, London; the chair was first held by Flinders Petrie, the greatest British Egyptologist of the century, under whom Margaret Murray studied. Also, the first woman professor at Cambridge, *Dorothy Garrod, was an archaeologist. Thus, Kenyon joined a small but very distinguished group of women who were successful in a field in which their male peers accepted them begrudgingly.

Kenyon's first experience with field archaeology was remarkable; rather than working on a British site, she joined (as an assistant and photographer) the 1929 expedition of Dr. *Gertrude Caton-Thompson to Southern Rhodesia, where Kenyon supervised part of the excavation of Zimbabwe. She also contributed an article to Caton-Thompson's *The Zimbabwe Culture*, "Sketch of the Exploration and Settlement of the East Coast of Africa," her first publication. Kenyon came to prominence as one of Britain's finest young archaeologists during the excavation of Verulamium, a Roman British town, from 1930 to 1935. Sir Mortimer and **Tessa Wheeler** ran the dig until 1933, after which they left to work on the reports for the site and to excavate at Maiden Castle. Kenyon was left in charge of the site for the final season, during which she uncovered the Roman theater, the only one of its kind in Britain. The theater was the second site on which Kenyon published, but she was not involved with the Wheelers' report on the site, which proved largely erroneous. Her work at Verulamium was the beginning of a long personal and professional relationship with Sir Mortimer Wheeler; between the two of them, they were to perfect new methodologies which revolutionized field archaeology.

While spending the summers working at Verulamium, Kenyon also spent parts of 1931 to 1934 as a member of the Crowfoot expedition to Samaria, her first work in Palestine. In an obituary for J.W. Crowfoot, she stressed the success of the excavation (1931–35) in view of the close superimposition of the remains of the successive periods. Samaria, founded in the early 9th century BCE, was the capital of the Kingdom of Israel, and remained an important community in Roman times, as Sebaste. It was Kenyon, however, who was largely responsible for the introduction, at Samaria, of new methods of excavation to Palestinian archaeology. She applied the stratigraphical techniques which Wheeler was developing on British sites to the tell (mound) of Samaria, with excellent results. While her pottery sequence for Samaria was considered questionable by her peers, there was no doubt that her work was "one of the most remarkable achievements in the history of Palestinian excavation," wrote G.E. Wright. She was surprised to find that buildings in Palestinian excavations were being dated by means of the material above their floors; this contrasted strongly with the British methodology of dating buildings on the basis of the most recent material found in the fill associated with the actual construction. Wheeler became the most vocal champion of the new methodology and, in fact, using Kenyon's work as his proof, denounced all archaeological work in Palestine prior to 1952. This created certain animosities, which slowed to some extent the spread of the Wheeler-Kenyon method in Near Eastern archaeology.

From 1935 to 1948, Kenyon worked on a number of sites in Britain and also became involved in matters of administration and organization, another area of her field in which she would excel. She excavated at, and published on, the following sites: the Jewry Wall site, Leicester, 1936–39; Viroconium, Shropshire, 1936–37; the Wrekin, Shropshire, 1939; Southwark, 1945–48; Breedon-on-the-Hill, Leicester, 1946; and Sutton Walls, Herefordshire, 1948–51. Thus, in addition to the extensive work in Palestinian archaeology which was to form the foundation of her reputation, she also made substantial contributions to the study of Iron Age and Roman Britain. During the Second World War, she worked for the British Red Cross, first as a divisional commandant and secretary (1939–42), and then as the director of the Youth Department, from 1942 to 1945. Between the years 1944 and 1949, she served as secretary of the new Council for British Archaeology; in this capacity, she helped to maintain British archaeology during the difficult war and postwar years. She was involved with Wheeler's 1937 establishment of the University of London Institute of Archaeology, for which she was secretary from 1935 to 1948, and then acting director from 1942 to 1946. She is credited with holding the Institute together during the war years, largely by force of personality. From 1948 to 1962, she was lecturer in Palestinian archaeology at the Institute and was a powerful force in supporting it; Max Mallowan, in his memoirs, wrote that Kenyon "was a dragon in promoting its welfare."

In 1948–49, and again in 1951, she directed the excavation of the Phoenician and Roman site at Sabratha in Tripolitania (now Libya). Also in 1948, she began a seven-year tenure as the treasurer of the Palestine Exploration Fund, an organization which she remained involved with throughout her life. In 1951, she became the director of the British School of Archaeology in Jerusalem, a position in which her organizational gifts were again utilized to good effect. The school, officially founded in 1919 but languishing from lack of funding until 1951, came to new prominence under Kenyon. The two principle reasons for this were the funds which she was able to secure from international sources, and her work on the site of Jericho, in Jordan. The excavation of Jericho (1952–58) is a landmark event in Near Eastern archaeology both because of the importance of the finds to our understanding of the development of civilization, and because of the impact of Kenyon's methods on other excavators.

The fact that an important Biblical story was attached to Jericho made it an obvious choice for the pioneers of archaeology in Palestine to test the usefulness of the new discipline in supporting the Biblical version of history. No more impressive find could be uncovered than the very walls which Joshua caused to collapse, after all. Work on the site (Tell es-Sultan) by John Garstang in the 1930s did indeed uncover collapsed walls and evidence of fire; these walls were identified as those of the Biblical period, and Jericho became a touchstone of the movement to use archaeology to support the history contained in the Bible. At the time when Kenyon arrived at Jericho, much work was being done in the Near East which sought to revise the theories which had been established in the '30s. The Biblical picture of a Hebrew invasion of Canaan, which had been supported by the work done by Garstang and his peers, was being refined to reflect new ideas and evidence suggesting a more extended, less military process. Kenyon's excavation of Jericho contributed to this movement in a number of ways, one being that the walls attributed to the Biblical era were discovered to be in fact those of an Early Bronze Age settlement of about 2350 BCE. The entry into Canaan is generally considered contemporary with the Late Bronze Age, of which period of occupation little remained at Jericho due to massive erosion. The most surprising discovery at Jericho, however, was evidence of extensive domestic architecture dating back to the 7th millennium BCE. Carbon fourteen testing yielded a date of roughly 6800 BCE for the earliest Neolithic occupation of Jericho, making it the oldest known community in the world. The discoveries at Jericho led to a new understanding of the importance of urbanization to early civilization in the Near Eastern region.

The archaeological techniques which Kenyon rigorously applied to her excavations, and which are consequently known as the Wheeler-Kenyon method, depend on the careful observation and recording of stratigraphy. For most of the early history of archaeology, excavation was carried out in what can be called an architectural manner; that is, buildings and walls were excavated in their entirety, without their connections to the surrounding soil being recorded. Wheeler and Kenyon, on the other hand, advocated a system of excavation which followed the actual stratigraphy of a site, and emphasized the provenance of objects within the stratigraphy. Also, Kenyon insisted that "side by side with the recording of objects from the layers must go the interpretation of the significance of the layers." Thus, a wall would be excavated at right angles in order to maintain the connections between it and the associated floors and fill. When a site is excavated using the grid method, which Wheeler pioneered, the areas of earth left between the squares are known as baulks; it was these that Kenyon used for her always meticulous study of a site's stratigraphy. Precise stratigraphical control and systematic recording are the hallmarks of the Wheeler-Kenyon system.

While the principles of the system had been anticipated to some extent by excavators such as Petrie, W.F. Albright, and G. Reisner, it was Kenyon who had the largest share in popularizing it. The system spread gradually but inexorably through the Near East, aided by the many colleagues and students of Kenyon's who directed excavations, such as Peter Parr at Petra and **Diana Kirkbride** at Beidha. Archaeologists of many nationalities were influenced by Kenyon and adapted her methods to their needs; the exception to this, initially, were Israeli archaeologists, who were not able to observe firsthand the excavations at Jericho and later Jerusalem. Kenyon did manage to maintain professional relationships with her Israeli peers, although with some difficulties.

It was as a field archaeologist that Kenyon excelled, and it seems as though it was in the field that her true personality was most evident. Regarded as unyielding by some academic colleagues, she was seen as patient and open minded by those who worked with her in the field. As some recall, "she consulted us, as equals, and tried out her ideas on us, encouraging us to suggest counter-explanations if we disagreed with her." This can be contrasted with her administrative persona, which Max Mallowan recalls from their time together at the Institute of Archaeology: "Woe betide those who opposed her, or were not of the same mind." Even so, Mallowan remarks that "though often offensive in confrontation she spoke good behind one's back, and belied an occasional rough manner by great kindliness of heart." The dig at Jericho was marked by frequent festive occasions, including the "lowest Boat Race on record," which took place on the

Dead Sea; on these occasions, Kenyon "participated with great zest" in the festivities.

From 1958 to 1961, Kenyon and Wheeler were both members of the committee (of six men and Kenyon) which the British Academy, with the sponsorship of the Rockefeller Foundation, created to study the provisions for research in the humanities and social sciences. The report, released in 1961, had the desired effect of generating a program for funding of the humanities through the Academy. Following this, Kenyon returned to excavating, this time at Jerusalem. Another important Biblical site, Jerusalem also had in common with Jericho a history of traditional excavation, and thus proved another excellent testing ground for Kenyon's methodologies. Although the site was a difficult one to excavate, she succeeded in establishing a coherent sequence for the walled cities.

By 1962, it seemed as though Kenyon, then at the height of her reputation as an excavator, would likely become the director of the Institute of Archaeology; instead, she became the principal of St. Hugh's College, Oxford. In his memoirs, Mallowan suggests that the reason why she did not become the director had less to do with qualifications than choice of pets. According to him, Kenyon (an acknowledged animal lover) was in the habit of taking in numerous stray dogs, who were not looked upon with favor by the rest of the Institute. This lead to a confrontation between Kenyon and the director, which was apparently only resolved with the offer of the St. Hugh's post. Despite this unusual origin, her appointment at St. Hugh's was to prove extremely successful, as she saw the college through more than a decade of growth and expansion.

In 1967, during the final year of her excavation at Jerusalem, Kenyon found herself involved in an administrative dispute with Wheeler, which apparently strained their relationship. Wheeler had spoken of retiring from his position as chair of the Council of the British School of Archaeology in Jerusalem, and Kenyon decided to run for the position; a heated debate broke out between those who supported her and those who preferred that Wheeler remain in the position. In the end, Wheeler preferred to withdraw, but not before suggesting that Kenyon was unsuitable for the position because of her political involvement with the Arabs (this occurred in the wake of the Six-Day War in June, during which Israel occupied Western Jordan), an opinion which she bitterly resented.

In 1969, Kenyon gave the Galton Lecture at the annual symposium of the Eugenics Society, their theme that year being biosocial aspects of sex. In speaking on "Women in Academic Life," her remarks were pointed, although often mixed with humor. She made it clear that the progress of female students and also female administrators was being held up largely due to "the surviving nineteenth-century attitude of men." She was not, she said, a "dyed-in-the-wool woman academic." Certainly, the events of her life show that she demanded equal treatment with her male peers and was not inclined to defer to them. While this may not always have endeared her to them, it did contribute to her becoming one of the most successful and influential archaeologists of the century.

SOURCES:

The Times (obituary). August 25, 1978.

*Hawkes, Jacquetta. *Adventurer in Archaeology: The Biography of Sir Mortimer Wheeler.* NY: St. Martin's Press, 1982.

Kenyon, Kathleen M. *Digging Up Jericho.* London: Ernest Benn, 1957.

———. "The Galton Lecture 1969: Women In Academic Life," in *Biosocial Aspects of Sex.* Oxford: Blackwell, 1970.

Mallowan, Max. *Mallowan's Memoirs.* NY: Dodd, Mead, 1977.

Moorey, P.R.S. "Kathleen Kenyon and Palestinian Archaeology," in *Palestine Exploration Quarterly.* January–June, 1979. pp. 3–10.

Moorey, Roger, and Peter Parr, ed. *Archaeology in the Levant: Essays for Kathleen Kenyon.* England: Aris & Phillips, 1978.

William MacKenzie,
Graduate Student, Department of History,
University of Guelph, Ontario

Keopuolani (c. 1778–1823)

Sacred chiefess, the mother of kings, who was the wife of Kamehameha I. Name variations: Keopulani. Born to parents who were half brother and sister of high rank around 1778; died on September 16, 1823; raised by grandmother Kalola; became first wife of Kamehameha I the Great (1758–1819), king of Hawaii (r. 1810–1819), around 1795; children: Liholiho (1797–1824), later known as Kamehameha II, king of Hawaii (r. 1819–1824); Kauikeaouli (1814–1854), later known as Kamehameha III, king of Hawaii (r. 1824–1854); Princess Nahienaena (c. 1815–1836).

Raised on Maui by her grandmother **Kalola**, Keopuolani was born around 1778 of high rank, making her a prime bridal candidate for Kamehameha I when she was still a teen. She was a woman of power, like Kamehameha's chief wife *Kaahumanu, and, like Kaahumanu, also rebelled against the old ways. When Keopuolani's daughter *Nahienaena was born, she kept her near, rather than hand her over to another chief to raise, as was the custom. On the day after her husband's death in 1819, Keopuolani broke other taboos, wrote **Marjorie Sinclair**: "She ate coconuts previously forbidden to women, and she sat down with the chiefs for a meal." Keopuolani was among those who approved of the work of the missionaries and had her two younger children learn to read and write. She began to don Western clothes, study Christianity, and had furniture in her house. When her health began to fail in 1823, Keopuolani pursued a warmer climate, moving her family to Lahaina, on the island of Maui. Baptized while on her death bed, she was considered "the first fruit of the mission."

SOURCES:

Sinclair, Marjorie. "Keopuolani," in *Notable Women of Hawaii*. Edited by Barbara Bennett Peterson. Honolulu: University of Hawaii Press, 1984.

Keppel, Alice (1869–1947)

*English aristocrat and influential mistress of King Edward VII. Name variations: Alice Edmonstone; Mrs. George Keppel. Born Alice Frederica Edmonstone in 1869 in Stirlingshire, Scotland; died on September 11, 1947, in Florence, Italy; youngest daughter of Admiral William Edmonstone and Mary (Parsons) Edmonstone (d. 1902); great-grandmother of *Camilla Parker-Bowles (b. 1949); married George Keppel (1865–1947, an army officer and brother of the earl of Albemarle), on June 1, 1891; paramour of Charles Windsor, prince of Wales, the future King Edward VII; children: (paternity uncertain) Violet Keppel Trefusis (1894–1972); Sonia Rosemary Keppel (1900–1986); and others.*

The English aristocrat Alice Keppel was best known for being the mistress of Edward VII, king of England. The youngest daughter of **Mary Parsons Edmonstone** and Sir William Edmonstone, a Scottish admiral in the British navy, Alice was born in 1869 and grew up in a comfortable but not wealthy home in the old castle of Duntreath in Stirlingshire. Her education was good but not extensive, typical for a woman of her class.

In 1891, Alice married the Honorable George Keppel, youngest son of the earl of Albemarle. They were a loving couple throughout their marriage. They had two daughters, the writer *Violet Keppel Trefusis and Sonia Keppel, both of whom adored their mother. (The paternity of Violet is in dispute.) Acquaintances describe Alice Keppel as humorous and charming, but with a shrewd intelligence and a keen grasp of British politics and economic events. All of these qualities attracted the attention of the Prince of Wales when he met Mrs. Keppel in February 1898 (he was 57, she 29). Albert Edward, called "Bertie" by his family and friends, was the outgoing and genial heir to the throne of his mother Queen *Victoria.

Similar in personality despite their age difference, they began a romantic relationship which lasted beyond Edward's accession in 1901 until his death in 1910. Soon Alice was recognized as Edward's mistress, although neither ever spoke publicly of it, nor displayed any affection in public. But they were seen together frequently, attending social functions as a couple. Perhaps contrary to expectations, Edward and Alice each maintained good relationships with their spouses. Alice's husband George, an officer and a gentleman, handled his wife's indiscretion with upper-class aplomb for which he was awarded the Royal Victorian Order. George remained on friendly terms with the king, while Queen *Alexandra of Denmark welcomed the arrangement. The queen preferred a quiet home life with her seven children to the constant parties, social engagements, and outdoor activities enjoyed by her husband. Restless and easily bored, Edward needed constant activity and new diversions. Alexandra was content to let Alice act as a second queen, as long as the affair remained discreet. The prudent Alice was a kind woman, and she seems to have gotten along well with Alexandra. In fact, they became friends and allies. When years later a grieving Edward VIII abdicated the throne to marry *Wallis Warfield Simpson (1895–1986), Keppel remarked: "Things were done better in *my* day."

Before long those closest to Edward, including his wife and ministers, recognized that Alice had an unusual degree of positive influence over him. Of all of Edward's mistresses, including *Lillie Langtry and *Frances Evelyn Greville, Alice Keppel had the most influence. She was capable of calming him during his infrequent but violent fits of anger and knew how to keep him in good humor with gossip, card games, and other amusements. Known for her wit, beauty, good nature, deep voice, flair for cigarette smoking, and her ability to control the temper of the king, Keppel once apologized to her card-partner, an angry Edward, for a miscalled play with the line: "I never could tell a king from knave." Consequently, those around the king began to rely on her ability to handle him. They also appreciated her tact and discretion; although the relationship was widely known, she kept it as quiet as possible, so important in an era valuing outward appearances above all else. The king's ministers also used Alice's political knowledge and influence to their advantage, invoking her aid in convincing Edward to heed their policy advice. Keppel was known to have smoothed over one or two diplomatic matters and to have acted as an intermediary between the king and the Liberal regime of Prime Minister Sir Herbert Asquith.

In the course of the affair, Alice (and her husband) became quite wealthy. "Mrs. Keppel," notes **Diana Souhami**, "regarded adultery as a sound business practice." Edward showered her with gifts of clothing and jewels in addition to a large income. Since neither the Edmonstones nor the Keppels were particularly well off, the king's gifts allowed members of both families to be part of England's wealthiest elite. The Keppels also traveled extensively with the king, spending months at a time abroad, most often in France.

In May 1910, when King Edward died at age 70, Alice was deeply grieved, as were George and Alexandra. Alice decided to go abroad with her family during the transition to the reign of George V. In November 1910, the Keppels and their two daughters sailed to Ceylon, then to China, not returning to London until 1912. There Mrs. Keppel emerged once again as a popular hostess to London's high society. During World War I, George Keppel served in France; Alice followed him there, serving as a nurse in a field hospital.

Following the war, the Keppels retired to Italy, purchasing the villa known as L'Ombrellino in the hills overlooking Florence. Life at L'Ombrellino was leisured and slow-paced, spent entertaining friends, mostly English, French, and Italian aristocrats. The outbreak of World War II caused them to flee Italy for England by way of France, causing Frances Greville to sniff, "To hear Alice talk about her escape from France, one would think she had swum the Channel with her maid between her teeth." The Keppels returned to Florence in 1946. There Alice Keppel died in September 1947, at age 78. In 1995, Britain issued a stamp that had been approved by Queen *Elizabeth II, featuring a mother and child; the mother was Alice Keppel.

SOURCES:

Phillips, John, *et al. The Last Edwardians: An Illustrated History of Violet Trefusis and Alice Keppel*. Boston, MA: The Boston Athenaeum, 1985.

Souhami, Diana. *Mrs. Keppel and Her Daughter*. NY: St. Martin's Press, 1996.

Laura York,
Riverside, California

Keppel, Mrs. George (1869–1947).

See Keppel, Alice.

Keppel, Violet.

See Trefusis, Violet Keppel.

Keqing, Kang (1911–1992).

See Kang Keqing.

Ker-Seymer, Barbara (b. 1905)

British photographer. Born in 1905, probably in England; studied painting at the Royal College of Art and Slade School of Art, London, mid-1920s.

Barbara Ker-Seymer was one of a number of innovative British women photographers who emerged between 1920 and 1940, and included **Violet Banks**, Edith Plummer (later known as *Madame Yevonde), **Lettice Ramsey, Helen Muspratt, Ursula Powys-Lybbe**, and **Winifred Casson**. Ker-Seymer intended to become a painter, and by her own admission went into photography by accident. After studying painting at the Royal College of Art and the Slade School of Art during the mid-1920s, she apprenticed with London society portrait photographer **Olivia Wyndham**, the former partner of American photographer Curtis Moffatt. "Olivia was a socialite, also a leader of the 'Bright Young Things,'" Barbara said of her mentor, "so there was always plenty going on and she was invited to a lot of parties where the press were barred but she was allowed to take photographs as she was a friend of the various hosts. My job was to stay up all night after the parties, developing and printing the films in order to take them round to the *Tatler, Sketch* and *Bystander,* etc." In 1931, Ker-Seymer was contracted by *Harper's Bazaar* to photograph theatrical and society celebrities as well as people in the news, and she later moved on to do fashion work with the prestigious Colman-Prentice agency.

Strongly influenced by the German cinema and the seminal book *Köpfe des Alltags (Everyday Faces)* by Helmar Lerski, Ker-Seymer was known for her experimentation with poses and lighting. She was strictly an interior photographer, working out of a studio on Bond Street, where she often collaborated with Brian Howard, who was known for his bizarre images of society girls encircled in wire. While her work for *Harper's,* as well as her fashion spreads, reflect some of her innovations, it is the portraits of her friends (*Nancy Cunard, Frederick Ashton, David Garnett, and Eddie Sackville-West, among others of the "new intelligentsia") that most clearly defines

Photograph of Nancy Cunard by Barbara Ker-Seymer.

her style. In a 1932 portrait of **Nancy Moore**, an oiled profile shot emphasizing the muscular construction of the face and neck, Ker-Seymer adopts Lerski's method of presenting faces of working people in extreme close-ups. A profile portrait of Raymond Mortimer against corrugated iron (head tilted upward toward the light source while an outstretched hand holds a cigarette in the same light) is dramatic in pose and illumination, as are images of Frederick Ashton against tapestry and Nancy Cunard against a tiger skin. "Here was the new, post-Bloomsbury generation in a setting of industrial metal and soft embroidery," notes **Val Williams** in *The Other Observers*, "encompassing the modernists' interest in industrial forms with the aesthete's love of luxuriant surface. It was the quintessential new British photography."

At the outbreak of World War II, Ker-Seymer abandoned photography and joined Larkin and Company, an enterprise that made instructional films for the armed services. "It seemed to be the end of things as we knew them," she said. After 1947, she disappeared from both film and photography. "Ker-Seymer's photography was based almost entirely on her love of experimentation," writes Williams in an

effort to explain Ker-Seymer's disappearance. "She never saw herself as a professional photographer, and thrived in the adventurous climate of the early thirties. Without that climate, her work seemed purposeless."

SOURCES:
Rosenblum, Naomi. *History of Women Photographers.* NY: Abbeville Press, 1994.
Williams, Val. *The Other Observers: Women Photographers in Britain 1900 to the Present.* London: Virago Press, 1966.

COLLECTIONS:
Correspondence (1925–81) held in London's Tate Gallery.

Barbara Morgan,
Melrose, Massachusetts

Kerenhappuch (fl. 2000 BCE)

Biblical woman. Name variations: Keren-Happuch. The youngest of Job's three daughters; sister of *Jemima and *Keziah.

The youngest of Job's three daughters, Kerenhappuch was probably born after his restoration to health and prosperity.

Kerima (1925—)

Algerian actress. Born in Algiers in 1925.

Selected films: An Outcast of the Islands *(UK, 1951);* La Lupa *(The She Wolf, Italy, 1952);* La Nave delle Donne Maledette *(The Ship of Condemned Women, Italy, 1953);* Cavalleria Rusticana *(Fatal Desire, Italy, 1953);* Tam Tam Mayumbe *(Italy/France, 1955);* Land of the Pharaohs *(U.S., 1955);* Fuga nel Sole *(Italy/France, 1956);* The Quiet American *(U.S., 1958);* Il Mondo dei Miracoli *(1959);* Jessica *(U.S./France/Italy, 1962).*

Exotic Algerian actress Kerima played leads and supporting roles in international films during the 1950s and early 1960s. Her screen debut in the British film *An Outcast of the Islands* (1951), directed by Sir Carol Reed, is considered her most memorable role.

Kéroüalle, Louise de (1649–1734)

Duchess of Portsmouth and Aubigny and mistress of the English king Charles II. Name variations: Louise de Keroualle or Kerouaille, Duchess of Portsmouth; Louise de Querouille or Louise de Querouaille; (in France) variously spelled Queroul, Kéroual and Kéroël. Born Louise Renné in 1649 (some sources cite 1650) in Brittany; died in 1734; daughter of Guillaume de Penancourt and Marie de Plaeuc de Timeur;

mistress of Charles II, king of England (r. 1649–1685); children: (with Charles II) Charles Lennox (1672–1723), duke of Richmond.

Born in 1649, Louise de Kéroüalle was the daughter of Guillaume de Penancourt and **Marie de Plaeuc de Timeur**, impoverished nobles in Brittany. The name Kéroüalle was taken from an heiress whom her ancestor François de Penhoët had married in 1330, but the form Querouailles was commonly used in England, where it was derisively corrupted into Carwell, Carewell, or Cartwheel. In France, it was variously spelled Queroul, Kéroual and Kéroël.

Early in life, Louise was placed in the household of *Henrietta Anne, duchess of Orléans, who was the sister of England's king Charles II and sister-in-law of France's king Louis XIV. Saint-Simon asserts that, since Louise's parents could offer no dowry for their daughter, they threw her at Louis XIV in the hope that she would be promoted to the place of *maîtresse en titre* (royal mistress).

In 1670, Louise accompanied the duchess of Orléans across the Channel on a visit to Charles II at Dover. The sudden death of Henrietta Anne because of peritonitis, dubiously attributed to poison, left Kéroüalle unprovided for, but the king placed her among the ladies-in-waiting of his own queen *Catherine of Braganza. It was later said that Louise had been selected by the French court to captivate the king of England, but there seems to be no evidence for this. Yet when the king seemed interested, the affair was energetically pushed by the French ambassador, Colbert de Croissy, and England's secretary of state, Lord Arlington. Louise, who concealed her wit and her strong will under an appearance of weakness, showed her true colors only after she had established a strong hold on the king's affections. When her son Charles, ancestor of the dukes of Richmond, was born in 1672, Charles II gave her the title duchess of Portsmouth, a pension of £10,000 per annum, and a suite of 24 rooms in Whitehall, described as having "ten times the richness and the glory of the Queen's."

Nicknamed Fubbs by Charles and Squintabella by her competitor *Nell Gwynn, Louise set about providing Charles with comfortable domesticity, excellent food, and a sympathetic ear, and manipulated him with enough temper tantrums that Gwynn also dubbed her the "weeping willow." In so doing, it is said that Louise dominated Charles. "No body shall come to Court or to any preferment," said Louise, "but those who will be my creatures." Unpopu-

lar with the populace of England, Louise returned to France following the king's death and lived at Aubigny, beleaguered by debt. She died in Paris on November 14, 1734, "very old, very penitent and very poor," wrote Saint Simon. (*See also Gwynn, Nell.*)

SUGGESTED READING:

Forneron, H. *Louise de Kéroualle*. Paris, 1886.

Louise de Kéroüalle

Kerr, Anita (1927—)

American singer, pianist, and musical arranger who formed the Anita Kerr Singers. Born Anita Jean Grilli in Memphis, Tennessee, on October 31, 1927; her mother hosted a local radio program in Memphis; married second husband, Alex Grob.

A major contributor to the Nashville country-pop sound of the 1960s, Anita Kerr grew up in music, performing on her mother's Memphis radio show as a child and leading her own trio in high school. She was first heard in Nashville on radio station WSM's "Sunday Down South," heading up the program's eight-member choir. In 1949, she organized the Anita Kerr Singers, which debuted on the Red Foley recording "Our Lady of Fatima" (1950) and made later appearances at the

Anita
Kerr

Grand Ole Opry. During the early 1960s, Kerr provided arrangements and back-up for such country-pop singers as Jim Reeves ("He'll Have to Go" and "Welcome to My World"), Floyd Cramer ("Last Date"), **Skeeter Davis** ("End of the World"), and Bobby Bare ("Detroit City"). For some time, the Anita Kerr Quartet, including Gil Wright (tenor), **Dottie Dillard** (alto), and Louis Nunley (baritone), was one of the busiest vocal groups in Nashville. Kerr also did orchestral arrangement for RCA and produced several country records. Based in Hollywood after 1967, she made the charts with her LPs *The Anita Kerr Singers Reflect on the Music of Burt Bacharach and Hal David* and *Velvet Voices and Bold Brass.* She also wrote the instrumental music for several poetry albums by Rod McKuen. Her later work included television and film music, and the formation of yet another singing group, the Mexicali Singers. Kerr moved to Switzerland with second husband Alex Grob to compose music for films. Eventually, she returned to Memphis.

Kerr, Deborah (1921—)

English actress who received an honorary Academy Award in 1994 for being "a dedicated actress whose motion picture career has always stood for perfection, discipline and elegance." Name variations: christened Deborah Kerr-Trimmer, always acted under the name Deborah Kerr, and kept her maiden name through two marriages. Pronunciation: CARR. Born Deborah Jane Kerr-Trimmer in Helensburgh, Scotland, on September 30, 1921, but grew up mainly in England; only daughter of Arthur Kerr-Trimmer (a civil engineer and architect); trained as a dancer at her aunt Phyllis Smale's drama school in Bristol; granted a scholarship to Sadler's Wells ballet school; married Anthony Charles Bartley (an aviator), on November 28, 1945 (divorced 1959); married Peter Viertel (a writer), in 1959; children: (first marriage) **Melanie Jane Bartley**; **Francesca Bartley**.

Made BBC radio debut (1936); made London stage debut (1939); shot first film (1941); shot first Hollywood film, The Hucksters *(1947).*

Selected filmography: Major Barbara *(UK, 1941);* Love on the Dole *(UK, 1941);* Penn of Pennsylvania *(Courageous Mr. Penn, UK, 1941);* Hatter's Castle *(UK, 1941);* The Day Will Dawn *(UK 1942);* The Avengers *(UK, 1942);* The Life and Death of Colonel Blimp *(UK, 1943);* Perfect Strangers *(Vacation from Marriage, UK, 1945);* I See a Dark Stranger *(The Adventuress, UK, 1946);* Black Narcissus *(UK, 1947);* The Hucksters *(1947);* If Winter Comes *(1948);* Edward, My Son *(1949);* Please Believe Me *(1950);* King Solomon's Mines *(1950);* Quo Vadis *(1951);* The Prisoner of Zenda *(1952);* Thunder in the East *(1953);* Young Bess *(as Catherine Parr, 1953);* Julius Caesar *(1953);* Dream Wife *(1953);* From Here to Eternity *(1953);* The End of the Affair *(UK, 1955);* The Proud and the Profane *(1956);* The King and I *(1956);* Tea and Sympathy *(1956);* Heaven Knows, Mr. Allison *(1957);* An Affair to Remember *(1957);* Bonjour Tristesse *(UK, 1958);* Separate Tables *(1958);* The Journey *(1959);* Count Your Blessings *(1959);* Beloved Infidel *(as* **Sheilah Graham**, *1959);* The Sundowners *(1960);* The Grass is Greener *(1960);* The Naked Edge *(1961);* The Innocents *(1961);* The Chalk Garden *(1963);* The Night of the Iguana *(1964);* Marriage on the Rocks *(1965);* Eye of the Devil *(1967);* Casino Royale *(1967);* Prudence and the Pill *(UK, 1968);* The Gypsy Moths *(1969);* The Arrangement *(1969);* A Woman of Substance *(1984);* The Assam Garden *(1985);* Reunion at Fairborough *(1985);* Hold the Dream *(1986).*

In the early years of her movie career, British actress Deborah Kerr played the part of distinguished ladies, and she was a staple figure in the historical epics of the 1950s. Occasionally, she was cast against type and demonstrated that she was an actress of genuine range and ability. One of her most notable roles was as the adulterous officer's wife in *From Here to Eternity* (1953). Her famous frolic in the surf with Burt Lancaster tested Hollywood's skittishness about sex, and paved the way for bolder sensuality in the future, so that by the time she acted in film roles in the late 1960s she was required by some scripts to appear naked.

Deborah Kerr-Trimmer was born in Scotland on September 30, 1921, but grew up mainly in England, having an unhappy childhood at joyless boarding schools but conceiving early the ambition to be an actress. Her father was a disabled veteran of the British army who had lost a leg in the trenches of the First World War and worked as the inventor of mechanical gadgets; he died when she was only 16. From her dismal boarding school, she went to a much more likeable drama school run by her aunt **Phyllis Smale** in Bristol in 1936; the same year, she was auditioned by the British Broadcasting Corporation as a reader. Her polished elocution won her a position reading children's stories on the air for the next few years. In 1938, then in her late teens, Kerr studied ballet at the Sadler's Wells Company in London, but at 5'7" she was too tall to become a prima ballerina. She realized, besides, that she did not have the kind of outstanding talent and dancing ability necessary to make her a star.

Kerr's radio work helped her make contacts in the theater world, however, and she had her London stage debut in 1939, moving to the prestigious West End the following year in *Heartbreak House*. Staying in London despite the hazards of the German bombing, then at its height, she met a Hungarian film director, Gabriel Pascal, who gave her a small role in his superb film of George Bernard Shaw's *Major Barbara* (1941). Her role was that of Jenny Hill, a morally resolute Salvation Army woman; to prepare for the role, the director told Kerr to spend a few weeks working with the real Salvation Army. She found their work serving food and giving shelter to the destitute of London inspiring, but found her own religious inclinations better served by Christian Science, which she studied ardently in the early 1940s.

Major Barbara was a success, and Kerr spent the rest of the war years acting in other films by Pascal and his friends. Her second role was as Sally Hardcastle in *Love on the Dole*, based on a popular novel about life in Britain's industrial north during the Great Depression.

Other roles followed, including *Hatter's Castle* (1941), where she was matched with James Mason, and *The Life and Death of Colonel Blimp* (1943), in which she proved her versatility by playing three different roles. While filming *The Day Will Dawn,* where she had the unlikely role of a Norwegian seacaptain's daughter, she and Rex Harrison, who had joined the cast for a social drink at the end of a day's work, were almost killed by a German bomb. Despite a terrible scare and concussion, they emerged with nothing worse than scratches and a coating of dirt from the adjacent vegetable garden where the bomb had exploded. In the last year of the war, Kerr joined a theater company which performed *Gaslight* at British army camps in Western Europe following the D-Day invasion. In 1945, she married Anthony Bartley, a Royal Air Force squadron leader and hero of the Battle of Britain, who had shot down 15 enemy planes. By then, she was fully established as a major figure in British film and theater.

In ***Rumer Godden**'s *Black Narcissus*, her first postwar film, Kerr played the Sister Superior at a bewitched convent in a remote part of the Himalayan mountains, where one of her flock falls in love with an Englishman who lives nearby. The film traces the Sister Superior's transition from spiritual pride to genuine humility. Acclaimed by many American critics, the movie won the New York Film Critics Award and prompted Louis Mayer, head of MGM, to offer her a Hollywood contract. Not all American reviewers were impressed. The acerbic James Agee wrote: "The head nun, Deborah Kerr, just makes Sisterly sheep's eyes at [the man] as he lunges around the sanctuary in his shorts."

Kerr and her husband, who was willing to give up his job as a test pilot and aviation promoter to accompany her to stardom, emigrated from England during the bitter winter of 1946–47, when wartime rationing was still in force. She was dazzled by the opulence of New York, the luxury of the trains, and the splendid way of life in Hollywood, and said she had not eaten so well in all her life. Mayer, sure he had found a money spinner, began paying her $3,000 per week, which he later raised to $7,000. Her first MGM role was as an advertising executive's wife in *The Hucksters* (1947), where she played alongside Clark Gable, ***Ava Gardner**, and Sydney Greenstreet. Kerr followed with *If Winter Comes* (1948), and then *Edward, My Son* (filmed back in England, 1949) in which she co-starred with Spencer Tracy and played the role of a deceived woman descending into alcoholism. In these years, Kerr also gave birth to two daughters but managed to juggle filming schedules around her pregnancies.

Despite her success in playing a heavy drinker in *Edward, My Son,* MGM mainly reserved her for ladylike parts, and in the 1950s she adorned a long succession of historical epics, usually as the wife of a king or an emperor. Among these were *Quo Vadis* (1951), *Young Bess*—in which she played Henry VIII's last wife, ◆❧ **Catherine Parr**—(1952), and *Julius Caesar* (1953), playing *Portia opposite James Mason's Brutus. These were the years when British and American actors appeared unselfconsciously side by side, despite the clash of national and regional accents. In 1953, bored with the repetition these roles implied, Kerr sought a complete change, arranged to end her contract with MGM even though it cost her almost $1,000 per week, and took on a new agent, Bert Allenberg.

Allenberg persuaded the producers at Columbia to cast her in the role of Karen Holmes, an unfaithful and libidinous army wife in the film version of James Jones' popular novel *From Here to Eternity,* which was then being planned. The role had originally been offered to *Joan Crawford, but the temperamental star disliked many aspects of the planned production and withdrew, so Allenberg was able to get the role for Kerr, even though it meant a complete change in the film persona she had exhibited since coming to America. Now, says her biographer Eric Braun, she was "transformed into the American conception of how a sexy blonde should look. *Marilyn Monroe was currently at her peak in films like *River of No Return* . . . and some of the publicity stills of Deborah Kerr at that time could actually be taken for Monroe herself." The film, one of the first to criticize the American army, was a terrific success, and Kerr was highly praised for her convincing role, winning an Oscar nomination.

❧◆
Parr, Catherine.
See Six Wives of Henry VIII.

A reddish-blond with noble features, [Deborah] Kerr possessed a quiet glamour that had nothing to do with Hollywood's definition.

—**Richard Sater**

Deborah Kerr had begun her career on stage and in 1953 returned to it in the Broadway play *Tea and Sympathy,* directed by Elia Kazan. It ran for more than a year before making a successful national tour, with Kerr in the leading role throughout. Like *From Here to Eternity,* the play broke new ground by portraying sympathetically the affair of a mature woman with a

teenaged boy at a repressive boarding school. Now independent of the studio system and at the height of her fame and powers, Kerr could vary her work by choosing occasional movie roles which took her fancy. She explained to an interviewer when she left MGM: "In the future, parts I choose are going to be about real women; they may not be pleasant, but they will be real people." One such "real person" was Sarah Miles, her role in the film version of Graham Greene's novel *The End of the Affair,* which was released in 1955. Greene himself had worked on several films and wrote movie reviews for the English press but usually deplored the results when his own novels were filmed. This one he gave relatively high praise by saying that it was the "least unsatisfactory," adding that "Deborah Kerr gave an extremely good performance" but that her good work was destroyed by the miscasting of Van Johnson to play a man who was meant to be much older.

Another great success was *The King and I* (1956), a corny musical adaptation of English governess *Anna Leonowens' memoirs about her life as tutor to the king of Siam's children. Yul Brynner played the king, after a four-year run on stage in the same part had brought him stardom. Kerr was a reasonably good singer, but she had a voice-double in the film, **Marni Nixon**, who filled in on the sustained high notes and complicated passages. The next year, Kerr was paired with Robert Mitchum in John Huston's film *Heaven Knows, Mr. Allison,* again playing a nun, as she had in *Black Narcissus.* This time, she was cast adrift in a lifeboat with a tough marine in the middle of the Pacific War, surviving through a savvy combination of divine and mundane ideas and beating a Japanese army into the bargain. As film historian Brandon French notes, the film was in some ways a rehash of Huston's earlier success *The African Queen,* but whereas the *Katharine Hepburn figure had been on terms of full equality with her man in facing jungle hazards, Kerr now played a far more passive role. French suggests that the shift symbolizes the cramping social restriction many American women felt in the 1950s. In the same year, 1957, Kerr made *An Affair to Remember,* a classic "weepie" with Cary Grant, which was recently parodied in the Tom Hanks-**Meg Ryan** film *Sleepless in Seattle.*

Kerr's marriage to Anthony Bartley had become strained during the 1950s as she toured with plays or filmed on location. To compound their long separations, he had become a European representative of CBS television. Rumors of infidelities in the press heralded their divorce

in 1959, but gossip columnists found Kerr far more private and self-contained than many of the stars and her divorce correspondingly less sensational. In 1960, after success in an Australian film, *The Sundowners,* in which she was again paired with Mitchum, Kerr married Peter Viertel, a writer who had worked on the script of her 1959 film *The Journey* and was the son of *Salka Viertel. Throughout the 1960s, Kerr and her husband lived mainly in his home country, Switzerland, where she enjoyed publicity as a prominent member of the "jet set," flying frequently back and forth to New York, Hollywood, London, and Paris, when the idea of flying still seemed more romantic than irksome. In *The Innocents* (1961), based on Henry James' story *The Turn of the Screw,* Kerr won high praise from *The New Yorker* critic *Pauline Kael, who wrote: "Deborah Kerr's performance is in the grand manner—as modulated and controlled, and yet as flamboyant, as almost anything you'll see on the stage. And it's a tribute to Miss Kerr's beauty and dramatic powers that, after twenty years in the movies—years of constant overexposure—she is more exciting than ever." Kerr herself felt it was one of her best films but added to an interviewer: "It was also one of the hardest; in a very long schedule I was in virtually every shot [and I] worked every single day of the sixteen week schedule."

By contrast, her later films of the 1960s, when cinema was coming under intense competitive pressure from television, were less compelling. In *Night of the Iguana* (1964), a film based on Tennessee Williams' play in which Kerr played "a frustrated spinster awakened to life by Richard Burton," remarks one critic, "The production publicity for the film so far exceeded what emerged on the screen that everything about the film, including Deborah's neurotic performance, was a disappointing anticlimax." The film, which also starred *Elizabeth Taylor, Ava Gardner, and Sue Lyon, was shot on location at Puerta Villarta in Mexico and directed by John Huston, who had to overcome great technical and logistical difficulties to finish the production at all. Kerr, who was paid a quarter of a million dollars for her role, wrote for *Esquire* magazine an ironic article about the difficulties the production faced, in which she deplored efforts by the press to whip up false tales of feuding and adultery among the cast.

In the late 1960s, film nudity came into fashion as the censorious Production Code which had kept a puritanical ban on film sex breathed its last. By then, Kerr was 47 but willingly shed her clothes for *The Gypsy Moths,* a parachuting film, and then for *The Arrangement* (1969), director Elia Kazan's adaptation of his own bestselling novel. *The Arrangement* proved to be her last movie role before a 15-year retirement. Playing the wife of a Los Angeles advertising executive (Kirk Douglas), Kerr, sounding as English as ever, was miscast. Deploring the result, Pauline Kael wrote one of the most stinging reviews Kerr had ever received:

> Deborah Kerr is wrong in every nuance as a conventional Los Angeles matron. She's even less at home than she was as the adulterous Kansas housewife in *The Gypsy Moths.* The understanding-unloved-wife role she plays here (and she's hideously made up) wears out an actress's welcome faster than anything else; it just about convinced me that I didn't ever want to see her again. Miss Kerr used to play against her overemotional voice; now she lets it use her for a constant neurotic nagging that is revolting.

In view of Kael's eminence and her earlier praise for Kerr's work in *The Innocents,* this review probably carried a particularly sharp sting. Kerr claimed to have enjoyed making the film, but this and other negative reviews must have convinced her that the time had come to quit. She took a "leave of absence," saying she felt "too young or too old" for any role offered.

Kerr showed in the following years that she still had plenty of resilience, however. Always a strong character, immune to the more chaotic side of Hollywood life, she returned to the stage in England and America and enjoyed a long series of acclaimed performances, including a nine-month London run with *The Day After the Fair* in 1972, along with occasional television work. She also appeared in Edward Albee's *Seascape* on Broadway and returned to sporadic filming in 1984. Her increasing leisure time was spent with her husband and friends in Switzerland and a new home in Marbella, Spain.

During her film career, Deborah Kerr was nominated for an Academy Award as Best Actress a record-breaking six times; no other actress had had the misfortune to be nominated so many times without winning. But nominations are cherished compliments from the Hollywood community, and she had been singled out for her performances in *Edward, My Son, The King and I, Heaven Knows, Mr. Allison, From Here to Eternity, Separate Tables,* and *The Sundowners.* In March 1994, as she was awarded an honorary Oscar at the *Dorothy Chandler Pavilion, the 72-year-old Kerr received a standing ovation. "Thank you, thank you," she said, obviously moved. "There should be some more words for thank you, shouldn't there." Poised patiently center stage, in frail health, Kerr once again lent her grace and dignity to the world of the movies, contributing the most touching moment of the evening.

SOURCES:

Agee, James. *Agee on Film: Reviews and Comments.* Boston, MA: 1958.

Braun, Eric. *Deborah Kerr.* NY: 1977.

Greene, Graham. *Mornings in the Dark.* Manchester, England: 1993.

Kael, Pauline. *Deeper Into Movies.* Boston, MA: 1973.

———. *I Lost it at the Movies.* Boston, MA: 1965.

Parish, J.R., and R.L. Bowers. *The MGM Stock Company: The Golden Era.* New Rochelle, NY: 1973.

SUGGESTED READING:

French, Brandon. *On the Verge of Revolt: Women in American Films of the Fifties,* 1958.

Patrick Allitt,
Professor of History, Emory University, Atlanta, Georgia

Kerr, Jean (1923—)

American playwright and author of the bestselling **Please Don't Eat the Daisies.** *Born Jean Collins on July 10, 1923, in Scranton, Pennsylvania; eldest of two daughters of Thomas J. Collins (a construction engineer) and Kitty (O'Neill) Collins; attended Marywood Seminary, Scranton, Pennsylvania; Marywood College, Scranton, Pennsylvania, B.A., 1943; Catholic University of America, Washington, D.C., M.F.A., 1945; married Walter Kerr (a drama professor and later drama critic of the* New York Herald Tribune*), on August 9, 1943; children: Christopher Kerr; (twins) Colin Kerr and John Kerr; Gilbert Kerr; Gregory Kerr;* **Katharine Kerr.**

Selected works: (dramatized by Kerr) The Song of Bernadette *by Franz Werfel (1944); (dramatized by Kerr)* Our Hearts Were Young and Gay *by* ***Cornelia Otis Skinner** *and* **Emily Kimbrough** *(1946); (play)* Jenny Kissed Me *(1948); (revue with Walter Kerr and J. Gorney)* Touch and Go *(1949); (play with E. Brooke)* King of Hearts *(1954, film version,* That Certain Feeling, *1956); (essays)* Please Don't Eat the Daisies *(1957, film version, 1960, television series, 1965–67); (musical comedy with W. Kerr and L. Anderson)* Goldilocks *(1958); (essays)* The Snake Has All the Lines *(1960); (play)* Mary, Mary *(1961, film version, 1963); (play)* Poor Richard *(1964); (essays)* Penny Candy *(1970); (play)* Finishing Touches *(1973); (essays)* How I Got to Be Perfect *(1978); (play)* Lunch Hour *(1980).*

Once described by Whitney Bolton as "a Lazzeroo beauty with a brain of surgical precision and a gleaming sense of humor," playwright and author Jean Kerr was born in 1923 in Scranton, Pennsylvania, and attended Marywood Seminary and Marywood College in her hometown. While working as the stage manager for a college production of *Romeo and Juliet,* she met Walter Kerr, who at the time was a drama professor at the Catholic University of America in Washington, D.C. (He later became the drama critic of the *New York Herald Tribune.*) The two married in 1943, shortly after Kerr graduated from college. She received her M.F.A. from Catholic University in 1945, the same year that the first of the six Kerr children arrived. Jean said she started to write because it would enable her to pay for someone to help with the children, and was also something she could do at home "among the cans of Dextri-Maltose." It was a chance compliment from her father years earlier, wrote Kerr, that centered her interest on playwriting. "'Look,' he exploded one evening over the dinner table, 'the only damn thing in this world you're good for is *talk*.' By talk I assumed he meant dialogue—and I was off."

Her career had a bumpy start, however. Her first play, an adaptation of Franz Werfel's novel about ***Bernadette of Lourdes**, *The Song of Bernadette* (1946), written in collaboration with her husband, ran for a mere three performances, while her first solo comedy, *Jenny Kissed Me* (1948), fared only slightly better with 20 performances. A collaboration with Walter, the revue *Touch and Go* (1949), was more favorably received, as was *King of Hearts* (1954), a collaboration with **Eleanor Brooke** that Walter directed. Though most critics felt that the play was weak, Brooks Atkinson credited the collaborators with having "a sense of humor and a gift of gab," and William Hawkins noted their "breezy disdain for pomposity."

Jean Kerr

Although Kerr considered her essays a mere diversion from her true calling as a playwright, her book *Please Don't Eat the Daisies* (1957), an autobiographical collection of comic sketches on domestic life (some of which had appeared in various magazines), was highly regarded by the critics and topped the nonfiction bestseller list for 20 weeks. "Whatever Mrs. Kerr is up to," wrote Dan Wickenden in the *New York Herald Tribune Book Review,* "she keeps startling laughter out of us, making the minor vicissitudes of life more bearable in the process." Whitney Bolton of the *New York Morning Telegraph* concurred, noting that "Mrs. Kerr is the kind of woman whose writing is diverting even when turned to so prosaic a chore as a memo to the grocer." The book spawned a movie in 1960, with *Doris Day, and a television series which ran for two seasons.

Of all Kerr's plays, *Mary, Mary* (1961) was her biggest hit and one of Broadway's longest-running productions (1,572 performances). Starring *Barbara Bel Geddes, for whom Kerr wrote the part, and Barry Nelson, the play examines the highs and lows of marriage, divorce, and reconciliation. (A film version was made with Debbie Reynolds in 1963.) Like all of her plays, it is a "realistic comedy," focusing on educated, affluent professionals coping with the trials of everyday life. Kerr's characters are brought to life with witty dialogue that Harold Clurman called "agile, shrewd, light and literate." Although popular with audiences, Kerr's later plays were often viewed as old-fashioned and predictable. Critics urged her to leave the 1950s and 1960s behind and tackle more substantial themes. In a *Newsweek* article on *Finishing Touches* (1973), Jack Kroll wondered if Kerr was "fighting her own intelligence." "What we see in [this] well-produced play is in fact a Lost Paradise," he wrote, "and it's the loss rather than the Paradise that would make a good theme for this writer who really knows the terrain." There were those, however, that delighted in Kerr's consistency. In reviewing her last play, *Lunch Hour* (1980), Frank Rich of *The New York Times* called it the kind of old-fashioned comedy one would expect from Kerr. "And why not?," he queried. "There's nothing wrong with the old forms when they're in loving hands. "

Subsequent collections of Kerr's essays included *The Snake Has All the Lines* (1960), *Penny Candy* (1970), and *How I Got to Be Perfect* (1978), a collection of some of the author's old work, as well a six new pieces. In her later essays—like her plays—Kerr harkened back to simpler times, ignoring more contemporary issues like Watergate, the women's movement, and the war in Vietnam. **Phyllis Theroux**, who reviewed *How I Got to Be Perfect* for *The New York Times Book Review,* wished for less nostalgia and more bite. "It is somewhat mystifying to me," she wrote, "that Mrs. Kerr is still making daisy chains when it's quite evident, from the random, dart-to-the-other-side-of-the-room allusions she allows herself now and then, that she really could play a different song if she wanted to. . . . Beneath her cleverness lies a sizable literary talent, equal to the heart of the writer and the matter that she never quite squares up to." On the other hand, the *Washington Post's* **Katherine Evans** referred to Kerr as an endangered species that should be protected. "It may be unreal," she wrote, "but it certainly is soothing to make your way through a contemporary book about kids and parents without reading one word about grass, speed, coke, the counter culture, abortion, live-in girlfriends or the sexual revolution."

The Kerrs raised their large family in the converted stables and coach house of a large estate in Larchmont, New York. Dubbed "the Kerr-Hilton," the property boasted a medieval courtyard and a 32-bell carillon that played the duet from *Carmen* every day at noon. Kerr claimed she did her writing in the family car, parked some distance from the hubbub of family activities. She was the recipient of numerous awards during her career, including honorary degrees from Northwestern and Fordham universities, the Campion Award (1971), and, with her husband, the Laetare Medal from the University of Notre Dame (1971).

SOURCES:
Candee, Marjorie Dent, ed. *Current Biography.* NY: H.W. Wilson, 1958.
Contemporary Authors. Volume 7. New Revision Series. Detroit, MI: Gale Research.
Mainiero, Lina. *American Women Writers.* NY: Frederick Ungar, 1980.
McHenry, Robert, ed. *Famous American Women.* NY: Dover, 1983.

Barbara Morgan,
Melrose, Massachusetts

Kerr, Sophie (1880–1965)

American novelist, short-story writer, and editor. Name variations: Mrs. Sophie Kerr Underwood. Born in Denton, Maryland, on August 23, 1880; died in 1965; daughter of Jonathan Williams Kerr and Amanda Catherine (Sisk) Kerr; Hood College, Frederick, Maryland, B.A., 1898; University of Vermont, M.A., 1901; married John D. Underwood, on September 6, 1904 (divorced 1908).

Selected works: Love at Large *(1916);* The Blue Envelope *(1917);* The Golden Block *(1918);* The See-Saw *(1919);* Painted Meadows *(1920);* One Thing Is Certain *(1922);* Confetti *(1927);* Mareea-Maria *(1929);* Tigers Is Only Cats *(1929);* In for a Penny *(1931);* Girl Into Woman *(1932);* Stay Out of My Life *(1933); (play, with A.S. Richardson)* Big-Hearted Herbert *(1934);* Miss J. Looks On *(1935);* There's Only One *(1936);* Fine to Look At *(1937);* Adventure with Women *(1938);* Curtain Going Up *(1940);* Michael's Girl *(1942).*

Writer Sophie Kerr began her career in the newspaper business, spending successive years as the women's editor of the Pittsburgh *Chronicle-Telegraph* and *Gazette Times.* She subsequently was managing editor of the *Woman's Home Companion* for several years. Kerr's writings—short stories, magazine serials, and novels—have been categorized as professionally executed, "but lightly skimming the surface of life." Wrote Gerald Hewes Carson: "She might tell us much about human nature as it peers out from beneath its humdrum shell of business. But she is ambitious only to amuse. One must grant that she can do that to perfection." Kerr also wrote one play, *Big-Hearted Herbert,* a collaborative effort with A.S. Richardson. Successfully produced in 1934, it was called "good clean fun, laid on with a steam-shovel" by one critic. Sophie Kerr, who was married and divorced from John D. Underwood, made her home in New York, but traveled widely. She entertained frequently and was known as a delightful host and a gourmet cook.

Kersee, Jackie Joyner (b. 1962).
See Joyner-Kersee, Jackie.

Keshko, Nathalia (1859–1941).
See Nathalia Keshko.

Kestner, Charlotte (1753–1828).
See Buff, Charlotte.

Kéthly, Anna (1889–1976)
Hungarian Social Democratic leader and a major force in the Hungarian revolution of 1956. Name variations: Anna Kethly. Born in Budapest, Hungary, in 1889; died in Blankernberg, Belgium, in September 1976.

Served as minister of state in the short-lived government of Imre Nagy that was overthrown by Soviet troops during Hungary's 1956 national uprising; lived the remainder of her life in exile.

Born in Budapest in 1889 into a family of nine children, Anna Kéthly would become a leader of Hungary's Social Democratic Party for more than half a century, opposing all forms of intolerance and totalitarianism including those practiced by the Horthy dictatorship, native and foreign fascists, and the Communist Party. She received her education in her home city, as well as in Vienna's Sacré-Coeur School, and then worked in an office. During this time, she became an active member of the Social Democratic Party, a powerful working-class organization founded in 1890. Drawn to journalism, Kéthly also became involved in feminist and trade-union activities. By 1920, she had become head of the Women's Secretariat of the Social Democratic Party and in 1922 was elected to Parliament, serving as the only woman in that body until 1937.

From 1919, when a short-lived Soviet Republic was suppressed, until 1945, Hungary was a half-fascist dictatorship headed by Admiral Nicolas Horthy. Kéthly was fearless in her criticism of this regime, both in speeches and in print. A gifted journalist, she was editor of the journal *The Female Worker* during the years 1926 through 1938. In the early years of her political career, she worked to improve conditions for, and to free if possible, the thousands of "Red" political prisoners the Horthy regime held in prisons and concentration camps.

Throughout the 1920s and 1930s, Kéthly worked to advance the causes of free trade unions and human rights. By the early 1940s, Hungary had fallen into the orbit of Nazi Germany. Although the Horthy regime tried to retain a measure of sovereignty, each passing year witnessed ever more repressive measures unleashed against both the political Left and the Jewish community. Kéthly courageously protested against the state's brutal anti-Semitism and suppression of dissent. In March 1944, German troops occupied the country and within months a radical faction of pro-Nazi Hungarian fascists, the Arrow Cross Party, seized power; among other things, they butchered political opponents and handed the country's Jewish population over to the Germans for annihilation. Kéthly went into hiding during this perilous time, keeping in contact with leaders of the banned Social Democratic movement.

Although hostilities would not end on Hungarian soil until April 1945, Kéthly returned to political life in February of that year. Immensely popular with the masses because of her fearless political record, she was returned to her old seat in Parliament and within months was elected deputy speaker of the Hungarian Legislative Assembly. In the first democratically elected Parliament in Hungary's history, the Communist Party was able to win 70 out of 409 seats, with Kéthly's Social Democrats doing almost as well, winning 17.4% of the national vote in the 1945 elections. At first, the Communists insisted that they supported democratic ideals and that they would work to rebuild the nation as part of a broad anti-fascist coalition. Soon, however, it became clear that Hungary's Communists, with the backing of the Soviet Union, were intent on creating a monopoly of power for themselves. Relying on "salami tactics" which took thin slices of human rights over an extended period of time, the Communists destroyed Hungary's hard-won freedom and created a one-party state over the course of three years.

The elimination of the Social Democrats, traditional champions of both social reform and political democracy, was an important part of the Communist totalitarian agenda. Kéthly strongly opposed her party's bowing to pressure from the Communists, and she spoke out in public against such moves by members of the party's left wing, individuals whose mixed motives ranged from the idealistic and realistic to the

*Anna
Kéthly*

mercenary. Kéthly's definition of democratic socialism was in harmony with that of the British Labor Party, members of which she met on several occasions when they visited Hungary. She also made trips to London in April 1946 and traveled to the International Socialist Conference in Zurich, Switzerland, in June 1947, in order to keep in touch with developments within the global democratic socialist community.

Despite encouragement from foreign colleagues and friends, Kéthly could do little to halt the inexorable growth of Communist power in Hungary. She was increasingly isolated and powerless to stop elections rigged by the Communists which guaranteed defeats for democratic parties like her own, and her protests carried little weight with a demoralized public. Her voice also had small impact on the growing number of her fellow Social Democrats who managed to convince themselves that a merger of their party with the Communists was not only inevitable but even desirable.

In 1948, Kéthly was forced out of the leadership of the Social Democratic Party. In June of that year, the pro-Communist elements within her party merged with the Communists to form a new and totally Communist-dominated entity, the Hungarian Workers' Party. Kéthly was among a small group of Social Democrats who risked their own safety by refusing to recognize this shotgun marriage. One of her colleagues, former Minister of Justice Istvan Ries, was arrested and eventually beaten to death in prison.

The late 1940s was a time of terror and fear in Eastern Europe, and Hungary was no exception. The danger extended beyond "reactionaries" and "bourgeois-nationalist elements" who found themselves subject to persecution and surveillance, or worse. Even Communists, many of them Jewish, were accused of being Zionists, Western spies, or Trotskyites, and a number of Communist leaders were purged and executed in 1949. Social Democrats, too, now found themselves targeted. Along with a number of other Social Democrats who had refused to accept the Communist dictatorship, Anna Kéthly was arrested in June 1950. Her sentence was harsh: life imprisonment at hard labor. This vindictive act of political justice soon became a cause célèbre around the world, and many prominent individuals and important organizations in democratic nations raised their voices in protest. In July 1953, the Socialist International strongly condemned Kéthly's sentence and imprisonment.

The death of Joseph Stalin in 1953 created a new international climate as well as a cautious atmosphere of thaw in the Soviet Union. In 1954, the British Labor Party brought the Kéthly case to the attention of the new post-Stalinist Soviet government. The international protests on her behalf very likely hastened her release from prison in November 1954. Although she would remain under house arrest for the next two years, Kéthly was now able to regain her health and reestablish contacts with the informal network of Social Democrats that still remained in Hungary.

By 1956, Communism in Eastern European had entered a profound stage of crisis. In his secret address to the 20th Congress of the Soviet Communist Party early that year, Nikita Khrushchev had revealed the immensity of Joseph Stalin's crimes. By implication, the philosophical and moral foundations of the Soviet system were now open to all forms of scrutiny and criticism. Long-festering grievances against Soviet occupation forces, economic failures, and the corrupt and brutal nature of Communist rule erupted later that year, first in Poland in the spring and then in Hungary during October 1956. Within a few days, protests by intellectuals in Budapest ignited the entire nation in a spontaneous revolutionary upheaval. A new government, headed by a reform-minded veteran Communist, Imre Nagy, demanded that Soviet forces leave Hungary and announced the creation of a democratic multiparty system. Amidst this euphoria, the banned Social Democratic Party reconstituted itself, choosing Kéthly as its leader on October 31, 1956.

On November 1, 1956, she went to Vienna to bring the latest news of the Hungarian revolution to her Western colleagues at a meeting of the bureau of the Socialist International. Kéthly's pleas for support of the Nagy government met with sympathy from Western Social Democrats, but their actual power was quite limited. The horrible reality of Hungary's geopolitical status as a pawn of the great powers became only too clear on November 4, when Soviet forces in Hungary went on the offensive, crushing the popular uprising in a sea of blood. Immediately, Kéthly flew to New York to make an appeal on behalf of democratic Hungary before a special session of the United Nations Security Council. While in the United States, she brought Hungary's case to the attention of world and wrote a detailed report on the causes and events of the Hungarian revolution. Kéthly's impassioned advocacy of her nation's right to exist free of Cold War pressures impressed many, but the concrete results of her testimony were meager. A special meeting of the United Nations in September 1957, and a special report on events in Hungary,

became part of the historical record, but the reality remained that, at least in the short term, Soviet power had prevailed. A fiery Hungarian patriot as well as a Social Democrat, Kéthly was incensed by those individuals who attributed the 1956 uprising to incendiary propaganda by Radio Free Europe and meddling by Western intelligence agencies. Her response to an American journalist at the time of the revolt was a curt one: "What kind of people do you think we are that we need some radio broadcasts to tell us to resist Russia?"

In June 1958, Imre Nagy and several of his associates in the 1956 revolution were executed, not in Hungary but in Rumania. Speaking as one of the most respected Hungarian leaders in exile, Kéthly condemned this deed in the most powerful terms possible. Refusing to be discouraged, she settled down as a political emigre in Brussels. In October 1957, the first anniversary of Hungary's failed bid for freedom, she founded and became president of the Hungarian Social Democratic Party in Emigration. That same year, the Council of Europe headquartered in Strasbourg awarded her a special prize of 10,000 German marks to commemorate her life's work of dedication to the causes of freedom and human rights. Kéthly announced that she would contribute the prize funds to support the activities of exiled Hungarian youth organizations.

Despite her advanced age, Kéthly was determined to make a new life for herself in exile. Falling back on her skills as a seasoned journalist, she became editor of an exile journal, *Voice of the People*, which was published in London between 1957 and 1963. In 1962, the Communist government of János Kádár, securely in power and able to point to significant economic reforms, "forgave" Kéthly for her past transgressions and rehabilitated her, but she chose not to return to Hungary even for a visit. Instead, she continued to criticize the Communist regime and the ideology it used to justify its deeds. In Brussels, she played a key role in founding the Imre Nagy Institute, a research center that monitored the situation in Hungary, and over the next decades she published several studies of the 1956 revolution and its aftermath.

Anna Kéthly died in Blankernberg, Belgium, in September 1976, almost two decades after the start of the Hungarian uprising. By the time of her death, her name was largely forgotten in the West, as were most details of the tragic revolt in which she had been a leader. In Hungary, however, her name remained well known, at least among aging Social Democrats who continued to hope for a time when the Communist system would collapse of its own contradictions. When this finally did take place in 1989 in Hungary and other Soviet satellite states, Kéthly's name and achievements once more served to inspire those individuals who believed that freedom and social justice were inseparable ideals. In November 1989, the Hungarian Social Democratic Party opened its first congress in over four decades by declaring null and void its forced absorption by the Communists in 1948. On the platform during this moving occasion was a blue screen bearing the portrait of the party's last leader before its demise, Anna Kéthly.

A year later, in November 1990, Kéthly's ashes were returned from Belgium and placed in Hungarian soil in Budapest's Rakoskresztur Cemetery near the grave of Imre Nagy and his martyred associates. With intellectual freedom restored, Hungarians could read about her life, and several books about Kéthly appeared in print during the 1990s. In October 1994, a centrist and non-Marxist faction within the Hungarian Social Democratic Party was announced, calling itself the Anna Kéthly Social Democratic Party. Party chair Sandor Bacskai named as his new party's goal the creation of an organization resembling that of the Social Democrats of Germany, whose 1959 Bad Godesberg program marked a final break with Marxist dogmatism and theories of class struggle. It is likely that Anna Kéthly would have been flattered to have a political party named after her. It is safe to speculate that she would have been even happier, however, in the knowledge that this took place in a Hungary where citizens enjoyed strong guarantees of political freedom and fundamental human rights.

SOURCES:

Aczél, Tamás, and Tibor Meray. *The Revolt of the Mind: A Case History of Intellectual Resistance behind the Iron Curtain.* NY: Frederick A. Praeger, 1959.

"Anna Kethly," in *Der sozialistische Kämpfer* [Vienna]. No. 9–10. September–October, 1976, p. 8.

"Anna Kethly—85. Geburtstag," in *Der sozialistische Kämpfer* [Vienna]. No. 11–12. November–December, 1974, p. 15.

"Anna Kethly: Former Hungarian Minister," in *The Times* [London]. September 10, 1976, p. 16.

"Anna Kethly Reburied in Hungary," in *BBC Summary of World Broadcasts.* November 6, 1990.

"Anna Kethly Sprach in New York," in *Wiener Zeitung* [Vienna]. November 10, 1956, p. 1.

Beichman, Arnold. "Hungary Not a Case in Point," in *Washington Times.* April 17, 1991, p. G4.

Benkö, Péter. "Szociáldemokrácia '56-Ban," in *Múltunk.* Vol. 35, no. 3, 1990, pp. 143–160.

Haraszti-Taylor, Eva, ed. *Britain and the Hungarian Social Democrats, 1945–1956: A Collection of Documents from the British Foreign Office.* Nottingham. UK: Astra Press, 1996.

———, ed. *The Hungarian Revolution of 1956: A Collection of Documents from the British Foreign Office.* Nottingham, UK: Astra Press, 1995.

Held, Joseph. *Dictionary of East European History Since 1945.* Westport, CT: Greenwood Press, 1994.

Kéthly, Anna. "Die Entspannung in Ungarn im Lichte der Tatsachen," in *Jahrbuch des Deutsch-Ungarischen Kulturkreis.* Mainz, 1965, pp. 68–77.

———. "Radio Free Europe," *The Times* [London]. March 6, 1972, p. 15.

———. *Szabadsagot Magyarorszagnak: Irasok, Beszadek, Tanusagtetel a Magyar Szabadsagert a Szamuzetesben.* Budapest: Kethly Anna Alapitvany, 1994.

———. *Valogatott Irasai es Beszedei.* Edited by Erzsebet Strassenreiter. Budapest: Keszult az Elektroplaszt Kisszovetkezet Nyomdajaban, 1990.

———. *Why? The History of a Mass Revolt in Search for Freedom.* Vienna: International Union of Socialist Youth, n. d.

Kovrig, Bennett. *Communism in Hungary: From Kun to Kadar.* Stanford, CA: Hoover Institution Press, Stanford University, 1979.

Ravasz, Károly, ed. "Szociáldemokrata Kibontakozási Terv: 1956–1957," in *História.* Vol. 11, no. 1–2, 1989, pp. 61–63.

John Haag,
Associate Professor of History,
University of Georgia, Athens, Georgia

Kettle, Alice (fl. 1324).

See Kyteler, Alice.

Keturah (fl. 3rd, 2nd, or 1st c. BCE)

Biblical woman. Flourished in the 3rd, 2nd, or 1st century BCE; married Abraham also known as Abrahim ("father of a multitude"), although his original name appears to have been Abram ("exalted father"); children—six sons: Zimran, Jokshan, Medan, Midian, Ishbak, and Shuah.

Keturah's dates cannot be secured since the historical era of Abraham cannot be established with any certainty (indeed suggestions range widely, from the 3rd to the 1st millennium BCE). Keturah married Abraham, the first great patriarch of the nation of Israel, after his wife *Sarah's death. She has also been called Abraham's concubine. Keturah had six sons—Zimran, Jokshan, Medan, Midian, Ishbak, and Shuah—all of whom were the founders of six Arabian Tribes in Palestine.

Key, Ellen (1849–1926)

Swedish teacher, writer, lecturer, and feminist. Born Ellen Carolina Sophia Key on December 11, 1849, at Sundsholm, her father's estate in Småland, southern Sweden; died on April 25, 1926, at Strand, her country home on Lake Vättern in the province of Ostergotland; daughter of Emil Key (a gentleman farmer and politician) and Sophie (Posse) Key (daughter of an old noble family); tutored at home; attended a Stockholm boarding school for one year; completed three years of study at Jenny Rossander's Teaching Course for Ladies in Stockholm, 1872; never married; no children.

Functioned as secretary and housekeeper to her father, an Agrarian party member of the Swedish Parliament; employed as teacher at Anna Whitlock's private school for girls and at the People's Institute; retired from teaching to devote herself to writing and lecturing (1903); traveled and lectured abroad, particularly in Germany; was a pacifist during World War I.

Selected publications: (in English translation) Love and Ethics, Love and Marriage, The Woman Movement, The Century of the Child, The Renaissance of Motherhood, War, Peace and the Future, *and* *Rahel Varnhagen; *(in Swedish) other books, numerous essays of literary criticism and social comment, voluminous correspondence.*

Ellen Key was always a figure of controversy. In her mature years, she called herself an individualist, a monist (she considered humankind and nature, body and spirit to be one), and an evolutionist. Her enemies called her a corrupter of youth, "the High Priestess of Vice." Feminists of various persuasions and at various times proudly claimed and bitterly disclaimed her. One newspaper article called her "the witch of Strand." Another, more friendly, paper labeled her "liberal Europe's great aunt." Toward the end of Key's long life, many in Sweden honored her as the heir of Saint **Bridget of Sweden** (1303–1373), "our spiritual mother."

The Sweden of 1849 into which Ellen Carolina Sophia Key was born was a conservative society with a population of some three and a half million. The country was a constitutional monarchy with limited suffrage and significant power for the king and nobility. The riksdag or Parliament was made up of a single house with representation based on the feudal Four Estates. Communication throughout the sprawling northern land was undeveloped. No railroads had yet been built nor had plans for their future financing and construction been determined. Ninety per cent of the people were country dwellers.

Fathers exercised strict control over their families and guardianship of all unmarried daughters. A daughter might not marry without her father's consent. Once married, she was under the legal guardianship of her husband. In families of some means, boys and girls were edu-

cated at home as young children. In their early teens, boys were sent away to academies to prepare them for university. Girls in their mid-teens were sent to boarding school for a year to prepare for confirmation in the state Lutheran Church, then returned home to domestic duties. Key, who detested sewing, would later write about the bright daughter doomed to stay at home stitching fine shirts for her stupid brother away at the academy.

> God, let me be one of the radiators of the sun . . . a voice in the time's song about honor, peace and good will.
>
> —Ellen Key

Key's upbringing was not in fact illiberal for her time and place. Her father Emil Key was descended from a distinguished military officer and immigrant to Sweden from Scotland during the Thirty Years' War. The clan name had probably been MacKay. Emil's given name, and that of his father before him, honored Emile, the protagonist of Jean-Jacques Rousseau's radical book on education. Emil was a graduate of the University of Lund and something of a poet. During his early 20s, he was the lover of Sweden's most glamorous young actress. Upon her untimely death, he left Stockholm and purchased Sundsholm, a country estate in Småland, where he meant to carry on agricultural experimentation.

In the reforms of 1865, when the riksdag became bicameral, he entered politics as a representative of the new Agrarian party and was, until 1883, absorbed in its activities. Public affairs and the books in his well-stocked library at Sundsholm were his passions. He did not hunt and fish like his country neighbors and, in a society where alcohol was a major problem, he did not drink or play cards. This abstemiousness and devotion to what he considered to be the public good would be repeated in the life of his daughter.

Ellen Key's mother was **Sophie Posse Key**, the daughter of an old Swedish noble family. Sophie's parents were not happy at first about their daughter's choice of a husband. Emil was a commoner and, at the time of his proposal, not long or solidly settled in the Småland countryside. According to family tradition, however, Count Posse at length announced that *he* had married for love and his daughter should do the same.

Ellen Key was, so she would later write, "the first child of young and happy parents." Yet the Sundsholm world was a sober one. For people of their station, the Keys were determinedly democratic. The six children were severely punished for discourtesy to servants. They served themselves at breakfast and supper with milk and coarse bread and ate standing. At the mid-day family dinner table, little ones did not speak.

The young Keys lived in an attic area of the manor house removed from their parents' rooms. There they were left free to busy themselves and to settle their own childish disputes and problems. Ellen, as the first and favorite child, became "the little mother" and apparently acted as intermediary between parents and children. The brothers and sisters were instructed at home by their mother and by hired tutors. Their studies included French, German and—an innovation—English. There was no forgiveness for unlearned lessons.

In this strict regimen, there were compensations for the shy and introspective oldest daughter, who was early given a gable room of her own. She always remembered her delight in the blue walls and window looking out upon trees

Ellen Key

and meadow. Key loved the out-of-doors, and rode and swam. She also loved her father's library and was well supplied with books, beginning in her very early years with Scandinavian myths and epics. She would later say that she was more influenced by nature and books than by people. The intense soul-searching of her childhood and adolescence she confided not to people but to her own "Thought Book," a kind of diary which she kept until her mid-20s.

At 14, Key was sent, as was customary, to Stockholm for a year's limited academic work and preparation for confirmation. Her parents were not frequent churchgoers. Rationalists in religion, they observed the outer forms of the state church. Their young daughter was deeply interested in religion but found the confirmation lessons cold and sterile. She would be only briefly an orthodox Lutheran.

Stockholm had other attractions for Key, however. When her father was elected to the Second House of the riksdag, she privately vowed to devote herself, too, to furthering the freedom which this governmental reform seemed to promise the Swedish people. She, her mother, and sisters accompanied her father to the city each winter when the riksdag was in session.

In 1869, Key enrolled in **Jenny Rossander**'s Teaching Course for Young Ladies which offered a three-year liberal arts course. For the first time, she encountered the natural sciences which had never been a part of her instruction at home. She studied Darwin and other scientific thinkers. Though at first repelled by evolution, she soon began to feel that she could not ignore the facts it presented.

At a "reading salon," Key met the editor of *Tidskrift for Hemmet* (The Home Journal), a magazine which advocated the liberation of women. In the early 1870s, she began contributing to the journal, writing book reviews, translations, biographical sketches of English writers (she was particularly attracted to the English woman novelist George Eliot [***Mary Anne Evans**]), and essays about her own developing feminist thought. Key was also inspired at this time by the Norwegian poet and dramatist Bjørnstjerne Bjørnson, who lectured in Stockholm. With her father, she took long trips to Europe, especially to Italy, where she discovered great classical art.

In 1876, Sophie Key was in such poor health that she could no longer accompany her husband to Stockholm. Ellen Key became her father's housekeeper and secretary. She prepared the articles which Emil submitted to *Dagen's Nyheter* (the Daily News) and began to write some of those articles herself, with special concern for the legal status of married women.

But Emil Key's career and the family prosperity were soon to end. Times were difficult for Swedish agriculture, and the devoted riksdag member had paid too little attention to his own estate. In 1888, the family was obliged to give up Sundsholm. Even the treasured books were sold. Compelled to find a way to support herself and help her family, Key settled in Stockholm and, having already done volunteer teaching, became an instructor in her friend **Anna Whitlock**'s private school for girls. Soon, she also became a lecturer on Swedish civilization at the newly formed People's Institute, where she would spend 20 dedicated years speaking to audiences of working-class men and women. Shy in ordinary social life, Key was a highly effective public speaker. She began to lecture throughout Sweden and ventured abroad, particularly to Germany where she attracted enthusiastic audiences.

In her new and independent life, Key was important to "young Sweden," the new liberal intellectual and literary life of Stockholm. She did not join the feminist *Fredrika Bremer Society, but she greatly admired Bremer, author of *Hertha*, Sweden's first feminist novel. Key formed close friendships with the novelist ❧▶ **Victoria Benedictsson**, "the wild bird of Skane," and with *Sophia Kovalevskaya, the Russian novelist and mathematician who, denied higher education in her own country because of her sex, fought her way to an academic degree in Germany and received an appointment at Stockholm University. As a liberal, Key defended the right of free speech for the controversial dramatist August Strindberg and for less gifted rebels. She applauded Nora, the heroine (based on *Laura Kieler) of Henrik Ibsen's *A Doll's House,* whose abandonment of husband and children signaled a search for personhood.

Key's views, expressed in a steady flow of articles, literary criticism, and widely translated books, opposed the views of the majority of Swedes. Citizen of a monarchy, she disapproved of royalism and proclaimed herself a lifelong democrat. A politician's daughter, she came to feel that politics corrupted. In a society which was 95% Lutheran, she retained her love of Jesus but rejected Christianity. Eve's fault was not tasting forbidden fruit but betraying her sex, Key declared. Christianity, with its doctrine of original sin, was a religion without hope or backbone. Influenced by the German philosopher Friedrich

Nietzsche who foresaw a superman, Key preached a religion of faith in life. A stronger and finer race of human beings could be created, she wrote, through the care of loving parents and a new and wiser educational system.

Although a believer in Scandinavianism, Key supported Norway's break from Sweden in 1905. She initially supported women's suffrage. There was no reason why a woman's hands should be more soiled by a ballot paper than by a cooking recipe, she said. Yet she came to regard suffrage as too narrow a goal, diverting attention from the larger task of developing woman's true individuality.

Despite wide-ranging interests, Key devoted most of her attention to three major issues—the need for a new and free relationship between men and women, the importance of mother-

---

❧▶ **Benedictsson, Victoria** (1850–1888)

Swedish novelist. Name variations: Ernst Ahlgren. Born Victoria Maria Bruzelius in Skåne, Sweden, on March 6, 1850; died in Copenhagen, Denmark, on July 22, 1888; daughter of Helena Sophia Finérus and Thure Bruzelius; married Christian Benedictsson (a postmaster), in 1871; children: two.

Selected works: Från Skåne *(From Skåne, 1884);* Pengar *(Money, 1885);* Fru Marianne *(Mrs. Marianne, 1887);* Stora Boken *(The Big Book, 1978).*

Victoria Bruzelius moved from her childhood home, where her parents' relationship was volatile and her father refused her permission to study art in Stockholm, to an unhappy marriage with Christian Benedictsson, a widower 30 years her senior. During their marriage, Victoria added two children to her husband's five with his previous wife. Though their union was businesslike, providing little emotional warmth, it left room for the artistic existence Benedictsson had longed for as a teenager. Under the pseudonym Ernst Ahlgren, she wrote gothic thrillers for the daily newspaper and began writing novels in the 1880s. Benedictsson kept a personal journal, published in 1978 as *Stora Boken,* which documents her friendship and romantic liaison with Danish critic Georg Brandes. In 1888, following Brandes' rejection of her and his negative review of her work *Fru Marianne,* she checked into a cheap Copenhagen hotel, where she committed suicide by slitting her throat. *Stora Boken* was republished in the 1980s in its multivolume entirety.

SOURCES:
Buck, Claire, ed. *The Bloomsbury Guide to Women's Literature.* NY: Prentice Hall, 1992.
Steinberg, S.H., ed. *Cassell's Encyclopedia of World Literature.* London: Cassell, 1973.
Zuck, Virpi, ed. *Dictionary of Scandinavian Literature.* Westport, CT: Greenwood Press, 1990.

Crista Martin,
freelance writer, Boston, Massachusetts

---

hood, and the demand for a new educational system. In *The Woman Movement,* Key wrote: "Now marriage has become only an affair of custom, a common death or comatose condition, because neither party needs trouble himself to keep the love of the other." Key looked on sexual life as essential to human happiness. Sexual love should be given freely without legal or other motivations. Individual needs change with time. The love which is compelling at 20 may not be a love which will satisfy at 30 or 40. Divorce should be available, since individual fulfillment is the prime consideration. Key also fought against labeling the children of unmarried mothers "illegitimate."

Paradoxically, so it seemed to some feminists, Key, the advocate of "free love," regarded motherhood as woman's truest vocation. A woman should have the right to reject motherhood, but most women would and should choose family life. A mother should have state financial support. At least during the first important years of her child's life, the mother should not seek work outside her home since "No woman has ever been at the same time all that a wife can be to a husband, a mother to her children, a housewife to her house, a working woman in her work."

Yet "motherliness is not a spontaneous natural instinct, but the product of thousands of years not merely of *child-bearing,* but also of *child-rearing* and it must be strengthened in each new generation by the personal care which mothers bestow upon their children." To further this end, the year's military service which the state required of 20-year-old men should be balanced by a year's training for young women in economics, household matters, hygiene, child care, and eugenics (then a fairly new and not yet discredited school of thought).

Key called the Swedish educational system of her time "soul murder," and thought that its sterile religious instruction should be abolished. Kindergartens should be abolished, too; young children should be taught at home by their mothers. Later, in school, they should be placed in small groups so that the teacher could know the personality and individual needs of each pupil. Studies should not be routine but made attractive to children.

No child who was old enough to remember should ever be struck. Corporal punishment was illogical, teaching violence and creating resentment, deception, and a gulf between children and adults. Key wrote feelingly of the little boy who was spanked—only once, she assured her readers—and that evening prayed that God would tear out his mother's arms so that she could not beat him again.

Like John Ruskin, the English writer whom she admired, Key believed that competition in school should be eliminated. In *The Century of the Child,* she insisted that "Every contest decided by examination and prizes is ultimately an immoral method of training."

Not surprisingly, Key paid a high price for her views. Rumors about her personal life spread. In a book which one critic declared should never have been written, Strindberg caricatured her savagely. Others insisted that she had borne an illegitimate child. In fact, she had no child and never married. In 1876, she met and fell deeply in love with Urban von Feilitzen, a Swedish literary critic, whose ideas attracted her. The 11-year affair was in considerable part conducted through letters on literature and social issues. Feilitzen was married with children and in the end was unwilling to leave his family.

From her girlhood, Key had rejected casual relationships and social life. She was unwilling even to take part as a lady bountiful in charitable events. In her *Thought Book,* she called herself "ugly." Photographs of Key suggest that to have been an overly harsh judgment, but she was not a beautiful woman and always wore austere clothing and a simple hair style.

After 30 years in Stockholm, Key left her teacher's life to devote herself full time to writing and lecturing. She determined to leave Sweden. Like Ibsen, who exiled himself from Norway for 25 years because of the hostility of his compatriots, Key may have been in search of a more congenial world. Abroad, she lectured widely and was received cordially by such noted writers as the German Gerhard Hauptmann and the Belgian Maurice Maeterlinck. But Sweden haunted her, and after several years she returned.

In 1910, the state granted her property in a government park reservation on the shores of Lake Våttern. It was a beautiful site near the old Alvastra Cloister, founded long ago by Sweden's Saint Bridget. There, Key built Strand, her long-dreamed-of home, which looked down from its slope through oak and beech and elm to the waters of the great lake.

With its red tile floors and snowy white walls, its frieze of the same red and green wreaths which had decorated her books and the reversed motto from Goethe "Remember to live" placed above the entrance door, Strand offered an hospitable welcome to friends and refugees in need of shelter. Among the guests were some of the Tolfterna or "dozens" which Key had first organized in Stockholm to bring women of different social classes together. During World War I, Key, a pacifist, used her home as a clearing house for correspondence from both sides in the long conflict. She died at Strand in 1926, willing the house to the use of working women who might need a temporary retreat for creative work. Years later, when conditions in Sweden changed, Strand became a haven for impoverished university women.

Ellen Key had never been an organization woman. She had joined no major feminist groups, held no high office, and won a problematic fame. Though, for a time, some of her contemporaries ranked her with Strindberg, Ibsen, and Bjørnson, she was never offered membership in the Academy of Letters, Sweden's literary "establishment." Fame and fortune would not seem to have been her goals. She struggled rather to be a prophet of "the religion of love," to become, in the words of her own youthful prayer, "one of the radiators of the sun . . . a voice in the time's song about honor, peace and good will."

SOURCES:

De Angelis, Ronald William. *Ellen Key: A Biography of the Swedish Reformer*. Ph.D. dissertation, University of Connecticut, 1978.

Key, Ellen. *The Century of the Child*. NY: Putnam, 1909.

———. *Love and Ethics*. NY: B.W. Huebsch, 1912.

———. *The Renaissance of Motherhood*. NY: Putnam, 1914.

———. *The Woman Movement*. NY: Putnam, 1912.

Meyer, Donald B. *Sex and Power: The Rise of Women in America, Russia, Sweden and Italy*. Middletown, CT: Wesleyan University Press, 1987, 1989.

Nystrom-Hamilton, Louise. *Ellen Key: Her Life and Work*. NY: Putnam, 1913.

SUGGESTED READING:

Anthony, Katharine Susan. *Feminism in Germany and Scandinavia*. NY: Henry Holt, 1915.

Key, Ellen. *Rahel Varnhagen, a Portrait*.

COLLECTIONS:

Ellen Key Collection at the Royal Library in Stockholm includes books, newspapers, letters, journals, etc. (well catalogued, extensive and accessible).

Margery Evernden,
Professor Emerita, English Department,
University of Pittsburgh, and freelance writer

Keynes, Lady (c. 1892–1981).

See Lopokova, Lydia.

Keys, Martha Elizabeth (1930—)

American politician who served in the U.S. Congress (1974–78). Born Martha Elizabeth Ludwig in Hutchinson, Kansas, on August 10, 1930; daughter of S.T. Ludwig and Clara (Krey) Ludwig; attended Olivet College, Kankakee, Illinois, 1946–48; University of Missouri at Kansas City, Mus.B., 1952; married second husband Andrew Jacobs, on January 3, 1976; children: (previous marriage) Carol, Bryan, Dana, Scott.

Martha Keys was born in 1930 in Hutchinson, Kansas, and raised and educated in Kansas City, Missouri. A 1951 graduate of the University of Missouri, Keys gained her early political experience as the Kansas state coordinator of the George McGovern presidential campaign in 1973. Future senator Gary Hart, her brother-in-law at the time, was McGovern's national campaign manager. In 1974, when Second District Republican William Roy resigned from the House of Representatives to challenge Senator Robert Dole, Keys ran for and won the vacated congressional seat. As a freshman member of Congress, she was appointed to the prestigious Ways and Means Committee but spent the majority of her time drumming up support in her

Martha Elizabeth Keys

district for a difficult reelection bid. Narrowly defeating her Republican opponent, she served a second term but lost her seat in 1978 to Jim Jeffries. From 1979 to 1980, Keys was a special adviser to the secretary of health, education and welfare, and then served as assistant secretary of education from 1980 to 1981. She stayed on in Washington as a political consultant and headed the Center for the New Democracy from 1985 to 1986.

SOURCES:

Office of the Historian. *Women in Congress, 1917–1990.* Commission on the Bicentenary of the U.S. House of Representatives, 1991.

Keys, Mary (1545–1578).

See Grey, Lady Jane for sidebar on Mary Grey.

Keziah (fl. 2000 BCE)

*Biblical woman. Daughter of Job; sister of *Keren-happuch and *Jemima.*

The second daughter of Job, Keziah was born after his restoration to health and prosperity.

Khadijah (c. 555–619)

Muhammad's first wife and the first convert to Islam, who supported her husband when his revelations began in 610. Name variations: Kadijah or Khadija. Born Khadijah bint Khuwaylid around 555 CE; died in 619 CE; third cousin to Muhammad once removed; married and widowed twice by the age of 40; hired Muhammad to manage one of her caravans to Syria in 595, and proposed marriage to the future Prophet shortly thereafter; children: (six with Muhammad) two sons, al-Qasim and Abdallah, who both died as infants; four daughters, Zaynab, Ruqaiyah, Umm Kulthum, and Fatimah.

Khadijah bint Khuwaylid, wealthy merchant of the important Quraysh (or Kuraysh) clan in Arabia, played a critical role in the origin and development of Islam. Her marriage to Muhammad in 595 provided the Prophet with the material resources to pursue his reflective inclinations, and her reassurance and emotional support of her husband in the early stages of his revelations gave him the strength and confidence to proclaim his religion's tenets. Khadijah's prominent role as Muhammad's beloved wife and supporter suggests that pre-Islamic Arabian women were capable of significantly influencing affairs and events—a point of view that surprises some in the modern West, who hold preconceived notions about the subordinate position of females in Middle Eastern societies and assume that it was always so.

Despite the important role Khadijah played in the Prophet Muhammad's career, very little is known about her early life. She was born around 555 during a period when matrilineal and polyandrous marriage practices existed side by side with patrilineal and polygamous forms. The presence of varied marital practices in pre-Islamic Arabia is significant in a consideration of Khadijah's life, because it suggests a social climate that allowed for her later career as a wealthy businesswoman. Matrilineal marriage customs allowed some women to remain with their own families, and thus a measure of independence from their husbands was possible in the pre-Islamic period. Khadijah's family, the Asad clan of the Quraysh tribe, was prominent in Mecca. She was married and widowed twice before 595, and had children with each of her husbands.

By the time Khadijah met Muhammad, she was approximately 40 years old and he was a young caravan worker aged 25. His background was one of disadvantage, as he had been orphaned at age six when his widowed mother **Amina** died. According to early Arabic writers in the century or so after Muhammad, Khadijah was impressed with the future Prophet's personality and honest business practices, and she commissioned him to conduct a caravan to Syria. Muhammad's first biographer, Ibn Ishaq, gave an 8th-century account of this trip's impact on Khadijah's decision to propose marriage to the future Prophet. According to Ibn Ishaq, a Christian monk recognized Muhammad as the future Prophet of the Arabians, and one of Muhammad's fellow workers on the caravan reported to Khadijah that he had observed angels protecting Muhammad from the hot sun. Khadijah conferred with one of her Christian cousins, Waraqa ibn Naufal, who enthusiastically affirmed the likelihood that Muhammad was indeed the Prophet of the Arabian people. When Khadijah proposed marriage, Muhammad accepted.

As the husband of the wealthy Khadijah, Muhammad enjoyed greater economic opportunity and security than he had experienced as an orphan. He spent considerable time in solitude, reflecting on religious matters. Arabic sources indicate that their marriage was a happy one. One *surah* (verse) in the Qur'an (or Koran, meaning the recitation) refers to Muhammad's deliverance from his impoverished state to the life of relative ease as Khadijah's husband:

Did He not find thee
An orphan and give thee
Shelter (and care)? . . .

And He found thee
In need, and made
Thee independent.

(Surah 93, 6 and 8)

Despite her age at the time of her marriage to Muhammad in 595 CE, Khadijah had two sons, al-Qasim and Abdallah, and four daughters, **Zaynab, Ruqaiyah, Umm Kulthum**, and *****Fatimah**. The sons died while they were still infants, and only one of the daughters, Fatimah, outlived her father.

When Muhammad's revelations commenced around 610, Khadijah provided invaluable assistance to her husband. The Prophet was terrified when the messages from the angel Gabriel began, and he feared for his sanity—indeed, three *surahs* of the *Qur'an* specifically deny that Muhammad was "mad or possessed" (7:184; 68:2; and 81:22). Yet it was Khadijah who provided the emotional and physical affirmation of her husband's startling new path: she wrapped him in her blanket in his moments of terror and doubt, and expressed her unwavering belief in the veracity of his revelations. Thus, Khadijah was the first convert to the new religion of Islam.

Khadijah enlisted the further support of her elderly relative Waraqa, who assured Muhammad that he was sane and a great Prophet given by God to the Quraysh people of Arabia. Many of the richer members of the Quraysh were extremely alarmed at the social and economic implications of his message, and resisted his attempts to enlist converts to Islam. By 616, when the stern monotheistic nature of Islam had been firmly proclaimed by Muhammad, violent clashes between the various clans of the Quraysh erupted. The Prophet and his family and supporters found it necessary to constantly guard against physical confrontations with Meccans who denied both the idea that God is singular, and the egalitarian message of socially responsible concern for the poor and weak that Muhammad insisted was God's command. While Khadijah shared her husband's difficulties in this turbulent period, the powerful Hashim clan leader, Abu Talib, Muhammad's uncle, protected the Prophet from his Meccan enemies.

In 619, the powerful Abu Talib became ill and died, and Muhammad lost his only political buffer against the angry Quraysh of Mecca. An even deeper source of sorrow to the Prophet was the death of his beloved wife Khadijah, aged 64

or 65, earlier in 619. Muhammad's early biographers designated this year the Prophet's "Year of Sadness." Perhaps she died as a result of the hardships and food deprivation she shared with her husband from 612 on. It is noteworthy that while Khadijah was his wife, Muhammad refrained from marrying other women, although he would go on to wed ten, perhaps twelve, women, and took a concubine as well. But only Khadijah had his children, and such was his affection for this remarkable woman that, years later, when his favorite wife *****A'ishah bint Abi Bakr** jealously referred to Muhammad's first wife as a "toothless old woman," the Prophet rebuked her. According to one of his biographers, Muhammad denied A'ishah's assertion that God had given her to the Prophet as an improved replacement for Khadijah: "He has not given me a better one. She believed in me when no one else did. She considered me to be truthful when the people called me a liar. She helped me with her fortune when the people had left me nothing. Allah gave me children from her while he gave me none from other women." Khadijah thus influenced the Prophet more deeply than any other woman, and stands apart from his later wives in this regard just as she remained his only wife during the 25 years she shared with her husband.

A perfect woman, the mother of those
that believe.

—From 'Abdullah Yūsuf 'Alī's commentary to the Holy Qur'an.

SOURCES AND SUGGESTED READING:
'Abdullah Yūsuf 'Alī. *The Meaning of The Holy Qur'an.* New edition with revised translation and commentary. Brentwood, MD: Amana Corporation, 1412 A.H./1992.
Ahmed, Leila. *Women and Gender in Islam.* New Haven, CT: Yale University Press, 1992.
Armstrong, Karen. *Muhammad: A Biography of the Prophet.* San Francisco: Harper Books, 1992.
Keddie, Nikki R., and Beth Baron. *Women in Middle Eastern History: Shifting Boundaries in Sex and Gender.* New Haven, CT: Yale University Press, 1991.
Muir, William. *The Life of Muhammad from Original Sources.* Edinburgh: J. Grant, 1923.
Walther, Wiebke. *Women in Islam From Medieval to Modern Times.* Princeton: Markus Wiener, 1993.

Cathy Jorgensen Itnyre,
Professor of History at Copper Mountain College, Joshua Tree, California

Khaizaran (d. 790)

Arabian queen. Name variations: Khaizuran; al-Khaizurān. Birth date unknown; died in 790 CE; married al-Mahdi, 3rd Abbasid caliph of Baghdad (pre-

sent-day Iraq); children: Musa al-Hadi (4th Abbasid caliph, r. 785–786); Harun al-Rashid also seen as Haroun al-Raschid (763/5–809, 5th Abbasid caliph); and a daughter (name unknown); (stepdaughters) *Ulayya and Abassa.

During the 8th century, Baghdad was the center of a world market: ships arrived with porcelain, silks, spices, mirrors, linen, dyes, and jewels, as well as slaves taken in war. Its wharves were busy with the selling of uprooted boys and girls; the most beautiful of the Greeks, Turks, Scandinavians, Russians, Africans, and fair, doe-eyed beauties from the Caucasus were saved for the caliph or Baghdad's nobility. **Alev Croutier** in *Harem* reprints a customs declaration of 1790: "Circassian girl, about eight years old; Abyssinian virgin, about ten; five-year-old Circassian virgin, Circassian woman, fifteen or sixteen years old; about twelve-year-old Georgian maiden, medium tall negro slave, seventeen-year-old Negro slave. Costs about 1000–2000 kurush." At that time, a horse was worth around 5,000 kurush.

Khaizaran was a slave girl from Yemen. One story maintains that she was first noticed by the powerful Abu Jafar (known as al-Mansur), 2nd Abbasid caliph of Baghdad, who brought her to the imperial household of his son, al-Mahdi. Another suggests that al-Mahdi, while crushing a revolt in Tabaristan in Persia, had absconded with two Persian "maidens" as trophies of conquest from the house of the defeated governor. One of them gave birth to his daughter *Abassa; the other was Khaizaran who, as a slave, bore Mahdi two boys at Raiy near Teheran—Musa al-Hadi and Harun al-Rashid—as well as another daughter, name unknown.

In 775, when al-Mahdi became caliph on the death of al-Mansur, he freed and married Khaizaran. Women of 8th- and 9th-century Arabia enjoyed considerable liberty. It was not until the end of the 10th century that the system of seclusion became commonplace. Those of the early Abbasid period could achieve great distinction, and exercised influence in state affairs. Arab maidens not only composed poetry, but competed with men in literary and musical undertakings; they also went to war and commanded troops.

Since it was also not uncommon for slaves in Baghdad to become extremely powerful, Khaizaran exerted considerable influence over her husband. She convinced al-Mahdi to place her favorite son Harun first in line of succession over his elder brother Musa. When Musa, who

was fighting a campaign in Persia, balked at the idea, his father set out with an army from Baghdad to teach him some paternal respect. But on the way, Mahdi was mistakenly given poisoned fruit and died. Surprisingly, Harun, who had been accompanying his father and was now leader of the army, did not take advantage of his position. Instead, he diplomatically sent a message to Musa to come at once to Baghdad and claim the caliphate.

Under Musa al-Hadi, Khaizaran was confined to quarters and her influence was greatly diminished—until Musa foolishly set aside Harun's generosity, named a son next in line for succession, and dropped his brother to third place. Furious, Khaizaran began to make plans with her ladies-in-waiting. When Musa fell ill during the second year of his reign (786), he was smothered to death by his concubines. Other versions say Khaizaran poisoned him. The 23-year-old Harun was now caliph. Four years later, Khaizaran died.

SOURCES:
Croutier, Alev Lytle. *Harem: The World Behind the Veil.* NY: Abbeville Press, 1989.

Khamerernebty I (fl. c. 2600 BCE)

Egyptian queen. Name variations: Khamerernebti. Flourished around 2600 BCE; daughter of Khufu or Cheops (Greek), king of the 4th dynasty; sister of Merisankh III; married King Khafre also known as Chephren (Greek), who was probably her half-brother; children: number unknown, including son Menkaure (Menkure or Mykerinos [Greek], who built the Third Pyramid at Giza) and daughter Khamerernebty II.

Egyptian queen Khamerernebty I was the daughter of the builder of the great pyramid at Giza, King Khufu of the Fourth Dynasty. As he had more than one principal queen during his lifetime, it is not certain which gave birth to Khamerernebty who was destined to carry on the royal line. Khamerernebty was married, not to the immediate successor of her father, but to his son King Khafre (builder of the Second Pyramid of Giza). Khamerernebty and Khafre had a son Menkaure who would also reign and build the Third Pyramid at Giza.

Kings' mothers were powerful and influential women in ancient Egypt. During her life, Khamerernebty I fulfilled priestly duties in the cults of major deities, such as the god of wisdom Thoth, and bore queenly titles, such as "Mother of the King of Upper and Lower Egypt, Daughter of the King of Upper and Lower Egypt, Greatly Loved Wife of the King" and "Great One of the *Hetes* scepter," the significance of which is not clear. Although queens of Khufu were provided with smaller pyramids at the base of their husband's, the wives and families of Khafre had their tombs cut into the sides of the quarry on the Giza plateau that supplied most of the building stone for the pyramids. Khamerernebty's tomb was discovered in 1907–08 by excavators working for the Count de Galarza, but indications are that it was not used by her but taken over by her eldest daughter, *Khamerernebty II. This may indicate that the mother was able to have an even more splendid tomb built; certainly she should have been the most powerful woman of her time, but the politics of this family were apparently tumultuous (though poorly recorded), and thus the personal story of this woman and her fate is not known.

Barbara S. Lesko,
Department of Egyptology,
Brown University, Providence, Rhode Island

Khamerernebty II (fl. c. 2600 BCE)

Egyptian queen. Name variations: Khamerernebti II. Flourished around 2600 BCE; daughter of Khamerernebty I and King Khafre or Chephren (Greek); married her brother King Menkaure (Menkure or Mykerinos [Greek]), who built the Third Pyramid at Giza); children: son Khuenre (died prematurely).

Egyptian queen, the eldest daughter of Queen *Khamerernebty I and King Khafre, Khamerernebty II is believed to have been married to her brother King Menkaure and had a son Khuenre who died prematurely. Like her mother, Queen Khamerernebty II served the cults of important deities and bore the titles of a major queen, such as "God's Daughter of his Body, One Who Sits with Horus, Greatly loved Wife of the King." However, she either died long before her husband or, as seems more likely, fell from his favor before her death. This is suggested by her statement in her tomb that she paid the artisan from her own largess. She enlarged the tomb begun by her mother and added many statues, among which is one more than twice life-sized, the earliest known colossus of a woman. In the tomb inscriptions, Khamerernebty II emphasizes her closeness to the king, although the fact that she was not buried at his funerary complex but instead had to use the tomb built for her mother, suggests otherwise.

Barbara S. Lesko,
Department of Egyptology,
Brown University, Providence, Rhode Island

Khan, Begum Liaquat Ali
(1905–1990)

Pakistani diplomat and much-beloved women's rights activist who in 1954 became one of the first Asian women to serve her nation as an ambassador.
Name variations: Begum Raana Liaquat Ali Khan; Rana Liaquat Ali Khan. Born in Almora, India, on February 13, 1905, as Miss Pant; died in Karachi, Pakistan, on June 13, 1990; grew up in a Hindu Brahmin family but converted to Islam when she married; earned a degree in economics from Lucknow University; was second wife of (Zada) Liaquat Ali Khan (1895–1951), the first prime minister of Pakistan; children: two sons.

Played a crucial role in organizing the All Pakistan Women's Association (1949); appointed delegate to the United Nations (1952); served as an ambassador (1954–66); appointed governor of Sind by Zulfikar Ali Bhutto (1973); resigned (1976).

During a 1952 visit to Pakistan, *Eleanor Roosevelt was told by the president of the All Pakistan Women's Association, Begum Liaqat Ali Khan, that the human rights of women were highly respected in her country, asserting, "to us it is of great pride that the human rights principles are the very basis of Islam" and that these concepts had been adopted by the nation's Parliament. Although that ideal has often failed to measure up to the realities of daily life for the great majority of Pakistani women, the life of the begum continued to provide inspiration that one day women would be able to enjoy full equality in an essentially patriarchal society.

Born in 1905 in Almora, India, the daughter of a senior government official of the then British Indian administration, the future begum, then known as Miss Pant, was raised a Hindu in a prominent Brahmin family. Fortunately, her father believed that women should be exposed to higher education if they desired careers; as a result, she was able to earn a degree in economics from Lucknow University. Upon graduation, she became a lecturer in economics in Delhi. At this time, she met and fell in love with Liaquat Ali Khan, a Muslim lawyer from an affluent and aristocratic Punjabi family. A lawyer and rising political star, Liaquat Ali married Miss Pant in 1933; she became his second wife and also converted to the Islamic faith.

Determined not to play the role of a traditional Muslim wife, and encouraged by a husband whose outlook was secular and modern, the Begum Liaquat Ali Khan, as she was now known, worked together with her husband to achieve the independence of the Indian subcontinent from British rule. While on honeymoon in London, she and her husband encountered Mohammad Ali Jinnah, a leader of the Muslim League, who had migrated to England because of his frustrations with the political infighting in the Indian independence movement. Both the begum and her husband pleaded with Jinnah, then practicing law in London, to return to India immediately in order to revitalize the Muslim League. Not completely convinced, Jinnah suggested that upon their return home they sound out the leaders of the organization. This was done, and Jinnah did in fact go back to India to become, along with Mohandas Gandhi and Jawaharlal Nehru, one of the key leaders of the successful struggle for independence. Within the Muslim League, the role of Liaquat Ali Khan was comparable to the one Nehru played to Gandhi—that of a trusted friend and collaborator.

As her husband's career advanced—he became general secretary of the All India Muslim League (1937) and was named finance minister of the interim government of India that prepared for independence (1946)—the begum too became more active in public affairs. Convinced that true national independence required greater emancipation for women, she advocated social and economic advancement for Muslim women, arguing that their talents and energies would be crucial for social and economic progress once political freedom had been realized.

Tragically, the achievement of independence from the British in August 1947 brought not peace and prosperity but bloody massacres as Hindus and Muslims butchered each other across the subcontinent. Millions of Muslims fled India, arriving destitute and traumatized in the new Islamic Republic of Pakistan. The begum's husband Liaquat Ali Khan became the new nation's first prime minister. While he tackled the country's immense economic and political problems, the begum worked to bring assistance to the refugees, persuading the rich to donate significant sums for relief programs. She personally visited the refugee camps to see that food and other necessities were being fairly distributed, and the Pakistani public, and many refugees, began to call her the "*Florence Nightingale of the camps." But the begum was aware that the weakest and most vulnerable members of the refugee population, and indeed of Pakistani society in general, were the women. Thus, she played a key role in founding the All Pakistan Women's Association in 1949. Over the next decades, this organization would help millions of desperate women escape from the worst aspects of poverty and discrimination.

In October 1951, personal tragedy transformed the life of the begum. While addressing a public meeting in Rawalpindi, her husband was assassinated. The grieving begum was able to find solace by devoting her energies to several programs for the poor. These included helping set up the Pakistani Cottage Industries in Karachi, and the Health and Nutrition Association, as well as sponsoring industrial and health centers for women throughout the country. As a result of the begum's lobbying, Colleges of Home Economics were also established during this period in Daccam, Karachi, and Lahore. The many organizations she helped create or push forward in their reform agendas included the Pakistani International Women's Club and the Pakistani Federation of University Women. Concerned about the need to improve public health conditions, she spent considerable time as the chief patron of the Pakistani Nurses Association as well as with the Liaquat Memorial Hospital. As a member of the management committees of a number of important social welfare organizations, she was often called on to deliver persuasive speeches. The begum was also a skilled journalist, often writing articles for the national press.

Regarded as a radical feminist by many conservative Muslims, Begum Liaquat Ali Khan minced no words in her opposition to laws and traditions she saw as discriminatory to women. In 1949, while her husband was prime minister, she had been appointed a brigadier in the newly formed Women's National Guard. This organization, based on the notion that Pakistani women should be permitted to participate in both the defense and the modernization of their new nation, was viewed with suspicion from the start by Islamic fundamentalists, particularly hard-line mullahs. Some years after its creation, the Women's National Guard was disbanded. To dramatize her firm belief that the advancement of women's social, political and economic rights was fully compatible with the tenets of Islam, in 1952 she helped organize and presided over the first international conference of Muslim women, which was held in Pakistan that same year.

In 1952, the begum became Pakistan's delegate to the United Nations (as well as to the International Labor Organization), then only the second Muslim woman to have served in this capacity. Starting in 1954, she began serving as her nation's ambassador to a number of nations including Italy, the Netherlands, and Tunisia. Her diplomatic career ended in 1966, and she returned home to continue her activities on the social and economic front. From 1973 through 1976, the begum served as governor of Sind Province. During this period, she received national recognition during the silver jubilee celebrations honoring the All Pakistan Women's Association, which by that time had been able to render significant assistance to over one million women. In 1979, her reform efforts brought her international recognition when she received the Human Rights Award of the United Nations.

Greatly beloved by both Pakistanis and those who met her abroad, and affectionately called Begum Sahiba in the final decades of her life, this remarkable woman could display charm and grace, but was also tenacious when advocating a cause she deemed just and necessary for her nation's advancement. In the last years of her life, she struggled with ill health but continued to play a significant role in Pakistani public life. The begum was particularly incensed when the dictatorial regime of General Zia ul-Haq made attempts to erode the hard-won women's rights. She minced no words in attacking the discriminatory legislation, allegedly inspired by the spirit of the Koran, that became a central theme of the fundamentalist Pakistani political agenda beginning in the 1970s. In her view, the legislation was profoundly inimical to the true ideals of Islam. Using her immense prestige as a founding mother of the nation, she spent her final years attempting to halt the spread of those elements and ideas she was convinced were not only un-Islamic in their religious content but profoundly bigoted in their attitude toward one of Pakistan's greatest and often under-appreciated resources, its women. Begum Liaquat Ali Khan died in Karachi, Pakistan, on June 13, 1990.

SOURCES:

Burki, Shahid Javed. *Historical Dictionary of Pakistan.* Metuchen, NJ: Scarecrow Press, 1991.

Haq, Mushirul. "Liaqat Ali Khan (1895–1951)," in Siba Pada Sen, ed., *Dictionary of National Biography.* Vol. 2 (1973). Calcutta: Institute of Historical Studies (1972–1974), pp. 411–412.

James, Michael. "Islam Rights Told to Mrs. Roosevelt," in *The New York Times.* February 22, 1952, p. 3.

"Raana Liaquat Ali Khan," in Deborah Andrews, ed., *The Annual Obituary 1990.* Chicago, IL: St. James Press, 1991, pp. 378–379.

"Raana Liaquat Ali Khan," in *The Times* [London]. June 22, 1990, p. 14.

Reber, Karin. "Women in Pakistan," in *Swiss Review of World Affairs.* November 1993.

Wolpert, Stanley. *Jinnah of Pakistan.* NY: Oxford University Press, 1984.

John Haag,
Associate Professor of History,
University of Georgia, Athens, Georgia

Khan, Noor Inayat (1914–1944)

Courageous wireless operator, known as "Madeleine," who worked for the British Special Operations Executive in occupied France in 1943, was executed at Dachau, and earned a posthumous George Cross in 1949. Name variations: (code name) Madeleine, as well as Babuly, Nora, Jeanne-Marie Regnier, Rolande, Nora Baker, Marie-Jeanne. Pronunciation: Nur In-AY-at Cawn. Born Pir Zadi Noor-un-Nisa Inayat Khan on January 1, 1914, in the Kremlin, Moscow, Russia; died in Dachau concentration camp, Germany, on September 13, 1944; daughter of Inayat Khan (an Indian mystic and teacher of Sufism) and Ora Ray Baker; sister of Pir Vilayat Inayat-Khan (a writer and lecturer on Sufism); attended College Moderne de Filles, Suresnes, France; École Normale de Musique, Paris, France; Sorbonne Université de Paris, École des Langues Orientales of the University of Paris; never married.

Parents moved from Moscow to London (1916), then to Paris, France (1920); entered the University of Paris (1937); fled from wartime France to England (1940); enlisted in the British Women's Auxiliary Air Force (WAAF), a branch of the Royal Air Force (1940); assigned to the Air Ministry, Directorate of Air Intelligence (February 1943); dispatched as a Special Operations Executive agent into occupied France (June 1943); captured by the German Gestapo (October 1943); transported and executed at Dachau (September 1944); posthumously awarded the British George Cross and French Croix de Guerre; designated a saint by the Islamic Sufi order.

Noor Inayat Khan had evaded her Nazi pursuers for months before they captured her in Paris, France. Her behavior as a prisoner confirmed her loyalty to the British cause and enmity towards the Germans. Despite rigorous interrogations, she revealed nothing of use to her enemies, and after two unsuccessful attempts to escape, the second time with other prisoners, she refused to sign a pledge promising to curtail her escape efforts. Her angry captors shipped her to Pforzheim, Germany, where she was kept in chains and solitary confinement. When she again refused to break or cooperate, she was shipped to the infamous Dachau concentration camp. On September 13, 1944, Khan and three other female agents were forced to kneel by a wall, shot from behind, and their bodies cremated. The Germans never did discover her identity. This was the fate of Noor Inayat Khan—also known as "Madeleine"—one of the most courageous British agents operating in Nazi-occupied France. Like many of her female compatriots, her heroic story remained virtually unknown outside official circles long after the war.

Noor Inayat Khan was born on January 1, 1914, in the Kremlin, Moscow, Russia. Her father Inayat Khan was the leader of the Sufi sect of Muhammad mystics and a direct descendant of Tipu Sultan, the 18th-century sultan of the Indian state of Mysore. Impressed with Sufist mysticism, Gregori Rasputin had invited Inayat Khan to the Kremlin to instruct Tsar Nicholas II and establish a Sufi order in Moscow. Noor's mother, **Ora Ray Baker**, was a grandniece of

*Mary Baker Eddy, the founder of Christian Science. The political unrest and riots leading to the Russian Revolution forced Inayat Khan's family to flee Russia in 1916, in a sledge provided by Leon Tolstoy. They settled in London, where three more children—Vilayat, Hidayat, and Khair-un-Nisa—completed the family. In 1920, they moved to France and eventually settled in Suresnes, a suburb of Paris, in a large house called "Fazal Manzil" (the House of Blessings); they also made many sidetrips to India. In 1926, Noor's father made preparations for another trip to India and instructed his family and disciples

Noor Inayat Khan

that he would never return. Several months later, on February 5, 1927, Inayat Khan died of pneumonia in Delhi, India. This left Noor's mother, known to the Sufist faithful as the begum, with full responsibility for the family. When her mother became ill, Noor, a student at the Lycée Saint Cloud, took over the family management.

In 1931, 17-year-old Noor left the Lycée Saint Cloud with her diploma and entered the École Normale de Musique de Paris, where her studies for the next six years would include harp and piano. In 1932, she also took a course in the psycho-biology of the child at the Sorbonne, Université de Paris. Though Khan was engaged to another music student during this period, her family's opposition successfully ended the relationship.

By 1935, her mother's health had improved to the point that Noor and her brother, Vilayat, were able to travel to Italy and Switzerland. They were still deeply absorbed in Sufism, and spoke in their native Hindustani dialect. Khan even studied the language for two years at the École des Langues Orientales in Paris in 1937–39. In 1938, she successfully passed her examinations and received her license in the psycho-biology of the child. Noor and the **Baroness van Tuyll**, one of her father's disciples, collaborated in writing and illustrating children's stories based on the Jataka Tales, legends about the incarnations of Buddha. At the same time, Khan wrote freelance children's articles for the *Sunday Figaro* and had some of her stories broadcast on French radio. *The Jataka Tales* by Khan and van Tuyll was published in 1939, and one of these tales, "The Fairy and the Hare," would be broadcast over the BBC during the war.

Noor's family, like most French families, saw their peaceful lives shattered by the aggression of Nazi Germany. Noor was shocked by the German persecution of the Jews, but she believed Sufism, based on the idea of love, tolerance, and non-violence, would triumph over Nazism. Anticipating the need for nurses, she undertook nursing and first-aid training with the French Red Cross. The rest of her family decided to flee to Britain as fighting neared Paris. Caught in the panic of evacuation, they finally found space on a Belgian cargo-boat, the *Kasonga,* in June 1940. Noor, still in Paris when the Germans invaded, escaped with the help of her London publisher.

In England, she lived for a few weeks with her mother and sister in Oxford. In September 1940, she used her French Red Cross certificate to obtain a position at Fulmer Chase Maternity Home for Officers' Wives at Slough. Unchallenged by hospital work, she tried to join the Women's Auxiliary Air Force (WAAF), a branch of the Royal Air Force (RAF). When she was turned down because she was not a British citizen, she reapplied under her "British Protected Person" passport. She was accepted and enlisted on November 19, 1940, as Nora Inayat Khan, while stating her religion to be Church of England. She was 25 years old.

That same autumn, writes William Stevenson in *A Man Called Intrepid,* the British had a "new medal struck to recognize the changed nature of war. It was the George Cross, valued above all orders of knighthood, awarded sparingly to civilians now drawn into front-line emergencies caused by German terror bombing, and given 'for the most conspicuous courage in circumstances of extreme danger.' The citation would become her epitaph."

> *I* have served my country.
> That is my recompense.
> —**Noor Inayat Khan**

Quick, intelligent, and dependable, Khan was posted to Harrogate for training. She and 40 other women were the first of the WAAF to be taught wireless operations. "Such women were needed as radio operators to work with small guerrilla groups," writes Stevenson. "The radio war . . . was not only defensive. There was a need to build up circuits of agents and networks of saboteurs and partisans, providing them with radio contacts that would integrate their efforts. Nothing like this had been attempted in the history of the war."

On December 23, the entire WAAF group was assigned to Edinburgh where the General Post Office directed their communications training. On June 10, 1941, Khan and another woman, **Joan Clifton**, were posted to the Royal Air Force Bomber command at Abington. At first, Khan disliked the drill and "spit-and-polish" of her new assignment but that soon gave way to boredom. Near the end of 1941, the two women applied for commissions. Clifton entered a commission course in 1942, but Khan was reassigned as a wireless operator to Compton Basset in Wiltshire. While there, she was chosen for a seven-week secret course in more sophisticated wireless training. Khan finally met the Commission Board on August 28 but was reassigned to Abington without an evaluation concerning her performance before the board. In April 1942, she received orders to attend an interview at the Victoria Hotel in London.

Khan's interview was conducted by Captain Selwin Jepson of British Special Operations Executive (SOE), a top-secret military organization. It was Jepson's responsibility to recruit people for service in enemy-controlled countries. The conversation with Khan was wide-ranging, and she talked of being somewhat rootless as a result of her Russian birth, American mother, Indian father, French childhood, and attraction to Indian philosophy. Jepson, who normally took his time with potential recruits, trusted Khan instantly and was impressed with her integrity when she candidly told him, in answer to his question, that she would struggle for India's freedom from British rule. He then explained the purpose of their interview, and Khan volunteered for SOE service on the spot.

This presented two problems. There was a regulation in the Royal Air Force preventing women from taking part in military operations, and women agents were required to wear some kind of uniform during training to prevent speculation about their duties. For this reason, Khan, like other SOE women recruits, was transferred to the First Aid Nursing Yeomanry (FANY), which *did* have military combat duties. While entitled to wear the FANY nurses' khaki uniform, the women agents secretly held honorary military commissions from the RAF. Khan was therefore discharged from the RAF and enrolled in FANY as she prepared for her training in the French Section of the SOE.

She remained at Abington until she was ordered in February 1943 to begin intensive training at Wanborough Manor in Surrey. Khan was later trained as a covert wireless operator, the first woman selected for that duty, at Aylesbury, and received field security training at New Forest. She was provided with a new identity, that of Jeanne-Marie Regnier, a children's nurse. The SOE French Section, known as the Baker Street Irregulars, would know her only by the code name of *Madeleine*. Khan received carefully forged identity papers, ration books, and a new Parisian wardrobe. Her transmitter, which was installed in a suitcase, had to be light and compact since she was a small woman at 5'3", weighing 108 pounds. Her final training included confinement to test her mental fitness. She was taught in the use of various types of pills, unarmed self-defense, and the use of knives and pistols. Code omissions to signify forced transmissions by her potential captors were also part of her training.

Although there were some doubts from instructors about Khan's stability (fellow trainees, fearful for her life, felt that she was "emotionally fragile and in many ways too innocent"), Khan and ❧▶ **Vera Atkins**, her final conducting officer, convinced director Maurice Buckmaster that she was ready. Khan was assigned to the PROSPER network, one of the largest, most important, and more hazardous secret operations in France. Headquartered in Paris, PROSPER provided weapons, explosives, and money to the French underground guerrillas. This required almost daily contact with the British covert operations group at Bletchley Park and SOE headquarters at Baker Street in London. "Its demands were insatiable," writes Stevenson. "Its rural circuits were disrupting lines of communication by sabotage. Its guerrillas were arming for the day of liberation." Khan was given the assignment because the network desperately needed a new wireless operator in Paris. Her major assets were her knowledge of French and familiarity with the environs of the city.

In preparation, Noor's cover story, writes Stevenson, "was tested by her instructors in fake Gestapo interrogations under blazing lights, accompanied with snarled commands. Her reactions were noted by a FANY conducting officer whose job was to watch for slips and continually review the trainee's mental fitness." Noor "never deviated from her story, but her conducting officer reported later that" the mock interrogators "found their task almost unbearable because of her terrified reactions."

One of her superiors' major concerns was that her elegant appearance could attract attention. She was hauntingly beautiful, with olive skin, dark eyes, and long dark hair. For most agents, continues Stevenson, "it was difficult to submit unquestioningly to the dictates of others. Madeleine had this submissive quality. Her attitude was expressed in her story of the river that reached the sea by going *around* obstacles instead of attacking head on. She liked and wrote about gentle animals. She meditated a great deal on metaphysical matters. Her childhood friends remembered that she peopled her garden with small figures of her own imagination and was in despair when told there was no world of small benevolent spirits. She described her philosophy as oriental. She saw action and inaction intertwined in the Buddhist circle of life."

Khan and two other female agents were flown to France aboard a Westland Lysander on the night of June 16–17, 1943. When the airplane touched down briefly near LeMans, Khan quickly scrambled out and moved away from the dangerous landing field. She walked to the railroad station in LeMans, boarded a train, and arrived at her first contact's residence at 40 rue Erlanger in the Paris suburb of Auteuil late on June 17. Khan's PROSPER sector-chief, Émile Garry, was wary at first, because he had received no notification from England concerning her arrival. After security checks, she was accepted by the PROSPER agents, and the following day they moved her to their headquarters, the École Nationale d'Agriculture at Grignon, near Versailles. Khan lived briefly with **Madame Balachowsky** and her husband Professor Alfred Balachowsky, the PROSPER section chief at Grignon. Two days after her landing, Khan transmitted her first message from a greenhouse on the Grignon section transmitter. A few days later, her own transmitter was delivered in another supply drop.

Khan had been dropped into a very dangerous situation. Only a week after her arrival, the Nazi Gestapo arrested the chief of PROSPER and several couriers and agents. A few days after Khan left Grignon, Professor Balachowsky was arrested. Except for a few scattered agents, the PROSPER network was in shambles. "In London, a signal was delivered to Maurice Buckmaster at Baker Street," writes Stevenson. "It reported the destruction of the PROSPER network. All the leaders and their equipment had been captured, and only one transmitter remained in operation." The message came from Madeleine. For Khan's safety, London offered to send a plane to retrieve her. But Khan argued that since she carried the only remaining transmitter in operation, she was the only source of communication for the French resistance. "Buckmaster made a hard decision," notes Stevenson. If she stayed, she would eventually be caught. "Yet the catastrophe had left her as the most important 'station' in France." Buckmaster reluctantly accepted her position but warned her not to transmit; all German efforts would be concentrated on her sole transmitter.

Khan was on her own, and the next few months of her life are difficult to reconstruct chronologically. It is known that she visited or briefly stayed with several people from her past, including former music teachers, old family friends, and even her former family doctor. In July, she made contact with French resistance members known as X, Y, and Vaudevire. Khan was known as Rolande by this group, and they met several times weekly at the Tuileries. The agents would take her by car into

Atkins, Vera (c. 1908–2000)

British officer for the SOE during World War II who recruited and trained nearly 500 secret agents and also made sure that murderers of agents were eventually brought to trial for war crimes. Name variations: Adkins. Born in Rumania around 1908; died in Hastings, England, in July 2000.

During World War II, Vera Atkins was considered the "hear t and brain of the Baker Street Irregulars' French section," writes William Stevenson, in charge of reinforcing an agent' s cover. Young and incredibly organized, she was a conducting officer at Orchard Court, second in command to Colonel Maurice Buckmaster, head of the British SOE (Special Operations Executive). Atkins had an eye for detail, notes Stevenson, "an encyclopedic memory for local regulations in odd corners of Europe, and subtleties of behavior that a stranger might fatally ignore." She made sure to include in the agent' s gear, "tram tickets fr om the region where the agent was going, concert programs, crumpled French cigaret packs" and she could catch potentially fatal slips: "the way the agent poured tea or the use of improper jargon."

the Paris suburbs where she could use her aerial to transmit to London. She eventually established a safe house at 3 Boulevard Richard Wallace, Neuilly-sur-Seine, under the name Jeanne Regnier, and sometimes used the home of a family friend, **Madame Prénat**, near the old Inayat home "Fazal Manzil" to transmit her messages. The Prenats remember the diminutive Noor, with her hair dyed blonde, lugging around her heavy suitcase containing the transmitter. Though she continued to broadcast from several locations, she was always on the lookout for other safe places from which to transmit and tried not to compromise the safety of those who helped. Khan was beginning to wear down. Her acquaintances began to notice carelessness due to fatigue. One of them, a friend untrained in espionage, even lectured her for falling asleep and leaving her codebook lying open on the kitchen table.

In August, Vaudevire introduced Noor, under the name Rolande, to Monsieur P. Viennot, a resistance member who was director of the Société Radio Electrique. A complex man whose company did work for the Germans, Viennot used his position to infiltrate the German police and Gestapo. Though impressed with Noor's courage and devotion to duty, he was concerned about her English accent, her personal appearance, and her notebook containing all of her previous transmissions. Since she refused to destroy the notebook and there was nothing to be done about her accent, Viennot took her to a professional hairdresser who changed her hair color to light-brown, eliminating the brittle, dyed look. A visit to fashionable shops provided Khan with several current and more subtle dresses, hats, scarfs, and a new coat. The group also agreed that she would use Marie-Jeanne instead of Jeanne-Marie to partly assume a new personality.

In early October, as more resistance members were being arrested, Khan's fellow agents arranged and supplied a train ticket to send her to a farmhouse in Normandy. Even though they took her to St. Lazare station, she did not go. After nearly four months in the field, her incredible operation came to an end when she was betrayed for money by the relative of a former agent. On October 13, Noor Khan, arrested in her Paris apartment, put up a fierce struggle and had to be handcuffed before she could be taken to Gestapo Headquarters at 84 Avenue Foch. "She was working with a rebuilt circuit, a group of saboteurs, when arrested," writes Stevenson. "The group had traced underground sewers in which the Germans stored torpedoes to be shipped to the U-boat pens at Brest, and Madeleine had conveyed their request to London" for new explosives. Noor was confined on the fifth floor in cells specifically reserved for important prisoners. The Germans also found her transmitter, cipher codes, and the notebook containing every message she had transmitted from France.

Khan, who refused to answer any questions at Gestapo headquarters, requested permission to take a bath. Within minutes, the Gestapo, which had permitted her some privacy, found her crawling along the fifth-story roof gutter in an effort to escape. She was quickly apprehended and afterwards watched closely by her captors. Noor was interrogated by a courteous, amicable, non-uniformed interpreter but, while she gossiped, she never provided useful information. Her interrogations are a matter of record because they were included in evidence given at war-crime trials. During her incarceration, the Germans and British played cat-and-mouse. Her captors used her codes and style of transmission to mislead the British, but the British grew increasingly suspicious of the bogus broadcasts and acted accordingly. Arguments continue about the effectiveness of both sides in this intrigue.

Khan made a second attempt to escape with two other agents, British Captain John A.R. Starr and French Major Leon Faye, in mid-November 1943. Succeeding in removing bars from their windows, they escaped to the roof of Gestapo headquarters. They then lowered themselves on blankets used as ropes and dropped in the darkness of night onto the flat roofs of adjacent buildings. Despite their careful planning, they were recaptured before they could leave the area. Gestapo Sturmbannfüher Hans Kieffer demanded that they sign declarations promising not to attempt to escape in the future. When Khan refused, Kieffer notified Berlin that she was a dangerous and desperate case. She was transported on November 26 to a prison in Pforzheim, in Germany's Black Forest.

When Khan arrived at Pforzheim at 2:30 in the afternoon of November 27, she was the first political prisoner assigned to that prison. Registered as Nora Baker, she was confined to a ground floor cell and chained like an animal in a crouching position, day and night, with her hands in handcuffs, her feet in leg-irons, and a chain from the handcuffs to the leg-irons. She was segregated from other women prisoners, and the cells on both sides of her were kept empty. "She depended on male jailers to deal with her sanitary and feeding problems," notes Stevenson. After many months, Wilhelm Krauss, the prison governor, ordered the chains removed and permitted her to walk in the courtyard a few minutes each week. She briefly established a clandestine contact with three imprisoned Frenchwomen, who later related how they were impressed with the courage and faith expressed in her secret notes.

After some ten months at Pforzheim, Khan was suddenly removed from the prison and transported to the concentration camp at Dachau. On September 13, 1944, she and three other SOE women, **Yolanda Beekman, Eliane Plewman** and **Madeleine Damerment**, were forced to face a wall and were shot at the crematorium by their guards. For her valor and sacrifice, Noor Inayat Khan was posthumously awarded France's Croix de Guerre, and, on April 5, 1949, she received the George Cross. The citation read in part:

> Following her arrival the Gestapo made arrests in the Paris Resistance groups to which she had been detailed. She refused to abandon what had become the principal and most dangerous post in France, although given the opportunity to return to England. She did not wish to leave her French comrades without communications and she hoped also to rebuild her group. The Gestapo had a full description of her but knew only her code name Madeleine. They deployed considerable forces in their effort

to catch her and so break the last remaining link with London. After 3½ months she was betrayed to the Gestapo and taken to their HQ in the Avenue Foch. The Gestapo had found her codes and messages and were in a position to work back to London. They asked her to co-operate, but she refused and gave them no information of any kind.

The woman codenamed Madeleine has long been a heroine in intelligence circles but only in recent years have her sacrifice and remarkable accomplishments been related to the general public.

SOURCES:
Brown, Anthony Cave. *Bodyguard of Lies*. NY: Harper and Row, 1975.
Foot, M.R.D. *S.O.E. in France*. London: HMSO, 1966.
Fuller, Jean Overton. *Madeleine: The Story of Noor Inayat Khan*. London: Victor Gollancz, 1952.
Stevenson, William. *A Man Called Intrepid: The Secret War*. NY: Ballantine, 1976.

SUGGESTED READING:
Foot, M.R.D. *S.O.E.* London: British Broadcasting Corp., 1984.
Fuller, Jean Overton. *Double Webs*. NY: Putnam, 1958.
———. *The Starr Affair*. London: Victor Gollancz, 1954.
Nicholas, Elizabeth. *Death Be Not Proud*. London: Cresset, 1958.
Rossiter, Margaret L. *Women in the Resistance*. NY: Praeger, 1986.

Phillip E. Koerper,
Professor of History,
Jacksonville State University, Jacksonville, Alabama

Khansa (c. 575–c. 645)

Arabian poet. Name variations: al-Khansa. Born Tumadir bint Amr ibn al Harith ibn al Sharid in Najd, a central plateau in Arabia, around 575; died around 645 or 646; of the tribe Sulaim, a branch of Qais; sister of Sakhr and Mu'awiya (also seen as Moawiya); married Mirdas ben Abi 'Amir; children: six, including at least four sons and a daughter 'Amra who also wrote poetry.

Khansa, an Arabian poet of the tribe Sulaim, a branch of Qais, was born around 575 and raised in an atmosphere of wealth and privilege. Refusing the offer of Duraid ibn us-Simma, a great poet, warrior, and prince, because he had been chosen for her, she married Mirdas and had six children; her daughter 'Amra also wrote poetry. Before 632, the first year of the Muslim calendar, Khansa lost her brothers Sakhr and Mu'awiya in battle with warring tribes. Her elegies written about them, as well as those about her father, made Khansa the most famous poet of her time. In a poetry contest at the fair of 'Ukaz Nabigha Dhubyani, it is said that *A'isha was first among the poets then present and Khansa was second above Hassan ibn Thabit.

Along with her tribe, Khansa accepted Islam somewhat late. Though she led a delegation to Medina in 629, she persisted in wearing a hairshirt, the heathen sign of mourning, against the precepts of Islam. Her four sons fought in the armies of Islam and were slain in the battle of Kadisiya (Qadisiya). Omar wrote her a letter congratulating her on their heroic end and offered her a pension. Khansa died in her tent around 645. Opinion was divided among later critics as to whether Khansa or *Layla al-Akhyaliyya was the greater poet. About 1,000 of Khansa's verses are extant. Her *dewan* (account book) was edited by L. Cheikho (Beirut, 1895) and translated into French by De Coppier (Beirut, 1889).

Khentkawes (fl. c. 2510 BCE)

Egyptian queen of the Old Kingdom, who carried the legitimate line from the 4th to the 5th Dynasty as mother of the Two Kings of Upper and Lower Egypt. Name variations: Khentkaues. Flourished around 2510 BCE; probably daughter of King Shepseskaf; married King Userkaf; children: Sahure (Egyptian king) and Neferirkare (Egyptian king).

Probably the daughter of King Shepseskaf, Khentkawes was the wife of King Userkaf and mother of the two 5th Dynasty rulers Sahure and Neferirkare. She may have ruled as regent for her under-aged sons because her funerary monument is impressive and has often been called the Fourth Pyramid of Giza. It stands between the causeways of Khafre and Menkaure at Giza and took the unusual form of a sarcophagus mounted on a high podium of natural rock. The fact that she did not imitate her predecessors and their queens who had pyramid tombs has suggested to some that she deliberately was trying to break away from the influence of the powerful priesthood of the sun god Re.

Barbara S. Lesko,
Department of Egyptology,
Brown University, Providence, Rhode Island

Khirniq (fl. late 6th c.)

Iraqi poet. Name variations: al-Khirniq. Flourished in the late 6th century; sister of Tarafa; married Bishir ibn 'Amr.

Sister of the Iraqi poet Tarafa, poet Kirniq largely wrote of love and mourning for her husband, Bishir ibn 'Amr, who was killed on Mount Qudab by a neighboring tribe.

Khoklova, Olga (d. 1955)

Russian ballerina and wife of Pablo Picasso. Name variations: Khokhlova. Born in Russia; died in Cannes, France, in 1955; married Pablo Picasso (the painter), in 1918 (separated 1935); children: one son, Paulo (b. 1921).

Born into the lower echelons of Russian nobility, Olga Khoklova was a dancer with the Ballets Russes when she met and married artist Pablo Picasso, who designed sets and costumes for the ballet during World War I. Although Olga was beautiful, Picasso's attraction had more to do with her social status than aesthetics, and the marriage was doomed from the start. Picasso believed that he could maintain his independent bohemian lifestyle on a slightly grander scale, while Olga was intent upon molding her new husband into something more presentable. The newlyweds set up housekeeping in an apartment near the Champs-Élysées in Paris, and Olga gave birth to a son Paulo in 1921. During the 1920s, Olga introduced Picasso to Parisian high life, and the artist became distracted from his painting because of their rigorous social calendar.

In 1935, Picasso asked for a divorce. He had also taken a new mistress, **Marie-Thérèse Walter**, who was pregnant at the time with his daughter **Maya Picasso**. The dissolution of the marriage was complicated by Spanish law, however, so the couple separated but remained legally married until Olga's death in 1955. In her book *Life with Picasso*, *****Françoise Gilot**, another of the artist's mistresses and the mother of two of his children, recalled that Picasso took her to visit both the apartment and a house at Boisgeloup where he had lived with Olga. Gilot described going into one of the deserted rooms at the house. "There was nothing in it but a chair, the one that appears in the rather Ingresque 1917 portrait of Olga sitting in a chair, holding a fan. I began to have the feeling that if I looked into a closet, I would find half a dozen ex-wives hanging by their necks. The atmosphere was all dust, decay, and desertion, and it gave me a chill."

Khoklova, who had never wanted a divorce, became obsessed with Picasso, following him around France and taking up residence in hotels not far from his quarters. In 1947, she was in Midi, where Picasso was living with Gilot and their newborn son Claude. Olga's son Paulo frequently visited his father and Gilot during the summer, and Olga would follow the entourage to the beach, where she would try unsuccessfully to gain the attention of Picasso, whom she claimed, rightly so, was still her husband. She also followed Françoise on the street, demanding attention and swearing and yelling if she was ignored. Gilot writes that although she found Olga's behavior disturbing, she felt only pity. "She was a very unhappy, unfortunate creature, incapable of coping with the situation in which she found herself. I have never seen a more solitary person than she. Everyone avoided her. People were afraid to stop and speak to her, knowing what they would be letting themselves in for."

During her later years, Olga Khoklova lived in Cannes, and it was there that she died of cancer in 1955. At the time, Paulo was recovering from complications from a hernia operation and could not be with his mother, so she died alone. Ironically, she was buried in Vallauris, a place she hated after Picasso moved there with Françoise Gilot.

SOURCES:
Gilot, Françoise, with Carlton Lake. *Life with Picasso.* NY: McGraw-Hill, 1964.

Barbara Morgan,
Melrose, Massachusetts

Kholodnya, Vera (1893–1919)

Russian actress. Name variations: Kholodnaya; Kholodnaia. Born in Russia in 1893; died in Odessa, Russia, in 1919; married a military officer.

Selected films: Song of Triumphant Love *(1915);* Thief *(1916);* A Life for a Life *(1916);* The Woman Who Invented Love *(1918);* A Living Corpse *(1918).*

Vera Kholodnya was one of Russia's most popular pre-revolutionary film actresses, although her career was cut short by her untimely death at the age of 26. The wife of a military officer, Kholodnya was employed as an extra at Moscow's Alexander Khanzhonkov film studio in the spring of 1915. A stand-out with dyed black hair, bottle-green eyes, and pale skin (accentuated with dead white make-up), she caught the attention of director Yevgeni Bauer, who gave her the leading role in the film *Song of Triumphant Love* (1915), which established her as a star. In 1918, Kholodnya moved to Odessa, where many of the studios had relocated during the Civil War that followed the Russian Revolution. Not long after her arrival, she succumbed to a fatal attack of influenza, a war-born epidemic which took the lives of many of the city's inhabitants.

Khomiakova or Khomyakova, Valeriia (d. 1942).

See Litvyak, Lidiya for sidebar.

Khorandzem (c. 320–c. 364).

See *Pharandzem*.

Khostaria, Anastasia Eristav
(1868–1951).

See *Eristavi-Xostaria, Anastasia*.

Khurrem, sultana (c. 1504–1558).

See *Roxelana*.

Kiddle, Margaret (1914–1958)

Australian historian. Born Margaret Loch Kiddle in South Yarra, Melbourne, Australia, on September 10, 1914; died on May 3, 1958; daughter of John Beacham (a solicitor) and Mauna Loa (Burrett) Kiddle; attended Melbourne Church of England Girls' Grammar School; University of Melbourne, B.A., 1937, Diploma of Education, 1938, M.A., 1947; never married; no children.

An Australian, born and raised in South Yarra, Melbourne, Margaret Kiddle was awakened to history by her social studies teacher in grammar school. She received both her baccalaureate and master's degrees from the University of Melbourne, where she later taught history. Kiddle first published a series of children's books, beginning with *Moonbeam Stairs* in 1945. It was followed by *West of Sunset* (1949), and *The Candle* (1950). A biography, **Caroline Chisholm*, which served as Kiddle's master's thesis, was published in 1950.

Kiddle's most acclaimed work, *Men of Yesterday* (1961), traces the history of the western district of Victoria in the 19th century, from the native Aboriginal inhabitants to the large-scale immigrations in the 1830s and 1840s, and is based largely on the records of pioneer families. The work, started in 1949, was finished just six weeks before Kiddle died of congenital kidney disease in 1958. The manuscript was edited for publication by Kiddle's university colleagues. During the nine years that Kiddle labored on the project, she spent one year on a fellowship at the Australian National University and also toured the UK with her sister, seeking papers and records of descendants of the original western settlers. **Lindsay Gardiner**, in *200 Australian Women*, describes Kiddle's work as rich in its use of voices from the past. "Here the voices are those not only of the men but also of the women of yesterday, revealed from their letters and diaries in their loneliness, their frailties, their determination and their triumphs." The book, considered a major contribution to Australian historical research and writing, sold 15,000 copies in 20 years. The University of Melbourne continues to honor the memory of Margaret Kiddle by awarding an annual prize in her name for the best final Honors essay in history.

SOURCES:

Radi, Heather, ed. *200 Australian Women*. NSW, Australia: Women's Redress Press, 1988.

Wilde, William H., Joy Horton, and Barry Andrews, ed. *Oxford Companion to Australian Literature*. Melbourne: Oxford University Press, 1994.

Barbara Morgan,
Melrose, Massachusetts

Kieler, Laura (fl. 1860s)

German writer who served as the inspiration for Nora in Henrik Ibsen's A Doll's House. *Flourished in the 1860s; married a schoolteacher.*

Beginning in 1877, Norwegian poet and playwright Henrik Ibsen (1828–1906) wrote a series of social or thesis plays that were instrumental in changing the course of written drama. These works, including *The Pillars of Society* (1877), *A Doll's House* (1879), *Ghosts* (1881), and *An Enemy of the People* (1882), were departures from traditional drama not only in their treatment of serious social issues, but in their use of ordinary language and realistic settings. *A Doll's House*, first performed at the Royal Theater in Copenhagen on December 21, 1879, was written in response to the growing movement for the emancipation of women and explores through plot and character women's dependent status in society. In the groundbreaking drama, Ibsen for the first time applied the concept of individuality to women as well as to men. "Women also shall be themselves, be human beings, and not merely their husbands' wives, and their children's mothers," wrote Henrik Jaeger, explaining Ibsen's theme in a critical biography of the playwright. In the course of the drama, Nora, a doll-like creature completely dependent on her husband, is forced into a moral conflict which she solves in the end by walking out on her marriage.

While historians frequently credit the Norwegian novelist **Camilla Collett* with influencing Ibsen in the writing of *A Doll's House*, few mention that the character of Nora was based on another woman known to the playwright, a writer by the name of Laura Kieler whom he met in Dresden in the late 1860s. Kieler had written a sequel to one of Ibsen's plays and sent it to him, after which the two met and stayed in touch for several years. The events in Kieler's life during those interim years became Nora's experiences in *A Doll's House*, although Ibsen somewhat altered characters and events and also manipulated the outcome to support his theme.

Sometime after her meeting with the playwright, Kieler's schoolteacher husband contracted tuberculosis and was told by his doctors that a warmer climate might be the only thing to prolong his life. Without consulting her husband, but with the assistance of a friend, Kieler took out a loan to finance the necessary trip. The couple then traveled to Italy where Kieler's husband made a full recovery. Sometime later, Kieler related these events to Ibsen and his wife **Susannah Thoresen Ibsen** during a visit in Munich, at which time Ibsen noticed that the young woman seemed mentally burdened. Early in 1878, Kieler sent Ibsen the manuscript of her newest novel with a letter asking him to submit the book to his publisher. Ibsen, who was unimpressed by the work, wrote back to Kieler telling her that he felt the book did not warrant publication.

What Ibsen did not know was that Kieler was now being forced to pay back the loan she had negotiated and that the manuscript was her last hope of raising the money without involving her husband. When she received Ibsen's letter rejecting her work, she became desperate and forged a check to pay back the debt. The forgery was eventually discovered, and Kieler was forced to confess everything to her husband, who was less than sympathetic. He accused her of a criminal act and sought a legal separation to keep her from her children. As a result, Kieler suffered a nervous breakdown and was confined to a mental institution for a month. Upon her release, her husband took her back, but only after a considerable amount of pleading on her part.

When *A Doll's House* was published and produced in 1879, starring *Betty Hennings, Laura Kieler was recognized as the inspiration for the play, but little is known of her after that time. The play, as might be expected, unleashed a flurry of protest. Ibsen's departure from the classic rules governing tragedy (elevated characters and poetic language), to say nothing of his radical ending, angered the critics and outraged the audience. The moral outcry over Nora's flagrant disregard of her duties as a wife and mother was such that some theaters refused to produce the play. When it reached Germany two years later, one actress decided to change the ending herself, proclaiming, "I would never leave *my* children." (Copyright laws between countries did not then protect the playwright.) Ibsen, backed into a corner, grudgingly wrote an alternative ending in which Nora does not leave, but called it "a barbaric outrage on the play."

While Laura Kieler slipped into obscurity, the work she inspired became one of the most important plays in the history of the theater. *A Doll's House* was first performed in America as early as 1882, by an amateur group in Milwaukee, Wisconsin; a year later, *Helena Modjeska presented an adaptation of the play in Louisville, Kentucky, but it closed after only one performance. *Minnie Maddern Fiske revived the play in 1894, 1895, and 1902, and the Russian actress *Alla Nazimova provided a riveting performance of her own in 1907, although by that time Ibsen had been embraced by most of the country's literary critics. *A Doll's House,* along with the entire body of Ibsen's work, has since become a standard in American theater repertory.

SOURCES:

*Andreas-Salomé, Lou. *Ibsen's Heroines.* Translated by Siegfried Mandel. Redding Ridge, CT: Black Swan Books, 1985.

Gassner, John. *A Treasury of the Theater.* NY: Simon and Schuster, 1950.

Jaeger, Henrik. *Henrik Ibsen: A Critical Biography.* From the Norwegian by William Morton Payne. NY: Benjamin Blom, 1972.

Wilmeth, Don B., and Tice L. Miller, eds. *Cambridge Guide to American Theater.* Cambridge, England and NY: Cambridge University Press, 1993.

Barbara Morgan,
Melrose, Massachusetts

Kielland, Kitty L. (1843–1914).

See Backer, Harriet for sidebar.

Kielmansegge, Sophia Charlotte von (1673–1725)

Countess of Platen, Brentford and Darlington. Name variations: Baroness von Kielmansegge; Countess Leinster; Baroness of Brentford. Born around 1673; died in 1725; daughter of Ernest Augustus, duke of Brunswick-Luneburg, and **Clara Elizabeth Meisenburg**; *associated with George I (1660–1727), king of England (r. 1714–1727).*

Kiesler, Hedy (1913–2000).

See Lamarr, Hedy.

Kilborn, Pam (1939—)

Australian hurdler. Born in Melbourne, Australia, on August 12, 1939.

Won the bronze medal in the 80-meter hurdles at the Tokyo Olympics (1964); won the silver medal in the 80-meter hurdles at the Mexico City Olympics (1968).

A hurdler from the age of 16, Australian Pam Kilborn captured the attention of the track-and-field world during the 1962 British Empire and Commonwealth Games, winning the 80-meter hurdles by an impressive four meters and placing first in the long jump with a 6.268-meter leap, a career best. At the 1964 Olympics, Kilborn finished third in the 80-meter hurdles, but equaled the world record for the event just a few days later. She retained her hurdles crown at the 1966 British Empire Games and won a silver medal in the 80-meter hurdles at the 1968 Olympics. At the 1970 British Commonwealth Games, weeks shy of her 31st birthday, Kilborn won two gold medals in the 100-meter hurdles and relay event. Pam Kilborn was the first woman selected to carry the Australian flag at the opening ceremony of the 1970 Olympics, but she did not medal at those Games.

SOURCES:

The Oxford Companion to Australian Sports. Melbourne: Oxford University Press, 1992.

Barbara Morgan,
Melrose, Massachusetts

Kildare, Lady (1731–1814).

See Lennox Sisters.

Kilgallen, Dorothy (1913–1965)

American columnist and radio and television personality. Born Dorothy Mae Kilgallen in Chicago, Illinois, on July 3, 1913; died under mysterious circumstances in New York City on November 7, 1965; eldest of two daughters of James Lawrence Kilgallen (a journalist) and Mae (Ahern) Kilgallen; attended grade school in Chicago, Indianapolis, and New York; graduated from Erasmus Hall High School, Brooklyn, 1930; attended the College of New Rochelle, New York; married Richard Kollmar (an actor and producer), on April 6, 1940: children: **Jill-Ellen Kollmar**; *Richard Kollmar;* **Kerry Kolmar**.

Considered by some to be the greatest woman reporter of her era, Dorothy Kilgallen was born in 1913, the daughter of famous journalist James Lawrence Kilgallen and **Mae Ahern Kilgallen**, an attractive red-head who at one time had a promising career as a singer. Dorothy and her younger sister **Eleanor Kilgallen** grew up in Chicago, Indianapolis, and Brooklyn, New York, where the family settled when James Kilgallen's career with Hearst's International News Service brought him East. Not much is known of Dorothy's childhood. Since her mysterious death of a barbiturate overdose in 1965, her family has

withheld information about her. Her biographer **Lee Israel** found that Kilgallen's immediate family, teachers and schoolmates had little to relate about her early life, except that she was a good student and a voracious reader. Kilgallen, it seems, seldom reminisced with her friends about occurrences prior to her first job as a cub reporter with the New York *Evening Journal,* at age 17. Intending only to work during summer break from the College of New Rochelle, she won a byline for a story on a hospitalized child and decided to leave college and begin a career in journalism. James "Red" Horan, who worked with Kilgallen during her "sob-sister" days at the *Journal,* recalls that she stood out from the other young women who populated the newsroom at the time. "[T]here was something about the way Dorothy handled herself," he said. "I had the opinion that she was born for the business. That soft, quiet way of hers hid a steel ambition and a drive and also a very keen intelligence."

By age 20, Kilgallen, who had already covered a myriad of grisly murders and notorious trials (the *Journal*'s specialty), had earned substantial stature at the paper. She first won national acclaim, however, for her "Girl Around the World" series, the chronicle of a competing round-the-world flight the paper sent her on in 1936. Vying with Leo Kieran of *The New York Times* and Bud Ekins of United Press International, Kilgallen, traveling only commercial routes, made her trip in 24 days, 12 hour, and 52 minutes and only placed third in the race, but the junket launched her as a celebrity and brought the paper some notoriety as well. Her dispatches later appeared in a book, *Girl Around the World,* and she was the subject of the song "Hats off to Dorothy."

In November 1937, Kilgallen went off to the West Coast, ostensibly to report on the movies for the new *Journal-American* (the result of a merger between Hearst's *American* and the *Evening Journal*). While in Hollywood, she also visited Warner Bros. to promote an autobiographical screenplay about her globe-trotting experiences, *Fly Away Baby.* The movie, with **Glenda Farrell** in the role of Torchy Blane, the "smart blonde" reporter, opened in New York in July 1937 to a "Fair-Good" rating. Kilgallen also tested and was given a small role as a reporter in the forgettable *Sinner Take All,* an experience she found boring, and one she would seldom mention in later life. In her role as a Hollywood gossip columnist, however, Kilgallen proved to be no competition for *Louella Parsons, who had the Hollywood beat pretty much to herself by virtue of her chummy relationship with William Randolph Hearst and his mistress, actress *Marion Davies. Kilgallen made a hasty retreat.

Upon returning to New York, the young reporter aligned herself with the city's flourishing Café Society. Instead of stories about crime and trials, she now covered such events as the wedding of Franklin Delano Roosevelt, Jr. to Ethel du Pont and the coronation of George VI. The *Journal-American*, however, had other plans for its talented reporter. Envisioning Kilgallen as a kind of female Walter Winchell, the newspaper officially awarded her the Broadway beat in 1938, promoting her as "the first and only woman Broadway columnist" and assuring readers that, though it was a man's job, Dorothy was up to the task. Indeed she was. Her daily column, "Voice of Broadway," was soon appearing in 24 out-of-town papers and, by 1950, was syndicated in 45 newspapers throughout the country. According to Israel, Kilgallen was no innovator and followed the style set by Winchell. The columns, writes Israel, dealt with "declarative name-naming, hard-core gossip about marriage, divorce, nose bobs, public drunkenness, pregnancy, brouhahas, comebacks, broken kneecaps, hairline fractures, lost dogs, nervous breakdowns, gambling losses, political shenanigans, hiring, firing, trysting, fisting, overnight success, and terminal self-destruction among the famous and the notorious." Though Kilgallen eventually eclipsed Winchell during the 1950s, and wielded a great deal of power in her heyday, she never adopted the mean-spirited approach that made Winchell such a formidable journalistic presence.

Kilgallen made her radio debut in 1941, on a Saturday morning chat show also called "Voice of Broadway," which *Newsweek* reviewed as "crisp and sparkling." She became better known, however, for her daily (except Saturday) program "Breakfast with Dorothy and Dick," which was launched in 1945 with her husband Dick Kollmar, an actor and Hollywood producer whom she had married in 1940. The program, unrehearsed, was broadcast live from the large dining room of the Kollmars' 16-room apartment on Park Avenue and took the form of an impromptu exchange of small talk centering on the couple's glamorous lifestyle. Topics included theater and opera performances, celebrity parties (including their own), and items gleaned from their nightly rounds of the city's posh restaurants and night clubs, notably The Stork Club. On occasional Sunday mornings, the Kollmar children, Jill-Ellen and Dick, joined in the broadcast. (Another son, Kerry, was born in 1954.) The fact that the Kollmars were a few so-

cial notches above their audience, and made no pretense about it, gave the show an edge over other programs with a similar format, explains Israel. "They were rich, mobile, quintessentially cosmopolitan," she writes. "If Dorothy endorsed a food product—and she endorsed more and more as the show blossomed—she did not pretend to have cooked it. It had doubtless been served to her. As the months went by, their loyal listeners knew the names of their staff, the dimensions of their table, the quality of their glassware, a good deal about the extremely social permutations of the couple, and the names of most of their close, equally privileged friends." Israel also points out that the success of the show had nothing to do with the Kollmars' popularity as a couple. "On the contrary," she writes, "the Kollmars were compelling irritants to whom a large part of their audience was drawn in spite of itself, as tongue to a septic tooth."

Although the Kollmar marriage reverberated with good cheer on the air—"Good morning, darling," Kilgallen chirped daily at the show's opening—it was a troubled union. There were questions at the onset as to whether Kollmar had married Kilgallen because of her ability to advance his acting career, although he achieved moderate status as an actor and producer on his own. Later, his alcoholism and philandering drove a wedge between the couple, who would have probably divorced had it not been for their strong Catholic beliefs. As a compromise, the two increasingly adopted separate emotional lives, while remaining united on matters involving the children or their professional partnership. Kilgallen's name was frequently linked with other men, including the singer Johnny Ray, with whom she had a long-term affair beginning in 1956.

In 1949, Kilgallen made her television debut on "Leave It to the Girls," which featured a group of successful New York career women dispensing advice on life, love, and the battle between the sexes. Kilgallen reached a much larger audience, however, when she joined the pioneering "What's My Line?," a weekly game show in which a panel of celebrities, including Fred Allen, *Arlene Francis, and Bennett Cerf, attempted to guess the occupations of guests. The show, moderated by John Daly, also featured a weekly mystery guest for whom the panel was blindfolded. Premiering on February 2, 1950, the show became a national institution and made Kilgallen one of the most visible journalists of her time. In turn, she brought to the show a love of the game and a fierce competitiveness that cast her in the role of villain. Her seriousness eventually came to be balanced by Arlene Francis' more ebullient and playful personality. Kilgallen disliked the role of the heavy and often complained. "Why can't I be the adorable one?," she frequently asked Francis during pre-show make-up sessions.

During her period as a successful columnist and television celebrity, Kilgallen also occasionally covered news stories, including the coronation of *Elizabeth II and the trial of Wayne Lonergan, who was accused of bludgeoning his socialite wife **Patricia Lonergan** to death with a

candelabra. During the mid-50s, Kilgallen began accepting assignments from the city desk, which, according to Israel, she turned into stories of great impact. "Flashy, skilled, rapturously or peevishly reflective of her own world view," writes Israel, "they are among the best examples of colorful, personal reporting." Among them was Kilgallen's coverage of the 1954 trial of Sam Sheppard, who was accused of brutally murdering his wife **Marilyn Sheppard** in their Ohio home, and who steadfastly claimed innocence and was later released from prison. Kilgallen's stories of the trial appeared on the *Journal's*

Dorothy
Kilgallen

front page and were characterized not so much by the reporting of the events themselves, but by Kilgallen's reactions to the events. "We momentarily expected to hear that she had been chosen to deliver the summation or, at least, to be a surprise witness," commented *Time* magazine about her coverage of the Sheppard case. Kilgallen also covered the trial of society surgeon Bernard Finch, who was accused of shooting his wife **Barbara Finch** while his mistress hid in a clump of bushes, and that of Dr. Stephen Ward, who was part of England's notorious John Profumo-*Christine Keeler scandal. Bennett Cerf then asked her to write a book for Random House on the trials she had covered. She agreed, thinking she could produce it within a year, but the book, *Murder One*, was not published until 1967, two years after her death. Allen Ullman, who was ultimately assigned to the project, never knew that Kilgallen had been working on it, and he assembled his manuscript entirely from old newspaper clippings.

Kilgallen, who was fascinated by illness and accident, had her own health woes beginning in 1959, when she collapsed in her bathroom and was hospitalized for more than two weeks. That was the first in a series of episodes that were never really clarified, although Kilgallen told her closest friends that her condition was a form of anemia. The columnist also drank increasingly and came to use barbiturates to help her sleep. Although her health never prevented her from working, it often concerned her friends. In March 1965, Kilgallen fractured her left shoulder in what was reported as a fall, but the two lengthy hospital stays after the incident may have been associated with her alcohol and barbiturate dependency. Meanwhile, Kilgallen was purportedly preparing a chapter for *Murder One* on Jack Ruby, who had been charged with the televised murder of Lee Harvey Oswald, and with whom she had had a private interview. During the summer of 1965, the columnist also took an extended vacation in Europe, returning home looking and feeling better than she had in years.

On Sunday, November 7, 1965, after her usual appearance on "What's My Line?", Kilgallen had a drink with a friend, then made her way alone to the Regency Hotel where she sat down at a table in the cocktail lounge. The bartender there was the last person to admit seeing her that evening. Kilgallen was found dead the next morning, November 8, sitting up in bed in the master bedroom of her five-story townhouse. Cause of death was initially attributed to a heart attack, but a subsequent autopsy credited "acute ethanol and barbiturate intoxica-

tion—circumstances undetermined." Her family deemed the death an accident, and there was no further investigation of the matter. Ironically, Kilgallen's husband Dick Kollmar died in much the same manner in January 1971. His death, too, was first thought to be a heart attack, but eventually was attributed to a drug overdose.

There are some, Lee Israel included, who believe that Kilgallen may not have taken her own life, but may have been murdered because of information she had obtained from Jack Ruby about the Kennedy assassination. Although Israel's own exhaustive three-year investigation turned up many ambiguities surrounding Kilgallen's death, it did not yield proof of a murder. In addition, nothing of what Kilgallen learned in her private talk with Jack Ruby, or on trips she made to Texas and New Orleans to investigate the Kennedy assassination, has ever come to light.

SOURCES:

Candee, Marjorie Dent, ed. *Current Biography*. NY: H.W. Wilson, 1952.
Israel, Lee. *Kilgallen: A Biography of Dorothy Kilgallen*. NY: Delacorte Press, 1979.

Barbara Morgan,
Melrose, Massachusetts

Kilgore, Carrie B. (1838–1908)

American lawyer. Born Caroline Burnham in Craftsbury, Vermont, on January 20, 1838; died in Swarthmore, Pennsylvania, on June 29, 1908; served a medical apprenticeship in the Hygeio-Therapeutic College of Bellevue Hospital, New York, and earned a medical degree; first woman graduate of the Central Pennsylvania Law School (now University of Pennsylvania), 1883; married Damon Kilgore (a lawyer), in 1876 (died 1888); children: two daughters.

In 1864, Carrie Burnham Kilgore graduated with the degree of doctor of medicine from Bellevue Hospital in New York City; a year later, she went to Philadelphia and began reading Blackstone. After considerable time spent knocking at the door, she managed to graduate from law school in 1883, inspiring the ridicule of the press, bar and bench. When she argued her right to vote before the state Supreme Court, the chief justice pronounced her address "an able and exhaustive argument." In 1886, she was allowed to practice in the federal courts and, in 1890, in the U.S. Supreme Court. After her husband's death in 1888, Kilgore took over and managed his law practice. At age 70, Carrie Kilgore was the only woman passenger in the first hot-air balloon flight of the Philadelphia Aeronautical Recreation Society.

Killigrew, Anne (1660–1685)

English poet, painter, and maid of honor to Mary of Modena, who was celebrated in one of Dryden's odes: "To the pious memory of the accomplished young lady, Mrs. Anne Killigrew." Pronunciation: Kill-LI-grew. Born in 1660; died of smallpox, age 25, on June 16, 1685; daughter of Judith Killigrew and Henry Killigrew (both royalist supporters of the Stuart kings, closely associated with the court of Charles II, in the early years of the Restoration); never married; no children.

Selected poetry: Poems by Mrs. Anne Killigrew (London: S. Lowndes, 1686, published posthumously by her father; republished as Poems [1686] by Mrs. Anne Killigrew: A Facsimile Reproduction, with an introduction by Robert Morton, ed., Gainesville, FL: Scholars' Facsimiles and Reprints, 1967).

*Portraits and still-lifes: three of which are mentioned in her poems, including self-portraits and paintings of both James II and Mary of Modena. The portrait of James II is now in the possession of Her Majesty Queen *Elizabeth II, and an engraving by Blooteling from a self-portrait and a mezzotint by B. Lens from Killigrew's painting Venus and Adonis are in the Paul Mellon Collection. The Venus and Adonis itself was recorded as in a private collection in Folkestone in 1915. A miniature in mezzotint, done from Killigrew's self-portrait, was prefixed to the 1686 edition of her Poems.*

Anne Killigrew's life, though short, was in many ways exemplary of a 17th-century gentlewoman born into the upper classes of the English gentry. Reading her poems and examining her paintings offer insights into what 17th-century English life might have been like for a lively and observant young girl at the court of Charles II. Setting these poems and paintings in the context of what we know of that court life confirms some of our assumptions while challenging others.

The details of Killigrew's life, though scant, are suggestive. She was the daughter of Henry and **Judith Killigrew**, both royalist supporters of the Stuart kings and connected by marriage to an illegitimate branch of the royal family. Thomas Killigrew, uncle of Anne, had been a page to Charles I and had accompanied the Prince of Wales (later Charles II) into exile during the years of the English Civil War and Republic. With the Restoration, the three Killigrew brothers, William, Thomas and Henry, were rewarded for their loyalty with offices at court. Henry, who had been a chaplain in the king's army, was appointed Master of the Savoy Hospital in Westminster. His daughter Anne Killigrew, born just months before the Restoration in 1660, was christened privately, as offices of the common prayer were not publicly allowed by the Puritan government of the Commonwealth.

Killigrew's family was not only associated with the court but also distinguished through its literary achievements and associations. As young men, all three of the Killigrew brothers wrote plays, and later in life Henry Killigrew published his sermons. Thomas Killigrew, with William Davenant, another playwright, was granted a patent for two theatrical companies, the Duke's Servants and the King's Servants. That same uncle, by all accounts a witty and lively courtier, introduced guitar playing to London society when he sent a group of Italian singers and musicians from Venice to entertain the king. The guitar rapidly became popular, and skill with this instrument was quickly added to the list of accomplishments desirable for fashionable women of the court. Killigrew's Italian singers continued to perform at the court where they were received with great enthusiasm.

> *A* Grace for beauty, and a Muse for wit.
>
> —Anthony Wood (1820)

We know nothing specific about Anne Killigrew's social training or her formal education, but we can make some inferences based on our knowledge of her family setting and drawn from allusions made in her poems and paintings. Despite the musical and dramatic interests of her father and uncles, neither music nor playwriting attracted her, but painting and poetry evidently did.

While most young women of Killigrew's social situation probably received some instruction in painting and would most likely have been introduced to sufficient reading to make them pleasing conversationalists, Killigrew seems to have profited from a more extensive and perhaps more formal education. Her paintings in their choice and handling of topic imply an engagement with Greek and Roman mythology and literature that goes beyond the superficial, and the development of classical allusions in her poetry implies an intellect capable of philosophical and moral insights. Her technical skill in both arts is immediately apparent, suggesting that she had competent teachers and was able to profit from their instruction. Killigrew had a number of brothers and sisters, yet she is the only member of that large family whose work was acknowledged by her contemporaries or continues to be read. While posthumous publication as a means of memorializing someone was not unusual in the 17th century, Anthony Wood, Killigrew's first, rather informal, biographer is emphatic in his assertion that if the praises her poems received had been no more than compliments, her father would not have permitted their publication.

At some point, when Killigrew had completed her childhood education, her father secured a position for her as maid of honor in the household of *Mary of Modena, second wife of the duke of York (later King James II). There she joined a circle of women who were to become known for their intellects and accomplishments. *Catharine Sedley, *Sarah Jennings (Churchill), and *Anne Kingsmill (Finch) were all members of this circle and women who would become influential in court life in the years to follow.

Mary of Modena has been praised by historians for the disciplined and serious nature of her household, in contrast to the increasingly dissolute court of Charles II. It is misleading, however, to conclude that so serious an atmosphere dictated the tone of Killigrew's poetry. A careful reading of the poems suggests instead that Killigrew was less "pious" than Dryden described her and more of an amused observer than the didactic moralist that membership in such a household might imply.

We have no way of knowing who determined the ordering of Killigrew's poems in her published volume or what criterion was used, but because the first poems in the collection refer to the writer as inexperienced, we might guess that the poems were ordered chronologically. If so, they allow for a tone of witty self-deprecation, implying a writer who takes her work, not herself, seriously.

The first poem, for example, is devoted to a curious choice of topic for a young female writer, suggesting that Killigrew thought of herself as a poet first and as a woman writer only secondarily. It celebrates Alexander the Great, in a confident tone, and begins in true epic fashion, "I sing the Man that never Equal knew/ Whose Mighty Arms all Asia did subdue." Although Killigrew does acknowledge her gender at one point ("Nor will it from his Conquests derogate/ A Female Pen his Acts did celebrate"), she certainly does not apologize for it, and part of the wit of the poem arises from the fact that the gorgeous rival troops, who with "Scarlet Plume" and "haughty Crest" challenge Alexander, turn out to be Amazons. The poem does break off, unfinished, and the editor (probably Killigrew's father) comments that the epic mode proved too challenging for the young poet, but both his comment and the self-deprecating wit of the poem are addressed to deficiencies in literary experience, not gender.

The arrangement of the poems that follow, while apparently still chronologically ordered, also seems to have been designed to display Killigrew's versatility as a poet; the poems are often grouped by poetic genre, thus emphasizing their variety. Epigrams appear together as do pastoral dialogues and some philosophical pieces. Occasional poems are scattered throughout, but another set of linked poems seems to emphasize personal rather than generic affinities. Killigrew's poems on her own paintings, for example, appear together. Viewed as a collection, Killigrew's *Poems* suggests that she tried her hand at a variety of poetic genres—heroic, pastoral, epigrammatic, occasional, panegyric—from a variety of stances, old and young, male and female, engaged by or disenchanted with the court. The arrangement of her verse, then, reinforces the impression that she viewed herself not as a female writer but as a serious beginning poet, exploring all the facets of her craft.

While all of the poems in the collection are intriguing, some deserve particular mention in filling out an impression of Killigrew's life and personality. The short verse titled "On My Aunt Mrs. Anne Killigrew Drown'd under London-bridge, in the Queen's Barge, Anno 1641," for example, while clearly notable for the startling nature of its title, also gives us a sense of Killigrew's own royalist sympathies and the intensity with which she maintained them. The stanza which specifically marks the drowning incident—

When angry Heav'n extinguisht her fair Light
It seem'd to say, Nought's Precious in my fight;
As I in Waves this Paragon have drown'd,
The Nation next, and King I will confound

—is sufficiently emphatic in its royalist sympathy as to leave no doubt that Killigrew's political affiliations were based on strongly held personal convictions and not simply a matter of family connections.

In similar fashion, the poem titled "To the Queen" clarifies Killigrew's moral stance as self-chosen rather than as a non-reflective product of familial and courtly influence. Moreover, while her moral position is delivered emphatically, it is tempered by humor and realism, and its tone, even when denouncing vice, is decidedly not "pious."

Appearing second in the collection, the poem begins by making an amused reference to the failure of the first poem, on Alexander. While the poet does acknowledge her own technical inadequacy in the earlier poem, she also observes that the fault there was not only that a young poet, in violation of decorum, chose an epic mode too early, but that that epic subject was not of true epic proportion after all. Alexander's force, set against the queen's virtue, is no longer impressive but comic, and he is seen as flailing with "Frantic Might" against "Windmills" in contrast to the queen's quiet "Prowess" of "Grace and Goodness." The poet "smile[s] . . . at his Unequal (though Gigantick) State" and is moved to "Pitty" for "him the world called Great." Yet the poem is more serious than amusing and, as it shifts its attention to the virtues of the queen, is even grim in its indictment of the corruption of the court, the moral equivalent of venereal disease which "dares its Ulcerous Face appear." These lines in particular dramatize Killigrew's own strongly felt indignation at court attitudes and practices which, as documented elsewhere, were indeed seriously corrupt.

More individual notes can also be found in Killigrew's poems on her own paintings, although again the reader must depend on inference as Killigrew is rarely direct about her own personal beliefs. The titles of the three poems— "St. John the Baptist Painted by her self," "Herodias' Daughter . . . also painted by her self," and "On a Picture representing two Nimphs of Diana's . . . Painted by her self"—tell us little and were probably in fact selected by someone else. The references to Biblical and mythological subjects sound conventional until one recalls that the Savoy Hospital where Killigrew's father held the post of Master included a chapel dedicated to John the Baptist (in the chancel of which Killigrew herself was to be buried and where her family erected a monument to her). This chapel may well have held personal and familial meaning for Killigrew, and thus the selection of John the Baptist as a topic may not have been dictated by convention at all.

What is most interesting about the painting poems, however, is Killigrew's attitude toward the relative merits of the two arts. While her contemporaries, as reported by Wood and Horace Walpole, appear to have valued her at least as much as an artist, Killigrew herself praised the poet. "If you ask where such heights do dwell," she concludes of the heroic beings celebrated in the visual arts, "the Poets only that can tell." Thus she implies that only poetry can deliver the special knowledge which is the key to the kind of virtuous behavior needed to offset the corruption of the contemporary world.

Killigrew's love poems, too, might well be rewarding when read more in the context of her own life than from the perspective of the conventions of her age. While they are, of course, conventionally pastoral and offer the expected counsel of caution to the various nymphs whom they invoke or to whom they are addressed, one might also profitably view them as referring to the various courtship experiences of Killigrew's own circle of friends. The images of Alinda and her shepherd suitor Amitor in the second pastoral dialogue, for example, might well correlate with the historical figures of Anne Kingsmill and Heneage Finch whose courtship, in 1684, was generally seen as exemplary and in just the serious and reciprocally respectful terms that Killigrew's poem promotes.

One last grouping of poems might finally be examined in the light of learning about Killigrew's life in Mary of Modena's household. The poem titled "Upon the saying that my Verses were made by another" which is frequently anthologized and read alone, could sound much like the lament of a female poet, excluded from acknowledgement by her peers and unfairly valued because of her gender. "The Envious Age" the poet complains, "only to Me done,/ Will not allow, what I write my Own" and instead, while commending her verses, sees them as more likely springing from "An other's Brow, that had so rich a store/ Of sacred Wreaths, that circled it before." The more experienced male poet is given credit that belongs to the female as the others "'gainst a Maide Conspire."

As the editors of *Kissing the Rod,* one anthology in which the poem appears, point out, such a poem is a commonplace in female writing. Nevertheless, when this poem is read in conjunction with the lines addressed to "My Lord Colrane," a rather different picture emerges. The second poem, evidently written in response to lines by Colrane written to Killigrew and probably prompted in turn by a poem of hers, makes clear that Killigrew practiced her craft not as an isolated female writer but rather within an established manuscript culture. Such an impression is reinforced by the delicate mixture of tact and strategy which Killigrew brings to what must have been a fairly sensitive undertaking. Lord Colrane (Henry Hale, 2nd Baron Colrane, 1638–1708) was a fairly influential individual, well-educated and scholarly in his interests. An antiquary of Tottenham, Middlesex, he evidently was acquainted with all of Killigrew's verse as a copy of her *Poems* bearing his bookplate survives (now in the possession of the University of Michigan libraries). Killigrew, in responding to Colrane, had to be respectful yet not obsequious. She had to demonstrate her understanding of the conventions of compliment and courtly exchange that verse circulated in manuscript called forth. She succeeds in meeting these requirements quite skillfully, exchanging compliment for compliment in such a way that inequities of gender, age, and possibly social standing which might have existed at the beginning of the poem are gently adjusted by its conclusion. The poem closes by invoking the exemplary goals of complimentary verse, instancing both Colrane's lines and Killigrew's as efficacious moral instruments in accordance with proper complimentary decorum.

It would be satisfying to be able to round out a discussion of Killigrew's life by assessing her paintings against known cultural contexts as well, but all we have for now are one or two portraits (including the one of King James II), possibly the *Venus and Adonis* and several titles. Walpole reports that six of Killigrew's paintings were sold from her brother Admiral Killigrew's collection. These included the *Venus and Adonis, A Satyr playing a pipe, Judith and Holofernes, A woman's head, The Graces dressing Venus* and one of Killigrew's self-portraits. Walpole, however, did not see them and thus comments at second hand when he reports that Killigrew painted "in the style of Sir Peter Lyly." The self-portraits we do have, one appended to the *Poems* and another attached to Walpole's *Anecdotes of Painting*, show us a rather elegant young woman, fashionably dressed and poised in expression and posture. The portrait done by John Lyly reinforces this impression. She looks at home in her age and place.

Taken altogether, then, the poems and paintings of Anne Killigrew confirm our impression that life for a 17th-century woman at court was comfortable, though also both personally and socially demanding. What her poems challenge is the stereotype of female authorship, particularly that it was isolating and handicapped by deficiencies in education and opportunity. Killigrew seems to have been a confident young woman, observant in her daily life and successfully serious about developing the skills of a poet and painter. It is ironic that even the official appointments and public acts of her father, uncles, and brothers might still have left them unknown. We have retrieved the names of Henry, William, Thomas and Admiral Killigrew not for their accomplishments, but because they had the good fortune to be related to a young poet named Anne.

SOURCES:

Ballard, George. *Memoirs of Several Ladies of Great Britain*. London: J. Noon, 1752, pp. 337–345.

Cibber, Theophilus. *Lives of the Poets*. Vol. 2. London: R. Griffiths, 1753, pp. 224–226.

Clayton, Ellen Creathorne. *English Female Artists*. Vol. 1. London, 1876, pp. 59–70.

Granger, John. *Biographical History of England*. Vol. 4. London, 1775, p. 129.

Morton, Richard, ed. *Poems (1686) by Mrs. Anne Killigrew, a Facsimile Reproduction*, with introduction. Gainesville, FL: Scholars' Facsimile Press, 1967.

Reynolds, Myra. *The Learned Lady in England 1650–1750*. 1920 (reprinted 1964).

Walpole, Horace. *Anecdotes of Painting in England*. Vol. 3. London: Shakespeare Press, 1828, pp. 52–55.

Wood, Anthony. *Athenae Oxonienses*. 3rd ed. with additions. Ed. by Philip Bliss. Vol. 4. London, 1820, pp. 622–623.

SUGGESTED READING:

Doody, Margaret. *Daring Muse*. Cambridge, MA: Harvard University Press, 1985.

Ezell, Margaret J.M. *The Patriarch's Wife: Literary Evidence and the History of the Family*. Chapel Hill, NC: University of North Carolina Press, 1987.

Greer, Germaine, Susan Hastings, Jeslyn Medoff, Melinda Sansone, eds. *Kissing the Rod: An Anthology of Seventeenth-Century Women's Verse*. NY: Farrar, Straus, Giroux, 1988.

Hobby, Elaine. *Virtue of Necessity: English Women's Writing 1649–1688*. Ann Arbor, MI: University of Michigan Press, 1990.

Messenger, Ann. *His and Hers: Essays in Restoration and 18th-Century Literature*. Lexington, KY: University Press of Kentucky, 1986.

Mulvihill, Maureen E. "Essential Studies of Restoration Women Writers: Reclaiming a Heritage, 1913–1986," in *Restoration: Studies in English Literary Culture, 1660–1700*. Vol. 11, Fall 1987, pp. 122–131.

Pohli, Carol Virginia. "Formal and Informal Space in Dryden's Ode, 'To the Pious Memory of . . . Anne Killigrew,'" in *Restoration: Studies in English Literary Culture, 1660–1700*. Vol. 15. Spring 1991, pp. 27–40.

Rogers, Katharine, and William McCarthy, eds. *Anthology of Early Women Writers 1600–1800*. NY: New American Library, 1987.

Silber, C. Anderson. "Nymphs and Satyrs: Poet, Readers and Irony in Dryden's 'Ode to Anne Killigrew,'" in *Studies in Eighteenth-Century Culture*. Vol. 14, 1985, pp. 193–212.

Straub, Kristina. "Indecent Liberties with a Poet: Audience and the Metaphor of Rape in Killigrew's 'Upon the Saying that My Verses,' and Pope's Arbuthnot," in *Tulsa Studies in Women's Literature*. Vol. 6. Spring 1987, pp. 27–45.

Ann Hurley,
Assistant Professor of English,
Wagner College, Staten Island, New York

Killigrew, Catherine (c. 1530–1583)

English noblewoman. Name variations: Lady Catherine Killigrew; Katherine. Born around 1530; died in 1583; fourth daughter of Sir Anthony Cooke (1504–1576, a politician and tutor to Edward, the prince of Wales); married Sir Henry Killigrew, in 1565.

Lady Catherine Killigrew was born around 1530, the fourth daughter of Sir Anthony Cooke, a politician and tutor to Edward, the prince of Wales (the future Edward VI). She was said to have been a lady of learning, proficient in Hebrew, Greek, and Latin.

Killigrew, Elizabeth (c. 1622–?).

See Gwynn, Nell for sidebar.

Kilmury, Diana (1948—)

Canadian union activist. Born around 1948; raised in Vancouver, British Columbia; married and divorced; children: three.

Raised in Vancouver, British Columbia, Diana Kilmury was a young, divorced mother of three when she went to work for a small trucking firm. She joined Local 213 of the Teamsters Union three years later, the first woman member to work in heavy construction, and, in 1977, came to the aid of Jack Vlahovic, a dissident British Columbian union representative who had been ousted for whistle-blowing on corruption in the union ranks. Kilmury helped Vlahovic raise $40,000 for his legal fund, then joined the Teamsters for a Democratic Union, crisscrossing Canada, urging union members to get rid of mob-controlled officials and demand democratic elections. "These people had pension money stolen, three presidents indicted—it's not like you had to tell anyone the union was corrupt," she said. "We just needed to tell them, 'You have the right to vote.'" For speaking out, Kilmury was the target of heckling and even death threats, but she refused to be intimidated. Her efforts paid off in 1989, when the union rank and file won the right to elect their leadership. Kilmury was subsequently elected a Teamsters vice-president and took office in February 1992, the first woman member of the Teamster General Executive Board. The Teamsters Human Rights Commission that she chairs held the first Teamsters Women's Conference (1994), the first Civil Rights Conference (1995), and has sponsored many regional seminars and events. "This time," she said, "the people with the white hats won." Kilmury's crusade was the subject of the 1996 TNT television movie, "Mother Trucker: The Diana Kilmury Story."

SOURCES:

Eftimiades, Maria. "Spotlight On . . . Diana Kilmury," in *People Weekly.* October 21, 1996.

RELATED MEDIA:

"Mother Trucker: The Diana Kilmury Story" (television docudrama), starring **Barbara Williams**, script by **Anne Wheeler**, directed by Sturla Gunnarsson, 1996.

Kim, Nellie (b. 1957).

See Comaneci, Nadia for sidebar.

Kimball, Martha G. (1840–1894)

American philanthropist and war nurse. Born in Portland, Maine, in 1840; died in 1894.

Martha Kimball accompanied her husband, who was an appraiser of captured cotton, to the front in the Civil War, acted as a nurse during Sherman's campaign in Georgia, and was appointed inspector of hospitals. Acting on her suggestion, General John Logan, as head of the Grand Army of the Republic, introduced the observance of Decoration Day.

Kinau (c. 1805–1839)

Hawaiian kuhina nui (co-ruler) during the reign of her half-brother Kamehameha III. Name variations: Kaahumanu II. Born in Waikiki around 1805; died in Honolulu, on April 4, 1839; daughter of Kamehameha I the Great (1758–1819), king of Hawaii (r. 1810–1819), and Kaheiheimalie; sister of Kauikeaouli (1814–1854), later known as Kamehameha III, king of Hawaii (r. 1824–1854), and Queen *Kamamalu (c. 1803–1824); educated by missionaries; married Liholiho known as Kamehameha II (1797–1824), king of Hawaii (r. 1819–1824); married Kahalaia (died); married Kekuanaoa, on September 19, 1827; children: (with Kahalaia) one son, Kamehameha; (with Kekuanaoa) David Kamehameha (b. 1828); Moses Kekuaiwa (b. 1829); Lot Kamehameha (1830–1872), later known as Kamehameha V, king of Hawaii (r. 1863–1872); Alexander Liholiho (1834–1863), later known as Kamehameha IV, king of Hawaii (r. 1855–1863); Victoria Kamamalu (1838–1866); (adopted) Bernice Pauahi Bishop (1831–1884), the great-granddaughter of Kamehameha I the Great (1758–1819), king of Hawaii (r. 1810–1819).

The daughter of **Kaheiheimalie** and King Kamehameha I, Kinau was born around 1805 in Waikiki and lived in Oahu until 1812, when her father moved his court to Kailua-Kona. She was one of the earliest pupils of the missionaries who arrived in Hawaii in 1820 and thus learned to speak English and became a devout Christian. At a young age, Kinau became one of the five primary wives of Liholiho, the future Kamehameha II, in 1819. Following Liholiho's death in 1824 (he succumbed to measles while visiting England), Kinau was given in marriage to Kahalaia and had one son Kamehameha. Soon after his son's birth, Kahalaia died of whooping cough, and Kinau was once again a widow. Her third husband was Kekuanaoa, whom she married in 1827. This marriage produced four sons and a daughter and Kinau also adopted a daughter *Bernice Pauahi Bishop.

Upon the death in 1832 of *Kaahumanu, who was *kuhina nui* and regent for the boy king Kamehameha III (Kauikeaouli), Kinau became *kuhina nui* and regent by succession. Under the arrangement, all the decisions made by the king, who was now 19, were subject to her approval. Unfortunately, the king was wild and extravagant in his behavior and refused to be restrained. He promptly ended Kinau's regency and embarked on a two-year period of revelry. He repealed all the laws except those concerned with theft and murder, and threw himself into merry-making with abandon. Kinau was so alarmed and distressed over the king's behavior and the immorality it fostered that she considered taking her family to America. After consulting friends, however, she decided to stay and make the best of the situation. Kinau's relationship with the king steadied, and in 1835 he named her fourth son, Alexander Liholiho (b. 1834), heir to the throne. In addition, he turned over a large part of the governing powers to Kinau and appointed her husband, Kekuanaoa, governor of Oahu.

With her power restored, Kinau undertook a serious program of reform. She held frequent prayer meetings and attempted to abolish alcohol from the islands (an impossibility, in actuality, since the king obtained revenues from three distilleries and a public drinking hall). Strongly opposed to Catholicism, she also made it her duty to banish priests from the islands. (Catholicism had previously been banned under the rule of Kaahumanu, possibly because its use of idols was reminiscent of the Hawaiian religion and because it caused division among the people.) Kinau apparently had no difficulty in making her presence known. Weighing an estimated 250 pounds and frequently sporting a large black hat with a drooping ostrich feather, she was described by American naturalist John Townsend as "one of the great rotund beauties." Friends **Laura Fish Judd** and her husband Dr. Gerrit Judd further characterized Kinau as "sedate, courteous, and reliable, a little haughty in her deportment toward strangers, but a loving, exemplary wife, a tender mother and a warm-hearted friend."

In November 1838, Kinau gave birth to her last child, daughter *Victoria Kamamalu. Shortly after, Kinau contracted mumps (brought to the island aboard a ship from Valparaiso) and died of complications from the disease. Upon her death, the *Sandwich Island Gazette* wrote that the nation had lost "a chief whose firmness and strength of mind has been of late its greatest support." Present at her elaborate funeral, missionary **Juliette Cooke** (1812–1896) wrote: "How dreadful to hear a nation wail."

Kinau's son Alexander succeeded Kauikeaouli as Kamehameha IV in 1854, and her son Lot Kamehameha succeeded as Kamehameha V in 1863. Her daughter Victoria Kamamalu was appointed *kuhina nui* in 1855.

SOURCES:
Peterson, Barbara Bennett Peterson, ed. *Notable Women of Hawaii.* Honolulu: University of Hawaii Press, 1984.

Barbara Morgan,
Melrose, Massachusetts

Kincaid, Jean (1579–1600)

Scottish murderer. Born in Scotland in 1579; beheaded in 1600; daughter of John Livingstone of Dunipace; married John Kincaid of Warriston.

Jean Kincaid paid to have her husband John Kincaid, a man of some influence in Edinburgh, Scotland, murdered. For her efforts, she was beheaded in 1600.

Kind, Marien (1871–1955).

See Handel-Mazzetti, Enrica von.

King, Alberta Williams (1903–1974)

African-American church organist and mother of Martin Luther King, Jr. Name variations: Mama King. Born Alberta Christine Williams in 1903; assassinated in 1974; daughter of Reverend Adam Daniels Williams, pastor of Ebenezer Baptist Church; married Martin Luther King, Sr. (b. 1899, a prominent Baptist preacher); children: Martin Luther King, Jr. (1929–1968, who, employing the doctrine of civil disobedience, led the crusade that toppled segregation).

In 1926, Alberta Williams, daughter of Reverend Adam Daniels Williams, pastor of Ebenezer Baptist Church in Atlanta, married Martin Luther King, Sr., who had pastored two small churches in Atlanta and was taking courses at Morehouse College. The couple moved into her parents' home in a prominent black neighborhood while her husband continued his education. Martin, Sr., also joined his father-in-law as assistant pastor at Ebenezer. When Alberta's father died in 1931, her husband was elevated to pastor. Martin Luther

King, Sr., had a distinguished career and created a secure middle-class life for his family.

The Williams-King union produced a caring extended family that had a strong influence on their son, Martin Luther King, Jr. They taught him that he could transcend the bonds of segregation, within the limits allowed by whites, and he soon learned that he did not have to internalize the indignities of discrimination. But much to his confusion, young King was allowed to play with his white friends until they reached school age, when they were separated by his friends' parents. By way of explanation, Alberta King provided a short history of the black experience in America, then admonished him: "You must never feel that you are less than anybody else. You must always feel that you are somebody."

On June 30, 1974, six years after the 1968 assassination of her son in Memphis, Alberta King was playing "The Lord's Prayer" on the new organ at the morning service in the Ebenezer Baptist Church, when she was gunned down by African-American Marcus Wayne Chenault, Jr. Chenault, who had just been publicly welcomed to the church by the 400 worshippers, had risen from his place in the front pew, pulled out two pistols, and fired. The 69-year-old church deacon, Edward Boykin, was also fatally wounded. The killer told police that his mission was to kill Martin Luther King, Sr., but he shot Alberta King instead because she was the closest to him. Chenault told police that he hated Christianity. He had decided months earlier that black ministers were a menace to black people and God told him to kill them. Chenault was tried, convicted, and condemned to die. Though his sentence was upheld on appeal, he was resentenced to life in prison without parole because of the King family's strong opposition to the death penalty and doubts about Chenault's mental competency.

SOURCES:

Bennett, Lerone, Jr. *What Manner of Man: A Biography of Martin Luther King, Jr.* Johnson Publishing, 1976.

Oates, Stephen B. *Let the Trumpet Sound: The Life of Martin Luther King, Jr.* NY: New American Library, 1982.

Witherspoon, William Roger. *Martin Luther King, Jr.: . . . To the Mountaintop.* NY: Doubleday, 1985.

King, Billie Jean (1943—)

American champion tennis player and founder of the Women's Tennis Association who fought to ensure women's access to equal purses in major tournaments and helped establish a separate professional women's tennis tour. Name variations: Billie Jean Moffitt; Mrs. L.W. King. Born Billie Jean Moffitt on November 22, 1943, in Long Beach, California; daughter of Willard J. Moffitt (a firefighter) and Betty (Jerman) Moffitt; attended school in Long Beach; graduated from Long Beach Polytechnic High School, 1961; attended California State College (now University), Los Angeles, 1961–66; married Larry King, on September 17, 1965; no children.

Member of the Southern California Junior Wightman Cup team (1959–60); achieved first national tennis ranking (1959); won women's doubles at first Wimbledon (1961); named Associated Press Women's Athlete of the Year (1967); turned professional (1968); suspended by U.S. Lawn Tennis Association (1970); played key role in establishing the first Virginia Slims tournament (1971); named Sports Illustrated Sportsperson of the Year (1972); named Top Woman Athlete of the Year (1972); founded the Women's Tennis Association, played Bobby Riggs at the Houston Astrodome, and repeated AP Women's Athlete of the Year award (1973); co-founded and published WomenSports magazine (1974); named Time magazine Woman of the Year (1976); named in controversial palimony suit (1981); international television sports commentary for NBC was expanded to coverage of male players (1982); elected to International Tennis Hall of Fame (1987); elected to National Women's Hall of Fame (1990).

Major championships: Wimbledon singles (1966–68, 1972, 1973, 1975), doubles (1961, 1962, 1965, 1967, 1968, 1970–73), mixed doubles (1967, 1973); U.S. Open singles (1967, 1971, 1972, 1974), doubles (1965, 1967, 1974, 1980), mixed doubles (1967, 1971, 1973); French Open singles and doubles (1972), mixed doubles (1967, 1970); Australian Open singles and mixed doubles (1968); Italian Open singles and doubles (1970); U.S. Hard Court singles (1966); West German Open singles (1971); South African Open singles (1966, 1967, 1969); U.S. Indoor singles (1966–68, 1971); U.S. Clay singles.

On September 20, 1973, the circus came to the Astrodome in Houston, Texas. The event featured Chinese rickshaws, Egyptian litters, and a crowd of 30,472 in the stands, in addition to 50 million television viewers, a baby pig named Larimore Hustle and a giant Sugar Daddy sucker. But the main attraction, large enough to draw heavyweight boxing champion George Foreman to Houston to present the winner's check, was a five-set tennis match scheduled between Wimbledon champion Billie Jean King and aging hustler and Wimbledon champion Bobby Riggs. How did a tennis match between this superlative player in her prime and a man 26 years her elder come to take on such importance? And what was the significance of King's 6-4, 6-3, 6-3 victory for women's tennis, women athletes in general and, in a larger sense, the women's movement in 1973? To understand fully takes a review of King's entire career.

Born in 1943, at the height of World War II, Billie Jean Moffitt grew up during the 1950s in Long Beach, California, in a family that she herself has described as "Exhibit A: American Dream, Southern California Division." Her father worked as a firefighter, and her mother worked inside the home, raising Billie Jean and her younger brother Randy, born in 1948. As she remembers it, the young Billie Jean Moffitt always knew that she would do something important with her life, preferably in athletics, a realm in which both she and her brother were gifted (he would later be a pitcher for the San Francisco Giants). Growing up, Billie Jean played football, ran track, and played softball on a team for girls 15 and younger in Long Beach's Houghton Park. After realizing that there was no future for a woman in football or softball, she asked her father what sports would be open to her as she grew older, and he suggested golf, swimming, or tennis. Billie Jean found golf too slow and never liked the water, so tennis became her choice.

After purchasing her first racquet for eight dollars with money she made doing odd jobs for the neighbors, ten-year-old Billie Jean began taking tennis lessons from Clyde Walker on the public courts at Houghton Park. She soon fell in love with the sport. After only three months of training, she reached the finals in her first tournament before losing 6-0, 6-0. From then on, Billie Jean was a fixture in Southern California tennis. She got her first taste of the tennis snobbery she would struggle against throughout her career when she played in the Girls' 13-Under singles at the Southern California Junior championships in June 1955. Perry T. Jones, president of the Southern California Tennis Association, refused to allow her to have her photograph taken with the other players because she was not wearing a tennis dress.

Over the next few years, Billie Jean played in and around Los Angeles while reading extensively about the game. In 1958, she was invited to attend the National Girls' 15-Under championships, and, thanks to financial support from the Long Beach Tennis Patrons, she and her mother made the trip to Middletown, Ohio, where she lost in the quarterfinals. Following that, she began to take lessons from *Alice Marble, Wimbledon and U.S. champion during the

1930s, who encouraged Billie Jean to think like a winner. By 1959, she was a member of the Southern California Junior Wightman Cup team, traveling regularly on the Eastern tennis circuit, playing against teams of girls from other parts of the United States. That year, Billie Jean attained her first national ranking, placing #19 on the U.S. Lawn Tennis Association (USLTA) charts. In 1961, she made her first trip to England with doubles partner **Karen Hantze**. After winning the Queen's Club, the tournament immediately preceding Wimbledon, the two began to feel that they might have a chance at that most prestigious of tournaments. They were right. They beat *Margaret Smith Court and ✤ Jan Lehane of Australia in straight sets, launching an unprecedented record of Wimbledon championships for Billie Jean.

In 1961, there were few opportunities for women tennis players to make money in their profession. The sport was in the grip of what Billie Jean has called "shamateurism," with top players receiving money under the table from tournament sponsors for appearances, as well as free racquets and other equipment from manufacturers, and small per diem fees from the national federations that controlled the sport. A few men had been able to earn a living by turning professional, at the cost of further chances at the major championships, but women were typically unable to accomplish even that. That autumn, Billie Jean entered Los Angeles State College, planning to play tennis part time. While there, she met her future husband and business partner, Larry King, and in the fall of 1964 she left for Australia to spend three months being coached by Mervyn Rose, determined to devote herself to tennis full time.

By the fall of 1965, King was sure she could be the #1 tennis player on the women's circuit, a position she achieved the following year when she won her first Wimbledon singles title. In 1967, she adopted a new stance, vocally representing all tennis players struggling to put forth the idea that they would play just as hard as professionals as they had as "ostensible" amateurs. "Nobody considers an amateur painter, or an amateur writer, or an amateur inventor necessarily more talented or dedicated than a professional," she said, so why insist that athletes not be paid for the entertainment they provide to a sports audience? In 1967, she expressed these views during her press conferences at the 1967 National championships at Forest Hills and was threatened with suspension by the USLTA if she continued to speak out against the rules of the game. Ultimately, King was not suspended, and she never hesitated thereafter to insist that athletes have the right

✤▶

Lehane, Jan.
See Court,
Margaret Smith
for sidebar.

to earn a living through sport and to govern themselves through professional organizations.

Less than a month later, the British Lawn Tennis Association voted for open tennis, allowing both amateurs and professionals to compete against each other. Ironically, with the coming of the era of the open, the disparity between what the men and women could earn and the prize money they were offered became yet another injustice for King to address. In a shrewd assessment of the situation, she saw that professional women players must prove that they could attract an audience. Accordingly, she joined with *Françoise Durr, Ann Jones, *Rosemary Casals and six male touring professionals in the National Tennis League in traveling throughout Europe for the next two years, learning the business of tennis, promoting tournaments and handling the press at each stop. According to King, those two years taught crucial lessons that she applied in 1971, when the women began to run their own tour. Unfortunately, the stress put on her knees by that tour and the major tournaments she played during 1967 and 1968 also forced her to undergo the first of many knee operations in October 1968.

When I die, at my funeral, nobody's going to talk about me. They're all just going to stand up and tell each other where they were the night I beat Bobby Riggs.

—Billie Jean King

By the fall of 1970, the new era of the tennis open had demonstrated to King and other women professionals that they were going to have to stand together to assert their right to fair treatment at tournaments. In a sport controlled by men, with tournaments run by men, the women often found themselves playing on outside courts in not-so-prime time and receiving relatively little public or financial credit despite their high-quality games. By that autumn, it was also evident that promoters were cutting back the number of tournaments that included women in order to reduce the women's share of the purses they would have to pay. According to King, the women players were initially not even asking for an equal share of tournament money, since they played best-of-three sets rather than the best-of-five sets played by the men. The fact that the women were not as physically strong as the men, and their games therefore not typically as heavy-hitting, was also seen as a justification for the lower purses. On the other hand, people did want to see the women play, which meant in King's mind that women's tennis was equal in entertainment value to men's tennis. During the last week of September 1970, to establish this point, King joined with Casals, *Julie Heldman, Val Ziegenfuss, Kristy Pigeon, Nancy Richey, Peaches Bartkowicz, Kerry Melville, and Judy Dalton in signing contracts with *World Tennis* magazine to play in what was to become the first Virginia Slims tournament, to be held in Houston. Because the tournament was not sanctioned by the U.S. Lawn Tennis Association, all nine players were suspended. They responded by announcing an eight-tournament women's profes-

sional tennis circuit to be sponsored by *World Tennis* and Virginia Slims, to begin play in January 1971. King then took it upon herself to recruit other women to join the Virginia Slims tour, and although it was a struggle for the tour to survive through the early years, the players involved continued to promote their matches and encourage the growth of professional women's tennis for the sake of the next generation of women players.

By 1971, the money had begun to come in for Billie Jean King, who earned for the first time more than $100,000 playing tennis that year. The next year, she won over $100,000 in prize money again, regained her #1 ranking, and became the first Sportswoman of the Year ever named by *Sports Illustrated*. Thanks to her success and the arrival of new young tennis stars like *Chris Evert, the women on the tour gained enough clout to require their own professional organization, the Women's Tennis Association (WTA), which King helped to found in 1973.

As King and other women tennis professionals forced the sports world to accept them as athletes and entertainers deserving fair treatment, women in other fields were demanding an end to sex discrimination. This so-called second wave of feminism demanded equal pay for equal work and, significantly for women athletes, equal access to opportunities for young girls to compete, breaking down the tradition that had limited girls' intramural games to times when boys were not using the facilities. As athletics had historically been extolled as a means for young boys to acquire the competitive spirit they would need later in life, people began to ask why girls should not also benefit from such competition. Those opposing women's sports argued that since women could not successfully compete with men, money and facilities should not be provided for young girls to perform in competitions that would necessarily be of inferior quality. In 1972, in response to demands that girls and young women be afforded more sports opportunities, Congress passed Title IX of the Civil Rights Act, which made it illegal to discriminate on the basis of sex in any federally funded educational institution. Thus, schools and colleges had to provide equal opportunity for sports involvement for all students. (Thousands of women active in college sports today have Title IX to thank.)

In light of the debate over the meaning and value of athletics for women and girls, the contest that took place at the Houston Astrodome between Bobby Riggs and Billie Jean King in the fall of 1973 had broad significance—especially because Riggs had soundly beaten his first woman challenger, Margaret Smith Court, earlier that year. King believes that her victory over Riggs was not just a victory over one man but over the things for which he stood, including the notion that women could not compete equally with men in tennis or any other professional endeavor. "We proved we don't choke under pressure," she said. Fortunately for King, her experiences as a speaker for women's rights and the nascent Virginia Slims tour prepared her for the circus-like atmosphere of the Riggs match. She would need those skills once more.

In 1981, just as her tennis career was winding down, King was faced with a lawsuit brought by her former lover, **Marilyn Barnett**, who accused King of backing out of a commitment to support her for the rest of her life. The suit brought to public attention a matter in her private life that King would have preferred to keep private. Determined to handle Barnett's accusations in a straightforward manner, King once again showed courage in the face of adversity and an understanding of the importance of her place as a public representative for women's athletics. She handled the issue honestly before the press. By refusing to hide or avoid confrontation, King thus defused the situation with Barnett, whose suit was ultimately thrown out of court by a California judge. She also helped other athletes, such as *Martina Navratilova, to face the media when their own sexual orientation became the subject of controversy. King acknowledged that the Barnett lawsuit cost her a great deal of money in endorsements, including a contract to represent an exclusive line of Wimbledon clothing that was never finalized and the cancellation of other clothing contracts. On the other hand, in 1982 the NBC network not only kept Billie Jean King as an announcer for its Wimbledon coverage but broke with tradition by using her for commentary on some of the men's matches.

After the 1973 Riggs match, King continued to play championship-caliber tennis throughout the decade. In 1975, she won her last Wimbledon singles final, but won the U.S. Open doubles title as late as 1980, 19 years after her first Wimbledon championship. Besides playing in major championships, she remained actively involved in the organization and promotion of TeamTennis, which she envisioned as an alternative way of showcasing tennis. Indeed, King argued that TeamTennis was a forum for new systems of scoring and for demonstrating that tennis should not be the sport of second chances that it tradi-

tionally had been. In recognition of her contributions to the game, Billie Jean King was elected to the International Tennis Hall of Fame in 1987; in recognition of her work on behalf of women, she was elected to the Women's Hall of Fame in Seneca Falls, New York, in 1990, and received the *Elizabeth Blackwell award in 1998. "Everything I do is about equal opportunity," she said. "Race, gender, sexual orientation. Let's get over it. Let's celebrate our differences."

SOURCES:
Bartlett, Michael, and Bob Gillen, eds. *The Tennis Book*. NY: Arbor House, 1981.
"The Battle of the Sexes," in *Newsweek*. September 21, 1998, p. 90.
King, Billie Jean, with Cynthia Starr. *We Have Come a Long Way: The Story of Women's Tennis*. NY: McGraw-Hill, 1988.
—— with Frank Deford. *Billie Jean*. NY: Viking Press, 1982.
—— with Kim Chapin. *Billie Jean*. NY: Harper & Row, 1974.

SUGGESTED READING:
Guttmann, Allen. *Women's Sports: A History*. NY: Columbia University Press, 1991.
King, Billie Jean, and Fred Stolle, with Greg Hoffman. *How to Play Mixed Doubles*. NY: Simon and Schuster, 1980.

Wanda Ellen Wakefield, historian, State University of New York at Buffalo

King, Carol Weiss (1895–1952)

American lawyer and civil libertarian. Born on August 24, 1895, in New York City; died on January 22, 1952, in New York City; one of four children of Samuel Weiss (a lawyer) and Carrie (Stix) Weiss; graduated from the Horace Mann School, New York City, 1912; graduated from Barnard College, 1916; New York University Law School, J.D., 1920; married Gordon Congdon King (a writer), in 1917 (died 1930); children: one son, Jonathan.

Devoting her career to those usually victimized by the law, attorney Carol Weiss King specialized in cases involving immigration legislation and was frequently pitted against officials of the U.S. Immigration Service. King, who had been inspired by a frightening glimpse of fascism in Germany during the 1930s, was further impelled to preserve human rights in America at all costs.

Born into a wealthy and cultured family in 1895, King was one of four children of Samuel Weiss, who started one of the first corporate law firms in New York, and **Carrie Stix Weiss**, the daughter of a wealthy merchant. Carol attended the Horace Mann School in New York City and graduated from Barnard College in 1916, after which she took a job as a research fellow for the American Association for Labor Legislation. Coming to believe she could better serve the labor movement as a lawyer, she entered New York University Law School in 1917, the same year she married Gordon King, a writer. (The marriage would endure until Gordon's death in 1930 and produce one son, Jonathan.) After receiving her law degree in 1920 and being admitted to the bar, King could not find a job in a labor law firm, so she rented an office from Hale, Nelles, and Shorr, one of the more liberal law firms in the city. It was there that she gained experience in civil liberty and deportation cases involving immigration law. In 1925, she became a head partner in a successor firm, Shorr, Brodsky, and King.

King eschewed the courtroom, working mainly behind the scenes, researching and preparing briefs. When her partner Joseph Brodsky helped organize the International Labor Defense, King became a member, serving on its legal advisory committee. In that capacity, she worked on numerous cases, notably the defense of nine black youths arrested in Alabama (the "Scottsboro Boys") who were accused of raping two white women, *Ruby Bates** and **Victoria Price**. For that case, she prepared an argument for the Supreme Court which objected to the exclusion of blacks from juries trying black defendants, and advocated that indigents had the right to receive counsel provided by the state.

King's best-known client was Harry Bridges, the radical president of the International Longshoremen's and Warehousemen's Union, who was twice arrested and tried for deportation on the basis of his membership in the Communist Party. On appeal after the second trial, the Supreme Court reversed the deportation order. She also represented Communist Party leader William Schneiderman against the government, which sought to revoke his citizenship. When the case reached the Supreme Court, King enlisted lawyer Wendell Willkie, who eventually won the case in 1943.

King's frequent defense of Communists led some to brand her a Communist sympathizer, particularly during the Cold War hysteria of the 1950s. A *Saturday Evening Post* article (February 17, 1951) referred to her as "Communism's dearest friend," an epithet she chose to ignore. King never answered questions concerning her political affiliations, believing that in a free country they were entirely inappropriate.

In addition to her professional work, King was active in a number of civil libertarian organizations. She helped found the National Lawyers Guild (1936) and was a member of the Joint Anti-Fascist Refugee Committee. In 1932, she founded the *International Juridical Association Bulletin*, which tracked developments in constitutional theory and the practice of labor, civil rights, immigration, and landlord-tenant law. King edited the monthly journal—called "by far the best legal publication in this country" by the dean of a leading law school—until 1942, when it merged with the *Lawyers Guild Review*. In 1949, King entered politics, making an unsuccessful bid for municipal judge on the American Labor Party ticket.

Following her political defeat, she returned to defend a fresh clientele of aliens and activists being arrested by the Immigration Service for deportation. Her job became more difficult as judges began to deny bail to aliens charged only with deportation. In January 1952, shortly after making her first and only appearance before the Supreme Court, arguing a deportation case which she lost, Carol King died of cancer.

SOURCES:
McHenry, Robert. *Famous American Women*. NY: Dover, 1983.
Sicherman, Barbara, and Carol Hurd Green, eds. *Notable American Women: The Modern Period*. Cambridge, MA: The Belknap Press of Harvard University Press, 1980.

SUGGESTED READING:
Ginger, Ann Fagan. *Carol Weiss King: Human Rights Lawyer, 1895–1952*. Niwot, CO: University Press of Colorado, 1993.

COLLECTIONS:
The Carol King Collection, containing correspondence, briefs, transcripts, legal documents, and periodicals, is housed at the Meiklejohn Civil Liberties Institute, in Berkeley, California.

Barbara Morgan,
Melrose, Massachusetts

King, Carole (1942—)

American composer and performer who won four Grammy awards for her album Tapestry. *Born Carole Klein on February 9, 1942, in Brooklyn, New York; attended Queens College in New York City; married Gerry Goffin, in 1960 (divorced 1968); married Charles Larkey (divorced); married Rick Evers (died after one year of marriage); married Richard Sorenson; children: (first marriage) two daughters, Louise Goffin and Sherry Goffin-Kondor; (second marriage) daughter Molly.*

After studying piano as a child, wrote songs and organized her first band in high school, changing last name to King; dropped out of college to marry and went to work part-time for a New York music publish-

ing company, composing with her lyricist husband the music for a string of Top 40 hits; had first #1 song, "Will You Still Love Me Tomorrow?" (1960); after a divorce (1968), began to promote herself as a solo performer; released album Tapestry *to great acclaim (1971), winning four Grammy awards; has continued to write and perform ever since, as well as composing music for film scores and occasionally acting in films and on the stage; is also an outspoken environmentalist.*

One afternoon in 1960, chemist Gerry Goffin was surprised to see his fiancée appear at the New York lab in which he worked, and even more startled to see a shiny black limousine waiting outside. More astounding still was Carole King's news that one of the four dozen songs they had written together, "Will You Still Love Me Tomorrow?," had been received so enthusiastically by a music publisher that they had each been given a $10,000 advance. It was the first substantial money either of them had made from their passionate devotion to writing music; and for Carole, it was the beginning of a career that would help define the shape of the music industry for the next 40 years.

Born Carole Klein on February 9, 1942, to a middle-class family in Brooklyn, she developed an early love for music through the piano lessons she began taking at the age of four, and was so intent on a life in the music business that she had formed her first group, a vocal quarter she called The Co-Sines, while still in high school, even going so far as to legally change her name to the more commercial-sounding King. It was a time of poodle skirts and pompadours, of cars with tailfins and abundant chrome, of "sock hops" and televised dance parties like the weekly show hosted by pioneering rock 'n' roll disc jockey Alan Freed. Along with most of her generation, King danced to the records of Elvis Presley and Jerry Lee Lewis, the Coasters and the Chordettes, and rhythm-and-blues artist Ben E. King. But unlike many of her contemporaries, King realized these performers owed their stardom to the people who supplied their material, for very few of the recording stars of the day wrote their own songs. Carole was especially taken with the work of Jerry Lieber and Mike Stoller, who had written "Blue Suede Shoes" for Elvis.

Arriving at Queens College after graduating from high school, King met others who shared her admiration for writing teams like Lieber and Stoller. One of her college acquaintances, Neil Sedaka, found early success in 1959 with a song he had written for her, "Oh, Carol!" (Carole's answer song, "Oh, Neil!," failed to meet similar success), while a young Paul Simon was beginning to explore writing and performing as well. Of more significance to King's future was her relationship with Gerry Goffin, who was earning a degree in chemistry at the time he and Carole met. Planning on marrying and starting a family, both of them dropped out of school, moved to a basement apartment in Manhattan, and found jobs in New York—Goffin at his chemistry lab and Carole as a secretary—while they dedicated their evenings to songwriting. Goffin supplied the lyrics while King set them to music, and their efforts seemed rewarded when Neil Sedaka introduced them to the publishers who had handled "Oh, Carol!"

> *I'm a songwriter first, have always been, and probably always will be.*
>
> —Carole King

Aldon Music, owned by Don Kirschner and Al Nevins, was one of scores of such enterprises housed in the legendary Brill Building on 57th Street, then the heart of a vibrant music business jolted into frenetic growth by the arrival of rock 'n' roll. Huddled in cubicles, puffing on cigarettes, and living on Coca-Cola and hot dogs, young composers dreamed of writing the next hit for Elvis or Dion. The few that sold songs to the publishing houses were rarely paid royalties, but the arrangement did not stop King and Goffin from cranking out nearly 50 unsold songs before Kirschner agreed to buy "Will You Still Love Me Tomorrow?," a somewhat controversial song for its day, with its innocent speculation about the consequences of a first kiss ("Is this a lasting treasure/ Or just a moment's pleasure?"). It was Kirschner's good fortune to decide to let his young writing team arrange and record a demo of the song, which was promptly bought by a popular "girl group" of the time, **The Shirelles**. Their recording of the song shot to the top of Billboard's charts within a week of its release in 1960, giving Carole and Gerry reason enough to celebrate by marrying.

The success of "Will You Still Love Me Tomorrow?" established a pattern for the writing team of King and Goffin, with a string of hits over the next five years for African-American "girl groups" like **The Cookies** (with 1962's "Chains") and **The Chiffons** (with 1963's "One Fine Day"), and for solo artists like **Eva Boyd**, who, at the time she recorded the demo of Carole and Gerry's "The Loco-Motion" as Little Eva, was working as the Goffins' babysitter. Kirschner liked King's arrangement for the demo, with its fat tenor sax line doubling the bass, and decided to release it commercially. It promptly took over Billboard's #1 slot on the Top 40 charts. The Drifters' recording of "Up on the Roof" remains a classic of the King-Goffin style which came to be called "uptown R&B," marked by King's silky-smooth arrangements and sophisticated chord changes which highlighted Goffin's introspective lyrics. But it was their great genius to be able to tailor music for other kinds of artists, too. Steve Lawrence's 1962 version of "Go Away, Little Girl" appealed to a somewhat older and less urban audience, while King's first recording as a solo artist of one of her own songs, 1962's "It Might as Well Rain Until September," swept the European charts, although it only reached #22 in America. King's arrangements for the demo recordings of her songs were so admired that many artists merely replaced her vocals with their own, finding it difficult to imagine the song any other way. King never objected at the time, or later in her career, when her songs were covered in their own versions by artists as varied as James Taylor and **Aretha Franklin**. "Making the demo is a natural product of writing a song," King once told a journalist. "After that, I'm happy to hear other people do it in other ways." By the mid-1960s, King and Goffin's style was so widely admired that Paul McCartney claimed his and John Lennon's most fervent wish was to write songs "as good as Goffin and King." (The Beatles included a version of "Chains" on their first album.)

It was the Beatles' success with their film *A Hard Day's Night* that indirectly opened an entirely new market for King. Columbia's television arm, Screen Gems, took note of the popularity of the film and decided to tailor a TV series around a manufactured American group to be called The Monkees. With as many as four new songs needed for each weekly show, and with only one member of the new group, Mike Nesmith, actually a songwriter, Columbia turned to Don Kirschner for help. The series premiered in 1965 with three songs penned by Goffin-King. As well, "Pleasant Valley Sunday," with its wry condemnation of middle-class hypocrisy, was King and Goffin's first socially conscious song to rise into the top ten on the charts, and was a sharp break from their earlier, rhythm-and-blues dominated style.

By the late 1960s, in fact, the entire music business was heading in a new direction, driven by recording artists who were now writing their own material. While Goffin was content to write lyrics for others, King noted the trend and determined to begin promoting herself as a performer. The inevitable strains on the partnership led to a separation in 1967, following the couple's last collaboration—(You Make Me Feel Like a) "Natural Woman," written for Aretha Franklin. With the divorce finalized the next year, Carole moved to Los Angeles with her two daughters, Louise and Sherry, and settled in Laurel Canyon in the Hollywood Hills. She joined a group of new young artists intent on preserving their artistic independence to write and record songs with an intensely personal flavor—artists such as **Joni Mitchell, Melanie**, David Crosby, Stephen Stills and, most important, James Taylor, who became a close friend and encouraged her efforts to create a solo career. "Those were remarkable days in Laurel Canyon," Taylor once said. "Exceptional was commonplace." King had met Taylor through her association with singer and guitarist Danny Kortchmar, who had played with Taylor in a mid-1960's group called the Original Flying Machine. Kortchmar, along with bass guitarist Charles Larkey (who would become King's second husband) and drummer Jim Gordon, formed Carole's first group since her high school days in Brooklyn. The new group, called The City, recorded only one album, 1969's *Now That Everything's Been Said*, which failed to attract attention. Its only distinction was the first recording of the song that would become so closely identified with King (as well as Taylor), "You've Got a Friend." Adding to the group's short life was King's reluctance to tour; her finely tuned studio ear told her that The City was nowhere near ready for live appearances. The City was disbanded after barely a year together.

Still, James Taylor and others continued to urge her on. Among the support group was record producer Lou Adler, who finally coaxed King into a studio in 1970 to record the basic tracks for a solo album, to be called *Writer*. It proved to be another failure, criticized for a lack of focus and indifferent production—a result of King's leaving the project before the tracks were mixed to take on a writing project for **The Mamas and the Papas**. *Writer* sold only 10,000 copies. But then came *Tapestry*, King's breakthrough album and the work still cited as the highwater mark of her career. The album blended original songs like "So Far Away" and "I Feel the Earth Move," several tunes written in collaboration with ex-husband Gerry Goffin ("Smackwater Jack") and with lyricist Toni Stern ("It's Too Late"), and her own versions of "Will You Still Love Me Tomorrow?" and "Natural Woman." Backed by Kortchmar's guitar work, Charles Larkey's bass, Jim Gordon's drums, and backup vocals by, among others, James Taylor,

King's soulful vocals and distinctive piano sent *Tapestry* skyrocketing up the charts. King was on tour, opening for Taylor, when the album made its debut; by the end of the tour, Taylor was opening for her. (King returned the favor when Taylor's own release of "You've Got a Friend" brought him his first #1 single.) *Tapestry* broke all sales records of the time at 22 million copies, remained on Billboard's list of the 200 bestselling albums for six years, and was the bestselling solo album by a female vocalist for an astonishing 25 years. Nearly every song on the album met success as a single release, with "It's Too Late" remaining in the #1 spot for five weeks. In all, *Tapestry* brought King four Grammy awards—for Best Song of the Year ("You've Got a Friend," in James Taylor's rendition), Best Record of the Year ("It's Too Late"), Best Pop Vocal for a Female Artist (for the album's title song) and Album of the Year. Critics cited the album for breaking new ground for female pop singers, freeing them from the white gloves and sequined gowns of the 1960s and opening the door to a more natural, honest style. The triumph for King, however, was the acceptance of her work as a composer by a wider audience. "I don't consider myself a singer," she said two years after *Tapestry*'s release. "The main reason I got into performing and recording on my own was to expose my songs to the public in the fastest way."

But the success of *Tapestry* carried a price, which became evident with the release of *Carole King Music,* also in 1971, and containing songs written with Toni Stern. Although one of the numbers, "Sweet Seasons," became a Top Ten single and the album itself briefly hit #1, reviewers inevitably compared it to its predecessor and found it lacking. "Anyone who failed to follow up an album [like *Tapestry*] with a very similar album would have to be either a fool or Bob Dylan," wrote one critic for *Rolling Stone.* "Carole King is neither. The middle ground where she is now standing isn't good enough for her, and the sooner she moves, the better." 1972's *Rhymes and Reasons,* which also reached #1 for a brief period, fared no better; and King's third post-*Tapestry* effort, *Fantasy*—a "concept" album with overtones of social protest—never even made it past the #6 slot on the charts. Fans pointed out that the negative reaction almost always concerned the lyrics written by collaborators and not King's melodies; and her popular acceptance remained high enough for an estimated 70,000 fans to crowd Central Park in New York for a live concert in 1973. Although the performance was well received, the press was more impressed by her plea to the audience at the end of the concert to pick up their trash and throw it away properly.

King seemed to regain her critics' favor with the release in 1974 of *Wrap Around Joy,* a jazz-tinged album written in collaboration with David Palmer and featuring instrumentals by jazz saxophonist Tom Scott, who had graced Joni Mitchell's *Court and Spark* a year earlier. *Wrap Around Joy* settled in for a respectable stay at #1 and produced a #2 single, "Jazzman." The versatility of her days in the Brill Building with Gerry Goffin returned with King's next

album, a collection of children's songs based on Maurice Sendak's story *Really Rosie,* about the adventures of a New York schoolgirl and her friends. (Sendak was a fellow Brooklynite and had known King in high school.) The album was later turned into the score for an animated film and, later still, a Broadway play. Her work with Sendak led to several offers of work on film scores, including *Pocket Money* and the title song for *Murphy's Romance.*

By the mid-1970s, King's iconic status in the music industry seemed assured, even if she never produced another album as popular and influential as *Tapestry*; and her carefully guarded personal life survived the upheaval of her divorce from Charles Larkey and the early death from a drug overdose of her third husband, Rick Evers, who had contributed lyrics to two of her albums. The ardent environmentalism she had developed by this time was reflected in 1979's *Touch the Sky,* released just as she was moving from California to Idaho (where she met and married her fourth husband, rancher Richard Sorenson), and in her appearances in public support of several environmental initiatives in state legislatures and in Congress. *Touch the Sky,* unfortunately, turned out to be one of her worst-selling albums, prompting a reviewer for *Melody Maker* to note that while King's environmental advocacy was certainly laudable, "these laments from Tin Pan Alley hipsters are not instantly affecting." Perhaps stung by the reaction, King looked to the past for her next effort, collaborating with Gerry Goffin on *Pearls,* which included new versions of their hits from the 1960s and which fared much better commercially. Her subsequent work during the last two decades of the 20th century also fared respectably, much of it drawing on the talents of contemporary artists who were barely in grade school when King and Goffin were slaving away in the Brill Building. *City Streets,* released in 1989, was noted for its harder-edged arrangements and guitar work by Eric Clapton; while Guns N' Roses guitarist Slash appeared on 1993's *Color of Your Dreams*—also notable for including King's song "Now and Forever," written for the film *A League of Their Own.* **Faith Hill**, Rod Stewart and Aretha Franklin all appeared on 1995's *Tapestry Revisited,* a re-recording of the original album's songs which, in a back-handed compliment to King's solo work 25 years earlier, failed to find an audience. A more apt tribute came in the form of the 1996 film *Grace of My Heart,* based on the story of the King-Goffin legend and starring **Ileana Douglas** in a role drawn heavily from King's life.

Although she and Goffin were inducted into both the Songwriters' Hall of Fame and the Rock and Roll Hall of Fame, and although she has been featured on programs as varied as VH-1's *Rock Divas Live* and on *Oprah Winfrey, Carole King famously keeps a low public profile and rarely grants interviews. It is her support of environmental issues, particularly the Northern Rockies Ecosystem Protection Act, that now bring her most often to the public's attention. Still, it is her contributions to contemporary music that may prove more lasting than her ecological dedication. "The simplicity of the singing, composition and ultimate feeling achieve the kind of eloquence and beauty I had forgotten rock is capable of," *Rolling Stone* critic John Landau once wrote. "She reaches out towards us and gives us everything she has. And this generosity is so extraordinary that perhaps we can give it another name: passion."

SOURCES:

Perone, James. *Carole King: A Bio-Bibliography.* Westport, CT: Greenwood Press, 1999.

Snyder, Louise. "Will You Still Love Me Tomorrow?" in *Salon.* June 19, 1999.

RELATED MEDIA:

Grace of My Heart, starring Ileana Douglas and directed by **Allison Anders**, Gramercy Pictures, 1996.

"Tapestry Revisited: A Tribute to Carole King," Lifetime Television, produced by David Foster, aired in 1995.

Norman Powers,
writer-producer, Chelsea Lane Productions, New York

King, Coretta Scott (1927—)

African-American activist, and wife of civil-rights leader Martin Luther King, Jr., who took on an independent role in the civil-rights movement in the years following her husband's assassination in 1968. Name variations: Corrie or Cora; Mrs. Martin Luther King, Jr. Born Coretta Scott on April 27, 1927, in Heiberger, Alabama; daughter of Obidiah "Obie" Scott (a farmer, independent truck driver, and small store owner) and Bernice McMurry (also seen as McMurray) Scott; attended public and private schools in Alabama; attended Antioch College, 1945–51, and New England Conservatory of Music, 1951–54; married Martin Luther King, Jr., on June 18, 1953; children: Yolanda Denise King (b. 1955, an actress); Martin Luther King, III (b. 1957); Dexter Scott King (b. 1961); Bernice King (b. 1963).

Received Antioch College Race Relations Committee scholarship (1945); received Jesse Smith Noyes fellowship to New England Conservatory of Music (1951); met Martin Luther King, Jr. (1952); moved to Montgomery, Alabama (1954); start of Montgomery bus boycott (1955); was present with her baby daughter when the King home was bombed (1956); gave concert performance in New York (1956); moved to Atlanta, Georgia (1960); taught at Morris Brown College and attended Geneva disarmament talks (1962); accompanied husband to Norway to receive Nobel Peace Prize (1964); was trapped with family in Chicago riots (1966); assassination of her husband (1968); spoke at St. Paul's Church, began planning for Martin Luther King, Jr., Memorial (1969); founded Center for Non-Violent Change (1971); toured South Africa (1986); resigned as head of Center for Non-Violent Change (1994).

Coretta Scott King, wife of Martin Luther King, Jr., the most influential African-American leader of the 20th century, served largely as a witness to the development of the struggle of black Americans for equal rights until the death of her husband at the hands of an assassin in June 1968. Thereafter, she took on an independent role in the civil-rights movement, and, at the same time, worked to preserve her husband's legacy. Scholarly accounts of the movement by historians Taylor Branch and David Garrow have illuminated the complex and sometimes troubled relationship Coretta Scott King had with her husband.

We were united during all the years we were together, not only as man and woman, but also in our belief in the rightness and justice of the civil rights movement and the continuing battle to end war, poverty, and racism.

—Coretta Scott King

Unlike Martin Luther King, Jr., who grew up in Atlanta, Coretta Scott was a product of the rural South. She was born on April 27, 1927, on a family farm outside Marion, Alabama, the daughter of Obie Scott and **Bernice McMurry Scott**. Her father, a substantial figure in the black community, worked as a barber and a driver for the local lumber mill in addition to farming. As she recalled in her memoirs, Coretta Scott grew up tending the family garden and was nourished by the food her parents grew. Part of her childhood was spent picking cotton to help meet her school expenses. In the rigidly segregated South of that time, her father was threatened by poor whites who resented his ownership of a truck and his work as an independent driver. "I learned very early to live with fear for the people I loved," she later wrote, noting how this advance training prepared her to cope with the danger her husband faced in his fight against segregation.

Coretta Scott's education began in a segregated one-room country schoolhouse in the nearby village of Heiberger. She walked the six-mile round trip each day. But she entered a different environment at Lincoln High School in Marion. There, in an institution founded after the Civil War by northern missionaries, she and her older sister **Edythe Scott** were taught by an integrated faculty, half of whose members were white. Her parents stretched their resources to pay the annual fee of $4.50 per child.

Coretta Scott's musical interests blossomed at Lincoln, where she learned the trumpet and took voice lessons. In 1945, she followed Edythe to Antioch College in Ohio. The recently integrated school had a total of six black students. Scott was not attracted to the one young black man in her class, and her steady boyfriend for a year was a Jewish student from New York. Nonetheless, even in this liberal northern environment she experienced a palpable racism. Required to complete a stint as a practice teacher for her degree in elementary education, she was not permitted by the local school board to seek a place in a white school. Such experiences pushed her to become an active member of the Antioch chapter of the National Association for the Advancement of Colored People (NAACP). In all, she found Antioch a crucial experience in expanding her self-confidence and ability to function in a multiethnic world.

While at Antioch, Scott decided to continue her voice training, and she was admitted to Boston's New England Conservatory. Ironically, some of her financial support came from the state of Alabama, which used such grants to promote segregation by encouraging talented black students to leave the state.

In her second semester at the conservatory, Coretta Scott met Martin Luther King, Jr., a young Baptist minister who was studying for a doctorate in theology at Boston University. The two were introduced by a mutual friend, one of Scott's fellow students at the conservatory. On their first date, Martin told Coretta that she had all the qualities he was looking for in a wife: "character, intelligence, personality, and beauty." He explained to her that he was involved with a woman in Atlanta, but that the relationship was one that their respective families were sponsoring, and he wanted to choose his future spouse himself. Martin expected a wife to be primarily a homemaker who would deal comfortably with all segments of his future congregations, including the many simple and uneducated parishioners she would encounter.

In the end, Coretta Scott put aside her musical ambitions, her "dissimilar plan for my life," to fulfill the young Martin's wishes. She visited the King family in Atlanta in the summer following her first acquaintance with Martin. A few months later, when his parents, Martin Luther King, Sr., and ***Alberta King**, were visiting Boston, Martin announced his plans to marry Coretta. She in turn shifted the direction of her studies at the conservatory so that she could teach music rather than pursue a career as a performer. The two were married at Coretta Scott's Alabama home on June 18, 1953, with Martin's father performing the ceremony. She convinced her future father-in-law to omit from the ceremony the customary promise from the bride to obey her husband.

In 1954, with his doctorate almost completed, Martin Luther King, Jr., accepted a position as minister at the Dexter Avenue Baptist Church in Montgomery, Alabama. Coretta King was initially opposed to his decision. While she accepted the fact that they would return to the South someday, she hoped to enjoy living in the more racially liberated atmosphere of the North for some time longer. She was particularly reluctant to settle in Montgomery with its rigid racial segregation.

During the year following their arrival in Montgomery, the Kings found their circumstances changing rapidly. In November 1955, they had their first child, a girl they named Yolanda Denise. Only a few months before, Martin had received his doctorate in systemic theology from Boston University. Meanwhile, the civil-rights movement in Montgomery began to focus around the issue of segregation on the city's buses. The refusal of ***Rosa Parks**, an African-American woman, to give up her seat to a white passenger in accordance with the racial requirements of the time led to the boycott of the bus lines by members of the black community. Martin, who soon emerged as the leader of the boycott organization, was arrested and held in the city jail overnight for an alleged traffic violation. At home, Coretta was confronted with up to 40 threatening and obscene phone calls each day.

On January 30, 1956, while Coretta and her baby daughter were present and Martin was away giving a speech, the King home was bombed. Although no one was injured in the attack, their families implored Martin and Coretta King to leave Montgomery. They both refused. While they accepted the fact that members of their congregation were guarding their house, the Kings, as devotees of nonviolence, refused to permit them to be armed. As she later recalled, "I was able to draw strength from my religious faith. . . . If you are doing what God wants you to do you will be successful and fulfilled in the process."

In the difficult days of the early civil-rights movement, Coretta King took on the roles that she would continue for more than a decade. The King house, with Coretta as cook and host, became a meeting ground for civil-rights workers. When Martin could not speak at a meeting, Coretta often filled in for him. She became a featured performer at money-raising concerts to support the cause of civil rights and integration. The first such performance was in New York on December 5, 1956, the anniversary of the start of the Montgomery bus boycott. Perhaps most crucially, she provided emotional support and encouragement for her seriously burdened husband. One of her close friends later described her during these years as "a very strong woman, the best wife and partner Martin could have had." She added, however, that no other woman "could have lived with him and kept any kind of personal identity at all. Cora did."

After the success of the bus boycott, Martin and other black leaders founded the Southern Christian Leadership Conference (SCLC) to expand the effort to end racial segregation. Meanwhile the King family grew with the birth of a son, Martin Luther III, in October 1957. While Coretta King watched as her husband achieved national acclaim as a civil-rights leader, such prominence came at a heavy price. In September 1958, she received a phone call informing her that Martin had been stabbed by a deranged black woman in New York City. Visiting him at the hospital, Coretta learned that he had missed being fatally injured by a mere fraction of an inch.

The King family moved to Atlanta in 1960. Martin had decided to devote all his energies to the struggle for civil rights, and thus he gave up his work as the full-time minister of the church in Montgomery. It was an opportune moment; young black students in the South, partly inspired by the success of the bus boycott in Montgomery, were staging sit-ins to challenge restaurant segregation. The cost for Martin's growing role in the civil-rights movement was a series of jail sentences, and Coretta found herself repeatedly consoling her children for their father's absence and explaining the motives behind his actions to them. Martin Luther King's activities placed an increasing strain on his family. Writes David Garrow, "He was not intentionally uncaring, but sometimes it seemed that way."

In the fall of 1960, after Martin Luther King, Jr., had been sentenced to a long term in

an Alabama jail, Coretta King received a call from Senator John F. Kennedy, who was in the final stages of his campaign for the presidency. Kennedy offered the Kings his assistance, and the storm of publicity resulting from the call helped to free Martin on bail. Coretta King later wrote that she shared the view of many historians that the votes Kennedy won by this action were decisive in electing him to the presidency that year.

Coretta King again became a mother in January 1961 with the birth of a third child, a son whom the parents named Dexter. In the early 1960s, already a veteran of peace groups during her college days at Antioch, she now joined the Atlanta chapter of the Women's International League for Peace and Freedom. In March 1962, she accepted an invitation from another peace group, the Women's Strike for Peace, to attend a disarmament conference in Geneva, Switzerland. As a member of a delegation of 50 American women, she joined with delegates from other countries in trying to influence atomic test ban negotiations taking place in the Swiss city.

In the spring of 1963, Martin was involved in the effort to stage massive civil-rights demon-

Coretta
Scott
King

strations in Birmingham, Alabama, one of the most important and most segregated cities in the South. Meanwhile, in March, Coretta gave birth to their fourth child, a daughter they named **Bernice**. When she found that her husband had not only been arrested but was being held without any contact with the outside world, Coretta King tried to telephone the president of the United States, then the vice-president, for help in assuring Martin's safety. After a flurry of calls, she received an answer from President Kennedy, who assured her that the FBI was being sent to Birmingham. When she spoke to Martin thereafter, he remarked on how suddenly his treatment in prison had improved.

The mass demonstrations at Birmingham not only led to a settlement starting the desegregation of the city, they also pushed the Kennedy administration to propose a sweeping civil-rights bill. Coretta King remembered Birmingham "as a turning point almost too significant to be grasped at the time of its happening." She also recalled suggesting to her husband that the momentum of the civil-rights movement could be promoted by "a massive March on Washington."

The March on Washington, for which the most important impetus had come from such leaders as A. Philip Randolph, head of the Negro American Labor Council, took place on August 28, 1963. Coretta King was disappointed to learn that she would not be able to march alongside her husband. The front row of marchers was to be given to the top leadership of the civil-rights movement. She did manage to sit behind Martin Luther King, Jr., on the platform for his stirring "I have a dream" speech. She later recalled she was also hurt, however, when she was excluded from her husband's meeting with President Kennedy. David Garrow put it more strongly, noting that her "pleasure with the event was replaced by fury" when she learned she would not accompany Martin to the White House.

Despite the triumphant success of the gathering in Washington, Coretta King had growing reason to fear for her husband's life. In June 1963, the head of the Mississippi NAACP, Medgar Evers, had been shot to death at the door of his home. Shortly after the March on Washington, murderers set a bomb at a Birmingham church that killed four young black girls, ◀ **Denise McNair** (11), **Cynthia Wesley** (14), **Addie Mae Collins** (14), and **Carol Robertson** (14). The final tragedy of the year was the assassination of President Kennedy in November. At that moment, Martin warned his wife, "This is what is going to happen to me also." She found

that she could not refute his thinking once he had pronounced the grim words. When she watched ***Jacqueline Kennedy** at the president's funeral, Coretta had the feeling that she was "steeling myself for our own fate."

In 1964, Coretta King, taking her 1956 stage appearance in New York as a model, began a series of "Freedom Concerts." They combined her skills as a singer and public speaker in order to raise money for various parts of the civil-rights movement, and they gave her a chance to resume her abandoned singing career. She persisted in the face of her husband's skepticism that such events would be a financial success. He admitted his mistake, she recalled, when the concerts brought in more than $50,000. A year later, in another public act in support of her political beliefs, she insisted on joining her husband in one of the marches in Selma, Alabama, aimed at obtaining voting rights for black Americans.

In late 1964, the Kings learned that Martin Luther King, Jr., had been awarded the Nobel Peace Prize. In her memoirs, Coretta King recalled that she was the first to receive the news when the Associated Press called the family home. She accompanied her husband and her in-laws, along with a number of colleagues from the civil-rights movement, to Oslo for the ceremony.

Despite such occasional roles in public, Coretta found, often to her frustration, that her life centered on home. Her husband was too often absent to play a steady role in raising their four children. It became her responsibility, for example, to deal with the children's health problems. While she described her relationship with her husband in mild language in her memoirs, historian Taylor Branch indicates a more difficult situation. He refers to the "mutual recriminations" the Kings exchanged in phone calls during their separations in the early 1960s as "Coretta King complained bitterly from home about his constant and prolonged abandonments." She was embittered by her husband's insistence, notes Garrow, that "she take care of the home and family and not become involved in movement activities."

In her memoirs, Coretta King recalled briefly that, by 1965, she and her husband were aware their phone lines were being tapped by the FBI. She left unmentioned the type of information such spying brought and the use to which it was put. Even at the time of their courtship, Coretta King had discussed with her future husband his attractiveness to large numbers of women. She later wrote that he explained this

❧▶
McNair, Denise,
et al. See Davis,
Angela for
sidebar.

simply: "You know that women are hero-wor-shippers." Soon after Martin Luther King had risen to prominence through the Montgomery bus boycott, rumors about his extramarital affairs had appeared in print in a prominent black newspaper, the *Pittsburgh Courier*. Now, as a result of their telephone surveillance, J. Edgar Hoover and other leading FBI officials had clear evidence that Martin was engaged in extensive sexual activity outside his marriage. They circulated this material among government officials and threatened Martin with public exposure as an adulterer.

After passage of the Federal Voting Rights Bill in 1965, Martin now directed much of his energy in an effort to improve the lives of black Americans living outside the South. For a time in the summer of 1966, Coretta King and their children joined him in living in a slum apartment in Chicago as they tried to familiarize themselves with life in a northern ghetto. During a riot that broke out in that city in July, Coretta and her children found themselves trapped in their apartment as police clashed with rioters and shots rang out in the neighborhood.

In April 1967, Martin made his first major speech opposing the Vietnam War. Coretta helped defend her husband against the storm of criticism that followed, and she herself became prominent as a speaker against the war. When he spoke to a massive demonstration in New York that month, she went to San Francisco to address a large crowd there.

Coretta King remembered the early months of 1968 as a time when she and her husband had "a sense of fate closing in." Martin had long spoken openly about the personal danger in which he found himself: he was convinced that men who took clear moral stands risked their lives and that he could not worry about his own safety. Coretta King now had the feeling he was "preparing himself for his fate" as "the last few months before his death were lived at a frantic pace." In March, in an unaccustomed gesture, he gave her a bouquet of artificial flowers, the last flowers he ever bought his wife. "Somehow, in

Coretta Scott King with first ladies Rosalynn Carter, Betty Ford, and Lady Bird Johnson.

some strange way," she believed, "he seemed to have known how long they would have to last."

On Thursday, April 4, 1968, in Memphis, Tennessee, Martin Luther King, Jr., was fatally shot by an assassin. Coretta King received the first terrible news that her husband had been wounded in a phone call from Jesse Jackson. She had just returned from a shopping trip to buy Easter clothing for the King children. She rushed to the airport and, while waiting for her plane, learned that her husband had died. The following Monday, she and her three oldest children took part in a civil-rights march in Memphis. It was the march Martin Luther King, Jr., had been scheduled to lead.

In the aftermath of her husband's death, Coretta King emerged as a powerful, and sometimes controversial, personality in her own right. She saw to it that her four children received psychiatric care following the loss of their father. She was granted the signal honor of being invited to preach from the pulpit of St. Paul's Cathedral in London, the first woman in history to have such an opportunity. She began to plan a monument for Martin. Her book of memoirs, *My Life with Martin Luther King, Jr.*, was published in English in 1969 and subsequently appeared in 14 other languages.

At the same time, some workers in the civil-rights movement found her manner so imperious that they began to call her "The Queen," or, linking her loss to that of the Kennedy family, "Black Jackie." In a highly critical article that appeared in 1972, *The New York Times* writer Henry R. Leifermann noted the affluence in which Coretta King seemed to live, a marked contrast from the modest standard of living Martin had insisted on.

In 1971, after three years of planning, Coretta King opened the memorial to her late husband, the Martin Luther King Jr. Center for Non-Violent Social Change in Atlanta. She raised more than $10 million for the Center, and served as the founding president and the chief executive officer until 1994. She also took the lead in the successful movement to have her husband's birthday, January 15, declared a national holiday beginning in 1985. The following year, she toured the Union of South Africa, meeting with black civil-rights leaders there. In recent years, she pursued, and lost, a law suit over the rights to a large portion of her late husband's papers held by Boston University. To help expose the truth about her husband's murder, she called for a public trial of the convicted killer James Earl Ray (whom the King family believes did not act alone) before his death. She also became embroiled in conflict with the U.S. Park Service over a plot of land the Park Service wishes to use for a memorial to her late husband; the King family wanted the land for a museum tied to the life of Martin Luther King, Jr. In 1994, as Coretta King moved toward retirement, she saw her son Dexter Scott King take over as CEO of the Center for Non-Violent Social Change.

SOURCES:

Branch, Taylor. *Parting the Waters: America in the King Years, 1954–63.* NY: Simon and Schuster, 1988.
———. *Pillar of Fire: America in the King Years, 1963–65.* NY: Simon and Schuster, 1998.
Current Biography Yearbook, 1969. NY: H.W. Wilson, 1969.
Diamonstein, Barbaralee. *Open Secrets: Ninety-four Women in Touch with Our Time.* NY: Viking Press, 1972.
Garrow, David J. *Bearing the Cross: Martin Luther King, Jr., and the Southern Christian Leadership Conference.* NY: William Morrow, 1986.
King, Coretta Scott. *My Life with Martin Luther King, Jr.* Rev. ed. NY: Henry Holt, 1993.
Leifermann, Henry R. "Profession: Concert Singer, Freedom Movement Lecturer," in *The New York Times Sunday Magazine.* November 26, 1972.
The New York Times. 1985–1997.
Nugent, Lynn. "Coretta Scott King: The Woman Behind the King Anniversary," in *Ebony.* January 1990, pp. 116–121.

Neil M. Heyman,
Professor of History,
San Diego State University, San Diego, California

King, Debra Flintoff (b. 1960).

See Flintoff, Debra.

King, Mrs. Frances (1863–1948).

See King, Louisa Yeomans.

King, Grace Elizabeth (c. 1852–1932).

See Dunbar-Nelson, Alice for sidebar.

King, Helen Dean (1869–1955)

American biologist. Born Helen Dean King in Oswego, New York, in 1869; died in Philadelphia, Pennsylvania, in 1955; elder of two daughters of George (a businessman) and Leonora (Dean) King; graduated from Oswego Free Academy, around 1877; Vassar College, B.A., 1892; Bryn Mawr College, Ph.D., 1899; never married; no children.

Known for her pioneering research on the breeding of rats, biologist Helen Dean King was the subject of more than a little controversy during her career. Like recent experiments in cloning, King's research on inbreeding laboratory rats was greeted by hysterical headlines and public denunciation.

Helen King was born in 1869 and raised in Oswego, New York, the daughter of a successful businessman. She graduated from Oswego Free Academy and received her B.A. from Vassar before pursuing doctoral studies at Bryn Mawr. There, she majored in morphology under Thomas Hunt Morgan, known as the "father of modern genetics," and minored in physiology and paleontology under J.W. Warren and *Florence Bascom. Completing her degree in 1899, she remained at the college for five years, serving as an assistant in biology. From 1906 to 1908, she was an assistant in anatomy at the University of Pennsylvania, after which she took a teaching post at Philadelphia's Wistar Institute of Anatomy and Biology. She remained at Wistar for the next 41 years, working her way up from assistant to assistant professor and finally to professor of embryology. In addition to teaching, she served on the Institute's advisory board for 24 years. In 1932, she was awarded the *Ellen Richards Research Prize of the Association to Aid Scientific Research for Women.

King's research on albino and Norway rats was considered controversial partly because she was a woman. One amazed reporter commented on "the spectacle of a woman holding a rat in the palm of her hand," and further noted that he could hardly "believe that one of the greatest authorities of rats in the country is a very human and thoroughly feminine woman." The results of King's experiments in inbreeding were also somewhat misinterpreted. After studying 25 generations of albino rats to determine the effects of inbreeding, King concluded that brother-sister matings produced animals that were superior in body size, fertility, and longevity. "I do not claim that this superiority is due solely to the fact that the animals were inbred," she added, "neither do I wish to assert that, in general, inbreeding is better than outbreeding for building up and maintaining the general vigor of a race." Some newspaper reports, however, implied that King considered incest taboos unnecessary. "Dr. King Quizzed on Kin Marriage Theory: Home Folk Shocked by Advocacy of Human Inbreeding," shouted one headline. Public responses to the reports ranged from amusing to violent. A California woman wrote asking King to find her a husband. A young man from Clark University, calling himself a "Christian and a student," wrote that "he wished someone would kill her, and if they didn't he would do it himself."

From 1919 to her retirement in 1949, King devoted herself to research involving domestication of the Norway rat, which was considered too wild to breed in the laboratory. Again, she captured the public's imagination by producing a variety of mutant breeds, including curly-haired rats, waltzing rats, and chocolate-colored rats. More important, however, King succeeded in producing rats with the specific genetic characteristics required for particular research projects. Her work also made it possible to maintain a pure strain of laboratory animal. Helen King died in Philadelphia in 1955, age 85.

SOURCES:

Bailey, Brooke. *The Remarkable Lives of 100 Women Healers and Scientists.* Holbrook, MA: Bob Adams, 1994.

Ogilvie, Marilyn Bailey. *Women in Science.* Cambridge, MA: The MIT Press, 1986.

King, Henrietta Chamberlain

(1832–1925)

American cattle rancher and philanthropist. Born Henrietta Maria Morse Chamberlain in Boonville, Missouri, on July 21, 1832; died in Santa Gertrudis, Texas, on March 31, 1925; daughter of Hiram Bingham Chamberlain (a preacher) and Maria Chamberlain; attended a female institute in Holly Springs, Mississippi; married Captain Richard King (a steamboat master turned rancher), in December 1854 (died in April 1885); children: five, including **Alice King Kleberg***.*

Henrietta King, the wife of world-famous rancher Richard King, inherited 500,000 acres of Texas land and $500,000 of debt from her husband in 1885. At the time of her own death in 1925, she left an estate of nearly one million acres and almost 95,000 head of cattle. Credited with building one of the largest ranching enterprises in the United States, King also helped foster the use of scientific techniques in cattle breeding, thus producing a safer, more abundant beef supply.

The daughter of a preacher, Henrietta King was born in Boonville, Missouri, in 1832, and was educated at a female institute in Mississippi. When King was 17, her father relocated the family to Brownsville, a remote outpost on the Texas Rio Grande, where he established the first Presbyterian mission and where Henrietta taught school and served as a devout member of her father's church. Characterized as a self-reliant and remote young woman, she did not socialize much until she met and fell in love with Richard King, a former boat captain who had come to Brownsville in 1847 and had established a cattle ranch on the Santa Gertrudis Creek, 40 miles inland from Corpus Christi. After a long and sedate courtship, the two were married by Reverend Chamberlain in early December 1854 and honeymooned at King's Rancho Santa Gertrudis. Henrietta's expectations were somewhat dashed when her first house turned out to be so small that she had to hang her large serving platters on the outside walls.

Richard King's dream was to increase his empire by purchasing all the land along the Gulf of Mexico between the Nueces River and the Rio Grande, 150 miles to the south. While he acquired acreage and cattle, Henrietta became "La Patrona" of the homestead, raising a family (which grew to include five children) and frequently defending the ranch against outlaws and renegades in her husband's absence. In 1863, during the Civil War, the ranch was attacked by the Union army and Henrietta, seven months pregnant, was forced to flee with the children to San Antonio, while her husband joined Captain

Henrietta Chamberlain King

James Richardson's company of home guards. Following the war, Richard used the money he had earned supplying the Confederate army with food and services to purchase more land and livestock. Henrietta, possessed of strong Puritan scruples, had some difficulty accepting the trappings of the family's increasing wealth. When her husband presented her with a pair of diamond earrings, she agreed to wear them only after having their brilliance dulled with a coat of enamel.

By 1885, Richard was well on the way to realizing his dream when he was diagnosed with stomach cancer in its final stages. Before he died in April of that year, he willed all his land, property, and livestock to Henrietta to be "used and disposed of precisely the same as I myself might do if I were living." Henrietta's first business decision was to hire her husband's lawyer Robert Kleberg to manage the ranch. Kleberg, who would later marry Henrietta's daughter Alice, not only possessed legal skills but also shared Henrietta's deep love of the land, and he ultimately proved worthy of the trust she placed in him. Kleberg made it a point to confer with Henrietta on all major decisions, the first of which was to sell off several thousand acres of Richard's beloved land to pay off the most pressing debts.

As Henrietta grew older and her health started to decline, she began to spend winters at her Victorian mansion in Corpus Christi, where she launched a program of philanthropy to improve the community. She donated funds for a hospital, the Presbyterian church, and the public schools. Although she eventually gave Kleberg her power of attorney, she still remained involved in all the decisions regarding the ranch. Together, they encouraged a rail line through the property by contributing land for the right of way and for a new town called Kingsville, three miles east of the ranch headquarters. Henrietta planned much of the new community herself, donating land and money for churches as well as for a milling company, a cotton gin, and a weekly newspaper. She provided funds for the community's first public school, and also subsidized the Texas-Mexican Industrial Institute, which was located near Kingsville and provided for the vocational training of Mexican-American young people. Apparently, the only facility lacking in Kingsville was a saloon. Henrietta, a lifelong supporter of temperance, saw to it that her town remained dry by including a clause forbidding the sale of liquor in every deed she issued.

King was a forward-thinking woman for her time and moved easily into the future. When the automobile replaced the work horses that had been bred on the ranch, she and Kleberg began developing race horses, and bought or bred three Kentucky Derby winners—Bold Venture, Assault, and Middleground. King was also quick to adopt the newest scientific advancements in order to solve many of the problems of ranching. After the drought of 1891, during which they had to ship 12,000 cattle to Indian Territory in order to save them, she authorized purchase of one of the new heavy well-drilling machines. A local driller struck water in 1899, thus protecting the ranch from subsequent droughts. The King ranch became a leader in taking precautions against tick fever and in experimenting in breeding techniques. Crossing Brahmas and shorthorns, they produced the only authentic new breed of cattle to be developed in North America. The Santa Gertrudis breed, as it was known, was resistant to disease, thrived in unfavorable conditions, and yielded a high proportion of usable meat. King Ranch, Inc., later introduced the breed to many other countries.

After paying off her husband's debts, Henrietta continued to expand her landholdings, until she had one million acres. Although the ranch became a huge enterprise, she continued to visit her outlying properties at least twice a year. The King ranchhouse also became a gathering place for visitors and the scene of Henrietta's annual Christmas party for the ranchhands and their families. When the homestead burned to the ground in January 1912, a massive white stucco ranchhouse was built to replace the old wooden structure. (Its fortress-like design would later serve as protection, when border disputes put ranchers in constant danger of attack by marauders.) Henrietta continued to extend her hospitality to all, demanding only that women wear dresses and men wear coats at dinner. Another inflexible rule was that everyone, family and guests alike, eat cereal at breakfast, and to that end she kept some 80 varieties on hand.

In 1916, Kleberg became ill and his sons (her grandsons) Robert, Jr. and Richard took over the running of the ranch under his direction. During her final years, Henrietta deeded the Santa Gertrudis ranch headquarters and the land surrounding it to her daughter Alice, who had lived her entire life on the ranch. Henrietta died on March 31, 1925, at age 92, and was escorted to her final resting place in the Kingsville cemetery by all 200 of the King Ranch vaqueros, dressed in range clothes and mounted on horseback.

SOURCES:

Bird, Caroline. *Enterprising Women*. NY: W.W. Norton, 1976.

Crawford, Ann Fears, and Crystal Sasse Ragsdale. *Women in Texas*. Austin, TX: State House Press, 1992.

Barbara Morgan,
Melrose, Massachusetts

King, Isabella (1886–1953).

See Greenway, Isabella Selmes.

King, Jessie Marion (1875–1949)

Scottish artist and graphic designer. Born in New Kilpatrick, Scotland, in 1875; died in Kirkcudbright, Scotland, in 1949; attended the Glasgow School of Art; married E.A. Taylor (an artist).

Associated with the British version of Art Nouveau, Jessie Marion King was trained at the Glasgow School of Art and developed a style strongly influenced by Charles Rennie Mackintosh (1868–1928), a Scottish architect and designer who was at the forefront of modernism. King produced watercolors, wallpaper, jewelry, and tile and textile designs which she actively exhibited, from 1897 to 1940, at the Royal Scottish Academy, the Glasgow Institute of Fine Arts, and Bruton Galleries. In 1902, she won a gold medal for her drawings and watercolors at the Turin International Exhibition of Modern Decorative Art. Jessie King authored several books, and also produced book illustrations and jacket designs. The artist was married to E.A. Taylor and lived in Paris and Scotland.

King, Joyce (b. 1921).

See Blankers-Koen, Fanny for sidebar.

King, Julie Rivé (1854–1937).

See Rivé-King, Julie.

King, Katie (b. 1975).

See Team USA: Women's Ice Hockey at Nagano.

King, Louisa Yeomans (1863–1948)

American gardener. Born Louisa Boyd Yeomans in Washington, New Jersey, on October 17, 1863; died in Milton, Massachusetts, on January 16, 1948; elder of two daughters of Alfred Yeomans (a Presbyterian cleric) and Elizabeth Blythe (Ramsay) Yeomans; educated in private schools; married Francis King, on June 12, 1890; children: Elizabeth King; Henry William King; Frances King.

Louisa King was drawn into gardening by her mother-in-law, whom she called "one of the ablest and most devoted gardeners of her generation." Louisa planted her first garden in 1902 and devoted the rest her life to horticultural pursuits. She was a founding member of the Garden Club of America (1913) and served as president of the Woman's National Farm and Garden Association from 1914 to 1921.

Beginning in 1910, King wrote magazine articles on gardening and, in 1915, published the first of her nine books, *The Well-Considered Garden.* King advocated artistry over practicality, particularly when it came to groupings and color considerations. "I can admire a perfect Frau Karl Druschki rose, a fine spray of Countess Spencer sweet pea," she wrote in the June 1910 issue of *Garden Magazine,* "but never without thinking of the added beauty sure to be its part if a little sea-lavender were placed next to the sweet pea, or if more of the delicious roses were together." In 1921, Louisa King became the first woman to receive the George White Medal of the Massachusetts Horticultural Society, the highest gardening award in America. She was also a fellow of the Royal Horticultural Society of Great Britain.

SOURCES:

Edgerly, Lois Stiles. *Give Her This Day.* Gardiner, ME: Tilbury House, 1990.

Read, Phyllis J., and Bernard L. Witlieb. *The Book of Women's Firsts.* NY: Random House, 1992.

SUGGESTED READING:

James, Edward T., ed. *Notable American Women, 1607–1950.* Cambridge, MA: The Belknap Press of Harvard University Press, 1971.

Barbara Morgan,
Melrose, Massachusetts

King, Mrs. L.W. (b. 1943).

See King, Billie Jean.

King, Mrs. Martin Luther, Jr. (b. 1927).

See King, Coretta Scott.

King, Maxine (b. 1944).

See King, Micki.

King, Micki (1944—)

American diver who won a gold medal in the Munich Olympics. Name variations: Captain Maxine King; team manager under name Micki Hogue for the U.S. Olympic divers in 1988. Born Maxine King on July 26, 1944, in Pontiac, Michigan; graduated from University of Michigan, 1966; enlisted in U.S. Air Force, 1966.

Won gold medal in the Munich Olympics (1972); competed against men in the World Military Games (1969); appointed diving coach at the Air Force Acad-

emy *(1973); was the first woman to hold a faculty position at a U.S. military academy.*

Micki King's mother wanted her to be a figure skater, but the little girl found this sport tedious. She loved the thrill of jumping into a pool off an elevated platform and began training at the local YMCA at age ten. In high school, King played water polo and was a member of the swim team. Though she did not enter her initial diving competition until age 15, she won on her first attempt. In 1963, then a journalism sophomore at the University of Michigan, King decided to take diving more seriously, very late for a competitive diver. "I would like to know what makes people jump," she once said. "A lot don't at first, you know. They stand there on the edge and finally walk away. Height is the big psychological thing that scares people off. When you hit the water after jumping off the tower, you're going about 40 miles an hour. Sometimes you hit with such force that your shoulders and upper arms turn black-and-blue. I was scared for three years." Her coach Dick Kimball encouraged King, and for those three years she led the university diving team. After winning many competitions, she placed fifth in the Olympic tryouts in 1964.

When Micki King graduated from college in 1966, she faced an uncertain future as an athlete, particularly as a female athlete. If she planned to devote herself full-time to diving, she needed support in order to afford the expense of training for international competition and the 1968 Olympic Games. Although the ongoing Vietnam War did not make the military a popular option, King enlisted in the U.S. Air Force in 1966 as an officer candidate. When she received her commission as a second lieutenant, she returned to the University of Michigan Reserve Officer Training Corps and to her coach Dick Kimball. At the Mexico City Olympics in 1968, King was determined to win the gold. In her next-to-last dive off the springboard, she jumped too high on the inward reverse 1½ layout, one of her best dives. Attempting to correct her mistake, she broke her left arm when she hit the board. "The thud was so loud it echoed through the whole building," she said later. "I can still hear it now, and it makes me sick." She returned for her last dive with a broken arm although she dropped from first place to fourth. **Sue Gossick** of the U.S. took the gold medal.

Older than many diving champions, King decided to retire after this setback. However, the national indoor championships in Los Angeles in the spring of 1969 fired her competitive spirit, and she was soon back on the board. She en-

Opposite page

Micki
King

tered the World Military Games in Pescara, Italy, in 1969 where she competed against men. King performed dives no woman had ever attempted before and placed fourth in platform and third in springboard. Between 1969 and 1972, she won ten national springboard and platform diving championships. She competed in the Pan American Games, the World University Games, and the International Invitational.

At 28, King was one of the more seasoned athletes at the 1972 Munich Olympics. Fellow divers called her "Mother Max." Nonetheless, she believed in herself: "It takes years to perfect the mechanics and form and to attain that essential consistency. I started later than most girls, so I'm attaining my goals later." Ten years of hard work paid off and Micki King, heavily favored, won a gold medal in the springboard event. In 1973, Captain King became the first woman appointed to a faculty position at a U.S. military academy when she became the diving coach at the Air Force Academy. She continued to coach and was a founding member of the Women's Sports Foundation.

SOURCES:

Sabin, Francene. *Women Who Win.* NY: Random House, 1975.

Woolum, Janet. *Outstanding Women Athletes: Who They Are and How They Influenced Sports in America.* Phoenix, AZ: Oryx Press, 1992.

Karin L. Haag,
freelance writer, Athens, Georgia

Kinga.

Variant of Cunegunde.

Kingsford, Anna (1846–1888)

British physician and religious writer. Born Anna Bonus in 1846; died in 1888; studied medicine in Paris; awarded M.D. degree, 1880; married Algernon Godfrey Kingsford (vicar of Atcham, Shropshire), in 1867.

Anna Kingsford had established herself quite well as a writer before taking up the study and practice of medicine. She began publishing miscellaneous works as early as 1863 and contributed stories to the *Penny Post* from 1868 to 1872. Kingsford converted to Roman Catholicism in 1870 and, in 1872, purchased the *Lady's Own Paper* which she edited for a year. She began her medical studies in Paris in 1874 and received her M.D. degree in 1880. She practiced in London for only eight years before her death in 1888. Kingsford was also the president of the Theosophical Society (1883) and founded the Hermetic Society (1884).

Kingsley, Dorothy (1909–1997)

American screenwriter who wrote scripts for over 25 movies, including Pal Joey, Can-Can, Kiss Me, Kate, *and* Seven Brides for Seven Brothers. *Born Dorothy Kingsley on October 14, 1909, in New York City; died of a heart ailment on September 26, 1997, in Carmel, California; daughter of Alma Hanlon (a silent-screen actress) and Walter Kingsley (a Broadway press agent); first marriage ended in divorce; married William Durney (d. 1989); children: (first marriage) three sons.*

Academy Award nomination for Seven Brides for Seven Brothers; *Writers Guild best script nominations for* On an Island with You; Angels in the Outfield; Kiss Me, Kate; Don't Go Near the Water; Pal Joey; *and* Can-Can.

Filmography: Look Who's Laughing *(1941); (uncredited)* Girl Crazy *(1943); (uncredited)* Here We Go Again *(1944); (co-credit)* Broadway Rhythm *(1944); (co-credit)* Bathing Beauty *(1944);* Easy to Wed *(1946); (co-credit)* On an Island with You *(1948); (cocredit)* A Date with Judy *(1948);* Neptune's Daughter *(1949); (co-credit)* Two Weeks in Love *(1950);* Skipper Surprised His Wife *(1950); (co-credit)* Angels in the Outfield *(1951); (co-credit)* Texas Carnival *(1951);* It's a Big Country *(1951); (uncredited)* Cause for Alarm *(1951);* When In Rome *(1952);* Small Town Girl *(1953);* Dangerous When Wet *(1953); (co-credit)* Kiss Me, Kate *(1953);* Seven Brides for Seven Brothers *(1954);* Jupiter's Darling *(1955);* Pal Joey *(1957); (cocredit)* Don't Go Near the Water *(1957);* Green Mansions *(1959);* Pepe *(1960);* Can-Can *(1960); (co-credit)* Valley of the Dolls *(1967); (co-credit)* Half a Sixpence *(1967);* Angels in the Outfield *(remake, 1994). Also was a radio writer for Bob Hope and created the television series "Bracken's World," 1969.*

Dorothy Kingsley was born in New York City in 1909 and spent her childhood on Park Avenue as the only daughter of successful show-business parents. Walter Kingsley was a press agent who represented major stars of the Broadway stage, including *Sarah Bernhardt, George M. Cohan and Florenz Ziegfeld. Kingsley's mother, **Alma Hanlon**, was an actress who appeared on Broadway and in a dozen motion pictures. When Kingsley was 13, her parents divorced. Alma Hanlon gave up her career and moved with her daughter to Grosse Point, Michigan, an affluent suburb of Detroit, where she married a wealthy real estate developer. Kingsley's adolescence was spent as a socialite in the company of the daughters of the nation's leading industrialists.

Kingsley's own first marriage ended in divorce. Left with three sons to raise, she had to find a way to support her young family. While recuperating from a bout of measles, Kingsley spent her time listening to the radio. It was the heyday of such comics as Jack Benny, Bob Hope and Edgar Bergen, and Kingsley became convinced that she too could write gags. After several false starts, she moved to Hollywood where she was hired as a $50-a-week gag writer for Edgar Bergen. Not long after, she decided the better move would to be to work in the motion-picture business. She began writing screenplays "on spec" and submitting them, through her agent, to the studios.

In 1943, Kingsley was hired as a staff writer at Metro-Goldwyn-Mayer. Though she wrote some original material, she was most often brought onto movies to rewrite them. It was her ability to fix scripts in trouble that made her reputation and kept her working for two decades. In a 1991 interview with Pat McGilligan for *Backstory*, Kingsley said she never considered herself a "real writer. I only wrote because I needed the money. I had no desire to express myself. I couldn't have cared less."

Kingsley remained active in show business until the early 1970s. In 1969, she created the television series "Bracken's World," a dramatic show revolving around the inner workings of a motion-picture studio. The show ran a couple of seasons after which Kingsley went into semi-retirement. She and her second husband, William Durney, moved to Carmel, California, and founded Durney Vineyards. In 1994, Dorothy Kingsley came out of retirement to co-write the remake of *Angels in the Outfield*. She remained a resident of Carmel, where she died of heart failure less than three weeks before her 88th birthday.

SOURCES:

McGilligan, Pat. *Backstory 2.* Berkeley, CA: University of California Press, 1991.

Deborah Jones, Studio City, California

Kingsley, Mary H. (1862–1900)

Victorian Englishwoman, famous for her adventures in West Africa, who wrote several books detailing her trips and caused considerable controversy with her ideas about how West Africa should be governed. Born Mary Henrietta Kingsley on October 13, 1862, in Islington, England; died on June 3, 1900, in South Africa, of typhoid fever; daughter of George Kingsley (a physician) and Mary (Bailey) Kingsley; educated mostly through reading her father's library of travel books; never married; no children.

Following the death of both parents, used her inheritance for a visit to the Canary Islands (1892); inspired by the previous journey, set sail for Freetown, West Africa (August 1893); spent 11 months in West Africa leading an expedition of Africans in exploring the Ogooué River, crossing overland from the Ogooué to the Ramboé River, and becoming the first person, along with her African assistants, to ascend the southeast side of Mount Cameroon (1895); after four years back in England, departed in March for South Africa, where she nursed military prisoners of the Boer War (1900).

Selected publications: Travels in West Africa, Congo Français, Corisco and Cameroons *(Macmillan, 1897);* West African Studies *(Macmillan, 1899);* The Story of West Africa *(Horace Marshall, 1900).*

In the small grass hut where she lay dozing, Mary Kingsley was awakened suddenly by a violent smell, later described in her book *Travels in West Africa,* as being of "an unmistakably organic origin." Inside the hut cleared for her by the village chief, she found a small bag hanging from the roof. In it, she found a human hand, three toes, four eyes, and two ears. "The hand was fresh," she later wrote, "the others only so so."

Kingsley was deep in Fang country, the lands of a West African tribe known for ritual cannibalism. The year was 1895, and she was crossing a 50-mile stretch of land between the Ogooué and Ramboé rivers, unspectacular except for the fact that no white man—and certainly no white woman—had ever set foot on this part of the "Dark Continent." During this period, West Africa was also known as the "white man's grave" because of the abominable rate at which disease claimed traders, missionaries, and government officials sent off to this part of Africa from Europe as if sentenced to a very short life in prison.

Though Kingsley spent barely spent two years traveling in West Africa, it was the highlight of her life. The activities of her first 30 years hardly indicated that this singular woman would go on to become a daring adventurer or a famous spokesperson for West African affairs. She was born in Islington, England, in 1862. Until her parents' death in 1892, she lived entirely at home, caring for her invalid mother and looking after the needs of her father during his infrequent stays. Except for a trip to Paris when she was in her mid-20s, she never stepped outside Great Britain, and there is no record that she traveled much there. Her experience was confined mostly to London and to Cambridge, where the family moved in 1886.

Voluminous reading, however, allowed Mary Kingsley to explore the world mentally. Her father, a physician, generally worked in the service of aristocrats and spent much of his life traveling with his wealthy patients to such far-off places as the South Pacific and the American "Wild West." George Kingsley had a passion for travel and a library filled with the serious travelogues of his time, written by such famous adventurers as Sir Richard Burton and Mungo Park. Dr. Kingsley even co-authored his own travel book, *South Sea Bubbles by the Earl and the Doctor,* recounting his journeys in the South Seas with the Earl of Pembroke. It was from this library of books about far-off lands that Kingsley filled her developing mind.

On his returns from abroad Dr. Kingsley brought back strange tales and bags of exotic artifacts; his arrivals also ended Mary's use of the library and returned her to the rigid role that he felt all Victorian women should fill. Unlike her younger brother, Mary was never formally educated, but was relegated to helping her mother **Mary Baker Kingsley** with the housework while her mother was still well. Later, she became her mother's full-time nurse.

> *S*he dies at last a woman's death in the centre of civilisation, but perhaps that will only strengthen people's memories to recall that she had lived like a man in strange countries where civilisation had not gained mastery.
>
> —*The Lady,* June 21, 1900

Mary's mother had originally been George Kingsley's cook. They married when she learned she was pregnant with Mary, who was born only three days after the nuptials took place, and this near-illegitimacy was never publicly revealed during Mary's life. As an adult, she often lied about her age to aid in the deception, which she apparently found out about only at the death of her parents. Mary Baker Kingsley was from a working-class background and had little in common with her husband, which may help to explain why he spent so much time abroad. His absences probably played on his wife's frailty, however, and it is suspected that this life of bitter loneliness helped to erode her sanity and cause nervous attacks. When Mary was 28, one such attack left her mother paralyzed.

The constant attention that her mother required, sometimes through the night, put an end to Mary Kingsley's socializing within the small circle of stimulating friends she had begun to make in Cambridge. This full-time charge would have locked out any possibility of finding a suitor or husband, if that had been her desire, although there is little evidence to suggest that it was.

In 1892, when both her parents died within a few months of each other, Mary was nearly 30. In the next few years she would make up for the routineness of a life which had tied her to the confines of a few city blocks. The inheritance she received was not large, but it was enough to allow her to live independently and to indulge in some travel. In June 1892, therefore, just five weeks after her mother's death, she set off by ship due south, to "the closest least civilized part of the globe," the Canary Islands. She traveled alone, refusing requests from friends to accompany her.

The Canary Islands, just a hundred miles from the West Coast of Africa, were a gateway to that region as well as to Mary Kingsley's roaming, adventurous spirit which had been stifled for so many years. She wrote home that she had been having "a wild time since I left." On the island of La Gomera, she slept beneath a boulder at the center of an enormous volcanic crater. But most of her time was spent, she wrote, "on vessels going to and from the coast of Africa, on their way out with iron bedsteads, sperm candles and saltpeter or on their way home with black people of all ages and sexes, monkeys, parrots, snakes, canary birds, sheep, palm oil, gold dust and ivory." Taken with everything that went into trading as a line of work, she began to develop strong opinions about British traders in Africa.

When Kingsley returned to England she found that her brother Charley had rented a top-floor apartment for them in London. It was not to her liking, and she began to plan another journey. Since traveling to Africa as a single female tourist was not seen as appropriate behavior for a Victorian woman, she felt she needed a purpose for the trip. First she contacted the British Museum of Natural History and obtained a "collector's outfit"—bottles, nets, jars filled with liquids to preserve fish and insects—then she bought a revolver, and set off under the guise of doing scientific research for the museum. One of the last tasks she performed before embarking once more for the "white man's grave" was to make out her will.

This second trip to Africa lasted considerably longer than her first. It brought her initially to Freetown, Sierra Leone, a place she had seen so often in her mind's eye that she couldn't believe she was finally experiencing it firsthand. To be there, she later wrote in West African Studies, was "a thrill of joy." Aboard the Portuguese mailboat Lagos, she continued down the coast of Africa to Liberia, where, she wrote at one point to a friend, "there is another drenching sheet of rain wrapped round us."

On the West Coast of Africa, the sight of a white woman alone, dressed in mourning from head to foot, was as strange to the people she met as everything was to her. In this uncomfortably hot part of the world, there were no tourists, and when the only other white female on the boat got off in the Canary Islands, the white men on board were amazed that Kingsley remained. At first, they thought she was a missionary or perhaps a botanist—which was in fact the impression she tried to leave; she collected plants, fish, and rocks and took copious notes everywhere she went. Botanists from Kew had been known to explore the coast, but all of them were now dead.

Kingsley finally got off the Lagos in Cabinda, a trading station just north of the mouth of the Congo River. The European men at the station were astonished at her unexpected arrival. Kingsley's explanation was that she was waiting for the English mailboat to take her home, and hunting meanwhile for "fetish and fish." Sleeping in the same hut that the explorer Henry Morton Stanley had slept in on his first trans-African expedition, she stayed with the traders for two weeks. She shared their meals and came to trust these hard-living men. They in turn accepted her presence, calling her "Aunty." By the end of December, Kingsley arrived back in Britain with a trunkload of tales to tell and strolled irreverently in the streets of Liverpool with a pet monkey on her back.

Short trips upriver toward the heart of Africa had fueled her thirst for adventure. Kingsley wrote to a friend during this trip that she would cut all frivolous expenses out of her life when she returned to England, in order to save for another such journey. The sights, smells, the heat and the people of Africa had flooded her senses, and after this new world, a dream almost, the conventions of Victorian society clung to her like a damp rag. During the journey, when a fellow passenger asked if she was shocked upon seeing half-naked men paddling out to their boat in long canoes, she had become annoyed. Back in England she argued that her trip had not been a lark, and that "collecting" was a respectable pastime for a "middle-class spinster"; indeed, she had gathered a fine collection of fish, flies, beetles, plants and geological specimens. But her collection was too varied, and geological work was still considered the sole domain of men. Botany was a better bet, as there were several women who had already made names for themselves in the field, and she contacted the British Museum about her collection. She also contacted Macmillan, the publisher, about writing an account of her trip as a book.

A year after her return, she was back on the boat sailing south again toward Africa, this time accompanied by Lady **Ethel MacDonald**, who was going to join her husband, Sir Claude MacDonald, the first commissioner and consul general of the Niger Coast Protectorate. Because of her distinguished companion, Kingsley traveled this time in relative style and comfort. She was to stay for four months in Calabar, the site of the Colonial Government, helping to nurse men back to health who had succumbed to a smallpox epidemic. She also took short trips into the bush, pursuing her work as a naturalist and amateur anthropologist, studying the culture and legal systems of the indigenous peoples.

On one of several extended trips she took to visit missionaries, Kingsley was the guest of a French missionary couple at Talagouga when she decided to head up the Ogooué River in search of a species of fish she wanted to collect. She hired eight Galoas (Igaluas) as paddlers for her canoe. The French official protested that such a venture was unheard of, reminding Kingsley that the only white woman ever to go up the Ogooué had been accompanied by her husband and a number of other white men. Kingsley countered by making her own trip sound like a leisurely Sunday afternoon in the park. The **Madame Quinee** he mentioned had gone much further upriver than she planned; she would go a much shorter distance, for the purpose of collecting a few fish.

Once away from the mission, however, Kingsley ordered the men she now commanded to head towards the Alembe rapids at Kondo Kondo. In *Travels in West Africa,* she describes this whitewater journey:

> When we were . . . paddling about the Okana's entrance my ears recognised a new sound. The rush and roar of the Ogowé we knew well enough. . . . But this was an elemental roar. I said to M'bo: "That's a thunderstorm away among the mountains." "No, sir," says he, "that's the Alemba."

The rapids broke their paddles like matchsticks, but the voyagers lived to tell about it. For Kings-

Mary H. Kingsley

ley, the rapids were nearly as great a thrill as the freedom and power she felt in command of an expedition.

Her next expedition was the 50-mile overland crossing between the Ramboé and Ogooué rivers; as the first white person to do so, she could put herself in the category of amateur explorer, looking up to the such masters of the game as DuChailla, Dr. Barth, and Livingstone. In yet another first, climbing the 13,760-foot Mount Cameroon (known as Mungo ma Lobeth, or the Throne of Thunder, the first white climber of which had been Sir Richard Burton) began to seem too great a temptation for Kingsley to pass up. With the help of a number of porters, many of whom fell by the wayside along the trail during the week-long assault, Kingsley became the third English person to climb the mountain, and the first to reach the summit from the southeast face; she never mentioned in her books that she was undoubtedly the first woman to climb it.

Returning to England at the end of November 1895, Kingsley found she had been preceded by a flurry of press reports about her exploits. The public waited now with anticipation to hear more about the adventures of this daring traveler, touted by some as a "new woman." Despite her ability to excel in pursuits associated with the very essence of masculinity, Kingsley was no feminist, and on her return she stated bluntly, "I did not do anything . . . without the assistance of the superior sex." Ironically, she opposed female suffrage and believed throughout her life that a woman's place was in the home. In a profile article about Kingsley that appeared in *Young Woman* soon after her return, **Sarah Tooley** wrote:

> It affords [Kingsley] some amusement that her travelling exploits are spoken of as something extraordinary for a woman to have accomplished, while no one would have marvelled if she had continued the heavy strain of her home duties to the end of her days.

Kingsley felt the physical strain of nursing was far greater than any adventure she had been on in Africa.

But Kingsley's next four years in England were not spent professing the proper place of women in Victorian society. Taking up the cause of West Africans, she believed that the British government was mismanaging its holdings in that part of the continent and would soon ruin it. She was against interventionist colonial rule and favored a loose system of government resembling economic imperialism that would allow free trade to continue unfettered. In Kingsley's eyes, the traders were the only ones who really knew Africa, and they should have a say in deciding how it was governed. From this position it was natural that she should oppose the anti-liquor lobbyists, who wanted to ban the sale of trade gin to Africans. Kingsley argued that the liquor was used in West Africa almost as a currency, and that she had seen no more deleterious effects of it there than could be seen on the streets of London. Because of her strong support for the traders, she became the first woman ever to speak to the Manchester Chamber of Commerce, with a talk appropriately titled "The Administration of Our West African Colonies."

Almost two years on the African continent had made Kingsley something of an expert. Nearly everyone, from academics at Oxford University to the top echelons of government, was interested in hearing her views. While Joseph Chamberlain was Secretary of State for the Colonies, he corresponded with Kingsley and was occasionally influenced by her views. Meanwhile, Kingsley earned much of her income from lectures given throughout the United Kingdom on a wide range of topics related to the region she had explored.

During these four years, she also published three books. *Travels in West Africa* came out in January 1897 and was an immediate bestseller. *West African Studies*, a more scholarly work published two years later in January 1899, was not as widely received. *The Story of West Africa*, a history of that part of the world, in which Kingsley now rated as a specialist, came out in January 1900. Kingsley also wrote a number of articles for such periodicals as the *Spectator* and *Fortnightly Review,* and kept up a voluminous correspondence. The intense work led to severe headaches, and Kingsley suffered a breakdown in early 1898, then recovered and continued at the same pace as before.

After four years of planning, Kingsley finally got the chance to sail south again. This time her destination was South Africa, where the Boer War was in full swing by early 1900 and casualties were mounting. Nurses were needed to care for the injured soldiers, and Kingsley had volunteered, intending to do her duty and then travel from there to West Africa once the war was over. She set sail in March and was stationed at Simonstown, where, instead of treating the British wounded, she tended to the needs of captured prisoners. Conditions were miserable at Palace Barracks, where the diseased and injured were crowded together and the medical help was severely understaffed. Kingsley worked furiously, cleaning and caring for the sick, and wrote home, "I am down in the ruck of life again." Typhoid was raging throughout the camp, and Kingsley came down with it, dying three weeks later. A mere seven years had passed since the death of her parents had freed her, at the age of 30, to travel. At that time it would have been hard for anyone, including perhaps even Kingsley herself, to imagine what she would accomplish in the time she had left.

SOURCES:

Birkett, Dea. *Mary Kingsley: Imperial Adventuress.* London: Macmillan, 1992.

Kingsley, Mary H. *Travels in West Africa, Congo Français, Corisco and Cameroons.* London: Macmillan, 1897.

Taylor Harper,
freelance writer, Amherst, Massachusetts

Kingsmill, Anne (1661–1720).

See Finch, Anne.

Kingston, duchess of.

See Chudleigh, Elizabeth (1720–1788).

Kingston, Elizabeth (1720–1788).

See Chudleigh, Elizabeth.

Kinkel, Johanna (1810–1858)

German choral conductor, pianist, composer, poet, and writer. Born Johanna Mockel in Bonn, Germany, on July 8, 1810; died in London, England, on November 15, 1858; daughter of Peter Joseph Mockel (a singing teacher at the Royal Bonn Gymnasium); married Johann Paul Matthieux (a bookseller), in 1832 (marriage annulled after a few days); married Gottfried Kinkel (a poet), in 1843; children: four.

Johanna Mockel was born in Bonn, Germany, in 1810, the daughter of a singing teacher at the Royal Bonn Gymnasium who was her first music instructor. She also met Felix Mendelssohn, the composer, in Frankfurt; he encouraged her to compose. Johanna married Gottfried Kinkel, a poet and revolutionary, in 1843. She became involved with chamber and vocal ensembles until the Revolution of 1848 and her husband's subsequent arrest for political activities. Condemned to death, he escaped from Spandau Prison and went to London. Johanna followed him there, and supported her four children and husband as a choir director and composer. In addition, Kinkel wrote essays on music, and her writings on Chopin are still considered particularly valuable. Johanna Kinkel's life ended in 1858, ten years after the revolution, when she committed suicide.

John Haag,
Athens, Georgia

Kinnaird, Mrs. Arthur (1816–1888).

See Deng Yuzhi for sidebar on Mary Jane Kinnaird.

Kinnaird, Mary Jane (1816–1888).

See Deng Yuzhi for sidebar.

Kinsky, Countess (1843–1914).

See Suttner, Bertha von.

Kinue or Kinuye Hitomi (1908–1931).

See Hitomi Kinue.

Kinuyo Tanaka (1907–1977).

See Tanaka, Kinuyo.

Kira of Leiningen (b. 1930)

Princess of Leiningen. Born Kira Melita Feodore Mary Victoria Alexandra on July 18, 1930, in Coburg, Bavaria, Germany; daughter of Charles, 6th prince of Leiningen, and *Marie of Russia (1907–1951); married Andrei Karadjordjevic (son of Alexander I, king of Yugoslavia), on September 18, 1963 (divorced 1972, died in Irvine, California, in 1990, as a result of carbon monoxide poisoning); children: Lavinia Maria (b. 1961); Vladimir (b. 1964);

Dmitri (b. 1965). Andrei Karadjordjevic's first wife was *Christine of Hesse-Cassel (b. 1933); his third was Eva Maria Andjelkovich, known as Mitsi.

Kira of Russia (1909–1967)

Niece of Marie of Rumania. Name variations: Kira Cyrillovna. Born on May 9, 1909, in Paris, France; died on September 8, 1967, at St. Briac-sur-Mer, France; buried in Hechingen, Germany; daughter of Cyril Vladimirovitch (grandson of Tsar Alexander II of Russia) and *Victoria Melita of Saxe-Coburg (1876–1936); niece of *Marie of Rumania (1875–1938); married Louis Ferdinand Hohenzollern (1907–1994), prince of Prussia, on May 2, 1938; children: Frederick (b. 1939); Michael (b. 1940); *Marie-Cecile Hohenzollern (b. 1942, who married Frederick Augustus of Oldenburg); Kira Hohenzollern (b. 1943); Louis (1944–1977); Christian (b. 1946); Xenia Hohenzollern (b. 1949).

Kirby, Sarah (1741–1810).

See Trimmer, Sarah.

Kirch, Margarethe (1670–1720).

See Kirch, Maria Winkelmann.

Kirch, Maria Winkelmann (1670–1720)

German astronomer noted for calculating calendars and ephemerides as well as for discovering a comet. Name variations: Maria Winkelmann. Born Maria Margarethe Winkelmann on February 25, 1670, in Panitzsch, Germany; died of fever on December 29, 1720, in Berlin; taught by father, uncle, and private tutors; married Gottfried Kirch, in 1692; children: four, including Christfried Kirch, Christine Kirch, and Margaretha Kirch.

Awards: medal, Berlin Academy (1711). Publications: astrological pamphlets (1709–12), calendars, ephemerides.

Maria Winkelmann Kirch stands as an important example of a woman astronomer who, although she worked as partner to her astronomer husband, was not allowed to succeed him in his official capacity upon his death.

Kirch was born Maria Margarethe Winkelmann on February 25, 1670, in Panitzsch, near Leipzig, the daughter of a Lutheran cleric. Interested at a young age in astronomy, she was tutored by her father and by an uncle after her father's death. She became an advanced student of noted amateur astronomer Christoph Arnold and later Gottfried Kirch, Berlin Academy astronomer, whom she married in 1692. The couple spent most of their time calculating calendars and ephemerides, with Maria as an "unofficial" assistant. However, her role was widely known throughout astronomical circles, and she gained fame in her own right through her discovery of a comet in 1702, and publication of astrological pamphlets between 1709 and 1712. Upon Gottfried's death in 1710, Maria petitioned the Berlin Academy of Sciences for 18 months for an appointment as assistant astronomer and calendar maker. The academy, fearful of setting a precedent by hiring a woman for such an important position, refused her request, but allowed her six months' housing and salary. In what was perhaps a peacemaking gesture, the academy presented her with a medal in 1711.

Kirch moved her family to Baron von Krosigk's private observatory in Berlin and produced calendars as well as daily observations of the planets, eclipses and sunspots with the aid of two students. After Krosigk's death in 1714, Kirch worked briefly as an assistant to a professor of mathematics at Danzig and had a private position at the deceased Johannes Hevelius' observatory. In 1716, Kirch and her son Christfried turned down an invitation from Peter I the Great to become astronomers in Moscow when Christfried was appointed one of two observers for the Berlin Academy (his father's old position). Kirch became unofficial assistant to her son. In 1717, she was reprimanded by the academy for being too "visible" and warned to stay in the background. When she refused, she was removed from the observatory and, lacking her own equipment, was forced to end her observations. Maria Kirch died of fever in Berlin on December 29, 1720.

Christfied Kirch occupied the observer's position at the Berlin Academy until his death in 1740. His sister **Christine Kirch** was his assistant and, for many years, was the calculator of Silesia's calendar.

SOURCES:

Multhauf, Lettie S. "Kirch," in Gillispie, Charles Coulton, ed. *Dictionary of Scientific Biography.* Vol. 7. NY: Scribner, 1980.

Schiebinger, Londa. "Maria Winkelmann at the Berlin Academy," in *Isis.* Vol. LXXVIII, 1987, p. 174–200.

———. *The Mind Has No Sex?* Cambridge, MA: Harvard University Press, 1989.

Kristine Larsen,
Central Connecticut State University, New Britain, Connecticut

Kirchwey, Freda (1893–1976)

American editor and publisher of The Nation, *the oldest liberal journal in the United States. Born in Lake Placid, New York, on September 26, 1893; died in St. Petersburg, Florida, on January 3, 1976; daughter of George Washington Kirchwey (1855–1942, a lawyer, criminologist, and dean of the law school at Columbia University) and Dora Child (Wendell) Kirchwey; had one sister and two brothers; graduated from Horace Mann School, New York, 1911; Barnard College, A.B., 1915; Litt.D., Rollins College, 1944; married Evans Clark, on November 9, 1915; children: Brewster Kirchwey (died young); Michael Kirchwey; Jeffrey Kirchwey (died young).*

Began working for The Nation *(1918); became managing editor (1922), chief editor (1936), and publisher and owner (1937).*

Freda Kirchwey—a political activist, editor and publisher of *The Nation,* and a "militant liberal"—was a tireless defender of the underdog. She was a radical feminist in the 1920s as well as a champion of social justice domestically. Shifting emphasis in the 1930s, she emerged as one the first major public figures in the United States to warn of the threat posed by international fascism, and was a supporter of collective security and the cause of the Spanish Republic. After 1945, she fought successfully to maintain *The Nation* as a forum for Americans who challenged many of the basic assumptions of the Cold War.

Kirchwey was born in Lake Placid, New York, in 1893, into a family with a history of concern for social justice. Her German-born grandfather Michael Kirchwey had participated in the (unsuccessful) German liberal revolution of 1848, and her father George Washington Kirchwey was a reform-minded lawyer, criminologist, and dean of the law school at Columbia University. A well-known figure in the Progressive (Bull Moose) movement, George had a strong interest in prison reform, believing that many prisoners could be rehabilitated, and was willing to test some of his ideas when he served briefly as warden of Sing Sing prison in 1915–16. Believing that laws would only be respected if they were applied ethically, he publicly denounced the death penalty as a "demoralizing spectacle" that served no social purpose, and he actively campaigned for its abolishment, serving as president of the American League for the Abolition of Capital Punishment.

Freda attended the Horace Mann School, an experimental high school affiliated with Teachers College of Columbia University. The academically gifted student then entered Manhattan's Barnard College. Here, and at Columbia, she enrolled in courses taught by some of the most innovative scholars of the day, including Charles Beard, Franz Boas, and James Harvey Robinson, a pioneer of social history. With a sharp eye for hypocrisy and injustice, Kirchwey was a "rebel girl" from an upper-middle-class milieu who was in opposition to the discriminatory and exclusionary policies of Barnard's sororities (known at the time as women's fraternities). Incensed by the anti-Semitic rules that precluded Jewish participation in these organizations, she denounced such policies in the school paper and called for the sororities to be abolished.

While still a student, she wrote essays in favor of women's suffrage, read the then-radical authors H.G. Wells and George Bernard Shaw, was an active member of the Intercollegiate Socialist Society, and joined the garment workers' picket line. One of her instructors at Barnard described her as the prettiest, most intelligent, and most radical girl in her class. Her classmates agreed, voting her both "Best Looking" and "Most Militant." After her graduation from Barnard in 1915, she married Evans Clark, keeping her maiden name. Clark, who then taught economics at Princeton University, would eventually become a professional researcher, then director of the Twentieth Century Fund. The couple would have three sons, Brewster, Jeffrey and Michael. Tragically, Brewster died as an infant and Jeffrey died at age seven.

In 1915, when Kirchwey was hired by the sporting newspaper *Morning Telegraph* as its society columnist, she continued to write pro-suffrage pieces. In 1918, she worked briefly as an editorial assistant for the *New York Tribune*, as well as for the literary magazine *Every Week*. That August, she began working for *The Nation*, an influential liberal journal founded in 1865. Oswald Garrison Villard, an admirer of Kirchwey's father, had recently reorganized the crusading weekly. Impressed by Kirchwey's energy and intelligence, he hired her to read, clip, and file articles for the journal's international-relations section. Her creativity and initiative were quickly revealed, and in June 1919 she was promoted to editor of this section of the journal. In 1922, Villard recognized Kirchwey's talents by appointing her managing editor.

In her early years with *The Nation*, Kirchwey spent much of her time on women's issues. The achievement of suffrage in 1920 did not end her commitment to debates on gender roles, and she was part of the struggle for legalizing the dissemination of birth-control information. She believed that modern American women had an obligation to work in the political arena, and in the early 1920s she was a militant member of the left wing of the National Woman's Party (NWP). At the NWP inaugural convention, held in Washington, D.C. (February 1921), Kirchwey minced no words in attacking the fledgling organization's leadership, which boasted such names as *Alice Paul, as having been "a veritable tank" that was insensitive to the party's rank-and-file membership and intent on crushing all attempts to bring about equality for black women, birth control, or a maternity endowment.

During the following month, in a March 1921 article in *The Nation* entitled "Alice Paul Pulls the Strings," Kirchwey acerbically alleged that Paul was a racist who was indifferent to the appeals of black women and who so resented their presence at the convention that they had been denied use of the elevator. Kirchwey had suspicions that the NWP had agreed not to raise the race issue in return for support of women's suffrage in the Southern states. Abrasive on these and other issues, Kirchwey had a pragmatic side, which was manifested in her opposition to an Equal Rights Amendment for fear that it could lead to an undermining of legislation that protected women in the workplace.

During her first decade as managing editor of *The Nation*, she placed a strong emphasis on exploring issues related to changing roles of women in modern society. For a series of articles entitled "New Morals for Old," she recruited such noted writers as *Charlotte Perkins Gilman, Joseph Wood Krutch, H.L. Mencken, and *Beatrice M. Hinkle. The series brought forth a strong reader response, and in 1924 Kirchwey edited the articles into book format under the title *Our Changing Morality*. In another series published in *The Nation* in 1926–27 as "These Modern Women" and "Men—What of 'Em?," she asked a number of women (whose identities were not disclosed) to share their viewpoints on such matters as marriage, male-female relationships, children, and careers. Her approach to the data revealed a progressive attitude when she called on the women's autobiographical sketches to be analyzed in the journal by a neurologist, a behavioral psychologist, and a psychoanalyst of Jungian persuasion.

In her private life as well, Kirchwey employed modern notions. For a number of years, she and her husband experimented with "open marriage," a decision that would test and almost destroy their relationship. A two-career marriage, and the illnesses that had led to the deaths of two of their sons, also placed great strains on Kirchwey's personal life. Suffering from depression after her son Jeffrey died from tuberculosis and spinal meningitis, for a while she could not bring herself to work at The Nation. Eventually, however, she rallied emotionally and poured her energies into the journal. Her biographer **Sara Alpern** has suggested that after the deepest period of mourning had ended, Kirchwey "seems to have merged herself into the journal; she and the journal became one."

During the 1930s, there was a shift away from women's issues in the journal, and feminist concerns were rarely mentioned in The Nation after 1932. The appearance of the Nazi dictatorship in Germany during 1933 played a major role in this change. Welcoming articles on the most recent events in Germany and Europe by writers of various backgrounds, Kirchwey became one of the first American editors to fully recognize the immense threat posed by fascism. Readers were alerted from the start to the existence of Nazi concentration camps, the growing inhumanity of German anti-Semitism, and the rapid growth of the Third Reich's military might. In view of the fact that the Soviet Union was the most resolute anti-fascist power, Kirchwey regarded the Stalin regime, illiberal as it was domestically, as an indispensable bulwark against the threat posed by Adolf Hitler's powerful state. Criticism of Stalinism and its brutal governance of the USSR was often muted in The Nation during these years. Kirchwey, herself a militant liberal rather than a Communist, felt that with the threat of fascism as a clear and present danger, and with the Communists adopting a Popular Front strategy of collaboration with liberal and even conservative anti-fascists, the "unity of the left" would be best preserved by not emphasizing a divisive editorial policy.

In international affairs, she was ardently internationalist and a strong supporter of the idea of collective security. Only by implementing such policies, she was convinced, would the democracies be able to check the spread of fascism. This point of view was made even more relevant in the summer of 1936, when the Spanish Civil War began and a democratically elected Republic was attacked by Francisco Franco's fascist rebels, with significant military assistance from Nazi Germany and Fascist Italy.

Although former Communists who became passionately anti-Communist like Eugene Lyons regarded Kirchwey with a jaundiced eye as a gullible fellow traveler whose journal naively "hummed with hymns" praising Stalin's dictatorship, the reality of the matter was considerably more complex. The Nation initially saw the first Soviet purge trials in 1936 as a sign of a setback rather than a total repudiation of the democratic (on paper) Stalin Constitution of that year, but the Moscow trials that followed and the bloody purges in general were reported critically and with considerable skepticism. Kirchwey was also critical of the Communist Party, USA, which exhibited intellectual dishonesty when wrapping itself in the names of Jefferson and Lincoln and when calling the defense of democratic institutions a necessity while at the same time maintaining what she saw as its "intolerable control" over its members in all aspects of their political lives.

Many of the most distinguished contributors to The Nation during the 1930s and 1940s, while liberal in varying degrees, were also outspoken in their rejection of the intellectual straitjacket of Communism. Among these were John Dewey, Norman Thomas, Sidney Hook, Joseph Wood Krutch, Reinhold Niebuhr, and **Margaret Marshall**. Kirchwey, who became publisher and owner of The Nation in 1937, hired Marshall as editor of the cultural section, which included book reviews as well as art and film criticism. At times, particularly after the Soviet Union became an ally of the West in 1941, discerning readers noticed a split between the front of the magazine, which rarely criticized the Soviet state, and its back pages in which Margaret Marshall provided a safe haven for essays by anti-Stalinist stalwarts like Sidney Hook, Philip Rahv, and *Diana Trilling.

The Hitler-Stalin pact of August 1939 outraged Kirchwey, who had hoped that the Soviet Union might be able to continue to oppose Hitlerite aggression in Europe. In a sharp criticism of Stalin's dictatorship, she charged that the de facto alliance had been timed to give Adolf Hitler "the greatest possible benefit." The destruction and partition of Poland revealed itself as having been prearranged, and the Soviets' justifications for their actions were, in a word from Kirchwey, "sickening." She penned an equally harsh denunciation of the Soviets several months later when they invaded Finland to seize strategic territory. Unlike Communists and those intellectuals who found justifications for the Soviet foreign policy flip-flop, Kirchwey used her journal as a forum for harsh criticisms of Stalinist duplicity and betrayal of the anti-fascist cause. In its pages, one could read articles by Louis Fischer, Granville Hicks and Lewis Corey that were not only devastating critiques of Soviet realpolitik, but also sophisticated theoretical criticisms of Soviet realities as well as the Marxist foundations on which its state and society claimed to have been constructed.

With the Nazi attack on the Soviet Union, the editorial policy of *The Nation* once again took on a broadly sympathetic attitude to the Stalinist state, or at least to the courage and sacrifices being made by the Soviet people fighting against fascism. On the American domestic scene, Kirchwey voiced her belief in a 1944 editorial that liberals and progressives should seriously consider the creation of a permanent political federation resembling the Popular Front coalition of the previous decade. At this time, she had found much to admire in the work of militant labor's CIO political-action organizations.

Fearless of the critics and enemies *The Nation* already had or would likely make in the future, Kirchwey wrote and polemicized on many issues directly or indirectly related to World War II. In one instance that elicited considerable interest in intellectual circles, she vehemently criticized Time-Life publisher Henry Luce, who in 1941 had proclaimed the dawn of an "American century" in the world. Luce saw the peaceful globe that was to come as one that would be dominated by the United States, with a marginal amount of assistance by Great Britain and China. Pontificating that its ideas and ideals enabled it to transcend the crippling class divisions of other societies, Luce saw America's historical experience and achievement as "the key to the future."

Kirchwey tore into Luce's pronouncements with passion. She compared his "Lucite New Order" to the Nazi New Order and asserted that his "cult of American superiority is no whit less revolting and no less unjustified than the Nordic myth that provides the moral sanction for Hitler's brutal aggression." As she saw it, Luce's vision of a triumphant capitalist American-led world was profoundly insulting to the guerillas fighting Hitler's occupying armies, the inmates of concentration camps, and the soldiers of the Red Army who had shed their blood to halt the Nazi juggernaut. To Kirchwey, Luce was as myopic as he was culturally arrogant, revealing an "unconcealed contempt" for the peoples and cultures of Europe.

Throughout the war, the pages of *The Nation* mirrored Kirchwey's concern for the fate of the Jewish people. Her sympathy for the plight of the Jews dated back to the early years of her journalistic career when she had come to know and respect the Zionist leader Chaim Weizmann. This friendship had a significant impact on her attitude toward Jewish aspirations, including her strong support for the idea of the creation of a Jewish homeland in Palestine. With the start of World War II, *The Nation* kept its readers informed of

Freda
Kirchwey

the rapidly deteriorating situation for Jews in Nazi-occupied Europe. These included firsthand reports from the pen of Varian Fry, who in 1940–41 carried on a secret rescue mission in southern France as the head of the American Emergency Rescue Committee. Fry's articles provided details not only on the "massacre of the Jews" but also documented the pervasive anti-Semitism of United States consular officials who made it virtually impossible for threatened Jews to escape to America. Kirchwey wrote a number of eloquent articles contrasting the horrors engulfing Europe's Jewish population with the paltry efforts of Washington in rendering assistance. She exposed the deliberate roadblocks of U.S. policy, and in the article "Rescue Hungary's Jews!" (August 26, 1944) revealed a remarkable level of understanding of what only decades later has come to be more fully comprehended as the process of industrial mass murder called the Holocaust:

> Several million Jews in Central and Eastern Europe have met their death as a result of Nazi ferocity and Allied indifference. Millions of non-Jews have died, too, murdered as hostages or killed in guerrilla fighting or victims of the policy of depopulation practiced in every conquered country. But the Jews have died as Jews, selected for oblitera-

tion to satisfy the race mania that underlies the whole dogma of Teutonic fascism.

Done in cold blood, on a scale more impressive than any battlefield can equal, in centers specially constructed for extermination, this systematic murder of a race is without example in history. It is too vast and too terrible for the normal mind to grasp; indeed this is its protection. People react with anger to individual acts of cruelty; they hardly react at all to the impersonal horror of mass murder.

While Kirchwey believed that a better world could, and indeed had to, result from the second World War, she had few illusions about peace even after the defeat of fascism in 1945. She regarded the military triumph of the Allies not as the end, but only as "the beginning of the victory." Her reaction to the appearance of nuclear weapons was rational: "If anything is sure about the atom bomb it is that no physical protection against it will ever be possible." Permanent world peace would have to be based on something other than military force, and its moral and institutional foundations would have to be carefully crafted and passionately defended. During the war, Kirchwey had become active in a circle of intellectuals who were strongly influenced by the political emigre Louis Dolivet. Dolivet's International Free World Association and the magazine *Free World* both equated anti-fascism with postwar plans for a strong United Nations organization. Other influential members of Dolivet's inner circle included newspaper columnist Max Lerner and writer Archibald MacLeish.

As the Cold War seemed to sweep the world inexorably toward destruction in the late 1940s, Kirchwey attempted to make sense of an irrational universe. Although *The Nation* made every effort to understand Soviet actions from a perspective other than that of knee-jerk anti-Communism, she personally recognized that in the final analysis Joseph Stalin and the Stalinized American Communist Party had little to offer Americans but slogans and cynical ideological zigzags. Sometimes vilified by conservatives as a "totalitarian liberal," Kirchwey was driven by political impulses derived from her hatred of fascism and concern for the underdog. At the same time, she could be a political realist, regarding half as better than nothing at all. Accordingly, she supported Harry Truman in the 1948 election campaign and wrote highly critical pieces on the politically suicidal strategies of Henry Wallace's Progressive Party. When the Korean War erupted in June 1950, she backed U.S. intervention as part of a UN effort to repel aggres-

sion. In other areas, however, she remained a militant liberal, particularly in her spirited defense of civil liberties and courageous rejection of the smear tactics of Senator Joseph R. McCarthy. On the international stage, *The Nation* campaigned vigorously against the Argentine regime of Juan Peron, which Kirchwey saw as a relic of the fascist dictatorships she had despised.

Seemingly determined to thrive on controversy, Kirchwey could only smile when *Time* magazine described *The Nation* in 1943 as "a pulp-paper pinko weekly." In 1948, after a series of articles strongly critical of the Roman Catholic church by Paul Blanshard appeared in *The Nation,* the journal was banned from the official periodical list of the New York City public-school system. Incensed at what she saw as an infringement of free speech, Kirchwey took the matter to the courts. After a series of legal cases, she won in 1950 and the ban was lifted.

In 1955, a year when glimmers of hope began to suggest that the Cold War's worst tensions could be reduced if not eliminated, Kirchwey decided to retire and sell *The Nation* to Carey McWilliams. Still energetic and cause-oriented, she devoted herself to working for a number of liberal organizations including the Committee for a Democratic Spain, the Women's International League for Peace and Freedom, and the Committee for World Development and World Disarmament. She also was active in such time-tested organizations as the League of Women Voters and the NAACP. Moving to Florida, she attempted to write an autobiography but made little progress on it. Writes Alpern: "Kirchwey could never write that book, for there was no way that she could write the *Nation*'s history without writing her own." After her husband died in 1970, her own health deteriorated rapidly. Freda Kirchwey died in a nursing home in St. Petersburg, Florida, on January 3, 1976.

In 1944, on the 25th anniversary of Kirchwey's association with *The Nation,* she had been honored by 1,300 invited guests at a gala testimonial dinner. On that occasion, columnist and radio commentator *Dorothy Thompson praised her friend for having fought "to throw light into dark places and to defend the people versus those interests that in our society have repeatedly striven to defeat the full realization of the promises of democracy."

SOURCES:

Alpern, Sara. *Freda Kirchwey: A Woman of "The Nation."* Cambridge, MA: Harvard University Press, 1987.

———, ed. "In Search of Freda Kirchwey," in *The Challenge of Feminist Biography.* Urbana, IL: University of Illinois Press, 1992.

Cott, Nancy F. "Feminist Politics in the 1920s: The National Woman's Party," in *Journal of American History*. Vol. 71, no. 1. June 1984, pp. 43–68.

Denning, Michael. *The Cultural Front: The Laboring of American Culture in the Twentieth Century*. London and NY: Verso, 1996.

"Freda Kirchwey," in *The Times* [London]. January 19, 1976, p. 14.

"Freda Kirchwey, 82, Dies; Long Editor of The Nation," in *The New York Times Biographical Service*. January 1976, p. 57.

Geidel, Peter. "The National Woman's Party and the Origins of the Equal Rights Amendment, 1920–1923," in *The Historian*. Vol. 42, no. 4. August 1980, pp. 557–582.

Kirchwey, Freda. "Rescue Hungary's Jews!," in *The Nation*. Vol. 159, no. 9. August 26, 1944, p. 229.

Lyons, Eugene. *The Red Decade: The Stalinist Penetration of America*. Indianapolis and NY: Bobbs-Merrill, 1941.

Mark, Eduard. "October or Thermidor?: Interpretations of Stalinism and the Perception of Soviet Foreign Policy in the United States, 1927–1947," in *American Historical Review*. Vol. 94, no. 4. October 1989, pp. 937–962.

McWilliams, Carey. "The Freda Kirchwey I Knew," in *The Nation*. Vol. 222, no. 2. January 17, 1976, pp. 38–40.

Walker, J. Samuel. "'No More Cold War': American Foreign Policy and the 1948 Soviet Peace Offensive," in *Diplomatic History*. Vol. 5, no. 1. Winter 1981, pp. 75–91.

Warren, Frank A. *Liberals and Communism: The "Red Decade" Revisited*. Bloomington and London: Indiana University Press, 1966.

———. *Noble Abstractions: American Liberal Intellectuals and World War II*. Columbus, OH: Ohio State University Press, 1999.

Wrong, Dennis. "A Career in Causes," in *The New Republic*. Vol. 197, no. 10. September 7, 1987, pp. 38–41.

John Haag,
Associate Professor of History,
University of Georgia, Athens, Georgia

Kirkeby, Elizabeth (fl. 1482)

English goldsmith and merchant. Flourished around 1482 in London; married John Kirkeby, a goldsmith (died 1482).

Elizabeth Kirkeby made a fortune as a London goldsmith. Her family connections are unknown; she was born in London to an artisan family, and married the goldsmith John Kirkeby as a young woman. When he died in 1482, Elizabeth carried on their business and expanded it as well. She created and sold gold pieces, and subsequently used her profits to open a shipping firm and a mercantile shop. She did not remarry, preferring instead to manage her fortunes and business affairs herself. She did hire many assistants, especially to help with her transactions on

the Continent, as she preferred to remain in London. She was one of London's wealthiest women when she died.

Laura York,
Riverside, California

Kirkland, Caroline Matilda
(1801–1864)

American author who was an early exponent of frontier realism. Name variations: (pseudonym) Mrs. Mary Clavers. Born Caroline Matilda Stansbury on January 11, 1801, in New York City; died on April 6, 1864, in New York City; eldest of 11 children and one of two daughters of Samuel Stansbury (an insurance agent, book seller, and inventor) and Eliza (Alexander) Stansbury; attended Quaker girls' schools run by her aunt in Mamaroneck and Manhattan, New York; married William Kirkland (an educator and editor), on January 10, 1828; children: seven (three of whom died in childhood).

Selected works: A New Home—Who'll Follow? or Glimpses of Western Life *(1839);* Forest Life *(1842);* Western Clearings *(1845);* Holidays Abroad *(1849);* The Evening Book; or, Fireside Talks on Morals and Manners *(1851);* Garden Walks with the Poets *(1852);* A Book for the Home Circle; or Familiar Thoughts on Various Topics, Literary, Moral, and Social *(1853);* The Helping Hand *(1853);* Memoirs of Washington *(1857);* The School-Girl's Garland *(1864).*

Considered the first author to write about the American frontier in realistic terms, Caroline Kirkland grew up in a comparatively cosmopolitan setting. Born Caroline Stansbury in New York City in 1801, she attended Quaker schools run by her aunt in Mamaroneck and Manhattan, and after completing her own schooling in 1820, assisted her aunt in managing a succession of schools in Poughkeepsie, New Hartford, and Skaneateles, New York. In 1828, after a long engagement, she married William Kirkland, a tutor in classics at Hamilton College in Clinton, New York. Following her marriage, Kirkland assisted her husband in running a girls' school in Geneva, New York, and there gave birth to the couple's first four children. (They would ultimately have seven children, three of whom died in childhood.)

In 1835, the family moved to Michigan, where William took a job as the first principal of the Detroit Female Seminary. In 1836, when William purchased 1,300 acres of marshy land in Livingston County, Michigan, around 60 miles northwest of Detroit, the family moved to Pinckney, a tiny village that turned out to be little more than a clearing in the forest. Over the next six years, Kirkland, whose notions of the American wilderness had been shaped by such romantic authors as Chateaubriand, endured the most primitive of conditions. To ease her isolation and intellectual boredom, she wrote long, amusing letters to her friends back East, recounting her new life. The letters eventually grew into the extended narrative *A New Home—Who'll Follow? or Glimpses of Western Life,* which was published in 1839 under the pseudonym "Mrs. Mary Clavers." Thinly disguised as a novel, the work is an autobiographical and realistic account of frontier life in "Montacute," a settlement bearing remarkable similarities to Pinckney. Lacking in sentimental convention, the book set a new standard for frontier fiction and was followed by *Forest Life* (1842), a sequel of sorts, although it was written in the form of a series of essays.

In 1843, the Kirklands proclaimed their real estate venture a failure and returned to New York City, where William took up journalism, first working as an editor for the New York *Evening Mirror* and then founding and editing the *Christian Inquirer,* a Unitarian weekly. Meanwhile, Caroline ran a school from her home and pursued her writing, producing a second collection of stories on the frontier theme, *Western Clearings* (1845). Following her husband's death in October 1846, she became the sole support of her family and thus pursued her career more aggressively. Kirkland succeeded William as editor of the *Christian Inquirer,* then in 1847 began an 18-month tenure as editor of the *Union Magazine of Literature and Art.* In 1848, she visited Europe and upon her return published two volumes of letters she had contributed to the magazine during her journey, under the title *Holidays Abroad, or Europe from the West.* Her later work, including a series of gift annuals and compilations of her stories, as well as some memoirs of her school days, was more conventional.

Described as attractive, energetic, and full of good humor, Kirkland was a central figure in the New York

Caroline Matilda Kirkland

literary community. Her circle of friends included William Cullen Bryant and the novelist N.P. Willis, and she frequently attended the literary salon of author *Anne C.L. Botta. Kirkland was also a woman of social conscience. She served on the executive committee of the Home for Discharged Female Convicts and, in 1853, wrote *The Helping Hand* on its behalf. In 1864, during the Civil War, she devoted three months to the preparation of the Metropolitan Fair to aid the U.S. Sanitary Commission. On April 6, 1864, shortly after the fair opened, Kirkland died in her sleep. She was buried in Greenwood Cemetery in Brooklyn.

SOURCES:
Duyckinck, Evert A., and George L. Duyckinck. *Cyclopedia of American Literature.* Vol. I. Philadelphia, PA: Wm. Rutter, 1875.

James, Edward T., ed. *Notable American Women, 1607–1950.* Cambridge, MA: The Belknap Press of Harvard University Press, 1971.

McHenry, Robert, ed. *Famous American Women.* NY: Dover, 1983.

Barbara Morgan,
Melrose, Massachusetts

Kirkland, Gelsey (1952—)

American ballerina known for her legendary partnership with Mikhail Baryshnikov. Born on December 29, 1952, in Bethlehem, Pennsylvania; one of three children, two daughters and a son, of Jack Kirkland (a playwright) and Nancy (Hoadley) Kirkland (an actress); attended public school in New York; attended Professional Children's School, New York City; studied ballet at the New York City Ballet's School of American Ballet; married Greg Lawrence (a writer), on May 13, 1985.

"Speed was her natural pace and air her habitat," wrote one critic of American ballerina Gelsey Kirkland, who is credited in part with the renaissance of ballet during the 1970s. "Her equilibrium was uncanny in all those off-balance Balanchine postures," he continued. "She could turn on a dime, stand on one point forever, all slim curves like a Brancusi." Kirkland's professional success, from her meteoric rise as a soloist with the New York City Ballet to her legendary partnership with Mikhail Baryshnikov, was indeed the stuff of fairy tales. The enormous pressures of the ballet world, however, took an exacting toll on Kirkland, very nearly costing the young dancer her life.

The daughter of playwright Jack Kirkland (author of the long-running Broadway play *Tobacco Road*) and his fifth wife, actress **Nancy**

Hoadley, Gelsey spent her earliest years on the family farm in Bucks County, amid an extended family that included children from her father's former marriages and a constant parade of visiting friends. Kirkland, a contented but private child, did not talk until well into her second year. "Little did anyone suspect that someday I would speak with silence," she wrote in her autobiography *Dancing On My Grave,* "that I would make a career out of being seen but not heard."

When Kirkland was still a child, financial difficulties forced the family to give up the farm and move to an apartment in Manhattan. Her father, in the midst of a physical and literary decline, lapsed into alcoholism and outbreaks of fury which left Kirkland struggling between her intense love for him and her resentment over his behavior. Her mother, perhaps to compensate, was overprotective, fueling yet another kind of anger in her daughter. Kirkland later saw ballet as a creative arena in which to vent her rage. "By devoting myself to the discipline of dance, I was able to establish a measure of control that was otherwise lacking in my life, or so it seemed."

Gelsey was eight when she was taken by her mother to audition at the School of American Ballet, where her older sister **Johnna Kirkland** was already a student. When she earned a place in the first division, she was furious, thinking that the only reason she had been accepted was because of her sister. "The anger that I felt after that first audition became one of the guiding emotions for my entire career," she recalled. Throughout her early training, Kirkland remained fiercely competitive with Johnna, who went on to become a leading dancer with the Los Angeles Ballet Theatre.

Kirkland remained at the School of American Ballet for eight years, while working as a part-time child model to earn extra money. When she was 15, she officially joined the New York City Ballet's corps de ballet, becoming its youngest member. Now completely focused on dance, she gave up modeling and left school at the end of the 11th grade. Kirkland spent her first months with the company taking classes and learning the repertory. The following spring, she danced her first solo role as the Butterfly in *A Midsummer Night's Dream* and went on to perform leading roles in John Clifford's *Reveries* and in Balanchine's *Monumentum Pro Gesualdo.* In the annual performance of *The Nutcracker,* she played the Sugar Plum Fairy, winning accolades from Clive Barnes, the critic for *The New York Times* (January 3, 1970). "There is already such authority and breeding to this young

dancer," he wrote, "that you can hardly wait to see the dancer she must surely develop into in a few more years."

With her success in *The Nutcracker,* Kirkland was promoted to the rank of soloist and selected by Balanchine, then director of the company, to dance the title role in a revival of his 1949 triumph *Firebird.* The new production premiered at Lincoln Center's State Theater in New York on May 29, 1970. Although some critics found Kirkland's interpretation wanting, most were awed by her technical ability. "This Firebird is not Rima the bird-girl, but an honest-to-goodness magical bird, stripped of sentiment, grateful for freedom, always in flight except when the Prince cunningly and gently traps her," wrote Herbert Saal in *Newsweek* (June 8, 1970).

Just 17, Kirkland became the darling of the media. A six-page spread on her appeared in *Life* magazine, followed by articles in *Dance Magazine, Forbes, Seventeen,* and *Saturday Review.* "Everyone seemed to have an angle on me except me," Kirkland recalled in her autobiography. Indeed, Kirkland's young life was all about conforming to the rigorous demands of Balanchine, who held his dancers in what appeared to be an unyielding grip. In an effort to please her mentor, she starved herself through anorexia and bulimia, surgically altered her face and body, and danced through painful injuries. According to Kirkland, Balanchine's tyrannical approach stripped his dancers of their individuality. "He sought to replace personality with his abstract ideal of physical movement," she wrote. "Even in his choreography that retained plot and character, the drama was distilled and the passion of the dancers quelled. Those were his instructions. There were not supposed to be any stars in his theatre who might detract or steal thunder from his choreography."

During the 1970 and 1971 seasons, Kirkland danced leading roles in Jerome Robbins' *The Goldberg Variations,* John Clifford's *Tchaikovsky Suite,* and Richard Tanner's *Concerto for Two Pianos.* Her repertory further expanded to include *Brahms Schoenbert Quartet, Symphony in C, Theme and Variations,* and *Harlequinade.* She particularly delighted audiences in Jacques d'Amboise's *Irish Fantasy,* in which critic Don McDonagh of *The New York Times* noted marked improvement in her ability to combine characterization with her extraordinary technique. With a promotion to principal dancer in 1972, Kirkland took on additional roles, but by this time she had also begun to rebel against Balanchine's harsh demands. She took additional classes with British choreographer **Maggie Black**, who helped her with a placement and a linearity of movement designed to reverse the training of her earlier years. She eventually gave up her classes with Balanchine completely, stomping out of a session one day in 1971, after he made some particularly mean-spirited remarks about dancers Rudolf Nureyev and *Margot Fonteyn. Balanchine retaliated by shutting her out of new roles, thus setting the stage for Kirkland's final split with the New York City Ballet.

It was an offer to perform with *premier danseur* Mikhail Baryshnikov, who defected from the Kirov Ballet in 1974, that prompted Kirkland to change the course of her life. "Misha was more than the ultimate romantic fantasy . . . ," Kirkland wrote. "His very existence inspired me to clarify and confirm the direction in which I had been moving." Hired by the American Ballet Theatre as Baryshnikov's partner, Kirkland entered into a professional and romantic partnership with the dancer that turned out to be as dominating as her relationship with Balanchine had been. The pair first danced together at the Winnipeg Ballet, performing the grand *pas de deux* from *Don Quixote*. On October 22, 1974, they performed the piece with the American Ballet Theatre in Washington, D.C., an event which also marked Kirkland's debut with the new company. Notices were simply glowing, some suggesting that the partnership with Baryshnikov seemed to spark a new maturity and daring in Kirkland's performance. "Her dancing didn't just shine, it radiated," gushed Alan M. Kriegsman in the *Washington Post* (October 24, 1974). "Before this she seemed a youngster of exceptional promise. Now she looks and poses and moves like the star she has become." During the two-week Washington run, she and Baryshnikov made seven triumphant appearances, dancing *La Bayadère*, *Theme and Variations*, and *Coppélia*.

During the company's 1974 season in New York, Kirkland won particular acclaim in the role of Lise in *La Fille Mal Gardée*, which featured a breathtaking series of perfectly executed *fouettés*. Also spectacular was her debut in *La Sylphide*, in which she was partnered with Ivan Nagy. "Miss Kirkland made a lovely thing out of this Fokine ballet," wrote Clive Barnes in *The New York Times* (February 3, 1975). "Her softness and romanticism, yet also her spring and strength, looked perfect. Her jump was exceptional, as was her delicacy." In the title role of *Giselle*, one of the most difficult of all ballerina roles, Kirkland reached her zenith. She first danced the role during the American Ballet Theatre's two-week spring season in Washington, D.C., partnered with Baryshnikov. Barnes thought it one of the most memorable debuts of all time. "It was the coming together of a dancer and a role that had been made for each other. . . . Since her school days, Miss Kirkland has justifiably been the darling of the ballet's cognoscenti, but here irrefutably was the emergence of a great American ballerina. She did not put a foot, a hand or even a gesture wrong—it was the fairy-tale debut little girls dream about." (*The New York Times*, May 19, 1975.)

In July 1975, Kirkland returned to Lincoln Center in New York for the six-week summer session. In addition to her usual repertory, she appeared in two works by Antony Tudor: the premier of *Shadowplay*, in which she danced the role of the Queen of the Celestials, and a new work, *The Leaves Are Fading*, in which she danced the second of four linked *pas de deux*, partnered by Jonas Kage.

In 1976, Kirkland was contracted to play the young ballerina Emilia in the Herb Ross and *Nora Kaye film, *The Turning Point*, opposite Baryshnikov. Unhappy with the script and feeling increasingly out of control, Kirkland regressed into the anorexia and bulimia of her Balanchine days, starving herself down to barely 80 pounds and seriously jeopardizing her health. Eventually replaced by **Leslie Browne** (the goddaughter of Nora Kaye), Kirkland was demeaned and exhausted by the whole experience and barely pushed herself through the 1976 performance season. Just before the American Ballet Theatre's spring tour of 1977, Kirkland's mother was hospitalized, an event which shocked the dancer into making a concerted effort to overcome her problems. Her performances brought pronouncements from the critics that she had returned to top form, but shadows remained. Her personal relationship with Baryshnikov had soured because of his infidelities, and their dancing partnership suffered as she grappled with his criticism and her own increasing need to find direction and fulfillment. "Had I been able to speak as well as dance, I might have won the support of those who, like me, longed for a dance that portrayed the human drama with more depth and diversity," she explained. "Such a dance was a seemingly impossible dream. I never uttered such ambitious words about my art, even to myself, without feelings of absolute loneliness and derangement. The fanatical extremes of my commitment isolated me."

In 1978, Baryshnikov left the Ballet Theatre to join the New York City Ballet, after which Kirkland partnered with Patrick Bissell, Anthony Dowell, and Peter Schaufuss, among others. Her spirits continued to decline through the breakup of a new and promising romance and a brief but confusing reconciliation with Baryshnikov when he returned in 1980 to take over directorship of the American Ballet Theatre. Finally, her despair became so overwhelming that when an old ballet partner introduced her to cocaine she was a willing victim, "an accomplice in my own destruction," as she later recalled.

Through the nightmare of her increasing addiction to the drug, she continued to dance, fooling the audience and the critics for the most part. "Kirkland is like some lyrical phenomenon of nature, a willow bending beside singing water," wrote a critic for the *Boston Globe* in a review of *Other Dances*, which marked her first performance under the influence of cocaine. "I was a total wreck. I was dying," Kirkland remembered. "Both my brain and my body were out of order." A review of the *pas de deux* from *Don Quixote* by **Arlene Croce**, in February 1981, was one of the few that reflected her terrible de-

Gelsey
Kirkland

cline. "It was the saddest exhibition given by a dancer whose artistry is increasingly placed at the service of a gift for mimicry," wrote Croce. "She's dancing the public's idea of Gelsey Kirkland as a star."

Kirkland continued her downward spiral through a dismissal and a rehiring by the American Ballet Theatre, through visits to drug dealers, brain seizures, and confinement in a mental institution. In 1983, at the doorway of a Manhattan drug dealer, Kirkland met Gregory Lawrence, a writer and manager of a television production office, and a cocaine addict himself. Ironically, it was Lawrence who eventually convinced Kirkland to confront her addiction. After a final performance with the American Ballet Theatre on May 1, 1984, Kirkland resigned and took off with Lawrence to a farm in upstate New York, a refuge offered to the couple by a friend. There, over a two-year period, she withdrew from drugs and began to examine the destructive forces in her life. She also took up the education she had forsaken many years before, concentrating particularly on the arts. "My approach was not academic. I was looking for ideas and values that I could use in my life," she wrote. "It was not any particular work of art that helped me overcome drugs, but the continuous process of mobilizing my mental resources, supported by a man who needed to be saved as much as I did." The preparation of her autobiography provided the last therapeutic stage of her recuperation. (She has also written a second autobiography, *A Dance of Love*.)

Kirkland and Lawrence were married in May 1985, and in 1986 Kirkland returned to the stage, dancing *Romeo and Juliet* with the Royal Ballet. More important than the performance, however, was the fact that her life now had profound meaning off stage as well as on.

SOURCES:

"Ask the Globe," in *The Boston Globe.* January 30, 1999.

Kirkland, Gelsey, with Greg Lawrence. *Dancing On My Grave.* Garden City, NY: Doubleday, 1986.

Moritz, Charles, ed. *Current Biography.* NY: H.W. Wilson, 1975.

Barbara Morgan,
Melrose, Massachusetts

Kirkpatrick, Helen (1909–1997)

American journalist who was foreign correspondent for the Chicago Daily News. *Name variations: Helen Milbank. Born Helen Paull Kirkpatrick on October 18, 1909, in Rochester, New York; died on December 30, 1997; daughter of Lyman Bickford Kirkpatrick (a real estate broker) and Lyde (Paull) Kirkpatrick; attended private schools in Rochester and the Masters School, Dobbs Ferry, New York; graduated from Smith College, 1931; attended the Zimmern School, Geneva, summer 1931; attended the Geneva Institute of International Relations, 1932; married Victor Polachek, in 1934 (divorced 1937); married Robbins Milbank, in 1954; no children.*

During World War II, Helen Kirkpatrick was the sole woman correspondent on the Chicago *Daily News* foreign staff. Capturing a series of spectacular headlines and bylines, Kirkpatrick won the admiration and respect of her more seasoned male colleagues and was frequently compared with pioneering journalists *Dorothy Thompson and *Anne O'Hare McCormick.

Helen Kirkpatrick was born in Rochester, New York, in 1909, and educated at private schools. She graduated from Smith College in 1931 and pursued her studies at the Zimmern School in Geneva and the Geneva Institute of International Relations. In 1932, under the auspices of the National Student Federation of America, she was one of two student observers at the Disarmament Conference. Returning home, she worked for several years at Macy's department store in Manhattan before returning to the field of international relations in 1934.

While working as the executive secretary of the American Russian Institute for Cultural Relations with the Soviet Union and, later, in a position with the Foreign Policy Association in Geneva, Kirkpatrick realized that she wanted to share her experiences with others through journalism. Becoming friendly with the newspaper correspondents in Geneva, she occasionally filled in for them when they were ill or on vacation, and various newspapers began to notice her work. Before long, she was writing for leading British newspapers and magazines and acting as Geneva correspondent for the *New York Herald Tribune*. By 1939, she had published her first book, *This Terrible Peace* (in which she predicted war), and was a regular on the lecture circuit in the United States, giving talks with such titles as "The Future of the British Empire," "Careers for American Women in Europe," and "Behind the Scenes in London." In collaboration with Victor Gordon Maddox of the London *Daily Telegraph* and Graham Hutton of *The Economist*, she also edited the *Whitehall Letter*, a weekly digest of the news that warned of the takeover of Adolf Hitler. Published in London and distributed throughout the British Empire, it was read closely by such heads of state as Winston Churchill, Anthony Eden, and

<figure>Helen Kirkpatrick</figure>

Gustav V, the king of Sweden. To obtain material for the newsletter, Kirkpatrick commuted from one European trouble center to another.

In September 1939, Kirkpatrick joined the Chicago *Daily News'* London bureau and imme-

diately became known for her "exclusives"; her first was an interview with the duke of Windsor, the former King Edward VIII of England, who had for years shunned the press. With the outbreak of the war, Kirkpatrick's bosses went off on assignments, leaving the young journalist virtually in charge of the bureau. The promotion of sorts did not sit well with some of the editors of the *Daily News,* and on a brief trip to the states to promote her second book, *Under the British Umbrella,* Kirkpatrick was summoned to a meeting with Colonel Frank Knox, the newspaper's publisher, who explained that the daily simply did not have women on the staff. "I can't change my sex," she told him. "But you can change your policy."

The policy was never changed, but Kirkpatrick became a singular exception, winning over the hierarchy of the *Daily News* with a speech she delivered before the Council on Foreign Relations at the Palmer House in Chicago. Returning to London, she continued to acquire some of the best contacts of any American journalist at the time. Kirkpatrick encountered little of the hostility experienced by other women journalists during the war. Exceptionally tall and distinguished looking, with high cheekbones and blue eyes set into what was termed a memorable face, Kirkpatrick apparently discouraged insults by her very presence.

Like most wire service reporters during the war, Kirkpatrick covered "headquarters" stories, including communiqués, briefings, and press conferences, but she also wrote articles on military strategy, diplomacy, and eyewitness accounts of the fighting. When a Chicago subscriber objected to a woman reporting military strategy and a controversy ensued, the paper stood by her. In 1943, she spent six months in Algiers, covering the North African campaign, and she was present during the surrender of Italian forces in North Africa, flying to her destination aboard a one-seater P-38, wedged into a tiny space behind the pilot's seat. She also covered the surrender of the Italian Fleet in Malta, where she contracted "sandfly fever," an illness marked by high fever and diarrhea. In Naples in 1943, she reported from a field hospital a mile from the front where she observed surgeons performing 20 major operations on casualties too critical to be moved, while the war raged on around them.

In May 1944, Kirkpatrick was chosen to represent all newspapers on a committee assigned to arrange coverage of the landings in Normandy, although the U.S. War Department had ruled that no women correspondents would be allowed to accompany the armed forces during the invasion (June 6, 1944). Reaching the front within several days of the invasion, along with several other enterprising women, Kirkpatrick obtained an interview with General Dwight D. Eisenhower, the supreme allied com-

mander. Kirkpatrick also was the first correspondent assigned to the headquarters of Brigadier General Pierre-Joseph Koenig, commander of the French forces of the interior, the Free French forces operating inside France, and was one of the first correspondents to enter Paris on Liberation Day, August 25. She accompanied the Free French leaders when they entered Notre Dame Cathedral in Paris to give thanks to God and, while there, barely survived an attack by a group of French fascists. "For one flashing instant, it seemed a great massacre was bound to take place as the Cathedral reverberated with the sound of guns," she cabled the *Daily News.* "There was a sudden blaze, and machine guns sprayed the center aisle, chipping tiles to my left. Time seemed to have no meaning." Kirkpatrick also traveled to Frankfurt, Germany, with the first Allied tanks and visited the Berghof "Eagle's Nest," Hitler's famous retreat on a mountain above Berchtesgaden in Bavaria. There, she reportedly swiped a skillet from the kitchen to cook field rations.

After the war, Kirkpatrick covered the first of the war crimes trials in Nuremberg and, in 1947, reported on the meeting of the Council of Foreign Ministers in Moscow. By this time, the *Daily News* was under new ownership and the foreign service had come under the management of *Dorothy Schiff, publisher of the *Post,* and her husband, Ted Thackrey, the editor. Under a lucrative new contract, Kirkpatrick accepted a job as roving correspondent for the *Post.* She quit, however, when she learned that Thackrey was a Communist. There was a later investigation, and the *Post*'s foreign news service did not survive.

Kirkpatrick concluded her career by serving as chief of information for the French mission, Economic Cooperation Administration, Paris, where she worked to help implement the Marshall Plan. For her contributions, she was awarded the French Legion of Honor, the French Medaille de la Reconnaissance, the U.S. Medal of Freedom, and the Rockefeller Public Service award. She also received a Nieman fellowship to Harvard University, which she never used.

In 1954, Kirkpatrick, who had been married briefly during the 1930s, married Robbins Milbank, member of a prominent New England family. Over the next 30 years, the couple maintained homes in California and New Hampshire, and Kirkpatrick became active as a civic leader in both states, serving the causes of education, conservation, crime prevention, and world affairs. After her husband's death, she established a home in Williamsburg, Virginia.

SOURCES:

Belford, Barbara. *Brilliant Bylines*. NY: Columbia University Press, 1986.

Current Biography. NY: H.W. Wilson, 1941.

Barbara Morgan,
Melrose, Massachusetts

Kirkpatrick, Jeane (1926—)

American diplomat, political scientist and scholar, who was the first woman U.S. ambassador to the United Nations. Name variations: Mrs. Evron M. Kirkpatrick. Born Jeane Duane Jordan in Duncan, Oklahoma, on November 19, 1926; eldest of two children and only daughter of Welcher F. Jordan (an oil contractor) and Leona (Kile) Jordan; Stephens College, Columbus, Missouri, A.A., 1946; Barnard College, A.B., 1948; Columbia University, M.A., 1950; postgraduate studies at the Institut de Science Politique of the University of Paris, 1952–53; Columbia University, Ph.D., 1967; married Dr. Evron M. Kirkpatrick (a political science professor), on February 20, 1955 (died 1995); children: Douglas Jordan; John Evron; Stuart Alan.

A political scientist, scholar, and the first woman to serve as the U.S. ambassador to the United Nations, Jeane Kirkpatrick is a woman of outstanding achievement. She was born Jeane Duane Jordan in Duncan, Oklahoma, in 1926, the daughter of an independent contractor who drilled oil wells for large petroleum companies. Education was important to her parents, and she excelled in her studies and at her piano lessons. After high school, Jeane attended Stephens College in Columbia, Missouri, for a couple of years, then went on to Barnard College in New York City, where she received her B.A. in 1948. She received a master's degree in 1950, and a Ph.D. in 1968, both from Columbia, and also sandwiched in a year of graduate study at the University of Paris. Political science, however, was not Kirkpatrick's first love, and it took her years to fully embrace the field. "In college, I was originally interested in literature and philosophy," she has said. "As time went by, I got into political philosophy, and this finally developed into my focus of political science." While pursuing her education, Kirkpatrick worked variously as a research analyst at the Department of State, as assistant to the director of the Economic Cooperation Administration history project under the Governmental Affairs Institute, and as a research associate with the Human Resources Research Office at George Washington University in Washington, D.C. In 1955, Jeane married Evron M. Kirkpatrick, a political science profes-

sor who later served as the executive director of the American Political Science Association. Jeane blended her professional role with a traditional one, putting her career on hold for nine years to raise her three sons. "I felt it was important for my children—they're very dear to me—so I stayed at home," she said. When asked whether she regrets the years she lost to home and family, she claimed that she would do it all again. "I think it made me stronger to stay home, as a matter of fact."

In 1962, after her sons had grown, Kirkpatrick began her academic career as an assistant professor of political science at Trinity College. Five years later, she joined the faculty at Georgetown University, becoming a full professor in 1973. Between 1955 and 1972, Kirkpatrick also served intermittently as a consultant to the American Council of Learned Societies and to the departments of State, of Defense, and of Health, Education, and Welfare. A prolific writer, Kirkpatrick contributed to a number of political science journals and edited the volume *The Strategy of Deception: A Study in World-Wide Communist Tactics* (1963). With her books *Political Woman* (1974) and *The New Presidential Elite: Men and Women in National Politics* (1976), she began to attract a more general readership.

A lifelong Democrat, Kirkpatrick became politically active in response to the antiwar movement of the 1960s, which she viewed as a shift away from traditional American culture and institutions. In 1972, she helped found the Coali-

*Jeane
Kirkpatrick*

tion for a Democratic Majority, whose members, mostly writers and scholars, became known as "neoconservatives." She told *The New York Times* that the goal of the Coalition was to rescue to Democratic Party from the "antiwar, antigrowth, antibusiness, antilabor activists."

Kirkpatrick remained active within the party throughout the 1970s and, in 1977, became a resident scholar of the American Enterprise Institute for Public Policy, a conservative think tank in Washington. Although she had supported Jimmy Carter in the 1976 presidential campaign, she became increasing critical of his administration's foreign policy. When he failed to adopt a stronger anti-Soviet stance, she threw her support behind Ronald Reagan's 1980 presidential campaign, becoming a member of one of his advisory committees and serving on his interim foreign policy advisory board following his election victory. As president, Reagan appointed her U.S. Permanent Representative to the United Nations. She served until 1985, during which time she was also a member of the Cabinet and the National Security Council.

Following her service at the United Nations, Kirkpatrick was a member of the President's Foreign Intelligence Advisory Board (1985–90) and the Defense Policy Review Board (1985–93). Her many honors include the Medal of Freedom and two Department of Defense Distinguished Public Service Medals. Jeane Kirkpatrick has remained a voice of conservatism and has occasionally been considered a prospective presidential or vice-presidential candidate on the Republican ticket.

SOURCES:

"Kirkpatrick Headlines ISCS Luncheon," in *Las Vegas Business Press*. Vol. 15, no. 20. May 18, 1998, p. 20.

Moritz, Charles, ed. *Current Biography*. NY: H.W. Wilson, 1981.

Selle, Robert. "Current Issues: People in the News," in *World & I*. Vol 13, no. 8. August 1998, pp. 56–57.

Barbara Morgan,
Melrose, Massachusetts

Kirkus, Virginia (1893–1980)

American critic and author who founded Kirkus Bookshop Service. Born in Meadville, Pennsylvania, on December 7, 1893; died in Danbury, Connecticut, on September 10, 1980; daughter of the Reverend Frederick Maurice Kirkus and Isabella (Clark) Kirkus; attended Misses Hebbs School, Wilmington, Delaware; attended Hannah More Academy, Reisterstown, Maryland; graduated from Vassar College,

1916; attended Columbia University Teachers College; married Frank Glick (a personnel executive).

Born in Meadville, Pennsylvania, in 1893, Virginia Kirkus was educated in private schools and graduated from Vassar College in 1916. After completing additional teachers' training courses, she taught history and English at the Greenhill School in Delaware. In 1919, she left teaching to pursue an editorial career. She held a series of writing and editorial jobs in New York, including freelance work for Doubleday, for whom she wrote *Everywoman's Guide to Health and Beauty* (1922). From 1925 to 1932, Kirkus headed up the children's book department of Harper & Brothers, a job she later called "the most responsible position I ever had."

When the Depression hit, Kirkus, like so many others, found herself out of work. To keep her perspective and not jump at any job offered, Kirkus went ahead with plans for a trip abroad. On the return voyage, she hatched the idea for a liaison service between publishers and booksellers which she modestly launched as the Virginia Kirkus Bookshop Service in 1933. Providing booksellers with brief critical evaluations of new books in the form of a chatty bimonthly bulletin, Kirkus supplied prepublication information that had not been available before. When booksellers discovered that her predictions about new books were 85% accurate (particularly her identification of "sleepers," such as John Steinbeck's *Tortilla Flat* and *Rachel Field's *Time Out of Mind*), they began signing up in droves. Publisher participation also grew from an initial 20 ("optimists and progressives all of them," she said) to include practically every major firm in the industry. Many libraries also made use of the service, which, in addition to critical evaluations of new books, provided subscribers with information on changing titles, prices, and publication dates, and assisted them with promotion ideas.

In addition to heading the service, which required reading over 700 books a year and frequent travel, Kirkus also found time to write many articles and to collaborate (with Frank Scully) on two children's books, *Fun in Bed for Children* and *Junior Fun in Bed*, both published in 1935. With her husband Frank Glick, a personnel executive, she also remodeled and landscaped an old farmhouse in Redding, Connecticut, which she chronicled in *A House for the Week Ends* (1940). *First Book of Gardening* was published in 1956. At the time of her retirement in 1962, Kirkus reviewers were previewing books for some

4,000 subscribers. In 1971, the enterprise was sold to *The New York Review of Books.*

SOURCES:

McHenry, Robert, ed. *Famous American Women.* NY: Dover, 1983.

Moritz, Charles, ed. *Current Biography.* NY: H.W. Wilson, 1980.

Rothe, Anna, ed. *Current Biography.* NY: H.W. Wilson, 1941.

Barbara Morgan,
Melrose, Massachusetts.

Kirsten, Dorothy (1910–1992)

American opera and concert singer. Born on July 6, 1910, in Montclair, New Jersey; died on November 18, 1992, in Los Angeles, California; daughter of George W. Kirsten and Margaret (Beggs) Kirsten; attended Montclair High School; studied voice at Juilliard School, New York, and in Rome with Astolfo Pescia; married Edward MacKaye Oates (a broadcasting production expert), in January 1943 (divorced); married John Douglas French (a physician), on July 18, 1955.

American lyric soprano Dorothy Kirsten was born in Montclair, New Jersey, in 1910, into a musical family. She was the granddaughter of James J. Beggs, conductor of the Buffalo Bill Band and an early president of New York Local 802, and a grandniece of singer **Catherine Hayes*, known as the "Irish **Jenny Lind.*" Her mother **Margaret Beggs Kirsten** was an organist and music teacher, her two sisters played the piano, and a brother played the trumpet and was a professor of music. Kirsten set her sights on a stage career at an early age and, as a student at Montclair High School, took music, dance, and dramatics lessons. After high school, she financed her own voice lessons with a job at the New Jersey Bell Telephone Company, in Newark, as a "trouble-shooter" in the classified office. After appearing on several local radio programs, including her own five-day weekly feature, Kirsten had an opportunity to audition for **Grace Moore*, who was so impressed with the young singer that she financed her further training with Astolfo Pescia in Rome.

Kirsten's time in Italy was cut short by the turmoil that presaged World War II, and her family's insistence that she return home. She made her concert debut at the New York World's Fair in 1939, followed by her operatic debut with the Chicago Civic Opera in November 1940, in the minor role of Pousette in Massenet's *Manon.* She remained with the company for the rest of the season, singing various minor roles. During the next season, she appeared as Nedda in *Pagliacci,* Micaela in *Carmen,* and Musetta in *La Bohème,* a production that also featured her sponsor Grace Moore in the role of Mimi. Kirsten left Chicago in 1942 and joined the San Carlo Opera Company, making her New York debut with the troupe as Micaela in *Carmen.* From 1943 to 1944, in addition to opera and concert work, she had her own radio show, "Keepsake," and also appeared frequently as a guest artist on other radio programs.

Kirsten made her debut with the New York Metropolitan Opera on December 1, 1945, as Mimi in *La Bohème,* winning acclaim, if not raves, from the critics. "On the whole Miss Kirsten's vocalism entitled her to the enthusiastic reception accorded her after each of the acts," wrote Noel Straus of *The New York Times,* "as did her simple and direct, if not especially warm or tender, impersonation." Kirsten would sing with the Met for the next 30 years, distinguishing herself in the lyric roles of Verdi and Puccini, and steadfastly refusing roles that she felt were beyond her vocal capacity. Her first performance in *Madama Butterfly* (March 1947) was greeted enthusiastically by the critics. The reviewer from *The New York Times* called it "one of the most

$\mathcal{D}$orothy
$\mathcal{K}$irsten

distinguished performances of her career," and John Briggs of the *Post* praised Kirsten as "an artist in every fine sense of the word." The soprano subsequently performed in Met productions of *Roméo et Juliette, La Traviata, Tosca, Faust,* and in Charpentier's *Louise,* a role she prepared with the help of the composer.

Along with her regular performances with the Met, Kirsten continued to appear with the San Francisco, New Orleans, and Chicago opera companies, and she was a frequent guest at City Center. In 1962, at the height of the Cold War, Kirsten was the first American soprano to sing grand opera in the Soviet Union. At the time, the director of the Tbilisi Opera called her "the strongest link in the chain of friendship between the Soviet Union and the United States."

Kirsten retired from the Met in December 1975, after a farewell performance on New Year's Eve in *Tosca.* She continued to sing opera and give concerts ("I will sing as long as I sing well," she said), but also devoted time to her second love, painting. Dorothy Kirsten retired from singing completely in 1982, upon learning that her second husband, Dr. John Douglas French, head of the Brain Research Institute at University of California, Los Angeles (UCLA), had Alzheimer's disease. (Her first husband, Edward MacKaye Oates, was a Columbia Broadcasting System production expert.) From then on, until her own death in 1992, Kirsten devoted herself to raising funds for Alzheimer's research.

SOURCES:

Graham, Judith, ed. *Current Biography.* NY: H.W. Wilson, 1993.

McHenry, Robert, ed. *Famous American Women.* NY: Dover, 1983.

Obituary. *The Day* [New London, CT]. November 19, 1992.

Rothe, Anna, ed. *Current Biography.* NY: H.W. Wilson, 1948.

SUGGESTED READING:

Kirsten, Dorothy. *A Time to Sing,* 1982.

Barbara Morgan,
Melrose, Massachusetts

Kirszenstein-Szewinska, Irena (b. 1946).

See Szewinska, Irena.

Kishida Toshiko (1863–1901)

Writer and political activist for women's rights, who is known as Japan's first woman orator. Name variations: also known as Nakajima Toshiko; (pseudonym) Nakajima Shoen. Pronunciation: Key-SHE-dah Toe-SHE-koe. Born in Kyoto, Japan, in 1863, into a family of cloth merchants; died in 1901; mother was Kishi-

da Taka; married Nakajima Nobuyuki (a political activist), in 1884.

Because she had excelled in her study of the Chinese and Japanese classics, Kishida Toshiko was the first commoner to serve as a lady-in-waiting to an empress. She served Empress *Haruko, the consort of the Emperor Meiji. Kishida abruptly left court in 1882, however, to embark on a national lecture tour, sponsored by the Jiyuto (Liberal Party). On this tour, she drew standing-room-only crowds of mostly women and gained national fame. In her lectures, she spoke of women as participants in the establishment of a new Japanese society. She criticized the marriage system, in which women had no right to divorce; the concubine system, in which men could have multiple wives; and the lack of educational opportunities for girls. She attacked the traditional, Confucian values popularly expressed in the three obediences, in which women were under the control of their fathers, husbands, or sons throughout their lives. Kishida urged women to become educated as a basis for the promotion of equal rights for women and men. "I hope in the future there will be some recognition of the fact that the first requirement for marriage is education," she wrote. "Daughters must be taught basic economics and the skills that would permit them to manage on their own. Even a woman who expects to be protected during her husband's lifetime must be able to manage on her own, armed with the necessary skills, if he should die." The Peace Preservation Law of 1887, which prohibited women from publicly engaging in political activity (it is thought that Kishida, in particular, was meant to be the target of this law), effectively brought to an end her career of speaking for women's rights. She continued, however, to teach and write for *Jogaku zasshi,* and was said to have made a fortune in real estate dealings.

SOURCES:

Sievers, Sharon. *Flowers in Salt: The Beginnings of Feminist Consciousness in Modern Japan.* Stanford, CA: Stanford University Press, 1983.

Linda L. Johnson,
Professor of History, Concordia College, Moorhead, Minnesota

Kitson, Theo A.R. (1871–1932)

American sculptor. Born Theo Alice Ruggles in 1871; was first wife of Henry Hudson Kitson (an English sculptor).

The most talented pupil of her husband Henry Hudson Kitson, Theo Kitson later studied with Pascal Dagnan-Bouveret in Paris, became one of the few women members of the National Sculpture Society, and, at the time she received honors at the Paris salon, was the only American woman to have gained such distinction. The monumental statues which are her chief works are spirited, robust, and simple both in conception and execution. Among the best are the Massachusetts State Monument at Vicksburg, The Minute Man of '76 in Framingham, Massachusetts, the statue of Tadeusz Kosciuszko on Boston Common, an equestrian statue of victory in Hingham, Massachusetts, and various soldiers' monuments.

Kitt, Eartha (1928—)

African-American singer, dancer, and actress who, from the poverty of Southern U.S. cotton fields, created an international career that was almost derailed by her views on the Vietnam War expressed one afternoon at the White House. Nickname: Kitty Charles. Born Eartha Mae Kitt on January 26, 1928, in North Carolina (no records of her birth date exist; the January 26, 1928 date was an estimate given by her in the 1950s when she was required to do so); daughter of William Kitt (a sharecropper) and Anna Mae (Riley) Kitt; educated at New York School for the Performing Arts; married William McDonald, on June 9, 1960 (divorced 1965); children: daughter Kitt McDonald.

Toured U.S., Mexico, South America, England and France as a singer and dancer (1944–49); made European nightclub debut in Paris, France (1949); played in Orson Welles' production of Faust, *Paris (1951); had first American nightclub and Broadway successes, New York City (1952); recorded albums and made films and television appearances (1953–59); appeared on Broadway (1954–59); wrote first autobiography (1956); attended White House luncheon and denounced Vietnam War (January 1968); worked mostly overseas (1968–74); attended White House reception by invitation of President Jimmy Carter and returned to Broadway (1978); appeared at Carnegie Hall (1985).*

Awards: *Golden Rose First Place Award for best special of the year (*This is Eartha*) from Montreux Film Festival (1962); Woman of the Year Award from National Association of Black Musicians (1968).*

Plays: *Faust (1951); New Faces (1952); Mrs. Patterson (1954); Shinbone Alley (1957); Jolly's Progress (1959); Timbuktu (1978).*

Filmography: *Casbah (1948); New Faces (1954); Accused (1957); The Mark of the Hawk (1958); Anna Lucasta (1959); Synanon (1965).*

Television appearances: *"Batman" (1966); "The Ed Sullivan Show"; "Colgate Comedy Hour"; "I Spy" (1965); "Police Woman."*

Albums: *Eartha Kitt Album; That Bad Eartha (1955); Down to Eartha; St. Louis Blues; Thursday's Child; Bad But Beautiful (1961); At The Plaza (1965); I Love Men (1984).*

Writings: *Thursday's Child (1956); Alone With Me (1976). Recorded dramatic readings: Black Pioneers in American History: Nineteenth Century (1968); Folk Tales of the Tribes of Africa (1968).*

In January of 1968, *Lady Bird Johnson hosted the initial "Women Doers' Luncheon" at the White House. The discussion topic: "Why is there so much juvenile delinquency in the streets of America?" One of the guests, the popular and sultry singer and actress Eartha Kitt, had accepted her invitation with a keen interest. Kitt's own childhood in poverty had influenced every aspect of her life and had inspired her to help create many anti-poverty and anti-crime groups. Over the years, wherever she worked she had visited ghettos and talked with residents, and she had formed dance workshops in Harlem and Watts. Before the luncheon, she met with an organization called the "Mothers of Watts" about the discussion topic. These women felt the war in Vietnam was directly escalating youth street crime in several ways, but the most serious was the fact that law-abiding young men were being drafted while those with criminal records were deferred. Kitt flew to Washington with a "grave sense of personal commitment," paying her own travel expenses. At the luncheon, she quickly became disappointed with the air of frivolity she perceived among many guests and was annoyed by the staging of a "surprise" visit by President Lyndon Johnson. She later recalled, "I hadn't flown from Los Angeles to Washington D.C. to watch a show." Kitt's subsequent words were to transform her life. She remarked to the first lady, "I think we have missed the main point at this luncheon. We have forgotten the main reason we have juvenile delinquency . . . there's a war going on and America doesn't know why. Boys I know across the nation feel it doesn't pay to be a good guy. They figure that with a [criminal] record they don't have to go off to Vietnam . . . . [N]o wonder the kids rebel and take pot, and Mrs. Johnson, in case you don't understand the lingo, that's marijuana."

Almost immediately Kitt became *persona non grata* in her own country, she later said. Contracts with nightclubs were canceled or "lost." Her phone stopped ringing. Although she insisted she had "had no intention of launching a diatribe against the war in Vietnam," her opportunities in the United States dried up. Virtually ostracized, she had to work mostly overseas until the mid-1970s. It was not until 1974 that she again began to book nightclub appearances in America. In 1975, it was reported that following the 1968 incident, a Secret Service file on her had been assembled. The file was filled with gossip about her personal life, including CIA documents quoting a Paris source as saying Kitt had a "lurid sex life" and labeling her "a sadistic nymphomaniac with a vile tongue." Kitt rebutted the smears, saying, "I have always lived a very clean life. . . . I have nothing to hide." The file concluded, however, that she was no threat to the nation, and the exposition of the extensive investigation of Kitt's life by government agencies hastened the recovery of her U.S. career.

Overall, I've had a very good life, a life of cotton and caviar. And the cotton years have made the caviar years far more savory than they would have been had my early life been an easy one.

—Eartha Kitt

In the "Acknowledgments" at the beginning of her 1976 autobiography *Alone With Me*, Kitt expressed both her frustration with the treatment she received at the hands of her homeland and her unwillingness to be crushed by it. In that long list, she recognizes, "My country, which hasn't allowed me to work here but which takes a more than healthy chunk of my income because I refuse to be intimidated and leave it." Eartha Kitt was not to be defeated by difficult circumstances; she had weathered adversity before and come out on top. She was born in 1928 in a back-country town in North Carolina and named Eartha to "thank the earth" after her father's first good harvest in years. Kitt's parents, William Kitt, who was African-American, and **Anna Mae Riley Kitt**, who was half-Cherokee and half-black, were poverty-stricken sharecroppers. Because of her parentage, Kitt's unique image would one day be admired for the challenge it presented to mainstream racial stereotypes. Her childhood was full of racial conflict, and she was resented by other children for her light complexion. Her father disappeared when she was small and was reported dead two years later, and her mother went off with another man. Kitt later wrote that she believed her mother died from the effects of voodoo.

After losing both parents, she and her younger sister **Anna Pearl** picked cotton in ex-

change for food and shelter, and drifted between neighbors. When Kitt was eight, their aunt, **Mamie Lue Riley**, sent for the sisters to come and live with her. The girls traveled to New York City with just catfish sandwiches to eat, wearing all the clothes their aunt had sent them on their backs.

Living with her aunt in the Puerto Rican-Italian section of Harlem, Kitt was frequently alone, so she invented her own world of singing and dancing. She picked up several languages, and later won awards in dramatics at the New York School for the Performing Arts. A sports lover, she played baseball and became an excellent pole vaulter. At 14, she quit school to work in a Brooklyn factory sewing army uniforms, saving some money for piano lessons.

Kitt's first big break came at age 16 when she won a scholarship from the *Katherine Dunham Dance Group. With that troupe, she toured the United States, Mexico, and South America, and in 1947 danced in a sequence of the Hollywood film *Casbah*. Kitt was soon given more solo roles and became the group's vocalist, singing African, Haitian, and Cuban "ethnic" songs. The Dunham group toured in England and Europe, and Kitt was captivated by the cities of London and Paris. "Paris and London were the places that made me realise there is an Eartha Kitt inside of me somewhere," she said years later. When the Dunham troupe left Paris, she stayed behind and launched her nightclub career. Earning a reputation as "the rage of Paris," she traveled internationally and performed to wide acclaim. In 1951, upon returning to Paris from her aunt's funeral, Kitt was invited by Orson Welles to play Helen of Troy in his production of *Faust*. Although she had only two days to learn her part, her performance drew high praise from critics. She was grateful to Welles ever after for giving her her "first chance at a legitimate stage role."

Following *Faust*, she starred in two French films, and after a lukewarm reception at her first New York nightclub, she achieved her "first solid American success" at the Village Vanguard. Spotted by producer Leonard Sillman there, she went on to perform in his revue *New Faces* in 1952. As her fame snowballed, she sang at the after-dinner show at a local nightclub during the entire run of *New Faces*, breaking the all-time attendance record at the club. Her music recordings with RCA Victor made her a jukebox favorite of the time. After *New Faces*, she landed the lead role of Teddy Hicks, a 15-year old daughter of a Kentucky laundress, in Sillman's Broadway show *Mrs.*

Patterson. One reviewer was smitten with her cat-like style and wrote, "She has a fascinatingly alive face which can range from a savage look to one of tenderness. She prowls round the stage with a feline grace." While preparing for *Mrs. Patterson* in 1954, she made several television appearances. Her star had risen; she became a bona fide celebrity.

From the mid-1950s to the mid-1960s, Kitt, the 5'2" and 105-pound "sophisticated black seductress," was in high demand. She appeared in two more Broadway shows, wrote an autobiography, made several more records, appeared and starred in films and made several television shows. One of her most well-known roles was that of the Catwoman on the "Batman" television series of the mid-1960s. She was at the top of her profession when she articulated her opinion at that 1968 White House luncheon.

Eartha Kitt fit no one's stereotype, and opinions on what exactly she symbolized have varied widely. According to *Black Women in America,* interviews and articles on Kitt at the height of her career were preoccupied with her "urbane sophistication, linguistic fluency and haughty, aloof manner, all of which helped to shape a racially ambiguous image that stood at odds with the sambo stereotypes more commonly informing mainstream white perspectives." Her remarks to Lady Bird Johnson "castigating a group of prominent women for their myopic views of American racial and social problems and an unjust Vietnam War," shaped a portrait of her as a "pariah of conservative politics [and a] hero of the antiwar and civil rights movements." Yet her "feline seductiveness," her supposed predilection for white men, and her reported scorn of her own rural and racial past led some to feel her public persona also supported prevailing American social assumptions of male, urban, and white superiority. In 1972, she performed in South Africa and her "seemingly naive acceptance of white South African hospitality" garnered her the title of South Africa's "Honorary White" in a *Life* magazine essay.

"Knocked out of the box" in 1968, as she herself put it, Kitt did not return to Broadway until a brief stint in 1978 when she played "Sahleem-La-Lume" in *Timbuktu.* That year, a decade after the fateful luncheon, Kitt was invited to the White House by President Jimmy Carter for a reception for Ford's Theatre. She attended with her 16-year-old daughter **Kitt McDonald** and later said, "First I thought I shouldn't go. Now I'm very glad I went. Mr. Carter looked at me and smiled as though he understood." Since 1978, she has worked mainly as a cabaret singer. She appeared at Carnegie Hall in 1985 and made an album entitled *I Love Men* in 1984 which was popular in the gay disco communities of the time. In 1988, at age 60 or thereabouts, she appeared in the musical *Follies* to positive reviews. Throughout the early and mid-1990s she made several film and television show appearances.

Lon Tuck of the *Washington Post* wrote that Kitt "describes her life as a success story, in which disaster, for a citizen of the world, is only a temporary setback." Her extraordinary life trained her to survive personal disaster, while at the same time teaching her six languages, taking her to 92 countries, and showing her what it was like to make $10,000 a week. Kitt says simply, "In essence, I'm a sophisticated cotton picker."

SOURCES:

Candee, Marjorie Dent, ed. *Current Biography.* NY: H.W. Wilson, 1955.

Hine, Darlene Clark, ed. *Black Women in America: An Historical Encyclopedia.* Brooklyn, NY: Carlson, 1993.

Smith, Jessie Carney, ed. *Notable Black American Women.* Detroit, MI: Gale Research, 1992.

Washington Post. January 19, 1978.

Wolf, Matt. "She's Still Here," in *Plays & Players.* October 1988, p. 16.

SUGGESTED READING:

Kitt, Eartha. *Alone With Me.* Regnery, 1976.

———. *Thursday's Child.* Duell, Sloan & Pearce, 1956.

Jacqueline Maurice,
Ottawa, Ontario, Canada

Kittelsen, Grete Prytz (1917—)

Norwegian artist who specialized in enamel hollowware and jewelry in silver and stainless steel. Name variations: Grete Korsmo. Born Grete Prytz on June 28, 1917, in Oslo, Norway; daughter of Jacob Prytz (a goldsmith); trained at the Norwegian State School of Arts and Crafts and the Institute of Design, Chicago; married Arne Korsmo; remarried.

Grete Prytz Kittelsen trained at the Norwegian State School of Arts and Crafts and the Institute of Design, Chicago, as the recipient of a Fulbright scholarship. She followed her father, Jacob Prytz, into the leading Oslo firm of goldsmiths, J. Tostrup, in 1945. While working at Tostrup's workshop, she pioneered new methods of decorating silver with enamel, collaborating with the Central Institute for Industrial Research in the production of colored enamel. From the mid-1950s, she was a design consultant with her husband Arne Korsmo for the Cathrineholm firm in Halden, which collaborated with the Hadeland Glass Factory in the production of stainless-steel articles with transparent enamel, unique at that time. Her innovative techniques also resulted in serially produced jewelry of great novelty and artistry. She has stated that the play of light observed in her "glass house," the home designed for her by Arne Korsmo, has been the inspiration for many of her pieces.

Over several decades, Kittelsen's work was exhibited in Scandinavian and European countries and in the United States and Canada. She was an invited participant at the 1958 Biennale in Venice and exhibited at the World Fair in Brussels in the same year, in Paris in 1958, at George Jensen, New York in 1964, and the Montreal World Fair in 1967.

She was the recipient of many awards: the Lunning Prize (1952); the Grand Prix at the Milan Triennale (1954); gold medals at the same exhibition (1957 and 1961); a gold medal at the Munich Applied Art Fair (1960); and the Jacob Prize from the Norwegian Society of Arts and Crafts (1972). Kittelsen was also active on behalf of the applied arts. She became a member of the Advisory Board of the World Crafts Council in 1968 and from 1975 to 1978 was president of the Norwegian Society of Arts and Crafts.

SOURCES:

Aschehoug & Gyldendal. *Store Norske Leksikon* (Greater Norwegian Encyclopedia). Oslo: Kunnskapsforlaget, 1992.

Opstad, Jan-Lauritz. "Grete Prytz Kittelsen," in *Navn i norsk brukskunst nr. 3* (Names in Norwegian Applied Art, no. 3). English translation by Ruth Waaler. Oslo: Kunstindus-trimuseet i, 1978.

Elizabeth Rokkan,
translator, formerly Associate Professor,
Department of English, University of Bergen, Norway

Kittrell, Flemmie (1904–1980)

African-American educator and nutritionist. Born Flemmie Pansy Kittrell on December 25, 1904, in Henderson, North Carolina; died on October 3, 1980, in Washington, D.C.; seventh of nine children and youngest daughter of James Lee Kittrell and Alice (Mills) Kittrell; attended public school in Vance County, North Carolina; Hampton Institute, B.S., 1928; Cornell University, M.A., 1930, Ph.D., 1938; never married; no children.

Devoting her career to improving family welfare around the world, Flemmie Kittrell headed up the home economics department at Howard University for nearly 30 years, during which time she also conducted studies of nutrition problems in Liberia and India and established training programs in nutrition and child care for women in India and Zaire (now Republic of Congo).

One of nine children of parents of Cherokee Indian and African-American heritage, Kittrell was born in Henderson, North Carolina, in 1904, and grew up in a happy and supportive environment that contributed to her educational achievements in high school and later at the Hampton Institute in Virginia, where she received her B.S. degree in 1928. Few black women had the wherewithal to attend graduate school during the 1920s, but with the encour-

agement of her family and her professors at Hampton, she enrolled at Cornell University. Kittrell earned an M.A. in 1930 and a Ph.D. in 1938, both with honors.

Kittrell had spent a year teaching at Bennett College in Greensboro before entering Cornell, and she returned to teach at that institution briefly before accepting a position at her alma mater, Hampton Institute, to serve as the director of the home economics division and dean of women. In 1944, she was selected to head the home economics department at Howard University in Washington, D.C., where she immediately set out to implement a more comprehensive curriculum and to establish her field on sound scientific footing. In 1947, under the auspices of the Department of State, she instituted a research project in Liberia to study the country's living conditions and nutrition. Her findings confirmed that 90% of the population suffered from "hidden hunger" caused by a diet consisting mostly of rice and cassava. In a report to the Liberian government, she recommended expansion of the fishing industry and refinement of the agricultural industry to help balance nutritional intake.

In 1950, under a Fulbright exchange program, Kittrell assisted India's Baroda University in establishing a Home Economics College as well as a nutritional research program. In 1952, she traveled to the nation of Zaire to help organize the Congo Polytechnic Institute's School of Home Economics. Part of her goal in that developing country was to convince Congolese men that higher education for women would improve home life. This she achieved with persistence and diplomacy. In 1953, under the auspices of the Agency for International Development, she returned to India to conduct seminars in nutrition, teach courses in meal planning, and give home economics demonstrations. Kittrell's worldwide efforts took her to Japan, Hawaii, and West Africa in 1957, to West and Central Africa in 1959, and to Guinea in 1961.

At Howard University, Kittrell continued to work for improvement and expansion of the home economics program. For almost 15 years, she led the campaign for new facilities, finally obtaining approval for the construction of the School for Human Ecology, which was dedicated in 1963. The four-story building, in addition to providing classrooms, study centers, and laboratories, housed a nursery for the college's preschool program. Within its walls, the nation's Head Start program was conceived and tested.

Over her long career, Flemmie Kittrell received numerous honors and awards, including the Scroll of Honor from the National Council of Negro Women in 1961 and the establishment of a scholarship in her honor by the American Home Economics Association in 1974. Kittrell, who retired from Howard University in 1972, at age 73, continued to travel and lecture until two years before her death in 1980.

SOURCES:

Bailey, Brooke. *The Remarkable Lives of 100 Women Healers and Scientists.* Holbrook, MA: Bob Adams, 1994.

Smith, Jessie Carney, ed. *Notable Black American Women.* Detroit, MI: Gale Research, 1992.

Barbara Morgan,
Melrose, Massachusetts

Kitzinger, Sheila (1929—)

British pregnancy and childbirth expert. Born Sheila Helena Elizabeth Webster in Somerset, England, in 1929; attended Bishop Fox Girls' School, Taunton, England; attended Ruskin College, Oxford; B.Litt. in social anthropology from St. Hugh's College; married Uwe Kitzinger (an economist), in 1952; children: five daughters.

Sheila Kitzinger, a noted British pregnancy and childbirth expert, studied to become a drama teacher before eventually obtaining a degree in social anthropology from St. Hugh's College. During the early 1950s, she did research on race relations in the United Kingdom at the University of Edinburgh. During this period, she also married economist Uwe Kitzinger and began a family, which grew to include five daughters.

It was through her appointment as a member of the Advisory Board of the National Childbirth Trust in 1958 that Kitzinger undertook a mission to empower women in the childbirth process by arming them with information. "It's extremely difficult to act as your own advocate," she declared, "unless you have the information to challenge doctors who often treat women as if they were irresponsible, selfish, and concerned only with their own emotions."

As a National Childbirth Trust teacher, Kitzinger has lectured throughout the world and has produced a number of books, beginning with *The Experience of Childbirth* (1962), and including *Education and Counselling for Childbirth* (1977), *Women as Mothers* (1978), *Giving Birth: Emotions in Childbirth, Birth at Home, The Experience of Breastfeeding, The Good Birth Guide* (1979), *Pregnancy and Childbirth* (1980), *The Year After Childbirth: Surviving and Enjoying the First Year of Motherhood* (1992), and *Ourselves as Mother: The Universal Experience of Motherhood.* In the latter book, Kitzinger compares childbirth in different cultures and criticizes many childbirth practices in industrialized countries—such as induced labor and cesarean sections—that depersonalize the process. "Our society sets us up to feel socially isolated, guilty, as if we are failures as mothers," she states. "In many traditional societies there is much more woman-to-woman support in pregnancy, during the birth, and afterward."

Kitzinger, who is described as "outspoken, frank, and decidedly feminist," lives in a familial commune outside Oxford with her husband, two of her daughters, and their families. In addition to writing and lecturing, she runs the Birth Crisis Network, a telephone counseling resource for women who have suffered an invasive or humiliating birth experience. She also serves on the Board of Consultants of the International Childbirth Education Association of the United States.

SOURCES:

Findlen, Barbara. "Bold Type: Childbirth Is Powerful," in *Ms.* January 2, 1995.

Uglow, Jennifer, ed. *The Macmillan Dictionary of Women's Biography*, 2nd ed. London: Macmillan, 1989.

Klafsky, Katharina (1855–1896)

Hungarian opera singer, primarily of Wagner. Name variations: Katharina Lohse-Klafsky. Born at Mosonszentjános (St. Johann), Wieselburg, Hungary, in 1855; died in Hamburg, Germany, on September 29, 1896; daughter of humble parents; studied in Vienna with Mathilde Marchesi, then in Leipzig with Sucher; married three times; third husband was Otto Lohse (a conductor).

While employed in Vienna as a nurserymaid, Katharina Klafsky's fine soprano voice led to her being engaged as a chorus singer and to studies with the renowned *Mathilde Marchesi. Klafsky made her debut as a mezzo-soprano in Salzburg in 1875. By 1882, she had graduated from small roles and had become well known in Wagnerian roles at the Leipzig theater. She expanded her reputation at other German musical centers. In 1892, Klafsky appeared in London and enjoyed a huge success in Wagner's operas, notably as Brünnhilde and Isolde; her dramatic as well as vocal gifts were roundly praised. In 1895, Klafsky went on tour in the United States. She returned to Hamburg the following year, where she died suddenly of a brain tumor at age 41; it was said that she was at the height of her powers.

SUGGESTED READING:

Ordemann, L. *Aus dem Leben und Wirken von Katharina Klafsky (A Life)*. Leipzig: 1903.

Klarsfeld, Beate (1939—)

German-born French Nazi-hunter who, with her husband Serge Klarsfeld, exposed former Nazis, including the infamous Klaus Barbie. Born Beate Auguste Künzel in Berlin, Germany, on February 13, 1939; daughter of Kurt Künzel and Helene (Scholz) Künzel; married Jewish Holocaust survivor Serge Klarsfeld, in 1963; children: **Lida Klarsfeld**; *Arno Klarsfeld.*

In 1968, at a time when Germany had barely begun the process of coming to terms with its Nazi past, Beate Klarsfeld first came to world attention. She provoked several incidents directed against the West German chancellor, Kurt Georg Kiesinger, a man who had until that time largely succeeded in hiding the details of his career as a propaganda official in the Third Reich. Klarsfeld had come from an unlikely background for a Nazi-hunter. Born Beate Auguste Künzel in Berlin in 1939, on the eve of World War II, she was raised a Lutheran and knew little about the horrors of those years. Her father Kurt served in the Wehrmacht during the war and was one of the fortunate few to return home to his family. In 1960, she went to Paris to work as an au pair, ignoring her father's warning that if she left Berlin for Paris she would end up as a woman of the streets.

Soon after arriving in Paris, she met the young Frenchman Serge Klarsfeld on a Métro platform. Beate and Serge, who was then entering law school, fell in love, and he shared with her his family's past. His parents Arno and **Raïssa Klarsfeld** were Rumanian-born Jews who attempted to escape the Nazi dragnet that swept through occupied France during World War II. Until the summer of 1943, the Klarsfeld family escaped capture by living in the city of Nice. That summer Adolf Eichmann sent a Sonderkommando team headed by one of his "best men," Alois Brunner, to Nice. Brunner, commandant of the Drancy transit camp, was a notorious Jew-hater who had no regrets, he told an interviewer from the German magazine *Bunte* (1985), for "getting rid of all that garbage." On the night of September 30, 1943, one of Brunner's agents knocked on the door of Arno Klarsfeld's apartment. Arno told them that his children had been sent to the country because they suffered from head lice and that the apartment had been disinfected, ensuring that it would not be searched too closely. He then left with the Nazis, who did not detect that hidden behind a false closet wall were his wife, daughter, and eight-year-old son Serge, all of whom survived the Holocaust. Arno Klarsfeld saved his family and was murdered in Auschwitz.

Beate and Serge were married in November 1963. Beate took a job in Paris with the French-German Youth Service, an organization founded jointly by West German chancellor Konrad Adenauer and French president Charles de Gaulle. Serge earned his law degree and found a job with the French National Radio and Television System. For several years, life was rewarding for the Klarsfelds; they enjoyed their careers and were raising two children, son Arno and daughter Lida. In their leisure time, however, the couple continued to ponder the historical events that had shaped their lives. By the mid-1960s, only two decades separated Europeans from the horrors of fascism, World War II, and the Holocaust, yet few seemed to know or care about the events. Most Europeans wished to forget, and others, who had crimes of commission or omission to conceal, had good reason to let the past slip into oblivion. The capture and trial of Adolf Eichmann in Israel in the early 1960s had brought the Holocaust to world attention, but this too had started to fade from the public's consciousness. During these years, the Klarsfelds felt isolated from the rest of humanity as they struggled to make sense of a world that was seemingly indifferent to appalling injustice.

Their puzzlement over Germany's unresolved past turned to anger in December 1966, when Kurt Georg Kiesinger, a leading Christian Democratic politician and a strong advocate of improved French-German political and cultural relations, became the third chancellor of the Federal Republic of Germany. A lawyer, Kiesinger had joined the Nazi Party in 1933 "in the hope that it would become a good thing" and by 1940 was working for the radio department of the German Foreign Ministry; his assignment was to advise Joseph Goebbels' Ministry of Propaganda and Public Enlightenment as to the most effective means of spreading the Nazi message overseas. After the war, Kiesinger was interned by American occupation authorities as a Nazi leader for 18 months, but he was never formally charged with crimes or sentenced to a prison term. Incensed by the fact that a former Nazi now occupied the highest political post in West Germany, Beate Klarsfeld ignored the fact that her employer was effectively the West German government and penned a series of highly critical articles on Kiesinger's Nazi links in the Paris newspaper *Combat*. Her articles, which appeared over a period of eight months, described the chancellor as a Nazi and "murderer." In one of them, she asserted that if Adolf Eichmann represented the banality of evil, then "to me, Kiesinger represents the respectability of evil."

Not surprisingly, Beate's superiors thought ill of her strongly expressed opinions, and she was fired from her job at the French-German Youth Service in late August 1967. Serge's career at the national radio-television system was flourishing, however, so the Klarsfeld family was able to keep a roof over their heads. Beate's job loss served neither to discipline nor frighten her. The fact that she, now a French citizen, had been fired for "calling a Nazi a Nazi" set a dangerous precedent.

On the day she was fired, August 30, 1967, the Klarsfelds met in a café on the Rue des Saussaies. Recalled Beate, "We made up our minds then and there to fight. It was a decision reached in a moment and with scarcely a word spoken. But it was a total commitment. We would fight not to ease our conscience, but to win. Serge's career, our family life, our material security, all would take second place."

All my troubles began when that Klarsfeld woman came to Bolivia.

—Klaus Barbie, known as the "Butcher of Lyons"

The Klarsfelds undertook a systematic campaign to "out" Chancellor Kiesinger as a dyed-in-the-wool Nazi. They considered his guilt in the functioning of the Nazi regime to be at least as damning as that of any concentration camp official. "Clean" Nazis (*Edelnazis*) like Kiesinger, bureaucrats who carried out their deeds by signing documents in their offices, had ordered or inspired the inhuman cruelties of the Third Reich. When the Klarsfelds made their decision, it was almost impossible to find evidence to counter Kiesinger's claim that he had made a spiritual break with the Nazi state as early as 1934. Little in the way of negative documentation appeared to have survived in West German archives. Serge was convinced, however, that incriminating documents on Kiesinger were to be found in the East German archives in Potsdam, and he took the initiative to discover this data. He was aided by the Potsdam archivists. The fact that the East German government defined West Germany as "a neo-fascist state" doubtless induced the archivists to help track down as many incriminating documents as possible. Back in Paris with this material, which included Kiesinger's Nazi Party membership number

(2,633,390), the Klarsfelds analyzed the information and concluded that Kiesinger had in fact been an ardent Nazi and willing disseminator of anti-Semitic hatred, particularly in his role as director of Interradio, a Nazi propaganda agency that broadcast such items as "the Jew Roosevelt aspires to worldwide Jewish supremacy." Also found in the Potsdam files were Kiesinger's postwar de-Nazification records, which revealed the curious fact that he had been cleared by a panel that included his own father-in-law.

Determined to expose Kiesinger, Beate began to make overnight train trips to West Germany to speak in front of students and other Germans who at that time were asking harder questions about the older generation's unexamined past. With a suitcase bulging with documentation on Kiesinger, she campaigned against the distinguished-looking, silver-haired chancellor, pursuing him as if he had "a mongrel on his cuff." She spoke at countless New Left and labor rallies, relying on facts rather than slogans. Klarsfeld was a good, rather than a dramatic, speaker, and her audiences were at first strongly affected by her relentless pursuit-by-document of Kiesinger. In time, however, both she and her audiences tired of the thematic repetition. The press eventually also lost interest. Understanding the power of the media in modern society, Klarsfeld searched for a more dramatic approach to keep the issue alive.

Already well known by her married name, she used her maiden name to obtain a pass to the visitors' gallery of West Germany's Parliament, the Bundestag. There, one afternoon in April 1968, while Chancellor Kiesinger was delivering an address, she leapt up and shouted "Nazi! Nazi! Nazi!" at him until she was bodily removed from the chamber. Although most observers labeled her a born firebrand, she later claimed that this act went against her nature and that it had been incredibly difficult for her to get out the first shout. The incident was reported in the press, but she knew this action alone was insufficient. Then, Klarsfeld made a public promise that sometime in the future she would slap the chancellor in the face, the purpose being not to vent her own emotions but rather to express the conviction of many Germans that they were unwilling to accept a man like Kiesinger as their nation's head of government.

Beate was determined to make good on her word, but the idea proved to be a divisive one. Her mother-in-law Raïssa, a strong supporter of the Klarsfelds' work until now, wavered in her belief that such a deed could be effective. Raïssa pleaded with her daughter-in-law to drop the idea, but Beate was convinced that the only way to dramatize the issue of Kiesinger's Nazi past—and that of many other West German politicians and business leaders—was to humiliate him. On several occasions in the fall of 1968, she attempted to carry out her plan. At one campaign rally, the pro-Kiesinger crowd seemed to her to be so strongly partisan that her own fear prevented the action. But the time finally came. At 10:55 AM, on November 7, 1968, at a meeting of the Christian Democratic Party in West Berlin, she slapped Kiesinger full in the face, screaming once again, "Nazi!" Dragged away by security men, Klarsfeld did not learn until later that one of Kiesinger's security staff had drawn his gun but was unable to fire because the chancellor had blocked his line of sight. Although the chancellor played down the incident at an initial press conference (the slap had caused his left eye no more than a superficial injury), a few hours later Kiesinger apparently changed his mind, deciding to press charges. Later the same day, a summary trial took place. Charged with slander as well as assault and battery, Klarsfeld asserted that the reason for her action was Kiesinger's "continuing fascist attitude." By 8 PM, the highly unusual summary court handed down its verdict: one year's imprisonment. Klarsfeld was unrepentant and noted: "A summary court during the Nazi period could not have been very different." She also asserted that she was more convinced than ever that German courts were "protecting the Nazis" and vowed to the court that she would lodge a complaint with the French city commandant in Berlin.

The slap administered to Chancellor Kiesinger was heard around the world. The incident was reported in most of the international press and proved to be a public-relations disaster for Kiesinger and his party. His politically unwise decision to press charges, and the remarkably harsh punishment decreed by the summary court, served to dramatize the charges made by Klarsfeld and her husband, namely that West Germany was still harboring unrepentant ex-Nazis in the highest offices of the land. Important voices of the West German press, including the influential newsmagazine *Der Spiegel,* gave the event broad coverage, noting that, while Beate Klarsfeld had been sentenced to a year in prison, only a few weeks earlier the would-be assassin of student radical leader Rudi Dutschke (who had been almost fatally wounded in 1967) had received a mere fine of 200 marks for an infinitely more serious crime. The disparity between the two sentences was obvious and disturbing.

In a series of court appearances that followed the Berlin incident, Klarsfeld caused further consternation in government circles by bringing up the chancellor's Nazi past at every possible opportunity. Asked at one point why she had decided "to use violence against the Chancellor of our country?," her response was "Violence, your honor, is the imposition of a Nazi Chancellor on German youth." Kiesinger's attempt at damage control came much too late in June 1969, when, after he failed to appear in court in support of his own complaint, the case was dismissed. Running for reelection in 1969, he was unable to repair the damage he had inflicted on himself and his party because of the incident. In September of that year, Kiesinger and his party were defeated at the polls by Social Democrat Willy Brandt, a political leader who had fled Nazi Germany in 1933 and had risked his life throughout the Third Reich era as an anti-fascist emigre.

Refusing to rest after bringing down Kiesinger, Klarsfeld and Serge began orchestrating a publicity campaign against another West German politician with a Nazi past. Ernst Achenbach, an influential lawyer and Bundestag member, was being considered for the important

Beate Klarsfeld

post of West Germany's representative to the European Economic Community (EEC). Although Achenbach admitted to having been chief of political affairs at the German embassy in Paris during the war, he also insisted, as had Kiesinger, that he had no connection with the evils of Nazism. Assiduous searches in several Paris archives by the Klarsfelds revealed otherwise. They found documentation that linked Achenbach with crimes against humanity, including memos signed by him authorizing the deportation to death camps of at least 2,000 French Jews. Armed with these documents, they went to most of the capital cities of EEC member states, making it clear that if Achenbach were to be linked to that well-regarded international body, its reputation would be grievously harmed. Soon a storm of negative publicity appeared in the European media on the Achenbach nomination. Bowing to the pressure, he withdrew his name.

The Klarsfelds then turned to the arduous task of seeking justice in the cases of over 1,000 Nazi bureaucrats who had been tried, but not punished, for crimes they committed in France during the war. From 1945 to 1954, the French had tried 1,026 Nazis *in absentia,* under the assumption that they were back on German soil. Even if German courts had been inclined to prosecute these individuals, the Allies did not allow them to, arguing that, since many postwar German judges had also been Nazi Party members, in such trials ex-Nazis would be judging other ex-Nazis. Post-1945 France, increasingly conservative and anti-Communist, made no moves to return the former Nazis still on its soil, and in fact many were hired by French intelligence agencies because wartime Nazi knowledge of the Communist-led resistance made them useful agents in the Cold War. When the West German constitution was written in the 1950s, the Allies did not object to a provision forbidding extradition of German citizens. As a result of this, the 1,026 Nazis tried *in absentia* could neither be prosecuted in Germany nor punished in France. Although most were without a shadow of a doubt involved in war crimes and crimes against humanity, they remained free. This was the legal obstacle the Klarsfelds faced in the late 1960s, while working to show the public that so many men who had directly participated in genocide were neither punished nor in hiding. Not until 1975, after many years of agitation by the Klarsfelds, did West Germany and France ratify an extradition treaty making it possible for the French to punish Nazi war criminals.

Until the appropriate legislation was in place, the Klarsfelds hunted for former Nazis who were enjoying their lives in West Germany. In the case of Kurt Lischka, who had been an SS Obersturmbannführer and Gestapo chief in Paris during the war, Beate simply called information in Cologne to get a telephone number and address. Serge then traveled to Cologne, where he and a television photographer confronted Lischka with copies of documents he had signed in Nazi-occupied Paris. On that day, Lischka read the papers without emotion, but when Klarsfeld and the photographer caught Lischka two days later the old Nazi ran and zigzagged out of camera range, causing Beate to observe how strange it was to see this man behave like a trapped animal when chased by nothing more than a camera. In March 1971, the Klarsfelds and three trusted men attempted to kidnap Lischka; they planned to sedate him, put him in their car trunk, and take him back to France. The plot misfired when the wielder of the blackjack did not hit hard enough, and Lischka screamed for help from a passing policeman. Despite this setback, the Klarsfelds kept up their campaign against him. For her participation in the bungled kidnap attempt, Beate was sentenced to two months in jail in Cologne in July 1974. She served her sentence, realizing the immense publicity value of both the trial and her conviction. Eventually, Lischka was tried and sentenced to a long period in prison.

Also in 1971, the Klarsfelds began the complicated process of bringing the notorious Klaus Barbie to justice. Barbie, a member of the security service of the SS, was sent to Lyons in November 1942, where he eventually became head of the local Gestapo and was responsible for torturing and murdering members of the French resistance as well as deporting thousands of Jews and anti-fascists to concentration and death camps. To many then and later, Barbie was known simply as the "Butcher of Lyons." He had also authorized the rounding up on April 6, 1944, of 44 Jewish children at their place of refuge, the village of Izieu near Lyons; all were killed at Auschwitz. Initially eluding the Allies after the war, in 1947 Barbie began working for the U.S. Counter Intelligence Corps, because his knowledge of French Communists was deemed of vital interest in the early days of the Cold War. Shielded by the Americans until 1951, Barbie was permitted that year to flee first to Peru and then to Bolivia, where he took the name Klaus Altmann (originally Klaus Altmann Hansen) and became a prosperous businessman. By 1971, the Klarsfelds had tracked "Altmann" down to La Paz.

Although Beate realized that it might be years before he appeared before the bars of justice, a start had to be made. Again ready to use the power of publicity, she decided to go to Bolivia to draw attention to Barbie and the failure of the world to punish him for his crimes. She enlisted as an ally **Ita-Rosa Halaunbrenner**, a survivor of a Jewish family that Barbie and the Lyons Gestapo had almost totally wiped out. Murdered were her husband Jacob, son Léon, and daughters **Claudine** and **Mina**. Only Ita-Rosa, her daughter **Monique** and son Alexandre survived the Holocaust. Beate and Ita-Rosa left Paris on February 20, 1972. Although frustrated in La Paz in their efforts to initiate legal proceedings against Barbie, with Halaunbrenner pressing charges as an individual for the murder of four members of her family, the two women were nevertheless able to generate a great deal of publicity when, on March 6, 1972, they chained themselves for six hours to a bench on the Prado, the busiest street in La Paz. Opposite the bench were the offices of the Transmaritima Boliviana, of which Barbie was the managing director. A crowd formed and news of the event was broadcast on the local radio. A sympathetic Bolivian woman said to the chained women, "There is no such thing as justice in Bolivia. Kidnap him or kill him."

News of the La Paz demonstration appeared in the world's press, and Klaus Barbie would never again be free of the fear of being apprehended. In November 1972, anticipating that Bolivia would turn down France's request for the extradition of Barbie, the Klarsfelds, assisted by the radical French philosopher Régis Debray, devised a plan to kidnap Barbie in Bolivia with the assistance of army officers who were opponents of the current dictatorial regime. The idea was to smuggle Barbie to Europe through Chile. The plan was never carried out, however, because in March 1973 Barbie was taken into custody by the Bolivian authorities who feared he might flee the country. When he was released that October, it was too late to carry out the Klarsfelds' plan. There had been a change of government in Chile. Salvador Allende's democratic socialist administration had been overthrown in a bloody coup led by General Augusto Pinochet and the sympathetic army officers were no longer available.

Almost a decade passed and most of the world forgot about Klaus Barbie. But the Klarsfelds kept agitating for a change in the situation. This took place in the early 1980s, when a more liberal regime emerged in Bolivia. In 1983, Barbie was imprisoned in La Paz, ostensibly over a matter of tax delinquency. In reality, France had bought his extradition from Bolivia for $50 mil-

lion and 3,000 tons of wheat. He was taken to the scene of his crimes, Lyons, and it took four years to prepare a case of 23,000 pages of testimony against him. The trial, which lasted from May 11 through July 4, 1987 (*see also *Aubrac, Lucie*), resulted in Barbie being found guilty on charges of both war crimes and crimes against humanity. His conviction was a significant milestone in the evolution of international law, both reaffirming and refining the principle that there can be no statute of limitations, legal or moral, on crimes against humanity. Klaus Barbie died a prisoner in Lyons in September of 1991.

By the last decade of the 20th century, few Nazi-era war criminals remained alive, free, or unpunished. One of these was Alois Brunner, who had joined the Nazi Party in 1931 and started working for Adolf Eichmann in 1938, specializing in the deportation of Austria's Jews. Eichmann once described Brunner as "one of my best men." Among his crimes were the deportation of Berlin Jews in 1942, the virtual extinction of Salonika Jews in Greece, and the brutal regime he maintained at the Drancy transit camp outside of Paris. Historian **Mary Felstiner** has written that Brunner's "policy, his practice, and his personality constituted one unit, with no preoccupation but genocide." The Klarsfelds also had personal reasons for bringing Alois Brunner to justice. It was Brunner who was responsible for the death of Serge's father. As far back as 1954, Brunner had been sentenced to death *in absentia* in France for his crimes. In the late 1950s, Viennese Nazi-hunter Simon Wiesenthal tracked Brunner to Damascus, Syria, where he was living under the alias "George Fischer." Unlike Klaus Barbie, however, who was eventually betrayed by his host nation, Brunner remained safe in Damascus. On several occasions, nonetheless, the old Nazi suffered from acts of retribution. In 1961, Israel's Mossad (intelligence agency) sent Brunner a letter bomb which exploded, costing him four fingers on his left hand. Very likely Mossad was again at work in 1980 when a parcel from Vienna exploded, this time injuring Brunner's left eye.

Several times in the 1980s, Beate Klarsfeld traveled to Syria to find and perhaps even arrest Alois Brunner. On each occasion, she was recognized and not allowed to leave the Damascus airport. In December 1991, however, she was more successful. Using the passport of **Gertrude Baer**, one of her Jewish friends in Paris, Beate donned "a mousy brown wig" to cover her own red hair, wore black-framed eyeglasses, and was made up to look about a dozen years older. Normally a stylish dresser, Klarsfeld wore a shapeless car coat over baggy slacks. The ruse worked, and she was able to pass Syrian airport security. Immediately after unfurling her protest poster, she was arrested. While being interrogated, she explained the nature of her mission to Damascus: "Syria must stop protecting Alois Brunner, the last major Nazi war criminal at large. He must be delivered to justice." Although she was treated courteously by her Syrian captors, she did not get the interview she hoped for with President **Hafez al Assad**, and she was put on a plane back to Paris.

Not unexpectedly, 50 or more members of the press were on hand when Beate arrived back at Orly Airport. Serge Klarsfeld kissed his wife in the glare of television lights, then stood aside while she responded to the press. He held her hand tightly on the taxi ride back to their apartment, where she was greeted by the two family collies. More or less like many working women home from the office, she then examined her husband's shirts to decide which ones needed to be washed and put on her apron to make dinner from leftovers. Then the BBC called for a radio interview; they wanted to know more about Alois Brunner.

SOURCES:

Billig, Joseph. *La Solution finale de la question Juive: Essai sur ses principes dans le IIIe Reich et en France sous l'occupation.* Edited by Serge and Beate Klarsfeld. Paris: CDJC, 1977.

Binder, David. "Woman Hits Kiesinger in the Eye in Berlin and Gets Year," in *The New York Times.* November 8, 1968, pp. 1, 5.

Bower, Tom. *Klaus Barbie: Butcher of Lyons.* Rev. ed. London: Corgi Books, 1987.

Finkielkraut, Alain. *Remembering in Vain: The Klaus Barbie Trial and Crimes Against Humanity.* Translated by Roxanne Lapidus. NY: Columbia University Press, 1992.

"Ganz hübsch," in *Der Spiegel.* Vol. 22, no. 46. November 11, 1968, p. 30.

"Gaol for Slapping Kiesinger," in *The Times* [London]. November 8, 1968, p. 6.

Hellman, Peter. "Serge and Beate Klarsfeld: Nazi-Hunting is Their Life," in *The New York Times Biographical Service.* November 1979, pp. 1556–1560.

———. "Stalking the Last Nazi," in *New York.* Vol. 25, no. 2. January 13, 1992, pp. 28–33.

"The Just and the Unjust," in *Time.* Vol. 104, no. 4. July 22, 1974, pp. 47, 53.

Kent, George O. "Klaus Barbie, the United States Government, and the Beginnings of the Cold War," in *Simon Wiesenthal Center Annual.* Vol. 3, 1986, pp. 261–276.

Klarsfeld, Beate. *Wherever They May Be!* Translated by Monroe Stearns and Natalie Gerardi. NY: Vanguard Press, 1975.

Klarsfeld, Serge. *The Children of Izieu: A Human Tragedy.* Foreword by Beate and Serge Klarsfeld. Translated by Kenneth Jacobson. NY: Harry N. Abrams, 1985.

Lang, Kirsty. "Son of Nazi Hunter Puts France on Trial," in *The Times* [London]. September 28, 1997, p. 22.

Mauz, Gerhard. "'Den Bundeskanzler misshandelt,'" in *Der Spiegel.* Vol. 22, no. 46. November 11, 1968, p. 32.

Morgan, Ted. *An Uncertain Hour: The French, the Germans, the Jews, the Klaus Barbie Trial, and the City of Lyon, 1940–1945.* NY: Arbor House, 1990.

"Nazi Leader Brunner is Dead and Buried," in *Agence France Presse.* December 7, 1999.

Phillips, Ian. "How We Met: Serge and Beate Klarsfeld," in *The Independent* [London]. March 16, 1997, p. 58.

Proteus. "Two German Women," in *Midstream.* Vol. 21, no. 2, 1975, pp. 67–71.

Saxon, Wolfgang. "Klaus Barbie, 77, Lyons Gestapo Chief," in *The New York Times Biographical Service.* September 1991, pp. 998–999.

Wiss-Verdier, A. "Beate Klarsfeld, ou la Chasse aux Nazis," in *Documents.* Vol. 29, no. 5, 1974, pp. 6–13.

RELATED MEDIA:

Hanley, Jim, and Lee David. *Beate Klarsfeld: A Portrait in the First Person* (videocassette), Princeton, NJ: Films for the Humanities & Sciences, 1994.

Klarsfeld, Beate. "Wherever They May Be! One Woman's Moral Crusade Against Nazism" (videocassette), Ninth Annual Lipman Lecture, Colby College, April 29, 1987.

"Nazi Hunter: The Beate Klarsfeld Story," ABC-TV television drama, first aired November 23, 1986.

John Haag,
Associate Professor of History,
University of Georgia, Athens, Georgia

Kleeberg, Clotilde (1866–1909)

French pianist. Born in France in 1866; died in 1909; studied with Louise Aglae Massart at the Paris Conservatoire.

A student of **Louise Aglae Massart** at the Paris Conservatoire, Clotilde Kleeberg was a successful concert artist whose playing was described as unaffected and vigorous. She was one of the first to revive the old French clavecinist (harpsichord) composers.

John Haag,
Athens, Georgia

Kleegman, Sophia (1901–1971)

Russian-born gynecologist and obstetrician who was a pioneer in the study of infertility. Born Sophia Josephine Kleegman in Kiev, Russia, on July 8, 1901; died in New York, New York, on September 26, 1971; youngest of four daughters of Israel Kleegman (a Talmudic scholar) and Elka (Siergutz) Kleegman; University of Bellevue Hospital Medical College, New York, M.D., 1924; married Dr. John H. Sillman (an orthodontist), on December 31, 1932; children: Frederick (b. 1937); Anne Marice Sillman (b. 1942).

Born in 1901 in Kiev, Russia, Sophia Kleegman was the youngest of four daughters of Israel and **Elka Kleegman**. (Their four sons did not survive childhood.) Kleegman's two older sisters, **Mary** and **Rae**, immigrated to America ahead of the rest of the family, and worked in New York's garment industry to earn passage for their parents and younger sisters. The family was reunited in New York in 1906, although Kleegman did not become a naturalized citizen until 1923. While Kleegman's parents and her older sisters provided the family income, Sophia and her sister **Anna** were groomed for professional careers. Both chose to study medicine, and Sophia enrolled at the University of Bellevue Hospital Medical College, graduating in 1924 and taking a residency in obstetrics and gynecology at Chicago Lying-In Hospital. In 1929, she became the first woman appointed to the New York University College of Medicine faculty of obstetrics and gynecology, and that same year also joined the staff of Bellevue Hospital.

In 1932, Kleegman married Dr. John H. Sillman, an orthodontist, but, as an established professional, retained her maiden name. With the birth of her son (1937) and daughter (1941), she found it necessary to give up her obstetrical practice because of her increased family responsibilities. With the help of a full-time housekeeper and a babysitter, however, she was able to continue her work in gynecology while her children were small.

Kleegman began her research on conception early in her career, and was a pioneer in the study of infertility, including the diagnosis and treatment of sterility in both men and women. Straightforward in her approach, she confronted issues such as birth control and artificial insemination and was one of the few physicians of her time to incorporate psychological issues like performance anxiety, repression, and stress into her gynecological practice. Kleegman's rapport with her patients was such that it inspired confidence and trust, and in addition to responding to problems of conception, she often contributed to the improvement of a couple's total relationship.

Sophia Kleegman was an outspoken advocate of birth control and planned parenthood clinics, and toured the country lecturing on the subject before it was acceptable. She supported the early clinic established in New York by *Margaret Sanger** and served as medical director of the New York State Planned Parenthood Association from 1936 to 1961, after which she became a medical consultant to the Eastern Planned Parenthood League. She also fought for improved sex education and, after a 12-year battle, was able to convince New York University Medical Center to include sex education in its medical curriculum.

In addition to her social contributions to medicine, Kleegman is also remembered for her technical expertise, particularly her work with the "Pap smear" test for cervical cancer developed by Dr. George Papanicolau. Adding a endometrial aspiration test to the procedure, Kleegman further expanded the test's diagnostic capabilities.

Kleegman was active in a number of outside organizations, serving as president of both the Women's Medical Association of New York (1942–44) and the American Association of Marriage Counselors. In 1965, she was elected president of the NYU Medical Alumni Association, becoming the first woman to hold that post. Kleegman remained active in medicine until her death of cancer at the age of 70. Friends, colleagues, and patients honored her memory by establishing the Sophia J. Kleegman Professorship in Human Reproduction at the NYU Medical Center.

SOURCES:

Bailey, Brooke. *The Remarkable Lives of 100 Women Healers and Scientists.* Holbrook, MA: Bob Adams, 1994.

Sicherman, Barbara, and Carol Hurd Green, eds. *Notable American Women: The Modern Period.* Cambridge, MA: The Belknap Press of Harvard University Press, 1980.

Klein, Anne (1923–1974)

American fashion designer. Name variations: Hannah Golofski or Golofsky. Born Hannah Golofsky (also seen as Golofski) on August 3, 1923, in Brooklyn, New York; died on March 19, 1974; daughter of Morris Golofsky (owner of a fleet of cabs) and Esther Golofsky; married Ben Klein (divorced); married Matthew Rubinstein (a businessman), in 1963; no children.

Known as the mother of contemporary American style, designer Anne Klein reinvented the sportswear popularized by designers like *Claire McCardell** and Clare Potter in the 1930s and 1940s and brought it into the ranks of high fashion. Creating a simple "programmed wardrobe," consisting of blazers, skirts, pants, blouses, and sweaters that could be combined in a variety of different outfits, she led the way into the contemporary mode of dressing. "She always thought it through from the woman's point of view," said her close friend **Edie Locke**, a television fashion producer and onetime editor-in-chief of *Mademoiselle*. "Like, 'Am I going to wear this? If I buy it, will it go with the other things?' Today that seems normal, everyday kind of stuff, but it wasn't then." In 1974, at the height of her success, Klein would enter the hospital for what appeared to be a virus but it turned out to be cancer. Her death, at age 51, was a shock to all who knew her, and a particular loss to the fashion world.

Klein, known as Annie to her friends, was born in Brooklyn, New York in 1923, the daughter of Russian immigrants. Her father worked as a taxi driver when he first came to the United States, but he eventually acquired a fleet of cabs and then a garage. Klein was perhaps most influenced by her mother Esther, an extraordinary seamstress who transposed the fashions she saw in store windows into clothing for Anne and her three sisters. At age 15, Klein began working as a free-lance sketcher on Seventh Avenue in New York's fashion district. Her first full time job was with Varden Petites, where she updated their matronly image into something decidedly more chic. Klein, a small and ele-

Anne Klein

gant woman herself—and somewhat shy—was a hard taskmaster, even in the early days of her career. Award-winning designer Bill Blass, who assisted Klein at Varden for a year and then was fired, remembered that she kept extraordinary hours that did not much appeal to a bachelor just out of the army. "She was the perfectionist of all time," he said. "She was never satisfied and had a tendency to fit and fit and refit." Blass worked with Klein again in November 1973, when they both participated in the highly successful Versailles fashion show, which included designers Halston, Oscar de la Renta, and Stephen Burrows.

In 1948, Anne and her first husband Ben Klein started a firm called Junior Sophisticates, which specialized in updated, sleek styles for the smaller woman. "She was incredible to work with—her mind was always going," recalled Jerry Feder, who then assisted Klein. "There were times I felt like walking out—she was so demanding. But you just had to respect that woman. I didn't know how much I'd learned until I left her." Klein stayed on at Junior Sophisticates, even after her divorce from Ben Klein, but left in 1965 to open the Anne Klein Studio on West 57th Street. Three years later, she and her second husband Matthew "Chip" Rubinstein, along with Gunther Oppenheim and Sanford Smith, formed Anne Klein and Company, which began as a sportswear house but gradually expanded to include perfume, scarves, jewelry, handbags and belts, sleepwear, perfume, and menswear. The company went international in 1973, forming an alliance with Takihyo of Nagoya, a 200-year-old Japanese firm. **Donna Karan**, who had assisted Klein for nine months back at Junior Sophisticates, rejoined the designer in 1971 and co-designed what turned out to be Klein's last collection. She considered Klein both a teacher and a friend. "To watch Annie work was a trip in itself. She wouldn't ask anyone to do things she wouldn't do herself, including sweeping the floors."

Chip Rubinstein, Klein's husband for 12 years, claimed that in addition to being a perfectionist, his wife was an ever-flowing fountain of ideas. "An avid sketcher, she carried a voluminous bag filled with zillions of sheets of paper. She'd even sketch on the streets if she got an idea." Others who knew the designer speak of her almost childlike curiosity and her ability to draw inspiration from the most mundane items. "I remember going into the bathroom with her," recalled Klein's niece **Barbara Waldman**, who worked with her aunt from 1968 to 1974 as a salesperson and then in the design studio, "the one by the freight elevator; she never used the smart one by the showroom. We were standing washing our hands, and she picked up this old bar of soap, which was cracked and grimed with dirt, and took it off to the Xerox machine to make copies of it. Later it became a pattern on a fabric for a blouse."

Klein's concepts and philosophy of fashion are more popular than ever. Her label, designed by Louis Dell' Olio until 1993, when Richard Tyler took over, continues to flourish, and her influence is seen in the contemporary clothing lines of Calvin Klein (no relation), Ralph Lauren, and, of course, Donna Karan. "Anne allowed American women to find their own identity in dressing," explained designer **Hazel Haire**, who worked with Klein in the 1960s. "She offered them the comfort that didn't exist in fashion then. She gave them quality clothes that weren't available to women in the medium price range. And she taught them to recognize quality." **Bernadine Morris**, senior fashion writer for *The New York Times*, summed up Klein's contribution in simpler terms. "Clothes were loony," she said. "Anne instinctively understood it was time for a nice blazer."

SOURCES:

Brampton, Sally. "The House That Anne Built," in *Harper's Bazaar*. November 1993. No. 3384, pp. 190–194.

"Memories of Anne Klein," in *The Star-Ledger* [Newark, NJ]. March 9, 1975.

Barbara Morgan,
Melrose, Massachusetts

Klein, Melanie (1882–1960)

Controversial psychoanalyst whose revolutionary technique of "play analysis" and insights into early childhood development made an important and lasting contribution to the practice of psychoanalysis. Born Melanie Reizes in Vienna, Austria, on March 30, 1882; died in London, England, on September 22, 1960; daughter of Moriz Reizes (a medical doctor) and Libussa (Deutsch) Reizes (a shopkeeper); married Arthur Klein, in 1903 (divorced 1923); children: Melitta Klein; Hans Klein; Eric Klein.

Began analyzing children in Budapest (1919); moved to Berlin (1921); elected a full member of the Berlin Psychoanalytic Society (1923); developed the technique of "play analysis" (1921–23); moved to London (1926); became first European analyst elected to the British Psycho-Analytical Society (1927); analyzed last child patient (late 1940s).

Publications: The Psycho-Analysis of Children (1932); Contributions to Psycho-Analysis, 1921–1945 (1948); Envy and Gratitude (1957); (published posthumously) Narrative of a Child Psycho-Analysis (1961).

If the first page in the history of the psychoanalysis of children belongs to Sigmund Freud, whose 1909 "Analysis of a Phobia in a Five-Year-Old Boy" is the earliest published case of a child analysis, much of the rest of the story belongs to Melanie Klein. For more than 40 years, she was a highly original and controversial figure in the psychoanalytic community, who wrote, taught and conducted research in the field of child psychology. Her revolutionary techniques and theories about infantile sexuality and child development, outlined in four books and numerous published papers, evoked widespread admiration and respect, as well as shock and controversy. The fact that her theories continue to arouse strong reactions, debate and discussion is a testament to the lasting mark she has left on the practice of psychoanalysis.

> *There is little doubt that her work not only had a profound influence in technique but that it contributed to a change in the psychoanalytical approach to the understanding of the mind.*
>
> —Hanna Segal

Melanie Klein's lifelong passion for learning was formed early by the intellectually charged household in which she was raised. Born in Vienna on March 30, 1882, she was the youngest of four children of Dr. Moriz Reizes and **Libussa Deutsch Reizes**. Her father, though unsuccessful in his medical practice, was a brilliant, intellectually formidable man who read widely and taught himself ten European languages. His wife, 15 years his junior, was a beautiful woman who shared and supported his devotion to learning. Due to financial pressures early in the marriage, she operated a successful shop that sold exotic plants and animals. Though Klein preferred her loving mother to her remote father, there is little doubt that she was deeply influenced by him. His burning commitment to education and knowledge stoked the fires of her own intellectual ambitions.

Klein's early life was also tragically marked by the illnesses and deaths of two of her siblings. Her sister Sidonie, four years her senior, died at the age of nine of scrofula. Her brother Emanuel, to whom she was devoted, suffered from a rheumatic heart condition from which he eventually died in early adulthood. That Klein and her eldest sister, **Emilie Reizes**, were never close, made the illnesses and deaths of her two beloved siblings even more traumatic.

Klein made the decision to study medicine at the age of 14. With the help of Emanuel, who coached her in Greek and Latin, she passed the entrance exam to the Vienna Gymnasium, at that time the only school that prepared girls for university. But at the age of 19, she became engaged to Arthur Klein, an industrial chemist. Dazzled by his brilliance, she shelved her own plans to study medicine and during the period of their engagement studied art and history instead at the University of Vienna. They married when she was 21.

The following years were not satisfying ones for Klein. Her husband's work took them from one small industrial town to another. Despite the joy brought by the birth of two children, Melitta in 1904 and Hans in 1907 (a third child, Eric, would be born in 1914), she longed for the intellectual world she had left behind in Vienna.

In 1910, the family settled in Budapest, marking an important turning point for Klein. By chance, she picked up the book *On Dreams* by Sigmund Freud, and her intellectual life was reborn. Klein immediately embarked on a study of the new science of psychoanalysis and in 1914 entered analysis with Sandor Ferenczi, who became her first mentor. It was under his tutelage that she began analyzing children in 1919. Klein presented her first paper on child development to the Budapest Psychoanalytic Society on July 19, 1919. (The paper was expanded and published as "The Development of a Child.") Later that year, she was elected a member of the Budapest Psychoanalytic Society.

Klein met Karl Abraham, who was deeply impressed with her work, while attending the 1920 meeting of the Psychoanalytic Congress in The Hague. When Abraham invited her to practice in Berlin, Klein separated from her husband in January 1921 (they divorced in 1923) and moved there with her three children. The five years that Klein worked and studied in Berlin were important ones. It was here, under the auspices of the Berlin Psychoanalytic Society and with the support of Karl Abraham, that she began developing new therapeutic techniques and clinical insights that would affect the study of early childhood development forever.

From the time that Klein began analyzing her first patient, five-year-old "Fritz," she observed that children expressed fantasies and mastered their anxieties through play. She theorized that the elements of juvenile play were similar to the symbolic language of dreams. Accordingly, Klein began to apply the same technique of free association to children that Freud had used to uncover the unconscious in adults. By analyzing and interpreting play, she believed she could gain access to the child's unconscious. Thus her revolutionary technique of "play analysis" was born.

Until the time that Melanie Klein began constructing her theories, analysts had been unsure how to apply psychoanalytic techniques to children. As Klein herself realized, many of the mental conditions normally necessary for psychoanalysis seem to be absent in children. Yet it was precisely these differences in the infantile mind and the adult mind that led her to develop the technique of play analysis. As Klein wrote:

> By means of Play Analysis we gain access to the child's most deeply repressed experiences and fixations and are thus able to exert a radical influence on its development . . . . The whole kaleidoscopic picture, often to all appearances quite meaningless, which children present to us in a single analytic hour— the content of their games, the way in which they play, the means they use . . . and the motives behind a change of game . . . all these things are seen to have method to them and will yield up their meaning if we interpret them as dreams. . . . For play is a child's most important medium of expression.

An illustration of Klein's technique is contained in her account of the analysis of three-year-old Peter, a child who was strongly fixated upon his mother and difficult to manage. During the first hour, Peter "took the toy carriages and cars and put them first one behind the other and then side by side, and alternated this arrangement several times. He also took a horse and carriage and bumped it into another, so that the horses' feet knocked together, and said: 'I've got a new brother called Fritz.'" She then recounted how the child bumped two horses together, laid them down, covered them up with bricks and declared "Now they're quite dead; I've buried them." The child proceeded to play aggressively, knocking down the cars and horses and carriages. Klein interpreted the child's initial placement of the cars end to end as symbolizing his father's powerful penis. The horses bumped together represented parental intercourse, and the death of the horses symbolized the rage he felt at having on occasion witnessed his parents' coitus. The repeated falling over of the toys represented the child's own feelings of impotency.

Based on such clinical observations, Klein began to construct a theory of early childhood psychological development. From the beginning, she was interested almost exclusively in the internal conflicts and mechanisms affecting development, paying little attention to external factors such as home life and school life. (This exclusiveness remains a strong criticism of her work.) Her insights into infantile sexuality were, however, remarkable, and over the course of her life she continued to modify and expand them.

Klein traced childhood anxieties back to the infant's primitive ambivalent relationship with the mother, in particular a part of the mother's body, the breast. Early on, Freud had noted that an infant's first relationship is to the breast. Klein elaborated this point by attaching even greater significance to the development of object relations. She observed, for example, that in small children object relations (both real and fantasy objects) play an important role in the structure of the child's self.

According to Klein, an infant's relationship to its mother, who represents its whole world during the first months of life, is from the start one of both love and hate. The mother is the sole source of contact, comfort and food, and the child therefore demands her continuous presence and exclusive love. That its demands are not satisfied is a source of frustration which eventually leads to feelings of persecution and gives rise to aggression which is expressed through the desire to bite or devour cannibalistically. These hostile feelings in turn produce anxiety, which the child attempts to minimize through a process of introjection, projection, and splitting—a stage of development Klein termed the "persecutory phase."

Klein believed that a child introjects parts of the parents' bodies (first the breast and later the penis and other parts) into himself, often splitting them into ideal and persecutory objects, e.g. a gratifying "good breast" and a frustrating "bad breast." The child's relation to these internalized parts is extremely complex, involving elements of reality and fantasy. The goal for the child is to retain the introjected "good" parts, thus creating an idealized internal object, and project the "bad." She believed these processes were an important and natural part of a child's development and that they "participate in the building up of an ego and superego that prepare the groundwork for the onset of the Oedipus complex." Her views came to be known as "an object relation theory" due to the importance she placed on external and internal objects.

Klein's theory of "part objects" was, to some extent, a modification of Freud's theory of the superego. Freud described an internal object created when a child introjects his father, making him a part of himself. This internalized figure, the superego, is a figure of conscience responsible for self-observations and criticism, punishment and setting up goals. Klein's theory of part objects pointed to a superego that appeared much earlier and was far more complicated. Klein departed from Freud's belief that the construction of the superego occurred as a consequence of the Oedipus complex, insisting instead that the superego was a part of the Oedipus complex and was even evident in children much younger than five or six years of age, the period to which Freud ascribed the onset of the Oedipus complex. In fact, Klein came to believe that even a child under the age of a year could begin to experience and exhibit anxiety brought on by the beginning of the Oedipus complex.

In 1923, Klein analyzed her youngest patient, two-and-a-half year old "Rita," a child who suffered from *pavor nocturnus* (night terrors) and obsessive behavior. In Rita, she traced the source of her night terrors to the child's fantasies of parental intercourse and the Oedipal attacks she made toward her mother which, for the child, culminated in a terrifying fantasy of maternal retribution. It was precisely Klein's insistence that

Melanie Klein

very young children have a rich, often sadistic, fantasy life that ignited the controversy that would always surround her work. Many analysts continued to believe in the innocence of early childhood and were reluctant to attribute to children such complex and sophisticated perceptions.

During Klein's years in Berlin, her theories and investigations into early childhood anxiety increasingly evoked dissent and controversy. Though she received sharp criticism, the influence of her discoveries was far-reaching. Karl Abraham, still one of Klein's most vocal advocates, declared at a meeting in 1924 that "the future of psychoanalysis lies in play techniques." Earlier that year, she had persuaded Abraham to take her on as a patient, and with him she continued the analysis she began with Ferenczi. However, 14 months later, Abraham died. Klein was deeply affected by the loss of her friend and mentor. More important, the loss of his support found Klein increasingly at odds with members of the Berlin Psycho-Analytic Society.

In 1925, at the invitation of Ernest Jones, Klein spent three weeks in London delivering a series of lectures to members of the British Psycho-Analytical Society. Here she found a more receptive audience for her ideas. In 1926, when Jones invited her to move to England and work in the British Psychoanalytic Society, she accepted. Klein became the first continental European analyst admitted to the Society. With the support of Jones, her work flourished, and she began to train and supervise other analysts eager to learn her techniques.

The years from 1926 to 1936 were productive ones for Klein. In London, there was lively interest in the early stages of development, and her work was generally held in high esteem. In the early 1930s, Klein began analyzing adults as well. She found immense value in analyzing adults and children simultaneously, and much of her later theoretical conclusions were influenced by her work with adults. Her book *The Psycho-Analysis of Children,* published in 1932, elicited excitement and praise from her colleagues. In an enthusiastic review published in the *International Journal of Psycho-Analysis,* Edward Glover wrote: "In two respects her book is of fundamental importance for the future of psychoanalysis. It contains not only unique clinical material gathered from first-hand analytic observations of children, but lays down certain conclusions which are bound to influence theory and practice of analysis for some time to come."

In 1935, Klein introduced the concept of the "depressive position" which marked a crucial development in her theories. In the depressive position (a stage which follows the persecutory phase), the child begins to see and love the mother as a whole and separate object, rather than as part-objects. Thus, the child undergoes an important process of integration. The mother is now seen as an integral, external figure who embodies positive as well as negative traits. The growing integration of the ego is necessary so that the infant can begin to distinguish the external world and understand its contradictory nature. The anxiety produced is of a depressive nature as "the synthesis between the loved and hated aspects of the complete object gives rise to feelings of mourning and guilt."

By the mid-to-late 1930s, Klein's theories dominated the Society causing some members to view her work with increasing suspicion and hostility. At the same time, an influx of German-Jewish analysts from the Continent (first from Berlin, then Vienna) poured into London, including an ailing Sigmund Freud and his daughter Anna. *Anna Freud had begun analyzing children around the same time as Klein. However, she and Klein had distinct differences in technique and theory. Klein maintained that the most effective method of analyzing children was to reproduce the classic technique used with adults, and that close attention must be paid to the child's transference of negative impulses to the analyst. Anna Freud strongly believed, on the contrary, that standard psychoanalytic technique should be modified in the case of children and that the analyst should exert an educational influence over the young patient as well as work to gain the child's confidence. Moreover, Anna Freud dismissed the possibility of the transference situation occurring with a child since she regarded its emotional attachment to its parents as too complete. Their theoretical disputes widened the rift at the institute. A group of pupils, who became known as the "Kleinians," flocked to Klein championing her work with an almost fanatical zeal. An oppositional group formed, polarizing the institute. Ernest Jones, in an attempt to diminish the raging professional disagreements, initiated a series of discussions at the British Psycho-Analytical Society aimed at clarifying Klein's views. These occurred in 1943 and 1944 and came to be known as the "Controversial Discussions."

Despite the controversy raging around her, Klein continued to work feverishly in these years, producing some of her most important works. In 1942, she had introduced the term "paranoid-schizoid position" for the first time in an article entitled "Notes on Some Schizoid Mechanisms." The term denoted a further definition of the part-object phase of infantile development and emphasized the fact that the process of splitting and persecutory anxiety during the first few months of life coexisted with the mechanism of introjecting part objects. Klein believed that paranoia and schizophrenia in adulthood originates in this early period of development when persecutory anxiety interferes with the gradual formation of the ego.

Melanie Klein analyzed her last child patient in the late 1940s, but continued to treat adults and train students at the British Psycho-Analytical Society. In 1957, at the age of 75, she wrote *Envy and Gratitude,* her last major contribution to psychoanalytic theory. The book is an important study in early oral envy and the mutual interactions of envy, jealousy and greed. Shortly afterwards, she began work on one of her most ambitious works, "Narrative of a Child Analysis," a day-by-day account of her 1941 psychoanalysis of "Richard," a ten-year-old boy suffering from acute anxiety and depression. Klein believed that by presenting such a complete analytical record she could illustrate her therapeutic techniques more clearly and thus lay to rest certain misconceptions that she believed surrounded her work. Published posthumously, it remains a fascinating, detailed account of the process of psychoanalysis.

Melanie Klein remained actively engaged in intellectual debates, in writing, teaching and research even as her health began to decline. Following surgery to remove a malignancy, she died of a pulmonary embolus on September 22, 1960, at age 78.

SOURCES AND SUGGESTED READING:

Alexander, Franz, Samuel Eisenstein, and Martin Grotjahn, eds. *Psychoanalytic Pioneers.* NY: Basic Books, 1966.

Gross-Kurth, Phyllis. *Melanie Klein: Her World and Her Work.* NY: Alfred A. Knopf, 1986.

Klein, Melanie. *Contributions to Psycho-Analysis: 1921–1945.* London: Hogarth Press, 1948.

——. *Envy and Gratitude.* London: Tavistock, 1957; NY: Delacorte, 1975.

——. *Narrative of a Child Psycho-Analysis.* London: Hogarth Press, 1961; NY: Delacorte, 1975.

——. *The Psycho-Analysis of Children.* London: Hogarth Press, 1932; NY: Delacorte, 1975.

Segal, Hanna. *Melanie Klein.* NY: Viking Press, 1979.

COLLECTIONS:

Personal papers of Melanie Klein under the control of the Melanie Klein Trust are located at the Wellcome Institute for the History of Medicine.

RELATED MEDIA:

Mrs. Klein (play), opened on Broadway in Autumn 1995, starring *Uta Hagen, **Laila Robins,** and **Amy Wright,** written by Nicholas Wright.

Suzanne Smith,
freelance writer and editor, Decatur, Georgia

Klemencia.

Variant of Clementia.

Klier-Schaller, Johanna (1952—)

East German runner. Born on September 13, 1952.

East Germany's Johanna Klier-Schaller won the gold medal in the Montreal Olympics in 1976 for the 100-meter hurdles. In Moscow in 1980, she took the silver in the same event.

Klimova, Rita (1931–1993)

Czech political dissident, and the first post-Communist ambassador of her country to the U.S. (1990–1992), who coined the term "Velvet Revolution" to describe the bloodless collapse of Marxism in Czechoslovakia in 1989. Name variations: Rita Budin. Born in Jasi, Rumania, on December 10, 1931; died in Prague on December 30, 1993; daughter of Stanislav Budin (a journalist whose real name was Batya Bat) and Hana Coifman Budin; married Zdenek Mlynar (divorced); married Zdenek Klima, in 1978; children: (first marriage) daughter, Milena (Michaela Barlova); son, Vladimir (Vladya).

Upon arriving in Washington to take up her diplomatic post as Czechoslovakia's first ambassador to the U.S. after the collapse of the Marxist dictatorship in 1989, Rita Klimova spoke idiomatic American English and felt perfectly at home. Seven of her most formative years had been spent in America, a nation which in 1939 provided refuge from Nazism for her family. Rita and her Ukrainian-born parents fled Prague for their lives after Nazi Germany occupied Bohemia and Moravia in March of that year. The risk to them in Prague was so great because they were Jewish, and because her father, a journalist who used the pen name of Stanislav Budin (his real name was Batya Bat), was a Communist and militant anti-fascist. Rita's mother **Hana Budin** was also a journalist and like her husband had been attracted to Communism by a youthful spirit of idealism during her student years.

The family settled down in Manhattan and Stanislav Budin resumed his journalistic career. Rita attended grade school and then went on to junior high school. Over the next few years, she became fluent in English as well as a willing participant in the process of Americanization. As a student in Manhattan public schools, she pledged allegiance to the flag, listened to Frank Sinatra records, ate hamburgers and hot dogs, and joined the Girl Scouts. An American cousin often took her to see the Rockettes perform at Radio City Music Hall. As she grew into her teens, Rita learned to use lipstick and nail polish by reading *Seventeen* magazine. Although her parents remained passionately involved in political affairs and followed news of World War II with great interest, Rita was not emotionally touched by the bloodshed in Europe. She reluctantly attended Russian War Relief concerts with her parents but much preferred going to Carnegie Hall to hear the Count Basie band and *Billie Holiday.

The defeat of Nazism in Europe in 1945 was a signal for the Budin family to return to Prague. As Communists, Stanislav and Hana Budin were pleased that Czechoslovakia now had a coalition government in which the Communist Party had a leading voice, and they looked forward to the building of Socialism in a nation closely allied to the victorious Soviet Union. Although Rita pleaded with her parents to remain in the United States, in 1946 she accompanied them back to Prague. Because her Czech language skills had seriously deteriorated, she was enrolled at a private English-language *Gymnasium* where many of the students came from conservative families. In an act that was largely a sign of adolescent rebelliousness, she organized a few other students to form a Communist cell. By 1948, when the Czech Communists seized power in a coup d'état, Rita had joined the Communist Party. She missed the actual bloodless putsch, however, because her class was away on a skiing trip.

During the next few years, she and her parents were devotees of the Czech Communist dictatorship of Klement Gottwald, a slavish Stalinist. As a true believer, Klimova uncritically admired Joseph Stalin, believing the Soviet dictator to be "crucial to everything, and great, of course." After graduating from high school, she went to work for a year as a lathe-turner in a factory making engines for Soviet MiG jet fighter planes, at the same time advancing in the Communist Party by becoming an officer in the party's youth organization.

Even though the spectre of anti-Semitism was raised in the bloody Prague purges of 1952, neither Rita nor her parents lost their faith in the ultimate validity of their Marxist ideals, and the family survived these dark days unscathed. Fortunately for her father, his earlier critical attitudes within the Czech Communist Party had been largely forgotten, and after 1945 he was no longer considered to be a person of influence (he had resigned as editor of the party newspaper *Rudé Pravo* in 1936 over an ideological dispute, but had never rejoined the party). For these and possibly other reasons, Stanislav Budin was neither arrested nor executed in 1952, as were more than a dozen other Czech Communists of Jewish origins.

Rita enrolled at the Prague School of Economics, where she dutifully earned first a master's degree and then a doctorate with a dissertation on the U.S. economy during the Great Depression of the 1930s. As a party loyalist (she would admit decades later that throughout the 1950s she had "swallowed the ideology hook, line and sinker"), she then received an academic appointment as an instructor in the history of economic thought at Prague's venerable Charles University. At this time, she married Zdenek Mlynar, an up-and-coming Communist intellectual like herself, who had been Mikhail Gorbachev's roommate while studying at Moscow State University. Soon they had a daughter Milena and a son Vladimir.

For more than a decade, the family enjoyed the perquisites of being members of Communist Czechoslovakia's ruling elite. Klimova ignored or argued away evidence of the system's failings, continuing to believe that Marxism as an ideology and the Soviet model in politics and economics were both "inevitable and correct." The first glimmer of doubt appeared on her intellectual horizon in the early 1960s, when it became clear that the Czechoslovak economy was starting to stagnate, a phenomenon that could not be explained in any Marxist textbook and could only be understood in terms of the ideas she had discovered while reading Western economic and social theorists.

The Warsaw Pact invasion of Czechoslovakia in August 1968, engineered by the Soviet Union, ended the brief experiment in liberalization known as the "Prague Spring." For Klimova, who had divorced her husband the year before, the 1968 invasion was the "biggest shock" of her life. At first, the so-called process of "normalization" moved slowly and did not affect her, because she had not been a major figure during the brief months of liberalization. Her belief, however, that she was too much the expert in her field of economics to be replaced proved wrong. In 1970, when the Charles University faculty was purged of its less than 100% reliable members, she was expelled from the party and lost her teaching job; in fact, her entire department was dissolved.

She expected to become a cashier in a self-service restaurant—a typical fate for many of

Prague's intellectuals. One of her former students, Jiri Dienstbier, the future minister of foreign affairs, lost his job as a radio journalist and had to support himself doing manual labor as a stoker. Rita, however, was somewhat more fortunate and finally found work in the accounting department of Charles University. She supplemented her income by working as a freelance English interpreter at medical conferences. It was her aged father's signing of the Charter 77 petition in 1977 that started the process which made Rita a dissident. Charter 77, with its demand that the Czech government respect fundamental human rights, brought forth repressive measures from the regime.

In 1978, Rita married Zdenek Klima (hence her last name of Klimova). Zdenek was a former diplomat who had been purged from the party, and both he and his new wife soon suffered from harassment and felt the cruelties of a regime out of touch with its own people. Not only was their house searched, but they were required to move into a smaller apartment and take several tests to qualify for new driver's licenses.

By 1980, both of Klimova's parents had died, and her husband died suddenly of a heart attack. Demoralized, she had little interest in politics, and, with increasingly harsh restraints by the regime, the Charter 77 dissident movement had been largely repressed. It was Rita Klimova's teenaged son Vladimir, known to all as Vladya, who got his mother out of the doldrums in the early 1980s. Denied access to higher education because of his parents' politics, he worked as a hospital orderly in the daytime and in the evenings as a driver for counterculture musicians and other dissidents. Through these contacts, Vladya became part of a clandestine courier network that smuggled from West Germany into Czechoslovakia various forbidden manuscripts and books. Often this material was divided up at Klimova's apartment into small packages that were less likely to arouse suspicion by the secret police and informers. Among the many customers who received Vladya's late-night deliveries was the dissident playwright Václav Havel.

By the end of the 1980s, Rita Klimova's apartment had become a regular meeting place for the Czech dissident movement. In 1986, she became a member of the Czechoslovak Helsinki Committee, reporting human-rights abuses. She also worked closely with an emerging circle of non-Marxist economists, the most important of whom would turn out to be Václav Klaus, who eventually became Czech prime minister after the collapse of Communism. She also emerged as an important contact for foreign journalists and Western human-rights activists when they came to Prague. Klimova and her fellow dissidents wrote numerous articles on social and economic themes for the underground *samizdat* press. With tongue in cheek, she frequently signed her contributions with the pseudonym "Adam Kovár"—Czech for Adam Smith. At the urging of her former student Jiri Dienstbier, Klimova served occasionally as an interpreter for leading dissident Václav Havel. Although essentially a cautious person—"I was not one for going to prison," she later noted—she rarely said no to a request, and almost inevitably found herself drawn more and more into the dissident apparatus.

In 1989, the facade of Communism crumbled throughout Eastern Europe, but until the final weeks of that year the hard-line Czechoslovak regime tenaciously held onto its power. On November 17, 1989, while the police were bloodily suppressing a huge student demonstration in Prague, Klimova was in a small town in Hungary

Rita Klimova

negotiating with two Czech exiles to buy a small offset-printing machine for an underground newspaper. Listening to Radio Free Europe, she was aware of the demonstrations taking place in Prague. On her arrival back in Prague on the evening of November 19, she found a message from Václav Havel requesting that she be at his apartment at 9:30 the next morning.

Arriving at Havel's apartment building, she found it strange that no police seemed to be present outside, only a large number of taxis. After climbing five flights of stairs, Klimova was out of breath when she rang the doorbell. Havel's brother pulled her winter coat off and pushed her into the living room, where she was confronted by press photographers and television crews. Blinded by the bright lights, all she could see was Václav Havel signaling her to translate the proceedings into English. Klimova translated Havel's announcement of the formation of Civic Forum, the anti-regime coalition that within a few weeks would bring about the end of the dictatorship. By the time the offset machine from Hungary arrived in Prague, it was no longer needed.

By the last days of December 1989, a bloodless upheaval ended Communist rule in Czechoslovakia. Rita Klimova coined the phrase "Velvet Revolution" to characterize the transformation that she had described so well to the English-speaking world during those dramatic weeks. Havel became the new president, with Jiri Dienstbier chosen as minister of foreign affairs. Klimova, exhausted by several weeks of nonstop work as a translator, looked forward to a relatively low-key job as a member of the staff of Valtr Komarek, an economic forecaster who became a deputy prime minister in the new government. But this was not to be. After she meet with Meda Mladek, a prominent Czechoslovak emigre from Washington, Mladek was so impressed by Klimova's skill at dealing with the public that he urged Dienstbier to name her to the crucially important post of ambassador to the United States. Klimova was delighted by the offer, noting that it took her "30 seconds to accept."

From February 1990 to August 1992, she served as Czechoslovak ambassador to the United States. Shortly after arriving in Washington, she was diagnosed with leukemia. Aggressive medical treatment delayed the ravages of the disease but did not bring about a cure. Despite her illness and lack of previous diplomatic experience, she worked tirelessly at her job, in the words of Václav Havel using "her special combination of charm and intelligence, tact and forthrightness [to] quickly [win] many friends and supporters for Czechoslovakia in the US. By the time she stepped down in August 1992, she had done much to enhance Czechoslovakia's place in the world, and to strengthen its good name." Despite her declining health, Rita Klimova remained active after her retirement as ambassador, lecturing on Czech and Central European affairs at several universities including Manhattan's New School for Social Research. She died in Prague on December 30, 1993.

SOURCES:

Adelman, Ken. "End of an Error," in *The Washingtonian.* Vol. 27, no. 3. December 1991, pp. 47, 50–53.

Havel, Václav. "On Rita Klímová (1931–1993)," in *The New York Review of Books.* Vol. 41, no. 3. February 3, 1994, p. 6.

Lyons, Richard D. "Rita Klimova, 62, Czech Dissident Who Became Ambassador to U.S.," in *The New York Times Biographical Service.* December 1993, p. 1785.

"Rita Klimova: Czechoslovakia's Ambassador to the United States," in *Europe: Magazine of the European Community.* November 1990, pp. 9–11.

Ungar, Sanford J. "Rita Klimova: Havel's Choice," in *The New York Times Biographical Service.* April 1990, pp. 313–316.

John Haag,
Associate Professor of History,
University of Georgia, Athens, Georgia

Klothilde.

Variant of Clotilde.

Klumpke, Anna Elizabeth (1856–1942).

See Bonheur, Rosa for sidebar.

Klumpke, Augusta (1859–1927).

See Klumpke, Dorothea for sidebar.

Klumpke, Dorothea (1861–1942)

First American woman astronomer to receive a Ph.D. Name variations: Dorothea Klumpke Roberts. Born Dorothea Klumpke on August 9, 1861, in San Francisco, California; died on October 5, 1942, in San Francisco; daughter of John Gerard Klumpke and Dorothea Matilda (Tolle) Klumpke; sister of Anna Elizabeth Klumpke (1856–1942), Augusta Klumpke (1859–1927), and Matilda and Julia Klumpke; attended public and private schools in San Francisco and Europe; University of Paris, B.S., mathematics and mathematical astronomy, 1886, Ph.D., 1893; married Isaac Roberts (1829–1904), on October 17, 1901; no children.

Awards: Prix des Dames, Societe Astronomique de France (1889); Officer of the Paris Academy of Sciences (1893); fellow, Royal Astronomical Society; Helene-Paul Helbronner prize, French Academy of Sciences (1932); Chevalier of the Legion of Honor (1934).

Attachée, Paris Observatory (1887–1901), Head, Bureau of Measurements, Paris Observatory (1891–1901); assistant to husband Isaac Roberts (1901–04); private research (1904–34).

Selected publications: Isaac Roberts Atlas of 52 Regions *(1929).*

Dorothea Klumpke epitomizes the pioneering woman astronomer of the late 19th and early 20th centuries. From balloon observations of the Perseids to her Ph.D. in Paris, Klumpke's life was filled with "firsts."

She was born on August 9, 1861, in San Francisco, California, to wealthy German immigrant John Klumpke and **Dorothea Tolle Klumpke**. Klumpke, the middle of five daughters, also had two brothers, one of whom died in infancy. John Klumpke had made a fortune in real estate and boot-making, and sent his wife and children to Europe around 1877 in order to secure their best possible education. The results were remarkable: the son became a businessman, and the daughters became a physician ❧▶ **Augusta Klumpke**, an artist ❧▶ **Anna Elizabeth Klumpke**, a pianist **Matilda Klumpke**, a violinist **Julia Klumpke**, and a famous astronomer (Dorothea). Dorothea studied mathematics and mathematical astronomy at the University of Paris and received her B.S. in 1886 and Ph.D. in 1893, the first awarded to a woman at that institution, and the first Ph.D. awarded to an American woman on an astronomical topic (the rings of Saturn).

Klumpke was hired as an attachée at the Paris Observatory and became involved with the International Congress of Astronomers' Carte du Ciel, a photographic star chart project. She was appointed the head of the Special Bureau of Measurements at the Observatory in 1891, and was responsible for charting and cataloguing stars down to the 14th magnitude. Her work earned her the first award of the Prix des Dames of the Societe Astronomique de France (1889), and she was named an Officer of the Paris Academy of Sciences (1893). Klumpke became widely known for her selection as the observer for a November 16, 1889, balloon flight for the Perseid meteor shower.

On October 17, 1901, she married famed Welsh amateur astronomer and nebular astrophotography pioneer Isaac Roberts and became his assistant at his observatory in Sussex, England. After his sudden death in 1904, Klumpke moved Roberts' plate collection to France and lived with her sister Anna while continuing his work on charting and cataloguing nebulae. She published a number of articles in the *Monthly Notices of the Royal Astronomical Society* and in 1929 published the *Isaac Roberts Atlas of 52 Regions: A Guide to William Herschel's Fields of Nebulosity*, with a supplement in 1932. For this work, she received the Helene-Paul Helbronner prize of the French Academy of Science in 1932.

𝒫erseveringly we labour, taking little heed to the cares of the morrow, knowing that astronomy, like spiritual understanding, bears within her her own blessings.
—Dorothea Klumpke

In 1934, Klumpke was elected Chevalier of the Legion of Honor and was presented with the Cross of the Legion by Albert Lebrun, president of France, for her 48 years of service to French astronomy. She then returned to San Francisco with her sister Anna and became a philanthropist, endowing prizes for young astronomers at the Paris Observatory and students at the University of California, and donating to the Lecture fund of the Astronomical Society of the Pacific. Upon Klumpke's death on October 5, 1942, the Astronomical Society of the Pacific received an additional endowment and created the Dorothea Klumpke Roberts Award for the popularization of astronomy; recipients have included Isaac Asimov and Carl Sagan. Dorothea Klumpke is mainly recognized through these generous gifts to further astronomy, although her own astronomical work contributed to the field in ways that alone should justify her remembrance.

❧
Klumpke, Anna Elizabeth. See *Bonheur, Rosa for sidebar.*

❧▶ **Klumpke, Augusta** (1859–1927)

*American doctor. Name variations: Augusta Dejerine or Déjerine. Born Augusta Klumpke in 1859; died in 1927; daughter of John Gerard Klumpke and Dorothea Matilda (Tolle) Klumpke; sister of *Anna Elizabeth Klumpke (1856–1942) and *Dorothea Klumpke (1861–1942); educated in Switzerland and Paris; married Joseph Jules Dejerine.*

Born in the United States in 1859, Augusta Klumpke studied in Switzerland and Paris because she could not gain admittance to medical school in America. While in Europe, she and **Blanche Edwards** secured appointments for postgraduate training. Augusta was granted a prize from the Academy of Medicine for her discovery of Klumpke palsy, a partial paralysis of the arm, caused by injury to the lower brachial plexus nerve. Augusta married Joseph Jules Dejerine and the couple wrote a book on nervous pathology.

SOURCES:

Aitken, Robert G. "Dorothea Klumpke Roberts—an Appreciation," in *Publications of the Astronomical Society of the Pacific*. Vol. LIV, no. 321. December 1942, p. 217–222.

Bracher, Katherine. "Dorothea Klumpke Roberts: A Forgotten Astronomer," in *Mercury*. Vol. X, no. 5. September–October 1981, p. 139–140.

*Hoffleit, Dorrit. *The Education of Women Astronomers Before 1960*. Cambridge, MA: AAVSO, 1994.

Reynolds, J.H. "Dorothea Klumpke Roberts," in *Monthly Notices of the Royal Astronomical Society*. Vol. CIV, no. 2, 1944, p. 92–93.

SUGGESTED READING:

Klumpke, Dorothea. "A Night in a Balloon," in *Century Magazine*. Vol. LX, 1900, p. 276–284.

———. "The Work of Women in Astronomy," in *Observatory*. Vol. XXII, 1899, p. 295–300.

Weitzenhoffer, Kenneth. "The Triumph of Dorothea Klumpke," in *Sky and Telescope*. Vol. LXXII, no. 2, 1986, p. 109–110.

Kristine Larsen,
Associate Professor of Astronomy and Physics,
Central Connecticut State University, New Britain, Connecticut

Knape, Ulrika (1955—)

Swedish diver. Born on April 26, 1955.

Ulrika Knape won the Olympic gold medal in platform diving in Munich in 1972; she also took home the silver in springboard. In 1976, she won a silver medal in platform at the Montreal Olympics.

Knatchbull, Patricia (b. 1924).

See Mountbatten, Patricia.

Knef, Hildegard (1925—)

Award-winning German-born actress, author, and singer who built an international stage and film career. Name variations: name spelled "Neff" during her film career. Pronunciation: Nef. Born Hildegard Frieda Albertina Knef on December 28, 1925, in Ulm, Germany; daughter of Hans Theodor Knef and Frieda Auguste Groehn Knef; attended Wilmersdorf Peoples (Grade) School and High School, as well as the acting school of the German Film Studio UFA; married Kurt Hirsch (divorced); married David Cameron; married Peter Rudolph Schell, in 1977; children: (second marriage) daughter Christina Cameron.

Appeared in German propaganda films (1945); acted on stage in first German postwar stage productions at the Schlossparktheater, Berlin (1945); appeared in first German postwar film, The Murderers among Us *(1946); auditioned in Hollywood (1947); became major German film star with her role in* The Sinner *(1950); played the female lead role in the Broadway production of Cole Porter's* Silk Stockings, *New York City (1955–56); sang the role of Jenny in the German film of* The Three Penny Opera *(1962); began career as a night-club singer (1963). Prizes include the Bundesfilmpreis (1959 and 1977); the Edison Prize (1972); the Karlsbad film festival prize for best female role (1976); and the Golden Tulip award at the Amsterdam film festival (1981).*

Selected writings: The Gift Horse: Report on a Life *(translated from the German by David Palastanga, NY: McGraw-Hill, 1971);* The Verdict *(translated by Palastanga, NY: Farrar, Straus, 1975).*

"It has been my fate always to wander in new realms," Hildegard Knef wrote in 1970. Coming to adulthood during Nazi rule in her native Germany and surviving Allied bombings that destroyed her family's homes three times, Knef overcame the chaos and destruction of postwar Germany to create a career as an international stage and film actress. Her multilingual acting talents were showcased in German, French, British, and American films. Eventually, she added singing and writing to her repertoire, becoming a singing actress in an American musical comedy, as well as an internationally known author.

Knef did not remember her father, who died six months after her birth, though she was told that he was a "big, wild, restless, and red-haired man." He had served in the German army during World War I and fought in the battle of Verdun. She described her mother **Frieda Knef**, who was often absent because she worked to support the family, as "very beautiful, with the loveliest longest legs, greenest eyes—slender, tough, powerful, fearless." Knef remembered that she had a "lovely clear voice" but had not become a singer because there was not enough money for training or even to "go around begging for a scholarship."

As a child, Knef stayed much of the time at the farm of her maternal grandfather in eastern Germany—"really a glorified shack," she wrote, "with four rooms and a stove where we put the chicks at night to keep them warm." She also tied her pet goat to the bed post. Although her mother did not approve, Knef was allowed to run around "half naked," except during her mother's frequent visits.

In order to spend more time with her daughter, Frieda left her job with the Siemens Electrical Company and opened her own tobacco shop in Berlin, taking Knef with her. Hildegard later wrote that her mother changed to a candy shop after she realized that many of her male customers came to the shop only to see her, often tossing their newly purchased cigars into the street outside. When Frieda Knef remarried, to a shoe-repair man, the family moved to a shop near the Wilmersdorf railway station in Berlin.

Although Knef saw less and less of her grandfather, who was estranged from her stepfather for a time, both grandfather and stepfather impressed on Knef their dislike for the new Nazi government of Germany. She remembered her grandfather's saying that "the idiots should have done something in '33" (a reference to the Nazi accession to power) and, later, "we would have to pay for the death of the Jews." She was disappointed when, after she drew "Hitler is nuts" in sand, her stepfather forbade her to make any more such drawings. But when she came home from school and announced that she wanted to join the girl's branch of the Hitler youth, she was surprised to find her grandfather, stepfather, and mother all refusing to give her permission to do so. Her stepfather eventually joined the Nazi Party, but when asked to make a voluntary financial contribution to the faction, he thought a moment and then placed a one-mark piece (with a value of less than a dollar) on the table. Because of this, he lost his shop and had to search for a new one.

Knef was educated in schools where the students were subjected to a constant barrage of Nazi propaganda. She disliked both the teacher who began school by screaming "Heil Hitler" and the requirement that pupils study racial history and write essays on the theme, "I am Nordic because. . . ." When a teacher spoke of defending the Fatherland, Knef was disciplined for asking which country Germany should defend itself against, since it had not been attacked.

Gestapo arrests of other families in her neighborhood left a deep impression on Knef. In one case, a woman tried to escape across the roof and fell to her death. In another, members of a Jewish family were arrested despite their attempts to "appease" the government, such as their hanging of a swastika from their window on Hitler's birthday and the care with which the wife bleached her hair.

Upon graduation from high school, Hildegard was enrolled by her mother in a business school so that she would not have to do farm work for the national Labor Exchange. Knef was interested in working as a commercial artist, however, and showed samples of her drawings to a Labor Exchange official. She was sent to UFA, a major German film studio, where she worked as a studio artist and began attending the studio's acting school. The woman who hired her, **Else Bongers** of the Berlin film office, would be a lifelong friend. While at UFA, Knef was also required to work in a factory, where she painted the luminous instrument dials on German nightfighter aircraft.

Hildegard Knef began working on the other side of the camera when her beauty caught the eye of a UFA director, who decided to use her in two of his wartime propaganda movies. In her memoirs, she reported that propaganda minister Joseph Goebbels, the "patron of the film industry" and a notorious womanizer, invited her to dinner "privately, in order to get to know me personally," but that Bongers protected her by insisting that she was unavailable.

Wartime film work was hectic and difficult, though filming continued during the constant bombing by Allied planes. Knef's family replaced bombed-out windows of their home with cardboard, but still had to move three times. Two Hitler youth used one of their houses to fight Russian troops; Knef's grandfather, who escaped from the burning house but was badly burned, eventually committed suicide during the war, leaving a note saying that he could not "forget the horrors." Although Knef saw her mother infrequently and often worried about her safety, the two would be reunited at the end of the war.

The great film stars . . . were the . . . indomitables whom no make up, costume, or character could change and whose mystery was wrapped in an incorruptibility which only the camera was capable of measuring.

—Hildegard Knef

As Polish and Russian troops moved into the eastern section of Germany in 1945, Knef, attempting to flee, was convinced to join the German army by a 36-year-old soldier named Ewald Demandowsky, a fervent Nazi. Sporting a rifle and a grenade, she hid her hair under a hat, so that fellow soldiers did not know at first that she was a woman. She shot two enemy soldiers while in the middle of the fighting and saw two young German soldiers run over by a tank. She also fell in love with Demandowsky. Although the first lieutenant of their unit refused to marry them as they requested, Knef later referred to the period they were together as a "honeymoon." Captured and closely questioned by Polish and Russian soldiers, they were separated. Demandowsky, believing that Knef was endangered by her relationship to him, smuggled a note to her, telling her to flee, if possible, to the Berlin home of Viktor de Kowa, a filmmaker.

Knef's arrival at the Kowa house, which was in the American zone of occupation, proved fortuitous. Because Kowa was no sympathizer with Nazism, and because his wife knew one of the American generals occupying the area, he was able to vouch for Knef, who was being questioned by American authorities about her relationship with Demandowsky. Kowa was also able to convince occupation authorities to allow him to reopen playhouses in Berlin. To Knef's surprise, Bongers also vouched for her; Bongers revealed that her husband, an anti-Nazi, had fled Germany in the 1930s, but that the Nazi government had required Bongers to remain behind as a guarantee of her husband's silence.

At the start of the occupation, as Knef began appearing on the Berlin stage, authorities allowed her to travel within the country; she also began a career in postwar German film. "I busied myself with a fresh outbreak of dysentery and concentrated on the only thing I have ever really learned: survival, which now offered itself in the form of theater," she said. Her stage career in Germany was notable enough that among her visitors backstage was the distinguished conductor Wilhelm Furtwangler, whose presence left her speechless. Thus began a theater career of more than ten plays.

Knef also began a relationship with Kurt Hirsch, a Czech who had immigrated to the United States and now regularly visited postwar Berlin on business. Hirsch invited her to accompany him to see a film being shown in the Russian sector of postwar Berlin; it turned out to be photographs of Auschwitz. "I wanted to talk the picture away," she wrote, "wanted to hear that it wasn't true, wanted to think instead" of the German soldiers she had seen run over by a tank. At that point Hirsch told her, "I lost 12 relatives [in the Holocaust]." Although her official biographies in reference works do not list him as a husband, she has written in her memoirs that Hirsch began to help guide her career and eventually became her husband. When a German secretary criticized her for marrying a Jew, she replied, "Hold your tongue, you stupid cow." But she wrote that his family was not happy with the marriage, and they were later divorced.

Knef began to gather awards and international attention for her performances. While she was shooting exteriors in the desolation of postwar Berlin, a *Life* magazine photographer took a series of pictures of her which appeared under the theme "German girl makes good in the ruins of Berlin," and though she did not know it, her early films drew the attention of Hollywood. In 1947, the American producer David Selznick asked her to come to Hollywood for screen tests. Although Hirsch went along, helping her with the American press and American culture, the trip was a disaster. She refused to change her name to "Gilda Christian," although she later agreed to the new Anglicized form of her name, "Neff." (Even later in life, she stumbled over Neff and could not get used to it. She changed back to "Knef" in the late 1960s.) She refused to tell the American press that she was Austrian rather than German. When she reminded studio representatives that "Hitler was an Austrian," they replied, "but most Americans do not know that."

Studio executives were also unhappy with her outspokenness; she once remarked, "If the Nazis had been only half as dumb as they were portrayed [in American films], the thousand year Reich would have lasted a week." Knef refused to conform to studio heads' ideas of proper behavior for an actress and rebelled against advice on how she should behave. (Caught hurrying from one studio building to another, she was told, "A lady does not run.") "Especially in America," she later wrote, ". . . a man was never a woman's friend nor ever will be, [and] . . . the man-woman conflict has been retained and nurtured from the pioneer era and has led to an insurmountable rift, a setting of limits. . . . If in my conversations with American men, I went beyond the accepted giggling stage, they became suspicious and frightened and took me for a dangerous bluestocking who did not observe the rules, a busybody who might ask about politics or even money."

The studio offered no contract, and she returned to Germany feeling that she had failed. But this visit to Hollywood, and subsequent trips, left her with vivid impressions of some of the stars and filmmakers of the era. The director Billy Wilder struck her as "the embodiment of all that I held to be desirable at the time: a conqueror of the New World." She noted the mistreatment of *Marilyn Monroe by others, but added, "The camera loved her. The camera registered the honesty, candor, and naivete which disarmed the audiences and made her a star after a few appearances in mostly bad films." But her sharpest portrait was of *Marlene Dietrich, who took the younger Knef under her wing. Knef saw Dietrich as a regal figure surrounded by sycophants, a woman who sometimes wore her Legion of Honor with her formal clothes, and one whose silence could terrorize.

Upon her return to Germany, Knef appeared in *Film without a Name* (1948) before making her breakthrough motion picture, *The Sinner* (1950). In the movie, Knef portrayed a woman who turned to prostitution at the end of the war, quit, and then returned to prostitution to pay for an operation. Although the film gained a prize at the Berlin film festival, it also received condemnation from Catholic prelates. In Knef's words, the film brought her "illustrated proposals from sex maniacs and attacks from the pulpit."

Yet *The Sinner* returned her to the attention of studio executives in other countries, launching her into a multilingual acting career that would span more than 35 movies made by studios in four countries—France, Great Britain, Germany, and the United States. Although she never reached the level of top film "star," she compiled a series of firsts: she was in Germany's first postwar film, *The Murderers among Us* (1946); she was the first German woman to appear in a Paris film production after the war (1948): and, as she acknowledged with a laugh, she was the first actress to appear nude in a postwar German film. She was lured back to the American cinema by the film *Decision before Dawn* (1951); at first she rejected the film, until

Hildegard Knef

talked into it by director Anatole Litvak. During her second Hollywood period, she also appeared in the film adaptation of Ernest Hemingway's *The Snows of Kilimanjaro* (1952), co-starring Gregory Peck and *Susan Hayward.

Knef had an international lifestyle as well. She became an American citizen during the 1950s but changed to British citizenship in 1962 when she married a British citizen, David Cameron. She lived for various periods in several countries, including Great Britain. Knef believed that for much of her career she was treated with special hostility by the German press, partly because of the "immoral image" she was given by some of her films and partly because, as an international actress, she was suspected of not being German enough. After one particular round of hostile stories in the German press, a friend told Knef, "not even Hitler himself would get such bad reviews."

Knef was able to pursue her acting career despite almost constant medical problems. Added to a childhood battle with polio were adult bouts of hepatitis. After her daughter Christina was born by cesarean section in 1968, peritonitis set in, and Knef had to undergo numerous operations to correct resulting problems. In 1973, she would deal with a diagnosis of breast cancer.

During the 1950s, Knef added singing to her career. Despite daunting obstacles, she accepted a role in Cole Porter's 1955 Broadway musical *Silk Stockings*. She would have to sing nightly; speak clear and understandable English, but with a Russian accent; and risk comparison with *Greta Garbo, who had played the same role (as a Russian commissar) in the 1939 film *Ninotchka*. To make matters worse, during the run of the musical, Knef was mistakenly diagnosed with leukemia. Yet her performance in *Silk Stockings* was so widely praised that one critic labeled her "the thinking man's Marlene Dietrich."

Knef expanded her singing career by accepting the role of Jenny in the 1962 German film of *The Three Penny Opera*. In 1963, she began a new career as a nightclub singer, both in Europe and the United States. She wrote the lyrics to many of the wry and ironic songs she sang. After a highly successful tour with a five-man combo, she set out again with a big-band accompaniment and her husband as producer. Their daughter, only six months old when they started, often was taken along on the tours. The songs Knef sang are called *chansons* in Europe—in her words, "little stories where the lyric is more important than the music, [with the] melody . . .

serving the word." Out of her singing career came a large number of recordings.

Starting in 1970, Knef, who settled in Munich, also built an international career as a writer, including a book about the actress *Romy Schneider. Some of the most highly praised of her writings were her books of memoirs, particularly *The Gift Horse* (the original German version appeared in 1970) and *The Verdict* (1975). Praised for their frankness and sophisticated literary style—critics referred to them as "literature"—the books sold more than three million copies. Translated into more than 15 languages, they dealt with her early life, the birth of her daughter, and her constant hospitalizations, including the diagnosis of breast cancer. Her last film, *Checkpoint Charlie*, was released in 1980.

SOURCES:

Knef, Hildegard. *The Gift Horse: Report on a Life.* Translated by David Palastanga. NY: McGraw-Hill, 1971.

———. *Tournee, Tournee . . .* Munich: Goldman Verlag, 1980.

———. *The Verdict.* Translated by David Palastanga. NY: Farrar, Straus, and Giroux, 1975.

SUGGESTED READING:

Angst-Nowik, Doris. *One-Way Ticket to Hollywood: Film Artists of Austrian and German Origin in Los Angeles.* Los Angeles, CA: University of Southern California Library, 1986.

Ragan, David. *Who's Who in Hollywood: The Largest Cast of International Personalities Ever Assembled.* NY: Facts on File, 1992.

Wollenberg, H. *Fifty Years of German Film.* NY: Arno Press, 1972.

Niles Holt,
Professor of History, Illinois State University, Normal, Illinois

Knep, Mrs. (fl. 1670).

See Knipp, Mrs.

Knight, Laura (1877–1970)

Prolific English painter whose work stressed realistic portrayals of women, Gypsies, and circus performers, as well as scenes of Britain during World War II.

Name variations: Dame Laura Knight. Born Laura Johnson on August 4, 1877, in the town of Long Eaton, Derbyshire, England; died in London on July 7, 1970; third daughter of Charles Johnson and Charlotte Bates Johnson (an art teacher); attended Nottingham School of Art, 1890–94; married Harold Knight, on June 3, 1903 (died 1961); no children.

Father deserted family before her birth (1877); moved with family to live with her grandmother in Nottingham (1879); settled briefly in France (1889); won Princess of Wales scholarship (1894); settled in Staithes (1895); exhibited painting Mother and Child *at Royal Academy (1903); made trip to Holland (1906); settled in Newlyn (1907); moved to London and began studies of backstage life at the ballet (1919); made extended trip to the U.S. (1926); elected as associate to Royal Academy (1927); named Dame Commander of the British Empire (1929); toured with the circus (1930); made full member of Royal Academy (1936); witnessed Nuremberg War Crimes Trial (1946); retrospective exhibit of her work at Royal Academy (1965).*

Paintings: Self-Portrait *(Sotheby's, London, 1892–94);* Dressing the Children *(Ferens Art Gallery, Hull, 1906);* The Beach *(Laing Art Gallery, Newcastle-upon-Tyne, 1908);* The Green Feather *(National Gallery of Canada, Ottawa, 1911);* Self Portrait with Nude *(National Portrait Gallery, London, 1913);* The Penzance Fair *(private collection, 1916);* Two Girls on the Cliff *(Sotheby's, London, 1917);* Susie and the Wash-basin *(Harris Museum and Art Gallery, Preston, 1929);* Three Clowns *(Leicester Museums and Art Gallery, 1930);* A Ballet Dancer *(Nottingham Castle Museum, 1932);* A Gypsy *(Tate Gallery, London, 1938–39);* A Balloon Site, Coventry, *and* Ruby Loftus Screwing a Breech-ring *(Imperial War Museum, London, 1943);* The Dock *and* Nuremberg *(Imperial War Museum, London, 1946);* The Yellow Dress *(Worcester City Museum and Art Gallery, 1948).*

Etchings: Make-up *(Belgrave Gallery, London, 1925);* Three Graces of the Ballet *(Belgrave Gallery, London, 1926);* Zebras *(Laing Art Gallery, Newcastle-upon-Tyne, 1930).*

Laura Knight was one of the first prominent English women artists of the 20th century. At a time when the full curriculum of art schools was reserved for men, she broke through barriers with her talent, boundless energy, and ebullient personality. In the artistic world of the early decades of the century, writes biographer **Caroline Fox,** "she was extremely isolated and very much a pioneer." With such circumstances around her, Knight produced a body of work that was well-drawn and often brilliantly colored.

Knight's artistic training and her own inclinations separated her from the advanced artistic techniques on the Continent such as Cubism and Futurism. She clung throughout most of her career to a technique that emphasized colorful, dramatic, but realistic portrayals of the people around her. While her interests were wide-ranging, Knight had particular success in her depiction of girls and young women. She had no interest in probing deeply into the personalities of the subjects of her paintings, nor, with the exception

of her paintings during World war II, was she interested in expressing in her art the turmoil in the social and political world around her. "Her naturally extroverted personality and love of being in the limelight," as Fox has noted, "did not allow of much inner searching," while she was deeply influenced by "anxieties about money and memories of a childhood of deprivation."

Locked into an apparently passionless marriage with fellow artist Harold Knight, Laura Knight in the view of some critics put her sexual energies into her painting; many of her female nudes, for example, are vibrantly erotic. On the other hand, her works were so accessible to a broad public that some critics saw them as superficial. As one critic put it on the occasion of a major exhibition of her work in 1939, "This exhibition does not represent the apex of contemporary pictorial achievement in England." In his view, shared by others throughout her career, "Laura Knight paints jolly subjects in a fine, fresh, hefty way, but there is no intellectual stamp upon her work."

She wished to be remembered as the painter of modern life, and it is indeed the most consistent theme running through the wide range of subjects and styles she touched on in eighty years of painting.

—David Phillips

The future painter faced years of difficult circumstances in her youth and girlhood. Her father deserted her family shortly before Laura's birth in Long Eaton near the English city of Nottingham on August 4, 1877; he had married her mother because he was impressed by the fact that her family owned a lace factory. Upon learning that the factory was not profitable, Charles Johnson soon lost interest in both his marriage and the daughters he fathered. In 1877, by most accounts, he deserted the family for good, although some authors suggest it was his wife who left him. In either case, **Charlotte Bates Johnson**, a determined and energetic woman with a talent for art, was left alone to fend for herself and to care for the couple's three daughters. In 1879, she moved her fractured family to the Nottingham home of Laura's grandmother.

Despite her mother's efforts to care for them by teaching art in a girls' school and giving private art lessons, Laura and her sisters grew up in poverty. Nonetheless, their indefatigable mother encouraged all the girls to become interested in art, and Laura, most of all, shared Charlotte's enthusiasm. Even as a young child, according to biographer **Laura Dunbar**, Knight produced drawings that were "not scrawls but recognizable shapes of objects in the house," and the other members of her family recognized her remarkable talents.

In 1883, when Laura was only six, her mother received word that Charles Johnson, the husband who had left in 1877, had died. The news caused barely a ripple in the family to which he was a stranger. A more important development was the instruction in art and the painting expeditions that Charlotte provided for all three daughters, with Laura, as usual, showing the greatest interest and promise.

Knight went to study art in France in 1889 when she was only 12, but the family's ill fortune continued. Her sister Nell died, and her grandmother became sick as well, and Laura was forced to return to England. There she continued in her role as art student, beginning a productive period from 1890 to 1894 working at the Nottingham School of Art. Once again tragedy struck; in 1892, her mother became fatally ill with cancer. Thereafter, while still a student taking classes at night, Laura at the age of 16 had to claim to be an adult as she took on her mother's teaching responsibilities to help support the family.

The young woman's artistic ambitions were partially blocked by the educational conventions of the time. Women were not permitted to participate in the life-drawing classes open to male students, and she came to believe that her technique suffered for years thereafter as a result. On the other hand, she found a close friend and artistic confidant in Harold Knight, a talented fellow student at the art school. She received another boost to her ambitions when in 1894 she won the Princess of Wales scholarship, giving her a modest sum for two years. This allowed her to leave the school and to strike out on her own.

From the mid-1890s to 1918, the painter worked in two very different coastal towns. In 1895, she settled in Staithes, a small fishing village on the Yorkshire coast north of Whitby, where there was a small colony of artists. Laura supported herself by giving lessons to visiting students and through a small subsidy from her family. She concentrated on painting the seafarers and other villagers of Staithes along with views of the sea. A depressing feature of life at Staithes was the constant danger the weather posed to the village's fishing vessels, and she found the steady loss of life, with dead bodies and wrecked boats washed upon the shore, emotionally draining.

In these years, Laura Johnson remained the close companion of Harold Knight, and, in 1903, after seven years of working together at Staithes, they were married. That same year, her painting received its greatest recognition to date. A work she had done at Staithes, *Mother and Child,* was accepted for exhibition at the Royal Academy, the first time she had received this distinction. That piece of encouragement was soon augmented by the news that the painting had quickly been sold for £20. When Harold earned the princely sum of £100 for one of his paintings in 1906, the couple took the money and spent it on an extended stay to study the masterworks in Holland and to paint scenes of the countryside there.

In 1907, the Knights moved to the fishing town and artists' colony of Newlyn in Cornwall. Newlyn was a more active art center than Staithes, and its painters worked under the strong influence of the Impressionist school in France. Moreover, the area in Cornwall where it was located offered a pleasant climate. As Fox notes, "It was during the ten years spent in Cornwall (1907–18) that Laura's style reached maturity." Unlike Staithes, Newlyn offered an active social life based upon its lively gathering of artists, and Laura plunged into these activities with great enthusiasm. Harold, whose shy personality stood in marked contrast to that of his wife, held back from the spirited parties and other gatherings that typified these group activities. "Both the Knights were now well established," writes Dunbar, "sending pictures up to the Leicester Galleries [in London] and also selling them in Penzance [near Newlyn]."

During these years at Newlyn, Laura Knight's work took on some of the characteristics that were to mark her entire mature career. She adopted a palette of extremely bright colors, and she concentrated on painting individuals, often in a physical background marked by great beauty. Thus her picture of 1908 entitled *The Beach* featured a number of young girls playing on the sand, and *The Boys,* completed in 1910, showed male youngsters in a similar setting. Spectacular scenery became increasingly prominent in her paintings as she became more interested in the coast of Cornwall; *On the Cliff* and *Two Girls on the Cliff,* both finished around 1917, show two women on promontories above the ocean. Hiring female models from London who were willing to pose in the nude, Knight shocked the locals by painting these women as they modeled in public on the beaches and the adjoining rocks.

Both her professional and commercial reputations grew. *The Beach* and *The Boys,* as well as a third work entitled *Flying a Kite,* were also exhibited at the Royal Academy, and she found customers willing to pay handsomely for her work. A lush painting of a woman, finished in 1911 and named after the most prominent article of her clothing, *The Green Feather,* went to the National Gallery of Canada for £400.

The war years from 1914 to 1918 transformed Knight's life in a number of ways. Harold became a conscientious objector, and he was forced to work as an agricultural laborer in Cornwall. Laura found her favorite painting locales along the coast barred to her by military restrictions, and she and Harold moved to an inland town. She acted to evade the wartime measures by sneaking off and hiding in bushes near the sea long enough to make the sketches she needed; then she rushed home to do the corresponding painting. Despite her involvement in such escapades and her resentment at the restrictions on her movement, she accepted a generous commission from the Canadian government to paint a large picture of Canadian troops in their training camp in Surrey.

From 1919 onward, the Knights lived in London. Laura increasingly tried to look the part of the flamboyant woman artist; she ignored the fashion of the time to wear her blonde hair thickly coiled atop her head, and she favored brightly colored dresses and peasant blouses. In time, she would adopt a broad-brimmed straw hat and cloak as her personal emblems.

Knight's work continued to focus on individuals in interesting settings, now in locales like the backstage of the ballet and the dressing rooms of its dancers. Her longstanding interest in dance impelled her to ask permission to paint the dance world behind the scenes. As she came to know leading ballerinas like *Lydia Lopokova, Laura Knight gained increased access to dressing rooms as well as permission to draw dancers in various informal poses. She now overcame, by a combination of innate skill and extensive practice, her earlier deficiencies in sketching the human body. Her friendship with the theatrical magnate Sir Barry Jackson gave her comparable access to the world behind the scenes of the legitimate stage.

Fragment of The Dressing Room by Laura Knight.

An increasingly prominent member of the art world, Knight received an invitation from America's Carnegie Institute of Pittsburgh to visit the United States in 1922. The trip proved stimulating, and she was encouraged to accompany her husband for a second and longer trip across the Atlantic in 1926 when Harold received a commission to do paintings in Baltimore. She immersed herself in painting new subjects, such as members of the black population in the segregated wards of a city hospital.

During the 1920s, Knight gained some notable honors, while Harold's income as a portrait painter and her own sales gave the couple an increasing measure of financial stability. But her spreading fame put his own success in the shadows, and, according to Dunbar, there were further strains on the marriage due to his occasional strong attraction to other women. Writes Fox, "He inevitably found it difficult to cope with her success," even though she told family members that he was by far a greater artist than she. Knight gave frequent radio and newspaper interviews, and in 1927 found her career adorned when she was named an associate of the Royal Academy, only the second woman to receive such recognition in the 20th century. Harold received the same honor in 1928. But once again his wife outshone him: in 1929, she was named Dame Commander of the British Empire. Harold was apparently unwilling to escort her to the ceremony, and she was accompanied by Barry Jackson.

Meanwhile, her interests and enthusiasm flowed into studies of the circus. In 1930, she even joined one circus company as it toured central England. Her pictures of circus performers backstage, including her memorable *Three Clowns* from 1930, show Knight capturing the exotic energy of the circus troupe and the personalities of its performers. She also demonstrated her versatility with a continuing flow of powerful pictures of women and young girls. These ranged from intimate views of women, such as the nude *Blue and Gold* of 1927 and the partially dressed figure in *A Cottage Bedroom* done around 1929, to the striking portrayal of a young girl gazing confidently at the viewer in *Susie and the Wash-basin* from 1929. In Fox's view, these years of the late 1920s "coincided with the peak of her [artistic] achievements." Thereafter, according to Fox, the development of Knight's talent slowed.

In any case, her desire to extend her range of subjects into new areas continued during the decade of the 1930s. Friends suggested that the horse races might be another interesting locale, but on her visits to centers like Epsom she became acquainted with the Gypsies (Roma) who were a part of the race-track scene. She then visited Gypsy camps, persuaded members to pose for her, and produced such colorful works as *Romanies at Epsom* and *Gaudy Beggars,* both completed around 1938.

An important event in Knight's career in the 1930s was election to full membership in the Royal Academy in 1935. As usual, her husband lagged behind, receiving the honor in 1937. She took pride in the fact that she was only the second woman to receive this distinction, worked hard in helping to administer the Academy, and became uncomfortably involved in quarrels when the Academy offended the artistic community. She was estranged for a time from an old acquaintance, Augustus John, for example, when he protested against the Academy's decision not to accept a modern painting by Wyndham Lewis. That same year, an injury to her foot forced her into an extended convalescence; she used the time to write her autobiography, published the next year as *Oil Paint and Grease Paint.* It received mixed reviews, some critics finding the book too reticent to reveal anything about her inner struggles as an artist. The reviewer for the *Manchester Guardian,* however, was enthusiastic, advising, "he will be a dull reader who does not feel . . . that he has not only followed the varying fortunes of a remarkable artist but has also watched the development and unfolding of a great personality."

Laura Knight's greatest moment of popular esteem came during the years of World War II. Commissioned by the government's War Artists' Advisory Commission, she became a familiar sight at Britain's factories and military bases. Although she was in her 60s when the war broke out, she proved able to work in daunting physical conditions. Many of her most popular war subjects were portraits of women in the armed forces and pictures of factory workers and air crews doing their jobs. The clarity and color of her style was perfectly matched to the public's wartime tastes. Her morale-boosting work benefited from her ability to capture the precise detail of military and industrial equipment. At the same time, a less attractive feature of her work as an artist came forth: her concern about the level of her earnings. Fearful as always of sinking back into the poverty that had dogged her childhood and early years as a painter, she insisted on being paid a fee not too distant from the high commissions that she had enjoyed before the war.

Her work was worth the price for the government's War Office. She painted women crews taking care of the barrage balloons that helped protect crucial areas of the British Isles against air attack. What became her most famous wartime painting showed a talented young woman factory worker, **Ruby Loftus**, using her newly acquired machinist's skill to perform a crucial operation at the Royal Ordnance Factory. Since Ruby Loftus could not be spared from her work, Knight did the portrait in the dangerous setting of the factory. During one sitting, a loose wheel fell from an overhead conveyor belt down on the artist and her work; she instinctively threw herself forward to protect her painting, and the wheel missed her by a few inches.

Knight herself took the initiative in requesting an assignment to paint the war crimes trials at Nuremberg after the cessation of hostilities. She wrote to the Secretary of the War Artists' Advisory Committee that it would be "a pity for such an event to go unrecorded, and I feel that artistically it should prove exciting." Dispatched to Nuremberg, she lived in the shattered German city for three months in early 1946. Although Knight was deeply depressed by her surroundings, nonetheless she produced a striking picture that consisted mainly of the German defendants in the dock. At the work's top and left side, however, she pulled down the walls of the courtroom to show the physical devastation and the heaped corpses that she considered the essence of the German reality.

The aging artist continued to work steadily in the postwar years. She turned much of her energy to painting landscape scenes drawn from her country home in Worcestershire. Concerned as always about her earnings, she was disappointed to find that her works were out of style and no longer able to command top prices from buyers. Her health began to fail, and disease hindered her ability to hold a palette and brush. She found herself alone to face the problems of advancing age when Harold Knight died in 1961.

In 1965, she published a second autobiographical volume, *The Magic of a Line*. That same year, the Royal Academy gathered 250 of her paintings to honor her with an important retrospective exhibition of her works. The paintings, drawn from all the periods of her six decades of artistic production, constituted the largest assembly of her paintings ever achieved. But she approached the showing with trepidation, fearing that her work would received a hostile reception from the critics of the 1960s. In some cases this was true, and she had to read

new accusations that her work was superficial and vulgar.

Five years later, the Castle Museum in Nottingham, her childhood home, planned another gathering of her work, but it was one that Laura Knight did not live to attend. She died at age 93 in London, July 7, 1970, the day preceding the exhibit's opening.

SOURCES:

Dunbar, Janet. *Laura Knight*. London: Collins, 1971.

Fox, Caroline. *Dame Laura Knight*. Oxford: Phaidon, 1988.

Grimes, Teresa, Judith Collins, and Oriana Baddeley. *Five Women Painters*. Oxford: Lennard, 1989.

Knight, Dame Laura. *The Magic of a Line*. London: William Kimber, 1965.

———. *Oil Paint and Grease Paint*. London: Ivor Nicholson and Watson, 1936.

SUGGESTED READING:

Cole, Margaret. *Women of Today*, 1938 (reprint, Freeport, NY: Books for Libraries Press, 1968).

Foot, M.R.D. *Art and War: Twentieth Century Warfare as Depicted by War Artists*. London: Headline, 1990.

Harries, Meirion and Susie. *The War Artists*. London: Michael Joseph, 1983.

Neil M. Heyman,
Professor of History,
San Diego State University, San Diego, California

Knight, Margaret E. (1838–1914).

See The Inventors for sidebar.

Knight, Sarah Kemble (1666–1727)

Colonial diarist who provided an invaluable account of New England in the 18th century. Born Sarah Kemble on April 19, 1666, in Boston, Massachusetts; died on September 25, 1727, in New London, Connecticut; first daughter and second or third of five or six children of Thomas Kemble (a merchant) and Elizabeth (Trerice) Kemble; married Richard Knight, sometime before 1689; children: Elizabeth Knight (b. 1689).

Described by author **Hannah Mather Crocker** as "a smart, witty, sensible woman," Sarah Kemble Knight is remembered for her daring horseback journey from Boston to New York and back during the fall and winter of 1704–05. The diary of her travels, *The Journal of Madam Knight*, was first published posthumously in 1825, although it was some time before the author's identity was established. The diary has gone through numerous editions and provides an invaluable account of the early 18th century southern New England landscape and the customs and manners of the American colonists who lived there.

Knight was born in Boston, Massachusetts, in 1666, one of five or six children of Thomas, a merchant, and **Elizabeth Trerice Kemble**, the daughter of a shipmaster. Nothing is known of Sarah's childhood. Her marriage to Richard Knight (a bricklayer and carver by one account, a ship's captain by another, and an agent for a London business by yet a third) was not recorded, but was known to have occurred before her father's death in 1689. The couple had one daughter, Elizabeth, born on May 8, 1689. Records indicate that Knight resided on Moon Street in Boston, where she ran a shop and also took in boarders (possibly relatives). Frequent accounts that she founded a school attended by Benjamin Franklin are difficult to verify.

Knight set out on the journey chronicled in her diary on October 2, 1704, presumably to take care of business or family matters. Although a trip of this kind was unheard of for a woman of her day, there were apparently no objections voiced by her husband (absent from Boston at the time of her journey), her teenage daughter, or her "aged and tender mother." Her diary entries record daily rides from dawn to dusk and include all manner of harrowing experiences involving icy rivers and rickety bridges ("Buggbears to a fearful female travailer"), as well as accounts of each day's lodging, food, and encounters with the local inhabitants, who were not always hospitable. As **Doris Weatherford** reveals, Knight's diary is marked by keen wit and good humor, as when she had difficulty in getting potential guides to leave the tavern, "they, being tyed by the Lipps to a pewter engine." In addition to observations of societal mannerisms, Knight recorded information about business and economy, architecture, and transportation systems in the various colonies she visited. On a snowy stretch between New York and New Haven, for example, she saw "50 or 60 slays . . . so furious that they'le turn out of the path for none except a Loaden Cart." The diary concludes with her safe return to Boston in March 1705, "my Kind relations and friends flocking in to welcome mee and hear the story of my transactions and travails."

Widowed in 1706, Knight followed her married daughter to Connecticut in 1714, where she invested in real estate. Her later years were spent in New London, Connecticut, where she ran an inn on a farm she owned. She died there in 1727 and was buried in the town cemetery. Her diary passed into private hands and was discovered nearly 100 years later by Theodore Dwight, Jr., who published it in 1825. Since that first edition, it has been reissued many times. In 1995, **Janet**

Burnett Gerba wrote a novel based on the diary, *With No Little Regret: An Historical Novel Based on the Journal of Madame Knight.*

SOURCES:

James, Edward T., ed. *Notable American Women, 1607–1950.* Cambridge, MA: The Belknap Press of Harvard University Press, 1971.

Kimball, Carol W. "Novelist adds spice to narrative of Madam Knight's arduous trip," in *The Day* [New London, CT]. October 17, 1996.

Weatherford, Doris. *American Women's History.* NY: Prentice Hall, 1994.

Barbara Morgan,
Melrose, Massachusetts

Knipp, Mrs. (fl. 1670)

English actress. Name variations: Mrs. Knep. Flourished around 1670; married.

An English actress, Mrs. Knipp probably first appeared as Epicene in Ben Jonson's *Silent Woman* in 1664. What is known of her is principally from the entries in Samuel Pepys' diary, who found her "excellent company," despite her "horse-jockey of a husband." She acted in plays by Jacobean and Restoration dramatists and disappeared from the bills by 1678.

Knipper-Chekova, Olga (1870–1959)

Russian actress. Name variations: Olga Chekova; Olga Chekhova; Olga Knipper-Chekhova; Olga Knipper. Born Olga Leonardovna Knipper in Russia in 1870 (some sources cite 1868); died in 1959; aunt of composer Lev Knipper (b. 1898); studied drama with Alexander Fedotov and Vladimir Nemirovich-Danchenko; married Anton Chekhov (1860–1904, the dramatist), on May 25, 1901; no children.

A member of the first company of the Moscow Art Theater (founded in 1898), Olga Knipper-Chekova became famous for her portrayals of the heroines of dramatist Anton Chekhov, whom she married in 1901. She was first seen as Madame Arkadina in the Moscow Art Theater's revival of Chekhov's *The Seagull* (1898), which had initially been unsuccessfully performed at the Alexandrinsky Theater in St. Petersburg by actors who had not been trained in the subtle ensemble acting the play requires. In the hands of the Moscow Art Theater's actors, the play came to life. The company subsequently made Chekhov a mainstay, and Knipper went on to create the roles of Elena Andreyevna in *Uncle Vanya* (1899), Masha in *Three Sisters* (1901), and Madame Ranevskaya in *The Cherry Orchard* (1904).

Knipper's relationship with Chekhov was, for the most part, long-distance, as the playwright was forced to retreat to the warmer regions of Yalta for his tuberculosis. Letters reveal that she was insecure about her performances in his plays as well as her relationship with his mother **Yevgenia Chekhova** and sister **Maria Chekhova**, and he was frequently called upon to soothe her doubts and provide encouragement. After Chekhov's untimely death at age 44 in 1904, Knipper-Chekova continued to address him in her journal as a form of therapy. Some of Knipper-Chekova's contemporaries criticized her for continuing her career instead of devoting her days to nursing her husband. "The censure is clearly based on the assumption that every marriage should be like every other one," writes Simon Karlinsky. "The marriage of Anton Chekhov and Olga Knipper was a partnership of equals, and they arranged it to provide themselves with the independence they both wanted to be a part of that marriage. In the short time they had together, with all the occasional misunderstandings, with his deteriorating physical condition, and her severe illnesses, with all the separations, they managed to give each other more real happiness than many other couples achieve in a long lifetime together."

Before Anton's death, he had given his last will and testament to Olga for safekeeping. Anton had bequeathed his money, his dramatic works, and his house in Yalta to his sister Maria. To Olga, he left his house in Gurzuf and 5,000 rubles, and to his three brothers designated amounts of money. But after his death, because the document had not been notarized, the Russian probate court ruled that his estate be divided between his three brothers and his widow. Under Russian law, a sister could not benefit. The four heirs agreed to the decision. One month later, Olga and the Chekhov brothers legally awarded everything to Maria and empowered her to carry out Anton's will. Maria turned the Yalta house into a museum for her brother, then saved it from looters during the Civil War, protected it from nationalization in the mid-1920s, rebuilt it after a 1927 earthquake, and lived in it during the 1941 German occupation of the Crimea.

Olga Knipper-Chekova remained with the Moscow Art Theater, becoming best known for her dramatic roles, including her acclaimed performance as the lead in the revival of Turgenev's *A Month in the Country,* directed by Constantin Stanislavski. She was also delightful in comedies, including the role of Shlestova in *Woe from Wit* (1925). In 1943, Knipper-Chekova recreated the role of Madame Ranevskaya in *The Cherry Or-*

chard on the occasion of the 300th performance of the play. The actress died in 1959.

SOURCES:

Hartnoll, Phyllis, and Peter Found. *The Concise Oxford Companion to the Theatre.* Oxford and NY: Oxford University Press, 1993.

Karlinsky, Simon. *Letters of Anton Chekhov.* Translated by Michael Henry Heim. NY: Harper & Row, 1973.

Publishers Weekly. September 22, 1997.

SUGGESTED READING:

Ecco, Jean Benedetti, ed. and trans. *Dear Writer, Dear Actress: The Love Letters of Anton Chekhov and Olga Knipper,* 1997.

Barbara Morgan,
Melrose, Massachusetts

Knoll, Florence Schust (1917—)

American furniture and interior designer. Name variations: Florence Knoll Basset. Born Florence Schust in Saginaw, Michigan, on May 24, 1917; daughter of Frederick and M.H. (Haistings) Schust; trained at Cranbrook Academy; studied architecture at the Architectural Association in London; Illinois Institute of Tech-

$\mathcal{O}$lga $\mathcal{K}$nipper-$\mathcal{C}$hekova with $\mathcal{A}$nton $\mathcal{C}$hekhov nology, B.A., 1941; married Hans G. Knoll (a producer and distributor of modern furniture and founder of Knoll International), on July 1, 1946 (died October 1955); married Harry Hood Basset, on June 22, 1958.

One of America's leading designers of furniture and interiors, Florence Knoll trained at Michigan's Cranbrook Academy under Eliel and Eero Saarinen, and studied architecture in London and at the Illinois Institute of Technology under Ludwig Mies van der Rohe. In 1943, after working for both Marcel Breuer and Walter Gropius, she was employed by Knoll International in New York, a firm established by Hans Knoll in 1937 which was becoming a leading producer and distributor of modern furniture. In addition to adding to the product line with her own designs, Florence was put in charge of the Planning Unit, an interior design service that the firm offered to its furniture customers. The Unit quickly became a major asset to the firm, as many leading architects found that it offered interior design compatible with their work. Florence married Hans Knoll in 1946 and, after his death in 1955, took over as owner and chief designer of Knoll International. Under her management, the firm continued to prosper and grow, due in large part to the relationships she had already established with many noted architects of the time. Knoll International manufactured many classic furniture lines, including designs by Harry Bertola, Marcel Breuer, Ludwig Miles van der Rohe, and Eero Saarinen, whose sleek pedestal-based armchair became extremely popular. The firm was sold in 1959, and Knoll retired in 1965. Around that time, she also married Harry Hood Basset and went by the name Florence Knoll Basset.

SOURCES:
Candee, Marjorie Dent, ed. *Current Biography*. NY: H.W. Wilson, 1955.

Knollys, Elizabeth (fl. 1600)

*English noblewoman. Name variations: Lady Knollys; Elizabeth Howard. Born Elizabeth Howard; daughter of Thomas Howard (1561–1626), 1st earl of Suffolk (r. 1603–1626), and *Catherine Knyvett; married William Knollys (1547–1632), later earl of Banbury, Lord Vaux, comptroller of Queen *Elizabeth I's household; sister-in-law of *Lettice Knollys (c. 1541–1634).*

Knollys, Lettice (c. 1541–1634)

Countess of Leicester and Essex. Name variations: Lettice Dudley. Born around 1541; died in 1634; el-

dest daughter of *Catherine Carey (1529–1569) and Francis Knollys (c. 1514–1596, a diplomat); sister of William Knollys (1547–1632), comptroller of Queen *Elizabeth I's household; sister-in-law of *Elizabeth Knollys; married Walter Devereux, 1st earl of Essex; became second wife of Robert Dudley, earl of Leicester (c. 1532–1588, a favorite of Queen Elizabeth), in 1578 or 1579. Some accused Robert Dudley of bringing about the murder of his first wife, Lady *Amy Robsart.*

Knopf, Blanche (1894–1966)

American publisher, and full partner with her husband in one of the world's most successful publishing firms, who wielded power in an era when few women served as executives and brought authors of the stature of Albert Camus, Jean-Paul Sartre, and Simone de Beauvoir to America's attention. Pronunciation: KUH-noff. Born Blanche Wolf on July 30, 1894, in New York City; died on June 4, 1966, in New York; daughter of Julius W. Wolf (a jeweler) and Berta Wolf (both immigrants from Vienna); educated by governesses at home; attended the Gardner School and Columbia University; married Alfred A. Knopf (a publisher), on April 4, 1916; children: Patrick Knopf.

Helped husband to found Alfred A. Knopf publishing company (1915); traveled with husband to acquire European writing talent (1921); was vice-president of the firm (1921–56); was the first American talent scout to seek literary talent in South America (1943); named a Chevalier of the Legion of Honor for her literary work in France (1949); made a Cavaliero of the Brazilian National Order of the Southern Cross (1950); served as president of Alfred A. Knopf (1957–66); Knopf merged with Random House (1960); decorated a second time in Brazil, receiving the rank of Oficial in recognition of her literary contributions (1964).

The foyer of the glamorous Ritz Hotel in Paris has long been famous as a gathering place for fashionable women meeting in the afternoon for tea, but in the morning the room can usually be found empty. In the years leading up to and after World War II, however, a couple could sometimes be seen at one of its tables at mid-morning, speaking French over their coffee, bourbon, or Badois. He smoked the black Gaulois cigarettes beloved by the French, while she puffed on American Chesterfields. On the chair between them lay the raincoat which he often wore in photos for jackets of his books; she had had the coat made to order for him at Brooks Brothers in New York. The talk at the table was mostly about writing—American writers, English writers, Boris Pasternak—and about the past, the future, and themselves, for clearly these two people knew each other well. He was Albert Camus, the French existentialist writer and eventual winner of the Nobel Prize; she was Blanche Knopf, the American publisher who had made his works famous throughout the world. Camus was only one of many literary discoveries made by Blanche Knopf, and one of many great writers who counted her as a close friend.

Blanche Knopf was born Blanche Wolf in New York in 1894, the daughter of Julius W. Wolf, a prosperous jeweler, and **Berta Wolf.** Both had emigrated from Vienna. Educated at home by French and German governesses and at the Gardner School in New York, Blanche became fluent in several languages, especially French, which she spoke as if it were her native tongue. In 1911, she was 17 when she met Alfred Knopf, an undergraduate at Columbia and the son of a successful advertising executive and consultant, Samuel Knopf. Two years older than Blanche, Alfred graduated from Columbia in 1912 and went abroad before going to work for the publishing house of Doubleday, Page and Company. The couple were engaged by this time, and Blanche encouraged her fiancé's interest in publishing.

In 1913, while at Doubleday, Alfred was assigned the job of publicizing *Chance,* a novel by Joseph Conrad, who was relatively unknown in America. Alfred enlisted several notable American writers in praising the book, and the resulting publicity made *Chance* an enormous success, selling over 50,000 copies. Conrad wrote to Alfred, "If you had not happened along, all these books would have remained on the back shelves of the firm where they have been reposing for the last ten years."

At the beginning of his career, Alfred moved restlessly from job to job. In 1915, he was employed at the firm of Mitchell Kennerley when he was fired after the publisher learned that he was about to start his own company. With $5,000 from his father, Alfred set about launching his new firm, and Blanche rolled up her sleeves to help. Already knowledgeable about literature, she also began to learn a great deal about typography, paper, ink, and printing. On April 4, 1916, she married Alfred, cementing the bonds of marriage and work that would keep the two inextricably bound.

From the start, the Knopfs were noted for high standards of bookmaking. Their books were bound in bright cloth-covered boards and wrapped in jackets of arresting design; the typography was pleasing to the eye, the paper of exceptional quality. The logo of the new firm was an elegant borzoi, a long-haired Russian wolfhound. At the time of the founding, Blanche was particularly fond of her two wolfhounds, though she later grew to dislike the breed, preferring Yorkshire terriers for her canine companions. Whatever the borzois' deficiencies as pets, they were a striking symbol of an up-and-coming publishing firm, and the borzoi continues to grace Knopf books.

> *I* don't think a lady publisher is any different than a man publisher.
>
> —Blanche Knopf

A partner in every decision made at the top in the firm, Blanche Knopf was a vice-president after 1921. She and Alfred secured about two-thirds of the book contracts themselves. Only three people in the company were allowed to sign contracts—the Knopfs and their general manager. In weekly staff meetings, Knopf sat with her husband at one end of a conference table facing their gathering of employees; since the couple rarely agreed on the issues under discussion, the meetings were often heated. Seeing the two as rivals, employees often struggled to avoid taking sides, although the couple always reached a mutual objective in the end. Summing up their partnership, Alfred noted, "You have two heads, both with strong personal tastes, who often insist on publishing books that are almost sure to lose money." Although the first part of this statement was certainly correct, the second may be taken as poetic license, since the Knopfs ran an extremely profitable business.

The company's first major success was W.H. Hudson's *Green Mansions,* published in 1916, followed by Thomas Mann's *Royal Highness,* H.L. Mencken's *A Book of Prefaces,* *Willa Cather's *Youth and the Bright Medusa,* Max Beerbohm's *Seven Men,* and Clarence Day's *This Simian World.* In 1921, following World War I, the Knopfs took the innovative step of touring Europe in search of foreign authors, initiating a practice that would become standard among American publishers in future decades.

Their tours of Europe usually lasted three months, and Blanche felt very much at home there. In the couple's partnership, she was the one who possessed the charm and social graces that won over the European authors, including such notables as André Gide, Jules Romains, *Simone de Beauvoir, Jean-Paul Sartre, and Ilya Ehrenburg. Her enjoyment of conversation, travel and reading new works brought the firm a constant stream of new talent.

After Hitler came to power in Germany in 1933, Blanche Knopf saw a change in Europe that did not bode well for its future. After her travels in 1936, she claimed, "There is not a German writer left in Germany who is worth thinking about. The gifted writers and enterprising publishers who had any independence left Germany. Only the Nazi writers and publishers remain. They write to please the Nazi government." The outbreak of war ended her travels on the Continent, but she made several trips to war-torn Britain, risking danger in order to maintain contact with Knopf authors there.

In search of new authors, she blazed yet another literary path in 1943 by traveling to Latin America. Soon she had signed Eduardo Mallea, Germán Arciniegas, Jorge Amado, and Gilberto Freyre, among others, an effort that led to her being recognized as a Cavaliero of the Brazilian National Order of the Southern Cross in 1950. In 1964, Blanche was again decorated by Brazil, receiving the rank of Oficial. This followed similar recognition in France, where she had been named a Chevalier of the Legion of Honor in 1949.

Blanche Knopf also revolutionized the publishing of detective and crime novels by introducing writers in the genre who won mainstream critical respect. Her firm published all the major works of Dashiell Hammett, including *Red Harvest, The Dain Curse, The Maltese Falcon, The Glass Key,* and *The Thin Man,* and she introduced the first four books by Raymond Chandler, *The Big Sleep, Farewell My Lovely, The High Window,* and *The Lady in the Lake.* James M. Cain, author of *The Postman Always Rings Twice,* and Kenneth Millar (Ross Macdonald), who wrote *The Goodbye Look,* are two other Knopf discoveries whose works became enormously popular in Europe as well as the United States and are still recognized as classics.

The Knopf marriage was marked by the same individuality as their business relationship. Said Blanche, "A man and his wife don't become Siamese twins bent on identical pursuits and craving the same foods, friends, and diversions." Their differences in taste were particularly evident in dress, since Alfred enjoyed tailored silk shirts in dramatic shades worn with colorful jackets and ties, while Blanche preferred conservative designer clothes. While he collected and drank fine wines, she remained a bourbon drinker. During the week, the two were together at the office all day, but at night she retreated to a nearby apartment and spent evenings enjoying the concerts, parties, and other entertainments provided by the city, while he commuted to their country home in Purchase, New York. She would join him there on weekends. Sharing their love of people, travel, and the publishing of good books, the Knopfs recognized those areas where they were opposites in traits and tastes as a source of strength in their relationship.

"Book publishing is very hard for women in America," said Blanche. "In the early days, I commuted, ran a house, had a baby, read manuscripts all night and held open house (Were 5 coming or 30? It makes a difference)." At a time when few women were company officers, much less full partners in American firms, she worked in a world dominated almost entirely by men. Women in publishing were usually relegated to clerical tasks and rarely rose even to the position of editor. They were also excluded from membership in organizations like the Publishers' Lunch Club and the Book Table that might have helped to enhance their positions. When Knopf attempted to establish a female counterpart to the Publishers' Lunch Club, she attributed her failure to the fact that "there were never enough of us to make it work," and she freely expressed her resentment at the exclusion of women in the field. When a women's college invited her to speak about the future of women in publishing, she declined, saying there was "no future worth mentioning." Nevertheless, she was made president of Alfred A. Knopf in 1957, one of the few women of her era to attain such a position.

Blanche Knopf was a gracious hostess who enjoyed people, and, unlike Alfred, she was a good listener. She created social as well as working relationships with many of her authors, including Jean-Paul Sartre and Simone de Beauvoir, whom she introduced to the non-French public. At a time when she knew little about France's existentialists, she met with Sartre in Paris, declared that she wanted to know more about this group of French philosophers, and asked for a list its members. Sartre replied, "Well, there's Simone de Beauvoir and myself, and that's all."

Knopf also loved to give celebrity-studded parties which not only introduced the up and coming to the famous but also brought publicity to the firm. Alfred A. Knopf published women writers such as Willa Cather and *Katherine Mansfield, and black writers such as Langston Hughes and James Weldon Johnson. Some of its other U.S. authors included *Julia Child, Samuel Eliot Morrison, William Shirer, and John Updike.

In 1960, the head of Random House, Bennett Cerf, suggested Knopf merge with his company. One year previous, Patrick Knopf had decided to found his own publishing house, Atheneum, instead of inheriting his parents' firm. A distinguished veteran of World War II, Pat Knopf had frequently demonstrated a spirit of independence akin to that of his parents. Without a need to preserve family ownership, the couple welcomed the Random House merger, which allowed the firm to maintain its independence and its own imprint.

Inside Knopf, employees continued to address their bosses as "Blanche" and "Alfred," the couple continued to review all manuscripts chosen for publication, and their disagreements remained frequent. For a while, Blanche managed to keep secret from outsiders the fact that she had become virtually blind. Old friends in Paris, London, and Rome now scouted for works overseas, and her secretary read parts of manuscripts to her aloud. Her publishing sense and her awareness of trends and coming reputations remained strong, and some even felt that the handicap made her hunches better than ever. No one in the offices, including her husband, ever mentioned her handicap, and she never allowed it to intimidate her. One employee described the sight of her hailing a taxi: "She plunged five or six feet into the street with one thin, bangled arm upraised while brakes around her screeched. So far as I know, she was never injured."

On June 4, 1966, at age 71, Blanche Wolf Knopf died unexpectedly in her sleep at her New York apartment, having worked with her beloved books until the last. The *Borzoi Quarterly* was a Knopf publication devoted to a variety of in-house topics. The only exception came when Blanche Knopf died. Excerpts from more than 700 letters, cards, and telegrams sent in condolence from writers, editors, publishers, and public figures around the world were used to fill the entire issue.

Following Blanche's death, Alfred took a long trip West, filling his days with friends, conferences, and visits to national parks, but, without Blanche, his intense interest in books almost ceased to exist. Although he had been honored frequently for his immense contributions to the field, he described himself as "more a presence than a publisher" and appearances at his office became increasingly rare. Similarly, publication of the *Borzoi Quarterly* soon came to an end. (Alfred later married **Helen Hedrick** and lived with her happily until his death at 91.) The successful partnership forged by Blanche and Alfred Knopf had changed the world's literary landscape. The leaping borzoi on an Alfred A. Knopf book is still a reminder of the company's original elegance, creativity and style.

SOURCES:

"Alfred A. Knopf," in *American Literary Publishing Houses 1900–1980: Trade and Paperback*. Edited by Peter Dzwonkoski. Detroit, MI: Gale Research, 1986.

"Blanche Wolf Knopf," in *Publishers Weekly*. Vol. 189, no. 24. June 13, 1966, pp. 103–104.

Cerf, Bennett. *At Random: The Reminiscences of Bennett Cerf*. NY: Random House, 1977.

Commager, Henry Steele. "Speaking of Books: The Knopfs' Half Century," in *The New York Times Book Review*. October 31, 1965, pp. 2–3, 72.

"A Conversation with Alfred A. Knopf," in *U.S. News and World Report*. October 17, 1983, p. 88.

Fadiman, Clifton. *Fifty Years*. NY: Alfred A. Knopf, 1965.

Feldman, Gayle. "The Borzoi Three-Quarterly," in *Publishers Weekly*. Vol. 237, no. 43. October 26, 1990, pp. 46–51.

"Fifty Years of The Borzoi," in *Publishers Weekly*. February 1, 1965, pp. 48–54.

"Golden Anniversary of Excellence," in *Life*. Vol. 59, no. 4. July 23, 1965, pp. 37–38, 40.

Hellman, Geoffrey. "Profiles, Publisher—I: A Very Distinguished Pavane," in *The New Yorker*. November 20, 1948, pp. 44–57.

————. "Profiles, Publisher—II: Flair is the Word," in *The New Yorker*. November 27, 1948, pp. 36–52.

————. "Profiles, Publisher—III: The Pleasures, Prides, and Cream," in *The New Yorker*. December 4, 1948, pp. 40–53.

Hersey, John. "The Greatest Publisher This Country Ever Had," in *Publishers Weekly*. Vol. 226, no. 9. August 31, 1984, p. 316.

Kauffman, Stanley, "Album of the Knopfs," in *The American Scholar*. Vol. 56, no. 3. Summer 1987, pp. 371–380.

Knopf, Blanche, "Albert Camus in the Sun," in *The Atlantic Monthly*. Vol. 207, no. 2. February 1961, pp. 77–79, 84.

————. "An American Publisher Tours South America," in *The Saturday Review of Literature*. Vol. 26, no. 15. April 10, 1943, pp. 7–10.

————. "Impressions of British Publishing in Wartime," in *Publishers Weekly*. Vol. 144, no. 25. December 18, 1943, pp. 2232–2233.

"Mrs. Blanche Wolf Knopf of Publishing Firm Dies," in *The New York Times*. June 5, 1966, p. 86.

Schwed, Peter. *Turning the Pages: An Insider's Story of Simon & Schuster 1924–1984*. NY: Macmillan, 1984.

Scribner, Charles, Jr. *In the Company of Writers: A Life in Publishing*. NY: Scribner, 1990.

Tebbel, John. *Between Covers: The Rise and Transformation of Book Publishing in America*. Oxford: Oxford University Press, 1987.

————. "Publisher to an Era," in *Saturday Review*. Vol. 46, no. 35. August 29, 1964, pp. 131–133, 185.

Whitman, Alden. "Blanche W. Knopf," in *The Obituary Book*. NY: Stein and Day, 1971, pp. 69–73.

Karin Haag,
freelance writer, Athens, Georgia

Knox, Isa (1831–1903)

Scottish writer. Name variations: Isa Craig; Mrs. Knox. Born Isa Craig in Edinburgh, Scotland, in 1831; died in 1903; married John Knox (an iron merchant), in 1866.

Isa Craig was employed on the staff of the *Scotsman* for some time, contributing material under the name Isa, before moving to London in

1857. There, she was secretary to the National Association for the Promotion of Social Science until her marriage to her cousin John Knox, an iron merchant. She wrote the prize poem for the Burns festival at the Crystal Palace celebration on January 25, 1859, and went on to publish several novels, as well as *Tales on the Parables* (1872), *The Little Folks' History of England* (1872), and *In Duty Bound* (1881).

Knox, Rose Markward

(1857–1950)

American businesswoman. Born Rose Markward on November 18, 1857, in Mansfield, Ohio; died on September 27, 1950, in Johnstown, New York; youngest of three daughters of David Markward (a druggist) and Amanda (Foreman) Markward; attended public schools in Mansfield; married Charles Briggs Knox (a glove salesman), on February 15, 1883 (died 1908); children: Charles; James; Helen (died in infancy).

Businesswoman Rose Markward Knox was born in 1857 in Mansfield, Ohio, and received a public school education. In her 20s, she moved with her family to Cloversville, New York, where she found work in the glove factory which also employed her future husband Charles Briggs Knox, a salesman. The couple married in 1883 and had two sons, Charles and James, and a daughter Helen who died in infancy. In 1890, the Knoxes took their savings of $5,000 and invested in a gelatin business in Johnstown, New York. At the time, gelatin was still thought of as a dietary supplement for convalescents, so the Knoxes set out to bring their product into the mainstream. While her husband promoted the new product with a stable of race horses (the Gelatine String) and branched out into other enterprises, Rose concentrated on selling gelatin to the American housewife. From her home, she tested recipes, and in 1896, published the booklet "Dainty Dessert."

When Charles Knox died in 1908, Rose took over the business, although friends advised her to sell. Reluctant at first, she began by selling off the peripheral ventures and turning her attention to the sale of gelatin. She invested heavily in research, conducted in her own experimental kitchen and at the laboratories of Melon Institute. Directing her advertising to women, she prepared a second booklet, *Food Economy* (1917), and began a newspaper column of recipes and household hints, "Mrs. Knox Says." By 1915, the business was incorporated for $300,000 and ten years later was capitalized at $1 million. In the meantime, Knox purchased a half-interest in a plant in Camden, New Jersey, from which she had been buying gelatin, and in 1930, she became vice president of the newly organized Kind and Knox. She built a new plant in Camden for the production of flavored gelatin in 1936; the Johnstown plant was thereafter used for packaging and distribution. The Knox Company became the nation's top producer and distributor of gelatin, selling 60% for food and 40% for industry (photography in particular) and medicine. Knox remained modest about her success. "I just used common sense—a man would call it horse sense—in running my business," she said in an interview with *The New York Times* (May 23, 1937). "But from the first I determined to run it in what I called a woman's way."

In addition to her business acumen, Knox was a brisk but enlightened manager. Upon taking over the company in 1908, she had ordered the back door of the factory closed, saying to her employees, "We are all ladies and gentlemen working together here, and we'll all come in through the front door." In 1913, she instituted a five-day work week and later provided a two-week paid vacation and sick-leave policies. Her employees were reportedly "terrified of crossing her will," but the majority of them remained with the firm for 25 years or more. During the Great Depression, Knox was one of the few American companies that did not lay off a single employee.

Through the years, Rose Knox became known as one of the nation's outstanding businesswomen. A long-time member of the American Grocery Manufacturers' Association, in 1929 she became the first woman elected to its board of directors. She was also active in many civic and philanthropic activities in Johnstown. On the occasion of her 80th birthday, she distributed $50,000 among local institutions. She was the founder and first president of the Federation of Women's Clubs for Civic Improvement of Johnstown, and the founder of a home for women.

Knox continued to come to the office daily until the age of 88, when arthritis forced her to work from home. It was not until she was 90 that she agreed to let her son James assume the presidency of the company, although she stayed on as chair of the board. In 1949, James said of his mother, "She still runs things . . . She comes up with more bright ideas in a day than the rest of us produce in a month." Rose Markward Knox died at her home in Johnstown on September 27, 1950, just shy of her 93rd birthday.

SOURCES:

James, Edward T., ed. *Notable American Women, 1607–1950.* Cambridge, MA: The Belknap Press of Harvard University Press, 1971.

McHenry, Robert. *Famous American Women.* NY: Dover, 1983.

Weatherford, Doris. *American Women's History.* NY: Prentice Hall, 1994.

Barbara Morgan,
Melrose, Massachusetts

Knutson, Coya Gjesdal

(1912–1996)

U.S. Democratic congressional representative from Minnesota (1955–59). Born Cornelia Genevive Gjesdal on August 22, 1912, in Edmore, Ramsey County, North Dakota; died on October 10, 1996; one of five children of Christian Gjesdal (a farmer) and Christine (Anderson) Gjesdal; attended public schools in Edmore; Concordia College, Moorhead, Minnesota, A.B., 1934; postgraduate work in library science at Moorhead State Teachers College, Minnesota, and in music at the Juilliard School of Music, New York City;

Coya
Gjesdal
Knutson

married Andrew Knutson (a hotel owner), in 1940 (divorced); children: one son, Terrance.

Known as "the farm woman's Congresswoman," Coya Knutson was the first woman to represent the state of Minnesota in the U.S. Congress, although she did not enter politics until after a successful career in education, public relations, and social welfare. Raised on her family's farm in Edmore, North Dakota, Knutson knew firsthand the hardships of working the land. She liked to regale listeners of the time the grasshoppers stopped by the farm for lunch. "When they took off again," she explained, "our crops went with them." Knutson attended the local public schools and received an A.B. from Concordia College, where she majored in music and English. Following her graduation in 1934, she embarked on a 16-year high school teaching career, while pursuing graduate study in library science and music. Following her marriage in 1940, Knutson worked for the Agricultural Adjustment Administration in Minnesota, serving as a field agent investigating issues of price support and acreage allotments for farmers. A developing interest in social welfare led her to a job with the Red Lake County welfare board (1948–50); she also helped establish a local medical clinic, a Red Cross branch, and a community chest fund.

Knutson entered politics in 1948, when she chaired the Red Lake County Democratic-Farmer Labor Party and served as a delegate at the Democratic National Convention. In 1950, she was elected to the Minnesota House of Representatives where she served two terms. In 1954, buoyed by her success on the state level, she ran as Democratic-Farmer Labor candidate from the Ninth District to the U.S. House of Representative, winning over incumbent Harold C. Hagen with a "butter and egg campaign" that encouraged better support of farming families and was critical of the Eisenhower Administration's farm policy. During her freshman year in Congress, Knutson was the first woman to serve on the House Committee on Agriculture. Her tenure was further marked by her call for increased price supports for farm production, an extended food-stamp program for the distribution of farm surpluses, and a federally supported school-lunch program.

Knutson was preparing to campaign for re-election in 1958, when her husband Andrew (reportedly an alcoholic) published what came to be known as the "Coya, Come Home" letter, claiming that his wife's career had devastated their marriage and accusing her of having an affair with a young man who served as her administrative assistant. Although Andrew later maintained that political opponents of his wife had convinced him to write the letter, Coya's credibility had been irreparably damaged, and she lost the election. To no one's surprise, the marriage was dissolved.

Knutson attempted to win back her seat in 1960 but was unsuccessful. Under the Kennedy administration, she served as congressional liaison for the Office of Civilian Defense until 1970, and made yet another unsuccessful bid for a Congressional seat in nomination for a special election in 1977. She then retired to Arlington, Virginia, and died in October 1996.

SOURCES:

Candee, Marjorie Dent, ed. *Current Biography.* NY: H.W. Wilson, 1956.

Office of the Historian. *Women in Congress 1917–1990.* Commission on the Bicentenary of the U.S. House of Representatives, 1991.

SUGGESTED READING:

Beito, Gretchen Urnes. *Coya Come Home: A Congresswoman's Journey.* CA: Pomegranate Press, 1990.

Barbara Morgan,
Melrose, Massachusetts

Knyvett, Catherine (d. 1633)

*Countess of Suffolk. Name variations: Catherine Howard. Died in September 1633; daughter of Sir Henry Knyvett and Elizabeth Stumpe; married the Honorable Richard Rich; married Thomas Howard (1561–1626), 1st earl of Suffolk (r. 1603–1626), around 1583; children: (second marriage) Theophilus Howard (1584–1640), 2nd earl of Suffolk (r. 1626–1640); Thomas Howard, 1st earl of Berkshire; Henry Howard; Sir Charles Howard; Sir Robert Howard; Sir William Howard; Edward, Baron Howard; *Elizabeth Knollys; *Frances Howard (1593–1632); *Catherine Howard (d. 1672).*

Kobalskaya, Elizaveta (1851–1943).

See Kovalskaia, Elizaveta.

Kobrynska, Natalia Ivanovna (1855–1920)

Ukrainian writer and organizer of the feminist movement in Galicia, then a province of Austria-Hungary. Name variations: N.I. Kobrinskaia; Natal'ia Kobrynskaia; Natalia Kobryns'ka. Born in Belelui, Ukraine, on June 8, 1855; died on January 22, 1920, in Stanislav (now Ivano-Frankivs'k), Ukraine.

Despite harsh political and cultural repression by the tsarist state throughout the 19th century, Ukrainian intellectual life flourished. The awakening national consciousness was best expressed in the romantic poetry of Taras Shevchenko (1814–1861), which reached an ever-growing readership despite bans on Ukrainian publications in 1863, 1876, and 1881. Censorship was evaded by printing works in the Ukrainian language in the much more liberal environment of Galicia, then part of the Austro-Hungarian monarchy. Women became increasingly involved in the national cause during the closing decades of the 19th century, when they went in growing numbers to study in Vienna.

The writer Natalia Kobrynska was destined to be the central figure of the Ukrainian feminist movement for almost four decades. In her short story "Dukh chasu" ("The Spirit of the Times"), written in Vienna in 1883 and published in 1887, she presented an impassioned plea for equal rights for Ukrainian women. In 1884, Kobrynska turned her ideas into practical reality when she founded the Society of Ruthenian Women in the city of Stanislav.

In 1887, she and **Olena Pchilka** published the almanac *Pershyi vinok* (*The First Wreath*), which represented a major step forward not only for Ukrainian literature but for the Ukrainian women's movement. It contained important essays, articles and belletristic works by women to watch on the intellectual landscape, including not only the almanac's editors but such newcomers as the young *Lesya Ukrainka, Olena Pchilka's daughter. Encouraged by the positive responses to this work, Kobrynska published three additional almanacs from 1893 to 1896, collectively entitled *Our Fate*, all of which contained new writings by women authors. Aware of the often fragile state of cultural self-confidence among Ukrainian intellectuals, Kobrynska played a key role in persuading a number of young authors, the most important among them being *Olha Kobylianska, to write their works in Ukrainian rather than German.

In her own writings, Kobrynska depicted the poverty and backwardness of Ukrainian peasant life in Galicia, condemning the caste system and patriarchy which kept women ignorant and superstitious. The best known of her realistic short stories are "For a Piece of Bread" (1884) and "The Elector" (1889). Her 1890 novella *Iadzia and Katrusia* remains an important landmark in the development of Ukrainian realist literature. Convinced that World War I would only bring suffering to her people, Kobrynska took a strong stand against the war from its outset in 1914. Honored as both the initiator and organizer of the Ukrainian women's movement in Galicia, she died in Stanislav on January 22, 1920.

SOURCES:

Luckyj, George S.N. *Ukrainian Literature in the Twentieth Century: A Reader's Guide.* Toronto: Shevchenko Scientific Society-University of Toronto Press, 1992.

Pavlychko, Solomea. "Modernism vs. Populism in *Fin de Siecle* Ukrainian Literature," in Pamela Chester and Sibelan Forrester, eds. *Engendering Slavic Literatures.* Bloomington: Indiana University Press, 1996, pp. 83–103.

Shabliovs'kyi, Ievhen Stepanovych. *Ukrainian Literature Through the Ages.* Translated by Abraham Mistetsky, *et al.* Edited by Anatole Bilenko. Kiev: Mistetsvo Publishers, 1970.

John Haag,
Associate Professor of History,
University of Georgia, Athens, Georgia

Kobylianska, Olha (1863–1942)

Ukrainian modernist whose writings are celebrated for their lyrical descriptions and psychological portraits which struck a blow against prevailing populist myths about peasant life. Name variations: Olga Kobilyanska; Olha Yulianovna Kobylianska; Ol'ga Iulianovna Kobylianskaia. Born in Gura Humorului, Bukovina, Austria-Hungary, on November 27, 1863; died in Chernvitsi (Chernovitsy), Rumania, on March 21, 1942.

Olha Kobylianska was largely self-educated in a period when Ukrainian women lived under the dual burden of patriarchical traditions and tsarist Russian attempts to destroy Ukrainian cultural independence. Growing up in the southern part of Bukovina, then a province of the Austro-Hungarian monarchy, she was profoundly influenced by German literature and its idealistic values. Her first *novellen,* dating to the early 1880s, were all written in German, as were the first drafts of her novels *Liudyna* (*A Person,* written 1886, published 1891) and *Tsarivna* (*The Princess,* written 1888–93, published 1895). The Ukrainian versions of these two works are filled with quotations, imagery and epigraphs taken from German literature and philosophy, including the then-sensational writings of Friedrich Nietzsche. Kobylianska was also influenced by the works of *George Sand.

While some critics of the day faulted her for relying too much on German traditions and techniques, at least one perceptive contemporary, the writer *Lesya Ukrainka, detected the positive aspects of this influence. "Your salvation was in this Germany," said Ukrainka. "It led you to recognize *world* literature, it transported you out into the broader world of ideas and art—this simply leaps out at one, when one compares your writing with that of the majority of Galicians." Eager to embrace the new literary techniques of her day, Kobylianska was influenced in her writings by the neoromantic and symbolist currents. Her works depicted the struggle between good and evil, a natural subject for an author with a lifelong interest in philosophy.

Because of her interest in the lives of the Ukrainian peasantry in Bukovina, Kobylianska's writings treat the forces of nature—seen as far more accessible to illiterate peasants than to the most highly educated urban intellectuals—with great sympathy. An irrational world of magic and predestination is central to the storytelling in her important novels *Zemlia* (*The Land,* 1902) and *V nedilu rano zillia kopala* (*On Sunday Morn She Gathered Herbs,* 1909). The harsh, unforgiving aspects of peasant life were also shown from different angles in her short stories "At St. Ivan's" (1891, published 1896), "Rural Bank" (1895), "The Uncultured Woman" (1896), and "In the Fields" (1898).

Zemlia, a work which attacked a number of myths about the rural peasantry, reveals the harsh, oppressive nature of life in Bukovina at the start of the 20th century. An intellectually probing, even revolutionary work, the novel examines the ways in which the system of private ownership leads to a world in which brother kills brother. It tells an essentially simple story of the destructive power of the most basic element of peasant existence—their land. In *Zemlia,* land is shown to be a terrible force that enserfs and brutalizes all who desire it. Only the main character Anna, who is landless, is presented as having at least some chance of breaking free from these dehumanizing forces and thus moving to a higher state. In the end, however, she too falls victim to the all-encompassing dependence on the land, and her life is destroyed. Kobylianska showed that village life, rather than being a harmonious organic *Gemeinschaft* (a social relationship based on friendship or community), was in fact lacking in the most basic elements of peaceful existence. This struck a severe blow against the populist ideology that saw peasant existence in terms of happy patriarchical harmony.

With this one book, the author rocked a major pillar of Ukrainian thinking of the day, the notion that the Ukrainian village was an ideal social system. She demythologized the prevailing notions about the idealized woman by showing that there was little romantic purity in village women's lives. Unconstrained by culture or education, human nature in her Ukrainian village was deformed, cruel, and an abomination made up of raw human instincts, including incest. Family harmony was unveiled as a fantasy, with the village parental authority shown as crude and almost bestial at times. Kobylianska's writings represent important breakthroughs in the Ukrainian literature of the first decades of the 20th century toward a more realistic portrayal of ordinary people's lives.

Shocked and dismayed by the start of World War I, Kobylianska opposed its carnage from the very start. The brutality of the conflict is the subject of her short stories "Judas" (1915), "To Meet One's Fate" (1915), and "He Has Gone Mad" (1923). Although she never subscribed to Communist ideology, Kobylianska was generally sympathetic to the Soviet experiment after the Bolshevik Revolution of 1917. The dissolution of the Austro-Hungarian monarchy in 1918 gave Bukovina to Rumania, thus transforming Kobylianska into a citizen of that nation. Under Rumanian administration, the suffering of Bukovina's peasants was not ameliorated; if anything, it worsened.

The author's sense of moral outrage at the injustices taking place in Bukovina under Rumanian rule deepened with the passing years, and although her writings never reflected Marxist literary doctrines she was convinced that Soviet rule in the Eastern Ukraine, as she wrote in 1927, was making possible "great strides [so that] Ukrainian culture is thriving and developing." The Soviet government appreciated her positive assessment of the situation in Soviet Ukraine and provided her with financial assistance.

In September 1939, when the Nazi-Soviet Pact and the extinction of the Polish state made it possible for the Soviet Union to annex Western Ukrainian territories, Kobylianska rejoiced at the event, publishing an article some months later entitled "The Fruit of Culture is Developing." In the summer of 1940, Rumania was forced to surrender Northern Bukovina to the Soviet Union. As a result, Kobylianska's citizenship was again changed, and she became a Soviet citizen. She was feted as a veteran writer of social criticism and became a member of the Writers' Union of the USSR. In poor health, she was unable to flee from German Nazi and Rumanian fascist forces in June 1941, when Hitler launched his attack on the Soviet Union and quickly conquered Bukovina. Kobylianska was reviled as a dangerous "Red writer" despite her age and reputation, and the Rumanian fascist administration in Chernvitsi scheduled her to be tried by court-martial. Only her death on March 21, 1942, saved her from a more than likely fate of conviction and execution. In 1944, soon after the liberation of Bukovina from Nazi rule, a Kobylianska Museum was opened in Chernvitsi. Occupying a building where the writer had lived from 1928 until her death in 1942, the museum included exhibits with photographs, personal belongings, papers and editions of her works. Another memorial museum dedicated to Olha Kobylianska was established in the village of Dymka, where she had lived for many years in an earlier period of her life.

SOURCES:

Kopach, Alexandra. "Language and Style of Olha Kobylianska." Ph.D. dissertation, University of Ottawa, 1967.

Luckyj, George S.N. *Literary Politics in the Soviet Ukraine 1917–1934.* Rev. ed. Durham, NC: Duke University Press, 1990.

———. *Ukrainian Literature in the Twentieth Century: A Reader's Guide.* Toronto: Shevchenko Scientific Society-University of Toronto Press, 1992.

Pavlychko, Solomea. "Modernism vs. Populism in *Fin de Siecle* Ukrainian Literature," in Pamela Chester and Sibelan Forrester, eds. *Engendering Slavic Literatures.* Bloomington: Indiana University Press, 1996, pp. 83–103.

Shabliovs'kyi, Ievhen. *Ukrainian Literature Through the Ages.* Translated by Abraham Mistetsky, *et al.* Edited by Anatole Bilenko. Kiev: Mistetsvo Publishers, 1970.

John Haag,
Associate Professor of History,
University of Georgia, Athens, Georgia

Koch, Ilse (1906–1967)

German concentration camp overseer whose name has become a universal byword for sadism. Born Margarete Ilse Köhler in Dresden, Germany, on September 22, 1906; committed suicide at Aichach prison, Bavaria, on September 2, 1967; married Karl Otto Koch (1897–1945, a member of the SS and concentration camp commandant), in May 1937; children: two daughters (one of whom died in infancy); two sons.

Known to the world as the "Witch of Buchenwald," Ilse Koch remains the incarnation of Nazi savagery. She was born Margarete Ilse Köhler in 1906 in Dresden, Germany, into a working-class, Lutheran family. After eight years of basic schooling, she found work in a bookstore, later securing a more permanent job as a secretary. By chance, Ilse's secretarial work was at a factory that produced cigarettes (*Sturm-Zigaretten*) for the Nazi Party. Selling party-produced cigarettes was one of the many fundraising strategies utilized by the Nazi movement before it came to power. In the spring of 1932, Ilse Köhler joined the Nazi Party, receiving a membership card with her number, 1,130,836. In 1934, she met a man who would determine the course of her life, Karl Otto Koch. Born in Darmstadt in 1897, Karl was a veteran of World War I who became a bank clerk after the war. With the onset of the worldwide Depression, his bank collapsed, and he became unemployed. In 1931, embittered and economically insecure, he joined the Nazi Party, becoming a member of the elite SS a year later.

With the start of the Nazi dictatorship in the spring of 1933, Karl Koch's career flourished. As the SS tightened its grip on the scores of concentration camps the Hitler regime had created to terrorize the German population, Karl advanced rapidly in rank within the SS, becoming a senior commander at several concentration camps, including Esterwegen, Lichtenburg (Prettin), and Sachsenburg. In 1935, he became commandant of one of the most brutal of all concentration camps, the notorious Berlin prison Columbia Haus.

Ilse Köhler was quickly attracted to Karl. Captivated by men in uniform, she had been in love once before, with another SS man. Karl was also interested in the attractive Ilse, who was almost ten years his junior. The two became lovers, and Ilse spent much of her time in the several concentration camps Karl helped administer, including Sachsenhausen, of which he became commandant in July 1936. Because the SS expected its men to live "ordered lives," pressure grew on Karl to regularize his relationship with Ilse. In May 1937, the couple were married at midnight in a quasi-pagan SS ritual in an oak grove illuminated by torchlight. Soon after, Karl was promoted to lieutenant colonel.

Karl Koch's new assignment, which began officially on August 1, 1937, was to serve as the commandant of the newly established Buchenwald concentration camp. Located on the scenic Ettersberg mountain, it was a short distance from the historic town of Weimar, known for its association with two of the giants of German culture, Goethe and Schiller. By the end of 1937, Buchenwald had begun to function as another of the many camps into which political and religious opponents of the Nazi regime, as well as homosexuals, Sinti and Roma (Gypsies), Jews (particularly at the time of Kristallnacht, November 1938), and other so-called "undesir-

ables" were sent against their wills. The Kochs lived on the camp's grounds in a handsome villa built by prisoners.

Over the next several years, the prisoner population of Buchenwald would swell dramatically from 2,561 in 1937, to 10,992 in 1938, to 11,786 in 1939. By the time of the camp's liberation by the U.S. Army in April 1945, approximately 65,000 had lost their lives there as a result of being shot, hanged, poisoned, or denied proper medical treatment. Buchenwald became the personal kingdom of Karl as well as of Ilse, whose official title was that of SS-Aufseherin (female SS overseer). Despite the immense power the couple enjoyed, their private life soon deteriorated. One of their three children, a daughter of three months, died of pneumonia, and the couple went their separate ways. Karl had numerous affairs with women in nearby Weimar. Ilse too broke her marriage vows on countless occasions with a number of SS officers in the camp.

As an SS-Aufseherin, Ilse enjoyed her power. At her second trial in 1951, eyewitness testimony described how she beat prisoners with her own hands, or, in dozens of cases, with her riding whip. She would walk through Buchenwald in a provocative dress, intent on eliciting prisoner interest. If they even glanced at her, she demanded that punishment be severe—25 lashes of the whip. At her request, her husband ordered guards to beat prisoners, and a number of inmates were battered and kicked to death at her instigation.

At Ilse Koch's special request, a private riding stall was constructed for her during the first year of World War II. It was a costly, spacious rectangular wooden building, approximately 60 feet in height and 120 by 300 feet. Decorated with wall mirrors, it cost at least 250,000 reichsmarks even taking into account that it was built by unpaid and poorly fed slave laborers, at least 30 of whom died in accidents or took their own lives in despair during its construction. After its completion, Ilse would hold her morning ride there several times a week, during which an SS band provided her with appropriate musical accompaniment.

Among the many depraved aspects of the Buchenwald camp, one of the most grisly produced as evidence at postwar trials were the specimens of processed human skin, as well as shrunken human heads. Ilse Koch was accused of having singled out individual prisoners, particularly those who had unusual tattoos on their bodies, who were then murdered and their skin processed into various "souvenir" objects, including lampshades and bookbinding material.

Although Ilse was fully aware of this horrific project and was accused in her first trial in 1947 of having a lampshade made of human skin in her home, it could never be legally proven that she had been in charge of the project. Furthermore, since her husband had made a "hobby" of collecting patches of tattooed human skin and shrunken human heads, it proved to be difficult to separate his responsibility from her own in these deeds. There had in fact been several SS physicians working in Buchenwald who showed a strong interest in carrying out "medical research" along these lines, which had been officially forbidden by SS headquarters (at least on paper), most likely because of concern about negative propaganda if such information ever became public knowledge.

In September 1941, during the first phase of the German attack on the Soviet Union, Karl Koch was appointed commandant of Majdanek, at that time a Waffen-SS camp for Soviet prisoners of war. Under his regime, the camp was greatly enlarged and civilian prisoners, some of whom were Jews, were brought in. Soon prisoners were being murdered on a mass, systematic basis. In July 1942, after an outbreak of Soviet prisoners of war had taken place at Majdanek, Commandant Karl Koch was suspended from his post and placed on trial but was acquitted in February 1943. He was then assigned to administrative posts in postal service security units.

In August 1943, Karl was arrested by the SS on charges of embezzlement, forgery, making threats to officials, and unspecified other charges. These turned out to be the murder of prisoners who knew too much about his corruption, as well as an accusation that he had authorized the creation of the collection of human skins and shrunken heads. Ilse was arrested at the same time on charges of having been her husband's accomplice and of having stolen 710,000 reichsmarks. Strange as it may seem, Heinrich Himmler believed that the SS was an organization of honorable men that constantly had to be on guard against all manifestations of moral laxity and corruption. As early as December 1941, Karl Koch had been briefly arrested on suspicion of corruption, but Himmler had ordered his re-

Ilse Koch at her trial, 1950.

lease. Prince Josias Georg Wilhelm Adolf zu Waldeck-Pyrmont, an SS general and chief of police of the Weimar-Buchenwald district, who was an implacable foe of Karl's, was convinced that the Buchenwald commandant was guilty of gross corruption. The prince enjoyed great prestige in the SS, having been the first member of German royalty to join Himmler's fledgling elite Nazi corps in 1929.

The SS investigation that began with the arrests of Karl and Ilse Koch in August 1943 was a thorough one. Among the crimes discovered were Karl Koch's murders of Buchenwald prisoners, several of them killed by the injection of typhus into their bodies, because they knew too much about the commandant's massive embezzlement of money from Jewish prisoners. A search of the houses of several staff members uncovered large quantities of jewelry, cash, other valuables, and gold taken from the mouths of murdered prisoners. Himmler initially wanted to end the incident by sending Karl to serve at the front. He changed his mind, however, and the trial commenced. In 1944, Karl Koch was found guilty as charged by the SS Supreme Court in Munich and sentenced to death. Ilse was acquitted of all charges. After sentencing, ex-Commandant Karl Koch was returned to Buchenwald, this time as a prisoner. In early April 1945, a week before the American liberation, he was shot by the SS. On the last night of his life, he raved like a madman.

Ilse Koch moved to Ludwigsburg, where her two surviving children had stayed with relatives while she was on trial. During the next months, in which Germany surrendered, she drank heavily and behaved promiscuously. Recognized by chance on a Ludwigsburg street by a Buchenwald survivor in June 1945, she was arrested by Allied forces. After a long period of preparation by the prosecution, Ilse Koch and 29 other Buchenwald staff members were placed on trial starting on April 11, 1947. Fittingly, the trial took place at the former Nazi concentration camp of Dachau near Munich. As testimony in her part of the case became public, Ilse Koch became known in the press as the "Hexe von Buchenwald" (the Witch of Buchenwald), which ofttimes became the "Bitch of Buchenwald." The unimaginable horrors of Buchenwald, Majdanek and other Nazi concentration camps revealed by the trial shocked a world.

The bulk of testimony made it clear that Ilse was a sadist. Koch's American-appointed defense counsel, Captain Emanuel Lewis, who happened to be Jewish, argued in court that his client's "morality is nobody's business, and certainly not a matter for this court to judge, it is in fact a matter that she and she alone must come to terms with." Another American military lawyer, Leon Poullada, who had been chief of the defense team in the Nordhausen concentration camp trial, noted that "the documents reveal Frau Koch to have been a morally deviant woman lacking in human feelings . . . but in the United States such personality traits are not punishable offenses and they are certainly not war crimes under the rules of international law."

On August 17, 1947, the Buchenwald trial came to an end. Several prisoners were sentenced to death, with Ilse Koch receiving a sentence of life imprisonment at hard labor for having beaten Buchenwald prisoners and singling out others for execution. On October 29, 1947, Ilse added another bizarre element into her case when she gave birth to a fourth child, a son named Uwe Köhler. She refused to name the father but rumors swirled, some naming an American soldier, others suggesting that a German prison worker might have sired the baby. Soon, other matters dominated the front pages of the world's press, and Koch was forgotten.

In June 1948, General Lucius D. Clay, commander of U.S. Forces in Germany, commuted Koch's sentence from life to four years, which meant she could soon look forward to being a free woman. Clay's decision was based on the findings of a review board which had concluded that the bulk of the evidence against Ilse Koch was hearsay. Although the general defended his action in a secret memo as having been non-political and as one of the many "decisions of conscience" his job required him to make, the reality of the situation was that in 1948 American strategic interests called for an increasingly conciliatory policy toward Germany, which was urgently needed as a stable and prosperous ally in the Cold War.

Ilse Koch's impending release incited a public outcry in the United States, and a special Senate committee was created to investigate the matter. As before, the American public's interest in the Koch case soon faltered. At the same time, however, it was deemed ill-advised to release Koch when her four-year sentence had been served. In October 1949, upon her release from American custody, she was rearrested by a now semi-sovereign West German state. In November 1950, her new trial began in Augsburg, the charges being instigation to murder in 135 cases. The interrogation of 2,000 witnesses provided no proof of homicide charges, but she was found guilty on January 15, 1951, on two counts of incitement to murder of Buchenwald prisoners; the sentence was life imprisonment.

In the mid-1960s, Ilse Koch's last child Uwe Köhler discovered that his mother was the notorious Ilse Koch, then incarcerated at Aichach prison in Bavaria. Removed from his mother at birth, he had grown up in a foster home in Bavaria. At age eight, he happened to see his mother's name on his birth certificate and never forgot it. Eleven years later, he made a connection between himself and his mother after having by chance read a newspaper story about her. During the Christmas season in 1966, Köhler went to Aichach "with a creepy feeling" and met his mother in what he would later describe as a joyous reunion. They met regularly from then on, once a month according to prison rules, until she hanged herself on September 2, 1967, three weeks before her 61st birthday.

After his mother's suicide, Uwe began a campaign to clear her name. Noting that three different courts had not been able to convict her of major capital crimes and that none had found her guilty of ordering prisoners to be killed because she desired their tattooed skins, Köhler hoped to bring about a posthumous rehabilitation for his mother. At the same time, he seemed to be quite aware of the existence of the universe of evil in which she had lived. Uwe told a *New York Times* reporter in 1971: "I can't really imagine what it was like then in the war. I am not even convinced she was guiltless. But I feel that she just slithered into the concentration-camp world like many others without being able to do anything about it." Unlike the vast majority of those "others," however, who found themselves in the "concentration-camp world without being able to do anything about it" (the victims of Nazi brutality who suffered and were murdered there), Ilse Koch seems to have actively enjoyed herself.

SOURCES:

Binder, David. "Ilse Koch's Posthumous Rehabilitation Sought by Son," in *The New York Times Biographical Edition.* May 1971, p. 1531.

Bower, Tom. *Blind Eye to Murder: Britain, America, and the Purging of Nazi Germany—A Pledge Betrayed.* London: Granada-Paladin, 1983.

Buscher, Frank Michael. "The United States and the Problem of Convicted War Criminals, 1946–1955." Ph.D. dissertation, Marquette University, 1988.

Clark, J. Ray. *Journey to Hell: The Fiery Furnaces of Buchenwald.* Raleigh, NC: Pentland, 1996.

"Die rote Hexe von Buchenwald," in *Der sozialistische Kämpfer* [Vienna]. No. 11–12, November–December 1951, pp. 18–20.

Feig, Konnilyn G. *Hitler's Death Camps: The Sanity of Madness.* NY: Holmes & Meier, 1981.

Fitzgibbon, Constantine. *Denazification.* NY: W.W. Norton, 1969.

Grossmann. Kurt R. "The Trial of Ilse Koch," in *Congress Weekly: A Review of Jewish Interests.* December 18, 1950, pp. 7–9.

"The Guilty: The Butchers of Buchenwald Hear the Stern Judgment of Civilization," in *Life.* Vol. 23, no. 8. August 25, 1947, p. 39.

Hackett, David A., ed. *The Buchenwald Report.* Boulder, CO: Westview Press, 1995.

Koessler, Maximilian. "The Ilse Koch Senate Investigation and Its Legal Problems on Double Jeopardy and res judicata," in *Missouri Law Review.* Vol. 23, no. 1, 1958, pp. 1–23.

Konzentrationslager Buchenwald Post Weimar/Thür.: Katalog zu der Ausstellung aus der Deutschen Demokratischen Republik im Martin-Gropius-Bau Berlin (West), April–Juni 1990. Buchenwald: Nationale Mahn- und Gedenkstätte Buchenwald, 1990.

Mohler, Armin. *Der Nasenring: Die Vergangenheitsbewältigung vor und nach dem Fall der Mauer.* Munich: Verlag Langen Müller, 1991.

National Archives of the United States, Washington, D.C. Record Group 338, case 000-50-9, Box 426.

Segev, Tom. *Soldiers of Evil: The Commandants of the Nazi Concentration Camps.* Translated by Haim Watzman. NY: McGraw-Hill, 1987.

Smith, Arthur L., Jr. *Die Hexe von Buchenwald: Der Fall Ilse Koch.* Vienna and Cologne: Böhlau Verlag, 1983.

Smith, Jean Edward. *Lucius D. Clay: An American Life.* NY: Henry Holt, 1992.

——, ed. *The Papers of General Lucius D. Clay: Germany 1945–1949.* 2 vols. Bloomington, IN: Indiana University Press, 1974.

Sottile, Antoine. "Un Peu Plus de Justice, S.V.P.! (A Propos de Certains Verdicts et Acquittements Prononcés par les Tribunaux Militaires Internationaux)," in *Revue de Droit International de Sciences Diplomatiques et Politiques.* Vol. 26, no. 3, 1948, pp. 372–385.

Wistrich, Robert S. *Who's Who in Nazi Germany.* London and NY: Routledge, 1995.

John Haag,
Associate Professor of History,
University of Georgia, Athens, Georgia

Koch, Marita (1957—)

East German runner. Born on February 18, 1957, in East Germany.

Marita Koch, who once held world records in both the 200 meters and 400 meters, won the gold medal in the 400 meters in the Moscow Olympics in 1980, as well as the silver in the 4x100 meters. In 1982, she placed first in the 400-meter race in the European games in Athens, Greece, with a time of 48.16. In the 100 meters, her personal best time was 10.83. Koch's main rivals were *Irena Kirszenstein-Szewinska and *Evelyn Ashford.

Kochanska, Marcella (1858–1935).

See Sembrich, Marcella.

Ko-ching, Kang (1911–1992).

See Kang Keqing.

Kock, Karin (1891–1976)

Swedish economist and first woman member of the Swedish government. Name variations: Karin Kock-Lindberg. Born in Stockholm, Sweden, on July 2, 1891; died in 1976; daughter of Ernst Kock (chief supervisor in the Swedish Customs Office) and Anna (Aslund) Kock; graduated from the Whitlockska Samskolan, in Stockholm, in 1910; University of Stockholm, B.A., 1918, M.A., 1925, Ph.D., 1929; married Hugo Lindberg (a lawyer), in 1936.

One of Europe's foremost economists and the first woman Cabinet member in Sweden's history, Karin Kock was born in 1891 in Stockholm, where she attended the Whitlockska Samskolan, a combined high school and junior college. Shortly after graduating in 1910, she went to work as a statistical assistant with the Bureau of Statistics in Stockholm, leaving after three years to pursue her studies at the University of Stockholm. After receiving her B.A. degree in 1918, she was employed by a Swedish bank as a statistician and economic researcher. On her own time, she earned both her master's and Ph.D. degrees from the University of Stockholm, specializing in economics. Her doctoral thesis, a study of interest rates, was published in 1929 as the first of the "Stockholm Economic Studies" series. A second book on the Swedish banking system was published in 1930.

In 1932, Kock left the bank to become a professor of economics at the University of Stockholm, where she held teaching posts until 1946. During that period, she was also involved in a number of economic surveys for the Swedish government, one of which, in 1934–35, explored the economic and social trends of the period and proposed certain reforms in the compilation of statistics. Others included an investigation of salaries paid to Swedish women (for which she wrote a report on the theory of women's wages), a survey of the industries dependent on forest resources, and a study on private saving and the rate of consumption in relation to the financial state of the country. Kock also published a number of unofficial treatises and articles.

In 1947, Kock was appointed to the Swedish Department of Commerce as chief of one of its bureaus, and that April she was appointed consultative minister in the Social Democratic Labor Cabinet of Tage Erlander. The latter appointment marked the first time a woman was seated at the King's council table and was noted in the newspaper *Svenska Dagbladet* as "a high point in the striving of Swedish women toward full citizenship rights and recognition of the just principle that merit and skill, regardless of sex, should be decisive in appointments to high government positions." Kock's duties ranged from formulating the national budget to confronting issues of internal consumption versus foreign trade and the inflationary pressures of the postwar home economy. Kock was also named Minister of Supply in October 1948. She served until 1949. During the bicameral period (before the constitution was changed in 1971 and the number of houses of Parliament reduced to one) only four other women became ministers: **Hildur Nygren** (1951), **Ulla Lindström** (1954–66), *****Alva Myrdal** (1967–73), and **Camilla Odhnoff** (1967–73), all of them members of the Social Democratic Labor Party.

Kock was Sweden's delegate to the International Labor Organization Conference in Paris in 1947 and served for several years as the Swedish delegate to conferences of the Economic Commission for Europe. She was also a member of the Swedish Economic Society and the Swedish Federation of Business and Professional Women.

Kock was married in 1936 to Hugo Lindberg, a lawyer, but continued to use her maiden name in public life. Although an intimidating woman by reputation, she was apparently extremely approachable and down-to-earth. **Barbara Spinning** of the *New York Sun*, who met Kock when she was visiting the United States in 1948, remarked on her ability to put people at ease. "Her conversation slips effortlessly from a learned discussion on nation budgeting to a comparison of hemlines in Stockholm and New York." Karin Kock died in 1976. In May 1996, a Swedish postage stamp was issued in her honor.

SOURCES:
Information from the Swedish Parliament.
Rothe, Anna, ed. *Current Biography.* NY: H.W. Wilson, 1948.

Koen, Fanny Blankers (b. 1918).

See Blankers-Koen, Fanny.

Koesem (1589–1651).

See Reign of Women for Kösem.

Koestler, Marie (1879–1965).

See Köstler, Marie.

Koestlin, Josephine Lang (1815–1880).

See Lang, Josephine.

Kogan, Claude (1919–1959)

French mountaineer. Born in 1919; died in 1959; married Georges Kogan (a mountaineer), in 1945 (died 1951).

Ascended North Face of the Dru (1946); was first female lead of South Ridge of Aiguille Noire de Peuterey (1949); made second ascent of Quitaraju (1951); made first ascent of Salcantay (1952); made first ascent of Nun Kun (23,400 ft.) in Kashmir (1953); made first ascent of Ganesh Himal in Nepal, with Raymond Lambert (1955).

Made an honorary member of the Ladies' Alpine Club; lectured on her climbs to an unprecedented joint meeting of the men's and women's Alpine clubs in London.

Born in 1919, Claude Kogan began climbing in the Belgian Ardennes. During the German occupation of France, she moved to Nice and built up a small business, designing swimwear for women. While there, she met and married another mountaineer, Georges Kogan. After World War II, the couple joined the Groupe de Haute Montagne and made ascents in the Dauphine and Chamonix, as well as the North Face of the Dru (1946) and the South Ridge of the Aiguille Noire de Peuterey (1949) with Claude in the lead.

In 1951, Georges and Raymond Leininger made the first ascent of Alpamayo in the Andes; a few days later, Claude Kogan and **Nicole Leininger** went higher to Quitaraju (20,276 ft.). But six months after, Georges fell ill and died. A saddened Kogan returned to the Andes and made the first ascent of Salcantay (20,500 ft.) with Bernard Pierre.

On October 26, 1954, despite high winds and freezing temperatures, Claude Kogan, Raymond Lambert, Denis Bertholet, Jean Juge and two sherpas sat at Camp IV preparing for an attempt on Cho Oyu (26,906 feet) in the Himalayas. An Austrian team had made two failed attempts the week before. Of the Swiss team only Kogan and Lambert headed for the top. Wrote Lambert: "I was surprised to see how enfeebled the expedition was becoming, with the exception of Claude Kogan and myself. Our companions were no longer putting up a fight; they could hardly struggle against the cold and were letting death creep upon them without striking a blow to defend themselves. . . . [T]he wind was sweeping all before it corrupting moral strength as well as physical."

While the others and the sherpas retreated, Lambert and Kogan struggled on—with wind gusts at such high velocity that they sometimes had to crawl. "I tried to make the wind help me by leaning forward on it," wrote Kogan, "but immediately it dropped and I found myself face downwards on the snow with all my breath gone. . . . Never had I had so furious a struggle with the elements." They fought the wind for five hours but had to retreat to base camp. They had, however, reached 25,600 feet, the highest point ever attained by a woman.

But Kogan had unfinished business with Cho Oyu. In 1959, she suggested a Women's International Expedition (Expédition Feminine au Nepal) to the Himalayas. With Kogan as their leader, the powerful team included **Eileen Healey** (née Gregory), **Dorothea Gravina, Margaret Darvall, *Loulou Boulaz, Claudine Van der Stratten, Jeanne Franco, Collette le Bret, Micheline Rambaud** and two daughters and a niece of Sherpa Tensing, who had climbed Everest with Edmund Hillary.

On September 29th, Kogan and Van der Stratten, with **Ang Norbu** as sherpa, left Camp III

Claude Kogan

to establish Camp IV and attack the summit. But the weather turned warm the following day and waves of avalanches began to rumble down Cho Oyu. When contact with Camp IV and Kogan was lost, the other camps were forced to retreat to base camp. The weather improved on October 3rd and an exploring party set out for Camp IV. The report came back: "It was swept clean."

Lambert, one of mountaineering's greats, once wrote of Kogan: "For her an expedition is not an athletic feat; it is an essay in the poetics. She brings to it the same passion that filled the first seekers of gold or the companions of Magellan. For Claude, mountaineering is one long search for the Route to the Indies." She was considered one of the best.

SOURCES:

Birkett, Bill, and Bill Peascod. *Women Climbing: 200 Years of Achievement.* London: A. & C. Black, 1989.

Lambert, Raymond. *White Fury.* London: Hurst and Blackett, 1956.

Williams, Cecily. *Women on the Rope.* London: Allen & Unwin, 1973.

Kōgyoku-Saimei (594–661)

Japanese empress, the 35th and 37th sovereign of Japan, who witnessed her son commit murder. Name variations: Princess Takaru; (first reign) Empress Kōgyoku; (second reign) Empress Saimei; Kogyoku-tennō. Pronunciation: KOE-gyoe-koo Sigh-may. Reigned from 642 to 645 and from 655 to 661. Born in 594; died in Kyushu, Japan, in 661, while seeing off her forces to Korea to defend the Paekche kingdom from the Chinese invasion; grandmother of Empress *Jitō (645–702); married Emperor Jomei; children: Emperor Tenji; Emperor Oama; and the consort of Emperor Kotoku.

With the power struggles following the death of her husband, Emperor Jomei, Kōgyoku was installed as sovereign by the imperial counselors. The power struggles continued, however, and dramatically in 645 her own son Prince Naka (later Emperor Tenji) murdered an ambitious minister before her eyes. Stunned, she nevertheless questioned her son, who contended that the minister had committed treason. Kōgyoku left the murder scene without uttering a word and abdicated two days later. Nine years later, upon the death of her successor, Emperor Kotoku, she was again called upon to take the throne and served until her death in 661. During her second reign, Kōgyoku frequently sent military expeditions to the northern part of Japan to subdue the aboriginal people there.

SOURCES:

Aoki, Michiko Y. "Jitō Tennō: the Female Sovereign," in *Heroic With Grace: Legendary Women of Japan.* Chieko Irie Mulhern, ed. Armonk: NY: M.E. Sharpe, 1991, pp. 40–76.

Linda L. Johnson,
Professor of History, Concordia College, Moorhead, Minnesota

Kohary, Antoinette (1797–1862)

Aunt by marriage of Queen Victoria. Name variations: Antonia. Born on July 2, 1797; died on September 25, 1862; married Ferdinand of Saxe-Coburg (uncle of Queen *Victoria), on January 2, 1816; children: Ferdinand of Saxe-Coburg (1816–1885, who married *Maria II da Gloria, queen of Portugal); Augustus of Saxe-Coburg (1818–1881); *Victoria of Saxe-Coburg (1822–1857); Leopold Saxe-Coburg (1824–1884).

Kohut, Rebekah (1864–1951)

American social welfare leader and educator. Born Rebekah Bettelheim in Kaschau, Hungary, on September 9, 1864; died in New York City on August 11, 1951; youngest daughter and third child of three daughters and two sons of Albert Siegfried Bettelheim (a rabbi and physician) and Henrietta (Wientraub) Bettelheim (a teacher); attended high school and normal school in San Francisco; attended the University of California, San Francisco; married Alexander Kohut (a rabbi), on February 14, 1887 (died 1895); stepchildren: eight.

One of five children, Rebekah Kohut was born in Hungary and immigrated to America with her family in 1867. Her father Albert Bettelheim, who was also a physician, served as the rabbi of a synagogue in Philadelphia until 1869, when he took over a Reform temple in Richmond, Virginia. Her mother **Henrietta Bettelheim**, who died in 1870, was the primary role model for young Rebekah. One of the first Jewish women in Hungary to become a schoolteacher, Henrietta had been viewed as a radical in her day. "Her example inspired me," Kohut wrote in her autobiography *My Portion* (1925), "led me as a young girl to seek out all kinds of less sheltered activities, into which I entered with all the ardor of a cause, and I know I felt very brave and heroine-like to myself."

In 1875, the family moved to San Francisco, where Rebekah attended high school, normal school, and took courses at the University of California. It was at this time that she discovered her life's work. "It appeared to me that my real mission in life should be as a worker in the front ranks of American Jewish womanhood," she wrote. Thinking at first that she might forego marriage in order to devote herself to social service, Rebekah altered her plans somewhat upon meeting Alexander Kohut, a Hungarian rabbi 22 years her senior, and a widower with eight children. She married Kohut in February 1887 and moved to New York, where, in addition to caring for her ready-made family, she handled her husband's correspondence, translated his sermons for publication, and organized the women of the synagogue. Ignoring mild protests from her husband, she joined the New York Women's Health Protective Association and occasionally taught classes at the Educational Alliance, a school founded on New York's Lower East Side by a group of wealthy German-Jewish Americans. Life as she knew it changed abruptly in May 1894 when Alexander died, leaving her as the sole support of his family.

With characteristic resolve, Rebekah set out to establish a career as an educational and vocational expert. She lectured to groups associated with the Reform sisterhoods and taught confirmation classes to young Jewish girls. In 1899, with assistance from philanthropist Jacob Schiff, she founded the Kohut School for Girls, which she ran for five years. In addition to her full-time job, Kohut became a driving force behind the newly founded New York branch of the National Council of Jewish Women. "At the time the Council was founded," she recalled in her memoirs, "participation by women in public life was still a new thing, and there was an excitement, a heady sense of independence, a thrill, a feeling that one was taking part in the best kind of revolution, even if it involved nothing more at the moment than parliamentary debates about hot soup and recreation for children."

Kohut also became a patron of Jewish scholarship, which she endowed through Yale. In 1912, she established the Alexander Kohut Memorial Collection, donating her husband's numerous volumes of Near Eastern literature to the college. In 1915, the Kohut family and the college together instituted the Alexander Kohut Memorial Publication Fund to support the Yale Oriental Series, and in 1919, the family established a research fellowship for graduate students in Semitics.

Kohut was also involved with employment planning and counseling for women, establishing the Employment Bureau of the Young Women's Hebrew Association in 1914. During World War I, she served as chair of the Employ-

ment Committee of the Women's Committee for National Defense, which served as a clearinghouse for working women in New York. On the national level, she worked for the U.S. Employment Service and was a member of President Woodrow Wilson's Federal Employment Committee. She also served as the industrial chair of the National League for Women's Service.

Of her many activities, Kohut drew her greatest pleasure from her association with the National Council of Jewish Women, of which she served as president from 1894 to 1898. During the 1920s, the organization rallied to provide aid to Jews in Eastern Europe who had been devastated by the war. Kohut made numerous trips to Europe to view conditions firsthand and to determine how best to distribute aid. The council eventually grew to a membership of 600,000, a source of pride to Kohut, who called her sisters "conscientious, public-spirited women devoted to their communities and cooperating fully with other public bodies." In 1923, she was elected president of the World Congress of Jewish Women.

In 1931, Kohut was appointed by then governor Franklin D. Roosevelt to the New York State Advisory Council on Employment and to the Joint Legislative Commission on Unemployment. In 1934, at age 70, she returned to school administration, serving for several years as head of the Columbia Grammar School, a private boys' school. She also remained active in her organizations, including the National Council of Jewish Women, which honored her on the 50th anniversary of their founding with a banquet at the Hotel Commodore. Amid 900 guests, Kohut was presented with a check for $50,000, to be divided among her favorite charities. Rebekah Kohut died on August 11, 1951, at age 87.

SOURCES:

Henry, Sondra, and Emily Taitz. *Written Out of History: Our Jewish Foremothers*. NY: Biblio Press, 1990.

Sicherman, Barbara, and Carol Hurd Green, eds. *Notable American Women: The Modern Period*. Cambridge, MA: The Belknap Press of Harvard University Press, 1980.

SUGGESTED READING:

Kohut, Rebecca. *My Portion* (autobiography), 1925.

———. *More Yesterdays* (autobiography), 1950.

Barbara Morgan,
Melrose, Massachusetts

Koidula, Lydia (1843–1886)

Estonian poet and playwright who was a major figure in the Estonian national awakening of the 19th century. Born Lydia Emilie Florentine Jannsen in Vändra (Pärnu), Estonia, on December 24, 1843; died in Kronstadt, Russia, on August 11, 1886; daughter of

Johann Voldemar Jannsen (1819–1890), a teacher; married Eduard Michelson.

As the Soviet Union was crumbling in the late 1980s, the people of Estonia voiced their desire for national independence through poetry and music, creating what many would later call their "singing revolution." Among their favorite patriotic bards was the 19th-century poet Lydia Koidula, whose verse provided inspiration to make sacrifices for freedom. At times it appeared as if the entire Estonian nation was singing Koidula's words, "My love is my native country to whom I've devoted my heart."

The road to Estonian independence was long and difficult. Although independent in prehistoric times, the small Baltic nation fell under the domination of German and Danish feudal lords in the 13th century. While a rich folk culture of songs, fairy tales, proverbs, sayings and riddles flourished in the villages, a literary language and literature did not exist for many centuries and the urban intelligentsia was under strong German and later Russian influence. Poverty and ignorance stalked the countryside while foreign tongues and traditions took over the towns of Estonia.

Lydia Koidula

Inspired by traditional Estonian folklore and Finland's *Kalevala* epic, Friedrich Robert Fählmann (1798–1850) and Friedrich Reinhold Kreutzwald (1803–1882) spent three decades collecting their nation's ancient legends, myths and songs. By this time Estonian intellectuals, influenced by the spirit of Romantic nationalism, had called on scholars to "give the nation an epic and history; [then] the rest will be won." Encouraged by the Estonian Learned Society (founded in 1838), during the years 1857–61, Kreutzwald published the epic work in its final form of 18,993 verses under the title *Kalevipoeg* (The Son of Kalev). Powerful and stirring, *Kalevipoeg* ends with the prophecy that one day the son of Kalev, the father of heroes, will be freed by a fire from the rock that holds him prisoner, and Estonians will once again be a contented and prosperous people.

Lydia Koidula was born in 1843, the daughter of teacher Johann Voldemar Jannsen, and, as a precocious young woman, assisted her father in editing the country's first weekly newspaper, *The Postman of Pärnu,* founded in 1857. In 1864, Jannsen moved his newspaper to the larger city of Tartu and renamed it *The Estonian Postman.* Estonian cultural life flourished in Tartu, and Lydia responded enthusiastically to the spirit of the day. Her father was a leading cultural nationalist, and both he and Lydia took pride in his lyrics for "My Native Land," which were set to a melody by Finnish composer Fredrik Pacius and first sung at the Estonian Song Festival in 1869. (After 1918, both Finland and Estonia would adopt this song as their national anthems, Estonia's with J.V. Jannsen's lyrics.) As a sign of her patriotic fervor, Lydia changed her name from the Swedish-sounding Jannsen to the more Estonian Koidula.

In 1866, translating and adapting German poetry to the Estonian language, Koidula published her first volume of verse, entitled *Meadow Flowers.* The next year, she published a volume of original verse in Estonian, *The Nightingale of Emajögi* (1867), a work with strongly expressed nationalism. Over the next decade, she would publish a large number of verse works revealing her hatred of feudal oppression, social backwardness and national apathy.

Convinced that the stage could serve as an effective weapon in the struggle to win the national soul, Koidula began to write plays in the late 1860s. In rapid succession from 1870 to 1872, she wrote several plays including *The Cousin from Saaremaa, The Wooing Birches, or Maret and Miina,* and *Such a Mulk, or a Hun-*

dred Barrels of Coarse Salt. First presented in Tartu in the building of the Vanemuine Society—the nation's leading musical and cultural organization—in June 1870, *The Cousin from Saaremaa* was performed in Estonian, whereas all of the city's other theaters presented plays in the German language. Both this play and *The Wooing Birches* were adapted by Koidula from standard German plays, but *Such a Mulk,* a sharp social commentary on the educational backwardness of Estonia's peasants, was a completely original work. Koidula not only wrote but also produced and directed *Such a Mulk* at a theater soon to be called "Koidula's Theater." In this work, she gave voice to her hope that the Estonian nation would one day be free, prosperous and part of a world based on progressive ideals. Throughout the 1870s, her plays were performed in all of Estonia's cities and towns, and by 1880 performances were also given in the rural areas, usually in schoolrooms or threshing barns. By this time, many of Koidula's poems were rapidly being transformed into widely beloved popular songs.

A difficult change took place in Koidula's life in 1873. That year, she accompanied her husband, the physician Eduard Michelson, to his post at the imperial Russian naval base at Kronstadt near St. Petersburg. Over the next years, she longed to return to her native home, but Lydia Koidula died at Kronstadt on August 11, 1886. Her poems, however, lived on, continuing to inspire the people of Estonia. During her lifetime, when Estonia was part of a tsarist Russia determined to stamp out autonomous linguistic and cultural traditions in its Baltic Provinces, Koidula's nationalist sentiments often had to be expressed in veiled terms. Some two decades after her death, Estonia freed itself from the Russian yoke in 1918 and became an independent republic. Koidula's poems could then be read and enjoyed freely by all.

A new Soviet occupation, in 1940–1941 and 1944–1991, again pained Estonian nationalists, virtually all of whom drew inspiration from Koidula's verse. Most Estonian symbols were banned under Soviet rule, but during these years Koidula's poem "My Fatherland is Dear to Me," as set to music by Gustav Ernesaks, became a powerful means of expressing Estonian feelings. This was, and continues to be regarded as, an unofficial anthem, while her father's "My Native Land" is the official national anthem of post-Soviet Estonia. More than a century after her death, Lydia Koidula remains a revered Estonian author. In Tallinn, Lydia Koidula Street appears to have a particular magnetic appeal for women poets, for on this street have lived at least two major poets, **Betti Alver** (b. 1906) and **Anna Haava** (1864–1957). On December 14, 1993, Estonia honored Koidula by depicting her on a commemorative postage stamp.

SOURCES:

Aaver, Eva, Heli Laanekask, and Sirje Olesk. *Lydia Koidula 1843–1886.* Tallinn: Ilmamaa, 1994.

Harris, Ernest Howard. *A Glimpse of Estonian Literature.* Manchester: Sherratt & Hughes, 1933.

———. *Literature in Estonia.* 2nd ed. London: Boreas, 1947.

Ivask, Ivar. "A Home in Language and Poetry: Travel Impressions from Estonia, Latvia, Lithuania, and Russia, Autumn 1988," in *World Literature Today.* Vol. 63, no. 3. Summer 1989, pp. 391–405.

Janes, Henno. *Geschichte der estnischen Literatur.* Stockholm: Almqvist & Wiksell, 1965.

Kirby, William Forsell. *The Hero of Esthonia and Other Studies in the Romantic Literature of that Country.* 2 vols. London: J.C. Nimmo, 1895.

Nirk, Endel. *Estonian Literature: Historical Survey with Biobibliographical Appendix.* Translated by Arthur Robert Hone and Oleg Mutt. 2nd ed. Tallinn: Perioodika, 1987.

Puhvel, Madli. *Symbol of Dawn: The Life and Times of the 19th-Century Estonian Poet Lydia Koidula.* Tartu, Estonia: Tartu University Press, 1995.

Raun, Toivo U. *Estonia and the Estonians.* 2nd ed. Stanford, CA: Hoover Institution Press, Stanford University, 1991.

———. "Estonian Literature, 1872–1914: A Source for Social History?," in *Journal of Baltic Studies.* Vol. 12, no. 2. Summer 1981, pp. 120–127.

Rubulis, Aleksis. *Baltic Literature: A Survey of Finnish, Estonian, Latvian, and Lithuanian Literatures.* Notre Dame, IN: University of Notre Dame Press, 1970.

Scheller, Adolf. "Social Problems in Estonian Literature Under the Czar Regime and during the Epoch of Independence." Ph.D. dissertation, University of Montreal, 1962.

Thomson, Erik. *Estnische Literatur: Ihre europäische Verflechtung in Geschichte und Gegenwart.* Lüneburg: Nordostdeutsches Kulturwerk, 1973.

COLLECTIONS:

Lydia Koidula Library, Estonian National Museum, Tallinn; Lydia Koidula Papers, Estonian Archives of Cultural History, Tallinn.

RELATED MEDIA:

Lydia Koidula, 1843–1886: Sonalis-Muusikaline Kompositsioon, LP recording: Melodiia M40 38451, released 1989.

John Haag,
Associate Professor of History,
University of Georgia, Athens, Georgia

Kōken-Shōtoku (718–770)

Japanese empress who ascended the throne twice and played a significant role in popularizing Buddhism, which flourished as the national religion for centuries. Name variations: (first reign) Empress Kōken or Koken; (second reign) Empress Shōtoku or

Shotoku. Pronunciation: KOE-ken SHOW-toe-ku. Reigned from 749 to 758 and from 764 to 770. Born in 718 in Nara, Japan; died in 770 in Nara, Japan; daughter of Emperor Shomu and Empress Komyo; never married; no children.

The daughter and sole surviving child of Emperor Shomu and Empress **Komyo**, Kōken was one of only eight empresses of Japan to have been officially designated as heir apparent. Kōken was initially educated by her mother, until Kibi no Makibi, a brilliant scholar of institutional government, was appointed in 740 to teach Kōken the Chinese classics and train her in statecraft. In 749, Emperor Shomu abdicated in the midst of political controversies surrounding his project to construct Todaiji (Eastern Great Temple), and, within it, the huge statue of the Sun Buddha. It appeared to be a propitious time for rule by a woman, who could serve as the traditional female role of a spiritual medium to mollify the conflicting Shintō and Buddhist factions. Indeed, not long after her accession, Kōken received a divine message from a Shintō deity that it was his will that the Buddhist statue and temple be erected. This divine blessing made possible the completion of the project. Like her father, Kōken abdicated the throne to become more actively involved in propagating Buddhism, which she did by encouraging the casting of many Buddhist statues and the printing of Buddhist sutras for distribution throughout the country. She therefore played a significant role in the popularization of Buddhism outside the capital.

Following her abdication, Kōken created friction among the counselors at court, however, by declaring that, as a former empress, she would continue to make decisions regarding war, awards for meritorious service, and the punishment of criminals. She exacerbated tensions by seeking the counsel of a Buddhist priest, Dōkyo, whom, it was said, she would have married if that had been permitted of a retired empress. Opponents mounted armies to defeat her but her forces triumphed, and she returned to the throne for a second reign, as the Empress Shōtoku.

During her second reign, she consolidated the power of the throne and punished her opponents by prohibiting unauthorized persons from reclaiming land for private profit and officials from bearing arms. Involvement with the Buddhist priest Dōkyo, including a plan to name him as her successor, resulted in continued dissension. Seeking to evade the turmoil of the capital, Kōken-Shōtoku had a palace built in

Dōkyo's hometown in the provinces, where she lived with him for a time. "A male sovereign can marry at will," she supposedly said, "taking as many consorts as he wishes to have. Why is it that I, alone, because I am a woman and sovereign, cannot marry at all?" Upon her return to the capital, she fell ill and died in 770. Defamed for having been influenced by a male advisor, Kōken-Shōtoku became the ostensible reason why women were not permitted for centuries thereafter to rule as Japanese sovereigns.

SOURCES:

Aoki, Michiko Y. "Jitō Tennō: The Female Sovereign," in *Heroic With Grace: Legendary Women of Japan.* Chieko Mulhern, ed. Armonk, NY: M.E. Sharpe, 1991, pp. 40–76.

Linda L. Johnson,
Professor of History, Concordia College, Moorhead, Minnesota

Kolb, Barbara (1939—)

American composer of numerous contemporary pieces for chamber groups, ensembles, and orchestra. Born Barbara Anne Kolb in Hartford, Connecticut, on February 10, 1939; daughter of Helen (Lily) Kolb and Harold Judson Kolb (a director of music for a local radio station and conductor of many semi-professional big bands of the time); earned a bachelor of music at the University of Hartford in 1961 and a master's degree in 1965; studied with Lukas Foss, Gunther Schuller, and Arnold Franchetti.

Was first American woman to win the Prix de Rome (1969); was first woman to be commissioned by the Fromm Foundation to compose for concerts at Tanglewood (1970); received commissions from the Koussevitzky Foundation, New York State Council for the Arts, and the Washington Performing Arts Society among others; was first American woman to win the Prix de Rome (1970–71).

"Music is a matter of art not gender," according to Barbara Kolb. "If anything, composing a piece of music is very feminine. It is sensitive, emotional and contemplative. By comparison, doing housework is positively masculine." Kolb has specialized in compositional ideas of serialism, tone clusters, and other modern idioms, becoming one of the 20th century's most prolific composers. She began teaching as a professor of composition at Brooklyn College in New York during a time when there were less than 100 women teaching composition in the United States. In a sense, Kolb had two strikes against her—her gender and her love of modern music. "It is really a sad state of affairs when you think of the few orchestras that exist," said

Kolb, "and the limited number of conductors who would even think about programming a contemporary piece."

Despite these impediments, she continued to devote her energy to modern music. Some of these works were quite innovative. For example, *Soundings* was orchestrated for three orchestras which require two conductors. Two orchestras play on electronic music channels while one is live. Her composition *Trobar Clubs* also gained a worldwide reputation in modern music circles. Kolb made use of sound mass which minimizes the importance of individual pitches in preference for texture, timbre, and dynamics. She specialized in composing nontraditional chamber orchestras which often combined prerecorded nonelectronic sounds with various instruments. *Spring River Flowers Moon Night* was composed for two live pianists accompanied by a tape featuring an ensemble playing the mandolin, guitar, chimes, vibraphone, marimba, and percussion. Many orchestras increasingly perform 20th-century music, and Barbara Kolb's music is often featured on the program. Kolb is a pioneer in writing for ensembles outside the musical establishment.

SOURCES:

Cohen, Aaron I. *International Encyclopedia of Women Composers.* 2 vols. NY: Books & Music (USA), 1987.

Peyser, Joan. "Betsy Jolas and Barbara Kolb. Why Can't a Woman Compose like a Man?" in *The New York Times Biographical Edition.* June 1993, pp. 990–993.

SUGGESTED READING:

Henahan, Donal. "Rebel Who Found a Cause," in *The New York Times.* November 17, 1975, p. C–21 (illus).

COLLECTIONS:

Some of Barbara Kolb's music manuscripts are located at the New York Public Library, Music Division.

John Haag,
Athens, Georgia

Kollontai, Alexandra (1872–1952)

Russian revolutionary and feminist who was the first woman to be a member of the Bolshevik Central Committee and the Council of People's Commissars as well as the world's first female ambassador. Name variations: *Aleksandra Kollontay; (nickname) Shura.* Pronunciation: KOLL-lon-TIE. *Born Alexandra or Aleksandra Mikhailovna Domontovich in St. Petersburg, Russia, on March 19, 1872; died in Moscow on March 9, 1952; daughter of Mikhail Domontovich (a cavalry officer) and Aleksandra Masalina (daughter of a Finnish lumber merchant, she became an entrepreneur selling dairy products); tutored at home, leading to certificate, 1888; auditor, University of Zurich,* *1898–99; married Vladimir Kollontai, in 1893 (divorced); married Pavel Dybenko, in 1918; children: (first marriage) Mikhail.*

Did charitable and educational work in St. Petersburg (1895–98); joined Russian Social Democratic Labor Party (1899), associated with the Bolshevik faction (after 1915); wrote and lectured on Marxism and social issues (1900–05); promoted Marxist organization of Russian factory women (1906–08); fled abroad (December 1908), where she served as Russian representative to the International Women's Secretariat (1910–15), lectured at the Bologna Party School (1910–11), and wrote extensively on issues relating to maternity, sexuality and pacifism; returned to Russia (March 1917), elected to the Executive Committee of the Petrograd Soviet and to the Central Committee of the Bolshevik Party, and arrested (July 1917); served as commissar of Social Welfare (1917–18); was a member of Left Communist opposition (1918) and Workers' Opposition (1921–22); served as director, Women's Section (Zhenotdel) of the Central Committee of the Russian Communist Party (1920–22); performed diplomatic work in Norway (1922–25, ambassador 1927–30), Mexico (ambassador 1926–27) and Sweden (ambassador 1930–45).

Publications: over 230 newspaper and journal articles many of which have been reproduced in A.M. Kollontai, Izbrannye stat'i i rechi (Collected Articles and Speeches, Moscow, 1972), or in Selected Writings of Alexandra Kollontai (edited by Alix Holt, Westport, 1977). Also wrote 30 pamphlets, novellas and books among the more important being: Zhizn' finliandskikh rabochikh (The Life of Finnish Workers, St. Petersburg, 1903); Sotsial'nye osnovy zhenskogo voprosa (The Social Bases of the Woman Question, St. Petersburg, 1909); Obshchestvo i materinstvo (Society and Maternity, Petrograd, 1916); Komu nuzhna voina? (Who Needs War?, Bern, 1916); Novaia moral' i rabochii klass (The New Morality and the Working Class, Moscow, 1918); Sem'ia i kommunisticheskoe gosudarstvo (The Family and the Communist State, Moscow, 1918); Rabochaia oppozitsiia (The Workers' Opposition, Moscow, 1921).

On November 16, 1918, Alexandra Kollontai stood at the podium gazing out over more than 1,000 delegates representing female factory workers, peasant women, and Communist Party activists who had come from across Soviet Russia to attend the Congress of Working Women. As co-organizer, she had expected a third of that number. Her large and colorful audience, many wearing red kerchiefs and some with children in tow, was in marked contrast to the dispirited delegation of 45 women workers she had led at the First Congress of Russian Women only ten years earlier. In 1908, the male leadership of the party had dragged its feet at even sending a workers' delegation; now V.I. Lenin himself spoke at the 1918 Congress. None of Kollontai's resolutions had come to a vote on the earlier occasion; now the economic and political interests of working women received overwhelming support. In 1907 and 1908, the party had turned down her demands that it set up a women's bureau to coordinate work among women; in 1919, in large measure as a result of the recent congress, *Zhenotdel* or the Women's Section of the Central Committee came into being, and a year later Kollontai became its second director. While she had earlier been the first woman named to the Bolshevik Central Committee and the first female member of the Council of People's Commissars, this new position probably pleased her the most, it best suited her talents, and it offered her the greatest opportunity to affect the lives of Soviet women.

*W*e, the older generation, did not yet understand, as most men do and as young women are learning today, that work and the longing for love can be harmoniously combined so that work remains as the main goal of existence.

—Alexandra Kollontai

Alexandra Kollontai had been a rebel throughout her life. In the 1890s, she had rebelled against her family, her first husband, and her own aristocratic class. After the 1917 Revolution, she rebelled against Lenin over peace with Germany in 1918, and then against her party when she joined the Workers' Opposition in 1921. This action cost her her job as head of *Zhenotdel* and sent her into diplomatic exile. While she eventually became the world's first female ambassador, she continued to rebel against society's conventions. Following her death in 1952, it was finally recognized that Alexandra Kollontai, through her life and writings, had also been in the forefront of Europe's sexual revolution.

Kollontai, like many of the women who subsequently joined the Russian revolutionary movement, was raised in circumstances of wealth and privilege. "My childhood was a happy one," she later wrote in her *Autobiography*. "I was the youngest, the most spoiled, and the most coddled member of the family." Her father Mikhail Domontovich, who was to become a general in the Imperial Russian Army, was descended from an ancient, land-owning Ukrainian family. At the

time of Kollontai's birth on March 19, 1872, he was an instructor at the cavalry school in St. Petersburg. His home, as befitted his position in society, was comfortable and well-staffed with servants. The upbringing of Shura, as Alexandra was known to her family, was largely left in the hands of an English nanny. Her mother **Aleksandra Masalina** was from a mixed marriage of a Finnish peasant turned timber merchant and a Russian noblewoman. Her family estate in Finland provided an idyllic place for Shura to spend many of her youthful summers.

Kollontai's parents were in many ways unconventional in their lives and their thinking, and this in turn helped shape the subsequent development of their daughter. Because of the objections of Masalina's father, their initial courtship was terminated, and she was forced to marry an engineer named Mravinskii. Ten years and three children later, and following the death of the elder Masalin, Domontovich reappeared on the scene and convinced her to seek a divorce. Legal arrangements such as this were difficult for women in 19th-century Russia. Before the divorce was official, Shura was born out of wedlock. Her parents defied the conventions of the aristocracy in other ways as well. Domontovich, who had been interested in radical causes in his youth, was a widely read individual and surprisingly liberal for an army general. He was a firm believer in a constitutional monarchy in a country where constitutions were considered by many of his class to be revolutionary. When he suggested that Bulgaria, where he was stationed in 1878, be given a liberal constitution, he was ordered home in disgrace. Kollontai revered her father and later acknowledged that "if ever a man had an influence on my mind and development, it was my father." Her strong-willed mother was equally influential, though not as appreciated by her sometimes rebellious daughter. Following the death of her father, Masalina had taken over his business interests in Finland and developed a flourishing enterprise selling dairy products in St. Petersburg. Such independence was unusual for upper-class Russian women of her time. Somewhat more conventional were her charitable activities among the less fortunate in Russia's capital.

Aleksandra Masalina stressed that her daughter should get a good education and be self-reliant. "I was never sent to school," Kollontai recalled, "because my parents lived in a constant state of anxiety over my health and they could not endure the thought that I, like all the other children, should spend two hours daily far from home. My mother probably also had a certain horror of the liberal influences with which I might come into contact." With the aid of home tutors, she read voraciously. She learned to speak French with her mother and two half-sisters, English with her nanny, Finnish with peasants on her mother's estate, and German with one of her instructors. Her mother was less successful in developing her talents in the areas of music, art, and dancing. Nevertheless, Kollontai passed her examinations in 1888 and at the age of 16 received a certificate which would have allowed her to earn a living as a teacher.

The next decade was one of revolt and attempts at personal liberation for Shura. The first crisis came with her determination to marry her cousin, Vladimir Kollontai. Her parents opposed the match, since Vladimir, an engineering student at St. Petersburg's military academy, did not share her intellectual interests and had few financial resources. Shura was forbidden to see him and sent on an extended tour of Western Europe. In what she later admitted was a battle of wills with her parents, she won out. A year after her marriage to Vladimir in 1893, a son, Mikhail or

Misha, was born. While she had escaped the confines of the parental home and her mother's control, "the happy life of housewife and spouse" became a "cage" which limited her pursuit of new interests and of a more fulfilling career.

In part because of the role models of her parents and her own liberal education, Kollontai had by age 20 developed a social consciousness, an awareness of social and economic problems which the autocratic Russian state refused to address. This awakening was reinforced by her reading of populist and Marxist literature, which was in vogue among the young intelligentsia of the 1890s, and by her charitable and educational work among the poor of St. Petersburg. Vladimir, however, did not share these concerns; he had little interest in the conversations of her new radical friends, and he could not comprehend her desire for meaningful work outside of marriage and motherhood. Frustrated by these constraints, Kollontai rebelled once again—this time against her husband. In 1898, she took her four-year-old son to her parents, convinced her father to give her a modest

Alexandra Kollontai

monthly allowance, and left for the University of Zurich where she systematically studied the classics of European Marxism. A year later, after returning to St. Petersburg, she made the break with her past complete. Retrieving Misha from his grandparents, she moved into a small apartment and, as a single parent, began a new career as a writer. Kollontai rebelled yet again in 1899 by joining the illegal and revolutionary Russian Social Democratic Labor Party (RSDLP). In doing so, she turned her back decisively on the traditional life of an upper-class Russian woman; she rejected the political predilections of her parents and denied the efficacy of her own earlier charitable activities.

It was not unusual for women of Kollontai's background to join the RSDLP. Others had been attracted by Marx's scientific and revolutionary solutions to society's problems and by the sense of commitment and sacrifice which belonging to an illegal party provided. Such women accordingly took over many of the secretarial and organizational positions in the underground. Kollontai wanted more than this. She had undertaken her studies in Zurich because she wanted to be taken seriously as a theorist by her male colleagues in the party and because she wanted to write from an informed Marxist perspective. This determination, shown early in her revolutionary career, set her apart from almost all of her female counterparts and helps to explain the unique and important role she was to play in the RSDLP.

Her first project after returning to St. Petersburg was to begin a detailed study of the Finnish economy. Between 1900 and 1903, she published ten articles in Marxist newspapers or journals on the subject as well as a major statistical study entitled *The Life of Finnish Workers* which, wrote **Barbara Clements**, "established her intellectual credentials within the Social Democratic movement." She also began to hone her skills as a public speaker and agitator, another area where few Russian women excelled, by addressing working-class audiences. On January 9, she witnessed the beginning of the 1905 Revolution when she participated in a march to the tsar's residence at the Winter Palace which ended violently with the troops opening fire on the marchers. Kollontai survived "Bloody Sunday" and spent the rest of the revolutionary year raising money for the party among her wealthy friends and coordinating activities with the Finnish Social Democrats.

Prior to this time, Russian Marxists had ignored the special concerns of Russian factory women who were seen simply as the most back-

ward element of the proletariat, facing the same problems as male workers. As a result of this disinterest, the appeals of non-Marxist bourgeois feminists started to find a receptive audience among working women who made up almost a third of the labor force. Kollontai, who had not shown much interest in the "woman question" before 1905, recognized the feminist threat and started to speak out against alliances with bourgeois women to obtain such transitory gains as the right to vote. She also set up, in 1907, a Mutual Aid Society for Working Women in St. Petersburg, where women could read and hear lectures on subjects of interest to them, and organized a delegation of 45 women workers to attend the First Congress of Russian Women called by the bourgeois feminists in December 1908. To prepare the delegation and to undermine the arguments of the middle-class feminists, Kollontai wrote *The Social Bases of the Woman Question*—the first major study of women's issues by a Russian Marxist. In it, she suggested that not only should the capitalist system be overthrown but the family itself had to be restructured if women were to be truly free.

These activities aroused the ire both of the police, who forced Kollontai to flee the country during the course of the congress, and of her own party. Orthodox Marxists felt that trying to appeal specifically to women was simply another form of feminism and that setting up organizations for women was separatism which weakened the unity of the working class. The male hierarchy was particularly upset when Kollontai borrowed an idea from German Social Democratic women by suggesting that the RSDLP set up a Women's Bureau to coordinate party propaganda among women. As a result of these experiences in 1907 and 1908, "I realized for the first time how little our Party concerned itself with the fate of women of the working class," Kollontai wrote in her *Autobiography*, "and how meager was its interest in women's liberation." She was to spend the next 14 years seeking to correct this situation, and it is here that she made her greatest contribution to socialist feminism.

During the five and a half years before the outbreak of the First World War, Kollontai traveled extensively throughout Western Europe helping various Social Democratic parties. Her knowledge of five languages and her wide-ranging intellectual interests opened many doors for her. Now a handsome woman nearing 40, she eschewed the bohemian lifestyle of many emigre revolutionaries, preferring to dress stylishly and elegantly. She supported herself with a modest inheritance from her father, who had died in

1901, and with the fees she received from lecturing and the writing of her pen. Part of every summer was spent with her son Mikhail, who was a gymnasium student in Russia. But as she acknowledged, her existence, like that of many women who wanted to be independent, was a lonely one where work was the major ingredient in her happiness.

That work was now largely concerned with the "woman question." She lectured on the problem of prostitution and the organization of working women at the Bologna party school in 1910. She represented the St. Petersburg Textile Workers Union at the Second Conference of Socialist Women held in Copenhagen in 1910 and was elected to the International Women's Secretariat. At the request of the Menshevik faction in the Russian Duma (Parliament), she engaged in a lengthy study of maternity benefits offered to women in various European countries. Her proposals, which were ultimately incorporated into a 600-page report entitled *Society and Maternity*, advocated that maternity costs of all Russian women, including unwed mothers, be paid by the government rather than by employee contributions to group insurance funds. Kollontai's prewar writing also touched on the psychological side of female emancipation, on the double standard governing contemporary relationships, and on women's sexual needs. It was necessary, she argued, to break the constraints of bourgeois marriage and the bourgeois family wherein women were always economically and psychologically dependent on men. She talked about a "new morality" emerging in the proletariat after the revolution when women would be economically self-sufficient and, like men, free to have multiple sex partners.

While few of Kollontai's advanced views were shared by the male-dominated leadership of the RSDLP, she was quite clearly the most respected woman in the party and one whose opinions on political matters, at least, had to be taken seriously. As much as possible, she tried to avoid the factional squabbling which took up the energies of many Russian emigres. From 1906 to 1915, she was attracted to the Mensheviks in part because of her admiration of G.V. Plekhanov, the "father of Russian Marxism," and in part because she favored the mass movement they espoused over one led by professional revolutionaries as preached by Lenin and the Bolsheviks.

The outbreak of the First World War brought a temporary halt to Kollontai's pursuit of women's liberation and altered her political affiliation. "To me the war was an abomination, a madness, a crime," she wrote in 1926. Unlike many European socialists, she called for "a war on war" and advocated militant pacifism. As the conflict dragged into 1915, she became convinced that Lenin was right: only revolution could defeat war. In June 1915, she joined forces with him and for the next 20 months served as the Scandinavian link in Lenin's communications with Russia. She also made two trips to the United States in a vain attempt to find American allies for his defeatist policies.

Kollontai's commitment to Bolshevism became complete in 1917. In mid-March, two weeks after the abdication of Tsar Nicholas II and Empress ***Alexandra Feodorovna**, Kollontai returned to Russia with several of Lenin's communications hidden in her underwear. She immediately called for the overthrow of the new Provisional Government and was the only Bolshevik initially to defend Lenin's April Theses. If she had a regret about his program, it was that the Bolshevik leader said nothing about appealing to working women who had been so instrumental in the spontaneous demonstrations against the tsar in February. She revived an idea which she had proposed ten years earlier that the party create a bureau to direct and coordinate Bolshevik work among women. Once again, the male leadership showed no interest in a scheme which they saw as politically divisive to proletarian unity and of little importance in time of revolution. Frustrated, Kollontai turned her energies to work in the Executive Committee of the Petrograd Soviet of Workers and Soldiers Deputies. Her oratorical skills, first demonstrated during the 1905 Revolution, were once again evident in the Soviet and at the various meetings she addressed in the capital. To the Western press, she was "the Valkyrie of the Revolution"; to the Provisional Government, she was "the mad Bolshevik" who they slapped into jail in July 1917 following a premature and unsuccessful Bolshevik uprising. Charged with being a German spy and spreading antiwar propaganda, she spent six weeks in prison and another three weeks under house arrest. In recognition of her abilities, however, the Sixth Party Congress elected her *in absentia* to the Bolshevik Central Committee in August 1917. She had the distinction not only of being the only woman so honored but also of receiving more votes than Joseph Stalin.

After the successful overthrow of the Provisional Government two months later, Kollontai's unique position in the party was recognized once again when she was the sole woman selected to sit on the new Council of People's Commissars and given the portfolio of social welfare. This suited her interests if not necessarily her talents. Given the chaos caused by the revolution—the hunger, the dislocation of families, the antagonism of many of the professional people she had to work with—this was a difficult assignment for a woman who had no administrative experience and very little organizational ability. As she later recalled, these early months of the new regime were "rich in magnificent illusions, plans, ardent initiatives to improve life, to organize the world anew, months of the real romanticism of the Revolution." As commissar of social welfare, she was instrumental in instituting full state funding for maternity leave and child care. Her commissariat set up state-run orphanages and abolished the distinction between legitimate and illegitimate children. She backed efforts by the Council of People's Commissars to introduce legislation protecting female and child labor, to provide full political and legal equality for women, and to recognize civil marriage and divorce by mutual consent. Indeed, one of the first to take advantage of a civil ceremony was Kollontai herself when at the age of 45 she married Pavel Dybenko, a Bolshevik sailor of peasant origin who was now commissar of the navy and 17 years her junior.

Kollontai, who had rebelled against authority in her youth and was never subservient to party discipline, rebelled against Lenin in March 1918 when she joined the Left Communists in opposition to his proposed peace treaty of Brest-Litovsk with Germany. It was "opportunism," she declared, to seek a "breathing spell" for Russia at the expense of world revolution. For her insubordination, Kollontai was removed from the Central Committee, and in despair she quit her post as commissar of social welfare.

In the fall of 1918, her attention turned once again to organizing Russian women. Together with *Inessa Armand, a long-time Bolshevik and her sometime rival in the Russian women's movement, Kollontai organized the First All-Russian Congress of Working Women. The 1,147 delegates who showed up in Moscow in mid-November 1918 vastly exceeded expectations and restored her spirits. The resolutions passed reflected much of what Kollontai had been preaching since 1906, and the fact that even Lenin was in attendance seemed to indicate that for once the party leadership was listening to their voices. The congress reiterated her earlier calls that the party create a body to coordinate work among women. Less than a year later, Kollontai's long-sought women's bureau became a reality with the creation of *Zhenotdel* or the Women's Section of the Central Committee of the Russian Communist Party. The job of directing *Zhenotdel*, however, was initially given to

the more restrained and reliable Armand. Upon Armand's death in the fall of 1920, Kollontai was named director. For the next year and a half, she fought bureaucratic obstructionism, traditional male hostility, and a lack of resources in her efforts to create child-care facilities, to rehabilitate prostitutes, and to draw Muslim women into everyday Soviet life. She also promoted what a later generation would call "affirmative action programs" to get women into leadership positions in trade unions, government departments, and the party itself. While her achievements fell short of her goals, the economic, political, and legal position of Soviet women changed dramatically as a result of her work, as well as that of Armand and a handful of other socialist feminists.

Kollontai's rebelliousness and her belief in a democratic form of socialism came to the fore again in 1921. Several months after taking over *Zhenotdel*, she joined the Workers' Opposition, a group of Left-wing Communists who served as "the conscience of the revolution" by criticizing the drift toward authoritarianism in the party and the lack of trade union democracy in the workplace. She used her writing talents to set down their complaints in a pamphlet entitled *The Workers' Opposition*. For this, she and her colleagues were sharply criticized by the Tenth Party Congress in March 1921 and threatened with expulsion. When Kollontai continued to attack the party leadership, she was removed from her work in *Zhenotdel* in February 1922 and eight months later sent into political oblivion as a member of a Soviet trade delegation to Norway.

Kollontai remained abroad for most of the next 23 years, becoming the only important member of any opposition group to escape the purges. She spent 1923 writing semi-autobiographical novellas and articles dealing with erotic love and psychological problems associated with female liberation. Following renewed Soviet criticism of her views, she chose to concentrate on her diplomatic duties: first in Norway, then in Mexico, where she became the world's first female ambassador in 1926. She returned to Norway as ambassador in 1927, spending three years there, before being transferred to Sweden in 1930, where she represented Soviet interests for the next 15 years. Prompted by her own lifelong interest in Finland, she tried to seek diplomatic solutions to that country's conflicts with the Soviet Union in 1940 and again in 1944. After a distinguished career, Kollontai retired as dean of the diplomatic corps in 1945 to become a pensioner in Moscow. She died there, nearing the age of 80, on March 9, 1952.

Alexandra Kollontai did not receive the credit she deserved as a Marxist theorist, a socialist feminist, or as a Soviet diplomat during her lifetime. In her homeland, her Menshevik background and her opposition to Lenin were never forgiven until the Mikhail Gorbachev era. Her attempts to emancipate Soviet women were soon reversed by a Communist Party no longer interested even in paying lip service to women's liberation. *Zhenotdel* was closed by Stalin in 1930, and feminists such as Armand and Kollontai were quickly forgotten. In the West, popular attention was focused almost exclusively on Kollontai's colorful lifestyle. She wrote about free love and the sexual revolution and seemed to practice what she preached. She left her first husband after five years of marriage, had very public affairs with one married colleague and another 13 years her junior, and ended up marrying a 27-year old peasant-sailor when she was 45. Could such a woman—especially an attractive one of aristocratic birth who dressed flamboyantly and survived the purges in silence—be taken seriously? Titillation rather than scholarship was the norm when dealing with Kollontai until books by Barbara Clements, **Beatrice Farnsworth**, and Richard Stites appeared in the late 1970s. She is now recognized for what she was: a revolutionary sufficiently important to be a member of the Bolshevik Central Committee; the leading feminist in the early Soviet state; a surprisingly successful and durable diplomat; and a person whose writing on the psychological and sexual liberation of women is a significant contribution to the mainstream of 20th-century European feminism.

SOURCES:

Clements, Barbara Evans. *Bolshevik Feminist: The Life of Aleksandra Kollontai.* Bloomington, IN: Indiana University Press, 1979.

Farnsworth, Beatrice. *Aleksandra Kollontai: Socialism, Feminism and the Bolshevik Revolution.* Stanford, CA: Stanford University Press, 1980.

Kollontai, Alexandra. *The Autobiography of a Sexually Emancipated Woman.* Edited by Irving Fetscher; translated from the German by Salvator Attanasio. NY: Schocken Books, 1971 (unless otherwise indicated, all quotations are taken from this source).

SUGGESTED READING:

Itkina, A.M. *Revoliutsioner, Tribun, Diplomat: Stranitsy zhizni Aleksandry Mikhailovny Kollontai* (Revolutionary, Tribune, Diplomat: Pages from the Life of Aleksandra Mikhailovna Kollontai). 2nd ed. Moscow, 1970.

Kollontai, A.M. *Iz moei zhizni i raboty* (From My Life and Work). Moscow, 1974.

Stites, Richard. *The Women's Liberation Movement in Russia: Feminism, Nihilism, and Bolshevism, 1860–1930.* Princeton, NJ: Princeton University Press, 1977.

R.C. Elwood,
Professor and Chair of History,
Carleton University, Ottawa, Canada

Kollwitz, Käthe (1867–1945)

German artist whose Expressionist etchings, lithographs, woodcuts, and sculpture sympathetically and dramatically portrayed the German working class and victims of violence, making her the best-known German woman artist of the first half of the 20th century. Pronunciation: KAY-tee KOHL-witz. *Born Käthe Schmidt on July 8, 1867, in Königsberg, Germany; died at Moritzburg on April 22, 1945; daughter of Karl Schmidt (a lawyer) and Katherina (Rupp) Schmidt; educated at a girls' academy and by private tutors; attended art schools in Berlin and Munich; married Karl Kollwitz (a physician), on June 13, 1891; children: two sons, Hans and Peter.*

Began art studies with Rudolf Mauer, an engraver (1881); arrived in Berlin to study at the Women's School of Art (1885); took up residence, with husband, in slum area of North Berlin (1891); attended premiere of Gerhart Hauptmann's play The Weavers *and was inspired to do a series of prints (1893); received gold medal for her "Revolt of the Weavers" (1899); won Villa Romana prize (1907); became first woman elected to the Prussian Academy of Arts (1919); was co-founder of the Society for Women Artists and Friends of Art (1926); visited the Soviet Union as a guest of the Soviet government (1927); was forced to resign from the Prussian Academy by the National Socialist government, the beginning of the period when her works were condemned by the Nazis as "degenerate art" (1933); evacuated to Nordhausen because of bombing of Berlin (1943); moved to Moritzburg, located near Dresden, after that home was bombed (1944).*

Major works: Revolt of the Weavers *(1898);* The Peasant Wars *(1908);* Seed for the Planting Must Not Be Ground *(1942).*

Throughout history, many women artists learned their craft under the tutelage of a mentor, often a male relative, and many were born into families with a long artistic tradition. Neither was true of Käthe Kollwitz, who traveled her own path, balancing careers as a mother and an artist. Her rejection of a career as a painter led her to produce a series of memorable and highly distinctive etchings and lithographs portraying the working class and poor in the Germany of her day.

The fifth child in a family of seven children, Kollwitz was raised in an atmosphere of religious independence and high social ideals. Her grandfather, an ordained Lutheran minister, had left that church to found the first "Free Religious" Congregation in Germany, a church that sought to emulate early Christianity, even to the point of trying to create communal property among church members. Both her mother and father thought that thorough religious training would give their children high moral character.

Kollwitz' relationship with her mother **Katherina Rupp Schmidt** was uneasy. She later wrote that her mother was not friendly to her children, but Kollwitz came to admire Katherina's stoic suffering in the face of the early deaths of three of them. "I loved her terribly," Kollwitz wrote; she described the family atmosphere as loving and caring, despite her mother's emotional distance. What she admired in Katherina—emotional strength—she also noticed as a characteristic of the female friends of the family, particularly the ones who often came to their home to debate theology with her father.

It has been said many times that pure art does not have a purpose. But I want to have an influence with my art, as long as I can.

—**Käthe Kollwitz**

Kollwitz also came to admire the progressivism of her parents. Her mother, who had read Lord Byron and Shakespeare in the original English, was uncommonly well-educated for a Prussian woman of the middle class at the time. Katherina also taught her children that socialism, or concern for the working class, was a Christian duty. Her father's political views were similarly progressive. Although Karl Schmidt had a law degree, he refused to follow that profession because his political and social views placed him in conflict with the authoritarian state of the family's native Prussia. Among the writings that Karl Schmidt read to his children was a German translation of Thomas Hood's poem, "Song of the Shirt." The poem, a paean to a nameless seamstress and her never-ending work, proved to be an inspiration for much of Kollwitz' art work, which focused on the poor and the downtrodden.

The family's socialist sentiments were well-known. Her older brothers Karl, Hans, and Konrad were sympathizers with the Marxist party in Germany (the Social Democratic Party), and Käthe participated in family discussions about August Bebel, a co-founder of the party, who claimed that socialism would make women independent, both socially and economically. Her family's progressivism also created opportunities for Kollwitz that were unavailable to other women. Her father decided that both Käthe and her sister **Lisa Schmidt** should be encouraged to

Opposite page

Käthe

Kollwitz

pursue artistic careers. The girls' academy they attended proved to be a revelation for Käthe, who liked literature and history but was fascinated by the library, which included works of the English painter William Hogarth, and German writers such as Heinrich Heine and Johann Wolfgang von Goethe. Among the writers, Goethe, with his poem praising the powers and mysteries of nature, was Käthe's favorite.

Kollwitz felt a sibling rivalry with Lisa over their joint status as the family's future artists. Her fear that her sister would outpace her was a powerful motivation for her to achieve, at least until her sister's marriage in the late 1880s. Käthe realized that she had no family mentor for her artistic career, but she also acknowledged that the "blessed" atmosphere of her family had opened the door to a career that was denied to most German middle-class women.

In 1881, her father arranged for Rudolf Mauer, an engraver, to give Käthe lessons in art. When, at age 16, she was unable to enter the Königsberg Academy of Art because women were not admitted, her father arranged for a private tutor. Karl Schmidt's controlling influence also caused her to postpone a marriage to Karl Kollwitz, a medical student who proposed to her in 1884. Her father feared that marriage would ruin her prospects for a successful artistic career. When her brother Konrad, a student at the University of Berlin, discovered that the Berlin Academy of Art had an affiliated women's art school, Käthe was enrolled in it.

Her period of study in Berlin, which lasted just three years, influenced her in two ways. First, one of her art professors, a Swiss named Karl Stauffer-Bern, noticed that Kollwitz' drawings resembled the naturalistic style of the artist Max Klinger, whose works focused on human beings suffering in the social struggle for survival. He encouraged her to emphasize drawing, rather than painting, and Kollwitz tended to agree. She had discovered that she lacked the natural sense and appreciation for color shown by many of her fellow art students. She believed that drawing had closer ties "to reality" than did painting. Her work in the students' Etching Club convinced her that she had made the correct decision. She was impressed with Klinger's writing, which argued that drawing involved more imagination and creativity than painting—with "unfilled lines" and "holes" which had to be given meaning by subtleties of shading and angles of line.

Her Berlin studies also propelled her toward the idea that art should fulfill a social purpose. A close friend of hers in Berlin, **Helen Bloch**, met regularly with Kollwitz to read German Marxist writers and to discuss the "social question" and the "woman question." Kollwitz wanted to use arts to portray the suffering of the victims of German industrialization and urbanization. "Expression was all that I wanted," she later wrote, "and therefore I told myself that the simple line of the lithograph (and drawing) was best suited to my purposes."

In 1889, she entered the Munich Academy of Art, where teaching was less rigid and more progressive than at Berlin. Since the school believed that marriage and an artistic career were incompatible, celibacy was required of students. Women who married were condemned as traitors to art. When she graduated, Kollwitz discovered that she could not obtain a job as a commercial artist.

She married Karl Kollwitz in June 1891—when she was 24 and he was 28—both having agreed to continue their careers. The couple took up residence in North Berlin, where he opened a practice as a physician for slum residents as part of a government-sponsored medical program instituted by the German chancellor Otto von Bismarck. The marriage was, at first, more a union of mutual admiration than a love match, although it "grew slowly" toward the latter. Although she became pregnant with their son, Hans, during their first autumn together, Kollwitz was determined not to let marriage and motherhood spoil her chances to create art. While motherhood was special to her, she thought of herself as an artist rather than as a wife. Her *Self Portrait of a Young Couple,* begun in 1893, portrayed Kollwitz and her husband sitting in a double bed, facing different directions, and not touching.

Käthe set up a studio in a spare room of their apartment. Although initially she used her son Hans as a model, the subjects of most of her works would prove to be the working class in Germany and, in her words, the "downtrodden." "I did not see beauty in the upper, educated classes," she wrote. "I saw their superficiality and their lack of naturalness, integrity, and honesty." Working-class women, she noted, presented their feelings more "openly" and without disguises. "Bourgeois life on the whole struck me as stilted," she wrote, "whereas the proletariat had real grandeur and breadth in their lives."

She rejected the most popular styles in the art world of the time—Impressionism and Art Nouveau. If her art is to be classified as part of a school or movement, it fits most easily with Expressionism. She shared that movement's belief

that feeling was more important than form, but she was determined that figures in her work should be individuals—they never really represented types or categories of people—and that the picture should be dictated by the subject's feelings or emotions, rather than her own. Whether working in etchings, lithographs, or woodcuts, she also worked to achieve an economy of style, which would require the minimum number of lines and shading to portray a situation or an emotion.

Her first major art work, *Revolt of the Weavers,* was the result of a play she attended in 1893, Gerhart Hauptmann's *The Weavers.* The play dramatized a strike by weavers in Germany during the 1840s and the eventual shooting of several weavers by German troops. *Revolt of the Weavers* consisted of three etchings and three lithographs, depicting poverty, death (a portrait of a child dying of hunger), conspiracy, the weavers on the march, an attack on the boss' mansion, and the death of many weavers at the end. Contrasting dark areas were used to underline the emotions of the strike and the hopelessness of the strikers.

The series was condemned by the German emperor Wilhelm II (William II) as "gutter art," but the king of Saxony was persuaded to award her a medal. In fact, more of Kollwitz' art would eventually be on display in Saxony than in any other German state. Together with a later work entitled *The Peasant War,* the *Revolt of the Weavers* earned her the Villa Romana medal in 1907. Offered the job of teacher of life drawing and graphics at the Berlin School of Art for Women, she accepted only after hesitation, believing herself incompetent to teach etching.

The Peasant War, completed in 1908, was a series of seven prints about the peasant revolt of the early 1500s. Rejecting the idea that women had to be portrayed according to the prevailing standards of beauty, she depicted strong, enduring women whose physical presence was emphasized more than their sex. One of the most powerful prints was *Raped,* which depicted a shocked and humiliated woman lying on the ground after she had been attacked by mercenary soldiers. Flowers, which in an Impressionist painting might be objects of beauty, were here twisted menacingly with weeds, symbolizing tragedy, sorrow, and outrage. Kollwitz attacked the callousness of urban life with *The Downtrodden* (1900), which depicted urban poverty, and *Run Over* (1910), which portrayed parents furiously trying to save the life of a baby run over by a car as other children watch with looks of terror.

World War I brought triumph and sorrow. In 1917, a retrospective of her work, held in Berlin, was a great success. At the war's end, she became the first woman to be elected to the Berlin Academy of Art, winning the title of professor (which she rejected because she declared herself opposed to all titles) and the privilege of a free studio in the academy's building (which she accepted). But the war also brought the death of her son Peter while he was serving in the German army in Belgium in the early months of the conflict, plunging her into periodic fits of depression. Although she decided to make Peter's "spirit" pervade her work, she complained that her periods of depression became longer, and that the periods in between, which were periods of creativity, were becoming progressively shorter.

During the 1920s—when Kollwitz, like so many others, lived through periods of famine, very high inflation, and high unemployment in Germany—she devoted her work to specific social and political issues or situations. Although she never became a member of the Social Democratic Party, one of her first works after World War I was *From the Living to the Dead,* in honor of the party leader Wilhelm Liebknecht, who was killed by government-approved irregular troops ("Free Corps" troops) during an attempted revolution in 1919. Liebknecht was portrayed in the woodcut in a stylized and rather stately pose while grieving workers were bent at dramatically different angles, underlining their shock and sorrow.

Kollwitz increasingly tied her art to social issues, arguing that "I felt that I did not have the right to withdraw from the responsibility of being an advocate. It is my duty to voice the suffering of men." When an Austrian aid society asked her to do a poster to dramatize postwar famine in that country, she responded with a poster of death whipping masses of groaning, starving people. Feminist groups asked her help in a campaign to revoke an article in the German constitution which prescribed prison terms for women who had abortions. Her poster "Against the Abortion Law" portrayed a working-class woman with two children, looking hungry and very hopeless. In fact, her art during the 1920s made her a bit of a feminist icon, requiring her to hire a secretary to answer the volumes of mail pouring in from German, and even European, women.

A new theme in her work was a direct denunciation of the war, in memory of her beloved son. The antiwar movement drew her support. Her poster "Never Again War!," using the title of a book by the pacifist *Bertha von Suttner, reflected her belief that the idealistic energies of young people should be transformed into efforts to build a better German society, rather than be exploited to wage war.

A public opponent of National Socialism, she was not surprised when the new Nazi government of Germany began, in 1933, to include her work in the banned category of "degenerate art." Her public influence waned, and she suffered financially as the number of commissions she received dwindled. She decried the silence of those who she thought should speak out. "Scarcely anyone had anything to say to me about [the banning of my art]," she wrote. "Such a silence all around us."

Her etchings, lithographs, and woodcuts were increasingly removed from museums and consigned to museum basements. Nazi officials banned her small sculpture *Tower of Mothers,* completed in 1938, from appearing in an art show. Eventually even her husband's medical practice was banned, and the family increasingly relied on her small, and now infrequent, com-

Self-Portrait *by Käthe Kollwitz.*

missions. Kollwitz was generally left alone by the government, except for a visit in 1936 from Gestapo officers who wanted to know the name of an anonymous friend who had joined her in giving an interview to a foreign correspondent. Although their comments did not criticize the government, Kollwitz refused to identify the man. Thereafter, she always carried a vial of poison with her, to take if she were arrested by the Gestapo. When an American art collector offered to help her escape to the United States, she refused, not wanting to be removed from her family and friends.

World War II brought further blows. Her grandson Peter, namesake of her son, was killed during fighting in Russia. She condemned both the war and the American and British bombing of her homeland with a lithograph entitled *Seed for the Planting Must Not Be Ground,* which portrayed a mother holding firmly onto rambunctious 16-year-old boys—symbolizing, by implication, a mother who refuses to let her offspring go off to war. Her family twice changed residences because of the bombing. Once, just before their Berlin home was destroyed, they moved to Nordhausen. When bombs damaged

Woman Welcoming Death by Käthe Kollwitz.

WOMEN IN WORLD HISTORY

that, the family moved to Moritzburg, near Dresden, where Käthe Kollwitz died in 1945 at the age of 78.

SOURCES:

Kearns, Martha. *Kathe Kollwitz: Woman and Artist.* Old Westbury, NY: The Feminist Press, 1976.

Kollwitz, Käthe. *Briefe der Freundschaft und Begegnungen.* Edited by Hans Kollwitz. Munich: List Verlag, 1966.

————. *The Diary and Letters of Käthe Kollwitz.* Edited by Hans Kollwitz. Translated by Richard and Clara Winston. Chicago, IL: Henry Regnery, 1955.

————. *Drawings, Etchings, Lithographs, Woodcuts, Sculpture.* Jerusalem and Tel Aviv: Tel Aviv Museum and Israel Museum, 1972.

SUGGESTED READING:

Klein, Mina, and H. Arthur. *Kathe Kollwitz: Life in Art.* NY: Holt, Rinehart, and Winston, 1972.

Kollwitz, Käthe. *An Exhibition of Graphic Works by Kathe Kollwitz from the Permanent Collection of the Minnesota Museum of Art.* St. Paul, MN: Minnesota Museum of Art, 1973.

Timm, Werner, ed. *The Drawings of Käthe Kollwitz.* NY: Crown, 1972.

COLLECTIONS:

There is a Käthe Kollwitz archive in the Akademie der Kunste in Berlin.

Niles R. Holt,
Professor of History,
Illinois State University, Normal-Bloomington, Illinois

Kolmar, Gertrud (1894–1943)

"Poet of women and animals," gifted linguist, and writer whose works, mostly unknown at the time of her death, now identify her as one of the best German poets of the 20th century. Name variations: Gertrud Chodziesner. Born Gertrud Chodziesner on December 10, 1894, in Berlin; died after being sent to Auschwitz in 1943 (her date of death unrecorded); daughter of a prominent attorney in a wealthy German-Jewish family; studied linguistics after completion of high school; never married; no children.

Worked as a translator for the Foreign Office during World War I and published Gedichte, *a volume of poetry (1917); tutored sick and handicapped children while continuing to write poetry (1920s–30s); removed to Berlin ghetto (1939); was sent to Auschwitz (February 1943).*

Selected works: Gedichte *(1917);* Preussisch Wappen *(Prussian Arms, c. 1918).*

Gertrud Kolmar, Germany's "poet of women and animals," perished in Auschwitz in 1943. The power and beauty of her poetry outlived the evil that destroyed her.

Born on December 10, 1894, in Berlin, Gertrud Chodziesner was the eldest of four children in a typical upper-class German-Jewish family; they considered themselves German first and Jewish second. Her father was a well-to-do lawyer, and the Chodziesners' wealth allowed them to own an estate with large gardens, the spacious Villa Finkenkrug in the Brandenburg area, where the children spent a great deal of time. Gertrud loved animals and nature and felt a strong affinity for the Brandenburg peasantry and the fishermen who worked on the many lakes of the region.

After completing high school in 1911, Gertrud decided to study foreign language and literature. She soon proved a gifted linguist, fluent in French, English, and Russian, and was also interested in history, especially in Robespierre and the French Revolution. During World War I, she worked in the German foreign office as a translator and interpreter, as well as with prisoners of war; she also experienced an unhappy love affair. It is uncertain when she began to write poetry, but a volume of her verse, *Gedichte*, was published in 1917. As a poet, she used the last name Kolmar, the name of the city from which her father came.

In the postwar period, Kolmar became a teacher and private tutor, specializing in the education of deaf-mute, sick, or handicapped children. After her mother died in 1930, she took care of her aging father. Living in seclusion, detached from the literary mainstream, she has been compared to American poet *Emily Dickinson. Kolmar was influenced more by the natural world than by current literary fads, and her poems repeat none of the modish psychology so popular at the time as poetic themes. Describing the dark forests and landscapes inhabited by animals, she wrote as if from their inner experience. At times her poems appear closer to ballads than poetry, while some echo the work of Walt Whitman. In many, there appears to be a demonism at work, a feature considered unusual in the poetry of women. In her "Metamorphoses," for instance, she identifies with the feelings of a bat:

> Oh, man, I dream your blood; my bite is death.
> I'll claw into your hair and suck your breath.

Kolmar's frank expression of female sexuality is unprecedented for a woman writer of her time. Born in the late 19th century, when society's taboo-ridden moral code barely admitted to female sexual desire, she lived an extremely reserved life, and yet her poetry reflects a furious power elevated to a high plane of poetic art, unimpeded by feminine delicacy. Consider her poem "Troglodyte":

Nude, I crouch on taloned toes
Sharpened red on rendered meat;
In the reeds of swampy groves
I hide hunted and in heat. . . .

Suddenly, with howling moans
Out I leap from mud and weeds,
Claws and body dragging down
A wanderer who lost his way. . . .
Gasping, I devour my prey.

Kolmar's second book of poems, *Preussisch Wappen* (Prussian Arms), appeared at the end of the war. During the 1920s, she wrote furiously but did not publish much. Many of her poems were love poems and have been compared with the Biblical Song of Solomon. Being childless was one of Kolmar's great regrets and on numerous occasions she addressed the mother-child relationship, especially the mother who has lost her child, with poignancy. "Madness" reflects this theme:

The night outside the door, the cradle void.
And rocking it, a woman, pallid-faced,
With stringy hair as black and thick as tar,
and in her heart there gathers gray on gray. . . .

After Adolf Hitler came to power in 1933, his National Socialist Party espoused anti-Semitic beliefs that gradually brought the world as German Jews knew it to an end. Initially, however, few took the party's anti-Semitism seriously, including many Jews. The language of hate had been used before. For many both inside and outside Germany, Hitler represented economic stability and an alternative to communism. But when the Nuremberg laws were implemented in September 1935, declaring that citizenship in the Third Reich was determined by blood and forbidding marriage between Aryans and Jews, many members of Kolmar's family, including all her siblings, left Germany. Many Jews also chose to stay in Germany, however, since it was the only country they knew, and Kolmar remained behind with her father, who was old and frail. During their first years in power, the Nazis were sensitive to world opinion. For example, when the Olympic Games were held in 1936 in Berlin, the International Olympic Committee successfully pressured the Nazis to accept Jewish athletes on German teams. There was a lull in the country's anti-Semitic propaganda during the Olympics, which encouraged the belief that Hitler's regime would moderate or fail. There was some rationale for this thinking. A great deal of evidence points to the fact that although the German populace supported Nazi economic policies they were largely uninterested in the Jewish question. For its part, the National So-

cialist Party was not of one mind in this regard. Many "moderates" in the party wished to force immigration on the Jews while the more militant felt the entire race should be exterminated.

Unknown to average Germans, however, the Nazi regime had begun to gear up for war, and the extremist wing of the party felt that the Jewish question must be settled before the war was under way. In the late 1930s, there was still no mass extermination of Jews, but by this time German leftists and dissidents had perished in concentration camps. The Jewish question became more important after Hitler annexed Austria in 1938, because an additional 200,000 Jews were thereby added to the Third Reich. On November 9, 1938, Nazi extremists were dealt a favorable hand when a Polish Jewish student in Paris, Hershel Grynszpan, shot a bureaucrat in the German embassy to protest the deportation of Polish Jews from Germany to Poland. The murder became the Nazis' excuse for organizing a pogrom, the infamous Kristallnacht ("Night of the Broken Glass"), in which Storm Troopers and other thugs throughout Germany attacked Jews and destroyed their property. At this point, Kolmar's life and the lives of many Jews were changed forever. New laws required the sale of Villa Finkenkrug and forced Kolmar and her father to move from their large house and beautiful gardens into a shabby apartment in Berlin's Jewish ghetto, where other families soon joined them in sharing the small cramped flat. Kolmar was assigned to work long hours in a state factory and wrote to her sister, Hilde:

It seems to me that things are changing their face and shape today with a furious swiftness . . . and what once took years or decades to change now needs only a few days. And meanwhile I've withdrawn deeper and deeper into the lasting, the existing, that which happens eternally (this does not have to be only "religion," it can also be "nature," can also be "love").

Never having considered herself anything but German, Kolmar was forced to examine her identity because of the actions of the Nazis. In 1940, she began studying Hebrew, perhaps as a way of reclaiming her heritage. Because letters were censored, she could not refer directly to her daily experiences. What is clear in another letter to Hilde is her exploration of her own inner landscape:

The day before yesterday I was walking along Martin-Luther-Strasse and Neue Winterfeldstrasse, which I don't know very well. I suddenly realized with some bewilderment that contrary to my usual custom I hadn't really noticed the houses, the shops, or the people I encountered at all. "Be observant and pay attention," I commanded myself. Good. But five minutes later I stopped "seeing" again, and my gaze once more turned inward, as it were, like a day-dreaming and inattentive pupil in school. Soon we'll have been here for six months, and I simply can't establish a relationship—bearable or unbearable—with this neighbourhood. I'm as alien here as I was on the first day.

In a long letter written on Christmas Eve 1941, she wrote to her sister about an unconsummated love affair with a factory worker half her age. In the account, illusion and reality are difficult to separate, perhaps indicating a survival mechanism as circumstances grew increasingly grim.

On January 20, 1942, the Wannsee Conference was held (named after a Berlin suburb) and, not far from where Kolmar was writing and dreaming, her fate and that of the vast majority of other German Jews was decided by Reinhard Heydrich, Heinrich Müller, Adolf Eichmann and others. The fine points of "final solution" were conceptualized according to a simple basic plan: those Jews who could work would be worked to death; all others—the elderly, children, the handicapped—would be annihilated. Since the Einsatzgruppen, or mobile death squads, had already found individual killing tedious and demoralizing in the course of exterminating 1.4 million in the East, the plan heretofore was to use modern mechanized methods for the eradication of 11 million people. Soon the European ghettos began to be emptied into concentration and death camps, where rations were kept at starvation levels, prisoners who could work were often allowed no more than five hours' rest, and a lack of sanitation combined with starvation and exhaustion led to many deaths. Those who did not die in these ways were to be gassed and cremated.

Many Germans did not know what was happening to the Jews, only that they were being "resettled" in the East. The Nazis maintained the polite fiction that old people were being sent to rest homes and younger ones were being relocated, but from 1933 to 1945 a quarter of a million Germans (mostly German Jews), on average, were being imprisoned by the Nazis every year, and inquiries of any kind were considered foolhardy. The rest of the world remained ignorant or incredulous. For example, Kolmar's sister Hilde knew that both Kolmar and her father had been "relocated." Their father was sent to Theresienstadt concentration camp, five months before Kolmar went to Auschwitz, in late February 1943. A letter by Kolmar written in December 1942 suggests that she knew for some time the

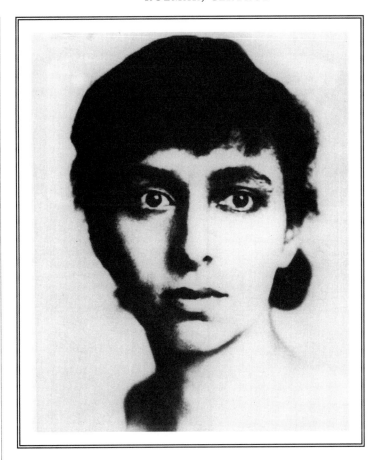

Gertrud Kolmar

end that awaited her: "I will also step up to accept my fate, be it high as a tower, black as a cloud." In her last letters and poems, written after midnight or before five in the morning despite her exhausting factory work, she raised a cry for justice. "Oh that I could raise my voice like a flaming torch in the dark desert of the world!"

No one knows when Gertrud Kolmar died. No one knows whether she was worked to death or gassed. But in 1943 all letters and poems to her sister ceased. After the war, Hilde arranged for the publication of the letters and poems that have ensured Gertrud Kolmar a place among Germany's greatest 20th-century poets. One wonders how poetry could come from such a time.

SOURCES:

Bauer, Yehuda. *A History of the Holocaust.* London: Franklin Watts, 1982.

Blumenthal, Bernhardt G. "Gertrud Kolmar: Love's Service to the Earth," in *The German Quarterly.* Vol. 42. September 1969, pp. 485–488.

Eben, Michael C. "Gertrud Kolmar," in *Twentieth-Century Literary Criticism.* Vol. 40. Edited by Paula Kepos and Laurie DiMauro. Detroit, MI: Gale Research, 1991, pp. 173–187.

———. "Gertrud Kolmar: An Appraisal," in *German Life and Letters.* Vol. 37, no. 3. April 1984, pp. 197–210.

Kolmar, Gertrud. *Dark Soliloquy: The Selected Poems of Gertrud Kolmar.* Translated by Henry A. Smith. NY: The Seabury Press, 1975.

Langer, Lawrence L. "Survival Through Art: The Career of Gertrud Kolmar," in *Leo Baeck Institute Year Book.* Vol. 23. London: Secker and Warburg, 1978, pp. 247–258.

Langman, Erika. "The Poetry of Gertrud Kolmar," in *Seminar: A Journal of Germanic Studies.* Vol. 14, no. 1. February 1978, pp. 117–132.

Picard, Jacob. "Gertrud Kolmar: The Woman and the Beasts," in *Commentary.* Vol. 10, no. 5. November 1950, pp. 459–465.

Ryback, Timothy W. "Evidence of Evil," in *The New Yorker.* Vol. 59, no. 38. November 15, 1993, pp. 68–81.

Shafi, Monika. "'Mein Ruf ist dünn und leicht' Zur Weiblichkeitsdarstellung in Gertrud Kolmars Zyklus 'Weibliches Bildnis,'" in *The Germanic Review.* Vol. 66, no. 2. Spring 1991, pp. 81–88.

Young, Gloria. "The Poetry of the Holocaust," in *Holocaust Literature. A Handbook of Critical, Historical, and Literary Writings.* Edited by Saul S. Friedman. CT: Greenwood Press, 1993, pp. 547–574.

Karin Loewen Haag,
freelance writer, Athens, Georgia

Kolstad, Eva (1918–1998)

Norwegian politician. Born Eva Lundegaard in Halder, Norway, in 1918; died on March 26, 1998; qualified as an independent chartered accountant, 1944.

Norway's Eva Kolstad trained as an accountant and worked as a bookkeeping teacher before becoming active in the cause of women's rights. She began her political career with the International Alliance of Women and was a member of the board from 1949 to 1958, from 1961 to 1968, and again in 1973. She served as president of the Norwegian Association for the Rights of Women (1956–68) and was a member of the UN Committee on the Status of Women (1969–75). She was also a member of the Oslo City Council from 1960 to 1975. Concurrently, Kolstad served two terms as a member of Parliament (1958–61 and 1966–69). Her last term was marked by her leadership on the Government Council on the Equal Status of Men and Women. Kolstad was later appointed as Ombudsman, serving from 1977 to 1988.

Komarovsky, Mirra (1906–1999)

Russian-born educator in America who produced significant sociological studies in the 1930 and 1940s. Born Mirra Komarovsky in Baku, on the Caspian Sea, in Russia, on February 4, 1906; died at her home in New York City in January 1999; daughter of Mendel Komarovsky (a Jewish banker and writer) and Anna (Steinberg) Komarovsky; attended high school for a year in Wichita, Kansas; graduated from Barnard College, A.B., 1926; Columbia University, M.A., 1927, Ph.D., 1940; married in 1926 (divorced 1928); married Marcus A. Heyman, in 1940 (died 1970).

Selected writings: (with George A. Lundberg and Alice McInerny) Leisure: A Suburban Study (Columbia University Press, 1934); The Unemployed Man and His Family (1940); Women in the Modern World: Their Education and Their Dilemmas (Little, Brown, 1953); Women in College: Shaping New Feminine Identities (1985).

Mirra Komarovsky was born in Baku, on the Caspian Sea, in Russia, in 1906, the daughter of Mendel Komarovsky, a Jewish banker and writer, and **Anna Steinberg Komarovsky**. In 1921, Mirra immigrated with her parents and younger sister to the United States. Five years later, she graduated from Barnard College in New York City, having studied under Franz Boas and *Ruth Benedict, and soon received her M.A. before being appointed an assistant professor at Skidmore College. She was later a research assistant at the Institute of Human Relations, Yale University (1930–31), and research associate at Columbia University's Council for Research in the Social Sciences (1931–35).

In 1938, Komarovsky was hired as an instructor in sociology at Barnard, where she rose rapidly to assistant professor, associate, and then chair of the department in 1947. Her contributions were in the study of leisure time, suburban life, the effect of unemployment on the status of the man within the family, and changing attitudes of women. Writing of the standards applied to women in 1944, Komarovsky called them a "veritable crazy quilt of contradiction" and asserted that "it is the girl with a 'middle of the road personality' who is most happily adjusted to the present historical moment. She is a perfect incarnation of either role (e.g. homemaker or career woman) but is flexible enough to play both." As a sociologist, she tried to remain impartial in the gender debate then underway: "Social changes have disturbed one type of equilibrium without as yet replacing it with another. Men as well as women are victims of the confusion." But Komarovsky was puzzled by Barnard's predilection for "extolling intellectual excellence while discouraging women from pursuing careers."

After 32 years on the Barnard faculty, Komarovsky retired in 1970, then returned to Barnard to chair its women's studies program. In 1985, using interviews with over 200 students from the Barnard class of 1983, she wrote *Women in College: Shaping New Feminine Identities.* Some of her conclusions echoed her 1981 *New York Times* editorial:

> Young women are becoming aware that the call to equal opportunities for women outside the home is an empty slogan as long as the society insists on traditional role segregation within the family. Some women react to this discovery with equanimity, others with frustration, resignation or indignation. But the real touchstone of their aspirations is the longing for a society in which the rhetoric of equality will be realized as fact. There is no denying that this would require major institutional changes.

In 1991, Mirra Komarovsky was given the Distinguished Career Award of the American Sociological Association.

SOURCES:
Candee, Marjorie Dent. *Current Biography.* NY: H.W. Wilson, 1953.
"Mirra Komarovsky, Authority on Women's Studies, Dies at 93," in *The New York Times.* February 1, 1999.

SUGGESTED READING:
Deegan, Mary Jo, ed. *Women in Sociology.* CT: Greenwood Press, 1991.

Komei empress.

See Yoshiko.

Komnena, Anna (1083–1153/55).

See Anna Comnena.

Kondakova, Yelena (c. 1955—)

Soviet cosmonaut. Name variations: Elena Kondakova. Born around 1955; married Valeri Ryumin (cosmonaut and director of Russia's end of the Mir-shuttle program who went on three space flights).

Yelena Kondakova's 169-day Mir mission in 1995 was the longest spaceflight by a woman until *Shannon Lucid topped the record in September 1996. "My life is easier on board," said Kondakova, "because you don't have to do laundry there, you don't have to cook there. So I think that for a woman, being in space is kind of a vacation from home work." In May 1997, Kondakova became the first Russian woman to fly on a U.S. spaceship; NASA considered her Mir experience and her English-language skills a great asset for the mission to ferry American astronaut Michael Foale to Mir.

Kondratyeva, Lyudmila (1958—)

Soviet runner. Born on April 11, 1958.

Russia's Lyudmila Kondratyeva won a gold medal in the 100 meters in the Moscow Olympics in 1980, beating East German champion *Marlies Göhr by a hundredth of a second. In 1988, in the Seoul Olympics, Kondratyeva won a team bronze in the 4x100-meter relay.

Konetzni, Anny (1902–1968)

*Austrian soprano. Born Anny Konerczny in Ungarisch-Weisskirchen, Austria, on February 12, 1902; died on September 6, 1968, in Vienna; sister of soprano *Hilde Konetzni (1905–1980); studied with Erik Schmedes in Vienna and Jacques Stückgold in Berlin.*

Debuted at the Vienna Volksoper (1925), Metropolitan Opera (1935), and Salzburg (1934); retired (1955); taught at the Viennese Music Academy until 1957.

Anny Konetzni was hired as a chorister at the Vienna Volksoper in 1923 but was let go because of lack of voice. Three years later, she made her debut in that same theater as contralto soloist in Wagner's *Rienzi.* Between 1931 and 1934, Konetzni was a member of the Berlin State Opera. She sang the first performance at that theater of Verdi's *I vespri Siciliani* in 1932. Her long association with the Vienna State Opera began in 1933, and soon she was one of that theater's best-known artists. She performed throughout Europe and North America. Anny Konetzni appeared frequently at Salzburg in 1934, 1935, 1936, and 1941. After World War II, she worked to revive opera in Vienna. She sang Lenore in the opening performance held under the baton of Josef Krips at the Theater an der Wien on October 6, 1945. She was an honored guest at a gala reopening of the Vienna Staatsoper in November 1955.

John Haag,
Athens, Georgia

Konetzni, Hilde (1905–1980)

*Austrian soprano. Born Hilde Konerczny on March 21, 1905, in Vienna; died on April 20, 1980, in Vienna; sister of soprano *Anny Konetzni (1902–1968); studied at the Vienna Conservatory; married Mirko Urbanic, in 1940; children: one daughter.*

Debuted at Vienna Staatsoper (1935) and joined the company; after her retirement (1974), continued to teach.

Hilde Konetzni and her sister Anny were both champion swimmers, which developed their breathing capacity and stamina. Hilde was three years younger than Anny and began her singing lessons at the New Vienna Conservatory. While Anny was engaged at the Chemnitz Opera, Hilde became a student and in 1929 was asked to take on the role of Sieglinde in *Die Walküre* with three days' notice, a feat she managed successfully. For three years, from 1933 to 1936, Hilde divided her time between Prague and Vienna before finally settling in her native city. Bruno Walter took her to Paris where she was cast as Donna Elvira. Anny Konetzni became jealous of her younger sister's success and tried never to appear in the same opera with her. Hilde's voice was strong, with great warmth and beauty of tone, but not enormous. She managed her voice carefully; as a result, it lasted throughout her long career, an example of vocal preservation. Hilde Konetzni lost everything in World War II, but recouped her fortunes as she was in great demand after the war. She continued to teach and perform at the Volksoper. Still in good voice, she gave her last performance in 1974.

John Haag,
Athens, Georgia

Hilde Konetzni

Kong, Madame H.H. (1890–1973).

See Song Ailing in The Song Sisters.

Königsmark, Aurora von (1662–1728)

Countess of Königsmark and mistress of Augustus II, elector of Saxony and king of Poland. Name variations: Maria Aurora von Konigsmark. Born Maria Aurora von Königsmark on May 8, 1662 (some sources cite 1668 or 1669), in Worms, Estonia, Russia; died at Quedlinburg, Prussia, on February 16, 1728; daughter of Swedish nobles; sister of Count Philipp Christoph von Königsmark (1665–c. 1694); had liaison with Augustus II the Strong ("Mocny"), elector of Saxony (r. 1670–1733) and king of Poland (r. 1697–1706 and 1709–1733); children: (with Augustus II) Count Maurice de Saxe, generally called Marshal de Saxe or Marshal Saxe (1696–1750, who served under Marlborough in the War of the Spanish Succession).

Aurora von Königsmark was born into a noble Swedish family on May 8, 1662. Having passed some years at Hamburg, where she attracted attention both with her beauty and her talents, Aurora went in 1694 to Dresden to look into the circumstances surrounding the sudden and mysterious disappearance from Hanover of her brother Philipp Christoph, count of Königsmark. (After entering into the service of the elector of Hanover, Philipp was accused of an affair with *Sophia Dorothea of Brunswick-Celle* [1666–1726], wife of the future George I, king of England. It is thought that Philipp was murdered in 1694.)

While in Dresden, Aurora caught the attention of Augustus, then elector of Saxony (and future king of Poland), and became his mistress. In October 1696, she gave birth to a son Maurice, afterwards the famous Marshal de Saxe. Augustus, however, soon tired of Aurora, who then spent her time in efforts to secure the position of abbess of Quedlinburg, an office which carried with it the honor of a princess of the Empire, and to recover the lost inheritance of her family in Sweden. She was made coadjutor abbess and lady-provost (*Pröpstin*) of Quedlinburg but lived mainly in Berlin, Dresden, and Hamburg. In 1702, she went on a diplomatic errand to Charles XII, king of Sweden, on behalf of Augustus, but her adventurous journey ended in failure. The countess, who was described by Voltaire as "the most famous woman of two centuries," died at Quedlinburg on February 16, 1728.

Konopnicka, Maria (1842–1910)

Polish poet, writer, and nationalist activist, who was one of the leading exponents of the realistic school of literature. Name variations: Marja Konopnicka; Marii Konopnickiej; (pseudonyms) Marko, Jan Sawa, and Jan Warez. Born Maria Wasilowska on May 23, 1842, in Suwalki; died on October 8, 1910, in Lemberg (Lvov), Austrian Galicia (now Lviv, Ukraine); daughter of Józef Wasilowski; married a landowner; children: six.

Maria Konopnicka was born the daughter of a lawyer into the restrictive small-town environment of Suwalki in 1842. She married at an early age, moved to her husband's rural estate, and had six children. Self-taught and seized by an urge to learn about the newest ideas of her day, she avidly read classic works by Montaigne and others as well as new books by such contemporary thinkers as John Stuart Mill. She was also strongly influenced by the writers of the Polish Positivist school of thought, whose works embraced the progressive social, political and economic ideals of the West. After some years, Konopnicka's marriage to her much older husband became strained, and when Russian repressive measures made life on the estate difficult, she moved with her children to Dresden, where they lived for two years.

After returning to Poland, she spent more and more time on her literary activities and made her debut as a poet in 1870. By 1876, her poems appeared in national journals, and her cycle of poems "In the Mountains" was published that year in the well-respected *Tygodnik Ilustrowany* (Illustrated Weekly).

In 1877, she separated from her husband and moved to Warsaw to be in the thick of Polish literary and intellectual life, supporting herself and her children as a private tutor. Accepted as a valuable addition to the city's cultural landscape, she took part in the many official as well as underground actions to assist both political and ordinary prisoners of the Russian regime that governed Warsaw. Konopnicka was committed to raising the educational level of the poor and devoted large amounts of her time to working in educational organizations for working-class women and men. The more she came into contact with the social realities of the poor, the more radicalized she became. As a passionate Polish nationalist, Konopnicka blamed some but not all of Poland's problems on the Russian and German empires which occupied much of the nation's territory (she was less critical of the Austro-Hungarian regime in Galicia, which had granted autonomy to the Polish population in that province).

She was convinced, however, that foreign occupiers were not solely responsible for Poland's woes. Konopnicka saw the lack of interest in the plight of the poor by the landowning *szlachta* (gentry) class as a major reason for Polish poverty and backwardness. She also attributed these problems to the reactionary attitude of the Roman Catholic Church, which she believed fostered a negative attitude toward progress with teachings based on superstition and civic passivity. As a result of the critical messages which permeated her poetry, she found herself constantly in trouble not only with Russian tsarist censors, who quite rightly considered her to be a Polish patriot, but also with Polish conservatives, who saw in her writings an open incitement to the peasants to revolt against their *szlachta* lords and masters. Equally sensitive to the horrific conditions suffered by both urban and rural proletarians, in her cycle *Obrazki* (Tableaux) she raged against the merciless exploitation of a virtually defenseless working class. Given the fact that Konopnicka rarely missed an opportunity in her works to present the clergy in a negative light, Poland's clergy also regarded her writings with great suspicion, considering them to be dripping with anti-clerical venom and harboring an impious spirit.

Confidently, Konopnicka ignored both foreign and domestic critics, increasingly writing not only poems but also short stories and children's books. After three collections of her poems appeared in print between 1881 and 1886, she authorized the publication of a volume of short stories. She also wielded her pen as a critic, publicist, and translator, crafting readable Polish versions of works by Heinrich Heine, Gerhart Hauptmann, Gabriele D'Annunzio, and Edmond Rostand.

Outspoken as a feminist in a society that had traditionally prayed to *Mary the Virgin but believed that mortal women should be silent and remain contentedly within the domestic sphere, Konopnicka experienced frustrations that were sometimes hard to contain. Her editorship of the women's magazine *Swit* (Dawn) from 1884 to 1886 served as one outlet. Frustrated by censorship and criticism from Polish conservative circles, in 1890 she lived in Western Europe and did not return to Galicia until 1902. From then until her death in 1910, she would live in Lemberg (now Lviv).

By the time Konopnicka returned from exile in 1902, she had gained universal recognition as a major poet and writer. Her short stories "Niemczaki" (German Boys), "Nasza szkapa" (Our Jade), "Dym" (Smoke), "Urbanowa" and "Milosierdzie gminy" (Township Charity), published between 1888 and 1897, are considered to be among the best in Polish literature. Vividly conceived and written, her literary studies, particularly that of the revered national poet Adam Mickiewicz, continue to be of interest to both readers and scholars alike.

As she grew older, Konopnicka grew increasingly belligerent in both her Polish nationalism and her desire to see the birth of a more just social order. While in exile, she had remained in close contact with her publishers, the press, and various organizations dedicated to the cause of national regeneration. She fell easily into the role of an activist and helped to organize protests opposing the repressive measures taken against Polish-speaking children by the Prussian government in Wrzesnia in 1901–1902. In 1903, to celebrate the 25th anniversary of her literary and social work, she was offered a house in Zarnowiec as a gift from the Polish nation. Although no longer young, on numerous occasions from 1905 through 1907 Konopnicka visited Russian-occupied Warsaw on missions of

Polish postage stamp honoring Maria Konopnicka, issued May 1952.

mercy to assist incarcerated political prisoners and their families. Her concern for the impoverished and socially marginalized extended not only to those Poles of Roman Catholic or Socialist persuasions, but also to Polish Jews. Unlike some intellectuals in Poland who began during this period to regard Jews as dangerous aliens, Konopnicka wrote sympathetically about Polish Jews both as individuals and as a people, the best of her writings on a Jewish theme being her 1897 story "Mendel of Gdansk (A Sketch)."

As German-Polish ethnic tensions became increasingly uncompromising in the years leading to World War I, Polish writers like Konopnicka accepted the challenge of inevitable Slav-Teuton clashes, at least on the printed page. Scholars and poets alike in both Germany and the occupied Polish lands re-fought the wars of the 14th and 15th centuries, when a growing Polish state had defeated the Teutonic Knights. History and literature became highly politicized, with the arts serving as simply another weapon in the bitter nationalist struggles of the day.

In 1910, to commemorate the 500th anniversary of the epic Battle of Grunwald, in which Poles decisively defeated Germans, a public subscription was launched to raise funds to erect a monument to recall Poland's hour of glory. Forbidden by Prussia to erect the monument on their sacred soil, the organizers had to content themselves with unveiling the monument in Cracow, in Austrian Galicia. When the ceremony took place on July 15, 1910, with the great pianist Ignacy Paderewski in attendance, the throng was thrilled to hear for the first time a rousing anthem specially composed for the occasion by Maria Konopnicka, which closed with the lines:

> By the very last drop of blood in our veins
> Our souls will be secured,
> Until in dust and ashes falls
> The stormwind sown by the Prussian lord.
> Our every home will form a stockade.
> May God so lend us aid.

In the final years of her life, Konopnicka invested much time and effort in writing an epic poem entitled *Pan Balcer w Brazylji* (Mister Balcer in Brazil, 1892–1906, complete edition 1910). Following a tradition set by other Polish poets like Krasicki and Slowacki, she wrote this work in *ottava rima* (used centuries earlier in the Renaissance by Tasso to depict exploits of chivalry). It centered on a topical issue of the early 20th century, the emigration of masses of impoverished Polish peasants to various parts of the New World. The author intended it to be the historical epic of the Polish peasant in the same way that

Adam Mickiewicz's *Pan Tadeusz* had been one for the proud Polish *szlachta*. While the lives of Polish emigrant workers were invariably difficult in Germany, France, the United States, and Canada, it was in Brazil, where they were brought to clear primeval forests for agricultural use, that their lot may well have been the hardest. Konopnicka's work, in which the hero of the poem, Mr. Balcer, is a simple village blacksmith, is now more of historical rather than literary interest, though some of its passages remain vivid and gripping for Polish readers. The poet's Ukrainian contemporary, the writer Ivan Franko, greatly admired her work in general and was so moved by *Pan Balcer w Brazylji* that he devoted a cycle of his own poetry, *Do Brazilii*, to it.

Honored by virtually all of her contemporaries as one of the leading representatives of the realist school of Polish literature, Maria Konopnicka died in Lemberg on October 8, 1910. Although many of her writings now appear dated to modern readers, the best of her poems and short stories remain living works of literature displaying both heart and soul. In the generations since her death, millions of copies of her books have been printed and reprinted in Poland.

SOURCES:

Brodzka, Alina. *Maria Konopnicka*. 4th ed. Warsaw: Wiedza Powszechna, 1975.

Czerwinski, E.J., ed. *Dictionary of Polish Literature*. Westport, CT: Greenwood Press, 1994.

Davies, Norman. *God's Playground: A History of Poland*. 2 vols. NY: Columbia University Press, 1982.

Gillon, Adam, and Ludwik Krzyzanowski, eds. *Introduction to Modern Polish Literature: An Anthology of Fiction and Poetry*. 2nd ed. NY: Hippocrene Books, 1982.

Kridl, Manfred, ed. *An Anthology of Polish Literature*. NY: Columbia University Press, 1964.

Milosz, Czeslaw. *The History of Polish Literature*. 2nd ed. Berkeley, CA: University of California Press, 1983.

Povsic, Frances F. "Poland: Children's Literature in English," in *The Reading Teacher*. Vol. 33, no. 7. April 1980, pp. 806–815.

Prymak, Thomas M. "Ivan Franko and Mass Ukrainian Emigration to Canada," in *Canadian Slavonic Papers*. Vol. 26, no. 4. December 1984, pp. 307–317.

Segel, Harold B., ed. *Stranger in Our Midst: Images of the Jew in Polish Literature*. Ithaca, NY: Cornell University Press, 1996.

Wawrzykowska-Wierciochowa, Dionizja. "Siedem melodii skomponowanych do tekstu Roty Marii Konopnickiej," in *Muzyka*. Vol. 29, no. 3, 1984, pp. 63–89.

Zamoyski, Adam. *The Polish Way: A Thousand-Year History of the Poles and Their Culture*. London: John Murray, 1987.

John Haag,
Associate Professor of History,
University of Georgia, Athens, Georgia

Konrads, Ilsa (b. 1944).

See Fraser, Dawn for sidebar.

Konstanz.

Variant of Constance.

Koñwatsi'tsiaiéñni (c. 1736–1796).

See Brant, Molly.

Koontz, Elizabeth (1919–1989)

American educator who was the first African-American to become president of the National Education Association. Born Elizabeth Duncan on June 3, 1919, in Salisbury, North Carolina; died on January 6, 1989, in Salisbury, North Carolina; youngest of seven children of Samuel E. Duncan and Lena Bell (Jordan) Duncan (both educators); graduated from Price High School, Salisbury; Livingstone College, B.A., 1938; Atlanta University, M.A., 1941; graduate work at Columbia University, Indiana University, and North Carolina College (now North Carolina Central University); married Harry L. Koontz (an educator), on November 26, 1947; no children.

Born in 1919, Elizabeth Koontz, the youngest of seven children, followed in the footsteps of her parents who were both educators. The product of segregated schools in her hometown of Salisbury, North Carolina, Koontz credited her family and an elementary school history teacher with giving her a strong sense of identity. After graduating with honors from Livingstone College in 1938, she took a position at Harnett County Training School in Dunn, North Carolina, teaching special education classes. Fired in 1940 for protesting against the high rents teachers were forced to pay at a school-owned boarding house, she went on to receive a master's degree from Atlanta University. Afterwards, she returned to pursue her teaching career in North Carolina, working primarily in special needs education. In 1947, she married Harry Koontz, also an educator.

In 1952, when black teachers were first permitted entry into the National Education Association (NEA), Koontz joined the North Carolina chapter. During the 1950s and 1960s, she became an outspoken leader in the organization, working for improved teaching conditions and higher wages, and urging teachers to take responsibility for their own destinies by becoming more politically active. By 1965, Koontz was president of the NEA's Department of Classroom Teachers, and in 1967 she was elected president of the organization at its

*Elizabeth
Koontz*

106th national convention. Her election was not only historic with regard to her race and gender, but also marked a change in NEA's leadership, away from the domination of mostly male administrators to a broader choice that included classroom teachers. Koontz continued to call for "teacher power" and even supported a strike of teachers in some 400 localities in 1968, saying: "Teachers who walk off the job after they have exhausted every other method of bringing needed improvement show dedication and commitment."

Koontz's tenure as president of the NEA was cut short when President Richard Nixon appointed her head of the Women's Bureau of the Department of Labor (his first appointment of an African-American), a post she held until 1973, when Nixon resigned. She used this position to speak out for black women's rights, and was particularly instrumental in helping to improve working conditions for domestic workers. After leaving the Bureau, Koontz returned to North Carolina, where she held various high-level educational positions, including assistant state superintendent for teacher education in the North Carolina Department of Public Instruction. From 1977 to 1979, she was a member of the North Carolina Council on the Status of Women.

A soft-spoken woman of great charm, Koontz was the recipient of numerous awards, citations, and honors, including over 30 honorary degrees from colleges and universities around the country. The educator retired in 1982, after which she and her husband made their home in Salisbury, North Carolina. Elizabeth Koontz died on June 6, 1989, following a heart attack.

SOURCES:

Diamonstein, Barbaralee. *Open Secrets: Ninety-four Women in Touch with Our Time*. NY: Viking Press, 1972.

Smith, Jessie Carney, ed. *Notable Black American Women*. Detroit, MI: Gale Research, 1992.

Weatherford, Doris. *American Women's History*. NY: Prentice Hall, 1994.

Barbara Morgan,
Melrose, Massachusetts

Koptagel, Yuksel (1931—)

Turkish composer and concert pianist known for her compositions of French and Spanish interpretation. Born in Istanbul, Turkey, on October 27, 1931; granddaughter of General Osman Koptagel, a famous commander from the Turkish War of Independence.

Yuksel Koptagel, a member of a prominent Turkish family, gave her first concert at age six. After studying piano, theory, and composition with the Turkish composer Cemal Resit, Koptagel journeyed to Madrid and Paris for further work with Joaquin Rodrigo, José Cubiles, Lazare Lévy, Tony Aubin, and Alexandre Tansman. At the Paris Conservatory, she won several first prizes and honorable mentions both for composing and for piano. Koptagel became a concert artist and performed with many international orchestras as a piano soloist. A member of the Istanbul State Symphony Orchestra, she also served on the jury of the Schola Cantorium and

the École Superieur de Musique. Yuksel Koptagel's compositions were written for small ensembles as well as the piano and voice. Her work has a continental European flavor.

John Haag,
Athens, Georgia

Korbut, Olga (1955—)

Soviet gymnastics star and medal winner in the 1972 Munich Olympics who, thanks to television, became a world famous athlete and helped her sport gain unprecedented popularity. Name variations: Olya Korbuta. Pronunciation: CORE-bit. Born Olga Valentinovna Korbut on May 16, 1955, in Grodno in the Byelorussian Soviet Socialist Republic of the USSR; daughter of Valentine Korbut (an engineer) and Valentina Korbut (a cook); graduated Grodno Teachers Training Institute, 1977; married Leonid Bortkevich (a Soviet pop singer), on January 7, 1978; children: Richard.

Enrolled at gymnastics school (1964); began work under coach Renald Knysh (1967); entered Soviet National championships (1969); won fourth place at Soviet National championships (1970); attained rank of "Master of Sports" (1971); at Olympic debut, won three gold medals and one silver medal in gymnastics (1972); named "Honored Master of Sports" and toured the U.S. and Europe (1973); competed at Montreal Olympics and toured the U.S. (1976); retired from competition (1977); inducted in absentia into International Women's Sports Hall of Fame (1982); exposed to nuclear radiation following nuclear accident at Chernobyl (1986); moved to the U.S. and toured with Mary Lou Retton (1989); tested for radiation sickness (1991).

Won Olympic gold medals in gymnastics for balance beam, floor exercises, and for all-around team competition, and Olympic silver medal for asymmetrical bars in Munich (1972); won Olympic silver medal for balance beam and gold medal for all-around team competition in Montreal (1976).

The Olympic Games held at Munich, Germany, in the summer of 1972 are remembered more for political turmoil and bloodshed than for athletic achievement. The world's controversies first appeared in a dispute about the right of Rhodesia, with its black majority and its white rulers, to be admitted to the competition. Overshadowing this and other issues was the phenomenon of political murder. Penetrating the extraordinarily lax security system, members of a radical Palestinian group took a number of Israeli athletes hostage in the Olympic Village. The terror ended in a bloody gunfight at an airport near Munich as the Palestinians tried to leave with their captives. In all, eleven Israeli athletes and five Palestinian terrorists died in the episode.

With the entire Olympic competition made somber by political murder, one individual provided a welcome image of youth, grace, and joy. The most colorful and popular figure to emerge at Munich was a 17-year-old girl who stood only 4'11" tall and weighed a mere 82 pounds. She was one of the most inexperienced members of the team from the Soviet Union. Nonetheless, she impressed a worldwide audience. Her brown hair done up in pigtails, her slight figure, and her open displays of exuberant emotion put her in a class by herself as a public figure.

*W*e had three coaches for each team and five KGB.

—Olga Korbut

Women's gymnastics has been a part of the Olympic competition since 1928. Starting in 1952, it came to include individual as well as team performances. The sport is an unlikely one to produce a world-famous figure. Gymnastics competition consists of four specific events: horse vault, floor exercises, asymmetric bars, and balance beam. Gymnasts sometimes compete as members of a team and sometimes individually. They sometimes appear in all-around events, which combine all four of the specific events listed above; sometimes they compete in an individual exercise.

Besides its complexity, gymnastics does not pit one contestant against another in direct fashion. Competition consists of exercises to be evaluated by a panel of judges using a complex scoring system. To the eye of someone who is not an expert, the exact level of skill the gymnast achieves is hard to see. Writes Korbut's biographer, Justin Beecham: "Nobody races anybody else . . . . The real competition takes place between the gymnast and his or her apparatus."

Korbut's home country was one of the powerhouses in world gymnastics competition, and her success at the Olympics ensured her the status of a national heroine. But she was a new kind of Soviet sports heroine. Starting with the Helsinki Olympics in 1948, Soviet teams played a central, often dominant role in Olympic competition. Even the most notable Soviet athletes seemed to fit a clear pattern. They did not exhibit strong emotions; they did not appear as distinct and colorful personalities. The growing force of television coverage, however, with its emphasis on dramatic scenes and vivid personal-

ities, was at odds with this tradition. With television playing a key role, Olga Korbut emerged as the first great Olympic personality representing the Soviets.

The future champion was born on May 16, 1955, in the quiet provincial city of Grodno. Now located in the republic of Belarus, Grodno was then a city in the Belorussian Soviet Republic; this was a part of the Soviet Union, and it is often known as White Russia. Located near the border with Poland, the region had been the scene of major fighting during World War II. During the war, Korbut's father Valentin fought and was wounded in the region as a partisan behind the German lines.

Olga distinguished herself at an early age as a promising athlete. The tiny child began to study gymnastics when she was nine. She stood out partly because of her diminutive size, but she was even more prominent because of her native ability and limitless enthusiasm. In 1964, she won a place in a school for athletes in Grodno where she could pursue gymnastics.

The special sports school in which she enrolled was part of a nationwide network of such institutions designed to produce star athletes. In them, Soviet youngsters continued their academic studies while receiving special training and coaching. There were only a few such schools in the country where training was available for gymnastics, but one of them was in Korbut's home city. Olga was also fortunate in having several former women champions as her teachers. But the most important guide to her career was her personal coach and senior gymnastics instructor at Grodno, Renald Knysh.

Korbut's strengths as a gymnastics student soon impressed instructors like *Yelena Volchetskaya, a member of the 1964 Olympic championship team. Olga combined coordination, timing, stamina, and body control with a natural grace and suppleness. Her size, a disadvantage in most sports, aided her in gymnastics: a gymnast must combine a maximum of physical strength with a minimum of body weight. Given her age, Korbut stood out because of her self-confidence; to some of her instructors and fellow athletes, she appeared too daring and sure of herself.

Under Knysh's direction, Olga concentrated on movements using her extremely supple spine. Thus, she was able to make a specialty of backward movements requiring a vast amount of agility. These skills were particularly suited to competition on the asymmetric bars, balance beam, and in the floor exercises. Her weakest

area was the competition on the horse vault where her short stature hindered her.

Starting in 1969, Korbut competed in a series of events designed to prepare her for the 1972 Olympics. She began with an appearance at the Soviet National championships, despite the fact that she was technically too young to compete that year. Her national debut fulfilled all expectations. She won fifth place overall, in some events overcoming Olympic medal winners. Her most notable achievement came on the balance beam, where she displayed her backward somersault. This movement utilized the spinal agility Knysh had recognized, and it now became her strongest competitive tool. In the National championships the following year, she raised her overall score to come in fourth. Her performances were already being characterized by daring, even dangerous movements like backflips; older Soviet women gymnasts, with their more mature bodies, did not attempt these.

In the aftermath of her 1970 success, the promising young gymnast suffered a personal setback. Soviet sports authorities did not allow Korbut to compete at the World championships that year in Yugoslavia. Only allowed to give a number of well-received exhibitions at this gathering, she turned her anger and frustration on her teammates, declaring that she had been unfairly excluded from competing. But her consequent unpopularity with her colleagues led her to an even greater concentration on developing her skills.

There were several previews of her stellar Olympic performance in the early months of 1972, including a tournament in Riga in which she placed first. In the two months just prior to the Olympics, *Larissa Latynina, the coach of the national women's team and the leading figure in Soviet women's gymnastics, directed her preparation.

Under the Olympic system in effect in 1972, Korbut would participate in a variety of gymnastic activities over a period of five days, from Sunday, August 27, through Thursday, August 31. A team competition would begin the gymnastics; in it, each team member would participate in an all-around event, with their scores being combined into a team score. This meant required exercises on each apparatus (balance beam, asymmetrical bars, horse vault) plus required exercises on the floor. Following would come original routines that each gymnast (and her coaches) had developed for each apparatus and the floor. The required exercises would test the basic competence of each individual, and the original routines would permit her to display special abilities and achievements. The competition would aim at winning a medal for the entire team.

Following the team competition, top-ranking gymnasts would compete as individuals using only original routines. Again there would be an all-around event combining all the varieties of exercise, which would produce the all-around champion. There would follow specific competitions to determine the champion for each exercise category: the balance beam, the horse vault, the asymmetrical bars, and the floor exercises.

The Olympics schedule placed women's gymnastics during the first week of the gathering at Munich. Korbut marched in as the last and tiniest member of her team, her first opportunity to start drawing the eyes of the audience. She looked so small that some newspapers described her as being only 15. She did well in the team all-around competition held on August 27 and August 28, then stumbled badly in the individual all-around event held on Wednesday, August 30. A serious mistake pushed her to tears. Performing on the asymmetric bars, she lost her rhythm, slipped completely off the bars, and found herself out of the running for the most prestigious award, the individual all-around championship. Even more seriously, her composure dissolved. To many of her teammates, Korbut's tears indicated that all her hopes for a medal were now gone.

On Thursday, August 31, the last day of the gymnastics, Korbut returned to the auditorium for the individual competitions with restored confidence and inimitable flair. Performing an original routine on the balance beam with supreme skill, she ended by dazzling both the judges and the audience with her backward somersault. This movement was normally done only when a gymnast performed on the floor, and, following the 1972 Olympics, the International Gymnastics Federation banned it as too dangerous. Nonetheless, on this occasion it gave her a decisive edge over her competitors and her first gold medal.

Next she took a silver medal during the individual competition on the asymmetric bars, which had been her nemesis on Wednesday. She finished the day with her greatest triumph for the entire Olympics. In floor exercises, she presented a brilliant performance, once again featuring her signature movement of backward somersaults. The floor exercises, which are performed to a musical accompaniment, present the greatest opportunity for a gymnast to exhibit her skills as a dancer and acrobat. Here Korbut's skills were unsurpassed. Again, the crowd went wild, and the judges, despite their professional demeanor, followed along. They awarded her the elevated score of 9.90 (out of a possible 10) and a second gold medal.

Korbut's success in the floor exercises was doubly remarkable because she had developed her routine only in the past week. With Olympic competition just a few days ahead, she had discarded as unsuitable a sequence of exercises she had been working on for months and persuaded both Knysh and Latynina to help her create a new routine. They considered it barely possible it might win her third place, but she made it into a first-place triumph.

The greatest novelty of Korbut's success was that it took place before a television audience of hundreds of millions of viewers. Her buoyant personality and girlish looks combined with her athletic skills to make her a memorable sight. Beecham has calculated that Korbut got only 30 minutes of television coverage. But, as he put it, "this was enough to establish her reputation—she was a thirty minute superstar." In the view of Allen Guttmann, Korbut owed her new fame to the television executive Roone Arledge. Recognizing the human interest value in her fall—and display of tears—during the individual all-around competition, he directed his camera crew to make her the star of the gymnastics coverage. Thus, writes Guttmann, "Roone Arledge of ABC-TV made diminutive Olga Korbut (USSR) the most famous woman in Munich."

The political implications of her performances were also significant. At a time of continuing tension between the Soviet Union and the United States, she became a heroine despite the lingering effects of the Cold War. Writes David Wallechinsky: "In the United States, despite antipathy to the U.S.S.R., little Olga Korbut's dramatic cycle of success, failure, and success captured the national imagination."

Thus, Korbut became one of the sensations of 1972 sports. She won two gold medals and one silver medal for individual performances, and she helped her six-woman team win a gold medal in the group competition. In terms of technical achievement, her teammate *Ludmilla Tourischeva did even better, winning the gold medal for the prestigious individual all-around category. Nonetheless, Korbut won the hearts of a worldwide audience. Sportswriters and other observers of the Olympics had long been impressed by the technical skill of Soviet athletes. They were doubly charmed by the gymnast who combined technical virtuosity with a bubbling personality, broad smiles, and friendly waves to the crowd.

Korbut's victory in the 1972 Olympics also helped to make gymnastics a popular sport, especially for women. Unprecedented numbers of girls took up the sport as participants, and large numbers of spectators began to follow the performances and results of gymnastic stars. Throughout America, young girls adopted Korbut's hairdo. According to *The New York Times*, private gymnastics clubs grew from about 50 in 1970 to almost 500 in 1976. American gymnasts, 45,000 at the start of the same period, numbered 500,000 by 1976.

Korbut herself made a tour of Europe and the United States in 1973 during which she was entertained by Prime Minister Edward Heath at 10 Downing Street and President Richard Nixon at the White House. Mayor Richard Daley of Chicago declared the day of her visit, March 26, "Olga Korbut Day." Prestigious foreign honors descended on the youngster, and she became perhaps the most famous teenage sports heroine in history. For example, the American Broadcasting Company designated Korbut its "Sports Personality of the Year," and Britain's BBC named her "Sportswoman of the Year." There were other tributes as well: Olga Korbut fan clubs formed in Los Angeles; Americans sported T-shirts with her name on them. At home, she received fan mail from all over globe. Like other athletes of worldwide reputation, she received letters addressed simply by her name and home country.

Soviet authorities apparently grew disturbed by the way in which the media in the West played up her personality. When she insisted on the right to go off on shopping trips and to enjoy other features of life in the U.S. and Western Europe, they considered it awkward to deny her such privileges. Nonetheless, she found herself increasingly under the shadow of official disfavor.

After her triumphal tour, Korbut returned to her schooling. She was, after all, still only in high school. With secondary school behind her, she studied at a training school for teachers in Grodno. Meanwhile, she continued her grueling schedule in preparation for 1976: five hours of practice a day in addition to her school work. In these years, she gave both exhibitions and public talks to audiences throughout the Soviet Union.

The 1976 Olympics showed that she remained a charismatic and popular performer as crowds applauded her wildly. Nonetheless, her results were disappointing: she won only a single silver medal for her individual performance. Just as she had been the tiny teenage sensation four years earlier, that role now fell to Rumania's *Nadia Comaneci. Television's coverage of Comaneci's performance continued the process begun by Korbut of making women's gymnastics one of the high points of the Olympics. Korbut had competed at the age of 17; Comaneci was only 14. Sports commentators now called Comaneci the successor to Korbut as "the little kid" of gymnastics. In the 1984 Olympics, the sport's popularity continued to grow with the spotlight now on the American teenager *Mary Lou Retton.

In January 1978, now 22, the former star gymnast married Soviet pop singer Leonid

Bortkevich, wearing a wedding dress she had purchased two years earlier during a tour of the United States. At her wedding, she announced that she was giving up performing. She now expected to devote herself to coaching younger gymnasts. In the spring of 1979, she gave birth to a son.

Korbut's public appearances became less and less frequent. Her teammate Tourischeva was honored by being named to membership to the Supreme Soviet, the Soviet legislative body, and appointed to the organizing committee for the 1980 Olympics. According to interviews Korbut gave more than a decade later, unlike Tourischeva, she had refused to cooperate with Soviet political authorities.

Wallechinsky has suggested that she had, in particular, shown unexpected independence during her tour of the United States in December 1976. This continued the pattern that had disturbed Soviet authorities in 1973 during the tour following her success at Munich. Certainly, she enjoyed and accepted the role of an individual celebrity in a way that other Soviet athletes had been encouraged to avoid. She paid the penalty by being denied what Tourischeva received and more. Korbut's hopes for a coaching job went unfulfilled, she was not permitted foreign travel, and she settled down in obscurity in the Byelorussian city of Minsk.

In 1986, Korbut found herself involuntarily involved in one of the great tragedies of the decade. The Soviet nuclear power plant at Chernobyl in the Ukraine became the scene of the world's worst nuclear accident, pouring radiation into the atmosphere. Korbut's home was less than 200 miles from the site of the calamity. She now became concerned about the danger to her health.

By the close of the 1980s, Mikhail Gorbachev's reforms had opened the way for Soviet citizens to travel more freely. Korbut visited the United States in 1988, her first trip abroad in more than a decade. In 1989, she left Minsk and settled in the U.S. to take up a career as a gymnastics coach. She now received formal induction into the International Women's Hall of Fame—an honor she had been forced to accept *in absentia* in 1982. At the close of 1989, with her famous pigtails no longer in evidence, she made an eight-city tour of the United States with American Olympic star Mary Lou Retton.

The shadow of Chernobyl remained with Korbut, however. She helped raise funds for the victims of the accident, and, in 1991, she suffered from apparently ominous bouts of fatigue. Medical tests conducted in the United States showed that, so far, she was not suffering from radiation exposure. She then turned her energies to writing an autobiography.

Although experts have rated her technical skills below those of Tourischeva, Korbut remains a renowned figure in the history of the Olympics. Her colorful and daring performances focused attention on a once obscure sport; since 1972, women's gymnastics has become a featured event in Olympic competition. At a time of Soviet-American rivalry, the smiling young girl bridged the gap between the two countries, becoming a sports heroine both at home and in the United States. To the chagrin of her nation's political establishment, she became a colorful, individual personality, far removed from the skilled but depersonalized athletes the system had previously produced.

SOURCES:

Beecham, Justin. *Olga.* NY: Paddington, 1974.

Brokhin, Yuri. *The Big Red Machine: The Rise and Fall of Soviet Olympic Champions.* NY: Random House, 1977.

Freeman, Simon, and Roger Boyes. *Sports behind the Iron Curtain.* London: Proteus, 1980.

Guttmann, Allen. *The Olympics: A History of the Modern Games.* Urbana, IL: University of Illinois Press, 1992.

Tatlow, Peter, ed. *The World of Gymnastics.* NY: Atheneum, 1978.

Wallechinsky, David. *The Complete Book of the Olympics.* NY: Viking, 1984.

SUGGESTED READING:

Associated Press and Grolier. *Pursuit of Excellence: The Olympic Story.* Danbury, CT: Grolier Enterprises, 1983.

Groussard, Serge. *The Blood of Israel: The Massacre of the Israeli Athletes, The Olympics, 1972.* NY: William Morrow, 1975.

Kanin, David B. *A Political History of the Olympic Games.* Boulder, CO: Westview Press, 1981.

Mandell, Richard D. *The Olympics of 1972: A Munich Diary.* Chapel Hill, NC: University of North Carolina Press, 1991.

Neil M. Heyman,
Professor of History,
San Diego State University, San Diego, California

Korchinska, Maria (1895–1979)

Russian-born British harpist who concertized widely. Born in Moscow, Russia, on February 16, 1895; died in London, England, on April 17, 1979; married Count Konstantin Benkendorff; children: a son and a daughter.

Maria Korchinska was the first harp of the Bolshoi Theater as well as a professor of harps at the Moscow Conservatory from 1918 to 1924. While at the conservatory, she won the first gold medal awarded to a harpist. In the musical world, instruments were often found acceptable or unacceptable depending on the gender of the person playing it. Most instruments such as the violin, drums, organ, and horns were considered male while the harp and piano were always considered female instruments. Until the 20th century, often the only female player in a symphony orchestra was the harpist. This scheme of gender classification gradually faded, although traces of it continue to exist.

Korchinska left Russia in 1926 when the upheavals of musical life in a revolutionary atmosphere proved to be too daunting. She quickly established herself in Great Britain and on the Continent as first harp in many orchestras. She also played contemporary chamber music with the Harp Ensemble and the Wigmore Ensemble. Korchinska gave the first performance of Arnold Bax's *Fantasy Sonata* for viola and harp which was dedicated to her. She also took part in the first performance of Benjamin Britten's *Ceremony of Carols* in which the harp is prominently featured. An advocate of the instrument, she founded the Harp Society of the United Kingdom. She and **Phia Berghout**, the Dutch harpist, organized annual international harp weeks in the Netherlands in 1960. Prominent as a musician, soloist, and teacher, Korchinska did a great deal to promote the instrument she played.

SOURCES:
"Maria Korchinska," in *The Daily Telegraph* [London]. April 18, 1979, p. 16.
Sadie, Stanley, ed. *New Grove Dictionary of Music and Musicians.* 20 vols. NY: Macmillan, 1980.

John Haag,
Athens, Georgia

Korea, queen of.

See Hong, Lady (1735–1815).
See Min (c. 1840–1895).

Korinna (fl. 5th or 3rd c. BCE).

See Corinna.

Kormlod (fl. 980–1015).

See Gormflaith of Ireland.

Korpus, Lilly (1901–1976).

See Becher, Lilly.

Korsmo, Grete Prytz (b. 1917).

See Kittelsen, Grete Prytz.

Korwin-Piotrowska, Gabriela (1857–1921).

See Zapolska, Gabriela.

Kosach, Laryssa (1871–1913).

See Ukrainka, Lesya.

Koschak, Marie Pachler- (1792–1855).

See Pachler-Koschak, Marie.

Koscina, Sylva (1933–1994)

Yugoslavian actress, best known for her supporting role in Fellini's Juliet of the Spirits. *Born on August 22, 1933, in Zagreb, Yugoslavia; died after a long illness complicated by heart problems on December 26, 1994, in Rome, Italy.*

Selected films: Il Ferroviere *(The Railroad Man, 1955);* Michel Strogoff *(Michael Strogoff, 1956);* Guendalina *(1956);* Le Fatiche di Ercole *(Hercules, 1957);* Gerusalemme Liberata *(The Mighty Crusaders, 1957);* Ercole e la Regina di Lidia *(Hercules Unchained, 1958);* Racconti d'Estate *(Love on the Riviera, 1958);* Erode il Grande *(1959);* L'Assedio di Siracusa *(Siege of Syracuse, 1960);* Le Mercenaire *(Swordsman of Siena, French-Italian, 1962);* Les Quatres Vérités *(Three Fables of Love, French-Italian-Spanish, 1962);* Jessica *(1962);* Copacabana Palace *(Girl Game, 1962);* Le Monachine *(The Little Nuns, 1963);* Judex *(French-Italian, 1964);* Hot Enough for June *(Agent 83/4, UK, 1964);* Giulietta degli Spiriti *(Juliet of the Spirits, 1965);* Made in Italy *(1965);* Deadlier Than the Male *(UK, 1966);* Three Bites of the Apple *(U.S., 1967);* Johnny Banco *(1967);* The Secret War of Harry Frigg *(U.S., 1978);* A Lovely Way to Die *(U.S., 1968);* Hornet's Nest *(U.S., 1970);* Battle of Neretva *(1970);* Homo Eroticus *(Man of the Year, 1971);* Uccidere in Silenzio *(1972);* La Mala Ordina *(1972);* Clara and Nora *(Spanish, 1975);* So Sweet So Dead *(1975);* House of Exorcism *(1975);* Delitto d'Autore *(1976);* Casanova and Co. *(1977);* Sunday Lovers *(1980);* Stelle emigranti *(1983);* Cinderella '80 *(1984);* Deadly Sanctuary *(1986);* Ricky and Barabba *(1993);* C'e Kim Novak al telefono *(1994).*

Known for her beautiful face and voluptuous figure, actress Sylva Koscina was born in Zagreb, Yugoslavia, in 1933 but began her career as a leading lady in Italian films. She was soon in demand internationally. Koscina spent her early years decorating costume melodramas and spectaculars, but her later work included romantic comedies and dramas. One biographer noted that her talent was such that at age 25, she was credible playing the mother of a 16-year-old. Koscina reached the peak of her popularity in the 1960s, and is most remembered for her supporting role in Federico Fellini's *Juliet of the*

Spirits (1965), the director's first full-length color film. Koscina played the beautiful sister of the hapless Juliet, who was portrayed by Fellini's wife *Giulietta Masina. Koscina's few American films include *Three Bites of the Apple* (1967) and *The Secret War of Harry Frigg* (1968). The actress died in 1994, following a long illness complicated by heart problems.

Kösem (1589–1651).

See Reign of Women.

Kosmodemyanskaya, Zoya
(1923–1941)

Soviet partisan who, after her capture and execution by German troops, became a symbol of heroism in the Soviet Union's war against Nazi Germany. Name variations: Tanya; Kosmodemjamskaja; Kosmodemianskia. Pronunciation: Kos-MO-dem-YAHN-sky-ah. Born Zoya Kosmodemyanskaya on September 13, 1923, in the village of Osinovye Gai, Tambov Oblast, near Moscow; executed by hanging on November 29, 1941, in the village of Petrishchevo, Moscow Oblast; daughter of an office worker and a mother widowed early; educated at Moscow's School No. 201; never married; no children.

Joined the Labor Front and worked in a factory; joined a sabotage unit engaged in guerrilla activities (autumn 1941), and captured within a few weeks by the Germans; tortured and hanged the next day.

On a bitterly cold morning in late November 1941, soldiers from Hitler's army led a young girl toward the town square of Petrishchevo, near the city of Vereya. A captured Soviet partisan, she had been savagely beaten and forced to walk barefoot in the snow. Under interrogation, flames had been held to her face to force her to reveal her name and the identities of her comrades; one young German officer left the room covering his face with his hands, no longer able to stomach the scene. Still nothing was learned—not the name of the 18-year-old partisan, nor any information about her fellow partisans, family or friends. Finally, the Germans ended her ordeal by hanging her in the village square, where her body was left for a month, in warning to all who dared defy the Nazi occupation.

German units passing through Petrishchevo jabbed at the body of the young woman with their bayonets and laughed. They did not realize that word of Zoya Kosmodemyanskaya's courage and martyrdom had spread throughout the Soviet Union, helping to sustain civilians starving in the siege of Leningrad, Red Army soldiers fighting to save Moscow, aviators trying to clear the air of Luftwaffe planes, and millions of other Soviet citizens in factories, mines, and farms. In early 1943, when the defeated German troops finally surrendered at Stalingrad, the spirit of Zoya Kosmodemyanskaya hovered over the city that sealed Adolf Hitler's doom.

The beginning of World War II went extremely well for Hitler's superbly trained forces. Using tanks and aircraft to a new advantage, his armies quickly occupied Europe after war was declared on September 1, 1939. Poland fell in a matter of weeks, followed by the collapse, in April 1940, of Denmark and Norway; the following month, the Blitzkrieg was launched against Belgium, the Netherlands, and Luxemburg, and soon engulfed France. The German Luftwaffe began massive air attacks on Britain, although that country did not fall, contrary to Hitler's predictions. In the meantime, Yugoslavia and Greece were overrun by German troops.

In August 1939, Joseph Stalin had signed a non-aggression pact with Hitler, so during the early part of the Blitzkrieg the Soviet Union was outside the fray. The Führer, however, was already planning to achieve what Napoleon had failed to accomplish over a century before—the occupation of Russia. Four million men, 3,300 tanks, and 5,000 planes were assembled for the German attack, and the battle was expected to be of short duration as it had been in the West. Conventional wisdom held that the Soviet army, decimated by Stalin's purges in the 1930s and equipped with outdated weapons, would soon collapse.

Although weaponry had changed since Napoleon's attempt to conquer Russia, other factors had not. The winters were as fierce as ever and so was the determination of the Russian people to defend the motherland. Soviet women especially personified the national determination to defend their country, volunteering for every kind of assignment. The Red Army was not prepared for so many women soldiers, who often had to wear oversize boots and overlong men's trousers, as smaller uniforms were not available. Proportionally, losses among women at the front were heavier than among the men, and German veterans of the Eastern Front were shocked by the numbers of Soviet women soldiers they found dead on the battlefield.

Over 800,000 women saw active duty, serving as combat pilots, navigators, snipers, gunners, paratroopers, sappers, cooks, and nurses; more than 300,000 women crewed anti-aircraft defenses, and the Soviet navy mustered 25,000 women. As combat pilots, women carried out low-level bombing and strafing attacks. Flying at night, these women became known as the "night witches." Describing their effort, one woman flyer said, "After a mission an aircraft stayed on the ground for a few minutes and then it was back in the air. Imagine how our girl armourers worked! During those few minutes they had to load the bomb racks with four bombs—400 kilos—by hand. . . . [T]he body reorganized itself to the extent that we ceased to be women throughout the war. . . . [W]e had no female functions at all."

Red Army women snipers took a tremendous toll against the enemy. There were many women like **Nina Pavlovna Petrova**, who was aged 48 when she first went to the front and notched up 122 kills. Lieutenant **Stanislava Volkova** was one of the Red Army's sappers, who had the dangerous and often fatal job of clearing minefields. Once, when a Soviet general bellowed for the sapper commander to clear a field, he brushed aside a grime-streaked and dishevelled woman only to learn she was the platoon commander. The mines were soon cleared so the tanks could advance.

In the Red Army, 41% of the doctors and 43% of the front-line medical personnel were women, and often as not they carried weapons as well as medical supplies. Engaged in an unequal battle with German troops, Dr. **Polina** and her assistants managed to carry 27 of the most gravely wounded into the woods. Cut off from Soviet troops, they built snow huts to shelter the wounded. Moss became cotton and razors were used as scalpels until they were rescued a month later.

Women also fueled the war machine in factories behind the front, serving as welders, machine operators, and painters. There was, for example, a "special women's brigade" which worked on moving flat-cars, painting artillery pieces as they sped to the front. Women even toiled as miners in the depths of the earth, working some mines entirely without men, while the war-torn country also depended to a great extent on women for its food supply. Because tractors had been turned into gun tows and fuel was an expensive luxury, the women harnessed themselves to plows in groups of half a dozen to prepare the soil for planting and did other work by hand. Special "tractor brigades" learned to operate the few machines and to keep them in working order.

Such determination was often fueled by horrifying experiences. **Pasha Prskovia Yermolenko** was sent to a work camp in Germany, from which she managed to escape. She returned to the Ukraine where she was met with further ravages of war. The German army in retreat from Kiev torched the thatched roofs of the village where she was hiding, setting 900 houses on fire, and hanged Yermolenko's best friend and killed her baby. Yermolenko's response to these atrocities was to plant potatoes. Soon, her *kolkhoz* (cooperative farm) was producing more than 14 tons of potatoes per acre. Women like Yermolenko fed Russia, not grandly or satisfyingly, but their efforts were critical to the winning of the war.

Partisans were another important group in the war effort. At least 100,000 women did that dangerous work, living in trenches and woods by day and sabotaging German war efforts by night. In actions that were highly effective at frustrating the enemy, they blew up bridges, destroyed roads, cut communication lines, derailed trains, and attacked garrisons using any means at their disposal. The partisans were the glue which held the resistance effort in the occupied country together. They published leaflets and newspapers reporting the latest war news and called on the people to unite in the war effort.

You won't hang us all. I will be avenged.

—Zoya Kosmodemyanskaya

Zoya Kosmodemyanskaya exemplified the spirit of all the partisans who fought for Mother Russia. She was born in the village of Osinovye Gai, in Tambov Oblast, southeast of Moscow, on September 13, 1923. Her father was an office worker. In 1938, when she was 15, Kosmodemyanskaya, like many students, joined the Komosomol (Communist Youth Organization). When the war broke out, she was living with her widowed mother and younger brother in Aleksandrovskii Prospect, near the gardens of the Timiryazev Agricultural Academy, in Moscow. Zoya was in the tenth form of School No. 201, where she was a model student. An idealist, she copied whole pages from *War and Peace* into her diary along with quotes from Chekhov and Chernyshevskii.

With the Soviet Union at war, Zoya and her brother joined the Labor Front, working in a factory as wood-turners, but her heart was not in this work. As the Germans drew ever nearer to Moscow, she decided to join in active service, applying in October for duty in a sabotage unit behind enemy lines. "Don't worry," she told her mother. "I'll either come back a hero or die a hero."

Kosmodemyanskaya chose Tanya as a new name and set off with a group of other young volunteers to the forested area between Mozhaisk and Moscow, deep behind German lines. At the time she joined her unit, partisan efforts were not well organized, and many lost their lives in these early days of the war. As time passed, however, the underground warfare became more refined and played an important role in ridding the country of the invaders.

According to Nazi ideology, Slavs were *Untermenschen,* inferior people, to be used in any way seen fit. During the German occupation, hundreds of thousands of men and women were enslaved and sent from the Soviet Union to Germany to be worked to death in factories. Those who were not enslaved were often executed outright; in one case, 60 wives of Red Army soldiers were hanged from telephone poles in Alexandria, in Kirovgrad District, and their corpses left as a warning. The wife of Senior Lieutenant Gabriel Kolesnikov was tortured before being hanged. Her six-month-old baby was impaled by a bayonet, and her two other children were also murdered while villagers were forced to watch.

As a woman, Zoya Kosmodemyanskaya faced particular horrors, as do all women in every war. If every victim of rape in wartime were awarded a Purple Heart, women would no doubt be the most highly decorated combatants on earth. Sexual slavery was also a common practice among the German invaders, who routinely gathered up the best-looking young girls to serve in brothels. One famous story was told of two lovely girls, Zina and Vera, who lived in a German-occupied village in the North Caucasus, where they were taken to the house quartering 12 Nazi officers. Knowing their fate, Zina maneuvered herself near a tank full of benzine while pretending to accept an officer's advances. After telling Vera to lock the door and throw the key into the stove, she asked for a cigarette and tossed it into the benzine tank. Only two German officers escaped the conflagration; they told the story later as military prisoners. Zina and Vera, whose last names do not survive, symbolized the fate of many women in the Soviet Union during the war, but also the courage that made them fight.

Stories such as these inspired Zoya Kosmodemyanskaya, who actually served her country only a few weeks. Her partisan group had been quite busy around the German-occupied village of Petrishchevo, where the invaders had thrown the villagers out of their huts, taken their food, and shipped many off to labor camps. In retaliation, the partisans had smoked the Germans out of the huts into the cold, attacked small groups of soldiers as well the unit headquarters, wrecked roads, and disrupted communications while acting as scouts for the Red Army. One night, Zoya Kosmodemyanskaya cut all the lines for the German field telephone, set fire to German headquarters, and burned a stable holding 17 German horses; the following evening, her target was a stable with more than 200 cavalry horses. Wearing a hat, fur jacket, quilted cotton pants, and felt boots, she crept forward with a bottle of gasoline and bent to strike a match, but was apprehended before the bomb could be thrown.

The Nazi soldiers began to beat her with belts; at one time four were beating her simultaneously. Kosmodemyanskaya was forced to remove her clothing and stand barefoot in the snow, but she gave no information. Brought inside a hut, she was punched by soldiers who held lit matches to her chin. One ran a saw across her back. The owners of the hut begged the Germans to stop for their children's sake. Still she refused to give any name but Tanya, named no friends or associates, and told nothing of movements of the Red Army. The torture continued through the night.

On the morning of November 29, 1941, a scaffold was erected in the town square. "Tanya" was allowed to put on her blouse, slacks, and socks, but her hat, fur coat, down-and-wool undershirt, and felt boots had disappeared. The soldiers hung bottles of gasoline on her chest and a sign around her neck that labeled her a partisan. Local inhabitants were ordered to attend the execution, but few showed up. More than a hundred German soldiers and several officers were present, and one officer began to focus his Kodak on the scaffold; the German military frequently photographed executions. Zoya Kosmodemyanskaya was picked up and placed on two orange crates, a noose around her neck, and while the executioners awaited the signal from the commandant, she took advantage of the moment to speak. "Hey, comrades! Why so glum? Be brave, struggle, beat the Germans, burn, poison! I'm not afraid to die, comrades. I'm happy to die for my people." Turning to the commandant she said, "You hang me now, but I am not alone. There are two hundred million of us. You won't hang us all. I will be avenged. Soldiers! Surrender before it is too late. Victory will be ours." The Russians wept. Some turned their backs so as not to see her death. The executioner tightened the rope, choking her, but she loosened it saying, "Farewell, comrades! Struggle, don't be afraid!" The executioner pushed his iron-tipped boot against the crate, someone cried out, and she died.

For a month, the body was left on the gallows as a warning. Finally the village elder called together some men to remove it, at the risk of losing their own lives, and a grave was hacked out of the frozen earth under a willow tree. Zoya's compatriots were never very far away. One cold winter night, the Red Army struck swiftly and savagely against the Germans. In retaliation, the Germans rushed to the neighboring village of Gritsovo and set fire to it. The following day, a German unit was sent back to torch Petrishchevo, but the soldiers, fearful of being separated from the main unit and left at the mercy of the partisans, fled after breaking a few windows.

While the Germans never knew her identity, the name of Zoya Kosmodemyanskaya was soon on every Soviet's lips. On February 16, 1942, hardly more than a year after her death, she was proclaimed a Hero of the Soviet Union, and her spirit came to symbolize the struggle against the Germans. Starving in Leningrad, fighting in Stalingrad, or manufacturing guns, Soviet citizens remembered her fearless courage. Wrote Isidor Schneider:

> They lashed her, beat her,
> Seared her skin.
> No word, no sound.
> They whined their frenzy;
> She was still. . . .
> In the unshuddering eye
> The Unbroken will!
>
> They hung on her breast
> The gasoline flasks
> And the sign, "GUERRILLA."
> They knotted the noose. . . .
>
> Then to the villagers
> Whipped to the gallows
> To see her die,
> She cried:
> "Keep courage, hold hope."
> To the hangmen:
> "You cannot hang a nation!"
> Thus she died. . . .

Ultimately, the German army was to prove no match for the determination of the Soviet people, and the fury of Soviet women. **Alexandra Zakharova**, a partisan from Byelo-Russia, summed up their efforts when she said, "We became a storm and the Germans were terrified [of] us." Zoya Kosmodemyanskaya has been reburied in the Novodevich'e Monastery in Moscow; a monument to her has been erected along the Minsk highway near the village of Petrishchevo, and many streets still bear her name.

SOURCES:

Drozdov, Georgii, and Evgenii Ryabko. *Russia at War 1941–45.* Edited by Carey Schofield. Vendome Press, 1987.

"Heroes—Kosmodemyanskaya," in *Time.* Vol. 39, no. 9. March 2, 1942, p. 23.

Keltinskaya, Vera. "Heroines," in *Soviet Russia Today.* March 1944, p. 21.

Lidov, Pyotr. "Tanya," in *World War II: Dispatches from the Soviet Front.* Edited by S. Krasilschchik. NY: Sphinx Press, 1985.

Mosely, Philip E. *Soviet Partisans in World War II.* Madison, WI: University of Wisconsin Press, 1964.

Myles, Bruce. *Night Witches.* Novoto, CA: Presidio Press, 1981.

Porter, Cathy, and Mark Jones. *Moscow in World War II.* London: Chatto and Windus, 1987.

Schneider, Isidor. "To Zoya, Martyered Heroine," in *Soviet Russia Today.* May 1942.

Smith, Jessica. "Soviet Women in the War," in *Soviet Russia Today.* April 1943, pp. 14–15, 33.

Winter, Ella. "Congress of Heroines," in *Soviet Russia Today.* October 1944, p. 9, 32.

John Haag,
Associate Professor, University of Georgia, Athens, Georgia

Kossak, Zofia (1890–1968)

Polish Roman Catholic writer of historical novels, which were popular both in Poland and the English-speaking world, who created the underground organization Zegota to save Jewish lives in German-occupied Poland during the Holocaust and survived imprisonment in Auschwitz. Name variations: Zofia Kossak-Szczucka; Zofia Kossak-Szatkowska; Zofia Kossak-Szczucka-Szatkowska; Zofdja de Szatkowska. Born in Kosmin, Volhynia, Polish Ukraine (then part of Russia), on August 8, 1890; died in Górki Wielkie on April 9, 1968; daughter of Tadeusz Kossak; married Stefan Szczucki; married Zygmunt Szatkowski; children: two sons.

Zofia Kossak was born in 1890 on a landed estate in Volhynia on the eastern border of the Polish Ukraine (then part of tsarist Russia). Hers was a talented, cultured, and socially prominent family. Zofia's father was an officer in the Austrian Army who in later years became a major in the cavalry corps of independent Poland, but many of her other relatives were acclaimed artists and intellectuals. These included her paternal grandfather Juliusz Kossak, one of Poland's greatest painters, as well as his brother Wojciech Kossak, also a distinguished painter. Zofia's cousin *Maria Pawlikowska was a prolific poet, while **Magdalena Samozwaniec** (Wojciech Kossak's daughter) also gained considerable fame as a writer.

With such talents apparently in her blood, Zofia at first chose to study art in Warsaw and Geneva and to prepare for a professional career as an artist. By 1913, however, she appeared to have chosen literature over art when she made her literary debut with the story "Bulli zaginal" (Bulli Disappeared), which was published in the journal *Wies Polska* (Polish Village). After her marriage to Stefan Szczucki, Kossak and her husband moved to Wolyn, Volhynia, where they were living when a bloody sequence of revolutionary upheavals and civil wars began in Russia in 1917.

In her first novel, *Pozoga (The Conflagration,* 1922, English translation, 1927), Kossak depicted the terrors and suffering that became part of her daily life during the violent years of 1917 through 1919. Although a narrative of events in Volhynia, the book also revealed her strongly pro-Polish and conservative beliefs; the work is permeated by an idealized view of life on the vast semi-feudal estates that dominated the lives of Volhynia's impoverished peasantry until the revolution. With her writing career successfully underway, she published a number of historical novels over the next years, including *Beatum scelus* (1924, subsequent editions entitled *Blessed Guilt*), which was set in Renaissance Poland; *Golden Freedom* (1928), a story of pre-partition Poland; *The Great and the Small* (1928), tales on Silesian themes; and *God's Madmen* (1929), a collection of biographies of saints.

In 1925, Kossak married a second time to Zygmunt Szatkowski. She moved to Górki

Zofia
Kossak

Wielkie in Beskid Slaski, Polish Silesia, and her literary productivity continued unabated. Successful historical novels followed, including *The Battlefield of Legnica* (1930), about the conflict between the Christian West and the Mongols, as well as *The Unknown Country* (1932) and *From the History of Silesia* (1933), both of which dealt with the struggles of Poles to retain their national identity. She also wrote several other books in the 1930s. The most important work Kossak produced during that decade was her monumental epic *The Crusaders*. Published in four volumes in Poznan in 1935, *The Crusaders* is in the tradition of the great historical novels of the 19th century. Filled with action, drama, battles, and adventure, the story starts in 1095 at the commencement of the First Crusade. Polish Silesian knights, called *Strzegonie,* set off on a pilgrimage to Provence, then join the Crusade. In the Holy Land, in addition to bloody battles and sieges, the knights experience famine, disease and the merciless forces of nature in the desert. The volumes conclude with an epilogue that takes the reader back to Silesia with the surviving knights' return home. The complex plot mixes a realistic depiction of events with fantasy and legend. Kossak's strongly traditional Catholic faith presents miraculous events as reality and vice versa. The vivid imagery and panoramic quality of this and her other historical novels suggests that Kossak's training in the visual arts sharpened her literary eye for spotting and recreating richness of detail and color.

Although not all critics praised her books— some saw her characters as being two-dimensional and her plots too sensationalistic—the Polish reading public loved Kossak's works, which they bought and read despite the poor economic conditions of the 1930s. Perhaps somewhat grudgingly, the literary establishment recognized her achievements in 1936 when she was crowned with the "golden laurel" of the Polish Academy of Literature.

The 1930s were good years for Kossak, but normalcy in her nation was soon to end. On September 1, 1939, Nazi Germany attacked Poland, defeating and subjugating a militarily unprepared nation within a month's time. Nazi rule in Poland was brutal and inhumane from the start. The Polish state was liquidated; deprived even of its name, it was simply called the *Generalgouvernement* as an occupied territory to be exploited by the German master race (*Herrenvolk*). Poland's cultural and moral leadership strata, the intelligentsia and clergy, were targeted almost immediately for humiliation and liquidation. Universities were shut down and intellectual life went underground, a long-established Polish tradition remembered from the oppressive decades of the 19th century. From the first days of the German occupation, Zofia Kossak was active in the underground, writing, teaching, and acting as a liaison.

By the end of 1940, it was clear that Poland's Jews were being targeted for particularly brutal treatment. Ghettos were created in the large cities in the first months of German rule, with the Warsaw Ghetto, by far the largest, established in October–November 1940. Conditions in all of the Polish ghettos were inhumane, resulting in hundreds of deaths a day from starvation, disease and lack of medical care. By early 1942, Nazi Germany had decided to effect its "Final Solution of the Jewish Question"—total annihilation of the Jewish people under their rule. Jews were to be killed on an industrial basis in a number of death camps established on occupied Polish territory. For Poland, this would result in the murder of about 90% of its prewar Jewish population—three million men, women, and children. Although the Third Reich envisaged "only" a future of enslavement and exploitation for Poland's Roman Catholics, who as Slavs were deemed to be *Untermenschen* (subhumans), as many as three million lost their lives during the more than five years of the brutal German occupation.

In Poland's history, powerful attitudes of anti-Semitism run through all aspects of public and private life. By the late 19th century, many Polish intellectuals had concluded that Jews could never be Poles and were in fact an inassimilable threat to the nation's moral and cultural integrity. Both conservative Roman Catholics and Right-wing nationalists like the National Democrats (Endeks) were convinced that "the Jews" were a hostile foreign body, a malignant tumor that was eating away at and destroying not only the national economy but the very essence of the Polish spirit (*Polskosc*). As a conservative Roman Catholic, Kossak shared many of these prejudices, which were common currency in the intellectual circles in which she moved.

From the earliest days of the German occupation, Zofia Kossak was the much-respected head of the Roman Catholic underground organization Front Odrozenia Polski (Polish Resistance Front), whose most important work was in organizing social and educational activities. With the onset of the Nazi assault on Poland's Jewish population, however, Kossak expanded her responsibilities to render assistance to this gravely endangered segment of the nation. In the summer

of 1942, she wrote an illegal pamphlet, entitled *Protest!* ("The Protest"), which received wide circulation in underground circles. Although its stated aim was to protest the bloody crimes of the Nazis against Poland's Jews, it is an unusual and in some ways disturbing mixture of outrage against the German atrocities, indignation against the indifference of the world in light of these crimes against humanity, and a reiteration of traditional anti-Jewish sentiments found so commonly in prewar Poland. Kossak condemns:

> [a] world [that] looks upon this murder, more horrible than anything that history has ever seen, and stays silent. . . . The perishing Jews are surrounded by Pilates who deny all guilt. This silence can no longer be tolerated. Whatever the reason for it, it is vile. In the face of murder it is wrong to remain passive. Whoever is silent witnessing murder becomes a partner to the murder. Whoever does not condemn, consents. Therefore we—Catholics, Poles—raise our voices.

Yet as the author continues she also notes emphatically:

> Our feeling toward the Jews has not changed. We continue to deem them political, economic, and ideological enemies of Poland. Moreover, we realize that they hate us more than they hate the Germans, and they make us responsible for their misfortune. Why, and on what basis, remains a mystery of the Jewish soul. Nevertheless, this is a decided fact. Awareness of this fact, however, does not release us from the duty of the damnation of murder.

Kossak, who had stated in *Protest!* that "we cannot help, nor can we rescue anybody," changed her mind dramatically between the summer and late September of 1942. Now believing that something could and must be done to save at least some of her country's Jews, on September 27, 1942, she officially founded the Tymczasowy Komitet Pomocy Zydom (Temporary Committee for Aid to the Jews). On December 4 of that year, after the Temporary Committee had provided evidence of its viability by bringing 180 threatened Jews under its care, Kossak expanded its responsibilities and made the organization a permanent part of the Polish underground landscape. Renamed Rada Pomocy Zydom (Council for Aid to Jews), the organization was generally known as Zegota.

Kossak's efforts to render assistance to Jews through the Zegota organization were supported both by a broad political spectrum of the underground movement and by the Delegatura, the representative of the Polish government-in-exile in Poland, which gave its official approval to Zegota's bold humanitarian agenda. Although Kossak's allegiance was Roman Catholic and conservative nationalist, the most active role in Zegota was assumed by the Socialists, who were split into a Right- and Left-wing party. Except for the extreme Right, which remained bitterly anti-Semitic even as the Holocaust progressed, and the excluded Communists, virtually all of Poland's prewar political groups, including several Jewish ones, were represented in Zegota's leadership. Those included the Bund, an important Jewish labor movement, the Jewish National Committee, the Peasant Party, and the Democratic Party. On the Zegota board sat representatives of five Polish and two Jewish political movements. Headquartered in Warsaw, the organization also had centers in Cracow, Lublin, and Lvov.

Zegota did not establish a regional clandestine network of its own, relying instead on the existing organizations of its member movements or of other groups with which it was in contact, including the headquarters group of the Armia Krajowa (Polish Home Army) and the Zwiazek Syndikalistów Polskich (League of Polish Syndicalists). Realizing that its work would be greatly enhanced with the help of more members of the Polish population, Zegota urged the Polish government-in-exile and the Delegatura to issue appeals for assistance and to impose severe sanctions on those Poles (*szmalcownicy* or extortionists) who made a living either by blackmailing or by turning Jews over to the Germans in return for money. Zegota published three leaflets on the fate Poland's Jews were facing and lodged protests against the anti-Semitic attitudes and actions of certain extremist factions in the Polish underground.

Always concerned about financing the work of Zegota, Kossak made impressive efforts in this area. The council received allocations in 1943 from the Delegatura that ranged from 150,000 to 750,000 zlotys a month ($4,000 to $8,000), and in 1944 from 1 million to 2 million zlotys a month ($7,000 to $8,000), for a total of 28.75 million zlotys ($215,000) during the entire period. Between July 1943 and June 1944, Zegota also received subsidies from two important Jewish organizations, the Bund and the Jewish National Committee, totaling 3.2 million zlotys. This money was repaid by the end of 1944, with Kossak approving a Zegota contribution in addition to the original amount that had been borrowed. From the start of its work, Zegota's finances were strictly supervised, so that as early as the autumn of 1943 the organization was able to repay a substantial sum—the equivalent of $23,000—to the International Organization of Polish Jews.

Zegota's aim of saving Jewish lives called for several strategies. One was to provide financial assistance to individuals who had been either confined in or had escaped from ghettos. In an environment that was often intensely anti-Semitic, and in which Polish informers made a living by turning over Jews to the Germans for money, Jews had to remain in hiding. Food had to be procured on the black market, and sometimes medications purchased, all of which was expensive. In January 1943, soon after its founding, Zegota provided financial assistance to 300 persons, a number that increased to 2,000 by the end of the year. By the summer of 1944, 4,000 Jews were able to live in hiding as a result of the organization's monetary support. Although the amount provided by the financially hard-pressed Zegota was pitifully small (400 to 700 zlotys monthly, about $15 on the black-market exchange rate), this modest sum was enough to provide a subsistence existence in hiding, and with it came a chance of survival in the Holocaust. Many Jews in hiding who came down with illness owed their lives to the clandestine Komitet Lekarzy Demokratów i Socjalistów (Democratic and Socialist Doctors' Committee), which created a remarkably efficient network to help Jews in hiding receive medical attention from specialists at short notice.

In addition to financial assistance, Zegota provided forged "Aryan" documents for the Jews under its care as well as for personnel of the Bund and the Jewish National Committee. The facilities of the Polish Home Army initially provided these life-saving documents, but as Zegota gained in experience as a clandestine organization it was able to create high-quality forgeries of its own, providing false baptismal and marriage certificates as well as identity and employment cards that turned Jews into non-Jews.

A special division of Zegota was devoted to saving the lives of Jewish children. Some of them were placed in the care of foster families, while others found safety in public orphanages or similar institutions maintained by Catholic convents. In Warsaw alone, Zegota found safe refuge for 2,500 children. All of the activities undertaken by Zegota members on behalf of Jews represented an extreme danger to those non-Jews caught in the act of assisting Jews. Under the German occupation regime, concealing Jews was an act punishable by death, not only for one individual but for all of the individuals, including children, living in a house or apartment where Jews had found refuge.

Zofia Kossak and her colleagues created in Zegota one of the very few organizations in

Nazi-occupied Europe that was run jointly by Jews and non-Jews from a broad spectrum of political ideals and ideological values. Despite the great risks to which its members were exposed, the organization survived as a functioning organism to the end of the Nazi occupation. The exact number of Jewish lives saved by the work of Zegota will never be known—it is probably less than 10,000—but one author has estimated that between 40,000 and 50,000 Polish Jews were positively affected by the various Zegota activities during the Holocaust.

In September 1943, Kossak was arrested by the Germans; her forged papers were excellent, however, and her real name was never discovered. Nevertheless, she was sent to Auschwitz, where she witnessed countless horrors which she would later describe in her 1946 memoir *Z otchlani: Wspomnienaia z lagru* (*From the Abyss: Memoirs from the Camp*). Released from Auschwitz by the Germans before their defeat, she left Poland in 1945, settling with her husband in the United Kingdom. Despite her detestation of Communism, Kossak remained profoundly Polish in spirit, and, often homesick, she yearned to return to her native country. The intellectual liberalization that began in 1956 was sufficient to lure her back, and she returned in 1957. Although critics had never been unanimous in appraising her work, and often criticized the less than academic knowledge of history and theology reflected in her novels, her books long remained popular with the Polish reading public because of their rich panoramic detail and her essentially Romantic view of human nature. During her last years, Kossak wrote a number of short stories for young people as well as several more historical novels, including a massive epic in three volumes, *Dziedzictwo* (*Heredity*, 1961–1967). Much beloved by the people of her country, she died in Górki Wielkie on April 9, 1968.

SOURCES:

Bartoszewski, Wladyslaw. *The Blood Shed Unites Us.* Warsaw: Interpress, 1970.

———, and Zofia Lewin. *The Samaritans: Heroes of the Holocaust.* Edited by Alexander T. Jordan. NY: Twayne, 1970.

Bejski, Moshe. "The Righteous Among the Nations and Their Part in the Rescue of Jews," in Yisrael Gutman and Livia Rothkirchen, eds., *The Catastrophe of European Jewry.* Jerusalem: Yad Vashem, 1976, pp. 582–607.

Berenstein, Tatiana, and Adam Rutkowski. *Assistance to the Jews in Poland, 1930–1945.* Warsaw: Polonia Foreign Languages Publishing, 1963.

Carroll, James. "The Silence," in *The New Yorker.* Vol. 73, no. 7. April 7, 1997, pp. 52–69.

Dmitrów, Edmund. "Die Polen über die Deutschen: Meinungen und Auseinandersetzungen aus den Jahren 1945–1948," in *Acta Poloniae Historica.* Vol. 70, 1994, pp. 127–150.

Dwork, Debórah. "*Lamed-Vovniks* of Twentieth-Century Europe: Participants in Jewish Child Rescue," in Michael Geyer and John W. Boyer, eds., *Resistance Against the Third Reich 1933–1990.* Chicago, IL: University of Chicago Press, 1994, pp. 89–118.

Friedman, Philip. *Their Brothers' Keepers: The Christian Heroes and Heroines Who Helped the Oppressed Escape the Nazi Terror.* NY: Holocaust Library, 1978.

Gillon, Adam, and Ludwik Krzyzanowski, eds. *Modern Polish Literature: An Anthology of Fiction and Poetry.* 2nd ed. NY: Hippocrene Books, 1982.

Gutman, Yisrael, and Efraim Zuroff, eds. *Rescue Attempts During the Holocaust: Proceedings of the Second Yad Vashem International Historical Conference.* Jerusalem: Yad Vashem, 1977.

Iranek-Osmecki, Kazimierz. *He Who Saves One Life.* NY: Crown, 1971.

Kossak-Szczucka, Zofia. "Komu Pomagamy?" (Whom do we help?), in *Prawda: Pismo Frontu Odrozenia.* August–September, 1943, p. 8.

Leuner, H.D. *When Compassion was a Crime: Germany's Silent Heroes, 1933–1945.* London: Oswald Wolf, 1978.

Prekerowa, Teresa. "The 'Just' and the 'Passive,'" in *Yad Vashem Studies.* Vol. 19, 1988, pp. 369–377.

———. "Rada Pomocy Zydom a Warszawskie Getto," in *Biuletyn Zydowskiego Instytutu Historicznego w Polsce.* No. 86–87, 1973, pp. 173–177.

———. *Zegota: Commission d'aide aux juifs.* Translated and edited by Maria Apfelbaum. Monaco: Rocher, 1999.

Sendlerowa, Irena. "CI KT: Zy Pomagali Zydom (Wspomnienia z czas okupacji Hitlerowskiej)," in *Biuletyn Zydowskiego Instytutu Historycznego.* No. 45–46, 1963, pp. 234–247.

Tec, Nechama. *When Light Pierced the Darkness: Christian Rescue of Jews in Nazi-Occupied Poland.* NY: Oxford University Press, 1986.

Tomaszewski, Irene, and Tecia Werbowski. *Zegota: The Council for Aid to Jews in Occupied Poland, 1942–45.* Rev. ed. Montreal: Price-Patterson, 1999.

Weiskopf, F.C. "St. Francis of Assisi," in *Saturday Review of Literature.* Vol. 27, no. 13. March 25, 1944, p. 11.

Zamojski, Jan E. "Konrad Zegota: Mityczny Patron Szlachetnej Sprawy," in *Kwartalnik Historyczny.* Vol. 90, no. 2, 1983, pp. 393–401.

RELATED MEDIA:

Rotter, Sy, and Andrzej J. Sikora. *Zegota: A Time to Remember* (video), Waltham, MA: National Center for Jewish Film, 1991.

John Haag,
Associate Professor of History,
University of Georgia, Athens, Georgia

Kossamak (r. 1955–1960)

Queen of Cambodia who reigned with her husband Prince Norodom Suramarit. Born Kossamak Nearirath also seen as Nearyreath, Nearrireak, or Nearirat;

daughter of Sisowath, king of Cambodia; sister of Monivong, king of Cambodia (died April 23, 1941); married Prince Norodom Suramarit, later king of Cambodia (died 1960); children: one son, Prince Norodom Sihanouk (b. 1922), prime minister and king of Cambodia.

Born into royalty, Kossamak Nearirath was the daughter of King Sisowath, who ruled Cambodia from 1904 to 1927, and the sister of King Monivong, who succeeded his father in 1927 and ruled until 1941. She married Prince Norodom Suramarit, and they had a son Prince Norodom Sihanouk, born in 1922. When her brother King Monivong died in 1941, Kossamak's son Sihanouk was appointed to the throne by Jean Decoux, then the French governor-general of Indochina. Sihanouk ruled until 1952, when, in an act designed to dramatize Cambodian demands for independence from France, he dissolved the government and fled into voluntary exile. After Cambodian independence was declared in 1954, Sihanouk was restored as king but abdicated in favor of his father, Prince Suramarit, serving instead as prime minister. Queen Kossamak ruled jointly with her husband from 1955 until his death in 1960, both having survived a bomb attack in an enclosure in the Royal Palace blamed on the Khmer Serei. In 1960, her son Sihanouk reclaimed his position as king. Ten years later, he was overthrown with the rise of the Khmer Rouge. Cambodia entered its darkest period, and Kossamak fled to Beijing (Peking) with the royal family on November 5, 1973.

Kostadinova, Stefka (b. 1965).

See Balas, Iolande for sidebar.

Köstler, Marie (1879–1965)

Austrian Social Democrat whose 40 years in public life included a turbulent period of exile politics in London during World War II. Name variations: Marie Kostler; Marie Koestler. Born in 1879; died in 1965.

In the 1920s, Marie Köstler was one of the first women to be elected to the Austrian National Assembly. A nurse by profession, she was a committed Social Democrat, convinced that workers deserved to enjoy the fruits of their labors. As did her party, she believed in constitutional democracy and rejected both the Leninist ideal of the dictatorship of the proletariat and the Nazi concept of a racist Führer state. When Nazi Germany ab-

sorbed independent Austria in the *Anschluss* of March 1938, Köstler fled to London.

Although no longer young, Köstler became one of the most active and energetic members of the politically active Austrian emigres in the United Kingdom. While remaining an ardent Social Democrat, she argued that in order to win the war against fascism a broad coalition had to be forged on the Left. She was not uncritical of the Communists within the Austrian exile community, but was convinced nevertheless that their cooperation within a united-front coalition was imperative if the full energy of anti-Nazi Austrians was to be harnessed to the war effort. These ideas were not popular with the strongly anti-Communist Social Democratic leadership. Neither was Köstler's conviction that with the defeat of Nazism, Austria should resume its status as an independent republic. The Social Democratic leadership rejected the concept of Austrian sovereignty, continuing to subscribe to an older Pan-German ideal of a united German-speaking state in the heart of Central Europe. Ironically, this had in fact been achieved in 1938 not by the Social Democrats but by Adolf Hitler's Third Reich.

Marie Köstler, **Annie Hatschek** and a number of other Social Democratic activists in London regarded a working coalition with the Austrian Communist exiles in wartime as both possible and necessary. Köstler attended Communist meetings and rallies, and as a result she was excluded from the Socialist Democratic Party in the fall of 1941. At that point, Köstler and Hatschek became the co-founders of a new organization, the League of Austrian Socialists in Great Britain. This association quickly found support from a significant number of dissatisfied Social Democratic Austrian emigres, including **Alice Graber, Greta Hauser, Grete Lichtenstein, Grete Mrak, Hedda Rattner, Elise Schwarzthal, Annie Steiner,** and **Paula Stieber.**

By the end of 1941, the League of Austrian Socialists in Great Britain was absorbed by a much larger organization, the Free Austrian Movement (FAM). Dominated by Austrian Communists, during the war years the FAM nonetheless emphasized a united-front policy, supporting the British war effort and raising funds for Soviet war relief. Köstler returned to Austria in 1945, hoping to resume an active political life within the Social Democratic Party. The conservative leadership there, however, regarded her wartime activities in a negative light and perceived her to be a dangerous fellow traveler. Denied readmittance to the party, she thereupon joined the small but well-organized Austrian Communist Party (KPÖ). Despite the vicissitudes of the Cold War, Köstler remained loyal to her new political home and was much admired in KPÖ party circles as the Grand Old Lady of Austrian Communism until the time of her death in 1965.

SOURCES:

Biographical files of Marie Köstler and Annie Hatschek, Arbeitsgemeinschaft "Biografisches Lexikon der österreichischen Frau," Institut für Wissenschaft und Kunst, Vienna.

Dokumentationsarchiv des österreichischen Widerstandes, Vienna, file folders 860, 3269, and 2604/1.

Maimann, Helene. *Politik im Wartesaal: Österreichische Exilpolitik in Grossbrittanien 1938–1945.* Vienna, Cologne and Graz: Böhlau Verlag, 1975.

John Haag,
Associate Professor of History,
University of Georgia, Athens, Georgia

Köstlin, Josephine Lang (1815–1880).

See Lang, Josephine.

Kostrzewa, Wera (1876–1939).

See Koszutska, Maria.

Koszutska, Maria (1876–1939)

Polish Socialist and Communist leader who was the most politically prominent non-Soviet woman killed during the Soviet purges of the 1930s. Name variations: (party names) Wera Kostrzewa; Vera Kostrzewa; Vera Kocheva; Vera Kostisheva; M. Zboinska; M.Z. Born Maria Koszutska in Glowczyn near Kalisz, Russian Poland, on February 2, 1876; secretly arrested in 1937 and killed in 1939; daughter of a landowner.

A professional revolutionary for virtually her entire adult life, Maria Koszutska was one of the founders and leaders of the Communist Party of Poland. Joseph Stalin attacked her views in 1924, and she bravely defended them as a delegate to a Congress of the Communist International. Like most of the Polish Communist leaders residing in the Soviet Union in the 1930s, she was secretly arrested (1937) and killed (1939).

Maria Koszutska, who would be known throughout most of her adult life as Vera or Wera Kostrzewa, was born on her parents' estate at Glowczyn near Kalisz, Russian Poland, on February 2, 1876. Like many members of the gentry (*szlachta*) class, she was raised in a tradition that fused literature and Romantic revolutionary fervor. She was trained as a teacher and drawn to the Socialist revolutionary movement early in life, as were many others of her generation. Already active in these circles by the dawn

of the 20th century, Maria joined the Polish Socialist Party (PPS) in 1902, carrying out her party assignments mostly in the industrial city of Lodz. After being imprisoned by the Russian authorities in 1903 and exiled in 1904, she resumed her revolutionary activities in Warsaw during 1905, when that city was at the epicenter of nationalist upheavals. Arrested again after the collapse of the revolutionary movement in 1906, she lived in Cracow, St. Petersburg, and Vienna following her release, using her party names— Wera Kostrzewa, Vera Kocheva, M. Zboinska, and M.Z.—to evade detection by agents of the tsarist secret police, particularly when she entered Polish territory to carry out party work.

Koszutska was interested in the fine points of ideology and played a major role in the events that led to the split within the PPS that resulted in the creation in 1906 of a new party, the PPS-Left. The nascent organization was grounded in a more orthodox and internationalist Marxist philosophy of action. The "official" PPS became increasingly nationalistic in both its theory and practice, and its leader Jozef Pilsudski—who ruled Poland as a dictator from 1926 until his death in 1935—in later years told one of his former comrades: "My friend, you and I caught the socialist train together. I got off at 'Polish Independence' station. I wish you good luck on your journey to . . . Utopia."

Koszutska was one of the leaders of the PPS-Left from its birth, serving on its central committee and playing a large part in the formulation of the organization's strategy and tactics. She was instrumental in drafting the official platform of the PPS-Left at its 10th Congress, held in 1908. Convinced that the Polish working class needed to be systematically educated in a broad framework of Marxist internationalism, she was active in various mass educational projects including the "University for All," the Society for Polish Culture, and the Prisoners' Aid Association. In 1915, these educational efforts for workers were formally organized in the Swiatolo (The Light) organization. In 1916, Koszutska helped to found the Rechniewski Workers' Club.

A tireless agitator and publicist, she served on many editorial boards and wrote innumerable polemical articles in both legal and underground journals and newspapers. From 1908 through 1914, she was associate editor of *Robotnik* (The Worker), the PPS-Left official organ. At the same time, she contributed to or was editorially involved with most of the illegal publications of the Polish revolutionary Marxist movement, including *Na barykady* (On the Barricades), *Mysla Socjalistyczna* (Socialist Thought), *Wiedza* (Knowledge), *Nowym Zyciem* (New Life), *Swiatlem* (The Light), *Glos Robotniczy* (Workers' Voice), and *Kuznia* (The Forge). Koszutska was a fervent believer in the historical validity of an internationalist perspective for the triumph of both the Polish and European working class, and she was a relentless critic of nationalism in the proletarian movement. Recognizing the destructive power of anti-Semitism, she attacked this Polish prejudice in a number of sharply written articles, including "Pseudo-Knowledge in the Service of Anti-Semitism" (*Kuznia*, No. 8, 1914).

The chaos and suffering of World War I, which impacted the lives of millions of Poles, only strengthened Koszutska's revolutionary spirit. During the war years, she was the de facto head of the entire PPS-Left organization in German-occupied Polish territory. Continuing to oppose the nationalistic line taken by the PPS, she was strongly against what she regarded as Jozef Pilsudski's Polish chauvinism, favoring instead a future Socialist society in which national independence and respect for ethnic diversity were basic postulates. Her viewpoints in many ways paralleled those of the leadership of the Social Democracy of the Kingdom of Poland and Lithuania (SDKPiL), founded by *Rosa Luxemburg and led by, among others, Adolf Warski (also known as Adolf Warski-Warszawski). In 1917, Koszutska hailed the Bolshevik Revolution in Russia, and in August 1918, in a series of articles published in *Glos Robotniczy,* she defended Lenin's proletarian dictatorship against its critics in Polish Socialist circles.

In November 1918, Poland regained its national independence after more than a century of foreign occupation. That December, Poland's Socialist left-wing parties, the PPS-Left and the SD-KPiL, joined to form a united Marxist revolutionary party, the Communist Party of Poland (KPP). Koszutska was elected both to the KPP secretariat and to its Central Committee. Realizing that the majority of Poland's working class supported the PPS rather than the freshly minted KPP, in the first months of the new party's existence she organized a council of workers' delegates to bring the new party, which had a disproportionate number of urban Jewish intellectuals in its leadership, more in touch with the working-class rank and file.

By 1920, Koszutska had established herself as one of the unchallenged leaders of the Polish Communist movement. Along with Adolf Warski and Henryk Walecki, she had established a high profile for herself as one of the KPP's "Three Ws" (Warski, Walecki, and Wera). The year 1920 brought both elation and heartbreak for Polish Communists like Koszutska. In the summer of that year, it briefly appeared likely that a war between Lenin's Russia and the Polish Republic would end with a victory for the Red Army; this conquest would guarantee the establishment of a Communist society in Poland, and possibly even the spread of the world revolution into Germany and the rest of Europe. When the "miracle of the Vistula" dashed these hopes and the Red Army retreated back into Russia, the KPP suffered a traumatic defeat. Koszutska was arrested twice during this period, and after her release from prison she went into exile, living in Danzig (now Gdansk) and Berlin.

Aware that the vast majority of the Polish people were impoverished peasants, Koszutska studied the agrarian question from both a theoretical and a tactical perspective. In April 1922, she delivered a report on this issue to the third KPP national conference. In November of the same year, she repeated this in Moscow at the Fourth Congress of the Communist International, or Comintern (the "general directorate of the world revolution"), where she served as a deputy representative of the KPP Central Committee to the Comintern's Executive Committee. In her reports, Koszutska emphasized that "in Poland the Revolution will be a worker-peasant revolution or none at all." Although the peasantry was in many ways a conservative social element, she argued, its grievances were deep, and the KPP could reap great benefits if it took advantage of the peasants' hunger for land by backing this demand for private property despite the contradiction to orthodox Marxist theory. Koszutska also believed that, given the relative numerical and organizational weakness of the KPP, it should strive where possible to create strategic alliances with the PPS, whose moderate socialist position remained popular with the majority of the working class.

Koszutska's power within the organization increased in 1923. That year, she was elected to the KPP Politburo, representing the party in exile (the party had been banned in Poland). In the early summer of 1924, she was once again in the Soviet Union to attend the Fifth Congress of the Comintern. This congress, the first of the Comintern held since the death of Vladimir Lenin in January 1924, revealed an entirely new political landscape in revolutionary Russia. Rapidly emerging as the most powerful personality in the Soviet Communist Party was Joseph Stalin (1879–1953), a professional revolutionary about whom Lenin had issued dire warnings in the final months of his life. At the 9th Congress of the Russian (later Soviet) Communist Party in 1922, Stalin had become general secretary, and he cunningly used that power to advance his own rise to an unchallengeable position. Ruthless and tactically brilliant, Stalin had yet to achieve absolute power in 1924, but he already revealed a colossal hunger for control and a remarkable ability to manipulate various party factions for his ultimate benefit.

An ultra-leftist group had accused the "Three Ws" of being too conciliatory on both the agrarian question and on the matter of alliances with the PPS, and Stalin used factional disputes within the KPP to create a Polish Commission within the Comintern to "rectify" the tensions within the Polish Communist Party. When it became clear that Stalin was siding with the ultra-leftists, Koszutska spoke out forcefully both on her own behalf and in defense of KPP policies. She addressed the commission twice, on July 1–2, 1924. The second time she spoke, on July 2, 1924, both her courage in defending her position and the intensity of her clash with Stalin was revealed. Demanding more time to speak than the five minutes she had been allotted, Koszutska noted drily, "Comrade Stalin has tried to sort our affairs out and to grasp what ails us. We must thank him for it, but I can't agree with him on everything." Asserting that, "We have never feared bitter clashes," she accused Stalin of having made "completely groundless" charges of opportunism against the KPP. At the same time, she accepted accusations of shortcomings, caused in her view by the fact that the party leadership lived abroad due to the illegality of the party on Polish soil.

At that meeting, Koszutska disagreed also with Stalin's ally Vyacheslav Molotov, telling him, "You cannot speak here about any single and absolutely reliable method as a principle which it is opportunistic to violate." Concerned by signs that many of the Comintern delegates had become little more than unquestioning puppets of Stalin, she addressed them boldly, "Comrades, broken bones knit in our Communist International. I fear something else altogether. Precisely because of your special privilege, it is not those people whose bones you may for whatever reason want to break who are a danger, but spineless people." Voicing her suspicions regarding the about-face of Comintern delegates whose former support had now turned into a repudiation of KPP leadership strategy, and suggesting that not principles but naked opportunism was at work, Koszutska challenged Stalin directly by asserting, "We must note that this is a dangerous thing which we cannot trust." Responding to this comment, surely an unwelcome one, Stalin asked her, "Do you regard this as unnatural?," to which she replied, "Yes, unnatural to say the least."

Determined to speak the truth as she saw it and not bend to the will of an assemblage of Stalinist loyalists, Koszutska defended the KPP's honor, describing the organization as "one of the more, if not the most revolutionary in the Comintern. Despite its clandestine status and the vicious persecution unleashed against it, it has succeeded in maintaining its ties with the masses and inspiring them with its militant spirit."

Then, addressing her Polish comrades in the Comintern, she minced no words in voicing her profound sense of disappointment: "My charge against you is not that you failed to defend us but that you failed to defend yourselves, your work and your achievements. This I will never forgive you. Because of you, the entire Comintern has a false impression of our work. It is your elementary duty before the party to present its image as it really is. You failed to do that."

The outcome was a foregone conclusion. The leadership of the "Three Ws" was eliminated, mainly because they had chosen not to support Stalin and his ally Grigori Zinoviev in the struggle against the faction led by Leon Trotsky. At the third KPP congress, held in January 1925, Koszutska's influence was further eroded when she was not reelected to the party's Central Committee. Nevertheless, she retained some support within the KPP and was invited to present a report on the agrarian question at the party's fourth national conference held in No-

Polish postage stamp honoring Maria Koszutska, issued in 1951.

vember of that year. Because Stalin's power, while growing, was by no means yet absolute, Koszutska again appeared at a Comintern meeting, the Sixth Congress, held in 1928, when she was even seen on the presidium rostrum and took part in the debates. In 1929, however, the replacement of Nikolai Bukharin by Molotov signaled the final Stalinization of the Comintern, and the residual influence still exercised by the "Three Ws" was swept aside once and for all with a thorough purge of the KPP.

Starting in 1930, Koszutska lived permanently in Moscow. She worked for the Peasants' International and other organizations but no longer had any political power or influence. Despite this, her old nemesis Joseph Stalin never forgot—nor forgave—her candor. In 1936, the great purges began to decimate the best and brightest women and men of the Soviet Union. These included hundreds of foreign revolutionary veterans who, like Maria Koszutska, had found refuge in the workers' state from their own oppressive fascist and reactionary regimes. Ironically, many more Polish Communists died at the hands of Stalin and his GPU (later NKVD) secret police than in the prisons of the Polish dictatorship. In August 1938, the Presidium of the Comintern officially dissolved the Communist Party of Poland, noting that it had allowed itself to be infiltrated with fascist and Trotskyite agents—a charge that was fabricated and absurd.

Sometime in 1937, Maria Koszutska, for four decades a dedicated professional revolutionary, was arrested on trumped-up charges. At an unknown date in 1939, she was killed by the security organs of the Stalinist state. It is not known with absolute certainty where she was buried after her murder. In 1990, Conor O'-Clery, Moscow correspondent for *The Irish Times*, wrote that the Memorial Society—an organization created during the Gorbachev era to commemorate the victims of Stalinist repression—discovered the remains of many hundreds and perhaps even several thousands of Polish, German, Hungarian, Rumanian, Yugoslav, Italian and other foreign Communist leaders who were buried in the late 1930s. These were found on the grounds of the Novospasski monastery, one of the ancient fortified churches that once guarded the southern approaches to the Russian capital. On the monastery's grounds, where even now nothing but weeds will grow, there is a stretch of about 100 feet that is believed to be the site of mass graves, and it is likely that Koszutska's remains are buried there. Wrote O'Clery: "If I take anyone to see the monastery now, it is to gaze at the scene of one of the hor-

rors of Stalin's Russia. I've noticed that even on the warmest weekends this summer, very few people sunbathe near the bank with no trees."

SOURCES:

Degras, Jane, ed. *The Communist International 1919–1943: Documents, Vol. II: 1923–1928.* London: Oxford University Press, 1960.

——, ed. *The Communist International 1919–1943: Documents, Vol. III: 1929–1943.* London: Frank Cass, 1971.

Dziewanowski, M.K. *The Communist Party of Poland: An Outline of History.* Cambridge, MA: Harvard University Press, 1959.

Gasiorowski, Prof. Zygmunt, personal communication.

Kasprzakowa, Janina. *Maria Koszutska.* Warsaw: Ksiazka i Wiedza, 1988.

Koszutska, Maria. "Maria Koszutska: 'Spineless People are Dangerous': The Polish Question at the 5th Congress of the Communist International," in *World Marxist Review: Problems of Peace and Socialism.* Vol. 32, no. 8. August 1989, pp. 82–85.

——. *Pisma i Przemówienia. Tom II: 1919–1925.* Warsaw: Ksiazka i Wiedza, 1961.

"Koszutska, Maria," in *Wielka Encyklopedia Powszechna PWN.* Vol. 6. Warsaw: Panstwowe Wdawnictwo Naukowe, 1965, pp. 99–100.

Lazitch, Branko, and Milorad M. Drachkovitch. *Biographical Dictionary of the Comintern.* Rev. ed. Stanford, CA: Hoover Institution Press, 1986.

McDermott, Kevin. "Stalinist Terror in the Comintern: New Perspectives," in *Journal of Contemporary History.* Vol. 30, no. 1. January 1995, pp. 111–130.

Medvedev, Roy. *Let History Judge: The Origins and Consequences of Stalinism.* Edited and translated by George Shriver. NY: Columbia University Press, 1989.

O'Clery, Conor. "Bones Beneath Moscow: The Buried Truth," in *The New Republic.* Vol. 203, Nos. 3944–3945. August 20–27, 1990, pp. 15–17.

Simoncini, Gabriele. *The Communist Party of Poland: A Study in Political Ideology.* Lewiston, ME: Edwin Mellen Press, 1993.

Weydenthal, Jan B. de. *The Communists of Poland: An Historical Outline.* Stanford, CA: Hoover Institution Press, 1978.

John Haag,
Associate Professor of History,
University of Georgia, Athens, Georgia

Kotanner, Helene (fl. 1440).

See Kottanner, Helene.

Köth, Erika (1925–1989)

German soprano. Born on September 15, 1925, in Darmstadt, Germany; died on February 20, 1989; studied with Elsa Blank in Darmstadt.

Debuted in Kaiserslautern (1948); sang in Karlsruhe (1950–53), in Munich (from 1954), in Berlin (from 1961), in Salzburg (1955–65); appeared at Bayreuth (1965–68); made a Bavarian Kammersängerin (1956) and a Berlin Kammersängerin (1970); professor at the Hochschule für Musik (1973).

Erika Köth was born in Darmstadt, Germany, in 1925, and sang with a dance orchestra in order to pay for her musical education. She won a singing competition sponsored by the Hesse Radio and made her debut the following year. From 1950 until 1953, Köth was engaged by the City Theater in Karlsruhe. Joining the Munich State Opera in 1954, she then appeared with the Vienna State Opera. Erika Köth sang Constanze in Mozart's *Die Entführung aus dem Serial* in 1955–57 and 1962–63 with sensational reviews. Between 1955 and 1960, she also sang the Queen of the Night. Köth appeared at Teatro alla Scala, the Opera in Rome, and Covent Garden. She toured Russia in 1961. From 1965 until 1968, she performed in the role of the Waldvogel in *Siegfried*. Erika Köth made many recordings of complete operas and appeared frequently on television. Her voice was described by one critic as "exquisitely beautiful with an especially luminous top." In addition to opera, she also sang coloratura waltzes and chansons. Her broad repertoire and beautiful voice made Köth one of Germany's important coloratura sopranos after World War II.

John Haag,
Athens, Georgia

Kottanerin, Helene (fl. 1440).

See Kottanner, Helene.

Kottanner, Helene (fl. 1440)

Austrian courtier and writer. Name variations: Helen Kottannerin. Born in Odenburg, Germany, and flourished around 1440 in Hungary; died in Hungary after 1440; married Peter Szekeles, a German merchant (died 1438); married Kotanner or Kottanner, a valet of Vienna.

Helene Kottanner came from Odenburg in Germany, where she married a wealthy merchant and local politician, Peter Szekeles. On his death in 1438, she married the valet of a Viennese provost. About this time, she gained a position as lady-in-waiting to Queen ***Elizabeth of Luxemburg** (1409–1442), wife of the Habsburg ruler of Germany and Hungary, Albert II.

Helene became the queen's primary aide and confidante, and was thus involved in the intrigues which followed Albert's death in 1439. The Germanic nobility did not support the succession of Elizabeth's 3-month-old son Ladislav (V), but Elizabeth did not want to lose the position and influence she would have as the mother of the king, so she approached her trusted lady-in-waiting with a plan. She asked Helene to steal the royal insignia, to keep this symbol of the throne out of the hands of her enemies and thus hopefully weaken their political position.

Helene, as she recounts in her biography, bravely did as she was requested and secured the throne for Ladislav for a few months. However, when Elizabeth died soon after, Helene lost her privileged position, and Ladislav was deposed. The autobiography Helene composed in her retirement relates the details of her life and focuses on her intimate contact with the royal family, giving us clues about the day-to-day functions of a female servant of a queen. Helene's writing does not relate much about the broader scope of the political struggles she witnessed, concerning itself only with her immediate experiences. Still, as the autobiography of a woman, it holds an unusual place among medieval writings.

SOURCES:

Uitz, Erika. *The Legend of Good Women: The Liberation of Women in Medieval Cities.* Wakefield, RI: Moyer Bell, 1988.

Laura York,
Riverside, California

Kovalevskaia, Sonia (1850–1891).

See Kovalevskaya, Sophia.

Kovalevskaya, Sophia (1850–1891)

Russian mathematician, teacher, writer, occasional nihilist sympathizer and the first modern woman to receive a doctorate in mathematics. Name variations: Kovalevskaya (or Kovalevskaia) is the feminized version of Sophia's married name, according to the Russian tradition; she is also referred to as Sonya, Sofya, or Sofia Kovalevsky or Kovalevski, or Sophia Korvin-Krukovsky or Corvin-Krukovsky. Born Sophia Vasilevna Korvin-Krukovsky on January 15, 1850, in Moscow; died in Stockholm on February 10, 1891, of pneumonia; daughter of Vasily Vasilevich Korvin-Krukovsky, or Corvin-Krukovsky (1801–1875, a noble who served in the army and later made a living managing his provincial estate) and Elizaveta (Schubert) Fedrovna (1820–1879); education began at the age of eight when she received instruction from personal tutors; married Vladimir Onufrievich Kovalevsky (1842–1883), in 1868; children: Sophia Vladimirovich Kovalevskaya (b. October 17, 1878).

Went to Germany to continue her higher education, specializing in mathematics (1869); earned Ph.D. from the University of Göttingen (1874); became a lecturer, then a professor, at the University of Stockholm; received a number of accolades for her work, including the Paris Academy's Prix Borodin and a corresponding membership in the Russian Academy of Sciences; minor participant in the Paris Commune of 1871, and an occasional supporter of Russia's nihilists, though she was never fully committed to their radical cause.

Selected writings: non-scientific writings that are available in English include her memoir of her early years, Recollections of Childhood, *and an unfinished novel entitled* Nigilistka (Female Nihilist), *which was translated into English as* Vera Vorontsoff.

Sophia Kovalevskaya was a renowned scientist who refused to remain satisfied with becoming the world's first female professional mathematician. In addition, she was a talented author who wrote a number of fiction and non-fiction pieces, many of which remained unfinished at the time of her premature death. Her strong interest in political matters also surfaced sporadically throughout her life. Though she rarely became actively involved in politics, she often supported young radicals by giving them money or helping them obtain travel documents. In the end, however, her love of mathematics always drew her back to the world of science.

Sophia's parents, Vasily Vasilevich Korvin-Krukovsky and **Elizaveta Fedrovna Schubert**, were married on January 17, 1843, in St. Petersburg, Russia. Their first child, ◄⚜ **Anna Vasilevna (Jaclard)**, was born in late 1843. Seven years later, Sophia was born, on January 15, 1850; five years after that, they had a son, Fedor.

Sophia's memories of her early years were unhappy ones. She later remembered feeling ignored and unloved during much of her childhood. Although it is true that she was never particularly close to her mother or brother, she was her father's favorite, and she maintained a strong, loving relationship with her sister throughout their lives.

In 1858, when Sophia was eight, the Krukovskys left their home in St. Petersburg and moved permanently to their estate at Palibino, near the present Russian-Belarus border, though they continued to spend winters in the capital. Sophia's education began at that time when her father arranged for private instruction for her and Anna. While she received a basic education from her tutor, Joseph Malevich, it was her uncle, Peter Vasilevich Korvin-Krukovsky, who piqued Sophia's interest in mathematics by introducing her to sophisticated theoretical concepts. Another early academic influence was a neighbor, physics professor Nikolai Nikanorovich Tyrtov. He appreciated Sophia's mathematical abilities when she was a teenager and convinced her father to allow her to study trigonometry and calculus, training that was highly unusual for a young girl.

General Korvin-Krukovsky was atypical of the era's nobles for the amount of attention he paid to his daughters' education. In 19th-century Russia, women of the nobility were generally schooled in painting, sewing, music, French and so forth, and did not receive a scholastic education in the arts and sciences; women of other classes usually received no education at all.

The Krukovsky girls expressed an early interest in literature, which brought them into contact with one of the greatest authors of the era, Fyodor Dostoevsky. In 1864, Anna sent him a story she had written in the hope that he would publish it in his journal *The Epoch*. Dostoevsky and Anna began to correspond about Anna's writings and other literary matters. When they met shortly thereafter, he began to court her. His eventual proposal was turned down, as Anna believed he would make an overly demanding husband. Sophia, who had herself developed an unrequited romantic affection for the writer, was unable to understand Anna's decision. Despite the complicated beginnings of the friendship, both sisters remained acquainted with Dostoevsky, and later his wife *Anna Dostoevsky, throughout their lives.

Sophia's lifetime interest in politics manifested itself early. During the Polish rebellion of 1863, she firmly proclaimed herself on the side of the Poles against the Russians, though at the age of 13 there was little she could do to actively support their cause. As the girls reached young adulthood, radical politics played a more important part in their lives when they became involved in Russia's nihilist movement. Russia of

⚜► **Jaclard, Anna** (1843–1887)

*Russian writer. Name variations: Anna Korvin-Krukovsky or Corvin-Krukovsky; Anna Krukovskaya or Krukovskaia. Born Anna Vasilevna Korvin-Krukovsky or Korvina-Krukovskaia in late 1843 in Moscow; died in October 1887; daughter of Vasily Vasilevich Korvin-Krukovsky (1801–1875, a noble who served in the army and later made a living managing his provincial estate) and Elizaveta (Schubert) Fedrovna (1820–1879); sister of *Sophia Kovalevskaya (1850–1891); received instruction from personal tutors; married Victor Jaclard (a French revolutionary).*

the 1860s and 1870s was teeming with groups and movements led by women and men hoping to find solutions to Russia's mounting social and political problems. Nihilism, less an ideology than a way of life, was one path open to politically aware young people. Nihilists held two strong beliefs—that science was capable of solving Russia's social ills, and that the struggle for personal fulfillment through economic and sexual liberation was necessary for both individual and social improvement. Nihilist women in particular sought freedom through "fictitious" marriages in which a man would volunteer to marry a woman on a platonic basis and thereby free her from her parents' house. This practice was popularized in Nikolai Chernyshevskii's 1863 novel *What is to be Done?*

Sophia was certainly influenced by nihilist precepts when she decided to engage in a fictitious marriage in order to pursue her scientific education in Europe. General Krukovsky would not permit either of his daughters to go abroad, and studying in Russia was virtually impossible, as higher education in that country was closed to women.

Sophia's sister Anna and their friend **Anna Mikhailovna Evreinova** were also interested in finding fictitious husbands so that they could leave their family households. The three young women therefore began screening candidates for this purpose while the Korvin-Krukovskys were spending the winter of 1867–68 in St. Petersburg. None proved suitable until Vladimir Onufrievich Kovalevsky presented himself, initially as a prospective husband for Anna. However, he decided that he would prefer to marry Sophia, and they became engaged in the summer of 1868. They were wed in September that year; she was 18 and he was 26.

Anna was not as fortunate as Sophia in finding a suitable husband, and the new couple decided to wait in St. Petersburg for Anna's luck to turn. Sophia tried to pursue her education there, but at that time women were only able to audit courses and were not formally admitted to university. A popular movement to protest this situation had been gaining strength since the 1850s, and Sophia was naturally a proponent of the cause, signing a petition that circulated the capital in 1867. Women were not allowed limited acceptance in special university courses until the 1870s, however, and Sophia therefore arranged to audit a number of courses and to be tutored independently as well. However, such measures were ultimately unsatisfactory, and in the summer of 1869, Sophia, Vladimir and Anna left

Russia so that Sophia could continue her education in Europe. Anna left the couple in Germany and continued to France, where she quickly became involved with French revolutionaries.

Sophia spent three semesters at the University of Heidelberg between 1869 and 1870, studying physics, physiology, and mathematics. Between semesters, she traveled around Germany, Italy, England, and France. In London, she met many of her era's distinguished scientists and authors, including Charles Darwin and George Eliot (*Mary Anne Evans). Extremely impressed with Eliot, in 1886 Sophia wrote a short biography of her for a Russian journal.

Sophia's personal life at this time was difficult. The status of the Kovalevsky marriage was never clear to either party, and both Vladimir and Sophia suffered numerous misunderstandings and a great deal of pain as a result. Their fictitious marriage was to remain in a constant state of flux for a number of years. In the fall of 1870, the couple moved to Berlin, where Sophia studied privately with Professor Karl Theodore William Weierstrass who worked at the University of Berlin. He initially opposed the idea of working with women students, but Sophia quickly convinced him of her abilities by solving some difficult mathematical problems he laid out for her at their first meeting.

Sophia's studies were briefly interrupted when she and Victor went to Paris in the spring of 1871 to visit Anna and her lover Victor Jaclard who were participants in the Paris Commune. They lived among the rebels for about six weeks, returning to Berlin in early May. Shortly thereafter, however, the Commune was disbanded by the French government and rumors reached Sophia that Anna and Jaclard had been arrested. The Kovalevskys rushed back to Paris, followed closely by the sisters' parents, to discover that Anna was free but that Jaclard was indeed in custody. Jaclard soon escaped from prison, and it is unclear to what extent, if any, the Kovalevskys were involved. However, Vladimir allowed Jaclard to use his passport, thereby helping him escape from France.

Following their adventure in France, Sophia and Vladimir returned to Berlin where, for the next three years, Sophia continued her studies with Weierstrass, and they developed an excellent professional and personal rapport. At this time, she wrote three papers that were worthy of serving as a Ph.D. dissertation. Two were on Saturn's rings and Abelian integrals, but it was the paper on partial differential equations that she eventually chose to present. Her work was a simplification of Augustin Cauchy's 1842 solution to a problem involving the conduction of heat; the solution is now known as the "Cauchy-Kovalevsky Theorum."

Because awarding a woman a Ph.D. was almost unprecedented, Weierstrass and Kovalevskaya had to consider carefully where they would present her work. They eventually decided on the University of Göttingen because Weierstrass knew a number of the researchers there. He also wanted Sophia to be spared the oral examinations that usually accompany Ph.D.s (though the reasons for this are unclear), and the university often awarded doctorates without them. The school administration was reluctant at first, but they finally awarded Sophia a Ph.D. summa cum laude in 1874.

"*People die, ideas endure*": it would be enough for the eminent figure of Sophia to pass into posterity on the lone virtue of her mathematical and literary work.

—**Karl Weierstrass**

Sophia and Vladimir returned to Russia that year; in her five years there, she devoted little time to mathematics. Sophia was unable to work in Russia's higher education system, as women were not permitted to sit for the exam to obtain the requisite Russian master's degree. Vladimir too had difficulty finding work in his field, paleontology. Instead, the couple spent a great deal of time among the St. Petersburg social elite and turned their efforts to a series of financial investments, most of which turned out to be shaky. The marriage, always on awkward ground, was made more difficult by their straitened circumstances.

In the fall of 1875, General Korvin-Krukovsky died. Except for Anna, Sophia had been closest to her father of all her family members, and she took the news hard. She turned to Vladimir for support, and the marriage was temporarily strengthened. Indeed, it was at approximately this time that the marriage ceased to be a fictitious one, though their "real" marriage proved eventually to be no more stable than their assumed one.

A few events of note mark Sophia's stay in Russia. She attended the Trial of the 193, a trial of young radicals, which later figured in her work *Nigilistka*. She also helped raise money for the St. Petersburg Higher Courses for Women that opened in 1878. Her talents as an author began to find expression as well when she wrote reviews and scientific articles for one of the journals in which she and Vladimir had invested. On a more personal note, Sophia gave birth to a daughter, also named Sophia, known by her nickname Fufu, on October 17, 1878.

Professionally, however, life in Russia was unsatisfying for Sophia, and she eventually decided to seek employment abroad. In November 1880, she left Russia for Berlin alone, leaving Fufu behind with her friend and fellow scientist *Julia Lermontova. Sophia hoped to re-establish her ties with the mathematical community, including Professor Weierstrass, whom she had neglected for the previous three years. The Kovalevskys' marriage had grown increasingly untenable during their stay in Russia, pushed to the breaking point by financial concerns. Vladimir, always somewhat unstable, was less able than Sophia to cope with the financial and professional difficulties they both faced. In March 1881, the couple agreed that they should continue to live apart. Fufu joined her mother in Berlin while Vladimir remained in Russia.

That fall, Sophia moved to Paris to be near her sister. She continued to correspond with a number of universities through her male colleagues in an effort to find a teaching position in any one of a number of European schools. Her contacts were not restricted to the academic community, however. She also met with many of the Russian political emigres living there, including Peter Lavrov and **Marie Jankowska-Mendelson**, with whom she developed a lasting friendship.

Sophia's disintegrating marriage came to a tragic end on April 15, 1883, when Vladimir committed suicide after months of increasingly erratic behavior. Sophia was devastated by her husband's death and refused to eat or see anyone for days. When she recovered from her grief, she returned to Russia to straighten out his affairs. She also managed to ensure that his name remained unsullied following his shaky, and sometimes legally questionable, financial dealings.

That same year, Sophia finally won a teaching position as a lecturer at the University of Stockholm, making her the first modern woman to receive a post at a European university. Her introductory lecture on January 30, 1884, was on partial differential equations, the subject of her dissertation. As a lecturer, she received no pay for her work and lived solely on her students' contributions.

Although she loved her work, Kovalevskaya did not particularly enjoy life in Sweden. While there, she began studying the problem of the rotation of a solid body around a fixed point, a question that would consume her for the next

Sophia Kovalevskaya

five years. She also worked as an editor of the mathematical journal *Acta Mathematica,* which had been founded by her colleague and friend Gösta Mittag-Leffler, brother of *Anne Charlotte Edgren. In June 1884, Kovalevskaya was offered a five-year term at the University of Stockholm as an "extraordinary (or assistant) professor." For the next few years, she traveled back and forth between her friends and family in Russia, Paris, Berlin, and Stockholm.

In the fall of 1886, Sophia was suddenly called to Russia to visit her sister who was very ill, likely with cancer. Kovalevskaya spent two months in Russia, sitting at Anna's bedside and discussing their childhood. The following summer, Sophia again returned to Russia to help Anna move to Paris to be with Jaclard. In October of that year, Anna died. Sophia reacted far differently to Anna's death than she had to Vladimir's. She did not suffer the near breakdown she had when her husband died, but continued with her work. As she once wrote to Mittag-Leffler, "I only bemoan and bewail when I am slightly unhappy. When I am in great distress, then I am silent."

It was at this time that Kovalevskaya began to devote more attention to her non-scientific writings. In 1887, she collaborated with the author Anne Charlotte Edgren on a play, "The

Struggle for Happiness." The hours spent discussing her youth at her sister's bedside also inspired Sophia to write about her childhood, and her memoir *Recollections of Childhood* was published in 1889. Kovalevskaya's last substantial literary work was a novel that she never completed about a nihilist girl in St. Petersburg during the politically turbulent 1870s, known as *Nigilistka* (female nihilist) in Russian or *Vera Vorontsoff* in English. The novel was not published in Russia until 1906, though it was published in Sweden in 1892. She was also working on a number of other projects at the time of her death, including a fictionalized biography of the author Nikolai Chernyshevskii.

Even as she devoted more time to her literary efforts in her final years, Kovalevskaya received increasing acclaim for her scientific work as well. In December 1888, she was awarded the Prix Borodin from the Academy of Paris (a first for a woman) for her work on the rotation of a solid body around a fixed point. In June 1889, she was awarded a permanent professorship at the University of Stockholm. That winter, she became the first woman elected as a corresponding member to the Russian Academy of Sciences, an honor to which she had been aspiring her entire professional life.

Personally, Sophia spent the last years of her life in an intense, turbulent relationship with Maxim Kovalevsky, a distant relative of her former husband. It is possible that during their last vacation together in France, they were making plans to marry. She left Maxim in France in January 1891. By the time of her arrival in Sweden on February 5, she was gravely ill. Over the next few days, she deteriorated rapidly, and on February 10, 1891, Sophia Kovalevskaya, the world's first woman professional mathematician, died of pneumonia. She was 41 years old.

SOURCES:

Donaldson, Christine F. "Russian Nihilism of the 1860s: A Science-Based Social Movement," unpublished Ph.D. dissertation, Ohio State University, 1979.

Kennedy, Don H. *Little Sparrow: A Portrait of Sophia Kovalevsky.* Athens, OH: Ohio University Press, 1983.

Koblitz, Ann Hibner. *A Convergence of Lives: Sofia Kovalevskaia, Scientist, Writer, Revolutionary.* Boston, MA: Birkhäuser, 1983.

———. "Science, Women and the Russian Intelligentsia: The Generation of the 1860s," in *Isis.* Vol. 79, no. 297. June 1988, pp. 208–226.

Kovalevskaya, Sofya. *A Russian Childhood.* Translated, edited and introduced by Beatrice Stillman. NY: Springer-Verlag, 1978.

Kramer, Edna. "Sonya Kovalevsky," in *Dictionary of Scientific Biography.* Edited by Charles Coulston Gillispie. NY: Scribner, 1973.

Naginski, Isabelle. "A *Nigilistka* and a *Communarde:* Two Voices of the Nineteenth-Century Russian *Intelligentka,*" in *Women as Mediatrix.* Edited by A. Goldberg. NY: Greenwood Press, 1987.

Rappaport, Karen. "S. Kovalevskaya: A Mathematical Lesson," in *The American Mathematical Monthly.* Vol. 88, no. 6, 1981, pp. 564–574.

Stites, Richard. *Women's Liberation Movement in Russia: Feminism, Nihilism and Bolshevism.* Princeton, NJ: Princeton University Press, 1978.

SUGGESTED READING:

Bell, E.T. *Men and Mathematics,* NY: Simon and Schuster, 1937, pp. 406–432 (for information on Weierstrass and his work with Kovalevskaya).

Cooke, Roger. *The Mathematics of Sonya Kovalevskaya.* NY: Springer-Verlag, 1984 (for information on Kovalevskaya's mathematics and a list of her writings in their original languages; most of Kovalevskaya's works have not been translated into English).

Keen, Linda. *The Legacy of Sonya Kovalevskaya.* Providence, RI: American Mathematical Society, 1987.

Susan Brazier,
freelance writer, Ottawa, Ontario, Canada

Kovalskaia, Elizaveta (1851–1943)

Russian feminist and revolutionary who was active in the Populist movement of the 1870s. Name variations: Elizabeth Koval'skaia or Kovalskaya; Kobalskaya. Pronunciation: Ko-VAL-sky-ya. Born Elizaveta Nikolaevna Solntseva on July 17, 1851 (o.s.) in Solntsevka, Russia; died in the Soviet Union in 1943; illegitimate daughter of Colonel Nikolai Solntsev (a landowner) and a female serf on his estate; educated by home tutoring, 1858–62; attended girls' gymnasium in Kharkov, 1862–67, and Alarchin courses in St. Petersburg, 1869–71; married Iakov I. Kovalskii, late 1860s; married M. Mankovskii, around 1900; children: none.

Was a serf until 1858 when she was adopted by her father and brought up as a noble's daughter; conducted women's courses in Kharkov (1867–69); was a member of female study circles in St. Petersburg (1869–71); lived in Zurich and became a follower of Bakunin (1872–73); was an active participant in the Russian Populist movement (1874–80); was a member of Chernyi Peredel (1879); was co-founder of South Russian Workers Union (1880); arrested (1880), tried (1881), and sentenced to exile and confinement in Siberia until 1903; immigrated to Switzerland (1903–07) and France (1907–17) where she was active in the maximalist wing of the Russian Socialist Revolutionary Party; returned to Russia after the October Revolution; was a researcher in the State Historical Archives in Petrograd (1918–23); was a member of the editorial board of Katorga i ssylka in Moscow (1923–35).

Selected publications: "Avtobiografiia" (Autobiography), in Entsiklopedicheskii slovar' (vol. XL, 1927, pp. 189–199, *reprinted in* Deiateli SSSR i revoliut-sionnogo dvizheniia Rossii *[Personalities of the USSR and the Revolutionary Movement in Russia], Moscow, 1989); Iuzhno-russkii rabochii soiuz, 1880–81 (South Russian Workers Union, Moscow, 1926).*

After midnight on a warm summer's night in 1880, Elizaveta Kovalskaia stood before more than a hundred workers in Baikov Grove outside Kiev. This was "an enormous number for those times," she later recounted in her autobiography, and even more remarkably the process was repeated every evening for a week with a different group of workers. The men and women who attended these all-night gatherings belonged to the South Russian Workers Union which Kovalskaia and Nikolai Shchedrin had organized the previous spring. They listened to their young agitators, both of whom were in their 20s, describe the causes of the oppression which beset tsarist Russia and the need for "economic terror" and social revolution. This was a message which Kovalskaia and other agrarian socialists had been preaching in the villages of Russia for over six years. Never before, however, had the Populists been so successful in tying the concept of armed struggle to a mass organization. Kovalskaia knew she was living on borrowed time. The union which she had helped establish was itself illegal and the nocturnal meetings she addressed were easily infiltrated by police agents. On October 22, 1880, the inevitable happened. She and Shchedrin were arrested as they left their home in Kiev; and the next May, shortly after the assassination of Tsar Alexander II by Populists in St. Petersburg, she was sentenced to a life of hard labor in Siberia. After 22 years confinement, she was released and resumed her revolutionary activity in Western Europe. In late 1917, Kovalskaia, now in her 60s, returned to a productive life in a new Soviet Russia.

It was not unusual that a woman should play a leading role in the Populist movement; many were attracted by the sexual equality and personal commitment which Populism offered. What set Elizaveta Kovalskaia apart was her origin. Unlike almost all of her revolutionary contemporaries, she was born a serf. Her father, Colonel Nikolai Solntsev, was a wealthy landlord who had an affair with a peasant woman on one of his estates near Kharkov in southern Russia. After her birth on July 17, 1851, a decade prior to the Emancipation, Elizaveta spent seven years as a serf before her father was persuaded to free her and her mother and to bring her up as a young lady in his own house.

Despite receiving a good home education from tutors hired by her father and having other belated advantages of wealth, Elizaveta never forgot the sexual exploitation of her mother, the stigma of her own illegitimacy, or her early childhood fear that she might be sold to another landlord. At the age of 11, she cajoled her repentant father into allowing her to enroll in a girls' gymnasium in Kharkov. For the next six years, she was exposed to the literature and ideas of the 1860s with their message of personal and political liberation. In her memoirs, she tells of setting up a "circle for self-education among the girls" where they discussed the "woman question." She also organized trips to a local court to observe trials of peasants accused of rebellion and of women who had murdered abusive husbands. According to **Barbara Engel**, by the time Kovalskaia graduated from the gymnasium in 1867 she was "already a committed feminist."

Elizaveta Kovalskaia

At about the same time, her father died, bequeathing her his substantial estate. She promptly turned one of his houses in Kharkov into an educational center for women. Osip Aptekman, who knew her during this period, described her as "young, beautiful, intelligent, sensitive to all social undertakings, a zealous defender of female emancipation." Kovalskaia sought to further the cause of women by offering informal courses to upper-class women seeking some form of higher education and by providing more basic skills to working-class women she met through her volunteer work at the Kharkov Society for the Promotion of Literacy. In these courses, she and the other lecturers called attention to the class and gender inequities of Russian society, but as she admitted, at this stage "I myself had no idea how injustice could be righted." One of her fellow teachers was Iakov Kovalskii who she married while still in her teens and who accompanied her to St. Petersburg in 1869 after the police had closed down her center.

Kovalskaia's intention in going to the Russian capital was to attend the Alarchin courses which for the first time provided advanced education for women but without conferring on them a university degree. Every evening from 6 to 9 PM, she and over 200 other women from diverse upper- and middle-class backgrounds attended lectures at a boys' high school given by well-known professors. Perhaps more important than this instruction were the contacts made with other women. These led to the formation of study circles made up exclusively of women in which they debated not only the "woman question" but also social and political issues. The two years Kovalskaia spent living alone in St. Petersburg—her husband had returned to Kharkov and was no longer a part of her life—were important in developing her self-reliance and in deepening her social understanding. They also served to change her focus from ways of helping members of her gender to means of achieving broader social change. Crucial in this transition from feminism to socialism was a year spent in Zurich. She does not appear to have attended classes in the medical faculty of the University of Zurich, as did so many other women denied a university education in Russia, but she was actively involved in the political debates between the Lavrovists and Bakuninists which raged in the emigre colony over the proper means of achieving peasant socialism. By the time she left Zurich in 1873, she considered herself an adherent to the more radical theories of Michael Bakunin.

ℒike a huge wave, the movement to liberate women [in the 1860s] swept over all the urban centers of Russia. I, too, was caught up in it.

—Elizaveta Kovalskaia (1925)

Kovalskaia returned to Russia intending to participate in the "To the People" movement of the "mad summer" of 1874 when several thousand students flocked to the villages to convince the peasantry of the virtues of socialism. Poor health, however, kept her from joining the pilgrimage but it did not prevent her from getting a job as a schoolteacher near Tsarskoe Selo outside St. Petersburg. During her spare time, she conducted propaganda circles and passed out leaflets among the local factory workers. Imminent police arrest forced her to move to St. Petersburg where she carried out the same illegal activity. Unlike most of her fellow Populists, she shunned formal organizations such as Land and Liberty and she was in the minority in concentrating her attention on urban factory workers rather than agitating the peasantry themselves. She felt that the more advanced workers, who themselves were often ex-peasants, were more susceptible to the ideas of agrarian socialism which they would spread when they returned periodically to their villages.

In 1879, when Land and Liberty split, she briefly joined Chernyi Peredel (Black Repartition) rather than the more extreme Narodnaia Volia (The People's Will). Early the next year, she left for Kiev with Shchedrin to establish the South Russian Workers Union. Not only did they succeed in organizing 700 workers and in holding a regular series of evening agitational meetings, they also printed three revolutionary leaflets and laid plans for an underground newspaper. In all of these endeavors, they preached the doctrine of "economic terror," i.e., attacks on police officials and factory administrators who had the closest contact with the workers as a means of building up the confidence of the masses. While she often carried a revolver, Kovalskaia does not appear to have been involved personally in any political assassinations.

At her trial in 1881, Kovalskaia denied the court's right to sit in judgment of her, and she refused either to have a lawyer defend her or to make a final statement on her own behalf. Her obstinacy continued during 22 years of exile and confinement in Siberia. On three occasions, she tried unsuccessfully to escape, and on another she attempted to commit suicide. She also engaged in a hunger strike, attacked a prison official with a knife for beating a fellow female prisoner, and refused to stand in the presence of the governor-general of the Amur Region. For this insubordination, she was abused by a prison administrator and transferred to a camp for common criminals.

Shortly before her scheduled release in 1903, Kovalskaia married M. Mankovskii, an Austrian citizen sent to Siberia for revolutionary activity in Poland. On the basis of his citizenship, she petitioned to go abroad with him rather than being forced to remain in exile in Iakutsk. The petition was grudgingly granted but she was forbidden to return to Russia. Kovalskaia had no intention of giving up her revolutionary work. She went immediately to Geneva where, in the absence of her second husband, she became involved in the publishing activities of the maximalist wing of the Russian Socialist Revolutionary Party. A botched assassination attempt by another female maximalist in 1907 forced Kovalskaia to flee to Paris. Undeterred, she helped form a new revolutionary group in the French capital and assisted in the publication of *Trudovaia respublika*. In 1914, her Austrian passport, which had been an asset 11 years earlier, suddenly became a liability as France went to war with the Central Powers. To escape detention, she was compelled to live illegally in southern France until Tsar Nicholas II was overthrown in February 1917. The new Provisional Government granted her a Russian passport in the name of her first husband, and with this she traveled back to her native land by way of England and Norway. She arrived in Petrograd shortly after the Bolsheviks seized power in October 1917.

Little is known about the life of this durable and fascinating woman after this point. Her brief autobiography written in 1925 mentions simply that she was employed as a researcher in the State Historical Archives in Petrograd from 1918 to 1923 and then moved to Moscow to join the editorial board of *Katorga i ssylka,* a journal devoted to the memory of exiles and political prisoners such as herself. While the journal was closed by the Stalinist regime in 1935, Kovalskaia's age spared her the fate of many former revolutionaries who perished during the purges. She died at the age of 92 in 1943.

SOURCES:

Engel, Barbara Alpern, and Clifford N. Rosenthal, eds. and trans. *Five Sisters: Women Against the Tsar.* NY: Alfred A. Knopf, 1975.

Engel, Barbara. "Koval'skaia, Elizaveta Nikolaevna," in *Modern Encyclopedia of Russian and Soviet History.* Vol. 18, 1980, pp. 7–9.

Koval'skaia, E.N. "Avtobiografiia," in *Entsiklopedicheskii slovar'.* Vol. XL, 1927, pp. 189–199.

SUGGESTED READING:

Engel, Barbara Alpern. *Mothers and Daughters: Women of the Intelligentsia in Nineteenth-Century Russia.* Cambridge, MA: Cambridge University Press, 1983.

Levandovskii, A. *E.N. Koval'skaia.* Moscow, 1928.

R.C. Elwood, Professor of History, Carleton University, Ottawa, Canada

Krahwinkel, Hilde (b. 1908).

See Sperling, Hilde.

Krainik, Ardis (1929–1997)

American opera administrator, under whose leadership the Lyric Opera of Chicago became one of the most important companies in the U.S. and a major force in world opera. Born in Manitowoc, Wisconsin, on March 8, 1929; died in Chicago on January 18, 1997; daughter of Arthur Krainik and Clara (Bracken) Krainik; never married.

During 16 years (1981–96) as general director of one of the world's leading opera houses, Ardis Krainik effected the rescue of the Lyric Opera from bankruptcy, bringing it to the heights of artistic quality and financial solvency. Although she would one day become a major figure in the musical life of the United States, music did not dominate her early years. Krainik was born in 1929 into a family of Norwegian, Czech and German ancestry. She was a gifted child who bored easily and would note years later, "My mother didn't know what to do with me." Homework was easy and left time for numerous activities, including swimming, tennis, and lessons in elocution, piano, and voice. She amused herself by singing opera arias, and sometimes danced in the basement to old recordings of *Amelita Galli-Curci, but had little interest during these years in serious music.

Krainik attended Northwestern University in Evanston, Illinois, and received a B.S. degree in drama in 1951. At first, she believed that a career as "a great dramatic actress" would present itself after graduation, but when reality intervened Krainik followed her father's wishes and took a job teaching drama at a high school in Racine, Wisconsin. Lonely in a strange town, she soon joined the choir of Racine's Congregational Church. The choir director spotted potential talent, insisting that Krainik not "just vegetate here in Racine," but instead take measures to "do something with this voice." That something turned out to be travel to Chicago, where Edgar Nelson of the Chicago Conservatory "flipped" when he heard Krainik sing. He not only accepted her as a student but also offered her a scholarship to his highly regarded special oratorio class. Soon, she was determined to become a professional singer and was busy learning such major operatic roles as Carmen and Isolde.

In 1953, Krainik quit teaching and became a graduate student at Northwestern University with hopes of emerging as a professional singer headed for an international career. As her skill grew, she appeared on stage on several occasions, including in the role of the Zia Principessa in a student production of Puccini's *Suor Angelica.* Krainik made her professional stage debut as the mother in Gian Carlo Menotti's *Amahl and the Night Visitors.* Not yet prepared for a full-scale career, in 1954 she completed her studies at Northwestern and sought ways to support herself while looking for career opportunities. A job in a church choir earned her five dollars a week, but additional income was required for survival.

In 1954, the course of Krainik's life was changed when a friend suggested that she might find work with a newly founded and apparently "fly-by-night opera company" calling itself the

Lyric Opera of Chicago. The Windy City's first resident professional opera company since the Depression, the Lyric Opera had been founded that same year by the conductor Nicola Rescigno, businessman Lawrence V. Kelly, and *Carol Fox. Its early days were stormy. After a power struggle among the founding trio, Carol Fox emerged in 1955 as general manager and undisputed master of the new company. Fox hired Krainik on the spot as a clerk-typist, noting that she was impressed by her "nice intelligent face" as well as the fact that she could already type. With this career move, Krainik became part of a great adventure in music.

At the start, she earned $55 a week typing. Within a year, Krainik had decided to audition with the company's chorus and was accepted. She soon stepped out of the chorus to appear in a number of small operatic roles including that of Giovanna, the duenna of Gilda, in Verdi's *Rigoletto*. Before long, she was regularly appearing in a string of supporting roles. "I sang everybody's maid or mother," she noted. She appeared on stage as *Renata Tebaldi's mother in Giordano's *Andrea Chénier*, as *Leontyne Price's slave girl in Massenet's *Thaïs*, and as the Valkyrie Rossweise. Krainik's voice, a lyric mezzo, was highly regarded and her acting skills were considered excellent. Nonetheless, even before 1960, when she became assistant manager of the Lyric Opera, she had abandoned her plans for a singing career. Management and administration, for all of their tensions and frustrations, made for a better career choice to Krainik, largely because she regarded the life of a professional singer as not only stressful but also lonely: "You're alone all the time. You study alone, you sit in your hotel room alone. And I love to be surrounded by people." Her by-now extensive knowledge of music and theater and her firsthand stage experience combined to give Krainik a broad understanding of the complex world of opera.

By the mid-1970s, her skill in financial matters had been revealed. Soon after starting with the company, she had become its office manager, with a budget of $5,000 that she never overspent. Frugal by nature, Krainik enjoyed saving funds in one area in order to have money left over for emergencies, particularly for the production department, in which unforeseen expenses were not unusual. In 1975, having become an indispensable partner to Fox in the administration of the Lyric Opera, Krainik received another promotion and began serving as the company's artistic administrator. For a number of years, she had worked with Fox in drawing up singers' contracts, a job which became hers alone in 1976.

By the late 1970s, the Lyric Opera of Chicago had earned an international reputation for the quality of its productions. Under the regime of Carol Fox, however, costs had almost always been ignored. Ever larger sums were lavished on star performers, and Fox thought nothing of outbidding everyone, even New York City's Metropolitan Opera, for the world's top vocal talent. (Its star-studded casts and costs-be-damned attitude earned the Lyric Opera the not always complimentary title of "La Scala West.") The company's achilles' heel—its almost total indifference to the budgets of its much-praised productions—was bringing it to the brink of a financial crisis. Now in declining health, Fox could no longer function effectively but refused to relinquish any of her powers, let alone consider the possibility of retirement. The disastrous 1976 production of *Paradise Lost,* an opera by the contemporary Polish composer Krzysztof Penderecki which ran nearly $1 million over budget, moved the Lyric Opera along toward fiscal ruin.

The company's financial problems, which were exacerbated by Fox's poor health and growing inability to focus on the day-to-day details of management, led to a lack of confidence on the part of Chicago's business community. While Fox refused to abdicate, mounting deficits made it increasingly difficult to raise any significant additional funds for the Lyric Opera, and the company's future became an open question.

Fox asked Krainik to run the entire production when the company toured Mexico in 1979, but the financial condition of the Lyric Opera remained in deep distress. Krainik, questioning whether her beloved company would survive the crisis, began to examine other professional opportunities at home and abroad. In December 1980, she flew to Australia for an interview with the Australian Opera, which was seeking a new general manager to work with conductor Richard Bonynge. She returned from Sydney to Chicago after having signed a "letter of intent to contract."

On January 5, 1981, the opera world was stunned when a seriously ill Carol Fox submitted her resignation to the Lyric Opera's board of directors. Fox would die only months later, on July 21, 1981. Offered the position of general director by the board, Krainik accepted it "instantaneously," and her appointment as impresario of one of the world's major opera companies was announced to the public on January 9, 1981.

The opera company she inherited was a pale shadow of its former glory, struggling with a deficit of $309,000 and having virtually no endowment (it had once been able to boast of nearly $3 million). The gravity of the situation was dramatized by the fact that the company's warehouse, which was full of largely obsolete costumes, sets, and props, had been mortgaged against a loan for current operating expenses. Within days of assuming power, Krainik instituted an across-the-board budget cut, slashing 1981 expenses by some $560,000. This move not only wiped out the deficit, but left the company with a sizable amount to use for dealing with the most pressing priorities. The endowment came back to life with a bequest of $500,000, and with 1982 ticket sales that filled the house to 97% of capacity (and turned out to be record-breaking), the Lyric Opera was resurrected and on the road to a full and lasting recovery. Artistic innovation linked to careful budgeting could be seen in the company's successful first operetta production, Lehár's *Merry Widow* in June 1982, which resulted in 80% box-office sales and a budget that was more than 20% below projected costs.

The Lyric Opera's sound fiscal footing was made possible by what Krainik described as "pinpoint budgeting." Every month—and more often during productions—she scheduled "budget responsibility meetings" in which the head of each of the company's departments, with computer printout in hand, went through each part of the budget line by line with her. In the margin of each printout, Krainik marked a letter "u," meaning unsatisfactory, if more was spent than budgeted. Such overspending, needless to say, required a full and convincing explanation. The Chicago press, reporting on the fiscal successes of her regime in its early years, nicknamed Ardis Krainik "Wonder Woman."

In her second season, Krainik produced a number of innovative but relatively low-budget productions. One was the opera *La Voix Humaine* by French composer Francis Poulenc. Attractive to any cost-conscious opera director because it is a one-act, *La Voix Humaine* is a one-character opera in which a jilted woman takes poison in a hotel room and then sings goodbye on the telephone to the man who betrayed her. Another work, Gilbert and Sullivan's classic *The Mikado,* was presented in a zany modernized version that was both popular with the public and cost-effective. In an interview, Krainik described it with obvious pride as having been "outrageous, courageous, and it came in under budget."

Artistically a woman of bold tastes, Krainik was unafraid to make hard choices. She showed her courage in 1989 when she dropped superstar Luciano Pavarotti from the Lyric Opera's company roster after he cancelled at short notice yet another date, a revival of *Tosca* (between 1981 and 1989, Pavarotti had bowed out of 26 of 41 scheduled Chicago performances). Krainik never asked Pavarotti back. In 1989, after less than a decade of management, Krainik announced an ambitious plan to stage more rarely heard 20th-century opera classics, as well as to commission and stage new pieces. One of the results of this policy was the triumphant 1992 premiere of William Bolcom's opera *McTeague,* with staging by Robert Altman. Krainik's enlargement of her company's repertory included a staging of Richard Wagner's *Ring* cycle; the Peter Sellars staging of *Tannhäuser*; an ambitious program of commissions for composers-in-residence; and the "Toward the 21st Century" artistic initiative, the goal of which was to bring 20 important contemporary works (including three premieres) into the Lyric Opera's repertory.

Because she appeared to be eternally cheerful and optimistic, some observers initially predicted Krainik would be a lightweight as the company's director. She was anything but that, first succeeding at keeping her company within budget and then slowly but surely building a solid endowment and running in the black on an

Ardis Krainik

annual basis. By 1993, she had raised much of the $100 million needed to purchase and restore Chicago's Civic Opera House, the Lyric Opera's home. A skilled political infighter, she sat on the National Council of the Arts, which oversees the National Endowment for the Arts, and thus played a role in securing for the Lyric Opera a grant of $1 million for its "Toward the 21st Century" program. A committed Christian Scientist, Krainik credited God for her successes: "I go to church, I read the Bible, and I pray a lot. I know it's unfashionable to say, but it's those angel ideas that come from elsewhere—that still, small voice in the middle of the night—that has made Lyric what it is."

Greatly mourned by her colleagues, friends and opera lovers worldwide, Ardis Krainik died in Chicago on January 18, 1997. Writing in *Opera News*, Patrick J. Smith praised her many achievements and remarked: "She was irreplaceable." In her honor, Chicago's huge Civic Opera House was renamed the Ardis Krainik Theater.

SOURCES:
"Ardis Krainik," in *Opera*. Vol. 48, no. 4. April 1997, p. 421.
"Ardis Krainik, 1929–97," in *Opera*. Vol. 48, no. 5. May 1997, pp. 533–534.
Belt, Byron. "There from the Start," in *Opera News*. Vol. 46, no. 4. October 1981, pp. 20, 22, 24.
Cox, Meg. "Born-Again Opera Company Hits a High Note," in *Wall Street Journal*. January 3, 1984, p. 32.
———. "Scaling Back: Under a New Manager, Chicago's Lyric Opera Thrives on a Shoestring," in *Wall Street Journal*. Eastern Ed. June 3, 1983, pp. 1, 19.
Kerner, Leighton. "Ardis Krainik, 1929–1997," in *Village Voice*. Vol. 42, no. 7. February 18, 1997, p. 70.
"Krainik, Ardis," in *Current Biography*. NY: H.W. Wilson, 1991.
Smith, Patrick J. "Ardis Krainik 1929–1997," in *Opera News*. Vol. 61, no. 11. February 22, 1997, p. 50.
Walsh, Michael. "Making Opera Pay, the Chicago Way," in *Time*. Vol. 143, no. 6. February 7, 1994, pp. 65–66.

RELATED MEDIA:
"As It Happened: Selected Backstage Stories from Lyric's 40 Years, as Told by Ardis Krainik and Danny Newman, with Norman Pellegrini" (audiocassette), Chicago: Lyric Opera of Chicago, 1994.

John Haag,
Professor of History, University of Georgia, Athens, Georgia

Kramer, Ingrid (b. 1943).

See Engel-Kramer, Ingrid.

Kramer, Leonie (1924—)

Australian educator and writer. Born in Melbourne, Australia, in 1924; educated at the universities of Melbourne and Oxford.

A professor of Australian literature and an expert on the works of *Henry Handel Richardson, Dame Leonie Kramer was a professor at the University of Sydney from 1968 and was also active in numerous community and educational organizations. Her works on Richardson include *Henry Handel Richardson and Some of Her Sources* (1954), *A Companion to Australia Felix* (1962), a guide to Richardson's work, and *Myself When Laura* (1966), concerning Richardson's novel *The Getting of Wisdom*. In collaboration with R.D. Eagleson, Kramer wrote *Language and Literature: A Synthesis* (1976) and *A Guide to Language and Literature* (1978). She also edited a number of scholarly volumes, including *Australian Poetry* (1961), *Coast to Coast* (1962), *Henry Kendall* (with A.D. Hope, 1972), and *The Oxford History of Australian Literature* (1981). Kramer was made OBE in 1976 and DBE in 1981.

Krasner, Lee (1908–1984)

Leading 20th-century American painter and one of the founders of Abstract Expressionism. Name variations: Leonore Krassner. Born Lena Krassner on October 27, 1908, in Brooklyn, New York; died on June 19 (sometimes given as June 20), 1984, in New York City; daughter of Joseph Krassner (owner of a small store) and Anna (Weiss) Krassner; attended Girls High School and Washington Irving High School, 1922–25, Women's Art School of Cooper Union, 1925–28, Art Students League, 1928, National Academy of Design, 1929–32; married Jackson Pollock (an artist), on October 25, 1945 (died, August 1956).

Worked as artist for Works Progress Administration (1935–43); met Jackson Pollock (1936); began to study with Hans Hofmann (1937); first exhibited paintings (1940); began to live with Pollock (1942); painted Little Image paintings (1946–49); presented first solo exhibition (1951); underwent psychoanalysis and presented collage exhibition (1955); painted Green Earth series (1956–57); held exhibition at Martha Jackson Gallery (1958); operated on for aneurysm (1963); had first retrospective exhibition of her work at Whitechapel Gallery, London (1965); picketed Museum of Modern Art to protest the museum's lack of interest in women artists (1972); was awarded Augustus St. Gaudens Medal by the Cooper Union Alumni Association (1974); received Ordre des Arts et des Letters from French government.

Major works: Self-Portrait (Miller Gallery, New York, 1930); Red, White, Blue, Yellow, Black (Marlborough Gallery, New York, 1939); Image Surfacing (Robert Miller Gallery, New York, 1945); Composi-

tion (Philadelphia Museum of Art, 1949); The City (Robert Miller Gallery, New York, 1953); Bird Talk (Robert Miller Gallery, New York, 1955); Triple Goddess (Robert Miller Gallery, New York, 1960); Gaea (Museum of Modern Art, New York, 1966).

Lee Krasner, a versatile and significant American painter whose works both reflected and helped to shape many of the most important artistic trends in the United States from the 1930s through the 1960s, produced more than 600 works. She painted in remarkably varied styles over the course of her career, and her failure to gain major recognition until she reached her 60s stems in part from this factor and in part because of her gender. In addition, Krasner possessed a complex personality that exposed her to the domination of abusive men. Two of them hindered, to one degree or another, the growth of her talent and her independent reputation.

The first was Igor Pantuhoff, a fellow art student she knew in the 1930s. More notable was her relationship with Jackson Pollock, who became her husband in 1945 and who emerged as the central figure in the development of Abstract Expressionism. Thus, at various times over several decades she put aside her own artistic ambitions in order to meet the needs of her male companions. Her years of caring for Pollock, combined with her role as the executor and caretaker of his artistic legacy following his death in 1956, caused her to be identified widely as "Pollock's widow." Nonetheless, despite such distractions, she invariably returned to her own career with talent and gusto. By the 1960s, a decade following Pollock's death, Krasner began to receive clear recognition as a significant figure in her own right. She was praised for both her paintings and her collages, but she is best known for her important contribution to the style known as Abstract Expressionism.

Developed in the New York area in the 1940s, Abstract Expressionism has been hailed as the major American contribution to the development of modern art. Departing from the tradition-bound American art world of the 1930s, artists like Krasner took ideas from the modernist painters of Europe, such as Piet Mondrian, Pablo Picasso, and Henri Matisse, then explored their own subconscious impulses, thus creating Abstract Expressionism. As Clifford Ross notes, Abstract Expressionism developed "highly charged images which force the viewer to recall and experience a range of powerful emotions and feelings." Instead of presenting a recognizable reality, "Abstract Expressionist images evoke; they do not depict. They confront;

they do not describe." With the development of Abstract Expressionism, New York became a lively gathering place for artists in the years after World War II. The new art, as **Anne Harris** and **Linda Nochlin** put it, "moved the center of the artistic avant-garde from Europe to America."

The future painter and pioneer in the growth of Abstract Expressionism was the daughter of an Orthodox Jewish family that had only recently immigrated to the United States from Russia. Her parents, Joseph and **Anna Krassner**, married in Russia, then Joseph left for the United States eventually to set up a grocery store. Anna joined him several years later. Lena—later to be known as Leonore, then Lee—was born on October 27, 1908, only nine months after her parents had been reunited in their new home. She was the fourth of her parents' five children, and she was the first to be born in their new country.

The Krassners showed the strains that characterized many such immigrant families. Her mother's hectoring nature and lack of patience, her father's emotional distance from his children, and the couple's continuing discomfort in American society created a tense, closed environment. Krasner later complained that she felt as if she had grown up in an atmosphere little different from a ghetto in Eastern Europe. In fact, she was surrounded by the languages that prevailed in Jewish communities there: Hebrew, Yiddish, and Russian. "Any member of the family could always break out in a language that I couldn't understand," she wrote.

Naifeth and Smith, Jackson Pollock's biographers, place heavy emphasis on the young girl's relationship with her older brother Irving in the shaping of her personality. Remote, brutal, and manipulative, he would attract the attention of his sister, then deliberately reject it. In their view, Lee "would always seek out men as remote, abusive, and implacable as Irving, and lose herself in them with the same guileless abandon." In general, her relationships with others were almost instantaneously antagonistic throughout her life.

It remains uncertain where Krasner's interest in art originated. In Orthodox Jewish families like hers, the Bible's condemnation of graven images was taken seriously. But her rebellious nature was evident here and elsewhere. By age 14, she was sufficiently committed to becoming an artist to apply—unsuccessfully, as it turned out—to Washington Irving High School, the only New York public secondary school where a girl could major in art. She had also dramatically announced to her parents that she was giving up Judaism.

Even when she succeeded in entering Washington Irving High School on her second try, Krasner was frustrated. Her grades in art classes were poor, and one teacher gave her a passing grade only because she was doing well in other subjects. Her continuing determination to become an artist led her to the Women's Art School of Cooper Union and then to the more prestigious National Academy of Design. These were institutions that promoted a traditional approach to painting, in which students had to proceed through a number of stages before they could even begin to work with live models, and she was notably uncomfortable at both.

For me, I suppose that change is the only constant.

—Lee Krasner

Much of Krasner's early work, such as a number of still lifes, reflect this academic training. It imbued her with the principles of the Impressionists and the Post-Impressionists. But her potential as an artistic rebel was already on display in her 1930 *Self-Portrait*. She completed it in order to present it to a faculty committee empowered to advance her out of the sterile exercise classes in which she was so frustrated. Painted in the outdoors (she claimed she nailed a mirror to a tree at her parents' Long Island home in order to use herself as a model), the work shows her as a powerful but unidealized figure standing at her easel.

Despite the energies and sacrifices Krasner had put into her artistic training, she abandoned her career in 1932. Her need to support herself as well as her alcoholic boyfriend, Igor Pantuhoff, led her to work as a Greenwich Village cocktail waitress. At the same time, in another step away from her ambition to become an artist, she entered a teachers' training program at the City College of New York.

In 1934, Krasner returned to painting. Three years later, along with Pantuhoff, she began to study with Hans Hofmann in his avant-garde school, a one-room establishment in Manhattan. A devotee of European modernism, Hofmann had begun teaching in Munich during World War I. He was a key figure in bringing the world of European modernist painting to the tradition-bound circles of American artists. His comments, given half in English and half in German, were nearly incomprehensible to Krasner, and she often had to ask another colleague to translate. Nonetheless, the young woman absorbed enough of his influence so that she redirected her energy to work in the style of Pablo Picasso's Cubism that Hofmann promoted.

Meanwhile, Krasner's relationship with Igor Pantuhoff went steadily downward. He had given up much of his own artistic ambitions years before, supporting himself by becoming a portrait painter for the rich. He often taunted her with anti-Semitic remarks, and his personal life was increasingly dominated by his alcoholism. Nonetheless, the final break between them came only in 1939 when he simply vanished from her life, turning up later when he joined his family in Florida.

Starting in the mid-1930s, Lee Krasner went to work for the federal government's Works Progress Administration (WPA). The artists she met there helped shape her political allegiance to left-wing causes, and she developed a particular admiration for Leon Trotsky, the Russian leader recently defeated and exiled by his rival Joseph Stalin. Krasner admired Trotsky's insistence that artists need not be mere propaganda tools but should be free to take up abstract artistic techniques. Nonetheless, the WPA did not prove to be a favorable environment for truly experimental art. Krasner worked on murals under the direction of Max Spivak, and these scenes of factories and city locales appeared in the style of Socialist Realism.

During the late 1930s, Krasner was drawn into numerous left-wing political causes, and her role in public demonstrations led to several arrests. "I was practically in every jail in New York," she later recalled. By the close of the decade, however, she had become disenchanted with organizations that she now saw were dominated by hardline Communists. She took particular exception to their view that art was primarily a mode of propaganda. "Painting," she said, "is not to be confused with illustration."

Still in her early 30s, Krasner—who changed her first name to Lee and Anglicized the spelling of her last name as well around this time—had notable success in combining Cubist forms, such as triangles, in studies of the human body. Her surviving paintings from the late 1930s are dominated by such works. Nonetheless, she received only grudging praise from Hofmann for her achievements, and found his comment that one of her drawings was "so good you would not know it was done by a woman" hard to forget.

Krasner's important liaison with Pollock began in the early 1940s. She had apparently met him several years before but they first became acquainted when both were scheduled to contribute to the fourth annual exhibit of an avant-garde group, the American Abstract Artists, in January 1942. Pollock was the more

810

isolated and lesser-known figure, and Krasner provided him with a valuable entry into New York's artistic world. Her willingness to subordinate her career to that of Pollock came after her initial visit to his studio: "I was totally bowled over by what I saw," she said. By the fall of 1942, they were living together, and, on October 25, 1945, they were married in Manhattan.

To the consternation of her friends who did not like either the raucous life Pollock led or his art, Krasner not only joined her personal life to his but abandoned her hopes for an independent artistic career. Her answer to their comments was that she felt he was leading the way in the direction she hoped her art could go: "He had found the way to merge abstraction with Surrealism." In later years, she equated her decision to come under Pollock's influence with her earlier shift, under Hofmann's direction, to draw inspiration from Picasso.

The two artists settled in the Long Island community of The Springs, near East Hampton, to live a primitive and impoverished life. Their home even lacked a usable bathroom, but, de-

Lee
Krasner

spite the pinch of poverty, they spent freely on art supplies. While The Springs was a modest community, it had the advantage of close proximity to East Hampton with that town's affluent art buyers. Pollock suffered from alcoholism and recurrent psychological crises, and one of his wife's key roles was trying to help him maintain his emotional equilibrium. Cultivating a vegetable garden for food and traveling by bicycle, they led a quiet life in which the once ebullient Lee became, as Robert Hobbs claims, "the plain, supportive, possessive, and at times hostile wife."

Krasner did only a small amount of painting during the first four years of their marriage. She painted in the morning, then left the studio to her husband during his customary working hours in the afternoon. Her dual role as a helper for her husband and an artist in her own right led to obvious strains. As she told **Cindy Nemser** more than two decades later, "Pollock being the figure he was in the art world it was a rough role seen from any view."

By now, Krasner's artistic interest had shifted to the exploration of her unconscious mind, and her art became increasingly divorced from realistic images and external models. Starting in the early 1940s, like other abstract artists appearing in increasing numbers in the United States, she used her inner sensations as a stimulus to put spontaneous forms on canvas. The scope of Krasner's painting, as well as her techniques, went through a spectacular evolution from the mid-1940s onward. Her important first works, to be found in the "Little Image" series from 1946 through 1949, consisted of tiny canvases covered with numerous abstract figures. Interpreted by critics like Hobbs as an effort to plumb the depths of her subconscious, their disciplined and discrete elements stand in marked contrast to the drip paintings that her husband was creating on canvases stretched across the floor of their home. The last of the "Little Image" paintings seem comprised of hieroglyphics, and critics of Krasner's works have alluded that its origins can be found in her long-standing interest in calligraphy. Others suggest that her early education in written Hebrew now found expression here.

Krasner began a program of psychotherapy in 1955 to help her troubled relationship with Pollock, but the two became increasingly estranged. While in Europe in mid-1956, on a trip designed to take her away from her marital difficulties, she received word that Pollock had died in a car accident. She dealt with his death for the next 18 months by painting a series of 17 works

known as the Green Earth paintings. Many of them, according to Hobbs, focused on such themes as "fecundity, growth, and harvest." In his view, her grief at Pollock's death was mixed with relief at her freedom from coping with his emotional turmoil, and "her art expresses a joy in being able to focus on herself and her growth."

Even before Pollock's death, Krasner had become still more versatile in her exploration of new forms. Around 1950, she had begun to paint on a larger scale. She had also become dissatisfied with some of her previous works, and she sliced them up to make the raw materials for a series of collages. Entering her studio in 1953, she found herself so disgruntled with her recent work that she tore all of her drawings, then many of her canvases, apart. The result was a series of collages that she put on exhibit in 1955.

In the aftermath of Pollock's death, Krasner returned to the modified use of figurative painting with works that featured eye-like forms as well as bright, rich colors. Her restlessness turned in a new direction in 1959 in what Nemser calls "a descent into wild despair" of "slashing, splintered strokes of raw umber and white." However, a new level of serenity in her work appeared by the late 1960s, featuring images that resembled birds and flowers painted in colors like red, blue, and yellow.

Despite the development of a brain aneurysm in 1963 that threatened her life, as well as later ailments such as arthritis, Krasner continued to paint in a variety of styles until her death. Returning to her earlier activism, in 1972 she participated in a public protest against the Museum of Modern Art for its limited showcasing of women artists. Much of her energy in the last decades of her life went to managing the legacy of her renowned husband. She permitted the works of Jackson Pollock to be shown only in selected museums, and she demanded high prices when she consented to sell anything in her collection. Some authorities believe that she thereby played a decisive role in raising the value of all works of American abstract art.

Lee Krasner died in New York City on June 19, 1984. Full recognition of her own achievements came only in the last two decades of her life. A major breakthrough for Krasner's reputation came first from abroad when, in 1965, a retrospective exhibit of her work was presented in London at the Whitechapel Art Gallery. She was honored with a similar exhibit at a venue in her own country only in 1973, when the Whitney Museum of American Art presented such a retrospective. Other retrospectives in Washington, D.C., in 1975, in New York in 1981, and in Houston in 1983, have strengthened her place in the art world.

SOURCES:

Abstract Expressionism: Creators and Critics: An Anthology. Edited and with an introduction by Clifford Ross. NY: Harry N. Abrams, 1990.

Harris, Anne Sutherland, and Linda Nochlin. *Women Artists: 1550–1950.* NY: Alfred A. Knopf, 1976.

Hobbs, Robert Carleton. *Lee Krasner.* NY: Abbeville Press, 1993.

Landau, Ellen G. *Lee Krasner: A Catalogue Raisonné.* NY: Abrams, 1995.

Naifeth, Steven, and Gregory White Smith. *Jackson Pollock: An American Saga.* NY: Clarkson N. Potter, 1989.

Nemser, Cindy. *Conversations with 15 Women Artists.* NY: HarperCollins, 1995.

SUGGESTED READING:

Chadwick, Whitney. *Women, Art, and Society.* London: Thames and Hudson, 1990.

Gabor, Andrea. *Einstein's Wife: Work and Marriage in the Lives of Five Great Twentieth-Century Women.* Penguin, 1996.

Wagner, Anne Middleton. *Three Artists (Three Women): Modernism and the Art of Hesse, Krasner, and O'-Keeffe.* Berkeley, CA: University of California Press, 1996.

Neil M. Heyman,
Professor of History,
San Diego State University, San Diego, California

Kraus, Lili (1903–1986)

Hungarian pianist who made dozens of recordings. Born in Budapest, Hungary, on March 4, 1903; died in Asheville, North Carolina, on November 6, 1986; studied with Béla Bartok, Edward Steuermann and Artur Schnabel.

Lili Kraus was born in Budapest, Hungary, in 1903, and studied at the Royal Academy there with, among others, Béla Bartok, and later Edward Steuermann and Artur Schnabel. By the early 1930s, she had made dozens of records. Captured and interned by the Japanese during World War II, Kraus had no access to a piano for more than three years. She became a British subject in 1948 but lived and taught in the United States in her later years. Kraus made her American debut in 1949; her appearances always summoned a devoted audience. On stage, she was the grande dame who had come to reveal the message of the masters. Starting in the 1950s, she re-recorded many of the works she had put on disc decades earlier, including the complete Mozart concerti, many solo sonatas, much of the Schubert repertoire, as well as some Bartok. In March 1978, Austria awarded her its Cross of Honor for Science and Art.

SOURCES:

"Kraus, Lili," *Current Biography.* NY: H.W. Wilson, 1975.

Nemy, Enid. "Pianist Talks but the Subject isn't Music," in *The New York Times.* April 6, 1971, p. 42.

Roberson, Steven Henry. "Lili Kraus: The Person, the Performer, and the Teacher," Ph.D. dissertation, University of Oklahoma, 1985.

John Haag,
Athens, Georgia

Krebs-Brenning, Marie

(1851–1900)

German pianist known for her performance of large-scale concertos. Born Marie Krebs in Dresden, Germany, on December 5, 1851; died in 1900; daughter of Karl Krebs (a music critic and philosopher).

Marie Krebs-Brenning was born in Dresden in 1851, the daughter of Karl Krebs, a music critic and philosopher. She toured Europe at an early age, was particularly well-liked in London, and had no fear of including the large-scale concertos in her repertoire, including Beethoven's *Emperor*. In 1870, Krebs-Brenning toured the United States as accompanist to the violin virtuoso Henri Vieuxtemps.

John Haag,
Athens, Georgia

Krějcárova, Milena (1896–1945).

See Jesenská, Milena.

Kremnitz, Marie (1852–1916).

See Elizabeth of Wied for sidebar.

Kreps, Juanita (1921—)

American economist, educator, and first woman appointed secretary of commerce. Born Juanita Morris on January 11, 1921, in Lynch, Kentucky; daughter of Elmer Morris and Cenia (Blair) Morris; Berea College, A.B., 1942; Duke University, M.A., 1944, Ph.D., 1948; married Clifton H. Kreps (an economist), on August 11, 1944; children: Sarah Blair Kreps; Laura Ann Kreps; Clifton H. Kreps.

An expert in labor economics, Juanita Morris Kreps has had a distinguished career in education, private industry, and public service. Born in a small coal-mining town in eastern Kentucky in 1921, Kreps was the daughter of a mine manager. The family had little money, and Kreps had to struggle to obtain an education. She worked and went to school part-time, finally completing her B.A. in economics at Berea College in Berea,

Kentucky, in 1942. An excellent student, Kreps then continued her education at Duke University in Durham, North Carolina. She received a master's degree in economics in 1944. In that year, she also married fellow Duke student Clifton Kreps, with whom she had three children. Kreps took a teaching position at Denison College in Granville, Ohio while working towards her doctoral degree from Duke University, which she completed in 1948.

She left Denison College to accept a faculty position at Hofstra University in Hempstead, New York, where she taught until 1954. After another brief teaching job at Queens College in New York City, Kreps returned to Duke University, this time as an assistant professor in the department of economics. She taught and performed research at Duke for over 20 years, becoming nationally recognized as an authority on the economics of labor in the United States. Her research included a focus on race and gender equity in the workforce, and she also contributed to the study of aging workers. Her book *Sex in the Marketplace,* published in 1971, described discrimination against women in the American workforce. Promoted to full professor at Duke in 1967, Kreps served as dean of the women's college from 1969 to 1972, when she was named as the first female director of the New York Stock Exchange. The following year, she became the first female vice-president of Duke. By the mid-1970s, she was among the most well-known of labor economists, and served on the boards of numerous large corporations.

In 1977, the newly elected President Jimmy Carter named Kreps as his secretary of commerce. She was the first woman to hold that office, as well as the first professional economist; Kreps was also only the fifth woman to hold any Cabinet post. As secretary, Kreps focused on U.S. trade issues and development of poor regions of the United States. She also maintained a strong interest in labor equity issues faced by women, who were by the late 1970s already a major sector of the American workforce and who were politically organizing to achieve government support against job discrimination. Having faced male prejudice in her own education and career, Kreps supported the U.S. feminist movement politically, while providing a role model for other professional women. Her high visibility in federal office and her efforts on behalf of women, minorities, and the poor led the *Ladies' Home Journal* to honor her as "Woman of the Year" for 1978. In 1979, President Carter appointed Kreps to lead a delegation to Beijing, making her the first secretary of commerce to visit China. There she helped bring about an important trade agreement.

Kreps resigned her Cabinet post following her success in China and returned to Duke University to teach again. She has been associated with Duke since 1979 and is currently the James B. Duke Professor of Economics, Emeritus and serves on the board of directors of the Duke Endowment. The author of many articles on economic development and job equity, Kreps continues to serve as an expert on labor issues on corporate boards, most recently with companies such as Eastman Kodak, AT&T, J.C. Penney, United Airlines, and R.J. Reynolds. She has also been appointed to national economic policy institutions, such as the National Council on Aging, and holds honorary doctorates from more than a dozen universities.

SOURCES:

Read, Phyllis J., ed. *The Book of Women's Firsts.* NY: Random House, 1992.

Zilboorg, Caroline, ed. *Women's Firsts.* Detroit, MI: Gale Research, 1997.

Laura York,
Riverside, California

Kristiansen, Ingrid (1956—)

Norwegian long-distance runner. Born Ingrid Christensen in Trondheim, Norway, on March 21, 1956.

Ingrid Kristiansen won the European championship (10,000 meters) in 1986, the World championship in 1987, and the cross-country World championship in 1987. She also placed first in the London Marathon (1984, 1985 and 1987), the Boston Marathon (1986), the Houston Marathon (1983 and 1984), and the Stockholm Marathon (1980, 1981, and 1982). She was the holder (in 1987) of world records in the 5,000 and 10,000 meters, the marathon and half-marathon. In the late 1970s, Kristiansen also participated in world and European ski events.

SOURCES:

Aschehoug and Gyldendal. *Store Norske Leksikon* (Greater Norwegian Encyclopedia). Oslo: Kunnskapsforlaget, 1992.

Elizabeth Rokkan,
translator, formerly Associate Professor,
Department of English, University of Bergen, Norway

Kristina.

Variant of Christina.

Kristina (fl. 1150)

Swedish royal. Name variations: Kristina Bjornsdottir. Flourished around 1150; daughter of Bjorn, prince *of Denmark, and Katerina Ingesdottir; married Erik or St. Eric IX, king of Sweden (r. 1156–1160); children: Knut Ericsson, king of Sweden (r. 1167–1195); Philipp; *Margaret (d. 1209); Katharina Ericsdottir (who married Nils Blaka).*

Kroc, Joan (c. 1929—)

American philanthropist. Born Joan Dobbins around 1929 in Minnesota; the daughter of a railroad telegrapher and a concert violinist; married and divorced; became third wife of Raymond Kroc (owner of the McDonald's fast-food chain), on March 8, 1969 (died 1984); children: one.

Joan Kroc, the widow of McDonald's CEO Raymond Kroc, made national headlines in 1997 when she was identified as the anonymous donor of $15 million to aid the flood victims of Grand Forks, North Dakota. Although her identity was closely guarded from the time her gift to the flood victims was first announced, reporters traced her through her private jet, which landed three times at the Grand Forks airport. Later, North Dakota senator Byron Dorgan confirmed that Kroc was indeed the donor.

The daughter of a railroad telegrapher and a concert violinist, Kroc grew up in St. Paul, Minnesota, but now lives in San Diego. She first met Ray Kroc in St. Paul in 1956. Ray, formerly a Chicago milkshake-machine salesman, had built McDonald's into the world's largest fast-food service company. Thirteen years later, she divorced her first husband, who ironically worked for the McDonald's enterprise, to marry Kroc in March 1969.

Apparently, Joan Kroc's generosity is as expansive as her fortune, which is estimated at over $2 billion, and includes the San Diego Padres baseball team. Since the death of her husband in 1984, she has donated millions to causes ranging from local theater to medical research. In 1996 alone, she reportedly gave $33 million to institutions, including the *Betty Ford Center and the University of San Diego. She has also contributed over $100 million to various Ronald McDonald charities and $80 million to the Salvation Army. Kroc, however, shuns publicity and prefers to make her contributions anonymously. "She has a big heart and a sort of Cinderella sense," said family friend Neil Morgan, who is also a columnist at *The San Diego Union-Tribune*. "She likes to surprise people with the golden slippers, but don't come after her. She's hard to approach. But when she gives, she gives with great spontaneity and generosity."

SOURCES:
Covarrubias, Amanda. "Mrs. Kroc is Flood Victims' Benefactor," in *The Day* [New London, CT]. May 20, 1997.
"Mystery No More: The Grand Forks Angel has a Name: Joan Kroc," in *People Weekly*. June 2, 1997.

RELATED MEDIA:
"Raymond Kroc," on "Biography," Arts and Entertainment Channel, first aired on Wednesday, March 24, 1999.

Barbara Morgan,
Melrose, Massachusetts

Krog, Cecilie (1858–1911).

See Thoresen, Cecilie.

Krog, Gina (1847–1916)

Norwegian champion of women's rights. Born Jørgine Anna Sverdrup on June 20, 1847, in Flakstad, Lofoten, Northern Norway; died on April 14, 1916; daughter of a Lutheran pastor; never married.

Gina Krog was born on June 20, 1847, in Flakstad, Lofoten, Northern Norway, a few months after the death of her father, a Lutheran pastor. Her family moved to the capital, Kristiania (Oslo), when Gina was eight years old. Influenced by the writings of *Camilla Collett, she became engrossed in the women's movement in the 1870s and '80s; she is quoted as having said that she did not wake up to the cause of women's rights but was born a supporter of the movement. Krog spent some time in England, where she came into contact with British women's organizations, but claimed that it was the struggle of American women for equality that gave her the courage to act.

After some years as a schoolteacher, she resigned from her profession in order to lead the women's movement and to argue the cause in newspaper and magazine articles. Together with journalist Hagbard E. Berner and his wife, she helped found Norsk Kvinnesaksforening (Norwegian Association for Women's Rights) in 1884. "Her well-poised personality and her unswerving confidence helped to disarm criticism and win respect," writes **Karen Larsen**. The following year, Krog established Kvinnestemmerettsforening (Association for Women's Suffrage), remaining its chair until 1897, when she resigned over the issue of giving voting rights to middle-class women only. Her principles demanded equal rights for all women, and her breakaway group represented rural and working-class women. From 1887 until her death, Krog edited the magazine *Nylaende* (New

Land). On the invitation of the International Council of Women, she established the National Council of Norwegian Women and remained its lifelong chair. These activities took her all over Norway on lecture tours, and to many international conferences. She supported Venstre (the Liberal Party) in politics, and was elected deputy member of its national committee in 1909.

Gina Krog has been described as the unchallenged leader of the women's movement in Norway from 1884 until her death on April 14, 1916, when she was given a state funeral by the Norwegian government.

SOURCES:

Aschehoug & Gyldendal's *Store Norske Leksikon.* Oslo: Kunnskapsforlaget, 1992.

Larsen, Karen. *A History of Norway.* NJ: Princeton University Press, 1948.

Norsk biografisk leksikon (Dictionary of Norwegian Biography), vol. 8. Oslo: Aschehoug, 1938.

Elizabeth Rokkan,
translator, formerly Associate Professor,
Department of English, University of Bergen, Norway

Kronberger, Petra (1969—)

Austrian downhill racer. Born on February 21, 1969, in Pfarrwerfen, Austria; her father drove a cement truck; her mother worked as a cleaning woman and dishwasher.

Won three consecutive World Cups (1990, 1991, 1992); won two Olympic gold medals in slalom and combined in Albertville (1992).

Petra Kronberger was born on February 21, 1969, in Pfarrwerfen, Austria, into a family of limited means: her father drove a cement truck while her mother worked as a cleaning woman and dishwasher. Petra took to the slopes early; by age six, she had won her first trophy. For four years, starting at age ten, she lived at a Skihauptschule in Bad Gastein, a special school for athletes. She then attended a similar school in Schladming. But Kronberger was not considered a strong skier because she had suffered a number of injuries. She took a job as a bank clerk.

In 1988, Kronberger placed 15th at Leukerbad, Switzerland, and was on the Austrian team for the 1988 Olympics in Calgary; she finished 11th in the combined and a respectable 6th in the downhill. Two years later, she was a superstar of the slopes.

In December 1990, Kronberger won a World Cup event in all four Alpine disciplines—slalom, giant slalom, Super G, and downhill—accumulating 276 points to the 195 points of the second place finisher; she followed that with a

victory in a combined event a month later. But starting in January of 1991, she was slowed by a knee injury, resulting from a crash in the World championships in Saalbach, Austria, causing her to miss a number of races in the second half of that season. Even so, she finished that tour with 312 points.

In the 1992 Olympics in Albertville, France, Kronberger took the gold medal in the downhill with a time of 1:32:68. **Anneliese Coberger** took the silver, the first time a New Zealander ever medaled in the winter Olympics. Also heavily favored in the Alpine combined, Kronberger easily took the downhill but skied conservatively on her first slalom run and placed sixth. But two months previous, Austria's slalom coach, Alöis Kahr, had been killed in an automobile accident, and Kronberger sensed Kahr offering advice as she prepared for her second slalom run. She aggressively attacked the course, beating all comers for another gold medal. But the pain in Petra Kronberger's knee grew worse and she retired soon after.

Krone, Julie (1963—)

American jockey who was the first woman to win the Triple Crown. Born Julieann Louise Krone in Benton Harbor, Michigan, on July 24, 1963; daughter of Judi Krone and Don Krone; married Matthew Muzikar (a television sports producer), on August 26, 1995.

Winningest female jockey, and one of the top jockeys—male or female—of all time; had $81 million in purse earnings and more than 3,500 wins.

Julie Krone was born in Benton Harbor, Michigan, in 1963, the daughter of Don and **Judi Krone**, an accomplished equestrian. Thus, it was not surprising that Julie learned to ride before she learned to walk. When Judi put her two-year-old daughter on a horse which promptly trotted off, she watched in amazement as the little girl picked up the reins and guided the horse back to her. It was the start of a life on horseback. As she grew, Krone began racing and jumping horses around the family farm in Eau Claire, Michigan (pop. 494). By age five, she began to win ribbons in horse shows.

More than anything, however, Krone loved to race. When she was 15, she wangled a job as a workout rider at Churchill Downs, home of the Kentucky Derby. On her return to Michigan, she began racing at local fairground tracks. Determined to become a winning jockey, Krone later left high school and went to live with her grandparents in Florida so that she could concentrate on racing.

Five weeks after Julie Krone arrived in Tampa, she won her first race on Lord Farkle at Tampa Bay Downs on February 12, 1981. In 48 races at Tampa, Krone won nine, finished second four times, and third ten times. She attracted the attention of Chick Lang, an agent who took her to race at Pimlico in Baltimore, home of the Preakness Stakes. Despite his endorsement, it was not easy for Krone to get jobs as a jockey. Racing had been closed to female jockeys until 1968, and Julie traveled up and down the Eastern seaboard in search of work. Her perseverance paid off; by 1982, she had won 155 races and more than $1 million in prize money, of which she kept 10%. Young and sometimes immature, Krone was suspended for 60 days for possession of marijuana. "It was pure torture," she commented. "I hadn't been off a horse for that long in 17 years. But I'm glad it happened. It gave me a chance to think about the talent I had been given. I almost threw it away." Settling down, she won the riding title in Atlantic City in 1982 and again in 1983. At the end of 1983, however, she fell off her mount during a race and broke her back. Four months were devoted to rehabilitation.

Krone continued to be a phenomenon on the racetrack. She competed at Garden State Park, the Meadowlands, and Monmouth Park in New Jersey and won 199 races, earning more than $2.3 million in prize money. In 1987, Julie Krone rode six winners in one day at Monmouth Park which equaled a previous record. At this point, she could no longer be ignored and was asked to race at Aqueduct in Queens, New York. On opening day, she won four races. In 1987, Krone was considered the sixth best jockey in the country, with 324 total wins. She won her 1,205th race on March 6, 1988, beating the record held by **Patricia Cooksey**. Krone was now the winningest woman jockey in history. Later that year, she defeated Willie Shoemaker, considered America's best jockey, in a match race. Krone was the first woman to participate in the annual Breeders' Cup races at Churchill Downs.

In 1988, she was the fourth leading rider in the U.S. and in 1989, she won more titles. At the end of 1989, a major spill at the Meadowlands left her with a shattered left arm, causing her to drop out for eight months, but as soon as she healed, Julie Krone was out of the starting gate. She was the first woman to ride in the Belmont Stakes on June 8, 1991. In June 1993, she won the Belmont Stakes aboard Colonial Affair, becoming the first woman to win the Triple Crown. That August, she became the third jockey to win five races in a day at the Saratoga Race Course. Angel Cordero, Jr., and Ron Turcotte were the

others. Ten days later at Saratoga, she went down in a spill, severely shattered her ankle, and suffered a cardiac contusion, but two plates and 14 screws later she returned to racing in May 1994.

Krone was injured once more at Gulfstream Park on January 13, 1995. Thrown from her horse, she broke both her hands and had a harder time regrouping; this time, she needed the help of a psychiatrist to "repair the damage." "While no other rider ever intimidated her, Krone admitted she had begun to lose some of her tenacity—some of her nerve," wrote *Sports Illustrated*. "When she returned to the race track again, she was more tentative than she'd ever been." In November 1999, Krone broke her right knee at the Meadowlands in a race that she won. She added two more winners that day before the fracture was diagnosed. After an 18-year career, Krone retired on April 8, 1999. That day, she had five races at Lone Star Park and had three wins, one second-place finish, and a third. "I'm on top, I'm 35 years old, and I don't want to do this anymore," she said. "I'd go to sleep at

Julie Krone

night, and my ankle hurt and my knee hurt and I'd think, 'I just want to get this over with.'"

With 3,546 wins out of 29,475 races, including 276 stakes, and over $81 million in purse earnings for a 16th place ranking in all-time earnings, Julie Krone put to rest any notions that women could not compete on the racetrack. In 2000, she became the first woman elected to racing's Hall of Fame.

SOURCES:

Callahan, Dorothy M. *Julie Krone: A Winning Jockey*. Minneapolis, MN: Dillon Press, 1990.

"Down the Bridal Path," in *People Weekly*. September 11, 1995.

"Going Out a Winner," CNN-Sports Illustrated (CNNSI.com). April 28, 1999.

"Julie Krone Rides Headlong into Racing's Record Books as the Winningest Woman Jockey," in *People Weekly*. May 2, 1988, pp. 111–114.

Virshup, Amy. "Reining Queen," in *New York*. Vol. 21, no. 24. June 13, 1988, pp. 46–50.

Woolum, Janet. *Outstanding Women Athletes: Who They Are and How They Influenced Sports in America*. Phoenix, AZ: Oryx Press, 1992.

Karin L. Haag,
freelance writer, Athens, Georgia

Krüdener, Julie de (1764–1824)

Russian writer, traveler, evangelist, and mystic whose career included a crucial encounter with Tsar Alexander I at the close of the Napoleonic wars which may have contributed to the formation of the postwar Holy Alliance. Name variations: Juliana de Krudener; Madame de Krüdener; Baroness von Krüdener. Pronunciation: CREW-de-ner. Born Barbara Juliana von Vietinghof on November 22, 1764, in Riga, a city in Livonia, which was a Baltic province of the Russian Empire; died, probably of cancer, in the town of Karasu-Bazar in the Crimea, December 24, 1824; daughter of Otto Hermann, Baron von Vietinghof (a landed noble and government official), and Countess Anna Ulrica von Münnich Vietinghof (granddaughter of a distinguished Russian military leader); educated, probably by governesses and private tutors; married Burchhard Alexis Constantine, Baron von Krüdener, in 1782; children: Paul (b. 1784); Juliette (b. 1787); (stepdaughter) Sophie.

Made first trip to Central and Western Europe (1777); made first trip to St. Petersburg and accompanied husband to Venice (1784); moved to Copenhagen (1786); began extended visit to France (1789); began love affair with the Marquis de Frégeville (1790); separated from husband, returned to Livonia (1792); began travels in Germany, Switzerland, and France, and met Jean Paul Richter (1796); published Valérie *in Paris (1804); had religious conversion in Livonia (1805); took on missionary work after battle of Eylau and visited Moravian Brethren (1807); met with Tsar Alexander I of Russia which may have contributed to formation of Treaty of the Holy Alliance (1815); occupied with missionary activities in Switzerland and Germany (1816–17); made final return to Riga (1818); journeyed to the Crimea (1824).*

Selected writings: Pensées d'une dame étrangère *(1802);* Valérie *(1804).*

The life of Baroness von Krüdener spanned the eventful age that extended from the second half of the 18th century through the first decades of the 19th century. She herself embodied, and perhaps influenced, several of the important trends of the time. Her early adult years were spent in the lively atmosphere and cosmopolitan environment of upper-class European society during the Enlightenment. She was an eyewitness to the horrors of Napoleonic warfare, and she underwent a religious conversion similar to that of many of her European contemporaries. In the most colorful episode of her life, her brief relationship with Tsar Alexander I of Russia, one of Napoleon's conquerors, may have influenced the political shape of Europe after 1815. In her final decade, her religious enthusiasm deepened into full-fledged mysticism with a tinge of social radicalism.

In the years after 1789, when a financial crisis had brought the French government to a halt and led to revolution, Europe was plunged into an era of turbulent political change. By the start of the 19th century, Napoleon, the French dictator who crowned himself emperor, was upsetting the political order throughout Europe. Only a powerful alliance of the existing monarchies, led by such figures as Tsar Alexander I, was able to bring Napoleon to bay in 1814 and, in 1815, to expel him from Europe permanently. These figures from the old order then had the responsibility of reconstructing a political system that would stabilize Europe after its quarter century of turmoil.

Within the intellectual and spiritual world, changes took place just as rapidly. Well before the outbreak of the French Revolution, the harshly critical, rational point of view that characterized the Enlightenment had given rise to a countermovement based upon feelings and spiritual values. This tendency was particularly evident in the writings of Jean-Jacques Rousseau. By the start of the 19th century, a religious revival was underway in many parts of Europe, led by such figures as René de Chateaubriand. It continued and intensified in the era of political conservatism that followed the fall of Napoleon.

Tsar Alexander I, with whom Madame de Krüdener is linked in European history, was one of the most complex and fascinating personalities standing in the midst of these events. His education had steeped him in the ideas of the Enlightenment. He came to power following the overthrow of his father Paul I, and he was psychologically devastated when the coup, which he had sanctioned, led to his father's murder.

The Russian leader had shown himself interested in the mystical religious currents of the time long before he met Madame de Krüdener, but he may have been particularly receptive to such views in 1815 and willing to place them in the world of politics. He had been shaken to the core by Napoleon's invasion of Russia in 1812, and he had turned to religion as a guide more forcefully than before. He now found himself in the heady position of the leading figure on the Allied side. Since the start of the century, at a time when Russia lacked the influence to put his plans into effect, Alexander had been promoting vague schemes pointing toward European unity.

Madame de Krüdener, as she is usually called, was born in the small, insular world of Russian Livonia. In this region along the Baltic coast, German conquerors had established sway over the local peasant population during the Middle Ages. The region came under Russian control at the start of the 18th century as a result of the military successes of Tsar Peter I the Great. Both of her parents came from the German nobility. Her father Otto Hermann, Baron von Vietinghof, was a landowner, government official, and patron of the arts. Her mother, **Anna Ulrica von Münnich Vietinghof**, was the granddaughter of a noted Russian general from the start of the century. Julie grew up in a privileged environment, dividing her time between the family's mansion in Riga and their country estate at Kosse. She apparently received her education from a series of tutors and governesses. The upper-class Livonian society of her childhood practiced the Lutheran religion, with some of its members, like her father, increasingly attracted by the freethinking of the Enlightenment. Nonetheless, more emotional varieties of Christianity, such as the Pietism practiced by the Moravian Brethren of Central Europe, had penetrated Livonia in the decades before her birth.

The Vietinghof family's comfortable lifestyle was disrupted by a number of factors. Julie's elder sister was a deaf mute, and her mother's grandfather, despite his military honors, had been forced into a prolonged period of exile in Siberia. In 1777, the family, including Julie, trav-

eled to Hamburg to place her sister in an institution; they then went on to Paris where she caught her first glimpse of the center of European culture.

In 1782, Julie's life took a turn when she married Burchhard Alexis Constantine, Baron von Krüdener. The young woman, not yet 18, now had a husband of 36, who was a rising figure in the Russian diplomatic service. As a consequence, she found herself in increasingly cosmopolitan circles: she entertained the future Tsar Paul, she was surrounded by enthusiasts immersed in French literature and ideas, and she soon accompanied her husband to increasingly important diplomatic posts: first Venice, then Copenhagen. The marriage was one of convenience rather than passion, although she gave birth to a son, Paul, in 1784, and a daughter, Juliette, in 1787.

Julie de Krüdener

In Venice, Alexander de Stakiev, a young member of her husband's entourage, became infatuated with Julie. The attraction was never consummated, and Stakiev, while serving the Baron de Krüdener in Copenhagen, confessed his passion to Julie's husband in 1787. More than a decade later, the incident provided the theme for her famous novel *Valérie*.

In the spring of 1789, due to her fragile health, Julie left for a stay in southern France. She reached Paris as the French Revolution was beginning and plunged into the literary world there and in the cities of the south. In Montpellier, she had a love affair with a young French officer of aristocratic lineage, Charles de Frégeville. Her husband refused her request for a divorce, but he agreed to a separation. She was required, however, to end the romantic liaison and return to Livonia. She did so in 1792.

Madame de Krüdener was an independently wealthy woman with an income based on an estate her father had given her shortly before her wedding. In the next years, she traveled widely in Germany and Switzerland. This was a region coming under the shadow of the rising military genius, Napoleon Bonaparte. Standing in a crowd in 1797, Julie saw the brilliant young general for the first time as he passed through the Swiss city of Lausanne. With only intermittent contact with her husband, she may have become involved in a number of love affairs. In 1802, she and her husband formally ended their marriage. He died less than a year later.

Madame de Krüdener's commitment to a literary career took shape in the first years of the new century. Working both in Paris and in Switzerland, she first produced a small work, *Pensées d'une dame étrangère* (*Thoughts of a Foreign Lady*), that appeared in the *Mercure de France* in 1802. Her personal, as well as her literary, connections allowed her easy entry into the literary salons of Paris.

> *She had the passionate and powerful charm of an inspired person.*
> —Ernst Moritz Arndt

Valérie, which appeared in 1804, was set in Venice and was told in the form of a series of letters. The novel tells the story of a junior diplomat from Scandinavia, much like the young man who had loved her from afar in Venice in the early 1780s, who serves as secretary to an aristocratic ambassador. The hero follows the events in the life of the noble's wife with fervor, but he cannot declare his love for her openly until he is fatally ill. The ambassador then finds and nurses the young man, seeing him through to death and burial. Critics have noted how the book borrows from prominent themes in the literature of the era as expressed in the work of Rousseau and Johann Wolfgang von Goethe. It also drew on the religious fervor stimulated by Chateaubriand's *Genius of Christianity.* Krüdener's biographer Ernest Knapton finds particular significance in the hero's exposure to religion, seeing this part of the novel as an indication of the spiritual fervor of its author. She apparently had found belief in God a consolation for the bouts of melancholy that accompanied her wanderings around Europe.

Although her first novel enjoyed substantial commercial success and drew a measure of praise from literary critics, Madame de Krüdener did not remain in Paris. A variety of factors, including a failed love affair, friction with fellow writers, and her easily overstressed emotional makeup, led her to return to Livonia. There, in 1804 and 1805, her life took its decisive turn toward religion. At this time, she lived both in Riga and at her country estate at Kosse. In the commonplace event of buying a pair of shoes, she was struck by the serenity of the cobbler with whom she was dealing. She then accepted

his invitation to attend meetings of the Moravian Brotherhood to which he belonged, and her conversion followed in short order. The noblewoman's physical exhaustion, the atmosphere of religious enthusiasm which she had encountered in France, and the growing spiritual interests she demonstrated in *Valérie* provide a partial explanation for this seemingly remarkable turn in her life. Some writers note that she was also traumatized by the sudden death of an acquaintance whom she had just greeted from the window of her house in Riga.

By late 1806, Krüdener was back Germany, possibly with the aim of visiting a spa for her health. At the East Prussian city of Königsberg, she found herself in the midst of one of Napoleon's military campaigns. It led to the brutally indecisive battle of Eylau in February 1807, and here Krüdener transformed her religious devotion into good works such as caring for the wounded. As one observer recalled, "We all loved this unusual woman and took pleasure in the radiant nature that revealed itself in all that she said."

In her subsequent travels in Central Europe, Krüdener visited the communities inhabited by the Moravian Brethren and became acquainted with Johann Heinrich Jung-Stilling, counselor to the grand duke of Baden, and the Protestant minister John Frederick Fontanes; both would be her spiritual mentors or companions in the following years. The Brethren's Pietist doctrines in which she was increasingly immersed proclaimed the ability of man to reach directly to God without the use of reason, as well as the imminence of Christ's Second Coming. Such beliefs had a strong influence in southern Germany, Switzerland, and Alsace. At the same time, her aristocratic background kept her in contact with some of the leading political circles of the time. One figure in those circles who became her friend was *Hortense de Beauharnais (1783–1837), the queen of Holland and Napoleon's stepdaughter.

For a time in early 1809, Julie de Krüdener joined a spiritual community in the village of Cleebronn, southwest of the German city of Heilbronn. Its leader was Fontanes, a charismatic minister of Pietist leanings, whom Julie had visited at length at his parish in Alsace. When the government of Württemberg expelled the group, Madame de Krüdener used her influence to secure a new home for them in the neighboring state of Baden. Her religious fervor deepened. In a letter she wrote to Fontanes from Riga in late 1811, she pointed out the flaws of both Catholicism and Protestantism. Devotees of the former were consumed in ceremonies; adherents to the latter were led astray by the use of reason. She looked to a newly reunited Christianity that would offer a spiritual satisfaction neither of the two could provide.

In the years following, her travels in Central Europe and her personal life once again connected with the great political events of the time. As the combined armies of Napoleon's opponents chased him across Europe and back to France in 1813, Madame de Krüdener and her colleagues began a campaign of spreading religious pamphlets to win over the rank-and-file soldiers in the Allied forces. In the following year, she renewed her acquaintance with Hortense de Beauharnais, who introduced Krüdener to her brother, Eugène Beauharnais. These imperial refugees, the stepson and stepdaughter of the recently deposed Napoleon, had taken refuge in Baden. They were partly shocked, partly amused, when Madame de Krüdener greeted them with an emotional speech setting out her religious beliefs.

Julie's passionate interest centered, however, on Tsar Alexander I. Since early 1814, she had been impressed by his public statements thanking God for the Allied victory over Napoleon. Thus, she welcomed the opportunity to become friends with **Roxane Stourdza**, a transplanted Rumanian who served as attendant to the tsar's wife *Elizabeth of Baden (1779–1826). On one occasion in 1814, Julie wrote Roxane that "I have known for a long time that the Lord will give me the pleasure of seeing" Alexander, and, she added momentously, "I have tremendous things to say to him."

Such emotional letters had their effect. Roxane, whose brother was Alexander's private secretary, sent the letters on to the tsar who expressed an interest in meeting Julie. The fateful encounter took place in the midst of an overwhelming political crisis. In the spring of 1815, Napoleon escaped from his place of exile on the island of Elba near the Italian coast. The tsar's forces and other Allied armies rushed toward France in preparation for the inevitable military encounter. Two weeks before the confrontation at Waterloo on June 18, 1815, Alexander was traveling across Bavaria and stopped at Heilbronn. Joining the crowd in front of the house where he was resting, Krüdener demanded to see the tsar and managed to get a message to him. He responded by calling her into his presence.

Madame de Krüdener's conversation with Alexander on the evening of June 4, 1815, is the most interesting and significant event in her life.

It initiated a period in which she touched on some of the great political questions of the era. Historians remain uncertain why Alexander decided to see her and what was said during their meeting. An account later published by one of her followers described a conversation in which she stressed how both of them were sinners; she, however, had succeeded in purging herself of sin. Presumably, he needed to do the same. Their meetings continued for several weeks while the tsar remained in Germany. After Napoleon had been defeated at Waterloo, Alexander invited Krüdener to follow him to Paris, where their meetings resumed. She became a public sensation on September 11, 1815, when he invited her to stand beside him during a huge review of the Russian army. An impressed observer was the French woman of letters *Germaine de Staël. She wrote a friend to describe Krüdener as "the forerunner of a great religious epoch which is dawning for the human race."

During the ensuing peace negotiations, the tsar presented the leaders of the other great pow-

Mme. de Krüdener with her son.

ers with a vague but provocative proposal pointing toward a united Europe. This Treaty of Holy Alliance mixed politics and religion in remarkable fashion, calling on the rulers of Austria, Prussia, and Russia to remain linked after the war in "a true and indissoluble brotherhood," as three branches of a common Christian family. Alexander called on them to rule that family with justice. To his biographer **Janet Hartley**, Alexander's language in this document was typically ambiguous and carelessly drafted; he had little appreciation of the idea's political consequences. Given the military and diplomatic weight of Russia at this time, however, no one could ignore the proposal.

To conservatives like Prince Clemens von Metternich, the Holy Alliance was both perplexing and dangerous. The full draft of the tsar's proposal seemed to raise the possibility that other countries, not just the great powers, would be brought into some kind of union. It also raised the issue of a common bond among the peoples, not just the rulers, of Europe. The Austrian diplomat moved quickly to alter or eliminate such phrases, which smacked to him of the ideas of the French Revolution. In its revised form, the treaty was signed by the rulers of Austria and Prussia on September 26, 1815.

Given Alexander's longstanding religious interests and his frequent earlier calls for a league of European states, recent historians refrain from identifying Madame de Krüdener as the inspiration behind the Holy Alliance. Moreover, its practical significance remains doubtful. The three great conservative powers of Central and Eastern Europe did in fact cooperate for several decades after 1815. But it was on the basis of other, more conventional international agreements, such as the Quadruple Alliance of 1815, which centered on the goal of preventing future French aggression.

The final decade of Madame de Krüdener's life saw her increasingly at odds with the political authorities of the time. Her missionary activities in Switzerland and several German states took place against a background of crop failures and famine. Her enthusiastic rhetoric about how the poor would inherit the earth, sometimes appearing in pamphlets that she and her followers published and distributed widely, seemed dangerously radical to local governmental officials. In one memorable talk she gave at Frankfurt-on-the-Oder, she referred to the devil's servants on earth and identified them as the police officers and customs agents of the time. Thus it is easy to see how, at the highest levels of European con-

servative leadership, Count von Metternich expressed his alarm at her teachings. Meanwhile, local religious leaders in Protestant regions objected to her use of Catholic practices such as appeals to *Mary the Virgin.

Expelled first from Switzerland, then from one German state after another, the aging evangelist suffered from declining health. The hardships of travel and preaching in the face of official disapproval sharply reduced the number of followers who accompanied her. One scholar who met her and her group in Saxony at this time wrote a poignant account of his reaction. He found it painful to see her trying to combine "so much heavenly goodness with such strange beliefs." In his view, she seemed to show how a world "addicted for so long to a frivolous enlightenment . . . was now reeling into mystical fanaticism and unintelligent superstition."

In the summer of 1818, she returned for the last time to Russia. At the border, her anomalous position as both a well-connected aristocrat and a religious fanatic under police supervision came to the fore. Russian authorities at the frontier were reluctant to admit the foreigners in her band of followers. She solved the problem by a direct appeal to her old acquaintance, Tsar Alexander I. The monarch refused to answer her directly, but he ordered that her party be admitted to his realm without further delay. Back at her estate at Kosse, Krüdener continued her missionary activity among the local peasantry. As usual, both local government officials and church leaders viewed all this with growing hostility.

In 1821, she paid a final visit to St. Petersburg in order to see her seriously ill son-in-law. Although the tsar had given permission for her trip to the capital, it is unlikely the two met. The only certain contact they had was over a political issue that led to a harsh rebuke for the baroness. She urged Alexander to support the Greek rebellion against the Turks that had begun in the spring of that year. He responded through one of his officials demanding that she refrain from comments on politics. She returned to her estate in the summer of 1822.

Following her arrival home, Julie de Krüdener's health continued to falter. Practices tied to her religious beliefs, including deliberate exposure to hunger and cold weather, further weakened her frail physical condition. In these personal circumstances, she made a typically dramatic decision in the spring of 1824: she would participate in founding a Christian colony in the Crimea. Traveling by river boat and sailing vessel, her party of settlers reached the Crimea in August. By this time, the baroness was so seriously ill that she could go no further. Cared for by her daughter, she lived out the last months of her life as an invalid in the small town of Karasu-Bazar. She died there on Christmas Eve, 1824.

Within a few years, several of her followers published accounts that established a vivid picture of Madame de Krüdener and her activities. They stressed her role in bringing the Holy Alliance into existence as well as her personal devoutness. In 1848, for example, an early biographer named Charles Eynard portrayed her life as a single, dramatic voyage that stretched from her years as a cosmopolitan aristocrat to a final status of saintliness. Her American biographer Ernest Knapton has analyzed the colorful baroness in more prosaic terms. He described her as "a natural product of her times," sharing the changing intellectual environment and swept along by great trends in the worlds of politics, literature, and religion that she could not fully understand. For him, her vast travels and broad range of acquaintances were astonishing. In the end, however, "she was one of those who mirrored rather than directed the tendencies of an age."

SOURCES:
Hartley, Janet M. *Alexander I.* London: Longman, 1994.

Herold, J. Christopher. *Mistress to an Age: A Life of Madame de Staël.* Indianapolis, IN: Bobbs-Merrill, 1958.

Knapton, Ernest John. *The Lady of the Holy Alliance: The Life of Julie de Krüdener.* 1939 (reprinted, NY: AMS Press, 1966).

Lincoln, W. Bruce. *The Romanovs: Autocrats of All the Russias.* NY: Dial Press, 1981.

SUGGESTED READING:
Gollin, Gillian Lindt. *Moravians in Two Worlds: A Study of Changing Communities.* NY: Columbia University Press, 1967.

Ley, Francis. *Madame de Krüdener: Romanticisme et Sainte-Alliance.* Paris: Champion, 1994.

Palmer, Alan. *Metternich.* NY: Harper and Row, 1972.

Sheehan, James J. *German History, 1770–1866.* Oxford: Clarendon Press, 1989.

COLLECTIONS:
Correspondence and papers located in Bibliothéque Nationale and Archives Nationale, Paris; and Bibliothéque Publique et Universitaire, Geneva.

Neil M. Heyman,
Professor of History,
San Diego State University, San Diego, California

Krull, Germaine (1897–1985)

Polish-born photographer who specialized in portraits, documentaries, industrial fashions, and advertising. Born in Wilda-Poznan, Poland, in 1897; died in Wetzlar, West Germany, in 1985; educated in Paris; studied photography at Bayerische Staatslehranstalt für Lichtbildwesen, Munich, Germany, 1916–18; married Joris Ivens (a filmmaker); no children.

Born in Poland in 1897 to German parents, photographer Germaine Krull studied photography in Germany and began her career as a portrait photographer in Munich and Berlin. From 1921 to 1924, she freelanced in the Netherlands, photographing architecture and industry. Around 1924, she married Dutch filmmaker Joris Ivens and moved to Paris, where she worked for such major French magazines as *Vu, Arts et métiers graphiques, Marianne,* and *Voilà.* She also associated with many of the avant-garde artists and writers of her day, including photographers *Berenice Abbott and Man Ray. Krull was the only photographer to exhibit in the 1926 Salon D'Automne in Paris, and her industrial photographs appeared in the book *Métal* (1927). In 1929, she was represented in the influential *Film and Foto* exhibition in Stuttgart, Germany.

After 1935, Krull lived in the south of France, but traveled widely in Europe on commercial and journalistic assignments. During World War II, she was accredited as a war correspondent and photographed for Free French publications in Africa, Germany, and Italy. After the war, she opened an Oriental Hotel in Bangkok, but continued to work on a freelance basis, making trips to Thailand, Burma, Nepal, India, and Tibet. From 1965 to the early 1980s, she lived with the Tibetan refugees in northern India and became a friend of the Dalai Lama. Her final years were spent in Wetzlar, Germany, where she died in 1985.

SOURCES:
Rosenblum, Naomi. *History of Women Photographers.* NY: Abbeville Press, 1994.

Barbara Morgan,
Melrose, Massachusetts

Krupp, Bertha (1886–1957)

German heiress to the Krupp armaments fortune and one of the richest individuals in Europe, who played a significant, if discreet, role in directing her family's enterprises during much of the 20th century. Pronunciation: Krupp rhymes with loop. Name variations: Bertha von Krupp; Bertha Krupp von Bohlen und Halbach. Born Bertha Krupp in March 1886 at the family home in Essen, a city in the Ruhr Valley region of Germany; died in Essen of a heart attack on September 21, 1957; daughter of Friedrich (Fritz) Krupp (a leading German industrialist) and Margarethe (von Ende) Krupp (a Prussian civil servant's daughter); at-

tended finishing school in Baden-Baden; married Gustav von Bohlen und Halbach, in 1906 (died 1950): children: Alfried von Bohlen und Halbach (1907–1967, who married Anneliese Bahr and Vera Hossenfeldt); Berthold von Bohlen und Halbach (b. 1913, who married Edith von Maltzan); Arnold von Bohlen und Halbach (1908–1909); Claus von Bohlen und Halbach (1910–1940); Irmgard von Bohlen und Halbach (b. 1912, who married Hanno Raitz von Frenz); Harald von Bohlen und Halbach (b. 1916, who married Doerte Hillringhaus); Waldtraut von Bohlen und Halbach (b. 1920); Eckbert von Bohlen und Halbach (1922–1945).

Became heiress to the Krupp fortune (1902); entertained Kaiser Wilhelm II at Krupp centennial (1912); saw first use of "Big Bertha" cannon in attack on Belgium (1914); her husband arrested by French occupiers of Ruhr (1923); opposed husband's conversion to Nazism (1933); Hitler made first visit to Krupp factory (1934); her husband decorated by Hitler (1940); her husband suffered his first stroke (1941); her firm granted special status by Hitler with the Lex Krupp *(Krupp Law, 1943); fled from Essen to Austrian Alps, while her sister was arrested following failed plot on Hitler's life (1944); arrest of her son Alfried by American authorities (1945); Alfried convicted of war crimes (1948); with death of husband, petitioned for return of her fortune (1950); Alfried released from prison (1951); Konrad Adenauer visited Krupps (1953); return of son Harald from Russian prison-of-war camp (1955).*

Bertha Krupp was the heiress to the great German armaments fortune established by her grandfather, Alfred Krupp. From 1902 onward, as one of the richest individuals in Europe, her role in the affairs of her country was generally discreet: she was always in the position of a privileged bystander to great events. Starting in 1914, she became famous throughout the world as the woman whose name was attached to the "Big Bertha" cannon employed in World War I. Her most visible role was to carry out a Krupp tradition by which the women of the family performed charitable works toward the company's workers and their families. Nonetheless, she was a circumspect but significant power behind the scenes in decisions about the massive family business. In the troubled years after World War I, she apparently had a significant role in determining the direction of the great industrial enterprise of which she was the legal owner. But while she was a potent force in the 1920s, Bertha Krupp saw her influence fade during the Nazi years

from 1933 to 1945. In the aftermath of World War II, however, she once again helped to direct the family fortune and the vast influence that came with it.

The Krupp family had its origins in the Rhineland city of Essen. As early as the era of the Thirty Years' War in the mid-17th century, one of Bertha Krupp's ancestors was in the business of selling weapons. The fortunes of the Krupps varied over the next 200 years. At one point, they were one of the wealthiest families in Essen. But, by the close of the 18th century, poor management had reduced the family's fortunes and its civic reputation.

In 1807, Friedrich Krupp, Bertha's great-grandfather and the family's pioneer in the making of steel, took over an iron works owned by his mother **Petronella Forsthof Krupp** (1757–1839). Eight years later, as a consequence of the territorial settlement reached at the Congress of Vienna, Essen became a part of the Kingdom of Prussia. Friedrich died in 1826. His son Alfred, who lived just long enough to see the birth of his granddaughter Bertha, brought the family's industrial empire into existence.

Alfred produced his first steel cannon in 1847. Ironically, it was the production of steel for the growing network of German railroads that made the family rich and made Krupp products famous. Moreover, much of his general business, as well as orders for arms, came from customers outside Prussia. Only in 1859 did he get his first substantial order for Krupp cannons from the Prussian government. When Austria and Prussia went to war in 1866, the future of Germany was in play. Prussia's victory at the Battle of Königgrätz in July 1866 paved the way for unification under Prussian leadership. But Krupp's weapons played only a minor role in Prussian success on the battlefield.

In the aftermath of the war, however, the Prussian army, as well as the new Prussian navy, began to rely on Krupp weapons. According to Krupp legend, the German victory in the Franco-Prussian War of 1870–71, which created a united Germany, was due to Krupp equipment. Even if this is an exaggeration, Krupp now became famous as the arms maker most responsible for German military power.

The new German Empire, ruled by Kaiser Wilhelm I and directed by Prime Minister Otto von Bismarck, became the major power within the European international system. Germany's military system remained the most potent as well as one of the largest on the Continent. The

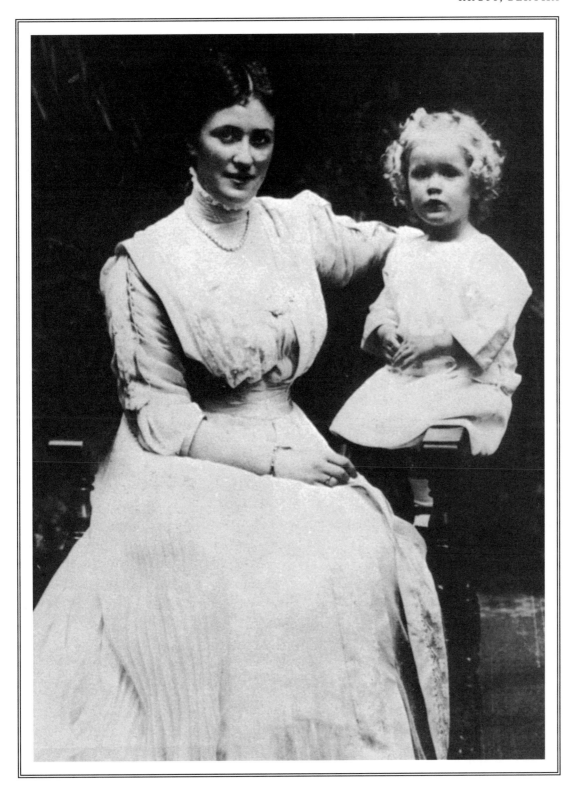

Krupp enterprises thrived on orders from the German government, and Krupp managers could point to those orders in appealing to arms buyers throughout the world. In 1905, George Bernard Shaw satirized the Krupps and their industrial empire in the play *Major Barbara*.

Bertha Krupp was born in March 1886 in Essen. She grew up in the family's vast residence, the Villa Hügel, outside the industrial city that her family dominated. By that time, her grandfather was one of the richest men in Europe, and the Krupp enterprises employed 21,000 workers. The Villa Hügel, with its 200 rooms and its twin castles, was a symbol of the newly acquired family wealth. The young girl received the meager education thought suitable for a European heiress. She attended a finishing school at Baden-Baden, along with other young girls from privileged families. The curriculum stressed horseback riding and the skills a wealthy female would need in meeting her family's social obligations. A plain young woman with a thin figure and cold blue eyes, she seemed to have drawn her features from Alfred, her grandfather, rather than from her pudgy father. She and her sister were raised under the strong influence of her mother, who seemed, as Bertha once put it, "infallible to us in every respect." Her father was only rarely present.

The Kaiser . . . addressed her on her wedding day, and Hitler . . . kissed her hand.

—Norbert Muhlen

Family scandal disrupted her girlhood. In November 1902, when she was only 16, Bertha received word of her father's sudden death. Fritz Krupp had been implicated in an ugly scandal. He reputedly conducted intimate liaisons with young Italian boys at his villa in Capri. As the scandal grew, Bertha's mother **Margarethe Krupp** had become sufficiently alarmed to appeal to the kaiser for help. The monarch responded by encouraging Fritz to put Margarethe into a clinic for the mentally ill. Biographers of the family agree that their marriage had broken down long before. At the close of November, a Socialist newspaper in Berlin published the full story of the scandal, and Krupp replied with legal action. In the midst of the uproar, he was found dying in the Villa Hügel. All of the evidence pointed to suicide.

An established Krupp tradition called for the eldest child to receive all of the family's properties. By her father's will, Bertha now inherited the Krupp fortune, thereby becoming the richest woman in Germany and one of the wealthiest individuals in Europe. Her mother was empowered to sign the crucial documents required for the firm's operation and expansion, and the Krupp board of directors determined policies. The board included bankers, former government officials, and an admiral with close personal ties to German emperor Wilhelm II.

In the following years, Margarethe Krupp continued an established policy that Bertha would take up in turn: by tradition, the leading woman in the family directed the company's welfare policies designed to benefit Krupp's workers and their families. Such efforts were particularly important to distract public attention from the scandal of Fritz's death. Moreover, they drew the public's eyes away from the deadly products that the firm made and sold to all comers.

The most important event for Bertha in the years after her father's death was her marriage to a young German diplomat. Gustav von Bohlen und Halbach, to whom Bertha became engaged in May 1906, was the descendant of a Rhineland family that had made its fortune in metal manufacturing in the 18th century. Gustav's great-grandfather had settled in Pennsylvania and prospered in the coal and iron business; Gustav's grandfather had died a heroic death fighting in the Union Army during the Civil War; and his father had returned to Germany to take up a diplomatic career. Historians believe that Gustav was the emperor's personal choice for Bertha's spouse. An energetic but unimaginative manager, he was likely to direct Krupp's activities in a way that suited the German government.

Bertha's wedding had political overtones, and the emperor attended. It was only his second visit to Essen since the death of Fritz Krupp. When the German monarch spoke at the young couple's wedding reception, he urged them to continue "to supply our German Fatherland with offensive and defensive weapons . . . unapproached by those of any other nation." He specifically granted Gustav the right to add the name Krupp to his own name, thereby becoming Gustav Krupp von Bohlen and Halbach. Bertha too adopted the new combination.

Bertha had Alfried, her first child and the heir to the family fortune, a year later. In a new mark of the link between the Krupp enterprises and the rulers of Germany, Wilhelm II stood as young Alfried's godfather. Meanwhile, the Krupp family, including Bertha, now found its existence dominated by Gustav. He directed both the family business and the household management with an obsessive concern for detail. Rooms in the family villa were kept at the cold temperature he preferred; meals proceeded at breakneck speed to match his personal preference for quick dining. Bertha joined in the obsessive effort to direct the household. She stayed up nights to make sure that the male and female servants did not violate family rules and creep across the bridge separating their quarters. And she fired on the spot any servant unfortunate enough to be caught in such activities. Moreover, she played a central role in the lavish entertaining the family conducted. A stellar example of such activities was the three-day centennial celebration of the first Krupp steel factory in November 1912, at which Bertha entertained both Prime Minister Theobald von Bethmann-Hollweg and Kaiser Wilhelm II. But it is likely that Fritz Krupp's daughter played more than the role of hostess to the nation's leaders. Observers behind the scenes noted that she had substantial influence in directing the firm's affairs. Gustav may have been the manager of the great set of enterprises, but, as biographer Norbert Muhlen notes, "she remained the steely queen of Kruppdom."

With the onset of World War I, Krupp became the arms supplier *par excellence* to imperial Germany. Even before 1914, the firm was the most favored arms maker in Germany, but much of its production had gone to other countries. Now, the weapons it made, ranging from cannon to submarines, went exclusively to Germany and Germany's allies such as Turkey and Bulgaria.

Bertha's name was attached to one such weapon. "Big Bertha" was a huge mobile mortar capable of firing a giant projectile of several thousand pounds at an enemy nine miles away. It played a crucial role in breaking down Belgian defenses in 1914, thus allowing the German army to sweep into northern France in the war's first great campaign. According to her brother-in-law, Krupp had not been enthusiastic about having such a weapon named after her. "She took it with resignation," he said.

As the war came to an end, Bertha and the other Krupps faced threats from both Germans and foreigners. The family fortified itself in the Villa Hügel in the first weeks of November 1918 as revolutionary workers took power in Essen. For a time, such radicals even threatened to seize and socialize Krupp enterprises. Shortly afterward, by the terms of the Treaty of Versailles, the military power of the German state was severely limited. The Krupp enterprises had to struggle through years of meager earnings. Neither Gustav nor Bertha seemed able to find a solution to the firm's difficulties.

In 1923, the French army invaded the Ruhr region, including Essen, to punish Germany for not making scheduled reparations payments. Gustav was arrested, and he remained imprisoned for seven months. Nonetheless, Krupp enterprises continued to exist. By the mid-1920s, a stream of American investment dollars was helping German industry recover, and Krupp shared in the economic surge. The factories shifted to profitable nonmilitary production in the Krupps' homeland. More ominously, arms development and manufacture went on in disguised fashion

elsewhere: non-German companies, partially owned by Krupp, operated in neighboring countries like Holland, Switzerland, and Sweden. Gustav directed these efforts, but it seems unlikely they went on without Bertha Krupp's knowledge.

The Nazi era arrived in 1933. Gustav had been less than enthusiastic about the Nazis before they were in power; in 1928, Hitler had not even been permitted to visit the huge Krupp factory at Essen. With the onset of the new political order, however, Gustav became one of its most avid supporters. Hitler was received at the Krupp steel factory with enthusiasm in June 1934, with Bertha's eldest daughter, **Irmgard von Bohlen und Halbach**, presenting him with a welcoming bouquet. He now visited the Krupp factories regularly. In August 1940, on Gustav's 70th birthday, Hitler personally decorated him with the Nazi Party's highest civilian award. By this point in the Krupp saga, however, Bertha and Gustav's eldest son, Alfried, was the driving force at the firm. A member of the Nazi Party since 1938, Alfried remained at home to carry out his industrial tasks while his brothers went off to fight in 1939.

Bertha disliked Hitler, and among trusted company she was daring enough to make her views clear. An event like the replacement of the Krupp family flag by the Nazi swastika above Villa Hügel outraged her. Her most consistent criticism of the Nazis was that they dominated the operation of the Krupp enterprises, removing decisions from the family's hands. She was apparently just as offended by Hitler's lower-middle-class background. Nonetheless, her personal feelings did not disrupt the close links between the Krupp enterprises and the German government. She may have been consoled by the family's growing wealth as government orders poured in. The firm's annual profits, which made up her personal income, increased tenfold between 1935 and 1939.

The Second World War put Krupp at the forefront of German miliary industry once more. Krupp tanks and Krupp submarines helped Germany come close to victory. But World War II also brought a number of painful blows to the Krupp family. Two of Bertha's sons died in the war. A third son was captured by the Soviet army in 1944 and spent 11 years in prison camp. Essen, and particularly the three square miles of the city occupied by Krupp factories, was one of the most heavily bombed areas in Germany. Bertha opened the rooms of the Villa Hügel to house key Krupp executives who had been bombed out of their homes. Most important of all, Krupp's use of slave labor tainted the company's reputation in what seemed an irreparable way.

In November 1943, Bertha consented to a fundamental shift in the nature of the Krupp holdings. To keep the ownership of Krupp enterprises permanently within the family, Gustav convinced Hitler to give the family firm special status via the *Lex Krupp* (Krupp Law). Krupp enterprises would no longer be subject to inheritance taxes; all the properties, which had traditionally been in the hands of the senior family member, would now pass to a single heir free of charge. As part of the new arrangement, Bertha gave up her ownership of the firm and passed it to Alfried.

In 1944, the family skirted the edge of deadly danger. One of Krupp's directors had ties to Carl Goerdeler, the mayor of Leipzig and a member of the July plot to assassinate Hitler. Bertha's younger sister, **Barbara Krupp** (b. 1887), as well as Barbara's husband, were caught up in the Nazi roundup of those connected to Goerdeler. Bertha was able to aid them only in small ways such as smuggling food to them during their confinement. Meanwhile, to escape the unrelenting bombing of Essen, Bertha and her husband fled to their summer castle at Blühnbach. Located in the Alps near Salzburg, it offered some measure of safety.

With the end of the war, Allied authorities arrested Alfried. While the Villa Hügel had escaped destruction, most of the city of Essen was in ruins. One English correspondent stated simply that the city "is just a chaos of burned-out, broken masonry and twisted ironwork." The Allies requisitioned Villa Hügel and transformed it into the headquarters of the North German Coal Control Commission. Bertha's bedroom now housed one of the Allied officials. The Allies made it clear that the Krupp industrial empire was slated to be destroyed for all time.

At war's end, Bertha and Gustav were at Blühnbach. The Allies also commandeered that castle, and the Krupps had to make do with the nearby servants' quarters. They remained there for the next five years. Gustav had been increasingly incapacitated by a series of strokes beginning in 1941; Bertha now devoted her days to nursing him.

In 1947, Alfried and 11 other key executives of the family firm went on trial for war crimes. Gustav Krupp, senile and immobile, was not considered healthy enough to be tried. Alfried was convicted in July 1948 and sentenced to 12 years' imprisonment. His property, the great set of Krupp enterprises, was declared confiscated.

The year in which Alfried was convicted and sentenced also saw the United States commit itself to Germany's economic recovery. The disintegration of the wartime alliance with the Soviet Union and the growth of Communism in France and Italy made it appear essential to Washington to strengthen Germany. In this new political environment, Bertha Krupp made an imaginative, although unsuccessful, stab at regaining the family property. She tried, in January 1950, to induce the Allies to set aside the *Lex Krupp* of 1943. Claiming Hitler had forced the family to accept it, she now tried to remove Alfried from the picture to gain title to Krupp property for herself and her other children. The effort failed.

In the new political environment, Alfried was released from prison in early 1951, and Bertha was soon welcoming her eldest son when he traveled to Blühnbach. At the start of 1953, an agreement between Alfried and the governments of the U.S., Britain, and France allowed the Krupps to resume most of their industrial activities.

When Gustav died in 1950, the widowed Bertha soon abandoned their modest home near Salzburg and returned to Essen. She resumed the social chores that Krupp women had always carried out, greeting such prominent visitors to Villa Hügel as the Shah of Iran. In the view of biographer Peter Batty, Alfried was uncomfortable with her presence. He believed that, in the public mind, she was a constant reminder of the role Krupp had played in World War I and World War II.

To the outside world, she remained the remote, somewhat forbidding figure who appeared only on ceremonial occasions. Nonetheless, her last years brought one more moment of high drama. On October 11, 1955, she learned that her son Harald, who had disappeared while serving on the eastern front and been given up for dead, was now home. After more than a decade as a prisoner of war in Soviet hands, he was back, a member of the final group of Germans returning home from Siberia.

The woman who had known Germany's leaders for more than half a century and been immortalized by the name of a World War I cannon died of a heart attack in Essen on September 21, 1957. She was stricken while preparing for her daily activity of visiting the widow of a deceased Krupp worker. Despite her immersion in charitable efforts, Bertha had remained a living link to an embarrassing past. A young generation of Krupps, led by Alfried, were busy restoring the family fortune. Thus, as Batty put it, her passing probably brought a sense of relief. Despite Alfried's personal loss when she passed away, Bertha's death "must nevertheless have made it that little bit easier for him to throw off his history."

SOURCES:

Batty, Peter. *The House of Krupp*. NY: Stein and Day, 1967.

Manchester, William. *The Arms of Krupp, 1587–1968*. Boston, MA: Little, Brown.

Muhlen, Norbert. *The Incredible Krupps: The Rise, Fall, and Comeback of Germany's Industrial Family*. NY: Henry Holt, 1959.

SUGGESTED READING:

Fielding, Gabriel. *The Birthday King: A Romance*. NY: William Morrow, 1963.

Von Klass, Gert. *Krupps: The Story of an Industrial Empire*. Translated by James Cleugh. London: Sidgwick and Jackson, 1954.

RELATED MEDIA:

The Damned (155 min.), fictionalized account of a German industrial family in the Nazi era based on the experience of the Krupps, starring Dirk Bogarde and *Ingrid Thulin, directed by Luchino Visconti, Warner Bros., 1970.

Neil M. Heyman,
Professor of History,
San Diego State University, San Diego, California

Krupskaya, Nadezhda (1869–1939)

Russian educator, writer, Marxist revolutionary, and wife of Vladimir Ilyich Lenin, who took on Stalin but was powerless to stop him. Name variations: N.K. Krupskaya; Nadya Krupskaia; Nadya Lenin. Pronunciation: NA-de-AH KROOP-skay-yah. Born Nadezhda Konstantinovna Krupskaya on February 26, 1869, in St. Petersburg, Russia; died on February 27, 1939, in Moscow; daughter of Konstantin Ignatevich Krupsky and Elizaveta Tistrova Krupskaya; attended Prince A.A. Obolensky Female Gymnasium and University of St. Petersburg; married Vladimir Ilyich Ulianov or Ulyanov later known as Vladimir Ilyich Lenin (Russian revolutionary), in 1899 (died 1924); no children.

Awarded a gold medal for academic excellence (1882); left University of St. Petersburg (1890); met Lenin (1894); arrested (1895); sentenced to three years' internal exile (1898); published first Marxist work on the emancipation of women (1899); endured foreign exile (1901–05); served as editorial secretary of Iska (1901–03); served as editorial secretary of Vpered and The Proletarian (1903–05); returned to Russia (1905); lived in exile (1907–17); treated for thyroid disease (1913); headed Commission for the Aid of Russian Prisoners of War (1915); returned to Russia (1917); elected to Vyborg Soviet (1917); became commissar for Adult Education (1918); Lenin shot (1918); Lenin's first stroke (1922); Lenin died (January 21, 1924); signed manifesto against Stalin's agricultural policy (1925); developed a heart condition (1925); supported Stalin (1927); was a member of the Central Committee (1927); served as deputy commissar of education (1929); was a member of the Soviet Academy of Sciences (1931); served as deputy of the Supreme Soviet (1937).

Selected publications: The Woman Worker *(1899);* Public Education and Democracy *(1915);* Memories of Lenin *(1930);* Soviet Woman: A Citizen with Equal Rights *(1937).*

On Shrove Tuesday, 1894, a small gathering was held at the home of an engineer in St. Petersburg. Anyone who looked in would have seen a typical pancake party in progress, like thousands of others being held across the city to celebrate the holiday. This festive scene was, however, carefully stage-managed. A meeting of young Marxists was in progress, the subject of which was the future of the Russian Empire.

Tall, pale, her hair in a bun, 25-year-old Nadezhda Krupskaya had been involved in radical politics since 1890. At the so-called pancake party, she met a young Marxist named Vladimir Ilyich Ulianov and was intrigued by his intellect and convictions. They soon became friends and colleagues. Vladimir Ilyich Ulianov would, in later years, become universally known as V.I. Lenin.

Born in February 1869, Nadezhda Krupskaya came from a family of the nobility. Her father, Konstantin Ignatevich Krupsky, was an army officer, whose career had suffered due to his involvement in radical politics. Her mother, **Elizaveta Tistrova Krupskaya**, was a teacher and a children's author. Nadezhda seems to have been a retiring, bookish child. She lived during a period in Russian history when the vocation of a professional revolutionary was an option open to women. She attended the Prince A.A. Obolensky Female Gymnasium in St. Petersburg, which had a reputation as a progressive institution. In 1882, Krupskaya won a gold medal for academic excellence. The Gymnasium produced many of Russia's pioneering female Marxists, including **Olga Grigoreva**, **Nina Gerd**, and **Lidya Davidova**. A fellow student, **Ariadne Tynkova**, described Krupskaya at the time:

> Earlier than any of us, more unyieldingly than any of us, she had defined her views, had set her course. She was one of those who are forever committed, once they have been possessed by their thoughts or feelings.

Krupskaya stayed on at the Gymnasium after her graduation, working as a part-time teaching assistant until 1891. She also enrolled in the Bestuzhev Courses, the first university program for women in St. Petersburg. Her true passion, however, soon became Marxist theory, and she left the University of St. Petersburg without completing her examinations. On evenings and weekends, she taught workers at a factory-school, where literacy, mathematics, history, and Russian literature were all part of the curriculum. As well, she recruited members for the revolution, disseminated propaganda, and assisted in the organization of strikes.

In 1895, Lenin was arrested for his involvement in labor unrest. Eight months later, Krupskaya's own arrest followed, for her subversive activities at the factory-school. Though sentenced to three years' internal exile in the town of Ufa in northern Russia, she soon petitioned the police for a transfer to Shushenskoye, in Siberia, where Lenin was serving a similar sentence.

Neither Lenin nor Krupskaya seem to have contemplated marriage, but their arrest contrived to bring that about. Permitted to travel to Siberia with her mother, Krupskaya was told by the authorities that unless she married Lenin promptly upon her arrival, she would be sent back to Ufa. Lenin wrote to his mother in May 1899, explaining the situation:

> At last I have received the so long awaited guests. . . . Nadezhda Konstantinovna does not look well at all and will simply have to take care of her health. . . . As you know, they put to Nadezhda Konstantinovna the tragic-comic condition: either get married immediately or go back to Ufa. I am not disposed to let her get away, and so have already begun the moves.

Although marriage was considered unfashionable in some revolutionary circles, particularly among nihilists and anarchists, a long-term commitment, with or without a ceremony, was the norm among most Marxists. Krupskaya and Lenin were married in an Orthodox ceremony. Although both were atheists, Krupskaya's mother, a deeply religious woman, was pleased to see her daughter married in church.

While in Siberia, Krupskaya not only acted as Lenin's secretary and sounding board, but also wrote on the subject of female emancipation. At the time, her pamphlet, *The Woman Worker,* was the lone Marxist text devoted solely to the topic. In it, she argued that women could only find true liberation through inclusion in the work force and could only gain equal access to the workplace through a proletarian revolution. When Lenin's term of exile ended in late 1899, he trav-

eled to Pskov, while Krupskaya returned to Ufa to serve the remainder of her sentence.

Between 1901 and 1905, Krupskaya and her husband lived abroad. She detested Western Europe, writing to a friend, "Akh, this emigration!," and referring to the West as a "dead sea." For several years, Krupskaya served as the editorial secretary of *Iska* (Spark), the periodical which Lenin had founded. During their first period overseas, Krupskaya was also responsible for coding and decoding sensitive communications between the party and activists inside Russia. It was a skill that Lenin had taught her in 1895. With the split of the Russian Social Democrats into Bolshevik (majority) and Menshevik (minority) factions in 1903, the Bolsheviks and Lenin lost control of *Iska.* However, he established a new journal, *Vpered* (Forward), as well as *The Proletarian,* of which Krupskaya naturally became secretary.

In 1905, Russia had just lost the Russo-Japanese War, the middle class wanted political reform, and continuous strikes rocked the nation, as workers demanded better treatment by employers. On October 17, Tsar Nicholas II announced the institution of limited civil liberties, and the creation of a consultative assembly, the Duma, in which the Bolsheviks were permitted to sit.

The 1905 Revolution gave Lenin and Krupskaya the opportunity to return to St. Petersburg. The government, weakened by the events of the summer and fall, was tolerant of political dissent. By the fall of 1907, however, the Bolshevik Party was still not strong enough to challenge the government, and the new administration of Premier Petr Stolypin was beginning to round up political opponents. Krupskaya and Lenin returned to Switzerland with the police at their heels.

This was followed by a three-and-a-half-year stay in Paris, where, together with Krupskaya's mother and Lenin's sister ◀ Marie Ulyanova, they lived in a large apartment on rue Bonier. It was during their stay in the French capital that Krupskaya met ◀ Laura Marx (Lafargue), the elderly daughter of Karl Marx. In July 1912, Lenin transferred the headquarters of the Bolshevik Party to Austrian Poland, in order to be close to the Russian frontier. "Almost in Russia," wrote Krupskaya. "It was only half emigration." Her old friends Gregory Zinoviev and Lev Kamenev also moved to Cracow.

During 1913, Krupskaya was increasingly afflicted by thyroid disease, and Lenin decided to have her treated in Berne. She gradually re-

Ulyanova, Marie. See Barkova, Anna for sidebar.

Marx, Laura. See Marx, Jenny for sidebar.

gained her health, though she admitted to being "pretty scared." The First World War caught Krupskaya and Lenin by surprise as she was recuperating in Austria. They both agreed that it was a capitalist conflict, in which the workers could only be harmed. Under the circumstances, the only safe harbor was back in neutral Switzerland. In 1915, Krupskaya became the head of the Commission for the Aid of Russian Prisoners of War, a Bolshevik organization designed to recruit party members. The Germans turned a blind eye to Bolshevik activities, always ready to encourage the enemies of the Russian tsar.

During the war, Krupskaya wrote widely on the subject of education, in magazines such as *Free Education*. No specific Marxist theory of education had yet been developed, and she sought to remedy this oversight. In a booklet entitled "Public Education and Democracy," she set forth her ideas for education in a socialist state. Like Marx, she argued that periods of physical labor should be part of the curriculum, in order to promote respect for proletariat values.

On May 12, 1917, while in Switzerland, Krupskaya wrote to a friend about the unexpected news leaking out of Russia:

Nadezhda Krupskaya with V.I. Lenin.

It is hard to make sense today because of the telegrams that have excited all the Russians here: about the victory of the Revolution in Russia, the seizure of Power by the Kadet-Octobrist bloc, the three-day battle, and so on. Perhaps it is another hoax.

The abdication of Tsar Nicholas II opened the way for the return of Krupskaya and her husband to Russia. Getting there, however, was no simple matter. It took an offer from the German government, anxious to encourage the antiwar movement, to provide safe railroad passage via neutral Sweden. Krupskaya and Lenin joined a group of 30 other socialists to make the trip across Germany. Late on the evening of April 3, 1917, they arrived at Petrograd's Finland Station, where the couple were greeted by a delegation from the Soviet of Workers' and Soldiers' Deputies.

From the time of their arrival to the end of the October Revolution, Krupskaya would see little of her busy husband. During much of this period, Lenin was preoccupied with the defense of his "April Thesis," which advocated the violent overthrow of the Provisional Government. In June, Krupskaya was elected to the local soviet of Vyborg, a suburb of Petrograd (St. Petersburg). She served as the head of public education and, from this period until October, was faced with the challenge of developing a new educational system for the district. On October 24, 1917, the night of the Bolshevik insurrection, while Leon Trotsky's Bolshevik Military Revolutionary Committee stormed buildings and seized bridges throughout the capital, Krupskaya went to the Smolny, where the Petrograd Soviets were headquartered, though in the confusion and excitement she missed Lenin.

With the downfall of the capitalist Provisional Government and the creation of the world's first socialist state, Krupskaya and Lenin moved to the new capital, Moscow. Krupskaya was not content to remain merely the wife of the new head of the Soviet state. Like the wives of many prominent Bolsheviks, she wanted to be an active participant in the building of a socialist society.

Thus, while blossoming into a prolific author and orator, Krupskaya also became the commissar for Adult Education. She envisioned an educational system similar to that of the United States, with locally elected school boards, but in which teachers would also be elected.

On August 30, 1918, a young woman named **Fanya Kaplan** shot Lenin at close range. He was taken, bleeding, to the Kremlin, where Krupskaya sat up with him all night. But Lenin's recovery was swift, and in 1919 and 1920 he kept up a furious work pace. In late May 1922, he suffered a stroke. Krupskaya gave up her heavy workload at the Commissariat for Adult Education and helped to nurse him at their country home. In mid-December, however, he suffered another stroke. As it became apparent that Lenin's illness would force him to give up the leadership of the party temporarily, if not permanently, a power struggle began in earnest. Lenin clearly favored Leon Trotsky, but the powerful alliance of Zinoviev, Leo Kamenev, and Joseph Stalin were aligned against him.

Krupskaya had acted as Lenin's personal assistant for many years, so it is hardly surprising that she did so again during his convalescence. She wrote letters on his behalf, some supporting the Trotsky faction. Krupskaya did, however, try to get Lenin to rest, but this was often a difficult task. Unfortunately, the succession struggle became increasingly bitter, and Stalin resented Krupskaya's interference. He telephoned her and ordered her not to meddle in party politics. Using abusive language, he threatened to have her arrested and brought before the party's disciplinary Control Commission.

Lenin's last will and testament was highly influenced by Stalin's treatment of his wife. In it, he wrote that "Stalin is too crude, and this fault, though tolerable in dealings among us Communists, becomes unbearable in a General Secretary. Therefore I propose to the comrades to find some way of removing Stalin from his position." On January 21, 1924, Lenin died. Krupskaya disapproved of the deification of her husband. In fact, she never visited his mausoleum in Red Square.

Nadezhda Krupskaya was poorly equipped to execute her husband's wishes. She was not a powerful political figure, although she did enjoy a prominent position in Soviet society. She had few political allies, and, in the end, it was easy for the party to suppress Lenin's politically embarrassing last wish. In the struggle for the succession, Krupskaya allied herself with Zinoviev and Kamenev, principally because she feared a split in the party, which might destabilize the nation. In an article in *Pravda* in December 1924, she criticized Trotsky for having "a purely administrative and utterly superficial view" of the party. When Stalin split with Zinoviev and Kamenev, Krupskaya found herself in opposition for the first time in her life. In October 1925, she took the unprecedented move of signing a manifesto against Stalin's and Nikolai Bukharin's moderate agricultural policies. At the same time, she also developed a serious heart condition.

Krupskaya consistently urged greater democracy and intellectual freedom within the party, both of which Stalin's autocratic methods precluded. She even went so far as to have a copy of Lenin's testament smuggled out of the country. Though published on October 18, 1926, in *The New York Times*, it had little effect in the Soviet Union, due to heavy press censorship. In her despair over Stalin's heavy-handed rule, she told Kamenev, "If Lenin were alive today, he would be in jail."

Stalin began to pressure Krupskaya to conform, at a time when her allies seemed to be faltering. He told her that if she did not stop supporting the opposition, he would "make someone else Lenin's widow." A whispering campaign began against her. Stalin was intent on depriving the opposition of its prestigious association with her. By the summer of 1927, she was forced to concede defeat, rationalizing her reluctant support of the regime by reasserting the need for party unity. Krupskaya had clearly failed in her bid to influence state policy and in her bid to influence the selection of a new leader.

In the last years of Krupskaya's life, she became the maternal symbol of Communism. By the 1930s, she even looked the part of an archetypal Russian grandmother. However, she did hold positions of considerable responsibility, including those of deputy commissar for education, member of the Central Committee, and member of the Soviet Academy of Sciences. She wrote and spoke at length on issues concerning the Soviet family. While many women considered legalized abortion and easy divorce important steps towards equality, Krupskaya held markedly conservative views on those subjects. On the issue of education, the Stalinist model of the '30s closely resembled the pre-revolutionary system, with school uniforms, subject specialization, and heavy discipline. The imposition of such a system shocked Krupskaya deeply, as did Stalin's forced collectivization policy and purges.

In 1937, she was elected to the Supreme Soviet. As one of the few women to attain high political office, Krupskaya became a figurehead for the party's traditional belief in the equal rights of women. In reality, however, while many Soviet women moved into the professions, they were exhausted by their dual roles as workers and homemakers. Thus, high political office remained largely a male preserve. Krupskaya did little to change this.

On February, 27, 1939, Nadezhda Krupskaya died in her apartment in the Kremlin, which had been her home for her last 20 years.

Stalin was one of the pallbearers at her funeral. An urn with her ashes was placed inside the Kremlin wall, where she rests with other heroes of the Soviet Union.

Women played a key role in the Russian revolutionary movement, and along with *Vera Zasulich and *Alexandra Kollontai, Nadezhda Krupskaya was a remarkable figure. Although she may be remembered primarily as Lenin's wife, she was instrumental as a party organizer and administrator. Krupskaya opposed Stalin's dictatorship, although she was often powerless to stop him. As well, her contributions to Soviet education should not go unmentioned, for while they were downplayed during the Stalinist period, they were recognized and celebrated in the post-Stalinist Soviet Union. Nadezhda Krupskaya was a woman of considerable intelligence and dedication, who remained true to the principal tenets of Marxist-Leninism, before and after the October Revolution.

SOURCES:

Goncharov, Lev, and Ludmila Kunetskaya. "Nadezhda K. Krupskaya, Founder of Soviet Public Education," in *School and Society*. Vol. XCIX, 1971, pp. 235–237.

Krupskaya, Nadezhda. *Memories of Lenin*. NY: International Publishers, 1930.

Payne, Robert. *The Life and Death of Lenin*. NY: Simon and Schuster, 1964.

Raymond, Boris. "A Sword with Two Edges: The Role of Children's Literature in the Writings of N.K. Krupskaya," in *Library Quarterly*. Vol. XLIV, no. 3, pp. 206–218.

Wolfe, Bertram A. *Three Who Made a Revolution*. NY: Dial Press, 1964.

SUGGESTED READING:

McNeal, Robert H. *Bride of the Revolution: Krupskaya and Lenin*. Ann Arbor, MI: University of Michigan Press, 1972.

Hugh A. Stewart, M.A.,
University of Guelph, Guelph, Ontario, Canada

Krusceniski, Salomea (1873–1952)

Ukrainian soprano. Name variations: Krushelnytska. Born in Bilavyntsy, Ukraine, on September 23, 1873; died in Lvov, on November 16, 1952; studied in Lvov with Wysocki and in Milan with Crespi.

A Ruthenian dramatic soprano, Salomea Krusceniski was born in Bilavyntsy, Ukraine, in 1873, and made her debut in Lvov in 1893 as Léonore in *Favorite*. An admired Isolde and Elektra, her singing at Brescia in 1904 was largely responsible for the early popularity of Puccini's *Madama Butterfly*. Krusceniski retired in 1920.

Krushelnytska, Salomea (1873–1952).

See Krusceniski, Salomea.

Krystyna Rokiczanska

*Queen of Poland. Name variations: Rokiczańska. Third wife of Kazimierz also known as Casimir III the Great, king of Poland (r. 1333–1370); children: possibly Elizabeth (who married Boguslaw V of Slupsk); Cunegunde; Anna. Casimir III was first married to *Aldona of Lithuania and Adelaide of Hesse; *Jadwiga of Glogow was his fourth wife.*

Kschessinska, Mathilde (1872–1971).

See Kshesinskaia, Matilda.

Ksenia or Ksenya.

Variant of Xenia.

Kshesinskaia, Matilda (1872–1971)

One of the foremost classical Russian ballerinas between 1890 and 1917. Name variations: at least nine different transliterations from the Russian, the most common being Mathilde or Matilde Kchessinska, Kcshessinskaya, Kschessinska, Kshesinskaia, Kshesinskaya, Kshessinskaya, Kshessinskaia; Princess Romanovsky-Krassinsky (after 1935). Pronunciation: Ke-SHES-in-sky-ya. Born Matilda Feliksovna Kshesinskaia on August 19, 1872 (o.s.) in Ligovo, Russia; died on December 6, 1971, in Paris, France; daughter of Feliks Ivanovich Kshesinskii (Krzhesinskii-Nechui), a ballet dancer, and Julia Kshesinskaia; attended Imperial Ballet School, 1880–90; married Grand Duke Andrei Vladimirovich, in 1921; children: Vladimir (b. 1902).

Was a member of the Maryinsky Theater company (1890–1917), as ballerina (1892–93), as prima ballerina (1893–95), as prima ballerina assoluta (1895–1904), as guest artist (1905–17); was mistress of the future tsar of Russia, Nicholas II (1892–94); danced in Vienna (1903), Monte Carlo (1895, 1912), Paris (1908, 1909), London (1911, 1912) and Budapest (1912); lived abroad near Monte Carlo (1920–28) and in Paris (1929–71); taught ballet (1929–64).

Roles: her best known and favorite roles were in La fille mal gardée, La fille du Pharaon, Esmeralda, La Bayadere, Le Talisman *and* Swan Lake. *Publication: (under the name Princess Romanovsky-Krassinsky)* Dancing in Petersburg: The Memoirs of Kschessinska *(London, 1960).*

"Where is Kshesinskaia?" bellowed Tsar Alexander III. The date was March 23, 1890, and the graduating class of the Imperial Ballet School had just completed their final examination dances before their teachers and the royal family. Matilda Kshesinskaia's rendition of a scene from *La fille mal gardée* had clearly been the best of the day. The 17-year-old dancer was taken to meet her imposing sovereign, curtsied, and was told, "Be the glory and the adornment of our ballet!" Much to everyone's surprise, the tsar then asked her to be his dinner partner at the graduation banquet, and he placed on her other side his 21-year-old son and heir, the tsarevich Nicholas (II) Aleksandrovich. The nonplussed dancer remembered little of the subsequent conversation except that Alexander, upon leaving the table, warned her: "Careful now! Not too much flirting!" These two imperial commands shaped the course of Kshesinskaia's life: one of them she obeyed, the other she did not. Within five years, she had risen to the rank of *prima ballerina assoluta*, the highest position in Russian ballet. During the same time, she was involved in a celebrated romance with the tsarevich. Although the affair came to an end when Nicholas married *Alexandra Feodorovna and became tsar of Russia in 1894, Kshesinskaia's dancing flourished for the next two decades while Russian ballet became the finest in the world. Long after Nicholas and Alexandra perished at the hands of the Bolsheviks in 1918, she continued to dance and teach ballet in Western Europe.

Matilda Kshesinskaia was born in Ligovo, near St. Petersburg, into a family of ballet dancers. Her father, Feliks Ivanovich Kshesinskii, was a Polish character dancer brought from Warsaw to perform in St. Petersburg's Maryinsky Theater. Her mother **Julia Kshesinskaia** and her two older siblings, Iosef and Julia, were also dancers. "I had a very happy childhood," Kshesinskaia later recalled. Her summers were spent at the family's country estate, and during the rest of the year they lived in a large, comfortable apartment in the capital. In this "marvellous enchanted atmosphere," her father taught the mazurka to members of St. Petersburg's high society. Matilda often watched her father dance professionally, began dancing herself when she was three, and at the age of eight passed the highly competitive entrance examination for the Imperial Ballet School. At her parents' insistence, she was one of the few students allowed to live at home. She nevertheless spent most of her time during the next ten years at the school, studying academic subjects, learning good manners and above all else being rigorously taught to dance by Russian and European masters. Upon graduating first in her class, she was given a coveted position in the corps de ballet at the Maryinsky Theater.

Her rise in the company was unparalleled. Within two years she was named ballerina, in

1893 prima ballerina, and in 1895 *prima ballerina assoluta*. Serge Lifar has called her "the best dancer of her time" and praised her for her lightness, purity and artistic instinct. Like most graduates of the Imperial School, she was well trained in classical techniques and was particularly adept at mime. What set her apart from her Russian contemporaries was her virtuosity, which up to this point had been the monopoly of Italian ballerinas brought in to star in Russian ballets. When Kshesinskaia successfully completed the 32 *fouettés* in the Black Swan *pas de deux* of Tchaikovsky's *Swan Lake*, it was hailed as a national triumph and a sign that Russian ballet had come of age.

There were some in St. Petersburg who uncharitably attributed Kshesinskaia's quick success to her "flirting" with various members of the royal family and in particular with Nicholas II, the official patron of the Maryinsky Theater. Kshesinskaia later admitted that when she first met Nicholas at her graduation dinner

> I fell in love with [him] on the spot! I can still see his magnificent eyes, his tender, kind expression. Almost from his first words he was something more to me than the Tsarevitch, heir to the throne. It was like a dream. . . . When we finally parted, we saw each other in a new light. In both of our hearts an attraction had been born impelling us irresistibly towards each other.

Several months later, in July 1890, she started dancing with her new company at Krasnoe Selo where Nicholas' regiment was conveniently stationed for the summer. He came to all of her performances, visited her backstage, and later confided to his diary that "ever since camp in 1890 I have loved little K passionately." His love was initially platonic, and then it was interrupted by a nine-month world tour dictated by his father. Upon his return, Nicholas resumed his intense interest in ballet, visited Kshesinskaia at her father's home, and began giving her expensive gifts. It suited both of them when she moved into an apartment with her older sister and later into a two-storey house on the English Quay purchased for her by the tsarevich. "I knew indeed that this was one of the things that 'just is not done,'" Kshesinskaia wrote in her memoirs:

> My father was shattered. . . . He listened to my account and merely asked me if I realised that I could never marry the Tsarevitch and that our idyll would be short. I replied that I fully understood, but that I loved him with all my heart, that I did not care what happened in the future. I wanted to take advantage of the happiness open to me, even if it proved of short duration.

She realized all too well that tsars of Russia married foreign royalty, not Russian ballerinas. Nicholas was in fact seeking the hand of Alexandra Feodorovna (then Princess Alix of Hesse-Darmstadt) at the same time that he was spending many of his nights on the English Quay. "I never imagined that two identical feelings, two loves could co-exist simultaneously in one's soul," he confessed to his diary in April 1892. Matilda's "idyll" ended precisely two years later when Princess Alix finally agreed to give up her Lutheran faith, took the name Alexandra, and by the end of 1894 married Nicholas, now the tsar of Russia. "It was something which I had foreseen, expected, known must happen," Kshesinskaia later wrote. "Nevertheless it brought me inconsolable sorrow." In subsequent years, she corresponded with the tsar on occasion but never again saw him privately.

*C*rowned with honors, rich in memories, hallowed by a great romance, [Kshesinskaia] represents a bygone century of ballet.

—Olga Maynard

Kshesinskaia's "dark curls and merry eyes" as well as the glamour of being a prima ballerina did, however, attract other members of the royal family to her side. In 1895, the Grand Duke Sergei Mikhailovich, Nicholas' cousin, became her "protector" and she his mistress. Five years later, she formed a lasting relationship with the tsar's nephew, the Grand Duke Andrei Vladimirovich, and gave birth to their son in 1902. It was in part because of these friends in high places that Serge Lifar has referred to "the all-powerful Kshesinskaia" as the "greatest and most influential of the stars of the Maryinsky Theatre."

During the first decade of the 20th century, she was widely considered to be the "doyenne of the traditionalists" and even *Isadora Duncan, anything but a traditionalist herself, said that Kshesinskaia danced "more like a lovely bird or butterfly than a human being." She helped spread the growing fame of Russian ballet by dancing in Vienna in 1903 and Paris in 1908 and 1909. As one critic wrote in 1904, "Kshesinskaia, with her great natural gifts, holds an exceptional place on the contemporary Russian stage, and even in Europe as a whole." Her salary of 3,000 rubles a year, plus the gifts of her many admirers, allowed her to live in considerable style. Grand Duke Sergei gave her a dacha on the Gulf of Finland where she spent many of her summers, and she purchased a villa on the

French Riviera for use when abroad. In 1907, she sold her house on the English Quay and built an opulent mansion on Kronversky Prospekt in St. Petersburg. Looked after by 14 servants, it soon became the focal point for much of the capital's social life. Perhaps wishing to surpass scenes from *The Nutcracker*, Kshesinskaia hired Russia's foremost clown and brought a large elephant into her ballroom to entertain guests at one of her son's Christmas parties.

This was also a decade of change and turmoil for Russian politics and Russian ballet. In 1905, an unsuccessful revolution broke out in St. Petersburg which even spread to the Maryinsky Theater. A number of the ballet company, including Kshesinskaia's brother Iosef but not Matilda herself, went on strike demanding better working conditions, less authoritarian control, and an end to what they considered to be growing artistic stagnation. Four years later, Serge Diaghilev harnessed some of these sentiments and started to revolutionize European dance. He proposed to take many of the Maryinsky company to Paris and to stage less tradition-

al ballets based on the innovative choreography of Michel Fokine. Initially, Kshesinskaia used her influence to get royal patronage and a subsidy for what came to be known as the Ballets Russes as well as permission to use Maryinsky sets and costumes. When she found out, however, that the major roles had been offered to her younger and more versatile colleagues, *Anna Pavlova and *Tamara Karsavina, she decided to stay home, and the royal family withdrew its patronage. In 1911 and 1912, Kshesinskaia did appear as a guest performer for the Ballets Russes in London. And while the conservative audience at Covent Garden showed more appreciation for her virtuosity in *Swan Lake* than for the soaring leaps of her partner Vaslav Nijinsky, it is indicative that she was not asked to dance the new roles from Igor Stravinsky's *Firebird*, *Petrushka* and *Rite of Spring* which Diaghilev had staged in Paris and which were to lay the groundwork for modern ballet of the 20th century.

The outbreak of the First World War varied the rhythm if not the substance of Kshesinskaia's privileged existence. Her foreign tours came to

Matilda Kshesinskaia

an end but the ballet still functioned every Wednesday and Sunday night at the Maryinsky Theater. In 1915, she traveled extensively in Russia, dancing in provincial cities and staying in a special railway carriage loaned to her by the Grand Duke Sergei. She contributed to the war effort by visiting the front to distribute gifts and by opening a temporary hospital near her mansion in Petrograd for recuperating soldiers. Unlike the British ambassador, who could not get coal to heat his embassy during the coldest part of 1916, Kshesinskaia was regularly supplied with fuel by army trucks. While most of the city was suffering from bread rationing, she had no difficulty feeding 24 guests off of her Limoges china at a special banquet on February 22, 1917. The next day people protesting their own lack of fuel and food as well as the continuation of the war began to demonstrate in Petrograd, and by the 26th the unrest had become so widespread that the chief of police urged Kshesinskaia to seek sanctuary elsewhere. Perhaps realizing that the mansion of the tsar's ex-mistress was a very visible symbol of the detested old order, she heeded this warning and 12 hours later fled with her fox terrier and a suitcase full of jewelry. It was a wise decision, for her house was soon sacked from top to bottom and then taken over by the Bolsheviks to serve as their temporary headquarters. The ballroom in which clowns and elephants had once entertained became the site of Lenin's Seventh Party Conference in April 1917.

As a result of the Bolshevik seizure of power in October, Kshesinskaia lost not only her mansion but also her dacha, her job, her pension, and a fortune in jewelry. Unlike her former lovers, Nicholas II and the Grand Duke Sergei, she did not lose her life. In the middle of 1917, using a safe-conduct pass issued to her by the Provisional Government, she and her son Vladimir left Petrograd and made their way to the Caucasus, where she spent most of the Civil War with the Grand Duke Andrei, trying to keep one step ahead of the Bolshevik forces. Finally accepting the fact that the monarchy would not be restored, they sailed from Russia on an Italian liner bound for France in February 1920. A year later Matilda and Andrei were married in Cannes. For the next eight years, they lived a comfortable emigre life in her villa overlooking the Mediterranean. In 1929, financial circumstances forced them to move to Paris so that Matilda could open a dance studio, where for 35 years she taught classical Russian ballet to several generations of aspiring ballerinas. Her long career as a dancer came to an end in 1936, at age 64, after 18 curtain calls before a standing audi-

ence at Covent Garden. She spent the postwar years in Paris teaching, writing her moving memoirs, caring for her aged husband, and taking an active role in the Federation of Russian Classical Ballet. Matilda Kshesinskaia died in her 100th year on December 6, 1971.

SOURCES:

Lifar, Serge. *A History of Russian Ballet.* Translated from the French by Arnold Haskell. London: Hutchinson, 1954.

Maynard, Olga. "Kchessinska at Ninety-Nine," in *Dance Magazine.* November 1971, pp. 22–24.

Romanovsky-Krassinsky, Princess (Matilda Kshesinskaia). *Dancing in Petersburg: The Memoirs of Kschessinska.* Translated from the French by Arnold Haskell. London: Victor Gollancz, 1960 (most of the quotations used above, unless otherwise indicated, come from this source).

SUGGESTED READING:

Massie, Robert K. *Nicholas and Alexandra.* NY: Antheneum, 1968.

R.C. Elwood,
Professor of History, Carleton University, Ottawa, Canada

Kuan, Lady (1262–1319).
See Guan Daosheng.

Kuan Fu-Jen (1262–1319).
See Guan Daosheng.

Kuan Tao-sheng (1262–1319).
See Guan Daosheng.

Kübler-Ross, Elisabeth (1926—)

Swiss psychiatrist and pioneer in the field of thanatology. Born Elisabeth Kübler in Zurich, Switzerland, on July 8, 1926; daughter of Ernest Kübler (a businessman) and Emma (Villager) Kübler; awarded M.D., University of Zurich Medical School, 1957; married Emanuel Ross, in 1958 (divorced); children: Kenneth; Barbara.

Moved to U.S. (1958); worked as rotating intern at Community Hospital, Glen Cove, New York (1958–59); became a naturalized citizen of the U.S. (1961); was a research fellow at Manhattan State Hospital (1959–61); was a resident at Montefiore Hospital, Bronx, New York (1961–62); was a fellow in psychiatry, Psychopathic Hospital, University of Colorado Medical School (1962–65); was an assistant professor in psychiatry, Billings Hospital, University of Chicago (1965–70); served as medical director of Family Service and Mental Health Center of South Cook County, Chicago Heights, Illinois (1970–73); was president and chair of the Board of Shanti Nilaya Growth and Health Center, Escondido, California (1977–83); moved to Virginia (1983); moved to Scottsdale, Arizona (1994).

Selected publications: On Death and Dying *(1969)*; Questions and Answers on Death and Dying *(1974)*; Death: The Final Stages of Growth *(1975)*; To Live Until We Say Goodbye *(1978)*; Working It Through *(1981)*; Living With Death and Dying *(1981)*; Remember the Secret *(1981)*; On Children and Death *(1985)*; AIDS: The Ultimate Challenge *(1988)*; On Life After Death *(1991)*.

A founding pioneer in the field of thanatology (the study of death), Elisabeth Kübler-Ross, a psychiatrist by training, is widely recognized as the 20th-century's foremost authority on death and dying. Her groundbreaking work with dying patients has transformed Western medicine's approach toward the terminally ill, affected public policy and scholarly research, and radically altered Western society's attitudes toward death and dying. While most of her work has dealt with the psychological effects of dying, in recent years Kübler-Ross has sparked controversy and professional criticism of her work by venturing into the study of spirituality and the speculative realm of life after death.

I still have so much to learn from the dying, who have become my best teachers.

—Elisabeth Kübler-Ross

Elisabeth Kübler-Ross was the first of triplet girls born to Ernest and **Emma Kübler** on July 8, 1926, in Zurich, Switzerland. Elisabeth and **Erika** (her identical twin) were both thin and sickly, each weighing a mere two pounds at birth. Doctors believed that of the three only **Eva** (a fraternal twin) would survive infancy. But Emma Kübler was a devoted and determined mother. She moved into the nursery with her daughters, nursing them every three hours around the clock for the next nine months. During the first few months, Elisabeth had to be fed through a doll's bottle as her tiny mouth was too small to allow her to breast-feed.

Her parents shared an enormous appetite for living and seemingly limitless energy, traits they passed down to their children. Her father Ernest Kübler was a successful businessman and part-time instructor at a technical college. He was also an avid mountain climber, hiker, and skier and instilled in his daughter a love of the outdoors.

The extraordinary origin of Elisabeth and her sisters led instantly to their domination of the Kübler household, with the result that their older brother, Ernest, was eclipsed and remained a distant figure throughout Kübler-Ross' life. The girls also became minor celebrities in Zurich, where their picture appeared in advertisements and on billboards. Although Elisabeth and her sisters each had highly distinctive personalities, in the hearts and minds of their parents, schoolteachers, and the public they were simply "the Kübler triplets." Kübler-Ross later recalled rarely being called by her first name at home, in school, or in the outside world. This lack of individual recognition affected her deeply and sparked an independent, rebellious streak and what she later referred to as her "strange beckonings." One such childhood beckoning was an obsession with a picture book on life in an African village that inspired her to create her own imaginary African village, "Higaland." She then devised a special Higaland language which she taught to her sisters.

As a child, Elisabeth Kübler-Ross also exhibited a bent toward science. She turned a section of the house cellar into a laboratory where she experimented with chemicals. Another area of the cellar she converted into a makeshift hospital for injured birds and animals. In a sixth-grade composition entitled "My Dream of What I Could Be," Kübler-Ross wrote that her first aspiration was to be "a researcher and explorer of unknown frontiers of human knowledge."

These precocious school-girl aspirations were temporarily sidetracked following the completion of her compulsory education in 1942. Her father decided that she should join his business rather than continue with her education. When Kübler-Ross refused, he ordered her either to join his business or go to work as a domestic servant. She defiantly chose the latter and for the next year was employed as a housekeeper in the French-speaking part of Germany.

She returned to her family in 1943 and, again against her father's wishes, accepted a three-year apprenticeship in a biomedical research laboratory. She also began attending classes in chemistry, physics, and mathematics in order to obtain her technician's certification. Kübler-Ross consistently ranked at the top of the class, and when the laboratory went bankrupt she won a coveted apprenticeship with Dr. Karl Zehnder, director of the dermatology department at Camden Hospital. At Camden, much of her work involved taking blood samples from prostitutes suffering from venereal diseases for an on-going study. This constituted Kübler-Ross' first direct contact with patients, and she quickly discovered that she had a natural empathy and compassion for those whom most physicians

Elisabeth
Kübler-
Ross

and hospital staff treated carelessly. It was, she later recalled, her first inkling that there was something greatly amiss "when the dispassionate technology of medicine could not be linked to the cries of the heart and an understanding of the mind." Kübler-Ross began to seek out the

sick children at the hospital, visiting and playing with them during her lunch hours.

Elisabeth Kübler-Ross' humanitarian instincts were aroused again in 1944 when scores of refugees from the war were sent to Camden hospital to be deloused. Without the approval of her department, she began working with the delousing team, counseling refugees rather than performing her duties at the lab. A desire to be more involved in relief work prompted her in the summer of 1945 to take a leave of absence from her apprenticeship and join the International Voluntary Service for Peace. Her first assignment as an unpaid relief worker concerned the rebuilding of the French town of Ecurcey. In the fall, she returned to Zurich and took her medical technician's exam, finishing first out of 32 students. After an unsatisfying stint in a research laboratory, Kübler-Ross was hired in 1947 by Professor Marc Amsler, head of the ophthalmology department at the University of Zurich. Once again, her main satisfaction derived from counseling the patients—many threatened by blindness—who came for treatment.

Kübler-Ross spent another few months in the summer of 1947 working as a relief worker in Belgium, Poland, and Stockholm, Sweden. Her experiences with refugees and Holocaust survivors strengthened her resolve to study medicine. She enrolled in the Medical School at the University of Zurich in 1952, after successfully passing the *Mature* examination, and continued to work full-time in the ophthalmology department. She received her medical degree in 1957 and early the following year married Emanuel Ross, an American medical student, after a lengthy courtship. The couple left Switzerland for the United States at the end of June 1958.

Upon arriving in America, Kübler-Ross accepted a one-year internship at the Glen Cove Community Hospital in Long Island, New York. The following year, she applied for and was accepted as a resident at the prestigious Columbia Presbyterian Medical Center, but an unexpected pregnancy (which later ended in a miscarriage) forced her to refuse the coveted residency. Instead, she accepted a research fellowship at Manhattan State Hospital, an underfunded, underequipped hospital that served indigent mentally ill patients. Kübler-Ross was originally hired to observe and record patient responses to a variety of experimental drugs (the drugs, she later discovered, were LSD, psilocybin, and mescaline). Appalled by the apathy of most of the staff and the horrendous conditions under which the patients lived, she worked tirelessly to clean up the wards, spoke out against the use of experimental drugs and shock therapy, and earned a reputation with the patients and the staff as a compassionate and empathetic doctor.

In 1960, she gave birth to her son Kenneth (daughter Barbara would be born in 1963), and

in 1961, after deciding on a career in psychiatry, she left Manhattan State Hospital and started a residency in psychiatry at Montefiore Hospital. Once there, she abandoned the classical Freudian technique of free association and interpretation preferred by the other physicians in favor of a less fashionable approach. She offered each patient individualized attention and based her diagnoses and treatment on intuition. Her colleagues criticized her unorthodox methods, yet her results were often extraordinary. Kübler-Ross later recalled that it was during these early years in New York that she began formulating some of the theories she would later pioneer. She noted that physicians at the hospital tended to regard the death of a patient as a personal failure and that the medical personnel's views of terminally ill patients were informed by their own fears of death. She also observed that physicians often showed a greater reluctance to accept a poor prognosis than did their patients.

In 1962, Elisabeth Kübler-Ross and her husband accepted joint positions at the University of Colorado. While there she worked, first as an assistant and then as an instructor, under the brilliant Vienna-trained psychiatrist Sydney Margolin. Margolin had a similarly independent nature and employed unusual techniques, including hypnosis. He became her mentor, encouraging rather than criticizing the spiritual dimension she brought to her work and her growing preoccupation with the psychological aspects of dying. Death was the subject of Kübler-Ross' first lecture to medical students. During the lecture, she interviewed a 16-year-old girl dying of leukemia, questioning her about her reactions to the prognosis. Then she invited the medical students to question the patient and observed their obvious discomfort as they avoided personal questions and instead asked questions related to symptoms and the patient's medical history. At the end of the emotionally charged lecture, Kübler-Ross challenged the students to confront their own fears of death and expressed her conviction that modern medicine's emphasis on technology and efficiency was undermining the genuine art of healing.

This lecture was a prototype of the seminars Kübler-Ross later developed at the University of Chicago's Billings Hospital, where she served as assistant professor in psychiatry from 1965 to 1970. She was considered a gifted teacher, and her lectures at the university were enormously popular. For each of her five years on the faculty, the students honored her with the "Most Popular Teacher" award. Though her main responsibilities were lecturing to medical students on psychiatry and caring for patients in the psychiatric in-patient unit, her interests were again drawn in another direction. She began conducting regular staged interviews with terminally ill patients for the benefit of medical students, nurses, chaplains, social workers, and therapists. The interviews served the purpose of alerting caregivers to the special psychological and spiritual needs of the terminally ill. By 1966, Kübler-Ross' Death and Dying seminars were gaining her larger audiences and academic popularity. She agreed to join the staff of the Lutheran Theological Seminary as a counselor in pastoral care in order to train future pastors to minister effectively to the ill or dying.

Elisabeth Kübler-Ross' years of research and work with the terminally ill culminated in her 1969 book *On Death and Dying*. In it, she systematically examined the human response to dying and identified the five "stages" of dying: denial, anger, bargaining, depression, and acceptance. Denial is typically the patient's initial reaction to the prognosis. Eventually the denial gives way to anger, as well as to displaced feelings of rage, envy, and resentment. The third stage, bargaining, is characterized by the patient's attempts to enter into an agreement, such as trading in good behavior, to put off or avoid the inevitable. Depression follows, in which the patient is overcome by feelings of loss. The final stage, acceptance, occurs when the patient experiences a void of feelings and quietly accepts his fate.

On Death and Dying became a bestseller, and Kübler-Ross' work won wide praise from physicians and specialists. Subsequent articles in popular publications like *Life* and appearances on national television catapulted her to international fame. Almost overnight, she was hailed as the foremost authority on death, and her work inspired a new field of study, thanatology. Following her example, theologians began devoting more time to exploring the meaning of death, while medical personnel started exhibiting greater compassion toward dying patients. Psychologists, sociologists, and anthropologists began researching death-related behavior, and universities like Harvard and Stanford began offering courses on the subject of death and dying.

Elisabeth Kübler-Ross' fame became so great that she received up to 3,000 letters a week and a steady stream of invitations to lecture and conduct workshops. She resigned from the faculty of the University of Chicago in 1970 so that she could to devote herself full time to her work with the terminally ill. Her "Life, Death and Transition" workshops, which she conducted

throughout the United States and abroad, attracted thousands of ill people, their families, and members of the medical profession. Though the first modern hospice to care for the dying was established in England by *Cicely Saunders, Kübler-Ross was largely responsible for bringing the concept to the United States, and she subsequently served on the boards of numerous hospices across the country.

By the mid-1970s, Elisabeth Kübler-Ross had begun delving into the spiritual aspects of death. In her 1974 book, *Questions and Answers on Death and Dying*, she wrote: "Before I started working with dying patients, I did not believe in life after death. I now do believe in life after death without a shadow of a doubt." Her vision of life after death included a happy, peaceful existence in which the physical and mental ailments of the body disappeared. This note of hope consoled her terminally ill patients and contributed greatly to the continued success of her workshops but also drew professional criticism. Further scientific skepticism was aroused by her claims that she had encountered "materialized" supernatural spirits, including a former patient. Countered Kübler-Ross:

> I have had many wonderful mystical experiences, from cosmic consciousness to the awareness and ability to be in touch with my own guides, although I come from a conservative Protestant, authoritarian European background and I have never sought or previously understood the concept of "higher consciousness." I have never been able to meditate regularly; activities of this nature do not accord with my personality. I have never had a guru. . . . I have lived a life of unremitting work; leisure has never had much part in it. Yet despite all this, I have had, very possibly, every mystical experience that human beings are capable of having. I have experienced the greatest highs without ever having taken any drugs. I have been able to see the light that my patients see in their near-death experiences, and I have been surrounded by that incredible unconditional love that all of us experience when we make the transition called death.

In 1977, she formed a fleeting professional alliance with self-proclaimed medium Jay Barham (a former Arkansas sharecropper who established the Church of the Facet of Divinity in 1975) and began participating in seances at Shanti Nilaya, a healing retreat she founded that year in Escondido, California. Kübler-Ross' reputation suffered a sustained blow when disgruntled participants alleged that sexual misconduct had occurred during the seances. The charges were ultimately dismissed, and Kübler-Ross continued to defend her belief that communication with the dead was a reality and that she could act as a visionary.

Throughout the 1980s, Elisabeth Kübler-Ross' efforts were focused on AIDS. She designed workshops in response to the special needs of AIDS patients and devoted a considerable effort on behalf of children with AIDS. In 1985, she sparked controversy again when she announced plans to build a hospice for children with AIDS at Healing Waters Farm, her 250-acre farm in rural Highland County, Virginia, where she had moved the base of her operations two years earlier. Her plan met with immediate resistance from local residents who staunchly opposed providing a haven for AIDS patients in their community. The local government supported the residents and denied her request to rezone the land. After much heated community debate, she abandoned the idea and instead set up a national network to place children with AIDS in other health centers across the country. In 1987, meeting with continued local disapproval, Kübler-Ross established a teaching center at the farm to train therapists working with the terminally ill and began operating workshops for grieving survivors. She detailed her struggles with the community in her 1987 book *AIDS: The Ultimate Challenge*. The book includes case histories of patients and explores the special needs and complex feelings associated with the disease; it also advocates a more compassionate and humane treatment of those stricken with AIDS and calls on society to meet the challenge of combating the disease. In the book, she writes:

> We can destroy ourselves with our own self-imposed fears, blame, shame, negativity. . . . Or we can make our choices based on love and begin to heal, to serve those with AIDS and other diseases, to show compassion and understanding, and finally, before it is too late, to learn the final lesson, the lesson of unconditional love.

The nine-year battle between Kübler-Ross and local residents over her attempts to found AIDS-related care or educational facilities in Highland County culminated in November 1994 when arsonists burned her farm and training center to the ground. Following the fire, she curtailed her professional activities in Virginia and moved to Scottsdale, Arizona.

Elisabeth Kübler-Ross is the recipient of numerous honorary degrees from universities, including Smith College, the University of Notre Dame, Amherst College, and Loyola University, as well as several awards including the Teilhard Prize from the Teilhard Foundation (1981). In an epilogue to her biography, written by Derek Gill, she wrote:

> Those years in the French part of Switzerland, in Poland, France, Germany, Belgium and Italy were gifts of awareness, gifts of sharing with other human beings who had survived the war but lost many loved ones under the most tragic of circumstances. By viewing the gas chambers, the concentration camps, the train filled with the baby shoes of murdered children in Maidanek, by talking with the Jewish girl who had lived through the nightmare of seeing her family march to their deaths, I learned that it is our choice, our own personal choice, whether we want to continue living as victims of resentment, negativity, the need for revenge; or whether we elect to leave the negativity behind and view such tragedies as the windstorms of life which can both strengthen us and help us to grow.

SOURCES:
Dempsey, David. "Learning How to Die," in *The New York Times Magazine*. November 14, 1971, pp. 58–81.
Gill, Derek. *Quest: The Life of Elisabeth Kübler-Ross*. NY: Harper and Row, 1980.
Kübler-Ross, Elisabeth. *AIDS: The Ultimate Challenge*. NY: Macmillan, 1987.
———. *On Death and Dying*. NY: Macmillan, 1969.
———. *Questions and Answers on Death and Dying*. NY: Macmillan, 1974.
———. *The Wheel of Life: A Memoir of Living and Dying*. NY: Scribner, 1997.
The New York Times. May 3, 1971; May 9, 1971; July 21, 1974.
Rosen, Jonathan. "Rewriting the End: Elisabeth Kübler-Ross," in *The New York Times Magazine*. January 22, 1995, pp. 22–25.
San Francisco Chronicle. November 14, 1976; November 22, 1979; November 27, 1983.
Washington Post. November 13, 1994.

Suzanne Smith,
freelance writer and editor, Decatur, Georgia

Kuchinskaya, Natalia (1949—)

Soviet gymnast. Name variations: Natalya. Born in March 1949.

In the 1968 Olympics in Mexico City, Natalia Kuchinskaya took two gold medals, for the balance beam and for the Team All-around; she also won a bronze medal in floor exercises and All-around individual.

Kuckhoff, Greta (1902–1981)

Member of the anti-Nazi resistance organization "Red Orchestra," in which her husband played a crucial role, who supported his espionage activities despite the danger involved. Born Greta Lorke on De-

cember 14, 1902, in Frankfurt an der Oder, Germany; died in 1981; married Adam Kuckhoff (1887–1943, a writer, editor and theater director), in 1937.

Born on December 14, 1902, in Frankfurt an der Oder, Greta Lorke grew up in modest circumstances, but her parents supported her desire for a higher education. After studying economics in Berlin and Würzburg from 1924 through 1927, she traveled to the United States, where she was enrolled at the University of Wisconsin, Madison from 1927 to 1929. While there, she became acquainted with Arvid Harnack (1901–1942) and *Mildred Fish (Harnack)— friendships that would prove to be fateful in later years. Returning to Europe, Greta worked in Zurich, then moved to Frankfurt am Main and Berlin where she taught courses in American business law and also did translations. In 1937, she married the writer, editor and theater director Adam Kuckhoff.

Adam despised the Nazi regime and was an active member of resistance circles, editing the underground newspaper *Die Innere Front*. Greta too desired the liberation of Germany and became an active member of the spy organization "Red Orchestra" which was led by her husband, Harro Schulze-Boysen (1904–1942) and Arvid Harnack (who had married her American-born friend Mildred Fish). Crucial military information radioed to Moscow by the Red Orchestra network may well have saved the Soviet Union and changed the course of World War II.

Greta Kuckhoff and her husband were arrested on September 12, 1942, and both were interrogated at the notorious Berlin headquarters of the Gestapo, Prinz-Albrecht-Strasse 8. The Kuckhoffs received death sentences, but while Adam's was carried out on August 5, 1943, Greta's was reduced to a term of ten years' hard labor. She was liberated from the Waldheim penitentiary in May 1945.

Following the war, Kuckhoff had a significant political career. In 1945, she joined the German Communist Party, which became the Socialist Unity party in 1946. In 1945–46, she was the highest civilian official in charge of food supplies in Soviet-occupied Berlin. In 1948, she was appointed to the German Economic Commission in the Soviet Occupation Zone of Germany, and the next year became a division chief of the newly created Foreign Ministry of the infant German Democratic Republic (GDR or East Germany). She also was elected to the People's Chamber in 1949, holding her seat until 1958. In December 1950, she became president of the German Bank of Issue, a post that entitled her to a vote in the Council of Ministers of the GDR. After leaving her bank post in 1958, she became a vice president of the German Peace Council. In 1963, she was appointed president of the German-British Society. Greta Kuckhoff published her memoirs in 1972; they were popular in the GDR, being reprinted many times in the 1970s and 1980s, and are a significant source of information on the Red Orchestra spy network. She died in 1981.

SOURCES:

Biernat, Karl Heinz, and Luise Kraushaar. *Die Schulze-Boysen-Harnack-Organisation im antifaschistischen Kampf.* Berlin: Dietz Verlag, 1970.

Kuckhoff, Greta. *Vom Rosenkranz zur Roten Kapelle: Ein Lebensbericht.* 7th ed. Berlin: Verlag Neues Leben, 1986.

Perrault, Gilles. *The Red Orchestra.* NY: Schocken Books, 1989.

Rürup, Reinhard. *Topographie des Terrors: Gestapo, SS und Reichssicherheitshauptamt auf dem "Prinz-Albrecht-Gelände": Eine Dokumentation.* 7th ed. Berlin: Verlag Willmuth Arenhövel, 1989.

Trepper, Leopold. *The Great Game: Memoirs of the Spy Hitler Couldn't Silence.* NY: McGraw-Hill, 1977.

U.S. Central Intelligence Agency. *The Rote Kapelle: The CIA's History of Soviet Intelligence and Espionage Networks in Western Europe, 1936–1945.* Washington, DC: University Publications of America, 1979.

John Haag,
Associate Professor of History,
University of Georgia, Athens, Georgia

Kuczinski, Ruth (1907—)

Captain in the Soviet army and spy known as Red Sonya, one of the most successful in the history of espionage, who transmitted the secret of the atomic bomb to the Soviet Union. Name variations: Ruth Kuczinsky; Ruth Beurton; Ruth Werner; (code name) Sonja or Red Sonia, Red Sonja, or Red Sonya. Born Ursula Ruth Kuczinski in Berlin, Germany, on May 15, 1907; daughter of Dr. Robert René Kuczinski (a well-known economist) and a mother who was an idealist and a Jew of Polish extraction like her father; sister of Juergen Kuczinski, also a spy; married Rudolf Hamburger, in 1930 (divorced); married Leon (Len) Beurton (a British Communist), in 1938; children: two.

Joined the Communist Party (1924); married Rudolf Hamburger and went with him to China (1930); recruited by Richard Sorge and sent to Moscow for training; worked in Peking and Poland; awarded the Order of the Red Banner for meritorious service to the Soviet Union (1937); became a captain in the Red Army; sent to Switzerland (1938) where she married Leon Beurton, a British Communist, after an earlier divorce from Hamburger; went to England with her children as a German refugee and began transmitting information to Moscow (spring 1941); sent large amounts of information including vital facts from Dr. Klaus Fuchs which allowed the Soviet Union to construct an atomic bomb after World War II; left Great Britain (1950) after serving as a spy for 20 years; retired in East Germany where she was joined by her husband; wrote a book about her life, Sonja's Rapport, *which sold over half a million copies.*

When World War II convulsed Europe, many were forced to flee to safety. In the spring of 1941, one refugee arrived in the Summertown district of Oxford where she moved into a cottage with her two small children. The woman's husband, Len Beurton, served in Britain's Royal Air Force (RAF) and the Coldstream Guards. He had been stranded in Switzerland, however, when war broke out, forcing her to flee to Britain alone with the children. The refugees were welcomed to the cottage at 50 George Street, just as thousands of others like them had been received with open arms by the British. Life soon became quite settled for the small family, though Mrs. Beurton did make one unusual request. She asked her neighbor, Judge Neville Laski, if she might place an aerial on his roof, to improve the radio reception in her cottage. He gladly complied with her request. The new resident was often seen shopping or chatting with a neighbor. No one suspected that this innocuous housewife was, in fact, a spy as well as a captain in the Soviet army. In fact, her cover was so good she would retire after serving 20 years with no one the wiser. Few spies have been more efficient than Ruth Kuczinski. (Kuczinski, however, never worked for the KGB and took umbrage when newspapers listed her as a KGB agent. "I was a member of the Red Army," she said, "in the reconnaissance service.")

*S*he is probably the bravest and most successful female spy in the history of the second oldest profession.

—Anne McElvoy

Ursula Ruth Kuczinski was born in Berlin on May 15, 1907. Her parents were German Jews of Polish origin. Her father, Dr. Robert René Kuczinski, was a well-known economist of some distinction. Her mother was a typical housewife of the period except that she, like her husband, had strong political beliefs. Ruth, as her parents called her, grew up believing that communism would be the world's salvation. The effects of inflation in Germany after World War I only reinforced her beliefs. Overnight, the capi-

talist system destroyed millions of lives due to horrific inflation. Savings of a lifetime were wiped out when a single loaf of bread cost millions of marks. People used wheelbarrows to carry the huge sums required to purchase life's bare necessities. Ruth was only 17 when she joined the Communist Youth Organization.

The roots of Ruth Kuczinski's ideological fervor grew deep in the soil of European history. During the late 19th and early 20th centuries, the old Europe began to crumble. Three multinational empires collapsed in a few short years. The Ottoman Empire, which had dominated part of Europe and the Middle East for over 1,000 years, was no more. The Austro-Hungarian Empire, ruled by the Habsburgs since the Middle Ages, became a group of new states—Austria, Hungary, Czechoslovakia, and Yugoslavia. The Russian Empire also collapsed and was replaced by the Soviet Union. Enormous economic change accompanied the disappearance of familiar empires as the industrial revolution swept across Europe. Family farms were replaced by agricultural complexes, forcing rural populations to urbanize. Small, traditionally home-centered industries were replaced by vast factories capable of manufacturing enormous quantities of goods. Working conditions in the new factories were frightful. Men, women, and young children were devoured by a system which often demanded 12-to-18 hours of work per day under appalling conditions.

Many rebelled against this new world. They felt international brotherhood should replace rampant nationalism. They believed that millions should not be forced to work as wage slaves in order for a few to enjoy enormous wealth. For them, capitalism was a system gone mad which would soon destroy the human race. One such individual was Karl Marx, the German idealist. His blueprint of "scientific socialism" provided an alternative to capitalism's ugly exploitation. According to Marx, the wealth generated by the industrial revolution should be used for the general good, providing ample food, shelter, medical care, and education for all. Under his scheme, moneys would be given "to each according to his need." The state, not individual capitalists, would own modes of production. As the old Europe crumbled, communist ideas engulfed the Continent. Communists were often highly idealistic people whose fervor could best be described as religious. They believed that in their lifetime a new world order would prevail. In the meantime, they must do battle with the evil forces of capitalism, fighting with every weapon at their disposal. A Communist government was established in the old Russian empire after World War I and more would be founded in Eastern Europe after World War II. The war between communism and capitalism would dominate the 20th century until the fall of the Berlin Wall in 1989. It was on this battlefield that Ruth Kuczinski fought, a warrior against what she deemed the evils of capitalism.

After joining the German Communist Party (KPD) in Berlin, Ruth Kuczinski worked at Ullstein Brothers, the well-known publishing house. Her job was of short duration, because her over-enthusiastic Communist activities caused her employers to dismiss her. Her father and brother were doing research in the United States so she joined them there, leaving her boyfriend, Rudolf Hamburger, behind. She obtained a job in a New York bookstore where she worked until 1929, when she returned to Germany to marry Rudolf. In the meantime, her father had visited Moscow thus cementing his relationship with Soviet Communists. In 1930, Rudolf applied for an architect's post with the Shanghai Municipal Council. Ruth was only 23 when the couple traveled to China via Moscow on the Trans-Siberian Express. At this point, the German Communist Party had become virtually a section of Soviet Intelligence. Moscow was enthusiastic about the prospect of converting millions of Chinese to communism.

Once in Shanghai, Ruth became friends with *Agnes Smedley, an American who was a veteran in the service of the Comintern, the Soviet agency for promoting worldwide revolution. Smedley served as a Far Eastern correspondent for the *Frankfurter Zeitung*, but her real objective was to assist the Chinese Communist Party. She soon introduced Kuczinski to Richard Sorge, a highly effective operative in China who arranged for the young woman to go to Moscow for training. There, Ruth took the code name Sonya. Returning to China, she organized Chinese partisan troops fighting the occupying Japanese army along the Manchurian border. While in Manchuria, she radioed reports back to Moscow about the Japanese invasion. She then served in Peking and Poland. In 1937, she was awarded the Order of the Red Banner for meritorious service to the Soviet Union.

In 1938, Ruth Kuczinski was promoted from lieutenant to major in the Red Army and sent to Switzerland. She was ordered to set up an espionage network there capable of providing extensive radio reports on Nazi Germany. She recruited Allan Alexander Foote to assist her in this task. By this time, her marriage to Ham-

burger had ended, and she was living alone with her two children, the first fathered by her husband and the second fathered by an individual she refused to name. In Switzerland, instructed to recruit and wed a British veteran, she chose to marry a young English Communist, Leon Charles Beurton, known as Len, and left for London on December 18, 1940.

The Soviet Union was extremely interested in gathering all the information it could from the British and the Americans. Although Adolf Hitler, Germany's Nazi leader, and Joseph Stalin, the Soviet Union's Communist dictator, had signed a non-aggression pact in 1939, the Soviets expected the Germans to attack them at any time. Western Europe and the United States had no love for Nazi Germany, but their dread of the Communist menace was even greater. The Soviets feared, quite rightly, that the West would allow Hitler to devour their country in the hopes that they themselves would remain free from attack. The safest course was to monitor the British and Americans as closely as possible.

Ruth Kuczinski first arrived in Glympton, a tiny Oxfordshire village three miles from the Palace of Blenheim, seat of the dukes of Marl-

Ruth Kuczinski with her husband.

borough. She told the vicar, the Reverend Charles Henry Cox, that she was a German refugee married to an Englishman called Len Beurton who was still in Switzerland. Having made a hazardous escape from the Continent with her two children, she sought temporary refuge. Her journey had been much more exciting than she described. She had stuffed some radio parts into her children's teddy bears in order to smuggle a transmitter into the country. When one customs officer inquired about a piece of electronic equipment in her luggage, she told him it was a toy. As soon as she settled in a bedroom at the rectory, she began to construct a radio transmitter. She then moved into that cottage in the Summertown district of Oxford.

As the war progressed, the Soviet Union and the Allies joined forces. Hitler's brutal attack on the Soviet Union almost brought the vast country to its knees, but millions fought bravely against the German invaders. The heroism of Soviet women and men impressed the Allies who had watched one country after another fall to Hitler's armies. In the meantime, Ruth transmitted a great deal of data to Moscow. Her husband Len provided information about British military forces, while her father René had important contacts inside the government. The Soviets were especially anxious to know if the Allies really intended to open a Second Front, and it was no doubt Ruth who told them this would happen. Her brother, Juergen, wrote reports on economic planning for the British which Moscow also found useful. Ruth's extensive network was augmented by many contacts in Britain who sympathized with the Soviet struggle and gave her information in order to aid an ally. Two or three times a month, Kuczinski sent her reports to Moscow using a Morse code transmitter and the aerial on Judge Laski's adjacent house to enhance the transmission signals. Never once were her activities suspected.

During the war against Germany, the Soviets were allies, and the British intelligence network shared information with the Soviet Union. In fact, most Allies realized that the war could never have been won had it not been for the valiant effort on the Eastern front. Yet even as the war on the Continent wound down, another conflict was beginning. Before the outbreak of World War II, nuclear fission had almost been discovered. Frèdèric and *Irène Joliot-Curie came so near to demonstrating fission in France that they stopped publishing papers on the subject in 1939 for fear Hitler might make use of this awesome power. Throughout the war, scientists in America worked frantically on the Man-

hattan Project to develop a nuclear bomb. Despite strict secrecy, rumors of the project were rampant. It was generally recognized that nuclear weapons would change the balance of power in the postwar world. In the meantime, Soviet and American troops rapidly occupied territory which had been held by the Nazis. Already arguments had broken out over whether the postwar world would be communist or capitalist. The United States struck quickly. On August 6, 1945, it exploded the first atomic bomb over Hiroshima. Three days later, on August 9, a second bomb devastated Nagasaki. No clearer signal of American intentions could have been sent as far as Moscow was concerned.

The Soviet Union was determined to acquire atomic technology, and Ruth Kuczinski would play a critical role in gathering this information. Although Soviet scientists had already made great strides toward creating a bomb, Stalin was determined to obtain information about atomic technology at all costs. Ruth Kuczinski had kept a low profile when Alexander Foote, a contact from China, re-defected to the West and revealed the names of many Soviet spies. When Moscow was certain her name was not on the list of suspects, she was reactivated and given the important assignment of transmitting information about building an atomic bomb. Kuczinski was instructed to obtain this information from Klaus Fuchs, a German physicist who had spent the war in Britain. Ruth would be Fuchs' control in espionage terms.

Klaus Fuchs, also known as the man who stole the atomic bomb, was a physicist who began reporting to Kuczinski in 1942. A German refugee like Ruth, Fuchs had also joined the Communist Party as a teenager. He fled to Britain in 1933 where he became a research assistant to Professor Neville Mott at Bristol University and received a Ph.D. in physics four years later. Mott then wrote Professor Max Born, a famous German physicist teaching at Edinburgh University, and asked him to take Fuchs on. This arrangement was quite happy for both Fuchs and Born until Fuchs was interned briefly as an enemy alien. Fuchs then went to Canada for a short period until another physicist, Rudolf Peierls, asked him to work on another project. So it was that Klaus Fuchs found himself at the heart of the British effort to build an atomic bomb.

In the summer of 1942, he began meeting Kuczinski, passing over his papers and other information about the bomb which she then transmitted to Moscow. Since Fuchs worked in Birmingham, the two often met in the English village of Banbury. This relationship would continue until 1948, when Kuczinski was questioned by MI5, the British intelligence agency. It is not known how much information Fuchs passed on to the Soviet Union through Ruth Kuczinski and others, but it did not take long after the war until the Soviets also had nuclear weapons.

Accurate historical accounts of a spy's life are all but impossible. Successful spies divulge little about themselves, and their own accounts are almost never to be trusted. This leaves others to piece together the true story as best they can. Since Ruth Kuczinski was extraordinarily successful, her story is especially difficult. Considerable evidence indicates that she had a powerful protector at MI5, the British intelligence agency, and that it may have been Roger Hollis, the head of the agency. She had met Hollis in China, so theirs was a longstanding relationship. Hollis lived near Oxford during the war, not far from her cottage. His department was responsible for listing dangerous Communists, a list Ruth Kuczinski's name never appeared on. It is established that Kuczinski transmitted thousands of messages to Moscow, and yet her powerful transmitter was never reported. Finally, when Kuczinski's activities did come to light in 1948, her interrogation by MI5 agents was a farce. She was allowed to stay in Britain and then to escape quietly to East Germany in 1950 completely unhindered. When Kim Philby's identity as a major spy was revealed, rumor persisted that an important "mole" remained at MI5. Whether or not this person was Hollis, many believe that individual was also Kuczinski's protector.

After Fuchs had confessed to his role in disseminating information about the atomic bomb in October 1949, Kuczinski had applied for permission to visit East Germany. As soon as her visa arrived, she left for the East. (Fuchs would serve nine and a half years in prison in Britain before also returning to East Germany.) The following summer, Len, her husband, cleared out the house, burned all incriminating papers, and followed his wife to where a new job awaited him with the East German News service. Although Moscow did not want Ruth to retire, she realized her espionage career had run its course. Rewarded for her many years of service, Kuczinski lived well in East Germany. In 1977, she published her autobiography, *Sonja's Rapport* (*Sonya's Report*) under the name Ruth Werner; it sold over half a million copies.

In 1993, London-based writer Norman Moss interviewed Kuczinski in her home in East Germany. He found a small, 85-year-old woman with "fluffy white hair and a prominent nose," and a way of "peering through her spectacles" as she talked. She entertained Moss with tea and cakes in her book-lined living room; her conversation centered on the "great lost cause": socialism. "Yes, we fought for communism," she told him. "We didn't know—I didn't know—about Stalin's crimes. I remember how shocked I was when we were told about them. Friends of mine were sent to prison, but I still didn't realize." She was also unhappy with the repressive policies in East Germany and welcomed Gorbachev's Glasnost. But Kuczinski maintained that distortions of socialism were what brought the system down. "For me, this is not a good time to be old," she said.

SOURCES:
Costello, John. *Mask of Treachery*. NY: William Morrow, 1988.
Frey, Gerhard. *Prominente ohne Maske DDR*. Munich: FZ-Verlag, 1991.
Knightley, Phillip. *The Second Oldest Profession: Spies and Spying in the Twentieth Century*. NY: Penguin Books, 1986.
McElvoy, Anne. *The Saddled Cow: East Germany's Life and Legacy*. London: Faber and Faber, 1992.
Moss, Norman. *Klaus Fuchs: The Man Who Stole the Atomic Bomb*. London: Grafton Books, 1987.
———. "'Sonya' Explains," in *The Bulletin of the Atomic Scientists*. July–August 1993.
Norton-Taylor, Richard. "Soviet Spy Denies MI5 Chief Link," in *Manchester Guardian*. July 7, 1990, p. 6.
Pincher, Chapman. *Too Secret, Too Long*. NY: St. Martin's Press, 1984.
———. *Traitors: The Anatomy of Treason*. NY: St. Martin's Press, 1987.
Shipley, Peter. *Hostile Action: The KGB and Secret Soviet Operations in Britain*. NY: St. Martin's Press, 1990.
Werner, Ruth. *Sonja's Rapport*. 4th ed. Berlin, DDR: Verlag Neues Leben, 1978.
Williams, Robert Chadwell. *Klaus Fuchs: Atom Spy*. Cambridge, MA: Harvard University Press, 1987.

John Haag,
Associate Professor of History,
University of Georgia, Athens, Georgia

Kuderikova, Marie (1921–1943)

Czech anti-Nazi activist and factory worker. Born on March 24, 1921, in Vnorovy-Hodonin, Czechoslovakia; executed in Breslau on March 26, 1943; leader of the illegal youth organization of the Czechoslovak Communist Party.

Born on March 24, 1921, in Vnorovy-Hodonin, in the Moravian province of Czechoslovakia, Marie Kuderikova had few economic advantages in her youth and despite her intelligence had to support herself from an early age by working in a factory. Like many of her fellow workers at the Racek factory in Brno (Brünn), she was strongly attracted to Marxism as a doctrine and a blueprint for a better life. These beliefs became a matter of life and death after March 1939, when what remained of the Czechoslovak Republic was taken over by Nazi Germany and became a puppet state, the "Protectorate of Bohemia-Moravia." Communist and Social Democratic organizations were brutally suppressed by the German occupying forces and their Czech collaborators, and membership in such groups in most cases made one liable to a death sentence.

Betrayed to the Gestapo, Kuderikova was arrested in Brno on December 5, 1941, transferred to the Pankrac prison in Prague, and then returned to Brno. Eventually she and others in her resistance circle were transferred to Breslau (now Wroclaw, Poland) in Germany. There a Nazi People's Court sentenced her and 11 members of her group to death. All were executed in Breslau on the same day, March 26, 1943.

SOURCES:

Gollwitzer, Helmut, Käthe Kuhn, and Reinhold Schneider, eds. *Dying We Live: The Final Messages and Records of the Resistance.* NY: Pantheon Books, 1956.

John Haag,
Athens, Georgia

Kudrun.

Variant of Gudrun.

Kuffner, Baroness (1898–1980).

See Lempicka, Tamara de.

Kuhlman, Kathryn (1907–1976)

American evangelist. Born on May 9, 1907, in Concordia, Missouri; died on February 20, 1976, in Tulsa, Oklahoma; daughter of Joseph Kuhlman and Emma (Walkenhorst) Kuhlman; married Burroughs Waltrip, in October 1938 (divorced 1948); no children.

Kathryn Kuhlman, whose ministry across the United States spanned five decades, was a nationally known evangelical preacher. Born on a small farm in Missouri in 1907, Kuhlman and her three siblings received minimal schooling. Their mother tried to raise them in the Methodist Church over the objections of their atheist father. At age 14, Kuhlman underwent a profound religious conversion at a Baptist revival meeting and began attending services regularly. In the summer of 1923, against her parents' wishes, she left Concordia for Oregon to help her evangelist sister and brother-in-law lead revival meetings. Though Kuhlman had planned to spend only the summer with her sister, she continued to help them with their ministry for the next five years.

In 1928, Kuhlman began preaching as her brother-in-law's substitute. Her popularity led to a five-year evangelist tour of the western U.S., arranging and conducting revival meetings and healing sessions with a pianist to assist her. In 1933, Kuhlman settled briefly in Pueblo, Colorado; soon, with the encouragement of the local Baptist community, she moved to Denver. She rented a warehouse, converted it into a center for worship services called the Kuhlman Revival Tabernacle, and hired a small staff. Her simple, direct style of preaching made her a household name in Denver. Her tabernacle came to include Sunday school services and a short radio program as well.

In 1937, Kuhlman met Burroughs Waltrip, an evangelist based in Iowa whom she had invited to preach at her Denver tabernacle. The meeting led to a business partnership and ultimately to their marriage in 1938. It was a turning point in Kuhlman's ministry. Soon after the marriage was made public, her congregation learned that Waltrip had abandoned his wife and children and had been divorced by his wife for desertion. Kuhlman's choice to marry Waltrip cost her most of her popularity in Denver, and several employees of her ministry resigned in protest. Her friends urged her to leave Waltrip but Kuhlman believed she was in love and that God had brought them together to preach.

They left Denver to settle in Mason City, Iowa, but the scandal of Waltrip's past eventually spread there as well and the couple picked up stakes once more to begin a nationwide preaching tour. They remained on the road for several years though they met with little success, again because of Waltrip's divorce. By 1944, the marriage was over, and Kuhlman separated from Waltrip, although they did not finalize their divorce for four years. From that point on, Kuhlman struggled to reestablish herself as a legitimate evangelical preacher. By 1946, the scandal of her marriage had faded, and Kuhlman became the host of a weekly radio prayer program in Franklin, Pennsylvania, which was soon picked up across Pennsylvania. She also initiated a series of prayer meetings and revivals which met with growing success in the late 1940s.

In 1947, Kuhlman changed her previous focus on the gospel of salvation and congregational singing to include a healing service. She was fascinated by the process of religious healing and believed strongly in its possibilities.

Kathryn
Kuhlman

However, she did not claim to actually perform healing miracles herself; instead, she saw herself as a vessel through which God acted to cure the ill. Soon the impromptu healing sessions became the standard ending to her worship services. She would ask members to come forward to describe their own healing, or she would lay hands on them and ask God to heal them.

By 1950, she had established a following strong enough to open a temple of her own in Pittsburgh, and also preached and performed healing sessions in cities across the state. Her regular revival meetings in Pittsburgh would continue until 1971. Throughout the 1950s, she steadily built a national following while defending herself against growing criticism from other leading evangelists, some of whom had lost congregation members to Kuhlman, over the veracity of her healing power. She consistently maintained that God had chosen her as an instrument of prayer and healing, and her growing audience in person and via radio testified to others' belief in her power to perform miracles. In 1957, her accountant Walter Adamack established the Kathryn Kuhlman Foundation in Pittsburgh, which administered her meetings and appearances and managed the sizable income she received from her followers' donations. The Foundation also made numerous gifts to aid other ministries worldwide.

Kuhlman brought her revival sessions to Los Angeles, California, where she preached regularly until 1975. Also in that year, Kuhlman made her first television appearances with her own weekly program on CBS. In addition, Kuhlman spread the gospel of salvation by publishing small booklets, many of which are still in print, that explained her message and provided testimonials from those who claimed to have been cured by her. As Kuhlman became an increasingly visible figure, the mass media began profiling her in mainstream magazines and talk shows, although she received both positive and negative treatments by the press for her message and style. Kuhlman's life became increasingly itinerant as she traveled several times a week across the United States, mainly between Pittsburgh and Los Angeles, but also, after 1973, throughout Canada as well. From her early days of arranging her own meetings Kuhlman progressed to a full-time staff of 11 accountants, managers, musicians, and vocalists. Yet it was not until her ordination by the Evangelical Church Alliance in 1968 that Kuhlman finally felt she had been given the legitimacy within her profession which she had long striven for.

By the early 1970s, Kuhlman's heavy schedule of travel and exhausting appearances had taken a toll on her health. Diagnosed with a heart condition, she continued to preach actively until she was hospitalized twice in 1975. She underwent open-heart surgery in Tulsa, Oklahoma, in February 1976 but died several days later, on February 20. After her death a considerable scandal followed the announcement that she had rewritten her will in 1975 and disinherited her family as well as her ministry. Her followers were surprised to learn that she did not intend the Kuhlman ministry to continue after her death. Instead, she left virtually all of her substantial personal wealth to two friends who had been her companions for the last year of her life. Kathryn Kuhlman is buried in Glendale, California.

SOURCES:

Buckingham, Jamie. *Daughter of Destiny: Kathryn Kuhlman . . . her story.* Plainfield, NJ: Logos International, 1976.

Warner, Wayne. *Kathryn Kuhlman: The Woman Behind the Miracles.* Ann Arbor, MI: Servant Publications, 1993.

Laura York,
Riverside, California

Kuhn, Irene Corbally (1898–1995)

American journalist who gained her reputation in the 1920s and 1930s as a foreign correspondent and feature writer. Born Irene Corbally on January 15, 1898, in New York City; died at the Brian Crest-Deaconess Nursing Home in Concord, Massachusetts, on December 30, 1995; daughter of Patrick J. Corbally and Josephine (Connor) Corbally; attended Packard Business School, Marymount College (Tarrytown-on-the-Hudson), and Extension Division, Columbia University; married Bert L. Kuhn, on June 11, 1922 (died 1926); children: Rene Leilani (b. 1923).

Started out as reporter on the Syracuse Herald *(1920); wrote for the* New York Daily News *(1920),* Chicago Tribune *(European edition, Paris, 1921–22),* Evening Star *(Shanghai, 1922–26); served as a foreign correspondent for Hearst Wire Service and International News Service, Honolulu and Shanghai (1923–26); worked as broadcaster, station KRC Shanghai (1924); wrote for the* New York Daily Mirror *(1926),* New York Daily News *(1927–28, 1930),* Honolulu Star-Bulletin *(1929–30); was a scriptwriter for 20th Century-Fox (1931–32), Metro-Goldwyn-Mayer (1932–33), Paramount (1939); worked as feature writer,* New York World-Telegram *(1933–35); was an executive and commentator, National Broadcasting Company (1940–49); was a columnist for King Features Syndicate (1953–69); was a columnist, Columbia Features, Inc. (1970); contributed reminiscences to* Gourmet *magazine (1970s–80s).*

Selected writings: Assigned to Adventure (Grosset and Dunlap, 1938); (with Raymond J. DeJaeger) The Enemy Within (Doubleday, 1952).

The story of Irene Corbally Kuhn transports one back to the whirlwind days of cutthroat journalism so ably portrayed in Ben Hecht and Charles MacArthur's 1928 play *The Front Page.* It was a world of glamorous aviators and sensational murder trials, of international playboys and Asian warlords, where journalists mixed copy-desk camaraderie and hard drinking with fierce competition. In this world, Irene Kuhn thrived. In her career, she gathered a number of "firsts" after her name, some quite unusual: the first woman ever to broadcast in the Orient; probably the first female announcer in radio; the first woman vice-president of the Overseas Press Club; the first individual to broadcast from a U.S. Navy vessel; the first person to broadcast from liberated Shanghai; the first woman reporter sent to Manila; and the first woman to write for the *Stars and Stripes*.

Irene Corbally Kuhn was born on January 15, 1898, in New York City, the daughter of Patrick J. and **Josephine Connor Corbally**. She grew up in Greenwich Village in a large brownstone house which her family shared with relatives. Writes her fellow journalist *Ishbel Ross, Greenwich Village then "really was a village, with backyard gardens, trees in the streets, band concerts in the parks and May parties in Central Park on Saturdays, reached by chartered trolley cars with ribbons flying from their poles. The horse cars used to jog and jingle through West Houston Street, where [Kuhn] was born, a stone's throw from her maternal grandfather's cooperage shop, established by him around Civil War time."

Irene received her early education in Roman Catholic schools. Her first journalistic experience was a column, "I'll Tell the World," in a neighborhood paper, the *Greenwich Village Home News*. Here, she acquired a taste for newspaper life that never left her. At age 16, before she had finished high school, she enrolled at New York's Packard Business School. Secretarial training, she believed, would provide her with writing skills while introducing her to that mysterious entity called "life." After seven months of studying stenography, she secured her first job at a salary of nine dollars per week.

After a series of minor positions, Kuhn became secretary to William J. Geis, professor of biological chemistry at Columbia University's College of Physicians and Surgeons. Geis not only convinced her of the need for a formal education, he obtained a fellowship for her at Marymount College in Tarrytown-on-the-Hudson, a school directed by French nuns for girls of wealthy families. Enrolling in the fall of 1918, Kuhn dropped out after a term, finding the school too elitist and upperclass. Returning to New York City, she took courses at the Extension Division of Columbia University.

By then she dreamed of working for a New York City newspaper. An acquaintance in the profession, Crosby Grant, recommended that she first obtain "cub" experience in an upstate city. Moreover, Grant was able to secure Kuhn her first reporting job. In 1920, she was hired by the *Syracuse Herald* at a salary of $18 a week. So green, she said, that "she didn't know copy paper from cleansing tissue," she began as a contributor to its "Inquiring Reporter" column. Thriving on the competition, she later wrote of "the old-school training":

> hard, unyielding discipline, little praise, much work, long hours, short pay. If you like the business you gloried in it and survived to prosper—at least, to have a swell time and do work that was a credit to yourself and your paper. If you didn't like the work and couldn't take the training you were fired before you had a chance to quit.

After six months in Syracuse, Kuhn was hired by the newly founded *New York Daily News*. City editor Philipp Payne taught her that the reactions of the "gum-chewers" were virtually the same as the upper classes "except that the former are more honest." Commenting about the *News*, she wrote:

> Here was the movie scenarist's dream of a newspaper, with everything moving at top speed, telephones jangling from every desk, voices shouting, boys scrambling for copy, everybody in the way, people slamming at typewriters, not enough chairs or desks to go around, reporters sitting in each other's laps. But not for long. For everybody, everything, was on the move in the fastest *tempo* I've ever seen.

I would not give up one heartache, or trade any part of the agony, for a chance to live my life again in security and peace. To live close to reality is really to live.

—Irene Corbally Kuhn

In 1921, laid off during a typical seasonal retrenchment, Kuhn went to Paris. For a brief time, she was hired to write advertising copy for an American manufacturer of perfumes and patent medicine, but the job was amorphous, her employer unreliable. She was soon fired. Armed with letters of recommendation from Payne to various American papers in Paris, she was hired by Floyd Gibbons, the flamboyant correspondent of the European edition of the *Chicago Tribune*. Her starting salary was equivalent to 90 American dollars a month. **Rosemary Carr**, the fashion editor, was just leaving the paper to marry poet Stephen Vincent Benét; Kuhn volunteered to fill the slot. Soon, she was covering fashionable Deauville in clothes borrowed from couturiers for modeling purposes. A general all-around reporter as well, Kuhn wrote on such topics as the marriage of a "tin plate" fortune heir to the daughter of a Russian grand duchess, an evening of music and Dada art at the Galerie Montaigne, and life among U.S. troops stationed in Germany. She chased a prominent draft dodger, Grover Cleveland Bergdoll, all over Switzerland to get his story.

In 1922, Kuhn resigned from the *Tribune* to accompany *Peggy Hull, a prominent war correspondent, to Shanghai. Arriving in the middle of the New Year holidays, Kuhn had about $50 in gold, of which $36 was spent on three days lodging. Just as the shutters were being taken down from the shop windows and businesses began to open, she met Herbert Webb, editor of the *China Press*, who hired her as feature editor for the *Evening Star*. Both the *Star* and *Press* were owned by a shady opium dealer who later found legitimacy as a civic leader and real estate operator. On her first day at work, she met a news editor, Bert L. Kuhn, who had written for the *Chicago Tribune*, had been city editor of the

Manila Bulletin, and was currently news editor of the *China Press*. Married in June, the couple lived in relative luxury. The household staff consisted of a Number One Boy, cook, cook's assistant, coolie, gardener, laundress, and personal rickshaw boy.

Soon after their marriage, the Kuhns obtained a year's leave of absence from their papers and sailed for Hawaii. Irene, now pregnant, wanted to have her baby on American soil. In Honolulu, both did newspaper work, Irene for Hearst's International News Service (INS) and Bert for the *Honolulu Star-Bulletin*. Three days before the baby (**Rene Leilani Kuhn**) was born, Irene scooped the Associated and United presses in covering a great tidal wave that crested at Haleiwa, 30 miles from Honolulu. The wave flooded many villages, damaged plantations, and tore out a section of the railroad. Writing her story on February 3, just as she was about to deliver her child, she then rushed to the maternity ward. Wrote Kuhn of her bonus from INS: "On March 2 the cheque arrived. It was for fifty dollars, and it paid for the baby."

Six months later, Bert's restlessness took the family back to Shanghai. When radio came to China in 1924, Kuhn was its first female voice. Facilities were primitive. They operated out of Shanghai's *China Press* offices. Wrote Kuhn:

> We draped heavy cambric sheets across walls and ceiling of a cubicle opposite the editorial room. We set up a wall telephone which had to be "cranked," and which was connected directly to the transmitting station a few miles away. [Roy] Delay [the station manager] installed a microphone and a wheezy portable gramophone with a dozen or so records.

In an article for the *China Press,* Kuhn predicted that "the introduction of a small instrument which can bridge this gap of the human voice may change the entire fortune of China." She interviewed a variety of people over the airwaves, including Chiang Kai-shek, the future Mme. Chiang Kai-shek (*Song Meiling**), and birth-control advocate *Margaret Sanger, who was in China to advance her cause.

On May 30, 1925, riots broke out in Shanghai after Sikh police shot into a mob of some 3,000 Chinese students storming a police station; they were protesting the convictions of Chinese strikers who had left their work in Japanese-owned cotton mills. "That volley of rifle-fire, dropping six students in sudden death," wrote Kuhn, "created such anti-foreign feeling as had not been known since the bloody days of the Boxer rising in Peking many years

Irene Corbally Kuhn

before." The next day, she said, the city was like an armed camp. Kuhn helped organize the Women's Volunteer Motor Canteen Service, which took food and drink to the international force of volunteers and marines doing outpost duty around the settlement.

The Kuhns felt themselves in danger. The household staff quit. Their nurse vanished one night, returning badly beaten. Taking four-hour shifts, one would work while the other stayed at home, watching the baby, cooking from cans set over electric grills, and guarding the house with a gun. To compound their troubles, new owners had taken over the *China Press* and were attempting to break their contracts. In the late fall of 1925, Irene sailed for America with her baby. During a stopover in Vancouver, just an hour before sailing time, she learned that her husband had died. The medical report simply mentioned "unknown causes." Bert had worked secretly for U.S. Naval Intelligence, and Irene could not help but link this activity to his death.

Irene Kuhn freelanced for six months in Chicago, then in July 1926 was hired by Phil Payne, who had moved to the *New York Daily Mirror,* a new Hearst tabloid. Now something of a celebrity, at least among reporters, Kuhn covered the Hall-*[Eleanor] Mills and Snyder-Gray murder cases, interviewing murderer *Ruth Snyder* in the process. Kuhn was assigned to the flight of Charles A. Lindbergh and the trial of Leonard Cline, a talented journalist who shot a friend while drunk and later committed suicide. A year later, she went back to the *New York Daily News,* where she remained for two years.

In the fall of 1929, Kuhn took a leave of absence. She and six-year-old Rene returned to Honolulu, spending a year there while Irene wrote a beach column and reported police news for the *Honolulu Star-Bulletin.* In March 1930, she returned once again to the *News,* where she was the only woman involved in rewriting on a New York paper. She also covered a major Washington social rivalry, the ✥➤ Frances ("Peaches") Heenan and Edward ("Daddy") Browning divorce, and various other scandals.

In 1931, Kuhn moved to Hollywood to write scenarios for the new "talking pictures." Attracted by the large salaries, she first worked for 20th Century-Fox, where she was "weaving plots which high-powered script writers embellished with dialogue and business," she said, "but getting nary a 'screen credit' with which to further my career elsewhere." In 1932, she began a year at Metro-Goldwyn-Mayer and in 1939 did a brief stint for Paramount. Her experiences, she remarked, ran true to form; she made a "grand entrance," then "suffered immediate and complete obliteration except on the payroll."

While vacationing in New York in 1933, Kuhn accepted an invitation from Roy W. Howard, head of the Scripps-Howard chain of newspapers, to become a feature writer for the *New York World-Telegram.* She stayed with the paper for two years. Out of her varied experiences came her autobiography, *Assigned to Adventure* (1938), the first such work ever written by a newspaperwoman. The book offered a rare view of American journalism during the interwar period, and included some deftly drawn portraits of press personalities.

In 1940, Kuhn joined the National Broadcasting Company (NBC), where she served as an executive and commentator until 1949. As director of program promotion, she visited Mexico in 1942 and broadcast from Rio de Janeiro. She also had her own radio column, "Irene Kuhn's Feature Page." In September 1945, Kuhn was the

---

✥➤ **Heenan, Frances** (b. 1911)

Subject of a 1926 scandal. Name variations: Peaches Browning. Born Frances Heenan in 1911; married Edward West Browning (a real estate magnate), on April 10, 1926 (divorced 1927).

Frances "Peaches" Heenan was attending the Textile High School in New York City when she met Edward West Browning, a real estate tycoon who had earned the nickname Daddy because he was generous with his money, especially with projects connected to poor children. Soon, Browning was squiring the young girl around town in his Rolls-Royce and arranging for a chorus-line job for her in Earl Carroll's *Vanities.* Ensuing publicity caught the attention of the Society for the Prevention of Cruelty to Children, who learned that Heenan had been allowed free rein for several years previous. In April 1926, when the Society began legal action in Children's Court against Heenan's mother for neglect, Browning married the young girl. She was 15; he was 51. Heenan's mother moved into Browning's 15-room mansion in Cold Spring, New York, and lived with them.

The marriage was front-page fodder for its duration: seven months. That October, Peaches sued for divorce, making particularly lurid accusations against him. She also accused him of being penurious, refusing to buy her the car, clothes, and jewelry she requested. The judge eventually dismissed her allegations in March 1927, claiming that "the defendant and her mother have falsified, exaggerated, and magnified to such an extent as to render their testimony entirely unbelievable." Browning then won a separation from her.

first person to broadcast from liberated Shanghai and a month later the first woman to broadcast from liberated Manila. At one point, she was broadcasting from a U.S. Navy vessel, the *Rocky Mount*, flagship of Admiral Thomas C. Kinkaid of the Seventh Fleet, anchored in the Whangpoo River in China. In 1945, she was an accredited NBC correspondent in the China-Burma-India theater of war, flying a total of 24,277 miles in planes of the Air Transport Command.

All this time, Kuhn was becoming more of a conservative activist. During the presidential campaigns of 1940 and 1944, she was associate director of publicity for the Republican National Committee. In 1952, in editing the memoir of a Roman Catholic priest who had served in China, she referred to "Communist control of China according to the Soviet viewpoint in their world conspiracy." She accused American policymakers of regarding the Chinese Communists as agrarian reformers and said that General George C. Marshall, who sought to negotiate a truce between the Communists and the Nationalists in 1946, "never really understood the true nature of communism." In an article written for the *American Mercury* in 1955, entitled "Geneva's Smile of Death," she blamed America's "defeat" in the Korean War on the United Nations and found the Eisenhower-Khrushchev summit riddled with Western appeasement.

From 1953 to 1969, Kuhn wrote a column, "It's My Opinion," for King Features Syndicate. Beginning in 1970, she was a columnist for Columbia Features, Inc. She contributed to a number of magazines, including *Reader's Digest*, *Town and Country*, *Cosmopolitan*, *Good Housekeeping*, *Sign*, *American Legion*, *Co-ed*, *Gourmet*, *Paradise of the Pacific*, *Vista*, and *Signature*. She also was travel editor for *American Labor Magazine* and wrote various travel and museum guides. On December 30, 1995, Irene Kuhn died, aged 97, at a nursing home in Concord, Massachusetts.

SOURCES:

Kuhn, Irene Corbally. *Assigned to Adventure*. NY: Grosset and Dunlap, 1938.

SUGGESTED READING:

Ross, Ishbel. *Ladies of the Press*. NY: Harper, 1936 (reprint, Arno, 1974).

Justus D. Doenecke,
Professor of History, New
College of the University of South Florida, Sarasota, Florida

Kuhn, Maggie (1905–1995)

American political activist and founder of the Gray Panthers. Born Margaret Eliza Kuhn in Buffalo, New York, on August 31, 1905; died on April 22, 1995, in Philadelphia, Pennsylvania; daughter of Samuel Kuhn (a businessman) and Minnie (Kooman) Kuhn; graduated from Flora Stone Mather College, B.A., 1927; never married; no children.

Served as assistant business and professional secretary, YWCA-Cleveland (1928–30) and YWCA-Philadelphia (1930–41); served as program coordinator for YWCA's USO Division (1941–48); joined the staff of the National Alliance of Unitarian Women (1948–50); became a member of the Department of Social Education and Action of the Presbyterian Church in the USA (1950–65); worked as program executive for the (Presbyterian) Church's Council on Church and Race (1969); formed ad hoc activist organization, the Consultation of Older Persons (1970); founded the political action group, the Gray Panthers (1971); held first Gray Panthers National Convention (1975); served on President Jimmy Carter's Commission on Mental Health (1978–80); published her autobiography No Stone Unturned: The Life and Times of Maggie Kuhn *(1991).*

A self-proclaimed "woman born to the task of organizing," Margaret "Maggie" Kuhn was an outspoken pacifist, political activist, and passionate advocate of the rights of older Americans. For more than 60 years, she concerned herself with the important social issues of the 20th century.

Margaret Eliza Kuhn was born on August 31, 1905, in the home of her maternal grandmother in Buffalo, New York. Her parents, **Minnie Kooman Kuhn** and Samuel Kuhn, had long yearned for a child but had been unable to conceive. When, after 12 years, a precious daughter was finally born to them, they became over-protective. Throughout Maggie's childhood, her activities were severely limited, and her meals, naps and play were all closely supervised.

Samuel Kuhn was a successful businessman whose career kept the family on the move during Maggie's childhood. In 1908 (the same year her brother Sam was born), the family moved from Memphis to Louisville. Seven years later, they moved to Cleveland. Yet summers and holidays were always spent in Buffalo with her maternal grandmother and two maiden aunts. Kuhn later credited her aunts, particularly her Aunt Pauline, a political activist and suffragist, with having an enormous influence on her life and work. "[My aunts] were both models to me in later life, demonstrating to me that a woman could lead a full life without a mate." Her independent-minded aunts also furnished a striking contrast to her own mother, who was utterly dependent on Maggie's father.

The Kuhn household was animated by two passions: a deep commitment to education and an abiding devotion to Christianity. The Kuhns were church-going Presbyterians who expected excellence of their children at school. Happily for Maggie, she proved to be a natural student—intelligent, hard-working, and popular—but her younger brother was as hopeless as she was successful. His abject failure in school seems to have produced in adulthood a sensitive and reactive temperament that eventually developed into severe mental illness. But the bonds of sibling attachment remained, and Maggie would care for and protect Sam from the time they were children until his death in 1975 at age 67.

In 1922, at age 16, Maggie graduated from West High School in Cleveland and immediately enrolled at Flora Stone Mather College. While there, she was deeply impressed by the work of John Dewey, the noted educator and philosopher, and began to train as a teacher, one of the few professions open to women at the time. However, her career focus soon shifted; by the time she graduated with a B.A. degree in 1927, she had decided to pursue a more activist career path.

Her first job was with the Cleveland office of the Young Women's Christian Association (YWCA). In the late 1920s, the YWCA was one of the most active and successful national organizations dedicated to improving the lives of women, particularly working-class women. It offered important community services, established affordable residences for working women, and served as a center for social activism, including unionizing and lobbying efforts to improve working conditions. Kuhn fully supported the moral mission of the YWCA, later calling it "one of the most successful feminist organizations" ever. She began as a volunteer, organizing programs and discussion groups for working-class women. After a year, she was hired full-time as the assistant business and professional secretary, in which capacity she supervised programs for "industrial" girls. Like many of her co-workers at the Cleveland YWCA, she joined and became active in the Young Socialists League.

When her father was transferred to Philadelphia in 1930, Kuhn accompanied her family and secured a job as the secretary in charge of programs for young business and professional women at the YWCA in the Germantown section of Philadelphia. Here she continued her work on behalf of women, organizing classes on consumer education, political awareness, and, more controversially, on marriage and sexuality. Her new position at the Germantown YWCA required additional training, so in the spring of 1929 she traveled to New York City to take a series of courses at the YWCA's national headquarters, Columbia University's Teachers College, and Union Theological Seminary.

It was also during this period that Kuhn became increasingly active in the Presbyterian Church. In 1935, at age 30, she became a church deacon, a position newly available to women. Later, she was nominated to become the first woman at her church to be elected to the session, the church's governing lay body.

Speak your mind—even if your voice shakes, well-aimed slingshots can topple giants.
—**Maggie Kuhn**

In the early 1940s, the YWCA was one of six social service organizations to form the United Services Organization (USO), a civilian coalition created to assist the Department of Defense in the war effort on the home front. In 1941, Kuhn was invited to New York to work at the national headquarters as program coordinator for the YWCA's USO division. Her work took her across the country, aiding in particular women defense workers, who often encountered unsafe working conditions and inadequate housing and childcare. In 1948, she moved to Boston and accepted a post with the National Alliance of Unitarian Women. Two years later, she returned to Philadelphia, the site of the national headquarters of the Presbyterian Church, to join the Department of Social Education and Action of the Presbyterian Church in the U.S.A. (which in 1958 would become the Department of Church and Society of the United Presbyterian Church in the U.S.A.). The department was responsible for conducting studies of secular issues and making recommendations that the church might adopt as official positions. It urged the governing body and churchgoers alike to take progressive stands on burning social and moral issues of the day such as desegregation, urban housing, McCarthyism, the Cold War, and nuclear arms proliferation. During the 1950s and 1960s, the Presbyterian Church came to be widely recognized for its enlightened policies on many issues, especially the civil-rights movement. As part of her duties, Kuhn managed a large leadership program, which trained the laity in social justice issues, and lobbied around the country on behalf of the church's positions on such issues as poverty and social health programs (such as Medicare). She also edited the journal *Social Progress*, which in the 1960s became *Church and Society Magazine*.

The Social Action Department was controversial from the start because it advocated a set of social and moral positions far more liberal than the church's mainstream and conservative membership, some of whom branded Kuhn's ideas as "socialistic." In 1954, for example, Kuhn wrote a pamphlet entitled "The Christian Woman and Her Household," which called for responsible consumerism and urged women to refuse to buy products produced under unfair labor conditions. The pamphlet was publicly burned in protest by a chapter of the Presbyterian Women's Organization in Lexington, Kentucky, and Kuhn was labeled a communist. Despite the controversy, Kuhn became a skilled grassroots organizer, well-versed in public policy, during her two decades of work in the Social Justice office. She took part in the fight for civil rights, advocated the creation of public housing and anti-poverty programs, and participated in important social policy conferences, including the 1961 White House Conference on Aging.

In 1965, she was transferred to New York to work on a program called Renewal and Extension of the Ministries. She continued to live in Philadelphia, however, in order to care for her brother, commuting each day to work. At the time there were few women occupying executive positions in the Presbyterian Church, and Kuhn and her female colleagues were paid less than their male counterparts. In response, Kuhn organized a group of women to work for sexual equality in the church, their efforts resulting in a three-year study on the status of women that eventually yielded changes in church policy. By 1969, she was the program executive for the church's Council on Church and Race and had become involved in a number of social-action projects, a few of which touched upon issues relating directly to the elderly. As Kuhn herself was advancing in years, her awareness and interest in the special needs of the aged was growing rapidly. In 1969, there were more than 20 million Americans over the age of 65, one quarter of whom lived below the poverty line. That same year, Kuhn was invited to sit on the board of several wealthy Presbyterian retirement homes. Stunned by the elderly residents' lack of control over their own lives, she tried unsuccessfully to transfer to them greater decision-making power in the running of these homes.

In 1970, Maggie Kuhn reached the mandatory retirement age of 65 and was forced to resign. Outraged over her dismissal by the church, she organized a meeting at Columbia University called "Older Persons and the Issues of the '70s." About 100 attendees of various ages decided to form an ad hoc activist organization under the name "the Consultation of Older Persons." Its slogan, "age and youth in action," expressed the group's inclusive spirit and was reflected in its first issue, opposition to the Vietnam war. The group joined younger protesters in marches and demonstrations. In 1971, officially organized as the Gray Panthers, the group began operating out of a church basement in Philadelphia. Its credo called for "fundamental social change that would eliminate injustice, discrimination and oppression in our present society."

By 1972, Maggie Kuhn's Gray Panthers were attracting the attention of the mass media. The Panthers exposed pension-plan frauds that prompted the federal government to impose new regulations. They also prepared a scathing indictment of the hearing-aid industry's abuses of the elderly. Kuhn gained wide visibility as she was interviewed in newspapers and on national television. By 1973, 11 chapters of the Gray Panthers had opened in such cities as New York, San Francisco, Washington, D.C., and Chicago. In the same year, consumer advocate Ralph Nader's Retired Professional Action Group moved its headquarters to Philadelphia and merged with the Gray Panthers. In 1975, the Gray Panthers held their first national convention during which they adopted a number of resolutions calling for a reduction in military spending, a reformed health system, an end to compulsory retirement and age discrimination in employment, and new housing initiatives for the old and young.

Throughout the 1970s and 1980s, the Gray Panthers lent their support to dozens of issues involving health care, pension rights, public transportation, voter registration, housing, and legal services for the poor. The group was directly responsible for a number of important reforms, including the 1978 Age Discrimination in Employment Act which raised the retirement age to 70, and an amendment to the Older Americans Act which removed barriers to senior volunteer service. They lobbied successfully for legislation to improve health-care access for older Americans and for nursing home reform. Spin-off organizations included the National Citizens Coalition for Nursing Care Reform and the Shared Housing Coalition. In 1976, Kuhn led a tour to the People's Republic of China in conjunction with the U.S. China People's Friendship Association. From 1978 to 1980, she served on President Jimmy Carter's Commission on Mental Health, and, in 1985, she was a member of the Philadelphia Delegation to the Soviet Union, sponsored by the Philadelphia-Leningrad Sister Cities Project. Kuhn also received a number of

awards and citations, including the Annual Peacekeeper Award of the United Presbyterian Peace Fellowship (1977); the Gimbel Award (1982); the Presidential Citation of the American Public Health Association (1982); and the Arthur Flemming Award (1994).

In addition to issues of public policy, for the last 20 years of her life Maggie Kuhn was deeply concerned with the wider cultural problems of aging: the social and psychological costs of isolating the elderly by forcibly excluding them from the workplace and propelling them into retirement communities which remove them from their families and the neighborhoods that give their lives meaning. She decried all forms of "ageism," the stereotyping and stigmatizing on the basis of age, advocated "intergenerational" living, and encouraged older Americans to remain active in the political and social life of their communities.

In 1995, in conjunction with the Gray Panthers' 25th anniversary celebration, Philadelphia Mayor Edward G. Rendell named April 1st "Maggie Kuhn Day" in recognition of her "unique combination of humanitarianism, social criticism, and leadership." Kuhn died three weeks later, on April 22, 1995, age 89.

SOURCES AND SUGGESTED READING:

Gray Panthers. "A Tribute to Maggie," in *Network Extra*, 1995, pp. 1–8.

Hessel, Dieter, ed. *Maggie Kuhn on Aging*. Philadelphia, PA: Westminster Press, 1977.

Kuhn, Maggie, with Christina Long and Laura Quinn. *No Stone Unturned: The Life and Times of Maggie Kuhn*. NY: Ballantine Books, 1991.

The New York Times. April 23, 1995.

Pratt, Henry J. *Gray Agendas: Interest Groups and Public Pensions in Canada, Britain and the United States*. Ann Arbor, MI: University of Michigan Press, 1993.

Suzanne Smith,
freelance writer and editor, Decatur, Georgia

Kukuck, Felicitas (1914—)

German composer and teacher who created many works for Protestant church services as well as chamber music. Born on November 2, 1914, in Hamburg, Germany; her mother was a singer; taught at home by her mother; studied at the Hochschule für Musik in Berlin, 1935–39.

Nazi racism not only forced many thousands of Germans, Jews, and non-Jews to flee their country, it compelled a smaller number of "racially unpure" individuals to be silent during the years of terror when the Third Reich dominated all aspects of life in a once-free culture. Felicitas Kukuck was one of the Germans of partially Jewish ancestry who lost her freedom but not her life during the Nazi years. She was born in Hamburg in 1914, the daughter of a singer. Her mother taught her at home and encouraged her to improvise on the piano at an early age. Her composition teacher was Paul Hindemith, who urged her to continue to develop her creative skills as a composer. Hindemith, though a "pure Aryan," perceived the evils of Nazism and fled Germany in the late 1930s.

Because of her part-Jewish ancestry, Kukuck was dismissed from her teaching position and struggled to endure both materially and spiritu-

ally. A devout Christian, she survived the war and went on to become one of Germany's most respected composers of music for Protestant church services. Also strongly influenced by Hindemith, Kukuck after 1945 concentrated on writing music of spiritual depth that addressed the needs of modern individuals in a complex world. Strongly influenced by the choral traditions of German musical history, she has written a Christmas Mass, a Reformation Cantata, and in 1986 conducted the world premiere of her church opera, *The Man Moses*.

John Haag,
Athens, Georgia

Kulcsar, Ilse (1902–1973).

See Duczynska, Ilona for sidebar.

Kuliscioff, Anna (c. 1854–1925)

Ukrainian-born political activist who began as an anarchist before turning to socialism, became renowned in Italy for her tenacious battle for the emancipation of Italian women, and was important in founding the Italian Socialist Party. Name variations: Anja Kulisciov. Pronunciation: KOO-lee-SHOF. Born Anja Moiseevna Rozenstein in the village of Moskaja, in the southern Ukraine, on January 9, around 1854 (the most reliable date, though some sources cite 1853 and 1857); died in Milan, Italy, on December 29, 1925; daughter of Moisej Rozenstein (a merchant); no information available about her mother; attended high school in Sinferopoli; became the first woman admitted to the Exact Science Department of Zurich Polytechnic (1871); enrolled with the Faculty of Medicine in Bern (1882), and moved two years later to the University of Naples; studied in Turin, Pavia, and Padua (1885-1888); married Petr Makarevich in Zurich, in 1873; had two other significant relationships, with Andrea Costa, and Filippo Turati (1857–1932), her companion for more than 30 years, beginning in the mid-1880s; children: (with Costa) daughter Andreina (b. December 8, 1881).

Left Russia for Zurich (1871); returned to Russia (1873); immigrated to Switzerland (1877); moved with Andrea Costa to Paris (1877); arrested and expelled from France (1878); arrested again in Florence (October 1878) and expelled from Italy; returned to Lugano (1880); moved to Imola (1881); expelled again by police authorities and returned to Switzerland (1881); lived in Naples (1884); with Turati, joined the Socialist League of Milan (1889); co-founded and contributed to the fledgling magazine Critica Sociale *and founded the Female Section of the Chamber of Work in Milan*

*(1891); lectured at Geneva Congress, where the Social-
ist Party of Italian Workers was born (1892); promoted a bill for women and children's working conditions
(1897–1900); arrested again in Milan (1898); lectured
to the Rome Congress (1900); promoted a campaign
for "great institutional reforms" at the Florence Congress (1908); fought within the Socialist Party for
women's right to vote (1910); founded the magazine*
La difesa delle lavoratrici *and the National Union of
Socialist Women (1912).*

Publications: Il Monopolio dell'uomo *(Milano
1890, reprint, Palermo: Tenerello, 1979).*

Anna Kuliscioff's youthful experience as a
revolutionary in Russia, coupled with a remarkable political intelligence, as well as an unconventional attitude toward her private life, lent a
charisma to her personality. As a political emigrant in Switzerland, France, and finally Italy,
she was able during the years 1870–80 to be introduced into the most exclusive cosmopolitan
circles of intellectuals and to meet the principal
figures of European socialism, men who were to
become the future leaders of socialist parties in
various countries by the end of the century.
Within the fledgling socialist movement, Anna
Kuliscioff was a lively presence at a time when
the movement remained rather provincial, while
her later achievements reach the level of myth.

Little information is available regarding the
early years of Anna's life. It appears that her father Moisej Rozenstein made a fortune in the
grain trade, allowing him to pay for his daughter's higher education and provide for her to live
comfortably for the rest of her life. The family
estate must have been conspicuous enough for
her to briefly mention in a letter to Andrea Costa
that she and her brothers were "drowned in
riches," causing them to resent and even hate the
family fortune. It is also worth noting that her
father had given up his Jewish religion to become an Orthodox Christian, and that the family therefore did not fit the description of a typical middle-class family as understood through
the literature of that period, nor of the Jewish
minority of the time, which had been severely
struck by anti-Semitic pogroms.

The purely rationalistic method of teaching,
typical of the Russian schools modeled on the
German example, and the literature imbued at
the time with romantic suggestions of egalitarian
utopias, undoubtedly helped to nurture a spirit
of rebellion in the younger generation of the
1860–70s, in contrast to the social reality of Russia, which was still practically feudal in its back-

wardness. Since Russian girls were forbidden access to university studies, many of them from
upper-middle-class families had begun to flock to
Switzerland. In Zurich, where Russians made up
the majority of the student colony, a strong revolutionary cell developed. In 1871, shortly after
Anna enrolled at the Zurich Polytechnic, she
abandoned her studies to join a revolutionary
group organized by the Zebunev brothers.

In 1873, when Anna was probably 19, she
married Petr Makarevich in Zurich. That same
year, following the edict of Tsar Alexander II
that resulted in the breakup of the Zurich students' colony, she returned to Russia. The following year, Makarevich was sentenced to hard
labor in Siberia. There is no further trace con-
necting him to her life; it is possible that their
marriage may have been the same fictitious ploy
used by a number of young women of the time
to obtain legal independence before officially
coming of age. In Russia, Anna went to Odessa,
where she joined a movement promoting the
practice of "going among the people," through
which many of Russia's young intelligentsia
shared the daily life of poor peasants while trying to instill in them the principles of socialism.

*As long as laws are made by men, even
though socialist men inspired by the best intentions, they
will always be to their advantage and against us.*

—A. Kuliscioff

After this "propagandistic" movement, inspired by the ideology of Peter Lavrov, resulted
in brutal police repression, Kuliscioff's political
attitude became more radical. In 1874, during a
visit to Kiev, she joined the "Buntary" group,
which rejected Lavrist pacifism and gradualism
in support of the insurrectionary extremism proposed by the anarchist Michael Bakunin. In fact,
the common people were not rising up in great
numbers to follow any of the revolutionaries at
the time Anna Kuliscioff's group in Kiev drew up
a false manifesto inciting peasants to revolt. In
summer 1876, Kuliscioff was sent to Switzerland to find a clandestine printer to make
posters to disseminate in the Cigrin countryside.
After the job was done, she became a suspect in
a judicial inquiry and succeeded in fleeing to
Char'kov together with two of her Kiev friends,
Frolenko and **Maria Kovalevskaya**. In 1877,
Kuliscioff returned to Kiev, where she lived for a
while under a false identity, before going back to
Char'kov. On April 14, using a false passport,
she crossed the Russian border to escape police
persecution and took refuge in Switzerland.

Switzerland was then the center for political emigration for all of Europe. There, Kuliscioff met the anarchist Andrea Costa, with whom she established an emotional and intellectual relationship. After a short stay in London with the famous Russian anarchist Peter Kropotkin, she joined Costa in Paris, where he wanted to establish an international anarchist federation. In 1878, she was arrested and then expelled from France. In Switzerland, she got in touch with a group of Italian anarchists, and in September of that year she went to Florence, where she was arrested again and was kept in prison for more than a year before being acquitted at trial due to lack of evidence.

In January 1880, Kuliscioff returned to Switzerland, where she and Costa founded the magazine *Rivista Internazionale del Socialismo* to express a significant shift in their political point of view. Repeated unsuccessful riots in Italy had convinced them to relinquish the use of armed insurrection in favor of more legalistic strategies. Known as Costa's "U-turn," this change in approach became famous and launched a new revolutionary strategy in Italy. Henceforth, entering the political struggle through institutional channels became the progressive approach.

In 1880, Kuliscioff was arrested again in Milan and fled to Lugano, where she undertook an intellectual collaboration with the anarchist Carlo Cafiero. In April 1881, she joined Costa in Imola, where she gave birth to their daughter, Andreina. Expelled from Italy again in December that same year, she spent a few months in Zurich, then moved to Berne to resume her university studies, this time in the Faculty of Medicine. In Berne, she got in touch with a group gathered around the socialist Georgi Plekhanov who exerted a decisive influence in directing her towards Marxism.

In the meantime Kuliscioff's relationship with Costa had gradually deteriorated. For health reasons, she moved to Naples, where she met Filippo Turati, the future leader of reformist socialism in Italy, with whom she was to live until her death. From 1885 to 1888, however, she remained outside the lively political debate in radical and republican Italian circles to which Turati had introduced her. In an effort to escape academic persecution, she kept moving on from one Italian university to another, forced from Turin to Milan, then to Pavia, and finally to Padua.

In 1889, she became active again, joining the Socialist League in Milan and promoting a conference about Paris Congresses and the birth of the II

International set. She believed in German Social democracy as a leader-party and fought to further clarify the difficult process of building up a political party of the Italian working class. In particular, she became engaged in the issue of the much-disputed role of intellectuals within the workers' movement. Kuliscioff, like Turati, held the conviction that the contribution of middle-class intellectuals was both decisive and unavoidable in the building up of a Socialist and Labour party. Experience had taught them not to believe in a spontaneous and independent surge of political socialist consciousness within the working class.

In 1891, Kuliscioff and Turati founded the magazine *Critica Sociale,* where she was to focus her collaborative efforts mainly on the conditions of women in Italian society for more than 20 years. During the previous year, she had single-handedly opened the subject to political debate with a conference, "Il monopolio dell'uomo," held at the Filological Circle in Milan, where she made strong claims for extending legal and equal rights to women and argued against reductive socialist economism for society in general. That year, Kuliscioff made Milan her base for her work as a doctor among the lower working classes, and helped to establish the foundations of the Women's Section of the Chamber of Work. At the International Socialist Congress, she introduced a point of discussion, together with German social democratic leader Karl Kautsky, inviting all European socialist parties to establish "total equality for both sexes" as essential points in their programs of reform, and to claim for women "the same political and civil rights enjoyed by men."

In August 1892, Kuliscioff was among the organizers of the Genoa Congress which saw the birth of the Socialist Party in Italy. Unfortunately, the conditions to guarantee the basic democratic freedoms of a true liberal state did not yet exist within the country, and the new group was doomed to an immediate clash with repressive government policy.

Kuliscioff's struggle in the interest of women led to her 1897 presentation of a bill to safeguard women and children's working conditions to the Italian Socialist Party Congress in Bologna. During political election periods, she campaigned through *Critica Sociale* for women's right to vote, an eight-hour working day, equal salaries for both sexes, and "women's right to spend their wages as they wished."

In May 1898, after riots broke out in Milan over the increase in the price of bread, Kuliscioff was again arrested, along with other members of the Socialist party, for a series of conferences held about the proposed bill regarding working mothers' leave. Eight months later, she was released through an amnesty agreement and again started to campaign for laws to protect working mothers. Her proposal, which included maternity leave on 75% pay, and one full day of rest a week and exemption from dangerous, unhealthy or night work, was presented to the Italian Parliament in 1902.

In these years, Kuliscioff rarely appeared on the Italian political scene; nevertheless, her opinion always represented the reformist side of party management, with which she identified until 1908. In that year, during the Florence Congress, she argued against Claudio Treves and Turati himself, siding with Gaetano Salvemini, who claimed the necessity to change the party's position from one of pacific cooperation with the government of Giovanni Giolitti to a fight for genuine institutional reforms such as universal suffrage. On that occasion, she submitted a motion for women's suffrage and followed it with a series of articles in *Critica Sociale*, again arguing against Turati, who was in favor of limiting the party's request to male universal suffrage. Kuliscioff's criticism was further directed against the political behavior of the Socialist party itself, which in her opinion was so ensnared by parliamentary maneuvers that it was becoming more and more distant from working people's problems and showing total indifference to the actual political struggle of the masses.

In 1912, after Italy had won male universal suffrage, Kuliscioff carried on a series of enterprises, promoted both through the magazine *La Difesa delle Lavoratrici* and through the steadfast exertion of pressure on the Socialist parliamentary group to submit a bill to gain the vote for women. In 1914, when the bill was finally elaborated and proposed, the outbreak of World War I put off discussion indefinitely. Now adhering to the position of democratic interventionists, Kuliscioff disagreed once again with the reformist party leaders, this time on the side of England and France, as she thought that a victory by Germany and Austria would result in the strengthening of Italy's militarist and reactionary forces.

Kuliscioff hailed the 1917 February Revolution in Russia, which caused the fall of the tsarist régime; later on, though ill, she received Russian delegates in Italy. She would not go so far as supporting the Bolshevik revolution, however, which she considered authoritarian and springing from the action of a restricted revolutionary élite who did not truly represent the masses. She disagreed with the Leninists as a "maximalist" faction of the party, exalting instead the American President Woodrow Wilson as a champion of those principles of freedom and democracy in which she believed.

In her 60s, and extremely ill, Kuliscioff observed the tense social period immediately following the end of World War I with apprehension. Skeptical about the possible revolutionary outcomes of the country's social troubles, she encouraged her fellow party members to break away from the revolutionary "maximalists" and co-operate with the Italian democratic forces. As virtually everybody in Italy did, she initially underestimated the real subversive power of Fascism, although she continued to fight for the alliance of the Socialist moderate wing and Catholic forces so as to create a barrier against Benito Mussolini's excessive power, which was well consolidated after the famous "March on Rome."

Though deeply disturbed by the 1924 murder of her friend, socialist deputy Giacomo Matteotti, Kuliscioff allied herself with Giovanni Amendola to rebuild a pool of democratic forces against Fascism until her death in December 1925, at her home in Milan. Although postwar disruptions had caused her to witness the political destruction in Italy of virtually all that she had fought for, Kuliscioff never lost an awareness that she had lived and played an active part in the events of her era. A few months before her death, she wrote a letter of encouragement to Turati, the last sentence of which may serve as an apt description of her own life:

> Even though the Fascist Regime continues to expand and consolidate itself we will fight it as long as we live. Whatever may happen, be assured that your conscience is clear because you have carried out to the best of your ability the political strategy which you considered useful and necessary.

SOURCES:

Anna Kuliscioff e l'età del riformismo. Atti del Convegno di Milano della Fondazione Brodolini, 1976. Milano: Mondo operaio e Avanti!, 1978.

Anna Kuliscioff: In memoria. Milano: Tipogr. E. Lazzari, 1926.

Casalini, Maria. *La Signora del Socialismo italiano: Vita di Anna Kuliscioff.* Roma: Editori Riuniti, 1987.

Kuliscioff, Anna—Turati, Filippo. *Carteggio.* voll. I–VI raccolti da A. Schiavi, a cura di A. Pedone. Torino: Einaudi, 1977.

Schiavi, Alessandro. *Anna Kuliscioff.* Roma: Edizioni Opere Nuove, 1955.

Venturi, Franco. "Anna Kuliscioff e la sua attività rivoluzionaria in Russia," in *Movimento operaio,* 1952, pp. 277–286.

SUGGESTED READING:

Pieroni Bortolotti, Franca. *Socialismo e questione femminile in Italia. 1892–1922.* Milano: Mazzotta, 1974.

Ragionieri, Ernesto. *Socialdemocrazia tedesca e Socialisti italiani*. Milano: Feltrinelli, 1976.

Maria Casalini,
Researcher Professor, Department of History,
University of Florence, Florence, Italy, and author of
La Signora del Socialismo italiano: Vita di Anna Kuliscioff

Kulthum, Umm (c. 1898–1975).

See Um Kalthum.

Kumaratunga, Chandrika Bandaranaike (1945—)

President of the Democratic Socialist Republic of Sri Lanka. Name variations: Chandra Bandaranaike. Born on June 29, 1945, in Colombo, Sri Lanka; daughter of S.W.R.D. Bandaranaike (founder of the Sri Lanka Freedom Party and prime minister of Sri Lanka from 1956 until his assassination on September 26, 1959) and Sirimavo Bandaranaike (b. 1916, first elected woman prime minister in the world); schooled at St. Bridget's Convent in Colombo, Sri Lanka; studied for LLB, law degree; awarded diploma in group leadership-EPHE

*C*handrika
*K*umaratunga

*from the University of Paris; studied for Ph.D. in development economics at the University of Paris; granted degree in political science from the University of Paris; married Vijaya Kumaratunga (a leading opposition figure and film idol), on February 20, 1978 (assassinated February 16, 1988); children: daughter, **Yasodara Kumaratunga**; son, Vimukti Kumaratunga.*

Chandrika Bandaranaike Kumaratunga was born on June 29, 1945, in Colombo, Sri Lanka, to S.W.R.D. Bandaranaike and *Sirimavo Bandaranaike, who both served as prime ministers of Sri Lanka. Chandrika received an excellent education, mostly in France, and is fluent in Sinhala, English and French. On February 20, 1978, she married Vijaya Kumaratunga; the couple had two children, a daughter Yasodara and a son Vimukti.

No stranger to violence, Chandrika Kumaratunga has seen both her father and her husband assassinated for their political beliefs. Following S.W.R.D. Bandaranaike's death in September 1959, Chandrika's mother, Sirimavo, assumed power. After holding a number of posts in the Sri Lanka Freedom Party (SLFP), which S.W.R.D. Bandaranaike had founded, and serving as president of the Sri Lanka Mahajana Party (SLMP), Kumaratunga emerged as a leader of the People's Alliance in the early 1990s. She was elected Sri Lanka's prime minister in August 1994 and a few months later, in November, became the first female president of Sri Lanka. She then appointed her mother to serve once again as prime minister. On December 21, 1999, Kumaratunga won a second term as president, although she was elected by a much smaller majority.

In 1994, Kumaratunga had campaigned with a promise to stop the bitter ethnic civil war between the Sinhalese, who are a majority of the population, and the Tamils (minority). She has met with mixed results. In 1995, talks with the Tamil Tigers, a separatist guerilla group also known as the Liberation Tigers of Tamil Eelam (LTTE), broke down and a cease-fire was called off. The result has been continued fighting in a war that has claimed more than 60,000 lives. Most seem to agree that any solution that keeps Sri Lanka whole will involve devolution of power to the Tamils. Failing to reach a peaceful solution, Kumaratunga vowed to wage an aggressive military campaign against the Tamils following her reelection in 1999. The outcome was an immediate upsurge in fighting with huge government losses of troops and territory.

Fearing for her life, Kumaratunga lives in a fortified house in Colombo. Her fears are well founded, for at her final campaign rally before the 1999 presidential elections, she was wounded in an explosion during a suicide bombing attack. After doctors removed shrapnel from her eye, she vowed to continue the fight against terrorism.

SOURCES:

"Injured Sri Lankan Leader Urges Tamils to Help End Terrorism," in *The New York Times*. December 20, 1999.

Mydans, Seth, "Wounded Sri Lankan Sees 'Gift of Gods' in Re-election," in *The New York Times*. December 23, 1999.

"Sri Lanka Wants Peace, Perhaps," in *The Economist*. December 18, 1999.

Jo Anne Meginnes,
freelance writer, Brookfield, Vermont

Kuncewicz, Maria (1899–1989)

Polish author whose essentially autobiographical works, particularly the novel Cudzoziemka *(The Stranger), are sensitive studies of alienation and otherness. Name variations: Maria Kuncewiczowa; Maria Kuncewicowa. Born Maria Szczepanska on October 30, 1899 (some sources state 1897), in Samara, Russia; died in 1989; daughter of Róza Szczepanska; married Jerzy Kuncewicz (1893–1984, an author and lawyer); children: one son.*

Regarded as one of interwar Poland's most respected writers, Maria Kuncewicz was born in 1899 in the Russian city of Samara, on the Volga, into a family typical of the patriotic Polish intelligentsia of the late 19th century; her father was a headmaster, and her mother a violinist. Although her family moved to Warsaw when she was only two, Maria would remember the sense of otherness that her family felt while living in Russia, to which they had been exiled after the failed Polish insurrection of 1863. Kuncewicz had both literary and musical talents, and studied French philology at the University of Nancy, Polish philology in the University of Warsaw and Cracow's Jagiellonian University, as well as voice at both the Paris and Warsaw Conservatories. For some years, she found it impossible to choose between music and literature as careers, and sang professionally on opera and recital stages in Poland and Germany while continuing to write in her leisure hours. As early as 1918, however, it became apparent to many readers and critics that a major new talent had surfaced in Polish literary life when her first published story appeared in the journal *Pro Arte et Studio*.

Living in Warsaw at a time in which cultural creativity in some ways rivalled that of Berlin and Paris, Kuncewicz had by the mid-1920s earned a strong reputation as a writer and was taking full advantage of the city. She was in the center of Polish intellectual life. Her daytime work at the office of the Polish section of the PEN Club, of which she was vice-president, enabled her to meet not only most of the nation's leading writers, but many foreign authors as well. By the end of the 1920s, Kuncewicz had published a number of stories which appeared in the collection *Przymierze z dzieckiem* (*An Alliance with a Child*, 1927) as well as her first novel, *Twarz mezczyzny* (*The Face of a Man*, 1928). In this work, she pursued the ideal of the "Skamander" school of writers, which was to create a "more normal" type of literature in Poland, focusing on the psychological uniqueness of individuals while moving away from any political or nationalistic agenda. These works, which enjoyed critical acclaim, told of women's experiences of love, marriage and maternity. The style was naturalistic, not overly analytical, and contained satisfying doses of lyricism and subtle humor.

In 1935, Kuncewicz published her novel *Cudzoziemka* (*The Stranger*, also translatable as *The Foreign Woman*) in the newspaper *Kurier Poranny* (Morning Courier). The definitive edition was published in Warsaw in 1936, and a translation into English appeared in 1945. In this novel, considered by critics to be her best work, Kuncewicz presents a subtle psychological portrait of a Polish woman who must confront the otherness of her Russian upbringing. Clearly based on the author's mother (even the name of the fictional protagonist and her real-life mother Róza are one and the same), the novel probes the tangle of emotions of an essentially egocentric woman who has built her life around dreams of an unrequited love. It has been suggested that the Polish heroine, whose existence has been distorted since childhood by the harsh forces of exile and cultural alienation, is essentially a symbol of Poland, and that her lack of inner peace, sharp memories of national defeat and humiliation, and profound lack of personal satisfaction are all reflections of the tragic history of the Polish people.

Despite personal turmoil and the rush toward chaos and war that marked the 1930s, Maria Kuncewicz was often able to find some serenity both in her life and writing. This is best reflected in her 1933 collection of stories, *Dwa ksiezyce* (Two Moons), which is set in the picturesque town of Kazimierz on the Vistula, a resort that enjoyed a reputation as a haven for Poland's artistic community. Now a highly respected artist, in 1936 she received the Literary Award of the City of Warsaw, followed the next year by the "golden laurel" of the Polish Academy of Literature. Having already won the approval of the nation's intellectual elite, in 1938 Maria Kuncewicz chose to place her art directly into the public sphere, creating Poland's first radio serials, *Dni powszednie panstwa Kowalskich* (The Ordinary Days of the Kowalskis), and *Kowalscy sie odnalezli* (The Kowalskis Have Returned). The nation's unsolved social, economic and moral problems were probed in two books of stories published in 1939, in the last months of an increasingly illusory peace: *Serce kraju* (The Heart of the Country) and *W domu i w Polsce* (At Home and in Poland).

In light of the tragic events soon to impact on Poland, very likely the most significant book Maria Kuncewicz published in 1939 was *Miasto Heroda: Notatki Palestynskie* (The City of Herod: Palestinian Notes). On cordial terms with fellow writers of Jewish origins, she was interested in Jewish culture and in the Zionist movement. Invited by the Hebrew branch of PEN to visit Palestine, she took extensive notes, which saw print just weeks before the German attack of September 1939. Her sympathetic comments on the problems and achievements of the Jewish renaissance taking place in Palestine, particularly on the role of Polish-born Jews, remain of historical as well as literary interest.

Maria Kuncewicz fled from German-occupied Poland in the early months of Nazi rule, arriving in Paris in the last days of 1939. After a few months in France, she escaped the Nazi juggernaut once more, finding refuge in England. The United Kingdom was a place of refuge for Polish soldiers, sailors and fliers who had escaped their defeated nation, vowing to fight until the defeat of the hated Nazi occupiers. A small but lively colony of Polish intellectuals flourished in London and several other British cities during the war years, and Kuncewicz quickly resumed her writing and publication in exile newspapers and journals. Her days were filled with her work as head of the Polish Section of the PEN Club in Exile. As early as 1942, one of her novels appeared in print in London under the title *Polish Millstones*. At the end of the war in 1945, she published an anthology, *Modern Polish Prose,* designed to introduce the English-speaking world to a largely unknown literary terrain.

Kuncewicz decided to remain in England when the Communists ruled Poland from 1945 to 1948. Concerned about the plight of the world's emigre artists and writers, in 1949 she sent an appeal to the United Nations to create a "world citizenship" status for this particularly vulnerable group of displaced persons. Despite considerable support from prominent Western intellectuals, her proposal was ignored. In 1956, she moved to the United States, where her considerable reputation had already preceded her. Her status as an expert on Polish literature was further enhanced in 1962 with the publication of her anthology *The Modern Polish Mind*. From 1963 until 1971, she taught Polish literature at the University of Chicago. At the time of her retirement in 1971, she was awarded the Medal of the Kosciuszko Foundation in recognition of her outstanding contributions to Polish and American cultures.

Starting in 1956, Poland underwent a process of considerable intellectual and artistic liberalization, and Maria Kuncewicz began to visit her mother country in the 1960s, living in her beloved town of Kazimierz while there. Upon her retirement from teaching in 1971, she settled permanently in Kazimierz. Despite advancing years, the venerable author remained productive, publishing two volumes of autobiography, *Fantomy* (Phantoms, 1971) and *Natura* (Nature, 1975). She wrote in *Natura* of her never-ceasing search for artistic and human truths: "I did not know then, as I don't know now, the nature of man or rather nature in general with all her hidden layers, fraudulent mimicry and mysteriousness of changes." She looked upon her efforts to create "world citizenship" for intellectuals as a noble failure: "I sift through the yellowed papers, and don't regret that I have amassed this pile of garbage."

Greatly respected in Poland—she received the Wlodzimierz Pietrzak Award in 1969 and the National Award (First Class) on two occasions, in 1974 and 1978—Maria Kuncewicz remained popular with a younger generation of readers, while at the same time literary scholars began to investigate facets of her lifetime achievement. A major personal loss was the death in March 1984 of her husband Jerzy Kuncewicz, who was not only a respected author but also a lawyer, natural historian, philosopher, leader of the prewar peasant movement, and a vice president of the exile Polish National Council in London during World War II. Maria Kuncewicz died in 1989, the year free elections finally ended the Communist regime in Poland. By the end of her long and productive life, her books had been translated into many languages, including English, Russian, Czech, French, Italian, Norwegian, Estonian, Spanish, Rumanian, and Slovak. In her will, she established the Kuncewicz Foundation, the goal of which is to help build bridges of understanding and friendship between the nations neighboring on Poland's borders.

SOURCES:

Becela, Lidia, *et al. Who's Who in Poland.* Warsaw: Interpress, 1982.

Czerwinski, E.J., ed. *Dictionary of Polish Literature.* Westport, CT: Greenwood Press, 1994.

Filipowicz, Halina. "Fission and Fusion: Polish Emigré Literature," in *Slavic and East European Journal.* Vol. 33, no. 2. Summer 1989, pp. 157–172.

Gasiorowski, Prof. Zygmunt. Personal communication.

Gillon, Adam, and Ludwik Krzyzanowski, eds. *Modern Polish Literature: An Anthology of Fiction and Poetry.* 2nd ed. NY: Hippocrene Books, 1982.

Kuncewicz, Maria. "A Polish Satanist: Stanislaw Przybyszewski," in *Polish Review.* Vol 14, no. 2, 1969, pp. 3–20.

——, ed. *The Modern Polish Mind: An Anthology.* Boston, MA: Little, Brown, 1962.

Kuncewiczowa, Maria. *The Stranger: A Novel.* Translated by B.W.A. Massey. NY: L.B. Fischer, 1945.

——. "A Turban," translated by George J. Maciuszko, in Alfred Bloch, ed. *The Real Poland: An Anthology of National Self-Perception.* NY: Continuum, 1982, pp. 136–142.

Milosz, Czeslaw. *The History of Polish Literature.* 2nd ed. Berkeley, CA: University of California Press, 1983.

Nowicki, Ron. *Warsaw: The Cabaret Years.* San Francisco, CA: Mercury House, 1992.

Schofield, Mary Anne. "Underground Lives: Women's Personal Narratives, 1939–45," in David Bevan, ed. *Literature and Exile.* Amsterdam and Atlanta, GA: Rodopi, 1990, pp. 121–147.

Segel, Harold B., ed. *Stranger in Our Midst: Images of the Jew in Polish Literature.* Ithaca, NY: Cornell University Press, 1996.

Smith, Mary C. "The Stranger: A Study and Note about Maria Kuncewicz," in *The Polish Review.* Vol. 17, no. 1. Winter 1972, pp. 77–86.

Uminski, Zdzislaw. "Mogliby byc soba gdyby nie byli mna" (They Could Have Been Themselves If They Hadn't Been Me), in *Kierunki.* March 10, 1974, p. 925.

*Yezierska, Anzia. "Casimir Comes Home," in *The New York Times Book Review.* September 12, 1954, p. 31.

Zaborowska, Magdalena. "Writing the Virgin, Writing the Crone: Maria Kuncewicz's Embodiment of Faith," in Pamela Chester and Sibelan Forrester, eds., *Engendering Slavic Literatures.* Bloomington: Indiana University Press, 1996, pp. 174–200.

Zaworska, Helena, ed. *Rozmowy z Maria Kuncewicowa* (Conversations with Maria Kuncewiczowa). Warsaw: "Czytelnik," 1983.

John Haag,
Associate Professor of History,
University of Georgia, Athens, Georgia

Kunegunda.

See Cunegunde or Cunigunde.

Kunegunde.

Variant of Cunigunde.

Kunehilda (d. 741).

See Sunnichild.

Kung, Madame H.H. (1890–1973).

See Song Ailing in The Song Sisters.

Kunigunde.

Variant of Cunigunde.

Kunke, Steffi (1908–1942)

Austrian teacher who, with her husband, was involved in anti-fascist underground work in Vienna during the Nazi occupation. Born Stefanie Jellinek in Vienna, Austria, on December 26, 1908; died of typhus in Auschwitz in December 1942; daughter of Marie (Ourednik) Jellinek and Ignaz Jellinek; married Hans Kunke (1906–1940).

Steffi Kunke was in many ways a typical Viennese Socialist of her generation, in that her working-class parents Marie Ourednik Jellinek and Ignaz Jellinek were of Czech background, and, though their formal education had ended early, were interested in politics and the arts. Steffi's mother was a hard-working dressmaker, and her father, who worked for the municipal brewery, was an amateur poet who was proud to see some of his works published in the *Heimgarten,* a popular journal edited by the famous Styrian folk-poet Peter Rosegger. Born in Vienna on December 26, 1908, young Steffi loved children and prepared in the 1920s for a teaching career. But the darkening political clouds of the early 1930s dictated that she and her husband Hans Kunke become increasingly active in the educational work of the Young Socialist movement. When the Social Democratic government of Vienna was overthrown in February 1934, the creation of the Dollfuss dictatorship only strengthened the Kunkes' resolve to fight Fascism. Hans was Jewish, and both he and Steffi regarded Nazism as the great enemy of humanity because of its racism and glorification of war. Though Steffi's work as a teacher gave her immense satisfaction, her dangerous assignments as the leader of the youth department of the Revolutionary Socialist underground became the core of her life.

Steffi and Hans Kunke had been arrested in July 1936 by the Viennese police for their political activities, but they were both free at the time of the Nazi Anschluss in March 1938. Now facing a much stronger and more cunning foe, they nevertheless continued their underground work. By 1938, the Kunkes had been able to create a well-organized underground Socialist youth movement in Vienna and the surrounding province of Lower Austria. But the Nazi takeover represented an infinitely greater threat to their own survival, and in the spring of 1938 they began to prepare to emigrate from Austria. False documents had already been procured by the Revolutionary Socialist leader Josef Buttinger, who was married to *Muriel Gardiner, a wealthy American-born sympathizer of the Austrian underground. But instead of departing immediately, Steffi and Hans made a fateful decision, to wait until a close colleague, Ferdinand Tschürtsch, had received his own papers. All three were arrested in May 1938, with Steffi being sent to the Lichtenburg concentration camp while Hans and Tschürtsch were transported to Buchenwald near Weimar. The terrible conditions at Buchenwald soon proved fatal for Ferdinand Tschürtsch, who suffered from a spinal deformity and had never been in robust health. Hans Kunke was physically stronger, but he eventually broke under the intense psychological torture, committing suicide in the quarry of Buchenwald in October 1940.

After a period at Lichtenburg, Steffi was transferred to the women's camp of Ravensbrück, where she displayed extraordinary courage. During its years of existence (1939–45), Ravensbrück held 132,000 women and children, of whom 92,000 died. While there, she served as secretary (*Blockschreiberin*) for the camp's political prisoners. Her fellow prisoner *Rosa Jochmann recalls in her memoirs how bravely Steffi Kunke bore the intense pain of 25 strokes of the lash after she refused to denounce a fellow inmate. The Nazi camp officials could not break her spirit despite two years of repeated solitary confinement and extreme physical punishment. As a consequence, she was sent to Auschwitz, where she died of typhus in December 1942.

SOURCES:

Buttinger, Joseph. *In the Twilight of Socialism: A History of the Revolutionary Socialists of Austria.* NY: Frederick A. Praeger, 1953.

Dokumentationsarchiv des österreichischen Widerstandes, Vienna, files 3188 and 3675.

Institut für Wissenschaft und Kunst, Vienna, "Biografisches Lexikon der österreichischen Frau."

Kerschbaumer, Marie Therese. *Der weibliche Name des Widerstands: Sieben Berichte.* Olten: Walter Verlag, 1980.

Neugebauer, Wolfgang. *Bauvolk der kommenden Welt: Geschichte der sozialistischen Jugendbewegung in Österreich.* Vienna: Europaverlag, 1975.

Spiegel, Tilly. *Frauen und Mädchen im österreichischen Widerstand.* Vienna: Europa Verlag, 1967.

Sporrer, Maria, and Herbert Steiner, eds. *Rosa Jochmann: Zeitzeugin.* 3rd ed. Vienna: Europaverlag, 1987.

Widerstand und Verfolgung in Wien 1934–1945: Eine Dokumentation. 2nd ed. 3 vols. Vienna: Österreichischer Bundesverlag, 1984.

John Haag,
Associate Professor of History,
University of Georgia, Athens, Georgia

Kuri, Rosa Guraieb (b. 1931).

See Guraieb Kuri, Rosa.

Kurtz, Carmen (1911—)

Award-winning Spanish author of children's literature. Name variations: Carmen de Rafael y Marés Kurtz. Born Carmen de Rafael y Marés in Barcelona, Spain, on September 18, 1911; married Pedro Kurtz Klein, in 1935; children: one daughter.

Born on September 18, 1911, a native of Barcelona, Carmen de Rafael y Marés married Pedro Kurtz Klein in 1935 and moved to France that year, on the eve of the Spanish Civil War. She returned to Spain only in 1943, during the Second World War. Between 1954 and 1964, she published nine novels, using her husband's surname. In the 1960s, she also turned to children's literature in the 1960s. Many of those works featured the protagonist Oscar, who experienced a great variety of adventures, including espionage, space travel, and exploring the Himalayas. Her children's books won the Lazarillo Prize in 1964 and the Children's Literature Prize of the Spanish Catholic Commission in 1964 and 1967.

Kendall W. Brown,
Provo, Utah

Kurys, Sophie (1925—)

Baseball player who played second base for the Racine Belles and had 1,114 stolen bases. Born Sophie Mary Kurys in Flint, Michigan, on May 14, 1925.

One of the original Racine Belles of the All-American Girls Baseball League (AAGBL), Sophie "Flint Flash" Kurys stayed with the team throughout its eight-year existence and distinguished herself by smashing every stolen base record in the league. In 1946 alone, Kurys stole 201 bases in 203 attempts, a league record that was never broken. During the course of her career, the 5'5", 120-pound second baseman chalked up an impressive record of 1,114 stolen bases.

Kurys, a native of Flint, Michigan, began playing baseball at 14 and was a veteran third baseman and shortstop by the time she signed with the Racine Belles in 1943. Johnny Gottselig, the hockey-star manager of the Belles, originally assigned Kurys to the outfield, but when the second baseman was injured after a few games, he moved her to second where she remained for the rest of her career. During her rookie year, Kurys stole only 44 bases, but increased her record to 166 the following year, seven of them in one game. In 1945, Leo Murphy, a 25-year veteran of the minor leagues, took over managing the Belles, and immediately recognized that Kurys should be batting lead-off so as to maximize her chances to steal and move to scoring position. Kurys played in 105 games that year, stealing 115 bases to lead the league in steals for the second consecutive year. "You pretend that you're not taking a big lead," she said about her technique. "I never took a big lead right away. Of course, they knew I was going."

Kurys hit her stride in 1946, but her record 201 stolen bases was only part of the story. Playing in 113 games, she also scored a league-high 117 runs and batted .286, second only to *Dottie Kamenshek's .316. She also had a record 93 walks and set a .973 fielding record for second base. In addition to Kurys' personal records, the league-leading Racine Belles won the best-of-five playoff series against the South Bend Blue Sox and moved on to compete in the Shaughnessy Series against the Rockford Peaches. The Belles won two games of the Shaughnessy Series at home, then dropped two of the three to Rockford. The seventh game, considered by some to have been one of the most dramatic games in baseball history, went a scoreless 14 innings. In the bottom of the fourteenth, Kurys, who had already stolen four bases in the game, led off with a single. While her teammate **Betty Trezza** was at the plate, Kurys stole third, and, as Trezza snapped a short single through the infield, headed for home, hooking a slide into the plate to score the winning (and only) run of the game. "It was such an exciting thing to see Sophie cross that plate," said teammate *Joanne Winter. "I'll never forget it." Neither would the Belles' fans, who surged onto the field and carried Kurys off on their shoulders. For her record as leading scorer for the season, and leading hitter and scorer for the postseason series, Kurys was elected Player of the Year.

One serious drawback to Kurys' specialty was the pounding her legs took from sliding into base. Not only was the field brick-hard, but the women of the AAGBL were forced to play in skirts. "They thought that having skirts would show that we were extremely feminine," Kurys said, "but I think all of us would have rather played in standard uniforms." The women suffered from constant abrasions that bled into their clothing, making it torturous to undress at the end of the game. To solve the problem, the league provided the players with sliding pads, which were taped to the thigh and hung down unattractively from under their short skirts. After trying the pads, the women unanimously rejected them. "They were too cumbersome," explained Kurys. "So I took them off and took my chances with strawberries. I had strawberries on strawberries. Sometimes now, when I first get up in the morning, I have problems with my thighs."

Kurys played with the Belles until they lost their franchise in 1950, and was elected to the All-Star team for four consecutive seasons, from 1946 to 1949. In 1950, she stole 120 bases and hit seven home runs to tie the year-high record with **Eleanor Callow**. After the team disbanded, Kurys played professional softball in Chicago for three years. She then played for Arizona for one year before retiring from the game at age 33.

After baseball, Kurys accepted a partnership with the Racine manufacturer she had been associated with for many years. She stayed with the firm until 1972, when she retired to Arizona. A modest woman who never liked the limelight, Kurys was quick to point out that there is more than one person on a baseball team. "I like the team concept," she said once, explaining her passion for the game. "You're in there helping each other."

SOURCES:

Gregorich, Barbara. *Women at Play: The Story of Women in Baseball*. NY: Harcourt Brace, 1993.

Macy, Sue. *A Whole New Ball Game*. NY: Holt, 1993.

Barbara Morgan,
Melrose, Massachusetts

Kurz, Selma (1874–1933)

*Austrian soprano. Born on November 15, 1874, in Bielitz, Silesia; died on May 10, 1933, in Vienna, Austria; studied with Johannes Ress in Vienna and *Mathilde Marchesi in Paris; married Josef Halban (a gynecologist), in 1910; children: daughter Desirée Halban (b. 1911).*

Debuted in Hamburg (1895); sang in Frankfurt (1897–99) and with the Vienna Staatsoper (1899–1927); appeared at Covent Garden (1904, 1905, 1907, and 1925).

Selma Kurz was born in Bielitz, Silesia, in 1874. She began her career in 1895 at Hamburg in the role of Mignon, but her contract was bought out by the Frankfurt Opera where she debuted as Elisabeth in *Tannhäuser*. Other roles included Marguerite in *Faust* and Queen of the Night in *Die Zauberflöte* (*The Magic Flute*). Kurz then met Gustav Mahler, the composer, and they had a brief affair. He arranged for her to be coached by *Anna Bahr-Mildenburg, the singer closely associated with his work. Kurz gave a highly successful performance of Mahler's songs in 1901 and became a member of his Vienna Opera ensemble where she remained until 1927, giving almost 1,000 performances. She often appeared at Covent Garden as well as in Paris and Monte Carlo. It was not until 1921 that she performed in the United States, although a serious illness forced her to cancel all but a few of the scheduled concerts. Kurz made a number of recordings from 1900 until 1925; her repertoire was extensive and included some 60 roles. These reveal that although hers was a beautiful voice, it lacked expressiveness. This flaw probably explains why Selma Kurz enjoyed a major career at one of the world's leading opera houses rather than international acclaim. Her daughter Desirée became famous as **Desi Halban** and specialized in the music of Gustav Mahler.

SUGGESTED READING:

Goldmann, H. *Selma Kurz*. Bielitz, 1933.

John Haag,
Athens, Georgia

Kathy
Kusner

Kusner, Kathy (1940—)

American equestrian who was the first licensed female jockey. Born in Gainesville, Florida, on March 21, 1940.

Won the President's Cup, the New York championships, the Prix des Amazones, and the Irish Trophy; also competed on the U.S. Olympic team; was the first woman in ten years to join the U.S. equestrian team (1961); filed a sexual discrimination suit against the Maryland Racing Commission for refusing to give her a license as a jockey (1967), a case which she won.

Kathy Kusner's love of horses was unique in her family. She was raised in the fox-hunting states of Virginia and Maryland, so horses became a part of her landscape. Her father, a mathematician who worked for the government, was mystified by his daughter's obsession, but he believed she should pursue her interests. At age ten, given her own pony, Kusner cleaned stables and groomed horses to earn its keep. Riding lessons at Mrs. Dillon's Junior Equitation School and show and ring events soon became central to her life. Her high school years were spent riding, grooming, and training, as well as showing horses for dealers.

At 18, Kusner set a women's horse-jumping record of 7'3". In 1961, she was the first woman in ten years to join the U.S. equestrian team; equestrian competition is the only Olympic sport in which men and women compete against each other. At this point, Kusner was a leading international dressage rider, an event in which the rider controls the horse through precise movements. She had won most of the world's major prizes—the President's Cup in Washington, D.C., the New York championships in Madison Square Garden, the Prix des Amazones in Rotterdam, and the Irish Trophy in Dublin. Kusner rode on the American gold medal team in the 1963 Pan-American games and again in the 1964 Olympics. In 1966, she won the International Grand Prix in Dublin for the second time in a row. She and her horse, Untouchable, were the only rider and horse in the history of the Dublin Grand Prix to win the event back-to-back.

By 1967, Kathy Kusner was an equestrian of top rank in the world, but she could not ride on American racetracks. In 1943, **Judy Johnson** had been granted a license to ride in the Pimlico track steeplechase, but women had not been granted jockey licenses, effectively keeping them off the track. When the passage of the Civil Rights Act in 1964 forbade discrimination on the basis of sex, race, national origin or religion,

Kusner believed the act could pertain to racing. "Horse-riding is more a game of technique and skill than strength," she commented. "It's the same as playing chess with men, so I don't intend to give up the fight." In 1967, she applied to the Maryland Racing Commission for a jockey license and was turned down.

The battle went to court for a year. In the end, Judge Ernest A. Loveless ordered the Maryland Racing Commission to grant Kusner the jockey license that had been denied on the basis of sexual discrimination. Though she was the first woman to receive a license, she was not the first to race professionally. Because Kusner was sidelined for much of 1969 with a broken leg, *Diane Crump rode into the history books at Hialeah on February 7, 1969. Kusner was victorious at Pocono Downs in September 1969. Continuing to compete as an amateur dressage rider, Kusner also won a silver medal in the 1972 Munich Olympics.

Women's proficiency on horseback is not a modern phenomenon. In the 20th century, women began to demand legal equality in an area in which they had long demonstrated their talent. Kathy Kusner raced for justice and won.

SOURCES:

Hollander, Phyllis. *100 Greatest Women in Sports*. NY: Grosset & Dunlap, 1976.

Read, Phyllis J., and Bernard L. Witlieb. *The Book of Women's Firsts*. NY: Random House, 1992.

Karin L. Haag,
freelance writer, Athens, Georgia

Kuti, Funmilayo Ransom- (1900–1978).

See Ransome-Kuti, Funmilayo.

Kuznetsova, Maria (1880–1966)

Russian soprano whose vast repertoire, expressive voice, and powerful acting place her in the highest rank of singers in the early 20th century. Name variations: Mariya Nikolayevna Kuznetsov; Marija Nikolaevna Kuznecova. Born Maria Nikolaievna Kuznetsova in Odessa, Russia, in 1880; died in Paris, April 26, 1966; daughter of Nikolai Kuznetsov; married to a son of Jules Massenet.

Maria Kuznetsova was born into the brilliant cultural universe of late tsarist Russia, a world of profound contrasts between glittering balls, ballets, and operas, and the oppressive poverty and illiteracy of the peasantry. From Maria's earliest years, the newest ideas in music, literature and the theater were discussed in her home. Her father Nikolai Kuznetsov was a highly regarded painter whose portrait of the composer Piotr Ilyitch Tchaikovsky has become universally recognizable. Initially, Maria showed great talent as a dancer, and she first appeared on stage in ballet at St. Petersburg's Court Opera. Soon, however, she decided to become a singer, studying for a number of years with Joakim Tartakov. Her 1905 operatic debut at the Mariinsky Theater as Marguerite in Gounod's *Faust* was an unqualified triumph. Acclaimed as a star, Kuznetsova took part in several operatic premieres, including that of Nikolai Rimsky-Korsakov's *The Legend of the Invisible City of Kitezh* on February 20, 1907. Her starring roles over the next few years included Tatiana in *Eugene Onegin*, Traviata, Madame Butterfly, and Juliette in the Gounod opera *Roméo et Juliette*. Starting in 1906, she began to sing outside Russia, performing in both Berlin and Paris.

Paris quickly became Kuznetsova's second artistic home. Much beloved at both the Grand Opéra and the Opéra-Comique, she appeared in various French roles, including Chabrier's *Gwendoline* (1910) and Massenet's *Roma* (1912), as well as in the standard roles of Aïda and Norma. In 1909, Kuznetsova's international reputation was further enhanced when she made her debut at Covent Garden. That same year, she crossed the Atlantic to perform at New York City's Manhattan Opera House as well as in Chicago. In 1914, Kuznetsova returned temporarily to dancing, appearing with great success both in Paris and in London, where she created the role of Potiphar's wife in the Richard Strauss ballet *Josephs-Legende*. She also sang the role of Yaroslavna in the first British performance of Aleksander Borodin's *Prince Igor*. Given at the Drury Lane Theater and conducted by Sir Thomas Beecham, this was the legendary "Russian season" that introduced a wealth of new Russian opera and ballet to the English-speaking public.

As a Russian patriot, Kuznetsova felt duty-bound to return home at the start of World War I, performing on stage as well as in benefit concerts for the war effort. In 1916, she braved the U-boat-infested Atlantic to perform once more in the United States. On her return to Russia in 1917, she saw her country first overthrow tsarist tyranny and then quickly descend into anarchy, with the year ending in a seizure of power by the Bolsheviks. Determined to escape the Communist regime and Vladimir Lenin's proletarian dictatorship, Kuznetsova succeeded in fleeing by ship to Sweden, having disguised herself as a cabin boy and then hiding in a trunk. Virtually penniless, she supported herself in her Swedish refuge for the next several years by giving song recitals with the tenor Georges Pozemofsky, also performing as a dancer during the same program.

By 1919, Kuznetsova's career was once more on track when she was invited to sing major roles at the Copenhagen and Stockholm opera houses. In 1920, she appeared again on the stage of Covent Garden, and the same year she settled in Paris, which had been transformed into a center of emigres from revolutionary Russia. Married to a son of the French composer Jules Massenet, Kuznetsova was a major personality in the social and artistic life of interwar Paris. Versatile as ever during these years, she not only sang operatic roles, but also appeared in operettas and even experimented with a new career as a motion-picture actress. In 1927, she took on another role, as impresario of a new opera company comprised largely of Russian emigres, the Opéra Russe, which survived until 1933 when it succumbed to the economic depression.

During the Opéra Russe's relatively brief but brilliant existence, Kuznetsova was not only its director but its unchallenged prima donna. Specializing in the Russian operatic repertoire, it had Paris as its base but made guest appearances at major opera houses throughout Europe, including Barcelona, London, Madrid, as well as at Milan's La Scala. In 1929, Kuznetsova and her company toured South America, presenting several previously unheard works in Buenos Aires, including Mussorgsky's *The Fair at Sorotchinsk* and Rimsky-Korsakov's *Snegourotchka (The Snow Maiden)*. As late as the mid-1930s, Kuznetsova was still singing professionally. In 1934, she replaced the celebrated *Conchita Supervia for a performance of Franz Lehár's operetta *Frasquita,* and in 1936 she undertook a strenuous and successful tour of Japan. After her retirement from the stage, she accepted an assignment as artistic advisor of the Russian operatic repertoire at Barcelona's Teatro Lirico. She lived the final decades of her life in Paris, dying there on April 26, 1966.

Boasting a repertoire ranging from the entire body of Russian opera to Salome, Aïda, Norma, Mimi and Gounod's Juliette, Kuznetsova not only possessed what critic Alan Blyth has described as a "gleaming voice and shimmering vibrato," but also was a famously beautiful woman whose stage charisma was legendary. Added to this were her talents as a dancer, which led some of her contemporaries to compare her artistry to that of *Isadora Duncan. Many have described her superb acting talent as being equal to that of the legendary basso Fyodor Chaliapin.

Highly expressive both as a singer and an actress, Kuznetsova left as a tangible legacy only 36 recordings, both acoustic and electrical, made between 1905 and 1928 for the Pathé and Odeon labels. Fortunately, all of these performances are of the highest artistic quality and have been transferred to the compact disc format in Pearl Records' compilation *Singers of Imperial Russia*. Critic Albert Innaurato has called Kuznetsova "one of the great singers on disc [whose] records have a fragile, tender allure, the glamorous magic in her sound closely fit to a musical sensitivity that is hard to match."

SOURCES:

Blyth, Alan. "'Singers of Imperial Russia,'" in *Opera.* Vol. 44, no. 5. May 1993, pp. 520–525.

Innaurato, Albert. "A Taste for Caviar," in *Opera News.* Vol. 57, no. 13. March 13, 1993, pp. 10–12, 14, 15.

Kinrade, D.C. "Marija Nikolaevna Kuznecova," in *The Record Collector.* Vol. 12, 1959–60, pp. 156–159.

Levik, Sergei Iurevich. *The Levik Memoirs: An Opera Singer's Notes.* Translated by Edward Morgan. With a foreword by the Earl of Harewood. London: Symposium Records, 1995.

Pokhitonov, Daniil Ilich. *Iz proshlogo russkoi opery* (From the Past of the Russian Opera). Edited by S.S. Danilova. Leningrad: Vseros. teatralnoe ob-vo, 1949.

Stark, Eduard Aleksandrovich ("Zigfrid"). *Peterburgskaia opera i ee mastera, 1890–1910* (The St. Petersburg Opera and Its Stars, 1890–1910). Leningrad: Gos. izd-vo "Iskusstvo," 1940.

RELATED MEDIA:

Singers of Imperial Russia. Vol. 3, Pearl CD 9004-6.

John Haag,
Associate Professor of History,
University of Georgia, Athens, Georgia

Kuzwayo, Ellen (1914—)

Teacher, social worker, Soweto community organizer, and children's rights activist who published Call Me Woman—*the first autobiography of a black South African woman—and was the first black to receive the prestigious Central News Agency (CNA) literary award. Name variations: Kuswayo. Pronunciation: koo-ZWY-o. Born Ellen Kate Merafe on June 29, 1914, on her grandfather's farm in Thaba'Nchu District, Orange Free State, South Africa; only daughter of Phillip Serasengwe (a businessman and civic leader in Johannesburg) and Emma Mutsi Makgothi Tsimatsima Merafe (a homemaker and farmer); homeschooled to Standard Four on her grandfather's farm; attended St. Paul's School in Thaba'Nchu, 1927, and St. Francis' College in Mariannhill, Natal, 1930; certified by Adams College in Durban as lower primary school teacher, 1933, and later as higher primary school teacher (highest certification that could be attained by a black at a teacher training college), 1935;*

additional education at Lovedale College in Cape Province, 1936; trained in social work at Jan Hofmeyr School of Social Work in Johannesburg (1953–55); awarded Diploma in Advanced Social Work Practice, University of Witwatersrand (1980); awarded Higher Diploma in Advanced Social Work Practice, University of Witwatersrand (1982); married Dr. Ernest Moloto, in 1941 (divorced 1947); married Godfrey Kuzwayo, in 1950 (died 1965); children: (first marriage) Matshwene Everington (b. 1942); Bakone Justice (b. 1944); (second marriage) Ndabezitha Godfrey (b. 1951).

Awards and honors: named Woman of the Year by the Johannesburg newspaper The Star (1979); nominated again as Woman of the Year by The Star (1984); was first black writer to win the prestigious bronze medal Central News Agency (CNA) Prize for literary achievement in an English-language work, for her autobiographical Call Me Woman (1985); granted honorary doctorate in law, University of Witwatersrand (1987).

Birth parents divorced (1916) and raised on grandparents' (Jeremiah and Segogoane Makgothi) farm at Thaba Patchoa with mother, aunts and cousins; death of both grandparents (1920); mother remarried to Abel Tsimatsima (1921) and continued to live on the farm at Thaba Patchoa; half-sister Maria Dikeledi born (1922); mother died (1930); stepfather remarried to Blanche Dinaane Tsimatsima (1933); took first teaching post at Inanda Seminary in Natal (1937); suffered nervous breakdown and returned to live with stepfather and stepmother (1937); taught at St. Paul's School in Thaba'Nchu (1938); forced to leave home by stepmother, moved first to Johannesburg and then Heilbron (1938); married and lived in Rustenburg (1941); became seriously ill following miscarriage; marriage broke down and was forced to leave her sons and flee to Johannesburg to live with her birth father (1946); appointed secretary of Youth League of the African National Congress (1946); after long separation, divorced first husband (1947); taught at Orlando East in Soweto, South Africa (1947–53); played role of a Skokian (beer brewing) queen in film Cry the Beloved Country (1949–51); married second husband and settled in Kliptown (1950); left teaching for first post as a social worker with Johannesburg City Council (1956); worked with Southern African Association of Youth Clubs in Johannesburg (1957–62); made first trip overseas to London (1961); served as general secretary of YWCA in the rural Transvaal region, assisting poor Tsonga-speaking women and children who had been uprooted and resettled by the South African government (1964–76);

made first trip to New York as representative of YWCA congress (1969); family farm at Thaba'Nchu dispossessed under Group Areas legislation (1974); appointed to faculty of School of Social Work, University of Witswatersrand (1976); elected only founding female member of Committee of Ten (community leaders elected during martial law of 1976) and founding board member of the Urban Foundation (1976); jailed for five months at Johannesburg Fort under the Terrorism Act but released without ever being charged (1977–78); appointed consultant to Zamani Soweto Sisters Council (umbrella body of Soweto women's self-help groups, 1978); appointed chair of Maggie Magaba Trust (1979); was subject of documentary film, Awake From Mourning (1981); appointed first president of Black Consumer Union (1984); was subject of another documentary film, Tsiamelo: A Place of Goodness (1985); at age 80, won a seat in the South African Parliament as an African National Congress (ANC) representative for Soweto (1994); appointed to the Truth and Reconciliation Commission (TRC) to investigate human rights abuses committed under the apartheid rule of the Nationalist Party (1995).

Publications: Call Me Woman (London: The Women's Press, 1985); Sit Down and Listen: Stories From South Africa (London: The Women's Press, 1990).

Ellen Kate Merafe Mokoena Cholofelo Motlalepule Nnoseng Moloto Kuzwayo is also known as Mama Soweto. The author of Call Me Woman—the first published autobiography of a black South African woman—answers to each of these names. Her birth parents chose the Christian name Ellen Kate, so that she might be baptized into the Christian Church and attend mission schools. Merafe is a family name from her mother's side, while Mokoena (crocodile) is her maternal clan name and family crest. Her mother gave her the endearing petname Cholofelo, which means "hope" in Setswana, Kuzwayo's first spoken language. Her maternal clan members also called her Motlalepule, a nickname meaning "the one who arrives on a rainy day." Rain is a blessing in the dry northern lands of South Africa, and Kuzwayo was born during a welcome downpour. As a young woman, Kuzwayo returned to her birth father's home and was given another name, Nnoseng, which translates as "give me water" but also implies that a woman's traditional role is to serve others in the home. Moloto and Kuzwayo are her married names and were passed on to her sons. Finally, Kuzwayo is affectionately referred to as Mama Soweto, an indication of the central role she has played for over four decades as a community developer in Soweto, a black township outside of Johannesburg, South Africa.

Each name carries a special significance and reveals part of Kuzwayo's life history; each name reflects the diverse responsibilities she fulfilled and the obstacles she conquered. But Kuzwayo is not alone in these achievements and struggles. The message of her powerful and profound autobiography, *Call Me Woman,* is that all black South African women answer to several different names, and these names reflect diverse personal histories and familial responsibilities as well as commonly won struggles. *Call Me Woman* may be the personal story of one extraordinary woman to educate herself and help others do the same, but it is also the story of *Annie Silinga, Nthaelone Manthata,* and **Mamazana Desiree Finca Mkhele,** women who faced similar obstacles but have yet to receive similar recognition. As Kuzwayo explained to **Wendy Davies,** a *New African* reporter, "the life of one black woman in South Africa depicts the life of another. We have all suffered injustice as women and as black women." Her eulogies of these "great mothers of South Africa" in *Call Me Woman* are offered in recognition of their contributions and achievements.

The life of Ellen Kuzwayo parallels the great transformation of rural, agrarian southern African society into the industrialized, modern nation-state of South Africa. In her memoir, Kuzwayo writes that as a child she moved "as freely on the farm as the birds in the air" and walked "single-file to the barn where they milked the cows in order to get our morning ration of fresh milk direct from the udder." As an adult, she survived five months of detention without charges in 1977–78 and struggled against the unjust apartheid laws of influx control which prohibited her third son, born outside of Johannesburg, from living with her in her home in Soweto, Johannesburg. At age 80, she won a seat in the South African Parliament as an African National Congress (ANC) representative for Soweto and in 1995 was appointed to the Truth and Reconciliation Commission (TRC) to investigate human rights abuses committed under the apartheid rule of the Nationalist Party. In her preface to *Call Me Woman,* South African novelist *Nadine Gordimer* wrote:

> Ellen Kuzwayo is history in the person of one woman. . . . She represents . . . wholeness attained by the transitional woman. . . . She is not Westernized; she is one of those who have Africanized the Western concept of woman and in herself achieved a synthesis with meaning for all who experience cultural conflict.

Education and community service are the central themes in Kuzwayo's life and directly reflect her extraordinary childhood growing up on a fertile farm in the northern regions of South Africa. From 1875 to 1883, her maternal grandfather, Jeremiah Makoloi Makgothi, attended Lovedale College, a Church of Scotland Missionary Society school for the black community, and he later became headmaster of one of the first boarding schools in the area for African boys. In addition to his church duties as preacher and steward in the Wesleyan Methodist Church, he served as secretary of the Native National Congress (later the African National Congress or ANC). As a result of his influence, some of Kuzwayo's most treasured childhood memories are of lessons and camaraderie enjoyed in the church-schoolhouse her grandfather had built just a three-minute walk from their homestead. "The highlights of those early schooldays were action songs and physical exercises which I was good at and loved," she writes. "My cousins and I looked forward to the tasty sour porridge dishes brought by our schoolmates from the village; they in turn loved the butter and jam sandwiches which we exchanged for their porridge."

Later, her stepfather Abel Phogane Tsimatsima supported and encouraged her schooling. He was "a great reader," continues Kuzwayo, "never without *The Friend,* magazines and other periodicals such as *The South African Outlook, The Farmers Weekly, The Government Gazette, The Homestead,* and others. In these, he always marked out what he saw as important and actively encouraged me to read and try to understand the gist of some of the articles. . . . He patiently coaxed me into reading, even if it was just for reading's sake." In an interview with **Cherry Clayton,** Kuzwayo explained: "Very early in my life I read Mary O'Reilly, who used to write fiction. . . . Then later on I started reading for reading's sake. And I enjoyed it. . . . I also used to sit down and do alot of sketching. Mountain scenery and so on, but I threw everything away. . . . Then drawing fell away and I became more interested in language. I've always been able to speak—address meetings, large groups of people." While Kuzwayo's family actively nurtured her intellectual and religious education, they also showed her how to respect herself when others did not. Kuzwayo's grandmother was an outspoken woman who once replied to a white Afrikaner woman's request for assistance in finding a kitchen maid, "I am also looking for that type of person—can *you* help me?" Kuzwayo's mother taught her to always think of others less fortunate than herself, and often sent her out to the edge of the homestead to offer meals to itinerant migrants moving along the roads in search of employment. Writes Kuzwayo: "Much as I resented this, as a child in the family I carried out instructions. . . . To this day, working with people, in particular women and young people, is a concern I cannot divorce myself from. I believe that I inherited my concern for people . . . from my parents."

At age 13, Kuzwayo left her beloved farm to continue her education and live with her mother's youngest sister, **Blanche Dinaane Tsimatsima**. This marked a new era in her life. "Being a pupil in a town school I felt different," she said. "I was a town girl and no longer a country girl." She attended St. Paul's Higher Primary School in Thaba'Nchu, where she faced competition from classmates who could show her up "as not so very intelligent as I believed myself to be at the farm school." In 1930, she left for boarding school at St. Francis' College in Natal Province which was unlike any of her previous educational experiences. The teachers were all white nuns, "rigid, cold and strict, dominating and disciplinarian," and Kuzwayo had difficulty understanding their English spoken with heavy German accents. Catholic ceremonies were confusing and the notion of confession conflicted with her Methodist upbringing. Although she excelled at her studies, Kuzwayo was unhappy and left for Adams College in Amanzimtoti, Natal Province, in 1932. She joined the debating society and traveled to other schools for competitions. "When the society was scheduled to compete with another college," she notes, "there would usually be several male students—and Ellen Merafe (Kuzwayo). The other girls did not seem to take an interest." By 1935, she had graduated from Adams College as a higher primary school teacher, the highest certification that could be attained by a black African at a teacher-training college.

After five years of intensive teacher's training, she felt confident about her ability to teach but was worried about the depth of her knowledge in such subjects as history, geography, and

Ellen
Kuzwayo

biology. In 1936, she enrolled at Lovedale College, the institution which had trained so many of her own relatives, to fulfill the plea of her stepfather to continue her education to at least the level of a university junior degree. Kuzwayo did not immediately fulfill his request; instead, she dropped out of Lovedale in 1937 to accept her first teaching post at Inanda Seminary in Natal. Due to failing health, however, she left Inanda and transferred the next year to teach at St. Paul's School in her childhood town of Thaba'Nchu. But teaching was not totally satisfying, and she found herself increasingly involved in community activities and national politics. She attended the All-African Convention in 1937, an umbrella body for groups working to improve the standard of living in the black community in South Africa. She was attracted to the organization "partly because of a sensitivity to community issues brought about by my early childhood learning to accept people as people. I was also deeply affected by my early exposure at the All-African Convention, which brought me into direct contact with individuals and groups who made a lasting impact on my personal guidelines." They encouraged Kuzwayo to attend the first national conference of the National Council of African Women (NCAW) in 1937. There she was inspired by the words of **Charlotte Manye Maxeke**: "This work is not for yourselves—kill that spirit of 'self' and do not live above your people, but live with them." The following year, Kuzwayo was elected secretary of the local branch of the NCAW in Thaba'Nchu and worked with many different women in the community to develop their homemaking and administrative skills.

During the next decade, Kuzwayo's life changed direction several times. She married in 1941 and gave birth to two sons, but was soon estranged from her abusive husband. She divorced him in 1947 and lost custody of the children. Kuzwayo eased the pain of separation from her young sons with continued teaching, community youth group organization, and political work with the African National Congress (ANC) Youth League. She remarried in 1950 and gave birth to her third son in 1951. By 1952, however, another incident would change her life. She had become increasingly dissatisfied with the callous attitude of her headmaster towards the education of delinquent boys in a nearby reformatory school. Despite his warnings, Kuzwayo continued to teach the reform-school boys from the same lesson plans used for the other schoolboys. One afternoon, the headmaster was cornered by a reform-school boy,

and Kuzwayo managed to defuse the conflict. "Everytime the Principal talks to us, he says we are criminals and murderers" the boy explained to her. "When you inflict corporal punishment on us for various offenses, we never fight back because you treat us as pupils." The incident convinced her that her calling was in social work, not teaching; in 1952, she resigned and "never looked back."

She attended Jan Hofmeyr School of Social Work from 1953 to 1955, excelled in her graduate work, and was appointed an instructor in physical education during her last year of studies. Her classmates and close friends included the future **Winnie Mandela** (Winnie Madikizela). Kuzwayo secured her first post as a social worker with the Johannesburg City Council in 1956 and devoted the next two decades of her life to serving the youth of Johannesburg through programs sponsored by the Southern African Association of Youth Clubs and the YWCA. This work culminated with a teaching appointment in the School of Social Work at the University of Witswatersrand in 1976.

Following the 1976 protest by youth in Soweto, a suburb of Johannesburg, against the marginalization of "Bantu" education for black South Africans, Kuzwayo's work became increasingly politicized. She was appointed a member of the Committee of Ten and a founding board member of the Urban Foundation. Her political activism resulted in a five-month detention in 1977–78; as was not uncommon, she was released from Johannesburg Fort without any charges. Near the end of her detention, she was called into the prison lieutenant's office. Kuzwayo quickly learned that her interrogator was Jimmy Kruger and realized that she "had been offered the chance of a life-time, that of a black woman in South Africa having an interview with the Minister of Justice and Prisons. It was without precedent, and one I intended using to the full. Our interview centered on the need for better communication between black people of South Africa and the Nationalist government." She concluded her prison conversation by declaring, "The day the government of this country agrees to sit round the table with the black people's own chosen leaders to learn about the political aspirations of that community, then and only then shall we all begin to see the dawn of a new day of anticipated peace and calm within the country." Much to her surprise, Kuzwayo was released within two weeks.

Kuzwayo's remarks to Kruger highlight her commitment to dialogue as a critical first step towards achieving peace and equality in South Africa. In an interview with Davies, she explained the goal of writing her autobiography: "Maybe I'm not given to taking a stone and throwing it at a person and this is how I throw my stones, through my book. I throw stones with my mouth. I stand up and I talk about things I don't like. . . . [M]y book is not a bomb. I'm trying to say '*Listen* to what we are saying.'" In a 1989 video interview with **Hilda Bernstein**, Kuzwayo commented about the effect of decades of injustice and apartheid rule: "This is what the government of my country does not understand, that everytime you bash a person, instead of that person withdrawing, that person comes out and the anger in you does not give you an opportunity to retreat. I should have retreated by now. I keep on asking myself why am I doing this at my age? But on the other hand, how do I withdraw and retreat under the circumstances? And this is the plight of all black women. Once you start to commit yourself, you cannot turn back. You find yourself doing things that you never thought you could do. I never thought I could write a book or make a film. What I am saying to the government of South Africa is, do look at us as we are human beings, the color of our skin does not make us any less human than you." Kuzwayo's book inspires an audience far beyond the borders of the new South Africa to challenge sexism and racism wherever they exist.

SOURCES:

Clayton, Cherry. "Interview with Ellen Kuzwayo," in *Between the Lines*. Edited by Craig MacKenzie and Cherry Clayton. Grahamstown, South Africa: National English Literary Museum, 1989, pp. 57–68.

Coullie, Judith L. "The Space Between the Frames: A New Discursive Practice in Ellen Kuzwayo's Call Me Woman," in *South African Feminisms: Writing, Theory and Criticism, 1990–1994*. Edited by M.J. Daymond. NY: Garland, 1996, pp. 131–153.

Davies, Wendy. "Not Weeping Behind the Door," in *New African*. Vol. 213, 1985, p. 42.

Kuzwayo, Ellen. *Call Me Woman*. London: The Women's Press, 1985.

———. "A Lone Persistent Voice," in *Values Alive: A Tribute to Helen Suzman*. Edited by Robin Lee. Johannesburg: Jonathan Ball, 1990, pp. 217–221.

———. *Sit Down and Listen: Stories From South Africa*. London: The Women's Press, 1990.

Lipman, Beata. *We Make Freedom: Women in South Africa*. London: Pandora Press, 1984, pp. 18–23.

SUGGESTED READING:

Goodwin, June. *Cry Amandla!: South African Women and the Question of Power*. NY: Africana Publishing, 1984.

Lazar, Carol (photographs by Peter Magubane). *Women of South Africa: Their Fight for Freedom*. Boston: Bulfinch Press, 1993.

Walker, Cherryl. *Women and Resistance in South Africa*. London: Onyx Press, 1982.

RELATED MEDIA:

Appeared as a Skokian Beer Brewing Queen in *Cry the Beloved Country* (100 min. film), directed by Zolton Korda, based on the novel by Alan Paton, 1951.

Awake from Mourning, Chris Austin, 1981. Chronicles the work of the Maggie Magaba trustees and the Zamani Soweto Sisters Council members in organizing literacy, self-help and crafts projects to improve the quality of life for black women in Soweto. Ellen Kuzwayo, **Joyce Seroke**, and others also speak about their experiences in detention.

Ellen Kuzwayo with Hilda Bernstein (45 min. video), Institute of Contemporary Arts Video (London) in conjunction with Trilion, 1989. Volume 23 in the series *Anthony Roland Collection of Films on Art: Writers Talk, Ideas of Our Time*, South African political activist Hilda Bernstein interviews Ellen Kuzwayo.

Tsiamelo: A Place of Goodness (58 min. film), directed by **Betty Wolpert**, produced by Ellen Kuzwayo, Wolpert, and Blanche Tsimatsima, London Contemporary Films, 1984. Available on video. This film examines Kuzwayo's life and the political and historical implications of the 1916 South African Land Act and the 1950 Group Areas Act which eventually dispossessed Kuzwayo of her family farm in 1974.

Kearsley Alison Stewart,
Instructor, Department of Anthropology and
Women's Studies Program, University of Georgia, Athens, Georgia

Kvitka, Larysa (1871–1913).

See Ukrainka, Lesya.

Kwan, Nancy (1939—)

Eurasian actress. Born on May 19, 1939, in Hong Kong.

Films include: The World of Suzie Wong *(1960);* Flower Drum Song *(1961);* The Main Attraction *(UK, 1962);* Tamahine *(UK, 1963);* Honeymoon Hotel *(1964);* Fate Is the Hunter *(1964);* The Wild Affair *(UK, 1965);* Lt. Robin Crusoe USN *(1966);* Drop Dead Darling *(Arrivederci Baby!, UK, 1966);* Nobody's Perfect *(1968);* The Wrecking Crew *(1969);* The Girl Who Knew Too Much *(1969);* The McMasters *(1970);* Wonder Women *(1973);* Supercock *(1975);* Project Kill *(1976);* Devil Cat *(*Night Creature, *1978);* Streets of Hong Kong *(1979);* Angkor *(1981);* Fowl Play *(1983);* Walking the Edge *(1983);* Night of Children *(1989);* Stickfighter *(1989);* Cold Dog Soup *(1990);* Dragon: The Bruce Lee Story *(1993).*

Nancy Kwan was born in Hong Kong in 1939 and trained with the British Royal Ballet before entering films. Exotically beautiful, she made a promising Hollywood debut as a Hong Kong prostitute who falls in love with an artist in the romantic melodrama *The World of Suzie Wong* (1960), co-starring William Holden, then was cast as a lead in the film version of the Rodgers and Hammerstein musical *Flower*

Drum Song (1961). Kwan's career leveled off during the 1960s and then went into a sharp decline, due at least in part to Hollywood's tendency toward casting myopia. By the late 1970s, she was limited to B movies out of Hong Kong. During the 1990s, Kwan did a series of television infomercials selling beauty products.

Kwast, Frieda Hodapp (1880–1949)

German pianist. Name variations: Frieda Kwast-Hoddap. Born on August 13, 1880, in Bargen, Germany; died in Bad Wiessee, Germany, on September 14, 1949.

Pianist Frieda Hodapp Kwast was born in Bargen, Germany, in 1880. She made a number of recordings at the turn of the century.

Kyme, Anne (c. 1521–1546).

See Askew, Anne.

Kyniska (fl. 396–392 BCE).

See Cynisca.

Kyo, Machiko (1924—)

Japanese actress immortalized in Kurosawa's **Rashomon.** *Born in Osaka, Japan, on March 25, 1924.*

Selected films: (bit part) Tengu-daoshi *(1944);* Final Laugh *(1949);* The Snake Princess *(Parts I & II, 1949–50);* Resurrection *(1950);* Rashomon *(1950);* Pier of Passion *(1951);* The Enchantress *(1951);* A Tale of Genji *(1951);* Beauty and the Bandits *(1952);* Saga of the Great Buddha *(1952);* Ugetsu *(1953);* Gate of Hell *(1953);* A Certain Woman *(1954);* The Story of Shunkin *(1954);* The Princess Sen *(1954);* Bazoku Geisha *(1954);* Whirlpool of Spring *(1954);* Princess Yang Kwei Fei *(1955);* The Teahouse of the August Moon *(U.S., 1956);* Street of Shame *(1956);* Itohan Monogatari *(1957);* Dancing Girl *(1957);* A Woman's Skin *(1957);* Flowers of Hell *(1957);* Night Butterflies *(1957);* The Hole *(1957);* Chance Meeting *(1958);* The Loyal Forty-seven Ronin *(1958);* A Woman of Osaka *(1958);* The Makioka Sisters *(1959);* Paper Pigeon *(1959);* Odd Obsession *(The Key, 1959);* Floating Weeds *(1959);* A Wandering Princess *(1960);* The Last Betrayal *(1960);* Assault from Hell *(1960);* Fan-

From the movie Rashomon, *starring Masayuki Mori and Machiko Kyo.*

tastico *(1961)*; A Design for Dying *(1961)*; The Black Lizard *(1962)*; The Life of a Woman *(1962)*; The Great Wall *(1962)*; Buddha *(1963)*; Sweet Sweat *(1964)*; The Face of Another *(1966)*; Daphne *(1966)*; The Little Runaway *(1967)*; Thousand Cranes *(1969)*; The Family *(1974)*; Yoba *(1976)*; Tora's Pure Love *(1976)*; Kesho *(1985)*.

A veteran of over 90 films, Japanese actress Machiko Kyo began her career as a dancer and made the transition to films on the strength of her beauty and grace. Possessing a compelling sensuality, Kyo was one of the first Japanese actresses to be exploited for her sex appeal. In 1950, however, she displayed surprising dramatic skill as the vulnerable wife of a samurai in *Rashomon*, the Akira Kurosawa masterpiece that reintroduced Japanese film to the world market. Set in medieval Japan, the film tells of a woman (Kyo) who has been raped and her husband (Masayuki Mori) who has been murdered, apparently by the notorious bandit Tajomaru (Toshiro Mifune). The story is told three times by each of the principals in flashback; each time, the tale shifts to benefit the teller. Capturing the Golden Lion at the Venice Film Festival and Hollywood's Academy Award as Best Foreign Film, the film brought Kyo international fame.

Machiko Kyo was subsequently featured in a string of movies during the 1950s and 1960s, in a wide variety of roles, from the traditional Japanese wife to a prostitute. Kyo worked with some of Japan's most notable directors, including Kenji Mizoguchi (*Ugetsu, Street of Shame,* and *Princess Yang Kwei Fei*), Kon Ichikawa (*Odd Obsession*), Yasujiro Ozu (*Floating Weeds*), and Shiro Toyoda (*Sweet Sweat*). Her only American film was *The Teahouse of the August Moon* (1956) with Marlon Brando.

Barbara Morgan,
Melrose, Massachusetts

Kyteler, Alice (fl. 1324)

Irish noblewoman tried for witchcraft. Name variations: Alice Kettle. Flourished in 1324 in Kilkenny; married William Outlawe (died); married Adam le Blund (died); married Richard de Valle (died); married Sir John le Poer (died).

The trial of Alice Kyteler represents one of the earliest prosecutions of a woman for witchcraft in Europe. She was an Irish noblewoman of Kilkenny who seems to have actually been a practitioner of the ancient Celtic pagan religion. She survived all four of her husbands, each wealthier than the previous. After her fourth husband John le Poer died, his entire estate fell to Alice and to his eldest son. His other children contested his will; when Alice refused to settle to their satisfaction, they accused her of witchcraft to discredit her. The local nobility supported Alice in her defense, but the bishop of Ossory believed the charges and excommunicated her. She was then indicted on charges ranging from animal sacrifice to prophecy.

Alice mounted a spirited defense, having her guards capture the bishop and imprison him in her castle. But she could not kidnap the entire church hierarchy and eventually she was forced to flee to England for refuge. She escaped to safety, though several of her fellow practitioners were arrested, and one of her servants was condemned to death for assisting her. Alice's house, the oldest in Kilkenny, has been restored and now serves as the Kyteler's Inn.

Laura York,
Riverside, California

ACKNOWLEDGMENTS

Photographs and illustrations appearing in *Women in World History, Volume 8,* were received from the following sources:

Courtesy of the American Ballet Theatre, **p.** 691; Portrait by Appiani, **p.** 319; Courtesy of Baron Studios, **p.** 99; Portrait by William Beechey, **p.** 307; Photo by Marcus Blechman, **p.** 484; Photo by A.K. Boursault, **p.** 462; Engraving by John C. Buttre, **p.** 242; Photo by J. Capstack, reprinted by permission of the National Portrait Gallery, **p.** 227; Courtesy of Celestial Arts, **p.** 839; Mme. Zoe-Laure de Chatillon, **p.** 187; © Cineguild, 1945, **p.** 233; Photo by George Cserna, **p.** 619; © Daiei, 1950, **p.** 876; © The Detroit Institute of Arts, 1994, **p.** 365; Courtesy of Elite International Sports Marketing and Management, **p.** 341; Courtesy of FAMJOY Enterprises, **p.** 335; Photo by David Gahr, **p.** 299; Courtesy of the Gray Panthers, photo by Julie Jensen, **p.** 857; Courtesy of Guerrero Photographic Group, **p.** 305; Courtesy of the Embassy of the Republic of Guyana, Washington, D.C., **p.** 63; Courtesy of the International Museum of Photography at the George Eastman House, **p.** 509; Courtesy of International Swimming Hall of Fame **p.** 675; Photo by James Ivory, **p.** 159; Courtesy of the John F. Kennedy Library, **pp.** 565, 579, 587; Courtesy of Elizabeth Jolley, **p.** 269; © Kathryn Kuhlman Foundation, 1975, **p.** 849; Courtesy of the King Center, **p.** 667; Courtesy of the King Ranch (Kingsville, Texas), **p.** 672; Courtesy of Anne Klein, a division of Kasper A.S.L., Ltd., **p.** 712; Courtesy of Alfred A. Knopf, Inc., **p.** 737; Courtesy of Lee Angle Photography (Fort Worth, Texas), **p.** 399; Courtesy of the Library of Congress, **pp.** 11, 25, 136, 249, 255, 289, 801; Courtesy of Barbara D. Livingston, Horse Racing Photography, **p.** 817; Courtesy of the Lyndon Baines Johnson Library (Austin, Texas), **p.** 245; Courtesy of Manya Igel Fine Arts, Ltd., **p.** 729; Courtesy of Matar Studio, **p.** 685; Courtesy of Maxine Barker Publicity, **p.** 5; Courtesy of Rollins Maxwell, **p.** 409; Courtesy of Musee Conde (Chantilly), **p.** 103; Courtesy of the National Softball Hall of Fame (Oklahoma City), **p.** 329; Courtesy of Hans Nemuth, **p.** 811; Photo by Bertram Park, **p.** 453; Courtesy of the Pennsylvania Academy of Fine Arts, portrait by Thomas Sully, 548; Courtesy of Mansah Prah, **p.** 165; Courtesy of Prominent Films, **p.** 433; © RKO, 1948, **p.** 191; Courtesy of Sean Gallup/CBS, **p.** 189; Courtesy of the Schlesinger Library, Radcliffe College, **p.** 776; © Selznick, 1946, **p.** 279; Courtesy of Sophia Smith Collection, Smith College (Northampton, Massachusetts), **p.** 693; Courtesy of the Embassy of Sri Lanka, **p.** 662; Courtesy of the Tate Gallery, **p.** 219; Courtesy of the U.S. House of Representatives. **pp.** 130, 419, 491, 524, 629, 740; Courtesy of United Artists, **pp.** 13, 511; Courtesy of the Sedgwick Collection, University Art Museum (Santa Barbara, California), **p.** 355; Courtesy of the College of Environmental Design, Documents Collection, University of California (Berkeley), **pp.** 117, 119; Courtesy of the United States Tennis Association/Russ Adams, **pp.** 51, 657; Painting by Phillippe Vignon, **p.** 613; © Warner Bros., 1956, **p.** 539; Photo by Eli Weinberg, **p.** 315.

ISBN 0-7876-4067-0

90000